CAMPING
AROUND AUSTRALIA

EDITION 2

EXPLORE
AUSTRALIA

CONTENTS

NORTHERN TERRITORY

QUEENSLAND

TASMANIA

INTRODUCTION

WHY CAMP?

It's the end of another sensational day in the outdoors. The sun slips towards the horizon, and birds and wallabies come out to feed in the twilight. A campfire is lit, and close friends and family gather around its glow to sink a sundowner, cook a meal and share the adventures of the day – waves that were caught, fish that got away, discoveries that were made.

The darkness deepens and the stars – much brighter away from the city lights – twinkle and shine over possums, gliders, owls, frogs and other creatures that begin to explore the night.

Around the campfire, senses are heightened so the meal tastes better, the jokes seem funnier and the ties that bind are strengthened.

Camping refreshes the mind, revives the soul and reminds us of what is special. Through it, we gain new experiences, visit parts of the world we otherwise wouldn't see, and relearn the importance of the simple things in life.

The incredibly comprehensive guide you hold in your hands is packed with great ideas of where to take your next camping holiday or weekend away. An experienced team of researchers has painstakingly scoured the country looking for top camping spots and their facilities, so you can start planning that next unforgettable excursion into the great outdoors.

WHERE TO GO?

Planning a trip is often the hardest part of camping. There are so many questions! Do you keep going to the same places that you know and love, or do you venture somewhere new? Will you go to a well-placed campground that has hot showers, flushing toilets and firewood supplied, or slip off the beaten track to an isolated, more rugged spot? Should you stay near the coast with its beaches, lush forests and nearby facilities, or venture into Australia's vast interior, where sites are usually quieter, and the landscape so spacious and vastly different? Do you need to camp in school holidays or public holidays when many campsites are overflowing, or can you slip away mid-week or at other non-peak times?

It's also worth considering what sort of a camping experience you want. Driving to a campsite is the most common way to get there, but have you considered hiking with a backpack? For a first hiking trip, it's best to start with an overnight walk over not too great a distance (no more than about ten kilometres each way). Many campers love this form of isolated camping so much, they disappear for weeks at a time on some of Australia's legendary, long-distance routes: the Larapinta Trail (Northern Territory), the Australian Alps Walking Track (east coast), the Bibbulmun Track (Western Australia) or the South Coast Track (Tasmania).

But if hiking isn't your thing, what about a canoe or kayak camping trip, a boat trip to an island, cross-country skiing or mountain-biking? All of these activities can deliver you to some exceptional out-of-the-ordinary camping experiences.

Whatever your method of transport, if your planned route takes you through or on to Aboriginal land, make sure you start applying for permits with the relevant Land Council well in advance, as it can take some time to have permits approved.

WHAT TO TAKE

It is almost impossible to define what any single individual will need on a camping trip – the amount and type of gear varies greatly with the style, length and location of the trip. A tough, three-day hike in a remote and cold area will require a vastly different list of essentials compared to a week spent with children at a well-established caravan park in summer by the beach.

Even when camping in the same conditions, people will choose to bring varying amounts and types of gear. Some campers (or 'glampers') bring along so much tonnage that you wonder why they left home at all: fairy lights, gas fridges, bikes, wine glasses, pillows and TVs. Others at the same campground may have decided to 'get back to basics' and bring little more than a 'hoochie', or mosquito net, and a billy.

Outdoor/camping shops will nearly always try to sell you more gear than you actually need. It isn't necessary to own the latest 'must-have' gizmo to have a satisfactory, fun and safe camping trip. The best advice is to start simply, with a few basic necessities, and to then add any extra items as you gain experience and discover what would be helpful or desirable for your style of camping.

Whatever style of camping trip you are undertaking, you will need to consider three key areas: bedding and shelter, food and cooking, and safety.

Bedding and shelter

Most people immediately think of a tent when contemplating camping, but in many situations a tent is unnecessary. If you are camping in a dry environment, such as Central Australia, a swag can be one of the nicest ways to spend the night. It's comfy and sleeping directly under the stars is blissful. Swags usually contain a warm layer or two (such as a sleeping-bag), a pillow, a rollable mattress and a canvas outer layer that keeps off the dew. Some even have a small flap that can be erected to keep off the rain.

In a hot, tropical environment, you are often better off with a mosquito net that lets through any whisper of breeze, rather than sweltering under potentially stifling plastic or canvas. If you don't have a suitable mosquito net, you can usually use a modern tent's 'inner tent' without a fly.

If you *are* going to buy a tent, think of the main purposes for which you will be using it. If backpacking, you will need the lightest tent you can buy, that is suitable for the conditions in which you will be travelling (for example, snow, heavy rain, high wind). If you will be setting up in a campground for a week or more with a family, a large walk-in tent with multiple rooms will be more suitable.

Many long-term car campers swear that camping becomes much more pleasurable with a large tarpaulin. A large tarp placed over the tent and extending out beyond it to provide an extra 'living space' gives you extra protection in rain, and also provides vital shade for the tent – and you – during summer holidays.

Although they are one of the most common camping items, sleeping-bags may not necessarily be the most appropriate bedding for your camping trip. They can be very hot, and if you are car camping with a trailer, it may be a better idea to bring sheets, a pillow and a comfy mattress, or even a camp bed.

Also remember that you will need to choose the most appropriate sleeping-bag for your trip. For example, a lightweight summer sleeping-bag will not be adequate if you are camping during winter in Central Australia.

Many air mattresses are very thin (particularly the self-inflating kind) but can still be surprisingly comfortable. If you are camping in very cold conditions, it is advisable to put a second layer – such as a foam mat or groundsheet – between the air mattress and the ground.

Food and cooking

Once again, the style of trip will greatly influence the cooking gear you bring – a backpacking trip will require a small gas-powered or methylated spirits cooker, but most car campers will have a larger, gas-powered cooker. Of course, cooking over a campfire, or using the coals for the camp oven, is often a great alternative, but it's a good idea to bring along another cooking source, in case of fire bans, lack of firewood or incessant rain. As you will see in this guide, many campgrounds now also have gas barbecues on-site.

When compiling your camp list, it is also worth thinking about the peripheral items relating to preparing food and maintaining hygiene: a cotton bag to hang your plates and cutlery can be helpful, alcoholic gel is a great tool for cleaning hands and, if you're staying at a campground with sinks, a plug can be helpful for washing up.

For great recipes, and more ideas on what to bring along for your campsite kitchen, pick up a copy of Explore Australia's *Camping Chef* by Heidi Marfurt.

Safety

No medical kit is useful if you don't know how to use its contents, or if it is left at home. Stock your medical kit with more medications than you think you will need (for example, antihistamines, pain killers) as well as bandages and saline solution. It is very worthwhile for at least someone in your group to do a first-aid course, particularly if you will be travelling in remote areas.

SELECTING THE TENT SITE

Many campers make poor choices when selecting where to set up camp. However, if you are arriving in a busy or pre-booked campground, your decision about where to camp will probably be limited.

Choosing a flat piece of ground is preferable, but if it is likely to rain make sure the ground isn't the lowest land around. Shade provided by trees is great in summer, but beware of river red gums and other lethal eucalypts that can unexpectedly drop huge branches.

Choosing a campsite with a great view can be ideal, but beware of how exposed the site is if the weather should turn nasty.

Before placing your tent or swag, always check for sharp rocks, sticks or insect nests that could make your night uncomfortable.

FIRES

Firewood that is gathered from bushland is not 'waste wood' waiting to be burned. Much of it provides habitat to a host of animals – in particular animals such as lizards, numbats, snakes and echidnas – and as it decays it also puts nutrients back into the soil. So, in many national parks, collecting firewood is illegal.

If collecting firewood is legal, be conscious of not using too much – restrict your fire to a size that's appropriate for your group.

Many national parks, particularly in bushfire-prone areas, do not allow fires at all. If you have chosen to camp in these areas, respect the park manager's wishes.

There are many other camping spots where fires are welcome, such as most state forests, and you will find those sites listed in this guide.

Fires should be lit in existing fireplaces where possible. If this isn't possible, dig a small pit or use rocks to contain the fire. Make sure your fire is lit in an appropriate place with no overhanging branches. Fires should be completely extinguished before you leave a site, preferably with water, as covering a fire in sand can make the sand ferociously hot for many hours, potentially causing serious burns to the next visitors to the campsite.

If you are likely to be lighting a fire with damp wood and kindling, it may help to use a fire starter or two.

CAMPING WITH KIDS

Taking children into the great outdoors provides them with positive experiences they will remember for life: seeing wildlife up close, enjoying the freedom of the outdoors and toasting marshmallows by the campfire. Many of today's keen adult campers were taken on camping trips when they were younger.

Initially, it's advisable to take young children on easy camping trips, where there are good amenities and help is nearby if necessary. However, as they gain experience and confidence, they will enjoy more varied and remote camping trips.

Generally, if the weather is good, children who become comfortable in the outdoors can quickly create their own fun, so there is no need to go overboard with prepared activities. In fact, it's often a great chance to get them away from video games and the television. However, it can be helpful to include card games, board games and books, particularly if you experience a stretch of bad weather.

Make sure all first-time little campers have their own torch to ward off night-time fear, and be extra vigilant with all safety hazards: in particular, fire, water and getting lost.

FIRST AID

There is no substitute for proper first-aid training, and the following advice is not definitive or comprehensive. Treatment regimes can

change with new information and regular campers are advised to update their first-aid training with suitable courses.

There are many great courses, including some specifically designed for camping and remote situations. A good starting point is a course through large, respected organisations such as St John Ambulance (www.stjohn.org.au), the Australian Red Cross (www.redcross.org.au) and Australian First Aid (www.australianfirstaid.com.au).

Burns

Cold, clean, running water is the best first-aid treatment for burns. Ideally, place the person or limb under a cold, running shower for at least ten minutes. Place a sterile, non-stick dressing over the wound, and seek medical assistance if the burn is severe.

Insect bites and stings

Ticks, sandflies and mosquitoes may all cause itchy bites. An antihistamine may be helpful in severe cases. Ticks can be almost microscopic, so check carefully and remove them with tweezers or a tick remover. Ice can be used to help dull the pain of bee and wasp stings, or the bites of other invertebrates such as ants, scorpions and centipedes.

Spider bites

The general rule of thumb with spiders is that if they are up high, in a web, they are almost certainly not dangerous. Spiders that live in burrows on the ground are most likely to be dangerous. With most dangerous spider bites, do not wash the wound, but apply a firm compression bandage, a splint if possible to immobilise the limb, and seek emergency help immediately. Try to identify the spider.

The exception is red-back spiders: do not bandage the bite, but apply ice and use painkillers while seeking urgent medical attention.

Bluebottles

Bluebottle stings can certainly take the enjoyment out of a summer ocean dip. The latest treatment is to first place the affected area in warm to hot water, to nullify the sting, then in cold water to help ease the pain, which should fade with time.

Other stings and bites

Although rare, other stings and bites may be caused by animals such as snakes and blue-ringed octopuses. Most animals, such as snakes, will flee from humans if given the chance. Generally, if there is a bite or sting with venom involved, the first-aid treatment is a compression bandage, keeping the patient or limb still, and seeking urgent medical attention. If the bite does not involve venom (such as a dog bite), keep the wound clean and stem the bleeding with bandages.

Sprains and breaks

The basic first-aid treatment for ankle and other sprains is remembered by the acronym RICE – Rest, Ice, Compression bandage (to immobilise and support it) and Elevation (placing it higher than the level of the heart when the patient is lying down).

If bones in a limb or elsewhere have been broken, the patient may well have other serious difficulties, so check breathing, circulation and stem any serious bleeding. Immobilise the limb with padding and a splint if necessary, and seek help.

CPR

Again, all regular campers should receive proper training on this resuscitation technique that can save lives. The current recommended CPR technique is two breaths, and then 30 chest compressions, repeated until the patient recovers.

RESPONSIBLE CAMPING

Many people who profess to love camping and the outdoors show little respect for the places they visit, and for other campers. Commonsense and courtesy should cover most issues, but all campers should think of the following.

Leave no trace

As a general rule, a campsite should look better when you leave than when you arrived. That means all rubbish needs to be removed, including fruit peel and lolly wrappers. Simply piling rubbish on top of or beside an already overflowing rubbish bin is ridiculous and leads to foraging by dogs, birds and other animals. If there is no suitable place to leave rubbish, take it with you. If you carried it in, you can carry it out.

And remember, just because you are camping doesn't mean you can ignore the principles of recycling. If possible, separate your recyclables and dispose of them accordingly.

For more information on the principles of 'leave no trace' camping, see www.lnt.org.au.

Toileting

If there are toilets at a campsite, use them. If not, dig a hole at least 20 centimetres deep, a long way from water sources (at least 100 metres) and other campers. As wild dogs and some other animals will dig up used toilet paper, leaving it to blow around unpleasantly, you should burn the used paper either in the hole, or place it in a small paper bag and burn it on the campfire. This will not be possible if a fire ban is in place. Used tampons, sanitary pads and disposable nappies should be carried out.

Camping with pets

You will see in this guide that many campsites allow pets, such as dogs on leashes, but that doesn't mean that every other camper will instantly fall in love with your animal. Keep pets under control, away from other campers, and clean up their faeces.

Noise and light pollution

Generators, loud music and wild parties can ruin the quiet ambiance that many seek when they camp. Only use generators in the places and times they are allowed, and be sensitive to the wishes of others.

CAMPING IN SENSITIVE AREAS

Some beautiful but vulnerable natural areas need extra protection – for example, above the snowline in the Australian Alps, or in the no-fire zones in many national parks – and so there are special rules and tips about camping in those areas.

In some areas, rather than burying toilet waste, you are encouraged or required to carry all human waste out. The easiest way is to bring along a chemical toilet, which you can buy at outdoor and camping stores.

In such sensitive areas, also consider the other chemicals you may be inadvertently leaving behind. Choose toothpaste with little or no fluoride (often children's toothpastes are best), and use biodegradable detergents and soaps or, preferably, none at all. (A combination of sand or grit and hot water can usually clean most things.) Never do the washing up directly in a water source, and make sure any fats and grease are poured out a long way from the water, preferably into a small hole.

If swimming in pristine waterholes or creeks, avoid the use of sunscreen as it can pollute the water. Swim in clothes if necessary to protect yourself from the sun.

BE PREPARED TO CHANGE PLANS

No matter how much planning you have done, some things can still go wrong. A camping trip may be plagued by sickness or injury, bad weather, or crowded or unpleasant campsites. Although most keen campers are prepared to put up with a little discomfort, being flexible can save a camping trip from complete disaster, and leave you keen and willing to camp again.

SAMPLE CAMPING LIST

The following list is intended as a helpful guide. You will need to modify it for your own trip.

Bedding/Shelter

- Tent, poles and pegs
- Tent repair kit
- Hammer/mallet
- Spring-loaded pegs
- Guy ropes
- Large tarpaulin
- Mozzie net
- Ground sheet
- Sleeping-bag
- Inner sheet
- Swag/airbed/camp bed/mattress
- Airbed repair kit
- Pump
- Pillow

Food/Cooking

- Stove and fuel
- Stove stand
- Gas bottle
- Gas attachments
- Barbecue plate or baking paper to place on the dirty hotplate
- Esky/car fridge/gas fridge
- Drink bottles
- Water supply if none available
- Plates/cups/bowls/mugs/cutlery
- Cooking utensils (e.g. a sharp knife)
- Barbecue tools
- Matches
- Water carrier
- Billies or pots and pans
- Camp oven
- Billy lifter or oven mitt
- Can opener
- Dishcloth
- Scourers/scrubbers
- Cutting board
- Washing-up bowl
- Detergent
- Garbage bags

- Tables/chairs
- Fire starters
- Firewood
- Folding saw
- Tomahawk

Safety

- First-aid kit
- Sunscreen
- Water purifying tablets or device
- Toiler paper
- Maps and compass
- Thermals
- Heat blanket
- Mirror and/or whistle for signalling

Extras

- Lights (e.g. solar or gas lantern, torches)
- Swimwear
- Rain gear
- Towels
- Hats
- Toiletries
- Fishing gear
- Shovel or trowel
- Brush and pan
- Doormat
- Camera
- Binoculars
- Water toys
- Ball games
- Card games
- Books
- Clothesline/pegs
- Mozzie coils
- Insect repellent
- Universal sink plug
- Hot-water shower bag
- Toilet system

CAMPSITE SYMBOLS

Facilities

A 4WD is required to reach the campsite.

Towed camper trailers can access the campsite.

There is an undercover camp kitchen area with some equipment.

A camping fee applies; you may need to pay it in advance or at the campsite.

Caravans can access the campsite.

Cold showers are available at the campsite.

The park, forest or conservation area charges a daily fee, which may be per person or per vehicle.

The toilets are wheelchair-accessible; showers at this campsite are not necessarily suitable for disabled visitors.

Some pets are allowed, usually small dogs, and they will need to be on a leash when outside. Always request permission before bringing your pet.

Drinking water is available. It may need to be boiled/treated before drinking; bore water may taste unpalatable, despite being safe to drink, due to high mineral content.

Vehicles of any kind (2WD or 4WD) can only reach the campsite in dry weather.

There is a facility to dump caravan toilet waste.

No campfires are allowed.

A gas or electric BBQ is at the campsite. It may be coin-operated.

Hot showers are available at the campsite. A fee may be charged for access to the shower block, or coins required to turn on the hot water.

Information about the area is available at, or near, the campsite.

The camping area or caravan park has a kiosk where basic food supplies or prepared food can be bought.

No pets are allowed.

There are no rubbish disposal facilities. Bring rubbish bags with you, and take rubbish away when you leave.

The camping area is not accessible to vehicles. All gear must be carried in; distances are usually indicated in the entry.

There is a sheltered picnic table at the campsite.

There is a picnic area with tables at, or near, the campsite.

The caravan park has sites with electricity, usually standard 240V.

There is a payphone at the campsite.

A ranger operates in the area. There may not be a permanent ranger station at the campsite, but one will visit regularly, or there will be a ranger station within reach.

This is one of our favourite campsites.

There is a toilet at the campsite. It may be a pit or composting toilet.

The campsite is suitable for a vehicle with a pop-up tent, or for a tent to be erected beside a vehicle.

When fire bans are not in place, fires can be lit at this campsite, generally in designated fireplaces or BBQs.

Activities

A boat ramp is within easy access of the campsite.

Canoeing or paddling is possible. BYO canoe/kayak, unless otherwise mentioned in entry.

Crocodiles live in waters near the campsite. Observe warnings.

Cycle trails are nearby, suitable for either normal bikes or mountain bikes.

Salt- or fresh-water fishing is allowed.

Hiking trails are nearby (these are more strenuous than walking trails). Recommended for fit adults.

A horseriding trail is nearby, or horses may be brought by float to the campsite; facilities are available.

The campsite is in a scenic area, or a scenic lookout is close by.

There is a walk near the campsite with information or signage about the flora and fauna in the area.

There is no swimming at, or near, the campsite.

The sea or reservoir near the campsite is suitable for sailing small boats. It does not mean there is a boat ramp.

There is a scenic drive within a reasonable distance of the campsite.

Swimming is allowed at, or near, the campsite.

A generally flat or gently sloping walking trail is nearby.

Facilities for waterskiing are available at, or near, the campsite.

HOW TO USE THIS BOOK

State or territory colour used in this section

State or territory name

State or territory key map shows regions covered in the text section, and map coverage with page numbers (*96–7*) in the atlas section

Contents for each state or territory, showing regions' names and page numbers

List of the best campsites in the state or territory, with region name and page number

Useful contacts gives information for authorities in charge of national parks, roads, permits and licences, and emergency services

Introduction provides information on national parks, state forests and reserves

Region name

Regional map shows the locations of the listed campsites (numbered), national parks, state forests and reserves

Regional introduction highlights the area's parks, activities and natural attractions

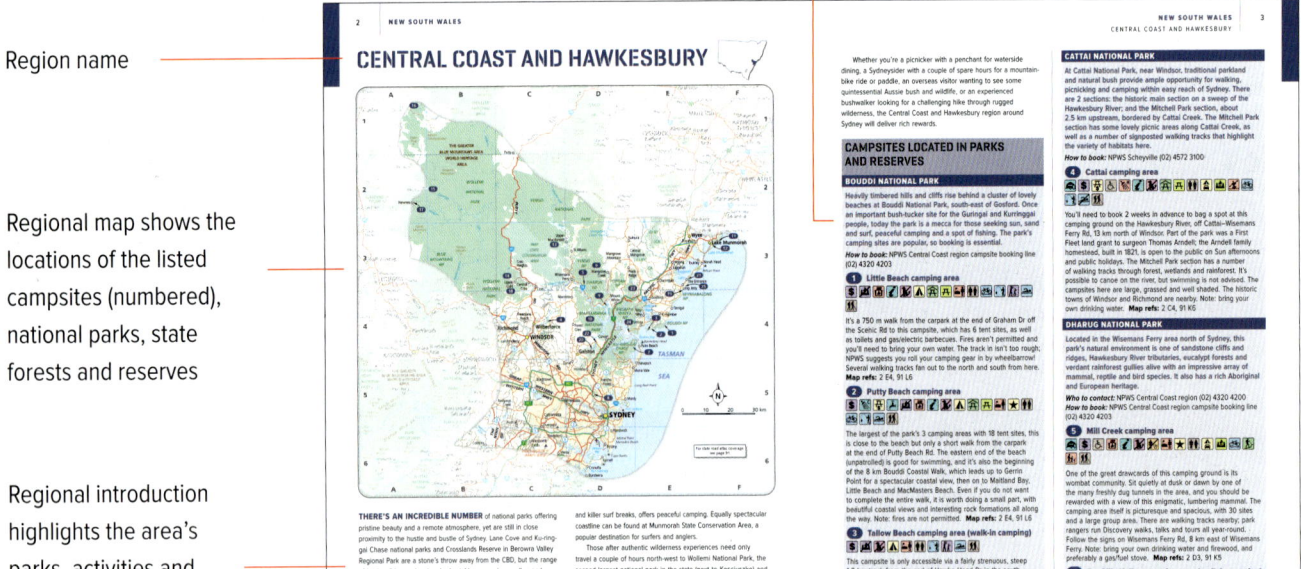

National parks, state forests and reserves are listed in alphabetical order within each region; campsites in these areas are also listed alphabetically

The number next to a campsite name corresponds to the number shown on the regional and atlas maps

Icons list the accessibility, facilities and activities at each campsite

Campsite entries provide information on individual campsites

Map references show the position of each campsite on the atlas pages located at the end of each state or territory section

Telephone contact details are provided for all entries

Campsites outside national parks, state forests and reserves are listed alphabetically in a section following those entries

Map title   Adjoining map page   State or territory location map

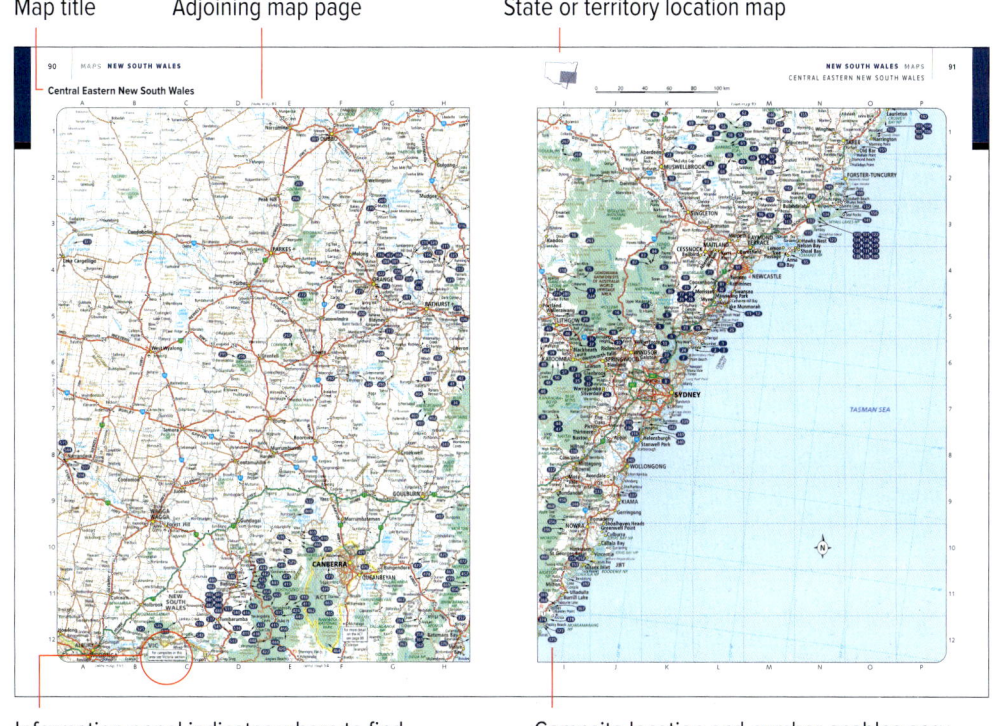

Index

There is an extensive index starting on p. 510. It includes place names and campsites, and lists both text and map references. For easy reference, campsite names include the national park, state forest or reserve in which they are located.

Information panel indicates where to find campsites for the adjoining state or territory

Campsite location and number enables easy cross-reference to campsite entry

NEW SOUTH WALES

CONTENTS

BEST CAMPSITES

Geehi Flats camping area (southern section)
Kosciuszko National Park (Capital Country and the Snowys), p. 70

Green Gully camping area
Oxley Wild Rivers National Park (New England and the North-West), p. 39

Homestead Creek camping area
Mutawintji National Park (The Outback), p. 86

Mungo Brush camping area
Myall Lakes National Park (Holiday Coast), p. 24

Polblue camping area (northern section)
Barrington Tops National Park (Hunter Valley and Coast), p. 13

USEFUL CONTACTS

Crown Land – Department of Primary Industries
1300 052 637
www.crownland.nsw.gov.au

Emergency
Dial 000 for police, ambulance and fire brigade

Environment ACT
13 2281
www.environment.act.gov.au

Fisheries – Department of Primary Industries
1300 550 474
www.dpi.nsw.gov.au/fisheries

Fossicking – Department of Primary Industries
1300 736 122
www.dpi.nsw.gov.au/minerals

NSW Rural Fire Service
1800 679 737
www.rfs.nsw.gov.au

National Parks and Wildlife Service
1300 361 967
www.nationalparks.nsw.gov.au

Roads and Traffic Authority
13 2213
www.rta.nsw.gov.au

State Forests of NSW Information Centre
1300 655 687
www.dpi.nsw.gov.au/forests

Campsite in Kosciuszko National Park, Capital Country and the Snowys region (p. 68)

CENTRAL COAST AND HAWKESBURY

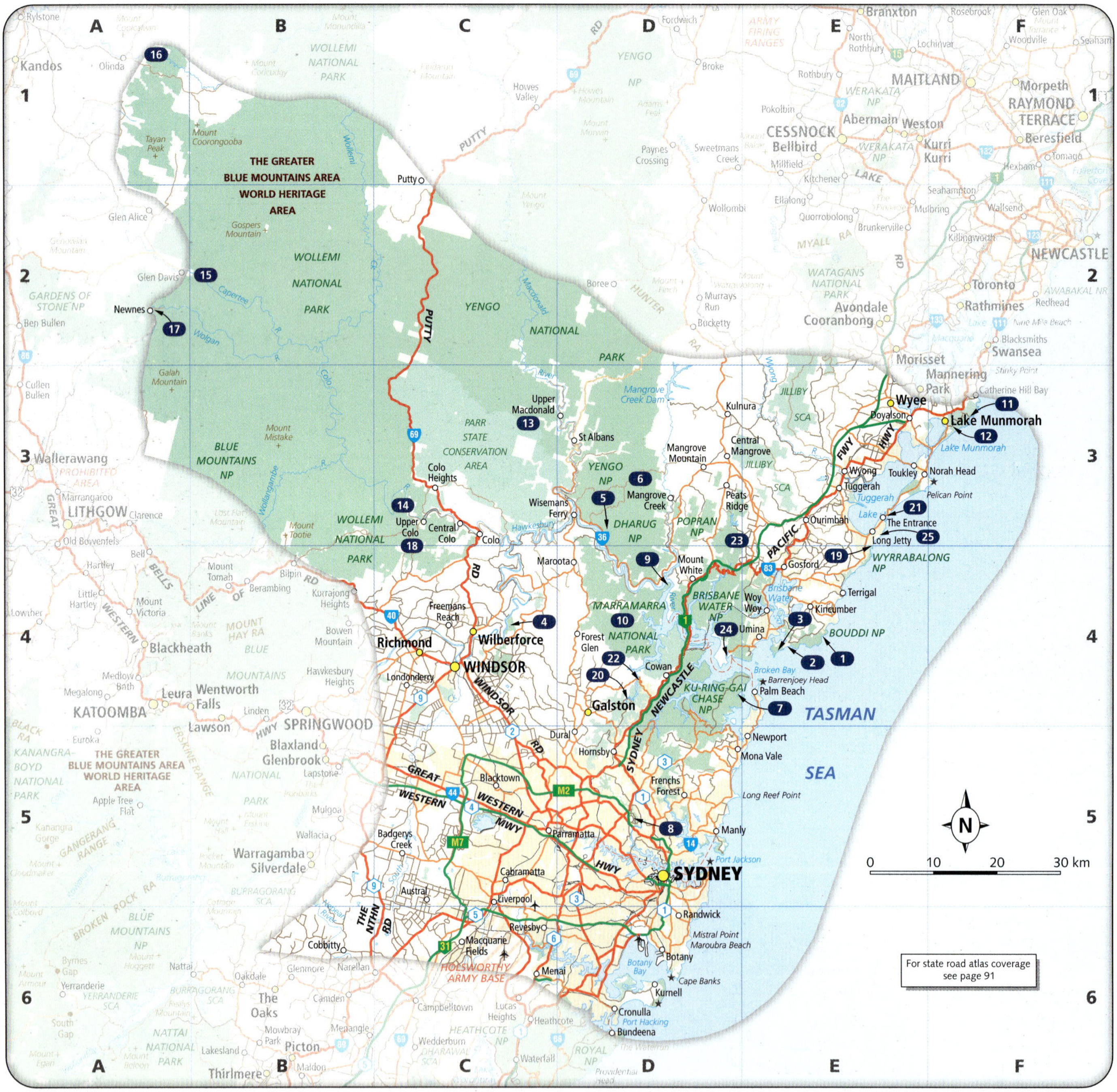

THERE'S AN INCREDIBLE NUMBER of national parks offering pristine beauty and a remote atmosphere, yet are still in close proximity to the hustle and bustle of Sydney. Lane Cove and Ku-ring-gai Chase national parks and Crosslands Reserve in Berowra Valley Regional Park are a stone's throw away from the CBD, but the range of bushwalking, swimming, birdwatching, canoeing, cycling and picnicking opportunities they offer are second to none.

Venture only a little further afield and you hit Dharug National Park, where you'll find an impressive array of wildlife amid rugged sandstone escarpments and magnificent forests. Bouddi National Park, with its panoramic coastal views, challenging walking tracks and killer surf breaks, offers peaceful camping. Equally spectacular coastline can be found at Munmorah State Conservation Area, a popular destination for surfers and anglers.

Those after authentic wilderness experiences need only travel a couple of hours north-west to Wollemi National Park, the second largest national park in the state (next to Kosciuszko) and its largest wilderness area. This is an awe-inspiring area, with a mosaic of diverse vegetation, dozens of native wildlife species and numerous signs of Aboriginal occupation. Experienced and fit bushwalkers will find demanding but richly rewarding walks across the rugged terrain.

Whether you're a picnicker with a penchant for waterside dining, a Sydneysider with a couple of spare hours for a mountain-bike ride or paddle, an overseas visitor wanting to see some quintessential Aussie bush and wildlife, or an experienced bushwalker looking for a challenging hike through rugged wilderness, the Central Coast and Hawkesbury region around Sydney will deliver rich rewards.

CAMPSITES LOCATED IN PARKS AND RESERVES

BOUDDI NATIONAL PARK

Heavily timbered hills and cliffs rise behind a cluster of lovely beaches at Bouddi National Park, south-east of Gosford. Once an important bush-tucker site for the Guringai and Kurringgai people, today the park is a mecca for those seeking sun, sand and surf, peaceful camping and a spot of fishing. The park's camping sites are popular, so booking is essential.

How to book: NPWS Central Coast region campsite booking line (02) 4320 4203

1   Little Beach camping area

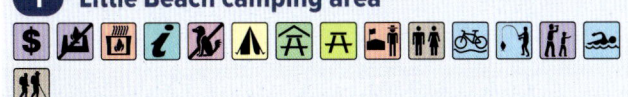

It's a 750 m walk from the carpark at the end of Graham Dr off the Scenic Rd to this campsite, which has 6 tent sites, as well as toilets and gas/electric BBQs. Fires aren't permitted and you'll need to bring your own water. The track in isn't too rough; NPWS suggests you roll your camping gear in by wheelbarrow! Several walking tracks fan out to the north and south from here. **Map refs:** 2 E4, 91 L6

2   Putty Beach camping area

The largest of the park's 3 camping areas with 18 tent sites, this is close to the beach but only a short walk from the carpark at the end of Putty Beach Rd. The eastern end of the beach (unpatrolled) is good for swimming, and it's also the beginning of the 8 km Bouddi Coastal Walk, which leads up to Gerrin Point for a spectacular coastal view, then on to Maitland Bay, Little Beach and MacMasters Beach. Even if you do not want to complete the entire walk, it is worth doing a small part, with beautiful coastal views and interesting rock formations all along the way. Note: fires are not permitted. **Map refs:** 2 E4, 91 L6

3   Tallow Beach camping area (walk-in camping)

This campsite is only accessible via a fairly strenuous, steep 1.2 km track from the end of Hawke Head Dr in the south-western reaches of the park. It's downhill to get there, which means a tough uphill walk back, and you need to carry your drinking water with you. But while there, there's an unpatrolled beach for swimming, surfing and fishing, and several walking tracks. Fires are not permitted. **Map refs:** 2 E4, 91 L6

CATTAI NATIONAL PARK

At Cattai National Park, near Windsor, traditional parkland and natural bush provide ample opportunity for walking, picnicking and camping within easy reach of Sydney. There are 2 sections: the historic main section on a sweep of the Hawkesbury River; and the Mitchell Park section, about 2.5 km upstream, bordered by Cattai Creek. The Mitchell Park section has some lovely picnic areas along Cattai Creek, as well as a number of signposted walking tracks that highlight the variety of habitats here.

How to book: NPWS Scheyville (02) 4572 3100

4   Cattai camping area

You'll need to book 2 weeks in advance to bag a spot at this camping ground on the Hawkesbury River, off Cattai–Wisemans Ferry Rd, 13 km north of Windsor. Part of the park was a First Fleet land grant to surgeon Thomas Arndell; the Arndell family homestead, built in 1821, is open to the public on Sun afternoons and public holidays. The Mitchell Park section has a number of walking tracks through forest, wetlands and rainforest. It's possible to canoe on the river, but swimming is not advised. The campsites here are large, grassed and well shaded. The historic towns of Windsor and Richmond are nearby. Note: bring your own drinking water. **Map refs:** 2 C4, 91 K6

DHARUG NATIONAL PARK

Located in the Wisemans Ferry area north of Sydney, this park's natural environment is one of sandstone cliffs and ridges, Hawkesbury River tributaries, eucalypt forests and verdant rainforest gullies alive with an impressive array of mammal, reptile and bird species. It also has a rich Aboriginal and European heritage.

Who to contact: NPWS Central Coast region (02) 4320 4200
How to book: NPWS Central Coast region campsite booking line (02) 4320 4203

5   Mill Creek camping area

One of the great drawcards of this camping ground is its wombat community. Sit quietly at dusk or dawn by one of the many freshly dug tunnels in the area, and you should be rewarded with a view of this enigmatic, lumbering mammal. The camping area itself is picturesque and spacious, with 30 sites and a large group area. There are walking tracks nearby; park rangers run Discovery walks, talks and tours all year-round. Follow the signs on Wisemans Ferry Rd, 8 km east of Wisemans Ferry. Note: bring your own drinking water and firewood, and preferably a gas/fuel stove. **Map refs:** 2 D3, 91 K5

6   Ten Mile Hollow camping area (walk-in camping)

This is a walk-in site and you'll only find wood fireplaces here, so you need to be self-sufficient with a gas/fuel stove and drinking water. You can reach the campground via the 2-day Great North Walk between Wisemans Ferry to Mangrove Mountain, or via the Simpsons Track. Mountain-bikers can also gain access via the Old Great North Rd up Devines Hill, or an easier ride can be had by using the Western Commission Track, a fire trail a few kilometres to the east of Wisemans Ferry. The impressive sandstone pylons of the convict-built Clare's Bridge are near this campsite. **Map refs:** 2 D3, 91 K5

KU-RING-GAI CHASE NATIONAL PARK

One of the state's best-loved and most visited parks, Ku-ring-gai Chase preserves an important stretch of natural bushland as well as the lower reaches of the Hawkesbury River and a number of its tributaries. This is a stunning recreational area, and it's only 30 km north of Sydney's bustling city centre. Bookings are essential for the camping area.

How to book: NPWS Basin booking line (02) 9974 1011

7   The Basin camping area

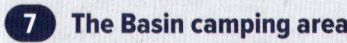

Camping for 400 visitors is permitted at this area only, near West Head. Vehicle parking is on West Head Rd; from there, it's a 2.8 km walk or cycle to the campground. There is also access by water, via private boat, ferry or water taxi from Palm Beach Wharf. Bring your own firewood. If everything's booked out, alternative accommodation is available at a YHA hostel at Towlers Bay. **Map refs:** 2 D4, 91 K6

LANE COVE NATIONAL PARK

Lane Cove River snakes its way through tranquil bushland at Lane Cove National Park, 10 km north-west of central Sydney via Plassey Rd off Delhi Rd or off Lady Game Dr. At the visitor centre you can learn about the area's natural and Indigenous heritage; other activities include picnicking, walking and rowboat hire. There are pleasant picnic areas near Delhi Rd, by the weir, and bushland walking tracks on both sides of the river.

How to book: Plassey Rd, Macquarie Park (02) 9888 9133, 1300 729 133 www.lcrtp.com.au

8   Lane Cove River Tourist Park

You'll find this topnotch park accommodation on Plassey Rd, off Delhi Rd in North Ryde. The 545 bus from Chatswood train station will drop you off at the corner. Ensuite and family cabins are available, as well as campervan and tent sites. There's a swimming pool, and boat and bike hire, and basic grocery items are available at reception. Other drawcards are a recreation room complete with internet kiosk and large-screen plasma TV, wireless internet, and a camp kitchen. Bookings recommended. **Map refs:** 2 D5, 91 K6

MARRAMARRA NATIONAL PARK

This is an uncut gem of a park 50 km north-west of Sydney, with a wide range of walking tracks, as well as cycling,

fishing and canoeing. Arrive by car via Canoelands Rd off Old Northern Rd; Bloodwood Rd; or from Wisemans Ferry along Singleton Rd. Water access is along Marramarra Creek, Berowra Creek and the Hawkesbury River.

Who to contact: Sydney North (Ku-ring-gai Chase National Park) Information Centre (02) 9472 8949 ***Note:*** for safety, visitors are advised to register and deregister with the information centre

9   Gentlemans Halt camping area (walk-in camping)

Perched on the banks of the Hawkesbury River, opposite Spencer, Gentlemans Halt is a 10 km walk from Canoelands Ridge Trail. Alternatively, you can paddle in by canoe as there are landing facilities here. Spare a few minutes to enjoy the mangrove forest. Note: you need to bring your own drinking water, and preferably a gas/fuel stove. **Map refs:** 2 D4, 91 K5

10   Marramarra Creek camping area (walk-in camping)

It's a 4 km walk from the locked gate at Canoelands Rd, off Old Northern Rd, to this basic bush site. As with Gentlemans Halt, you'll need to carry your drinking water with you, and preferably a gas/fuel stove. **Map refs:** 2 D4, 91 K6

MUNMORAH STATE CONSERVATION AREA

A stunning 12 km coastal ribbon 40 km north of Gosford, Munmorah State Conservation Area offers surfing, swimming, fishing, coastal walks and a kaleidoscope of wildflowers in spring. Follow the signs at the Pacific Hwy turn-off for Lake Munmorah.

How to book: NPWS Central Coast region campsite booking line (02) 4320 4203

11   Frazer camping area

The 6 sites here each fit 6 people, and you can stay for a maximum of 2 weeks. The camping ground is nestled in the Frazer Valley, close to the beach (only patrolled during Christmas and Easter holidays) and Snapper Point, a popular fishing spot. To get here, turn onto Frazer Beach Rd off Campbell Dr in the northern section of the park. It's a sought-after camping area in peak periods; bookings can be made up to 3 months in advance. Bring your own drinking water. **Map refs:** 2 F3, 91 L5

12   Freemans camping area

Freemans, a short walk to Birdie Beach, has 8 caravan sites and 28 tent sites. Note: the grounds close at 6pm in winter, 9pm in summer, and camping is limited to stays of 2 weeks. You can only use gas BBQs and gas/fuel stoves here. **Map refs:** 2 F3, 91 L5

PARR STATE CONSERVATION AREA

Named for early explorer William Parr, this is a harsh and hardy environment of rocky outcrops, cliffs and steep gorges. You can go it alone or take part in a Discovery walk, talk or tour through the park. To get here, travel 35 km north of Windsor via Putty Rd, or head 8 km west of Wisemans Ferry via St Albans Rd.

Who to contact: NPWS Gosford (02) 4320 4200

13 Heartbreak Hill camping area (walk-in camping)

Heartbreak Hill is walk-in only, but don't let the name put you off. It's a stopover point for hikers on the Womera Range Track, which also passes through adjacent Yengo National Park *(see p. 16)*. This is for self-sufficient campers only, although there are wood BBQs here – bring firewood, a gas/fuel stove, drinking water and good topographic maps, and let the parks office know when you intend to arrive and depart. **Map refs:** 2 C3, 91 K5

WOLLEMI NATIONAL PARK

Part of the Greater Blue Mountains World Heritage Area, Wollemi National Park is a sprawling, primeval landscape of precipitous escarpments and deep canyons, virgin forest, woodlands, flowering heath and pockets of rainforest. It's brimming with Aboriginal and European history, myriad wildlife and walking trails aplenty. While there is little formal access to the park from Putty Rd, one trail that is worth checking out is the Bob Turner Track, which is accessed via 3 km of unsealed road, 500 m north of the Ampol service station at Colo Heights. This is 16 km north of the Colo Bridge. A 3 km walk leads down to a lovely swimming hole on the Colo River, just above some rapids.

Who to contact: NPWS Blackheath (02) 4787 8877 for campsite nos **15**, **17**; NPWS Richmond (02) 4588 5247 for campsite nos **14**, **18**; NPWS Mudgee (02) 6370 9000 for campsite no. **16**
Camping fees: payable using self-registration

14 Colo Meroo camping area (walk-in camping)

Access to this camping site in the southern section of the park is by foot on the 24 km Mountain Lagoon Loop, which starts and finishes on Sam's Way in the town of Mountain Lagoon. A far less taxing method of transport is by rubber raft along the Colo River. Make sure you've got good topographic maps and you've checked track and river conditions with the parks office. You'll need to bring your own firewood and drinking water. **Map refs:** 2 C3, 91 J5

15 Coorongooba camping area

This basic camping area is set by the river at the start of the sandstone gorge gouged out by the Capertee River. Facilities are limited to picnic tables for sunset dining and wood BBQs. Bring your own firewood and drinking water. Access is 4WD only, via Glen Davis, 35 km north of Capertee. **Map refs:** 2 B2, 91 I4

16 Dunns Swamp–Ganguddy camping area

Camp by the tranquil Kandos Weir on Cudgegong River, accessed via Narrango Rd in the west of the park. There's a rock-art site nearby and you can explore the swamp and surrounding forest on a number of walking tracks. The rock art is thought to be over 7000 years old and other tracks give access to the eroded beehive-shaped sandstone formations known as pagodas. Swimming, canoeing and birdwatching is also popular here. Bring drinking water, or boil/treat water from the dam. **Map refs:** 2 A1, 91 I3

17 Newnes Ruins camping area

Close to this site are the ruins of the old shale-oil mining town of Newnes, as well as a glow-worm tunnel. With 80 campsites to choose from there's a lot of space, but keep in mind this is a very popular spot, particularly during holiday periods. The camping area is in the southern section of the park, on Wolgan River, en route to the ruins. Bring your drinking water and firewood or gas/fuel stove. There are also rustic cabins and camping sites at Newnes Hotel Cabins Historic Wilderness Retreat in the Wolgan Valley. **Map refs:** 2 A2, 91 I4

18 Wheeny Creek camping area

Wheeny Creek, in the southern section of the park, has 30 camping sites available. It's a spacious, picturesque medley of grassy terraces by the creek, which is a tributary of the Colo River. It's on Comleroy Rd off Bells Line of Road, 14 km north of Kurrajong, and is suitable for campervans and trailers. There is good mountain-biking here where Comleroy Rd heads on towards the Colo River. A few kilometres along there is a road to the left which gives access to Mountain Lagoon and then goes on to Bilpin. Come with your own firewood and water. **Map refs:** 2 C4, 91 J5

CAMPSITES LOCATED IN OTHER AREAS

19 Blue Lagoon Beach Resort

Camp at this Bateau Bay hideaway and you'll awaken to the sounds of the sea and an unobstructed view of the sunrise over the ocean. The beachfront resort has tent and caravan sites as well as cabins; a heated 25 m and toddler pools; 6 spas; tennis, basketball and volleyball courts; and best of all, a protected and inviting beach lagoon. It's a 20 min drive north-east of Gosford along The Entrance Rd; turn right into Bateau Bay Rd. Bookings are recommended year-round. **Map refs:** 2 E3, 91 L5

How to book: 10 Bateau Bay Rd, Bateau Bay (02) 4332 1447, 1800 680 036 www.bluelagoonbeachresort.com.au

20 Crosslands Reserve camping area

Set amid some of Sydney's best forest – peppermint, blackbutt, scribbly gum and blue gums – this family-friendly camping site is in Hornsby Shire in the city's north. You can drive in on Somerville Rd in Hornsby Heights, or walk in via Benowie Walking Track, part of the Great North Walk. Canoes and boats can also access the shores of the reserve via Berowra Creek. Visitors can partake in a number of activities including guided Aboriginal heritage tours, spotlighting and an eco-history walk. Note: bring your own drinking water and gas/fuel stove. **Map refs:** 2 D4, 91 K6

How to book: Hornsby Shire Council (02) 9847 6791

21 El Lago Waters Tourist Park

Enjoy views of Tuggerah Lakes at The Entrance on the picturesque Central Coast at this tourist park, which offers a range of accommodation options including camping. Don't get it confused with the adjacent resort of the same name, although you'll need to check in at the resort reception before heading to your campsite. **Map refs:** 2 E3, 91 L5

How to book: 11 The Entrance Rd, The Entrance (02) 4332 3955, 1300 664 554 www.ellago.com.au

Great North Walk

If you're passionate about getting to know NSW – its bushland, rural and urban settings – then the Great North Walk is for you. Stretching for 250 km from Sydney to Newcastle, the track can be covered in its entirety in 10–14 days. The track is divided into 4 sections, but the possibilities are endless.

■ *Please note that campsites are listed in alphabetical*
■ *order, not track order. Refer to the map on p. 2 for*
■ *further information.*

Who to contact: Walk coordinator Peter Corrigan (02) 4920 5074

22 The Benowie Walking Track

This 25 km slice of the trail leads from Thornleigh to Berowra, through Berowra Valley Regional Park. Stop off for a tasty meal with a view in one of the Berowra Waters cafes. There are 8 camping sites on this track. **Map refs:** 2 D4, 91 K6

23 The Hawkesbury Track

The Hawkesbury Track takes you 78 km from Berowra Waters to Somersby, supplying 7 camping areas along the way. It's centred around the beautiful Hawkesbury River and includes several magnificent vantage points of the region. **Map refs:** 2 D3, 91 K5

■ *This track continues through the Hunter Valley and Coast*
■ *region (see p. 17).*

24 Patonga Caravan and Camping Area

Nestled between Patonga Beach and an enticing river inlet, perfect for fishing or catching the currents on your boogie board, this serene camping area is located 25 km south of Gosford via Patonga Dr. Skirted by Brisbane Waters National Park, it's a great spot for swimming, bushwalking or whiling away lazy days to the tune of the ebb and flow of the ocean. There's a children's play area, tennis courts, amenities block and laundry in the park and a nearby general store sells the basics. An access code to enter the park is provided on payment. You can also catch a ferry here from Palm Beach. **Map refs:** 2 D4, 91 K6

How to book: Gosford Council (02) 4325 8222; or site manager (02) 4379 1287

25 Toowoon Bay Holiday Park

This well-appointed holiday park stretches along patrolled Toowoon Bay beach and is just south of The Entrance, via The Entrance Rd and Koongara St. There's an expanse of caravan and camping sites as well as cabins with killer views of the Pacific. There are 4 amenities blocks, 2 playgrounds, a pool, and a kiosk that sells the basics: groceries, ice, bait, coffee and gas refills. **Map refs:** 2 E3, 91 L5

How to book: Koongara St, Toowoon Bay (02) 4332 2834, 1800 241 342 www.toowoonbayhp.com.au

THE BLUE MOUNTAINS

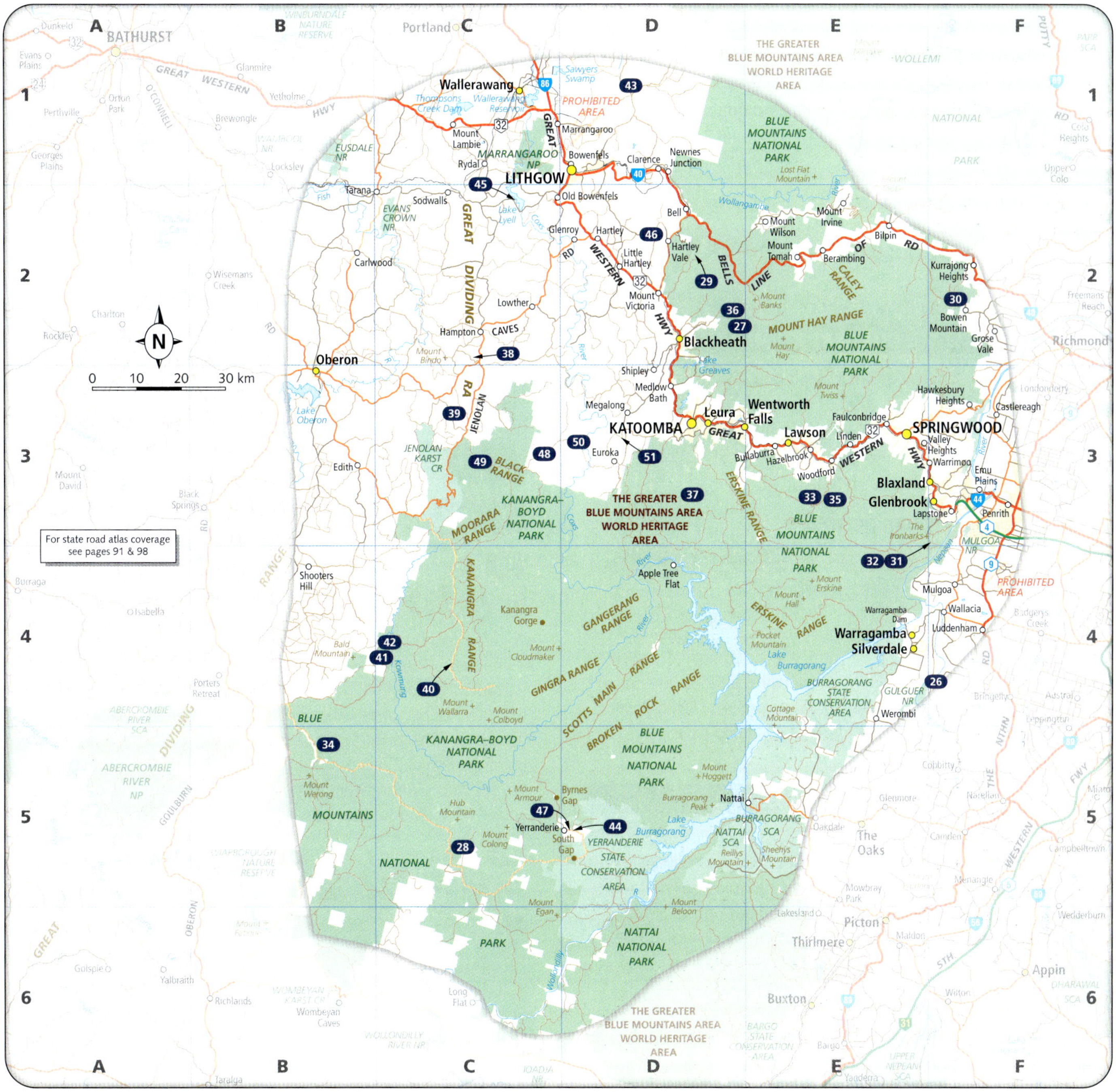

For state road atlas coverage
see pages 91 & 98

THE BLUE MOUNTAINS PRESENTS an astounding and unique landscape to its millions of visitors. The terrain ripples and folds, and there's a world of canyons, gorges and bizarre rock formations with golden sandstone breaking through a dense canopy of greenery. Waterfalls cascade from cliff-faces and a mystical blue haze – the result of permeating eucalyptus oil – hangs in the air.

Between 190 and 230 million years ago, layers of shale, coal, sandstone and claystone settled into the Sydney Basin, then 2–60 million years ago those layers were uplifted, buckling and warping to form the Blue Mountains. Over time the Grose River has gorged its way through the rock, creating the near-vertical

walls seen in Kanangra–Boyd National Park and elsewhere in the Grose Valley.

Meanwhile, underground, water has dissolved limestone and over hundreds of thousands of years created the stalactites, stalagmites and other beautiful shapes that can be found in the world-renowned Jenolan Caves. Not too far away, campers can put up a tent in Newnes State Forest and use it as a base from which to explore the caves, the Six Foot Track or the nearby glow-worm tunnel.

There is significant Aboriginal and European history woven into the Blue Mountains landscape. The region is the traditional territory of the Dharug people, and evidence of their occupation, including rock-art sites such as Red Hands Cave, dates back 14 000 years. In 1812 explorers Gregory Blaxland, William Wentworth and William Lawson forged a route across the mountains, opening up the fertile plains and mineral fields to the west. Townships emerged, railway workers settled and farmers and market gardeners set up business.

Today, this region provides almost endless opportunities for visitors to explore, walk and wonder at the scenery, climb or cycle, paddle or picnic and learn about the area's intriguing history.

CAMPSITES LOCATED IN PARKS AND RESERVES

BENTS BASIN STATE CONSERVATION AREA

Bents Basin is a waterhole that's formed in a gorge on the Nepean River, 25 km south of Penrith near Wallacia. It's a great natural swimming pool for Sydneysiders looking to escape the summer heat, and it's also a top picnicking spot.

How to book: NPWS Bents Basin (02) 4774 8662

26   Bents Basin camping area

You can get to the camping area by following Wolstenholme Ave off Greendale Rd from Wallacia. There are short walks from here to a lookout and the basin. It's well equipped and includes an amenities block with hot showers and flush toilets. Bring your own firewood; gas/fuel stove preferred. Bookings essential. **Map refs:** 7 F4, 91 J7, 98 H1

BLUE MOUNTAINS NATIONAL PARK

With wonderful walks, breathtaking views, idyllic picnic spots and many reminders of the area's Indigenous and European cultural history, this is one of Australia's most visited national parks. Call in at the Heritage Centre at Blackheath or visitor centres at Echo Point and Glenbrook for detailed information about walking tracks, camping and Discovery walks.

Who to contact: NPWS Blackheath (02) 4787 8877 for campsite nos **27**, **29**, **31**, **33**, **35**, **36**; NPWS Oberon (02) 6336 1972 for campsite nos **28**, **34**; NPWS Richmond (02) 4588 2400 for campsite nos **30**, **32**, **37** *How to book:* NPWS Richmond (02) 4588 2400 for campsite no. **32**

27   Acacia Flat camping area (walk-in camping)

This is a simply gorgeous bush camping area in Blue Gum Forest in Grose Valley. The modern conservation movement is reputed to have been born in this forest, and after a night spent sleeping beneath the majestic blue gums, you'll see why. It's a steep and strenuous walk in and out, however, and you need to be self-sufficient in gear, food and water. If you take water from the creek, boil or treat it before drinking. Note: gas/fuel stove only. **Map refs:** 7 D2, 91 I6

28   Batsh Camp camping area

One of the few camping areas in the southern end of the national park, Batsh Camp can be reached via the stunning Oberon–Colong Stock Route. Access by 2WD is possible in dry weather only. The campsite has fairly basic facilities – you'll need to bring your own drinking water and firewood, and while there are wood BBQs here, a gas/fuel stove is preferred. This is a good place to use as a base for some rugged wilderness walks. **Map refs:** 7 C5, 91 I7, 98 F1

29   Burra Korain Flat camping area (walk-in camping)

This is a walk-in bush camping site for self-sufficient walkers, reached from the Victoria Falls Lookout. It's a strenuous 6 km, 5 hr return trip, so you may as well take a tent with you and savour the experience. You can also gain access via Pierces Pass, off Bells Line of Road. Take this walk down into the Grose Valley, then cross the Grose River and head upstream for about 2 hr. The camp is at the junction of the Grose River and Victoria Creek. Boil/treat the water in the creek before you drink it, but better to bring your own, along with a gas/fuel stove. **Map refs:** 7 D2, 91 I5

30   Burralow Creek camping area

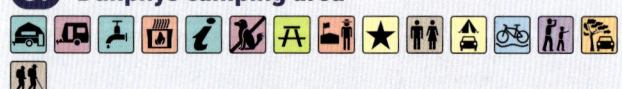

You can reach this spacious, family-friendly camping ground via a fire trail off Burralow Rd from Kurrajong Heights, or via the Patterson Range Fire Trail from Bilpin. Both these roads are 4WD only. The Bulcamatta Falls convict road (1 hr return, easy) leaves from here. The waterfall at the end of the walk cascades into a tiny box canyon, which is almost a cave. Keep your eyes peeled for the rare giant dragonfly, which zips around these parts. Bring your own firewood and drinking water. **Map refs:** 7 F2, 91 J6

31   Dunphys camping area

Located in a spectacular setting with escarpment views below Katoomba, Dunphys camping area is one of the best in the Blue Mountains. The site's openness catches the warming rays of the sun any time of year and provides spectacular sunsets. The 45 km Six Foot Track is accessed from Dunphys. You reach Dunphys via Blackheath. Coming from Sydney, turn left off the highway into Bundarra and then Station sts, right onto Shipley Rd and left onto Megalong Valley Rd. Follow for 19 km, passing through private gates (be sure to leave them as you found them). Water is limited here, so it is wise to bring your own. **Map refs:** 7 F3, 91 J6

32   Euroka Campground

This camping region, near the lovely Nepean River Gorge, can be reached via Bruce Rd in Glenbrook. It comprises 5 camping areas: Appletree Flat, Redgum, Nioka, Bennets Ridge and Durag.

Note that the access gate is locked from 6pm (7pm during daylight saving hours) to 8.30am and late arrivals will not be permitted. Bring your own firewood and drinking water, or use the tap near the ranger station. Note: you must book at least 2 weeks in advance. **Map refs:** 7 F3, 91 J6

33 Ingar Campground

At Ingar Campground you can swim or paddle in the dam on Ingar Creek, or strike out on a walking or mountain-biking track. From Wentworth Falls, take Tableland Rd and turn onto Queen Elizabeth Dr then Ingar Fire Trail. This is an unsealed road – follow it for about 9.5 km, then take the left fork. You'll need to bring your own drinking water; gas/fuel stove preferred. **Map refs:** 7 E3, 91 I6

34 Mount Werong Campground

A stone hut at this campground can be used as a cooking shelter (firewood not supplied), plus there are covered picnic tables. To get here, head south from Oberon on Shooters Hill Rd, turn left onto Gurnang Forest Rd, and left again at the Correctional Centre sign. There's a short walk from the carpark to the camping area. Bring your own drinking water, as the tank water here is limited. **Map refs:** 7 B5, 90 H7, 98 F1

35 Murphys Glen Campground

Murphys Glen Campground is tucked away among turpentine, angophora and eucalypt, 6 km south of Woodford via Bedford Rd off Railway Pde. Note that this is 4WD access only. It's a short walk from the carpark to the camping area, and there's a steep walk from here through rainforest to Bedford Creek. Fires aren't permitted, so bring your gas/fuel stove. There's water in a nearby creek, but you'll need to boil or treat it before drinking, otherwise bring your own. **Map refs:** 7 E3, 91 J6

36 Perrys Lookdown camping area

Perrys Lookdown campground has fabulous views of the Grose Valley and Mt Banks. Campers can only stay 1 night and no wood fires are permitted. It's 9 km from Blackheath via Hat Hill Rd, and there's a short walk from the carpark to the camping area. There's a smorgasbord of walking tracks to choose from in the Grose Valley below. You'll need to bring your own drinking water, and it's gas/fuel stove only. **Map refs:** 7 D2, 91 I6

37 Walk-in camping

Self-sufficient backpack walkers can camp in the national park to the south of the Great Western Hwy. Camping is not permitted within 200 m of any public access road, visitor facility or constructed walking track. Walk-in campers should take care to be sufficiently prepared for all weather, and bring plenty of food, water and good topographic maps. It's advisable to contact NPWS before setting off to register your intended route and obtain track and camping information. **Map refs:** 7 D3, 91 I6

HAMPTON STATE FOREST

Approximately 20 km east of Oberon, Hampton State Forest can be reached via Jenolan Caves Rd from the Great Western Hwy or via Duckmaloi Rd from Oberon. The forest offers good views of the Kanimbla Valley, Mt Victoria, Blackheath and Katoomba to the east and south-east.

Who to contact: Forests NSW Bathurst (02) 6331 2044

38 Millionth Acre picnic and camping area

Millionth Acre picnic area came into being in 1970, to celebrate the millionth acre of radiata pine to be planted in Australia. It's a pleasant camping site at the intersection of Jenolan Caves Rd and Oberon (Duckmaloi) Rd, 4 km south of Hampton and 33 km south of the Great Western Hwy. **Map refs:** 7 C2, 91 I6

JENOLAN STATE FOREST

It's about 15 km from Jenolan State Forest to the ethereal, world-renowned Jenolan Caves, which are dusted with astonishing stalactite and stalagmite formations. Jenolan Caves itself has no camping area; the state forest offers one of the closest. The native and pine forests here are also very popular with trail-bike riders.

Who to contact: Forests NSW Bathurst (02) 6331 2044

39 Jenolan camping area

Take the Jenolan Caves turn-off from the Great Western Hwy about 10 km past Hartley. The camping ground is another 20 km along the Jenolan Caves Rd. This is no longer maintained by Forests NSW as a designated camping ground, so facilities have been removed. Bring your own everything. **Map refs:** 7 C3, 91 I6

KANANGRA–BOYD NATIONAL PARK

Stunning views and remote walks are just some of the features of this mountainous park, much of which is declared wilderness. It's a majestic landscape of wild rivers, waterfalls and deep gorges rimmed by national park and state forests. The grand sandstone terrain is part of the Greater Blue Mountains World Heritage Area.

Who to contact: NPWS Blackheath (02) 4787 8877; or NPWS Oberon (02) 6336 1972

40 Boyd River camping area

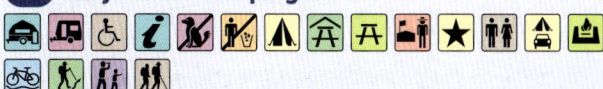

Boyd River camping area, set among snow gums, is accessible by 2WD but is subject to extreme weather and snowfalls. A highlight of camping here is the wildlife – at night gliders, brushtail possums, tawny frogmouths, wombats, red-necked wallabies and eastern grey kangaroos come out to feed. Access is via Kanangra Walls Rd, 20 km south of Jenolan Caves Rd. Some of the campsites are a short walk from the carpark. There is a shelter here built from reclaimed timber from the Sydney wharves; it has a large stone fireplace and is a welcome break from inclement weather. A few kilometres further down the road are the Kanangra Walls where there are walks out on to the plateau, taking in sensational views over the surrounding valleys. A short but steep trail also heads down to Kalang Falls. Bring firewood or a gas/fuel stove. **Map refs:** 7 C4, 91 I7, 98 F1

41 Dingo Dell camping area

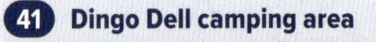

Dingo Dell campground, on Tuglow Hole Creek, has 14 tent sites and can only be reached by 4WD. To get here, follow Kowmung River Fire Trail from Kanangra Walls Rd or Banshea Rd. Consider avoiding the road altogether in wet weather: the trail is exceptionally steep in places and environmental damage to it can be considerable. There is also access from the west via fire trails to the Oberon–Goulburn Rd. Bring your own firewood or gas/fuel stove. **Map refs:** 7 C4, 90 H7, 98 F1

42 Kowmung Wild River camping area (walk-in camping)

This is a campsite for self-sufficient walkers only, 500 m downstream from the carpark at Kowmung River Fire Trail. Note: the access road is 4WD only. There's water in the creek but you'll need to boil or treat it before drinking; gas/fuel stove preferred. **Map refs:** 7 C4, 90 H7, 98 F1

NEWNES STATE FOREST

Newnes State Forest is a conglomeration of native forest and pine plantations adjacent to Blue Mountains, Wollemi and Gardens of Stone national parks. Access is from the south via State Mine Hill Rd from Lithgow or via Newnes Forest Rd from the Zig Zag Railway (accessible with 2WD in dry weather only).

Who to contact: Forests NSW Bathurst (02) 6331 2044

43 Bungleboori camping area

Bungleboori is predominantly a stop-off point for those driving through the state forest on their way to the impressive Glow Worm Tunnel or Gardens of Stone National Park. It's a pleasant spot amid towering pines, with walking tracks through rainforest nearby. To get here, turn off the Bells Line of Road at Clarence and follow the gravel road through Newnes State Forest. Note: the road is difficult to navigate at times – it's 2WD in dry weather only. Bring your own drinking water, and a gas/fuel stove Oct–Mar. **Map refs:** 7 D1, 91 I5

CAMPSITES LOCATED IN OTHER AREAS

44 Government Town camping area

Government Town camping area is in Yerranderie, a unique, NPWS-owned ghost town restored from its 1900s heyday, when it had a booming population of 3000 people. The town is on the edge of Blue Mountains National Park, so it's in spectacular

company, and access is via the Old Oberon–Colong Stock Route, a fabulous scenic drive in its own right. There's no firewood or drinking water at the campground, and a gas/fuel stove is preferred. **Map refs:** 7 D5, 91 I7, 98 G1

Who to contact: NPWS Yerranderie (02) 4659 6165

45 Lake Lyell camping area

Lake Lyell is a large water-storage area serving the dual purpose of supplying 2 nearby power stations and providing fabulous recreational opportunities to visitors. Swimming, fishing, waterskiing and paddling are just a few of the activities on offer. There are coin-operated showers and a kiosk where you can purchase firewood. **Map refs:** 7 C2, 91 I5

Who to contact: (02) 6355 6347

46 Lockyers Trackhead camping area (walk-in camping)

If you're a walker with a penchant for European history, you can follow part of the original route across the Blue Mountains on the Lawsons Long Alley and Lockyers Loop Rd (4 hr, 11 km return), setting out from either Mt York Rd in the town of Mount Victoria, or Hartley Vale. Keep an eye out for remnants of the original road. Lockyers Trackhead is midway between Hartley Vale and Collits Inn – it's walk-in only. **Map refs:** 7 D2, 91 I5

Who to contact: Lithgow Visitor Information Centre (02) 6350 3230, 1300 760 276

47 Private Town camping area

This camping area is situated, as its name implies, in a private town: Yerranderie, a restored silver-mining village that once rang with the voices of 3000 residents. The campground is well equipped – there's a camp kitchen with fridge, as well as toilets, hot showers and an undercover eating area with firewood and drinking water. Tours of Yerranderie can be arranged. **Map refs:** 7 D5, 91 I7, 98 G1

Who to contact: NPWS Yerranderie (02) 4659 6165

Six Foot Track

The Six Foot Track was established in the late 1880s as a bridle trail to convey tourists to Jenolan Caves from Katoomba. Today, it's a popular bushwalking track – walkers generally take 2–3 days to complete the 45 km route, beginning at the Explorers Tree, 2.5 km west of Katoomba, and ending at Jenolan Caves House. Once a year it hosts the Six Foot Track Marathon to raise money for the Rural Fire Service and the Six Foot Track Heritage Trust.

Please note that campsites are listed in alphabetical order, not track order. Refer to the map on p. 7 for further information.

Who to contact: Six Foot Track Heritage Trust (02) 6391 4306

Campsite along the Six Foot Track (p. 10)

48 **Alum Creek camping area (walk-in camping)**

This walk-in site is 22 km from the trackhead. Carry drinking water, and a gas/fuel stove is preferred. **Map refs:** 7 C3, 91 I6

49 **Black Range camping area (walk-in camping)**

A walk-in campsite 34.7 km from the trackhead. Campfires are not permitted, gas/fuel stove only. Carry in drinking water. **Map refs:** 7 C3, 91 I6

50 **Coxs River camping area (walk-in camping)**

At 15.5 km from the trackhead, you need to carry in drinking water to this walk-in campsite; gas/fuel stove preferred. This site is in a pleasant clearing above Coxs River. There is a swing bridge giving access to the trail upriver from here, or a ford just downriver. It is 15.5 km from the Explorers Tree and 7 km from where the trail crosses Megalong Rd. **Map refs:** 7 D3, 91 I6

51 **Old Ford Reserve camping area (walk-in camping)**

This is a flat, grassed camping area on Megalong Creek, about 500 m south of the Six Foot Track crossing with Megalong Rd. It's a little more than 8 km from the trackhead. There are toilets here, as well as good swimming holes. **Map refs:** 7 D3, 91 I6

HUNTER VALLEY AND COAST

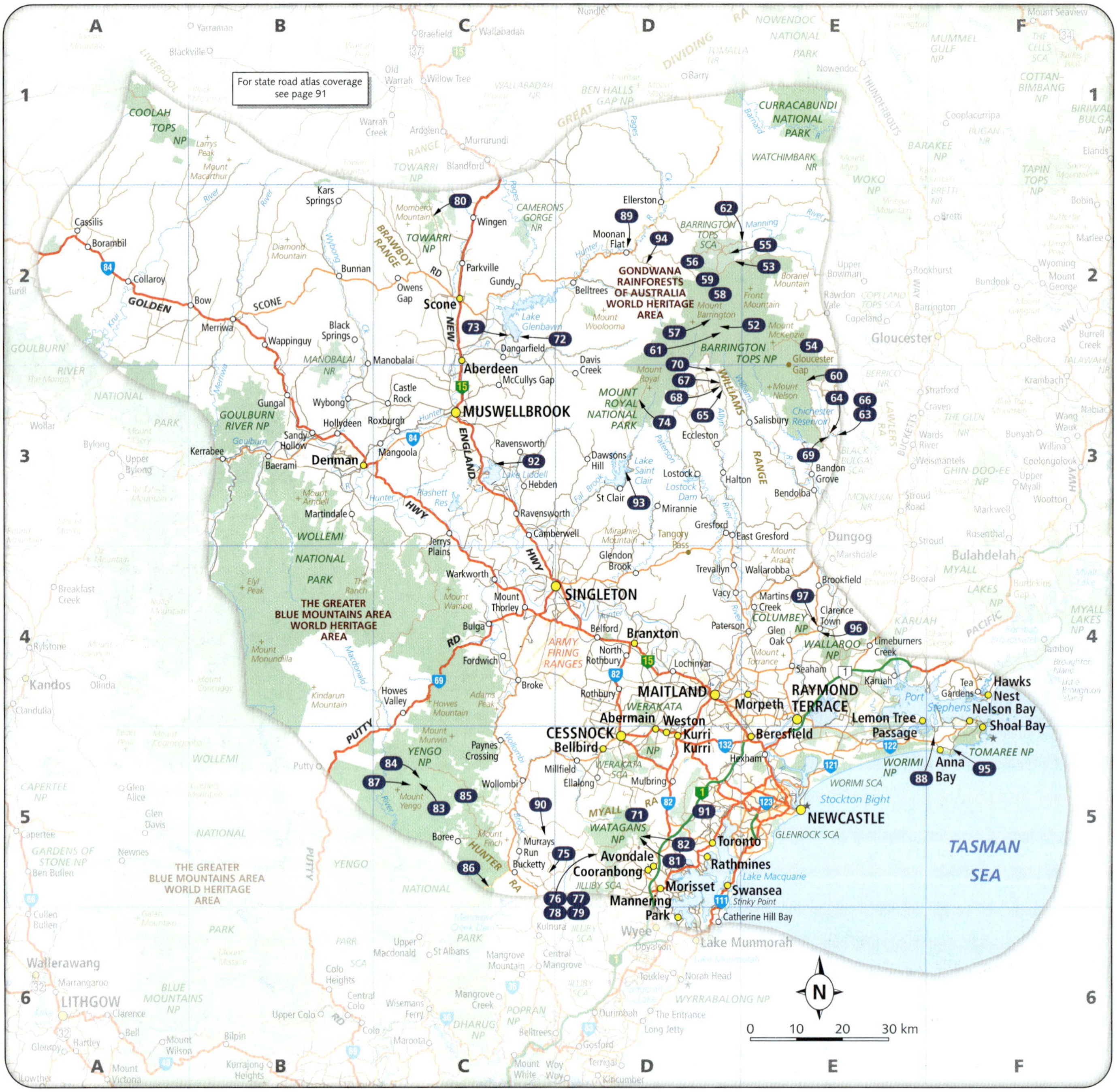

THERE'S SUCH A SMORGASBORD of landscapes and activities on offer in this region that your greatest difficulty will be deciding what 'dish' to tuck into. Barrington Tops National Park is a veritable *Lord of the Rings* landscape in Australia, with its magnificent forest-clad mountain peaks swathed in mist, eucalypt woodlands ringing with birdsong, plunging waterfalls and sun-filtered subtropical rainforests. Equally stunning is the dramatic sandstone country of Yengo National Park, where you can gaze upon Aboriginal rock engravings one day and walk along the convict-built Old Great North Rd the next.

You can bring your family and the dog on a fishing and swimming holiday on the banks of Telegherry or Allyn rivers in Chichester State Forest, or relax in the tranquil setting of historic Clarence Town, by Williams River. If you have a hankering for a bit of watersports action, such as sailing, waterskiing or boating, head for Lake Glenbawn, Lake Liddell or Lake St Clair, where you'll find comfortable camping accommodation and plenty of activities for the whole family.

For those who like to taste nature's wilder side, Towarri National Park offers an authentic, pristine environment where experienced walkers can explore the rugged landscape, steep hills and summits of the Liverpool Range.

Whether you've got an appetite for fishing, hiking, swimming, mountain-biking, birdwatching or just relaxing by a beautiful waterhole, the Hunter Valley and coast has all the ingredients for your perfect outdoor getaway – and it's all within easy access of Sydney and Newcastle.

CAMPSITES LOCATED IN PARKS AND RESERVES

BARRINGTON TOPS NATIONAL PARK

With its moss-cloaked, Tolkien-esque woodlands, subtropical rainforests, dramatic gorges, and wild thundering rivers, this World Heritage–listed wonderland ranges from near sea level to almost 1600 m. It's the ultimate destination for outdoor enthusiasts, with an endless choice of walking and cycling tracks, fishing and swimming holes, scenic drives and camping sites.

Who to contact: NPWS Scone (02) 6540 2300 for campsite nos **55**, **56**, **59**; or NPWS Gloucester (02) 6538 5300 for campsite nos **52**, **53**, **54**, **57**, **58**, **60**, **61**

52 **Black Swamp camping area (walk-in camping, northern section)**

The 2.6 km walk to this campground along Aeroplane Hill Track from Junction Pools will take you through beautiful montane forest alive with crimson rosellas to the highest large subalpine wetland in the area (1500 m). This is a bush campsite for self-sufficient walkers. **Map refs:** 12 D2, 91 L1, 93 I12

53 **Devils Hole camping area (northern section)**

It's a case of better the devil you know at this simple campground, on Barrington Tops Forest Rd, west of the Dilgry Circle Rd turn-off. With its lofty 1400 m vantage point, it's all about the views: spectacular subalpine forest, picturesque farmland at the foothills, and Devils Hole Lookout just across the road. At the lookout are picnic facilities, toilets and fireplaces; bring your own firewood and drinking water.
Map refs: 12 D2, 91 L1, 93 I12

54 **Gloucester River camping area (eastern section)**

There's a bit of everything available here, including walking tracks, swimming holes and plenty of wildlife. One of the few camping grounds in the east of the park, it lies 38 km south-west of Gloucester on Gloucester Tops Rd. A short drive away is Gloucester Tops, the starting point for a number of additional walking trails. There are 2 walks from the camping area itself: along Sharpes Creek and another along the Gloucester River. The wildlife that frequents the clearing here includes red-necked

pademelons, brush turkeys and lyrebirds. If you don't bring your own drinking water, boil or treat river water before use, and bring your own firewood. **Map refs:** 12 E2, 91 M1, 93 J12

55 **Gummi Falls camping area (northern section)**

Escape the caravanning brigade at this dry-weather, 4WD or walk-in campsite, set next to a small cascade 2.8 km along Bullock Brush Rd (via Tubrabucca Rd from the west). You'll need to bring your own firewood, stove and drinking water.
Map refs: 12 D2, 91 L1, 93 I12

56 **Horse Swamp camping area (northern section)**

This secluded site is tucked away 150 m to the south of Polblue Falls picnic area and Polblue Falls walk. Access is off Tubrabucca Rd, 2.3 km north-east of Barrington Tops Forest Rd. Bring your own firewood, stove and drinking water.
Map refs: 12 D2, 91 L1, 93 I12

57 **Junction Pools camping area (northern section)**

You'll be spoilt for choice at this campground, off Barrington Trail, 12 km south of Barrington Tops Forest Rd. Dip a toe or a fishing line into the Barrington River, strike out on one of several nearby walking tracks, or use it as a base for a spot of scenic drive touring. There are car-based sites here as well as some walk-in sites down the hill close to the river. A pleasant walk goes from here around Edwards Swamp and on to Careys Peak's expansive views. There is also the Aeroplane Hill Track, which goes to Black Swamp walk-in camping area. Mountain-biking on the fire trails can be fun, with access back to the Scone–Gloucester Rd, or on up to Mt Barrington. Bring firewood, gas/fuel stove and drinking water. Note: 4WD access only, closed to vehicles June–Sept. **Map refs:** 12 D2, 91 L1, 93 I12

58 **Little Murray camping area (northern section)**

This is a dry-weather, 4WD or walk-in access campground, closed to all vehicles June–Sept. It is a pleasant and secluded campsite at the end of the road, surrounded by snow gums. You'll find it 5 km south of Barrington Tops Forest Rd, 800 m south-east of Barrington Trail. Bring firewood, gas/fuel stove and drinking water. **Map refs:** 12 D2, 91 L1, 93 I12

59 **Polblue camping area (northern section)**

A late-afternoon or early-morning walk around the high-altitude swamp amid soaring snow gums is an experience that will remain with you long after you leave this spacious campground. It's along Barrington Tops Forest Rd, 68 km west of Gloucester and 16 km west of the Dilgry Circle Rd turn-off. It can also be accessed from the west via Scone and Moonan Flat. It is a great base from which to explore the Barrington Plateau, being central to many of the features, trails and walks. There is a shelter with a fireplace, which is pleasant on the frequent cold nights encountered at this high altitude. There's water in the creek, but it needs to be treated or boiled before it's safe to use. Bring your own firewood and gas/fuel stove. **Map refs:** 12 D2, 91 L1, 93 I12

60 Walk-in camping areas

Scattered throughout the park are established walk-in bush campsites with no facilities. These are for self-sufficient walkers carrying good topographic maps, their own drinking water and, preferably, a gas/fuel stove. **Map refs:** 12 E3, 91 M2

61 Wombat Creek Campground (walk-in camping, northern section)

A challenging but rewarding destination only for fit, experienced and well-prepared bushwalkers. It can be accessed via the Corker Trail (Lagoon Pinch to Careys Peak), a 20 km, 10 hr return walk; or the Link Trail (Gloucester Tops to Careys Peak), a 34 km, 10–12 hr return walk. Good topographic maps are necessary for both tracks, and you need to bring drinking water with you. When you reach the junction of the 2 trails, walk east for 1 km then turn left – the campground is a short walk from here. **Map refs:** 12 D2, 91 L1, 93 I12

BARRINGTON TOPS STATE FOREST

Perched on the northern boundary of Barrington Tops National Park, the state forest of the same name offers a swag of extra outdoor activities, including 4WD touring, mountain-biking and horseriding. This is a remote area, so bring good maps and come prepared for the highly changeable weather so typical of high-altitude regions.

Who to contact: Forests NSW Central region (02) 6585 3744, 1300 655 687

62 Manning River camping area

The trout in Manning River beckon: turn off Dilgry Circle Rd onto Pheasant Creek Rd, 15 km west of the junction of Dilgry Circle and Barrington Tops Forest rds. The scenic Manning River flows past the camping area, which is surrounded by cool temperate rainforest and tree ferns. Note: bring firewood and drinking water, or boil or treat the river water before use. **Map refs:** 12 E2, 91 L1, 93 J12

CHICHESTER STATE FOREST

To the south of Barrington Tops National Park is Chichester State Forest, which attracts family campers and those who want a bit more freedom for their dog, trail-bike or 4WD. It's divided into 2 distinct areas: to the west is the Allyn River section and to the east is the Telegherry River section.

Who to contact: Forests NSW Central region (02) 6585 3744, 1300 655 687

63 Coachwood camping area

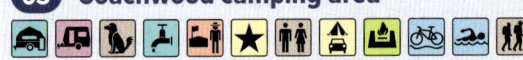

This is a cracker of a campsite next to Telegherry River, with a welcoming swimming hole as well as a 2 km return walking track to Problem Creek Falls. With dry-weather access only for 2WD vehicles, it's off Frying Pan Rd, about 2.3 km east of Middle Ridge Rd. Bring your own firewood and drinking water, or boil/treat water from the river. **Map refs:** 12 E3, 91 M2

64 Currawong camping area

This camping area is 4WD, dry-weather access only, as you need to cross Telegherry River via Telegherry Forest Park camping area on Middle Ridge Rd. It's closed in winter during the wetter months. It's possible to bring your off-road trailer, as long as the river level isn't too high. Bring your own firewood and drinking water, or boil/treat water from the river. **Map refs:** 12 E3, 91 M2

65 Dobbie Rim camping area

The spacious, grassy clearing here is ideal for families or groups. It's in the Allyn River section, at the southern limits of the forest, on Allyn River Rd. The best way to get onto this road is via Salisbury Gap Rd, which heads west from Salisbury, 31 km north-west of Dungog. Bring your own drinking water, or boil/treat water from the creek. **Map refs:** 12 D3, 91 L2

66 Frying Pan Creek camping area

A picturesque campsite on the banks of Telegherry River, this is a particularly popular spot for mountain-bikers. Note: dry-weather access only for 2WDs. Bring your own firewood and drinking water, or boil/treat water from the river. **Map refs:** 12 E3, 91 M2

67 Old Camp camping area

Travel a little further north from Dobbie Rim, along Allyn River Rd, and you'll reach Old Camp. The closest camping area to Allyn River, it provides spacious, shaded sites. Make sure you boil or treat water from the creek before drinking. There's a delightful swimming spot called Ladies Well close by, with a small waterfall and beautiful, deep pools. Allyn River Rd is reached via Salisbury Gap Rd, west of Salisbury. **Map refs:** 12 D3, 91 L2

68 Pademelon Park camping area

With its large, sheltered sites cordoned off with trees, this area in the Allyn River section is recommended for camping groups who don't wish to disturb other visitors. It's north of Dobbie Rim and Old Camp, and as at those sites you need to bring along your own drinking water or treat the river water before it can be used. **Map refs:** 12 D3, 91 L2

69 Telegherry Forest Park camping area

From this large grassed area on the banks of Telegherry River, you can go for a swim, bushwalk or bike ride, or take a look at the old logging machinery situated at the turn-off from Wangat Rd onto Middle Ridge Rd. The camping area is signposted along Middle Ridge Rd, and is dry-weather access only for 2WDs. It's closed in winter during the wetter months. Bring your own firewood and water for drinking; alternatively, you can boil or treat river water. **Map refs:** 12 E3, 91 M2

70 White Rock camping area

You can get here by either following Allyn River Rd north from Dobbie Rim camping area, or following Salisbury Rd north from Salisbury and turning onto Williams Top Rd. Bring drinking water, or boil/treat creek water. **Map refs:** 12 D3, 91 L2

HEATON STATE FOREST

Freed English convict and timber-cutter Richard Heaton gave his name to this forest. Today it offers visitors fabulous views of the coast from Newcastle to Lake Macquarie. It's adjacent to Watagan and Awaba state forests and Watagans National Park.

Who to contact: Forests NSW Central region (02) 6585 3744, 1300 655 687

71 Watagan Headquarters camping area

Once a forest workers' camp, this is now a quiet, grassy area ringed with protective native forest and blue-leaved stringybark. You'll find it off Watagan Rd, 3 km north of Watagan Forest Rd. Bring your own drinking water. **Map refs:** 12 D5, 91 L4

LAKE GLENBAWN STATE PARK

Fishing, birdwatching, bushwalking and watersports are all magnets for the families and nature lovers who flock to the shores of Lake Glenbawn – not to mention the beautiful setting. On the Hunter River 20 km east of Scone, Lake Glenbawn can be accessed from Aberdeen via Rouchel Rd. If you're coming from Scone, travel via Gundy Rd.

Who to contact: Lake Glenbawn Recreation Area, Eastern Foreshore Rd, Scone (02) 6543 7193

72 Lake Glenbawn camping area

The main camping area for Lake Glenbawn State Park is on the lake's eastern shore. There are also bungalows and cabins, a boat ramp, children's playground, and even archery. Other activities include canoeing, fishing, boating and waterskiing. A kiosk on this side of the lake sells basic grocery items. **Map refs:** 12 C2, 91 K1, 92 H12

73 Lake Glenbawn caravan park

This lake is camping paradise – you'll find everything you could possibly ask for here. The caravan park is on the western foreshore, near the tennis courts and golf course. There are tent sites here as well, but the main camping area is on the eastern shore. **Map refs:** 12 C2, 91 K1, 92 H12

MOUNT ROYAL NATIONAL PARK

Declared over former state forest in 1996, Mt Royal National Park, 50 km north of Singleton, protects a swathe of rainforest harbouring a number of rare and threatened animals, including the rufous scrub bird and the parma wallaby. The park, including the 40 km scenic drive along Mt Royal Rd, is suitable for 4WD vehicles only, and becomes inaccessible after rain.

Who to contact: NPWS Bulga (02) 6574 5555

74 Youngville camping area

On Mt Royal Rd, this camping area has 4WD dry-weather access only. From here, you can take the 5 km return hike down to Carrow Brook. If you're travelling north from Singleton, turn right off the New England Hwy onto Bridgeman Rd, which turns on to Mt Royal Rd. Bring your own firewood. There's a water tank, but the water needs to be boiled or treated before drinking, so you might prefer to bring drinking water with you. Note: it's generally 10°C colder here than on the valley floor. **Map refs:** 12 D3, 91 L2

OLNEY STATE FOREST

Forested and user-friendly, Olney State Forest is west of Lake Macquarie, bordered by Wyong and Watagan state forests, and Watagans National Park. Bushwalking, waterfalls, wildflowers and swimming holes are just a few reasons why this is such a popular recreation area.

Who to contact: Forests NSW Central region (02) 6585 3744, 1300 655 687

75 The Basin camping area (walk-in camping)

The Basin is open and grassy, and you can swim in the creek here if it's warm enough. The Rock Lily Walking Trail starts here – a pleasant trip through eucalypt forest, rocky overhangs and rainforest gullies. The camping ground is on Walkers Ridge Forest Rd, 8 km east of The Letter A on George Downes Dr. There's water in the creek, but you'll need to boil or treat it before drinking or bring your own. **Map refs:** 12 C5, 91 K4

76 Casuarina camping area

No prizes for guessing what trees you'll be surrounded by at this camping area, but wait until you hear the music the wind makes when it brushes through the casuarina leaves. This is a good spot for large groups as well as individual campers – you'll find signs along Watagan Forest Rd, 400 m from the junction of Watagan Forest and Walkers Ridge Forest rds. Boil or treat creek water before drinking or bring your own. **Map refs:** 12 D5, 91 L4

77 Olney Headquarters camping area

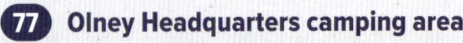

On Watagan Forest Rd, Olney Headquarters is ideal for a night's stay under a canopy of green. Bring drinking water and wood for the fire. **Map refs:** 12 D5, 91 L4

78 The Pines camping area

A nice shaded area under – you guessed it – pine trees, this is the starting point for several walks including Abbotts Falls Trail and the Pines Trail. Follow the signs along Watagan Forest Rd, 300 m north of the junction of Watagan Forest and Walkers Ridge Forest rds. Bring your own water or boil or treat the creek water before drinking. **Map refs:** 12 D5, 45 F3, 91 L4, 92 F11

79 Turpentine camping area

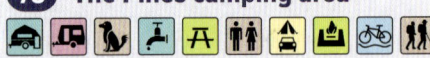

This is only 100 m from Casuarina camping area, and provides secluded camping sites that are perfect for small groups and families. Boil or treat water from the creek before drinking it or bring your own. **Map refs:** 12 D5, 91 L4

TOWARRI NATIONAL PARK

Towarri National Park, 25 km north-west of Scone, straddles the southern slopes of the Liverpool Range. It's a fascinating, rugged world of sandstone outcrops and dramatic mountain scenery peppered with abundant wildlife. Its relative newness makes it an attractive option for those looking for a more authentic natural experience.

Who to contact: NPWS Scone (02) 6540 2300; or NPWS Nelson Bay (02) 4984 8200 *Camping fees:* fees payable using self-registration

80 Washpools camping area

This secluded camping area is spacious, well shaded and good for families. You'll need to cross Middlebrook Creek to get here – there's a concrete causeway to make things easier, but flooding may occur after heavy rain, so keep an eye on the weather. Drive 13 km north from Scone on the New England Hwy and turn on to Cressfield Rd, then on to Middlebrook Rd. The campsite is 4 km north. While there are no official walking tracks, a wander along the banks of Middlebrook Creek when the water is low is worthwhile, with some interesting, eroded rock formations along the way. Bring your own drinking water. **Map refs:** 12 C2, 91 K1, 92 H12

WATAGANS NATIONAL PARK

Perched on Newcastle's doorstep, 30 km to the south-west, this rainforested wonderland protects the headwaters of small creeks feeding the Hunter River and Lake Macquarie. There are unpaved roads from Cooranbong via Martinsville Rd, Freemans Waterhole via Mt Faulk Rd or Cessnock via Watagan Rd. If the roads are wet, you'll need a 4WD.

Who to contact: NPWS Lake Munmorah (02) 4972 9000

81 Bangalow Road camping area

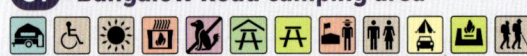

As its name suggests, you'll find this on Bangalow Rd, 3.8 km from the Mt Faulk Rd intersection, amid majestic blue gum and blackbutt forest. There are wood BBQs, although you'll need to bring your own firewood, and gas/fuel stoves are preferred. Bring your own water. **Map refs:** 12 D5, 91 L4

82 Gap Creek camping area

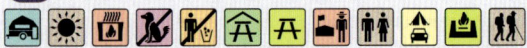

To get here, continue along Bangalow Rd for 1 km past Bangalow Road camping area. Bring your own firewood; gas/fuel stove preferred. Gap Creek is situated near 2 rainforest walks, one of which wends its way beneath red cedar and Illawarra flame trees to Gap Creek Falls, where you can gaze out at luxuriant rainforest gullies. Other highlights in the park include Monkey Face Lookout and Boarding House Dam. Bring drinking water. **Map refs:** 12 D5, 91 L4

YENGO NATIONAL PARK

Part of the Greater Blue Mountains World Heritage Area, Yengo National Park is a rich tapestry of rugged natural beauty, and Indigenous and European heritage. There's no shortage of ways to savour it, from 4WD touring to bushwalking, mountain-biking and horseriding (in the southern part of the park).

How to book: NPWS Central Coast (02) 4320 4203

83 Big Yango Homestead

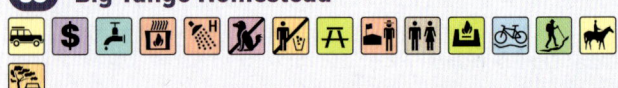

This sprawling homestead sleeps 9 people (with another 5 beds in an adjacent cottage), and supplies 240V power, hot showers, a wood fireplace and cooking equipment. There's a smorgasbord of things to do here, including bushwalking around Mt Yengo, horseriding, mountain-biking, 4WD touring, birdwatching and wildlife-spotting. The homestead is in the Big Yango Precinct, so you'll need to contact the parks office to get access through the locked gate; 2 weeks' advance booking and payment required. Note: 4WD access only. **Map refs:** 12 C5, 91 K4

84 Blue Gums camping area

This large camping area can accommodate large groups of up to 100 people as well as conventional vehicle-based campers. In Big Yango Precinct off Howes Valley Trail, 14 km west of Finchley Trig, the campsite can only be accessed via a locked

gate – contact the parks office for details. It's best if you have a 4WD vehicle, although conventional vehicles can make it here with care during dry weather. Bring drinking water; 2 weeks' advance booking and payment required. **Map refs:** 12 C5, 91 K4

85 Finchley camping area

A smaller site on the Yango Track, this is a great base for 4WD touring (check with NPWS for track details), and is only a 200 m walk to the Finchley Aboriginal Area. To get here from Wollombi and Laguna, follow the Yango Creek Rd, then take the Upper Creek Rd to the Finchley Track. Bring your own firewood or gas/fuel stove and water. Advance booking and payment preferred. **Map refs:** 12 C5, 91 K4

86 Mogo Creek Campground

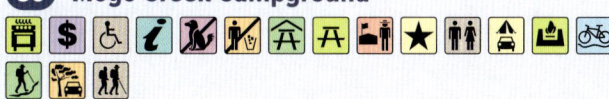

If you're a bit of a history buff, this is the campsite for you. It's situated on the Old Great North Rd, built using convict labour over a decade from 1825. Near here is the Circuit Flat Bridge, constructed in 1832. If coming here from Wisemans Ferry you will pass through St Albans, with its historic pub, and to the north is Bucketty, and more interesting remnants of the Old Great North Rd. You can explore the road on foot; alternatively, you can take a trip into historic Macdonald Valley, the majority of which was settled in the 1800s by convicts and their families. **Map refs:** 12 C5, 91 K4

87 Mountain Arm camping area

Mountain Arm is also in the Big Yango Precinct, so you'll need to pick up a key from the parks office to get through the gate. Once through, you'll reach Big Yango Homestead; turn left and you'll find the camping area. Bring your own drinking water; 2 weeks' advance booking and payment required. **Map refs:** 12 C5, 91 K4

CAMPSITES LOCATED IN OTHER AREAS

88 Bays Holiday Park

You can camp in style at this well-appointed caravan park on the Tomaree Peninsula in classy Port Stephens. As well as caravan and tent sites, there are 1- and 2-bedroom cabins and bunkhouse rooms sleeping 4 in each room. There's a camp kitchen, an amenities block and undercover BBQs, while a kiosk selling basic items is open during holidays. On top of all that, you're surrounded by the attractions of Port Stephens, which range from shopping and topnotch restaurants to fabulous beaches and outdoor activities. The park is off Nelson Bay Rd, on Port Stephens Dr in Anna Bay. **Map refs:** 12 F5, 91 M4

How to book: 23 Port Stephens Dr, Anna Bay (02) 4982 1438 www.baysholidaypark.com

89 Belmadar camping area

This comfortable camping ground is located in the picturesque town of Moonan Flat, on the Hunter River 50 km north-east of Scone. You can while away the hours fishing and swimming, and in the afternoon pop into the Victoria Hotel next door for a cold beer. **Map refs:** 12 D2, 91 L1, 93 I12

Who to contact: (02) 6546 3130

Great North Walk

If you're passionate about getting to know NSW – its bushland, rural and urban settings – then the Great North Walk is for you. Stretching for 250 km from Sydney to Newcastle, the track can be covered in its entirety in 10–14 days. The track is divided into 4 sections, but the possibilities are endless.

Please note that campsites are listed in alphabetical order, not track order. Refer to the map on p. 12 for further information.

Who to contact: Walk coordinator Peter Corrigan (02) 4920 5074

90 The Cedar Brush Walk

Beginning in Somersby and ending 61 km later at Flat Rock Lookout, this section of the Great North Walk includes 8 camping areas and takes in Jilliby State Conservation Area, farmland and Olney State Forest. **Map refs:** 12 C5, 91 K4

91 The Watagan Track

This 61 km track from Flat Rock takes you through rural farmland and Awaba State Forest, past the Sugerloaf Range and on to the town of Teralba on Lake Macquarie. There are 3 camping areas on this stretch, and accommodation at either end. **Map refs:** 12 D5, 91 L4

This track continues through the Central Coast and Hawkesbury region (see p. 6).

92 Lake Liddell Recreation Area camping area

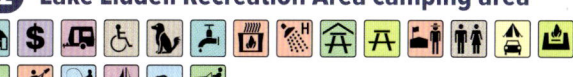

On a practical level, 1133 ha Lake Liddell supplies cooling water to 2 nearby power stations; on a recreational level, it's a haven for watersports, birdwatching, canoeing, boating, walking and fishing. It's approximately 15 km south of Muswellbrook. To get here, turn off the New England Hwy onto Hebden Rd and follow the signs. **Map refs:** 12 C3, 91 K2

Who to contact: (02) 6541 2010

93 Lake St Clair camping area

Nestled in the foothills of Mt Royal National Park, 25 km north of Singleton, picturesque Lake St Clair is about 16 km long and

Monkey Face Lookout, Watagans National Park (p. 16)

has a storage capacity of 283 megalitres – almost half that of Sydney Harbour. It's named for St Clair homestead, which was lost beneath the water upon the completion of Glennies Creek Dam in 1983. Ringed with vineyards and rolling green pastures, the lake provides myriad outdoor activities including fishing, boating, sailing and waterskiing. The camping area is on the lake's eastern shores, on Bridgman Rd off the New England Hwy. **Map refs:** 12 D3, 91 L2

Who to contact: (02) 6577 3370

94 Moonan Brook Forestry Cottage

This former 1800s schoolhouse in Moonan Brook, 3 km east of Moonan Flat, has been transformed into a comfortable cottage and bunkhouse sleeping up to 25 people. If your group is larger, there's space for tents in the grounds next to the cottage. The house includes a laundry, 2 bathrooms, a well-equipped kitchen, wood and gas BBQs, lounge room with fireplace, tank for drinking water, and septic and pit toilets. If you're coming from the west, follow Moonan Brook Rd from Moonan Flat; if travelling from the east, take Barrington Tops Forest Rd from Gloucester through Barrington Tops National Park. Bookings are essential. **Map refs:** 12 D2, 91 L1, 93 I12

How to book: Moonan Forestry Cottage Manager (02) 6546 3173 www.moonan-brook-cottage.com.au

95 One Mile Beach Holiday Park

Tucked in behind the crystalline sands of One Mile Beach, this holiday park includes over 4 ha of native bushland and sits adjacent to Tomaree National Park, which is scribbled with walking tracks. It's a 10 min drive from the tourist hub of Nelson Bay along Gan Gan Rd. You can stay in beachside apartments, villas or family beach houses, and there are caravan and tent sites. There's also a pool with waterslide, a heated spa,

minigolf, a tennis court, a games room and chatty resident birds! **Map refs:** 12 F5, 91 M4

How to book: 426 Gan Gan Rd, One Mile Beach (Port Stephens) 1800 650 035 www.onemilebeach.com.au

96 Wharf Reserve camping area

Ah, the serenity. Watch the sun set over the beautiful, tree-lined Williams River in historic Clarence Town, an old shipbuilding township 200 km north of Sydney and 50 km north of Newcastle. Coming from the south, take Clarence Town Rd from Raymond Terrace; from the east take Limeburners Creek Rd, which turns off Bucketts Way 5 km north of the Pacific Hwy. Find Queen St in Clarence Town and turn onto Rifle St. Note: no power; bring your own firewood. Bookings recommended, particularly during peak periods. **Map refs:** 12 E4, 91 M3

How to book: Williams River Holiday Park caretaker (02) 4996 4231

97 Williams River Holiday Park

This extensive and well-equipped holiday park in Clarence Town provides a range of accommodation styles, from tent-based camping to air-conditioned cabins. Clarence Town was an important trading port in the 1800s; today, the main action the river sees is swimming, fishing, boating, sailing and waterskiing. Bring your own firewood, and note that the park's gates close at 6.30pm in winter and 8pm in summer. To get here from the south, take Clarence Town Rd from Raymond Terrace; from the east take Limeburners Creek Rd, which turns off Bucketts Way 5 km north of the Pacific Hwy. Bookings recommended, particularly during peak periods. **Map refs:** 12 E4, 91 M3

How to book: Durham St, Clarence Town (02) 4996 4231

HOLIDAY COAST

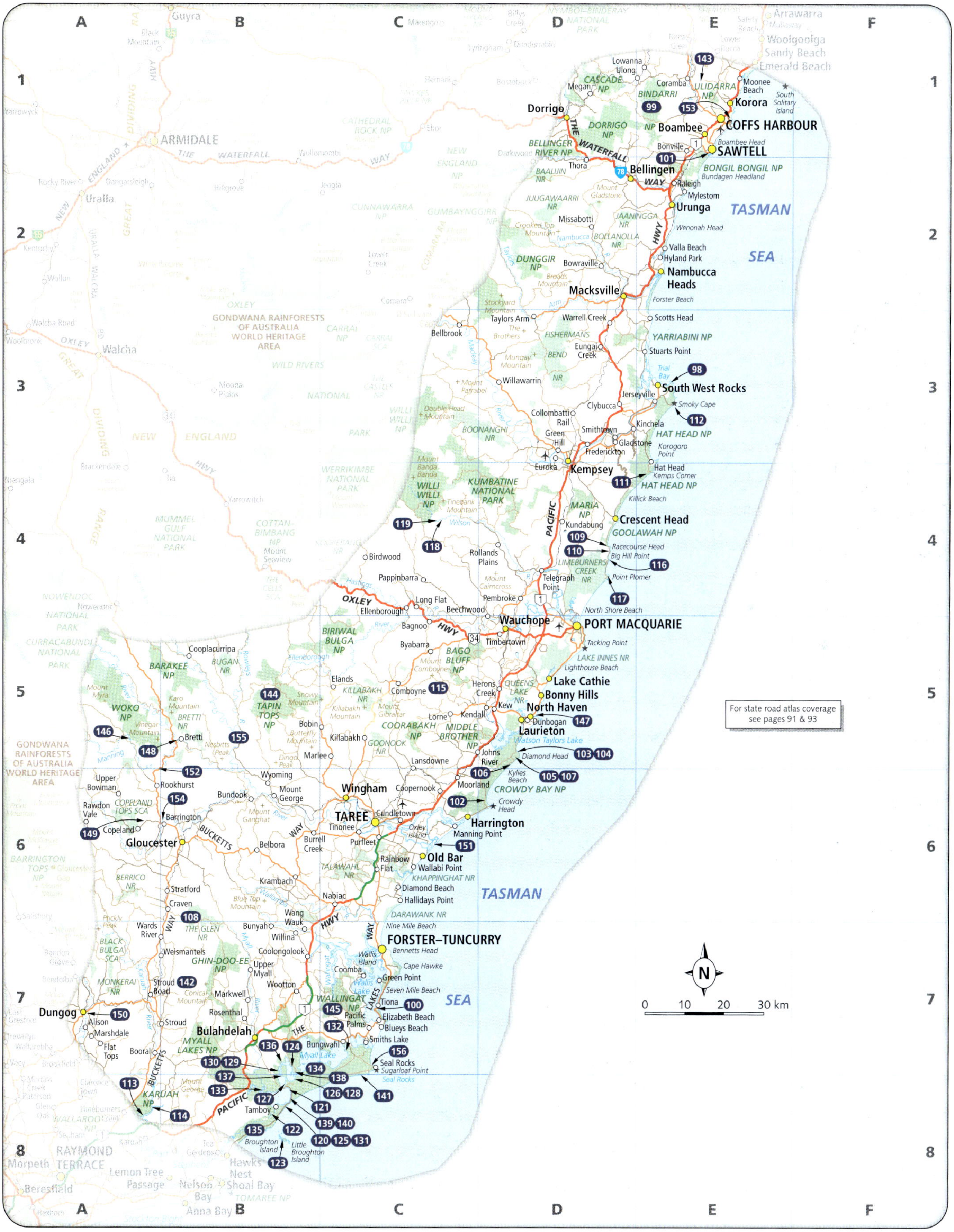

THE NATIONAL PARKS AND state reserves on Australia's mid-north coast are as rich and beautiful as a handful of emeralds scattered next to a sapphire sea. Stunning beaches, verdant rainforest, spectacular headlands, and fascinating estuaries and riverine systems cram in together between Myall Lakes National Park in the south and the Coffs Harbour hinterland in the north.

The long, windswept beaches of Myall Lakes National Park beckon beach anglers and 4WD aficionados, while its extensive, paperbark-ringed lake system is paradise to the boating or kayaking enthusiast. From here, the coastal gems just keep on rolling: Booti Booti, Wallingat and Crowdy Bay national parks and Limeburners Creek Reserve all deliver on surfing, swimming, fishing and a swag of other watersports.

Head inland and you'll find mountain-biking and horseriding in Kerewong or Orara East state forest. Dungog and the Gloucester areas, and Arakoon State Conservation Area, are perfect options for those with young families or a preference for the comforts of camping within reach of a town.

Whether you're here for a quick trip or a leisurely exploration, you'll soon see it's not called the Holiday Coast for nothing!

CAMPSITES LOCATED IN PARKS AND RESERVES

ARAKOON STATE CONSERVATION AREA

One of the historic drawcards of this pleasant and popular place, 3 km east of South West Rocks, is Trial Bay Gaol. In the late 1880s it was a Public Works Prison; during World War II it was used as an internment camp. Surrounding the headland are picturesque sandy beaches and easy walks.

How to book: NPWS South West Rocks (02) 6566 6168

98 Trial Bay Gaol camping area

This is a spectacular camping area on a sheltered surf beach, accessed via Cardwell St in South West Rocks. It's well appointed, with coin-operated showers, powered and unpowered sites, electric BBQs, a kiosk and even a restaurant. It is also popular, so bookings for peak periods are essential. There's a number of enjoyable walking trails, as well as all the water activities a beautiful beach can offer. **Map refs:** 19 E3, 93 M9

BINDARRI NATIONAL PARK

Rugged escarpments and waterfalls cascading through remote mountain ravines are the defining characteristics of this national park, 20 km west of Coffs Harbour. Access is via Dairyville from the east, and Corfes Rd off Eastern Dorrigo Rd from the west. Once in, most of the roads in the park are dry-weather, 4WD access only.

Who to contact: NPWS Coffs Harbour (02) 6652 0900

99 Bindarri camping areas (walk-in and bush camping)

Walk-in bush camping is possible throughout the park – facilities such as toilets, picnic tables and wood fireplaces are only available at Bindarray and Bangalore picnic areas, so you'll need to be self-sufficient if you plan to camp. Contact the parks office for recommended sites, and make sure you've got a good topographic map with you. **Map refs:** 19 E1, 93 M8

BOOTI BOOTI NATIONAL PARK

Booti Booti National Park protects a narrow strip of coastal land with one of the state's largest stands of littoral rainforest. Bordered by Wallis Lake on its western perimeter, this is ideal for those who like water- and nature-based activities in a magnificent natural setting.

Who to contact: NPWS Great Lakes (02) 6591 0300

100 The Ruins camping area

Cabbage tree palms and paperbarks surround this sprawling campground at the southern end of Seven Mile Beach, next to the parks office. There are a number of walks in the area, including the 7 km Booti Hill walking track, which connects the campground with Elizabeth Beach. A drive along the Lakes Way will take you through some of the park's main attractions. Drop in to the parks office for more details. **Map refs:** 19 C7, 91 N2

COFFS COAST STATE PARK

Luxuriant rainforest embraces beach after sparkling beach on this strip of mid-north coast between Bonville Headland and Park Beach. Fish off a beach, estuary or rocky headland; take your pick of surfing spots; duck underwater and explore Solitary Islands Marine Park; dine out in Coffs Harbour; or strap on a pair of boots and go bush.

How to book: 5 Lyons Rd, Sawtell (02) 6653 1379, 1800 729 835 www.coffscoastholidayparks.com.au

101 Sawtell Beach Holiday Park

This well-appointed caravan park is on Lyons Rd, about 8 km south of Coffs Harbour. You've got easy access to the beach and a wide range of accommodation options, including powered and unpowered sites, villas and cabins. Other drawcards include a TV and games room, children's playground, kiosk and tennis court for hitting a round of mixed doubles. **Map refs:** 19 E1, 93 N8

CROWDY BAY NATIONAL PARK

Crowdy Bay National Park is a coastal ribbon of lowlands with rocky outcrops and sandy beaches, set on the seaside 5 km south of Laurieton. The park is ideal for low-key, nature-based activities: camping, bushwalking, birdwatching, fishing, swimming and combing the rockpools. When camping, you need to bring drinking water and firewood.

Who to contact: NPWS Taree (02) 6552 4097 for campsite no. **102**; or NPWS Port Macquarie (02) 6588 5555 for all other campsites.

102 Crowdy Gap Cultural Camp

Turn off Crowdy Bay Rd north of Crowdy Head, and you'll find Crowdy Gap Cultural Camp nestled behind sand dunes on the site of an old dairy farm. There are 7 tent campsites, 2 trailer/caravan campsites and 1 group campsite. Crowdy Gap is also a place of great significance to the region's traditional owners, the Birpai. Bring your own water. **Map refs:** 19 D6, 91 O1, 93 L12

103 Diamond Head camping area

Located just off Diamond Head Rd (Coral Ville–Laurieton Rd) on the north side of Diamond Head, this 80-site spot has pride of place by the windswept beach. Take care when swimming, as beaches aren't patrolled. There's a short loop walk to Indian Beach, with gorgeous views along the coast, mountains and forest and there is 4WD beach access to Laurieton from here. Bring your own water. **Map refs:** 19 D5, 91 O1, 93 L12

104 Diamond Head camping area (walk-in camping)

This basic walk-in site is a short distance from the main camping area at Diamond Head. For those looking for privacy, particularly during the peak summer season, this is it. Access is via Diamond Head Rd. Bring your own everything. **Map refs:** 19 D5, 91 O1, 93 L12

105 Indian Head camping area

Sheltered at the base of the headland, 1 km south of Diamond Head camping area, is Indian Head camping area, which has 60 sites and no wheelchair access. Kangaroos frequent the grassy clearing here, and there are a number of good walks, one taking in the views from Diamond Head, and another through paperbark forest to the beach. Bring your own water. **Map refs:** 19 D5, 91 O1, 93 L12

106 Kylies Beach camping area

Australian writer Kylie Tennant lived and wrote in this lovely part of the world; her restored cabin can be found a short walk from this 70-site campground. There are secluded sites tucked away under trees up to 3 km from the road as well as car-based sites. This camping area is 1 km south of Indian Head, accessed via Diamond Head Rd (Coral Ville–Laurieton Rd). Bring your own water. **Map refs:** 19 D5, 91 O1, 93 L12

107 Kylies Hut camping area (walk-in camping)

This is a special, secluded camping site about 200 m walk from Indian Head camping area. It's small and basic. Bring your own water. **Map refs:** 19 D5, 91 O1, 93 L12

THE GLEN NATURE RESERVE

The Glen Nature Reserve is a densely forested haven 25 km south-east of Gloucester, reached via Glen Rd off Bucketts Way, south from Craven. This is a great place for hiking: the 220 km Tops-to-Myall heritage trail passes through the reserve. There are also a number of enjoyable scenic drives.

Who to contact: NPWS Nelson Bay (02) 4984 8200

108 Wards Glen camping area

A basic bush site with no facilities, Wards Glen is for self-sufficient campers only. It's dry-weather access only for 2WD vehicles, and set in the west of the reserve off Glen Rd. Bring drinking water and firewood with you. **Map refs:** 19 B6, 91 M2

GOOLAWAH NATIONAL PARK

A quiet coastal strip south of Crescent Head, the national park includes Goolawah Lagoon. The beaches are pristine and there's a surfing break at Crescent Head. Birdwatchers will be kept busy, as the lagoon attracts waders and waterfowl, while there are honeyeaters and seed-eating birds in the forest fringing the beaches.

Who to contact: NPWS South West Rocks (02) 6566 6168

109 Racecourse camping area

This is an unpatrolled beach, so be vigilant when swimming. It's 11 km south of Crescent Head via Point Plomer Rd, at Racecourse Headland. Bring drinking water. **Map refs:** 19 D4, 93 M10

GOOLAWAH REGIONAL PARK

Goolawah Regional Park, immediately south of Goolawah National Park, is a relaxed and friendly environment. Follow Point Plomer Rd from Crescent Head. Note: the road can be tricky going for caravans, so check road conditions before setting off.

Who to contact: NPWS Arakoon (02) 6566 6621

110 Delicate Beach camping area

This is a popular fishing spot, and a good place from which to head out for a spot of swimming, picnicking or wildlife-spotting. The beach isn't patrolled, so take care in the ocean. The camping area is 12 km south from Crescent Head and 1 km south of Racecourse Headland via Point Plomer Rd. Bring drinking water. **Map refs:** 19 D4, 93 M10

HAT HEAD NATIONAL PARK

This is a stunning slice of northern NSW coastline, complete with pristine beaches, rocky headlands, melaleuca wetlands, freshwater lagoons and forest. In case you're not moved by the promise of swimming, surfing, fishing, birdwatching and walking, there's also the chance to see migrating southern right whales May–July and Aug–Oct.

Who to contact: NPWS South West Rocks (02) 6566 6168
How to book: Smoky Cape Lighthouse (02) 6566 6301

111 Hungry Gate camping area

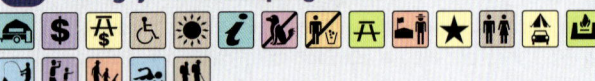

Tucked in behind sand dunes and ringed with heath and woodland, Hungry Gate is an attractive camping area just a hop, skip and jump from the ocean. It's 5 km south of Hat Head village – follow Hungry Rd off The Gap Rd. Bring your own firewood and water. There's a recycling station here, but it's best to take your garbage with you. **Map refs:** 19 E4, 93 M10

112 Smoky Cape camping area

To reach this small campground nestled in the rainforest at Smoky Cape, turn on to Arakoon Rd from South West Rocks Rd and head for Smoky Cape Lighthouse. Bring your own firewood and drinking water. There are plenty of walks to do around the cape, including one to the lighthouse itself, which delivers gobsmacking coastal views. In addition to camping, Smoky Cape Lighthouse has been transformed into a B&B, and self-catered accommodation is available at 2 assistant lighthouse keepers' cottages. **Map refs:** 19 E3, 93 M9

KARUAH NATURE RESERVE

There are 6 separate pieces of the Karuah Nature Reserve pie scattered either side of Karuah River. Turn off Bucketts Way on to Hobarts Forest Rd, 20 km north of Karuah. The camping areas are very basic, but what you lose in creature comforts you gain in privacy and outdoor adventures, including fishing, swimming and canoeing.

Who to contact: NPWS Nelson Bay (02) 4984 8200

113 Little Mountain camping area

Off Bucketts Way, just north of Limeburners Creek, Little Mountain camping area is perched on the banks of the Karuah River, the perfect spot to drop a line or paddle a canoe. Swimming, however, isn't encouraged. Bring your own water, firewood and portable toilet. 4WD access only. **Map refs:** 19 A8, 91 M3

114 Tattersalls camping area

Located on the Karuah River, access is via Hobart Rd from Limeburners Creek. The site is for self-sufficient campers only and access is 4WD only. Bring water and firewood. **Map refs:** 19 A8, 91 M3

KEREWONG STATE FOREST

Until 1964, this was the Swan family's privately owned dairy and beef farm. Since its amalgamation into Kerewong State Forest, it's become a popular place for walking, horseriding, mountain-biking and swimming. From Kendall, head west along Comboyne Rd and turn on to the unsealed Upsalls Creek Rd.

Who to contact: Forests NSW Wauchope (02) 6585 3744

115 Swans Crossing camping area

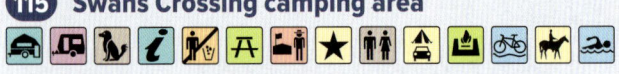

This camping area is signposted along Upsalls Creek Rd. It's surrounded by native forest and hardwood plantations; swimming is popular in the nearby shallows of Upsalls Creek. There are toilets and an information board at the camping area – bring your own drinking water. **Map refs:** 19 C5, 93 L11

LIMEBURNERS CREEK NATURE RESERVE

The natural gems just keep on rolling along the coast. At Limeburners Creek Nature Reserve, rainforest meets heathlands, banksia and blackbutt forest, which together embrace beaches popular for swimming, surfing or fishing. The reserve is a bumpy drive south from Crescent Head along Point Plomer Rd. There is also access along a rough, dry-weather only road from Port Macquarie to the south.

Who to contact: NPWS South West Rocks (02) 6566 6168

116 Melaleuca camping area

There's a short loop track through rainforest from the campground, which is on Point Plomer Rd about 12 km south of Crescent Head. It's a spacious area with 100 sites; bring your own drinking water and firewood. **Map refs:** 19 D4, 93 M10

117 Point Plomer camping area

This well-appointed, 100-site camping ground is 5 km south of Melaleuca camping area along Point Plomer Rd. There's bore water here, but you'll need to either treat or boil the water before drinking, or bring your own. You also need to bring your own firewood. Note: the comfortable Plomer Beach House on Plomer Point sleeps up to 12 people and has direct access to the beach. **Map refs:** 19 D4, 93 M11

MOUNT BOSS STATE FOREST

The Cobrabald Recreation Area in Mt Boss State Forest offers plenty of options for camping, as well as fishing and 4WD touring. It's 42 km north-west of Wauchope; to get here, take Beechwood Rd to Beechwood, then Bellangry Rd. The forest roads are unsealed but still suitable for conventional vehicles.

Who to contact: Forests NSW Wauchope (02) 6585 3744

118 The Bluff camping area

Kick back in one of 6 shady sites at this camping site, 1.4 km north of Wild Bull camping area. Access is via Cobrabald Rd. Bring your drinking water and firewood. **Map refs:** 19 C4, 93 L10

119 Wild Bull camping area

Throw a line in to see if you can snag a catfish, or cool off in a deep waterhole at Wild Bull camping area, 42 km north-west of Wauchope along Cobrabald Rd. You'll have to park then carry your gear over bollards to your tent site. Bring drinking water and firewood. **Map refs:** 19 C4, 93 L10

MYALL LAKES NATIONAL PARK

Myall Lakes National Park encompasses NSW's largest coastal lake system, with 100 000 ha of stunning waterways, 40 km of magnificent beaches washed by the Pacific Ocean, high sand dunes, dramatic headlands and a wealth of birdlife. With about 350 campsites scattered throughout the park, you're sure to find your own personal slice of heaven.

Who to contact: NPWS Great Lakes (02) 6591 0300 *How to book:* 1300 072 757 for campsite no. **123**

120 Banksia Green camping area

It might be a small site, but the power of Banksia Green lies in its close proximity to beach and lake, and it's not as far from Hawks Nest as some of the other sites. It's off Mungo Brush Rd, just south of Mungo Brush camping area. Bring drinking water; gas/fuel stove preferred. **Map refs:** 19 B8, 91 N3

121 Boomeri camping area

Boomeri's 20 sites are set away from the north-eastern banks of Bombah Broadwater, with a walking/cycling track to Johnsons and Shelley beaches. It's the next campsite north of the Wells camping area, off Mungo Brush Rd. Bring drinking water; gas/fuel stove only. **Map refs:** 19 B8, 91 N3

122 Brambles Green camping area (walk-in camping)

If you're after a quieter spot and don't mind missing out on ocean views, this walk-in campsite on the banks of the lower Myall River, south of Bombah Broadwater, is ideal for self-sufficient walkers and as a stopover point for kayakers or canoeists paddling the river. Bring your drinking water and gas/fuel stove or firewood with you. **Map refs:** 19 B8, 91 N3

123 Broughton Island camping area (boat-based camping)

Accessible by boat alone, Broughton Island's Poverty Beach camping area is said to be the only island-based site in NSW where you can camp among an active seabird colony – it's a vital breeding site for wedge-tailed shearwaters. The camping area includes 3 large timber camping platforms and 2 grassy sites. Wood and solid fuel fires are not permitted and you must bring your own water. Bookings are essential. **Map refs:** 19 B8, 91 N3

124 Bungaree Bay camping area

Tucked away on the banks of Boolambayte Lake beneath paperbarks and casuarinas, Bungaree Bay is accessible from Violet Hill Rd, off the Lakes Way. The turn-off to the Lakes Way is 18 km past Buladelah on the Pacific Hwy. Bring drinking water and firewood with you, and preferably a gas/fuel stove. **Map refs:** 19 B7, 91 N3

125 Dees Corner camping area

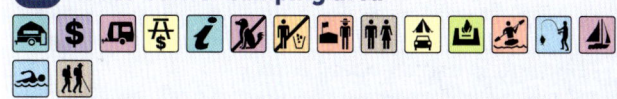

Dees Corner offers quiet camping under the dappled shade of melaleucas by Bombah Broadwater. It's north of Mungo Brush camping area, off Mungo Brush Rd. You need to bring drinking water and firewood, though gas/fuel stoves are preferred. **Map refs:** 19 B8, 91 N3

126 Freshwater camping area (walk-in and boat-based camping)

Freshwater is north of Joes Cove on the eastern shore of Two Mile Lake. It's a boat-based or walk-in site, a 2 km walk from Mungo Brush Rd – check with the parks office for track details. There are toilets here, but you need to bring your own drinking water, firewood and gas/fuel stove. **Map refs:** 19 B8, 91 N3

127 Joes Cove camping area (walk-in and boat-based camping)

Joes Cove is north of Bombah Point, on the eastern shore of Two Mile Lake. It's an 800 m walk in from Mungo Brush Rd. Bring your own drinking water, firewood and gas/fuel stove. **Map refs:** 19 B8, 91 N3

128 Johnsons Beach camping area (walk-in and boat-based camping)

One of the bigger boat-based camping areas in Myall Lakes National Park, Johnsons Beach camping area enjoys an embarrassment of riches – inviting sandy beaches and shallow, aquamarine waters. There are a number of walking tracks to explore, including the Johnsons Hill Track, which delivers you to a lookout with panoramic views of the Myall Lakes. Access is by boat or foot only. Moor at the boat ramp nearby at Violet Hill. Walkers access the camping area via the Old Gibber fire trail (from Mungo Brush Rd, 4 km). Bring firewood and drinking water. **Map refs:** 19 B8, 91 N3

129 Korsmans Landing camping area

You'll either need to get the car ferry across to Bombah Point from Mungo Brush Rd and continue north or come down Bombah Point Rd from the Pacific Hwy past Buladelah.

Situated on Two Mile Lake, this site has access to a wharf and boat ramp. Eastern grey kangaroos feed here at dawn and dusk. Bring your drinking water and firewood; gas/fuel stoves preferred. **Map refs:** 19 B7, 91 N3

130 Mackaway Bay (boat-based camping)

You'll find this site on the western shore of Two Mile Lake, between this and Boolambayte Lake. It's a good spot to choose if it's a windy day. Bring drinking water, firewood and gas/fuel stove. **Map refs:** 19 B7, 91 N3

131 Mungo Brush camping area

On the lake side of Mungo Brush Rd, about 22 km north of Hawks Nest, this is a popular campsite as it's close to the lake and the beach. There's a boat ramp here and a number of walking tracks, including the 1.5 km, 30 min Rainforest Loop and 4 km, 1 hr Tamboi walk. A campsite near the majestic paperbarks is perfect, with a view of the sun setting over the lake. There is also walking access through the forest and over the dunes to the beach. Bring drinking water; gas/fuel stove only. **Map refs:** 19 B8, 91 N3

132 Neranie Head camping area

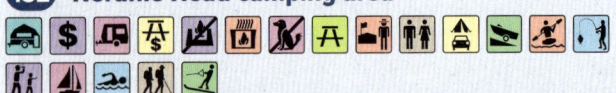

Neranie Head is at the far-north end of the national park, on the north-eastern shores of Myall Lake. There's a boat ramp nearby, and there is a short walk to the historic cemetery on Neranie Headland. You can get here via Seal Rocks Rd off the Lakes Way. Bring drinking water; gas/fuel stove only. **Map refs:** 19 C7, 91 N3

133 River Mouth camping area (walk-in and boat-based camping)

As its name suggests, this camping area's at the mouth of the Myall River. It's a good stopover for canoeists and kayakers on the Upper Myall River. Walkers can also access the camping area via the Rivermouth Fire Trail off Bombah Point Rd. You'll need to bring drinking water, firewood and gas/fuel stove. **Map refs:** 19 B8, 91 N3

134 Shelley Beach camping area (walk-in and boat-based camping)

This is a walk-in or boat-based campsite located 10 km north-east of Bombah Point on Myall Lake. If you're on foot, it's an 11 km walk via the Old Gibber fire trail, off Mungo Brush Rd. Bring drinking water and firewood; gas/fuel stove preferred. **Map refs:** 19 B7, 91 N3

135 Stewart and Lloyds camping area

This is the closest campground to Hawks Nest, 10 km along Mungo Brush Rd from town. It's tucked away behind sand dunes with easy access to the beach. You'll need to bring drinking water and firewood; gas/fuel stove preferred. **Map refs:** 19 B8, 91 N3

136 Sunnyside camping area (boat-based camping)

This charmingly named camping spot can be found on the western shore of Two Mile Lake, between this and Boolambayte Lake. Bring your own drinking water, firewood and gas/fuel stove. **Map refs:** 19 B7, 91 N3

137 Two Mile Sands camping area (boat-based camping)

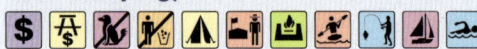

Sandy beaches and shallow waters greet boaters at this camping area on the western shore of Mackaway Bay. Bring your own drinking water, firewood and gas/fuel stove. **Map refs:** 19 B8, 91 N3

138 Violet Hill camping area

A great base for lakeside activities, Violet Hill camping area includes a boat ramp, a wharf and a smattering of boat moorings. There's space for campervans and trailers, although the main campsite area is closed to vehicles. Access is off Violet Hill Rd from the Lakes Way. Bring your own drinking water and firewood; gas/fuel stove preferred. **Map refs:** 19 B7, 91 N3

139 The Wells camping area

It's lakefront camping here, north of White Tree Bay camping area off Mungo Brush Rd. Located on the eastern shore of Bombah Broadwater, this is one of the few places where you can have a campfire, although you'll need to bring your own firewood. You'll also need to bring drinking water. **Map refs:** 19 B8, 91 N3

140 White Tree Bay camping area

On the eastern shore of Bombah Broadwater north of Dees Corner camping area off Mungo Brush Rd, this site includes a gas barbecue. Bring your drinking water; gas/fuel stove only. **Map refs:** 19 B8, 91 N3

141 Yagon camping area

This is a top location, sheltered behind the dunes, close to the beach, Seal Rocks and Sugarloaf Point Lighthouse, and away from the conglomeration of camping sites to the south around the lakes. To get here, turn on to the Lakes Way from the Pacific Hwy, 3 km north of Bulahdelah, then turn on to Seal Rocks Rd and follow the signs. Bring your own drinking water; gas/fuel stove only. **Map refs:** 19 C8, 91 N3

MYALL RIVER STATE FOREST

Bushwalking, mountain-biking, 4WD touring and camping are popular pastimes within this magnificent, mountainous reserve 10 km west of Bulahdelah. You can get here via Cabbage Tree Rd from Markwell Rd or Crawford Rd off Booral Rd.

Who to contact: Bulahdelah Visitor Information Centre (02) 4997 4981

142 Strike-a-light camping area

Although it's no longer managed by Forests NSW as a designated camping area, this is a large, grassy spot where you can put up a tent overnight. It's not far from Mammy Johnsons River and its tributaries, about 22 km north-west of Bulahdelah, via Cabbage Tree Rd. Bring drinking water. **Map refs:** 19 B7, 91 M2

ORARA EAST STATE FOREST

Travel 9 km west of Coffs Harbour on Bruxner Park Rd off the Pacific Hwy, and you enter the verdant subtropical paradise that is the mid-north-coast hinterland. Walking and mountain-biking are popular here, or you could just gaze into the forest canopy and enjoy the birdlife.

Who to contact: Forests NSW Coffs Harbour (02) 6652 0111

143 Bush camping areas

Self-sufficient campers armed with detailed, up-to-date topographic maps can access a number of good spots throughout the forest, either on foot, horseback or mountain-bike. **Map refs:** 19 E1

TAPIN TOPS NATIONAL PARK

This little-known national park, 30 km north-west of Wingham, protects swathes of old-growth forest as well as a number of threatened animal species including the parma wallaby, squirrel glider and sphagnum frog. Tapin means dingo in the local Kattang language, and the park has been identified as a dingo management area. Picnicking, walking, swimming, bushwalking and scenic drives are all popular pastimes here. Note: as is the case in all national parks, do not feed wildlife as it encourages reliance on humans and can attract unwanted attention.

Who to contact: NPWS Port Macquarie (02) 6588 5555

144 Dingo Tops Rest Area

Previously a forest workers' camp, Dingo Tops features old forestry machinery, including a dobbie (used to haul logs), a tractor and a horse-drawn grader. There are a couple of short rainforest tracks from the campground, and nearby Harry Browns Lookout offers imposing views of Rowleys Rock and Head and Shoulders Cliff. The campsite is at the junction of

Knodingbul Rd and Dingo Tops Rd. Bring drinking water and firewood with you. **Map refs:** 19 B5, 93 K11

WALLINGAT NATIONAL PARK

Located on the western shores of Wallis Lake, 30 km south of Forster via the Lakes Way and Sugar Creek Rd, Wallingat National Park is a vibrant mosaic of towering gum forest, pockets of cabbage palms and fascinating estuarine vegetation. The view from Whoota Lookout is one of the best on the mid-north coast.

Who to contact: NPWS Great Lakes (02) 6591 0300

145 Wallingat River camping area

Perched on the banks of tranquil Wallingat River, this site is small and peaceful; campers can fish, paddle, watch for wildlife and while away the hours in solitude. It's off River Rd, via Sugar Creek Rd. Note: bring your own drinking water and firewood with you; gas/fuel stove preferred. **Map refs:** 19 C7, 91 N2

WOKO NATIONAL PARK

With its striking rocky outcrops, luxuriant rainforested gullies and varied topography, Woko National Park is a good place to walk and watch for birds. Other wildlife includes pademelons, spotted-tailed quolls and brush-tailed wallabies. The park is 30 km north-west of Gloucester, accessible via Curricabark Rd off Thunderbolts Way.

Who to contact: NPWS Gloucester (02) 6538 5300

146 Manning River camping area

You'll find this camping area just inside the park on the banks of the Manning River, on the flood-detour road off Curricabark Rd. Bring your drinking water and firewood; gas/fuel stove preferred. **Map refs:** 19 A5, 91 M1, 93 J12

CAMPSITES LOCATED IN OTHER AREAS

147 Beachfront Holiday Park

Camp among the paperbarks here to the tune of surf washing on sand. About a 30 min drive south of Port Macquarie via Ocean Dr, this holiday park has myriad attractions, from its over 4 ha of shady bushland, 200 m walk to the beach, children's playground, cabins, fishing in the Camden Haven River and bushwalking in nearby national parks and reserves – be sure to walk the top-to-tail track on Middle Brother Mountain. It's a 5 min drive to Laurieton's Plaza Theatre, where Australian director Baz Luhrmann, as a boy, was first struck with the movie-making bug. **Map refs:** 19 D5, 91 O1, 93 M11

How to book: The Parade, North Haven (02) 6559 9193 www.northcoastholidayparks.com.au

148 Bretti Reserve camping area

Less than half an hour's drive north from Gloucester on Thunderbolts Way, Bretti Reserve has basic facilities, but it's spacious and the river is close by so it's good for swimming. Pets are allowed here. Note: bring your own firewood and drinking water. **Map refs:** 19 B5, 91 M1, 93 J12

Who to contact: Gloucester Visitor Information Centre (02) 6558 1408

149 Copeland Reserve camping area

Approximately 15 km west of Gloucester along the Gloucester–Scone Rd, you'll find this large open area near the creek, in which you can pan for gold. Bring drinking water, firewood, pets and your swimming costume. **Map refs:** 19 A6, 91 M1, 93 J12

Who to contact: Gloucester Visitor Information Centre (02) 6558 1408

150 Dungog Caravan Park

A quaint little spot by the Williams River, on Stroud Rd 700 m north of town, Dungog is a comfortable place to use as a base for exploring nearby Barrington Tops National Park and Chichester State Forest. There's an RV dump point at the showground. **Map refs:** 19 A7, 91 M2

How to book: Dungog Visitor Information Centre, cnr Dowling and Brown sts (02) 4992 2212 **Camping fees:** pay fees, make bookings and pick up keys to the amenities block at the visitor information centre

151 Farquhar Park Camping Ground

Farquhar Park is 8 km south of Manning Point, near the mouth of the Manning River at Old Bar. It's 4WD only at low tide across Smiths Beach; alternatively, there's boat access. Take your off-road camper trailer with care. For your trouble, you'll be rewarded with a secluded estuary and 25 camping sites. **Map refs:** 19 C6, 91 O1, 93 L12

Who to contact: Manning Valley Visitor Information Centre (02) 6592 5444, 1800 182 733

152 Gloryvale Reserve camping area

Pet-friendly, close to the river and only 23 km north of Gloucester along Thunderbolts Way, this camping area has a shallow, rocky swimming area suitable for small children. Note that it's 2WD access only in dry weather, and you need to bring your own firewood and water. **Map refs:** 19 A6, 91 M1, 93 J12

Who to contact: Gloucester Visitor Information Centre (02) 6558 1408

153 Park Beach Holiday Park

Located 3 km east of Coffs Harbour's city centre alongside an inviting stretch of sand and surf, Park Beach Holiday Park has a range of accommodation, including villas and cabins, as well as camping options – ensuite, ensuite drive-through and drive-through sites, and powered and unpowered sites. There's a pool with water slides, slippery dips and water fountains, a jumping pillow, children's playground, games and TV room, tennis court and internet with free wireless connection. **Map refs:** 19 E1, 93 N8

How to book: 1 Ocean Pde, Coffs Harbour 1800 200 555 www.coffscoastholidayparks.com.au

154 Poley's Place

Take the family camping on a working cattle property on the banks of picturesque Barrington River, 8 km north of Gloucester on Thunderbolts Way. Basic cabins, caravans and a bunkhouse are also available. Attractions include tube riding over rapids, an animal park for children and special country music hoedowns. **Map refs:** 19 B6, 91 M1, 93 J12

How to book: 814 Thunderbolts Way, Barrington (02) 6558 4220, 0438 584 220 www.poleysplace.com

155 Rocks Crossing Reserve camping area

At Rocks Crossing, 21 km north-west of Mount George Village beside Nowendoc River, you'll find toilets, BBQs and picnic tables. The river is great for canoeing and fishing. Note: bring your own firewood. **Map refs:** 19 B5, 91 N1, 93 K1

Who to contact: Manning Valley Visitor Information Centre (02) 6592 5444, 1800 182 733

156 Seal Rocks Holiday Park

Enjoy some much-needed R&R in the welcoming embrace of the fishing enclave of Seal Rocks, a coastal village that has managed to sidestep major development. Located across the road from the inviting sands of Number One Beach, the holiday park has a range of accommodation options, from cabins to grassy tent and caravan sites as well as amenities blocks. If you're a diver, don't miss the chance to visit the resident grey nurse shark population, and for bushwalkers, a hike to Seal Rocks Lighthouse is mandatory – it's a top spot to whale-watch in winter. Access is via Kinka and Seal Rocks rds and the Lakes Way off the Pacific Hwy. **Map refs:** 19 C7, 91 N3

How to book: Kinka Rd, Seal Rocks (02) 4997 6164, 1800 112 234 www.northcoastholidayparks.com.au

TROPICAL NORTH COAST

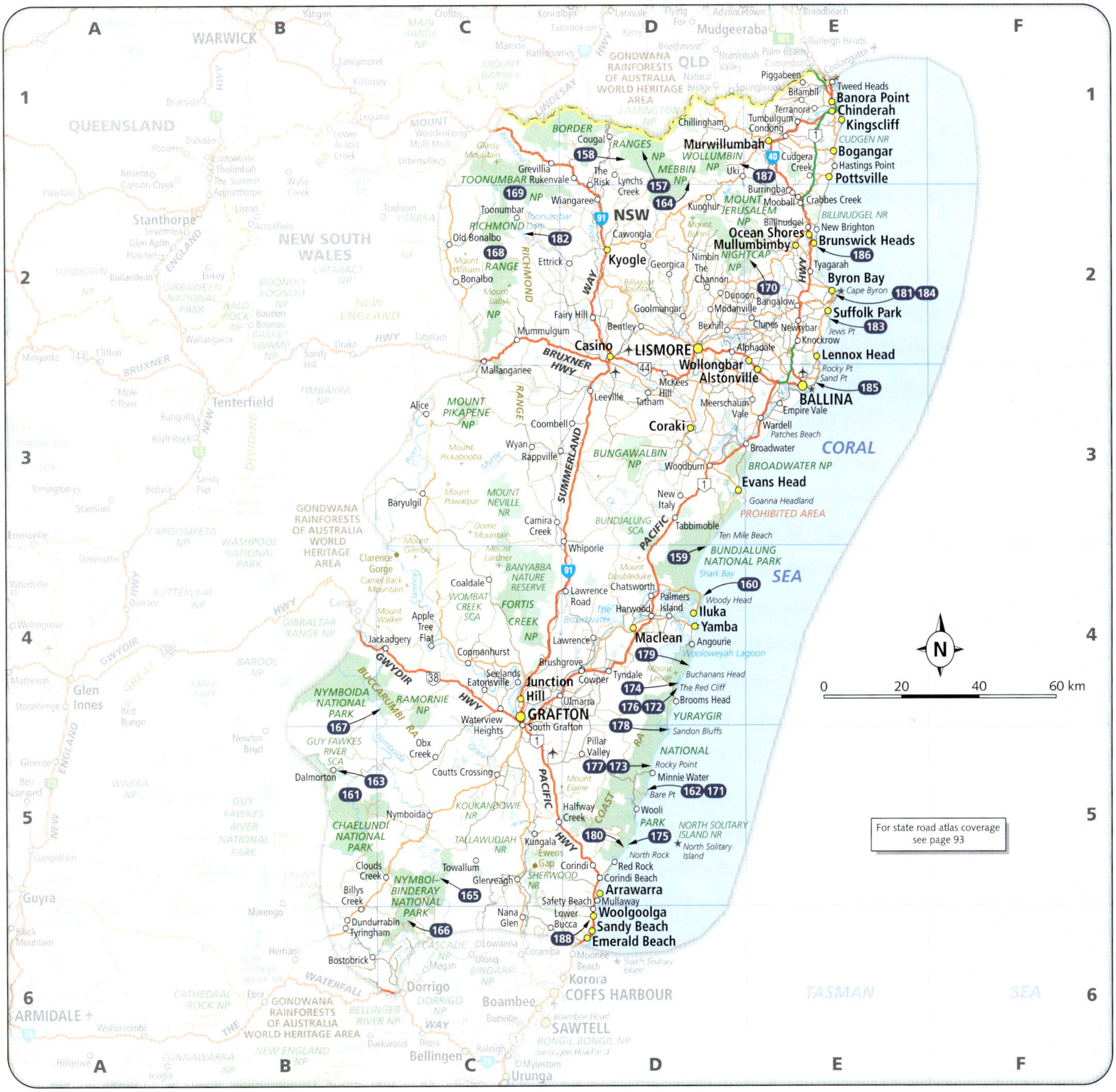

The map shows the Tropical North Coast region of New South Wales, with grid references A–F (columns) and 1–6 (rows).

Places and features (selection):

QUEENSLAND / QLD — WARWICK, Mudgeeraba, Burleigh Heads, Tweed Heads, Banora Point, Chinderah, Kingscliff, Bogangar, Hastings Point, Pottsville, Crabbes Creek, New Brighton, Brunswick Heads, Ocean Shores, Mullumbimby, Byron Bay, Cape Byron, Suffolk Park, Lennox Head, BALLINA, Empire Vale, Wardell, Broadwater, Evans Head

Murwillumbah, WOLLUMBIN, MEBBIN NP, MOUNT JERUSALEM NP, NIGHTCAP, Uki, Cudgera Creek, Burringbar, Mooball, Billinudgel, The Channon, Dunoon, Modanville, Bangalow, Clunes, Newrybar, Knockrow, Rocky Pt, Sand Pt, Patches Beach

BORDER RANGES NP, Cougal, Grevillia, TOONUMBAR NP, Rukenvale, The Risk, Lynchs Creek, Kunghur, Nimbin, NEW SOUTH WALES, RICHMOND RANGE NP, Toonumbar, Old Bonalbo, Bonalbo, MOUNT WILLIAM NP, Ettrick, Kyogle, Georgica, Cawongla, Mummulgum, Fairy Hill, Bentley, Bexhill, Alphadale

Casino, LISMORE, Wollongbar, Alstonville, McKees Hill, Tatham, Meerschaum Vale, Leeville, Coraki, BUNGAWALBIN NP, Woodburn, New Italy, BROADWATER NP, CORAL SEA, Goanna Headland, PROHIBITED AREA

MOUNT PIKAPENE NP, Alice, Coombell, Wyan, Rappville, MOUNT NEVILLE NR, Tabbimoble, Ten Mile Beach, BUNDJALUNG SCA, BUNDJALUNG NATIONAL PARK, Shark Bay

Baryulgil, Mount Powerpar, Camira Creek, Whiporie, New Doubleduke, Chatsworth, Lawrence Road, Palmers Island, Woody Head, Iluka, Yamba, Angourie, Maclean, Woolweyah Lagoon

BANYABBA NATURE RESERVE, WOMBAT CREEK SCA, FORTIS CREEK NP, Coaldale, Apple Tree Flat, Lawrence, Copmanhurst, Brushgrove, Cowper, Tyndale, Ulmarra, Buchanans Head, The Red Cliff, Brooms Head, YURAYGIR NATIONAL PARK, Sandon Bluffs

Clarence Gorge, Camel Back Mountain, Mount Glenreagh, Mount Walker, Jackadgery, Seelands, Eatonsville, Junction Hill, South Grafton, GRAFTON, Waterview Heights, Pillar Valley, Rocky Point, Minnie Water, Bare Pt

NYMBOIDA NATIONAL PARK, RAMORNIE NP, GUY FAWKES RIVER SCA, Newton Boyd, Dalmorton, Obx Creek, Coutts Crossing, Mount Elaine, Halfway Creek, Wooli, NORTH SOLITARY ISLAND NR, North Solitary Island

CHAELUNDI NATIONAL PARK, Nymboida, TALLAWUDJAH NR, Kungala, Ewens Gap, Corindi, Red Rock, North Rock, SHERWOOD, Corindi Beach, Arrawarra, Mullaway, Safety Beach, Woolgoolga, Lower Bucca, Nana Glen, Sandy Beach, Emerald Beach

Clouds Creek, Towallum, NYMBOI-BINDERAY NATIONAL PARK, Billys Creek, Marengo, Dundurrabin, Tyringham, Bostobrick, CASCADE NP, BINDARRI NP, Korora, COFFS HARBOUR, TASMAN SEA

ARMIDALE, Wollomombi, GONDWANA RAINFORESTS OF AUSTRALIA WORLD HERITAGE AREA, Ebor, CATHEDRAL ROCK NP, WATERFALL WAY, DORRIGO NP, Dorrigo, Boambee, SAWTELL, BONGIL BONGIL NP, Bellingen, BELLINGER RIVER NP, NEW ENGLAND NP, Thora, Raleigh, Urunga

Scale: 0 — 20 — 40 — 60 km

For state road atlas coverage see page 93

THE SUBTROPICAL CLIMATE AND rich, fertile soil of the coastal and hinterland region stretching from Coffs Harbour north to the Queensland border have given rise to a stunning range of national parks and reserves. Yuraygir National Park protects the largest stretch of undeveloped coastline in NSW – a seemingly endless string of sweeping beaches, rocky headlands, serene coves and tranquil estuaries. Not far north of this is Bundjalung National Park, with another 38 km of options for swimming, fishing, birdwatching and canoeing. Campers can learn about the Aboriginal history of the area, visiting middens and sites of cultural significance.

In this region, the Gondwana Rainforests of Australia reign supreme: the Border Ranges, Mebbin, Richmond Range and Toonumbar national parks are just a few of the 50 national parks between Newcastle and Brisbane that are included in this World Heritage listing – together, they protect more than 200 threatened plant and animal species. For the outdoor enthusiast, these parks offer infinite opportunities for camping, bushwalking, birdwatching, wildlife-watching, scenic driving and nature appreciation. Some of the forest experiences are second to none, such as Old Spotty, a spotted gum in Toonumbar National Park believed to be up to 300 years old.

Water, it seems, is never far away on the tropical north coast. It's not just the world-renowned beaches – Nymboida and Nymboi–Binderay national parks both offer spectacular whitewater rafting, and Toonumbar Dam, north-west of Kyogle, is a popular spot for boating, canoeing and fishing. And there are creeks and waterfalls aplenty, from beautiful Minyon Falls in Nightcap National Park, accessible by a short walk from Whian Whian State Conservation Area, to the cheerful Chaelundi Creek in Guy Fawkes River National Park.

No campers worth their salt could be bored exploring this region – whether their passion is wild and pristine forest, stunning beaches, laid-back coastal towns or wild rivers.

CAMPSITES LOCATED IN PARKS AND RESERVES

BORDER RANGES NATIONAL PARK

Sprawling across the very northern perimeter of NSW and extending for 85 km along the Queensland state border, this World Heritage–listed national park embraces 3 wilderness areas. It is an area of great biodiversity, with the border region said to have the highest concentration of marsupial, bird, snake and frog species in Australia. Bush camping is permitted in the park (keep 200 m from public roads, walking tracks and other facilities) but vehicle-based bush camping is prohibited. The Tweed Range Scenic Dr loops through the park and gives access to the camping areas, as well as a number of walks. Some lead to spectacular lookouts, such as the Bar Mountain and Pinnacle lookouts.

Who to contact: NPWS Kyogle (02) 6632 0000

157 Forest Tops camping area

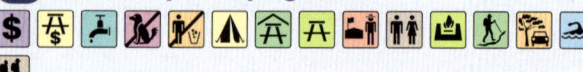

If you enter the national park along Tweed Range Scenic Dr, 30 km north of Kyogle, you'll see signposted access for this camping area. The medium–difficult 10.5 km Booyong Walk (5 hr) sets out from here and links Forest Tops and Sheepstation Creek, passing tumbling waterfalls and enticing swimming holes. The camping sites are a 10–50 m walk from your car. Access includes unpaved roads, reachable by 2WD. Boil or treat the water before use; gas/fuel stove preferred; bring your own firewood. **Map refs: 28 D1, 93 N2**

158 Sheepstation Creek camping area

With 40 sites, this sizeable camping area is just off Tweed Range Scenic Dr, 31 km north of Kyogle. The easy Rosewood Loop (6 km, 3 hr) and Palm Forest Walk (2 km, 1 hr) begin here: the former will take you through magnificent stands of old-growth flooded gum; the latter, luxuriant subtropical rainforest. Both of these walks cross the creek and also give access to views of Rosewood Falls. In the springtime, just after dark you may be treated to the forest around the camping

ground filling with fireflies – a truly magical sight. Access to the campsite includes unpaved roads, reachable by 2WD. Boil or treat the water before use; gas/fuel stove preferred; bring your own firewood. **Map refs: 28 D1, 93 N2**

BUNDJALUNG NATIONAL PARK

Bundjalung National Park protects a superb 38 km stretch of NSW's far-north coastline, including secluded beaches, sand dunes and headlands. The landscape is a mosaic of coastal cypress, freshwater lakes, mangrove mudflats and wetlands. In the south, the beautiful Esk River flows through undisturbed countryside – a marvellous area for self-reliant bushwalkers.

Who to contact: NPWS Lismore/Alstonville (02) 6627 0200
How to book: tent/cabin bookings essential during peak periods; (02) 6646 6134 for campsite no. **160**

159 Black Rocks camping area

Black Rocks is on Ten Mile Beach, via unsealed Gap Rd, 5 km south of Woodburn. There are concrete bunkers from World War II here – a section in the north of the park is still used by the military for target practice. A walk on the beach to the north of the camping area takes you to the unusual and interesting Black Rocks, soft, dark-brown stone eroded into intriguing shapes by the sea. There is also a walk along Jerusalem Creek from the camping area to the creek mouth where many shorebirds roost and nest. To get here from Grafton via the Pacific Hwy, take Gap Rd. Bring firewood and drinking water; gas/fuel stoves preferred. **Map refs: 28 D4, 93 O5**

160 Woody Head camping area

Surrounded by remnant subtropical rainforest, Woody Head is the larger of the park's 2 camping areas with more than 100 sites, 4 cabins, hot showers, a kiosk and a boat launch. Fishing, swimming, snorkelling and rockpool-hopping are visitors' favourite pursuits, and staff conduct regular Discovery activities. **Map refs: 28 D4, 93 O5**

CHAELUNDI NATIONAL PARK

Chaelundi National Park protects one of the largest swathes of old-growth forest in northern NSW. Sparkling creeks, gorges, ridges and delightful swimming holes make this a perfect backdrop for bushwalking, mountain-biking, birdwatching and 4WD touring. The park is north-west of Dorrigo, via Boundary Creek or Ellis rds from Waterfall Way, the Armidale–Grafton Rd. It is necessary to book and pay in advance to receive a permit and key.

How to book: Dorrigo Rainforest Centre (02) 6657 2309

161 Doon Goonge camping area

Tranquil and secluded, Doon Goonge is accessed by 4WD (off-road camper trailers permitted), mountain-bike or on foot – via

Chandlers Fire Trail or Quartz Rd. Once here, experienced bushwalkers can explore the Chaelundi Wilderness Area, provided they're self-sufficient and armed with detailed, up-to-date topographic maps. This is a dry weather access only campsite; bring your own firewood and drinking water. **Map refs:** 28 B5, 93 L6

DIGGERS HEADLAND RESERVE

Explore rocky headlands, swim, laze on the beach or paddle out on a surfboard at this sleepy and secluded area near Diggers Camp village, 45 km south-east of Grafton via Wooli Rd. During summer and school holidays the campground comes alive with beachgoers; at other times of the year it closes and blends into its pristine, natural surroundings.

Who to contact: Clarence Valley Council, Grafton (02) 6643 0200, (02) 6626 6858 after hours

162 Diggers Headland Reserve Camping Ground

There are up to 26 camping sites here, tucked in among coastal banksias, only a stone's throw from the beach. To get here, follow Diggers Camp Rd off Wooli Rd, about 12 km north of Wooli. It's a pretty basic setup, but it's quiet and attractive, and there's plenty of swimming, fishing and walking to keep you occupied. Note: camping is only permitted here Dec–Jan and NSW and Queensland school holidays. **Map refs:** 28 D5, 93 N6

GUY FAWKES RIVER STATE CONSERVATION AREA

The Guy Fawkes River State Conservation Area is adjacent to the national park of the same name, and it shares the same rugged, picturesque landscape. It comprises 2 sections with a total of a little more than 5200 ha. Dalmorton camping area is perched on the north-eastern edge of the conservation park, on the Boyd River.

Who to contact: Dorrigo Rainforest Centre (02) 6657 2309

163 Dalmorton camping area

Dalmorton camping area is a pleasant spot on the southern banks of the Boyd River. The nearby village of Dalmorton may look like a ghost town, but in the mid-1800s it was a bustling goldmining town of up to 5000 people. Access to the camping area is via Old Grafton–Glen Innes Rd, 66 km west of Grafton. Turn onto Chaelundi Rd at Dalmorton. Bring your own firewood and drinking water. **Map refs:** 28 B5, 93 L6

MEBBIN NATIONAL PARK

Adjacent to Border Ranges National Park, Mebbin forms part of the remains of the Tweed shield volcano, and it's also one of 50 national parks included in the World Heritage–listed Gondwana Rainforests of Australia. Its rich and rugged landscape can be enjoyed on foot or by 4WD.

Who to contact: NPWS Murwillumbah (02) 6670 8600

164 Cutters Camp camping area

You'll find Cutters Camp where Mebbin Forest and Caddell rds meet. Unsealed Mebbin Forest Rd is a 35 km scenic route with wonderful views of the region's volcanic, forest-clad landscape; you'll need a 4WD if it's been raining. Byrrill Creek walking track (450 m each way) leads from the camping area through subtropical rainforest down to the creek. Note: Cutters Camp is only suitable for small camper trailers and caravans. Bring along drinking water. **Map refs:** 28 D1, 93 O2

NYMBOI–BINDERAY NATIONAL PARK

Nymboi Binderay is the local Gumbaynggirr name for the river that cuts through this national park, 25 km north of Dorrigo, creating a dramatic backdrop for whitewater rafting. Access from Dorrigo is via Moonpar Rd off Tyringham Rd; or from the north via Nymboida–Kangaroo River Rd from Nymboida, 35 km south of Grafton. These roads are unsealed; you'll need a 4WD if it's wet.

Who to contact: Dorrigo Rainforest Centre (02) 6657 2309; or NPWS Grafton (02) 6641 1500

165 The Junction camping area

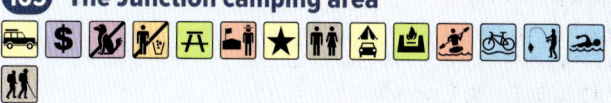

Take the Black Mountain Rd south from Nymboida, Glenreagh or Lowanna and turn onto Junction Rd, a 1.4 km unsealed road suitable for 4WDs only – unless you're prepared to walk or paddle in. Once there, you'll find a peaceful camping area by the Nymboida River, where you can launch your canoe or kayak or just kick back on the banks and look for platypus and river turtles. Bring your own drinking water and firewood. **Map refs:** 28 C5, 45 E5, 90 G4, 93 M7

166 Platypus Flat camping area

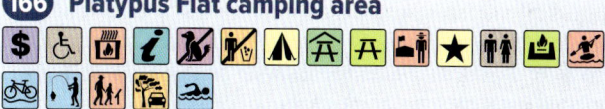

Perched on the banks of the Nymboida River, just off Moonpar Forest Dr, Platypus Flat provides tent sites in a grassy clearing beneath blue gums and river oaks, a short walk from your car. There are fabulous swimming holes within easy reach and you can launch your canoe or kayak here. If you're in the mood for a short walk, the delightful 300 m Red Cedar Track begins 1 km east. Note: this is 2WD access in dry weather only, and the roads are unsuitable for caravans. Bring drinking water and firewood. **Map refs:** 28 C6, 93 M7

NYMBOIDA NATIONAL PARK

If you're tiring of ocean vistas and coastal camping, you can venture deep into the rugged, pristine wilderness of Nymboida National Park, 55 km west of Grafton. Whitewater rafters revel in the twists and turns of the Nymboida River, while self-sufficient, experienced bushwalkers will enjoy the opportunity to explore a park with no marked walking trails.

Who to contact: NPWS Grafton (02) 6641 1500

167 Nymboida River camping area

You'll need a 4WD vehicle to get to this secluded camping area near Nymboida River, in the south-eastern corner of the park. Follow the T Ridge Rd 57 km west of South Grafton; take Dobby Rd, then Ramornie Rd from Glens Crossing. Swimming, fishing and canoeing are popular activities, as is bushwalking. There are no marked walking trails, however, so walkers need to be experienced and well prepared. Bring your own drinking water and firewood; gas/fuel stove preferred. **Map refs:** 28 C4, 93 M6

RICHMOND RANGE NATIONAL PARK

Richmond Range National Park, 40 km west of Kyogle and Casino, is a rich treasure trove of eucalypt, old-growth forest and World Heritage–listed rainforest. The park protects an astounding diversity of plants and animals, making it a fabulous destination for wildlife-watching, walking and 4WD touring. Note: roads may be closed when wet.

Who to contact: NPWS Kyogle (02) 6632 0000

168 Peacock Creek camping area

Located in a bend on the Peacock River, this is a grassy, sunlit camping area popular with birdwatchers, cyclists, walkers and 4WD enthusiasts. It's off Peacock Creek Rd, 36 km north of Mallanganee. To get here, take the Cambridge Plateau Scenic Dr from Mallanganee or Peacock Creek Rd from Bonalbo. Access for 2WD vehicles is in dry weather only. Bring your own drinking water and firewood. **Map refs:** 28 C2, 93 M3

TOONUMBAR NATIONAL PARK

Two World Heritage–listed rainforests, Murray Scrub and Dome Mountain, are contained within this park, 35 km north-west of Kyogle. It's a landscape rich with tropical and subtropical rainforest and a number of rare and threatened animals, including the sooty owl and red-necked pademelon. Access for 2WD vehicles in dry weather only. The land is co-managed by NPWS and the Githabul people.

Who to contact: NPWS Kyogle (02) 6632 0000

169 Iron Pot Creek camping area

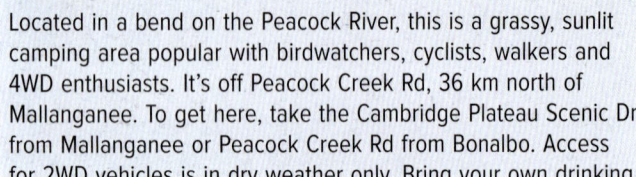

Rest in the dappled shade of flooded gums at this spacious, grassed camping area. There's a 750 m loop track leading to Iron Pot Creek; a night walk with a torch may reveal possums, native mice and gliders. To get here, follow Afterlee Dr from Kyogle for about 35 km and turn onto Toonumbar Forest Dr. Iron Pot Creek camping area is signposted along Murray Scrub Rd. Bring your own firewood and drinking water. **Map refs:** 28 C2, 93 M2

WHIAN WHIAN STATE CONSERVATION AREA

Established in 2003 to preserve a small area surrounded by Nightcap National Park, Whian Whian plays a vital role in the protection of koalas, platypus and spotted-tailed quolls. It's a relaxing place for a rainforest picnic or short walk. You'll find it 35 km north of Lismore, via Whian Whian Forest Dr off Lismore–Mullumbimby Rd.

Who to contact: NPWS Alstonville (02) 6627 0200

170 Rummery Park camping area

From this roomy, friendly camping area you can take a short walk following Boggy Creek to the beautiful Minyon Falls in Nightcap National Park. Other activities include birdwatching and car touring. To get here, turn off Whian Whian Forest Dr onto Peates Mountain Rd. You'll need to bring your own drinking water and firewood. **Map refs:** 28 E2, 93 O3

YURAYGIR NATIONAL PARK

Yuraygir National Park protects the longest stretch of undeveloped coastline in NSW: a glorious sweep of beaches backed by forest and heath. The state's coastal fringe is increasingly busy and developed, so this park's 60 km tract of largely untouched bushland is an important natural reserve. The 4-day, 65 km Yuraygir Coastal Walk follows the coast from Angourie to Red Rock. You can stay at the national park campgrounds along the way, or in accommodation at Brooms Head, Minnie Water and Wooli.

Who to contact: NPWS Grafton (02) 6641 1500

171 Boorkoom camping area

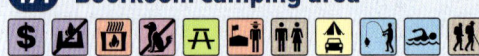

In the southern section of Yuraygir National Park, small and secluded Boorkoom is north of Wooli near Diggers Camp. The 10 campsites here aren't suitable for caravans or camper trailers; access is via the unsealed Diggers Camp Rd. There's an easy 3 km (1 hr) walk between the camping area and Wilsons Headland, where you'll be rewarded with sweeping ocean vistas. Bring your own water and gas/fuel stove as campfires are not permitted. **Map refs:** 28 D5, 93 N6

172 Grey Cliff camping area

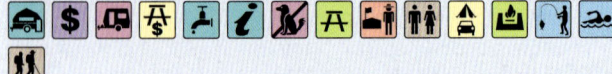

Next to Red Cliff camping area on the headland south of Lake Arragan, Grey Cliff is 5 km north of Brooms Head along the unsealed Brooms Head Rd. The campsites are big enough for camper trailers and caravans. Bring firewood or try the user-pays system. **Map refs:** 28 D4, 93 N6

173 Illaroo camping area

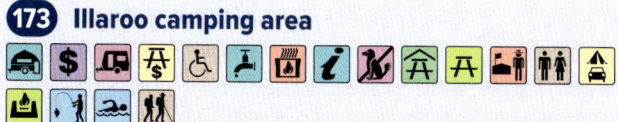

Just north of Minnie Water, via Minnie Water Rd off Wooli Rd, this is a large and spacious camping area with 60 sites shared between Illaroo north and Illaroo south. There's room for tents, campervans and trailers. The beach is close by, with 4WD beach access, and there are a couple of short tracks: the 30 min Angophora Grove Walk and the 2 km return Rocky Point Track, which leads to a walk-in camping area with no facilities. Bring your own firewood or try the user-pays system. **Map refs:** 28 D5, 93 N6

174 Lake Arragan camping area

Next to a small coastal lagoon ringed with paperbarks and nodding reeds, this camping area is just as popular with migratory and resident birds as it is with campers, but with 50 campsites there's room for everyone. The Angourie Walk (10 km, 3 hr return) is a medium-grade track that joins Mara Creek and Lake Arragan. The camping area is 5 km north of Brooms Head, along the unsealed Brooms Head Rd. Bring firewood or try the user-pays system. **Map refs:** 28 D4, 93 N6

175 Pebbly Beach camping area

This is a top spot in a bay north of Station Creek Beach, with 60 campsites surrounded by banksias and horse-tail she-oaks. Sites are large and spread out behind the beach. There is a pleasant walk north to Freshwater Beach. You'll need a 4WD to get here and you should plan to travel at low tide as there's a saltwater creek crossing and beach driving. It's at the end of Barcoongere Way. Station Creek Beach is a vehicle-free area (it's a breeding site for the endangered little terns), so it's a good place to bring children, along with your own drinking water. Firewood is provided. Not suitable for large caravans. **Map refs:** 28 D5, 58 D3, 91 I12, 93 N7, 98 F6

176 Red Cliff camping area

This is next to Grey Cliff camping area, on the headland south of Lake Arragan, 5 km north of Brooms Head along the unsealed Brooms Head Rd. The campsites are big enough for camper trailers and caravans. Bring firewood or try the user-pays system. **Map refs:** 28 D4, 93 N6

177 Rocky Point camping area (walk-in camping)

This is a walk-in camping area with no facilities, accessible via an easy 100 m walking track leading from Illaroo camping area. Campfires are not permitted, so bring your own gas/fuel stove and drinking water. **Map refs:** 28 D5, 93 N6

178 Sandon River camping area

You get the best of many worlds from here: sweeping sandy beach to the north; rockpools to the south at the base of Sandon Bluffs; and fine fishing in Sandon River. The 40 sites in the camping area are suitable for tents, caravans and camper trailers, and there's a boat ramp nearby. To get here, follow Sandon Rd off Brooms Head Rd south of Brooms Head. Bring firewood or try the user-pays system. **Map refs:** 28 D5, 93 N6

179 Shelley Head camping area (walk-in camping)

This walk-in selection of campsites is en route between Lake Arragan and Mara Creek on the Angourie Walk (10 km, 3 hr return). Campers need to bring their own drinking water and gas/fuel stove as campfires are not permitted. **Map refs:** 28 D4, 93 N5

180 Station Creek camping area

This is a popular spot in peak periods, positioned by a peaceful creek with access through the sand dunes to the beach. Bring a canoe and go for a paddle, or set out on the Corkwood and Scribbly Gum Walk (1.5 km, 1 hr loop, easy grade) upstream through coastal forest. There are 20 sites here; bring your own water. You can get here via Barcoongere Way, which is an unsealed road; if it's wet, a 4WD is recommended. **Map refs:** 28 D5, 93 N7

CAMPSITES LOCATED IN OTHER AREAS

181 The Arts Factory camping area

This relaxed backpacker-dominated site features a variety of accommodation options: tent sites, dorm and private rooms and even a tepee! Created in the 1970s by alternative lifestylers, the Arts Factory remains true to its roots with myriad options for self-expression – juggling, yoga, didgeridoo lessons, crystal healing and African drumming sessions. It's a 15 min stroll from the beach and the centre of Byron Bay; from town join Lawson St, turn left into Butler St and then follow the signs to the 'arts centre'. Bookings are essential in peak periods. **Map refs:** 28 E2, 93 O3

How to book: 1 Skinners Shoot Rd, Byron Bay (02) 6685 7709 nomadhostels.com/arts-factory

182 Bells Bay camping area

Situated beside picturesque Toonumbar Dam, 31 km north-west of Kyogle via Afterlee Rd, Bells Bay is a vision in green, surrounded by swathes of forest. Boating (8-knot limit), canoeing, swimming and fishing for Australian bass and east

coast cod are some of the popular pastimes here. Facilities on offer include sheds, rainwater tanks, a jetty and boat ramp. Take note of signs indicating water quality before heading in for a swim. **Map refs:** 28 C2, 93 N2

Who to contact: (02) 6633 9140 *Camping fees:* fees payable using self-registration

183 Broken Head Holiday Park

At Broken Head Nature Reserve, lush and fertile rainforests reach emerald tendrils all the way down to long, sweeping beaches, and this holiday park is tucked in right next to the reserve, 7 km south of Byron Bay. Villas, cabins, and powered and unpowered sites are all available at this beachfront haven, which also has a laundry, kiosk, barbecue facilities and showers. Bookings advisable during peak periods. **Map refs:** 28 E2, 93 O3

How to book: 184 Beach Rd, Broken Head (02) 6685 3245, 1800 450 036 www.brokenheadholidaypark.com.au

184 Clarkes Beach Holiday Park

Nestled on the sands of one of Australia's most famous holiday towns, Byron Bay, this park's serene environment is complemented by its modern facilities and amazing views. It's within walking distance of town and some of the country's most iconic beaches: Main Beach, the Pass and Wategoes Beach. An experience not to be missed is a picnic lunch on the park's viewing platform while watching migrating whales pass. There are cabins and villas, and tent and caravan sites as well as a playground and laundry. **Map refs:** 28 E2, 93 O3

How to book: Lighthouse Rd, Byron Bay (02) 6685 6496 www.clarkesbeach.com.au

185 Flat Rock Tent Park

This is a simple camping spot 4 km north-east of Ballina on the Coast Rd (Lennox Head Rd) but it's quiet and protected despite being about a 3 min walk to Angels Beach. With Ballina and Lennox Head close by, it's a great place to kick back and lose track of time over summer. Bookings recommended in peak periods. **Map refs:** 28 E3, 93 O3

How to book: 38 Flat Rock Rd, East Ballina (02) 6686 4848 www.flatrockcamping.com.au

186 Massey Greene Holiday Park

This is in a top location, right on the Brunswick River and minutes away from Brunswick Heads town centre. The river offers swimming, fishing, snorkelling and boating, and there's a surf beach only a 10 min walk away. You can choose from

tent and caravan sites and self-contained family cabins. Facilities include a laundry, camp kitchen, linen hire and free wi-fi internet. **Map refs:** 28 E2, 93 O3

How to book: Tweed St, Brunswick Heads (02) 6685 1329 www.masseygreene.com.au

187 Mount Warning Rainforest Park

Surround yourself with lush and up-tempo rainforest and mountain streams in this verdant mid-north-coast holiday park at the foot of Mt Warning. Accommodation options include deluxe, ensuite and budget cabins, and tent sites. There's a swimming pool, TV room and children's toy area, games room and camp kitchen, to name just a few of the facilities. Bookings are essential. To get here, take the Mt Warning Rd from Murwillumbah; less than 2 km along this road you'll see the turn-off to the left. **Map refs:** 28 D1, 93 O2

How to book: 153 Mt Warning Rd, Mt Warning (02) 6679 5120 www.mtwarningrainforestpark.com

188 Woolgoolga Beach Caravan Park

A great family holiday spot fronting the Pacific Ocean, Woolgoolga Beach Caravan Park's facilities include powered sites with beach views, villas with private verandahs, a camp kitchen complete with herb garden and a large children's playground. The town itself is well-known for its Indian community and Sikh temples (open to visitors on weekends). Woolgoolga Headland is the perfect spot to watch migrating humpback whales May–Nov. A 2 km riverside walk along Woolgoolga Creek wends through subtropical rainforest to a spectacular waterfall. Turn right off the Pacific Hwy onto Clarence St and follow the road to the beach. **Map refs:** 28 D6, 93 N7

Who to contact: 55 Beach St, Woolgoolga 1800 200 555 www. coffscoastholidayparks.com.au/woolgoolga-beach-caravan-park/

NEW ENGLAND AND THE NORTH-WEST

HEAD INLAND FROM THE mid-north coast and the natural tapestry of NSW becomes increasingly colourful and diverse: from quiet, riverside family-camping spots to rugged, remote granite and rainforest wilderness. The Fossickers Way follows the region's fortune-chasing history from Nundle in the south to Warialda in the north and east to Glen Innes. It brings such gems as the Burren Junction artesian bore reserve, Split Rock Dam and camping sites tucked into the choicest of places around Peel Valley, Barraba and Bingara. You can try your hand at hang-gliding in Manilla, or fossick for sapphires and other precious stones at Cranky Rock Recreation Reserve near Warialda.

This region boasts some incredible granite landscapes – from the staggering monolith of Bald Rock to the rock-climbing wonderland of Cathedral Rock National Park and the spectacular rocky outcrops of Mount Kaputar National Park. Mystery Face in Torrington State Conservation Area will have you scratching your head at the unique creativity of nature.

The exceptional northern NSW rainforest is still present in this region. New England National Park is lush and overgrown, an almost impenetrable tangle of vines, dripping tree ferns, delicate orchids and staghorn ferns, with a canopy of majestic red cedar and yellow carabeen. Oxley Wild Rivers National Park was given World Heritage status for its dry rainforest, a particularly rare vegetation type existing only in shaded gullies that are sheltered from fire. The biodiversity created by this dry rainforest provides a refuge for more than 180 plant species.

In a region as diverse as this, the recreational opportunities on offer are outstanding. Bushwalking, boating, fishing, waterskiing, wildlife-watching, rock climbing, picnicking and swimming are just a taste of what awaits the happy camper in New England and the North-West.

CAMPSITES LOCATED IN PARKS AND RESERVES

BALD ROCK NATIONAL PARK

Distracted by the beauty of Uluru in the NT, many Australians are unaware of its equally impressive cousin, Bald Rock, 27 km north of Tenterfield. At 750 m long, 500 m wide and 200 m high, the largest granite rock in the country is a mind-blowing tableau of stone arches, canyons and magnificent views.

Who to contact: NPWS Tenterfield (02) 6736 4298
Camping fees: fees payable using self-registration

189 Bald Rock camping area

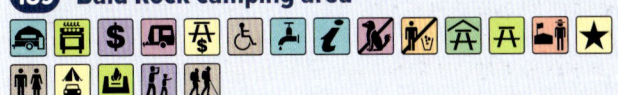

To get to Bald Rock, follow the Mt Lindesay Rd north about 30 km from Tenterfield, then take the park access road to the end. From the camping area you can take the short but strenuous Bungoona Walk (3 km, 2–3 hr) to the summit of Bald Rock; alternatively, there are a couple of other walks of varying difficulty that lead through diverse vegetation to viewing sites for Bald Rock and the surrounding granite landscape. The 14 campsites are sheltered and well shaded here. A walk up to Bald Rock at sunrise or sunset will be rewarded with fantastic views, and the changing colours of the rock in the early and late light offer many opportunities for the keen photographer. Bring your own drinking water, or boil/treat the creek water available. Some firewood supplied, but best to bring your own.
Map refs: 35 H2, 93 L3

BOONOO BOONOO NATIONAL PARK

The highlight of this national park in the state's north-eastern tablelands is the spectacular Boonoo Boonoo Falls. The Boonoo Boonoo River meanders through high country studded with granite domes before tumbling 210 m from the plateau into a lush rainforest valley. The park's name is said to mean 'big rock' in the language of the Juckambal.

Who to contact: NPWS Tenterfield (02) 6736 4298

190 Cypress Pine camping area

The national park is 24 km north-east of Tenterfield via Mt Lindesay and Woodenbong rds. Cypress Pine camping area is on the main park access road. There are several walks to do in the region – if you're time-poor, make sure you fit in the 30 min walk from the Boonoo Boonoo picnic area to the viewing platform overlooking the falls. A profusion of wildflowers carpets the region in spring. **Map refs:** 35 H2, 93 L3

BOONOO STATE FOREST

Adjacent to Basket Swamp National Park, Boonoo State Forest can be reached via Basket Swamp Rd off Lindrook Rd from Mt Lindesay Rd. Note: 2WD access is possible during dry weather only.

Who to contact: NPWS Tenterfield (02) 6736 4298

191 Basket Swamp camping area

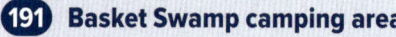

This is a basic site with toilets, tables and wood fireplaces. A track nearby leads to the Basket Swamp Falls, which are the main attraction for visitors to the forest. Nearby Basket Swamp National Park contains Woollool Woolloolni Aboriginal Place, named by the Bundjalung after a wuyangali, or clever man. To get to Basket Swamp camping area, take the Lindrook Rd turn-off from Mt Lindesay Rd; turn onto Woollool Woolloolni Rd and then Basket Swamp Forest Rd. Dry-weather access only for conventional vehicles. Bring your own drinking water.
Map refs: 35 H2, 93 L3

CARRAI NATIONAL PARK

Carrai National Park comprises an impressive granite plateau and steep escarpments dropping down to meet Kunderang Brook and the Macleay River. Self-reliant bushwalkers and campers will enjoy the solitude offered by the remote location. Note: as access roads are unsealed, a 4WD is recommended.

Who to contact: NPWS Walcha (02) 6777 4700

192 Daisy Plains Huts

There are 4 basic huts here, with pit toilets, a kitchen with an open fireplace (bring your own wood) and rainwater (boil/treat before drinking). Reservations aren't available. To get here, take the Kempsey–Armidale Rd west of Kempsey; 3 km north of Willawarrin, turn onto Carrai Rd, and the huts are just before the turn-off to Cochrane Rd. **Map refs:** 35 H5, 93 L9

CATHEDRAL ROCK NATIONAL PARK

Cathedral Rock National Park is great bushwalking and rock climbing territory, with myriad opportunities for photography. The rugged, granite landscape is punctuated with giant boulders, massive tors and curious rock formations, with 1584 m Round Mountain its highest point. It's 60 km west of Dorrigo via Waterfall Way, or via Ebor–Guyra Rd from the north.

Who to contact: Dorrigo Rainforest Centre (02) 6657 2309

193 Barokee camping area

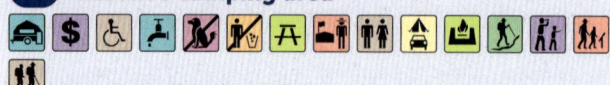

Barokee is the most popular campground, with secluded campsites amid eucalypts and banksia. There's water in a nearby creek, but it needs to be treated or boiled, otherwise bring your own. Walkers can take on the 5.8 km (2.5 hr return) Cathedral Rock Track, or the 10.4 km walk to Native Dog Creek, where they'll either need to stay the night before returning or organise a pick-up. This campsite can be reached via Waterfall Way south of Ebor. **Map refs:** 35 H4, 93 L8

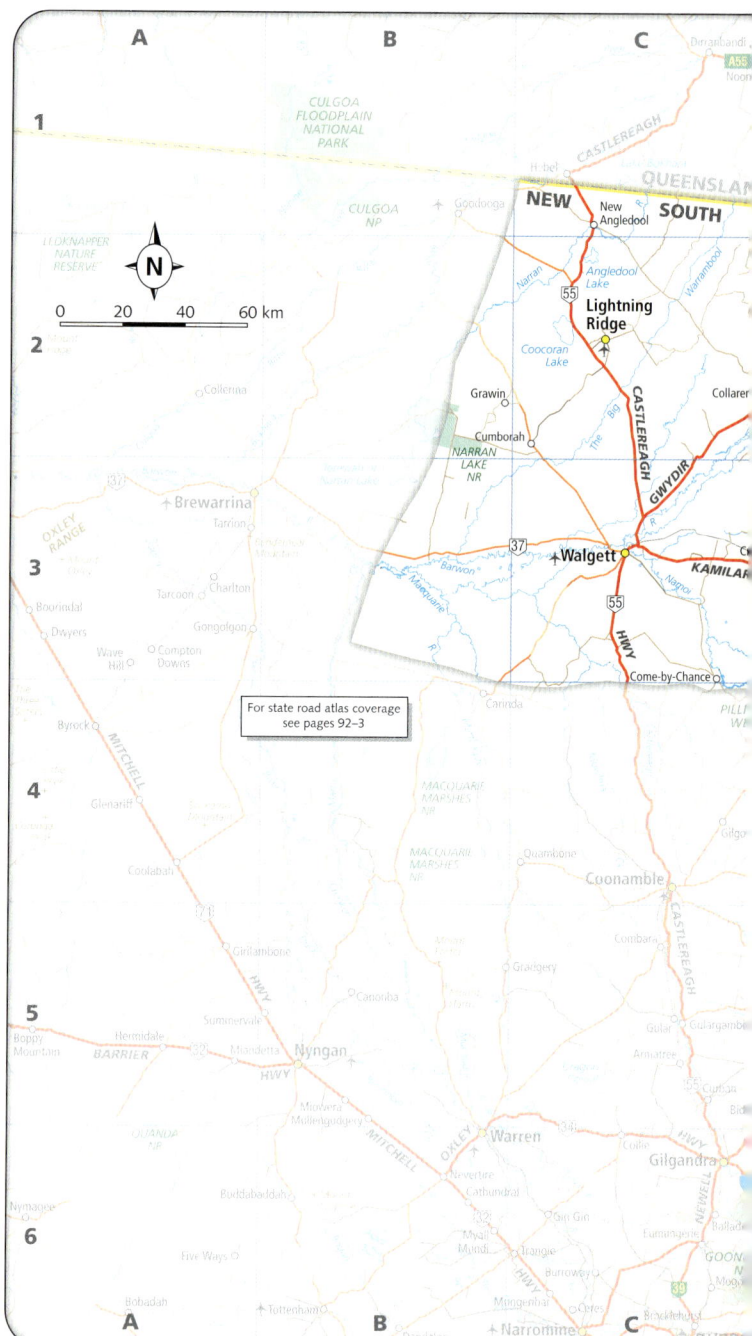

194 Native Dog camping area

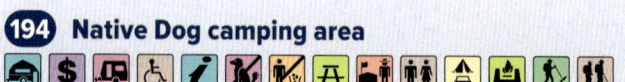

There's enough room at the campsite for your caravan or camper trailer, and a number of walks leave from here, including the easy Warrigal Track (1 km, 30 min return) and Woolpack Rocks (7.4 km, 3 hr return). There's a creek nearby but it can dry up in late winter and spring, so it's best to bring your own drinking water. Situated in the north of the park, this camping area is accessed via Guyra Rd. **Map refs:** 35 H4, 93 L8

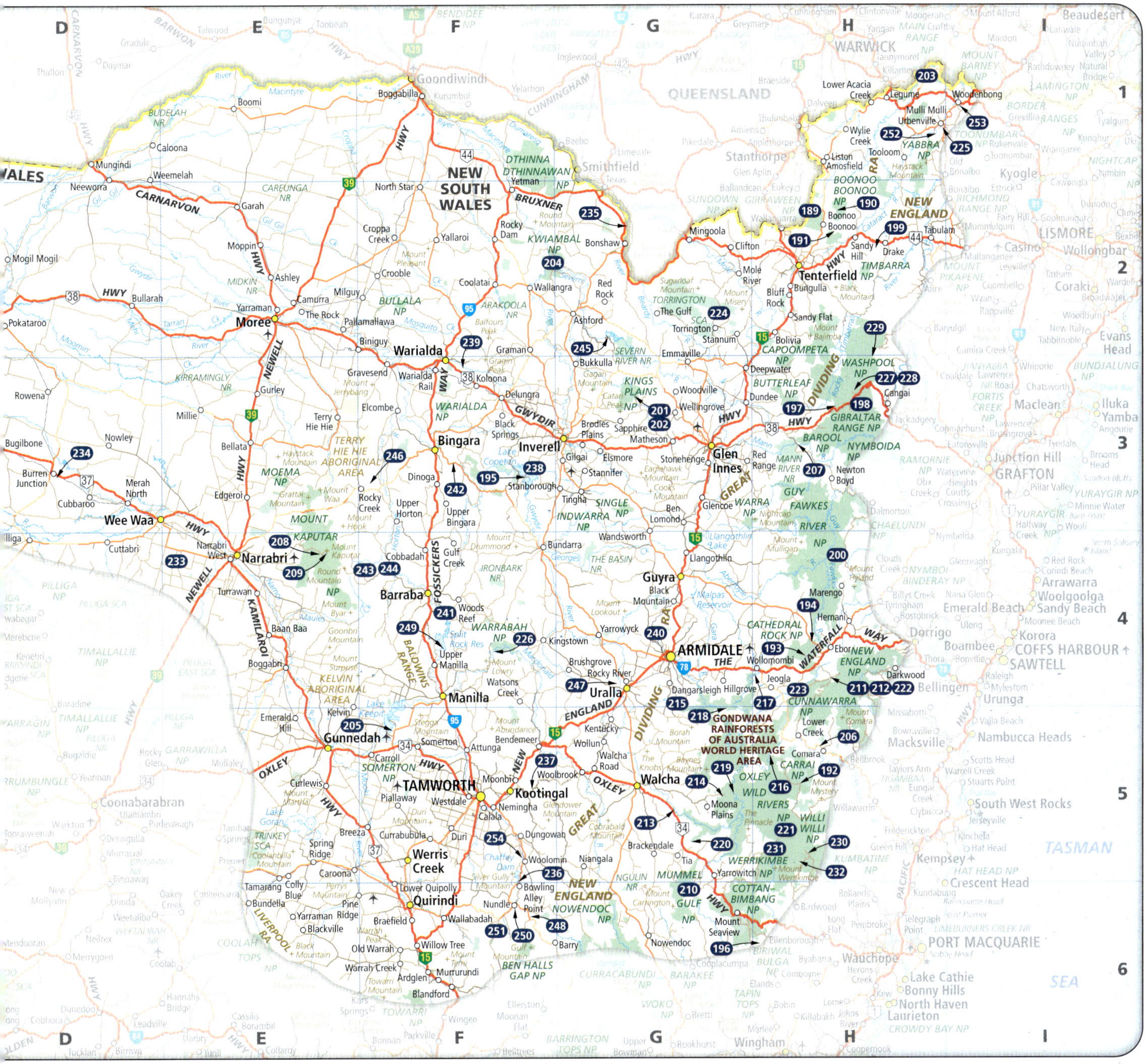

COPETON WATERS STATE PARK

Copeton Waters State Park is on the western shores of Copeton Dam, which holds enough water to fill Sydney Harbour 3 times. It's a recreational adventurer's paradise, with fishing, bushwalking, water activities and much more. The dam is about 40 km south-west of Inverell via Copeton Dam Rd. Bookings are essential at peak periods.

How to book: Copeton Dam Rd, Inverell (02) 6723 6269 www.copeton.com.au

195 Copeton Waters State Park camping area

What can't you do here? Canoeing, sailing, golf, fishing, walking and cricket are just a few of the activities on offer for daytrippers or multi-day visitors alike. There's even a waterslide. There are cabins and bunkhouses, amenities, boat ramps, a camp kitchen and laundry. **Map refs: 35 F3, 93 I6**

COTTAN–BIMBANG NATIONAL PARK

Walk under the jigsaw canopy of towering mountain forest, enjoy a scenic drive along Knodingbul Forest Rd and take in the beautiful view from Blue Knob, or roll along Myrtle Scrub Rd and unpack a picnic next to the historic forestry bridge over Cells River. You can reach this national park via Oxley Hwy, about 70 km west of Wauchope or 65 km east of Walcha. Roads in the park are unsealed, so if it's been raining call for information on road conditions.

Who to contact: NPWS Port Macquarie–Hastings (02) 6588 5555

196 Maxwells Flat camping area

Maxwells Flat is a secluded grassy area next to a small creek. You can reach it via Causeway Rd off Knodingbul Rd – the best approach is from the northern intersection of these roads. Bring your own drinking water, or boil or treat water from the creek before drinking. Note: access in wet weather can be difficult; 4WD recommended. **Map refs:** 35 H6, 93 K11

GIBRALTAR RANGE NATIONAL PARK

Gibraltar Range National Park preserves an area of immense natural beauty and spectacular scenery, 104 km west of Grafton on the Gwydir Hwy. Craggy granite outcrops, steep-sided valleys, a plethora of scenic creeks, tumbling waterfalls and pristine rainforest are among its many attributes. There's also more than 100 km of walking tracks to explore.

Who to contact: NPWS Glen Innes (02) 6739 0700

197 Boundary Falls camping area

There are 15 sites at this picnic and camping area, reached via Washpool Trail off the Gwydir Hwy, 60 km east of Glenn Innes. The magnificent Boundary Falls are nearby, and a number of walking trails lead off from here. You can time your visit to coincide with the flowering of the Gibraltar Range waratahs, in mid-Oct–Dec. Bring your own drinking water and firewood. **Map refs:** 35 H3, 93 L5

198 Mulligans camping area

Here you'll find 6 large camping areas for big groups as well as a number of smaller sites. There are several walking tracks fanning out from here, including the 5 km return Dandahra Falls Walk, which passes through towering eucalypt forest to rainforest before descending to the stunning 240 m Dandahra Falls. The camping area is 10 km along Mulligans Dr off Gwydir Hwy near the NPWS visitor centre. Ask at the visitor centre for information on walking tracks and ranger-guided spotlight tours. Tap water needs to be boiled or treated before drinking. **Map refs:** 35 H3, 93 L5

GIRARD STATE FOREST

Cycling, horseriding, bushwalking and 4WD touring are the main activities available in this former mining region, 30 km east of Tenterfield along the Bruxner Hwy.

Who to contact: Forests NSW Casino (02) 6662 0900

199 Crooked Creek Picnic Area

This natural clearing is just off the Bruxner Hwy, next to Crooked Creek. It's a pretty basic setup, but there are sheltered picnic tables, toilets and wood BBQs, which makes it a suitable spot overnight or for a short stay. **Map refs:** 35 H2, 93 L3

GUY FAWKES RIVER NATIONAL PARK

Guy Fawkes National Park in the state's north-east is a rugged landscape of mountain ranges, sheer gorges and narrow valleys. Well-equipped bushwalkers can get off the beaten track, but there is also vehicle access to campsites, waterfalls and picnic venues. Bushwalking, canoeing, rock climbing and wildlife-watching are key activities.

Who to contact: Dorrigo Rainforest Centre (02) 6657 2309

200 Chaelundi camping area

The burbling Chaelundi Creek, next to this small campground, is home to the rare New England tree frog, and echidnas and glossy black cockatoos will also occasionally make an appearance. A short walk leads to Chaelundi Falls; from there it's 1.5 km to Chaelundi Bluff, which offers excellent views across the valley. To get to the campground, follow the Armidale–Grafton Rd from Dundurrabin and turn onto Sheep Station Creek Rd, then Chaelundi and Misty Creek rds. It's a short walk from the parking area to tent sites. Bring your own drinking water or boil/treat water from the creek; bring a gas/fuel stove. **Map refs:** 35 H4, 93 L7

KINGS PLAINS NATIONAL PARK

One of the lesser known parks in the New England tablelands, Kings Plains is a wild and rugged region 50 km north-west of Glen Innes via Wellingrove and 48 km north-east of Inverell. Still pools, waterfalls, rapids and creeks make a beautiful backdrop for bushwalking and wildlife-watching.

Who to contact: NPWS Glen Innes (02) 6739 0700

201 Ironbark camping area

A small natural clearing amid woodland beside Kings Plains Creek, the Ironbark camping area is about 800 m along the road from Kings Plains Creek camping area. It's got vehicle-based camping (2WD in dry weather only) but no toilets – you'll need to walk or drive to the other camping ground for those. Bring your own drinking water and firewood. **Map refs:** 35 G3, 93 J5

202 Kings Plains Creek camping area

A broad, sweeping grassed area ringed with ironbark woodlands, this camping area can be reached via Jindalee Rd from Kings Plains Rd west of Wellingrove. Turn west about 2.5 km from Jindalee. There's a short walk from your car to the campsites, which are set out along the edge of a waterhole in a bend in Kings Plains Creek. This is a very pleasant place in the late afternoon, with the forest behind and the sun setting over the water to the west. The access road is 2WD during dry weather only. Bring your own drinking water and firewood. **Map refs:** 35 G3, 93 J5

KOREELAH NATIONAL PARK

Part of the Gondwana Rainforests of Australia conglomerate, 34 km north-west of Woodenbong, Koreelah National Park protects some of the most westerly rainforest in NSW. Beautiful deep, still pools beckon at Koreelah Falls; keep an eye out for the endangered double-eyed fig parrot and the eastern bristlebird.

Who to contact: NPWS Kyogle (02) 6632 0000

203 Koreelah Creek camping area

This is a dry-weather access only site – to get here, follow the Mt Lindesay Hwy 10 km west of Woodenbong and turn onto Mt Clunie Rd, then left onto White Swamp Rd. Look for Trough Creek Rd on the left. Both Koreelah Creek and Koreelah Creek Falls are close to the camping area. Bring your own drinking water and firewood. **Map refs:** 35 H1, 93 M1

KWIAMBAL NATIONAL PARK

The Macintyre and Severn rivers have chiselled drama and beauty into the granite landscape of Kwiambal National Park. Highlights include Macintyre Falls and the deep river gorge at Dungeon Lookout, both reached via short walking tracks. There is also a series of caves along Limestone Creek, and an easy walk through one of them, though you will need to bring a torch. When the water is low, rock hopping in the gorge above Macintyre Falls provides access to an unusual landscape of scoured and polished granite. And the walk down to the gorge below the falls is well worth it, with dramatic scenery and pleasant swimming. The park is 90 km north of Inverell and 40 km to the north-west of Ashford.

Who to contact: NPWS Tenterfield (02) 6736 4298
Camping fees: fees payable using self-registration

204 Lemon Tree Flat camping area

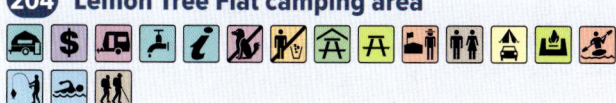

To reach the camping area, follow Wallangra Rd north from Ashford and turn onto Limestone Rd. Parts of the road are unsealed, so if it's been raining check with the parks office for road conditions. You can set up your tent next to the Severn River, where you can swim, explore up or downstream, or fish for Murray cod, golden perch and catfish. There's drinking water here, but you'll need to bring your own firewood. **Map refs:** 35 F2, 93 I3

LAKE KEEPIT STATE PARK

Off the Oxley Hwy around 50 km west of Tamworth, Lake Keepit State Park has activities and relaxation for all the family. Have a barbecue or picnic, take a bushwalk, go waterskiing or glide across the water in a pleasure boat. The park is also popular with anglers, who drop in a line to wait for yellow-belly, Murray cod and catfish to bite. Bookings are advisable for peak periods.

Who to contact: Lake Keepit State Park (02) 6769 7605

205 Lake Keepit State Park camping area

This is a great family camping spot, 54 km west of Tamworth and 38 km east of Gunnedah via Keepit Dam Rd off the Oxley Hwy. It's a little slice of outdoor paradise: everything from hang-gliding lessons and golf to a BMX and skateboarding park. And that's on top of the more traditional camping activities, such as birdwatching (there are 170 species in the region) and walking. Choose between luxury and standard cabins, and camping and caravan sites. There's also a laundry and kiosk. **Map refs:** 35 F5, 92 H9

MACLEAY RIVER PUBLIC RECREATION RESERVE

The beautiful Macleay River winds inland from the mid-north coast of NSW, from South West Rocks past Kinchela and Smithtown towards Kempsey. The Macleay River Public Recreation Reserve is on the upper reaches of the river, 71 km north-west of Kempsey along the Kempsey–Armidale Rd.

Who to contact: NPWS Armidale (02) 6738 9100

206 Blackbird Flat Reserve camping area

This is a spacious, friendly and free camping area on the banks of the Macleay River. Follow the Kempsey–Armidale Rd from Kempsey. There's fishing, swimming, mountain-biking and canoeing on offer – and you can bring your dog along. **Map refs:** 35 H5, 93 L9

MANN RIVER NATURE RESERVE

This is northern NSW at its best: quiet, lusciously green, fertile and mountainous terrain embellished with rivers and creeks. The nature reserve is accessed via the Old Glen Innes–Grafton Rd, 48 km east of Glen Innes and 129 km west of Grafton. Note: sections of this road are unsealed and steep.

Who to contact: NPWS Glen Innes (02) 6739 0700

207 Mann River Nature Reserve camping area

A picturesque and grassy space by the Mann River, this camping area is a top spot to kick back and relax. There are beautiful views from 1015 m Tommys Rock Lookout (4WD access only), named after a well-known Aboriginal bushman. It's a hard walk, however, so only take it on if you're fit (or in a 4WD). The Old Glen Innes–Grafton Rd is a scenic, winding 180 km route with a history dating back to the 1800s. Note: parts of this road are unsealed and only suitable for 4WDs. **Map refs:** 35 H3, 93 L5

MOUNT KAPUTAR NATIONAL PARK

Mt Kaputar looms 1510 m above the surrounding Western Plains – the highest point in the Nandewar Range, which formed when the Australian continent moved over a volcanic hot spot deep in the Earth's mantle. The result is a fascinating diversity of landscapes, plants and animals that can be explored via numerous walking tracks and fire trails. Be sure to leave time on the drive here to take in the views from various lookouts on the way, or stop for a walk up Mt Yulludunida – a dry, rugged escarpment where many ancient and twisted grass trees grow. The view, and the colours on the rocks, can be dramatic at sunrise, while at sunset, in the right conditions, the lookout at West Kaputar Rocks can provide good photographic opportunities.

Who to contact: NPWS Narrabri (02) 6792 7300

208 Bark Hut camping area

There are 15 camping spots here, on the main access road about 6 km from Mt Kaputar. This is the starting point for the demanding Scutts Hut walk (19 km, 6 hr), which should only be undertaken by fit, experienced and well-prepared walkers. An easy walk from the bottom of the camping area goes to the lookout over the dramatic volcanic plug of Euglah Rock. This is also a mountain-biking track. Less intrepid campers can drive to one of the many fine lookouts in the region. Note: bring your own firewood; gas/fuel stove preferred. **Map refs:** 35 E4, 92 G7

209 Dawsons Spring camping area

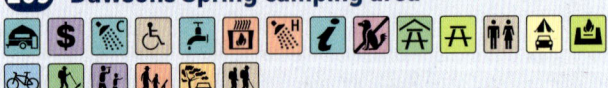

Just past the Mt Kaputar summit on the main access road, Dawsons Spring is a larger camping area with access to the medium–difficult Summit Walk (2 km, 1.5 hr) and Bundabulla Circuit Track (3 km, 3 hr), and the easy Dawsons Spring Nature Trail (1.4 km, 1 hr). Each of these will bring you great views of the park. Bring your own firewood; gas/fuel stove preferred. Limited cabin accommodation is also available. **Map refs:** 35 E4, 92 G7

MUMMEL GULF NATIONAL PARK

Perched on the edge of the Great Escarpment, this park's terrain plunges from 1450 m to 470 m. Old-growth rainforest offers protection to a number of threatened plant and animal species. The park is 50 km south-east of Walcha via the Oxley Hwy and Mummel Forest Rd. Access by 2WD is possible in dry weather only.

Who to contact: NPWS Walcha (02) 6777 4700

210 New Country Swamp camping area

A picturesque grassy area on Mummel Forest Rd (Enfield Rd), near a short and easy track to the edge of breathtaking Mummel Gulf. This is a good place for nature photography and birdwatching. Bring your own drinking water and firewood. Horseriding is allowed on the Bicentennial National Trail, which follows Enfield Rd to the east of the park. There are also opportunities for 4WD touring and trail- and mountain-biking in the region. **Map refs:** 35 G6, 93 K10

NEW ENGLAND NATIONAL PARK

Sweeping panoramas and vistas shrouded in mist, World Heritage–listed rainforest, moss-clad rocks, fern-filled valleys and tumbling waterways are some of the special treasures of New England National Park, 85 km east of Armidale. Walking tracks make some of the landscape accessible, but much remains an unspoiled and precious wilderness.

How to book: Dorrigo Rainforest Centre (02) 6657 2309

211 Park Entrance Rest Area camping area

For those with caravans, there's a basic camping site at Styx River, about 2 km outside the park entrance along Point Lookout Rd. Bush camping is also permitted; you must camp at least 500 m from park facilities. Bring firewood, drinking water and a fuel stove. The park also has 3 basic cabins for rent; bookings essential. **Map refs:** 35 H4, 93 L8

212 Thungutti Rest Area camping area

The campground at Thungutti is set amid towering eucalypts and snow gums. Cars have to be parked a short distance from the campsites. There are 18 sites; booking is not essential but fees apply. Firewood is supplied, and there's also a cold shower and an undercover cooking area with gas BBQs. **Map refs:** 35 H4, 93 L8

OXLEY WILD RIVERS NATIONAL PARK

Oxley Wild Rivers National Park, much of it World Heritage listed, is a stunning environment of majestic gorges, deeply incised river valleys and powerful waterfalls plunging over formidable escarpments on the eastern side of the Great Divide. The park encompasses 2 wilderness areas: Apsley Macleay Gorges and Kunderang Wilderness.

Who to contact: NPWS Walcha (02) 6777 4700 or Apsley Motors (02) 6777 2755 for campsite nos **213**, **214**, **219**, **220**, **221**; NPWS Armidale (02) 6738 9100 for campsite nos **215**, **217**, **218** *How to book:* NPWS Armidale (02) 6738 9100 for campsite no. **216**

213 Apsley Falls camping area

Follow the Oxley Hwy 19 km east of Walcha and you'll find this camping ground, a short walk from the Apsley picnic area and 2 tracks: the easy Apsley Gorge Rim Walk (1 km, 30 min) and Oxley Walk (1 km, 45 min). Both tracks incorporate spectacular views of Apsley Gorge. You'll need to boil or treat the tank water, or bring your own. **Map refs:** 35 G5, 93 J9

214 Budds Mare camping area

The view of Apsley River at Budds Mare is one of the highlights of the national park; to get here, follow Moona Plains Rd off the Oxley Hwy. There's a difficult 7 km walking track from the picnic shelter to the Riverside visitor area – it's very steep in places, and you'll need to camp at Riverside, organise a pick-up (4WD access only, permit required) or prepare for a strenuous 6 hr, 14 km return walk. Bring your own drinking water to the camping ground and firewood. **Map refs:** 35 G5, 93 K9

215 Dangars Gorge camping area

Located in the north-east of the park and accessed via Dangarsleigh, this popular 10-site spot delivers impressive views of the gorge; after rain, the falls are charged with water, and in springtime wildflowers carpet the area. The weather can be quite cold up here as it is at high elevation. Even in drier times the gorge is impressive. There are a number of walks from here ranging from a short 1.4 km return walk to longer day and overnight treks. Bring your own firewood. **Map refs:** 35 G4, 93 J8

216 East Kunderang Homestead

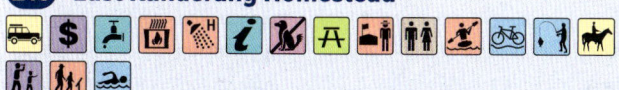

For another accommodation option within the park, this restored 1890s colonial homestead sleeps up to 10, with a possible 4 extra beds in adjacent quarters. It's fully furnished, complete with open wood fireplace, barbecue, well-equipped kitchen and 2 bathrooms – and surrounded by the wild and extravagant beauty of Oxley Wild Rivers National Park. It's a minimum booking of 2 nights; book in advance. Access is by 4WD via Raspberry Rd from Armidale–Kempsey Rd. Please note that camping is not allowed on the property. **Map refs:** 35 H5, 93 K9

217 Green Gully camping area

Just off Waterfall Way in the north of the park, Green Gully has short walks to lookouts over Chandler and Wollomombi falls – the latter being the largest single-drop waterfall in Australia (240 m). It's a small but well-appointed camping ground; some firewood is supplied, but it's better to bring your own. **Map refs:** 35 H4, 93 K8

218 Long Point camping area

Set amid forest in the north of the park, this camping ground is accessible via the old goldmining town of Hillgrove from Waterfall Way. The easy Cassinia Walk (1.5 km, 45 min) and medium Chandler View Circuit Walk (6 km, 2 hr) leave from here; hardened bushwalkers can strike out on the strenuous track to Wollomombi (33 km, 3 days). Track notes are available at the parks office. There's a short walk from car to tent; some firewood is supplied, but it's better to bring your own. **Map refs:** 35 G5, 77 I5, 90 D11, 93 K8, 98 A5

219 Riverside camping area

Riverside campground is only accessible by 4WD – to get here, you'll first need to get a key and permit from the parks office or Apsley Motors in Walcha, then head for Moona Plains Rd. It's a short walk from car to tent; bring your own drinking water. **Map refs:** 35 G5, 93 K9

220 Tia Falls camping area

To reach this camping ground, follow the Oxley Hwy from Walcha; the turn-off is 19 km past the Apsley turn-off. There are 2 walks fanning out from here: the easy Tia Falls (1.5 km, 45 min) and moderate Tiara (5 km, 3 hr). You'll need to bring your own drinking water and firewood. **Map refs:** 35 G5, 93 K10

221 Youdales Hut camping area

This camping area is 4WD only, accessed by key obtained from the parks office or Apsley Motors in Walcha. It's in the east of the national park near Kunderang Brook – a beautiful place for a picnic, swim or short walk. Nearby is the historic Youdales Hut and stockyards, restored in 1992. **Map refs:** 35 H5, 93 K10

STYX RIVER STATE FOREST

Wild landscapes, rushing rivers and stunning alpine woodland are just a few of the drawcards of Styx River State Forest, 65 km east of Armidale. With an elevation range of 200–1400 m, there's an endless variety of landscapes to explore – whether it be by foot, mountain-bike or 4WD.

Who to contact: Forests NSW Walcha (02) 6777 4100

222 Hyatts Flat camping area

This has 2WD access in dry weather only, and it's suitable for self-sufficient campers only as it's pretty thin on facilities and not officially managed as a camping site. To get here, follow Hardwood Rd from Styx River Forest Way. You're advised to bring your own chemical toilet; also bring drinking water and firewood. **Map refs:** 35 H4, 93 L8

223 Wattle Flat camping area

Named for the acacias that flower along the banks of the Styx River in early spring, Wattle Flat is a spacious, grassed area ringed with eucalypts, with welcoming river pools nearby. Turn onto Loop Rd from Styx River Forest Way. Bring your drinking water and firewood. **Map refs: 35 H4, 93 L8**

TORRINGTON STATE CONSERVATION AREA

Rugged landscapes, scenic outlooks and intriguing rock formations are the order of the day at Torrington State Conservation Area, an hour's drive from Tenterfield and Glen Innes. Wildflowers bloom Sept–Mar and the birdwatching is impressive year-round. Pull on your boots and stalk the views, or try your hand fossicking for gemstones.

Who to contact: NPWS Tenterfield (02) 6736 4298

224 Blatherarm Creek camping area

From Deepwater, north of Glen Innes on the New England Hwy, turn west onto the Stannum Rd and follow the signs to the conservation area. The campground is via Blatherarm Rd off Silent Grove Rd. It's not far from here to a range of lookouts and walking tracks of varying degrees of difficulty – contact the parks office for details. Bring your own drinking water and firewood; gas/fuel stove preferred. **Map refs: 35 G2, 93 K4**

URBENVILLE STATE FOREST

Just 25 km from the Queensland border, 80 km north-west of Casino via the Urbenville–Woodenbong Rd, Urbenville is a town of about 200 people. It's earned its place on the map due to the plethora of 4WD tracks in the vicinity, including at Urbenville State Forest, which is adjacent to town.

Who to contact: Urbenville Newsagency (02) 6634 1254
Camping fees: pay fees and pick up key to the amenities block at newsagency

225 Urbenville Forest Park camping area

This forest park on Urbenville–Woodenbong Rd has picnic tables and wood BBQs, but you need to bring your own firewood. **Map refs: 35 H1, 93 M2**

WARRABAH NATIONAL PARK

The Namoi River winds its way through the heart of this tranquil park and is the focus of most activities including canoeing, floating on li-los, swimming and fishing. Giant granite boulders, the river's deeply incised valley and the park's relatively remote location contribute to its charm.

Who to contact: NPWS Armidale (02) 6738 9100

226 Warrabah camping area

Hiking, swimming, fishing and canoeing are possible at this campground, on the Namoi River beside the park's southern boundary. Campers are asked to stick to numbered campsites. For those seeking some bush solitude, a 4WD track leaving from the camping area gives access to a number of secluded spots along the river. To get here, follow Namoi River Rd 35 km north-east of Manilla. Bring drinking water and firewood. **Map refs: 35 F4, 93 I8**

WASHPOOL NATIONAL PARK

World Heritage–listed Washpool National Park is an area of remote wilderness and magnificent warm temperate rainforest. It lies high on the northern tablelands, an expansive plateau that reaches almost 1200 m. Visitors can camp on the park's southern perimeter and enjoy shorter walks, while the more intrepid can trek into the interior.

Who to contact: NPWS Glen Innes (02) 6739 0700

227 Bellbird camping area

Located on unsealed Coachwood Dr off the Gwydir Hwy, Bellbird has drinking water, toilets, picnic tables, wood BBQs and private camping areas cordoned off from one another by vegetation. Relax and have a cuppa while you're serenaded by the sights and sounds of the rainforest. You can walk to the Coachwood picnic area from here (200 m). Both of these areas are good for spotting lyrebirds. **Map refs: 35 H3, 93 L5**

228 Coombadjha camping area

To get to this camping area, turn off the Gwydir Hwy onto unsealed Coachwood Dr and follow the road to the end. It's a short walk from car to tent. There are toilets and picnic tables and water in the creek (boil/treat before using, or bring drinking water). The medium–difficult Washpool Walk (8.5 km return, 3.5–5 hr) leaves from here, passing through several types of forest and crossing Coombadjha Creek. **Map refs: 35 H3, 93 L5**

229 Northern Washpool camping area

This is a basic camping area in the north-eastern section of the park. It's one of the few places in this part of the park that's accessible to visitors other than experienced bushwalkers who can penetrate the rugged interior. Access is by 4WD (dry weather only) via Washpool Rd, which runs off Lionsville Rd from Baryulgil, 74 km north-west of Grafton. **Map refs: 35 H3, 93 L5**

WERRIKIMBE NATIONAL PARK

A wild and magnificent landscape of rainforests, pristine rivers, cascading waterfalls, rugged escarpment and deep gullies greets visitors to the remote World Heritage–listed Werrikimbe National Park, 90 km south-east of Walcha.

Who to contact: NPWS Port Macquarie (02) 6588 5555 for campsite nos **230, 232**; NPWS Walcha (02) 6777 4700 for campsite no. **231**

230 Brushy Mountain camping area

In the eastern section of the park, Brushy Mountain camping area is accessed via unsealed Cockerawombeeba Rd or Hastings Forest Way. The former is 4WD only; the latter only suitable for caravans and 2WD vehicles in dry weather. Check with the parks office for road conditions. There's a variety of short and long walks branching out from here, including the easy 2.9 km Loop Walk and the medium-grade 9 km Scrub Bird Walk. You'll need to bring your drinking water and firewood. **Map refs:** 35 H5, 93 L10

231 Mooraback camping area

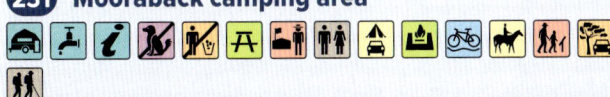

Mooraback is in the west of the park, accessed by 2WD in dry weather via Mooraback Rd off Kangaroo Flat Rd from the Oxley Hwy. If you have a 4WD, you can access it via the Racecourse Trail from Brushy Mountain. There are a number of enjoyable walking tracks leading from here, including the medium-grade Platypus Pools Walk (6 km) and Mooraback Trail (7 km, 2.5 hr). Firewood is supplied and there's water in the creek, but you'll need to boil or treat it before drinking. **Map refs:** 35 H5, 93 K10

232 Plateau Beech camping area

This campground is in the eastern section of the park on Plateau Beech Rd, 10 km south of Hastings Forest Way. Check with the parks office for road conditions before setting off, and note that the access roads aren't suitable for caravans and 2WD vehicles in wet conditions. There's a short walk from car to tent. The easy King Fern Walk (2 km) is hailed as one of the classics of the mid-north coast and a good introduction to the Gondwana Rainforests of Australia. Bring your drinking water and firewood. **Map refs:** 35 H5, 93 L10

YARRIE LAKE RESERVE

Yarrie Lake is a natural body of water that, when full, has a diameter of approximately 3 km. It's 28 km west of Narrabri and 18 km east of Wee Waa, on the Yarrie Lake Rd off Narrabri–Wee Waa Back Rd.

Who to contact: Narrabri Visitors Centre (02) 6799 6760

233 Yarrie Lake camping area

There are a number of camping areas around the shoreline. Note that the lake can be dry at times, so if you're keen to partake in the fishing, swimming, sailing and paddling that's available when the lake is full, it's best to check with the visitor centre beforehand. Those wanting to waterski must apply for a licence through the Yarrie Lake Flora and Fauna Reserve Trust. **Map refs:** 35 E4, 92 F7

CAMPSITES LOCATED IN OTHER AREAS

234 Artesian Bore Baths Reserve

If you're on Pilliga Rd between Walgett and Narrabri and feel like washing off the outback dust, pop in to Burren Junction, 55 km west of Wee Waa. You can put up a tent or book a cabin – and plunge into the refreshing artesian baths. Note: the baths are intermittently closed; check with the information centre before visiting. **Map refs:** 35 D3, 92 D6

How to book: Narrabri Visitor Information Centre (02) 6799 6760, 1800 659 931

235 Bonshaw Weir camping area

Tall eucalypts, mirror-still water and big, brazen blue skies are on offer at this camping site, up on the Qld–NSW border west of Tenterfield and 45 km north-east of Ashford. It's on Bonshaw Rd, off Bruxner Hwy. Visitors can swim, fish, or while away the hours at the water's edge. It's a fairly basic campsite: bring your own drinking water, firewood and fuel stove. **Map refs:** 35 G2, 93 J3

Who to contact: Inverell Visitor Information Centre (02) 6728 8161

236 Bowling Alley Point Recreation Reserve

This camping area is on the foreshore of Chaffey Dam, 14 km north of Nundle and 45 km south-east of Tamworth. The dam is a popular place for watersports such as waterskiing and powerboating, while fishing enthusiasts vie with pelicans and cormorants for yellow-belly, trout and catfish. Follow the signs along Fossickers Way east of Tamworth. Bring your own firewood. **Map refs:** 35 F5, 93 I10

Who to contact: Nundle Visitor Information Centre (02) 6769 3026

237 Cockburn River campsite

This pleasant, grassy, treed area makes a relaxing place to camp, swim and fish. The river's a bit chilly in winter, but very refreshing in hot weather. It's about 30 km north-east of Tamworth and 11 km east of Kootingal, accessed via the Kootingal–Limbri Rd. Bring your own drinking water and firewood. **Map refs:** 35 F5, 93 I9

Who to contact: Tamworth Visitor Information Centre (02) 6767 5300

238 Copeton Northern Foreshores Reserve camping area

On the northern shores of Copeton Dam, across the water from Copeton Waters State Park, this is a wonderful spot for fishing, waterskiing, fossicking, boating and birdwatching. At only 17 km south-west of Inverell via Auburn Vale Rd, this is closer than the state park and suitable for daytrippers keen to drop in from Inverell. **Map refs:** 35 F3, 93 I6

Who to contact: (02) 6723 6269

239 Cranky Rock Recreation Reserve

Located 8 km east of Warialda on the Gwydir Hwy, Cranky Rock Recreation Reserve is characterised by a visually arresting assembly of granite boulders, picnic facilities, a kiosk and bush shower. Visitors can follow a range of walking tracks, try their hand fossicking in the creek, or visit the wildlife sanctuary. **Map refs:** 35 F3, 92 H5

Who to contact: (02) 6729 1402

240 Dumaresq Dam camping area

This peaceful, relaxed setting is on the shore of Dumaresq Dam, 12 km north-west of Armidale, via Boorolong and Dumaresq Dam rds. Fishing, birdwatching and canoeing are all popular activities, and there's a walking track around the dam. The closest dump point is in Armidale Arboretum, on the south side of town. Bring your own firewood. **Map refs:** 35 G4, 93 J7

Who to contact: Armidale Visitor Information Centre (02) 6772 4655

241 Glenriddle Reserve camping area

Glenriddle Reserve is set in the northern reaches of Split Rock Dam, 15 km south of Barraba and roughly 100 km north of Tamworth on Fossickers Way. The dam is popular with fishing and boating aficionados, and the Barraba region is well known for birdwatching. Bring firewood and drinking water. You can reach the camping area via Crow Mountain Rd at the Black Springs turn-off on Fossickers Way. **Map refs:** 35 F4, 92 H7

Who to contact: Barraba Information Centre (02) 6782 1255

242 Gwydir River camping areas

Bingara is a quaint and friendly town, 100 km north-east of Narrabri on the Gwydir River. There's a 10 km area eastward from the town on Keera Rd where casual riverside bush camping is available. You can swim, fish and generally take it easy in a tranquil and secluded setting. Drop into Bingara Tourist Information Centre for a mud map; bring your own drinking water and firewood. **Map refs:** 35 F3, 92 H6

Who to contact: Bingara Tourist Information Centre (02) 6724 0066

243 Horton Falls camping area

This is a small and simple camping spot 39 km west of Barraba, which is on Fossickers Way. It's 2WD access in dry weather only, via Mt Lindsay Rd off Trevallyn Rd. Bring drinking water and firewood and be prepared for a rough road in. **Map refs:** 35 F4, 92 G7

Who to contact: Barraba Information Centre (02) 6782 1255

244 Little Creek Recreation Reserve

You'll find this small camping area 20 km north-west of Barraba via Trevallyn Rd. Barraba is on the Fossickers Way, and offers visitors plenty of activities such as swimming, boating and fishing at Split Rock Dam. You'll need to bring drinking water and firewood to this camping area. **Map refs:** 35 F4, 92 H7

Who to contact: Barraba Information Centre (02) 6782 1255

245 Pindari Dam camping area

Pindari Dam is 22 km east of Ashford on the Severn River, accessed via Pindari Dam Rd. The small camping area is perched just above the dam with lovely water views. It offers easy access to aquatic activities such as swimming, canoeing and fishing. There's a donation box on site. **Map refs:** 35 G2, 93 J4

Who to contact: Inverell Shire Council (02) 6728 8288

246 Rocky Creek Glacial camping areas

Rocky Creek is a picturesque string of placid waterholes formed by glacial activity about 290 million years ago. There are numerous camping areas scattered along the creek, but they're pretty basic; bring your own drinking water and firewood. **Map refs:** 35 F3, 92 G6

Who to contact: Bingara Tourist Information Centre (02) 6724 0066

247 Rocky River Fossicking Area camping area

Get into the spirit of the goldmining era – Rocky River Fossicking Area, 6 km to the west of Uralla, was the site of a major goldrush in the 1850s. Pop into the visitor centre for some equipment, then set up a tent and fossick for your fortune. To get to the camping area, follow Kingston Rd from Uralla, then Devoncourt Rd. Bring your own firewood. **Map refs:** 35 G4, 93 J8

Who to contact: Uralla Visitor Centre (02) 6778 4496

248 Sheba Dams Reserve

Originally built for sluicing gold, Sheba Dams Reserve, 11 km east of Nundle, is now a comfortable summer family-camping area. You can fish, swim or paddle and there's a 1.2 km walking track leading around the dam. There's an undercover cooking area here as well. To reach the reserve, take Nundle–Barry Rd from Nundle. Bring your own drinking water and firewood. **Map refs:** 35 F6, 93 I11

Who to contact: Nundle Tourist Information Centre (02) 6769 3026

249 Split Rock Dam camping area

Another worthwhile stop-off on the Fossickers Way, 64 km north of Tamworth. The town of Manilla, 20 km south of the dam, is a popular hang-gliding and paragliding spot. The dam is stocked with Murray cod and golden and silver perch – alternatively, visitors can paddle, swim, waterski or just relax by the water. There are picnic tables and shelter at the dam lookout, a short drive away. **Map refs:** 35 F4, 92 H8

Who to contact: Manilla Tourist Information Centre (02) 6785 1207; or Tamworth Regional Council (02) 6767 5555
Camping fees: honesty box on gate leading to camping area or pay fees to the council in Manilla on weekdays

250 Swamp Creek camping area

This popular gold- and gem-fossicking site is 4 km north of Nundle on Fossickers Way. If fossicking ain't your thing, you can head out for a walk or a swim instead. You'll need to bring your own drinking water and firewood. **Map refs:** 35 F6, 93 I10

Who to contact: Nundle Visitor Information Centre (02) 6769 3026

251 Teamsters Rest Camping Reserve

Next to Wombramurra Creek via Crawney Pass Rd (2WD in dry weather only), this is a popular spot for those wanting a bit of peace and quiet. There's water in the creek – not enough to swim in – but you'll need to boil or treat it before drinking, or else bring your own. **Map refs:** 35 F6, 93 I11

Who to contact: Nundle Visitor Information Centre (02) 6769 3026

252 Tooloom Falls camping area

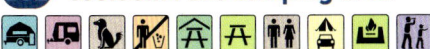

The beautiful Tooloom Falls (10 m high, 60 m wide) are found next to Tooloom National Park, 6 km south of Urbenville via Urbenville–Koorelah Rd and Tooloom Falls Rd. Tooloom is thought to have evolved from an Aboriginal word meaning headlice – but don't let that put you off! There's impressive subtropical rainforest here, which protects a number of

endangered animals including the powerful owl and the long-nosed potoroo. Note: you'll need to bring your own drinking water and firewood. **Map refs:** 35 H1, 93 M2

Who to contact: NPWS Kyogle (02) 6632 0000; or Tenterfield Shire Council (02) 6736 1744

253 Woodenbong camping area

With a dramatic backdrop of volcanic landscapes and World Heritage–listed rainforest, Woodenbong is a wonderful base from which to explore nearby national parks such as Border Ranges and Richmond Range. Woodenbong is just south of the NSW–Qld border, on Summerland Way from Kyogle or Mt Lindesay Rd from Tenterfield. The camping area is next to the local swimming pool at the western end of town. Bring your own firewood. Pick up the key to the amenities block from the Mobil Service Station in town or Fay's Takeaway, Unungar St (after hours). **Map refs:** 35 I1, 93 M2

Who to contact: Mobil Service Station, Woodenbong (02) 6635 1300

254 Woolomin Reserve

This is a spacious, grassy, treed area next to Peel River at Woolomin village, 21 km north of Nundle and 37 km south-east of Tamworth. There's a general store close by where you can pay for a powered site; otherwise, camping is free. Bring your own drinking water and firewood. **Map refs:** 35 F5, 93 I10

Who to contact: Nundle Tourist Information Centre (02) 6769 3026

THE CENTRAL WEST

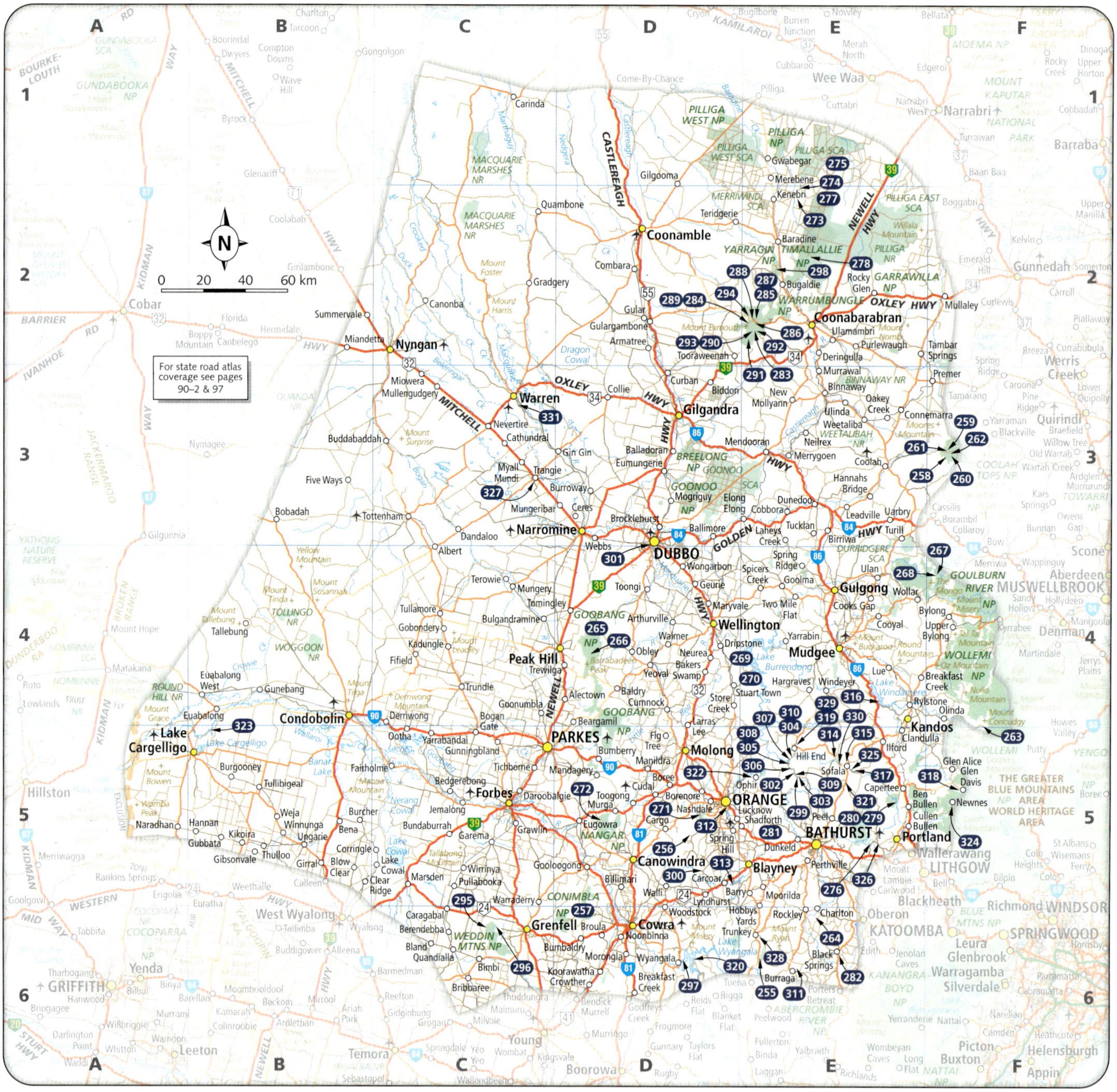

For state road atlas
coverage see pages
90–2 & 97

0 20 40 60 km

TRAVEL WEST OF THE Blue Mountains and you'll find that the NSW landscape grows harsher, its natural beauty more raw and rugged. Pioneering Australians built their livelihoods and communities on gold and copper mining, fossicking and agriculture, and many small villages and reserves retain traces of their pioneering legacy: from Sofala, Wattle Flat, Hill End and Ophir to Burraga. Drive the Bridle Track from Bathurst to Hill End and you'll be following the very hoofsteps of a much-used horse trail from gold-rush days. Take your time and you'll spot plenty of old gold workings and ruins.

Weddin Mountains National Park tips its hat to another kind of pioneer: the bushranger. You can camp half an hour's walk away from the very cave used as a hideout by notorious outlaw Ben Hall, before he was shot down by police in 1865. In the same park you can visit an historic homestead to see how a farming family weathered life during the Great Depression and beyond.

Nowhere is the beauty of a harsh landscape more evident than in Warrumbungle National Park. Violent volcanic activity 13–17 million years ago created a vast shield volcano, which gradually eroded away leaving tough volcanic plugs and fissures, and arresting landforms such as the shard-like Breadknife, domed Bluff Mountain, Belougery Split Rock and the majestic Grand High Tops. This is spectacular country indeed, with more than 17 peaks exceeding 1000 m.

For all this hardness, there's plenty of relaxation to be had in the Central West region. There are a number of fabulous places for swimming, fishing, paddling and other water-based activities – such as Grabine Lakeside, Lake Burrendong and Wyangala Waters state parks. The Turon River, running east and west of Sofala, offers numerous relaxing and secluded spots where you can tuck yourself in beside the river and while away the hours with a fishing rod or book.

Whatever your pleasure, you can be sure that a trip through the Central West region will reveal the inner workings of NSW, in all its rough-hewn glory.

CAMPSITES LOCATED IN PARKS AND RESERVES

ABERCROMBIE KARST CONSERVATION RESERVE

Time and water have crafted a stunning landscape of subterranean caves that rival the world-famous Jenolan Caves. Gaze upon the largest natural archway in the Southern Hemisphere, take a cave tour, hike to Mt Gray or fossick for precious gemstones in Grove Creek. The reserve is 70 km south of Bathurst and 15 km south of Trunkey Creek.

How to book: Abercrombie Karst Conservation Reserve (02) 6368 8603

255 **Abercrombie Caves camping area**

This is a fabulous set-up on the banks of beautiful Grove Creek, complete with a camp kitchen and dining room, 3 amenities blocks with hot showers, a laundry and kiosk. To get here, take the Trunkey Creek–Goulburn Rd south of Bathurst. Bring your own firewood; gas/fuel stove preferred. There are also a number of cabins – 2 standard, 2 deluxe – and one 3-bedroom house available in the reserve. **Map refs:** 45 E6, 90 G6

CANOBOLAS STATE FOREST

Canobolas State Forest surrounds the Canobolas State Recreation Area, home to Mt Canobolas, at 1395 m the highest peak between the Blue Mountains and the Indian Ocean. The state forest is 15 km south-west of Orange via Cadia Rd, off Forest Rd.

Who to contact: Forests NSW Bathurst (02) 6331 2044

256 **Canobolas Forest Park**

This is a peaceful picnicking and camping area surrounded by a 60-year-old pine forest. There are picnic tables, walking

tracks and trout in the creek nearby. It's 20 km south of Orange via Cadia Rd then Four Mile Creek Rd. Bring your own drinking water. **Map refs:** 45 D5, 90 F5

CONIMBLA NATIONAL PARK

Rising 500 m above the surrounding farming landscape of the central west, Conimbla National Park preserves a rare pocket of this region's original vegetation, including ironbark and scribbly-gum forest, and eruptions of wildflowers in spring. The national park is 20 km west of Cowra, via Barryrennie Rd off the Mid-western Hwy.

Who to contact: NPWS Forbes (02) 6851 4429

257 **Wallaby camping area**

Take a walk along the Wallaby Walking Track (4 km, 1 hr, medium difficulty) and you may catch a glimpse of a red-necked wallaby or swamp wallaby. Alternatively, sneak out after dark with a torch and see if you can catch nocturnal animals at their nightly foraging. The camping area is signposted from Barryrennie Rd. Bring drinking water and firewood. **Map refs:** 45 D6, 90 E6

COOLAH TOPS NATIONAL PARK

Located in the Liverpool Ranges, on the narrow Warung Plateau, Coolah Tops National Park enjoys spectacular views of Warrumbungle Range and Mt Kaputar, plunging waterfalls and a wealth of plant and animal life. The fire trails on the plateau make for good mountain-biking and the giant grass trees near the Barracks camping area are truly impressive, as is the view from the lookout at the end of Pinnacle Rd. The park is 120 km north-east of Mudgee and 30 km east of Coolah via Coolah Creek Rd.

Who to contact: NPWS Mudgee (02) 6370 9000 *How to book:* NPWS Mudgee (02) 6370 9000 for campsite no. **260**

258 **Bald Hills camping area**

This is a simple camping area reached via Bald Hills Rd, off Hildegard Rd from the Forest Rd (2WD access only in dry weather, 4WD recommended). You can also walk in from Norfolk Falls Picnic Area (approximately 4 km return, some steep sections). You can either boil or treat the water from the creek or bring your own drinking water. Bring your own firewood; gas/fuel stove preferred. **Map refs:** 45 F3, 92 F11

259 **The Barracks camping area**

The Barracks camping area is reached via Pinnacle Rd off the Forest Rd, 36 km east of Coolah. This is the most extensive of the park's camping areas, with an information bay and sites for caravans. A 600 m walk away is an stunningly impressive stand of grass trees. If you follow Pinnacle Rd to the end you'll find a lookout with fabulous views across to the Warrumbungle Range. There is a rainwater tank; bring firewood but gas/fuel stove is preferred. **Map refs:** 45 F3, 92 F11

260 Brackens Cottage

This restored 1930s farm cottage, 40 km east of Coolah along Hildegard Rd off the Forest Rd, is surrounded by a large, open grassy paddock, perfect for pitching a tent. There's a rainwater tank and firewood is supplied. Gas/fuel stove preferred. Advance bookings required via NPWS Mudgee. **Map refs:** 45 F3, 92 F11

261 Coxs Creek camping area

Turn off the Forest Rd onto Pinnacle Rd, and you'll soon reach a short track that leads to Coxs Creek camping area. There are a number of sites here, scattered along the pretty and sheltered Coxs Creek. You can either boil or treat the water from the creek or bring your own drinking water. Bring your own firewood; gas/fuel stove is preferred. **Map refs:** 45 F3, 92 F11

262 The Pines camping area

This quieter, less extensive camping area is popular with groups. You'll find it signposted along Hildegard Rd off the Forest Rd, 39 km east of Coolah. Bring your drinking water and firewood; a gas/fuel stove is preferred. **Map refs:** 12 D5, 45 F3, 91 L4, 92 F11

CORICUDGY STATE FOREST

Sharing a border with the sprawling wilderness of Wollemi National Park, Coricudgy State Forest is a great place for horseriding, bushwalking and 4WD touring. It's 2WD dry-weather access only from Rylstone via Narrango Rd. If it's wet, check road conditions before setting off.

Who to contact: Forests NSW Bathurst (02) 6331 2044

263 Kelgoola camping area

At the base of Mt Coricudgy, at the headwaters of the Cudgegong River, Kelgoola is a rustic bush-camping site for self-sufficient campers. You can get here via Narrango Rd from Rylstone. Bring your own everything. **Map refs:** 45 F4, 91 J3

DOG ROCKS STATE FOREST

Trout fishing in Campbells River is the main drawcard at Dog Rocks State Forest, 20 km west of Oberon and 15 km south-east of Rockley via Swallows Nest Rd from Dog Rocks Rd.

Who to contact: Forests NSW Bathurst (02) 6331 2044

264 Campbells River camping area

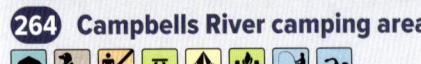

This is a simple but spacious camping spot in a grassy clearing on Campbells River. Throw a line in, dip a toe in, or kick back and enjoy the river from the comfort of your camp chair. To get here, take Rockley Rd from Rockley, turn onto Dog Rocks Rd and then Swallows Nest Rd. The campground is about 17 km south-east of Rockley. Bring your own drinking water and firewood. **Map refs:** 45 E6, 90 H6

GOOBANG NATIONAL PARK

A range of plant and animal life is preserved in Goobang National Park, along with picnic sites, views from Caloma Trig, bushwalking trails and bush-camping opportunities. You can also ride a horse through the park, as long as you have a permit. Roads are open to conventional vehicles, though heavy rain can make them boggy. The park is 30 km from Parkes, off the Newell Hwy.

Who to contact: NPWS Forbes (02) 6851 4429

265 Greenbah camping area

Pack your binoculars and bird-identification guide before heading to this camping area next to Greenbah Creek, as it's a top spot for birdwatching. To reach it, turn off Trewilga–Baldry Rd onto the Sawpit Gully Trail – this road is narrow and unsealed, so suitable for small caravans only, and it's 2WD access in dry weather only. There's a walking track leading to Burrabadine Peak, and cycling is possible along the access road. Bring your own drinking water and firewood. **Map refs:** 45 D4, 90 E2

266 Wanda Wandong camping area

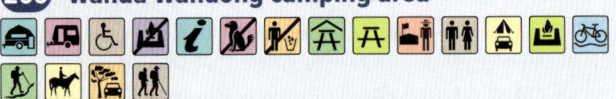

Let the children run free in this spacious, grassy camping ground, 700 m off the Tomingley–Obley Rd, 3 km north of Tomingley. This is the best section of the park to visit if you are towing a caravan with a 2WD vehicle; even so, it's only suitable in dry weather. You'll need to bring your own drinking water and firewood. **Map refs:** 45 D4, 90 E2

GOULBURN RIVER NATIONAL PARK

The Goulburn River is the larger-than-life figure on the stage of Goulburn River National Park. Its vast flood plains and rugged sandstone gorges create a wonderful camper's playground for bushwalking, kayaking, fishing, picnicking and wildlife-watching. The park is 35 km south of Merriwa, west of Muswellbrook and north-east of Mudgee.

Who to contact: NPWS Mudgee (02) 6370 900

267 Big River camping area

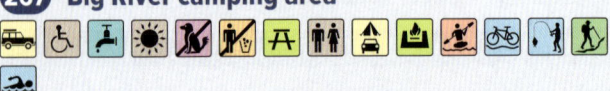

This sprawling grassed area is beside the Goulburn River, on Mogo Rd north of Wollar. Access is by 4WD only. Bring your own drinking water and firewood. Alternatively, you can boil or treat the river water. There is no wet-weather access. **Map refs:** 45 F4, 91 I1, 92 F12

268 Spring Gully camping area

On the banks of the Goulburn River on Mogo Rd, access to Spring Gully with a 2WD vehicle is possible in dry weather only. There is no vehicular access in wet weather. Boil or treat river

water before drinking or bring your own, along with firewood.
Map refs: 45 F4, 91 I1, 92 F12

LAKE BURRENDONG STATE PARK

Lake Burrendong State Park is an outdoor wonderland for people of all ages and interests. It's 27 km south-east of Wellington, a manageable hour's drive from Dubbo or Orange. There are 2 camping areas on the lake, and a 160 ha arboretum showcasing 2000 species of native plants.

How to book: bookings advisable during peak periods (02) 6846 7435

269 Lake Burrendong State Park camping area

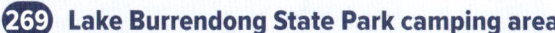

Turn onto Burrendong Rd off Wellington–Orange Rd north of Mumbil, and you'll soon find this camping area. Activities include golf, sailing, hiking, canoeing, fishing, waterskiing and a waterslide. There's a kiosk and laundry facilities, as well as cabin accommodation. Bring your own drinking water and firewood. If you manage to get bored here, you can always visit the Wellington Caves, about 30 min drive away.
Map refs: 45 E4, 90 G3

270 Mookerawa Waters Park camping area

To get here, follow Mookerawa Rd for 10 km from Stuart Town, off the Wellington–Orange Rd. Facilities and activities match those at the Lake Burrendong State Park camping area, but there are no powered sites here. Bring your own drinking water and firewood. A token is required to exit the park.
Map refs: 45 E4, 90 G3

MOUNT CANOBOLAS STATE CONSERVATION AREA

Mt Canobolas is a 1395 m remnant of an extinct volcano, and its slopes boast some of the largest remnants of subalpine vegetation in this region. There's a selection of walking tracks and lookouts, which take in the region's intriguing rock formations and surrounding agricultural land.

Who to contact: NPWS Bathurst (02) 6332 7640

271 Federal Falls camping area

The road in to Federal Falls camping area isn't suitable for caravans or camper trailers, although 2WD vehicles are permitted. To get here, follow Pinnacle Rd from Orange and turn onto Towac Rd. There are a number of walking tracks fanning out from the campground, including the Federal Falls Track. Note: there's a short walk from the carpark to the camping area. Bring your own drinking water and firewood. **Map refs:** 45 D5, 90 F4

NANGAR NATIONAL PARK

With its distinctive red siltstone cliffs and rare pockets of remnant central-west vegetation, Nangar National Park is of great value to naturalists and its traditional owners, and it also has much to offer visitors. The park is 70 km south-west of Orange and 40 km east of Forbes.

Who to contact: NPWS Forbes (02) 6851 4429

272 Terarra Creek camping area

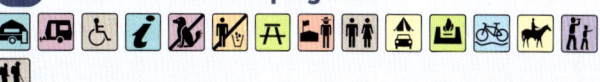

To get to this sole camping area in the park, follow the Escort Way from Eugowra and keep an eye out for a NPWS sign pointing to a dirt road. The campground is a little under 5 km from the park entrance. The road is 2WD, dry-weather access only, and not suitable for large caravans. Terarra Creek is a good base for exploring the park on foot or mountain-bike, and there's a 4WD track up to Mt Nangar Lookout. **Map refs:** 45 D5, 90 E5

PILLIGA STATE FOREST

Pilliga State Forest is a vast swathe of cypress pine and ironbark forest between Baradine, Narrabri and Pilliga. The main way in is via Pilliga Forest Way from Baradine, or the Newell Hwy south-west of Narrabri. Be careful when driving – the roads are labyrinthine and can become impassable after rain.

Who to contact: Forests NSW Baradine (02) 6843 1607

273 The Aloes camping area

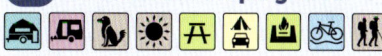

Keep your eyes peeled for koalas and plenty of aloe plants at this camping spot, 23 km north of Baradine near Etoo Creek. To get here, follow Cumbil Rd from Baradine and take the Pilliga Forest Way. Note: dry-weather access only; bring your own drinking water. Campfires not permitted during summer.
Map refs: 45 E2, 92 E8

274 Rocky Creek Mill camping area

Once the site of a thriving timber-mill community, this is now a quiet and spacious camping area 29 km north of Baradine. To get here, take the Cumbil Rd from Baradine and turn onto Pilliga Forest Way. Note: this is dry-weather access only. Bring your own drinking water. **Map refs:** 45 E2, 92 E8

275 Schwagers Bore camping area

This is a quiet spot tucked away near the bore, 51 km west of Baradine via Cumbil Rd and Pilliga Forest Way. It's dry-weather access only, and you'll need to bring your own drinking water.
Map refs: 45 E1, 92 E7

SUNNY CORNER STATE FOREST

Sunny Corner State Forest is 36 km east of Bathurst via Sunny Corner Rd off the Great Western Hwy at Meadow Flat. This is the heart of trail-biking and 4WD touring territory. There's also an arboretum showcasing the tree species that have been established in the region over the past 40 years.

Who to contact: Forests NSW Bathurst (02) 6331 2044

276 Mary's Park camping area

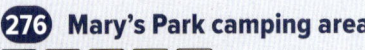

To reach this basic camping area, follow the signs on Sunny Corner Rd. It's about 2.7 km west of Sunny Corner village. There are no facilities here, so bring your own everything, including toilet, drinking water and firewood. **Map refs: 45 E5, 90 H5**

TIMALLALLIE NATIONAL PARK

Embedded within the 500 000 ha Pilliga Forest – the largest tract of native forest west of the Great Divide – is Timallallie National Park, accessed via No. 1 Break Rd off the Newell Hwy north of Coonabarabran. In an area rich with natural beauty – in particular, birdlife – Timallallie is one of the few places with visitor facilities.

Who to contact: Pilliga Forest Discovery Centre (02) 6843 4011

277 Salt Caves camping area

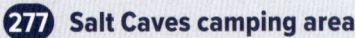

This is a relatively informal camping area with picnic tables and wood BBQs. There's a short walk to a nearby dam, where you'll have a chance to spot some of the 240 bird species found in the area. This is dry-weather access only along No. 1 Break Rd, Rocky Rd and Country Line Rd. Bring drinking water. **Map refs: 45 E2, 92 E8**

278 Sculptures in the Scrub camping area

Peg out your tent before exploring Sculptures in the Scrub, a permanent display of sculptures that sit on the edge of a cliff overlooking Dandry Gorge, a 2 km loop walk from the camping area. Four years in the making, Sculptures in the Scrub tells a story of local Aboriginal history and culture. There's rainwater available, but treat/boil it before using or bring your own. Dry-weather access only. **Map refs: 45 E2, 92 E8**

TURON NATIONAL PARK

Aboriginal and European history abounds in this national park, 5 km south-west of Capertee. The Turon River has its source here, the site of a major goldrush in the 1850s. Travel to and within the park is by 4WD or mountain bike.

Who to contact: NPWS Blackheath (02) 4787 8877

279 The Diggings camping area

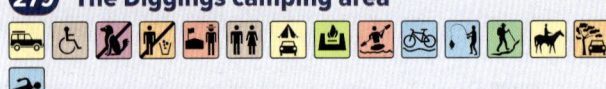

Where once the diggers panned for gold, now the campers fish for trout, swim or head out on a bushwalk. There are 20 sites here, with 4WD access only via Lochaber Creek Fire Trail, 9 km west of Capertee. Bring your own drinking water and firewood. **Map refs: 45 E5, 91 I4**

280 Woolshed Flat camping area

This is 4WD access only along the Turon River Track, 12 km south-west of Capertee. It's a peaceful, spacious spot next to the Turon River, where you can fish, swim or watch for birds by the water. Bring your own drinking water and firewood. **Map refs: 45 E5, 77 G2, 91 I4, 97 N6**

VITTORIA STATE FOREST

Macquarie Woods is situated within Vittoria State Forest, on the Mitchell Hwy midway between Bathurst and Orange. A variety of walking tracks, lookouts and picnicking areas can be found amid native forest and pine plantations.

Who to contact: Forests NSW Bathurst (02) 6331 2044

281 Heritage Grove camping area

Heritage Grove is one of 4 main areas in Macquarie Woods that have been established by Forests NSW to demonstrate sustainable forestry. This camping area can be accessed via Cashens La, off the Mitchell Hwy, 29 km west of Bathurst. Bring your own drinking water and firewood. **Map refs: 45 E5, 90 G5**

VULCAN STATE FOREST

Comprising mostly pine plantation, Vulcan State Forest is a popular spot for fishing, fossicking and seasonal mushrooming. It's 24 km west of Oberon via the Oberon–Black Springs Rd.

Who to contact: Forests NSW Bathurst (02) 6331 2044

282 Black Springs camping area

Surrounded by a large pine plantation, Black Springs is a popular picnicking area in Black Springs village, accessible via Oberon–Black Springs Rd. Eager fossickers can visit Sapphire Bend nearby, while anglers can try their luck in one of a few streams in the vicinity. There's a general store across the road from the camping area; bring your own firewood. **Map refs: 45 E6, 90 H6**

WARRUMBUNGLE NATIONAL PARK

At Warrumbungle National Park, rocky spires emerge from heavily forested valleys and peaks, and gorges slice deep into the landscape. With its strange volcanic terrain, fresh mountain air and excellent camping, this is one of NSW's most popular parks. It is definitely worth spending a few days here to give yourself a chance to do some of the many walks. For a truly special experience, hike out to Macha Tor to watch the rocky spires of the Grand High Tops come to life at sunrise. And though strenuous, the climb up to the Grand High Tops is rewarded with fantastic views.

Who to contact: Warrumbungle National Park Visitor Centre (02) 6825 4364 *How to book:* Warrumbungle National Park Visitor Centre (02) 6825 4364 for campsite nos **283, 294** *Camping fees:* pay fees and pick up permit at visitor centre

283 Balor Hut camping area (walk-in camping)

This old walkers' hut is at the base of the Breadknife and Grand High Tops, and is accessible via a fairly strenuous 6 km walk from Pincham carpark. The hut sleeps 8, but you'll need to bring everything with you. You must book ahead for the hut accommodation, as you need to obtain the key from the visitor centre. You can also pitch a tent in the adjacent camping area. It's a good base from which to tackle the steep walk up Bluff Mountain. Bring firewood if you want a fire, and boil or treat the tank water before drinking it. **Map refs:** 45 E2, 92 D9

284 Burbie Camp camping area (walk-in camping)

This walk-in only camping area has very basic facilities – pit toilets and wood BBQs – accessible along the fire trail to Mt Exmouth from Burbie Canyon carpark. Make sure you register with the visitor centre before heading here, and take good topographic maps with you. **Map refs:** 45 E2, 92 D9

285 Camp Blackman camping area

This is the big, main camping area in the national park, with 70 sites (32 with power), hot showers, gas/electric BBQs and a public telephone. Many of the park's walking tracks start a short drive away, and there are short walks and cycling routes fanning out from here. In the clear areas around the camp one can often see mobs of kangaroos, and birdlife abounds. Drinking water is supplied although boiling or treating it is advised; you'll need to bring your own firewood. To get here, take the John Renshaw Parkway to the national park, turn off for the visitor centre; the campground is just beyond. **Map refs:** 45 E2, 92 D9

286 Camp Pincham camping area

It's 200 m from the Pincham carpark to the camping area, one of the original Warrumbungle campgrounds. It's a good place to use as a base for walking to the Breadknife and Grand High Tops. There's a water tank here, but you'll need to boil/treat the water before drinking it. Bring your own firewood. Note: it's advisable to register with the visitor centre. **Map refs:** 45 E2, 92 D9

287 Camp Walaay camping area

It's not far from popular Camp Walaay to the many amenities of Camp Blackman. There are 5 spacious camping areas here that can fit up to 200 people; however, the road isn't suitable for camper trailers or caravans. It's advisable to book ahead. The park's main walking tracks are a short drive away. Note: there's water here, but you'll need to boil or treat it before drinking. Bring your own firewood. **Map refs:** 45 E2, 92 D9

288 Camp Wambelong camping area

Camp Wambelong is about 1 km past the visitor centre, and is close to the Split Rock, Grand High Tops and Mt Exmouth walking tracks. There are 30 sites here – if you're in a large group you'll need to book in advance; if you're in a small group, bookings are advisable in peak periods. There's untreated water here, so you'll need to boil it first before drinking. Bring your own firewood. **Map refs:** 45 E2, 92 D9

289 Danu Camp (walk-in and bush camping)

It's a long walk to Danu Camp from either Pincham, Split Rock or Burbie Canyon carparks. The camp is between the Grand High Tops and Mt Exmouth, on the Western High Tops. Campers must be self-sufficient with food and water (also available at Balor Hut or Burbie Camp), register with the visitor centre and take good topographic maps. Note: gas/fuel stove only. **Map refs:** 45 E2, 92 D9

290 Dows Camp (walk-in and bush camping)

Dows Camp is situated between the Grand High Tops and Mt Exmouth, at the junction of Bluff Mountain Trail and Western High Tops. It's a long walk from Pincham carpark – campers will need to be self-sufficient with food and water (also available at Balor Hut or Burbie Camp), register with the visitor centre and take good topographic maps. Note: gas/fuel stove only. **Map refs:** 45 E2, 92 D9

291 Gunneemooroo camping area (walk-in camping)

This is the only camping area in the southern end of the park – to get here, follow John Renshaw Parkway from Coonabarabran, turn towards Tooraweenah and then onto Dooroombah Rd. Access to the carpark is only possible by 2WD in dry weather. There's spring water here but you'll need to boil/treat it before drinking; bring your own firewood. Register with the visitor centre before setting out. Note: it's a long walk from the carpark to the camping area. **Map refs:** 45 E2, 92 D10

292 Hurleys Camp (walk-in and bush camping)

Sleep beneath the imposing monolith of Belougery Spire at this walk-in campsite, accessible from Pincham carpark. Named for famous Australian photographer Frank Hurley, this is a popular spot for walkers and climbers. Register with the visitor centre before setting out and take good topographic maps. Bring your own drinking water and gas/fuel stove. **Map refs:** 45 E2, 92 D9

293 Ogma Camp (walk-in and bush camping)

Ogma Camp is at the junction of the West Spirey Creek Trail and Western High Tops, between the Grand High Tops and Mt Exmouth. It's a walk-in campsite, accessed via the Pincham Trail and the Grand High Tops or West Spirey Creek Trail. Bring food and water (also available at Balor Hut), good topographic maps, and gas/fuel stove. Register with the visitor centre before setting out. **Map refs:** 45 E2, 92 D9

294 The Woolshed

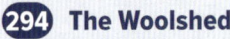

This is a spacious area for small- and medium-sized groups of up to 55 people. It has power, lighting and a composting toilet. Bookings are essential. Note: there's water here, but it'll need to be boiled or treated before use. Bring your own firewood. **Map refs:** 45 E2, 92 D9

WEDDIN MOUNTAINS NATIONAL PARK

Weddin Mountains National Park is a crescent-shaped pocket of rugged cliffs and gullies 390 km west of Sydney and 20 km south-west of Grenfell. Its claim to fame is that notorious bushranger Ben Hall hid out here. Highlights include walking tracks, great views and an old settlers' farm from the 1930s.

Who to contact: NPWS Forbes (02) 6851 4429

295 Ben Halls camping area

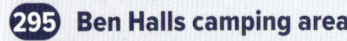
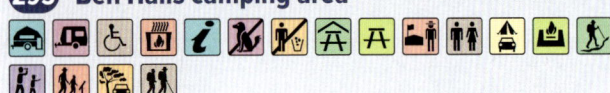

The grassy unpowered campsites here are set beside historic Seatons Farm, and are a 30 min walk from Ben Halls Cave. The farm is a well-preserved Depression-era structure, with interpretive signs that give a fascinating insight into life here in the 1930s. There are BBQs at the campsite, but you'll need to bring your own firewood and drinking water. To get here, follow Back Piney Range Rd and Weddin View Rd. **Map refs:** 45 C6, 90 D6

296 Holy Camp camping area

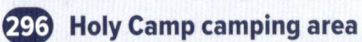

This is a nice, shaded spot 19 km south-west of Grenfell via Holy Camp Rd. From the camp you can do the Euladrie Walk, which follows an old logging road to the base of the escarpment and then climbs steeply to Peregrine Lookout, with fine views over the surrounding plains. Bring drinking water and firewood. **Map refs:** 45 C6, 90 D6

WYANGALA WATERS STATE PARK

Wyangala Waters is 37 km east of Cowra on the Darbys Falls Rd. Its capacity is more than double that of Sydney Harbour, ensuring plenty of space for myriad watersports, as well as bushwalking, mountain-biking and picnics.

How to book: (02) 6345 0877 www.wyangalawaters.com.au

297 Wyangala Waters camping area

This is a sprawling space on the shores of Wyangala Dam, offering powered and unpowered tent and caravan sites, bungalows, cabins, cottages and houseboats. Activities include waterskiing, sailing and fishing – the latter a particular drawcard given the abundance of silver and golden perch, brown and rainbow trout and Murray cod. To reach the camping area,

follow Darbys Falls Rd or Woodstock-Wyangala Rd from the Mid-Western Hwy. You'll need to bring your own firewood; gas/fuel stove preferred. Note: book ahead for peak periods. **Map refs:** 45 D6, 90 F6

YARRAGIN NATIONAL PARK

Yarragin National Park is one of many under the green-canopied umbrella of the Pilliga Forest. It's 15 km south of Baradine near Bulgadie, accessed via Bulgadie Rd or the Coonabarabran–Baradine Rd.

Who to contact: NPWS Baradine (02) 6843 4000

298 Yarragin picnic and camping area

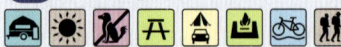

This is a very basic spot predominantly used for picnics – it's dry-weather access only and there are no toilets. To get here, take Ridge Rd south of Baradine. Bring drinking water and firewood. **Map refs:** 45 E2, 92 D9

CAMPSITES LOCATED IN OTHER AREAS

299 Amy Anderson Reserve camping area

On the Bridle Track, Amy Anderson Reserve is 42.7 km north of Bathurst and 1.3 km north of Bruinbun Reserve. Bring drinking water, firewood, a gas/fuel stove and a spare tyre. **Map refs:** 45 E5, 90 G4

Who to contact: Central Tablelands Heritage Lands (02) 6391 4330; or Bathurst Visitor Centre (02) 6332 1444, 1800 681 000

300 Bakers Shaft Reserve

This camping area is around 20 km west of the historic town of Carcoar. Follow the Mid-western Hwy through Mandurama, then turn north for Burnt Yards; take Bakers Rd then Junction Park Rd. This is 2WD, dry-weather access only. You can fish, swim and fossick in Belubula River. Bring your own drinking water and firewood. **Map refs:** 45 D5, 90 F5

Who to contact: Reserve Trust 0400 120 973

301 BIG4 Dubbo Parklands

Part of the BIG4 conglomerate, Dubbo Parklands is located on the Newell Hwy less than 2 km south of the town centre and supplies topnotch park facilities, including a recreation room with table tennis, movies and a big-screen TV, camp kitchen, children's playground and laundry. Accommodation options range from powered and unpowered tent sites to deluxe self-contained cabins. Dubbo's most famous drawcard is the Taronga Western Plains Zoo, but other attractions include Wellington Caves and Old Dubbo Gaol. **Map refs:** 45 D3, 90 F1, 92 C12

How to book: 154 Whylandra St, Dubbo (02) 6884 8633, 1800 033 072 www.big4dubboparklands.com.au

302 Black Gate Reserve camping area

On the Bridle Track, Black Gate Reserve is 45 km north of Bathurst and 4 km north of Bruinbun Reserve. Bring drinking water, firewood, a gas/fuel stove and a spare tyre. Note: this is as far as you'll get your trailer or caravan if you're coming from Bathurst. **Map refs:** 45 E5, 90 G4

Who to contact: Central Tablelands Heritage Lands (02) 6391 4330; or Bathurst Visitor Centre (02) 6332 1444, 1800 681 000

Bridle Track

This 60 km route from Duramana, north-west of Bathurst, to Hill End follows in the hoofsteps of an old horse trail. Camping sites and reminders of the region's goldmining past are scattered along the way. Off-road campervans and 2WD vehicles can travel this route in dry weather only, and they are not permitted between Black Gate Reserve and Johnsons Hole. After rain, some sections may be impassable even for 4WDs, so check road conditions before setting out. Note: the track is cut at Monaghans Bluff; access to the northern reserves is via Hill End.

■ *Please note that campsites are listed in alphabetical order, not track order. Refer to the map on p. 44 for further information.*

Who to contact: Central Tablelands Heritage Lands (02) 6391 4330; or Bathurst Visitor Centre (02) 6332 1444, 1800 681 000
Road conditions: Bathurst Regional Council (02) 6333 6111

299 Amy Anderson Reserve camping area
See p. 50.

302 Black Gate Reserve camping area
See above.

303 Bruinbun Reserve camping area
See below.

304 Cave Hole Reserve camping area
See below.

305 Grimleys Hotel Reserve camping area
See p. 52.

306 Johnsons Hole Reserve camping area
See p. 53.

307 Mary Flynn Reserve camping area
See p. 53.

308 Randwick Hole Reserve camping area
See p. 53.

309 Tattersalls Hole Reserve camping area
See p. 53.

310 Turon Crossing Reserve camping area
See p. 54.

303 Bruinbun Reserve camping area

On the Bridle Track, Bruinbun Reserve is 41 km north of Bathurst. Bring your own drinking water, firewood, a gas/fuel stove and a spare tyre. **Map refs:** 45 E5, 90 G4

Who to contact: Central Tablelands Heritage Lands (02) 6391 4330; or Bathurst Visitor Centre (02) 6332 1444, 1800 681 000

311 Burraga Dam camping area

Where once this dam serviced a large copper-mining operation, it now supplies water for agriculture and the residents of Burraga. It also provides a peaceful camping area, where visitors can swim, fish and picnic. Burraga is 70 km south of Bathurst via Rockley Rd; the camping area is 2 km north-east of Burraga via Arkstone Rd. You'll only be able to get a caravan in here during dry weather, and you'll need to bring your own drinking water and firewood with you. **Map refs:** 45 E6, 90 G6

Who to contact: Burraga Village Store (02) 6337 0255

312 Canobolas Caravan Park

This is a friendly and well-appointed caravan park on Bathurst Rd in Orange. There are shaded powered and unpowered tent sites as well as self-contained deluxe and standard cabins. Nearby attractions include wine-tasting and Mt Canobolas. **Map refs:** 45 D5, 90 G4

How to book: 166 Bathurst Rd, Orange (02) 6362 7279 www.caravanpark.canobolasmarine.com.au

313 Carcoar Dam camping area

Carcoar is a small and picturesque town, 12 km south-west of Blayney. On the National Heritage list for being the third oldest settled village west of the Blue Mountains, it certainly has a ye olde feel to it. The dam is about halfway between Blayney and Carcoar, 1 km from the Mid-Western Hwy, and is a popular spot for fishing and swimming. Sites here are in open forest spread along the hillside above the dam. Bring ye own firewood. **Map refs:** 45 D5, 90 G5

Who to contact: Blayney Shire Council (02) 6368 2104

304 Cave Hole Reserve camping area

On the Bridle Track, on the northern side of Monaghans Bluff, Cave Hole Reserve is about 9 km south of Hill End. Bring drinking water, firewood, a gas/fuel stove and a spare tyre. **Map refs:** 45 E5, 90 G4

Who to contact: Central Tablelands Heritage Lands (02) 6391 4330; or Bathurst Visitor Centre (02) 6332 1444, 1800 681 000

314 Coles Bridge camping area

Coles Bridge is about 15 km west of Sofala on the Turon River. Both the river and Sofala are historically significant: the river for the site of one of the first alluvial gold rushes in Australia; the town for being the oldest surviving goldmining town in the country (established in 1851). Take the Hill End Rd west from Sofala, turn onto Turondale Rd and follow it until you reach the bridge. Just over the bridge there's a track to the right leading to the camping area. Bring your own drinking water and firewood. **Map refs:** 45 E5, 90 H4

Who to contact: Bathurst Visitor Information Centre (02) 6332 1444, 1800 681 000

315 Crossley Bridge camping area

Crossley Bridge camping area is 500 m west of the historic goldmining town of Sofala, 45 km north of Bathurst, in a small bend on the northern banks of the Turon River. There's an access track 200 m north of the crossroads on the Mudgee–Bathurst Rd west of Sofala. Bring your own drinking water and firewood. **Map refs:** 45 E5, 90 H4

Who to contact: Bathurst Visitor Information Centre (02) 6332 1444, 1800 681 000

316 Cudgegong Waters Park

On the southern edge of Windamere Dam, Cudgegong Waters Park has all the activities and facilities a water-loving outdoor enthusiast could ask for. Fishing is a particular drawcard, with golden and silver perch, Murray cod and catfish on the menu. There are cabins and on-site caravans as well as campsites, and a kiosk sells bait, ice, petrol and groceries. The dam can be accessed via the Illford–Mudgee Rd, 35 km south-east of Mudgee. **Map refs:** 45 E4, 90 H3

How to book: bookings advisable during peak periods (02) 6358 8462

317 First Crossing camping area

This is one of several beautiful camping spots on the Turon River, a stone's throw from the famous gold mining town of Sofala, 45 km north of Bathurst (where you'll need to stock up on fuel). A picturesque spot beneath she-oaks, First Crossing is 5.9 km east of Sofala, at the first causeway crossing of the Turon River along Upper Turon Rd. There are toilets, wood BBQs and picnic tables here; bring your own drinking water and firewood. Note: that you will need a licence to fish here. **Map refs:** 45 E5, 90 H4

Who to contact: Bathurst Visitor Information Centre (02) 63321444, 1800 681 000

318 Glen Davis camping area

Perched on the edge of an escarpment overlooking Capertee Valley – one of the largest enclosed valleys in the southern hemisphere – Glen Davis is a spectacular Blue Mountains town. The camping area is in town, 32 km east of Capertee via Glen Davis Rd off the Castlereagh Hwy. It's a beautiful spot, set among white box and yellow box. While here, you can learn about the town's shale-mining history. **Map refs:** 45 F5, 91 I4

Who to contact: Lithgow Visitors Centre (02) 6350 3230, 1300 760 276

319 Glendora camping area

Glendora is one of 2 camping areas in the vicinity of Hill End, 85 km north of Bathurst via Sofala and 72 km south of Mudgee. Hill End's fascinating gold-rush history draws crowds of up to 35 000 annually, and it's well worth a visit. The spacious camping ground is 1 km north of town, on the way to the Bald Hill Lookout. There are coin-operated showers here; bring your own firewood. **Map refs:** 45 E5, 90 G4

Who to contact: NPWS Hill End Visitor Centre (02) 6337 8206

320 Grabine Lakeside State Park camping area

Grabine Lakeside State Park is on the north-eastern banks of the Wyangala Dam, 75 km north-west of Crookwell along the Crookwell–Bathurst Rd, or 120 km from Goulburn along Bigga Rd. The park offers endless boating, canoeing, swimming, windsurfing and other water-based activities, as well as golf, tennis, basketball, archery and a children's playground. There's also a large selection of accommodation options, from bungalow to bunkhouse and cabin to campsite. Bring firewood and drinking water to this popular park. **Map refs:** 45 D6, 90 F6

How to book: bookings advisable during peak periods (02) 4835 2345

305 Grimleys Hotel Reserve camping area

On the Bridle Track, this camping area is 14.7 km south of Hill End and 4.7 km south of Mary Flynn Reserve. Bring drinking water, firewood, a gas/fuel stove and a spare tyre. **Map refs:** 45 E5, 90 G4

Who to contact: Central Tablelands Heritage Lands (02) 6391 4330; or Bathurst Visitor Centre (02) 6332 1444, 1800 681 000

321 Heritage Grounds camping area

You'll find this basic camping area 1 km west of rustic Wattle Flat, 8 km down the road from Sofala. Both Wattle Flat and Sofala have a winning, down-to-earth charm born of their fascinating goldmining past, as well as the beauty of the surrounding countryside. Wattle Flat is 40 km north of Bathurst via the Bathurst–Kelso Rd. Heritage Grounds camping area is signposted on Thompson St. You'll need to bring firewood. Enjoy the 3 hr Buurree Walking Trail that meanders through the Heritage Lands. **Map refs:** 45 E5, 90 H4

Who to contact: Bathurst Visitor Information Centre (02) 6332 1444, 1800 681 000

306 Johnsons Hole Reserve camping area

On the Bridle Track, the Johnsons Hole Reserve camping area is 18.1 km south of Hill End and 3.4 km south of Grimley's Hotel Reserve. Bring drinking water, firewood, a gas/fuel stove and a spare tyre. **Map refs:** 45 E5, 90 G4

Who to contact: Central Tablelands Heritage Lands (02) 6391 4330; or Bathurst Visitor Centre (02) 6332 1444, 1800 681 000

322 The Junction camping area

This picnic and camping area is located in Ophir Recreation Area, which happens to be the site of Australia's first significant gold discovery. You can still see traces of the mine workings; in fact, you can relive the era and try your hand at fossicking. If that's not your thing, you can fish for trout instead, or stretch your legs on a walking track. The reserve is 30 km north-east of Orange via Ophir Rd or Ponds Rd. Camper trailers and caravans not recommended. Bring your own drinking water and firewood. **Map refs:** 28 C5, 45 E5, 90 G4, 93 M7

Who to contact: Orange Visitor Information Centre (02) 6393 8226, 1800 069 466

323 Lake Cargelligo Weir camping area

This camping area sits on the edge of Lake Cargelligo, 95 km west of Condobolin via Lachlan Valley Way. Pelicans, swans, wild ducks, geese and parrots are a few of the birds you may see here. Fishing and picnicking are also popular pastimes. It's 2WD, dry-weather access only; bring your own drinking water and firewood. **Map refs:** 45 B5, 90 A3, 97 N3

Who to contact: Lake Cargelligo Tourist Association (02) 6898 1501

307 Mary Flynn Reserve camping area

On the Bridle Track, you'll find the Mary Flynn Reserve camping area just over 10 km south of Hill End and 1.2 km south of Cave Hole Reserve. Bring drinking water, firewood, a gas/fuel stove and a spare tyre. **Map refs:** 45 E5, 90 G4

Who to contact: Central Tablelands Heritage Lands (02) 6391 4330; or Bathurst Visitor Centre (02) 6332 1444, 1800 681 000

324 Newnes private camping area

This is a small private area opposite the Newnes Hotel on the Wolgan River in Newnes, an old oil-shale-mining town 34 km

north of Lidsdale on the Castlereagh Hwy (Mudgee Rd). The camping area is adjacent to Wollemi National Park, so don't let your dogs wander over the boundary. Firewood is available for a fee; fuel stove recommended. **Map refs:** 45 F5, 91 I4

Who to contact: Newnes Hotel (02) 6355 1247

308 Randwick Hole Reserve camping area

On the Bridle Track, Randwick Hole Reserve is 15.2 km south of Hill End and 500 m south of Grimleys Hotel Reserve. Bring drinking water, firewood, a gas/fuel stove and a spare tyre. **Map refs:** 45 E5, 90 G4

Who to contact: Central Tablelands Heritage Lands (02) 6391 4330; or Bathurst Visitor Centre (02) 6332 1444, 1800 681 000

325 Ration Point camping area

This is one of a handful of delightful riverside camping spots along the Turon River, close to historical Sofala, one of Australia's oldest surviving goldmining towns. Ration Point can be reached via Upper Turon Rd – the turn-off is about 100 m past a small bridge, 2.8 km east of Sofala. Bring your own drinking water and firewood. **Map refs:** 45 E5, 90 H4

Who to contact: Sofala Souvenir Shop (02) 6637 7075; or Bathurst Visitor Information Centre (02) 6332 1444, 1800 681 000

326 Sunny Corner Recreation Reserve

This is a small camping area in Sunny Corner Village, a historic gold town 36 km east of Bathurst via the Great Western Hwy. The village is a good base from which to explore the surrounding forest by 4WD or trail bike. The camping reserve isn't hard to find in the village; bring your own drinking water and firewood. **Map refs:** 45 E5, 90 H5

Who to contact: Bathurst Visitor Information Centre (02) 6332 1444, 1800 681 000

327 Tandara Caravan Park

Located in Trangie, a friendly, small town on the Mitchell Hwy 72 km south-west of Dubbo, Tandara offers a range of accommodation including powered and unpowered tent sites, cabins and on-site vans. If you're travelling with a group, you can opt for an on-site train, which sleeps up to 12 people. If you're here during cotton season, you can take a tour of one of the local cotton gins. Facilities include a swimming pool, amenities block, dump point and laundry. If you want to bring a pet, advise at time of booking. **Map refs:** 45 C3, 92 B11

How to book: 55 John St, Trangie (02) 6888 7330 www.tandaracaravanpark.com.au

309 Tattersalls Hole Reserve camping area

On the Bridle Track, Tattersalls Hole Reserve is 44 km north of Bathurst and 2 km north of Amy Anderson Reserve. Bring

drinking water, firewood, a gas/fuel stove and a spare tyre.
Map refs: 45 E5, 90 G4

Who to contact: Central Tablelands Heritage Lands (02) 6391 4330; or Bathurst Visitor Centre (02) 6332 1444, 1800 681 000

328 Trunkey Creek Showground

Trunkey Creek is a little town about 13 km from Abercrombie Caves. Once a thriving goldmining village, it has retained some mud huts, abandoned mineshafts and other traces of its heyday. The showground is off Arthur St in the village. Bring your own firewood. Note: no camping during show weekend (2nd weekend in Oct). **Map refs:** 45 E6, 90 G6

Who to contact: Black Stump Hotel (02) 6368 8604

310 Turon Crossing Reserve camping area

On the Bridle Track, there are 2 campsites included in Turon Crossing Reserve: 7.3 km and 8.2 km south of Hill End. A concrete causeway crossing of Turon River 8 km south of Hill End may be impassable after rain, even for a 4WD, so check conditions before setting out. Bring your own drinking water, firewood, a gas/fuel stove and a spare tyre. **Map refs:** 45 E5, 90 G4

Who to contact: Central Tablelands Heritage Lands (02) 6391 4330; or Bathurst Visitor Centre (02) 6332 1444, 1800 681 000

329 The Village camping area

This is one of 2 camping areas in the vicinity of Hill End, a small village with a fascinating goldmining history. Hill End is 85 km north of Bathurst via Sofala and 72 km south of Mudgee; the campground is in the village, on Warry Rd, and there are plenty of non-camping options nearby. Unlike the Glendora camping area at Hill End, the Village camping area has powered sites for caravans and a laundry. Stay the night and take your time wandering through the historic buildings in the village. Bring your own firewood. **Map refs:** 45 E5, 90 G4

Who to contact: NPWS Hill End Visitor Centre (02) 6337 8206

330 Wallaby Rocks Crossing camping area

This is another of the small camping areas picturesquely set beside the Turon River close to the historic goldmining town of Sofala, 45 km north of Bathurst. Wallaby Rocks Crossing is on the eastern side of the bridge, 4.6 km west of Sofala on Hill End Rd. There's fishing and swimming in the river, and a large waterhole nearby. Bring your own drinking water and firewood. **Map refs:** 45 E5, 90 H4

Who to contact: Bathurst Visitor Information Centre (02) 6332 1444, 1800 681 000

331 Warren Weir camping area

Warren is a laid-back country town on the Macquarie River, 80 km west of Gilgandra on the Oxley Hwy. The weir is 5 km south of town; the camping and picnicking area is on the western side, accessed via Dubbo St. It's a good spot for fishing, but if you want to swim or paddle you'll need to head for the eastern flank of the weir. Campers should bring their own drinking water and firewood. **Map refs:** 45 C3, 92 A10

Who to contact: State Water Warren (02) 6847 4186; or Warren Visitor Information Centre (02) 6847 3181

SOUTHERN HIGHLANDS

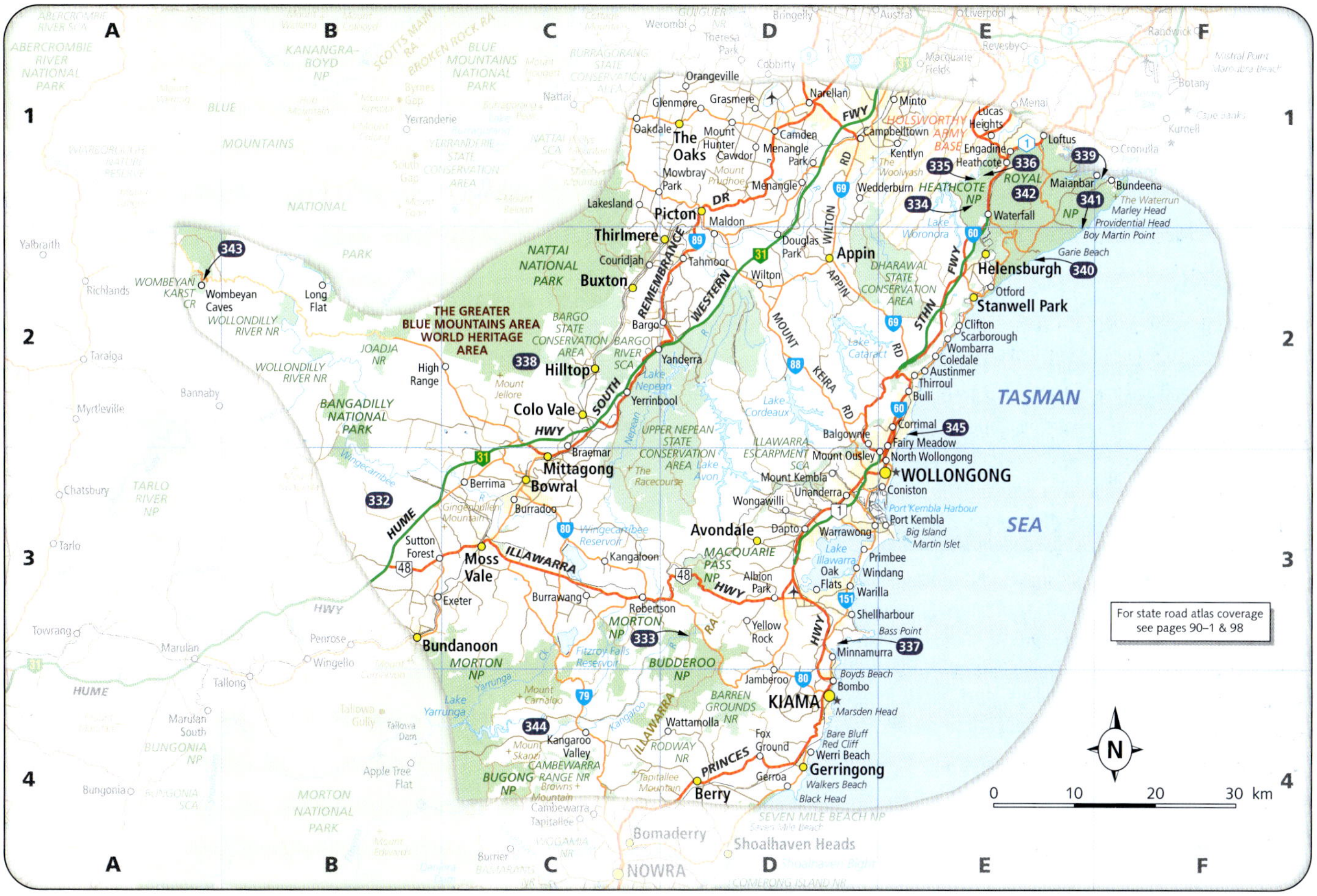

[Map of the Southern Highlands region of New South Wales, with grid references A–F across the top and bottom, and 1–4 down the sides. Features include Royal National Park, Heathcote National Park, Wollongong, Kiama, Bowral, Moss Vale, Mittagong, Bundanoon, and surrounding areas. A compass rose and scale bar (0–30 km) are shown.]

For state road atlas coverage
see pages 90–1 & 98

FOR SUCH A SMALL region, the Southern Highlands packs a pretty impressive punch when it comes to natural beauty. In the north is Royal National Park – the pride of NSW. The park is situated on a sandstone plateau deeply dissected by valleys, and in many ways it epitomises the distinctive Sydney landscape, both in its landforms and vegetation. Well over 1000 plant, 40 mammal and 40 reptile species have been recorded here, and birdlife is in abundance. More than 100 km of walking tracks traverse the park, and there are picnic locations scattered throughout.

Heathcote National Park, next door, is a wilderness wonderland right on Sydney's doorstep. With no public access roads into the park, its swimming holes, diverse vegetation, ocean and estuarine environments and sandstone heaths remain hidden to all but the most adventurous bushwalkers.

The south coast offers spectacular ocean views and winding coastal roads leading to such gems as Killalea State Park, with its excellent surf beaches, fishing and walking tracks. Head inland and you'll stumble onto Budderoo National Park, with its award-winning Minnamurra Rainforest Centre and awe-inspiring walking tour through the rainforest canopy. Not far from here is the picturesque and verdant Kangaroo Valley, a favourite secluded getaway for Sydneysiders and tourists alike.

And so the list goes on, from natural attractions to charming towns and seaside havens. There's little need for a map – in the Southern Highlands you rarely need to look further than the end of your nose to find a natural treasure.

CAMPSITES LOCATED IN PARKS AND RESERVES

BELANGLO STATE FOREST

Belanglo State Forest, 10 km west of Moss Vale, contains some of NSW's oldest radiata pine plantations, dating back to 1919. Just a 1 hr drive south of Sydney, it's a nice place for a weekend getaway. To reach the forest, take the Bunnygalore Rd west off the Hume Hwy.

Who to contact: Forests NSW Bombala (02) 6548 3177

332 Daley's Clearing camping area

Follow the signs along Bunnygalore Rd to this flat, grassy clearing surrounded by pine trees. Bring your own drinking water. If you're an adventurous type, you can strike out and camp in the bush, as long as you steer clear of pine plantation areas. **Map refs:** 55 B3, 91 I8, 98 F2

BUDDEROO NATIONAL PARK

Small but spectacular, Budderoo National Park is notable for its outstanding Minnamurra Rainforest, sandstone plateau country, sparkling waterfalls and superb views. Don't miss the chance to walk through the rainforest canopy at Minnamurra Rainforest Centre. The national park is 20 km west of Kiama via Jamberoo Mountain Rd and Minnamurra Falls Rd.

Who to contact: NPWS Fitzroy Falls (02) 4887 7270

333 Carrington Falls camping area

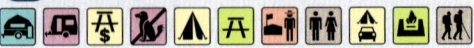

This small camping area can get crowded in peak periods, so think twice if you've got a campervan or trailer. You'll find it on Carrington Falls Access Rd, off Jamberoo Mountain Rd, 8 km east of Robertson. Bring your own drinking water and firewood, although a gas/fuel stove is a better alternative. **Map refs:** 55 D3, 91 J9, 98 G3

HEATHCOTE NATIONAL PARK

Heathcote National Park is a bushwalker's dream come true – with no internal public access road, you can only get here on the strength of your own 2 feet. It's 35 km south of Sydney on the western side of the Princes Hwy. Access is via tracks from Waterfall or Heathcote, both of which can be reached by train from Sydney. Advance booking and a NWPS camping permit are necessary.

How to book: NPWS Sydney South (Royal National Park) (02) 9542 0648

334 Kingfisher Pool camping area (walk-in camping)

On the Bullawaring Track in the middle of the park, this campsite is a fair walk in. It's only for self-sufficient campers carrying decent maps. Note: fires prohibited; gas/fuel stove only. **Map refs:** 55 E1, 91 J7, 98 H1

335 Lake Eckersley camping area (walk-in camping)

There are 2 camping sites here, near Lake Eckersley in the middle of the park, with enough room for up to 6 campers. You'll need to be self-sufficient in food and drinking water. Take a good map with you. Note: fires prohibited; gas/fuel stove only. **Map refs:** 55 E1, 91 K7, 98 H1

336 Mirang Pool camping area (walk-in camping)

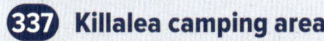

This is slightly larger than the other camping grounds in the park, with 4 campsites accommodating up to 12 people in total. Make sure you're self-sufficient in food and water, with a good map. Note: fires prohibited; gas/fuel stove only. **Map refs:** 55 E1, 91 K7, 98 H1

KILLALEA STATE PARK

Killalea State Park squeezes as much natural beauty as it can into its 265 ha. You'll find 2 excellent surf beaches, pristine wetland and rainforest environments, surfing, fishing, boating and birdwatching, 2 charming coastal towns – Kiama and Shellharbour – and all within an easy 90 km drive south of Sydney.

How to book: (02) 4237 8589

337 Killalea camping area

This is a well-equipped camping ground in prime position behind Mystics Beach. There are walking tracks, fishing spots and a golf course nearby; alternative accommodation is available in the form of a bunkhouse with 40 beds. Facilities include a kiosk, education centre for schools, amenities block and camp kitchen. Bookings are advised in peak periods. **Map refs:** 55 D3, 91 J9, 98 H3

NATTAI NATIONAL PARK

Nattai National Park plays an important role in the protection of the Warragamba Dam Catchment Area, which supplies Sydney's water, as well as the Greater Blue Mountains World Heritage Area. A good place for the adventurous camper, it's a pristine wilderness with little in the way of walking tracks or camping facilities.

Who to contact: NPWS Picton (02) 4640 0500

338 Starlights Trail camping area (walk-in and bush camping)

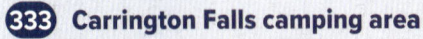

This is essentially a bush-camping site by the Nattai River, reached via the 12 km return Starlights Trail, which begins and ends in the carpark at the end of Wattle Ridge Rd. It's a strenuous walk for experienced, self-sufficient walkers only. Bring your own drinking water, food and up-to-date topographic maps. **Map refs:** 55 C2, 91 I8, 98 G2

ROYAL NATIONAL PARK

Royal National Park, Australia's oldest national park, has a rich cultural heritage, both European and Indigenous. It combines magnificent untamed sandstone country with Victorian-era gardens and memorable views to make it one of the state's favourite parks – and it's just a stone's throw from Sydney.

How to book: bookings essential; Sydney South (Royal National Park) (02) 9542 0648 *Camping fees:* payable in advance (02) 9542 0683

339 Bonnie Vale camping area

There are 74 sites here and it's the only designated camping ground that's accessible by vehicle. To reach it, take the Bundeena Rd from Bundeena and turn onto Seabreeze La. Note: fires are not permitted; gas/fuel stove and gas BBQs only. **Map refs:** 55 F1, 91 K7

340 North Era camping area (walk-in and bush camping)

On the stunning 26 km Coast Track (2 days, medium difficulty), this is a walk-in bush campsite with 12 sites. You'll need to be self-sufficient; bring food and drinking water with you. Wood fires are not permitted. Access is from Otford or Bundeena at either end of the Coast Track, or from the carpark at Garie Beach. **Map refs:** 55 E2, 91 K8

341 Providential Point camping area (walk-in and bush camping)

It's a 10 km southward-bound walk from Bundeena to this camping area or 17 km north from Otford on the Coast Track. While you can drive to the nearby picnic area, the campsite is for the exclusive use of walkers; a ranger checks the carpark at day's end and locks the access gate. Nestled near the beach, an inviting lagoon and your own private waterfall, Providential Point is coastal bush camping at its best. Bring your own water or treat before drinking. **Map refs:** 55 E2, 91 K7

342 Uloola Falls camping area (walk-in camping)

The medium-difficulty Uloola Falls Walking Track (11 km, 3 hr) is the only way in to this camping ground. The track can be accessed from Heathcote, Engadine or Waterfall, all of which are reachable by train. Make sure you've got a good map with you, as well as enough food and drinking water to cover the entirety of the walk. Fires aren't permitted. Note: alternative accommodation is available at the 3-bedroom Weemalah Cottage, on the shores of Hacking River, sleeping up to 8. **Map refs:** 55 E1, 91 K7, 98 H1

WOMBEYAN KARST CONSERVATION RESERVE

Wombeyan Caves is one of NSW's most stunning networks of subterranean limestone caves. The formations in Wollondilly and Kooringa caves are exquisite, and the self-guided Figtree Cave tour shouldn't be missed. The reserve can be reached via Wombeyan Caves Rd from Mittagong or, if you have a caravan or trailer, from Taralga.

How to book: Wombeyan Caves (02) 4843 5976

343 Wombeyan Caves Campground

While the caves are certainly the main drawcard, other activities in the reserve include swimming in the Wombeyan Gorge, hiking, canyoning and birdwatching. The extensive and well-equipped campground is along Wombeyan Creek near the visitor centre. You'll need to bring your own firewood, but pretty much everything else is taken care of. Book ahead for powered sites. Note: alternative accommodation is available in the form of cabins, dormitories and a cottage. **Map refs:** 55 A2, 90 H8, 98 F2

CAMPSITES LOCATED IN OTHER AREAS

344 Bendeela Recreation Area

In picturesque Kangaroo Valley, 20 km north of Nowra and 8 km west of Kangaroo Valley village, Bendeela is a hidden gem in a treasure chest of natural beauty. Camp in a secluded, shady grove next to the Kangaroo Riverand let the kids splash around in the river. Note: no open fires allowed here; gas stoves only. **Map refs:** 55 C4, 91 I9, 98 G3

Who to contact: Sydney Catchment Authority (02) 4886 4377, 1300 722 468

345 Corrimal Beach Tourist Park

Located on gorgeous Corrimal Beach, 5 km north of Wollongong, Corrimal Beach Tourist Park offers everything from tent sites through to standard, beachside and mountain-view spa cabins. Facilities include laundry, camp kitchen and kiosk. You'll find it right on the beach, via Lake Pde. Bookings essential in peak periods. **Map refs:** 55 E2, 91 J8, 98 H2

How to book: Lake Pde, Corrimal (02) 4285 5677 www.wollongongtouristparks.com.au

THE SOUTH COAST

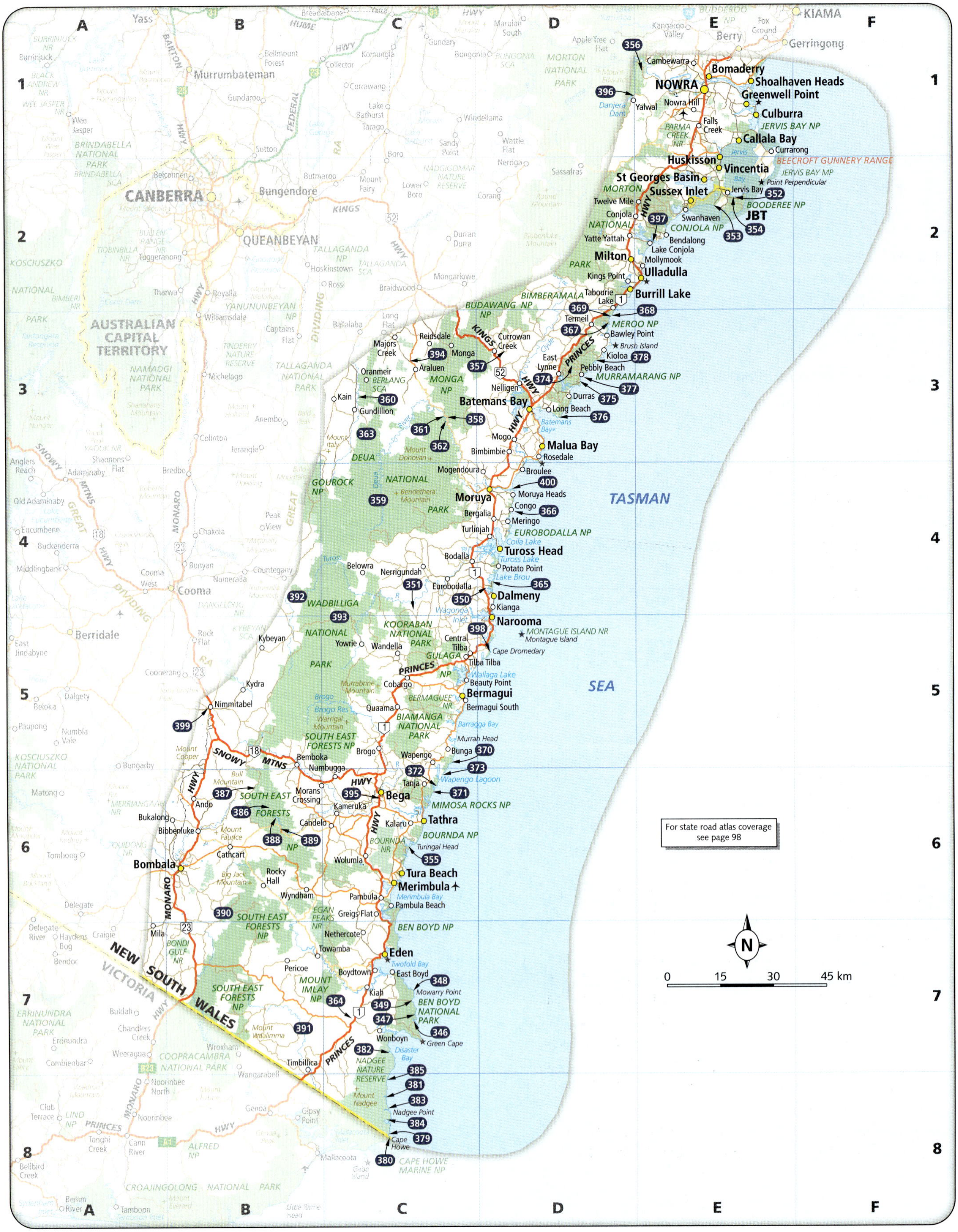

A
B
C
D
E
F
1
2
3
4
5
6
7
8
Yass
Murrumbateman
Gundaroo
Sutton
CANBERRA
Belconnen
QUEANBEYAN
Bungendore
Tuggeranong
Tharwa
Royalla
Williamsdale
Michelago
Colinton
Bredbo
Cooma
Berridale
Nimmitabel
Bombala
Delegate
Bellmount Forest
Collector
Currawang
Lake Bathurst
Tarago
Windellama
Braidwood
Captains Flat
Kain
Gundillion
Araluen
Majors Creek
Reidsdale
Monga
Mongarlowe
KIAMA
Gerringong
Berry
Kangaroo Valley
NOWRA
Bomaderry
Shoalhaven Heads
Greenwell Point
Culburra
Callala Bay
Huskisson
Vincentia
St Georges Basin
Sussex Inlet
JBT
Jervis Bay
Milton
Ulladulla
Burrill Lake
Batemans Bay
Malua Bay
Moruya
Tuross Head
Dalmeny
Narooma
Bermagui
Bega
Tathra
Tura Beach
Merimbula
Eden
BUDDEROO NP
MORTON NATIONAL PARK
JERVIS BAY NP
BEECROFT GUNNERY RANGE
BOODEREE NP
CONJOLA NP
MURRAMARANG NP
EUROBODALLA NP
MONTAGUE ISLAND NR
WADBILLIGA NATIONAL PARK
GULAGA NP
MIMOSA ROCKS NP
BOURNDA NP
BEN BOYD NATIONAL PARK
NADGEE NATURE RESERVE
CAPE HOWE MARINE NP
AUSTRALIAN CAPITAL TERRITORY
NAMADGI NATIONAL PARK
KOSCIUSZKO NATIONAL PARK
DEUA NATIONAL PARK
SOUTH EAST FORESTS NP
CROAJINGOLONG NATIONAL PARK
COOPRACAMBRA NATIONAL PARK
NEW SOUTH WALES
VICTORIA
TASMAN SEA
PRINCES HWY
KINGS HWY
MONARO HWY
SNOWY MTNS HWY
For state road atlas coverage see page 98
0 15 30 45 km
N

FROM NOWRA IN THE north to the Victorian border in the south, from the spectacular coast to the soaring plateaus and escarpments of the Great Dividing Range, there's not much that the South Coast doesn't deliver.

Beach lovers go barmy for the pearl-white sands around Jervis Bay and Booderee National Park, while families take pleasure in the quiet haven of Murramarang National Park, with its sheltered beaches and grassed camping areas shared with laid-back wallabies and grey kangaroos.

Mimosa Rocks National Park brings an element of rawness into the coastal equation, with its mix of slate, granite, basalt and volcanic rock folded, faulted and shaped by weathering over millions of years. Wildlife-watchers will be rewarded with glimpses of swamp wallabies, ringtail possums and long-nosed potoroos, while birdwatchers can keep a sharp eye out for sooty and masked owls and hooded plovers.

For true NSW coastal wilderness, Nadgee Nature Reserve wins hands down. Hardened bushwalkers revel in the remote, windswept beaches, coastal lagoons, heath and headlands on the 60 km, 4-day Nadgee Howe Wilderness Walk, which also takes in part of Croajingolong National Park in Victoria.

The inland national parks are just as spectacular. Morton National Park is a true treasure, with thundering waterfalls, mountainous terrain, diverse vegetation, and the dauntingly rugged Budawang Range. In Deua National Park you can go canyoning and caving in strikingly decorated limestone caves, or follow a 4WD track through the rugged wilderness of the park's central areas.

With the exception of high summer and mid-winter in Morton National Park, the South Coast region can be visited any time of year. Every season brings its own rewards, from carpets of wildflowers in spring to hot sunny summer days spent by beaches and swimming holes, to the warm colours and golden sunlight of autumn and the cold, clear beauty of winter.

CAMPSITES LOCATED IN PARKS AND RESERVES

BEN BOYD NATIONAL PARK

Ragged wave-worn cliffs, salt-pruned heath and banksia woodlands, beautiful beaches, historic buildings and a fascinating whaling heritage make Ben Boyd National Park a wonderful holiday destination. The northern part of the park is notable for its rocky coastline. Some of the highlights in the northern section of the park include North Long Beach, the coloured sands of the Pinnacles, Haycock Point and Terrace Beach. The southern part of the park has historic sites to explore, and includes highlights such as the sheltered Bittangabee Bay, Boyd's Tower, Davidson Whaling Station and Green Cape Lighthouse.

How to book: bookings essential during peak periods and for Green Cape Lighthouse; NPWS Far South Coast Region (02) 6495 5000

346 Bittangabee camping area

On the long-distance but easy Light to Light walking track (30 km, 3 days) in the southern section of the park, Bittangabee camping area offers swimming, snorkelling, fishing and diving. A shorter section of the track can be walked between Bittangabee and Saltwater Creek (9 km, 2.5 hr) camping areas. To get here, follow the Princes Hwy 18 km south of Eden and turn onto Edrom Rd, then Green Cape Rd. There are rainwater tanks but it's best to bring your own drinking water as well as firewood. **Map refs:** 58 C7, 98 E11

347 Hegartys Bay camping area (walk-in and bush camping)

This is a bush camping site with no facilities, along the Light to Light walking track north of Bittangabee Bay. Access either via Bittangabee Bay or Saltwater Creek to the north. Bring your own drinking water; gas/fuel stove preferred. **Map refs:** 58 C7, 98 E10

348 Mowarry Point camping area (walk-in and bush camping)

With no facilities, this bush camping site is along the Light to Light walking track, 3 km north of Saltwater Creek. You can also walk in from the end of the road to the north, which passes by scenic Leatherjacket Bay. Camping here is a delight, tucked in above beautiful, northerly facing Mowarry Beach. Bring your own drinking water; gas/fuel stove preferred. **Map refs:** 58 C7, 98 E10

349 Saltwater Creek camping area

To get to Saltwater Creek camping area, follow the Princes Hwy 18 km south of Eden and turn onto Edrom then Green Cape then Duckhole rds. Turn east onto Saltwater Rd and follow it to the end. There's fishing, swimming, snorkelling, sea kayaking, walking and diving on offer here, which makes it a popular spot for family campers. There are rainwater tanks, but it's best to bring your own drinking water just in case. Note: accommodation is also offered at the Green Cape Lighthouse; bookings essential. **Map refs:** 58 C7, 98 E10

BODALLA STATE FOREST

A gentle rainforest experience awaits those who enter Bodalla State Forest, south of Bodalla via Eurobodalla Rd. This is a good place to bring the family, with highlights including an easy 700 m rainforest walk through mossy, grey myrtle forest filled with birdlife, and a lookout offering impressive views across Narooma and the coast.

Who to contact: Forests NSW South Coast Region (02) 4472 6211

350 Bodalla Forest Park

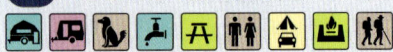

This shady picnic spot surrounded by spotted gums is 9 km north of Narooma via the Princes Hwy. There's some drinking water here, but best to bring your own. After lunch, you can stretch your legs on an easy walking trail that leaves from here. **Map refs:** 58 D4, 98 F7

351 Red Creek camping area (bush camping)

This is a basic bush-camping site with no facilities, next to Red Creek. Bring your own everything, including toilet, drinking water and firewood. It's 40 km south-west of Bodalla via Tuross River Rd and Red Creek Rd. Make sure you stick to the creek's eastern bank; it's national park on the other side. **Map refs:** 58 C4, 98 E7

BOODEREE NATIONAL PARK

On the southern side of Jervis Bay, Booderee is cloaked in coastal scrub and flowering heath, with cliffs fronting pale sandy beaches, clear blue waters and a wealth of Aboriginal archaeological sites. Its fascinating landforms, extraordinary plant and animal diversity and lovely coast make it a favourite destination for Canberra and Sydney residents. Advance bookings, which can be made up to 4 months before a visit, are essential.

How to book: Booderee Visitor Information Centre (02) 4443 0977

352 Bristol Point camping area

Wizened banksia, towering gums and coastal scrub meet the tranquil beauty of Bristol Beach at this medium-sized campsite off Jervis Bay Rd east of Green Patch. All sites require a short walk from car to tent (up to 50 m). Several walking tracks fan out from or near here. Bring your own firewood and a gas/fuel stove if you've got one. **Map refs:** 58 E2, 91 J10, 98 G4

353 Cave Beach camping area

It's a 300 m walk from carpark to tent site at this grassy camping area at the end of Cave Beach Rd off Jervis Bay Rd. It's a small and secluded spot suitable for the lightweight camper. Tents must be no larger than 3 m x 3 m and there's a maximum of 5 people per site. Bring your own gas/fuel stove. **Map refs:** 58 E2, 91 J10, 98 G4

354 Green Patch camping area

This spacious but discreet beachside camping ground can be accessed off Jervis Bay Rd. There are walk-in and vehicle-based campsites, which are allocated depending on your group size and requirements. The easy Telegraph Creek Nature Trail (2.4 km return, 1 hr) leaves from here and loops through eucalypt forest, woodland and heath and across fern-lined

creeks. Drinking water and firewood are supplied but limited, so best to bring your own, along with a gas/fuel stove. **Map refs:** 58 E2, 91 J10, 98 G4

BOURNDA NATIONAL PARK

This is a magically beautiful place of sea and freshwater lakes, an extensive lagoon, creeks, weather-worn cliffs and pale beaches fronting the breakers of the Tasman Sea. Families can enjoy walking, fishing, swimming, surfing and canoeing. It's 10 km north of Merimbula via Bournda Island Rd off the Sapphire Coast Dr.

How to book: bookings essential during peak periods; NPWS Merimbula (02) 6495 5000

355 Hobart Beach camping area

Spacious and well equipped, Hobart Beach camping area has shaded campsites, lovely picnic spots and excellent lookouts (Turingal Head is a favourite). A number of walking tracks fan out from here, and the park rangers run interesting tours over summer. The campground is 14 km north of Merimbula via Bournda Island Rd off Sapphire Coast Dr. It's recommended you boil or treat water before drinking. **Map refs:** 58 C6, 98 E9

BUNDUNDAH RESERVE

Inside Morton National Park, Bundundah Reserve is 22 km west of Nowra via Yalwal and Burrier rds. It's a picturesque spot offering bushwalking through eucalypt forest and gullies.

Who to contact: NPWS Nowra (02) 4428 6300

356 Grassy Gully camping area (bush camping)

You can reach this campsite via Grassy Gully Rd, which turns off Burrier Rd. It's basic bush camping here – bring your own everything, including water and a portable toilet. There are no wood BBQs, so also bring a gas/fuel stove. **Map refs:** 58 E1, 91 I9, 98 G3

CURROWAN STATE FOREST

You'll find this forest, noted for its flourishing burrawang cycads, between Clyde Mountain and beautiful Nelligen, about 10 km west of Batemans Bay. To get here, follow the Kings Hwy west from Nelligen and turn onto Lyons Rd.

Who to contact: Forests NSW South Coast Region (02) 4472 6211

357 Currowan Creek camping area (bush camping)

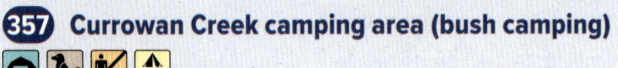

Basic bush camping is available by the Currowan Creek bridge in the forest. Bring your own portable toilet, food and drinking water. **Map refs:** 90 H12, 98 F6

DEUA NATIONAL PARK

Inland from Batemans Bay and Moruya, Deua National Park is a wilderness of densely clad mountains, limestone caves, deep valleys and fast-flowing pristine rivers. Access from

Moruya is via Araluen–Moruya Rd; from the west via the unsealed Krawarree–Snowball Rd. There's also 4WD access in the east and west.

Who to contact: NPWS Narooma (02) 4476 0800

358 Bakers Flat camping area

You can reach this camping area near the Deua River via Araluen Rd. There's a short walk (70 m) from the carpark to the tent sites, where you can camp under the trees on a hillside above the Deua River. Boil or treat the river water before use, and bring your own firewood. **Map refs:** 58 C3, 90 H12, 98 E6

359 Bendethera Valley camping area (bush camping)

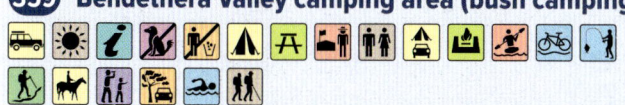

Bendethera is set in a picturesque, grassy valley, with bush-camping sites scattered along the Deua River. Kangaroos and wombats are numerous here and there is a walk to Bendethera Cave as well. It's 4WD dry-weather access only via Bendethera Fire Trail or Dampier Mountain Trail; the latter is not suitable for trailers. Bring your own drinking water and firewood. **Map refs:** 58 C4, 98 E7

360 Berlang camping area

For bushwalkers, a pleasurable easy walk from this camping area (4 km return, 1.5 hr) leads to the viewing platform for the Big Hole, a dramatic 110 m deep, 35 m wide crater created by the collapse of a limestone cave roof. More challenging is the medium Marble Arch walk (13 km return, 5.5 hr), which leads on from Big Hole. The camping site is in the north of the park, accessible via Krawarree Rd. Boil/treat river water before use; bring your own firewood. **Map refs:** 58 C3, 90 G12, 98 E6

361 Deua River camping area

There are 4 unmarked sites at this camping area on the Deua River, which make a great base for swimming, canoeing and fishing. The river crossing to the north end of the Bendethera Fire Trail is here as well. Access is via Araluen Rd. Boil or treat the river water before drinking, and bring your own firewood. Sites are a short (70 m) walk from the road. **Map refs:** 58 C3, 90 H12, 98 E6

362 Dry Creek camping area

It's 4WD access only to this camping spot, via Dry Creek Fire Trail off Araluen Rd. It's not dry, as the name suggests – if you plan to drink the river water, boil or treat it first. Bring your own firewood. **Map refs:** 58 C3, 90 H12, 98 E6

363 Wyanbene Cave camping area

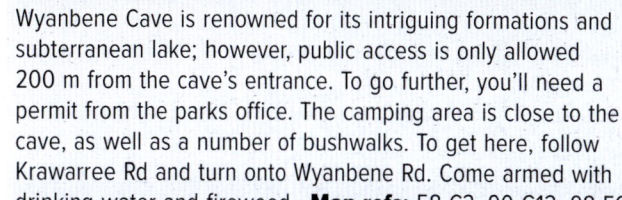

Wyanbene Cave is renowned for its intriguing formations and subterranean lake; however, public access is only allowed 200 m from the cave's entrance. To go further, you'll need a permit from the parks office. The camping area is close to the cave, as well as a number of bushwalks. To get here, follow Krawarree Rd and turn onto Wyanbene Rd. Come armed with drinking water and firewood. **Map refs:** 58 C3, 90 G12, 98 E6

EAST BOYD STATE FOREST

Head south of Eden along the Princes Hwy and you'll come to East Boyd State Forest, a leisurely patch of green abutting Mount Imlay National Park. It's a popular place for 4WD touring, bushwalking and horseriding.

Who to contact: Forests NSW South Coast Region (02) 4472 6211

364 Scrubby Creek camping area

The facilities here are pretty basic, but they include picnic tables, drinking water and wood BBQs, which is all you need for a comfortable overnight stop. Follow the signs from the Princes Hwy to East Boyd State Forest. **Map refs:** 58 C7, 98 E10

EUROBODALLA NATIONAL PARK

This sliver of national park runs in 3 sections along the south coast between Moruya Heads and Tilba Tilba Lake, just south of Cape Dromedary. It is particularly picturesque, with 30 km of lovely beaches broken by estuaries and backed by wetlands, lakes and forests of spotted gum. It's 12 km north of Narooma on the Princes Hwy.

Who to contact: NPWS Narooma (02) 4476 0800

365 Brou Lake camping area

In the middle of the coastal sweep of Eurobodalla National Park, Brou Lake offers swimming, beach walking, surfing, and lake and beach fishing. Anglers need to keep an eye out for signs depicting sanctuary zones where fishing isn't permitted. Bring your own drinking water and firewood. The campground is at the end of Brou Lake Rd off the Princes Hwy, about 10 km north of Narooma. Note: the campsite is only suitable for caravans and camper trailers capable of driving on unsealed roads. **Map refs:** 58 D4, 98 F7

366 Congo camping area

You'll find this camping area at the point where Congo Creek meets the ocean – which makes it a top spot for swimming, fishing, beachcombing and canoeing. To reach it, follow Congo Rd from South Head Rd, off the Princes Hwy south of Moruya. There's bore water supplied, but it'll need to be boiled or treated first. Campfires not permitted. **Map refs:** 58 D4, 98 F7

MEROO NATIONAL PARK

Meroo National Park is 5 km south of Ulladulla, and comprises 2 sections: a coastal area between Tabourie Lake Village and Bawley Point, and a region south-west of Burrill Lake on the western side of the Princes Hwy. The park is characterised by sandy beaches, coastal lakes and inland forest, all of which protect a variety of plant and animal species, in particular migratory waterbirds.

Who to contact: NPWS Ulladulla (02) 4454 9500

367 Meroo Head camping area

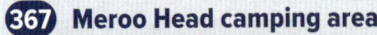

Follow Meroo Point Rd off the Princes Hwy to reach this camping area. Given the relative newness of the national park, facilities are underdeveloped, but this is part of the park's charm. You can walk to the beach from the camping ground, and explore the coastline as far as your feet and energy allow. There's a short walk from carpark to campsite; bring water and firewood. Stick to established fire pits. **Map refs:** 58 D3, 91 I11, 98 F5

368 Sunburnt Beach camping area (walk-in camping)

Walk-in bush camping is available at Sunburnt Beach, north of Termeil Point. There are no facilities at this site so bring your own everything. Access is off the Princes Hwy south of Ulladulla. **Map refs:** 58 D3, 91 I11, 98 F5

369 Termeil Point camping area

There are 11 sites at this car-based camping area. To reach Termeil Point turn east off the Princes Hwy on Blackbutt Rd, about 2 km south of Tabourie. Roads are unsealed, so check conditions in wet weather. Bring your own everything. **Map refs:** 58 D3, 91 I11, 98 F5

MIMOSA ROCKS NATIONAL PARK

At Mimosa Rocks National Park, 10 km north of Tathra along the Bermagui–Tathra Rd, a 16 km volcanic-rock coastline has been sculpted by weather and water into cliffs, rock stacks and jutting headlands, ideal for whale-watching. The beaches, bays and coves are perfect for swimming, surfing, fishing and snorkelling.

Who to contact: NPWS Narooma (02) 4476 0800

370 Aragunnu camping area

This northernmost campground can be accessed along Aragunnu Rd off the Bermagui–Tathra Rd, about 25 km south of Bermagui. There's a short, easy walk linking the northern and southern picnic areas, and a 200 m boardwalk leading to a lookout over the intriguing Mimosa Rocks. You can also walk to Aragunnu Beach from here. There is a variety of sites, some sheltered in among the bloodwoods and cycads at the south end, others being in a more open clearing near the path to Mimosa Rocks. Bring drinking water. Note: some sites require a short walk from the carpark. Fees are payable on site. **Map refs:** 58 C5, 98 E9

371 Gillards Beach camping area

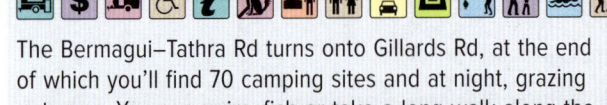

The Bermagui–Tathra Rd turns onto Gillards Rd, at the end of which you'll find 70 camping sites and at night, grazing potaroos. You can swim, fish or take a long walk along the beautiful sandy beach. Bring your own drinking water. Fees are payable on site. **Map refs:** 58 C6, 98 E9

372 Middle Beach camping area (walk-in camping)

Aptly named, this camping area is smack-bang in the middle of the national park's coastline. To get here, take the Haighs Rd turn-off from the Bermagui–Tathra Rd, and look for Middle Beach Rd. If you hit Bithry Inlet you've gone too far. There are 12 walk-in campsites here, 100 m from the carpark. Bring drinking water with you. **Map refs:** 58 C6, 98 E9

373 Picnic Point camping area

With only 18 sites and no bookings taken at this camping area, you'll just have to cross your fingers and hope for the best. Tent up amid gnarly banksias, then take your pick of swimming, fishing, picnicking or walking. This spot can be very busy during holiday periods. Bring drinking water and firewood. Picnic Point is located at the end of Wapengo Lake Rd off the Tathra–Bermagui Rd. The road leading to the camping area is private; leave gates the way you found them. **Map refs:** 58 C6, 98 E9

MURRAMARANG NATIONAL PARK

Murramarang National Park rims the south coast for 44 km and includes Darras Lake and several small offshore islands. The park features a string of lovely coves, sandy and shingle beaches, intriguing weathered sea stacks, rock platforms and a backdrop of low mountains. It's 10 km north of Batemans Bay via the Princes Hwy.

How to book: bookings are essential during peak periods; Fitzroy Falls Visitor Centre (02) 4887 7270 for campsite nos **374**, **376**; (02) 4478 6582 for campsite no. **375**; (02) 4478 6023 for campsite no. **377**; (02) 4457 2019 for campsite no. **378**

374 Bush camping areas

There are a number of opportunities for self-sufficient campers to strike out and find a site for themselves. The rules are you must camp more than 100 m from the coastline and roads, and 500 m from villages, and camping and picnic areas. Contact the parks office for maps and information. Campfires are not permitted. Bring your own everything. **Map refs:** 58 D3, 98 F6

375 Depot Beach camping area

You'll find plenty of grassy camping areas shaded by tall eucalypts at this well-appointed campground next to the beach. It's 20 km north of Batemans Bay via Mount Agony Rd off the Princes Hwy. Powered and unpowered sites are available – you may need to

share your space with the kangaroos. Bring your own firewood.
Map refs: 58 D3, 91 I12, 98 F6

376 North Head Beach camping area

Basic and very secluded, North Head Beach camping area is accessible via North Head Rd. Bring your own drinking water and firewood. **Map refs:** 58 D3, 90 H12, 98 F6

377 Pebbly Beach camping area

Pebbly Beach is sheltered and tranquil, ensconced in eucalypts, ringed with low hills and populated with laid-back wallabies, which wander through the campsite and lounge on the grass just behind the beach. The birdlife here is also abundant and friendly, with galahs, cockatoos and lorikeets often visiting. Fishing, swimming and canoeing are popular, as are the many coastal walking tracks nearby. The campground can be reached via Mt Agony Rd off the Princes Hwy. It's well appointed, with an amenities block, drinking water and firewood supplied.
Map refs: 28 D5, 58 D3, 91 I12, 93 N7, 98 F6

378 Pretty Beach camping area

Pretty by name, pretty by nature: grey kangaroos, wallabies, brush-tail possums and myriad birdlife against a backdrop of blue ocean, white sand and towering eucalypts. It's a well-equipped campground complete with an amenities block. To get here, take the Bawley Point/Kiola turn-off at the Princes Hwy, and Murramarang Rd from Bawley Point. Note: cabin accommodation is also available. Bring your own firewood; gas/fuel stove preferred. **Map refs:** 58 D3, 91 I12, 98 F6

NADGEE NATURE RESERVE

Nadgee Nature Reserve is the only remaining coastal wilderness in NSW; together with nearby Croajingolong National Park in Victoria, it forms a UNESCO Biosphere Reserve. Experienced walkers and sea-kayakers revel in its isolation and pristine, natural beauty, which includes old-growth eucalypt forest, extensive coastal heath, sea caves and diverse wildlife. Campers need a permit to bush camp, and walkers need to bring up-to-date topographic maps; contact the parks office for detailed track information.

How to book: advance booking and payment essential; NPWS Merimbula (02) 6495 5001

379 Bunyip Hole camping area (walk-in and bush camping)

From Nadgee Lake to Bunyip Hole is approximately 4.1 km – although if the lake is full it will be about 4.6 km. This is a bush-camping site for self-sufficient walkers only. Gas/fuel stove preferred. **Map refs:** 58 C8, 98 E11

380 Cape Howe camping area (walk-in and bush camping)

It's about 1 km from Bunyip Hole to Cape Howe. This is a designated bush-camping site for self-sufficient walkers only. Gas/fuel stove preferred. **Map refs:** 58 C8, 98 E11

381 Little Creek camping area (walk-in and bush camping)

From Newtons Beach to the designated bush-camping site at Little Creek is approximately 4.3 km. Gas/fuel stove preferred. For self-sufficient walkers only. **Map refs:** 58 C8, 98 E11

382 Merrica River Entrance camping area (walk-in and bush camping)

It's about 4.5 km from the trackhead to Merrica River Entrance camping area. This is a designated bush-camping site for self-sufficient walkers only. Gas/fuel stove preferred. **Map refs:** 58 C7, 98 E11

383 Nadgee Beach camping area (walk-in and bush camping)

From Little Creek to Nadgee Beach North is 4.2 km, then another 700 m to Nadgee Beach South. These are designated bush-camping sites for self-sufficient walkers only. Gas/fuel stove preferred. **Map refs:** 58 C8, 98 E11

384 Nadgee Lake camping area (walk-in and bush camping)

From the southern end of Nadgee Beach, it's about 2.4 km to Nadgee Lake camping area, a designated bush-camping site for self-sufficient walkers only. Gas/fuel stove preferred. **Map refs:** 58 C8, 98 E11

385 Newtons Beach camping area (walk-in and bush camping)

About 9 km from the trackhead, this camping site is a designated bush-camping site for self-sufficient walkers only. Gas/fuel stove preferred. **Map refs:** 58 C8, 98 E11

SOUTH EAST FORESTS NATIONAL PARK

South East Forests National Park sprawls across undulating hills and rugged, mountainous terrain, with tracts of precious old-growth forest, flowering heathlands, massive granite tors, tumbling waterfalls, fern-filled gullies and rare and threatened plant and animal species. Access throughout the park is on fire roads, which can become slippery in the rain. Devils Crossing on the Cattlemans Link Trail involves a water crossing of Tantawangalo Creek. Its southern boundary abuts the Victorian border.

Who to contact: NPWS Bombala (02) 6458 4080

386 Alexanders Hut

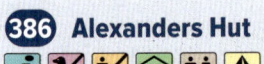

In the central section of the national park, Alexanders Hut is a simple slab dwelling that provides shelter and basic facilities for campers. You can also set up a tent in the grounds around the hut. The hut is situated picturesquely on a grassy hillside above a large dam; the camping area is adjacent, and nicely grassed. It's 2WD dry-weather access only. From Nunnock camping area continue south on Cattlemans Link Trail; at a fork in the road turn left and follow the road to the hut. From Postmans camping area, head across Devils Crossing and follow Cattlemans Link Track; turn east onto Cattlemans Link Trail and follow for 600 m to the hut. Bring drinking water and firewood. **Map refs:** 58 B6, 98 D9

387 Nunnock camping area

It's 2WD dry-weather access only to this camping ground. To get here from the north, follow the Snowy Mountains Hwy from Nimmitabel and turn onto Packers Swamp Rd. Turn left onto Cattlemans Link Trail, and follow it to the campsite. From the south, take Tantawangalo Mountain Rd from Mt Darragh Rd, turn left onto New Line Rd and then right onto Packers Swamp Rd. Head north to Cattlemans Link Trail and follow this to the campsite. It's a picturesque site with an easy 4 km loop walking track with lookouts over a high-altitude perched swamp. There are also some interesting pastoral ruins, including stockyards, in a clearing across the road from the start of the Nunnock Swamp walk. Bring drinking water and firewood. **Map refs:** 58 B6, 98 D9

388 Postmans camping area

Located on a sandy bend in Tantawangalo Creek, this camping area is 4WD dry-weather access only via Postmans Track off Tantawangalo Rd. There's a long walk from the car to the tent sites. There's water in the creek, but it'll need boiling or treating if you plan to drink it, otherwise bring your own. Bring firewood. **Map refs:** 58 B6, 98 D9

389 Six Mile Creek camping area

As you follow the Tantawangalo Mountain Rd to this campsite, you can inform your companions you're travelling on a road originally constructed more than 150 years ago. Six Mile Creek is a refreshing and scenic place to swim or picnic, and there's an easy 300 m return walk to a viewing platform over Tantawangalo Creek. Note: there are only 4 sites here, with limited space for trailers. If you're going to use the water in the creek, boil or treat it before drinking. Bring firewood. **Map refs:** 58 B6, 98 D9

390 Waratah Gully camping area

It's hard to beat the magic of old-growth forest, and you can experience it yourself at Waratah Gully camping area. It's in the Coolangubra section of the national park, accessible east of Bombala on Bucky Springs Rd, then Coolangubra Forest Way and Wog Way. Bring drinking water and firewood. Pheasants

Peak (4 km return, 4 hr, hard) and Myanba Gorge (2 km, 1 hr, medium) are 2 walking tracks that can be accessed from here. **Map refs:** 58 B6, 98 D10

TIMBILLICA STATE FOREST

Nestled in the far southern reaches of NSW, Timbillica is 30 km south-west of Eden via Imlay Rd from the Princes Hwy. Swimming and picnicking are popular here as is 4WD touring. There's a cracking good swimming hole at Newtons Crossing, on the Wallagaraugh River.

Who to contact: Forests NSW Eden 1300 880 548

391 Newtons Crossing camping area

Take Allan Brook Rd off Imlay Rd and follow the signs to Newtons Crossing. It's just a small spot, with 5 sites available. However, it is a lovely area, situated next to the Wallagaraugh River, which flows through a wide rocky clearing in the forest here. And being slightly inland you may find a break from the crowds at the coast, even in peak times. Bring your own firewood and drinking water or boil/treat the river water. **Map refs:** 58 B7, 98 D11

WADBILLIGA NATIONAL PARK

Abutting the northern boundary of South East Forests National Park, Wadbilliga is a rugged wilderness of plunging gorges and expansive rolling plateaus. It hosts a great diversity of plant and animal species, one of the state's largest untouched river catchments and the fascinating Brogo Wilderness Area.

Who to contact: NPWS Narooma (02) 4476 0800

392 Cascades camping area

The stunning Tuross Falls are accessible via 2 easy walking tracks from the carpark and camping ground. The camping area is beside the Tuross River off Peters and Badger rds. Most of the sites are spread around a large clearing, with a few just a couple of metres from a calm pool on the Tuross River. While the falls are at the end of a 3 km return walk, there are also good views of the cascades along the way. It's 4WD access only. Bring drinking water and firewood. **Map refs:** 58 B4, 98 D7

393 Lake Creek camping area

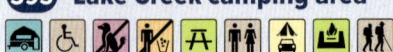

To get here, head west from Cobargo along Wandella Rd, then Yowrie Bourkes rds. It's 2WD, not suitable for caravans and only off-road camper trailers. Bring drinking water and firewood. **Map refs:** 58 C5, 98 D8

CAMPSITES LOCATED IN OTHER AREAS

394 Araluen Creek camping area

Nestled in a picturesque valley at the foot of Mt Araluen, Araluen is a small town known for its peaceful charm and

stone-fruit orchards. The village is 27 km south of Braidwood and 72 km west of Moruya on the south coast. The camping area is at the junction of the Araluen–Braidwood and Majors Creek rds. It's a simple set-up but you can swim in the river, let your dog run free, and enjoy a barbecue picnic for breakfast, lunch or dinner. Bring your own drinking water and firewood. **Map refs:** 58 C3, 90 G12, 98 E6

Who to contact: Braidwood Tourist Information Centre (02) 4842 1144

395 Bega Caravan Park

Nestled into the lush and verdant Bega Valley, Bega Caravan Park is a well-appointed, comfortable place with a range of accommodation options – including motel-style units, cabins, and powered and unpowered tent sites. There's a laundry and an amenities block here. Note: pets allowed except over Christmas and throughout January. **Map refs:** 58 C6, 98 E9

How to book: 256 Princes Hwy, Bega (02) 6492 2303 www.begacaravanpark.com.au

396 Danjera Dam camping area

The dam's waters cover an old gold-rush town called Yalwal; today, visitors come to the area for aquatic activities such as kayaking, swimming, fishing (the dam is stocked with rainbow trout and bass) and boating. The surrounding bushland makes it a picturesque camping spot and provides a variety of walking tracks. To get here, follow Yalwal Rd from Nowra and Burrier. The steep, unsealed road isn't suitable for caravans. Bring your own firewood and drinking water. **Map refs:** 58 D1, 91 I10, 98 G4

Who to contact: Shoalhaven Visitor Information Centre (02) 4421 0778, 1300 662 808

397 Lake Conjola Entrance Tourist Park

Set along the southern bank of sparkling Lake Conjola as it ambles towards the sea, this park enjoys both lake and beach access and is fringed by bushland. A 4 hr drive south of Sydney along the Princes Hwy and Lake Conjola Entrance Rd, the park has an array of cabins as well as tent and caravan sites, an amenities block, a jumping cushion, a playground, a tennis court and resident kangaroos. **Map refs:** 58 E2, 91 I11, 98 G5

How to book: Lake Conjola Entrance Rd, Lake Conjola (02) 4456 1141, 1300 133 395 www.conjolaentrancetouristpark.com.au

398 Mystery Bay Camp Ground (bush camping)

This is a gorgeous spot overlooking Mystery Bay, at the end of Mystery Bay Rd signposted off the Princes Hwy 15 km south of Narooma. Even your dog gets to enjoy this one. The

Tents and caravans at Congo camping area, Eurobodalla National Park (p. 61)

sites are shaded by tall and slender gums, there is plenty of room for vehicles of all shapes and sizes, and the views at the beach close by are fabulous. Firewood is available for sale on-site; gas and ice can be purchased at a nearby farm. **Map refs:** 58 D5, 98 F8

Who to contact: (02) 4476 8596, 0428 622 357

399 Nimmitabel Caravan Park

This caravan park is situated at the northern entrance to the small town of Nimmitabel, 40 km south of Cooma on the Monaro Hwy. What the town lacks in size it makes up for with character: many of its buildings date back to the mid-19th century. The caravan park is simple but sufficient; bring your own firewood. Pick up the key to the amenities block from the caretaker. **Map refs:** 58 B5, 98 D8

How to book: Boyd St, Nimmitabel 0427 406 668 www.nimmitabel.nsw.au

400 North Head Campground

A friendly and picturesque campground ringed with Norfolk pines and eucalypts, North Head is within walking distance of the beach and river. The other drawcard is the nearby town of Moruya, with its craft and novelty shops, Sat morning markets and Oct jazz festival. The town is 25 km south of Batemans Bay on the Princes Hwy; North Head Campground is 7 km east of town via North Head Dr. There's a dump point for caravans in town. Bring your own firewood or buy it from the caretaker. **Map refs:** 58 D4, 98 F7

Who to contact: 0428 633 447

CAPITAL COUNTRY AND THE SNOWYS

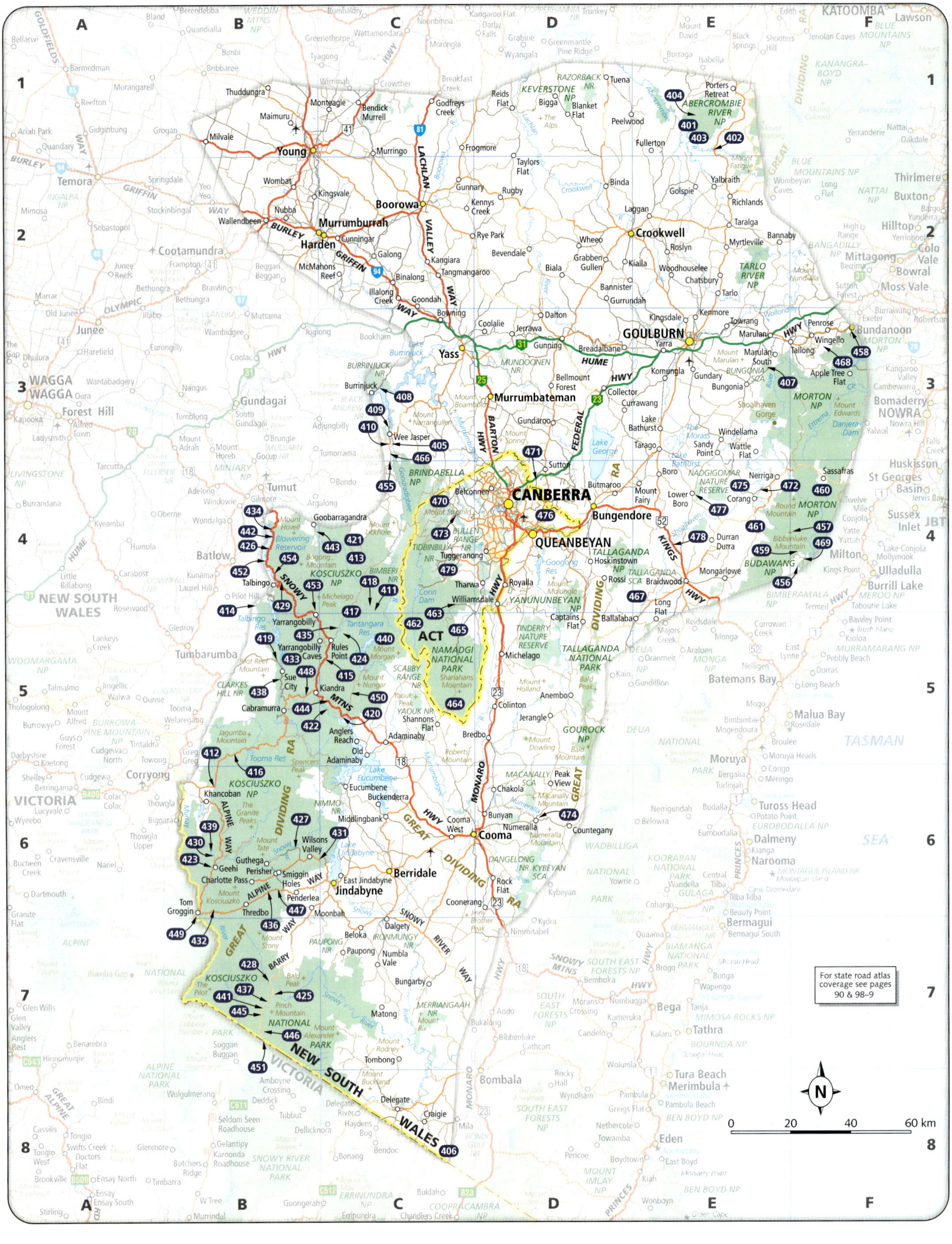

STRETCHING SOUTH FROM GOULBURN through the ACT, over the Snowy Mountains and down to the NSW–Vic. border, Capital Country is impressive in its variety and remarkable in its accessibility.

The jewel in the crown is without a doubt Kosciuszko National Park. The largest national park in NSW, Kosciuszko is expansive, dramatic and awe-inspiring. Situated on the highest land in Australia it has a rugged, wild beauty, yet up close it reveals many small treasures: delicate wildflowers, historic cattlemen's huts, and rare and endangered wildlife. In winter, when its peaks are blanketed with snow, it transforms into one of Australia's finest ski fields. In summer, wildflowers carpet the grassy meadows, and there are lovely walks and the chance to indulge in a range of outdoor activities. An outstanding natural feature is the spectacular Yarrangobilly Caves, with their dramatic limestone formations.

Sprawling across almost half the ACT is Namadgi National Park, with its stunning alpine scenery, diverse wildlife and opportunities for activities such as bushwalking, cycling, horseriding, 4WD touring, cross-country skiing and rock climbing. The name Namadgi is derived from an Aboriginal word for the ranges to the south-east of Canberra, and throughout the national park there are many clues to the long occupation of the land by Indigenous people.

The region's underground landscape is equally intriguing, with magnificent limestone caves at Wee Jasper, Kosciuszko National Park and Bungonia State Conservation Area. And then there are the towns, many of which have a unique brand of natural beauty. An overnight stay in campgrounds close to Braidwood, Numeralla or Nerriga provides a chance to learn about the region's history and rub shoulders with the characters who populate this rich and varied region.

CAMPSITES LOCATED IN PARKS AND RESERVES

ABERCROMBIE RIVER NATIONAL PARK

Abercrombie River National Park protects the largest tract of low open forest in the south-west central tablelands. Its 3 rivers are punctuated by deep waterholes suitable for swimming, fishing and paddling. The park is 40 km south of Oberon and 60 km north of Goulburn. The main access is via Arkstone Rd, from the Goulburn–Oberon Rd. Access throughout the park is on fire trails that, while not technically challenging, are very steep in some places and could be difficult if it rains.

Who to contact: NPWS Oberon (02) 6336 1972

401 The Beach camping area

This is a beautiful, quiet spot next to the Abercrombie River. The small campsite is sheltered on a bend in the river, deep in the valley. A short stroll upstream is a deep calm pool where you may be lucky enough to spot a platypus. Access is 4WD only along the Abercrombie Fire Trail via Arkstone or Emden Vale. There's water in the river, but you'll need to boil or treat it first. Bring your own firewood. **Map refs:** 66 E1, 90 H7, 98 E1

402 Bummaroo Ford camping area

This is the only camping area in the park that can be reached by 2WD. It's on Abercrombie Rd, at the crossing of the Abercrombie River, 29 km north of Taralga via the Goulburn–Oberon Rd. If the water levels are high enough, this is a good spot for swimming, fishing or paddling. Boil or treat water from the river, or else bring your own, plus firewood. **Map refs:** 66 E1, 90 H7, 98 E1

403 Silent Creek camping area

Silent Creek is aptly named, as the creek is often dry, but it's a spacious camping area suitable for large groups. This is 4WD access only, via Abercrombie Fire Trail. You can come in from either Arkstone or Emden Vale. Bring your own drinking water and firewood. **Map refs:** 66 E1, 90 H7, 98 E1

404 The Sink camping area

You'll need a 4WD to access this camping area, next to Retreat River on the Retreat Fire Trail via Arkstone Rd. If the river is running, it's a good spot for fishing and swimming, and there's also bushwalking to do here. Boil or treat water from the river before drinking, otherwise bring your own, along with firewood. There is a short walk from car to site. **Map refs:** 66 E1, 90 H7, 98 E1

BILLY GRACE RESERVE

Billy Grace is one of a handful of reserves near the small, picturesque town of Wee Jasper, which sits serenely at the foot of the Brindabella Ranges, 54 km south-west of Yass.

Who to contact: Wee Jasper Reserves (02) 6227 9626

405 Billy Grace Reserve

Perched on the banks of the Goodradigbee River, Billy Grace is 4.1 km south of Wee Jasper village via the Wee Jasper–Nottingham Rd. There's a playground for the kids and coin-operated showers. Bring your own firewood. Bookings are required for groups. **Map refs:** 66 C3, 90 E10, 98 C4, 99 A2

BONDI STATE FOREST

This pleasant native forest and pine plantation is 30 km south of Bombala via Bondi Forest Way from Monaro Hwy. There's a load of outdoor activities on offer, including bushwalking, horseriding, fishing, 4WD touring and swimming.

How to book: bookings essential; (02) 6458 7262

406 Bondi Forest Lodge

The Bondi Forest Lodge provides the only accommodation in the forest, in the form of twin bunk-bed rooms in 3 self-contained units, sleeping 72 in total. There's also a large recreation room

with a cosy log fire. It's on Buldah Rd, 32 km south of Bombala.
Map refs: 66 C8, 98 C10

BUNGONIA NATIONAL PARK

This region was first reserved for its limestone caves – a magnificent subterranean underworld that has become a magnet for canyoners and cavers. This combined with the dramatic gorges of Bungonia Creek and Shoalhaven River makes Bungonia National Park a place of great natural beauty. It's 35 km east of Goulburn and 25 km south of Marulan via Bungonia, on the Hume Hwy.

How to book: bookings essential; (02) 4844 4277, (02) 4844 4341

407 Bungonia camping area

This is a spacious, well-equipped camping ground in a stunning bushland setting. There's a conference room for hire, plenty of space for tents, caravans and camper trailers, and all the outdoor activities that the area has to offer. You can get here via the Lookdown Rd, 15 km from Bungonia. Make sure you bring water and, as fires aren't permitted, a gas/fuel stove too.
Map refs: 66 E3, 90 H9, 98 F3

BURRINJUCK WATERS STATE PARK

Lake Burrinjuck is a stunningly scenic spot: at times swathed in mist; at others, sun-kissed and sparkling. Bushwalkers can satisfy their cravings in the surrounding bushland, while water babies can choose from swimming, fishing, sailing, paddling and waterskiing. Burrinjuck Waters State Park is 50 km south-west of Yass via Burrinjuck Rd, off the Hume Hwy near Bookham.

How to book: (02) 6227 8114

408 Burrinjuck Waters State Park camping area

Situated on the western foreshore of Lake Burrinjuck, the state park camping area offers a huge array of facilities and activities. Accommodation options include self-contained cottages and cabins, and powered and unpowered caravan sites. Facilities and activities include volleyball and tennis courts, a kids' playground, conference centre, laundry and kiosk. You'll need to book ahead in peak periods. **Map refs:** 66 C3, 90 E9, 98 B3

CAREYS RESERVE

This reserve is named for John Carey, who discovered a beautiful limestone cave nearby in 1875. Careys Cave is on Caves Rd, not far past the reserve, and is open for guided tours.

Who to contact: Wee Jasper Reserves (02) 6227 9626

409 Careys Reserve camping area

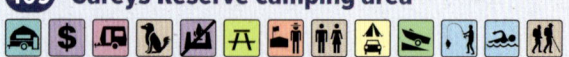

Careys camping area is 2.6 km north of Wee Jasper next to Burrinjuck Dam, via Caves Rd. You can fish, swim or strike out

on a walking trail, and launch a boat from the ramp as long as the dam is more than 60 per cent full. Bring your own drinking water and firewood. **Map refs:** 66 C3, 90 E10, 98 B4, 99 A2

FITZPATRICK TRACKHEAD RESERVE

Fitzpatrick Trackhead Reserve is one of 5 pretty reserves scattered around Wee Jasper, a small but picturesque town in a valley below the Brindabella Ranges. Although Wee Jasper's population is only 100, the town has had its share of history: Hume and Hovell trudged through here in 1824, and poet A. B. 'Banjo' Paterson was co-owner of the nearby Goodravale property until 1911.

Who to contact: Wee Jasper Reserves (02) 6227 9626

410 Fitzpatrick Trackhead camping area

This camping site is one of the major vehicle-access trackheads on the Hume and Hovell Walking Track. It's named for James Fitzpatrick, one of the men who accompanied Hume on the expedition. To get here, follow the signs on the Tumut–Nottingham Rd, 4 km south of Wee Jasper. There's tank water available here. **Map refs:** 66 C3, 90 E10, 98 B4, 99 A2

All other campsites on the Hume and Hovell Walking Track are in the Riverina and the Murray region, see p. 82.

KOSCIUSZKO NATIONAL PARK

Kosciuszko National Park embraces the majestic grandeur of the high country. A 450 km trip south of Sydney, this is one of the world's great national parks. Immerse yourself in alpine herbfields and soaring mountain peaks, the headwaters of the famed Snowy River and fascinating Aboriginal and European heritage.

Who to contact: NPWS Snowy Mountains (Tumut) (02) 6947 7000 for campsite nos **411**, **413**, **414**, **415**, **417**, **418**, **419**, **420**, **421**, **422**, **424**, **426**, **429**, **433**, **434**, **435**, **438**, **440**, **442**, **443**, **444**, **448**, **450**, **451**, **452**, **453**, **454**; NPWS Snowy Mountains (Khancoban) (02) 6076 9373 for campsite nos **412**, **416**, **423**, **430**, **432**, **439**, **449**; NPWS Snowy Mountains (Jindabyne) (02) 6450 5600 for campsite nos **425**, **427**, **428**, **436**, **437**, **441**, **445**, **446**, **447** *How to book:* (02) 6456 2224 for campsite no. **431**

411 Blue Waterholes Campground (northern section)

You'll need a 4WD in wet weather, and an off-road camper trailer to get to this cracking campsite. From here you can access multiple walking tracks, adventure caves, a waterfall and a spectacular lookout. Near the campsite is the historic Coolamine Homestead, built in the 1890s. With a number of preserved buildings and interpretive signs, it is well worth a look around. The walk through Clarke Gorge, which requires wading across the creek, is quite striking as it passes through a deep and sometimes narrow gorge. Take the Long Plain Rd off the Snowy Mountain Hwy, then the Blue Waterholes Trail. Note that Long Plain Rd is closed during the colder months, so be sure to check with the parks office before setting off. Bring your own water and firewood. **Map refs:** 66 C4, 90 E11, 98 B5

412 Bradneys Gap camping area (northern section)

Bradneys Gap camping area is 10 km north-east of Khancoban via the Cabramurra–Khancoban Rd. Bring drinking water and firewood. **Map refs:** 66 B6, 98 A7

413 Broken Cart camping area (northern section)

Set amid eucalypt forest, this is a very basic campsite with no facilities, near the intersection of Feints and Broken Cart trails in the north of the park. Access is via Broken Cart Track off Long Plain Rd, or Boundary, Bramina, Barnetts or Brindabella rds. Note: both Long Plain Rd and Broken Cart Track are likely to be closed June–Oct long weekends, so check with the parks office before setting out. **Map refs:** 66 C4, 90 E11, 98 B5

414 Buddong Falls camping area (northern section)

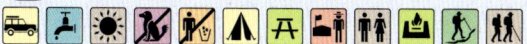

Located at the trackhead to Buddong (upper and lower) Falls, this camping area has basic facilities and no designated sites. Tracks to Buddong Falls follow forestry trails and are only suitable for 4WD vehicles in dry weather (summer) only. To get here from Batlow use Yellowin, Snubba and Browns rds and De Beaureville Track, which is narrow, steep and winding. Cattle, wild horses and other vehicles may be on these tracks so drive carefully. Bring your own firewood and water, or boil/treat water from Buddong Creek. **Map refs:** 66 B4, 90 D11, 98 A5

415 Bullocks Hill camping area (northern section)

Access this grassy camping area, which includes a horse yard, via Bullock Hill Trail off Snowy Mountains Hwy. The site is an ideal base for exploring the park on foot, horseback or mountain-bike. Bring your own water or boil/treat creek water. Note: Bullock Hill Trail is subject to closure June–Oct long weekends and a 4WD is required in wet weather. Check with the parks office before setting off. **Map refs:** 66 C5, 90 E12, 98 B6

416 Clover Flat camping area (northern section)

You'll need to bring drinking water and firewood to this camping area, 26 km north of Khancoban via the Cabramurra–Khancoban Rd. **Map refs:** 66 B5, 98 A7

417 Cooinbil Hut camping area (northern section)

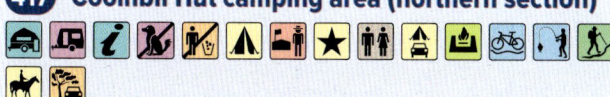

There are 2 sections to this camping area: a walk-in and vehicle-based camping site on the north side of historic Cooinbil Hut; and a vehicle- and horse-based camping site on the south side. The latter includes horse yards and a loading ramp. The hut, which was built in 1905, and camping area are surrounded by snow gums and are in a clearing on a hillside with expansive views back down over Long Plain. To get here, take the Cooinbil Hut access track from Long Plain Rd, 10 km

north of Long Plain Hut. Check road conditions before setting off; the road is closed in colder months and a 4WD is required in wet weather. Bring your own firewood and drinking water. **Map refs:** 66 C4, 90 E11, 98 B5

418 Cooleman Mountain camping area (northern section)

Surrounded by towering gums, this campground is on the Blue Waterholes access road, 2.6 km east of Long Plain Rd. A 2 km walking track will take you to historic Coolamine Homestead. Bring your own firewood and drinking water, or boil the tank water supplied before use. Note: Long Plain Rd is closed during the colder months; check with the NPWS before setting off. A 4WD is required in wet weather. **Map refs:** 66 C4, 90 E11, 98 B5

419 Coonara Point camping area (boat-based camping, northern section)

This boat-based campground offers waterskiing, paddling and fishing as well as camping. To get here, you can launch from boat ramps at Talbingo Dam Wall south of Talbingo, or O'Hares Rest Area off Elliott Way. Bring your own firewood and drinking water, or boil/treat reservoir water before use. **Map refs:** 66 B5, 90 D12, 98 A6

420 Denison camping area (northern section)

From this camping ground you can reach Eucumbene dam and river, where you can go fishing or motorboating. It's off the Snowy Mountains Hwy north of Gang Gang Creek. Bring your own drinking water and firewood. **Map refs:** 66 C5, 90 E12, 98 B6

421 Dubbo Flats camping area (northern section)

It's 4WD access only to Dubbo Flats, reached via Broken Cart Track in the north of the park. The road will be closed completely in bad weather, so check with the parks office before setting out. Note: there are no set sites here, and facilities are very basic. Bring your own drinking water and firewood. **Map refs:** 66 C4, 90 E11, 98 B5

422 Eucumbene camping area (northern section)

Camp near the Eucumbene River (no closer than 30 m) and try your luck with a fishing rod. There are no facilities or designated camping sites here. It's 4WD dry-weather access only via Four Mile Trail off the Snowy Mountains Hwy just north of the Rest House. Note: the road is likely to close June–Oct long weekends so check with the parks office before setting out. It's a short walk from your car to your camping site – bring your own everything. **Map refs:** 66 C5, 90 E12, 98 B6

423 Geehi Flats camping area (southern section)

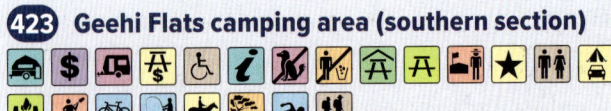

On the winding Alpine Way, 31 km south of Khancoban, Geehi Flats camping area isn't recommended for large caravans and camper trailers. Despite this, the old Snowy Mountains Hydro camp spot is popular in summer for its trout fishing and swimming. The views of the western escarpment of the Snowy Mountains are very good from here and at the nearby Scammell's Lookout. There is also a good 4WD track, linking some of the nearby huts via a track that crosses the Swampy Plain River a number of times. Bring your own firewood and drinking water. **Map refs:** 66 B6, 98 A8

424 Ghost Gully Horse Camp (northern section)

As its name suggests, this grassy camping ground allows horses, and provides a loading ramp and horse yard. You'll find it 9 km south-east of Rules Point, via Port Phillip Fire Trail off Long Plain Rd. Note: Long Plain Rd is closed during the colder months; check with the NPWS before setting off. You'll need a 4WD in wet weather. Bring your own firewood and drinking water. **Map refs:** 66 C5, 90 E11, 98 B6

425 Halfway Flat camping area (southern section)

This is a popular picnic and camping area offering swimming, fishing, paddling and walking. It's 55 km south of Jindabyne on the Barry Way near the Snowy River. You'll need to supply your own drinking water and firewood. **Map refs:** 66 B7, 98 A9

426 Humes Crossing camping area (northern section)

You'll need to bring drinking water and firewood to this camping area, 25 km south of Tumut near Blowering Dam, reached by the Snowy Mountains Hwy. There are loads of water-based activities to immerse yourself in during summer, including fishing, swimming and paddling. **Map refs:** 66 B4, 90 D11, 98 A5

427 Island Bend camping area (southern section)

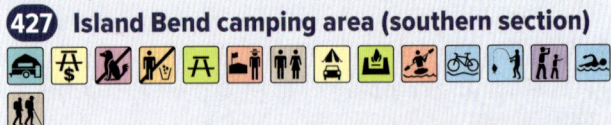

This former Snowy Mountains Hydro camp is located near the Snowy River, 23 km north-west of Jindabyne. Sites here are either in clearings where the old camp buildings were on the hill, or lower down near the upper reaches of the Snowy River, where there are scattered bush camps. To get here, turn on to Guthega Rd from Kosciuszko Rd. Bring your own drinking water and firewood – and fishing rod, if you're an enthusiast. **Map refs:** 66 B6, 98 B7

428 Jacob's River camping area (southern section)

Summertime offers fishing and swimming in the river next to this pleasant camping spot, 53 km south of Jindabyne. It's near the junction of the Jacobs and Snowy rivers, off Barry Way. You can boil/treat the river water or bring your own; and bring your own firewood. **Map refs:** 66 B7, 98 A9

429 Jounama Creek camping area (northern section)

This area has 2 parts. The main campground has picnic tables, BBQS and toilets; it's 300 m off the Snowy Mountains Hwy, opposite the Talbingo turn-off. There's a smaller area next to Jounama Creek, 1 km upstream, with no facilities. Bring your own firewood and drinking water, or boil/treat the creek water. **Map refs:** 66 B4, 90 D11, 98 B5

430 Keebles Hut camping area (southern section)

Renowned as one of the best huts in the national park, Keebles Hut was built in 1942 and has been an extremely popular camping area since its amalgmation into the national park in the 1970s. It's next to the Geehi Rest Area on Bears Flat. To access it you need either a 4WD to cross Swampy Plain River, or you can walk in from Geehi Rest Area via the Geehi Walls Trail. Bring drinking water and firewood. **Map refs:** 66 B6, 98 A7

431 Kosciuszko Mountain Retreat (southern section)

Kosciuszko Mountain Retreat offers a wide range of comfortable accommodation, from cedar cabins and chalets (some with spas) to caravan and tent sites. Facilities include a camp kitchen, drying room and laundry. It's 15 km from Jindabyne along Kosciuszko Rd, 500 m inside the national park entrance. Bookings required during peak periods. **Map refs:** 66 B6, 98 B8

432 Leatherbarrel Creek camping area (southern section)

You'll need to bring your own drinking water and firewood to this camping area, 16 km west of Thredbo on Alpine Way. Note: the Alpine Way is a narrow winding road, parts of which are unsuitable for large campervans or trailers. **Map refs:** 66 B6, 98 A8

433 Lobs Hole Ravine camping area (northern section)

Trout fishing, swimming and relative solitude are the drawcards of Lobs Hole Ravine camping area, which was once the site of a village supported by large-scale copper mining in the late 1800s to early 1900s. Access from the north is via Lobs Hole

Ravine Rd, which is fine for 2WD vehicles as far as the intersection with Blue Creek Trail. From there, Lobs Hole Ravine Rd is 4WD access only. From the south, Lobs Hole Ravine Rd is only suitable for 2WD vehicles as far as Wallaces Creek Lookout. Pack your snow chains in winter, and bring drinking water and firewood. **Map refs:** 66 B5, 90 D12, 98 B6

434 Log Bridge Creek camping area (northern section)

In summer these grassy woodlands make a great base for campers in the mood for paddling, sailing, swimming, fishing and walking. It's 18 km south of Tumut, near Blowering Dam, via the Snowy Mountains Hwy. Bring your own drinking water and firewood. **Map refs:** 66 B4, 90 D11, 98 A5

435 Long Plain Hut camping area (northern section)

There are horse yards here, to the east of Long Plain Hut, and there's another designated camping area to the north of the hut as well. It's a great spot for the active camper, with horseriding, mountain-biking, fishing and walking to choose from. Long Plain Hut is a nicely restored hut on a hillside overlooking Long Plain. Access is via Long Plain Rd, approximately 3 km north-east of the Snowy Mountains Hwy. Note: Long Plain Rd is closed during the colder months, so check with the parks office before setting out. Bring your own drinking water and firewood. **Map refs:** 66 C5, 90 E11, 98 B5

436 Ngarigo camping area (southern section)

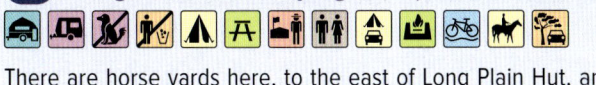

There's a short walk from car to tent here, although cars and small campervans and trailers can easily access the carpark. It's 3.6 km from Thredbo Diggings and 24 km south of Jindabyne. Access is via the Alpine Way. Bring your own firewood, drinking water – and fishing rod, if you're so inclined. **Map refs:** 66 B6, 98 A8

437 No Name picnic and camping area (southern section)

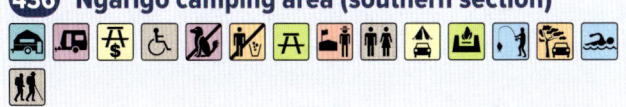

Bring your own drinking water and firewood to this small camping area, 57 km south of Jindabyne via Barry Way. **Map refs:** 66 B7, 98 A9

438 O'Hares camping area (northern section)

This old Snowy Mountains Hydro Scheme workers' campsite provides water access to the Talbingo Reservoir. As such, it's a popular spot for boaters, paddlers, sailors and anglers. To get here, take the Elliott Way from Cabramurra or Tumbaruma; it's more or less midway between these 2 villages. Bring your own drinking water (or boil/treat the reservoir water) and firewood. **Map refs:** 66 B5, 90 D12, 98 B6

439 Old Geehi Hut camping area (southern section)

The river here is a refreshing escape from the heat of summer; alternatively, you can drop a line in or go for a paddle. It's off the Alpine Way; access unsuitable for 2WD vehicles. Bring your own drinking water and firewood. **Map refs:** 66 B6, 98 A7

440 Old Snowy Camp (northern section)

You can get to this horse-camping area from the Snowy Mountains Hwy – turn on to Tantangara Rd and then Pocket Saddle Rd. Note: Pocket Saddle Rd is apt to close during June–Oct long weekends, so check with the parks office before setting out. There's not much in the way of facilities, so bring everything you need with you. **Map refs:** 66 C5, 90 E12, 98 B6, 99 A9

441 Pinch River camping area (southern section)

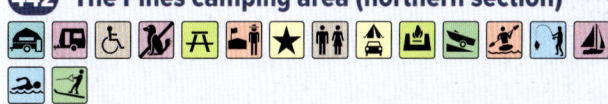

You'll find this spacious creekside camping area straddling Barry Way, 60 km south of Jindabyne. Bring your own drinking water and firewood. **Map refs:** 66 B7, 98 A9

442 The Pines camping area (northern section)

Put up a tent at the Pines and head out on the water at Blowering Dam for a spot of fishing, waterskiing, swimming or kayaking. The camping area is 22 km south of Tumut via the Snowy Mountains Hwy. Bring your own drinking water and firewood. **Map refs:** 66 B4, 90 D11, 98 A5

443 Rock Flat camping area (northern section)

Follow Lacmalac Rd for about 25 km south-east of Tumut and you'll be here before you can say Goobarragandra River, which is what you'll see when you arrive. Fishing, swimming and kayaking are all on offer here. Bring your own water or boil/treat the river water before use. Bring firewood. **Map refs:** 66 B4, 90 E11, 98 B5

444 Rocky Plain camping area (northern section)

This is a horse-camping area with loading ramp about 300 m off the Snowy Mountains Hwy just south of the Rest House (Sawyers Hill). The road is accessible by camper trailers and 2WD vehicles, but only in good weather and it is subject to closures during June–Oct long weekends, so check with the parks office before setting out. Bring drinking water and firewood. **Map refs:** 66 C5, 90 E12, 98 B6

445 **Running Waters camping area (southern section)**

You'll need to bring drinking water and firewood to this campground, but it'll supply the picnic tables, wood BBQs and top swimming, fishing and paddling spots. It's 63 km south of Jindabyne via Barry Way. **Map refs:** 66 B7, 98 A9

446 **Scotchies Yards camping area (southern section)**

Accessed via Barry Way, 71 km south of Jindabyne, Scotchies Yards offers swimming, paddling, fishing and walking. Bring your own drinking water and firewood. **Map refs:** 66 B7, 98 A9

447 **Thredbo Diggings camping area (southern section)**

Steer clear of drinking the river water here – bring your own water, along with firewood. Access is via the Alpine Way, 1.4 km from the park entrance. **Map refs:** 66 B6, 98 A8

448 **Three Mile Dam camping area (northern section)**

Three Mile Dam, 14 km north-east of Cabramurra, was built in 1883 to service gold mining in the Kiandra region. Come in early to mid-summer and you'll catch a kaleidoscopic display of wildflowers; in winter, the place is covered in snow and closed to vehicles. Access is via Kiandra–Cabramurra (Link) Rd. Bring your own drinking water and firewood. **Map refs:** 66 B5, 90 E12, 98 B6

449 **Tom Groggin camping area (southern section)**

On the south-western border of the national park, Tom Groggin is a large grassed area next to the Upper Murray River, with its good trout fishing. Access is via the Alpine Way, which is unsuitable for large campervans and trailers. There's also 4WD access from here to Alpine National Park in Victoria. This involves a crossing of the Murray River. Bring your own firewood and drinking water; alternatively, you can boil/treat the river water before use. **Map refs:** 66 B6, 98 A8

450 **Wares Yards camping area (northern section)**

You can get to this horse-camping ground via Tantangara Rd off the Snowy Mountains Hwy, although the track in may be closed during the June–Oct long weekends. Bring drinking water and firewood, and check road conditions with the parks office before setting out. Other activities here include mountain-biking and walking. **Map refs:** 66 C5, 90 E12, 98 B6

451 **Willis camping area (southern section)**

Just inside the NSW border is Willis camping area, 74 km south of Jindabyne via Barry Way. Bring your own drinking water and firewood. **Map refs:** 66 B7, 98 A9

452 **Yachting Point camping area (northern section)**

There are water activities galore during summer at this aptly named campground, 30 km south of Tumut near Blowering Dam. Take your pick of swimming, boating, fishing, waterskiing and paddling. Bring your own firewood and drinking water. **Map refs:** 66 B4, 90 D11, 98 A5

453 **Yarrangobilly Village camping area (northern section)**

This is the perfect place to stay if you're interested in visiting the startlingly beautiful Yarrangobilly Caves. You can also see Cotterill's Cottage, which dates back to the 1890s, making it one of the oldest buildings in the national park. To get here, follow the Snowy Mountains Hwy, 62 km south of Tumut. You can drink river water as long as you boil/treat it first; bring your own firewood. **Map refs:** 66 B5, 90 E11, 98 B5

454 **Yolde camping area (northern section)**

One of several camping spots on Blowering Reservoir, Yolde offers a great selection of water-based activities during summer: swimming, fishing, boating, paddling and waterskiing. It also has a boat ramp. It's 34 km south of Tumut, via the Snowy Mountains Hwy. Bring your own drinking water and firewood. **Map refs:** 66 B4, 90 D11, 98 A5

MICALONG CREEK RESERVE

Micalong Creek Reserve is one of a handful of well-maintained camping areas scattered around the small town of Wee Jasper, in the foothills of the Brindabella Ranges, 54 km south-west of Yass. Wee Jasper's picturesque beauty and nearby limestone caves make it a popular camping destination.

Who to contact: Wee Jasper Reserves (02) 6227 9626

455 **Micalong Creek Reserve camping area**

Micalong Creek is about 10 km south of Wee Jasper along Nottingham Rd. There's fishing and swimming here, as well as walking tracks and picnic facilities. Bring your own drinking water and firewood, or boil/treat the tank water supplied. **Map refs:** 66 C4, 90 E10, 98 B4, 99 A3

MORTON NATIONAL PARK

Morton National Park is a world of dense bush, spectacular sandstone country, deep gullies and thundering waterfalls. This national park has been a popular retreat for more than a century – well-developed visitor sites are a feature in the northern section, while the south, which includes the rugged Budawang Ranges, caters for the wilderness-savvy walker. While Pigeon House Mountain is better known, the strenuous hike up to the Castle is spectacular, with incredible views over the Budawang Ranges.

Who to contact: NPWS Fitzroy Falls Visitor Centre (02) 4887 7270; or NPWS Ulladulla (02) 4454 9500 *How to book:* NPWS Fitzroy Falls Visitor Centre (02) 4887 7270 for campsite no. **458**

456 Bluegum Flat camping area (bush camping)

It's a short 30 m walk from the carpark to this camping ground in the park's south. It's on the Clyde River, accessed via Blue Gum Flat Rd off Yadboro Rd. A short walk along the river brings you to a wonderful swimming hole, and a few kilometres east along Yadboro Rd is the trackhead for the walk to the famous Pigeon House Mountain, named in 1770 by Captain James Cook as he sailed up the east coast. Bluegum Flat is a bush-camping site with no facilities so bring your own everything. **Map refs:** 66 F4, 90 H11, 98 F5

457 Bush camping areas

To experience the true spirit of Morton National Park it's necessary to strike out on one of the many walking tracks in the area and camp remotely. Note: this region is not for the faint-hearted; walkers must be fit, experienced and self-sufficient with plenty of food, water and good-quality topographic maps. Contact the parks office for details, and always advise someone of your departure, intended route and return time. **Map refs:** 66 F4, 90 H11, 98 F5

458 Gambells Rest camping area

This is the only designated camping ground in the north of the park, and it's a good springboard for 10 walking tracks. It's less than 1 km south of Bundanoon via the Gullies Rd. No fires are allowed, so you'll need to bring a gas/fuel stove, and your own drinking water. Bookings are essential. **Map refs:** 66 F3, 91 I9, 98 G3

459 Long Gully camping area

You can camp with your vehicle at this spot in the park's south, accessed via Long Gully Rd off Yadboro Forest Rd, or via the Western Distributor. It's next to Yadboro River at the foot of the mighty Budawangs. Nearby Monolith Valley is considered the Budawangs' pièce de résistance, but it's pure wilderness, so make sure you're well prepared before you go exploring. There are toilets and picnic tables at the camping area. Bring your own wood. **Map refs:** 66 F4, 90 H11, 98 F5

460 Sassafras camping area (walk-in camping)

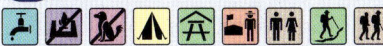

At the central northern boundary of the national park, Sassafras camping area has walk-in access from the end of the

Endrick River Fire Trail (off Turpentine Rd). It's about a 5 km walk. Visitors generally use it as a starting point for a number of overnight walks, including the continuation of the Endrick River Fire Trail. Fires are not permitted; gas/fuel stove only. Boil or treat the water before drinking. **Map refs:** 66 F4, 91 I10, 98 F4

461 Wog Wog camping area

This is one of the park's 4 main entrances, on the central-eastern boundary of the park off Charleys Forest Rd. It's a good place to regroup before and after an extended walk. There are a number of overnight walking tracks you can take from here, including the Wog Wog to Bibbenluke track. Contact NPWS for detailed track information. Bring your own drinking water or boil/treat the creek water. Bring a gas/fuel stove. **Map refs:** 66 E4, 90 H11, 98 F5

NAMADGI NATIONAL PARK (ACT)

Rolling grassy hills unfold towards the horizon, hardy snow gums create woodlands on the subalpine slopes and higher still are alpine meadows with fragile wildflowers in season. Namadgi National Park is only 32 km from Canberra, but a world away from city life. It covers almost half of the ACT.

Who to contact: Namadgi Visitor Centre (02) 6207 2900; or Canberra Connect 13 2281

462 Bush camping areas

Contact the Namadgi Visitor Centre for advice and information about bush camping in Namadgi National Park. **Map refs:** 66 C5, 90 E11, 98 C5, 99 B9

463 Honeysuckle camping area

From the 1960s to the 1980s, a space-tracking station operated at Honeysuckle Creek; today, it's the site of a well-developed campground that comfortably accommodates small and large groups. It's 16 km south-west of the visitor centre via Honeysuckle Rd from Naas Rd. Bring your own firewood, although a gas/fuel stove is preferred. **Map refs:** 66 C4, 90 F11, 98 C5, 99 C8

464 Mount Clear camping area

Access to this campground is via an unsealed road – it's a good idea to check conditions before setting out. The campground is 42 km south of the visitor centre via Boboyan Rd. There are wood BBQs here, but you'll need to bring your own firewood and campers are encouraged to bring a gas or fuel stove as an alternative. You can walk into Naas Valley from here, via the Horse Gully Walk. **Map refs:** 66 C5, 90 F12, 98 C6, 99 C12

465 Orroral camping area

Suitable for smaller groups, Orroral Campground is 18 km south of the visitor centre via Orroral Rd. It's situated near a creek, from which you can get water as long as you boil or treat it before drinking. You can bring your own firewood, but campers are encouraged to use a gas or fuel stove instead. **Map refs:** 66 C5, 90 F11, 98 C5, 99 C9

SWINGING BRIDGE RESERVE

This delightful reserve is near Wee Jasper, a small but pretty town of roughly 100 people, 54 km south-west of Yass at the foot of the Brindabella Ranges. The town and its surrounds are popular with travellers, due in large part to the beautiful limestone formations of Carey's Cave nearby.

Who to contact: Wee Jasper Reserves (02) 6227 9626

466 Swinging Bridge Reserve camping area

Positioned 7.3 km south of Wee Jasper village along Nottingham Rd, Swinging Bridge Reserve is a green and grassy glade on the banks of the Goodradigbee River. Throw a line in or go for a paddle along the river. Bring your own drinking water and firewood. **Map refs:** 66 C3, 90 E10, 98 B4, 99 A3

TALLAGANDA STATE FOREST

You'll be visited by the spirit of loggers past at this state forest, 10 km east of Captains Flat. Some of the relics here are up to 170 years old, including a waterwheel that was used to generate electricity. Today the towering brown barrel forest hosts picnickers, mountain-bikers and 4WD enthusiasts.

Who to contact: Forests NSW South Coast Region (02) 4472 6211

467 Lowden Forest Park

To get to Lowden Forest Park, follow Lowden Rd 25 km east from Captains Flat. There are walking tracks here, as well as a picnic area and approximately 50 campsites, a 50 m walk from the carpark. Bring your own drinking water. **Map refs:** 66 E4, 90 G11, 98 E5

WINGELLO STATE FOREST

Wingello State Forest is a mix of pine plantation and hardwood forest in the Southern Highlands between Goulburn and Sydney. A popular destination for mountain-biking enthusiasts, it's 9 km south of Bundanoon, via Forest Rd from the town of Wingello.

Who to contact: Forests NSW Bombala (02) 6458 3177

468 HQ Camp

The forest's HQ Camp is 4 km south-east of Wingello via Forest Rd. Camping is only allowed between Easter and the Oct long weekend. There's a map here displaying mountain-biking trails. Bring your own drinking water. Gas/fuel stove preferred. The

roads in are unsealed, so check accessibility in wet weather. **Map refs:** 66 F3, 91 I9, 98 F3

YADBORO STATE FOREST

Tucked in against the southern reaches of Morton National Park, Yadboro State Forest is close to the famous Pigeon House Mountain and the strikingly rugged Budawangs. Walkers often use it as a base from which to strike out into the national park. The forest is 30 km south-west of Milton via Yadboro Rd.

Who to contact: Forests NSW South Coast Region (02) 4472 6211

469 Yadboro Flat camping area

Situated on the clear and sparkling Clyde River, which offers swimming and fishing, Yadboro Flat enjoys the beauty of Morton National Park without its fees and regulations. Don't let your dog wander into the national park, though. The challenging trail up to the Castle, with its stunning views over the rugged Budawang Ranges, starts near here. Bring drinking water and firewood. **Map refs:** 66 F4, 90 H11, 98 F5

CAMPSITES LOCATED IN OTHER AREAS

470 Blue Range camping area

You'll find this campground in Blue Range Recreation Area, inside Uriarra Forest, 35 km west of Canberra via Brindabella Rd and Blue Range Rd. This is the site of the heritage-listed remains of a World War II Italian internment camp; Blue Range Hut was the galley. Today, the hut sleeps up to 6 people – you can book the hut or a campsite, or the whole recreation area for exclusive use. You'll need to carry your gear from the carpark to the camping area. Bring firewood. Bookings essential; an access code to the locked gate is given on confirmation of booking. **Map refs:** 66 C4, 90 F10, 98 C4, 99 B4

How to book: Canberra Connect 13 2281

471 Capital Country Holiday Village

Choose from powered and unpowered tent sites through to cabins, bungalows and lakeside villas at this holiday park, 14 km north of Canberra on Bidges Rd, just off Federal Hwy on the ACT border. Facilities include a laundry, swimming pool, minigolf course, volleyball and basketball courts, and an ornamental lake. **Map refs:** 66 D4, 90 F10, 98 D4, 99 F4

How to book: 47 Bidges Rd, Sutton (02) 6230 3433, 1800 664 269 www.holidayvillages.com.au

472 Corang River camping area

There's beautiful forest in the Nerriga area, 50 km north-east of Braidwood and 55 km south-west of Nowra. Corang River

camping area is 8 km south-west of Nerriga on the Nerriga Rd at Corang River crossing. There aren't any facilities here, so you'll need to bring everything, including water and firewood. There's usually a total fire ban over summer. **Map refs:** 66 E4, 90 H10, 98 F4

Who to contact: Braidwood Tourist Information Centre (02) 4842 1144

473 Cotter Campground

Hailed as 'the most highly serviced bushland camping area in the ACT', Cotter Campground is set beside the iconic Murrumbidgee River, 22 km west of Canberra. The river corridor is a great spot for swimming, canoeing and fishing, as well as bushwalking and picnicking. The campground can be reached via Cotter Rd. There's limited firewood provided, so best to bring your own. The maximum stay is 2 weeks, which tells you something about its popularity. **Map refs:** 66 C4, 90 F10, 98 C4, 99 C5

Who to contact: Canberra Connect 13 2281

474 Numeralla camping area

Set beside the sparkling river of the same name, Numeralla is the site of an annual folk festival each Jan. The camping ground is in the village, 22 km north-east of Cooma. Camping here is basic – bring your own drinking water and gas/fuel stove. **Map refs:** 66 D6, 98 D7

Who to contact: Cooma Visitors Centre 1800 636 525; or Cooma–Monaro Shire Council (02) 6455 1777

475 Oallen Ford camping area

This is a simple set-up at the Shoalhaven River crossing, 18 km west of Nerriga on Nerriga–Tarago Rd. There are no facilities here, so bring your own gas/fuel stove and drinking water. There's usually a total fire ban over summer; in the colder months you can have a fire if you bring your own firewood. **Map refs:** 66 E4, 90 H10, 98 F4

Who to contact: Braidwood Tourist Information Centre (02) 4842 1144

476 Old Kowen Homestead camping area

Situated within the Kowen Forest Pine Plantation east of Canberra, this camping area attracts horseriders, mountain-bikers and picnickers. To get here, follow Yass Rd east of Canberra Airport and turn onto Sutton Rd then Kowen Rd. Kowen Forest is locked, so make sure you organise your booking in advance. Bring your own firewood and water. **Map refs:** 66 D4, 90 F10, 98 D4, 99 F5

How to book: Canberra Connect 13 2281

477 Stuart Crossing camping area (bush camping)

This camping area is on Mayfield Rd, 35 km north of Braidwood. There are no facilities but the fishing's good. Note: there's usually a total fire ban over summer; in the colder months you can have a fire if you bring your own firewood. Bring drinking water. **Map refs:** 66 E4, 90 H10, 98 E4

Who to contact: Braidwood Tourist Information Centre (02) 4842 1144

478 Warri Camping Reserve

This is a picturesque spot on the sandy banks of the Shoalhaven River, 13 km north-west of Braidwood off the Kings Hwy. It's a good place for swimming and fishing, but you'll need to bring your own firewood and drinking water, or else boil/treat the river water. The nearby village of Braidwood is worth visiting for its historic value and beautifully restored buildings. **Map refs:** 66 E4, 90 G11, 98 E5

Who to contact: Braidwood Tourist Information Centre (02) 4842 1144

479 Wood's Reserve camping area

A spacious and user-friendly camping area on Gibraltar Creek, Wood's Reserve is 30 km south-west of Canberra and close to Tidbinbilla Nature Reserve. There are hot showers here, as well as picnic facilities. A short drive south on Corin Rd brings you to Gibraltar Falls; a short walk from the carpark takes you to the lookout. You'll need to bring your own firewood and drinking water, or boil/treat the river water before use. Bookings are essential. **Map refs:** 66 C4, 90 F11, 98 C5, 99 C7

How to book: Canberra Connect 13 2281 *Access:* code for the amenities block provided on payment

RIVERINA AND THE MURRAY

THE PIONEERING HISTORY OF inland NSW follows the twists and turns of 2 great rivers: the Murrumbidgee and the Murray. These rivers have witnessed much change since the 1800s. Where riverboats once traversed the mud-brown waters transporting wool and beef, waterskiers, boaters and anglers enjoy the wide, still waterways, basing themselves in a number of state forest camping grounds along the rivers' banks. Where once the weary feet of famous explorers Hamilton Hume and William Hovell trod, bushwalkers flock to set up tents, boil billies and spin yarns by campfires. Cocoparra National Park now protects the Whitton Stock Route, where the wheels of the famous Cobb & Co. coaches once rumbled, delivering mail, goods and people to far-flung places.

The three Murrumbidgee Irrigation Areas (MIA) in Murrumbidgee Valley National Park hug the northern banks of the Murrumbidgee east from Narrandera, offering visitors water-based activities as well as scenic drives through the forest. There's also a handful of reserves from Darlington Point upstream to Wagga Wagga.

Similarly, the string of national park precincts along the Murray River provides plenty of space to pitch a tent, pull out your fishing rod and while away the hours in the company of iconic river red gums. It's worth remembering, too, that this is one of the country's most important areas of food production. Take some time to visit some wineries and tuck into some fruit, and wander through the region's classic country towns, where stately buildings and heritage pubs have also seen their share of change.

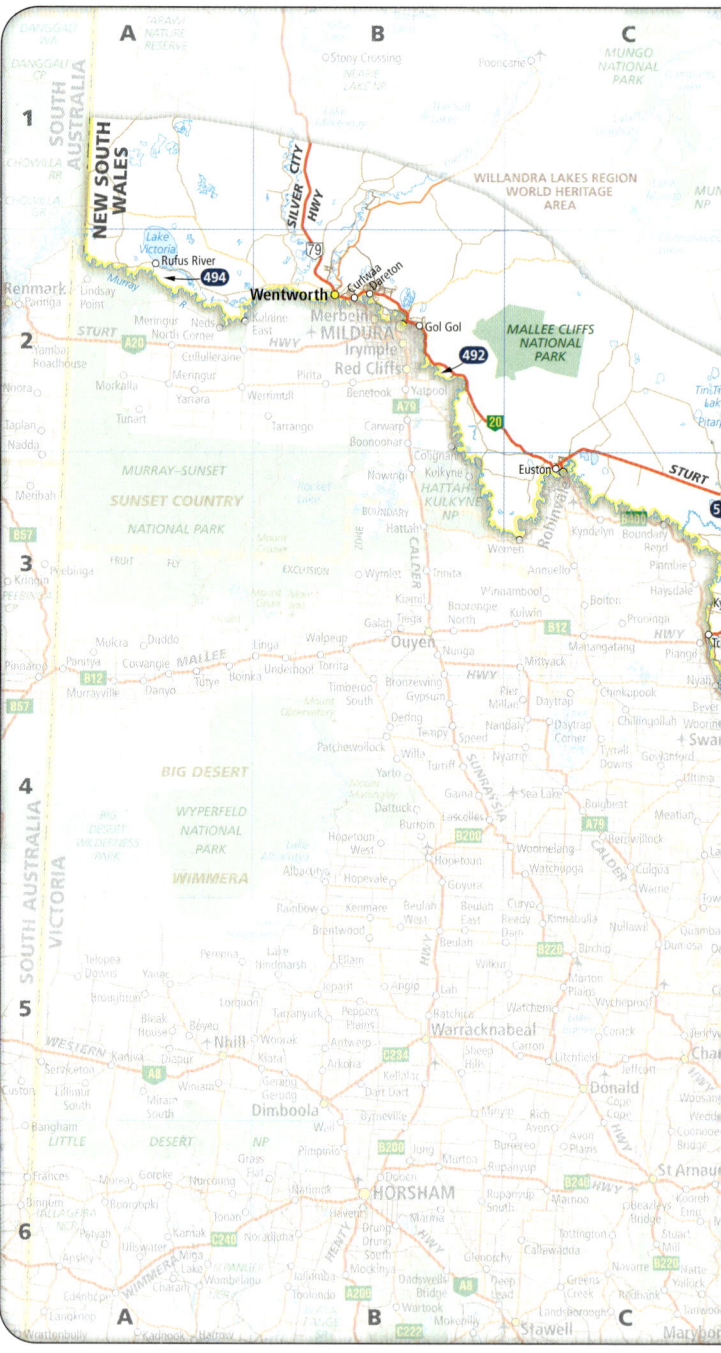

CAMPSITES LOCATED IN PARKS AND RESERVES

BAGO STATE FOREST

Visitors to Bago State Forest can take their pick of camping spots scattered around the foreshore of Blowering Dam and Jounama Pondage. The forest is 10 km south-east of Batlow; a handful of ways in follow unsealed roads between Batlow and Tumbarumba.

Who to contact: Forests NSW Tumut (02) 6947 3911 **How to book:** (02) 6947 5271 for campsite no. **480**

480 Blowering Forest Holiday Camp

You'll find this well-equipped camping ground on the western shore of Blowering Dam, accessed via Blowering Camp Rd, 27 km east of Batlow. Bring your fishing rod, swimming costume, canoe, sailboat and waterskis. There's also a bunkhouse sleeping 58 and cabin accommodation. Bookings essential. **Map refs:** 77 I5, 90 D11, 98 A5

481 Dormans Point camping area

One of a handful of camping areas dotted along the western shore of Blowering Dam, 20 km east of Batlow. Follow Blowering Foreshore Rd. If you're bringing a caravan from Batlow, check road conditions before setting off. Bring drinking water and firewood, but note that there's a fire ban from late in the year to Easter, so you'll need a gas/fuel stove during this time. **Map refs:** 77 I5, 90 D11, 98 A5

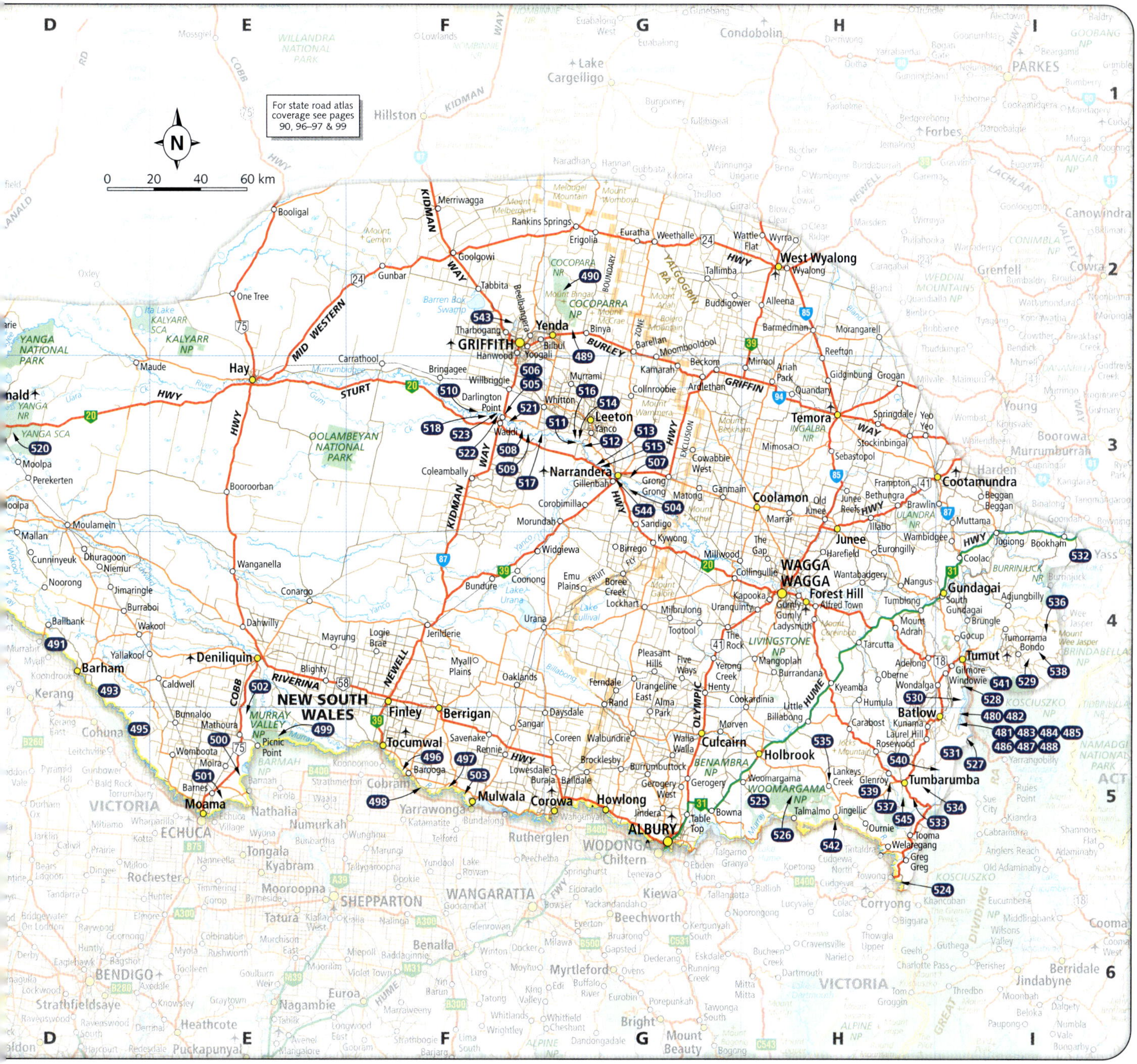

For state road atlas coverage see pages 90, 96–97 & 99

482 Island Forest Park camping area

This camping area is on the western shore of Blowering Dam, via Blowering Foreshore Rd, 20 km from Batlow. Check road conditions before setting off with a caravan. Bring drinking water, firewood and gas/fuel stove from Dec to Easter.
Map refs: 77 I5, 90 D11, 98 A5

483 Junction Park camping area

One of a handful of camping areas along the western shore of Blowering Dam, 20 km east of Batlow. Follow Blowering Foreshore Rd; check road conditions if you're bringing a caravan. Bring drinking water and firewood; a fire ban operates from late in the year to Easter, so you'll need a gas/fuel stove during this time. **Map refs: 77 I5, 90 D11, 98 A5**

484 Long Point camping area

One of a handful of camping areas along the western shore of Blowering Dam, 20 km east of Batlow via Blowering Foreshore Rd. Check road conditions before setting off from Batlow with a caravan. Bring drinking water and firewood; note that a fire ban operates from late in the year to Easter, so you'll need to bring a gas/fuel stove during that time of year. **Map refs:** 35 G5, 77 I5, 90 D11, 93 K8, 98 A5

485 Platypus Bay camping area

On the western shore of Blowering Dam, via Blowering Foreshore Rd, 20 km from Batlow. Check road conditions before setting off from Batlow with a caravan. Bring drinking water, firewood and gas/fuel stove from Dec to Easter. **Map refs:** 77 I5, 90 D11, 98 A5

486 Platypus Park camping area

One of a handful of camping areas dotted along the western shore of Blowering Dam, 20 km east of Batlow. Follow Blowering Foreshore Rd. Caravanners bringing a caravan from Batlow should check road conditions before setting off. Bring drinking water and firewood, but note the fire ban from late in the year to Easter, when you'll need a gas/fuel stove. **Map refs:** 77 I5, 90 D11, 98 A5

487 Willow Bay camping area

This camping area is on the western shore of Blowering Dam, via Blowering Foreshore Rd, 20 km from Batlow. Check road conditions before setting off from Batlow with a caravan. Bring drinking water, firewood and gas/fuel stove from Dec to Easter. **Map refs:** 77 I5, 90 D11, 98 A5

488 Windy Point camping area

One of a handful of camping areas dotted along the western shore of Blowering Dam, 20 km east of Batlow. Follow Blowering Foreshore Rd. Check road conditions before setting off from Batlow with a caravan. Bring drinking water, firewood and gas/fuel stove from Dec to Easter. **Map refs:** 77 I5, 90 D11, 98 A5

BINYA STATE FOREST

Binya State Forest is dressed in lovely cypress pine and decorated with wildflowers in spring. It's a popular birdwatching area, with twitchers coming from far and wide to spot species such as the masked and white-browed woodswallow, red-capped robin, turquoise parrot and

numerous honeyeaters. It's 30 km east of Griffith, near Yenda.
Who to contact: NPWS Griffith (02) 6966 8100

489 Binya camping area

This simple but pretty camping spot is accessible via the Binya Forest Dr. You'll need to bring your own drinking water and firewood, although there's a total fire ban throughout summer, during which time it's gas/fuel stove only. **Map refs:** 77 G2, 97 N6

COCOPARRA NATIONAL PARK

Cocoparra is a colourful tapestry of vibrant red rocks, green forest, scenic gullies, ephemeral waterways and striking wildflowers after rain. It's one of the few remnant forested areas in the Riverina region, and it offers several good walking tracks. It's 2WD dry-weather access only on Myall Park Rd via Yenda, 25 km north-east of Griffith.
Who to contact: NPWS Griffith (02) 6966 8100

490 Woolshed Flat camping area

Take Whitton Stock Route, a historic trail formerly used by the famous Cobb & Co. coaches, off Mt Bingar Rd and follow the signs to this camping area. There is a pleasant walk to Woolshed Falls, which only flows after heavy rains. It's 2WD dry-weather access only. Fires are permitted during winter, but gas BBQs are supplied; bring your own drinking water. **Map refs:** 45 E5, 77 G2, 91 I4, 97 N6

MURRAY RIVER STATE FORESTS

Scattered beneath stately river red gums along the Murray, these forests invite visitors to strike camp and stay awhile. Here you'll fall asleep to the sounds of cockatoos roosting and the gurgling flow of one of the country's most iconic waterways. Note: there's a fire ban from late in the year until Easter, so use gas/fuel stoves only during this period. You need to come equipped with drinking water when staying at these camping areas.
Who to contact: Forests NSW Deniliquin (03) 5881 9999 for campsite nos **491, 493, 495**; Forests NSW Mildura (03) 5019 8414 for campsite nos **492, 494**

491 Campbells Island State Forest camping areas

This state forest is about 5 km downstream of Barham via Little Murray Rd off North Barham Rd. **Map refs:** 77 D4, 96 H10

492 Gol Gol State Forest camping areas

This forest with camping areas is 24 km east of Mildura via the Sturt Hwy. **Map refs:** 76 B2, 96 E6

493 Koondrook State Forest camping areas

This is actually the western end of what's known as Koondrook–Perricoota Forest: Perricoota Forest is on the eastern end of the NSW side of the forest. Koondrook Forest is accessed via Murray St from Barham. **Map refs:** 77 D4, 97 I11

494 Lake Victoria State Forest camping areas

Lake Victoria State Forest is 55 km west of Wentworth via Rufus River Rd. **Map refs:** 76 A2, 96 C5

495 Perricoota State Forest camping areas

This forest is adjacent to Koondrook State Forest, accessible via Nineteen Mile Rd, Yarraman Access Rd or Belbins Rd from Perricoota Forest Rd. **Map refs:** 77 D5, 97 I11

MURRAY VALLEY NATIONAL PARK

River red gums arch drought-weary boughs over the sleepy Murray River, while flocks of cockatoos screech overhead. This is one of Australia's most iconic riverine landscapes and there are a number of national park precincts scattered along its banks that enable campers to sit and drink it all in. Note: there's a fire ban from Oct until Easter, so use gas/fuel stoves only during this period. You need to come equipped with drinking water when staying at these camping areas.

Who to contact: NPWS Griffith (02) 6966 8100

496 Barooga precinct camping areas

This precinct is located next to the town of Barooga, accessible via the Tocumwal–Barooga Rd. **Map refs:** 77 F5, 97 L11

497 Boomanoomana precinct camping areas

Part of a newly amalgamated national park, Boomanoomana precinct is accessed by following the Mulwala–Barooga Rd 16 km west of Mulwala. Bring your own drinking water. **Map refs:** 77 F5, 97 L12

498 Cottadidda precinct camping areas

Cottadidda is only 2 km west of Barooga off the Tocumwal– Barooga Rd. **Map refs:** 77 F5, 97 L12

499 Millewa precinct camping areas

Formerly Millewa State Forest, this area is now part of Murray Valley National Park. You can get here via Tocumwal Rd, 10 km east of Mathoura, or from Lower River Rd onto Tocumwal Rd south-east of Deniliquin. **Map refs:** 77 E5, 97 K11

500 Moira precinct camping areas

Formerly one of the Millewa group of state forests (which included Barmah Forest in Victoria, and Millewa and Gulpa Island forests in NSW), this recently became part of Murray Valley National Park. It's 4 km south-east of Mathoura, via Moira Forest Dr off Cobb Hwy. **Map refs:** 77 E5, 97 J12

MURRAY VALLEY REGIONAL PARK

Established in July 2010 to protect the majestic river red gum forests of the region's Ramsar-listed wetland, this park hosts a unique ecosystem with 40 threatened plant species and more than 60 threatened native animal species. It's also a great place to camp, walk, fish, canoe or birdwatch; keep an eye out for the park's yellow rosella.

Who to contact: NPWS Griffith (02) 6966 8100

501 Bama precinct camping areas

Downstream from the town of Barmah, this precinct is accessible via Barmah Forest Rd, 13 km north-east of Moama. **Map refs:** 77 E5, 97 J12

502 Gulpa Island precinct camping areas

Formerly Gulpa Island State Forest, Gulpa precinct is now part of Murray Valley Regional Park. It is accessed via Millewa Rd, 9 km north-east of Mathoura. The precinct's Edward River camping area, which has toilets, is accessed from Tocumwal Rd. **Map refs:** 77 E5, 97 J11

503 Mulwala precinct camping areas

This precinct is 8 km west of Mulwala, via Mulwala–Barooga Rd. **Map refs:** 77 F5, 97 M12

MURRUMBIDGEE RIVER RESERVES

Between Darlington Point and Wagga Wagga there are several good camping areas where you can pitch a tent, bait your line and enjoy the beauty of the Murrumbidgee River. Other activities include boating, waterskiing and canoeing.

Who to contact: Narrandera Visitors Centre (02) 6959 1766, 1800 672 392

504 Buckinbong Reserve camping area

There's a small, very basic camping area close to the Inland Fisheries Research Station and next to the river. It's about 16 km south-east of Narrandera via Buckingbong Rd off the Sturt Hwy. Bring your own drinking water and firewood. **Map refs:** 77 G3, 90 A8, 97 N8

505 Bunyip Hole Reserve camping area

A simple camping spot by the river, there is dry-weather access only via King St from Darlington Point. There are toilets here. Bring drinking water. **Map refs:** 77 F3, 97 M7

506 Common Beach camping area

There are picnic tables and wood BBQs at this dry-weather access only camping area next to Darlington Point township. It's off King St. Bring your own water and firewood. **Map refs:** 77 F3, 97 M7

507 Five Mile Reserve camping area

There's a boat ramp here, which makes it a popular camping spot for boat-based anglers. It's 8 km east of Narrandera next to Bundidgerry Creek. To get here, take Old Wagga Rd from Narrandera. Bring drinking water and firewood. **Map refs:** 77 G3, 90 A8, 97 N8

MURRUMBIDGEE VALLEY NATIONAL PARK

Defined by river red gums and the grand Murrumbidgee River, this park protects swathes of riverine habitat and its inhabitants, including koalas, cockatoos and migratory birds. Encased within its boundaries are many former state forests, today known as precincts, that both promise and deliver delightful camping experiences for those wanting to connect with nature.

Who to contact: NPWS Griffith (02) 6966 8100; Leeton Tourism (02) 6953 6481 for campsite no. **516**

Cuba precinct

This is a sprawling forested area with good access to a range of riverine habitats on the Murrumbidgee River, including sandy beaches and riverside cliffs. This makes it a popular spot for shore-based and boat fishing. It's 40 km south of Griffith near Darlington Point; 2WD dry-weather access only via Cuba Forest Rd.

508 Cuba Beach camping area

You'll find this spot 19 km east of Darlington Point via Cuba Forest Dr. Swimming, fishing and paddling are a few of the activities possible here on the Murrumbidgee River. Bring your own drinking water. Note: there's a fire ban Oct–Easter, when it's gas/fuel stoves only. **Map refs:** 77 F3, 97 M8

509 Tims Beach camping area

Follow Cuba Forest Dr a little further past the turn-off for Cuba Beach, and you'll find Tims Beach with much the same facilities and activities as Cuba Beach camping area. Bring drinking water and gas/fuel stove Oct–Easter, when there's a solid fuel fire ban. **Map refs:** 77 F3, 97 M8

Dunnoon Lagoon precinct

Just downstream from Darlington Point on the Murrumbidgee River is Dunnoon Lagoon, a forest-wetland region rich with birdlife and popular with anglers. It's dry-weather access only from Murrumbidgee River Rd; check road conditions before setting out.

510 Nobles Beach camping area

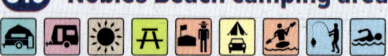

Follow the signs in the state forest off Murrumbidgee River Rd to reach this camping area. Note: it's dry-weather access only, so check road conditions before setting out. There are a number of water activities to enjoy, including fishing, swimming and paddling. Bring your own drinking water. There's a fire ban in

place Oct–Easter, so bring a gas/fuel stove during this period. **Map refs:** 77 F3, 97 M7

Euroley precinct

The Euroley precinct flanks the Murrumbidgee River. This camping area is on the river's southern banks, 8 km south-west of Yanco. Take the turn-off onto Euroley Rd, 6 km south of Yanco, and travel approximately 2 km past Euroley Bridge. It's dry-weather access only.

511 Euroley Beach camping area

This is a good spot for swimming, fishing, paddling and even waterskiing; dry-weather access only via Euroley Rd. Bring drinking water, and note that there's a fire ban Oct–Easter, when you'll need to bring a gas/fuel stove. **Map refs:** 77 G3, 97 N8

MIA precincts

512 Long Beach (MIA I precinct) camping area

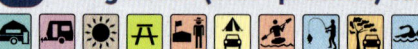

Coming from Yanco, the turn-off onto MIA Forest Dr is about 3.5 km along Trunk Rd. The road to Long Beach camping area is about 8 km east of Yanco. Bring drinking water. Note: gas/fuel stove only Oct–Easter. **Map refs:** 77 G3, 97 N8

513 Markeys Beach (MIA I precinct) camping area

The turn-off to this riverside camping spot is a couple of kilometres further along the MIA Forest Dr from the Sandy Beach turn-off. Bring your own drinking water. Note: there's a solid fuel ban Oct–Easter, so it's gas/fuel stove only during this period. **Map refs:** 77 G3, 97 N8

514 Middle Beach (MIA II precinct) camping area

As the most spacious and accessible beach on the Murrumbidgee River, this spot gets plenty of visits from school, fishing and community groups. Access is via Murrumbidgee Forest Dr, 6 km south-west of Yanco. Turn off before Euroley Bridge. Bring your own drinking water. Note: there's a fire ban Oct–Easter, so it's gas/fuel stove only during this period. **Map refs:** 77 G3, 97 N8

515 Sandy Beach (MIA I precinct) camping area

Turn off MIA Forest Dr onto Red Gum Rd, about 17 km west of Narrandera. Bring your own drinking water. Note: it's gas/fuel stove only Oct–Easter due to a fire ban. **Map refs:** 77 G3, 90 A8, 97 N8

516 Ski Beach (MIA II precinct) camping area

The facilities here are maintained by Leeton Ski Club, and include a concrete ramp, toilets and shaded picnic tables. Access is via the Murrumbidgee River Rd. Bring drinking water. Note: there's a fire ban Oct–Easter, so it's gas/fuel stove only during this period. **Map refs:** 77 G3, 97 N8

517 Whitton Beach (MIA III precinct) camping area

This camping area is 22 km south-west of Yanco, accessible via Forest Dr past Golgelderie Weir. It's well-shaded, flat and open. Bring drinking water, and note that it's gas/fuel stove only Oct–Easter. **Map refs:** 77 F3, 97 M8

Uri precinct

Hugging the southern bank of the Murrumbidgee River, Uri has a lot to offer, including waterskiing, canoeing, swimming and fishing. It's 9 km south-west of Darlington Point; access via Britts Rd from Hay Rd. Some of it is dry-weather access only, so check road conditions before setting out.

518 Beaumont Beach camping area

This is situated off Britts Rd in the state forest. Bring your own drinking water. Note: there's a fire ban from late in the year until Easter, so bring a gas/fuel stove for use during this time. **Map refs:** 77 F3, 97 M7

Yanga precinct

One of NSW's newest parks, Yanga has a long and significant history – from Indigenous families to colonial explorers, shearers to rabbit trappers and fishermen. There are also more than 150 species of birds to acquaint yourself with and fishing by the river to enjoy. Reach the park via the Sturt Hwy, 5 km south-east of Balranald.

519 Mamanga camping area

Mamanga, 8 km south-west of Balranald on the Sturt Hwy, is a large, secluded camping area on the banks of the Murrumbidgee River shaded by river red gums and black box. It's divided into 2 sections – one for tents, the other for caravans and camper trailers. Go fishing, swimming, kayaking or canoeing in the river here or explore on mountain bikes. Bring your own water and firewood. Solid fuel fires are not permitted. **Map refs:** 77 D3, 96 G7

520 The Willows camping area

A birdwatcher's haven, the Willows is located 24 km east of Balranald along the Sturt Hwy. Once your camp's set up, explore nearby Wilga Woolshed or paddle, swim or fish in the river. Campfires are permitted Apr–Sept, but there's a solid fuel fire ban year-round so bring your own wood. Tank water is available, but unsuitable for drinking so bring your own supplies. **Map refs:** 77 D3, 96 H8

MURRUMBIDGEE VALLEY REGIONAL PARK

Created in July 2010 by amalgamating Hay, Narrandera, Willbriggie and Wooloondool state forests, Murrumbidgee Valley Regional Park protects the Riverina bioregion and covers an area of 1197 ha.

Who to contact: NPWS Griffith (02) 6966 8100

Willbriggie precinct

Willbriggie straddles the town of Darlington Point – on both sides of the town there are lovely sandy beaches, solid river red gums and good fishing. Some roads are dry-weather access only, so check road conditions before setting out. You can reach Willbriggie's camping areas via Willbriggie Forest Dr from Whitton Rd, and Black Box Rd from Whitton Rd. Note: there's a fire ban from late in the year until Easter, during which time you'll need to use a gas/fuel stove.

521 Boomerang Beach camping area

You'll keep coming back to this lovely little camping spot, 7 km east of Darlington Point off Black Box Rd. Bring your own drinking water, fishing tackle and canoe. **Map refs:** 77 F3, 97 M8

522 Horries Beach camping area

Horries is 4 km west of Darlington Point via Willbriggie Forest Dr. Bring drinking water. **Map refs:** 77 F3, 97 M7

523 Swaggys Beach camping area

Unroll your own swag at this camping spot, 7 km west of Darlington Point via Willbriggie Forest Dr. Bring your own drinking water. **Map refs:** 77 F3, 97 M7

TOWONG RESERVE

This is a small reserve 2 km north-east of the Victorian town of Towong. It's a quaint little riverside town hiding a little-known fact: parts of the movie *Phar Lap* were filmed at Towong Racecourse. Fishing, swimming and canoeing are popular activities here.

Who to contact: Tumbarumba Visitor Centre (02) 6948 3333

524 Towong Reserve camping area

Come and tickle the trout from this large, level, grassed area on the Murray River. It's 2 km north-east of Towong village, which is in Victoria, near the bridge that crosses the Murray River. Bring your own drinking water and firewood. **Map refs:** 77 H5, 98 A7

WOOMARGAMA NATIONAL PARK

Woomargama National Park is the largest protected area west of the Great Dividing Range in south-eastern NSW and has wonderful views over the Murray River, Riverina and South West Slopes regions. It is a haven for a large number of threatened and endangered species, such as the regent honeyeater, superb parrot, powerful owl, Booroolong frog and carpet python. It is an ideal place for bushwalking, birdwatching, 4WD touring and motorcycling. It's only 4WD access during dry weather (not accessible when wet).

Who to contact: Office of Environment and Heritage, Tumut (02) 6947 7025

525 **Samuel Bollard camping area (walk-in camping)**

Samuel Bollard was one of Hovell's servants. This is a walk-in only campsite on the Hume and Hovell Walking Track. Set amid eucalypts, it is 12 km south-east of Woomargama and 28 km west of Tin Mines campsite. Bring your own drinking water. **Map refs:** 77 H5, 90 B12, 97 O12

526 **Tin Mines camping area**

This is a campsite on the Hume and Hovell Walking Track about 40 km west of Jingellic and 28 km east of Samuel Bollard camping area. It has 4WD, dry-weather access only via Tin Mines Rd from Tunnel Rd. If there's water in the creek, make sure you boil/treat it before drinking, but it's a good idea to bring your own, just in case. Bring your own firewood. **Map refs:** 77 H5, 90 B12, 97 P12

CAMPSITES LOCATED IN OTHER AREAS

Hume and Hovell Walking Track

This 440 km walking track, stretching from Yass to Albury, follows in the footsteps of explorers Hamilton Hume and William Hovell, who in 1824 journeyed from Appin near Sydney to Port Phillip in Victoria. The entire track takes approximately 21 days to complete, or can be broken up into smaller sections. Note: the track is closed between Wee Jasper and Henry Angel Trackhead due to flooding, which washed away bridges, etc. Work is being undertaken to reopen this section; please check with the track coordinator for updates.

Please note that campsites are listed in alphabetical order, not track order. Refer to the map on pp. 76–7 for further information.

Who to contact: Hume and Hovell Walking Track coordinator (02) 6937 2700

527 **Ben Smith camping area (walk-in camping)**

Ben Smith was Hovell's servant. This is a walk-in campsite, 37 km south of Browns Creek camping area, on the banks of Jounama Pondage. Boil/treat water from the dam before drinking. **Map refs:** 77 I5, 90 D11, 98 A5

528 **Blowering camping area**

It's a 250 m walk from the carpark at Blowering Dam to this campsite near the Blowering Dam wall, accessed via the Snowy Mountains Hwy south-east of Tumut. Those in the mood for a short walk can do a return trip from here to Browns Creek. **Map refs:** 77 I4, 90 D10, 98 A5

529 **Bossawa camping area (walk-in camping)**

This campsite has walk-in access from Brindabella Rd, 49 km east of Tumut. Boil/treat water in the creek before drinking.

There are wood BBQs here; bring your own firewood. **Map refs:** 77 I4, 90 E10, 98 B4

530 **Browns Creek camping area (walk-in camping)**

This campsite is 9.5 km south of Blowering camping area on the Blowering Reservoir foreshore and 37 km north of Ben Smith camping area. It's a long but manageable return walk from Blowering camping area if you're only in the mood for an overnighter. You can also paddle here. Boil/treat water from the dam before drinking. **Map refs:** 77 I4, 90 D11, 98 A5

531 **Buddong Hut camping area**

Walk to this campsite – it is the next campsite on the track south of Ben Smith camping area – or 4WD in via Buddong Rd. The campsite is 3.5 km south of Buddong Falls, so if you've got a 2WD you could park at the falls and walk in. Boil/treat the creek water before drinking. **Map refs:** 77 I5, 90 D11, 98 A5

532 **The Captain camping area (walk-in camping)**

This is the first campsite on the track leading from Yass. It's walk-in access from Black Range Rd, 28 km west of Yass. Boil/treat water from the creek before drinking. **Map refs:** 77 I4, 90 E9, 98 C3

410 **Fitzpatrick Trackhead camping area**

See p. 68.

533 **Henry Angel Trackhead camping area**

Named for another of Hume's men, the Henry Angel Trackhead marks the end of the track's second main section. It's a vehicle-access site, 7 km south-east of Tumbarumba via Tooma Rd. Here, walkers can wash off in the Burra Creek, catch some fish for dinner, and set off refreshed the next day. Boil/treat the creek water before drinking. **Map refs:** 77 H5, 90 D12, 98 A6

534 **Junction camping area (walk-in camping)**

This is 6.5 km north of Henry Angel Trackhead; walk-in access only. If you had no luck fishing at Henry Angel, you can try again for trout here. Boil/treat the creek water before drinking. **Map refs:** 77 H5, 90 D12, 98 A6

535 **Lankeys Creek camping area**

It's only a short walk from the carpark off Holbrook–Jingellic Rd to this campsite, about 16 km north of the small town of Jingellic. Boil/treat the creek water before drinking. **Map refs:** 77 H5, 90 C12, 97 P12

536 Log Bridge Creek camping area (walk-in camping)

It's about 14 km from the Fitzpatrick Trackhead to the walk-in Log Bridge Creek campsite. If there's water in the creek, it'll need to be boiled or treated before use. **Map refs:** 77 I4, 90 E10, 98 B4

537 Mannus camping area

Mannus can be accessed by vehicle via Linden Roth Dr, 8 km west of Tumbarumba. You can swim and fish in the creek; boil/treat the water before drinking. **Map refs:** 77 H5, 90 C12, 98 A6

538 Micalong Creek camping area (walk-in camping)

It's about a 14 km walk from the Log Bridge Creek camping area to Micalong. Walk-in access only; boil/treat water in the creek before drinking. **Map refs:** 77 I4, 90 E10, 98 B4

539 Munderoo camping area (walk-in camping)

It's a 12.5 km walk west from Mannus to Munderoo. If there's water in the creek you can boil/treat it first before drinking, but be sure to bring enough to sustain yourself if the creek is dry. **Map refs:** 77 H5, 90 C12

540 Paddys River Dam camping area

You can get here by car – it's 2WD dry-weather access only via Bullongra Rd from JDX and Perkins rds off Tumbarumba–Batlow Rd. Catch a trout for dinner; boil/treat the water before drinking. Note: there's a fire ban Dec–Mar, so it's gas/fuel stoves only during this period. **Map refs:** 77 I5, 90 D11, 98 A5

525 Samuel Bollard camping area (walk-in camping)

See p. 82.

541 Thomas Boyd Trackhead camping area

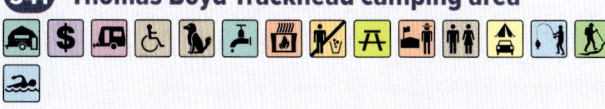

Thomas Boyd, a member of the Hume and Hovell expedition, ended up settling in the Tumut region. His namesake campsite is one of the major trackheads on the walking trail. There's vehicle-based camping available, accessible via Goobarragandra (Lacmalac) Rd. It's a well-rounded campsite with gas BBQs and picnic tables, drinking water and activities such as swimming and fishing. You can also camp with your dog. **Map refs:** 77 I4, 90 E10, 98 B4

526 Tin Mines camping area

See p. 82.

542 Jingellic camping area

Jingellic is about 27 km south-west of Tumbarumba, on the banks of the upper Murray River. During summer happy campers flock to this pretty, shaded spot on the banks of the river for swimming, fishing and canoeing. It's next to the Bridge Hotel in Jingellic, where you can pay to have a shower. You'll need to bring your own firewood, although there are also gas BBQs here. **Map refs:** 77 H5, 90 C12, 97 P12

Who to contact: Tumbarumba Visitor Centre (02) 6948 3333; or Bridge Hotel (02) 6037 1290

543 Lake Wyangan camping area

You'll find BBQ facilities and an amenities block at this camping area on the shores of Lake Wyangan, 10 km north of Griffith via Wyangan Ave. Fishing, swimming, canoeing, waterskiing and sailing are all possible on the lake; there's a boat ramp as well. There's a wading pool and playground for children, and a kiosk that's open in summer. Maximum stay 2 nights; bring drinking water and firewood. **Map refs:** 77 F2, 97 M6

Who to contact: Griffith Visitor Information Centre (02) 6962 4145, 1800 681 141

544 Narrandera Caravan Park

A great stopover on your way to Sydney, Melbourne, Brisbane or Adelaide, this neat park offers cabin accommodation as well as powered and unpowered caravan and camping sites. There's a pool to wash away the heat in summer, a laundry, plenty of room for pets, including a dog-walking track, and a playground. Access is via either the Newell or Sturt hwys. **Map refs:** 77 G3, 90 A8, 97 N8

How to book: Junction of Sturt and Newell hwys, Narrandera (02) 6959 2955 www.narranderacaravanpark.com.au

545 Paddys River Falls camping area

Watch the early-morning mist rise off the surface of Paddys River at this lovely grassed camping area, 18 km south of Tumbarumba via the Tumbarumba–Tooma Rd. You can swim and fish here; not far away are opportunities for horseriding, mountain-biking and bushwalking. Bring your own firewood and boil/treat the river water before drinking. There are dump sites in Tumbarumba and Khancoban. **Map refs:** 77 H5, 90 D12, 98 A6

Who to contact: Tumbarumba Visitor Centre (02) 6948 3333

THE OUTBACK

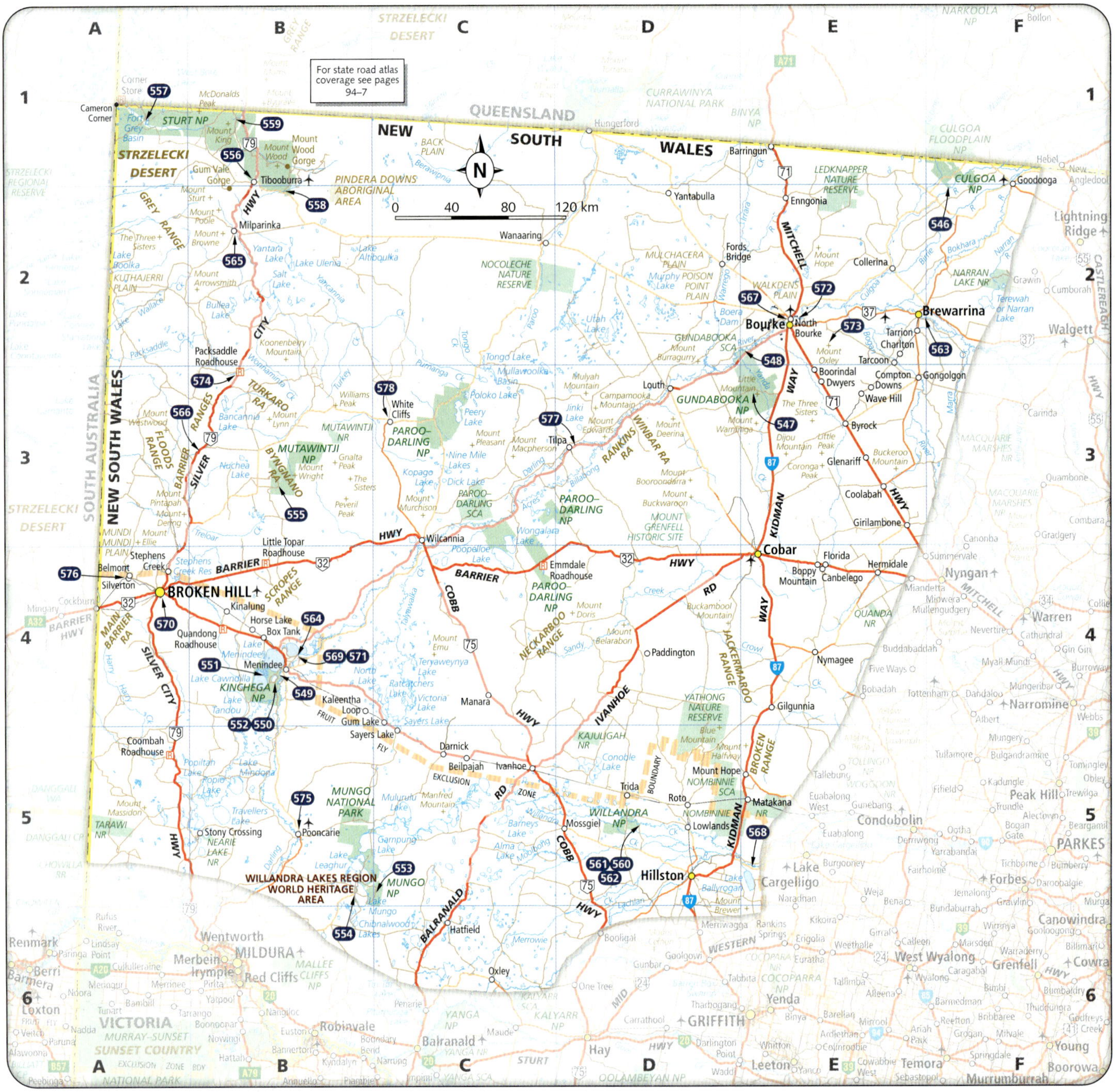

For state road atlas coverage see pages 94–7

''TIS SAID THE LAND out West is grand, do not care who says it', wrote poet Henry Lawson in 'The Paroo River' in 1893. Grand it is indeed – with its broad gibber plains and sun-cracked clay pans, rugged 'jump up' country and riverine landscapes laced with river red gums, brazen blue skies and larger-than-life Aussie characters.

It takes a bit of brawn to explore the outback – you need to come prepared with a good, well-serviced vehicle, plenty of water, spare tyres, stores of food and petrol, good maps and a willingness to let the countryside slowly reveal itself. In return, you'll be rewarded with a swag of unforgettable memories: a flock of cockatoos screeching across a late-evening sky above the Darling River; a sunset painting the world red from on high at Mt Oxley; a euro grazing quietly beneath a river red gum by the banks of the Murray River.

Visit Aboriginal rock-art sites in Mutawintji or Gundabooka national parks and feel the presence of the country's Indigenous ancestors. Explore the old pastoral homesteads at Sturt or Willandra national parks, and marvel at how the early European pioneers survived before communications, air-conditioning or refrigeration. Spend a night at the Burke and Wills Campsite near Menindee and try to imagine what our earliest explorers must have experienced, traversing this unfamiliar and inhospitable land.

Of course, no trip to the outback is complete without a stop at the local watering hole. Be entertained by decades of graffiti at the Tilpa Hotel on the way to Tilpa Weir camping area; try a steak sandwich at the Packsaddle Roadhouse on your way up to Tibooburra and Corner Country; or spin a yarn with the locals at the Albert Hotel in Milparinka. Wherever you travel, the spirit of the great Australian outback is part of the adventure.

CAMPSITES LOCATED IN PARKS AND RESERVES

CULGOA NATIONAL PARK

Butting up against the Qld border, 180 km north-east of Bourke or 100 km north of Brewarrina along unsealed roads, this is a sprawling, rugged region shaped by the Culgoa River and its floodplains. It's a stunning outback landscape of claypans, gibber plains, brigalow-gidgee woodlands and stands of coolibahs.

Who to contact: NPWS Bourke (02) 6830 0200

546 Culgoa River camping area

Don't get too excited about fishing and swimming, as the river here is often dry. Instead, you can camp among the gidgee trees and take the Riverbank Walk to the river, or the Connellys Walk through stands of tall cypress pines. To get here, take the Weilmoringle–Byra Rd from Weilmoringle. Note: this is a remote area, so bring plenty of petrol and drinking water. Wood fires are not permitted. Roads are unsealed and often impassable after rain. Contact the parks office for access details. **Map refs: 84 F2, 95 O2**

GUNDABOOKA NATIONAL PARK

The Gunderbooka Range rises majestically from this spectacular national park, 50 km south of Bourke. The range makes such a dramatic contrast to the flatness of the surrounding landscape that it's hardly surprising it holds sacred significance for the Ngemba Aboriginal people, who have adorned its flanks and foothills with rock art.

Who to contact: NPWS Bourke (02) 6830 0200

547 Dry Tank camping area

Follow Kidman Way 50 km south of Bourke and turn right onto the main park road; alternatively, turn onto East Toorale Rd 10 km south of Bourke and follow the signs. There's a 2.4 km walk from here leading to a spectacular vista of the northern end of Gunderbooka Range. Bring plenty of drinking water, and advise the parks office of your intended visit. Gas/fuel stove preferred. Note: alternative accommodation is available in the Belah Shearers' Quarters (sleeps up to 12) and Redbank Homestead (sleeps up to 12). Contact NPWS Bourke for information. **Map refs: 84 E3, 95 L6**

548 Yanda camping area

Camp right on the Darling River at this newly established site on the north-western side of Louth Rd. From Bourke, head south along the Kidman Way and turn right onto Louth Rd. Follow the road about 45 km and watch for a sign to the right. Bring your own drinking water and advise parks of your intended visit. Wood fires aren't permitted, so bring a gas/fuel stove. **Map refs: 84 E2, 95 L5**

KINCHEGA NATIONAL PARK

Kinchega National Park hugs the southern end of the fascinating Menindee Lakes system, which after rain becomes a haven for waterbirds. Visitors can fish or swim when the lakes are full, or explore the region's rich Aboriginal and European history. The Old Kinchega Woolshed still stands here and interpretive signs give a fascinating insight into the pastoral history of the area, as do the ruins of the old homestead nearby. The national park is 5 km south of Menindee and 110 km south-east of Broken Hill. Note: access roads are closed when wet, and a total fire ban is in place annually from 31 Oct – 1 Mar. Carry in your own firewood and drinking water.

Who to contact: NPWS Broken Hill (08) 8080 3200 *How to book:* NPWS Broken Hill (08) 8080 3200 for campsite no. **552**

549 Darling River camping areas

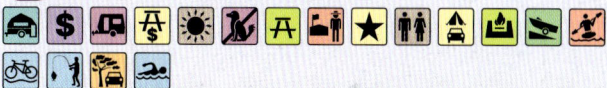

There are 34 campsites scattered along the Darling, accessible from 10 km south of Menindee along River Dr. Many of the sites are on groves of ancient river red gums, and while you should not set up camp directly beneath them, camping among these amazing trees, next to the river, is a truly magical experience. Most of the sites are well away from neighbours and the birdlife along the river is abundant. Rain can make the access roads here very slippery. **Map refs: 84 B4, 94 D11**

550 Emu Lake camping area

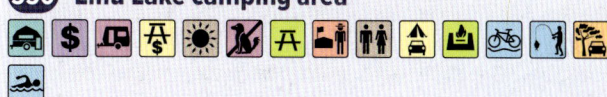

This camping area is on Woolshed Dr, near the park visitor centre. **Map refs: 84 B4, 94 D12, 96 E1**

551 Lake Cawndilla camping area

On Lake Dr off Old Pooncarie Rd, this camping area is right on the lake's foreshore, which offers beautiful early-morning or late-evening views. Following years of drought that saw the lake dry out, it is now full again, so the views from the shore, through the drowned river red gums, is as special as ever. Birdlife is abundant and watching the sun set over this oasis in the outback is something not to be missed. Note: it's 2WD access in dry weather only. **Map refs: 84 B4, 94 D11**

552 Shearers Quarters

The rooms in these shearers' quarters each have 2 bunk beds, 3 with additional trundle beds, sleeping a total of 27 people. There are hot showers here, as well as toilets, communal kitchen and gas BBQs. Advance booking essential. Access is via Emu Lake Dr, off Old Pooncarie Rd. **Map refs:** 84 B4, 94 D12, 96 E1

MUNGO NATIONAL PARK

At the heart of the Willandra Lakes World Heritage Area in the state's remote south-west, Mungo National Park is a wild and arid moonscape. Many photo opportunities exist here among the eroded clay and sand formations called the Walls of China. At sunrise and sunset, especially in the winter, some amazing colours light up the sky and landscape. Scattered remains recall human occupation over 40 000 years, making the area one of immense international archaeological significance. Note: no petrol is available at the park; the nearest fuel is at Pooncarie, 80 km away.

Who to contact: NPWS Buronga (03) 5021 8900 *How to book:* NPWS Buronga (03) 5021 8900 for Shearers Quarters and Mungo Lodge *Camping fees:* fees payable at self-registration stations

553 Belah Camp camping area

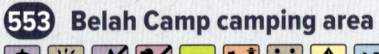

Belah Camp is a small campground 11 km from Vigars Well, the site of a natural water soak. It's around the halfway point along the 70 km Mungo Drive Tour, which leaves from the Mungo Visitor Centre. No wood fires are allowed here; there are hot showers available at the visitor centre. Note: some access roads are unsealed, and not suitable for driving on after rain. **Map refs:** 84 C5, 96 G4

554 Main Camp camping area

There are 33 sites here, 2 km from the Mungo Visitor Centre on Arumpo Rd. Hot showers and firewood are available at the visitor centre. The Zanci Pastoral Loop is a 10 km scenic drive or cycle from the visitor centre to the site of the old Zanci homestead. You can also drive or cycle along the road over the ancient lake bed to the Walls of China (20 km one way). Alternative cabin accommodation is available at Shearers Quarters (sleeps up to 26 people) or Mungo Lodge, on Arumpo Rd, 2 km from the park entrance. **Map refs:** 84 B5, 96 G4

MUTAWINTJI NATIONAL PARK

Tranquil valleys and rugged gorges cut through the craggy Bynguano Range, the dominant landform in Mutawintji National Park. On the fringe of the Central Arid Zone, this is a landscape of red dirt and woodlands, precious creeks and waterholes, and some of the finest Aboriginal rock-art galleries in the country at Mutawintji Historic Site; contact the Broken Hill visitor centre for tour details.

Who to contact: NPWS Broken Hill (08) 8080 3200 *Road conditions:* RTA Broken Hill (08) 8082 6660

555 Homestead Creek camping area

Homestead Creek offers all the facilities you need, including gas/electric BBQs and hot showers. The nearby walk up Homestead Creek passes by some good rock-art sites, and on to the ridge top for views over a rugged, red rock landscape dotted with cypress pines. A short drive leads to the start of the Mutawintji Gorge Walk, where you first cross open range land, then enter a picturesque gorge that ends at a shady rockpool. No bookings are taken and there's no fuel or firewood, so bring your own. There's bore water, but it's best boiled before drinking. Homestead Creek is 130 km north-east of Broken Hill, via the Silver City Hwy then the Broken Hill–White Cliffs Rd. Note: check road conditions beforehand as roads can be closed in wet weather. **Map refs:** 84 B3, 94 D8

STURT NATIONAL PARK

Sturt National Park is one of Australia's driest, most remote national parks. It's a sea of sand, seemingly endless gibber plains, red rock and mulga bushes. Lake Pinaroo, near Fort Grey in the park's east, was placed on the Ramsar list in 1996 – when it fills it is a significant refuge for large numbers of waterbirds and waders.

Who to contact: NPWS Tibooburra (08) 8091 3308

556 Dead Horse Gully camping area

Dead Horse Gully camping ground, set among enormous granite boulders, is about 2 km north of Tibooburra via the Silver City Hwy. The campground is close enough to pop into town for a dinner at one of the friendly outback pubs. Emus are a common sight in and around the camp. Wood fires are not permitted. There's a short signposted walking track taking you through the unusual landscape – undertake the walk at sunrise or sunset and not only will the boulders seem to smoulder and glow, but you'll also have a chance of seeing reptiles and roos. Bring your own water. **Map refs:** 84 B1, 94 D2

557 Fort Grey camping area

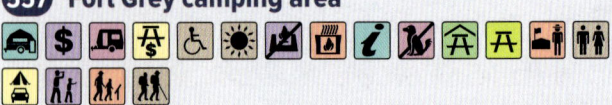

On the road to Cameron Corner from Tibooburra, on roads that are unsealed and only accessible in dry weather, this campground is near the ephemeral Lake Pinaroo, providing terrific birdwatching when the lake is filled with water. There's an informative nature walk starting at the campground and leading to the lake. Wood fires are not permitted, but there are gas/electric BBQs. Cameron Corner, 30 km away, has basic meals and accommodation. **Map refs:** 84 A1, 94 B1

558 Mount Wood camping area

Mt Wood camping area is on gibber downs, in view of the historic Mt Wood homestead. You can get here by following the Gorge Loop Rd, just off the Tibooburra–Wanaaring Rd, but be aware that this road is unsuitable for driving in wet weather. Bring your own water. **Map refs:** 84 B2, 94 E2

559 Olive Downs camping area

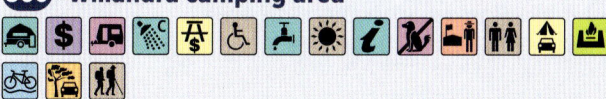

Set among mulga trees, this campground has a short walking track and a good lookout over jump-up country. This is a lovely, secluded and serene place with abundant birdlife. Going west along this road, you see some fantastic scenery and wildlife; wallabies and wedge-tailed eagles are a common sight. Access is via the Jump Up Loop Rd, off Silver City Hwy about 55 km north of Tibooburra. Bring your own water. **Map refs:** 84 B1, 94 D1

WILLANDRA NATIONAL PARK

In its heyday, Willandra was one of the country's great sheep stations; today, sheep properties surround the park and remnants of the pastoral era linger. Walking tracks, a 20 km scenic drive, canoeing, fishing and picnicking are popular pastimes. The park is 64 km north-west of Hillston via dry-weather access only roads.

How to book: NPWS Griffith (02) 6966 8100

560 Willandra camping area

There are 2 camping spots on Willandra Creek, one of which is a large-group camping spot. The other is for individual campers and isn't suitable for caravans. Follow the signs from the Hillston–Mossgiel Rd, but note that the access roads will be closed in wet weather. Firewood is supplied, but you'll need to treat drinking water. **Map refs:** 84 D5, 97 K3

561 Willandra Homestead Cottage

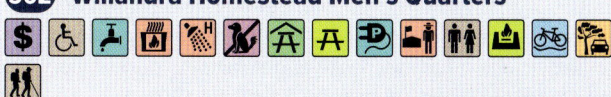

This small fibro cottage has 2 bedrooms with bunk beds sleeping up to 8 people. Self-contained, it has a kitchen stocked with cooking utensils, air conditioning and wood heating. It's near Willandra Creek and surrounded by the beautiful gardens of Willandra Homestead. Bookings are essential. Bring your own linen. **Map refs:** 84 D5, 97 K3

562 Willandra Homestead Men's Quarters

This corrugated-iron 1960s building has 6 bedrooms sleeping up to 24 people, with a gauzed verandah to keep the flies out. It's surrounded by the lovely formal gardens and fragrant, old-world peppercorn trees of the original 1918 Willandra Homestead. Bookings are essential. **Map refs:** 84 D5, 97 K3

CAMPSITES LOCATED IN OTHER AREAS

563 4 Mile camping area

At 4 miles, or approximately 6.5 km, east of Brewarrina along Carinda Rd, this is a top spot for fishing and swimming in the Barwon River. You'll be joining a tradition stretching back thousands of years – one of the drawcards of Brewarrina is its Aboriginal fish traps, an elaborate network of stones designed to catch fish swimming through the river; tours run from the visitor centre. Bring drinking water and firewood. **Map refs:** 84 E2, 95 O5

Who to contact: Brewarrina Visitor Information and Cultural Centre (02) 6830 5152

564 Burke and Wills Campsite

The famed 1860 Burke and Wills expedition saw the first successful north-south crossing of the continent between Melbourne and the Gulf of Carpentaria. The expedition's leader, Robert O'Hara Burke, and his third in command, William John Wills, were 2 of 7 men to die in the attempt. The expedition camped for some time at this spot on the Darling River, 20 km north-east of Mendindee near the Main Weir. To get here, take the Menindee–Broken Hill Rd north of Menindee, and after 8 km take a right turn-off and follow the signs. Bring your own drinking water and firewood. **Map refs:** 84 B4, 94 E11

Who to contact: Menindee Visitor Information Centre (08) 8091 4274

565 Evelyn Creek camping areas (bush camping)

This is a good place to get away from it all, if you're so inclined. Evelyn Creek is about 1 km east of Milparinka, which is in turn 42 km south of Tibooburra in Corner Country. Turn off Silver City Hwy onto Milparinka Rd, about 40 km south of Tibooburra. This is remote bush camping – bring your own everything, including plenty of water and spare petrol. **Map refs:** 84 B2, 94 D3

Who to contact: (08) 8091 3862

566 Fowlers Gap Rest Area

This isn't much to write home about, and it's not suitable for tents, but it's a good place to stop overnight if the long drive is making you sleepy. It's 108 km north of Broken Hill on the Silver City Hwy. Bring your own everything. **Map refs:** 84 B3, 94 C7

Who to contact: Broken Hill Visitor Centre (08) 8080 3560

Camping in Sturt National Park (p. 86)

567 Kidmans Camp

This is a neat and friendly caravan park in North Bourke, not far from the famed Darling River. It's got a swimming pool, which is heavenly in the high heat of summer, as well as powered and unpowered tent sites, cabins, caravan sites and a camp kitchen.
Map refs: 84 E2, 95 M5

How to book: Cunnamulla Rd, North Bourke (02) 6872 1612
www.kidmanscamp.com.au

568 Lake Brewster Weir camping area

This is a family-friendly spot by the Lachlan River, 42 km west of Lake Cargelligo town. Facilities are basic – a wood fireplace and picnic table only – but there's space for the kids to run around, and it's a tranquil setting. It's 2WD access in dry weather only, via Ballyrogan Channel from Hillston Rd. You'll need to bring drinking water and firewood. **Map refs:** 84 E5, 97 M4

Who to contact: State Water Lake Cargelligo (02) 6898 1009; or Lake Cargelligo Tourist Association (02) 6898 1501

569 Lake Pamamaroo camping area

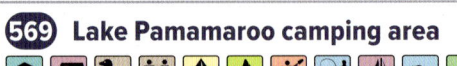

Lake Pamamaroo camping area is 16 km north of Menindee, and comprises part of the Menindee Lakes system. Take the Menindee–Broken Hill Rd north of Menindee, and after 8 km you'll see the turn-off to Lake Pamamaroo and Main Weir on the right. Activities at the lake include fishing, paddling and swimming. Bring your own drinking water and firewood.
Map refs: 84 B4, 94 E11

Who to contact: Menindee Visitor Information Centre (08) 8091 4274

570 Lake View Caravan Park

Don't get overly excited about the 'lake view' part – you can see it, but it's not open to the public. Focus instead on the attractions of Broken Hill, a vibrant outback Australian town saturated with history. The caravan park offers powered and unpowered camping sites, caravan spots, cabins and villas. Facilities include a laundry, kiosk and swimming pool. It's on Mann St, off Argent St. **Map refs:** 84 A4, 94 C10

How to book: 1 Mann St, Broken Hill (08) 8088 2250
www.visitbrokenhill.com.au

571 Main Weir camping area

To get to this camping spot in the Menindee Lakes area, take the Menindee–Broken Hill Rd north of Menindee, and after 8 km you'll see the turn-off to Lake Pamamaroo and Main Weir on the right. Bring your own drinking water and firewood. There's a plaque on a tree here pointing you in the direction of the Burke and Wills Campsite. **Map refs:** 84 B4, 94 E11

Who to contact: Menindee Visitor Information Centre (08) 8091 4274

572 Mays Bend camping area

Gaze across the Darling River to towering red gums at this spot, just 11 km north of North Bourke. Facilities are non-existent, but it's quiet and beautiful, and you can fish, paddle, or go for a swim if you don't mind the mud. Follow the Kidman Way from North Bourke and keep an eye out for a small sign pointing right. Bring your own drinking water. **Map refs:** 84 E2, 95 M5

Who to contact: Bourke Tourist Information Centre (02) 6872 1321

573 Mount Oxley camping area

Mt Oxley is a tabletop mountain with spectacular views over the broad and sunburnt plains surrounding Bourke. This camping area is on private property; to get here, follow the road to Brewarrina for 28 km and take the Tarcoon turn-off. After 4 km, take a right and follow the road to the gate and then on to the summit. There's a wonderful covered BBQ spot at the top, where you can kick back and watch the sun set over the outback. Bring your own drinking water or boil the tank water. **Map refs:** 84 E2, 95 M5

Who to contact: Bourke Tourist Information Centre (02) 6872 1321 *How to book:* Bourke Tourist Information Centre (02) 6872 1321; or property owner 0428 723 275 *Camping fees:* pay fees and pick up permit and key from tourist centre

574 Packsaddle Rest Area

This is a small rest area 177 km north of Broken Hill on Silver City Hwy, about 500 m north of Packsaddle Roadhouse. You'd really only want to stay here for a night as there isn't much to do – although the roadhouse makes a mean steak sandwich. You need to bring your own firewood and drinking water. **Map refs:** 84 B3, 94 D6

Who to contact: Broken Hill Visitor Centre (08) 8082 3560

575 PADDA Park

This is a nice little spot on the Darling River, where you can fish, swim or canoe. There are 5 powered sites and as many campsites as you'd care to throw a tent at. Dogs are allowed on a lead. It's in Pooncarie on Tarcoola St. Bring drinking water and firewood. **Map refs:** 84 B5, 96 F3

Who to contact: Telegraph Hotel (03) 5029 5205 *Camping fees:* pay fees and deposit for key to powered sites at the hotel

576 Penrose Park

Penrose Park is in Silverton, an old goldmining town that's retained an enormous amount of character – as well as some interesting characters. The park offers a goodly amount of facilities, including hot showers and bunkhouse accommodation (bring your own linen), laundry, tennis courts and a bush golf course. Silverton is 25 km north-west of Broken Hill. Bring your own drinking water and firewood. **Map refs:** 84 A4, 94 B10

Who to contact: Penrose Park Trust (08) 8088 5307

577 Tilpa Weir camping area

This is a nice little campsite overlooking the Darling River, 140 km north-east of Wilcannia and 6 km east of Tilpa on the Tilpa–Louth Rd. Don't miss the chance to stop in for a cold drink or a meal at the Tilpa pub, a quintessential Aussie watering hole with walls covered in travellers' graffiti. You'll need drinking water and firewood at the campsite. **Map refs:** 84 D3, 95 I7

Who to contact: Tilpa Hotel (02) 6837 3928

578 White Cliffs Opal Pioneer Tourist Park

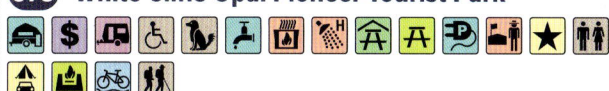

You'll find this caravan park in the opal-mining town of White Cliffs, 95 km north of Wilcannia. The town is popular among tourists for its underground accommodation and businesses, as well as its opals. The park, sadly, is above ground, but it's got coin-operated showers and laundry facilities, powered sites, gas BBQs and a children's playground. If you want to use the wood fireplaces, you'll need to bring firewood. **Map refs:** 84 C3, 94 F7

How to book: Johnston St, White Cliffs (08) 8091 6688 www.whitecliffsopalfield.com

Central-eastern New South Wales

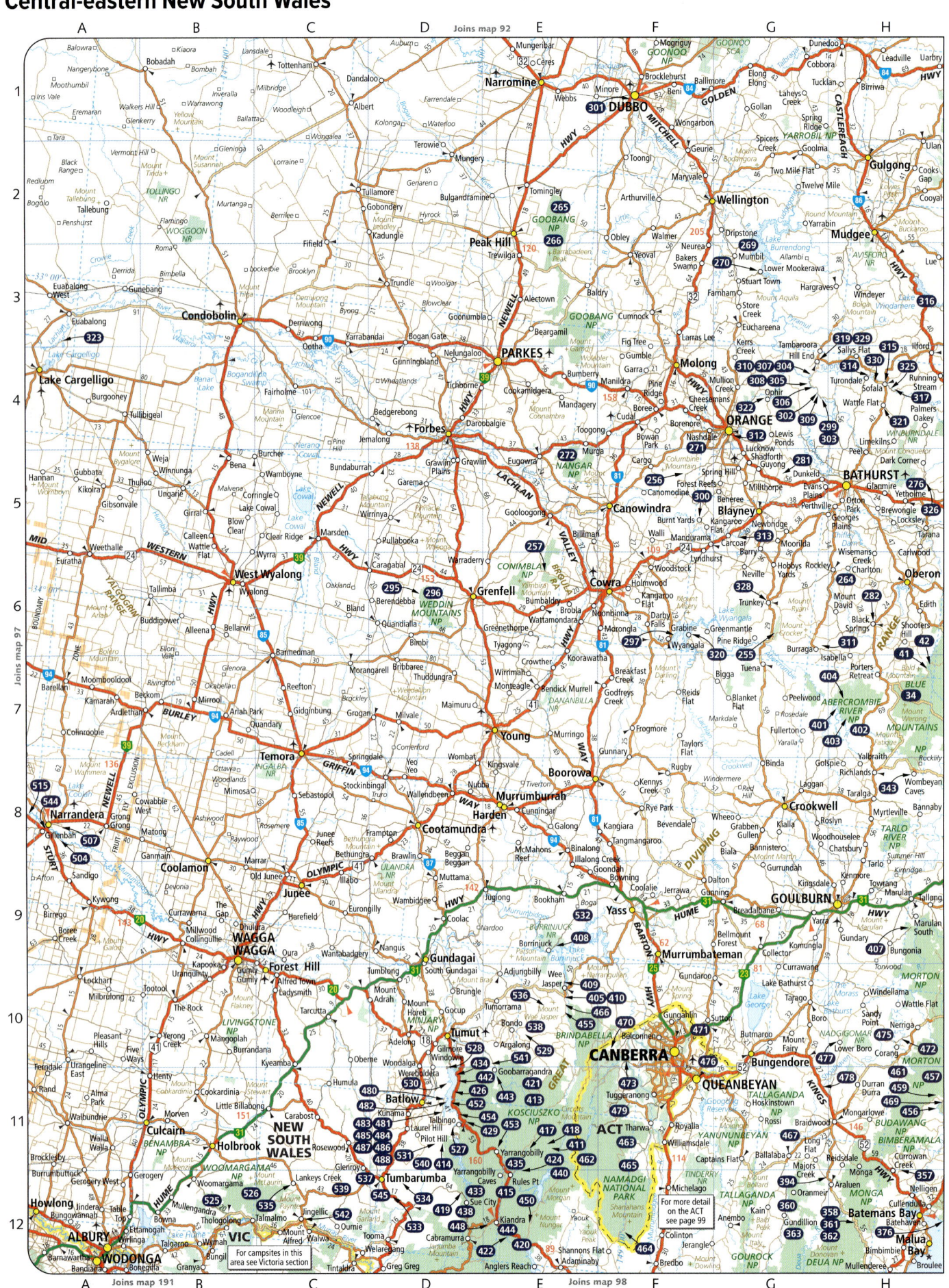

Joins map 92

Joins map 191

Joins map 97

Joins map 98

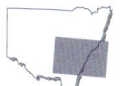

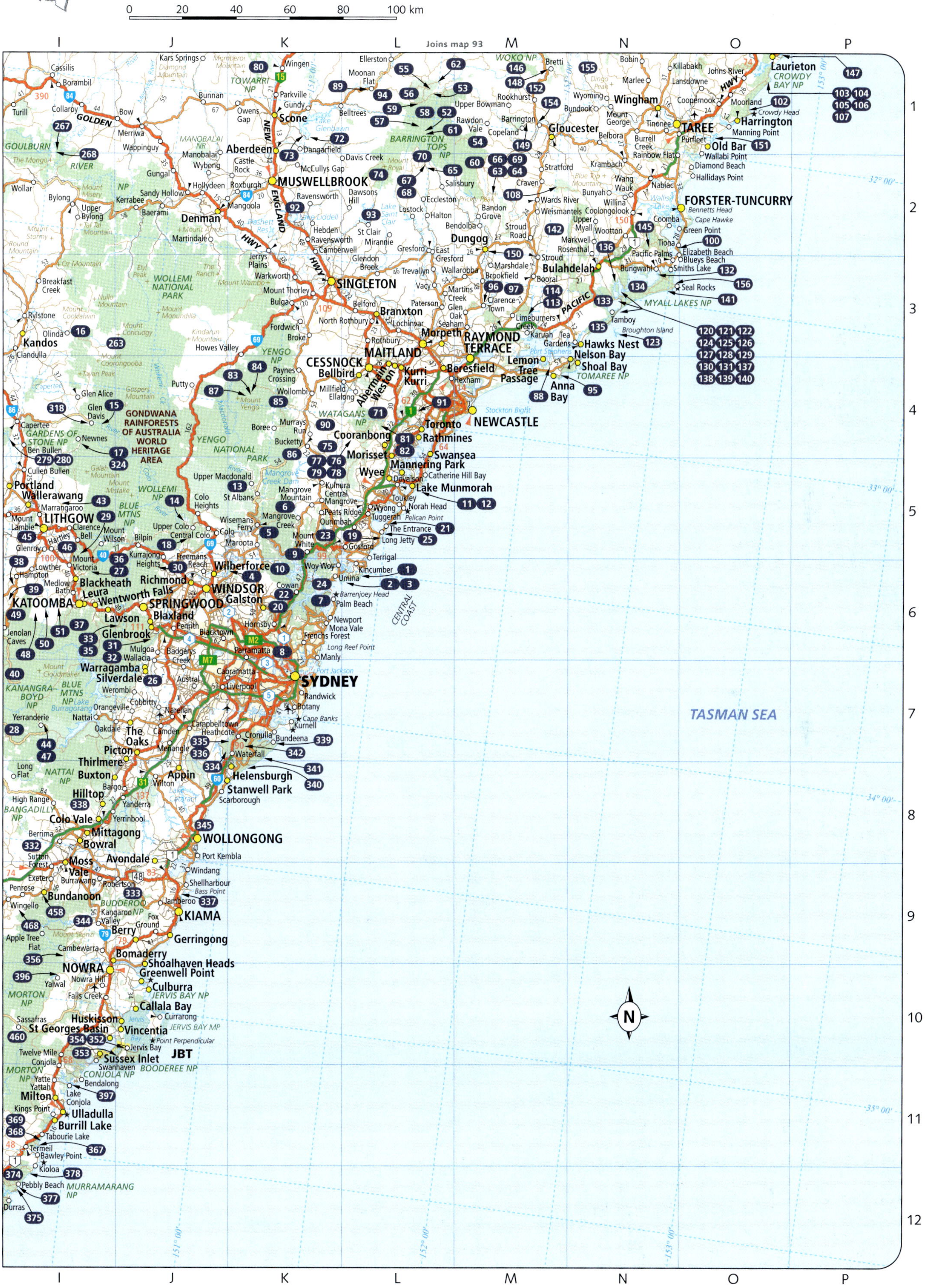
0 20 40 60 80 100 km
Joins map 93
I J K L M N O P
1 2 3 4 5 6 7 8 9 10 11 12
TASMAN SEA
N
SYDNEY
NEWCASTLE
WOLLONGONG
MAITLAND
CESSNOCK
SINGLETON
MUSWELLBROOK
TAREE
FORSTER-TUNCURRY
RAYMOND TERRACE
KATOOMBA
LITHGOW
WINDSOR
SPRINGWOOD
NOWRA
KIAMA
Scone
Aberdeen
Denman
Dungog
Gloucester
Wingham
Laurieton
Harrington
Old Bar
Bulahdelah
Hawks Nest
Nelson Bay
Shoal Bay
Anna Bay
Lemon Tree Passage
Morpeth
Branxton
Kurri Kurri
Beresfield
Toronto
Rathmines
Swansea
Cooranbong
Morisset
Wyee
Mannering Park
Lake Munmorah
Gosford
Wilberforce
Richmond
Blaxland
Lawson
Glenbrook
Blackheath
Wentworth Falls
Leura
Warragamba
Silverdale
The Oaks
Picton
Thirlmere
Buxton
Appin
Helensburgh
Stanwell Park
Hilltop
Colo Vale
Mittagong
Bowral
Moss Vale
Avondale
Bundanoon
Berry
Gerringong
Bomaderry
Shoalhaven Heads
Greenwell Point
Culburra
Callala Bay
Huskisson
St Georges Basin
Vincentia
Sussex Inlet
JBT
Milton
Ulladulla
Burrill Lake
Kandos
Portland
Wallerawang
GOLDEN HWY
NEW ENGLAND HWY
PACIFIC HWY
BARRINGTON TOPS NP
WOLLEMI NATIONAL PARK
YENGO NATIONAL PARK
GONDWANA RAINFORESTS OF AUSTRALIA WORLD HERITAGE AREA
BLUE MTNS NP
KANANGRA-BOYD NP
MYALL LAKES NP
TOMAREE NP
MORTON NP
MURRAMARANG NP
JERVIS BAY NP
BOODEREE NP
CONJOLA NP
CENTRAL COAST

North-eastern New South Wales

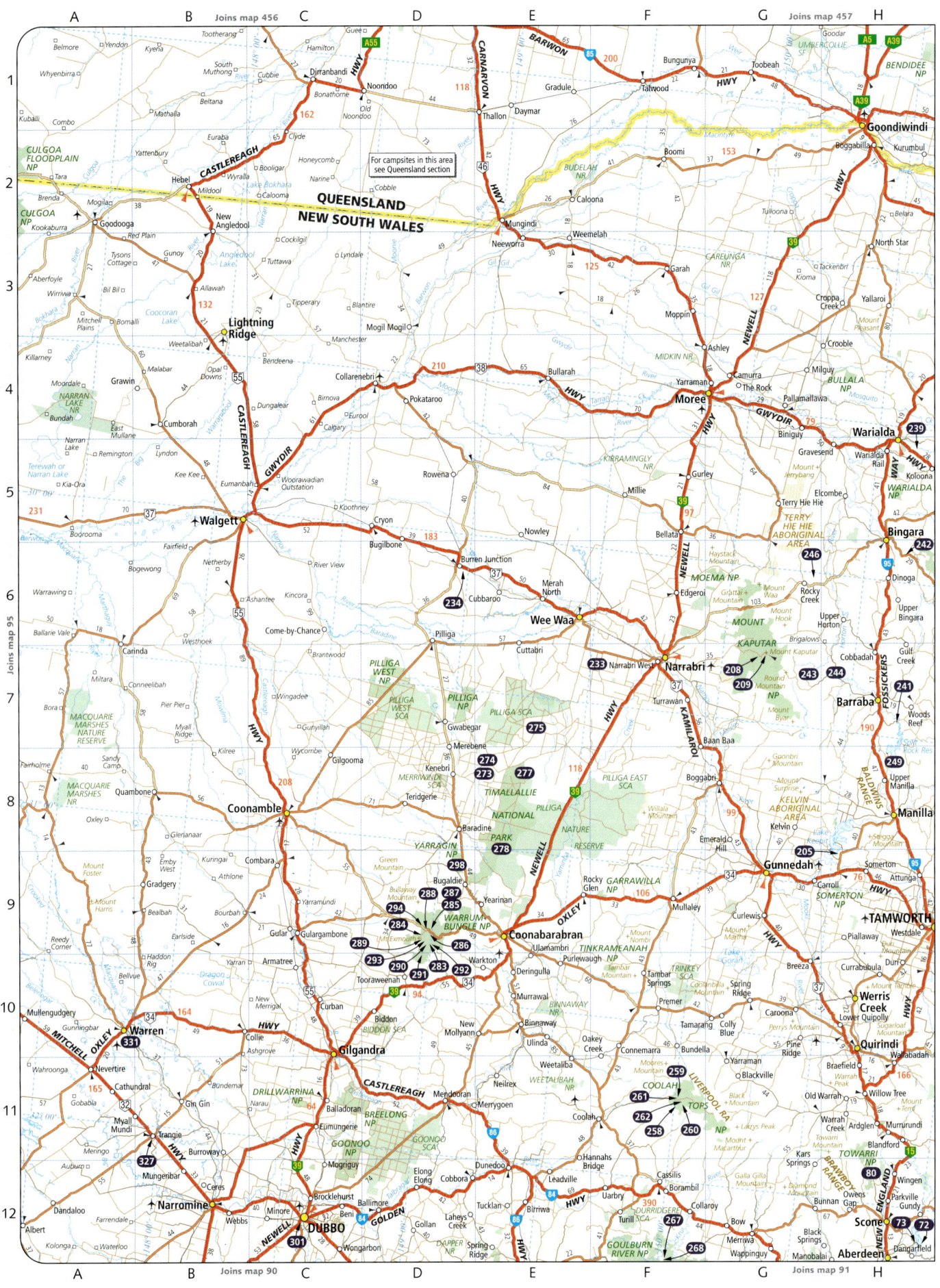

North-western New South Wales

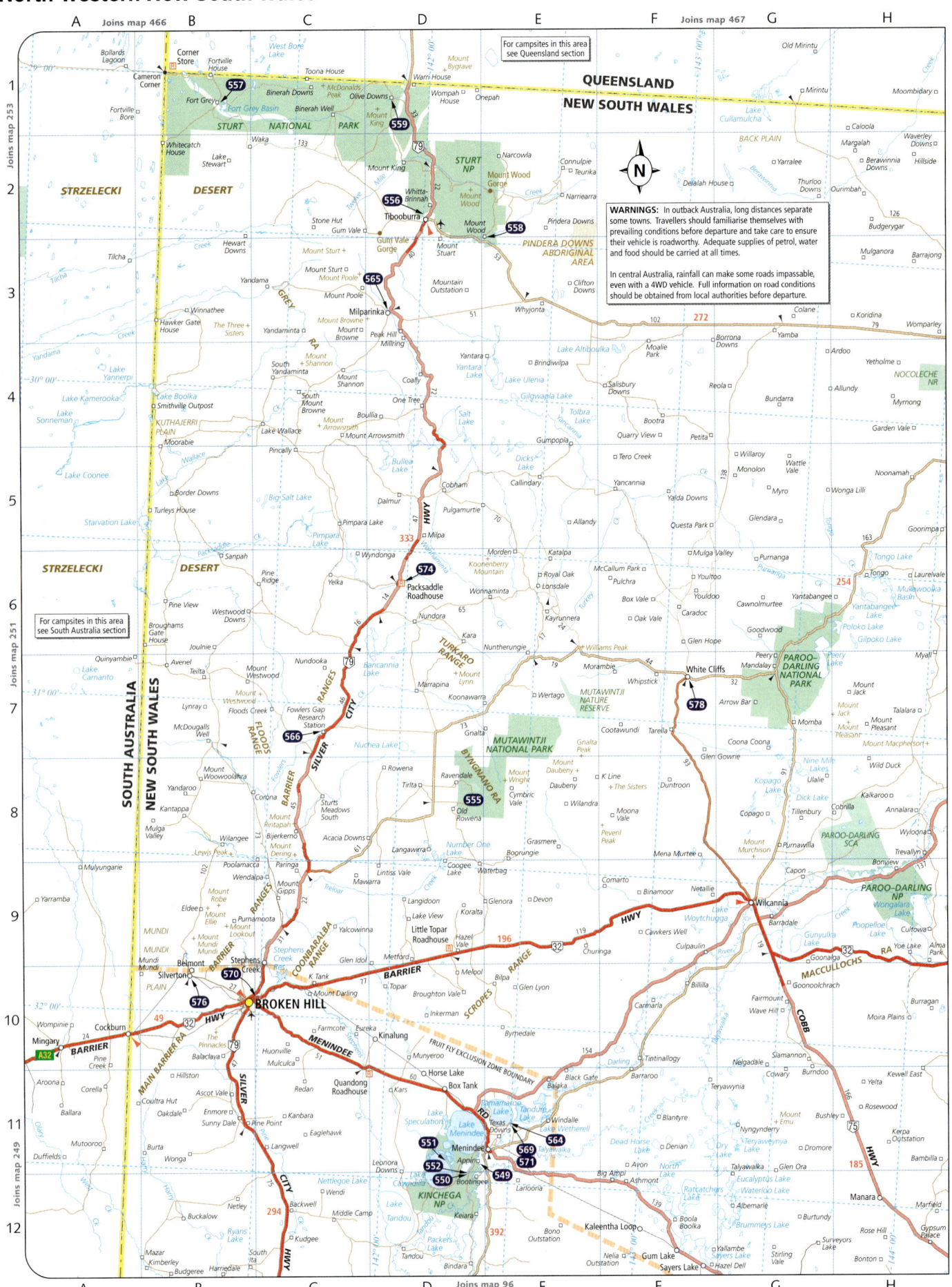

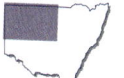

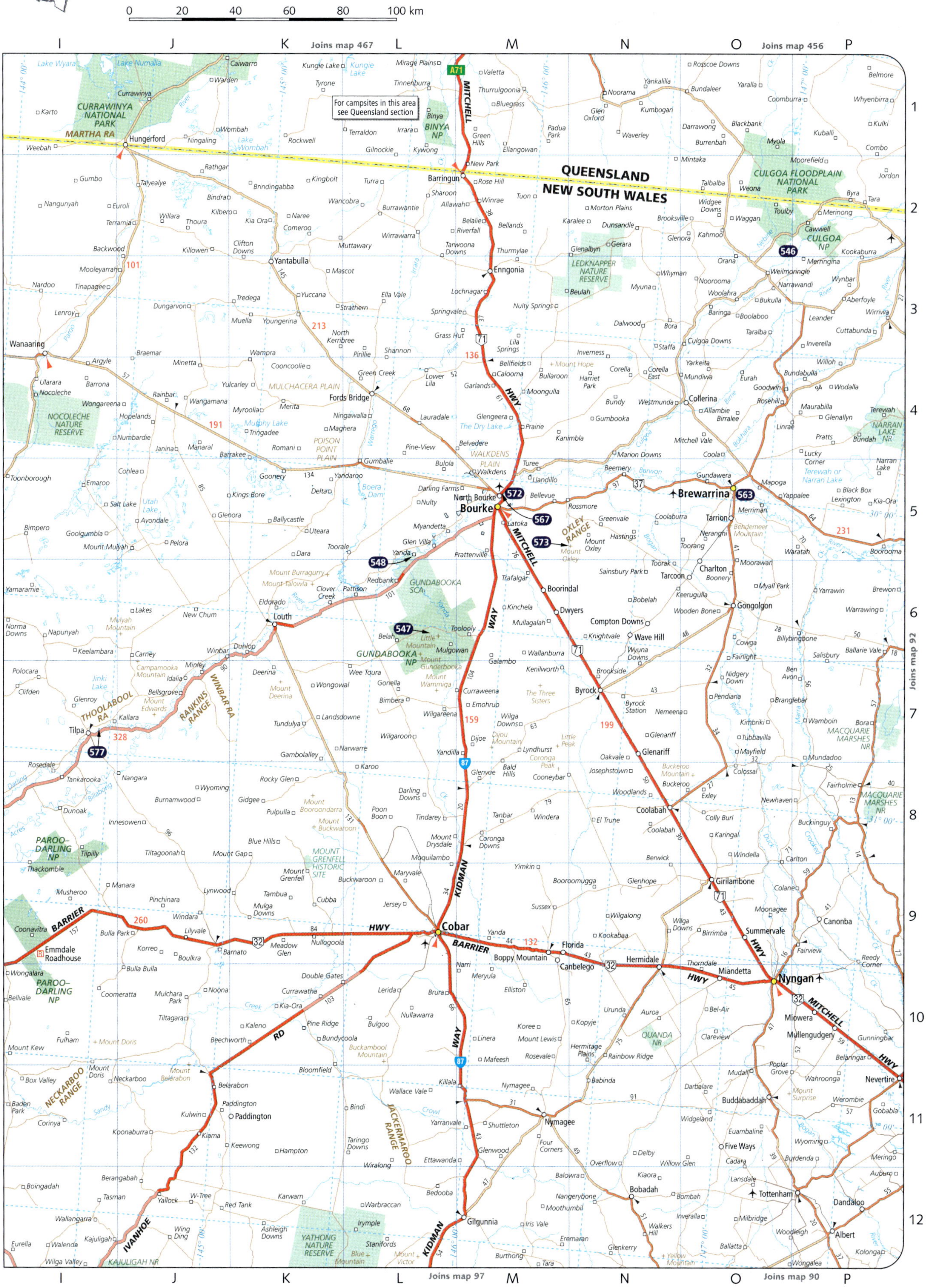
0
20
40
60
80
100 km
I
J
K
L
M
N
O
P
Joins map 467
Joins map 456
Joins map 97
Joins map 90
Joins map 92
1
2
3
4
5
6
7
8
9
10
11
12
For campsites in this area see Queensland section
QUEENSLAND
NEW SOUTH WALES
CURRAWINYA NATIONAL PARK
MARTHA RA
Hungerford
Wanaaring
Lake Wyara
Lake Numalla
Caiwarro
Warden
Currawinya
Karto
Weebah
Wombah
Ningaling
Lake Wombah
Rockwell
Kungie Lake
Kungie Lake
Tyrone
Mirage Plains
Tinnenburra
Terraldon
Irrara
Gilnockie
Kywong
BINYA NP
Binya
A71
MITCHELL
Valetta
Thurrulgoonia
Bluegrass
Green Hills
Ellangowan
Padua Park
Noorama
Glen Oxford
Waverley
Yankalilla
Kumbogan
Bundaleer
Rosscoe Downs
Yaralla
Belmore
Coomburra
Whyenbirra
Darrawong
Blackbank
Kulki
Kuballi
Burrenbah
Myola
Combo
Mintaka
Moorefield
Jordon
CULGOA FLOODPLAIN NATIONAL PARK
Talbalba
Weona
Byra
Tara
Widgee Downs
Toulby
Merinong
Rathgar
Gumbo
Talyealye
Brindingabba
Kingbolt
Turra
Barringun
New Park
Rose Hill
Sharoon
Winrae
Tuon
Nangunyah
Euroli
Bindra
Wancobra
Allawah
Burrawantie
Morton Plains
Brooksville
Waggan
Cawwell
CULGOA NP
Terramia
Willara
Thoura
Kilbero
Kia Ora
Naree
Comeroo
Belalie
Riverfall
Bellands
Karalee
Dunsandle
Glenora
Kahmoo
Backwood
Killowen
Clifton Downs
Wirrawarra
Muttaway
Tarwoona Downs
Thurmylae
Glenalbyn
Gerara
546
Kookaburra
Mooleyarrah
101
Yantabulla
Mascot
Enngonia
LEDKNAPPER NATURE RESERVE
Whyman
Orana
Merringina
Weilmoringle
Nardoo
Tinapagee
Beulah
Myuna
Noorooma
Narrawandi
Wynbar
Tredega
Yuccana
Ella Vale
Lochnagar
Woolahra
Bukulla
Aberfoyle
Lenroy
Dungarvon
Strathern
Springvale
Nulty Springs
Baringa
Boolaboo
Wirriwa
Muella
Youngerina
213
Dalwood
Bora
Leander
Taralba
Grass Hut
Lila Springs
Culgoa Downs
Cuttabunda
North Kerribree
Pirillie
Shannon
136
Inverness
Staffa
Inverella
Braemar
Wampra
Bellfields
Mount Hope
Argyle
Minetta
Cooncoolie
Yarkeita
Willoh
Ularara
Barrona
Yulcarley
MULCHACERA PLAIN
Green Creek
Lower Lila
Caloona
Bullaroon
Harriet Park
Corella
Corella East
Mundiwa
Eurah
Bundabulla
Nocoleche
Rainbar
Wangamana
Garlands
Moongulla
Goodwin
Wodalla
Wongareena
Myroolia
Merita
Fords Bridge
Collerina
Bundy
Westmunda
Rosehill
NOCOLECHE NATURE RESERVE
Hopelands
191
Murphy Lake
Ningawalla
Lauradale
Glengeera
Allambie
Birralee
Maurabilla
Terewah
Tringadee
Maghera
The Dry Lake
Prairie
Gumbooka
Linrae
Glenallyn
NARRAN LAKE NR
Numbardie
POISON POINT PLAIN
Kanimbla
Mitchell Vale
Pratts
Bundah
Janina
Manaral
Romani
Pine-View
Belvedere
Barrakee
WALKDENS PLAIN
Marion Downs
Coola
Lucky Corner
Narran Lake
Toonborough
Conlea
Gumbalie
Bulola
Turee
Beemery
Terewah or Narran Lake
Goonery
134
Yandaroo
Walkdens
Llandillo
Gundawera
Mapoga
Emaroo
Kings Bore
Delta
Boera Dam
Darling Farms
Bellevue
Brewarrina
563
Black Box
Yappalee
Lexington
Kia-Ora
Nulty
North Bourke
572
Bourke
567
Rossmore
Merriman
Salt Lake
Utah Lake
Glenora
Latoka
Coolaburra
Tarrion
Avondale
Ballycastle
Myandetta
Greenvale
Bimpero
Goolgumbla
Utearra
OXLEY RANGE
Hastings
Nerangh
Bendemeer Mountain
231
Mount Mulyah
Pelora
Glen Villa
573
Mount Oxley
Toorong
Warratah
Booroomа
Dara
Tooral
Yanda
Prattenville
Toorak
Charlton
Moorawarri
548
Sainsbury Park
Tarcoon
Boonery
Mount Burragurry
Redbank
GUNDABOOKA SCA
Trafalgar
Myall Park
Mount Talowla
Clover Creek
Pattison
Boorindal
Keerugulla
Yarrawin
Brewon
Yamaramie
Eldorado
Bobehah
Gongolgon
Lakes
Kinchela
Dwyers
Wooden Bone
Warrawing
New Chum
Louth
Mullagalah
Compton Downs
Norma Downs
Mulyah Mountain
Napunyah
547
Toolooly
Belah
Little Mountain
Knightvale
Wave Hill
Cowga
Billybingbone
Ballarie Vale
Keelambara
Carney
Winbar
Dunlop
Mulgowan
Wallanburra
Wyuna Downs
Fairlight
Salisbury
GUNDABOOKA NP
Mount Gunderbooka
Galambo
Polocara
Campamooka Mountain
Minley
Idalia
Deerina
Wee Toura
Kenilworth
Brookside
Nidgery Down
Ben Avon
Jinki Lake
Bellsgrove
Mount Deerina
Wongowal
Gonella
Mount Wammiga
Curraweena
The Three Sisters
Byrock
43
Pendiana
Branglebar
Clifden
Mount Edwards
WINBAR RA
RANKINS RANGE
Emohruo
Byrock Station
Nemeena
Glenroy
THOOLABOOL RA
Kallara
Bimbera
Wilgareena
Wilga Downs
Kimbriki
Wamboin
Tilpa
328
Tundulya
Landsdowne
159
63
199
Tubbavilla
MACQUARIE MARSHES NR
577
Wilgaroon
Dijoe
Dijou Mountain
Little Peak
Glenariff
Glenariff
Bora
Rosedale
Gambolalley
Narwarre
Yandilla
Lyndhurst
Coronga Peak
Oakvale
Mayfield
Mundadoo
Tankarooka
Nangara
Karoo
87
Glenvue
Bald Hills
Cooneybar
Josephstown
Buckeroo Mountain
Colossal
Fairholme
Wyoming
Rocky Glen
Buckeroo
Exley
Dunoak
Burnamwood
Gidgee
Pulpulla
Mount Booroondarra
Darling Downs
Poon Boon
Tindarey
Tanbar
Windera
Woodlands
El Trune
Coolabah
Newhaven
Colly Burl
Innesowen
Mount Buckwaroon
Coolabah
Karingal
Buckiinguy
PAROO-DARLING NP
Tilpilly
Blue Hills
Mount Drysdale
Coronga Downs
Windella
Carlton
Thackombie
Tiltagoonah
Mount Gap
MOUNT GRENFELL HISTORIC SITE
Moquilambo
Yimkin
Berwick
Manara
Mount Grenfell
Maryvale
KIDMAN
Booroomugga
Glenhope
Girilambone
Colane
Musheroo
Lynwood
Tambua
Buckwaroon
Canonba
Pinchinara
Mulga Downs
Cubba
Jersey
Sussex
Wilgalong
Moongee
Windara
Lilyvale
Wilga Downs
Birrimba
Summervale
Coonavitra
BARRIER
157
Bulla Park
260
32
Meadow Glen
Nullogoola
84
HWY
Cobar
Yanda
132
Florida
Kookabaa
Fairview
Emmdale Roadhouse
Korreo
Boulkra
Barnato
Boppy Mountain
Canbelego
Hermidale
Thorndale
Miandetta
Nyngan
Reedy Corner
Wongalara
Bulla Bulla
Double Gates
Narri
Meryula
PAROO-DARLING NP
Bellvale
Coomeratta
Mulchara Park
Noona
Currawatha
Lerida
Brura
Elliston
Tiltagara
Kia-Ora
Urunda
Auroa
Bel-Air
Miowera
Mullengudgery
Gunningbar
Kaleno
Pine Ridge
Bulgoo
Nullawarra
Koree
Kopyje
QUANDA NR
Clareview
Fulham
Mount Doris
Beechworth
RD
Bundycoola
Linera
Mount Lewis
Hermitage Plains
Mount Kew
Buckambool Mountain
Mafeesh
Rosevale
Rainbow Ridge
Poplar Grove
Belaringar
Box Valley
Mount Doris
Mount Belarabon
Bloomfield
Mudall
Wahroonga
Nevertire
Neckarboo
Killala
Babinda
Darbalare
NECKARBOO RANGE
Belarabon
Wallace Vale
Nymagee
Mount Surprise
Baden Park
Paddington
Bindi
Buddabaddah
Weronbie
Gobabla
Corinya
Kulwin
Paddington
JACKERMAROO RANGE
Yarranvale
Shuttleton
Nymagee
Widgeland
Koonaburra
Kiama
Taringo Downs
Four Corners
Euambaline
Keewong
Hampton
Glenwood
Five Ways
Wyoming
Wiralong
Ettawanda
Overflow
Delby
Willow Glen
Cadara
Burdenda
Meringo
Berangabah
Balowra
Kiaora
Lansdale
Auburn
Boingadah
Tasman
W-Tree
Karwarn
Bedooba
Nangerybone
Bobadah
Bombah
Tottenham
Dandaloo
Yallock
Red Tank
Warbraccan
Moothumbil
Inveralla
Milbridge
Wallangarra
Wing Ding
Ashleigh Downs
Irymple
Gilgunnia
Iris Vale
Walkers Hill
Woodleigh
Albert
Eurella
Walenda
Kajuligah
IVANHOE
YATHONG NATURE RESERVE
Stanifords
Eremaran
Glenkerry
Ballatta
Kolonga
Wilga Valley
KAJULIGAH NR
Blue Mountain
Mount Victor
Burthong
Tara
Yellow Mountain
Wongalea

South-western New South Wales

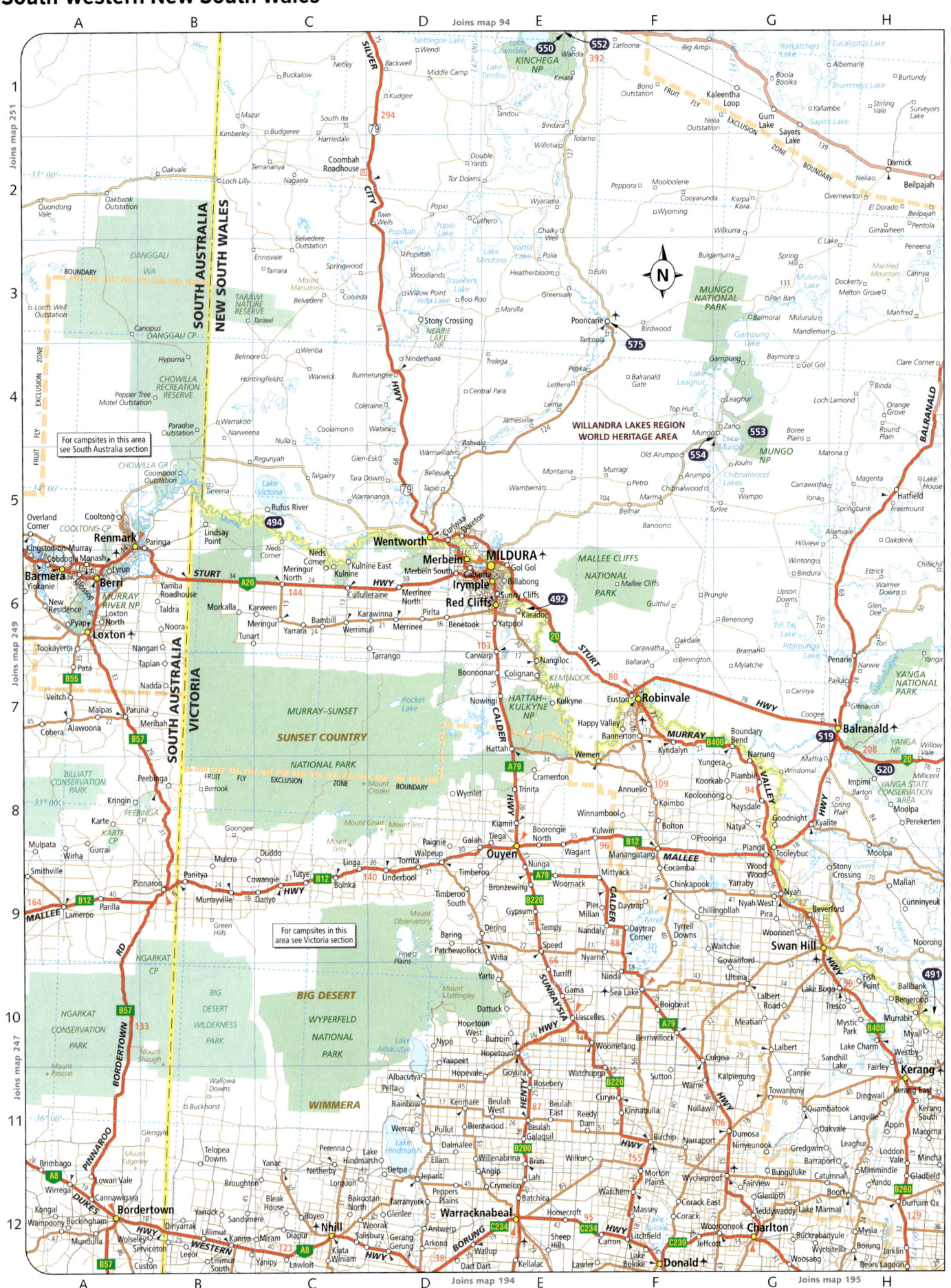

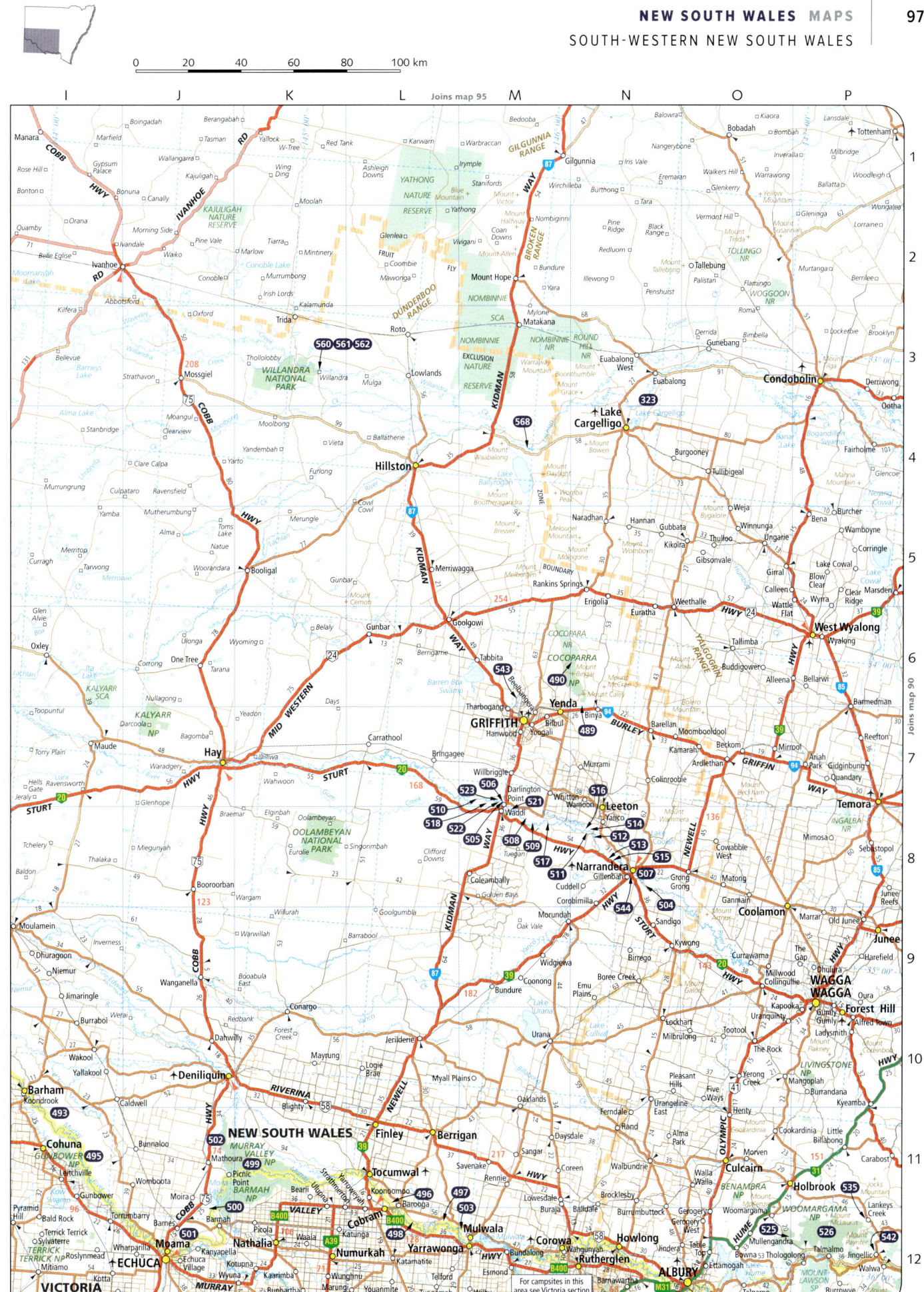

South-eastern New South Wales

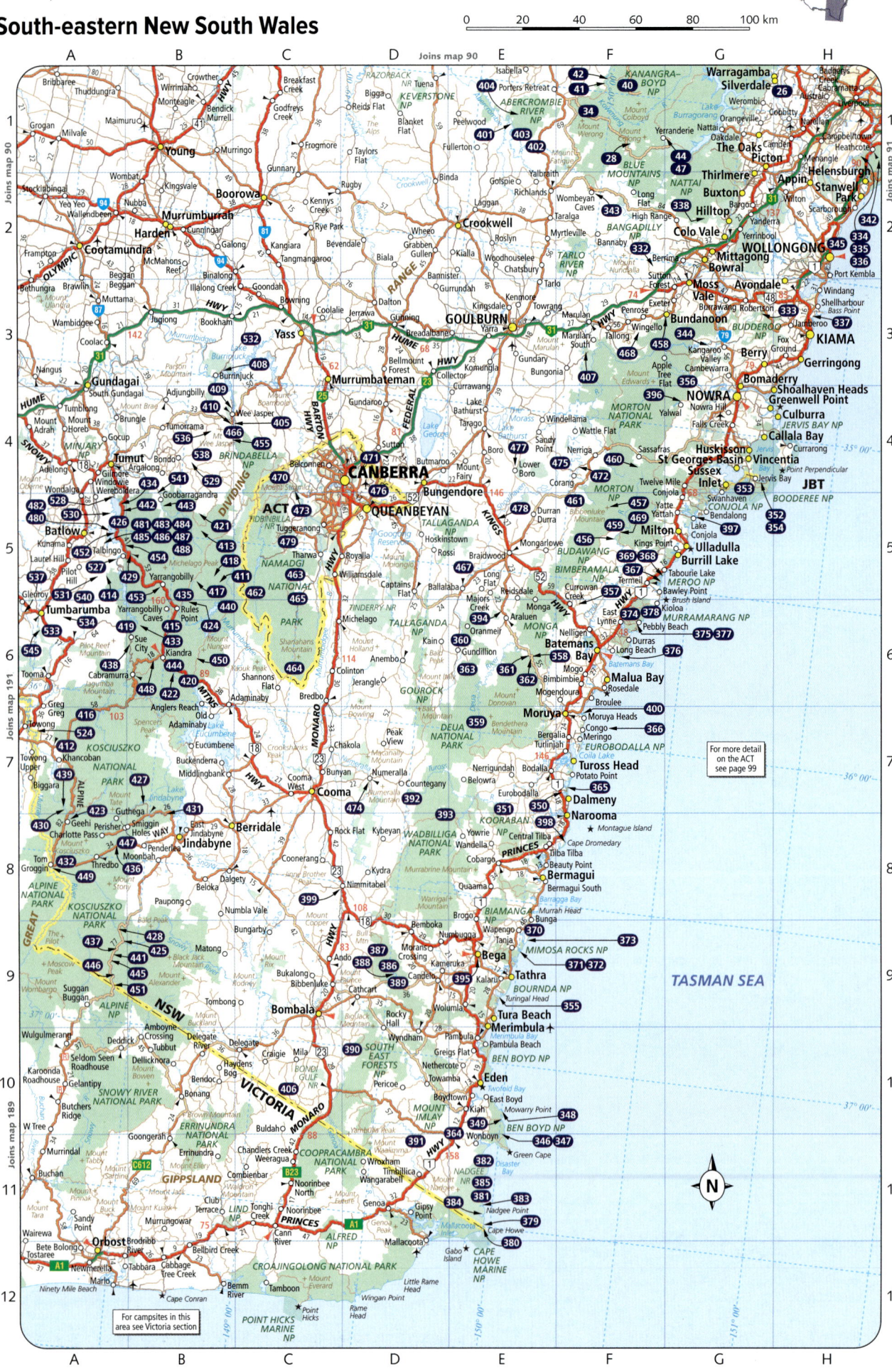

Australian Capital Territory

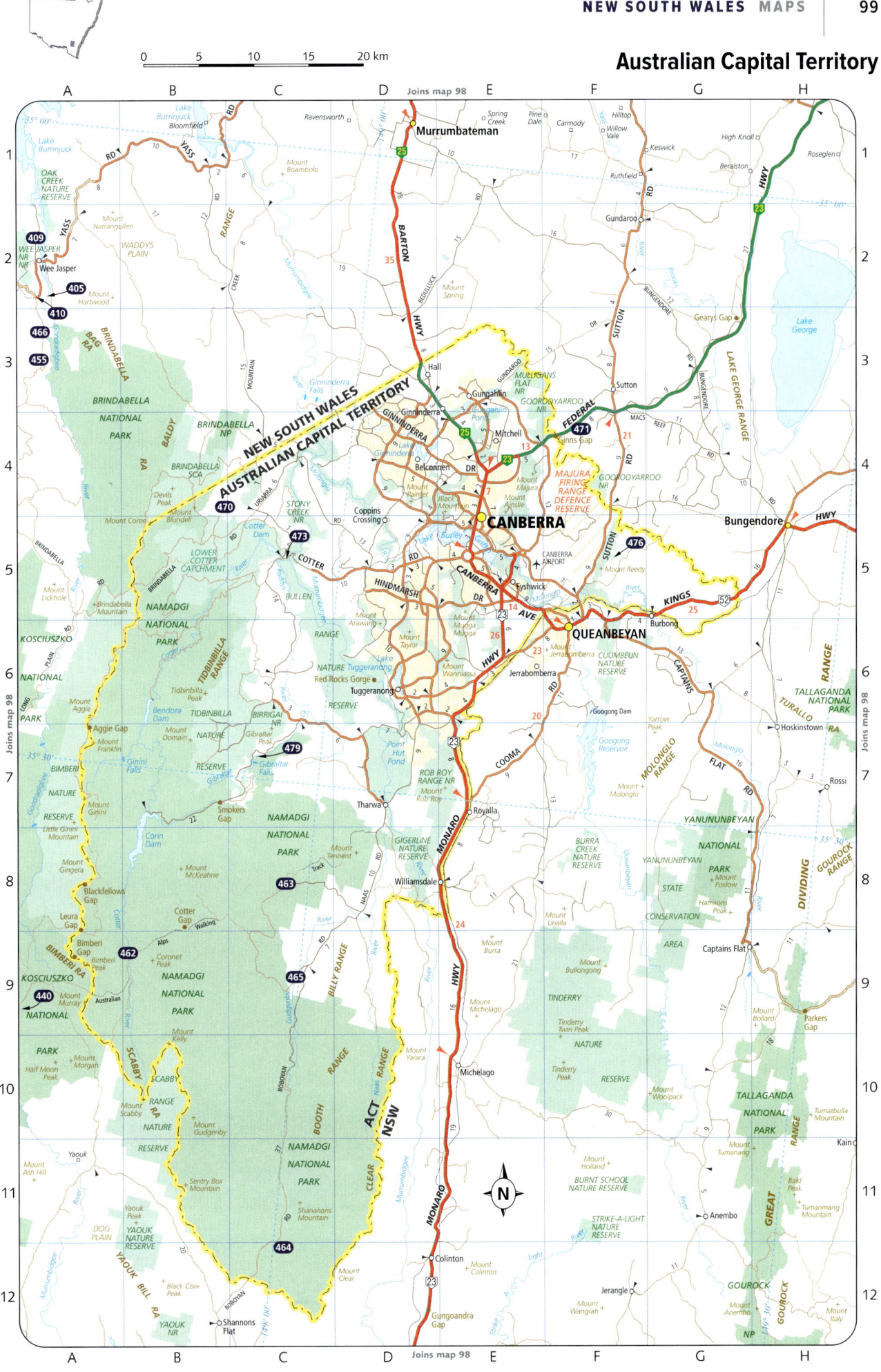

VICTORIA

CONTENTS

BEST CAMPSITES

Buandik camping area
Grampians National Park (Grampians and Central West), p. 174

Buttercup Creek campsites 1–3
Buttercup Creek Reserve (High Country), p. 138

Lake Hattah camping area
Hattah–Kulkyne National Park (Mallee Country), p. 181

Thurra River camping area
Croajingolong National Park (East Gippsland), p. 124

Tidal River camping area
Wilsons Promontory National Park (Gippsland), p. 116

USEFUL CONTACTS

Country Fire Authority – Fire Restrictions
Bushfire Information Hotline
1800 240 667
www.cfa.vic.gov.au

Department of Sustainability and Environment
13 6186
www.dse.vic.gov.au

Emergency
Dial 000 for police, ambulance and fire brigade

Fisheries – Department of Primary Industries
13 6186
www.new.dpi.vic.gov.au/fisheries

Parks Victoria
13 1963
www.parkweb.vic.gov.au

VicRoads
13 1171
www.vicroads.vic.gov.au

Camping on Mount Clear, Alpine National Park, High Country region (p. 131)

MORNINGTON PENINSULA

[Map of Mornington Peninsula region showing Melbourne, Port Phillip Bay, Western Port, French Island and surrounding areas with grid references A–F and 1–6]

For state road atlas coverage
see pages 188 & 197

N

0   10   20   30 km

THE MORNINGTON PENINSULA CURVES away to the south-east of Melbourne to cup the placid waters of Port Phillip Bay, and provide a natural barrier against the rough-and-tumble antics of Bass Strait. On the peninsula's eastern side is the smaller harbour of Western Port, which swirls like a moat around bucolic French Island. The bays' sheltered waters are perfect for stress-free sailing and swimming, and are regularly visited by pods of bottle-nosed dolphins taking a well-earned break from the ocean currents. Australian fur seals also make themselves at home here, and several species of whale – including the minke and southern right varieties – pass through as well.

Strung out along the western edge of the Mornington Peninsula, facing across Port Phillip towards the distant Bellarine Peninsula, are several extensive foreshore reserves where campers can claim a patch of grass and then turn their attention to the cool but inviting waters of the bay. Rosebud, Rye and Sorrento collectively make hundreds of campsites available, which tells you something about the region's popularity. Sorrento also boasts a picturesque streetscape of historic limestone buildings that turn golden when the sun dips towards the horizon.

The south-eastern edge of the Mornington Peninsula has relaxed foreshore camping at Point Leo, Balnarring and Shoreham, though the water is much rougher here because it's exposed to the ocean swells sweeping in from the strait. From Stony Point you can catch a ferry over to French Island, a peaceful domain of walkers and cyclists. There's a staggering array of birdlife to be glimpsed here, plus healthy populations of koalas and potoroos, and heaps of fresh air to breathe in. From the settlement of Tankerton, take another ferry trip over to Phillip Island to see its famous fairy penguins scrambling back to their dens after a busy day of fishing.

CAMPSITES LOCATED IN PARKS AND RESERVES

BALNARRING BEACH CAMPING RESERVES

There are 3 separate camping reserves at Balnarring Beach, which is on the eastern side of the Mornington Peninsula between Hastings and Flinders, some 80 km south of Melbourne. This ocean beach is at the entrance to Western Port, and a variety of watersports can be enjoyed here. From Balnarring, take the Balnarring Beach Rd down to the seashore. Note: these reserves are closed between mid-June and the end of Aug.

How to book: advance bookings recommended during peak periods; (03) 5983 5582

1 Balnarring East Beach C Reserve

This is the easternmost of the 3 beach reserves at Balnarring – you can get to it from Feathers Rd. It's just over some dunes from yet another idyllic beach in this area, where swimmers and members of the local yacht club congregate. If you're after some solitude, wander further up the beach in the direction of Somers. **Map refs:** 102 D5, 188 C8

2 Balnarring Koala B Reserve

Located opposite the Balnarring General Store, the Koala B Reserve is one of 3 beachside parks here. It comprises a nicely laid-out campground that's only a hop, skip and a jump from the beach – for the record, it's the closest ocean beach to Melbourne. Ideal for families, it has the added bonus of a little creek where young ones can try their luck fishing. BBQs are close by, and the park manager's office is also located in this reserve. Access is from Balnarring Beach Rd. **Map refs:** 102 D5, 188 C8

3 Balnarring South Beach A Reserve

South Beach A is accessed via Mason Smith Rd. It's opposite a protected beach that's ideal for young children, and there's also a toddlers' playground to keep the under-five brigade amused. Keep an eye out for koalas, which can often be seen snoozing in the gum trees overhead. **Map refs:** 102 D5, 188 C8

CAPEL SOUND FORESHORE RESERVE

Facing Port Phillip Bay on the western side of Mornington Peninsula is the Capel Sound Foreshore Reserve. The reserve's campsites are sprinkled along the beach at 2 locales: Rosebud West and Tootgarook – access to both sites is from the waterfront Port Nepean Rd. Arthurs Seat State Park is close by, as are some excellent wineries.

How to book: bookings essential at peak periods; (03) 5986 4382

4 Capel Sound Foreshore Reserve camping areas

There's plenty on offer for water lovers at Capel Sound, including fishing, swimming, canoeing and boating, the latter aided by a boat launch. Note: Tootgarook is only open seasonally Nov– Apr, while Rosebud West is open year-round. All campsites are accessed from Point Nepean Rd. **Map refs:** 102 C5, 188 B7

FRENCH ISLAND NATIONAL PARK

This little gem of a park comprises serene French Island in Western Port. The mangrove saltlands and open woodland play host to a range of wildlife, including hundreds of birds. The park is accessed by a 15 min ferry ride from Stony Point on the Mornington Peninsula; individuals and bicycles are transported, but not vehicles.

Who to contact: Parks Victoria 13 1963

5 Airs Farm camping area (walk-in camping)

Toast your toes around the open fire (wood supplied) at this private campground, nestled in bushland some 10 km east of Tankerton. The owners will pick you up or you can walk or cycle along Bayview Rd to reach the farm. Also located here is Bayview Chicory Kiln, a historic 1890s building containing a large display of memorabilia. The owners run guided walking tours of French Island. **Map refs:** 102 E5, 188 D7

6 Fairhaven camping area (walk-in camping)

The Fairhaven campsites are in a beautiful natural setting on the western shore of French Island, 5 km north of Tankerton off Coast Rd. It's a great spot to kick back for a few days. While you have your feet up, look out for long-nosed potoroos and also for koalas, which are prolific on the island. Bring a bike or walking boots with you so you can explore the island's undulating terrain. For great views over Phillip Island, head up to the Pinnacles. **Map refs:** 102 E5, 188 D7

POINT LEO FORESHORE RESERVE

The Point Leo Foreshore Reserve is situated on the shoreline of Mornington Peninsula around 70 km south of Melbourne. From here you look across the mouth of Western Port towards Phillip Island. Comprising banksia woodlands, smooth-running creeks and sand dunes, it offers decent surf breaks and walks through wetland areas, while the Point Leo Boat Club provides opportunities for sailing.

How to book: (03) 5989 8333

7 Point Leo Foreshore camping area

There are plenty of activities for campers on the Point Leo foreshore. Top of the list is a refreshing dip just off the beach or a surf at one of the 7 local breaks. Canoeing, fishing and waterfront strolls will also help you to while away most days. There are plenty of camping sites, although some are closed during winter. This camping area is located on Point Leo Rd, which runs off the Frankston–Flinders Rd – take the Red Hill–Shoreham Rd from Red Hill. **Map refs:** 102 D5, 188 C8

ROSEBUD FORESHORE RESERVE

The Rosebud Foreshore Reserve lies 5 km south-west of Dromana, on the appealing curve of Mornington Peninsula. Locals and visitors alike come down here to swim and sail in the sheltered waters of Port Phillip Bay. One of the reserve's features is the 34 m high McCrae Lighthouse, built in 1883, while another is the 1851 wreck of the *Rosebud*.

Who to contact: Mornington Peninsula Shire 1300 850 600
How to book: (03) 5950 1011

8 Rosebud Foreshore Reserve camping area

There are literally hundreds of campsites scattered throughout the Rosebud Foreshore Reserve, which stretches for 7 km between Anthonys Nose in McCrae to Chinamans Creek in Rosebud West. Wander along the bayfront or take a boat out and go fishing. Note: camping areas are only open Nov–Apr. All sites are accessed off Point Nepean Rd. **Map refs:** 102 C5, 188 C7

RYE FORESHORE RESERVE

The foreshore at Rye is a flat, hassle-free stretch of waterfront land on which to raise a tent or park a caravan. Fronting the calm waters of Port Phillip Bay between Tootgarook and Blairgowrie, it suits watersports lovers and anglers. From here it's only a short distance to the upmarket holiday town of Sorrento, with its chi-chi cafes and convivial old limestone pub.

Who to contact: Mornington Peninsula Shire 1300 850 600
How to book: (03) 5950 1011

9 Rye Foreshore camping area

There are 300 sites at Rye Foreshore Reserve, which are split between 2 areas: Rye East and Rye West. Needless to say, there's lots of activity in the area during peak holiday periods, when you may want to consider booking well in advance of your visit. Those who stay here are usually torn between boat-related activities like waterskiing, and another dip in the calm bay. Note: camping is only permitted here Nov–Apr. Access is off Point Nepean Rd. **Map refs:** 102 C5, 188 B7, 197 P9

SHOREHAM FORESHORE RESERVE

The sleepy town of Shoreham is on the south-eastern edge of Mornington Peninsula, facing Phillip Island and its famous penguins across a channel of Western Port. The town's foreshore reserve is a comfortable, relaxing spot for a bit of camping – swimming, fishing and boating round out the activities in the area. The Frankston–Flinders Rd will get you here from the Moorooduc Hwy.

How to book: bookings essential; (03) 5989 8325

10 Shoreham Foreshore Reserve camping area

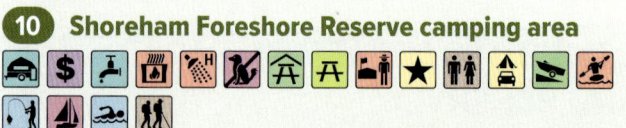

You can camp all year long at this restful foreshore reserve. Take long walks along the nearby cliffs, cool off in the waters of Western Port, or spend the afternoon sampling fine vintages at a local winery. There's a boat ramp off Beach Rd, though you'll need a 4WD to reach it across some sand. The reserve is off the Prout–Webb Rd in Shoreham. **Map refs:** 102 D5, 188 C8

SORRENTO FORESHORE RESERVE

At the very tip of Mornington Peninsula, with the rough swells of Bass Strait on one side and the sheltered sweep of Port Phillip Bay on the other, lies the Sorrento Foreshore Reserve. It faces across the bay, while behind it are the historic limestone buildings of Sorrento township. All manner of watersports are enjoyed here, as is cycling along the picturesque waterfront. Follow Point Nepean Rd to get here.

Who to contact: Mornington Peninsula Shire 1300 850 600
How to book: (03) 5950 1011

11 Sorrento Foreshore camping area

There are plenty of campsites to choose from here alongside the bay. If you're lucky you'll catch sight of the bottle-nosed dolphins that sometimes frequent the area. You can also catch a ferry from Sorrento across the mouth of Port Phillip Bay to the attractive town of Queenscliff on the Bellarine Peninsula. Camping is only permitted here Nov–Apr. **Map refs:** 102 B5, 188 B7, 197 P8

YARRA AND DANDENONGS

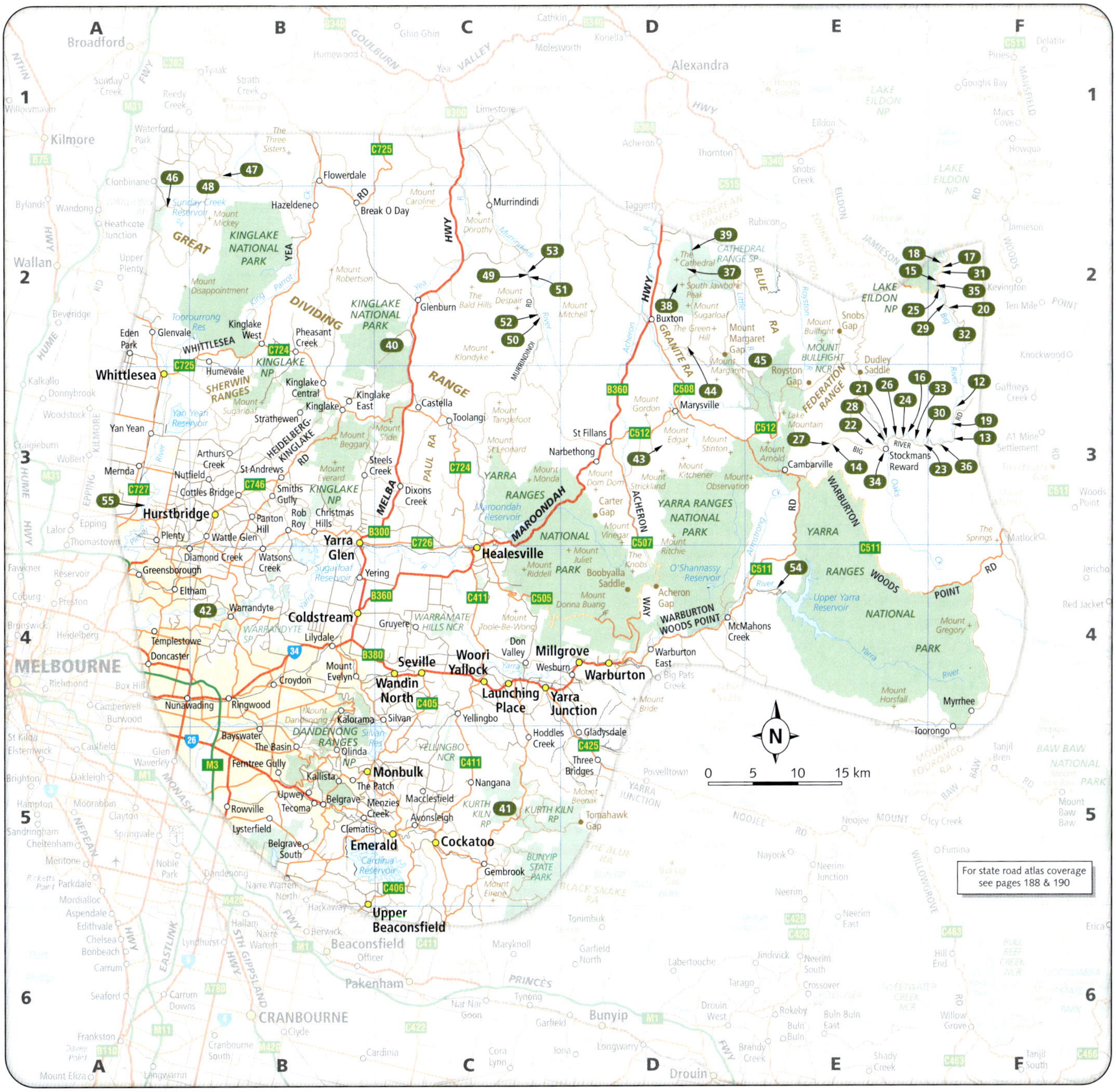

THE LOVELY YARRA VALLEY and the picturesque mountain ranges that surround it, including the diminutive Dandenongs, inspire Melburnians to travel a short distance east of their urban homes to wander through lush rainforests and groves of majestic mountain ash. The forests and townships in this and neighbouring regions, such as the Kinglake and Murrindindi areas, suffered terrible damage during the 2009 Black Saturday bushfires, and their rejuvenation, although well underway, will be ongoing for a long time. But the natural beauty of the landscape through which the Yarra River lazily flows has reasserted itself, with spectacular scenes of floral regeneration contrasting with the greenery of untouched woodlands.

The literal high point of these magnificent forests is the centuries-old Ada Tree, a mountain ash that towers above its neighbours in Yarra State Forest, though it has plenty of fellow giants to keep it company. Camping within these old-growth woods is a special experience, one that's heightened by the scenery you encounter when strolling along the local network of tracks. The regenerated foliage that blankets Kinglake National Park, the Cathedral Range and the erroneously named Mt Disappointment is just as striking. Even in a state of recovery, these places still beguile visitors with the views from atop their assorted crags and peaks.

There's plenty of wildlife to be spied too, from swamp wallabies and eastern grey kangaroos to echidnas, bats, powerful owls and many other colourful bird species. At Kurth Kiln Regional Park, to the east of the pretty Dandenong Ranges, you can turn your attention to an interesting man-made artefact in the form of a furnace used to create charcoal to fuel gas-powered vehicles during World War II. On the Yarra River itself, try camping in the cosy shadow of the reservoir that serves as Melbourne's biggest water supply.

CAMPSITES LOCATED IN PARKS AND RESERVES

BIG RIVER STATE FOREST

An expansive forest blankets the hills and gullies surrounding Big River as it wriggles down from Lake Eildon past the Yarra Ranges. This rugged area was the setting for 19th-century goldmining exploits, and now it's popular with bushwalkers, anglers and 4WD enthusiasts. Access the river's upper reaches via Big River State Forest Rd just east of Cumberland Junction, 19 km east of Marysville down the Marysville–Woods Point Rd; its lower reaches are accessed via the Eildon–Jamieson Rd or Big River State Forest Rd. Note: the Big River camping areas are usually very popular during holiday periods; you can't book any of the sites in advance, so you should try to arrive early to claim one.

Who to contact: DSE 13 6186

12 25 Mile Creek camping area (bush camping, upper section)

This is the end of the road as far as camping in the upper part of the Big River State Forest is concerned. It's the furthest you'll get from Marysville and still be able to pitch a tent. There's only 4WD access north of 25 Mile Creek; conventional vehicles can follow the enigmatic Big River no further. **Map refs:** 133 F6, 189 L2, 191 L12

13 Big Bend Creek camping area (bush camping, upper section)

True to its name, this collection of campsites is near a big bend of Big River, which turns the waterway due west. Get here early during holiday periods, as the forest's camping spots tend to fill up quickly. North of here, there are only 2 more camping options before Big River Rd becomes a 4WD track. **Map refs:** 105 F3, 188 H3

14 Big River Camp camping area (upper section)

This is one of the first camping areas you'll encounter after entering the upper section of Big River State Forest from Marysville. It's also one of only 3 places in the area that can comfortably accommodate large groups – the other 2 are the Stockmans Reward and Frenchmans Creek sites. Big River Camp is at the junction of Big River Rd and the Eildon–Warburton Rd, almost 6 km north-east of the Marysville–Woods Point Rd. **Map refs:** 105 E3, 188 G3

15 Big River camping area (lower section)

These campsites are on an attractive bend of the river off the Eildon–Jamieson Rd, near the junction with Big River Rd. Just across the river is the scenic fringe of Lake Eildon National Park. If you're planning on lighting a campfire, remember that it's illegal to cut any standing vegetation into firewood – you can only use fallen dead wood. **Map refs:** 105 F2, 188 G2

16 Bobuck Ridge camping area (bush camping, upper section)

Bobuck Ridge is where Big River wanders off on a bit of a loop before steadying itself to continue west. This camping area is in-between Gang Gang Gully and Specimen Creek. It only accommodates tent campers, and is off limits to conventional vehicles when the weather is wet. Anglers will usually have some success here. **Map refs:** 105 E3, 188 G3

17 Bulldog Flat camping area (lower section)

Bulldog Flat is accessed off the Eildon–Jamieson Rd between Burnt Bridge and the Pines, either of which are a better bet if you're towing a caravan or a camper trailer. While venturing to and from Bulldog Flat, you may encounter the odd group of horseriders from the horse camp just down the road. **Map refs:** 105 F2, 188 G2

18 Burnt Bridge camping area (lower section)

Burnt Bridge is one of the first camping areas you reach when entering the forest from the direction of Jamieson along the Eildon–Jamieson Rd. In spring, you may spy canoeists negotiating rapids on the stretch of Big River between here and the Big River bridge. Bring your own drinking water and firewood. **Map refs:** 105 F2, 188 G2

19 Catford camping area (bush camping, upper section)

Catford is almost as far as campers can go for an overnight stay in the upper section of Big River State Forest. Beyond this point, heading north, only 25 Mile Creek offers the possibility of camping. The access track to Catford, which gets you down close to the river, can be negotiated by standard 2WD vehicles, but only during dry weather. **Map refs:** 105 F3, 188 G3

20 Chaffe Creek camping area (lower section)

Out of all the overnight options in the lower section of Big River State Forest, the large flat areas at Chaffe Creek, which lie off Big River Rd south of the Old Coach Rd site, are arguably the most suitable for large groups of tent and caravan/trailer campers. South of here, beyond Railway Creek, are the camping areas of the upper Big River. **Map refs:** 105 F2, 188 G2

21 Dairy Flat camping area (bush camping, upper section)

This is one of the nicest spots along the river in which to set up camp. The only catch is that you'll need a 4WD to negotiate the access track, which leads off Big River Rd between the Miners Flat and McClelland camping areas. Drop a line in the water to see if you can hook one of the local brown trout. **Map refs:** 105 E3, 188 G3

22 Fishbone Flat camping area (bush camping, upper section)

Fishbone Flat is near Arnold Creek, between the Petroffs and Stockmans Reward camping areas. Numerous narrow tracks branch off Big River Rd to the east of here, inviting 4WD exploration. The campground itself is accessed via a rough track that requires a 4WD vehicle. **Map refs:** 105 E3, 188 G3

23 Frenchmans Creek camping area (upper section)

Frenchmans Creek is well up Big River, on another of the peaceful waterway's myriad bends. The site caters to camper trailers and small caravans as well as tent campers, and has enough space for large groups to make themselves at home. It's signposted off Big River Rd about 6 km east of the Stockmans Reward camping area. **Map refs:** 105 E3, 188 G3

24 Gang Gang Gully camping area (bush camping, upper section)

This is one of the many camping spots in the upper part of Big River State Forest that allows you to pitch a tent near the slow-flowing river. Make sure to bring in your own supplies of drinking water and firewood, and note that the access track to Gang Gang Gully is only negotiable by 2WD in dry weather. **Map refs:** 105 E3, 188 G3

25 Jimmy Bullocks camping area (lower section)

The origin of the name Jimmy Bullocks is a mystery, but the campground itself is easy enough to track down – it's at the northern end of Big River Rd right near the junction with the Eildon–Jamieson Rd. **Map refs:** 105 F2, 188 G2

26 McClelland camping area (bush camping, upper section)

The McClelland camping area is located right beside Big River, just before the waterway bends away from its westerly course and starts heading south. If you're driving a conventional vehicle,

note that you'll only be able to work your way down the access track when the weather is dry. **Map refs:** 105 E3, 188 G3

27 Married Mens camping area (bush camping, upper section)

This may well have once been a place where a fraternity of married men gathered to indulge in some bromance. Regardless, everyone is now welcome here – bar those towing caravans or camper trailers, which are not accommodated. The Married Mens site is signposted off Big River Rd near the Big River Camp. The access track can only be negotiated by conventional vehicles in dry weather. **Map refs:** 105 E3, 188 G3

28 Miners Flat camping area (bush camping, upper section)

Miners Flat is another of the camping areas off Big River Rd that can only be accessed with a 4WD. It's situated on the eastern side of a sweeping bend in Big River, and is one of the first riverside campsites you'll reach on the drive into the forest from the direction of Marysville. **Map refs:** 105 E3, 188 G3

29 Old Coach Road camping area (lower section)

The Old Coach Rd camping area is located south of Jimmy Bullocks, several kilometres down the unsealed Big River Rd from the intersection with the Eildon–Jamieson Rd. Bushwalkers may want to check out the nearby Bald Spur Track, while trail-bike riders can make their way over to Newmans Track. **Map refs:** 105 F2, 188 G2

30 Peppermint Ridge camping area (bush camping, upper section)

Peppermint Ridge lies to the north of Frenchmans Creek, and can be accessed by 2WD vehicles in dry weather. It's an out-of-the-way spot that tends to attract repeat visits from keen anglers and others who appreciate the peaceful atmosphere and the fresh forest air. **Map refs:** 105 E3, 188 G3

31 The Pines camping area (lower section)

The Pines is south of Bulldog Flat off the Eildon–Jamieson Rd, near Newmans Track. You may have some luck fishing for trout in the river here. **Map refs:** 105 F2, 188 G2

32 Railway Creek camping area (lower section)

This camping area is located just to the north of the picnic area at Enoch Point, and is accessed from Point Rd, which runs off Big River Rd. This spot is accessible only by 4WD, and you should bring firewood and drinking water with you. Catching your dinner in Railway Creek is a possibility, while at Enoch Point there are remnants of the alluvial mining that once took place here. **Map refs:** 105 F2, 188 H2

33 **Specimen Creek camping area (bush camping, upper section)**

The 4WD track heading north to Specimen Creek branches off Big River Rd between the Bobuck Ridge and Frenchmans Creek tracks. As with all of the camping areas in the upper part of Big River State Forest, the sites here are filled on a first-come, first-served basis – arrive as early as possible during peak holiday periods or you may miss out on a place to camp. **Map refs:** 105 E3, 188 G3

34 **Stockmans Reward camping area (upper section)**

The Stockmans Reward camping area is well-suited to larger groups and those who are towing their accommodation. The only other place east of here that can receive camper trailers and small caravans is Frenchmans Creek. Stockmans Reward is signposted off Big River Rd some 7.7 km east of Big River Camp. **Map refs:** 105 E3, 188 G3

35 **Taponga camping area (lower section)**

Surrounded by peppermint forest is a large clearing set by the Taponga River – the first of the Lower Big River sites (travelling from Eildon). Lots of shade and tea-trees in the understorey make for pleasant camping. Access is on the eastern side of Eildon–Jamieson Rd. Watch for overhanging tea-tree branches. **Map refs:** 105 F2, 188 G2

36 **Vennells camping area (bush camping, upper section)**

One of the more secluded bush-camping areas in the upper section of Big River State Forest, Vennells is a notably quiet spot that rewards those who travel out this way with a refreshing riverside experience. Drop a line in the water to see what you can catch. **Map refs:** 105 F3, 188 G3

CATHEDRAL RANGE STATE PARK

The splendid, high-peaked ridge of the Cathedral Range offers spectacular walks and rock climbing routes to suit all levels of fitness and ability. To get here, take Cathedral La off the Maroondah Hwy between Taggerty and Buxton. The Cathedral Range is recovering from the extensive damage caused by the 2009 Black Saturday fires when 92% of the park was burnt. Although accessibility to most areas has been restored, contact Parks Victoria for the latest information. Advance bookings for campsites are requested.

How to book: Parks Victoria 13 1963

37 **Cooks Mill camping area**

This camping area is off Little River Rd in the centre of the park and can accommodate a handful of caravans when the

pine harvest is not taking place. The Friends Nature Trail is an easy route through manna gum forest, while the Saint Bernards Track to Jawbone carpark is a little more strenuous. Note: bring your own wood, as firewood cannot be collected anywhere in the park. Also note that the fireplace here doesn't have a cooking plate. **Map refs:** 105 D2, 188 F2

38 **The Farmyard camping area (walk-in camping)**

To reach the small camping area at the Farmyard, you need to walk in from Jawbone carpark on Cerberus Rd along the steep Jawbone Creek Track, which will take you about an hour. The park's ultimate physical challenge is south of here – the Wells Cave Track is a very difficult and exposed route linking Sugarloaf Saddle with Sugarloaf Peak, the area's highest point. You can also reach Sugarloaf Peak via the Razorback Ridge Track. **Map refs:** 105 D2, 188 F2

39 **Neds Gully camping area (walk-in camping)**

Neds Gully is off Little River Rd at the northern entrance to the park; it's a 50 m walk from the carpark to the campsites via a swing bridge. An easy walk leads from Neds Gully to Cooks Mill along Little River. If you're after something a bit more challenging, follow another trail to Neds Saddle, from where you can take the steep, difficult track heading west to Cathedral Peak. **Map refs:** 105 D2, 188 F2, 190 F12

KINGLAKE NATIONAL PARK

A staggering 98% of the forested Kinglake National Park was burnt in the 2009 Black Saturday bushfires, with visitor access slowly returning to normal, although there are significant ongoing recovery works. Some walking tracks and picnic areas remain closed – check with the rangers as to which facilities visitors can use. Entry to the park is via the Maroondah Hwy near Kinglake.

How to book: Parks Victoria 13 1963

40 **The Gums camping area**

The Gums camping area can be reached by travelling 4 km down Glenburn Rd from Kinglake, and then continuing for another 6 km down Eucalyptus Rd. While the campsites here in the midst of the Great Dividing Range have been restored, check out the national park's spectacular regeneration from the Andrews Hill section of the Wombelano Block. **Map refs:** 105 C2, 188 E2

KURTH KILN REGIONAL PARK

Kurth Kiln Regional Park is a short distance east of Melbourne. Check out the remnants of Kurth Kiln, with its tall iron chimney, and then take to one of the park's many great walking tracks.

Who to contact: Parks Victoria 13 1963

41 Kurth Kiln camping area

This camping area is accessed via Soldiers Rd, which branches off the Gembrook–Launching Place Rd. As you stroll through the mountain ash, keep your eyes peeled for swamp wallabies and echidnas. **Map refs:** 105 C5, 188 E5

LONGRIDGE PARK

Located in Warrandyte on flat ground between the Yarra River and the adjacent slopes, Longridge Park is a great place to go birdwatching and fishing, or to meet and greet the local eastern grey kangaroos. Its spacious environs are perfect for large groups who want room to play. Access is via Warrandyte Rd – more specific directions will be provided by Parks Victoria once the obligatory booking is made.

How to book: Parks Victoria 13 1963

42 Longridge Park camping area

A one-time cattle-grazing area set within the pretty Yarra Valley Parklands, the turf at Longridge can now be booked through Parks Victoria (by phone or online) by individuals or groups of up to 40 for relaxing camping stints. Go swimming and canoeing in the river, and at night keep an eye out for powerful owls and eastern free-tail bats. **Map refs:** 105 B4, 188 D4

MARYSVILLE STATE FOREST

Marysville State Forest, which lies to the north-east of Marysville and contains numerous walking tracks and the superb Steavenson Falls, was one of the worst-affected areas on Black Saturday in early 2009. Fortunately, wet winters in subsequent years have meant that the rate of forest regeneration has been phenomenal, and the DSE has completed works to facilities at picnic areas and campsites. Walking tracks have been improved too – try to pick up the DSE brochure detailing walks in the forest.

Who to contact: DSE 13 6186

43 Andersons Mill camping area

Located about 6 km south of Marysville and accessed from Andersons Mill Rd is this attractive little campsite with room for just 5 or 6 tents. You can walk or cycle along a shared pathway to/from town. **Map refs:** 105 D3, 188 F3

44 Keppel Creek camping area

There are no toilets at this informal campsite, 6 km north of Marysville. Access is from Cerberus Rd, which runs off Mt Margaret Rd. The campsite is located right next to the Cathedral Range, which is reached by continuing down Cerberus Rd. There are half a dozen spots to pitch a tent. **Map refs:** 105 D2, 188 F2

45 Keppel Hut camping area

The original Keppel Hut was built on this site around 1940 but burned down in 1983, as did its predecessor on Black Saturday 2009. The hut has since been rebuilt. This remote site can only be accessed by 4WD – take Keppel Hut Track off Lady Talbot Dr. During the winter months it is a walk-in site, accessible only on foot. **Map refs:** 105 E2, 188 G3

MOUNT DISAPPOINTMENT STATE FOREST

Nestled within the Great Dividing Range to the south-east of Broadford, the Mt Disappointment State Forest was a popular bushwalking, mountain-biking and horseriding area prior to the 2009 Black Saturday bushfires, when the region was extensively burnt. By mid-2012 an extensive government-sponsored bushfire-recovery program had been implemented, including the rebuilding of visitor facilities and the reopening of campsites. The regeneration of the forest is also well underway, aided by some wet winters following the bushfires.

Who to contact: DSE 13 6186

46 Andersons Garden camping area

A lovely site on Sunday Creek, 9 km off the Hume Fwy. There are good facilities under the towering mountain ash and wattle abounds in the undergrowth. Access to the campsite is south from the town of Clonbinane along Clonbinane Rd, which changes name to Westcott Creek Rd at the forest. **Map refs:** 105 A2, 188 D2, 190 D12

47 No. 1 Camp camping area

Gatherings of horseriders and other large groups often base themselves at No. 1 Camp, which is a spacious open site – you're likely to have company if you stay here. Turn east on North Mountain Rd at Heathcote Junction on the Hume Fwy, then follow Main Mountain Rd to its intersection with Flowerdale Rd, where the camping area is located. **Map refs:** 105 B1, 188 D2, 190 D12

48 Regular Camp camping area (walk-in camping)

This camping area, a short distance south of No. 1 Camp on Main Mountain Rd, is surrounded by bollards so you can't park beside your tent. At the southern end of the park is the short, easy walk from Blairs Hut to the top of Mt Disappointment, from where you can look back towards Melbourne and Port Phillip Bay. **Map refs:** 105 B2, 188 D2, 190 D12

MURRINDINDI SCENIC RESERVE

The 815 ha Murrindindi Scenic Reserve, situated to the east of Glenburn on the Melba Hwy, was devastated during the 2009 Black Saturday bushfires. DSE authorities have since rebuilt facilities and the reserve along with its campsites and walking tracks have now all reopened. Thanks to some wet

Walking through Yarra Ranges National Park

winters since the bushfires, the regeneration of the forest has been remarkable.

Who to contact: DSE 13 6186

49 Blackwood camping area

Around 1 km from the forest boundary along Murrindindi Rd is signposted access to the Blackwood campsites.
Map refs: 105 C2, 188 E2

50 Bull Creek camping area

From the Melba Hwy, turn east on Murrindindi Rd to the south of Devlins Bridge. The Bull Creek camping area is signposted off this road at the southern end of the Murrindindi Scenic Reserve.
Map refs: 105 C2, 188 F2

51 Cassinia camping area

Close to Blackwood camping area, this small camping spot is about 1.5 km from the forest boundary along the Murrindindi Rd. It's tent camping only and it's a good spot to throw a fishing line in for trout. **Map refs:** 105 C2, 188 E2

52 The Ferns camping area

This camping area beside the Murrindindi River is signposted off Murrindindi Rd, about 100 m south of Falls Creek Rd.
Map refs: 105 C2, 188 F2

53 SEC camping area (walk-in camping)

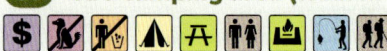

The SEC camping area is a walk-in site. It's signposted off Murrindindi Rd. **Map refs:** 105 C2, 188 E2

UPPER YARRA RESERVOIR PARK

Centred on one of Melbourne's largest water storages, this park allows the uppermost access to the Yarra River. Although no swimming is permitted here, you can do some walks up to local viewpoints, and the facilities will ensure a very comfortable stay. The park is 24 km east of Warburton, off the Woods Point–Warburton Rd.

How to book: Parks Victoria 13 1963

54 Upper Yarra Reservoir Park camping area

This camping area is spacious and wheelchair-accessible and, if the weather is wet, you can take shelter in a large hall equipped with electric BBQs. For a fine view over the reservoir, take the steep 2 km track to the Doctor Creek Lookout, but note that walking tracks are off limits to dogs. You can also inspect a restored waterwheel. Advance bookings are essential.
Map refs: 105 E4, 188 G4

CAMPSITES LOCATED IN OTHER AREAS

55 Nioka Bush Camp

The tiny 1.2 ha Nioka Bush Camp is a Parks Victoria site beside the Plenty River on the outskirts of Melbourne. It's a peaceful retreat where you can fish, bushwalk or just hang around doing not much at all. Advance bookings are required, whether you pitch a tent or sleep in the bunkhouse. To get here, turn onto Gordons Rd from Plenty Rd in South Morang. **Map refs:** 105 A3, 188 D3

How to book: Parks Victoria 13 1963

GIPPSLAND

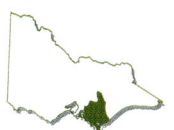

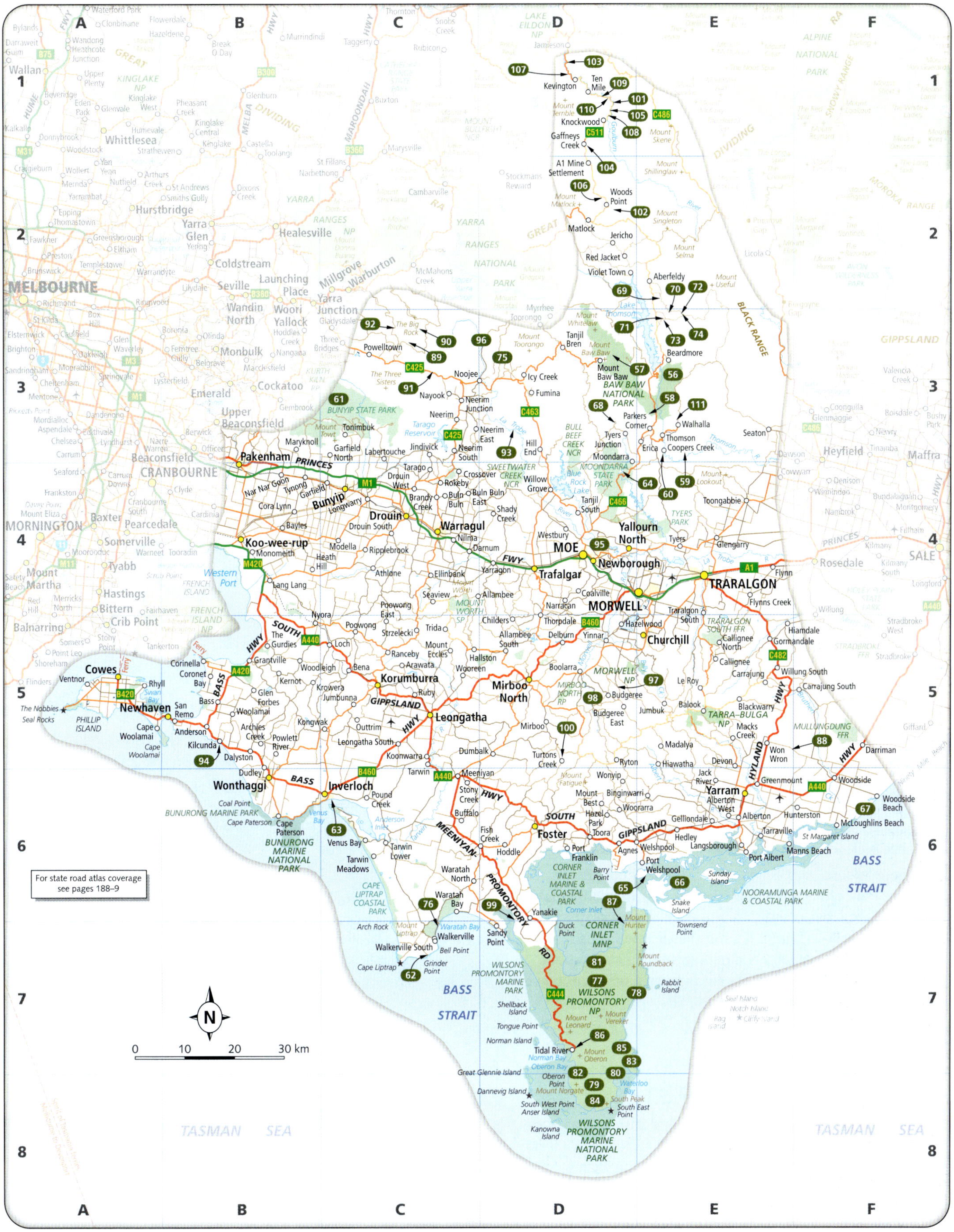

For state road atlas coverage see pages 188–9

THE GIPPSLAND REGION EXTENDS from Western Port across a pastoral area anchored by the service towns of Warragul, Morwell and Traralgon. The landscape gets taller to the north of the Princes Hwy, culminating in the dazzling subalpine plateau of Baw Baw National Park, where cross-country skiers point themselves across frosty fields in winter. The southern edge of Gippsland is dominated by one of Australia's best-known national parks – Wilsons Promontory, a granite-peaked continental appendage that gives campers the chance to sleep at the edge of utterly beautiful ocean coves and bays.

The northern reaches of Gippsland are a picturesque collage of quiet forests, still lakes and low-slung mountain ranges. Bunyip State Park has a clutch of fine camping spots embedded in rainforest and stands of mountain ash – the area is named after a legendary critter that doesn't tolerate any wrongdoing, so campers should be on their best behaviour here. Other regional forests that offer shady places for sojourns include Tanjil and Boola Boola. An added attraction of the latter is that it's close to the Walhalla Historic Area, a fascinating repository of goldmining relics and prospecting tales. Directly north of here is Mount Baw Baw, where the cross-country crowd are followed by wildflower fanciers and the thrill-seekers who go whitewater rafting down the Thomson River.

The Gippsland coastline east of Phillip Island jags its way around pretty locales like Venus Bay and Cape Liptrap, the rugged shoreline giving surfers plenty of waves. Further east are Shallow Inlet and Nooramunga, a pair of coastal parks where you can strand yourself on sand islands and practise your surf-fishing technique. Between them are the outstanding wilds of Wilsons Promontory. Walk down the length of the promontory to the elements-battered lighthouse at its southern tip, clamber up through tea-tree thickets to Norman Point to spy the islands of the adjacent marine park, and sit on a deserted beach at night to count the stars.

CAMPSITES LOCATED IN PARKS AND RESERVES

BAW BAW NATIONAL PARK

The mountainous, sub-alpine environment of Baw Baw National Park offers stunning views, invigorating bushwalking and excellent cross-country skiing. Wildflowers delight visitors in summer, while in winter it's the snowy woodlands that create some chilly magic. The park is near Rawson, about 40 km north from Moe. Access roads branch off the Thomson Valley Rd north of Erica.

Who to contact: Parks Victoria 13 1963

56 **Aberfeldy River camping area**

Located up in the north-eastern arm of Baw Baw National Park, the Aberfeldy River camping area is close to where you'll find some of Victoria's best whitewater rafting: on the Thomson River downstream from the Thomson Dam. For great views of the valley that the Aberfeldy River has carved out for itself, climb up

to the top of Mt St Gwinear. This campground is 17 km north of Walhalla, off the Walhalla–Aberfeldy Rd. **Map refs:** 111 E3, 189 I5

57 **Baw Baw Plateau camping area (walk-in camping)**

The long-distance Australian Alps Walking Track that traverses the grand landscape between Walhalla and the ACT passes through the far north of the national park. Using this means of access, you can go bush camping in this picturesque area. Talk to the ranger if you're interested in camping here. A 2-night limit will likely apply to your stay. **Map refs:** 111 D3, 188 H5

58 **Eastern Tyers camping area (walk-in camping)**

This walk-in camping area in the extreme south of the national park is the first overnight stop for intrepid hikers coming down the long-distance Australian Alps Walking Track from Walhalla. There's a horseriding track nearby along the old tramway that shadows Thomson Valley Rd. While you're here, keep an eye out for endangered species such as the Leadbeaters possum and Baw Baw frog. **Map refs:** 111 E3, 188 H5

BOOLA BOOLA STATE FOREST

Boola Boola State Forest is a wild arboretum to the south-east of Rawson, just below the southern edge of spectacular Baw Baw National Park. It's a one-time mining area and remnants of this activity can be glimpsed at various places, though most people come here to indulge in some isolated four-wheel driving, fishing and bushwalking. South of Rawson on the Walhalla–Tyers Rd, turn east on Walhalla Rd.

Who to contact: DSE Erica 13 6186

59 **Bruntons Bridge camping area**

This peaceful site beside the Thomson River is reached via the signposted route from Walhalla or via Bruntons Bridge Rd off Cowwarr Rd. There is ongoing work at this campsite, which includes significant road upgrades, firepits being put in and proper stone steps leading to the river. To reward yourself when you finally get here, have a refreshing swim in the river. **Map refs:** 111 E3, 189 I6

60 **Coopers Creek camping area**

This camping area (actually 2 camping areas) is sheltered within the diverse Boola Boola forest. It's accessed by conventional vehicles along Coopers Creek Track, which you'll find signposted off the Erica–Walhalla Rd. The facilities include toilets and fireplaces. Consider paying a visit to the bucolic Boola Boola Winery, where you can slurp some locally produced fruit wines and liqueurs. **Map refs:** 111 E3, 189 I6

BUNYIP STATE PARK

Just 65 km east of the Victorian capital, Bunyip provides some rural relief for over-urbanised Melbournites. The rugged bush landscape is best explored on foot or by mountain bike.

While doing so, keep a watch out for the fierce-eyed bunyip, a hirsute mythological creature that, according to Aboriginal people, is intent on punishing naughty folk. You can get here from Gembrook, which lies just outside the park's western perimeter, or turn off the Princes Fwy at Tynong North.

Who to contact: Parks Victoria 13 1963

61 Nash Creek camping area

In the heart of the park, Nash Creek has an isolated feel. It's reached via Black Snake Creek Rd, west of the junction with Bunyip River Rd. From the nearby Dyers Picnic Ground you can undertake the 17 km Dyer Circuit, which passes the impressive Four Brothers Rocks. If you're after something easier, try the Buttongrass or Mortimer nature trails in the south-western corner of the park. **Map refs:** 111 C3, 188 F5

CAPE LIPTRAP COASTAL PARK

This windswept coastal park protects a curving, slender peninsula overlooking Bass Strait. There's swimming here in sheltered coves and in body-bashing surf, as well as excellent fishing. The park, which extends from Point Smythe to Waratah Bay, is accessed from the Tarwin Lower–Waratah Rd – take the turn-off onto Cape Liptrap Rd.

Who to contact: Parks Victoria 13 1963

62 Bear Gully camping area

At the bottom of the cape, just to the east of its historic lighthouse, the Bear Gully camping area is the only overnight option in the park, its shady campsites nestling among tall banksias. From here you can rock-hop along small sheltered coves all the way to Walkerville – you'll be rewarded with fine views of the peaks and islands of Wilsons Promontory National Park. To reach the campsite from Walkerville, 10 km away, take Walkerville Rd and turn onto Bear Gully Rd. **Map refs:** 111 C7, 188 G11

INVERLOCH FORESHORE RESERVE

Sited right beside Anderson Inlet, this foreshore reserve is a great place for families, with the expansive beach and shallow water being particularly good for young kids. The reserve is accessed off The Esplanade in the town of Inverloch, 12 km east of Wonthaggi. In Inverloch itself, visit the Bunurong Environment Centre, which has information on the local environment, plus a huge shell collection.

How to book: bookings required Dec–Feb; (03) 5674 1236

63 Inverloch Foreshore Reserve camping area

Camping is available year-round at the foreshore reserve, but it does get popular. For views over the inlet, take the Screw Creek Walk which includes a boardwalk section and a trail through a paperbark forest. If you prefer waves in your water, head to nearby Venus Bay, which also has good surf-fishing. **Map refs:** 111 C6, 188 F9

MOONDARRA STATE PARK

Crowding the northern edge of the Latrobe Valley, this native forest protects significant plots of flora and the diverse fauna that shelter within it. You can explore the park at your leisure on scenic drives and bushwalks, and there are also plenty of opportunities for picnicking and mountain-biking. The park is 13 km north of Moe; the Moe–Erica Rd passes directly through the park.

Who to contact: Parks Victoria 13 1963

64 Seninis camping area

This well-shaded campground, the only one in the park, is set on the grassy banks of Tyers River. Access is from Seninis Track, which runs off the Moe–Erica Rd and leads through an area noted for a wildflower display that includes 16 species of orchid. Koalas can be spotted snoozing in tree branches here, and you can also see echidnas, bandicoots, swamp wallabies and gliders – although you'll need to have a good torch and a night-time stroll for a chance to spot most of these. **Map refs:** 111 D4, 188 H6

NOORAMUNGA MARINE AND COASTAL PARK

The Nooramunga Marine and Coastal Park lies 200 km south-east of Melbourne and is framed by the glorious, rugged peaks of Wilsons Promontory. The islands of the park provide a natural buffer for some of the Gippsland coastline from the relentless pounding of Bass Strait. Fish the network of waterways for Australian salmon or peer at old shipwreck sites. The South Gippsland Hwy provides access.

How to book: Parks Victoria 13 1963 *Permits:* camping permit required

65 Little Snake Island camping areas (boat-based camping)

Little Snake Island is closer to the Gippsland coast than its larger neighbour; it's just offshore from Port Welshpool. As with Snake Island, the only access is by boat, and a permit is needed to camp here. The campsites can be found at the Bluff in the south-western corner of the island. Don't forget to bring a lemon to flavour the snapper or King George whiting that you'll be landing on the beach. **Map refs:** 111 E6, 188 H10

66 Snake Island camping areas (boat-based camping)

The largest sand island in Victoria has 3 official places for campers: Swashway, Gulf and Huts. None has facilities, so you need to be self-sufficient. Surf-fishing and walking to the remote reaches of the island, including on an overnight hike, tempt most visitors. Access is by boat and depends on the tide – Port Welshpool has the closest boat launch. A camping permit is required. **Map refs:** 111 E6, 189 I10

REEVES BEACH COASTAL RESERVE

This small reserve's reason for existence is the fine strip of sand that wanders along the coastline 13 km south-east of the town of Woodside, and which lies at the southern end of the fantastic Ninety Mile Beach. Swim and surf fish here to your heart's content. From Woodside, follow Woodside Beach Rd, turn south on Balloong Rd and then head east on Reeves Beach Rd.

Who to contact: Parks Victoria 13 1963

67 Reeves Beach camping area

From this scenic camping area, you can walk into the sunrise along Ninety Mile Beach, the sand barrier that stops the Gippsland Lakes from becoming part of Bass Strait. At Reeves you might spot dolphins or whales frolicking offshore, or you can throw in a fishing line and land something a bit smaller. Access is via Reeves Beach Rd. **Map refs: 111 F6, 189 J9**

TANJIL STATE FOREST

Tanjil State Forest is a hilly, densely wooded tract of land where trail-bikers and those in a 4WD lose themselves on many a weekend. Bushwalkers are also attracted to the forest's peaceful isolation, while anglers make return trips to fish for trout in mountain streams. Take Telbit Rd from the Moe–Rawson Rd just south of Erica.

Who to contact: DSE Erica (03) 5165 2200, 13 6186

68 Western Tyers camping area

This camping area beside the Western Tyers River is perfectly suited to those whose idea of happiness is sitting on a riverbank in the forest waiting to see what will bite. The facilities here are limited to a picnic table and fireplace. Access to the campsites is off Western Tyers Rd, which leads off Telbit Rd. **Map refs: 111 D3, 188 H5**

THOMSON STATE FOREST

Thomson State Forest, 40 km north of Walhalla, is riddled with rough tracks that off-road vehicles and trail bikes negotiate with practised abandon. Note: it also includes a new 4WD Heritage Trail that begins in nearby Walhalla and takes in Donnelly Creek and many historic sights in the forest. The trees that have taken root here occasionally open out into expansive campsites where large groups settle around blazing fires, and local streams hold plenty of promise for keen anglers. Access is provided by Walhalla Rd, which is narrow and rarely straight.

Who to contact: DSE Erica (03) 5165 2200, 13 6186

69 Andersons camping area

Andersons is one of the smaller camping areas in Thomson State Forest (with room for 3 or 4 tents) taking up a compact plot of bushland beside the Aberfeldy River. So, if you're towing a caravan or camper trailer, head for one of the other sites scattered throughout the region. You can reach Andersons by turning onto Donnelly Creek Track from Walhalla Rd. **Map refs: 111 E2, 189 I4**

70 Jorgenson Flat camping area

Set beside Donnelly Creek, Jorgenson Flat is one of several spacious and open overnight options in Thomson State Forest – great when you don't feel like being too close to other people, or if there's a large contingent that needs to be accommodated. You'll need a 4WD to make the trip down Donnelly Creek Track from Walhalla Rd. Note: a couple of creek crossings will be involved in getting here. **Map refs: 111 E3, 189 I4**

71 The Junction camping area

A 4WD is the vehicle of choice (but not a necessity) for the enjoyable trip through the forest to the campground. The campsites are arrayed alongside the Aberfeldy River, where you can drop a fishing line or heave yourself in for a refreshing swim in the large waterhole. From Walhalla Rd, take the turning down Merringtons Track, continue for 1.3 km and then wheel onto the Junction Track. **Map refs: 111 E3, 189 I4**

72 Little O'Tooles camping area

The Little O'Tooles site is a beautiful spot right on the river, lying off Donnelly Creek Track – the turning for which is signposted off Walhalla Rd. A 4WD is required to negotiate the route here – note that this is subject to seasonal access. Swimming and fishing are the best ways in which to occupy yourself here, although snoozing under the nearest tree isn't a bad option either. **Map refs: 111 E3, 189 I4**

73 Merringtons camping area

Although a conventional vehicle can roll its way down to Merringtons, a 4WD is recommended. And if you're going to tow, make it an off-road camper trailer. This large camping area is south of Cast Iron Pot Lookout, reached by following Merringtons Track as it veers off Walhalla Rd. **Map refs: 111 E3, 189 I4**

74 O'Tooles camping area

The O'Tooles site is a large, grassy area encircled by a natural barrier of tall trees. The openness of the area is perfect for gazing up at the broad night sky and tracing the stars. This relaxing camping spot is reached via Donnelly Creek Track, which you'll find signposted off Walhalla Rd. A 4WD is needed to reach O'Tooles, and also to enjoy the surrounding network of cool forest tracks. **Map refs: 111 E3, 189 I4**

TOORONGO FALLS RESERVE

This hushed reserve contains a number of waterfalls and is a great place to toss down a picnic blanket. A couple of fine walks highlight the beauty of the forest, one of them leading to a platform looking over Toorongo Falls. Travel 8 km north-east of Noojee to get to the reserve, which can be reached by following Toorongo Falls Rd off Baw Baw Tourist Rd.

Who to contact: DSE 13 6186

75 Toorongo Falls camping area

These bushy camping sites are close to the swirling Toorongo River. They can't be booked in advance, so get here early during peak holiday periods. A walking track bends about 1.5 km north-east from the camping area to the falls. If your legs need more of a workout, you can continue north to the Amphitheatre Falls. The Toorongo Falls Rd will get you here. **Map refs:** 111 D3, 188 G5

WALKERVILLE FORESHORE RESERVE

In the shadow of Wilsons Promontory's hulking peaks lies Walkerville Foreshore Reserve, which stretches languidly along the shore of Waratah Bay. It has a fabulous coastal perspective, and there's good swimming in the bay's sheltered waters. The reserve is 30 km south-west of Foster and is reached via the Walkerville–Fish Creek Rd.

How to book: 1 Loop Rd, Walkerville North (03) 5663 2224

76 Walkerville camping area

Popular with many families who return year after year, this camping reserve has great facilities and is kept neat and tidy by the staff. Close by are surf beaches for adults, as well as safe beaches for kids. Walking tracks give a sense of the area's history, including a visit to an old lime kiln at Walkerville South. **Map refs:** 111 C7, 188 G10

WILSONS PROMONTORY NATIONAL PARK

The hook of land that is mainland Australia's most southerly point is also one of the most enchanting wilderness regions you could wish for. Half the park is still recovering from a bushfire early in 2009, but that hasn't deterred visitors from funnelling through Tidal River to bushwalk across rainforests, heathlands and golden dunes, all the while gazing up at the park's granite heights or towards an oceanic horizon. Potoroos, koalas, wombats and damselflies keep visitors company as they explore the area. Access is via Wilsons Promontory Rd from Fish Creek. A 2-night maximum stay applies to all walk-in campsites. There are day walks, visitor sites and overnight hikes that remain closed since flooding in early 2011 – check the current situation with Parks Victoria.

Who to contact: Parks Victoria 13 1963

77 Barry Creek camping area (walk-in camping)

As with the other campsites around the national park, you can't stay at the Barry Creek camping area for more than 2 nights. From the carpark on Five Mile Rd, which leads east off Wilsons Promontory Rd, it's a walk of 6.2 km to Barry Creek. Along the way, take the easy detour up to the Vereker Lookout for some fine views of the surrounding wilderness. **Map refs:** 111 D7, 188 H11

78 Five Mile Beach camping area (walk-in camping)

Five Mile Beach arrows along the eastern coast of Wilsons Promontory between Monkey Point and the headland that hides gorgeous Sealers Cove. This generous sweep of sand is a great place to go beachcombing, swimming or just nap while the ocean laps the shore. The camping area is a 16.7 km hike from the Five Mile Rd carpark, accessed off Wilsons Promontory Rd. **Map refs:** 111 D7, 188 H11

79 Halfway Hut camping area (walk-in camping)

Walkers keen on getting to the lighthouse perched on the south-eastern tip of the promontory stride down Telegraph Track from Telegraph Saddle and stop for a breather after 7 km at Halfway Hut. Along the way, some choose to detour east to Waterloo Bay for a refreshing dip. From the hut, it's another 4.5 km to Roaring Meg camping area. **Map refs:** 111 D8, 188 H12

80 Little Waterloo Bay camping area (walk-in camping)

The campsites at Little Waterloo Bay are within easy reach of the beautiful, sheltered stretch of water between Cape Wellington and Waterloo Point, with Mt Wilson as a backdrop to the west. The track leading here from Refuge Cove is 7 km in length and has some taxing sections, so stock up on rest before you tackle it. **Map refs:** 111 D7, 188 H12

81 Lower Barry Creek camping area (walk-in camping)

From the Five Mile Rd carpark, you'll need to walk for 9.7 km to reach Lower Barry Creek – the route leads east down Five Mile Rd before branching north on a separate trail that starts just to the west of Barry Creek. Lower Barry Creek is a serene streamside camping spot. **Map refs:** 111 D7, 188 H11

82 Oberon Bay camping area (walk-in camping)

Oberon Bay is just around Norman Point from Tidal River, and makes a wonderful introduction to camping on the promontory. You can reach Oberon by walking south from Telegraph Saddle down Telegraph Track and then taking another track west to the bay – a distance of around 17 km. You can also walk here directly from Tidal River, which involves a mixture of walking trails and plodding along pristine beaches.

The coastal route from Tidal River makes a good day walk, even if you are not camping overnight. The views from Norman Point are striking, and the huge granite boulders covered in bright orange lichen at Little Oberon Bay are fantastic photographic subjects, as are the white sand and clear turquoise waters. **Map refs:** 111 D7, 188 H12

Bush camping in Wilsons Promontory National Park (p. 115)

83 Refuge Cove camping area (walk-in camping)

Refuge Cove is around Horn Point from the equally sublime Sealers Cove. There's a fine lookout just south of here up Kersop Peak on Cape Wellington. The 6.4 km trail from Sealers down to the camping area at the southern end of Refuge Cove is a relatively undemanding hike that exposes walkers to some great coastal scenery. **Map refs:** 111 D7, 188 H12

84 Roaring Meg camping area (walk-in camping)

Roaring Meg is the southernmost camping area in Wilsons Promontory National Park, a 4.5 km walk down Telegraph Track from Halfway Hut. From here, you can veer south-west to have a squiz at the rough coastline around South Point, or head south-east to the historic lighthouse built on South East Point in 1859. It's possible to stay overnight in the lighthouse's restored cottages; bookings are essential. **Map refs:** 111 D8, 188 H12

85 Sealers Cove camping area (walk-in camping)

From the carpark at Telegraph Saddle, it's a hike of just over 10 km past the Wilson Range to reach magical Sealers Cove, nestled on the eastern coast of the promontory. Before you set out, follow the steep 3.4 km track to the top of Mt Oberon for a grand panorama of the national park and the ocean that cradles it. **Map refs:** 111 D7, 188 H12

86 Tidal River camping area

Tidal River, at the end of Wilsons Promontory Rd, is a large, well-equipped campground back behind the dunes of stunning Norman Bay. There are myriad short walks you can do in the area, including the Lilly Pilly Gully Nature Walk and the stroll alongside the tannin-stained Tidal River. Watch the sun set over the ocean from Norman Lookout. Note: a ballot is used to allocate campsites from the week before Christmas to the end of January.

Visit outside of peak times if you're hoping to find a site with a bit of privacy in this large campsite. With all facilities available, including hot showers and a kiosk, a few days here is recommended to explore the many bays and beaches. Coastal tracks from here give access to Whisky Bay to the north and Little Oberon Bay and beyond, to the south. **Map refs:** 111 D7, 188 H12

87 Tin Mine Cove camping area (walk-in camping)

Tin Mine Cove is at the north-eastern tip of Wilsons Promontory, west of Mt Hunter. It requires 11 km of very difficult walking to get here from Lower Barry Creek. Have a swim in Corner Inlet or at the nearby Chinaman Long Beach, or just sit still and enjoy the isolation in this remote neck of the national park. **Map refs:** 111 D7, 188 H10

WON WRON STATE FOREST

The Won Wron State Forest is flush with yellow stringybark, while a variety of gums crowd into the area's damp gullies. A scenic driving circuit takes you past remnants of the region's logging history, such as sawmills and pits, fire towers and a tramway bridge. Situated 15 km north of Yarram, the forest is accessed from the South Gippsland or Hyland hwys.

Who to contact: DSE Yarram (03) 5183 9100, 13 6186

88 White Womans Waterhole camping area

This is a large, shady area and the only place in the forest where you can camp. Several walks radiate out from this site: the White Womans Walk highlights the diverse vegetation, while the Old Railway Walk retraces what was once part of the Great Southern Railway. According to local legend, the waterhole got its name from the single survivor of a shipwreck off Ninety Mile Beach, who was subsequently cared for by local Aboriginal people. Access to the camping area is signposted off Napier Rd (Won Wron Rd), reached via Carrajung Rd, which is south from Woodside. **Map refs:** 111 E5, 189 J9

YARRA STATE FOREST

The mighty mountain ash trees swaying gently in the breeze are a big drawcard for visitors to Yarra State Forest, located 75 km east of Melbourne via the Eastern Fwy. Walking trails reveal waterfalls and the majesty of the local tree line, and show the route of an old logging-industry tramline. From Yarra Junction or Warburton, drive into the forest to Powelltown.

Who to contact: DSE Powelltown (03) 5965 9900, 13 6186

89 Ada No. 2 Mill camping area (walk-in camping)

Tucked away deep in the forest, this is a walk-in bush-camping spot on the 33 km, 2-day Walk into History Trail that leads from Warburton to Powelltown. The section of the track heading from the mill up to Highlead carpark is the most difficult part of the walk, and you'll see evidence of past bushfires that have swept through this region. The Highlead carpark is accessed off the Noojee–Powelltown Rd. **Map refs:** 111 C3, 188 F5

90 Federal Mill camping area (walk-in camping)

Like Ada No. 2 Mill, Federal Mill is an overnight camping option for hikers who are tackling all or part of the Walk into History Trail between Powelltown and Warburton. It's not far south of the soaring, 300-year-old Ada Tree, which sits in myrtle beech rainforest. The Federal Mill site is accessed from the Highlead carpark up on the Noojee–Powelltown Rd. **Map refs:** 111 C3, 188 F5

91 Latrobe River camping area

This camping area is sited next to the Latrobe River in the south of the park. If you find the surrounding mountain ash mesmerising, make sure you hunt out the sky-scraping Ada Tree,

a real giant – one of the largest trees in the state. The Latrobe River camping area is located on Ada River Rd, via the Noojee–Powelltown Rd. **Map refs:** 111 C3, 188 G5

92 Starlings Gap camping area

Starlings Gap is in the path of 2 excellent forest walking tracks, with the 9 km walk to Big Pats Picnic Area, which follows the 1933 federal tramway, arguably the highlight. In the camping area itself, take a look at the old winch and boiler, 200 m past the toilet block. From the Yarra Junction–Noojee Rd take the signposted Black Sands Rd and then Big Creek Rd to reach Starlings Gap. **Map refs:** 111 C3, 188 F5

CAMPSITES LOCATED IN OTHER AREAS

93 Hawthorn Bridge camping area

Hawthorn Bridge, which was recently rebuilt, crosses the Latrobe River some 25 km north-east of Neerim South. You can camp on either side of the bridge site to make the most of the swimming and fishing on offer. Get there by following Neerim East Rd from Neerim South, and then taking Latrobe River Rd. **Map refs:** 111 D3, 188 G6

Who to contact: DSE 13 6186

94 Kilcunda Oceanview Holiday Retreat

Dramatic coastal views are the norm at this quiet beachside caravan park, located between Wonthaggi and San Remo. The beaches here are safe for kids, plus there are good spots for a snorkel and plenty of walking options, including the winding George Bass Coastal Trail. If you need some elevation to better enjoy the stunning views, try your luck at hang-gliding from the nearby cliffs. For those more interested in nature, make your way over to nearby Phillip Island for the famous penguin parade. **Map refs:** 111 B5, 188 E9

How to book: 3560 Bass Hwy, Kilcunda (03) 5678 7260 www.kilcundaoceanview.com.au

95 Lake Narracan Caravan Park

When its water levels are high enough, Lake Narracan, 5 km north-east of Moe, is a popular watersports venue. Besides sailing and canoeing, waterskiing is also conducted here under the auspices of what's believed to be Australia's oldest waterskiing club. The lake's caravan park is on North Moe Rd. **Map refs:** 111 D4, 188 H7

How to book: bookings required for peak periods; South Shaw Rd, Moe (03) 5127 8724

96 Loch Valley (The Poplars) camping area

Loch Valley is a peaceful spot to the north of Noojee, a small town between Yarra Junction and Baw Baw National Park. About 7 km from Noojee and accessed via Henty St from Powelltown Rd, which leads off Bennett St, you'll find dispersed bush camping beside the Loch River. An old logging company tramway used to run between Noojee and Loch Valley, and the first few kilometres have been turned into a fine walk through stands of tall trees and ferns. Closed mid-June to end-Oct.
Map refs: 111 D3, 188 G5

Who to contact: DSE 13 6186

97 Middle Creek camping area (bush camping)

From the small town of Yinnar, south of the Strzelecki Hwy, get onto Middle Creek Rd and follow it for 10 km to the south-east. Here, at a secluded spot beside Middle Creek, you'll find a small bush-camping area with no facilities. One reason for trying this place out is that you may want to use it as a base to visit nearby Morwell National Park, a beautiful region in the Strzelecki Ranges where no camping is permitted. **Map refs:** 111 D5, 188 H8

Who to contact: Parks Victoria 13 1963

98 Morwell River camping areas

Blackfish, trout and crayfish are the prime targets for anglers when they set themselves up along the banks of the Morwell River. If you're a like-minded soul, head for one of the campsites strung out along Morwell River Rd about 5 km south-east of Boolarra. If you're planning to come here in Feb, try to make your trip coincide with the annual and mightily popular Boolarra Folk Festival. **Map refs:** 111 D5, 188 H8

Who to contact: Parks Victoria 13 1963

99 Shallow Inlet camping area

This campground is 4 km west of Yanakie at the end of Lester Rd, just outside the boundary of the marvellous Shallow Inlet Marine and Coastal Park. The sheltered waters of the park are ideal for swimming, canoeing and fishing – catch some King George whiting or watch migratory birds doing their own spot of trawling. Note: the campground is only open Nov–Easter.
Map refs: 111 D6, 188 G10

Who to contact: (03) 5687 1365

100 Turtons Creek camping area

You can camp without facilities beside Turtons Creek about 18 km north of Foster. Near the campsite, reached via Turtons Creek Rd, which branches off the Boolarra–Foster Rd, you'll find a lovely little waterfall framed by ferns and eucalypts. There are lots of animals in the surrounding bush, and the creek yields trout and eels. **Map refs:** 111 D5, 188 H9

Who to contact: Parks Victoria 13 1963

Upper Goulburn Historic Area

From the town of Jamieson, the Goulburn River makes several sweeping turns on its way south past Woods Point. This was where the second of Victoria's gold rushes took place, and its history is now contained within the Upper Goulburn Historic Area. One-time mining settlements, eerie cemeteries and numerous historic buildings await visitors, who can also indulge in recreational fossicking and canoeing. Note: new and improved facilities, including fireplaces, picnic tables and toilets, were due to be installed at many of the campsites in late 2012. Call the DSE for the latest updates on this. Access to points of interest is via the Mansfield–Woods Point Rd.

Who to contact: Mansfield DSE (03) 5733 1200

101 Blue Hole camping area

As suggested by the name, swimming is the primary attraction at this campsite, while fishing is another popular distraction. There are pit toilets here but no other facilities – if you're going to draw drinking water from the river, boil or treat it before consuming it. Another in the string of camping options accessible from the Mansfield–Woods Point Rd, Blue Hole is 1 km south of the Twelve Mile camping area. **Map refs:** 111 D1, 188 H2

102 Comet Flat camping area

Comet Flat is stretched out along a riverbank about 4 km south-east of Woods Point. A 4WD is recommended to access the camping area from that township – take the Johnson Hill Track. Swimming and fishing are the main activities here, and there's also bushwalking in the area. On chilly nights, toast your toes and some marshmallows by an open fire. **Map refs:** 111 D2, 188 H3

103 Doctors Creek camping area

This is one of many camping reserves in the upper Goulburn River area. It's only 4 km south of Jamieson, off the Mansfield–Woods Point Rd, which is great for history buffs who want to check out the township's heritage-listed courthouse and get information on the disused goldmines in the region. Its proximity to town, however, may see its dozen or so campsites snapped up quickly during holiday periods. **Map refs:** 111 D1, 188 H2, 190 H12

104 Gaffneys Creek camping area

This reserve is 37 km south of Jamieson, with the entry point along the Mansfield–Woods Point Rd. There's fishing in the river and picnic tables for dining. The nearby Lauraville settlement site is where gold was first discovered in the region in 1859. Historic dwellings and other remnants of this mining-era town pepper the local hills. **Map refs:** 111 D1, 188 H3

105 Picnic Point camping area

Once again, the name pretty much says it all. Fresh fish plucked from the river could be the perfect addition to your picnic basket. And if it's hot, a dip is a great way to cool off. If you prefer the excitement of gold prospecting, try sifting the sand that blankets the riverbed. This camping reserve is located 2 km south of Blue Hole and is similarly accessed from the Mansfield–Woods Point Rd. **Map refs:** 111 D1, 188 H2

106 Scotts camping area

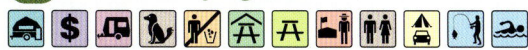

The Mansfield–Woods Point Rd provides access to this camping area, which lies just 2 km north-west of Woods Point. It has 40 campsites, shaded picnic tables for those inevitable hot days, and an adjacent river in which to cool down. The nearby town of Woods Point and the surrounding area retain some historical facades from their long association with goldmining, dating back to 1862, including the hotel and local store. **Map refs:** 111 D2, 188 H3

107 Skipworth camping area

Skipworth is the largest of the camping areas that dot the Upper Goulburn Historic Area, hosting around 50 campsites and related amenities. It's also one of several places run by local management committees, who charge a small camping fee to help cover their activities – fees are usually collected by volunteers on-site. It's located about 7 km from Jamieson down the Mansfield–Woods Point Rd. **Map refs:** 111 D1, 188 H2

108 Snakes camping area

Although it may not have the most comforting name, this is an appealingly spacious campground that's spread out on the riverbank about 26 km south of Jamieson, off the Mansfield–Woods Point Rd. Take one of the walks winding through the Upper Goulburn Historic Area, which include sections of the Australian Alps Walking Track and treks past old mine sites and through former settlements. **Map refs:** 111 D1, 188 H2

109 Tunnel Bend camping area

This camping spot, hosting around 20 sites, is 19 km south of Jamieson via the Mansfield–Woods Point Rd. The significance of the area centres on a water-diversion tunnel, now a historic relic, that was fashioned so that the old river bed here could be mined. The settlement of Ten Mile, established in the 19th century, used to be close but was destroyed by the fierce bushfires of 1939. **Map refs:** 111 D1, 188 H2

110 Twelve Mile camping area

With only 10 campsites, Twelve Mile affords peaceful riverside camping. Floating down the Goulburn River in a canoe is a good way to get around, and trout are fun to catch (and even better to eat) if you want to throw in a line. This relaxing place is a bit further on from Tunnel Bend, and 20 km from Jamieson, and is also accessed via the Mansfield–Woods Point Rd. **Map refs:** 111 D1, 188 H2

Walhalla Historic Area

Exploration of the historic goldmining town of Walhalla, 184 km east of Melbourne, reveals fascinating buildings as well as old tramways, mines and tunnels, all of which are best discovered on foot. Just in case you're tempted by a long walk, Walhalla is also the start of the 650 km Australian Alps Walking Track to the ACT. From Moe on the Princes Hwy, head north to Rawson and then go east on Walhalla Rd.

Who to contact: Parks Victoria 13 1963

111 North Gardens camping area

North Gardens is located in the history-ridden centre of Walhalla township on Stringer Creek. This campground was once the end of a tramway used to bring timber fuel to the mines. It has limited space for vans and camper trailers; so, if you're towing, get here early during peak holiday periods. A signposted walking track leading from North Gardens provides some good views of the town. **Map refs:** 111 E3, 189 I5

EAST GIPPSLAND

EAST GIPPSLAND IS FRAMED in the south by the gentle arc of Ninety Mile Beach and in the north by the fabulous peaks and gorges of the Snowy River and Mitchell River national parks. At the midpoint of the region's sandy coastline is the bustling holiday town of Lakes Entrance, perfectly positioned to make the most of the grand ocean beach that soaks up the energetic swells of Bass Strait. West of Lakes Entrance is Gippsland Lakes Coastal Park, where you can camp among the sand dunes of Ninety Mile Beach or plant yourself on the shoreline of peaceful Lake Victoria. If you have a boat, you'll want to explore the extremity of Bunga Arm, where no access roads intrude.

Wedged into the far south-eastern corner of Victoria is a gorgeous strip of forested coastline shared between Cape Conran Coastal Park and Croajingolong National Park. The rockpools and sands of Cape Conran are paradise for beachcombers, while Croajingolong has undisturbed wetlands and inlets, and some of the best remote campsites in the state. Another grand national park, Mitchell River, lies to the north of Bairnsdale. Walkers can spend several days following the contours of the river through a series of deep gorges, taking breaks to camp on isolated riverbends and splash around in the cool water.

Up towards the NSW border is the marvellous wilderness region negotiated by the landmark Snowy River. Paddle a canoe or raft down stretches of this magical waterway – McKillops Bridge is a favoured starting point for such excursions – or just pitch a tent in peaceful bushland occupied by rock wallabies and lyrebirds. At the southern tip of the national park are the spectacular Buchan Caves, where you can gaze at surreal limestone sculptures and swim in the outflow of underground springs before retiring to your tent or campervan.

CAMPSITES LOCATED IN PARKS AND RESERVES

AVON–MOUNT HEDRICK SCENIC RESERVE

The forests of the 5700 ha Avon–Mount Hedrick Reserve, 20 km north-west of Maffra, are fed by the lovely Avon River and contain abundant wildlife, including grey kangaroos, sugar gliders, water dragons and tawny frogmouth owls. Take long walks along the river's rocky channel, or have an extended picnic among the eucalypts. From Maffra, head to Boisdale. Three km past the town, turn onto Luckmans Rd, north onto the Warrigal–Tom Rd, then follow the signs.

Who to contact: DSE Heyfield (03) 5139 7777, 13 6186

112 Dermody Camp camping area

Dermody Camp is in the north-eastern section of Avon–Mt Hendrick Scenic Reserve and offers campers flat sites next to easy swimming in the Avon River. From here you can walk

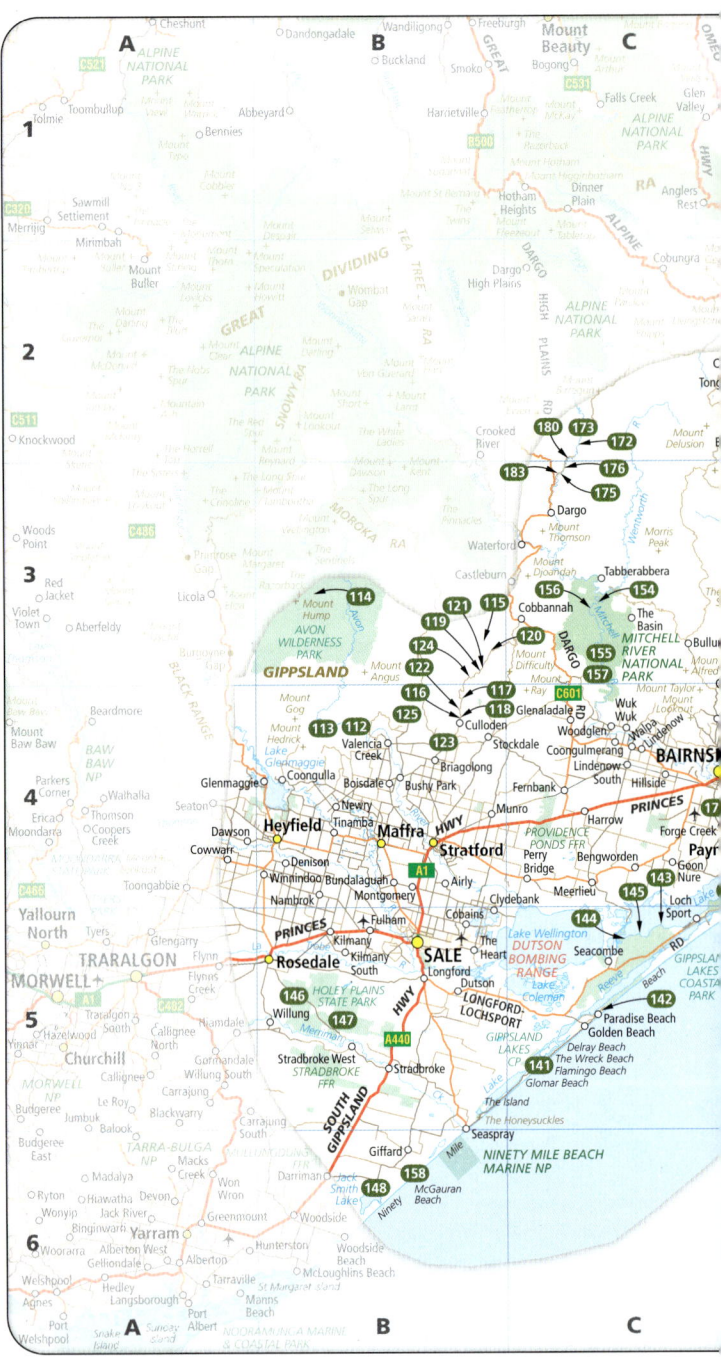

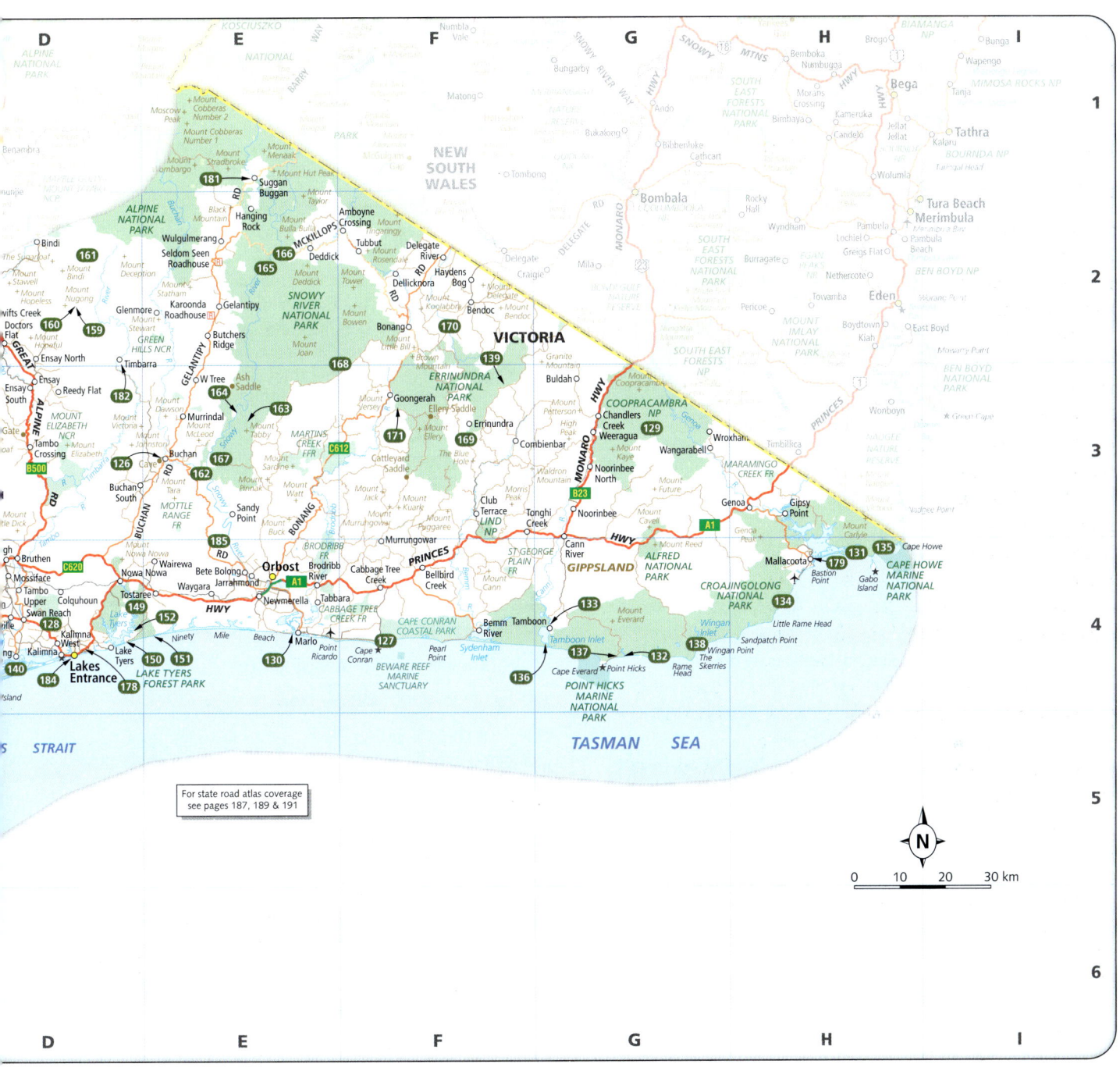

For state road atlas coverage
see pages 187, 189 & 191

N

0   10   20   30 km

westwards for 9 km along the Avon River Trail to Huggetts Crossing. Take Dermody Rd off the Warrigal–Tom Rd to reach this peaceful, shady spot. **Map refs:** 120 B4, 189 K5

113 Huggetts Crossing camping area

This camping area is at the western edge of the reserve, and is connected to Dermody Camp by the enchanting Avon River Trail. South of here you can get superb forest views from the Green Hill and Huggett lookouts, or head further south to Bulldog Junction to do the walk up to the picturesque summit of Mt Hendrick. Huggetts can only be accessed with a 4WD from Green Hill via the Huggett–Mt Angus Track. **Map refs:** 120 B4, 189 J5

AVON WILDERNESS PARK

Avon Wilderness Park is a vast, undisturbed wonderland of forest-smothered ranges, just the place for adventurous bushwalkers to get right away from any beaten tracks. There are no facilities here and no vehicle access, just pristine wilderness to tramp through on your own. The park is 40 km north of Heyfield.

Who to contact: Parks Victoria 13 1963

114 Avon Wilderness camping area (walk-in camping)

Only fit and experienced hikers should attempt to go bush camping in this area. Talk to the ranger about the lie of the land, and don't forget to register before you set out on your hike. You can reach the perimeter of the park via Mt Margaret Track off Licola Rd, or Mt Wellington Track off Moroka Rd. **Map refs:** 120 B3, 189 J4

BRIAGOLONG STATE FOREST

Delightful Briagolong State Forest is 15 km north of the town of Stratford – which is on the Avon River, of course. It was once filled with excitable gold prospectors and is now a magnet for nature-struck bushwalkers and picnickers. Signposted off the tracks that squirm through the forest are numerous pleasant campsites. Take Briagolong Rd north from Stratford, which is on the Princes Hwy.

Who to contact: DSE Heyfield (03) 5139 7777, 13 6186
Camping fees: fees charged for campsite no. **123** only, payable at the Briagolong store

115 Alistair Fieldings camping area

This camping area is accessed via Lee Creek Track from the Lee Creek camping area on Freestone Creek Rd. This route is only accessible by 4WD. Besides enjoying some splendid isolation, you can take the 3 km return Alistair Fielding Walking Track (named after a park ranger who was based at Briagolong), past remnants of 1890s gold diggings and settlements. **Map refs:** 120 B3, 189 K4

116 Blue Pool camping area

Blue Pool is a fantastic, deep swimming hole in a gorge on Freestone Creek, and one of the most popular spots in the state forest on a hot day. After your swim, you can walk a couple of hundred metres to a lookout over the creek, or stroll through a cheery fern gully. Blue Pool is 10 km north of Briagolong off Freestone Creek Rd. Note: this is the only campground in the forest that has a toilet. **Map refs:** 120 B4, 189 K5

117 Carney Creek camping area

Carney Creek is a small camping area signposted off Freestone Creek Rd just to the north of McKinnon Point. When you've had your fill of swimming in the creek, why not drive or hike up to the lookout on nearby Mt Moornapa, which overlooks an adjacent flora reserve. Note: there are no facilities at Carney Creek. **Map refs:** 120 B4, 189 K5

118 Froam camping area

The Froam camping area is 500 m beyond Blue Pool along Freestone Creek Rd, close enough that you can make the most of the popular swimming hole, as well as the engaging walks that radiate out from it. That said, Froam is also beside Freestone Creek, so you can just stay put and throw yourself into the creek here. **Map refs:** 120 B4, 189 K5

119 Johnstones Flat camping area

Only 1 km north of Shadys Place, and a full 20 km from Briagolong, is Johnstones Flat. It's one of a clutch of camping areas huddled around this section of Freestone Creek. The facilities at Johnstones Flat are limited to picnic tables and fireplaces – bring the necessary wood and water with you. **Map refs:** 120 B3, 189 K4

120 Lee Creek camping area

Confusingly, the Lee Creek camping area is beside Sportsman Creek on Freestone Creek Rd. The Lee Creek area was the focus of intensive alluvial goldmining during the last decade of the 19th century, and it's worth heading over to Alistair Fieldings to do a walking tour of old water races, dams and housing sites. This campground is 28 km north of Briagolong. **Map refs:** 120 B3, 189 L4

121 Lloyd Knob camping area

With the trickle of Winkie Creek to the east, this campsite is named for the rocky Lloyd Knob to the west. As with the area's other camping spots, the centrepiece is still the lovely Freestone Creek, which veers off to the south-west at this stage of its journey. **Map refs:** 120 B3, 189 K4

122 McKinnon Point camping area

Between the Froam and Carney Creek camping areas sits McKinnon Point, some 14 km north of Briagolong along Freestone Creek Rd. If you feel like disappearing on a long walk into the gums and stringybarks, consider following some or all of the 60 km of trails that make up Track 96, named after an old miner's track and which begins just north of Blue Pool. **Map refs:** 120 B4, 189 K5

123 The Quarries camping area

The gravel Freestone Creek Rd slices roughly north-south through Briagolong State Forest, and it's off this thin thoroughfare that the majority of the forest's campgrounds lie. The first one you reach when heading north from Briagolong is the Quarries, a favourite local swimming spot and the only camping area in the forest for which a fee is charged. **Map refs:** 120 B4, 189 K5

124 Shadys Place camping area

Shadys Place camping area is 19 km north of Briagolong along Freestone Creek Rd. During the day, try to spot some of the dozens of bird species that live in the forest; at night, when you're stretched out beside the campfire, listen to the frog calls that fill the evening air. Cyclists will sometimes pedal through here on their way to or from Dargo. **Map refs:** 120 B3, 189 K5

125 Valencia Creek camping area

On the other side of Briagolong State Forest from Freestone Creek is the equally fetching Valencia Creek. Alongside this waterway, 8 km north of tiny Valencia Creek township and reached via the Valencia Creek–Morgan Rd, you'll find a good, quiet spot to set up camp for the night. **Map refs:** 120 B4, 189 K5

BUCHAN CAVES RESERVE

The sublime formations in the Buchan Caves were formed by rainwater seeping down through the limestone and depositing calcite, which progressively built up – it's amazing to see what can be achieved with a leaky roof. These famous caves are adjacent to Buchan township and are a hugely popular destination. Motor down Buchan Road from town to reach them.

How to book: bookings essential during peak periods; Parks Victoria 13 1963

126 Buchan Caves camping area

A fantastic subterranean world is only one of the attractions in the Buchan Caves Reserve. Here you'll also find a swimming pool fed by an underground stream, an informative display in the visitor centre, and lots of kangaroos, lyrebirds and owls. Cave tours are conducted daily except on Christmas Day. **Map refs:** 121 E3, 187 A10, 189 O4

CAPE CONRAN COASTAL PARK

This coastal park contains nearly 12 000 ha of banksia woodlands and heathlands, plus some lovely rough-sea beaches. Swimming, fishing, beach bumming and wading through rockpools will all occupy you here. The main access road extends 19 km east from Marlo, but you can also reach the park via interlinked tracks that head south from the Princes Hwy.

Who to contact: bookings by ballot at Christmas, and advance bookings advisable during other peak periods; Cape Conran Coastal Park Cabins and Camping (03) 5154 8438

127 Banksia Bluff camping area

Banksia Bluff is the campground at Cape Conran, where over 60 km of Bass Strait beaches are yours to explore. Plod around the boardwalk at East Cape and follow the nature trail to Joiners Channel, or take the Heathland Walk and try to spot some local goannas. Swamp wallabies frequent the campground, and birdlife is abundant. **Map refs:** 121 F4, 187 C12

COLQUHOUN REGIONAL PARK

What's now known as Colquhoun Regional Park was traversed by the Indigenous Gunai people for thousands of years before Europeans built a tramway here in the early 20th century to transport granite to Lakes Entrance. Now cyclists and walkers cross the forest on the Gippsland Lakes Discovery Trail. It's 12 km north-west of Lakes Entrance, and accessed off the Princes Hwy via Log Crossing Rd.

Who to contact: DSE Bairnsdale (03) 5152 0600, 13 6186

128 Colquhoun camping area (bush camping)

While enjoying the dispersed bush camping available around the forest, campers can familiarise themselves with forest bats, tree goannas, lyrebirds and koalas. The Forest Discovery Drive takes you past such historical highlights as the enormous, century-old Stony Creek Trestle Bridge and Costicks Weir. There are toilets at the trestle bridge and the Log Crossing picnic area. **Map refs:** 121 D4, 189 N5

COOPRACAMBRA NATIONAL PARK

In the isolated far east of Victoria, 30 km north of Cann River, lies Coopracambra National Park. Beehive Falls and the red sandstone gorge carved out by the Genoa River are two of the park's standout attractions, along with enormous grey box trees, brilliant wildflowers and a sense of nature at its most pristine. The Monaro Hwy is the park's main access route.

Who to contact: Parks Victoria 13 1963

129 Coopracambra camping area (bush camping)

Bush camping in Coopracambra is an option for hikers or those steering 4WD vehicles. Experienced walkers literally go wild here, navigating their way up Mt Denmarsh and Mt Kaye, and stepping off the tracks to see what they can find. Note: the nearest facilities are in Cann River, so make sure

you're well-equipped to spend a night or more in the wild.
Map refs: 121 G3, 187 F9

CORRINGLE FORESHORE RESERVE

Set amidst knotted tea-trees at the mouth of the Snowy River, 18 km south of Newmerella, you can go surf-fishing in Bass Strait here and scramble along the foreshore opposite Marlo township, or take a boat back up the Snowy to Lake Corringle. To get here from Newmerella, take Corringle Rd from the Princes Hwy.

Who to contact: advance bookings are necessary at Christmas and Easter; Parks Victoria 13 1963

130 Corringle Slips camping area

These restful beachside campsites are in particularly great demand over Christmas and Easter, and it's worth calling the ranger to check availability at other times. You can go boating and canoeing in the Snowy backwater and in Frenchs Narrows. Note: taking a dip at Corringle's ocean beach is not recommended due to the strong rips. **Map refs:** 121 E4, 187 B11

CROAJINGOLONG NATIONAL PARK

Beautifully remote Croajingolong National Park stretches for 100 km along Victoria's untamed south-eastern coastline. The only disturbance at the beaches here is the tide, and the glassy inlets provide superb canoeing. Walkers will enjoy seeing the waterbirds that thrive in the wetlands and the wildlife that roams in the soaring forests. You can reach the park from Mallacoota or via a number of tracks leading south of the Princes Hwy; check conditions after heavy rain.

How to book: bookings for campsite nos **132**, **137** necessary late Dec–Jan and Easter, through the Point Hicks Light Station office (03) 5158 4268; bookings for campsite nos **133**, **134**, **138** by ballot at Christmas and Easter; Parks Victoria Mallacoota (03) 5161 9500, 13 1963

131 Lake Barracoota camping area (bush camping)

Designated bush-camping site for self-sufficient walkers only. Gas/fuel stove preferred. **Map refs:** 121 H4, 187 H11

132 Mueller Inlet camping area

There are 8 campsites at Mueller Inlet, sheltered by heath-covered sand dunes; 3 of these are reached on foot from the carpark. No open fires are allowed to be lit here. For a good 4WD excursion, take the nearby Cicada Trail. Get to Mueller Inlet by following Tamboon Rd from the Princes Hwy and turning onto Point Hicks Rd and finally Bald Hills Track. Note: the gravel access roads may be inaccessible after heavy downpours.
Map refs: 121 G4, 187 E12

133 Peachtree Creek camping area

Peachtree Creek is one of Croajingolong's more popular camping destinations. There's good swimming in the adjacent

Tamboon Inlet, but note that the mouth of the inlet can be subject to strong currents. You can bring a caravan to Peachtree Creek, but be cautious on the rough gravel access roads. Follow Fishermans Track off Point Hicks Rd. **Map refs:** 121 G4, 187 E11

134 Shipwreck Creek camping area

Shipwreck Creek only has 5 campsites, set in forest above an isolated cove. The flat ground here makes setting up camp a breeze. Take a walk along the ocean beach and gaze out towards Gabo Island. You can also follow the 3 km trail over to Seal Creek, which is decorated with rockpools. From nearby Mallacoota, take Betka Rd and then Centre Track. **Map refs:** 121 H4, 187 G11

135 South of Cape Howe (bush camping)

Designated bush-camping site for self-sufficient walkers only. Gas/fuel stove preferred. **Map refs:** 121 H4, 187 H11

136 Tamboon Inlet camping areas
(boat-based camping)

There are a number of designated bush campsites scattered around the shoreline of Tamboon Inlet. These can only be reached by boat and, needless to say, only entirely self-sufficient campers should head out to them. Note: the islands of the inlet are used as nesting sites by various birds, and you shouldn't land on them Oct–Feb. **Map refs:** 121 G4, 187 E12

137 Thurra River camping area

The large camping area at Thurra River is in prime position for excursions to the nearby historic Point Hicks Light Station, whose tower (complete with Hitchcockian spiral staircase) was finished in 1890; you can stay in the lightkeepers' cottages. Croajingolong's rough gravel roads are mostly not conducive to towing in, but small vans will make it to Thurra River along Cape Everard Rd, which runs off Tamboon Rd. The sheltered campsites here are dispersed along the peaceful Thurra River, a perfect place for a swim, kayak or canoe. There is no tap water, so you need to bring your own. **Map refs:** 121 G4, 187 E12

138 Wingan Inlet camping area

Its beautiful sandy beaches and encircling rainforest make Wingan Inlet a wonderful place to stay. Take a walk through fern gullies to see some of Wingan River's rapids, stroll over boardwalks to Fly Cove, and traverse banksia woodland to find the (not so) Elusive Lake. Take West Wingan Rd off the Princes Hwy, but leave the caravan at home. **Map refs:** 121 G4, 187 F12

ERRINUNDRA NATIONAL PARK

The largest area of temperate rainforest in Victoria is protected within the confines of the tranquil but rugged

Camping in Croajingolong National Park (p. 124)

Errinundra National Park. Set atop a plateau about 90 km north-east of Orbost, the park has brilliant lookouts and bushwalks. Visit during the warmer times of year, as the region is often sealed off by the weather in winter. Errinundra Saddle features signs detailing the history of the park, as well as a boardwalk through cool temperate rainforest.

Who to contact: Parks Victoria 13 1963

139 Frosty Hollow camping area

Frosty Hollow is the only camping area within Errinundra National Park, although there are a couple of other sites just outside the park boundary. South of here down Hensleigh Creek Rd is Waratah Lookout, but the best views are from atop Mt Ellery in the south of the park. The star attraction, however, is the magical old forest – drive down Goonmirks Rocks Rd to see old-world mountain plum pines. Frosty Hollow is signposted off Coast Range Rd, or get here via Back Creek Rd from Bendoc. **Map refs:** 121 F3, 187 D9

GIPPSLAND LAKES COASTAL PARK

This activity-laden coastal park favours a glorious stretch of Ninety Mile Beach extending from Seaspray to Lakes Entrance. It also takes in some watersports-happy lakes. Indulge in surf fishing, beach walking and waterskiing in this highly relaxing oceanfront environment. The Longford–Loch Sport Rd will take you to the western part of the park; the lake- and sea-fringed eastern section has boat access only.

Who to contact: Parks Victoria 13 1963; Parks Victoria Bairnsdale (03) 5152 0600

140 Bunga Arm (boat-based camping)

Bunga Arm, in the road-free western part of Gippsland Lakes Coastal Park, is a spit of sand that has built up between the ocean and Lake Victoria. There are 7 designated camping areas, each with a dozen campsites and basic facilities. The sites are only accessible by boat, and you need a permit to camp here (bookable through Bairnsdale office). Keen anglers will fix their sights on mullet, flathead and skipjack, and there's also a designated waterskiing area offshore. **Map refs:** 121 D4, 189 N6

141 The Honeysuckles to Golden Beach camping areas

Numerous restful campsites are spread out among the dunes between the Honeysuckles and Golden Beach, many backed by thickets of tea-trees. Just to the west of Delray Beach you can spy the remains of the *Trinculo*, a ship that was wrecked here in 1858. Conditions are often too rough for safe swimming, but there are patrolled swimming areas nearby at Seaspray. You can access these sites by driving east along Shoreline Dr from Seaspray. Note: you can take dogs to campsites 1–6 at Golden Beach. **Map refs:** 120 C5, 189 L8

142 Paradise Beach camping area

This oceanfront camping area does resemble paradise; nonetheless, take care when swimming in the often-rough waters of Bass Strait. Behind this beach are the internationally recognised Lake Reeve wetlands, where waterfowl congregate in large numbers. Paradise Beach is one of a handful of places in the coastal park where you can bring your dog. Get here via Shoreline Dr. **Map refs:** 120 C5, 189 L7

143 Red Bluff camping area

Red Bluff is just north of Beacon Swamp at the edge of Lake Victoria. Besides going swimming or paddling out in a canoe, you can go driving or horseriding along the tracks that run riot between here and Lake Reeve – though note that you're not allowed to take your vehicle onto the lake bed when it's dry. You can reach this camping area via Lakeside Track or Track No. 10. **Map refs:** 120 C5, 189 M7

144 Spoon Bay camping area

Spoon Bay, off Lakeside Track, is on the gently curving western foreshore of Lake Victoria. The water is quite calm here, which makes it a good place to launch a canoe. You'll probably spot ringtail possums and black wallabies in the surrounding trees and undergrowth, but you're less likely to lay eyes on the rare New Holland mouse. **Map refs:** 120 C5, 189 M7

145 Thalia Point camping areas

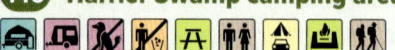

You can plant yourself in the bushland alongside Lake Victoria at Thalia Point, between the Spoon Bay and Thalia tracks. The catch is that you can only do so during the designated hunting seasons for duck, quail and deer. If this doesn't discourage you, confirm dates and requirements with the ranger. There are no facilities out here; bring your own firewood and drinking water. **Map refs:** 120 C5, 189 M7

HOLEY PLAINS STATE PARK

Holey Plains is a great place for nature lovers due to its nearly 11 000 ha of diverse vegetation and the numerous easygoing walking tracks winding through it. Wallabies, emus and a multitude of airborne birds also crowd the park's lovely environs. Holey Plains lies between the Princes and South Gippsland hwys south of Rosedale – take Limestone Quarry Rd off the Rosedale–Willung Rd.

Who to contact: Parks Victoria 13 1963

146 Harrier Swamp camping area

The short walking track around Harrier will provide a good introduction to swamp life. This low-key camping spot is at the western edge of Holey Plains State Park, and can be accessed by turning off Limestone Quarry Rd onto West Boundary Track, then onto Long Ridge Track. To see more of the park, take a scenic drive via the West Boundary, Long Ridge and Wildflower tracks. **Map refs:** 120 B5, 189 J7

147 Holey Hill camping area

Holey Hill is only 200 m high, but that's enough to make it the highpoint of this low-lying state park. While camping here you can stroll down the 1 km Banksia Forest Walking Track or take the Long Swamp Walking Track over to the area's largest marsh – this is a good place to hear the many local species of frog at full croak. From Limestone Quarry Rd, turn onto Holey Hill Track to get here. **Map refs:** 120 B5, 189 J7

JACK SMITH LAKE STATE GAME RESERVE

This game reserve is well-known to birdwatchers, who come here to marvel at the amazing variety of waterbirds that descend on the area's marshes and lagoons. Set up camp on a grassy plain and listen to the birdsong, or go surf fishing off nearby Ninety Mile Beach. Follow Stringy Bark La off the South Gippsland Hwy at Woodside; alternatively, take Middle Rd off the highway near Darriman.

Who to contact: Parks Victoria 13 1963

148 Jack Smith camping area (bush camping)

Camping in the exposed bushland around shallow Jack Smith Lake allows you to observe cormorants, swans, pelicans, teals, egrets and many other waterbirds as they pursue insects and other food around the lake; sea eagles and falcons can also be spied soaring overhead. The remnants of Aboriginal camps, dusted with charcoal and shells, lie throughout the reserve. There are no facilities in the vicinity of the lake, so come well-equipped for your stay. **Map refs:** 120 B6, 189 K9

LAKE TYERS FOREST PARK

Placid Lake Tyers is fringed with eucalypts on one side, and on the other it's separated from Bass Strait by a thin ridge of sand. Only 20 km north-east of Lakes Entrance, the lake's sheltered waters attract canoeists, anglers and swimmers, while walkers tramp cheerily through the nearby rainforest. The lake can be accessed off the Princes Hwy via Burnt Bridge Rd, 10 km north of Lakes Entrance, or Lake Tyers Rd, 6 km east of Nowa Nowa.

Who to contact: Parks Victoria 13 1963

149 Camerons Arm camping area

This is the northernmost camping area in the park, the closest to Nowa Nowa – take Lake Tyers Rd off the Princes Hwy east of the township, then turn west on Camerons Arm No. 1 Track. Canoeists can roam up and down Nowa Nowa Arm, on the lookout for azure kingfishers and herons. If you feel like a stroll, head west down the Princes Hwy to the Cherry Tree picnic area and take the pretty 2 km Tooloo Arm Walk. **Map refs:** 121 D4, 189 O5

150 Glasshouse camping area

Glasshouse is one of several camping spots east of Nowa Nowa Arm. It's on Glasshouse Beach at the southern end of Lake Tyers Rd and has no facilities to speak of – perfect for those who want to play castaway for a night. The site is named after an early 20th century factory that made glass telegraph insulators in a special furnace. **Map refs:** 121 D4, 189 O6

151 Pettmans Beach camping area

This beach is at the end of Pettman Rd, which runs off Lake Tyers Rd. This is the only camping area in Lake Tyers Forest Park that has toilets. Coupled with the fact that it's beside the ocean, this means that there's often stiff competition for the sites here, particularly from those who like surf-fishing. If you're a surfer rather than a surf-fisher, try the swells over at Red Bluff. **Map refs:** 121 E4, 187 A11, 189 O6

152 Trident Arm camping area

You'll find this tranquil spot at the end of Trident Arm Track, off Lake Tyers Rd. As with the park's other campsites, it's east of Nowa Nowa Arm – the area to the west of the arm has several decent walks, including the Lonely Bay Walk through old-growth forest. Trident Arm only has room for a couple of tents, so head here for some privacy. Check out nearby Gibbs Beach for some good surf fishing. **Map refs:** 121 D4, 189 O6

THE LAKES NATIONAL PARK

This park is a serene bushland oasis centred on Lake Victoria and Lake Reeve, and has great family-friendly walks. Rotamah Island is ideal for watching the region's prolific birdlife, and you may also spot kangaroos, swamp wallabies, possums, echidnas and wombats. Lakes National Park is 60 km east of Sale, via the Longford–Loch Sport Rd.

Who to contact: Parks Victoria 13 1963

153 Emu Bight camping area

On Sperm Whale Head, Emu Bight is the only place to camp in the Lakes park. It's 5 km east of Loch Sport, beside Lake Victoria and accessed from Lake Victoria Track; campsites must be booked in advance through Parks Victoria. Grass Tree Walking Track starts near Emu Bight and links up with other walking tracks in the south of the peninsula. It also leads to a lookout tower that provides great views over the Gippsland lakes system. **Map refs:** 120 C4, 189 M6

MITCHELL RIVER NATIONAL PARK

Mitchell River National Park is a favourite of canoeists and rafters for its centrepiece network of rocky gorges, complete with rapids. If you're a hiker who wants to stride out for a few days, hop onto the long track that follows the Mitchell River through the park's densely forested terrain. You can also confront an ancient Aboriginal story at the Den of Nargun. This national park is 25 km north-west of Bairnsdale via the Bairnsdale–Dargo Rd. Check with Parks Victoria regarding the current status of track closures within the park, often due to weather damage or upgrades.

Who to contact: Parks Victoria 13 1963

154 Angusvale camping area

Angusvale is scenically sited at the northern edge of the national park, beside the Mitchell River some 16 km east along the Mitchell Dam Rd from the junction with the Bairnsdale–Dargo Rd. From here you can follow the Mitchell River Walking Track for 18 km to the other end of the park, a hike of around 2 days. Look to the skies for peregrine falcons, swift parrots and other fascinating local birds. **Map refs:** 120 C3, 189 L4

155 Billy Goat Bend camping area

Billy Goat Bend has a spectacular curving cliff as a backdrop, and the small rapids here are a great place to test the durability of your air mattress. If you're planning on canoeing to this spot, note that the best time for a long-distance paddle is July–Dec. Those with vehicles can get here via Billy Goat Bend Rd direct from the Bairnsdale–Dargo Rd. **Map refs:** 120 C3, 189 L4

156 Rock Creek Track camping area

There are only 2 campsites at Rock Creek Track, so have a backup plan in case they're taken when you arrive. From Mitchell Dam Rd, head east on Mitchell Rd and then north-east on Angusvale Track to get here. You can also paddle a canoe here, or hike in along the walking track that follows the river. No open fires are allowed at this camping spot, so bring a gas or fuel stove with you. **Map refs:** 120 C3, 189 L4

157 Woolshed Creek camping area (walk-in camping)

Woolshed Creek is a walk-in campsite close to the southern end of the Mitchell River Walking Track. It's only a short hike from here to the deep gully that hides the Den of Nargun, a cave where a fierce ancient creature resides, according to Aboriginal legend. The Gunai/Kurnai people request that you don't enter this important Indigenous site, but simply admire it from outside. From the den, another walk leads up to the Bluff Lookout, which has views over the striking Mitchell River Gorge. **Map refs:** 120 C3, 189 L4

NINETY MILE BEACH MARINE NATIONAL PARK

This marine national park protects 2750 ha of pristine reefs and seabed off Ninety Mile Beach, which stretches north-east from Woodside towards Lakes Entrance. Included in this area of staggering marine diversity is 5 km of coastline around Lake Denison, part of which is taken up by the lovely sands of McGaurans Beach.

Who to contact: Parks Victoria 13 1963

158 McGaurans Beach camping area

McGaurans Beach is 21 km north-east of Woodside. North of the township, take Giffard Rd off the South Gippsland Hwy, and after 9 km take the signposted turning onto McGaurans Beach Rd. Note: while you can enjoy observing the marine life offshore, it's illegal to fish in the waters of the park, and to remove any object from the beach. **Map refs:** 120 B6, 189 K9

NUNNIONG STATE FOREST

Birdwatchers, hikers and 4WD-tourers flock to eucalypt-filled Nunniong, 35 km east of Swifts Creek via Nunniong Rd. There's plenty of history in these hills, notably Moscow Villa Hut, built by forestry man Bill Ah Chow back in the 1940s. Nunniong Rd is off Bindi Rd, 8 km from Swifts Creek via the Omeo Hwy.

Who to contact: DSE Swifts Creek (03) 5159 5100, 13 6186

159 Bentleys Plain Reserve camping area

Only a few hundred metres east of the better known Moscow Villa Hut, down Bentley Plain Rd, is the Bentleys Plain Reserve camping area. There's a rustic old picnic shelter here on a grassy chunk of land corralled by a timber railing. Large gums dot the area and the enclosing bushland is as peaceful as can be – a good night's sleep is practically guaranteed. **Map refs:** 121 D2, 189 O2

160 Moscow Villa Hut camping area

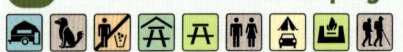

Bushman Bill Ah Chow finished this log and stone gem in 1942, on the day the Battle of Moscow was won. When local officials objected to the name, he allegedly told them it was actually an acronym for 'My Own Summer Cottage Officially Welcome Visitors Inside Light Luncheon Available'. You can camp near the hut and enjoy the forested surrounds. From Nunniong Rd, follow Bentley Plain Rd for 3.3 km. **Map refs:** 121 D2, 189 O2

161 Nunniong Plains camping areas

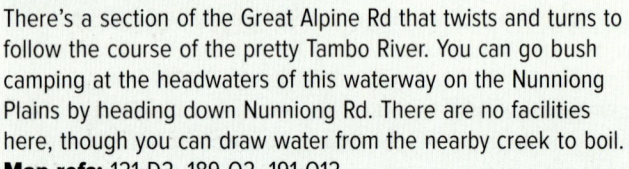

There's a section of the Great Alpine Rd that twists and turns to follow the course of the pretty Tambo River. You can go bush camping at the headwaters of this waterway on the Nunniong Plains by heading down Nunniong Rd. There are no facilities here, though you can draw water from the nearby creek to boil. **Map refs:** 121 D2, 189 O2, 191 O12

SNOWY RIVER NATIONAL PARK

Flanking the iconic Snowy River, and with deep forested gorges, this enormous slice of Victorian wilderness is a breathtaking treat. Canoeing or rafting the Snowy River are highly rewarding experiences, and there are numerous walking tracks to follow. The main access routes run off the Buchan–Jindabyne Rd and the Princes Hwy at Nowa Nowa.

Who to contact: Parks Victoria 13 1963

162 Balley Hooley camping area

Balley Hooley sits on the south-western fringe of the national park, due east of Buchan – access is signposted off the Buchan–Orbost Rd. Canoeing is a real treat along the Snowy River here, with its rapids, rugged gorges and sand bars amidst sublime forest scenery. One of the best river sections runs from McKillops Bridge to the Buchan River junction at Balley Hooley – leave yourself 3–4 days to complete it. **Map refs:** 121 E3, 187 A10, 189 P4

163 Hicks camping area

Hicks camping area is in the south of Snowy River National Park, beside the Yalmy River. It's accessed off Varneys Track, which runs off Yalmy Rd. A 4WD is required to reach this spot, and note that access is seasonal, restricted to dry weather. Keep a lookout for the rare brush-tailed rock wallaby, which occasionally makes an appearance in the area. There are also hiking, horseriding and mountain-biking trails nearby that you can tackle. **Map refs:** 121 E3, 187 B9, 189 P3

164 Jacksons Crossing camping area (bush camping)

This is a delightful camping area. Access to the bush-camping site, on the banks of the Snowy River, is via Varneys Track, off Yalmy Rd. A 4WD is needed to reach this isolated spot in the south of the park, although it's also possible to get here by canoe. There are no facilities – don't forget to bring drinking water. Jacksons Crossing contains some Aboriginal relics; it's believed the Kruatungulung group of the Kurnai people used to hunt in the area. **Map refs:** 121 E3, 187 A9, 189 P3

165 Little River Junction camping area

Located where the Snowy and Little rivers meet, this camping area is not far from Victoria's deepest cleft. At the spectacular Little River Gorge, stroll out to the cliff-top viewpoint for scenic splendour on your way to the campsite. If temperatures are starting to get high, cool off with a swim at Little River Junction. Turn off the Bonang–Gelantipy Rd to access the camping area or, alternatively, paddle here in a canoe. **Map refs:** 121 E2, 187 B8, 189 P2, 191 P12

166 McKillops Bridge camping areas

McKillops Bridge provides an entry point to the Snowy River by conventional vehicle and is a popular place for launching canoes. The self-guided 18 km Silver Mine Walking Track starts from the bridge, which is also a stop on the Snowy River Iconic 4WD Adventure Trail that winds through the heart of the surrounding forest. Just upstream from the bridge are sandy beaches and shallow rock pools, ideal for a dip. The McKillops Bridge camping areas are located in the north of the national park – the Bonang–Gelantipy Rd provides access. **Map refs:** 121 E2, 187 B7

167 Raymond Creek Falls camping area

This tiny campground, comprising just 4 sites, is situated near a waterfall (it's about 1.5 km from the camping area to the falls) that pitches 20 m into a deep foaming pool, accessed off Yalmy Rd – turn onto Moresford Track to get here. While on the track to the viewing area, keep a close eye (and ear) out for lyrebirds. At the pool itself you may be lucky enough to spot the rainbow-flecked azure kingfisher darting around. Normally visitor-shy platypus have even been sighted here. **Map refs:** 121 E3, 187 A10, 189 P4

168 Waratah Flat camping area

If you're looking for peace and quiet, make a beeline for the Waratah Flat camping area beside Rodger River. To get there, cruise through big-tree country admiring forests of grey gum, alpine ash and native pine along Yalmy Rd, skirting the Yalmy River, and then turn off at Waratah Flat Rd. To really enjoy this wooded wonderland, pull on a pair of hiking boots. **Map refs:** 121 F2, 187 C9

CAMPSITES LOCATED IN OTHER AREAS

169 Ada River camping area

The campground at Ada River lies close to the southern boundary of enchanting Errinundra National Park, with its vast temperate rainforest, rocky viewpoints and clear streams. Check out the panorama from the Ocean View Lookout and wander through ancient groves of trees at Errinundra Saddle. From Club Terrace, north of the Princes Hwy, follow the Club Terrace–Combienbar Rd and then turn onto the Errinundra Valley Rd. **Map refs:** 121 F3, 187 D9

Who to contact: Parks Victoria 13 1963

170 Delegate River camping area

From the small town of Bendoc near the NSW border, follow Gap Rd for 8 km south-west of town to reach this camping spot beside the Delegate River. Fishing and swimming are the prime activities here. There are several old goldmine sites you can inspect in this region, including the Jungle King Mine with its deep shaft. **Map refs:** 121 F2, 187 D8

Who to contact: Parks Victoria 13 1963

171 Goongerah camping area

A pretty place for a stopover, this camping area is signposted off the Bonang–Orbost Rd at Goongerah, a small township roughly 78 km north of Orbost. Immediately east of here is Errinundra National Park, with its gorgeous plateau-top rainforests and outstanding walks. **Map refs:** 121 F3, 187 C9

Who to contact: DSE 13 6186

172 Black Flat camping area

Black Flat is midway between the Ollies Jump-Up and Collins Flat camping areas on the Dargo River. It's more of a private, enclosed site than its neighbours, fringed by tall trees and scrub, but it's similarly equipped with pit toilets, a fireplace and picnic table. The access track runs off Upper Dargo Rd some 11 km from where this thoroughfare branches off Dargo High Plains Rd. **Map refs:** 120 C2, 189 L3

Who to contact: DSE Heyfield (03) 5139 7777, 13 6186

173 Collins Flat camping area

Collins Flat is signposted about 15.7 km down Upper Dargo Rd from the junction with Dargo High Plains Rd. It's a small site down by the Dargo River, with leafy vistas all around and the occasional trout taunting would-be anglers from the water. You need a 4WD to get to the campsites. Note: bring your own drinking water and firewood. **Map refs:** 120 C2, 189 L2

Who to contact: DSE 13 6186

174 Haunted Stream camping areas

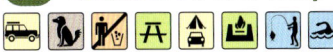

Not named to conjure up visions of a romantic night under the stars, Haunted Stream is an old goldmining region about 25 km south of Swifts Creek. It's accessed along 4WD tracks – try Brookville or Angora Range roads from Swift Creek, or detour from the Omeo Hwy at Tambo Crossing onto Haunted Stream Track. The camping area with fireplace and picnic table is at Dawson City (the junction of Witch Creek and Nightmare Creek, which form the Haunted Stream). **Map refs:** 121 D3, 189 N3

Who to contact: DSE 13 6186

175 Italian Flat camping area

This camping area is on river flats up towards the Dargo High Plains, making it an adventurous trip for an overnight stay. You can reach it by taking Dargo High Plains Rd for 5.7 km north of its namesake township and then veering north-east on Upper Dargo Rd – Italian Flat is 3 km from the junction. You can bring caravans and camper trailers up this way, but take great care while towing on the narrow, winding access road. **Map refs:** 120 C3, 189 L3

Who to contact: DSE 13 6186

176 Jimmy Iversons camping area

Jimmy Iversons is a relatively open area of gently sloping ground, set on the flats beside the slender, burbling Dargo River. The access track off Upper Dargo Rd is steep and the clay can become quite slippery when wet, so it's not suitable for caravans or camper trailers. You'll find the signposted turning off Upper Dargo Rd about 4.2 km from the junction with Dargo High Plains Rd. **Map refs:** 120 C3, 189 L3

Who to contact: DSE Heyfield (03) 5139 7777, 13 6186

177 Lake King Waterfront Caravan Park

Water activities including sailing, fishing and waterskiing abound at this lakeside caravan park. One of Victoria's best koala reserves is nearby on Raymond Island. Unpowered and powered campsites are well-located, right by the water. The park is off Paynesville Rd, 10 km from Bairnsdale, and is also on the Howitt Bicycle Trail. **Map refs:** 120 C4, 189 M6

How to book: 67 Bay Rd, Eaglepoint (03) 5156 6387 www.lakekingwaterfront.com.au

178 Lakes Entrance Tourist Park

There is plenty of room for kids to run about at this caravan park, along with a playground and games room to keep them amused. It's situated 2.5 km from the town of Lakes Entrance and is close to Eastern Beach. The camping area is spacious,

kept very clean and has excellent amenities. There are beach walks nearby along with sublime views of the coastline.
Map refs: 121 D4, 189 O6

How to book: 127 Princes Hwy, Lakes Entrance (03) 5155 1159 www.lakesentrancetouristpark.com

179 Mallacoota Foreshore Holiday Park

This holiday park is beautifully sited on Mallacoota Inlet, with a dozen jetties staked out along its grassy, well-tended perimeter. With 650 campsites, it gets crowded at peak times of the year, but the scenery, free use of the BBQs, and its proximity to the centre of town make it worth the crowds – try for one of the waterfront sites. **Map refs:** 121 H4, 187 G11

How to book: Allan Dr, Mallacoota (03) 5158 0300, 1800 637 060 www.mallacootaholidaypark.com.au

180 Ollies Jump-Up camping area

This is one of several well-grassed and open camping areas to be found beside the sleepy Dargo River. The access track off Upper Dargo Rd is signposted just under 7 km from the intersection with Dargo High Plains Rd, which heads north from the township of Dargo. The river supplies a refreshing swim, and you can also wander off through the gums to stretch your legs. This camping area is often on the itinerary of 4WD parties.
Map refs: 120 C2, 189 L3

Who to contact: DSE 13 6186

181 Suggan Buggan camping area (bush camping)

For those wanting to get off the beaten track, bush camping can be found at various points off the Snowy River Rd between the old Suggan Buggan township and the NSW border. These sites are accessed along various tracks, many of which lead directly to the Snowy River – some have better facilities than others. Suggan Buggan is about 70 km north of Buchan. Take your time on the narrow, twisting road, and allow a bit of extra time to check out a few of the campsites: some give good access to the river, while others do not. **Map refs:** 121 E1, 187 B7, 189 P1, 191 P11

Who to contact: Parks Victoria Omeo (03) 5159 0600, 13 1963

182 Timbarra camping area (bush camping)

The Timbarra bush-camping sites are tucked away beside the Timbarra River about 23 km north-west of Buchan. There is little in the way of facilities, which leaves you free to prioritise fishing and swimming in the river. The sites are located downstream from Timbarra Community – take Nunnett Rd and turn onto Timbarra Rd. **Map refs:** 121 D2, 189 O3

Who to contact: Parks Victoria 13 1963

183 Two Mile Creek camping area

Along Dargo High Plains Rd, about 5.7 km north of the tiny community of Dargo, with its groves of old walnut trees, the Upper Dargo Rd branches off to the north-east. If you follow this narrow, twisting road, you'll find some relaxing, out-of-the-way campsites, including at Two Mile Creek. There's a table and fireplace here, and you can swim and fish in the creek.
Map refs: 120 C3, 189 L3

Who to contact: DSE 13 6186

184 Waters Edge Holiday Park

This high-standard camping and caravan park is located in the centre of Lakes Entrance, the holiday town sited behind the magnificent sweep of sand known as Ninety Mile Beach. It's opposite an arm of the Gippsland Lakes, hence the name. The kids will keep themselves occupied here with the games room, playground and small heated swimming pool, while the oldies can cook up a storm on the BBQs. It's right on The Esplanade, which is a short section of the Princes Hwy in disguise.
Map refs: 121 D4, 189 O6

How to book: 623 The Esplanade, Lakes Entrance (03) 5155 1914 www.watersedgepark.com

185 Woods Point camping area

This idyllic campground is beautifully positioned on the shores of the Snowy River. Water-based activities include canoeing and rafting, while throwing in a line may reward anglers with Australian bass. There are also horse yards for day or overnight use. From Orbost, head west along McLeod St, which becomes the 'B' road and then Garnett's Track. Head into state forest and turn left at Woods Point Track. Leave all gates as you find them.
Map refs: 121 E4, 187 A10, 189 P5

Who to contact: DSE Orbost (03) 5161 1222, 13 6186

HIGH COUNTRY

THE VICTORIAN ALPS, MIGHTY chunks of which are protected within the confines of Alpine National Park, are a source of sheer delight for alpine hikers, high-plains horseriders and wild-river canoeists. These steep-sided ranges at the southern end of the aptly named Great Dividing Range also put big smiles on the faces of skiers and snowboarders when snow dusts their slopes over winter. Those who settle down for the night in meadows and forests will find themselves captivated by the expansive night skies and a refreshing sense of solitude.

Mt Buffalo is a popular skiing destination come winter, but it's equally attractive in spring, when brilliant wildflowers reveal themselves to visiting walkers. A drive up Mt Stirling showcases more of the region's entrancing flora, from rainforest ferns on the lower slopes right through to mountain ash and beautifully pale ghost gums further up. Alpine National Park contains some of the state's most remote and spectacular terrain. Four-wheel-drivers, mountain-bikers and hikers roam across the Bogong and Davies high plains. They also immerse themselves in gold-rush and grazier history, inspecting old homesteads, rustic huts and long-vanished townships.

CAMPSITES LOCATED IN PARKS AND RESERVES

ALPINE NATIONAL PARK

Alpine National Park is a sublime patchwork of landscapes that extend from Lake Dartmouth in the north to the Snowy Range in the south, and between Mt Buller in the west and the Murray River in the east. One of Victoria's biggest national parks, at 646 000 ha, it hosts myriad activities for all seasons, including skiing and snowboarding, hiking, cycling and rock climbing. It also has magnificent vistas, ranging from brilliant wildflowers to spectacular summits. Note: some of the region's roads are closed during winter.

Who to contact: Parks Victoria 13 1963

186 4WD and walk-in bush camping

There are walk-in and 4WD-access campsites scattered throughout Alpine National Park. Camp in the wild forests and bushlands around Lake Dartmouth, or watch out for the unique Bogong moth on the high plains Nov–Apr. Many of the campsites lie near the huts that provide emergency shelter. Talk to the ranger and equip yourself with reliable large-scale maps before setting out on your trip. **Map refs:** 133 H4, 191 N9

187 Barkly River camping area (Heyfield region)

Some 15 km from Licola, there's serene bush camping and mountain river fishing right at the south-western edge of Alpine National Park. From Licola, take Target Creek Rd, which winds around to the north-west of town, and follow it into Glencairn Rd.

The camping area is situated at the bridge where this road crosses over the Barkly River. Note: Glencairn Rd is steep and narrow, and is not suitable for caravans or camper trailers. **Map refs:** 133 D7, 189 I3

188 Bennies camping area (Whitfield region)

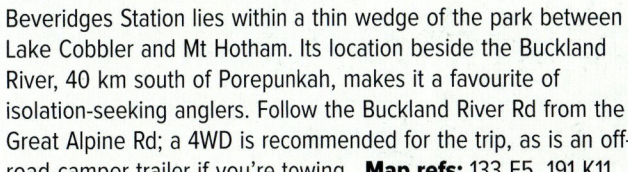

Bennies is situated in the south-western branch of Alpine National Park, between the towns of Mt Buller and Whitfield – from the latter, follow the Rose River Rd (the Whitfield–Myrtleford Rd), then the Upper Rose River Rd, then turn down Lake Cobblers Rd; a total distance of 29 km. The campsites lie near the Rose River, and there's a pleasant walk you can do here along the watercourse. If you have a 4WD, head down Little Cobbler Track and peer up at the bluffs of Mt Cobbler. **Map refs:** 133 D5, 191 I11

189 Beveridges Station camping area (Bright region)

Beveridges Station lies within a thin wedge of the park between Lake Cobbler and Mt Hotham. Its location beside the Buckland River, 40 km south of Porepunkah, makes it a favourite of isolation-seeking anglers. Follow the Buckland River Rd from the Great Alpine Rd; a 4WD is recommended for the trip, as is an off-road camper trailer if you're towing. **Map refs:** 133 E5, 191 K11

190 Bindaree Hut camping area (Mansfield region)

To reach Bindaree Hut, which lies in the shadows of Mt Buller and Mt Stirling and was built by well-known bushman Fred Fry, take Bindaree Rd off Circuit Rd and continue for 10 km to the signposted turning. The hut is situated 1.4 km down the access track, and near it, on the Howqua River flats, are the campsites. An off-road camper trailer or a 4WD can make this trip – Bindaree Rd is a popular 4WD route. **Map refs:** 133 D6, 189 I1, 191 I12

191 Bluff Hut camping area (Mansfield region)

There's bush camping among snow gums within a few hundred metres of Bluff Hut; a reconstruction of the original 1950s hut that burnt down in 2007. It's on a well-worn path that begins at Eight Mile Flat, wanders over the summit of the Bluff – from where you can gaze at Mt Buller – and then meanders through alpine meadows before descending via a 4WD track (Bluff Track, which runs off Brocks Track) to the hike's starting point. Horseriders also head up this way. **Map refs:** 133 D6, 189 I1, 191 I12

192 Buckety Plain camping area (Bogong area)

The camping area at Buckety Plain is situated near Faithfuls Hut, which is for emergency accommodation only. Buckety Plain is 18 km south of Falls Creek, and a couple of kilometres beyond the Raspberry Hill camping area. **Map refs:** 133 F5, 191 M11

193 Buckwong Creek camping area (Davies High Plain area)

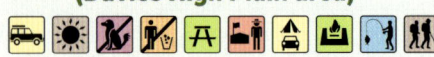

Buckwong Creek is one of several possible stopovers on the 4WD Davies Plain Track, which heads north from near Mt Cobberas (access is off Limestone Creek Rd) to eventually hit the Murray River near the Alpine Way. It's only a small site, but if it's full there are other options at Dogman Hut to the north and Davies Plain Hut to the south. A 4WD vehicle is needed to reach this isolated bush-camping site, which is only 3 km from the Murray.

Crossings of the Murray River and Buckwong Creek are required to reach this site from the north, so heavy rain can make access impossible. Note: the camping area is subject to seasonal closure. **Map refs: 133 I4, 187 A4, 191 P9**

194 Buenba Flat camping area (Davies High Plain area)

This is a novelty in the Davies High Plain area – a bush-camping area that can be reached with a conventional vehicle. The dispersed sites are 44 km north-east of Benambra, off Beloka Rd. Nearby is the junction of the Benambra and Buenba creeks, so anglers have plenty of water to fish. **Map refs: 133 H4, 191 O10**

195 Bullock Flat camping area (Heyfield region)

Bullock Flat is popular with anglers because of its location beside the Wonnangatta River. It's about 8 km south-east of the Eaglevale camping area and can be accessed along Wonnangatta Rd. Consider detouring up to the fire tower-topped Pinnacles lookout for some excellent panoramic views. There are no toilets at Bullock Flat, but there are picnic tables and fireplaces. **Map refs: 133 E7, 189 K3**

196 Charlies Creek Plain camping area (Davies High Plain area)

The campsites of Charlies Creek Plain are at the southern end of the 4WD Davies Plain Track, which heads north from here to reach the Murray River at Tom Groggin on the NSW border. It's 2.5 km north of the junction with McCarthys Track, which has been incorporated into the Bicentennial Nature Trail, a long and adventurous horseriding trail that extends from Healesville all the way to Cooktown in Queensland. **Map refs: 133 I4, 187 A5, 191 O10**

197 Craigs Hut camping area

Craigs Hut is situated on Mt Stirling, about 40 km east of Mansfield. There are 2 ways to get here: by driving down Mt Buller Rd, turning onto Circuit Rd and looking for the signposted access 20 km east of Telephone Box Junction, then walking in from the Circuit Rd carpark; or by taking your 4WD down Clear Hill Track off Circuit Rd. The drive in is a botanically scenic route that takes you from fern-lined gullies up through stands of mountain ash and into snow gum territory. **Map refs: 133 D5, 189 I1, 191 I11**

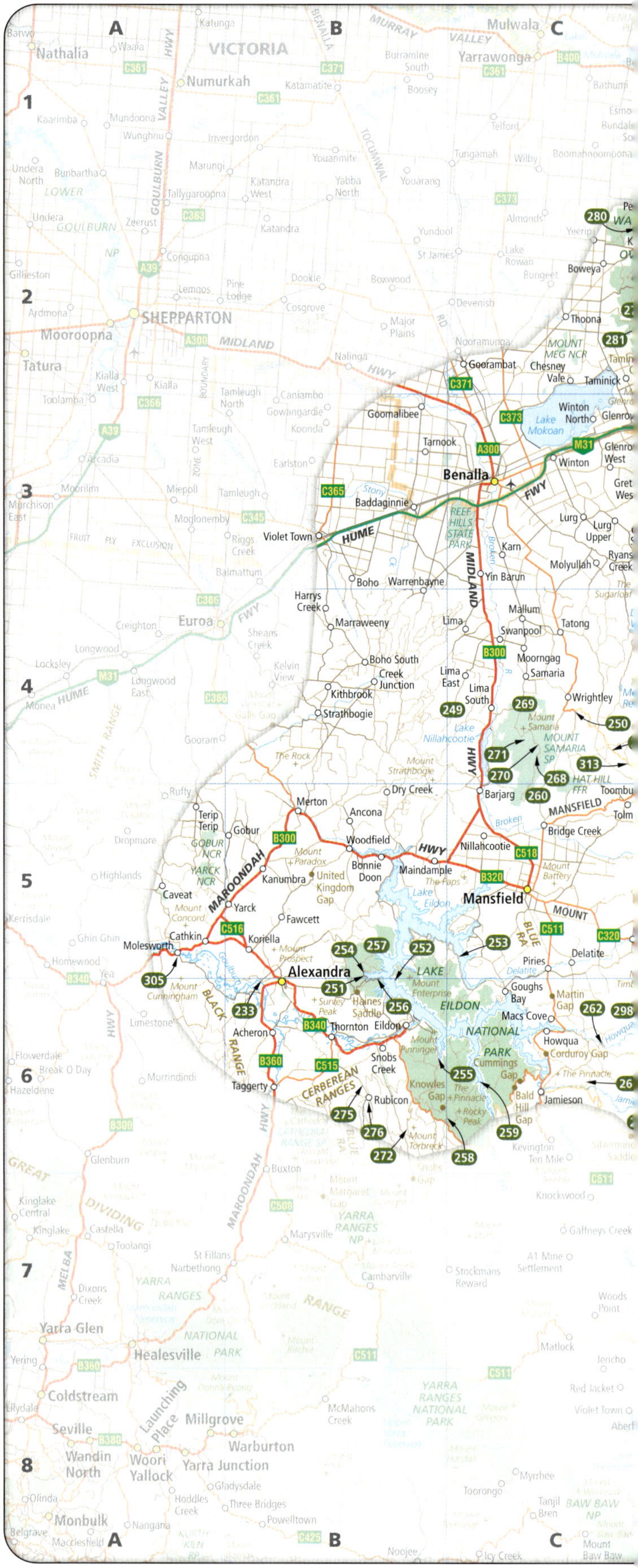

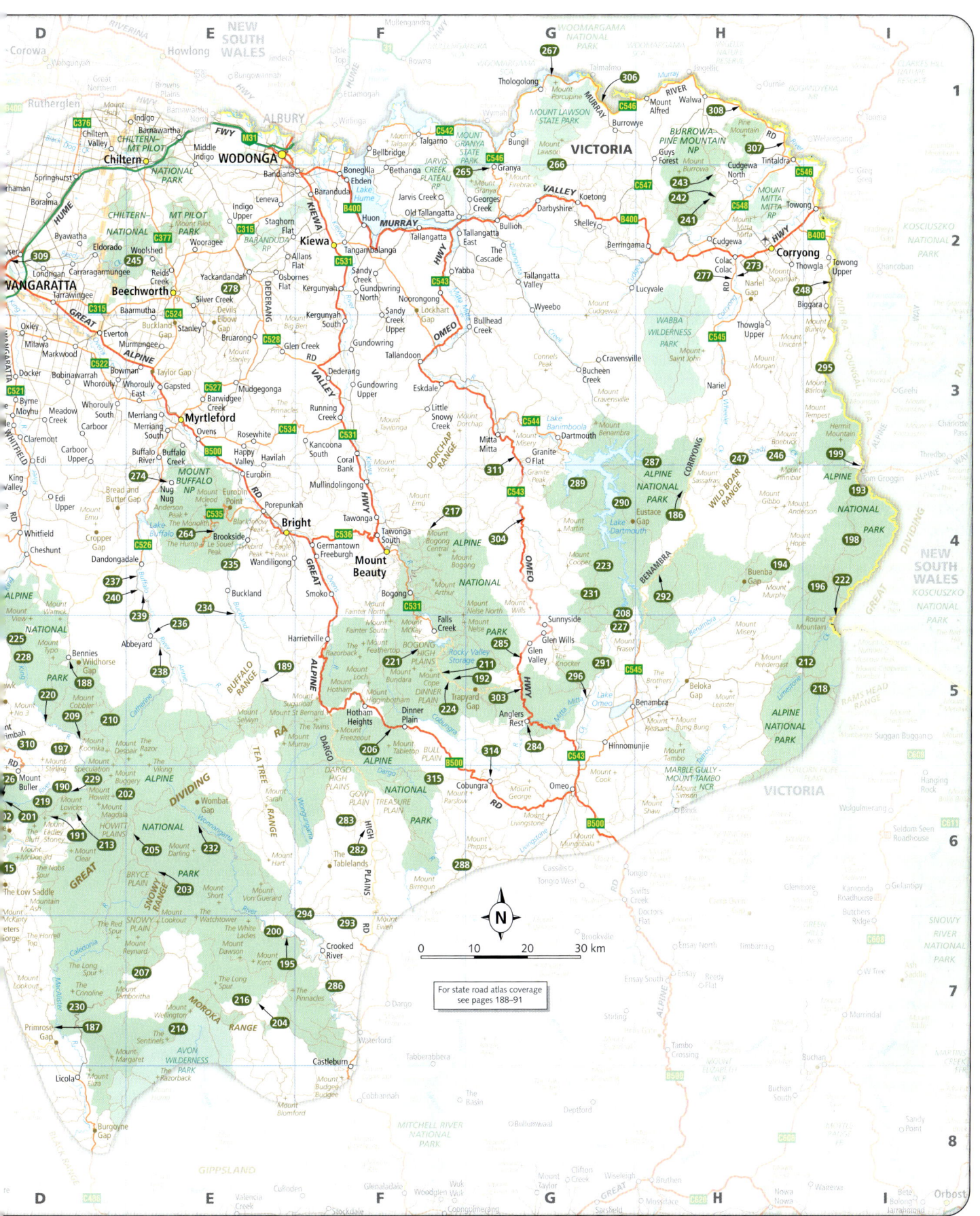

For state road atlas coverage
see pages 188–91

198 Davies Plain Hut camping area (Davies High Plain area)

Camping is possible among the snow gums near the historic Davies Plain Hut, which is just over 16 km south of the nearest Murray River crossing, and 13 km north of Charlies Creek Plain. Located on the Davies Plain Track, this is the domain of 4WD vehicles and horseriders – the latter take advantage of the nearby horse yards. If you're lucky, you may even see some wild horses up here. This site makes a good stopover on a tour or a pleasant base from which to explore to the north and south. **Map refs:** 133 I4, 187 A5, 191 P10

199 Dogman Hut camping area (Davies High Plain area)

Dogman Hut is in the far north-east of the park, not far from the Murray River, and is a nice place to set up camp and watch the setting sun. Four-wheel-drivers often use this area as a staging post for the run up nearby Mt Pinnibar. Access for 4WD vehicles is provided by Tom Groggin Track; from NSW you can reach Dogman via the Alpine Way. **Map refs:** 133 I4, 187 A4, 191 P9

200 Eaglevale camping area (Heyfield region)

The Eaglevale campsites are beside the Wonnangatta River, overshadowed by Snowy Bluff and Mt Kent. There's a track you can follow north-east to the eerie remains of Talbotville and the one-time gold-rush town of Grant. Eaglevale is 54 km north-west of Dargo and accessed via Wonnangatta Rd. **Map refs:** 133 E7, 189 K3

201 Eight Mile Flat camping area (Mansfield region)

Not surprisingly, Eight Mile Flat is just beyond Seven Mile Flat along Brocks Track, off which it's signposted. This access road, which leads off Howqua Track off Mt Buller Rd, is a 4WD affair – off-road camper trailers can be towed down this way too. The camping area is beside the Howqua River, and you'll need to cross a small creek to reach it. Note: Eight Mile Flat is subject to seasonal closure. **Map refs:** 133 D6, 189 I1, 191 I12

202 Gantner Hut camping area (Heyfield region, walk-in camping)

The A-frame Gantner Hut, built as emergency shelter in the 1970s, is situated on the walking track that leads from Howitt Rd up to the summit of Mt Howitt. This peak reputedly has some of the finest views in the national park. Near the hut are such enticing formations as the Devil's Staircase, the Terrible Hollow and the Cross-Cut Saw. The hut is 37 km north of Arbuckle Junction, and roughly 5 km from the carpark on Howitt Rd. **Map refs:** 133 D6, 189 J1, 191 J12

203 Guys Hut camping area (Heyfield region, walk-in camping)

Guys Hut is a 1940s structure on a walking circuit that begins at Howitt Rd, skirts the cliffs of Bryce Gorge and passes several waterfalls, including one on Pieman Creek, and then loops back to the main road. The walk in from the carpark is about 1 km, and immediately beyond the hut you'll encounter stands of snow gums. Several horseriding trails also connect the waterfalls in the area. **Map refs:** 133 E6, 189 J2, 191 J12

204 Horseyard Flat camping area (Heyfield region)

Horseyard Flat is on the banks of the Moroka River, 30 km east of Arbuckle Junction down Moroka Rd. There aren't actually any horse yards here – horseriders can find those to the west at Wellington River. After crossing a footbridge over the river, you can follow an at-times steep path to several waterfalls and into the narrow, rocky Moroka Gorge. You can also drive up to the nearby Pinnacles, where there's a fire tower and sweeping views of the region. **Map refs:** 133 E7, 189 K3

205 Howitt Hut camping area (Heyfield region)

Camping at Howitt Hut is centred on a cattleman's hut built in the early 20th century, making it one of the oldest such structures in this section of the park. You can reach this site, beside the Caledonia River, by following the scenic Howitt Rd for 30 km north of Arbuckle Junction. There are horse paddocks here, used mainly by those riding east towards Wonnangatta Homestead. There's also a testing walk nearby up Mt Howitt. **Map refs:** 133 E6, 189 J2, 191 J12

206 J B Plain camping area (Bogong area, walk-in camping)

J B Plain is a walk-in campsite 11 km south-east of Mt Hotham, just off the Great Alpine Rd. From here you can take a great 5 km walk due south to the aptly named plateau of Mt Tabletop. While exploring this region, learn how to identify a Bogong daisy bush, which grows nowhere else in the world. **Map refs:** 133 F5, 189 L1, 191 L11

207 Kellys Lane camping areas (Heyfield region)

Dispersed bush camping is permitted along Kellys Lane, off Tamboritha Rd about 8 km south-west of Arbuckle Junction. The sites are bordered by Shaws Creek and Holmes Plains. Nearby is the Bennison Lookout, just to the south of Tamboritha Saddle. There are great views from here of alpine hills rolling away into the distance. **Map refs:** 133 E7, 189 J3

208 Kennedys Hut camping area (Lake Dartmouth area)

Like Taylors Crossing camping area to the south, Kennedys Hut is located on the banks of the Mitta Mitta River. The campsites are arrayed near the hut, which is a rustic log cabin straight out of a wilderness adventure story. Sit by the river and admire the surrounding forest, or throw a line in and see what you catch. A 4WD can get you here via Wombat Track and then Four Mile Creek Track. **Map refs:** 133 G4, 191 N10

209 King Hut camping area (Whitfield region)

King Hut is perched on the western edge of the park, about 35 km east of Mt Stirling. The dramatic 4WD-access route follows the King River Track for 7 km from the junction with Speculation Rd, which is itself reached via a turn-off on Circuit Rd about 6 km east of the Craigs Hut turn-off. There are horse yards here for use by intrepid explorers. The hut itself is in excellent condition, having been recently rebuilt. **Map refs:** 133 D5, 189 J1, 191 J11

210 Lake Cobbler camping area (Whitfield region)

Lake Cobbler is around 47 km south of Whitfield along Lake Cobblers Rd, which is accessed from the Upper Rose River Rd; you'll need a 4WD or high-clearance 2WD to negotiate the stretch of road south of Bennies, and an off-road camper trailer if you want to tow your accommodation in. On the way in you'll see Dandongadale Falls, which have an impressive drop of over 200 m. There's also a challenging walk from Lake Cobbler up to the summit of Mt Cobbler. **Map refs:** 133 D5, 189 J1, 191 J11

211 Langford West camping area (Bogong area)

This camping area is right up on the fabulous Bogong High Plains, about 14 km south of Falls Creek via Bogong High Plains Rd. Mountain-bikers will want to head north from here up the Langford West and Langford East aqueducts, while equestrian types can make use of the horse yards (make advance bookings). Also nearby is the start of the walk across grassy plains to the summit of Mt Cope. **Map refs:** 133 F5, 191 L11

212 Limestone Creek camping area (Davies High Plain area)

Limestone Creek flows within untouched woodlands on the Davies High Plain. Horseriders plod slowly through the area along the Bicentennial Nature Trail, while others camp beside the creek to float a fishing line, or let their feet lead them down nearby vehicular and walking tracks. The Limestone Creek camping area is accessed via Limestone Creek Track, 2.4 km north of the junction with Black Mountain Rd. **Map refs:** 133 I5, 187 A6, 191 O11

213 Lovicks Hut camping area (Mansfield region)

Lovicks Hut, on Mt Lovick, marks the spot where one of the original cattlemen's huts stood until 2003. Horseriders and 4WD vehicles head over from the Bluff to check out the area, while hikers walk in from the east from the direction of Mt Howitt. Lovicks Hut is accessed via the 4WD Bluff Track off Brocks Track – it's 300 m from the junction of Bluff and Cairn Creek tracks. **Map refs:** 133 D6, 189 I1, 191 I12

214 Millers Hut camping area (Heyfield region)

Millers Hut is one of many emergency shelters in the park, and there's a camping area nearby for those who are just passing through. You'll need a 4WD to get here along Mt Wellington Track, which branches off Moroka Rd about 17 km south-east of Arbuckle Junction. A rough vehicle track leads from here to the viewpoint on top of Mt Wellington. **Map refs:** 133 E7, 189 J3

215 Mitchells Flat camping area (Mansfield region)

Mitchells Flat is right at the western edge of the park. It was the site of a gold find in the 1860s and subsequently became home to the Mitchell family homestead. It's now the eastern end of the 2-day Mitchells Bridle Trail, which follows the Jamieson River from Grannys Flat in Mansfield State Forest. Get here via the 4WD Mitchells Track, off the Jamieson–Licola Rd, or (in dry weather only) from Mansfield via Sheepyard and Tobacco flats. **Map refs:** 132 D6, 189 I2, 191 I12

216 Moroka Bridge camping area (Heyfield region, bush camping)

There's back-to-basics bush camping at Moroka Bridge, which is accessed by Moroka Rd and situated about 26 km south-east of Arbuckle Junction. There's nothing in the way of facilities, just plenty of time to fish and snooze. Visit the Moroka Valley Lookout for some fine views of the area. **Map refs:** 133 E7, 189 K3

217 Mountain Creek camping area (Bogong area)

Mountain Creek is about 15 km east of Tawonga, which is down the road from Mt Beauty – from the Kiewa Valley Hwy south of Tawonga, head east for 10 km on Mountain Creek Rd. Most people come here to climb Victoria's highest peak, Mt Bogong, which stretches upwards for almost 2000 m. This is a difficult hike that seasoned walkers complete in one long day via the Staircase Spur. There are also much gentler walks, like the Shady Gully Nature Walk. **Map refs:** 133 F4, 191 L9

218 Native Dog Flat camping area (Cobberas–Tingaringy area)

Native Dog Flat, 45 km east of Benambra and at the southern end of the Snowy Mountains, is in one of the most remote and rugged regions of Alpine National Park. The local high point is Mt Cobberas, which is scaled by the Australian Alps Walking Track. A less difficult climb, but one that still leads to excellent views, is the Rams Horn Track to the south of the camping area. Native Dog Flat is off the Benambra–Black Mountain Rd.

This camping area is accessible to conventional vehicles, but would also make a great base to explore some of the many challenging 4WD tracks nearby, such as Davies High Plains to the north or the tracks to the east that head towards Suggan Buggan. **Map refs:** 133 I5, 187 A6, 191 O11

219 Pikes Flat camping area (Mansfield region)

Pikes Flat is a short distance west of Bindaree Hut on a track that branches off Bindaree Rd, which leads south from Circuit Rd. Like Bindaree, the campsites at Pikes Flat are on the flats beside the Howqua River, which has a good reputation when it comes to fly fishing. This is an appealing spot for bush camping. **Map refs:** 133 D6, 189 I1, 191 I12

220 Pineapple Flat camping area (Whitfield region)

Pineapple Flat is 10 km north of Mt Stirling in the western reaches of the park. It is reached via Burnt Top Track, which branches off King Basin Rd, which in turn runs off Circuit Rd. This route is 4WD only. Those with a taste for isolated mountain tracks usually do a circuit of the area that involves the Sandy Flat, Longspur, Stockyard and Burnt Top tracks, the latter providing some wonderful views of Buckland Spur. **Map refs:** 133 D5, 189 I1, 191 I11

221 Pretty Valley camping area

Essentially a picnic ground also used for camping, this scenic spot overlooks Pretty Valley pondage and also gives access to the high plains via walking tracks. There is room for roughly 20 tents, and caravans will squeeze in too. Nearby is a historic hut and horse yards. The camping area is located 3 km south-west of Falls Creek, and you access the Pretty Valley turn-off after Falls Creek Village. **Map refs:** 133 F5, 191 L10

222 The Poplars camping area (Davies High Plain area)

The Poplars site allows you to camp on the banks of the Murray River at the eastern edge of the park. To the south is the rugged terrain surrounding Mt Cobberas, while across the Murray in NSW is wild Kosciuszko National Park. Fishing usually occupies campers here, but 4WD touring also keeps them busy. The Poplars is off the 4WD McCarthys Track, 1.2 km east of the junction with Limestone Creek Track. **Map refs:** 133 I5, 187 A6, 191 P10

223 Quartpot Flat Hut camping area (Lake Dartmouth area)

Quartpot Flat is near one of the southernmost tendrils of Lake Dartmouth. To get here, steer a 4WD off the Omeo Hwy onto Razorback Spur, just north of the Mt Wills Historic Area, and then head east on Limestone Gap Track. You can camp near the hut, and the site (and access road) is suitable for an off-road trailer. **Map refs:** 133 G4, 191 N10

224 Raspberry Hill camping area (Bogong area)

About 3 km south of Langford West lies Raspberry Hill, off the Bogong High Plains Rd. Use this as a base while you decide which of the area's fine walking tracks to tackle next. For a view out over Falls Creek and the high country that cradles the resort, backtrack to the Rocky Valley Dam Wall, from where you can hike up through the snow gums to Ropers Lookout. **Map refs:** 133 F5, 191 L11

225 Sandy Flat camping area (Whitfield region)

Sandy Flat is another of the camping areas accessible only by 4WD in the section of the national park south of Whitfield. Off-road vehicles tend to make the most of the many tracks that wind around Mt Pleasant, Mt Cobbler and the pink sandstone of Mt Typo. To get to this dispersed camping area beside King River, take the Sandy Flat Track from Lake William Hovell, which is linked to Cheshunt by Upper King River Rd. **Map refs:** 133 D5, 191 I10

226 Seven Mile Flat camping area (Mansfield region)

Seven Mile Flat is in the section of Alpine National Park directly south of looming Mt Buller and 45 km east of Mansfield. A 4WD is required to reach this campground – from Mt Buller Rd, head south on Howqua Track and then continue on Brocks Track. The small grouping of campsites is beside the Howqua River, which is good for swimming and fishing. **Map refs:** 133 D6, 189 I1, 191 I12

227 Taylors Crossing camping area (Lake Dartmouth area, walk-in camping)

The Mitta Mitta River is a great place for swimming and fishing. At Taylors Crossing, you can camp right beside this waterway. There are 2 ways of getting here: in a 4WD along Four Mile Creek Track, or in a 2WD from the direction of Uplands. The latter route requires you to carry your camping gear across a pedestrian swing bridge to the campsites. Note: the toilets are on the other side of the river from the campsites, in the day-use area. **Map refs:** 133 G5, 191 N10

228 Top Crossing Hut camping area (Whitfield region)

Grassy camping spaces can be found beside the King River at Top Crossing Hut, built in 1951, which lies in a branch of the national park just south of Whitfield. From Whitfield, head towards Cheshunt and then detour south-west along Upper King River Rd and finally down Top Crossing Track. These tracks are suitable for 4WD only; note that several crossings of King River are involved, which may be impassable after rain. If you like trout fishing, stop off at Lake William Hovell on the way in. **Map refs:** 133 D5, 191 I11

229 Upper Howqua camping area (Mansfield region)

From the Circuit Rd that winds around Mt Stirling, take Bindaree Rd and follow it for 10 km to reach the turn-off to the lovely Upper Howqua camping area; the trip will require a 4WD. Spend your time fishing in the Howqua River, or walk up to the summit of Mt Howitt via the Upper Howqua Rd and several waterway fordings. **Map refs:** 133 D6, 189 I1, 191 I12

230 Wellington River camping areas (Heyfield region)

The south-western section of the park, north of Heyfield, is crisscrossed by mountain waterways where you can go swimming and fishing. These include the Wellington River, which has 13 dispersed campsites (some with recently upgraded facilities) shaded by manna gums and peppermint trees; the sites start 10 km north of Licola down the Tamboritha Rd. Horseriders can follow a track from here to Lake Tali Karng, though the horses can't be taken onto the lakeshore itself. **Map refs:** 133 D7, 189 I3

231 Wombat PO camping area (Lake Dartmouth area)

The Wombat PO camping area is located alongside Wombat Creek some 30 km north of Benambra. This creek is no rival for the large expanse of Lake Dartmouth to the north, but you can still while away the hours fishing here. Whether or not letters were ever sorted here remains a mystery; but, for what it's worth, wombats are indeed numerous in this region. Four-wheel drives can get here via Wombat Creek Track. **Map refs:** 133 G4, 191 N10

232 Wonnangatta Valley camping area (Heyfield region)

The Wonnangatta Valley, 65 km north of Arbuckle Junction, is popular for the 4WD trips conducted between here and Zeka Spur. A well-used horseriding trail also winds through here. You can camp near the site of the Wonnagatta Homestead, a symbol of when cattle grazing was allowed in the valley. One access route is down Zeka Spur Track, off Howitt Rd from Licola, while another is via Wombat Spur Track off Crooked River Rd near Dargo. Off-road camper trailers can be brought in from Myrtleford via Abbeyards Rd. **Map refs:** 133 E6, 189 J2, 191 J12

BROOKS RIVER RESERVE

The Goulburn River flows alongside Brooks River Reserve, a small recreation area on the eastern outskirts of Alexandra. This area is popular with anglers who vie with each other to hook the local trout. If you're not interested in fishing, head into town to inspect some gold-rush-era buildings.

Who to contact: Parks Victoria 13 1963

233 Brooks River Reserve camping area

To reach this compact camping area, head north-west out of historic Alexandra township on the Maroondah Hwy and turn west on Swanns La, which leads down to the banks of the Goulburn River. There are fireplaces here but you'll need to lug in your own firewood. The fishing gets competitive when the trout season begins. **Map refs:** 132 B6, 188 F1, 190 F12

BUCKLAND VALLEY STATE FOREST

The valley hewn by the Buckland River stretches between a pair of great wilderness areas: Mt Buffalo National Park to the north, and Alpine National Park to the south. Few camping facilities are on offer in the forest here, 22 km south-west of Bright, but it's a good place for 2WD touring, as well as swimming and fishing.

Who to contact: DSE 13 6186

234 Buckland River Valley camping areas

It's permissible to pitch a tent between Buckland River Rd and the river itself, except on privately owned land. Once you've selected your campsite, you can concentrate on enjoying the fresh mountain air and water. From Porepunkah on the Great Alpine Rd, head south-west on Buckland Valley Rd – the first of the access tracks will appear after 14.5 km, and the last another 19 km from this point. **Map refs:** 133 E4, 191 K10

235 AH Youngs camping area

It was gold that drew people to the Buckland River in the 1850s, but now it's the scenic landscape of Victoria's High Country. AH Youngs at Maguire Point, 18 km down Buckland River Rd from the Great Alpine Rd intersection, is a spacious riverside camping area. Note: the access road can be rough depending on weather conditions. **Map refs:** 133 E4, 191 K10

BUFFALO RIVER STATE FOREST

The scenic Buffalo River winds its way along the western edge of Mt Buffalo National Park, south of Myrtleford, pooling into Lake Buffalo before continuing towards Alpine National Park further south. The campsites in the state forest bordering the river give access to great fishing spots and 4WD tracks.

Who to contact: DSE 13 6186

236 Abbeyards camping area

Riverside tent and camper trailer sites are on offer at Abbeyards, another of the camping areas scattered off Abbeyards Rd in Buffalo River State Forest. Go fishing for trout, have a refreshing dip or just laze by the water's edge. **Map refs:** 133 E5, 191 J10

237 Blades camping area

Blades is one of several riverside camping areas you can access by following Buffalo River Rd south from Myrtleford, turning onto Abbeyards Rd, and then watching for the signposted access tracks about 14 km beyond Lake Buffalo. The trails in this area are popular with the 4WD crowd. **Map refs:** 133 E4, 191 J10

238 McIver camping area

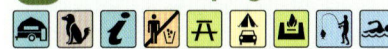

Camp down by a fresh mountain river in the Buffalo Valley at the McIver camping area. Tents and camper trailers are accommodated here. The area attracts its share of 4WD tourers searching for challenging, scenic tracks. **Map refs:** 133 E5, 191 J10

239 Manna Gum camping area

The Manna Gum camping area is accessed off Abbeyards Rd in Buffalo River State Forest, which is 35 km south of the township of Myrtleford. Bring firewood and water with you on the drive down to the Buffalo River. **Map refs:** 133 E4, 191 J10

(240) Tea-Tree camping area

This is another of the fine riverside camping areas signposted off Abbeyards Rd south of Lake Buffalo. Anglers pursuing the stocks of trout in the Buffalo River are common visitors to this part of the tangled state forest. **Map refs:** 133 E4, 191 J10

BURROWA–PINE MOUNTAIN NATIONAL PARK

Dominated by the twin peaks of Mt Burrowa and Pine Mountain, this national park occupies a rugged plot of land beside the NSW border. Its remote location is one of its drawcards, as are the numerous bushwalks that range from ambles to demanding hikes. Mountain-bikers and people in 4WDs also love it here, though the smaller vehicle tracks tend to be inaccessible in the wet. From the Murray Valley Hwy, detour through Cudgewa, then turn onto Cudgewa North Rd.

Who to contact: Parks Victoria 13 1963

(241) Blue Gum Camp camping area

Blue Gum Camp is off Bluff Falls Rd about 1 km past Bluff Creek. Walk westwards to Campbells or Ross lookout for great views out over the surrounding region. Alternatively, try driving up a fire trail towards the peak of Black Mountain, from where you can gaze northwards towards the silhouettes of the Snowy Mountains. **Map refs:** 133 H2, 191 O6

(242) Bluff Creek camping area

This camping area is on Bluff Falls Rd, close to the park entrance. There aren't too many sites, so arrive early in peak holiday periods. From here, walk the 2 km trail through blue gum forest to Bluff Falls, which are at their spectacular best in spring, or prepare for an attempt on the park's highest summit via the difficult 7.5 km Mt Burrowa Walking Track. **Map refs:** 133 H2, 191 O6

(243) Hinces Creek Camp camping area

To reach Hinces Creek, follow Cudgewa North Rd past the Bluff Creek turn-off and then veer onto Hinces Creek Track. Up at the northern end of the national park is the monolithic Pine Mountain and its wondrous botany, which includes several types of grevillea and the phantom wattle. You can hike to the summit via a very strenuous 6 km walking track. **Map refs:** 133 H2, 191 O6

BUTTERCUP CREEK RESERVE

This restful reserve is embedded in forest about 25 km east of Mansfield. Touring by 4WD is popular on nearby trails, as is fishing in the local waterways. You can take a conventional vehicle and caravan down the Mansfield–Mount Buller Rd and turn onto Carters Rd east of Merrijig; or there's a tougher route in from the east via Buttercup Rd.

Who to contact: DSE Mansfield (03) 5733 1200, 13 6186

(244) Buttercup Creek campsites 1–3

Three sites with varying facilities have been staked out next to Buttercup Creek, each of them signposted off Buttercup Rd. Go rambling or cycling down the trails in the surrounding forest. While you're in the area, also take the time to drive over to Mt Buller for a look-see. Note: bring your own drinking water and firewood. **Map refs:** 132 D5, 189 I1, 191 I11

CHILTERN–MOUNT PILOT NATIONAL PARK

There's a feast of goldmining history in this region, dating back to the claims that were taken up here in the late 1850s – places to visit include the Indigo Goldfields Cemetery and the open-cut Magenta Mine. Also here is the Yeddonba Aboriginal Cultural Site, at the base of Mt Pilot. Natural highlights include Woolshed Falls. The park has 2 sections: one around Chiltern, the other to the south of town.

Who to contact: Parks Victoria 13 1963

(245) Reedy Creek camping area

In the southern section of the national park, several bush-camping sites are scattered alongside Reedy Creek, which winds from near Woolshed Falls to the fancifully named Eldorado gold dredge. To get here, take the road towards Beechworth from Chiltern and then head west on Woolshed Rd – a worthwhile detour is the Gorge Scenic Drive just north of Beechworth. **Map refs:** 133 E2, 191 J7

CORRYONG DISTRICT FOREST

This forest contains enough nature to keep visitors satisfied, but it has some wild neighbours as well: to the west is the wriggly shoreline of Lake Dartmouth, and to the east is Mt Kosciuszko and its surrounding national park. Corryong District Forest is a prime 4WD area. It's 65 km south of the town of Corryong and is accessed by following the Benambra–Corryong Rd and turning onto Wheeler Creek Logging Rd.

Who to contact: DSE Corryong (02) 6076 3100, 13 6186

(246) Bush camping areas

You can set up camp in various bushy places in the state forest, some of which are accessible by 2WD and others which can only be reached with a 4WD. There are a number of such sites along Dunstans Logging Rd, a few of them located near logging huts. Contact the ranger for information on the best places and how to access them. **Map refs:** 133 H3, 191 O9

(247) Wheelers Creek Hut camping area

Wheelers Creek Hut was built about 30 years ago for timber industry workers. It's now a prime destination for 4WD tourers who ramble down a scenic stretch of Wheeler Creek Logging Rd to reach it. The area for campers has facilities that include toilets and picnic tables. As with other camping spots in Corryong District Forest, a 4WD is recommended for access; check with the ranger about road conditions. **Map refs:** 133 H3, 191 O9

INDI BRIDGE RESERVE

Indi Bridge is one of many delightful small reserves scattered along the upper reaches of the stately Murray River. Fishing and birdwatching are just a couple of the leisurely activities enjoyed here. The reserve is to the east of the Murray Valley Hwy township of Corryong.

Who to contact: Corryong Tourist Information Centre (02) 6076 2277

248 Indi Bridge Reserve camping area

The relaxed camping at Indi Bridge can be accessed via Upper Murray Rd, some 4 km south of Toowong Upper. If you have a hankering for a clear view of the neighbouring Kosciuszko Range, head up past Toowong and follow Ranch Rd into Mt Mittamatite Regional Park, where you'll gain excellent views from Emberys Lookout. **Map refs:** 133 I2, 187 A3, 191 P7

JAMES CAMPING RESERVE

This reserve is hidden away within the confines of the Strathbogie Ranges, 25 km north-west of Mansfield. Its claim to historical fame is that it served as a hiding place for the Kelly Gang, but visitors are more interested in the area's walking and cycling tracks, and in the trout that swim in the local creeks. At Swanpool, turn off the Midland Hwy onto Lima East Rd.

Who to contact: DSE Benalla (03) 5761 1611, 13 6186

249 James camping area

The campsites in this small reserve are only 50 m from the fishing in Moonee Moonee Creek. There are toilets here and you can draw water from the creek, though obviously boil or treat it before use. Horseriders and 4WD regularly trek through this area on their way to distant tracks. **Map refs:** 132 C4, 190 G10

JONES CAMPING RESERVE

Jones Camping Reserve is a quiet slice of bushland in the Toombullup Ranges. These ranges are very popular with horseriders, walkers and 4WD excursions, due to the network of tracks snaking through the foliage. The reserve is 18 km south of Tatong – take the road from Tatong to Tolmie and turn off onto Jones Rd.

Who to contact: DSE Mansfield (03) 5733 1200, 13 6186

250 Jones camping area

This small camping area is sited next to Hollands Creek, where rainbow and brown trout can be hooked and then cooked by hungry anglers. To the west is Mt Samaria State Park, which has some fine lookouts and waterfalls to share. Note: the road leading into Jones Camping Reserve is generally fine for conventional vehicles, but not when it's wet. The camping reserve is closed mid June–Oct. **Map refs:** 132 C4, 190 H10

LAKE EILDON NATIONAL PARK

Nearly 30 000 ha of wild, hilly territory is protected within the beautiful confines of Lake Eildon National Park. The lake itself accommodates waterskiing, canoeing and fishing, while the tracks in the surrounding forest are used by bushwalkers and mountain bikes. No camping fees are levied at walk-in and other sites accessed without a vehicle. To get here, follow the signs from Alexandra on the Goulburn Valley Hwy.

Who to contact: Parks Victoria 13 1963

251 Candlebark camping area

Candlebark is located in the popular Fraser Camping Area, on the western edge of Coller Bay and accessed via UT Creek Rd. Each of its 70 or so campsites should be booked in advance through the Parks Victoria website. To find out about the national park's ecology and history, take the self-guided Candlebark Gully Nature Trail. While walking, you may spot some of the eastern grey kangaroos that roam through the local woodlands. **Map refs:** 132 B5, 188 G1, 190 G12

252 Coopers Point camping area (boat-based camping)

A boat trip is your only option for getting out to Coopers Point on the eastern shoreline of Lake Eildon, just to the west of Mt Enterprise. Before paddling or motoring out of Coller Bay, check with the national park ranger as to the best route and what to expect when you reach Coopers Point. Bring your own drinking water. **Map refs:** 132 B6, 188 G1, 190 G12

253 Delatite Arm Reserve camping areas

There are some far-flung campsites adjacent to the softwood plantations on Delatite Arm, at the north-eastern extremity of Lake Eildon National Park. You can reach these dispersed lakeside sites by travelling to Goughs Bay from either Jamieson or Mansfield, and then heading west along Walsh Rd. **Map refs:** 132 C5, 188 G1, 190 G11

254 Devils Cove camping area

Devils Cove is one of several scenic camping spots at Collers Bay, in what's known as the Fraser Camping Area. Sites here can be booked online via the Parks Victoria website. Take the gentle 3.5 km walk around the bay to the Lakeside camping area. East of Devils Cove is the Merlo Lookout, named after an old homestead now submerged in the lake's waters, which makes a dramatic reappearance when water levels are low. **Map refs:** 132 B5, 188 G1, 190 G11

255 Jerusalem Creek camping area

There are a half-dozen designated camping areas at Jerusalem Creek, each with about 10 sites. Three of these – areas 1, 5 and 6 – need to be pre-booked using the Parks Victoria website. Pet lovers, note: this is the only camping spot in the national park in which dogs are permitted. This place is on Jerusalem Inlet, 10 km south of the township of Eildon and reached by following Jerusalem Creek Rd. **Map refs:** 132 B6, 188 G2, 190 G12

256 Lakeside camping area

The boat ramp at the Lakeside camping area gets a workout during holiday periods, when sundry anglers, waterskiers and sightseers take to the water. This is one of the popular Fraser camping area destinations on the edge of Coller Bay, and sites have to be booked in advance through Parks Victoria's online booking service. Lakeside is 12 km north-east of Alexandra via UT Creek Rd. **Map refs:** 132 B6, 188 G1, 190 G12

257 Mountaineer Creek camping area (walk-in and boat-based camping)

Mountaineer Creek is up in the northern section of Lake Eildon National Park, where you can really get away from it all. The camping area is situated on peaceful Stone Bay and can only be accessed by boat or on foot. Whether you're contemplating canoeing here across the lake or hiking in along a network of bushy tracks, first talk to the ranger about access and conditions. **Map refs:** 132 B5, 188 G1, 190 G11

258 O'Toole Flat camping area

If you want to avoid the bustle of the popular places around Coller Bay, head south of Eildon towards Jamieson and then veer north on Pinnacle Track for 1 km to O'Toole Flat. It's a suitably basic site, equipped only with fireplaces. Orchids and other wildflowers are known to blossom on the surrounding hillsides in spring. **Map refs:** 132 C6, 188 G2, 190 G12

259 Taylors Creek camping area (walk-in and boat-based camping)

Taylors Creek is in the isolated Jerusalem Block, down at Big River Arm, and can only be reached by boat or a decent bushwalk. This is where you should head if remote bush camping is your preference. **Map refs:** 132 C6, 188 G2, 190 G12

MANSFIELD STATE FOREST

Stretching roughly between the towns of Mansfield and Jamieson, Mansfield State Forest has trails rough enough to excite those who are fond of a 4WD or of mountain-biking, and access to enough creeks and rivers to satisfy the choosiest angler. Horseriders are also frequent users of the forest tracks.
Who to contact: Mansfield DSE (03) 5733 1200, DSE 13 6186

260 Blue Range camping area

Follow the Mansfield–Whitfield Rd north from Mansfield, continue north on Walker Rd, then turn onto Blue Range Creek Rd and you'll soon come to the Blue Range camping reserve. This is a small creekside site dominated by manna gums, with orchids and grevillea hiding in the undergrowth. Horseriders and trail-bikers frequent this area. **Map refs:** 132 C5, 190 H10

261 Grannys Flat camping area

The Grannys Flat camping area near the banks of the Jamieson River is a good spot for swimming, but take care as there can be strong currents here. For something a little more strenuous, consider walking the Mitchells Bridle Trail, a 24 km, 2-day hike to Mitchells Flat via the historic Quicksilver mercury mine. Grannys Flat is 8 km east of Jamieson, signposted off the Jamieson–Licola Rd. **Map refs:** 132 C6, 188 H2, 190 H12

262 Running Creek camping area

Peppermint, blue gum and stringybark trees intermingle in this forested area north-east of Jamieson. One appealing characteristic of the campsites here is that they lie beside the Howqua River, but watch out for quickly rising water levels when thunderstorms hit the catchment upstream. Look for signposted access about 10 km down the Howqua River Rd from the Mansfield–Jamieson Rd junction. **Map refs:** 132 C6, 188 H1, 190 H12

263 Wrens Flat camping area

Suitable for camper trailers but not caravans, Wrens Flat is 44 km to the east of Jamieson down Mt Sunday Rd, which branches off the Jamieson–Licola Rd. There's decent fishing in the Jamieson River. Up Mitchells Rd to the north is Mitchells Flat, which is one end of the 24 km Mitchells Bridle Trail that leads hikers past an old mining site. **Map refs:** 133 D6, 189 I2

MOUNT BUFFALO NATIONAL PARK

Mt Buffalo's spectacular granite cliffs are tailor-made for some adventurous hang-gliding and rock climbing, while the alpine plateau is also an excellent skiing destination when the winter snows drift in. In spring, bushwalkers flock here to walk among the wildflowers and take in some fantastic views of the Australian Alps. At Porepunka, turn off the Great Alpine Rd onto Mt Buffalo Rd.

Highlights of this spectacular park include Ladies Bath and Eurobin Falls, the view over the Ovens Valley from the cliff-tops near the Chalet, and the exposed granite peaks of the Cathedral and the Horn. These last two can be quite spectacular at sunset as the rich light paints the grey stone in varying tones of pink, red and orange.

Who to contact: Parks Victoria 13 1963

264 Lake Catani camping area

It's possible to camp among the snow gums on the eastern side of Lake Catani. From Lake Catani, cycle or stroll the 2 km track leading to the Gorge, where there are some sublime views of distant mountains. The camping area is open Nov–Apr only; bookings via website essential from 1 Sept.

Due to its elevation, nights can be cool here even in the warmer months. Camping is quite pleasant nonetheless, with brightly coloured crimson rosellas being common visitors to many camps. And if you have a canoe or kayak you can take it for a paddle on Lake Catani. The nearby Monolith Track, accessible from the Gorge Lake Catani Trail, offers fantastic views over the lake and surrounding forests. **Map refs:** 133 E4, 191 K9

MOUNT GRANYA STATE PARK

Rising up beside Lake Hume are the steep slopes of Mt Granya, the summit of which affords great views of faraway mountain ranges. Bushwalkers wend their way up and down the park, as do many a mountain bike and 4WD. Follow the Murray Valley Hwy east of Tallangatta and turn north on Murray River Rd.

Who to contact: Parks Victoria 13 1963

265 Cottontree camping area

This lovely camping area is west of the town of Granya, down Webbs La. Take the short walk from here to the seasonal Granya Falls, which passes by a Scout hut built in the 1930s. A tad more challenging is the 6 km Georges Walking Track, which leads from Cottontree Creek up to the summit of Mt Granya. While you're up there, take the Lyrebird Loop Nature Trail, where you'll more than likely hear the bird's distinctive call. **Map refs:** 133 G2, 191 M6

MOUNT LAWSON STATE PARK

The impressive bluffs of Mt Lawson rear up near the Murray River some 70 km east of Wodonga. The mountain's summit provides a great viewpoint from which to count off the region's other peaks. Koetong Creek is the highlight of the park as far as anglers are concerned. You can access the area from Murray River Rd in the north or Murray Valley Hwy from the south.

Who to contact: Parks Victoria 13 1963

266 Koetong Creek camping area

This campground is near its namesake creek – from the Murray Valley Hwy, head north on Firebrace Track, continue along Mt Lawson Rd, then turn west on Koetong Creek Track. Back near the highway is a historic railway trestle bridge that was built almost 100 years ago; today, it's a good place for a picnic. To the north is the summit of Mt Lawson, where a nature trail enhances the fantastic lookouts. **Map refs:** 133 G1, 191 M6

267 Kurrajongs camping area

The Kurrajongs is located up near Lake Hume at the peaceful northern edge of the park, and is accessed via Murray River Rd.

Hikers will love the 7 km Flaggy Creek Gorge Walking Track that traverses this area. It first passes the excellent Valley View lookout before winding down to the gorge proper. **Map refs:** 133 G1, 191 M5

MOUNT SAMARIA STATE PARK

Retreat into the coolness of the eucalypt forest in Mt Samaria State Park. Apart from enjoying the spectacular views from atop granite outcrops, and some plunging waterfalls, visitors also get to see the vivacious local bird life and historic remnants of old logging sites. From Mansfield, the park is 14 km away via Tolmie Rd; from the north, head in along Samaria Rd from Swanpool.

Who to contact: Parks Victoria 13 1963

268 Camphora camping area (walk-in camping)

After taking the signposted access route of Mt Samaria Rd, you'll need to park the car or bike and walk the remaining 500 m to the Camphora site. After you've set up your camp, continue south down Mt Samaria Rd to the beginning of the Wileman Track, from where you can reach the soft splashing of the Back Creek Falls. **Map refs:** 132 C4, 190 H10

269 Samaria Well camping area

The level camping area at Samaria Well is situated in the midst of serene bushland at the northern perimeter of the park. Head south of here down Mt Samaria Rd to tackle the steep climb up to the summit of the park's rocky centrepiece – unobstructed views greet you on all sides. **Map refs:** 132 C4, 190 H10

270 Spring Creek Sawmill camping area

At the Spring Creek Sawmill site, you'll find what's left of the substantial timber-cutting operation that began working the forest here in the 1920s, including several kilns. Near here is the beginning of a walk that trails alongside an old wooden tramway. The ruins of the sawmill and the campground are accessed off Mt Samaria Rd in the middle of the park. **Map refs:** 132 C4, 190 H10

271 Wild Dog Creek Falls camping area (walk-in camping)

Along the walking track leading from Mt Samaria Rd over to Wild Dog Falls is the falls campground, set within a grove of blue gums. The cascades themselves are well worth a look, particularly as there's an unimpeded view from above them east towards the Strathbogie Ranges. You can also trek from here up to the summit of Mt Samaria via the Summit Link Track. **Map refs:** 132 C4, 190 H10

MOUNT TORBRECK SCENIC RESERVE

This reserve surrounds the 1500 m high Mt Torbreck, which lies about 15 km south of Eildon. Most visitors come here to walk up to the mountain's summit for the breathtaking views of the region. Follow Barnewall Plains Rd from its junction with the Eildon–Jamieson Rd to get here. Note: access roads are closed at times during winter.

Who to contact: DSE Alexandra (03) 5772 0200, 13 6186

272 Barnewall Plains camping area

You can camp on small grassy sites in the Barnewall Plains camping area, which is 6 km down Barnewall Plains Rd from the Eildon–Jamieson Rd turn-off. This is the start of the superb 2 km Mt Torbreck Walking Track. It leads up through alpine ash into snow gum forest before reaching the summit, with its panoramic views. Note: snow and heavy fog can descend on the area in winter and the camping area is closed from mid-June to end Oct. **Map refs:** 132 B6, 188 G2

NARIEL CREEK RECREATION RESERVE

This creekside reserve is about 12 km south of Corryong – access is provided by the Corryong–Benambra Rd, which branches off the Murray Valley Hwy 7 km west of the town of Corryong. There's good safe swimming in the creek, and shade is provided by the numerous trees on-site.

Who to contact: Corryong Visitor Centre (02) 6076 2277

273 Nariel Creek Recreation Reserve camping area

This is a large and lovely camping area on a bank of Nariel Creek. You'll be doing well to get a campsite here between Christmas and 2 Jan, which is when the annual, long-running Nariel Creek Folk Festival fills the reserve with the sounds of concerts and jam sessions. You should be fine at other times of year, though, when this makes a great base for regional exploration. **Map refs:** 133 H2, 191 O7

NUG NUG RESERVE

Nug Nug Reserve sounds like it's straight out a children's story, but it's a real-life place beside the Buffalo River, 15 km south of Myrtleford. You can swim and fish in the river, and then head south to Lake Buffalo to repeat the process, or go waterskiing. From Myrtleford, follow Buffalo River Rd for 13 km and then swing east on Nug Nug Rd for another 1.5 km.

Who to contact: Nug Nug Reserve Campers Association Inc. (03) 5751 1255, (03) 9551 1178

274 Nug Nug Reserve camping area

This picturesque camping area has plenty of sites to spread out in, and facilities that include cold showers. There are also concrete tennis courts if you tire of water-based activities. Right next door is Mt Buffalo National Park, though to reach the mountaintop itself you'll need to double back to the Great Alpine Rd. Note: you pay a few dollars extra per site for power. **Map refs:** 133 E4, 191 J9

RUBICON VALLEY HISTORIC AREA

Nestled within Rubicon State Forest, 150 km north-east of Melbourne, is the Rubicon Valley Historic Area. This 1470 ha area protects the historic remnants of a once thriving logging industry, including old wooden tramways and sawmills, as well

as a still-operational hydro-electric scheme built on the cusp of the Great Depression. From Taggerty on the Maroondah Hwy, take the Taggerty–Thornton Rd and then Rubicon Rd.

Who to contact: DSE 13 6186

275 Kendalls A camping area

This is one of a pair of camping areas just off Rubicon Rd, to the north of the power station. Directly east of here are Snobs Falls, a fetching 100 m cascade over tumbledown rocks. Unfortunately, there's no dependable route across the forest to the falls; you'll need to backtrack to the Taggerty–Thornton Rd, swing onto the Goulburn Valley Hwy, then take Snobs Creek Rd and follow it for 7 km from the turn-off. **Map refs:** 132 B6, 188 G2, 190 G12

276 Kendalls B camping area

The Kendalls B camping area is near the entrance to the hydro-electric power station, and 1.5 km from Kendalls A – the 2 campgrounds are linked by a walking/cycling track. During the warmer months of the year, drive up to Morris Lookout for great views of nearby townships; the track leading here from Rubicon Rd is subject to restricted access during winter. **Map refs:** 132 B6, 188 G2, 190 G12

STACEYS BRIDGE RESERVE

Staceys Bridge Reserve is a quiet waterside spot at the head of the Nariel Valley, 46 km south of Corryong. Swimming and fishing in the local creek are highly recommended. From Corryong, head straight down the Corryong–Benambra Rd and watch for the signposted access.

Who to contact: Corryong Visitor Centre (02) 6076 2277

277 Staceys Bridge camping area

The level ground at Staceys Bridge is good for pitching tents, and there's plenty of shade for when the weather heats up. You may spot some wildlife around here, in particular the local kangaroos. Bring your own firewood to use in the fireplaces provided, and a good supply of water. **Map refs:** 133 H2, 191 O7

STANLEY STATE FOREST

A few kilometres south of the pretty little town of Yackandandah, and just over 30 km south of Wodonga, you'll find the eucalypt-dominated Stanley State Forest. You can drive a 14 km forest circuit that starts and finishes in Yackandandah, passing an old sawmill, a deep tailrace and a stand of native pines. Enter the forest via Bells Flat Rd from Yackandandah.

Who to contact: DSE Beechworth (03) 5720 8190, 13 6186

278 Stanley Forest camping areas

Numerous camping areas have been cleared alongside Yackandandah Creek – access is off Yack Gate Rd and Number One Rd. Make sure your chosen campsite is at least 20 m away from the creek or any other watercourse. There is a composting toilet located on the corner of Yack Gate Rd and Gravel Pit Track. Stop by Yackandandah Junction, where a goldmining community once thrived, and detour down Cohns Track to see where a local prospector worked himself into the ground. **Map refs:** 133 E2, 191 K7

WARBY–OVENS NATIONAL PARK

The steep Warby Range, 12 km west of Wangaratta, has lots of energising bushwalking tracks and excellent ridge-top viewpoints. Visitors follow in the footsteps of Ned Kelly, who used the range as an open-air hideout at the end of the 19th century. Take Wangandary Rd west from Wangaratta; from the south, try Taminick Gap Rd heading towards Lake Mokoan.

Who to contact: Parks Victoria 13 1963

279 Bush camping (walk-in camping)

It's permissible to go bush camping in the park by following your nose down secluded pathways – mountain-bikers can pedal themselves down any of the vehicle tracks. Anyone intending to pitch a tent among the stringybark and box trees will need to contact the local ranger first to make the necessary arrangements. **Map refs:** 132 C2, 190 H7

280 The Forest Camp camping area

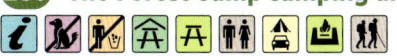

Located in the far north of the Warby–Ovens National Park, this basic campground has pit toilets and wood BBQs. There are walking tracks that head north and south from the campsite. To access the campsite turn off the Tungaamah–Peechelba Rd from the north, Forest Rd from the west or the Wangaratta–Yarrawonga Rd to the east. **Map refs:** 132 C2, 190 H6

281 Wenhams Camp camping area

Wenhams Camp is at the Glenrowan (southern) end of the park. From here, you can take a 4.5 km self-guided stroll along the Friends Track to learn about the local vegetation; detour down the side track to Kwat Kwat Lookout, where there's a stupendous view of the Victorian Alps. The best vantage point, however, is afforded by Mt Glenrowan – courtesy of a 9 km return walk along Ridge Track from Taminick Gap. The campground is off Booth Rd, accessed from Gerrett Rd off Wangaratta Rd.

There are a number of pleasant bushwalks that start from this campground, and mobs of eastern grey kangaroos frequent the forest and grassy clearings nearby. **Map refs:** 132 C2, 190 H7

CAMPSITES LOCATED IN OTHER AREAS

282 25 Mile Creek camping area

Reaching this appealingly isolated camping area entails a long drive from the small alpine township of Dargo. Head north for 45 km along the Dargo High Plains Rd and then turn onto Ritchie Rd; 25 Mile Creek is a further 10 km down the road. The creekside campsites are only accessible in dry weather.

Come equipped with plenty of drinking water and firewood. **Map refs:** 133 F6, 189 L2, 191 L12

Who to contact: DSE 13 6186

283 30 Mile Creek camping area

For a taste of high plains life, follow Dargo High Plains Rd to the junction with Ritchie Rd, 45 km north of Dargo, and then continue down Ritchie Rd for 22 km to 30 Mile Creek. Here you can fish and daydream to your heart's content. Note: the road in is only accessible in dry weather, and you need to bring supplies of water and firewood. **Map refs:** 133 F6, 189 L2, 191 L12

Who to contact: DSE 13 6186

284 Anglers Rest camping area

Anglers Rest is a highwayside stopover in the middle of an arm of Alpine National Park. It's almost 30 km north of Omeo off the Omeo Hwy, along a snaking section of road near the confluence of the Bundarra, Cobungra and Mitta Mitta rivers – all 3 waterways are known for their trout fishing, hence the name of the camping area. Nearby is the historic Blue Duck Inn Hotel, a popular refreshment break for motorcyclists enjoying the area's sweeping bends. **Map refs:** 133 G5, 189 M1, 191 M11

Who to contact: Parks Victoria 13 1963

285 Big River Bridge camping area

The Glen Valley area is squeezed between 2 chunks of Alpine National Park forest. The Omeo Hwy negotiates this valley and you can camp just off the road here near Big River Bridge, 42 km north of Omeo. It's common for canoeists to use this spot as a starting point for extended paddles along the river. North of here is a section of the Australian Alps Walking Track that leads to the top of scenic Mt Wills. **Map refs:** 133 G5, 191 M11

Who to contact: Parks Victoria 13 1963

286 Black Snake Creek camping area

About 25 km north-west of Dargo, in an isolated area, is the Black Snake Creek campsite. It may not sound terribly enticing, but it's a peaceful bush-camping site that's well off the beaten track. Anglers will appreciate its location at the junction of 2 watercourses: the Wonnangatta River and Black Snake Creek. Head down Wonnangatta Rd from Crooked River Rd to reach this place. **Map refs:** 133 F7, 189 L3

Who to contact: DSE 13 6186

287 Dart Arm camping area (boat-based camping)

You'll find Dart Arm on the eastern shoreline of Lake Dartmouth, an immense reservoir surrounded by the grand forests of Alpine National Park. The only way to get here is by boat, which limits the amount of company you're likely to have – put your vessel into the lake via the boat ramp at Six Mile Creek, off Dartmouth Rd just east of Dartmouth township. **Map refs:** 133 H3, 191 N9

Who to contact: Goulburn-Murray Water (03) 5833 5500, 13 1963

288 Dogs Grave camping area

The Dogs Grave monument site could be called the Tomb of the Unknown Dog – does it mark the grave of Boney the cattle dog, or Angus the Smithfield heeler? Regardless of which local story is true, this remains a decent off-the-beaten-track camping spot. There are 2 fireplaces with BBQ plates. It's 35 km west of Swifts Creek – from Cassilis Rd, take Upper Livingstone Rd and then Birregun Rd. **Map refs:** 133 F6, 189 M2, 191 M12

Who to contact: DSE Swifts Creek (03) 5159 5100, 13 6186

289 Eight Mile Creek camping area (boat-based camping)

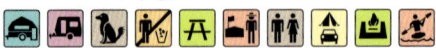

Eight Mile Creek is a camping area on the southern shoreline of Lake Dartmouth, where it's only accessible by boat. The lake is encircled by, but not technically part of, the stunning Alpine National Park, and the lack of car access only enhances the peace and quiet. Go fishing for Macquarie perch and trout, or paddle a canoe around Victoria's largest-capacity water storage. **Map refs:** 133 G4, 191 N9

Who to contact: Goulburn-Murray Water (03) 5833 5500; or Parks Victoria 13 1963

290 Eustace Creek camping area

You can enjoy a variety of watersports on Lake Dartmouth, 20 km east of Mitta Mitta – except for waterskiing, which isn't allowed. At the southern end of the lake is the Eustace Creek camping area. Of the 3 campgrounds around the lake, this is the only one accessible by car; Eight Mile Creek and Dart Arm can only be reached by boat. From the Benambra–Corryong Rd, head south-west along Eustace Gap Track. **Map refs:** 133 G4, 191 N9

Who to contact: Goulburn-Murray Water (03) 5833 5500; or Parks Victoria 13 1963

291 Ferny Flat camping area (bush camping)

To reach this peaceful spot in the Omeo Valley, head north from Omeo on the Omeo Hwy and, before the road winds into Alpine National Park, veer north-east on Omeo Valley Rd. Ferny Flat is a bush-camping site, so there's nothing in the way of facilities. Canoeists can outnumber anglers on the nearby Mitta Mitta River. **Map refs:** 133 G5, 191 N11

Who to contact: Parks Victoria 13 1963

292 Gibbo River camping areas

The Gibbo River camping areas are just south of the Exhibition Creek Bridge, around 30 km north of Omeo on the Corryong–Benambra Rd. These pleasant dispersed camping sites are not conducive to caravans or camper trailers, but those with tents will find them cosy enough. You'll need to be fully self-sufficient to stay here; the only facilities are some picnic tables and wood-fired BBQs. **Map refs:** 133 H4, 191 N10

Who to contact: Parks Victoria 13 1963

Grant Historic Area

If you follow the Dargo High Plains Rd for 17 km north of Dargo and then turn down McMillan Rd, you'll soon reach Grant – a boom town during the 19th-century gold rush but now a town of ruins. Walk or drive around the local goldfields, and don't forget to bring a picnic and fishing rods.

Who to contact: Parks Victoria 13 1963 for campsite nos **293**, **294**

293 Grant camping area

The small Grant camping area is behind the information shelter in the one-time ridge-top township. After using your imagination to re-create the 15 hotels that operated here at the height of the gold rush, walk over to the Jolly Sailor Mine and battery site. Also nearby is the water-filled Jeweller Shop Mine. The Crooked River Lookout is west of here down McMillans Rd. **Map refs:** 133 F7, 189 L2

294 Talbotville camping areas

You'll find dispersed camping on grassy sites at Talbotville down by Crooked River, almost 16 km along McMillan Rd from the Dargo High Plains Rd turn-off. Wander around the old Talbotville Cemetery or inspect the rusty ore carts at the nearby New Good Hope Mine. Note: reaching the latter entails numerous river crossings. You can also follow McMillans Track into adjacent Alpine National Park. Note: McMillans Rd is suitable for 2WD only in dry weather; off-road camper trailers can be towed in by a 4WD. **Map refs:** 133 F6, 189 K2

295 Hairpin Bend camping area

South of Bunroy Junction in the Biggara Valley is Hairpin Bend, where campers enjoy access to the Murray River for refreshing swims, canoe trips and fishing sessions. From the stretch of the Murray Valley Hwy leading east to Khancoban, detour south down Upper Murray Rd, then take Bunroy Rd and finally Bunroy Creek Track. **Map refs:** 133 I3, 187 A3, 191 P8

Who to contact: Corryong Tourist Information Centre (02) 6076 2277

296 Hinnomunjie Bridge camping area

There's bush camping beside the Mitta Mitta River at Hinnomunjie Bridge, north up the Omeo Valley Rd from Omeo township. Fishing for trout and canoeing are both highly popular activities in this neck of the Victorian woods. The bridge is one of only a handful of historic timber truss bridges in the state. It was built using hand-cut wood around 1910, and looks pretty good for its age. **Map refs:** 133 G5, 191 N11

Who to contact: DSE Swifts Creek (03) 5159 5100, 13 61 86

Howqua Hills Historic Area

Remnants of the goldmining that took place in the Howqua Hills are scattered about the area, including an old water race and a smelting furnace. A particularly poignant historic sight is the former home of bushman Fred Fry, who left his mark in the form of many huts around the region. Horseriders join bushwalkers in exploring this lovely area. Turn onto the signposted Howqua Track from the Mansfield–Mount Buller Rd just east of Merrijig.

Who to contact: Parks Victoria 13 1963

297 Davons camping area

Davons is located about 600 m east of Sheepyard Flat down Brocks Rd. On the other side of the Howqua River is state forest, while a kilometre or so to the south is the perimeter of Alpine National Park. Bring in a load of firewood and plenty of drinking water when you camp here. **Map refs:** 133 D6, 189 I1, 191 I12

298 Frys Flat camping area

A well-known bushman called Fred Fry hand-built his home here in the 1930s. His reputation was such that in 1950 author Neville Shute wrote a novel about Fry's Howqua Valley existence – *The Far Country*. Note, however, that while you can admire Fry's former home, you can't use it for an overnight stay. There are some popular horse yards just south of here and this is a designated horse camping area Nov–May, attracting large groups. Frys Flat is about 2.5 km south of Sheepyard Flat along Howqua Hills Track. This area is subject to seasonal closure. **Map refs:** 132 D6, 189 I1, 191 I12

299 Noonans Flat camping area

Like Pickerings Flat, 700 m to the west down Brocks Rd, Noonans has a private hut on-site. The access track, signposted off Brocks Rd, is subject to seasonal closure – check with Parks Victoria about its condition if you plan to stay here. **Map refs:** 133 D6, 189 I1, 191 I12

300 Pickerings Flat camping area

Pickerings Flat is 400 m east of Davons Flat and 700 m from Noonans Flat. There's signposted access off Brocks Rd. Fishing and swimming in the Howqua River are some of the recommended activities here. Avoid going off any of the local tracks, as there are some open mineshafts in these hills. Note: there's a private hut here. **Map refs:** 133 D6, 189 I1, 191 I12

301 Sheepyard Flat camping area

This camping area boasts open, grassy campsites on either side of Brocks Rd, about 2.5 km north of Frys Flat; needless to say, it's popular with large groups. There's an information shelter here, along with toilets, picnic tables and wood-fired BBQs. An easy, self-guided walk shadows the Howqua River from here down to Frys Flat. **Map refs:** 132 D6, 189 I1, 191 I12

302 Tunnel Spur Flat camping area

This area was named after a 100 m tunnel dug between the Howqua River and a lengthy water race that terminated at

a now-defunct water wheel 4 km south of Sheepyard Flat. Horseriders can make use of the horse yards here Nov–May, as well as the ones further south at Frys Flat; bookings must be made in advance through Parks Victoria. **Map refs:** 133 D6, 189 I1, 191 I12

303 Joker Flat camping area

Joker Flat is just off the Omeo Hwy almost 40 km north of Omeo, not far south of the junction with Bogong High Plains Rd. Flowing nearby is Big River, which is very popular with trout anglers. The waterway is also well-attended by canoeists paddling through the various rapids sprinkled between Big River Bridge and Anglers Rest, where it merges with the Mitta Mitta River. **Map refs:** 133 G5, 191 M11

Who to contact: Parks Victoria 13 1963

304 Lightning Creek camping area

This roadside camping area is a nice spot to pull over for a snooze while admiring the great scenery along the Omeo Hwy. It's beside Lightning Creek some 20 km south of the small settlement of Mitta Mitta, and is equipped with toilets and fireplaces. The local waterway is good for a swim or fishing. **Map refs:** 133 G4, 191 M9

Who to contact: DSE Mitta Mitta (02) 6072 3410, 13 6186

305 Molesworth Caravan Park

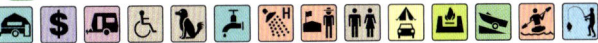

There are decent facilities at Molesworth Caravan Park, including a laundry, showers and BBQs. It's located in a riverside reserve, signposted north off the hwy to the west of the bridge over the Goulburn River. Anglers look for signs of trout from the riverbanks here, or launch small boats from the informal ramp, while others take short walks through the reserve. You'll need to bring a supply of firewood, which will be easy enough to arrange in town. **Map refs:** 132 A5, 188 F1, 190 F11

How to book: Goulburn Valley Hwy, Molesworth (03) 5797 6278

Murray River – Granya to Towong

Between Granya and Towong, two small towns north of the Murray Valley Hwy, a number of small camping areas sit beside the Murray River. Take an overnight break from the highway and enjoy camping among the river red gums and taking a cool swim. The camping areas are signposted along Murray River Rd linking Granya and Towong.

Who to contact: Parks Victoria 13 1963

306 Burrowye Reserve camping area

The Burrowye Reserve is adjacent to the densely treed Mt Lawson State Park – the summit of the mountain at the centre of the park provides fantastic views of the surrounding region. Burrowye is about 24 km west of Walwa, off Murray River Rd; you can also reach it from the Murray Valley Hwy by taking Burrowye Rd from Koetong. **Map refs:** 133 G1, 191 N6

307 Clarke Lagoon Reserve camping area

This reserve is 6 km north of Tintaldra, off Murray River Rd. It's a decent spot to pitch a tent and have a swim. If approaching the site from the west, keep a lookout for Pine Mountain, a tree-covered monolith that's one and a half times the size of Uluru. South of Clarke Lagoon, in Mt Mittamatite Regional Park, is a great lookout called Emberys. **Map refs:** 133 H1, 191 O6

308 Neils Reserve camping area

Neils Reserve is a good choice for camping for several reasons. It has a great location beside the Murray River, between the small townships of Walwa and Tintaldra, so you can enjoy your favourite river-based activities. It's well off the Murray Valley Hwy, so it's peaceful – in fact, between it and the highway are extensive forests. And it's adjacent to Burrowa–Pine Mountain National Park, which has a wonderful variety of plants, animals and bushwalks. **Map refs:** 133 H1, 191 O6

309 North Cedars Holiday Park

On the northern fringe of Wangaratta, off the Old Hume Hwy, is the North Cedars Holiday Park. This is a tranquil spot, with plenty of trees and a reasonable amount of space allowed between each of the campsites. The pool, playground and games room will keep the kids out of your hair. The Ovens River isn't far away and provides a bit of scenery and a place to fish. **Map refs:** 133 D2, 191 I7

How to book: Old Hume Hwy, North Wangaratta (03) 5721 5230, 1800 333 410 www.northcedars.com.au

310 Razorback Hut camping area

In recent times, Razorback Hut, up on Mt Stirling, was still being used by its owners during their annual cattle muster. Get onto Circuit Rd from Mt Buller Rd and take the track just before the No. 3 Rd intersection – the hut is 5 km north of Telephone Box junction. You may be able to get here during dry weather in a conventional vehicle, but a 4WD is highly recommended for the trip into this beautiful and remote alpine region. There are horse yards nearby. **Map refs:** 133 D5, 189 I1, 191 I11

Who to contact: DSE 13 6186

311 Snowy Creek camping area

If you're wandering down the Omeo Hwy, consider detouring onto Holloways Log Rd, 12 km south of Mitta Mitta, and stopping for the night at the Snowy Creek camping area. Cool yourself in a mountain stream or go fishing for blackfish, trout and spiny crayfish. Note: caravans can only make it through to the creek in dry weather. **Map refs:** 133 G3, 191 M9

Who to contact: DSE Mitta Mitta (02) 6072 3410, 13 6186

312 Stringybark Creek camping area

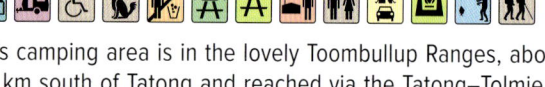

This camping area is in the lovely Toombullup Ranges, about 30 km south of Tatong and reached via the Tatong–Tolmie Rd. It's adjacent to a reserve centred on the spot beside Stringybark Creek where the Kelly Gang shot and killed 2 constables, dooming themselves in the process. Note: logging trucks are regular users of the Tatong–Tolmie Rd, so drive carefully along this thoroughfare. **Map refs:** 132 C4, 190 H10

Who to contact: DSE Mansfield (03) 5733 1200, 13 6186

313 Toombullup East School Site camping area

The Toombullup East School Site camping area is one of several overnight sites that have been established in the low-key Toombullup Ranges, which lie to the south-east of the small town of Tatong, south of Benalla. The former school site is in bushland about 30 km from Tatong down the Tatong–Tolmie Rd, about 2 km beyond another campground at Stringybark Creek. Forest walkers will enjoy the isolation here, while those with 4WD vehicles will find plenty of local territory to explore. **Map refs:** 132 C4, 190 H10

Who to contact: DSE Mansfield (03) 5733 1200, 13 6186

314 Victoria Falls Historic Area camping area (bush camping)

This basic camping area is surrounded by snow gum and mountain gum woodlands, and has two rivers for company – the Victoria and the Cobungra – that provide plenty of decent fishing nearby. Camping close to a defunct hydro-electric plant may not sound like the most compelling reason to stay somewhere, but the Victoria Falls plant is nonetheless an interesting part of the state's early 20th-century history. **Map refs:** 133 G6, 189 M1, 191 M12

Who to contact: Parks Victoria Omeo (03) 5159 0660, 13 1963

315 Victoria River Track camping area

A true bush-camping option, the Victoria River Track is accessed off the Great Alpine Rd some 20 km west of Omeo, just past Cobungra. You won't find any facilities here, only the Victoria River and plenty of solitude. In the nearby Victoria Falls Historic Area are the remnants of Victoria's first hydro-electric power scheme, established in 1908 to power the goldfields south of Omeo. **Map refs:** 133 F6, 189 L1, 191 L12

Who to contact: Parks Victoria 13 1963

GOULBURN AND MURRAY

THE LANDSCAPE OF VICTORIA'S central-north is defined by two big rivers: the majestic Murray, which sketches the state's northern border as it wiggles past bucolic communities like Yarrawonga, Echuca and Cohuna; and the equally snaky Goulburn River, which flows down past Shepparton and Seymour. An extended camping excursion along the Murray gives you the chance to become acquainted with one of the country's great watercourses, as well as the pastoral endeavours and picturesque countryside that it sustains. Bush-camping spots are secreted off the hwy between Barnawartha North and Cobram, allowing access to photogenic billabongs and sandy riverbend beaches.

This landscape is dominated by the thick-set limbs of river red gums, in particular the Barmah forests, which are crammed with more of these large trees than any other place in the world. Although comfortingly familiar, the river red gum occasionally wreaks havoc at campgrounds. Its heavy branches can crack off the trunk without warning, so avoid erecting your tent or parking your car directly underneath the shady canopy. More freshwater camping can be had at Echuca near the confluence of the Murray and Goulburn rivers, where you can try an old-fashioned form of transport by boarding a paddle-steamer, and north-west of here on pretty Gunbower Island.

Away from the rivers, there are Aboriginal heritage sites and lots of colonial history to explore. In Heathcote–Graytown National Park there's an old gunpowder magazine and the foundations of a former gold-rush boom town. More history is enshrined nearby in the sombre remains of a World War II POW camp. And there's plenty more for nature lovers to enjoy at the internationally recognised Kerang Lakes wetlands, where an amazing variety of waterbirds congregate.

CAMPSITES LOCATED IN PARKS AND RESERVES

BARMAH NATIONAL PARK

Some of the river red gums in Barmah National Park took root here half a millennium ago. This extraordinary national park is the world's largest sanctuary for the river red gum, located beside the Murray River near the town of Barmah. There's cool swimming in the river. Some visitor sites and tracks within the national park were closed due to flood damage in early 2012 – check with Parks Victoria on the current status.

Who to contact: Parks Victoria 13 1963

316 Barmah camping area (bush camping)

You can choose your own bush-camping site beside the Murray among (though never under, because of the possibility of falling branches) the towering red gums here. From Picola, which lies off the Murray Valley Hwy, take Picola North Rd,

then Murrays Mill Rd and finally Gulf Rd, from where there's signposted access. **Map refs:** 149 E3, 190 D4

317 Barmah Lakes camping area

Just east of the relatively flat ground of the Barmah Lakes camping area is the Dharnya Interpretative Centre (closed indefinitely), where a number of bushwalks begin. These include the self-guided Yamyabuc Discovery Trail, which passes remnants of Indigenous culture, and the longer Lakes Loop Walk. If you don't feel like walking, try boating or canoeing on the lakes. Drive here from Barmah via Moira Lakes Rd. **Map refs:** 149 E3, 190 D4

318 Ulupna Island camping area

The perimeter of Ulupna Island has been staked out by the flow of Ulupna Creek and that of the Murray River. Look for platypus in the quieter stretches of water. Take Bourchiers Rd from the Murray Valley Hwy at Strathmerton, turn left on Mywee Rd, then right on Ulupna Bridge Rd. **Map refs:** 149 F3, 190 E4

BENWELL STATE FOREST

Benwell State Forest is a 500 ha grove of towering red gums that have flourished alongside the stately flow of the Murray River. Swimming, fishing and canoeing are all favoured by visitors to the area. The forest lies to the east of the small town of Murrabit, which is itself situated due north of Kerang on the Murray Valley Hwy.

Who to contact: DSE 13 6186

319 Benwell camping area (bush camping)

Follow Murray Rd from Murrabit township, or Hall or Watsons lanes from the Koondrook–Murrabit Rd, and you'll soon find yourself surrounded by river red gums. Fishing in the river is focused on Murray cod and yellow-belly, while back in Murrabit a huge regional-produce market takes place on the first Sat of each month. **Map refs:** 148 B1, 195 N3

ECHUCA REGIONAL PARK

This sprawling riverside park is situated about 6 km east of Echuca, signposted off Simmie Rd. Needless to say, the cooling waters of the Murray River here are very popular during school holidays and pretty much any time when the weather is hot.

Who to contact: Echuca Moama Visitor Information Centre 1800 804 446

320 Christies Beach camping area

There are lots of shaded bush-camping options on flat ground at Christies Beach, which makes it a good choice for large groups.

There's also easy access to the river here, and it's only a short trip into Echuca if you have a hankering to see some well-preserved colonial history or to catch a paddle-steamer. Note: the road leading in should be negotiated in dry weather only. **Map refs:** 149 D4, 190 C5

GOORAMADDA STATE FOREST

Gooramadda is one of the many river red gum forests that border the Murray River, giving you access to plenty of swimming and fishing. Travel 2 km east of the centre of the wine-soaked township of Rutherglen, and then veer north off the Murray Valley Hwy onto Police Paddocks Rd.

Who to contact: Parks Victoria 13 1963

321 **Gooramadda State Forest (Police Paddocks) camping area**

The Police Paddocks are so named because police horses used to have a rest in the vicinity in the late 19th century. Nowadays it's campers who put themselves out to pasture here to take a break from heavy activity. This camping area lies only 10 km north-east of Rutherglen, so stocking up on drinks won't be a problem. **Map refs:** 149 I3, 191 J5

GUNBOWER NATIONAL PARK

Measuring 50 km in length, Gunbower National Park is on Gunbower Island, framed by the Murray River to the east and Gunbower Creek to the west. Most of the island is covered in river red gum and black box forest, within which over 100 peaceful bush-camping sites are secreted. The island extends between Torrumbarry and Koondrook, and tracks lead to it from various points along the Murray Valley Hwy; most visitors take Cohuna Island Rd from Cohuna.

Who to contact: Parks Victoria 13 1963

322 **Gunbower Island camping area (bush camping)**

Only a few of the many bush-camping sites on Gunbower Island have any facilities – one to note is the toilet with disabled access near Twin Bridges. Canoeing and swimming in the (often cold) water of the Murray River are the preferred activities here. A walking track circumnavigates the island; allow about 7 hrs for the round trip. Note: dogs are allowed into some parts of Gunbower and not others – call ahead to check. Also, formal campsites will be established in the park over the next couple of years. **Map refs:** 148 C2, 190 A3, 195 O5

GUTTRUM STATE FOREST

Like the neighbouring Benwell State Forest, and the Campbell Island State Forest directly across the Murray River, the Guttrum forest is devoted to the river red gums that loom over the local wetlands. Guttrum lies to the north of the twin towns of Koondrook and Barham.

Who to contact: DSE 13 6186

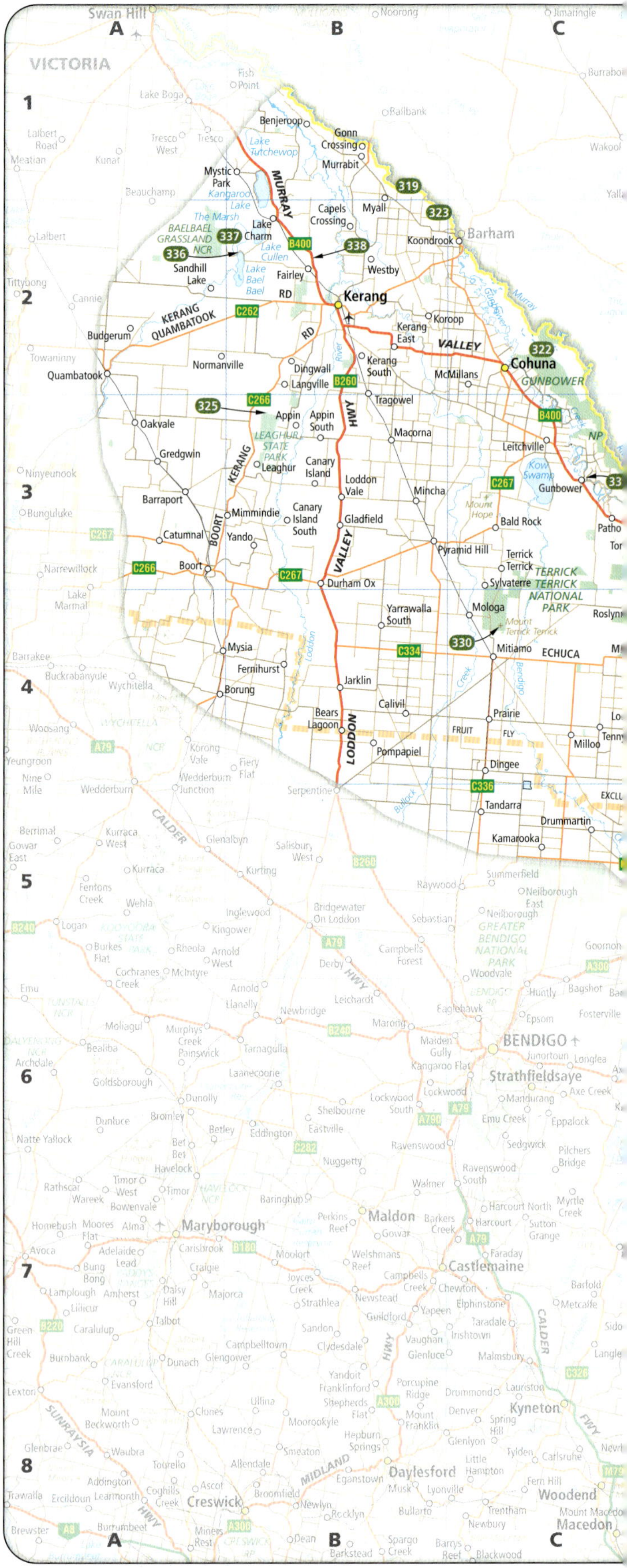

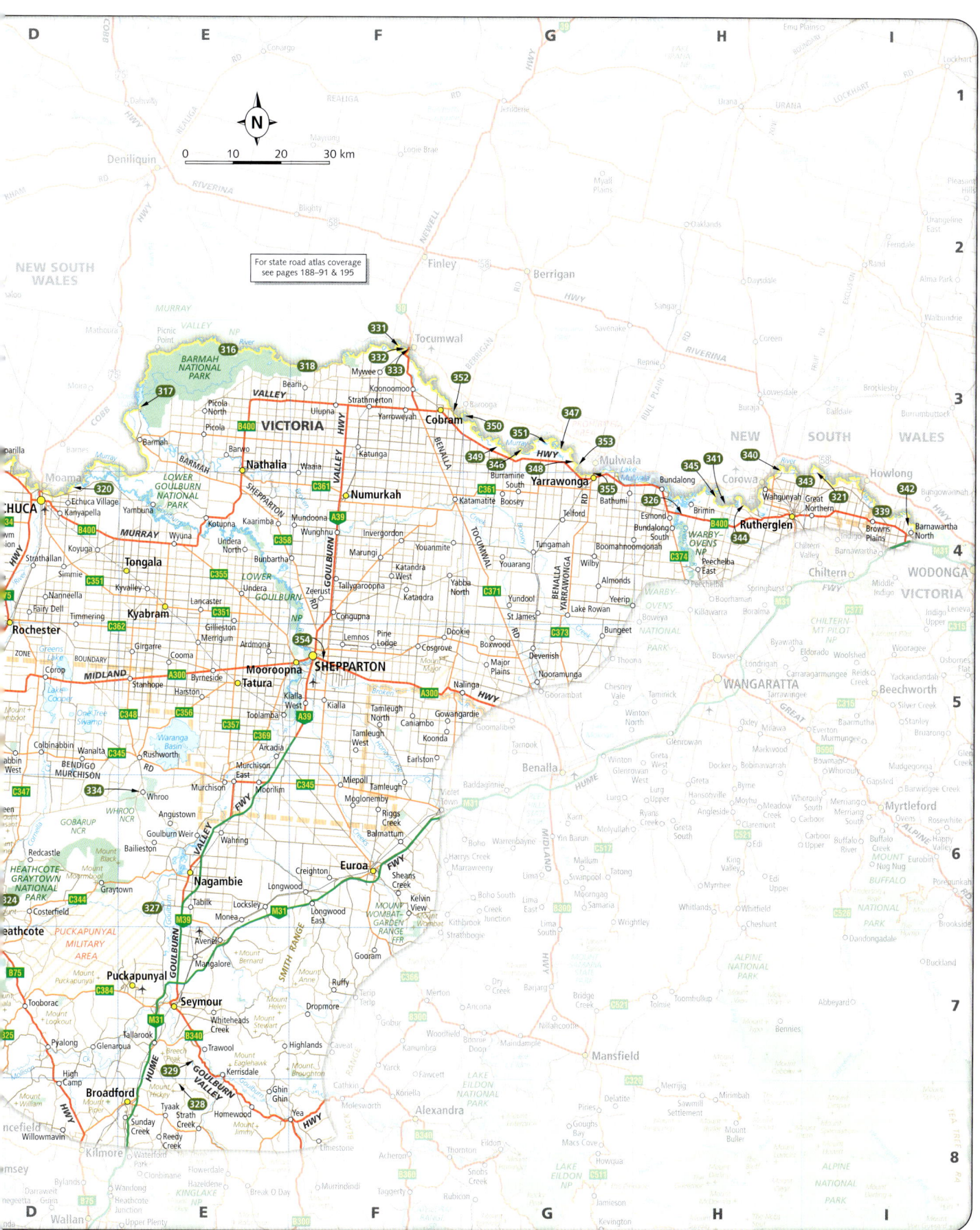

323 Guttrum camping area (bush camping)

Bush-camping sites are scattered throughout Guttrum State Forest, where campers while away the hours, and the days, by swimming, canoeing and fishing in the waters of the Murray River. From Koondrook, follow Cassidys La and then turn onto River Track; alternatively, try Millers Rd, which branches to the north off the Koondrook–Murrabit Rd. **Map refs:** 148 B2, 195 N3

HEATHCOTE–GRAYTOWN NATIONAL PARK

The declaration of this land as national park in 2002 ensured the protection of the state's biggest forest of ironbark and box, and the diverse flora and fauna that is found there, including endangered orchid and parrot species. The region's fascinating human history is embodied by significant Aboriginal sites and the ruins of gold-rush structures and a World War II POW camp. The park is north of Heathcote and can be reached via the Heathcote–North Costerfield Rd or the Heathcote–Nagambie Rd.

Who to contact: Parks Victoria 13 1963

324 Dargile camping area

The Dargile camping area is accessed from the Heathcote–North Costerfield Rd. On the way there, head up Mt Ida or to the Viewing Rock Lookout in the McIvor Range for some great views; from the latter you can hike down to the Heathcote Powder Magazine, where explosives were kept during the gold rush. The remains of the Graytown POW Camp are in the eastern section of the park, accessed off the Heathcote–Nagambie Rd. **Map refs:** 149 D6, 190 C9

LEAGHUR STATE PARK

Situated on the flood plain of the Loddon River, Leaghur State Park is the preserve of black box woodlands and is a great place for a picnic and an overnight camp. A relaxing scenic drive follows a roughly triangular route around the area. The park is 25 km south-west of Kerang, signposted off the Kerang–Boort Rd. At the time of writing, there was a blue-green algal bloom affecting Lake Meran, south-west of Kerang. As a result, activities such as swimming and fishing were being strongly discouraged by Parks Victoria. Call them for the latest.

Who to contact: Parks Victoria 13 1963

325 Lake Meran camping area

The only camping area in Leaghur State Park is at the southern end of Lake Meran, at the northern edge of the park. You get here by following the Chamberlain and Lake Meran tracks from the park entrance, and then turning north onto Vallance Track. To complete a tour of the flood plain, from the Vallance Track intersection, continue south-east down Dairy Track and then veer south-west down Main Track. **Map refs:** 148 B3, 195 M5

LOWER OVENS REGIONAL PARK

This park is centred on the confluence of the Ovens and Murray rivers, just east of Lake Mulwala and 20 km from Yarrawonga. It's a scenic place to go fishing, boating and camping, with its old-growth river red gums, flocks of pelicans and black swans, and a handful of overgrown islands. Access is off the Murray Valley Hwy.

Who to contact: Parks Victoria 13 1963

326 Lower Ovens camping area (bush camping)

There's dispersed bush camping along the picturesque Ovens and Murray rivers – try Parolas and Camerons bends. Check the local riverbanks for platypus and water rat burrows, and watch kingfishers go after their supper. Look for the signage off the Murray Valley Hwy near the Parolas Bridge, which stretches across the Ovens River. **Map refs:** 149 H4, 191 I6

MAJOR CREEK RESERVE

Drive 25 km north of Seymour, beyond the northern edge of the large Puckapunyal Military Training Area, to get to the low-key Major Creek Reserve. Take a break from negotiating Victoria's highways to go fishing or canoeing here.

Who to contact: Parks Victoria 13 1963

327 Major Creek Reserve camping area

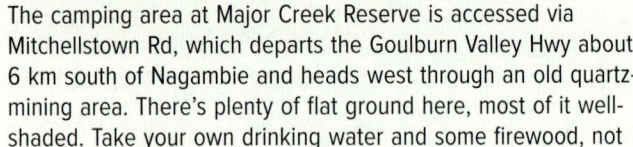

The camping area at Major Creek Reserve is accessed via Mitchellstown Rd, which departs the Goulburn Valley Hwy about 6 km south of Nagambie and heads west through an old quartz-mining area. There's plenty of flat ground here, most of it well-shaded. Take your own drinking water and some firewood, not to mention some fishing gear. **Map refs:** 149 E6, 190 D9

TALLAROOK STATE FOREST

This 5000 ha forest is threaded by dirt trails and so is understandably popular with those in a 4WD and motorcyclists. It lies to the east of the Hume Fwy between the towns of Broadford and Seymour. Access to the network of tracks within the forest is via Ennis Rd.

Who to contact: DSE Broadford (03) 5784 0600, 13 6186

328 Freemans camping area

Formerly the site of a forestry camp, Freemans is now regularly occupied by picnickers and other daytrippers. The open nature of the site makes it good for families and other large groups. Get onto Main Rd from Ennis Rd, which branches off the Hume Fwy just south of the Tallarook township exit – the campground is 11 km east of the Hume. Note: while conventional vehicles can access Freemans, other areas of the forest require a 4WD. **Map refs:** 149 E8, 188 D1, 190 D11

329 Trawool Reservoir camping area

You'll need a 4WD to get out to Trawool Reservoir, an old water storage at the northern edge of the forest. Drive along Main Rd and turn onto East Falls Rd. For some good views of the surrounding area, head up Mt Hickey Rd to the summit of Mt Hickey, also known as Mt Tallarook. Hang-gliders launch themselves from Meadow Hill Lookout. **Map refs:** 149 E7, 190 D11

TERRICK TERRICK NATIONAL PARK

The expansive grasslands of Terrick Terrick National Park are where wildlife-watchers go to catch glimpses of black wallabies, tree goannas, the endangered legless hooded scaly-foot lizard and over 100 species of birds. The park also contains some rare flora, such as the yellow daisies known as annual buttons. Head 4 km north of Mitiamo on Mitiamo Forest Rd.

Who to contact: Parks Victoria 13 1963

330 Terrick Terrick camping area

This is the only place in the national park where you are allowed to camp. Nearby is a granite outcrop known as Mt Terrick Terrick, the summit of which affords some wonderful views – the walk up here is short but steep. From the Mitiamo Forest Rd, head east along Cemetery Track at the entrance to the park, or take the Allen Track turn-off further north. **Map refs:** 148 C4, 190 A5, 195 O7

TOCUMWAL REGIONAL PARK

Tocumwal Regional Park encompasses a pretty tract of land beside a winding stretch of the Murray River. This area lies to the north-west of Cobram, and directly across the Murray from the NSW town of Tocumwal. There's plenty of bush camping here, and also plenty of river beaches to sink your toes into. Access roads run off the Goulburn Valley Hwy.

Who to contact: Parks Victoria 13 1963

331 Apex Beach camping area

Apex Beach is downstream of the Tocumwal Bridge, about 2 km south-west of Tocumwal township; Pumps Bend Track will lead you there. This beach is frequented by locals and out-of-towners alike, who all come here to enjoy the rural riverside ambience. **Map refs:** 149 F3, 190 F4

332 Finley Beach camping area

This is another one of the relaxing beaches that line the Murray River. You'll find it 2 km upstream of Tocumwal Bridge – pretty much due south of the township. Turn east off the Goulburn Valley Hwy at Finely Track to reach it. **Map refs:** 149 F3, 190 F4

333 Pebbly Beach camping area (bush camping)

There's dispersed bush camping around Pebbly Beach, which is located opposite Tocumwal township on a sweeping bend of the Murray River. Pull out your camera and explore the local billabongs or just take a long snooze beside the river. **Map refs:** 149 F3, 190 F4

WHROO HISTORIC RESERVE

Secreted within Rushworth State Forest, Whroo Historic Reserve protects the site of an 1850s goldmining town and the fields where prospectors staked their claims. Balaclava Hill was where the biggest finds were made. Take a long walk through this gold-rush history, and also see the rock well that was important to local Aboriginal people. The reserve is 7 km south of Rushworth.

Who to contact: Parks Victoria 13 1963

334 Greens Campground

From Rushworth, follow the Rushworth–Nagambie Rd and then turn onto Green Rd to reach the campground. Once you've settled in, walk through the Balaclava open-cut mine and past the remains of puddling machines and the quartz reef that was mined here. Then head south to Whroo's sombre hillside cemetery, which contains 400 gravesites. **Map refs:** 149 E6, 190 D8

CAMPSITES LOCATED IN OTHER AREAS

335 Gunbower Caravan Park

With well-grassed campsites and within easy walking distance to shops, Gunbower Caravan Park is a convenient stop on the Murray Valley Hwy. If you enjoy peace and quiet, this country caravan park ticks the boxes. River activities such as waterskiing and boating are close by. There's a solar-heated swimming pool and the fishing around town is usually very good. **Map refs:** 148 C3, 190 A4, 195 O6

How to book: 74–80 Main Rd, Gunbower (03) 5487 1412 www.gunbowercaravanpark.com.au

336 Lake Bael Bael camping areas

Lake Bael Bael is one of the largest of the 50 or so bodies of water that make up the Kerang Lakes, an internationally recognised wetland district. It's fed by the Avoca River and, in turn, sustains a bewildering assortment of waterbirds; bring your binoculars. Bush camping is permitted on the north-western fringe of the lake. Turn off the Murray Valley Hwy at the township of Reedy Lake onto Fairley Rd. **Map refs:** 148 B2, 195 M4

Who to contact: Parks Victoria 13 1963

337 The Marshes camping areas

Though they sound rather unappealing, the marshes in question are in fact significant wetlands with a thriving population of birds; eagles' nests are scattered throughout the area. There's dispersed camping around the marshes. You can reach them via the Bael Bael–Boga Rd west of the township of Lake Charm, which sits on the Murray Valley Hwy. A 4WD is recommended for the trip. **Map refs:** 148 B2, 195 M4

Who to contact: Parks Victoria 13 1963

338 Middle Reedy Lake camping area

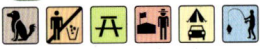

This is one of the 3 freshwater bodies that make up the Reedy Lakes system, which is in turn part of the renowned Kerang Lakes wetlands. Middle Reedy Lake is famous for its extensive ibis rookery, but it also attracts many other species of waterbirds, making it a prime destination for twitchers (birdwatchers). You can camp at various points around the lake, which is located north of Kerang township – take Pratt Rd from the Murray Valley Hwy. **Map refs:** 148 B2, 195 N4

Who to contact: Parks Victoria 13 1963

Murray River – Bundalong to Barnawartha North

The stretch of the Murray River between the old town of Barnawartha and the equally well-aged township of Bundalong harbours numerous small reserves where you can pitch a tent in the bush – so long as the tent is set up at least 20 m from any watercourse, that is. If you like wine, the vineyards around nearby Rutherglen may tempt you away from the riverbank. Signposted access roads appear frequently along the Murray Valley Hwy.

Who to contact: Parks Victoria 13 1963

339 Doolans Bend camping area

Doolans Bend is one of many twists and turns in the Murray River to the immediate north-west of Barnawartha North. Fishing, canoeing and swimming tend to make up the daily agenda here, with long breaks between activities for eating and sleeping. You can access this camping area off Barnawartha–Howlong Rd. **Map refs:** 149 I4, 191 J5

340 Granthams Bend camping area

From Lake Moodemere, the Murray River doglegs north past Corowa before taking another turn to the east. It's up this way, 5 km north-east of Wahgunyah, that you'll find Granthams Bend. There are walks along the riverbank here – one heads south to the John Foord Bridge that links Wahgunyah with Corowa, and another takes you 2 km upstream to the St Leonards Winery. From the centre of Rutherglen, take Hopetoun Rd, which becomes Carlyle Rd. **Map refs:** 149 H3, 191 I5

341 Lumbys Bend camping area

Lumbys Bend is another of the tranquil twists of the Murray River enjoyed by overnighting motorists and intrepid canoeists. It's also utilised by swimmers, though the water can get quite cold. This camping area is 15 km west of Rutherglen. From the Murray Valley Hwy, head north on Raitts Rd, which will take you through tiny Dugays Bridge. **Map refs:** 149 H4, 191 I5

342 Richardsons Bend camping area

Take Kings Rd off the Old Barnawartha Rd to reach Richardsons Bend, which lies a few kilometres north-west of Barnawartha

North. Note: like many of the tracks leading to sites beside the Murray River, this route is accessible in dry weather only. Bring your own drinking water. **Map refs:** 149 I4, 191 K6

343 Shaws Flat camping area

This camping spot is only 7 km north of Rutherglen, forcing visitors to choose between another swim or more fishing, and a trip to a local winery for a glass of fine wine and a long lunch – tough decisions must be made. From the Murray Valley Hwy just east of Rutherglen, head north on Gooramadda Rd and, just past the Barkly St turn-off, stay left rather than following Gooramadda Rd north-east – this becomes Shaws Flat Rd. **Map refs:** 149 I4, 191 J5

344 Stantons camping area

Stantons camping area is only 5 km from Rutherglen, where the delicious tastes of locally bottled shiraz and muscat await, as well as the fine fare offered in the local cafes and restaurants. Access is via Moodemere Rd, which branches off the Murray Valley Hwy and angles around the eastern edge of Lake Moodemere. **Map refs:** 149 H4, 191 I5

345 Taylors Bend camping area

This slight crook in the flow of the Murray River is 18 km west of Rutherglen, near the township of Dugays Bridge. Turn north off the Murray Valley Hwy onto Brimin Rd, which meets the Murray near Collendina State Forest. Car campers may be joined here by canoeists taking leisurely paddles along the river. **Map refs:** 149 H4, 191 I5

Murray River – Cobram to Yarrawonga

Yarrawonga is a community on the southern edge of Lake Mulwala, where the Murray River briefly widens before continuing west towards the holiday destination of Cobram. Between the 2 towns are some nice riverside reserves with dispersed bush camping, some of which are equipped with boat launches. Look for the various access roads signposted off the Murray Valley Hwy.

Who to contact: Parks Victoria 13 1963

346 Bourkes Bend camping areas

The fine beach at Bourkes Bend is located about 20 km south-east of Cobram. Follow the Bourkes Bend Track off the Murray Valley Hwy. Nearby Duffys Beach is also worth a visit. Canoeists are a fairly common sight as they go with the flow along the Murray River from Yarrawonga to Cobram. **Map refs:** 149 G3, 190 G5

347 Bruces Bend camping areas

River beaches and calm backwater billabongs are what you'll find at and around Bruces Bend. The dispersed bush camping here is embellished by some fireplaces and picnic

tables. To get here, head west out of Yarrawonga along the Murray Valley Hwy for 8 km and turn north onto Bruces Rd. **Map refs:** 149 G3, 190 G5

348 Chinamans Bend camping area

Chinamans Bend is very close to the centre of Yarrawonga, making it an ideal camping area for those who want quick access to the township's attractions. These include a mine-shaft complex and leisurely cruises around Lake Mulwala. Head west out of town on the Murray Valley Hwy for 3 km and take the Brears Rd turn-off. **Map refs:** 149 G3, 190 H5

349 Cobrawonga Island camping areas

Travel 16 km south-east of Cobram to get to Cobrawonga Island, where you'll find some spacious bush-camping sites. This area is dominated by river red gums – tents should not be set up underneath the branches of these impressive trees, as they are notorious for snapping without warning. Access is via Grinter Rd, which heads north off the Murray Valley Hwy. **Map refs:** 149 G3, 190 G5

350 Horseshoe Beach camping area

This camping area lies beside Horseshoe Lagoon, which is located about 5 km south-east of Cobram on another gentle bend of the Murray. There are no facilities at this bush-camping site, but the local sandy beach and the grassy turf more than make up for this. Turn off the Murray Valley Hwy at Horseshoe Track. **Map refs:** 149 G3, 190 G5

351 Nevins Bend camping areas

A drive or cycle of 11 km to the west of Yarrawonga will bring you to the camping areas at Nevins Bend – turn off the Murray Valley Hwy onto Thoms Rd. If you were to continue down the highway for a few kilometres past the turn-off, you'd reach Byramine Homestead. Set within a grove of elm trees, Byramine was built in 1842 and has an octagonal central room, designed so that bushrangers and other enemies could be seen approaching from any direction. **Map refs:** 149 G3, 190 G5

352 Scotts Beach camping area

Just a few kilometres to the south-east of Cobram is Scotts Beach, which has a large and popular camping area. On the way to Scotts Beach down River Rd, stop off at the Quinn Island wetlands, a nesting area for waterbirds that's accessed by a footbridge. First, though, have a walk around Cobram and check out its attractive historic buildings, including several old pubs. **Map refs:** 149 F3, 190 F4

353 Yarrawonga Bends camping areas

The Yarrawonga Bends, a mere 5 km from Yarrawonga township, offer some nice beaches and freshwater swimming,

all courtesy of the Murray River. There are also a number of dispersed bush-camping sites in the vicinity with differing facilities. Take the Murray Valley Hwy west out of Yarrawonga and turn onto Forges Pump Track. **Map refs:** 149 G3, 190 H5

354 Strayleaves Caravan Park

Strayleaves is a peaceful park in Shepparton with flat, grassy campsites that are scrupulously tended, and – as befits the name – lots of foliage. Each of the sites has sullage, and there's a well-stocked shop on-site where you can buy the daily newspaper and basic supplies. Strayleaves is located on Mitchell Street, which runs off the Midland Hwy at the eastern edge of the town centre. **Map refs:** 149 F5, 190 E7

How to book: cnr Mitchell St and Old Dookie Rd, Shepparton (03) 5821 1232 www.strayleavescaravanpark.com.au

355 Yarrawonga Holiday Park

On the banks of the Murray River, downstream from Yarrawonga Weir, the clipped lawns and ample shade at Yarrawonga Holiday Park make for a pleasant camping experience. There are tennis courts, a football oval and a golf-putting green to get you outside and active, and of course you can always splash about in the river. Kids will love the jumping pillow. Dogs are permitted during off-peak times but not at waterfront sites or in cabins. **Map refs:** 149 G4, 190 H5

How to book: cnr Piper St and Burley Rd, Yarrawonga (03) 5744 3420 www.yarrawongaholidaypark.com.au

GOLDFIELDS

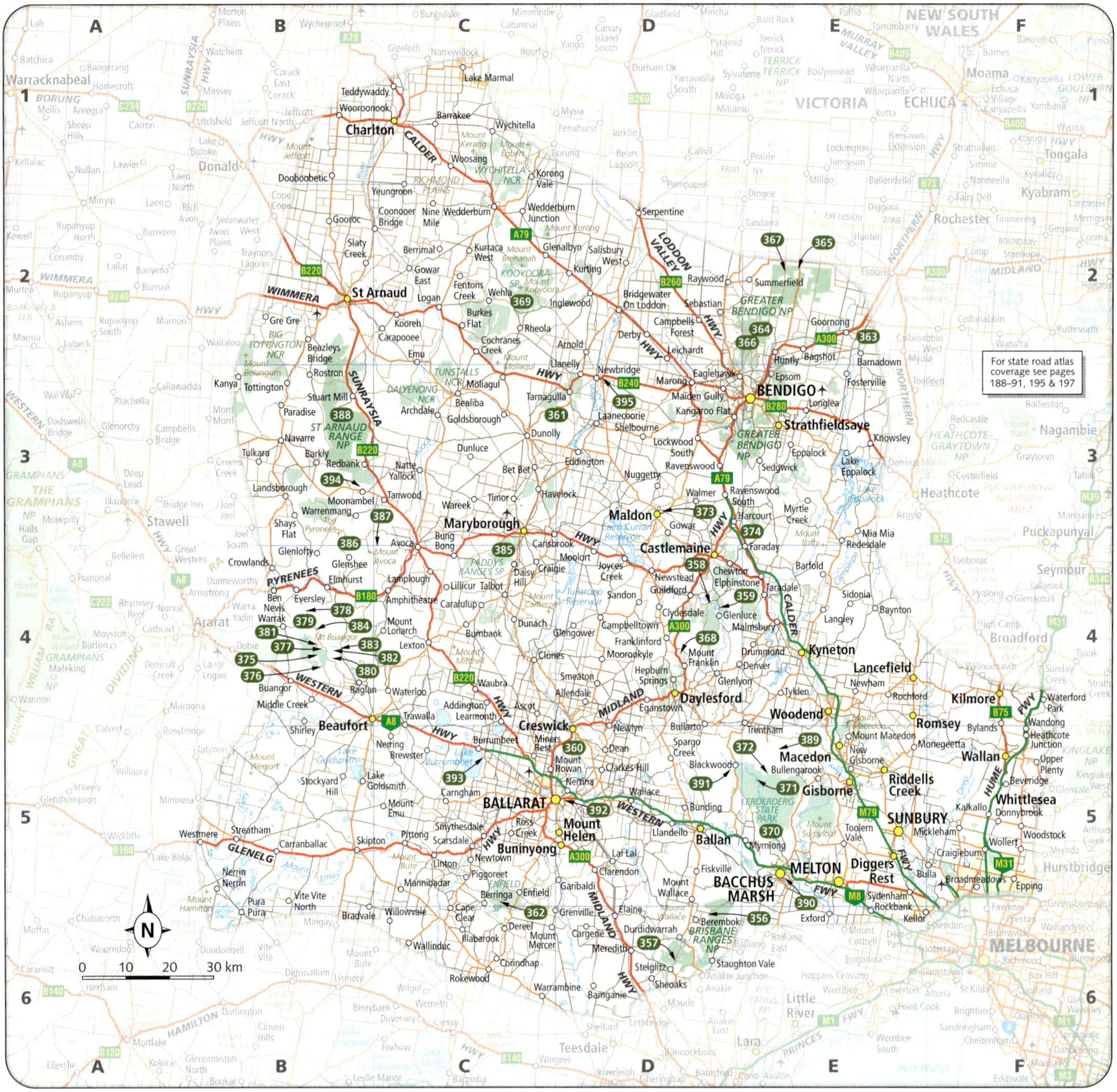

For state road atlas coverage see pages 188–91, 195 & 197

THE VICTORIAN GOLDFIELDS WERE the scene of great human drama in the second half of the 19th century. When that most precious of metals was discovered in the state's central soils, thousands of fortune-seekers were prompted to begin panning the rivers and ploughing the ground with picks, shovels and bare hands. Greater Bendigo National Park is littered with fascinating remnants of the gold rush, including atmospheric mines and creaking water races. Recreational fossickers still pick at the land here, searching for those undiscovered veins. At Castlemaine Diggings National Heritage Park, you can wander around an old cemetery filled with the marked graves of prospectors and their families, and ponder what life must have been like in the now-abandoned diggings.

There's more goldmining history on show at the decrepit workings in Paddys Range State Park, and in the ruined shafts and structures at Maldon Historic Reserve – you can ride a steam train from here across the once-crowded goldfields, letting your imagination bring the past to life. Human excavations are not the only attractions of this region: scattered across the area are a number of parks and reserves where you can set up camp and then embark on long, peaceful rambles over wildflower-dotted hills, through serene forests and up panoramic peaks.

Lerderderg State Park is split by a stunning sandstone gorge that can be explored on foot over the course of 2 to 3 days. The Brisbane Ranges can also be traversed in a couple of days via the Burchell Trail, giving you plenty of time to observe the local wildlife. Rough track-threaded areas such as the Wombat and Mount Cole state forests supply the challenges so keenly sought by those on a mountain bike or in a 4WD. And if your priority is relaxation rather than exertion, go no further than Hepburn Springs.

CAMPSITES LOCATED IN PARKS AND RESERVES

BRISBANE RANGES NATIONAL PARK

The Brisbane Ranges are easily accessible from Melbourne, which lies only 80 km to the east. Swamp wallabies and eastern grey kangaroos roam the bush here, while the flora includes a type of grevillea that is unique to the region. Bushwalkers love this park for its range of walks, from the 1 hr Anakie Gorge Walk to the 3-day Burchell Trail. Access is off the Ballan–Geelong Rd.

Who to contact: Parks Victoria 13 1963

356 Boar Gully camping area

The campsites at Boar Gully need to be booked in advance. Boar Gully is at one end of the 3-day Burchell Trail that traverses the park; the other is at the Steiglitz Courthouse. While navigating this track, bushwalkers can camp overnight at the Old Mill and Little River campsites. From the Ballan–Geelong Rd, turn east on Brisbane Ranges Rd, then south on Reids Rd. **Map refs:** 154 D6, 197 N5

357 Fridays camping area

Fridays is located at the western end of the national park and has basic facilities. There are a number of great walks to the east of here around Stony Creek. The 3 km Anakie Gorge walk is a good leg-stretcher. For a bit more of a work-out, tackle the 8 km Ted Errey Nature Circuit. To get to Fridays camping area, head north from Steiglitz on Duroidwarrah Rd. **Map refs:** 154 D6, 197 N6

CASTLEMAINE DIGGINGS NATIONAL HERITAGE PARK

Goldmining still takes place in the region around Castlemaine, but it's a lot less frenzied than it was at the peak of the 1850s gold rush. Scattered within the forests that now cover most of the 7500 ha Castlemaine Diggings National Heritage Park are ruined dwellings and workings, an evocative cemetery, and mineral springs. From Yapeen on the Midland Hwy, take Vaughan Springs Rd; you can also take the Vaughan–Chewton Rd from the Pyrenees Hwy at Chewton.

Who to contact: Parks Victoria 13 1963

358 Vaughan Springs camping area

There's only space at Vaughan Springs for a few caravans and a half-dozen tents, so get there early if you want to stay during holiday periods. To the north are the old Spring Gully Junction Mine and a walk along the Eureka quartz reef. And don't forget to try the local mineral water while you're here. The turn-off to the campground is on Vaughan Springs Rd. **Map refs:** 154 D4, 195 N12, 197 N2

359 Warburtons Bridge camping area

This basic campground is accessed off the Vaughan–Drummond Rd. It's in the same part of the park as the Vaughan Springs camping area, which may prove useful if Warburtons Bridge is full. Up in the north of the park are the foundations of what was one of the world's largest waterwheels – the Garfield Wheel – and also the well-preserved Pennyweight Cemetery. **Map refs:** 154 D4, 195 N12, 197 N2

CRESWICK REGIONAL PARK

Besides viewing gold-rush remnants in Creswick Regional Park, such as the stone-and-earth Eaton Dam, you can also scan the trees of Koala Park for dozing marsupials, go mountain-biking down narrow trails, and take the informative self-guided trail around the Landcare Centre and Nursery – just one of many walks in the area. Access is off the Bungaree–Creswick Rd, which leads off the Midland Hwy 18 km north of Ballarat.

Who to contact: Parks Victoria 13 1963

360 Slaty Creek camping area

There are actually 3 camping areas spread around Slaty Creek in the south of the park: Number 1, Number 2 and Number 3 camping areas. After you've taken a nap under a manna gum and panned for gold in the creek, head up to St Georges Lake to go bird- and platypus-watching, or just to enjoy this placid body of water. The camping areas are accessed via Slaty Creek Rd, which is off Bungaree–Creswick Rd. **Map refs:** 154 D5, 197 M3

DUNOLLY STATE FOREST

About 10 km north-east of Dunolly township is eucalypt-dominated Dunolly State Forest, centred on the remains of the one-time gold-rush town of Waanyarra. Drivers will enjoy the 4.2 km Waanyarra Forest Dr, which passes the old township site, its cemetery and Mortons Old Hotel; cyclists can tackle the 24 km Golden Triangle Bicycle Track.

Who to contact: DSE Maryborough (03) 5461 0800, 13 6186

361 Waanyarra Recreation Area

This recreation area is sited between the original Waanyarra town site, where gold-rush miners set up their tents, and the cemetery. Over spring and summer, wildflowers will burst into colour here. To take a close look at old gold workings, follow the 3 km Wet Gully Walking Track, which begins 2 km south of Waanyarra. **Map refs:** 154 D3, 195 M10

ENFIELD STATE PARK

The setting for furious excavation work in the Victorian gold-rush days, the Enfield region is now explored by bushwalkers and horseriders – horses must keep to vehicle tracks. Nature lovers will really enjoy the surroundings: dozens of orchid species and many eucalypts have taken root here, and the area resounds with the calls of numerous birds and frogs. Take Misery Creek Rd off the Ballarat–Colac Rd, 25 km south of Ballarat.

Who to contact: Parks Victoria 13 1963

362 Surface Point camping area

A Chinese settlement was located at Surface Point in the gold-rush days, and there's still some evidence of it scattered throughout the bush. Try your hand at fossicking along Misery Creek – don't let the name deter you – or take long walks around the park. Note: when walking, stick to the tracks, as mine shafts are hidden in the surrounding terrain. **Map refs:** 154 C5, 197 L5

ENGLISHS BRIDGE STREAMSIDE RESERVE

This small reserve has been established beside the Campaspe River about 48 km north-east of Bendigo, within a larger wedge of land framed by the Midland and Northern hwys.

Who to contact: Parks Victoria 13 1963

363 Englishs Bridge camping area

The Campaspe River, which flows out of the Great Dividing Range to eventually join the Murray River to the north, makes a nice setting for an overnight stop. The camping area in the Englishs Bridge Streamside Reserve is east of the Midland Hwy – turn off the highway about 500 m north of Goornong onto Corner La, or get to the reserve via the Axedale–Goornong Rd. **Map refs:** 154 E2, 190 B8, 195 P9

GREATER BENDIGO NATIONAL PARK

This interesting national park extends north and south of Bendigo, and has a number of significant Aboriginal sites plus remnants of the gold rushes that swept through the area in the mid-19th century – amateur prospectors still try their luck here. There's a great wildflower show in spring, a highlight being the colours of the whirakee wattle, only found around Bendigo. Access roads branch out from the Calder, Loddon Valley, Midland and McIvor hwys.

Who to contact: Parks Victoria 13 1963

364 Loeser camping area

The Loeser camping area is located on Loeser Rd, which runs off Hartlands Rd. For some great views over Bendigo and the surrounding region, head across town into the Mandurang

section of the park and scale the steep heights of One Tree Hill. Closer to Loeser is the Shadbolt picnic area, which is the starting point for a 1 km walk around Flagstaff Hill. **Map refs:** 154 E2, 190 A8, 195 O9

365 Mulga Dam camping area

Small Mulga Dam is in the far north of the national park. A short walk past old charcoal pits starts from the picnic area here. Along the way you may hear some of the many songbirds that thrive in the region. To reach the camping area, head north-east from Bendigo along the Midland Hwy, then veer due north on the Bendigo–Tennyson Rd and turn west on Camp Rd. **Map refs:** 154 E2, 190 A7, 195 O9

366 Notley camping area

Notley is the only overnight option in Greater Bendigo National Park that has pull-through sites suitable for caravans. You'll find this camping area off Nuggety Rd, which branches off the Neilborough–Eaglehawk Rd to the north of Eaglehawk township. Bring your own firewood, but note that you aren't allowed to light any fires here over summer. Horseriding is allowed in this region of the park, which formerly comprised an area known as Whipstick State Park. **Map refs:** 154 E2, 190 A8, 195 O9

367 Rush Dam camping area

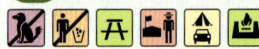

Like its neighbour Mulga Dam, Rush Dam is up near the northern boundary of the park. Closer to Bendigo, near the Shadbolt picnic area, you can check out some goldmining history at Old Tom Mine; if you'd like to do some recreational fossicking here, you'll need a Miners Right permit. The campground is west of Mulga Dam down Camp Rd. Note: bring your own drinking water and firewood. **Map refs:** 154 E2, 190 A7, 195 O9

HEPBURN REGIONAL PARK

Bushwalking, mountain-biking and horseriding down old logging tracks are just some of the adventurous activities you can do in this fascinating park, which hosted gold diggers in the mid-19th century and nowadays encompasses the mineral springs of Hepburn and Daylesford. A highlight is the 16 km Tipperary Walking Track that runs between Lake Daylesford and the Hepburn Mineral Springs.

Who to contact: Parks Victoria 13 1963

368 Mount Franklin Reserve camping area

The crater of the extinct Mt Franklin volcano makes a wonderful setting for an overnight camp. Separated from Hepburn Regional Park proper by the Midlands Hwy, the reserve is an enclave of large conifers that makes a great base from which to explore the area's many springs and walking tracks. Note: only short-term camping is allowed here. **Map refs:** 154 D4, 197 N2

KOOYOORA STATE PARK

Rugged Kooyoora State Park, 15 km west of Inglewood, is an entrancing jumble of granite, grassy hills and big trees. Its system of roads is used by bushwalkers, motorists and horseriders, while its peaks entice rockclimbers and provide the setting for lofty lookouts; don't miss the brilliant view from atop Mt Brenanah.

Who to contact: Parks Victoria 13 1963

369 Melville Caves camping area

This campground is off Melville Caves Rd, signposted off the Wedderburn–Dunolly Rd; the caves were once used as a hideout by bushranger Captain Melville. From the picnic area there's a short walk to the Southern Lookout, which continues to McLeods Lookout – there's no shortage of superb views here. If you're really into rocks, do the 4.5 km Eastern Walking Circuit, which takes in all manner of interesting formations. **Map refs:** 154 C2, 195 M9

LERDERDERG STATE PARK

This park takes up a Tasmania-shaped chunk of land between Blackwood in the north and Bacchus Marsh in the south. Its centrepiece is the 300 m deep gorge carved out of sandstone by the Lerderderg River. Well-defined walking tracks expose you to goldmining relics and the local koalas, wedge-tailed eagles and swamp wallabies. Main access is via Lerderderg Gorge Rd, which leads off the Bacchus Marsh–Gisborne Rd.

Who to contact: Parks Victoria 13 1963

370 Bush camping (walk-in camping)

Walk-in camping is allowed within the conservation zone that covers most of the park; confirm which areas you can stay in with the rangers. Remember that the river can rise quickly after heavy rain, which will affect crossings and where you choose to camp. Vehicle-based camping is also allowed at some sites outside the 2 official camping areas. **Map refs:** 154 E5, 188 A3, 197 O4

371 O'Briens Crossing camping area

O'Briens Crossing is a lovely picnic spot in the north of the park. From here you can walk west to Shaws Lake and Sweets Lookout. Experienced bushwalkers should consider shadowing the Lerderderg River across the park on the 2 to 3 day walk to Mackenzies Flat – the hike involves several river crossings. Head south from Blackwood on the Greendale–Trentham Rd, then turn east on O'Briens Rd. **Map refs:** 154 E5, 188 A2, 197 O4

372 Upper Chadwick Campground

The camping area at Upper Chadwick is on the border between Lerderderg State Park and Wombat State Forest, close to O'Briens Crossing – continue east from the crossing on O'Briens Rd and then head north on Upper Chadwick Track. If you want

a break from the solitude up here, head back around to the southern edge of the park and join daytrippers in swimming at Mackenzies Flat and Graham Dam. **Map refs:** 154 E5, 188 A2, 197 O4

MALDON HISTORIC RESERVE

This small reserve surrounds Maldon and was created to protect the remnants of the gold rush that gave birth to the town. The most prominent are the Beehive Mine Chimney and the ruins of the North British Mine, but old shafts, dams and other relics are scattered throughout the reserve.

Who to contact: Parks Victoria 13 1963

373 Butts Reserve camping area

Butts Reserve is west of town on Mt Tarrengower Rd. After visiting the collection of artefacts at the North British Mine and exploring the adjacent Carmans Tunnel, climb the fire tower on Mt Tarrengower and also scale Anzac Hill to check out the surrounding landscape. Train enthusiasts will want to take a ride on the historic railway that crosses Smiths Reef, bound for Castlemaine. **Map refs:** 154 D3, 195 N11, 197 N1

MOUNT ALEXANDER REGIONAL PARK

This regional park is centred on the steep-sided, 350 m Mt Alexander. Put aside a half-day and do a circuit of the best viewpoints up on the mountain's granite peaks via the 4 km West Ridge Walking Track. The park is 3 km east of Harcourt and 8 km north of Castlemaine.

Who to contact: Parks Victoria 13 1963

374 Mount Alexander camping area (bush camping)

You can go bush camping throughout this park. Talk to the ranger about the best places to pitch a tent on the slopes of Lanjanuc, which is the Aboriginal name for the mountain. Along with Dog Rocks, the Langs and Shepherds Flat lookouts provide great panoramas. To get here, turn onto the Mt Alexander Tourist Rd from the Calder Hwy at Faraday, or from the Harcourt North Rd. **Map refs:** 154 E3, 190 A10, 195 O11, 197 O1

MOUNT BUANGOR STATE PARK

About 20 km west of Beaufort, and reached via Ferntree Gully Rd from the Western Hwy, is 2500 ha Mt Buangor State Park. The mountain itself, decorated with snow gums, looms over the surrounding area. A web of walking tracks is strung between the park's 2 camping areas, and more trails delve into neighbouring Mt Cole State Forest.

There are major projects underway to repair roads, walking tracks and visitor facilities in Buangor State Park, which were damaged by fire in 2010 and torrential rainfall and storms in 2011. Check with Parks Victoria regarding areas not open to visitors.

Who to contact: Parks Victoria 13 1963

View from Langs Lookout, Mount Alexander Regional Park (p. 157)

375 Ferntree camping area

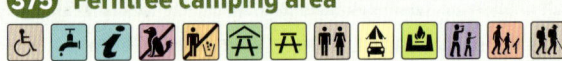

Ferntree is located in the centre of the park and has only 5 sites for campers, arrayed alongside the picnic ground. Take the short nature walk from here to the Ferntree Waterfalls, wander over to the Sugarloaf viewpoint, or take an enjoyably aimless drive around the western section of the park. You can also venture due east into Mt Cole State Forest. **Map refs:** 154 B4, 197 K2

376 Middle Creek camping area

If you're part of a large group, or are towing a caravan or camper trailer, head for relatively flat ground at Middle Creek. You can walk right across the park from here. A particularly steep and demanding trail is the Cave Walking Track, which heads north-east to an impressive rock overhang. The campsites are on Jimmy Smith Rd, which is signposted off Ferntree Gully Rd. **Map refs:** 154 B4, 197 K2

MOUNT COLE STATE FOREST

Sizeable Mt Cole State Forest is bordered by Mt Buangor State Park to the west, and cedes some territory in the south to pine plantations. Four-wheel-driving is a popular activity in the thick of the forest, while horseriders also make their way along the local tracks. Some excellent bushwalks round out the area's attractions. The forest is 25 km north-west of Beaufort. Turn off the Western Hwy towards Raglan, where you pick up the Mt Cole Rd.

Who to contact: DSE Beaufort (03) 5349 2404, 13 6186

377 Beeripmo camping area (walk-in camping)

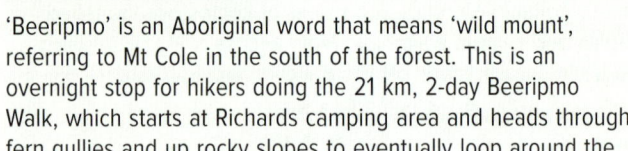

'Beeripmo' is an Aboriginal word that means 'wild mount', referring to Mt Cole in the south of the forest. This is an overnight stop for hikers doing the 21 km, 2-day Beeripmo Walk, which starts at Richards camping area and heads through fern gullies and up rocky slopes to eventually loop around the southern section of the forest. **Map refs:** 154 B4, 197 K2

378 Ben Nevis camping area

Located at the site of a hut, there is room here for a couple of caravans or a handful of tents. The cosy hut has been recently refurbished and comes with table and seating. Ben Nevis is near a fire tower which provides great views of the surrounding landscape. The camping area is well-signed off a loop track called Sandys Pinch, which runs off Mt Cole Rd. If you're towing, keep in mind the access road is pretty rough **Map refs:** 154 B4, 195 J12, 197 J2.

379 Chinamans camping area

Birdwatchers are very fond of the 5 km Borella Walk that leads north from Chinamans camping area to Ben Nevis, due to the 120-plus species that fly around the forest. This walk has a couple of steep sections, so allow yourself plenty of time to complete it. Crowned with a fire tower, Ben Nevis is also equipped with toilets and picnic tables. Chinamans is accessed from Warrak via Mt Cole Rd. **Map refs:** 154 B4, 195 J12, 197 J2

380 Ditchfields camping area

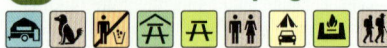

From Mt Cole Rd, take the signposted Camp Rd to reach Ditchfields camping area in the far south of the forest. Manna and blue gums are the most abundant trees here. This spot is suitable for camper trailers as well as tent dwellers. When you've exhausted all the other walks in the area, step out along the challenging 9 km Paradise Walk. **Map refs:** 154 B4, 197 K2

381 Mugwamp camping area

Mugwamp is in the centre of Mt Cole State Forest, near Mugwamp Creek. It's on the Beeripmo Walk – a decent stretch of the walk to the south, beyond the Beerimpo camping area, detours through the eastern fringe of neighbouring Mt Buangor State Park. Turn off Mt Cole Rd onto Dawson Rock Rd to reach Mugwamp. **Map refs:** 154 B4, 197 K2

382 Richards camping area

There are several excellent walks you can take from the Richards camping area, which is situated beside Fiery Creek. The 21 km overnight Beeripmo Walk makes a fine introduction to the diversity of plants and trees at Mt Cole. Another option, the Grevillea Walk, comprises a short trail to the Glut picnic area – along the way, you might spot the rare local species of grevillea. Follow Glut Rd to reach the campground. **Map refs:** 154 B4, 197 K2

383 Smiths Bridge camping area

The Smiths Bridge camping area, located on the Elmhurst–Beaufort Rd, is often used as a base by the horseriders who frequent the forest. Note: horseriders can only access existing vehicle roads, not walking tracks; also, some roads may be subject to seasonal closures in the latter months of the year. **Map refs:** 154 B4, 197 K2

384 Victoria Mill camping area

Nestled in old-growth forest, Victoria Mill is a scenic area to pitch a tent, and camping is based around its hut and separate picnic area. There are bollards around the hut, making it suitable for tents only. The hut is well-signed off a loop track called Sandys Pinch which runs off Mt Cole Rd, while the picnic area is a bit further along. **Map refs:** 154 B4, 195 K12, 197 K2

PADDYS RANGES STATE PARK

The spring wildflower display is arguably the natural highlight of this area, although the gold prospectors who feverishly dug up the ground here in the mid-19th century may have begged to differ. You can go recreational prospecting in certain areas if you have a Miners Right permit; otherwise, occupy yourself with some gentle bushwalks. About 3 km south-west of Maryborough, follow Old Avoca Rd off the Pyrenees Hwy.

Who to contact: Parks Victoria 13 1963

385 Karri Track camping area

There's not much space at this camping area in the west of the park, so it's best to contact the ranger beforehand to check

the availability of sites, particularly if you have a caravan. You can walk across the park to its main picnic area, where you can continue along a self-guided wildflower trail or take a wheelchair-accessible track to Reserve Dam. **Map refs:** 154 C4, 195 L12, 197 L1

PYRENEES STATE FOREST

The Pyrenees Ranges, lying to the immediate west of Avoca and accessed via Vinoca Rd, are replete with grand picnic spots, lookouts and walking tracks. The foothills of the range are dotted with gold-rush remnants and coloured by orchids and lilies. You may see echidnas and goannas wandering through the undergrowth, or wedge-tailed eagles soaring overhead.

Who to contact: DSE 13 6186

386 Camerons Track Campground

This camping area, located on Camerons Track some 20 km from Avoca, is suitable for camper trailers, but the Waterfalls camping area is a better option for caravans. Camerons Track is the midpoint of the Pyrenees Endurance Walk, a testing 18 km hike across the forest from east to west – only those with a high level of fitness should tackle this trail. A few kilometres to the north-east, Governor Rock Lookout has fine views. **Map refs:** 154 B3, 195 K12, 197 K1

387 Waterfalls camping area

The Waterfalls site, on the eastern fringe of the forest, is easily accessed from Avoca. Several easy bushwalks start here, including the 1 km Valley Walk along No. 2 Creek, and another that heads towards Sugarloaf Reservoir. This is also the starting point of the challenging 18 km Pyrenees Endurance Walk, which should only be attempted by fit, experienced hikers. **Map refs:** 154 C4, 195 K12, 197 K1

ST ARNAUD RANGE NATIONAL PARK

This mountainous national park contains nearly 14 000 ha of pristine box and ironbark forest. Go bushwalking or take a 4WD along the steep ridge tops, or go fishing for trout in the local reservoirs. Follow Teddington Rd off the Sunraysia Hwy at the town of Stuart Mill.

Who to contact: Parks Victoria 13 1963

388 Teddington camping area

You can camp beside the Upper Teddington Reservoir as long as you set up your tent no closer than 40 m to the water. Fishing and canoeing are popular pursuits here, but note that swimming is not allowed in the reservoir. You can also camp at nearby Teddington Hut – book a hut stay in advance through Parks Victoria's Inglewood office. **Map refs:** 154 B3, 195 K10

WOMBAT STATE FOREST

The rough tracks that crisscross Wombat State Forest between Macedon and Daylesford are a favourite destination for those with a 4WD, trail bike or mountain bike, and for horseriders. The pretty Nolans Creek picnic area on Lerderderg Rd is a nice place to stop for lunch – Lerderderg Rd is part of the Wombat Forest Dr that guides motorists on a scenic 65 km round trip from Daylesford.

Who to contact: DSE Ballarat (03) 5348 2211, 13 6186

389 Firth Park camping area

Firth Park is an old sawmill site in the northern section of Wombat State Forest; there are visible remnants of the logging that was done here. There's plenty of room for tents, but the space available for caravans and camper trailers is limited. From the Bacchus Marsh–Gisborne Rd, turn onto Carrolls La and then onto Firth Rd. **Map refs:** 154 E5, 188 A2, 190 A12, 197 O3

CAMPSITES LOCATED IN OTHER AREAS

390 Bacchus Marsh Caravan Park

Bacchus Marsh is on the Western Hwy just outside Melbourne's city limits. West of here is the scenic Werribee Gorge State Park, while to the north is the equally striking sandstone gorge of the Lerderderg River. The Bacchus Marsh Caravan Park is on gently undulating ground off Main St, and is equipped with grassy sites, a disabled toilet, a playground and a clutch of cabins. Pets are allowed at the manager's discretion, so have a chat to them when booking if bringing an animal. **Map refs:** 154 E5, 188 A3, 197 O5

How to book: 26 Main Street, Bacchus Marsh (03) 5367 2775 www.bacchusmarshcp.com.au

391 Blackwood Mineral Springs Caravan Park

Blackwood struck it big (albeit briefly) as a goldmining area in the 1850s and visitors can still pan for gold here. They can also take numerous walks in the area, including to the springs, along the Lerderderg River and to nearby Shaws Lake. Adjacent to Blackwood is Lerderderg State Park and its beautiful, deep-throated gorge. The caravan park is about 400 m east of town, signposted off Golden Point Rd. **Map refs:** 154 D5, 188 A2, 197 O3

How to book: bookings recommended during peak periods; 41 Golden Point Road, Blackwood (03) 5368 6539 www.blackwoodcrownreserves.websyte.com.au

392 Eureka Stockade Holiday and Caravan Park

This caravan park is in a great location if you're planning on exploring some of Ballarat's myriad attractions. It is right next to the Eureka Stockade monument and reserve, and Sovereign Hill and the wildlife park are also close by. This is camping luxury-style with clipped lawns and some sites containing their own ensuite bathroom. There is also a huge outdoor heated pool and plenty on offer to keep the kids amused. **Map refs:** 154 D5, 197 M4

How to book: 104 Stawell Street South, Ballarat (03) 5331 2281 www.eurekaholidaypark.com.au

393 Lake Burrumbeet Caravan Park

When it holds water, Lake Burrumbeet attracts watersports lovers from around the region, and anglers keen on catching trout and redfin. It's situated on the western fringe of Ballarat, the town centre of which is 15 km to the east down the Western Fwy. The caravan park is on the lake's northern shoreline, off the Western Hwy. **Map refs:** 154 C5, 197 L3

How to book: bookings required for Christmas and Easter; 1185 Remembrance Dr, Burrumbeet (03) 5344 0583 www.lakeburrumbeetcaravanpark.com

394 Mountain Creek camping area

This campground is a few hundred metres north of the small town of Moonambel in Victoria's Pyrenees, which encompasses a winemaking district. In the vicinity of Mountain Creek is the Warrenmang Vineyard, which specialises in shiraz and has its own restaurant on-site. Access to the camping area is signposted via Greens La. **Map refs:** 154 B3, 195 K11

Who to contact: DSE Maryborough (03) 5461 0800, 13 6186

395 Newbridge River Reserve camping area

You'll find the compact Newbridge River Reserve camping area next to the township's main street, the Bendigo–St Arnaud Rd. Anglers set themselves up on the riverbank, while canoeists occasionally push themselves across the water; the birdwatching is reputedly good here too. **Map refs:** 154 D3, 195 M10

How to book: Bendigo–St Arnaud Rd 0487 703 434
Camping fees: fees payable at Newbridge General Store, Lyons St, Newbridge

SOUTH-WEST COAST

A JOURNEY THROUGH SOUTH-WESTERN Victoria takes you along the spectacular stretch of coastline between Geelong, on the western edge of Port Phillip, and the charming town of Nelson down near the SA border. The region is best known for the Great Ocean Rd, a sublimely scenic route that winds its way along the limestone cliffs shaped by the crashing waves of the Southern Ocean. Off this road you'll find some wonderful places to camp, from the surf beaches at Torquay to the beautiful forests of Great Otway National Park. West of Cape Otway, which is crowned by a splendid lighthouse, are the Twelve Apostles, rocky towers that jut above the ocean swells and glow in the setting sun.

But the Great Ocean Rd is only one part of the camping adventure in this corner of the state. Inland from the Otway Ranges are several lakes – Colac, Purrumbete, Bullen Merri – that attract lovers of watersports when water levels are adequate. Or to get to know as much of the region as possible, consider tackling the Great South West Walk. Beginning and ending in Portland, this superb trail follows the course of the Glenelg River west as far as Princess Margaret Rose Cave, the star attraction of the surrounding national park, before swinging down to Discovery Bay to trace its serene shoreline.

CAMPSITES LOCATED IN PARKS AND RESERVES

ANNYA STATE FOREST

This peaceful swathe of forest is north of Heywood, beyond the small town of Drumborg and only a few kilometres from the attractive foreshore of Portland Bay. It's a tranquil area for BBQs and quiet rambles through the undergrowth.

Who to contact: DSE Heywood (03) 5527 0444, 13 6186

396 Annya Camp camping area

This quiet spot is nestled in the forest just off the Portland–Casterton Rd, between Drumborg and Casterton. Plentiful shade is provided by the surrounding trees, while an abundance of sites on relatively level ground make it a good place for large groups. Note: make sure to bring your own drinking water in with you. **Map refs:** 162 C2, 196 D6

COBBOBOONEE NATIONAL PARK

Cobboboonee is an attractive mixture of forests, heathlands and wetlands accessed from the Princes Hwy between Portland and Dartmoor. The area is a well-established favourite of hikers and horseriders. Walkers avail themselves of numerous tracks, including the Great South West Walk, which winds through the landscape between Portland and Nelson. Equestrians can explore the 60 km of trails that make up the Great Cobboboonee Horse Trail.

Who to contact: Parks Victoria 13 1963

397 Jackass Fern Gully camping area

Don't take the name personally: it's actually a wise move to pitch a tent on this peaceful stretch of flat ground. From Portland, drive west for 22 km along the road to Nelson and take the signposted turn-off north onto the T&W Rd. Drive a further 20 km to the signposted turn-off to Jackass Fern Gully, 300 m off the T&W Rd. **Map refs:** 162 B2, 196 C6

398 Surry Ridge camping area

The Great South West Walk passes straight through this serene picnic and camping area. To get here, follow the Portland–Nelson Rd for 22 km west of Portland and take the signposted turn-off north onto the T&W Rd. Head up the T&W Rd for just over 6 km and turn onto Cut Out Dam Rd. Surry Ridge is a further 3.6 km along Cut Out Dam Rd, 300 m south of the turn-off. **Map refs:** 162 B3, 196 D7

CRAWFORD RIVER REGIONAL PARK

This park encompasses nearly 2500 ha in a valley carved out by the Crawford River to the north of Portland. There are a number of delightful picnic spots on the north side of the river, beside the gently winding thoroughfare called The Boulevard. When not having a long lunch, visitors enjoy scenic drives through stands of big gums, birdwatching, bushwalking through fern-lined gullies and trying to snare freshwater crayfish.

Who to contact: Parks Victoria 13 1963

399 Hiscocks Crossing camping area

A rewarding nature trail does a 2.5 km loop from this camping area along the Crawford River and through several types of forest. It's located off The Boulevard. To get here, head north from Hotspur towards Casterton and follow the park signage; alternatively, follow the signs from the Princes Hwy 22 km north-west of Heywood, near Greenwald. Note: the access road is not suitable for caravans; camper trailers will need to be towed by a 4WD. **Map refs:** 162 B1, 196 D5

CUMBERLAND RIVER RESERVE

Signposted off the Great Ocean Road 7 km south-west of Lorne, this small reserve encompasses the pretty landscape beside the narrow Cumberland River.

How to book: bookings recommended during peak periods; 2680 Great Ocean Road, Cumberland River (03) 5289 1790 www.cumberlandriver.com.au

400 Cumberland River Holiday Park

The grassy, flat campsites at Cumberland River are overlooked by impressive cliffs that rise up across the water – ask the

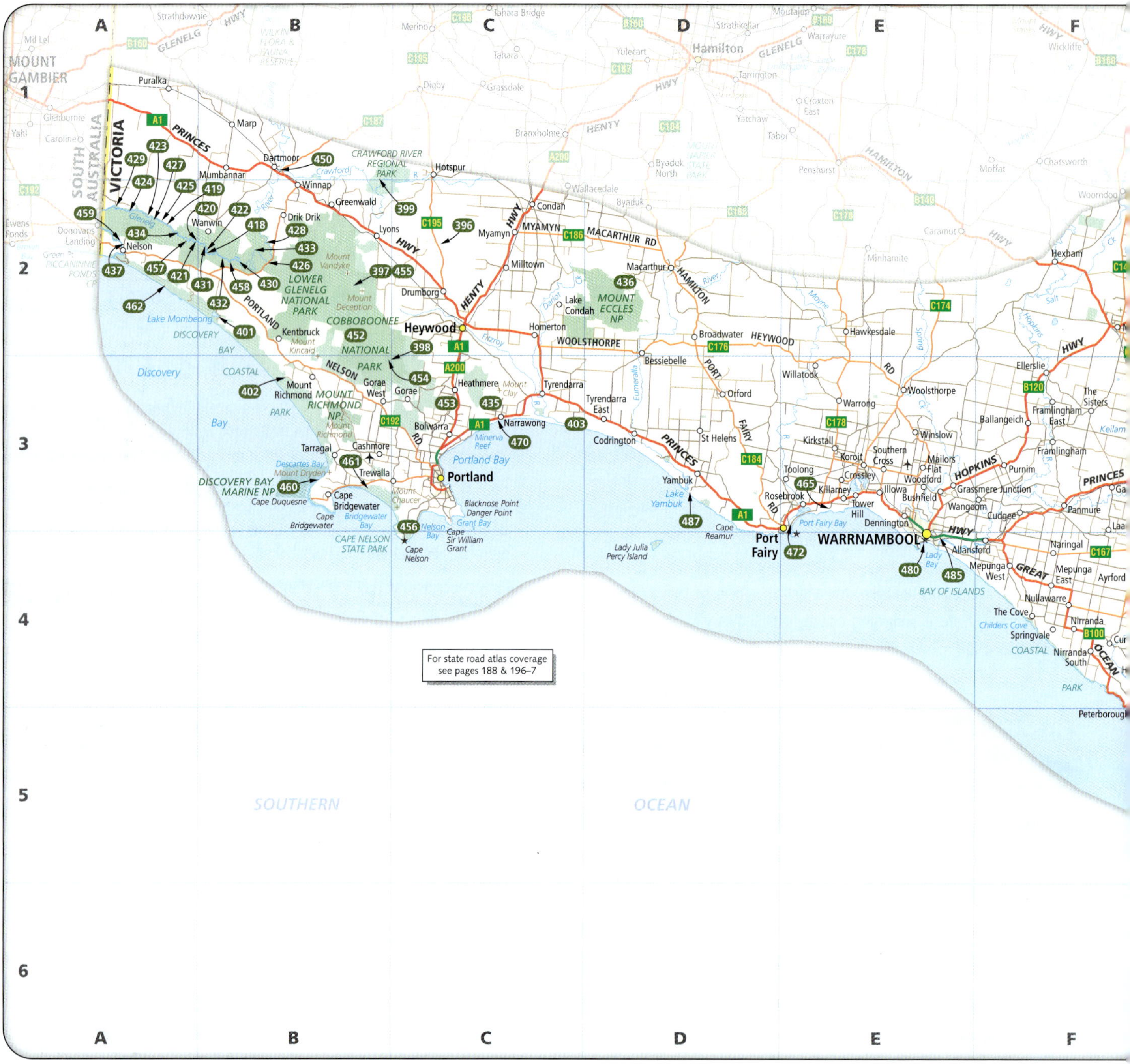

(Map of Victoria South-West Coast region)

For state road atlas coverage
see pages 188 & 196–7

park's managers about the trail that climbs the bluff, and about the many other local walking options. Swim in the river or head across the road to the surf beach. Note: fires are permitted in the drums provided, though this is subject to any fire bans that may be in force. Pleasant camping is to be had next to the river, which is frequented by ducks and other waterbirds. **Map refs:** 163 I5, 197 M9

DISCOVERY BAY COASTAL PARK

The glorious oceanfront that stretches west from Cape Bridgewater for 50 km, almost to the South Australian border, is protected within the confines of Discovery Bay Coastal Park. The region's natural attractions include Victoria's highest sea cliffs, pristine beaches and a network of massive sand dunes. The fur seal colony at Cape Bridgewater is one of the highlights.

Who to contact: Parks Victoria 13 1963 *Camping fees:* advance bookings and fees payable through Nelson Visitor Information Centre (08) 8738 4051

401 Lake Monibeong camping area

With flat, grassy ground and basic facilities, this camping area is 7 km along Lake Monibeong Rd, signposted 16 km south-east of Nelson on the road to Portland. Go swimming or sailboarding in the lake or tackle the 1 km walk to the ocean beach at Discovery Bay. The site is on the Great South West Walk, 13 km from White Sands Camp. Caravans will need to be towed by a 4WD. **Map refs:** 162 B2, 196 B6

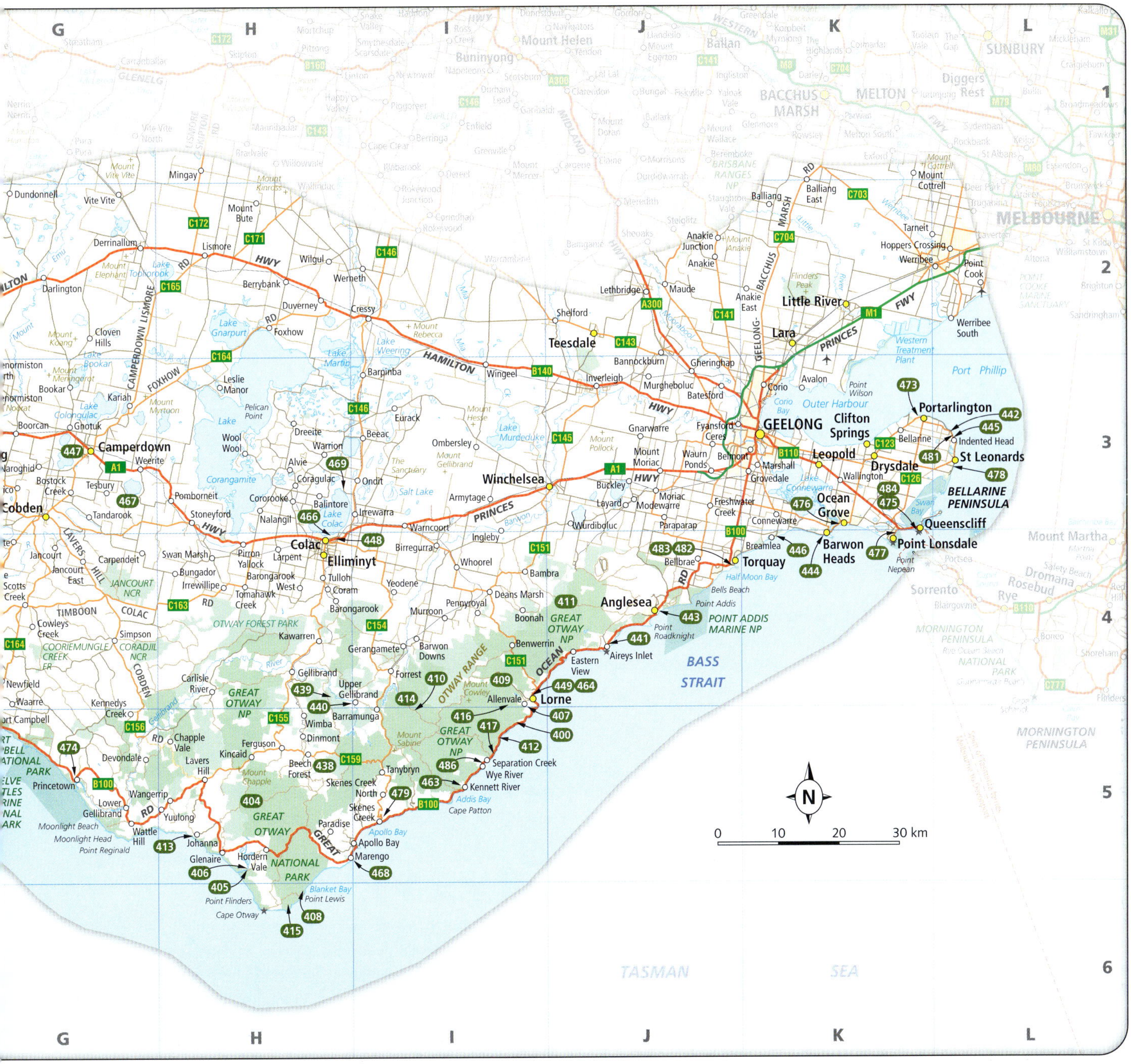

Map labels

G H I J K L

1
SUNBURY
Diggers Rest
MELTON
MELBOURNE
Mount Cottrell
Hoppers Crossing
Werribee
Point Cook

Mount Helen
Buninyong
BACCHUS MARSH

2
Derrinallum
Lismore
C171
C172
Mingay
Vite Vite
Mount Bute
Wilgul
C146
Werneth
Berrybank
Duverney
Cressy
Shelford
Teesdale
C143
Lethbridge
Maude
Anakie Junction
Anakie
Anakie East
C141
Little River
Lara
PRINCES FWY
Werribee South

3
Camperdown
447
A1
Weerite
467
466
Balintore
469
Colac
448
Elliminyt
Winchelsea
GEELONG
Clifton Springs
Leopold
Drysdale
Ocean Grove
Queenscliff
Point Lonsdale
Portarlington
442
445
Indented Head
481
St Leonards
478
BELLARINE PENINSULA
484
475
476
Barwon Heads
446
477
444

4
TIMBOON
COLAC
C163
OTWAY FOREST PARK
C154
C151
Deans Marsh
411
Anglesea
443
POINT ADDIS MARINE NP
441
Aireys Inlet
BASS STRAIT
MORNINGTON PENINSULA
C777

5
474
B100
Princetown
GREAT OTWAY NP
439
440
414
410
Barramunga
416
417
486
463
B100
438
459
409
449
464
407
400
412
Lorne
Wye River
Kennett River
Cape Patton
Apollo Bay
0 10 20 30 km

6
406
405
413
404
GREAT OTWAY NATIONAL PARK
468
Cape Otway
408
415
TASMAN SEA

G H I J K L

402 Swan Lake camping area

Though not quite as magical as a Russian folk tale, this is a nice spot. The lake is nestled among sand dunes and is a good place for a picnic and a lie-down. Travel west of Portland on the road to Nelson for 30 km and you will find the turn-off for Swan Lake Rd, a steep, loose-gravel road with a number of sharp twists. Caravans will need to be towed by a 4WD. The site is on the Great South West Walk, 16 km from Lake Monibeong. **Map refs:** 162 B3, 196 C7

FITZROY RIVER PUBLIC PURPOSES RESERVE

This private reserve is on the edge of Portland Bay near the township of Tyrendarra.

Who to contact: Portland Visitor Information Centre (03) 5523 2671

403 Fitzroy River Public Purposes Reserve camping area

Surrounded by coastal scrub at the mouth of the Fitzroy River, this campground is only a short walk from lovely ocean beaches. You'll find it 4 km down Thompsons Rd, which is 32 km east of Portland on the road to Port Fairy. **Map refs:** 162 C3, 196 E7

GREAT OTWAY NATIONAL PARK

Named after the mountain range that stretches along the rugged coast of the Southern Ocean, Great Otway National

Park is blanketed by pristine rainforest and stands of mountain ash, while the seashore is covered in pretty heathlands. The park extends west from Torquay to Princetown, and the ocean has fashioned the coastal limestone here into world-famous coves and rock formations. Beachcombing, walking in cool forests and driving the curvaceous Great Ocean Rd are must-dos for visitors.

Who to contact: Parks Victoria 13 1963

404 Aire Crossing camping area

Just north of this riverside campground is the magnificent Triplet Falls, cascading down through untrammelled old-growth forest. Also in the vicinity is the walk to Little Aire Falls, which weaves through rainforest to end at a cantilevered viewing platform. To get to this camping area, take the Aire Crossing Track from the Great Ocean Rd or turn onto Wait-A-While Rd from Colac–Lavers Hill Rd. **Map refs:** 163 H5, 197 K10

405 Aire River East camping area

This shady campground is about half the size of the camping area on the other side of the river, and so may afford a little more peace and quiet. It's accessed via Horden Vale Rd, signposted south off the Great Ocean Rd just over 3 km west of the turn-off to the Cape Otway Lightstation. The campground is 5.5 km down Horden Vale Rd. **Map refs:** 163 H5, 197 K11

406 Aire River West camping area

This camping area on the western side of the Aire River, near the mouth of the watercourse, is big, flat and open, making it ideal for large groups. You can reach it by travelling 5.3 km down Sand Rd (seasonal access); the turn-off for Sand Rd is signposted off the Great Ocean Rd at Glenaire. Alternatively, drive to the smaller Aire River East campground (see that entry for directions) and continue for another 700 m. **Map refs:** 163 H5, 197 K11

407 Allenvale Mill Site camping area (walk-in camping)

The old Allenvale Mill site lies just beyond the outskirts of Lorne, which is handy for campers who like to have all the conveniences of a modern township within easy reach. This is a walk-in campsite, but it's only a few minutes from the road. It's located 2 km south-west of Lorne along Allenvale Rd. **Map refs:** 163 I4, 197 M9

408 Blanket Bay camping area

This is a very popular camping area with shaded sites near an ocean beach to the south-west of Apollo Bay. A little further around the coast is the historic Cape Otway Lightstation. About 20 km west of Apollo Bay, turn onto Cape Otway Lighthouse Rd. Then, after 9 km, take the signposted turning onto Blanket Bay Rd and drive for another 6 km. Note: the campsites at Blanket Bay are booked through a ballot system during summer and over the Easter holiday period, and fees apply during this time. **Map refs:** 163 H6, 197 K11

409 Cora Lynn camping area (walk-in camping)

The 2 campsites at Cora Lynn offer intimacy and tranquillity. They are accessed on foot via a track leading from the Blanket Leaf picnic area – you can take a walk from the carpark here to scenic Erskine Falls. The picnic area is reached via the road to the falls, which winds up into the hills behind Lorne. **Map refs:** 163 I4, 197 M9

410 Fork Paddock camping area (bush camping)

There's seasonal, dry-weather access only to this remote spot, as the track leading in becomes treacherous after rain. The reward for those who venture to the half-dozen or so sites here is relative isolation. There are also some fine waterfalls nearby, including the iconic Stevenson Falls on Gellibrand River, accessed by a lovely walking track. Fork Paddock is on the West Barwon Track, 6.4 km north of Benwerrin Rd and 100 m south of the Barwon River crossing. Note: this is a bush-camping site with no facilities. **Map refs:** 163 I5, 197 L9

411 Hammonds Road camping area

There's plenty of open space at this campground up in the far north of the national park. Back towards the coast, close to Aireys Inlet, nice short walks include the easy Distillery Creek Nature Trail and the Moggs Creek Circuit. To get here, drive up from Aireys Inlet on Bambra Rd and turn onto Hammonds Rd, a distance of 10 km. **Map refs:** 163 J4, 197 M9

412 Jamieson Track camping area (bush camping)

Jamieson Track is a remote bush camp with only a handful of sites and no facilities, and is subject to seasonal access. You'll need a 4WD to reach it. Turn onto Jamieson Track from the Great Ocean Rd about 10 km south from Lorne. **Map refs:** 163 I5, 197 M10

413 Johanna Beach camping area

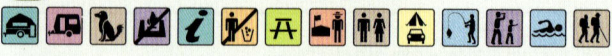

This large campground is nestled behind the dunes at Johanna Beach, a popular surfing spot to the north-west of Cape Otway. There are 2 ways to reach it. The first is to turn off the Great Ocean Rd onto Red Johanna Rd, signposted 12 km south of Lavers Hill, and keep going for nearly 5 km. The second is to take Blue Johanna Rd, 3.5 km south of Lavers Hill off the Great Ocean Rd, and follow it for just over 8 km. Note: the second option is a steep, narrow road unsuitable for caravans or camper trailers. **Map refs:** 163 H5, 197 K10

414 Lake Elizabeth camping area (walk-in camping)

Lake Elizabeth had an unusual genesis, forming in 1952 after heavy rains caused a landslide that dammed the East Barwon

River. It's a very pretty place, with a campsite you walk to via a 50 m path from the carpark. A nature trail guides you around the submerged valley, and mountain-bikers will enjoy the 12 km trail that does a loop between the lake and the West Barwon Reservoir. Take Kaanglang Rd from Forrest and look for the signage. **Map refs:** 163 I4, 197 L9

415 Parker Hill camping area

A small collection of campsites on Parker Hill look out over a sparkling inlet between Cape Otway and Point Franklin, where the Parker River empties into the ocean. From Cape Otway Lighthouse Rd, travel for 1 km east along Blanket Bay Rd then 1.5 km south down the signposted track to the hill. **Map refs:** 163 H6, 197 K11

416 Sharps Track camping area

This site is up in the hinterland behind Lorne. To stretch your legs, head to the nearby Sheoak Picnic Area and follow the well-graded trail to Upper and Lower Kalimna Falls. To reach the camping area from Lorne, take Allenvale Rd, then the turn-off onto Garvey Track, then the signposted turn onto Sharps Track. A 4WD is recommended to negotiate the route, but a conventional 2WD should be fine during dry weather. **Map refs:** 163 I4, 197 M9

417 Wye River Road camping area

Wye River is a peaceful beachfront settlement on the Great Ocean Rd between Lorne and Apollo Bay. An even more peaceful campground is almost 2 km inland on the Wye River Rd; camper trailers will need to be towed here by 4WD. Note: there are no facilities, although the proximity of the township means this isn't really an issue. **Map refs:** 163 I5, 197 M10

LOWER GLENELG NATIONAL PARK

The centrepiece of this lush national park is the tranquil Glenelg River. Just before reaching Discovery Bay, the river washes through a spectacular limestone gorge, while the stalactites glowing in the depths of Princess Margaret Rose Cave provide more evidence of the river's erosive powers. Besides hiking along part of the Great South West Walk, intrepid visitors can paddle across the park in canoes. To reach the river's southern shore, take Glenelg Dr, signposted 2 km north of Nelson; for the northern shore, head south of Dartmoor on Wanwin Rd for 15 km and turn onto River Fire Line Track.

How to book: advance bookings and permits required for all sites in Lower Glenelg National Park; Parks Victoria 13 1963; or Nelson Visitor Information Centre (08) 8738 405; (08) 8738 4171 for campsite no. **429**

418 Battersbys camping area

Located in the central section of the national park, this is a cosy camping area with only a couple of sites. Just to the south of here are the Bulley Ranges, which afford nice views of the surrounding countryside. The 300 m access track is signposted

off Glenelg Dr some 16 km east of North Nelson Track. **Map refs:** 162 B2, 196 B6

419 Bowds camping area (canoe-based camping)

Bowds is one of a number of camping areas in the park that are primarily for canoeists making their way down the Glenelg River, although these sites can be made available to powerboat operators at the ranger's discretion during quiet periods. Note: camping permits are required for all riverside sites. **Map refs:** 162 A2, 196 B6

420 Forest Camp North camping area

The simple name belies the attractive riverside location. This large campground is accessed via a steep vehicle track, for which a 4WD is recommended. From the signposted turning off River Fire Line Track, it's 200 m to Forest Camp North. Alternatively, you can get here by boat. **Map refs:** 162 A2, 196 B6

421 Forest Camp South camping area

This encampment is a good deal smaller than its neighbour directly across the river. The access road leads 200 m off Glenelg Dr – the turn-off is 13 km east of North Nelson Track. Note: bring your own drinking water. **Map refs:** 162 A2, 196 B6

422 Georges Rest camping area (canoe-based camping)

Georges Rest is only accessible by boat. Located plum in the middle of the national park, it's used as an overnight camp by canoeists who are working their way along the lower reaches of the Glenelg River. **Map refs:** 162 B2, 196 B6

423 Hutchessons camping area

There's not much to see at Hutchessons beyond the reed-lined riverbank and the surrounding trees – which is just the way that visitors like it. The turn-off for the 250 m track to the campground is on River Fire Line Track about 1 km west of the McLennans Punt access track. **Map refs:** 162 A2, 196 B6

424 Lasletts camping area (canoe-based camping)

Canoeists beach themselves at Lasletts to stage impromptu picnics, or to rest for the night before setting out for Princess Margaret Rose Cave. It's one of the handful of campsites in Lower Glenelg National Park that can only be accessed from the river. **Map refs:** 162 A2, 196 B6

425 McLennans Punt camping area

Nestled on the northern shore of the Glenelg River, McLennans Punt has only a couple of sites on offer and is a peaceful spot to erect a tent. The fishing is often very good due to the large numbers of finned creatures that tend to congregate here. The campground is 250 m from the signposted turning off River Fire Line Track. **Map refs:** 162 A2, 196 B6

426 Moleside Camp (walk-in camping)

Moleside Camp is 22 km west of Fitzroy Camp and 17 km east of Battersbys Camp. The trail to Moleside crosses into Lower Glenelg National Park, where it passes the Inkpot, a mysteriously black waterhole whose colouring is due to decayed vegetation. Another way to get here is by canoe along the Glenelg River. **Map refs:** 162 B2, 196 C6

427 Pattersons Camp (walk-in camping)

From Battersbys, it's a hike of 13 km to Pattersons Camp and a further 17 km to Simsons Camp. Along the way the trail passes Sapling Creek, where you can detour onto a nice short nature walk. You can also paddle a canoe along the Glenelg River to this spot. **Map refs:** 162 A2, 196 B6

428 Pines Landing camping area

Pines Landing is usually the first overnight stop for the adventurous canoeists who drift down the Glenelg River from Dartmoor on the first leg of their trip through the national park. There's also vehicle access via Hedditch Track, which branches off Nelson–Winnap Rd. For views, drive a short distance south to Jones Lookout. **Map refs:** 162 B2, 196 C6

429 Princess Margaret Rose Caves camping area

Underground pools, cave coral, shawls and delicate, unpredictable helictites are just some of the memorable sights within Princess Margaret Rose Cave, one of the star attractions of the national park. A number of walking trails begin at the information centre, including one that leads to the Glenelg River gorge. Signposted on the Princes Hwy 10 km east of Mt Gambier is Princess Margaret Rose Caves Rd – the caves are 19 km from the turn-off. **Map refs:** 162 A2, 196 B5

430 Pritchards camping area

This is one of the few campgrounds in Lower Glenelg National Park that can receive caravans and camper trailers – the best options are the sites numbered 11 to 20. To reach Pritchards, turn north off Portland–Nelson Rd at Wade Junction onto Nelson–Winnap Rd, then drive 9 km and take the signposted turn onto the campground's 1 km access road. **Map refs:** 162 B2, 196 C6

431 Red Gum camping area

Drive south for 15 km along Wanwin Rd from Dartmoor and turn onto the road signposted 'Red Gum'. After 3 km, turn west onto River Fire Line Track and follow it for 2 km to reach the campground's signposted access track. You'll find the big,

open Red Gum camping area 200 m off River Fire Line Track. **Map refs:** 162 B2, 196 B6

432 Skipworth Springs camping area (canoe-based camping)

Trees crowd the shoreline of the Glenelg River at Skipworth Springs. As there's no vehicle access, the only traffic noise out here comes from the occasional passing motorboat and canoeists taking a break from their journey along the waterway. **Map refs:** 162 B2, 196 B6

433 Wild Dog Bend camping area

Wild Dog Bend is in the eastern reaches of the national park, where the Glenelg River almost doubles back on itself to head southwards. This is one of the few overnight options in the national park for those towing camper trailers. The turn-off to this campground is on Nelson–Winnap Rd, just over 5 km north-east of the Pritchards camping area turn-off. Note: the 3 km access track may not be signposted. **Map refs:** 162 B2, 196 C6

434 Wilson Hall camping area

If you're towing a boat and coming into the national park from Dartmoor, you may want to take advantage of the boat ramp here – there are a limited number of launching places on this side of the river. The 350 m access track is signposted off River Fire Line Track, almost 3.5 km west of the trail to Forest Camp North. **Map refs:** 162 A2, 196 B6

MOUNT CLAY STATE FOREST

Thick eucalypt forest surrounds Mt Clay in the hinterland behind Portland Bay, 15 km east of Portland. Mountain-bikers of all levels of experience make the most of the many trails that squeeze their way through the dense foliage here. A highlight is the walk to Whalers Lookout, from where you can spy Lady Julia Percy Island.

Who to contact: DSE Heywood (03) 5527 0444, 13 6186

435 Sawpit camping area

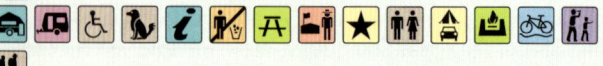

This old sawmill site attracts campers because of its access to ocean views. Take the easy track to Whalers Lookout and see if you can spot some passing cetaceans. To reach the site, follow the signposted Boyers Rd from Narrawong north for 1.2 km and turn left at the T-intersection onto Goodes Rd. After another 1.6 km, take the signposted 200 m track to the campground. **Map refs:** 162 C3, 196 D7

MOUNT ECCLES NATIONAL PARK

Mt Eccles, also known as Budj Bim and situated 10 km west of Macarthur, is a dream destination for budding vulcanologists. Ancient eruptions resulted in lava flows and caves that visitors can explore via a network of invigorating walking tracks. A trio of craters now holds the waters of Lake Surprise, which have bubbled up from underground springs.

Who to contact: Parks Victoria 13 1963

436 Lake Surprise camping area

Set in serene manna gum forest not far from an equally serene crater lake, this is a delightful place to stay. Walking tracks guide you along lava canals, around the rim of a crater and down to Lake Surprise itself. Bookings are obligatory for the main public holidays. To get here, follow Mt Eccles Rd from Macarthur. **Map refs: 162 D2, 196 E6**

NELSON RESERVE

Nelson Reserve comprises 10 ha of bird-filled bushland near the winding Glenelg River, just shy of the South Australian border and within striking distance of the Historic Shipwreck Trail and the Great South West Walk. It's also close to the many attractions of neighbouring Lower Glenelg National Park, which include enigmatic caves, river cruises and superb bushwalks.

How to book: bookings recommended during peak periods; North Nelson Rd, Nelson (08) 8738 4174 www.kywongcp.com

437 Kywong Caravan Park

At Kywong Caravan Park, you can spend your days swimming, fishing and saying hello to the local kangaroos and wallabies. Don't forget to pay your respects to beautiful Lower Glenelg National Park while you're here. The caravan park is 500 m down North Nelson Rd from the signposted turn-off on Portland–Nelson Rd. **Map refs: 162 A2, 196 B6**

OTWAY FOREST PARK

This widely scattered park brushes up against the twisting perimeter of lush Great Otway National Park, encompassing forests on the slopes and in the foothills of the Otway Ranges to the north of the mountains' spine. Hidden within this densely wooded landscape, which is home to owls, eagles and bats, are appealing waterfalls and uncrowded bushwalking tracks.

Who to contact: Parks Victoria 13 1963

438 Beauchamp Falls camping area

There are only half a dozen campsites here, which will suit those who prefer small encampments to big ones. A walking track leads through the cool rainforest to the waterfall, where a viewing platform provides a close-up view. Head north from Skenes Creek on Skenes Creek Rd, then head west for 17 km on Beech Forest Rd to Aire Valley Rd. Your next turn is onto Flannagan Rd, then onto Beauchamp Falls Rd. **Map refs: 163 H5, 197 L10**

439 Dandos camping area

This sizeable bush camping area has several dozen campsites scattered among a cluster of pines and silver birch trees. Close to the Gellibrand River, it's a good location for anglers who just want to sit and fish away the hours. Dandos is due south of Gellibrand township – access is via Lardner Track. **Map refs: 163 H4, 197 L9**

440 Stevenson Falls camping area

The drawcard here is the walking track that shadows the Gellibrand River and negotiates groves of Douglas firs before arriving at the viewing platform at lovely Stevenson Falls, where you can take a plunge in the rock pools. Note: only the section of the track between the falls and the day-visitor area is wheelchair accessible. The site is 4 km west of Barramunga, signposted off Upper Gellibrand Rd. **Map refs: 163 I4, 197 L9**

CAMPSITES LOCATED IN OTHER AREAS

441 Aireys Inlet Holiday Park

This small caravan park, wedged between the bush and the beach, makes a good stopover on forays deeper into Great Ocean Rd territory. Situated on a beautiful stretch of the famous road, the small township here is quiet and without the glamour of nearby Lorne. Some of the powered sites come with private bathrooms, while unpowered tent sites have a decent green carpet. The park is pet friendly outside of peak times. **Map refs: 163 J4, 197 N9**

How to book: 19–25 Great Ocean Rd, Aireys Inlet (03) 5289 6230 www.aicp.com.au

442 Anderson Reserve camping area

Anderson Reserve is one of 3 foreshore camping options at Indented Head on the Bellarine Peninsula, the others being Batman Park and Taylors Reserve. John Batman, Melbourne's founder, set up camp at Indented Head in the 1830s. Accessed from The Esplanade, Anderson Reserve snakes along the edge of Port Phillip Bay, its campsites spread out rather than being clustered together in the one spot. Note: the reserve is open mid-Dec to mid-Mar. **Map refs: 163 L3, 188 B6, 197 P7**

How to book: bookings essential during peak periods; Bellarine Bayside (03) 5259 2764, 1800 222 778

443 Anglesea Beachfront Family Caravan Park

In Anglesea, turn off the Great Ocean Rd onto Cameron Rd to access this waterfront campground, where you can choose

between a splash in a river and chasing waves off a surf beach. Anglesea township is only a short walk away, while the park itself has plenty of distractions for kids, including a toddlers' playroom, a games room and a huge open-air 'jumping pillow'. Cabin accommodation is available, and adults can enjoy an indoor spa. **Map refs:** 163 J4, 197 N9

How to book: bookings recommended during peak periods; 35 Cameron Rd, Anglesea (03) 5263 1583 www.angleseabeachfront.com.au

444 Barwon Heads Caravan Park

The campsites here are sprinkled alongside the Barwon River, right where the watercourse flows out into Bass Strait. Aside from the picturesque views, the park offers safe freshwater swimming, quick access to a surf beach and good fishing. Those who prefer land-based activities can play tennis and basketball, organise a team sport on the adjacent oval, or just stroll along the foreshore. **Map refs:** 163 K4, 188 A7, 197 O8

How to book: bookings essential during peak periods; Ewing Blyth Dr, Barwon Heads (03) 5254 1115 www.barwoncoast.com.au

445 Batman Park camping area

This park is situated off The Esplanade within the tiny town of Indented Head, which occupies a small wedge of land on the western shore of Port Phillip Bay. It's one of 3 camping options in Indented Head: the others are Anderson Reserve and Taylors Reserve. Book early to claim one of the string of sites positioned opposite the sand. Beachcombers should keep their eyes peeled for the wreck of a paddle-steamer just offshore. The reserve is open Nov–Apr. **Map refs:** 163 L3, 188 B6, 197 P7

How to book: bookings essential during peak periods; Bellarine Bayside (03) 5259 2764, 1800 222 778

446 Breamlea Caravan Park

Fringed by tea-trees and sand dunes, this caravan park is located on Horwood Dr in the small, low-key town of Breamlea, near the beginning of the Great Ocean Rd. A patrolled surf beach is only a short walk away and there's an on-site store where you can stock up on camping provisions. There are excellent fishing spots nearby. **Map refs:** 163 K4, 188 A7, 197 O8

How to book: bookings recommended during peak periods; Horwood Dr, Breamlea (03) 5264 1352

447 Camperdown Lakes and Craters Holiday Park

This scenic park is wedged between a pair of extinct volcano craters. Part of one crater has been flooded by Lake Bullen Merri, which is perfect for watersports such as sailing, waterskiing and

swimming. The scenery is just as good in the adjacent Botanic Gardens. You'll find the park 3 km south-west of Camperdown, on Park Rd; just follow the signs from town. **Map refs:** 163 G3, 197 J7

How to book: 220 Park Rd, Camperdown (03) 5593 1253

448 Central Caravan Park

True to its name, this caravan park is located close to the centre of Colac, at the township's showgrounds. It's also close to the largest botanic gardens in country Victoria, and at the end of the street are the placid waters of Lake Colac, which are great for cooling off or a leisurely boat trip (note that water levels may be low). The volcanic plain on which Colac sits is also worth a tour. **Map refs:** 163 H4, 197 L8

How to book: bookings preferred; Bruce St, Colac (03) 5231 3586 www.centralcaravanpark.com.au

449 Erskine River Caravan Park

This park has several dozen sites right beside the Erskine River, which flows through the busy seaside holiday town of Lorne. Tackle the walking trail to Erskine Falls, dive into the surf off Lorne's main beach or cradle a coffee in one of the town's many cafes. This is one of 5 local campgrounds that are collectively referred to as the Lorne Foreshore Caravan Park, and are accessed off the Great Ocean Rd. **Map refs:** 163 I4, 197 M9

How to book: bookings required during peak periods; Lorne Foreshore Caravan Park, 2 Great Ocean Rd, Lorne (03) 5289 1382, 1300 364 797 www.lornecaravanpark.com.au

450 Fort O'Hare camping area

Set on the northern bank of the Glenelg River in the low-key town of Dartmoor, this camping area is where canoeists set off on a popular 4 day, 75 km paddle through Lower Glenelg National Park to the river mouth beyond Nelson. Non-canoeists can check out the carvings hewn from the Atlantic cedars lining Greenham St, a local tribute to those who served in World War I. Turn off the Princes Hwy onto Ascot St, then turn right on Greenham St. **Map refs:** 162 B1, 196 C5

Who to contact: Portland Visitor Information Centre (03) 5523 2671

451 Great Ocean Road Tourist Park

Situated at Peterborough on the Great Ocean Rd, 12 km west of Port Campbell and within easy reach of the Twelve Apostles, is the Great Ocean Road Tourist Park. It's next to the tranquil Curdies Inlet, which offers safe, turbulence-free swimming and sailboarding; anglers can try their hand at surf-fishing over the dunes. There are some good views out over the water, and campsites are sheltered from the worst of any wind. A camp kitchen and free BBQs are just some of the facilities

here. Note: no pets on school holidays or long weekends.
Map refs: 162 F4, 197 I9

How to book: Great Ocean Rd, Peterborough (03) 5598 5477, 1800 200 478 www.gortp.com.au

Great South West Walk

This outstanding 250 km hike heads inland from Portland and makes its way through dense forests and across languid rivers to Nelson, before looping back to Portland along the beautifully rough limestone coast. Walkers should register the details of their trip with either the Portland Visitor Information Centre or the local police; they must also sign out once they've finished the walk. Note: carry some water as supplies at the campsites aren't always reliable.

Please note that the campsites are listed in alphabetical order, not track order. Refer to the map on pp. 162–3 for further information.

Who to contact: Parks Victoria 13 1963; or Portland Visitor Information Centre (03) 5523 2671

452 Cobboboonee Camp (walk-in camping)

Just south of Cobboboonee camp is the Heathland Nature Trail, an easy walk that reveals colourful wildflowers in springtime. Cobboboonee Camp is in the centre of the national park between Cut-out Camp (9.4 km) and Fitzroy Camp (12.5 km). **Map refs:** 162 B2, 196 C6

453 Cubbys Camp (walk-in camping)

Cubbys Camp is a 20 km trek north-west of Portland. It's located in the eastern fringe of Cobboboonee Forest. **Map refs:** 162 C3, 196 D7

454 Cut-out Camp (walk-in camping)

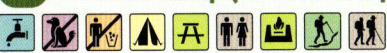

The 15 km walk between Cubbys Camp and Cut-out Camp leads you into Cobboboonee National Park. It's 9.4 km from Cut-out Camp to Cobboboonee Camp. **Map refs:** 162 B3, 196 D7

455 Fitzroy Camp (walk-in camping)

Situated on a bank of the Fitzroy River, this camp is a 12.5 km walk from Cobboboonee Camp and 22 km to Moleside Camp. **Map refs:** 162 B2, 196 C6

401 Lake Monibeong camping area

See p. 162.

456 Mallee Camp (walk-in camping)

Mallee Camp is 15 km from Trewalla Camp, a hike that takes you around Cape Nelson. Portland is another 21.7 km to the north. **Map refs:** 162 C3, 196 D8

426 Moleside Camp (walk-in camping)

See p. 166.

457 Murrells Camp (walk-in camping)

Murrells Camp is between Battersbys and Pattersons campsites. Note: this campsite has been earmarked for decommissioning; check with Parks Victoria before camping here. **Map refs:** 162 A2, 196 B6

427 Pattersons Camp (walk-in camping)

See p. 166.

458 Post and Rail Camp (walk-in camping)

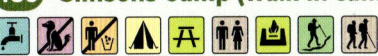

This camp is located between Moleside Camp and Battersbys Camp. The trail here follows the Glenelg River as it wriggles its way through the heart of the national park. Note: this campsite has been earmarked for decommissioning; call Parks Victoria to check if it's still open. **Map refs:** 162 B2, 196 C6

459 Simsons Camp (walk-in camping)

The 17 km trail that leads from Pattersons Camp to Simsons Camp affords some spectacular views of the limestone cliffs of the Glenelg River Gorge. From this point on, you leave the environs of the Glenelg River behind and head down to the shoreline of the Southern Ocean. Continuing on from here it is 13 km to White Sands Camp. **Map refs:** 162 A2, 196 B6

460 The Springs Camp (walk-in camping)

White Sands to Swan Lake is 28.5 km, from Swan Lake to the Springs is 32 km, and from there to Trewalla is 15 km. The Springs camp is on Cape Bridgewater, not far from some spectacular blowholes and a petrified forest. The offshore waters are part of Discovery Bay Marine National Park. **Map refs:** 162 B3, 196 C8

402 Swan Lake camping area

See p. 163.

461 Trewalla Camp (walk-in camping)

From the Springs Camp, a walk of 15 km takes you around the edge of the cape, past its famous fur seal colony, and skirts Bridgewater Bay before reaching Trewalla Camp. It's a further 15 km to Mallee camp. **Map refs:** 162 B3, 196 D8

462 White Sands Camp (walk-in camping)

White Sands Camp is a 13 km walk from Simsons Camp. The track departs Lower Glenelg National Park and cuts through the town of Nelson to eventually hit the sandy beaches of Discovery Bay Coastal Park. From White Sands, you continue along the ocean for 13 km to the campsite at peaceful Lake Monibeong, then a further 3.5 km to the campsite at Swan Lake before proceeding to The Springs Camp. **Map refs:** 162 A2, 196 B6

463 Kennett River Caravan Park

This orderly park is just across the Great Ocean Rd from the popular surf beach at Kennett River. Rising up behind it are the Otway Ranges, which are threaded by numerous walking trails. You can feed the local rosellas and parrots, or go searching for koalas in the surrounding trees. Those who like to bring the world with them when they camp will appreciate the free wireless internet at the campground. Note: if you want to use a fireplace, talk to the managers beforehand. **Map refs:** 163 I5, 197 M10

How to book: bookings required during peak periods; Great Ocean Rd, Kennett River (03) 5289 0272, 1300 664 417 www.kennettriver.com

464 Kia-Ora Caravan Park

Kia-Ora is one of several campgrounds next to the Erskine River in Lorne that are collectively managed by the Lorne Foreshore Caravan Park. It's located on the river's southern bank close to the Great Ocean Rd, with the Lorne Visitor Centre and the town's main strip only a short walk away. Kia-Ora has over 100 sites, so you'll have plenty of company here. **Map refs:** 163 I4, 197 M9

How to book: bookings required during peak periods; Lorne Foreshore Caravan Park, 2 Great Ocean Rd, Lorne (03) 5289 1382, 1300 364 797 www.lornecaravanpark.com.au

465 Killarney Beach Camping Reserve

Killarney Beach has grassy, sheltered campsites. There's safe swimming here, while the surrounding rural region is notable for its peacefulness. A short drive east is Tower Hill Reserve, a shallow crater of an extinct volcano that now contains a lake and several islands linked by self-guided walks. Note: the caretaker of the camping reserve is only resident over summer. **Map refs:** 162 E3, 196 G8

How to book: bookings recommended at Christmas; Mahoneys Rd, Killarney 0428 314 823

466 Lake Colac Caravan Park

When its water levels are high, the namesake body of water next to the town of Colac, 73 km west of Geelong on the Princes Hwy, is used for all manner of watersports: from swimming and sailing to waterskiing. The caravan park, which is on Fyans St, provides direct access to the lake's southern shoreline. It also has lots of grassy campsites and lies directly opposite the township's pretty botanic gardens. **Map refs:** 163 H4, 197 L8

How to book: bookings recommended during peak periods; 51 Fyans St, Colac (03) 5231 5971

467 Lake Purrumbete Caravan Park

Lake Purrumbete is a prime destination for anglers chasing chinook salmon and rainbow and brown trout, as attested to by the heavy-duty boat ramps and jetties at the caravan park. The park is on the foreshore at the lake's southern end. To reach it, turn off the Princes Hwy 10 km east of Camperdown to access the Purrumbete Estate Rd. **Map refs:** 163 G3, 197 J8

How to book: bookings recommended during peak periods; 540 Purrumbete Estate Rd, Camperdown (03) 5594 5377

468 Marengo Holiday Park

Off Marengo Cres on the headland at Marengo, a little south of Apollo Bay, this holiday park is freshened by sea breezes and affords fine views over the ocean. Just off Marengo Beach is a marine sanctuary containing a sandstone reef that snorkellers will want to explore, while surfers will enjoy the local swells. Needless to say, the swimming and fishing here are also good. **Map refs:** 163 H5, 197 L11

How to Book: bookings required during peak periods; off Great Ocean Rd, Apollo Bay (03) 5237 6162 www.marengopark.com.au

469 Meredith Park camping area

On the northern shore of Lake Colac, this simple camping area attracts hordes of anglers when the water level is good. From Colac, head north on the road to Ballarat for 10 km and turn onto Meredith Park Rd. **Map refs:** 163 H3, 197 L8

Who to contact: Colac Visitor Information Centre (03) 5231 3730

470 Narrawong Holiday Park

This scenic place is 13 km east of Portland on the Princes Hwy. It has its own natural moat, the Surry River, which circles the campground before flowing out past the local beach. Many of the grassy campsites are bordered by stately Norfolk Island pines, with the most popular boasting riverfront positions. The playgrounds, recreation room and outdoor movie screenings will keep the kids well-occupied. **Map refs:** 162 C3, 196 D7

How to book: off Princes Hwy, Narrawong (03) 5529 5282; 1800 005 066 www.narrawongcaravanpark.com.au

471 Port Campbell Holiday Park

It's only a short drive from Port Campbell east down the Great Ocean Rd to the landmark Twelve Apostles, a spectacular but slowly diminishing offshore grouping of limestone towers sculpted over countless centuries by wind and sea. This holiday

park occupies a plot of land on Morris St alongside Campbells Creek, just back from the oceanfront. Ask for a site next to the creek, or for one behind the beachside surf lifesaving club. **Map refs:** 163 G5, 197 I9

How to book: bookings required during peak periods; 1 Morris Street, Port Campbell (03) 5598 6492, 1800 781 871 www.pchp.com.au

472 Port Fairy Gardens Caravan Park

This large caravan park is huddled around a sportsground off Griffiths St in the pretty town of Port Fairy, famous for its 19th-century cottages and the hugely popular folk festival it stages in Mar. Flowing along the park's eastern boundary is the Moyne River and at its southern end is the township's botanical gardens, while a few hundred metres east is the sandy sweep of East Beach. **Map refs:** 162 E3, 196 F8

How to book: bookings required during peak periods; 111 Griffith St, Port Fairy (03) 5568 1060

473 Portarlington Seaside Resort

You'll usually need to book well in advance of your visit to get one of the campsites arrayed along the beachfront at this sprawling holiday complex, located on Sproat St in Portarlington. Popular activities here include taking constitutionals up and down the foreshore, playing a round of golf at the local club, buying fresh seafood down at the pier, and having a refreshing drink at the Grand Hotel. **Map refs:** 163 K3, 188 B6, 197 P7

How to book: bookings essential during peak periods; Bellarine Bayside (03) 5259 2764, 1800 222 778

474 Princetown Recreation Reserve

This campground has its fair share of peace and quiet, but the main reason for staying near Princetown is the fact that the beautiful Twelve Apostles are only a few minutes to the west of the tiny settlement by car. **Map refs:** 163 G5, 197 J10

How to book: 99 Old Coach Rd, Princetown 0429 985 176 www.princetownrecreationreserve.com

475 Queenscliff Recreation Reserve camping area

This foreshore reserve has lots of shady sites and plenty of wide open spaces for playing games. Go for a wander through the streets of the historic township or watch enormous tankers and cargo ships navigate the Rip, the thin waterway that separates the Bellarine and Mornington peninsulas. Note: pets are only allowed May–Oct. **Map refs:** 163 K4, 188 B7, 197 P8

How to book: bookings essential during peak periods; Queenscliff Tourist Parks (03) 5258 1765

476 Riverview Family Caravan Park

The beach here at Ocean Grove is a lovely stretch of sand that's very popular with holidaymakers when the summer sun is shining. Equally popular is the nearby nature reserve, where there is over 140 ha of native bushland to explore. The campsites in the park are well-sheltered, with several dozen of them fringing the slow-flowing Barwon River. You'll find them off Ocean Grove Rd. **Map refs:** 163 K3, 188 A7, 197 O8

How to book: bookings essential at Christmas; Barwon Heads, Ocean Grove Rd, Ocean Grove (03) 5256 1600 www.barwoncoast.com.au

477 Royal Park camping area

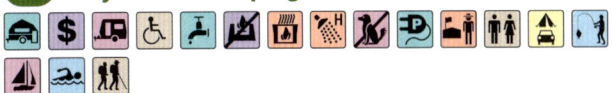

Point Lonsdale is joined to Queenscliff by a narrow isthmus and shares the same ocean-wide view. It's here you'll find snug Royal Park. Stroll the promenade behind the seawall down to the point itself, or wander over to Queenscliff to check out the rugged entrance to Port Phillip Bay. Note: Royal Park is only open from the last weekend in Nov to 30 Apr. **Map refs:** 163 K4, 188 B7, 197 P8

How to Book: bookings essential during peak periods; Queenscliff Tourist Parks (03) 5258 1765

478 St Leonards Foreshore caravan and camping area

You can camp in two parks on the foreshore at St Leonards, off The Esplanade. This is a useful base from which to explore the other lovely towns of the Bellarine Peninsula, or you can just sit and stare across placid Port Phillip Bay towards the distant outline of the Mornington Peninsula. The larger of the 2 parks is open Nov–Apr, while the smaller is open from 21 Dec–3 Feb. You'll pay a bit more for a beachfront site than for one that's away from the water. **Map refs:** 163 L3, 188 B6, 197 P7

Who to contact: bookings essential during peak periods; Bellarine Bayside (03) 5259 2764, 1800 222 778

479 Skenes Creek Beachfront Caravan Park

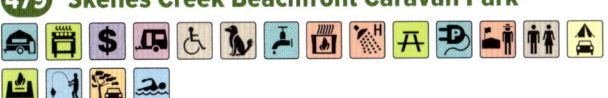

Skenes Creek is a small place on the Great Ocean Rd at the northern edge of Apollo Bay, only 6 km from its much bigger neighbour and opposite the turn-off to Colac. Over half the campsites here run along the edge of the beach, where you can swim or go fishing. The swells afford good surfing and boards can be hired for the occasion. Drums are provided for open fires; wood is also sold here. **Map refs:** 163 I5, 197 L10

How to book: bookings required during peak periods; 2 Great Ocean Rd, Skenes Creek (03) 5237 6132 www.skenescreek.com

480 Surfside Holiday Park

Across the road from this campground is a huge family-friendly park, centred on a lake and festooned with playgrounds. Nearby is the Merri River, beyond which you'll find the enticing sheltered waters of Stingray Bay. Southern right whales can usually be spotted offshore between June and Sept. Note: pets are not allowed in the holiday park at certain times of year, such as at Christmas and Easter; check when booking.
Map refs: 162 E4, 196 G8

How to book: bookings required during peak periods; Pertobe Rd, Warrnambool (03) 5559 4700 www.surfsidepark.com.au

481 Taylors Reserve camping area

Several dozen campsites are congregated at Taylors Reserve, off The Esplanade in Indented Head. Like the 2 other campgrounds in the bayside township, Batman Park and Anderson Reserve, this place is popular with holidaymakers. Note: the reserve is only open from mid-Dec to the beginning of Feb.
Map refs: 163 L3, 188 B6, 197 P7

How to book: bookings essential during peak periods; Bellarine Bayside (03) 5259 2764, 1800 222 778

482 Torquay Caravan Park

A stop on the Great Ocean Rd, Torquay Caravan Park is within walking distance to beaches and is also close to the shops and restaurants of Torquay township. Powered sites are well-shaded and located in the middle of the park, while unpowered tent sites are to the rear and used at peak times only. Minigolf, a jumping pillow and a playground are distractions for the kids, while grown-ups can run around on the tennis courts or beach volleyball court.
Map refs: 163 J4, 197 N8

How to book: 55 Surfcoast Hwy, Torquay (03) 5261 2493 www.torquayholidaypark.com.au

483 Torquay Foreshore Caravan Park

Torquay is the centre of the Victorian surfing scene, so it's no surprise that this caravan park is adjacent to a great surf beach at the southern end of Paterson Bay – not very far from the best known surf spot of them all, Bells Beach. The park has lots of shade and a playground for the kiddies. If you're in need of a boat ramp, head to Fisherman's Beach. The park is pet friendly from May–Aug. **Map refs:** 163 J4, 197 N8

How to book: bookings required during peak periods; 35 Bell Street, Torquay (03) 5261 2496, 1300 736 533 www.torquaycaravanpark.com.au

484 Victoria Park caravan and camping area

Victoria Park is on Hesse St, near Queenscliff's main street with its quaint cafes and shops, and is almost as close to the dramatic entrance to Port Phillip Bay. Its campsites are arrayed opposite the town's pleasant recreation reserve, with the ocean only a short walk beyond. Book well ahead for school and public holidays, when the sites are in great demand. Note: Victoria Park is only open from the last weekend in Nov to 30 Apr.
Map refs: 163 K4, 188 B7, 197 P8

How to book: bookings essential during peak periods; Queenscliff Tourist Parks (03) 5258 1765

485 Warrnambool Holiday Park

Filled with amenities, this holiday park is situated 2 km east of the centre of Warrnambool. Within its confines you'll find a reasonable number of sites shaded by large trees, as well as a playground, a pool and a grassy communal area to laze on. The town's main beach is a short drive or cycle away.
Map refs: 162 E4, 196 G8

How to book: cnr Raglan Pde and Simpson St, (03) 5562 5031, 1800 650 441 www.whpark.com.au

486 Wye River Foreshore Camping Reserve

The patrolled beach at the mouth of Wye River is great for all manner of surfing, from body to board, while those who prefer calmer waters can wade into the creek. Next-door to the campground is a relaxed pub where you can ask the locals about the best fishing spots in the area. Note: the campground is open from late Nov–Apr. **Map refs:** 163 I5, 197 M10

How to book: (03) 5289 0412

487 Yambuk Lake Caravan Park

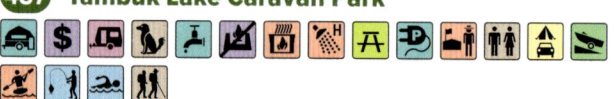

In Yambuk township, take the signposted turn off the Princes Hwy onto Yambuk Lake Rd and drive for 3 km; alternatively, take the Carrolls Rd turn-off to the east of Yambuk. This campground is at the southern end of Lake Yambuk, which comprises reed-fringed wetlands, and is also close to the mouth of the Eumeralla River. Taking long, aimless strolls along the beach and fishing in the lake are the activities of choice here.
Map refs: 162 D3, 196 F8

How to book: bookings essential at Easter and Christmas; off the Princes Hwy, Yambuk 0419 006 201 www.portfairycaravanparks.com

GRAMPIANS AND CENTRAL WEST

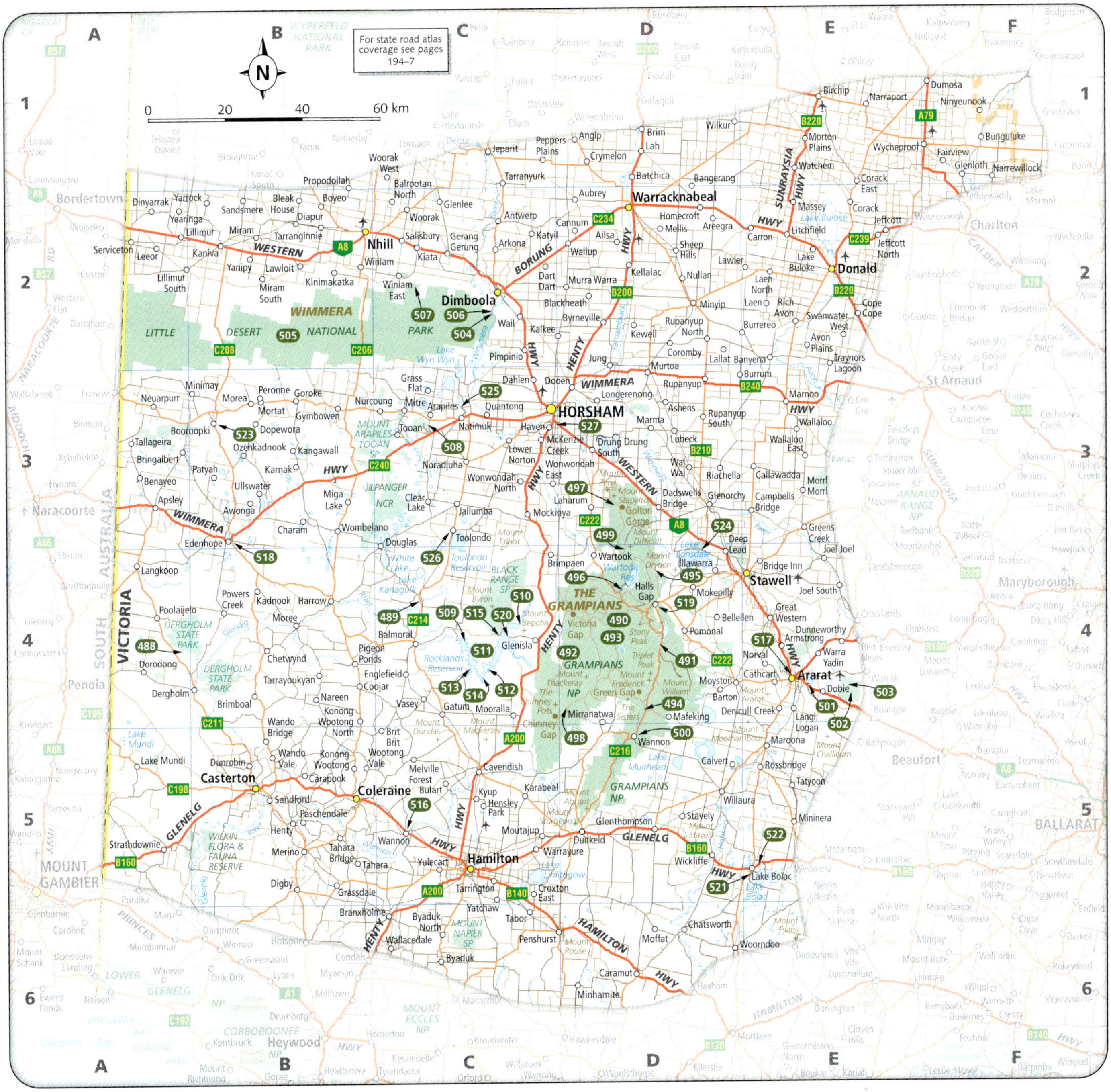

For state road atlas coverage see pages 194–7

GRAMPIANS (OR GARIWERD) NATIONAL Park is one of Victoria's, if not Australia's, prime bushwalking and camping destinations. The park's sandstone ridges rise up dramatically from the state's central-west plains, providing plenty of steep terrain for demanding hikes, as well as unforgettable views of the surrounding region from mountain-top lookouts. Between the ridges' enormous folds lie pristine rivers and waterfalls, and some fascinating Aboriginal heritage sites where ancient rock art is on display. Also sheltering here are some marvellous spots for bush camping, from where you can admire the park's natural grandeur at your leisure.

More impressively rocky terrain is to be found east of the Grampians in Langi Ghiran State Park, its thick forests studded with granite peaks. The park's trail-free terrain is perfect for hikers who want to make their own way into the wild. On the other side of the Grampians is the rock enthusiast's ultimate destination – Mt Arapiles–Tooan State Park. The area boasts myriad free-climbing routes, allowing anyone so inclined to heave themselves up cliffs and dangle from overhangs to their heart's content. Not far from here are the forest-shrouded environs of the Rockland Reservoir, where campers gaze across the water while waiting for the next tug on the fishing line.

For a change of scenery, intrepid and well-equipped campers should head north to explore the remote scrublands and sand dunes of Little Desert National Park. Stretching west of Dimboola, Little Desert, the country town made famous by David Williamson's alcohol-drenched tale of an outback wedding, is a haven for Australian flora – it's home to hundreds of species of plant life indigenous to the park. Its rough, sandy tracks also make a good introduction to the continent's dry, enigmatic interior.

CAMPSITES LOCATED IN PARKS AND RESERVES

DERGHOLM STATE PARK

A drive of 40 km north-west of Casterton will take you to Dergholm State Park, an area of gentle hills where you can picnic among the red gums and brown stringybarks. The 10 400 ha park is split into 2 blocks: the southernmost is called Youpayang, while the northernmost is called Bogalara.

Who to contact: Parks Victoria 13 1963

488 Baileys Rocks camping area

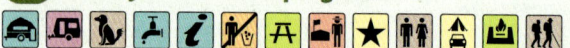

Baileys Rocks, in the Bogalara block of Dergholm State Park, are so-called for the ancient granite tors found here. Aside from ogling the impressive stonework, you can also follow the Rocky Creek walking track, which does a 5 km loop from the campground. In the neighbouring Youpayang block is what's been deemed the world's largest river red gum, Bilston's Tree. To get to the campground, turn onto Baileys Rocks Rd from the Casterton–Naracoorte Rd. Note: boil the tank water before drinking it. Dogs permitted in picnic area. **Map refs:** 173 A4, 194 C12, 196 C2

FULHAM STREAMSIDE RESERVE

This reserve is set alongside a river – the Glenelg River – rather than a stream, and abounds in native orchids in springtime. It's about 10 km north of the town of Balmoral, to the west of Grampians National Park.

Who to contact: Parks Victoria 13 1963

489 Fulham Streamside Reserve camping area

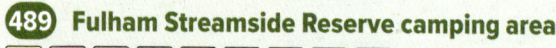

A 4WD vehicle is needed to reach this camping area. The access road is signposted off the Natimuk–Hamilton Rd, just south of Kanagulk. There are no facilities to speak of, but the campground's pleasant riverside location makes it a good spot for canoeists. Note: the sandy track leading to the reserve is subject to seasonal closure. **Map refs:** 173 C4, 194 E11, 196 E1

GRAMPIANS NATIONAL PARK

The sublime Grampians, also known as Gariwerd, are a series of steep, spectacular sandstone ridges adored by campers and bushwalkers. The region is home to over 800 species of plants – the wildflowers are a kaleidoscopic sight in spring.

There are also numerous Aboriginal heritage sites, and stupendous views from places like The Pinnacle. The Henty Hwy and Grampians Rd off the Western Hwy are the main access roads.

The park was extensively damaged following a significant storm in January 2011, resulting in the closure of many areas, so contact Parks Victoria before planning your trip.

Highlights of the large park include the unusual rock formations at The Balconies, Mackenzie Falls and the views to the east from the summit of Mt William. Sunrise here can be spectacular. There are also many worthwhile bushwalks ranging from easy short strolls to strenuous overnight hikes. Visit the Brambuk National Park and Cultural Centre, at the south end of Halls Gap, to get information about drives, walks and camping.

Who to contact: Parks Victoria 13 1963 *Camping fees:* permit from, and fees payable to, Brambuk National Park and Cultural Centre, Halls Gap (03) 5361 4000

490 Boreang camping area

For those who want to camp right in the middle of the national park, this is the place for you. Nearby are the Balconies, a pair of sandstone shelves that jut out spectacularly from a sheer cliff – the views are dizzying. The Balconies are reached by a 1 km track that weaves through gum tree forest from the carpark at the superb Reed Lookout. To get to Boreang from Halls Gap, head west on Victory Rd and then turn onto Victoria Valley Rd. **Map refs:** 173 D4, 194 G12, 196 G1

491 Borough Huts camping area

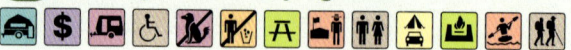

Borough Huts is 10 km south of Halls Gap, just off Grampians Rd. In between these 2 places you'll find lovely Lake Bellfield, which makes for a fantastic canoeing trip, due in no small part to the grand views of the surrounding mountains. The campground's dozen or so sites are down by picturesque Fyans Creek; despite the name, there are no huts here. Birdlife is abundant and this is the closest camping area to Mt William, which is useful if you wish to catch the sunrise from the summit, though a drive is still necessary to the end of the summit road. **Map refs:** 173 D4, 194 H12, 196 H2

492 Buandik camping area

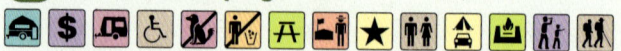

The Buandik camping area, at the western boundary of the Grampians, is bookended by two Aboriginal heritage sites – Billimina to the north, and Manja to the south. Manja is fringed by heathlands which are traversed via a boardwalk, making for a pleasant outing. The campground itself is in forest beside Billimina Creek. Turn onto Billywing Rd from the Henty Hwy at Glenisla. **Map refs:** 173 D4, 194 G12, 196 G2

493 Bush camping (walk-in camping)

You can go bush camping almost anywhere in Grampians National Park. The exceptions are the Wonderland Range, the watershed of Lake Wartook, and within 1 km of a campground or 50 m from a sealed road; check the regulations with the rangers. If you're going to go on an extended walk, don't forget to register your intentions at Brambuk National Park and Cultural Centre, located just outside Halls Gap. **Map refs:** 173 E4, 194 G12, 196 G1

494 Jimmy Creek camping area

The campground at Jimmy Creek is in the south-eastern slice of the park, wedged between the Serra and Mt William ranges. To the east along Jimmy Creek Rd is Mafeking, a one-time goldmine site you can explore via the self-guided Brownings Loop Walk. Strike out southwards from Halls Gap on Grampians Rd to reach Jimmy Creek; if you're coming from the Glenelg Hwy end, the campground is north of Wannon. **Map refs:** 173 D4, 196 H2

495 Plantation camping area

The Plantation area is the Grampians' biggest campground, providing around 30 sites in a pine forest at the northern edge of the national park (technically, just outside of it), at the foot of the Mt Difficult Range. In eucalypt forest just north of here is the historic Heatherlie Quarry, where prized freestone was dug up a century ago. Head north from Halls Gap on the Halls Gap–Mt Zero Rd and turn east on Pines Rd. **Map refs:** 173 D4, 194 H11, 196 H1

496 Smiths Mill camping area

This pine tree-fringed old mill site is just south of Wartook Reservoir. It has over 2 dozen campsites but not much allowance has been made for compact vans and camper trailers. East of here is the Boroka Lookout, which affords fantastic views over the aptly named Wonderland Range. You can reach Smiths Mill on Old Mill Rd via Wartook Rd. **Map refs:** 173 D4, 194 G11, 196 G1

497 Stapylton camping area

This large campground has a mixture of sheltered and open sites, and is situated in the far north of the national park. You can take a short, self-guided walk to Ngamadjidj Shelter, a one-time Aboriginal campsite where some fascinating rock art is on display. A more testing walking track leads from the nearby Golton Gorge picnic area down into the gorge proper. From Northern Grampians Rd, head east down Plantation Rd to reach Stapylton. **Map refs:** 173 D3, 194 G10

498 Strachans camping area

The south-western branch of Grampians National Park is shaped around the curvaceous Victoria Range, and it's at the foot of these mountains, on the site of an old timber mill, that you'll find Strachans camping area. West of here are the Chimney Pots, an eye-catching rock tower that can be scaled via a steep track; the views from the summit are fantastic. Take Glenelg

River Rd to get to Strachans. Note: there are bollards around the camping area. **Map refs:** 173 D4, 196 G2

499 Troopers Creek camping area

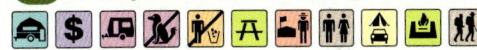

The forested campground at Troopers Creek can be used as a base camp by those who want to rest up before tackling the precipitous but highly recommended climb up Mt Difficult. If you'd prefer something less strenuous, try the nearby gentle ascent to the seasonal Tilwinda Falls. At Wartook, turn off Mt Victory Rd onto Roses Gap Rd and follow it for about 10 km. **Map refs:** 173 D4, 194 H11

500 Wannon Crossing camping area

At Wannon Crossing you'll find a quartet of campsites on a forested patch of turf beside the Wannon River. It's a good choice for keen hikers as it's the closest camping area to the trio of invigorating walks clustered in the far south of the national park – the hard 6–7 km return climbs up Mt Sturgeon and Mt Abrupt, and the easier 2.5 km return track to The Piccaninny. Wannon Crossing is off Grampians Rd south of Jimmy Creek. Whether for a picnic or a few nights, this is a pleasant place to stop for great views of the falls, which can be spectacular after rain. **Map refs:** 173 D5, 196 H3

GREENHILL LAKE RESERVE

A few kilometres east of the township of Ararat is placid Greenhill Lake, where locals and visitors alike come to go fishing, boating, waterskiing or just cool off when the weather gets too hot.

Who to contact: Ararat and Grampians Visitor Information Centre (03) 5355 0281, 1800 657 158

501 Greenhill Lake Reserve camping area

The campsites here on the shoreline of Greenhill Lake are relatively flat, and there's reasonable shade. From the centre of Ararat, drive for 4 km along the Western Hwy towards Beaufort and turn north on Greenhill Lake Rd; the camping area is 200 m further on, over the railway line. Note: camp only where sites are signposted. **Map refs:** 173 E4, 197 J2

LANGI GHIRAN STATE PARK

Located 13 km east of Ararat, 2500 ha Langi Ghiran State Park has impressive granite peaks that rise up from peaceful forests of yellow box and red gum. There are fine views from the main lookout, and you can inspect Aboriginal rock art on the Lar-ne-Jeering walk. Experienced hikers have plenty of opportunities to head off-track.

Who to contact: Parks Victoria 13 1963

502 Bush camping (walk-in camping)

Bush camping is permitted in the mountainous section of the park. Hidden Lagoon, which lies between Mt Langi Ghiran and

the slightly shorter Mt Gorrin, is a popular spot for off-track hiking. Make sure you're well-equipped for the walk, including having a plentiful supply of water. Talk to the rangers before setting out. **Map refs: 173 E4, 197 J2**

503 Langi Ghiran camping area

This camping area is equipped with picnic tables where you can have a long lunch among the candlebark gums. Afterwards, take a slow, pleasant drive south along the Langi Ghiran Track, which links up with several walking trails. The campground is accessed via Kartuk Rd, which branches off the Western Hwy. **Map refs: 173 E4, 197 J2**

LITTLE DESERT NATIONAL PARK

This national park has a wonderfully diverse landscape that ranges from the Wimmera River to desert dunes, and is crammed with hundreds of native plants. It's divided into western, central and eastern blocks, accessible from Natimuk Rd in the south and the Western Hwy in the north. The eastern section is riddled with walks lasting from 30 min to a few days. Campgrounds can be reached with 2WDs, but elsewhere you'll need a 4WD to tackle the sandy tracks.

Who to contact: Parks Victoria 13 1963

504 Ackle Bend camping area

Ackle Bend is on the Wimmera River in the eastern block of Little River National Park, just south of Horseshoe Bend. The walk north along the river yields some great views. Other leisurely pursuits available here include swimming and fishing. Drive down Horseshoe Bend Rd from the Western Hwy in Dimboola and keep an eye out for the signage. **Map refs: 173 C2, 194 F8**

505 Bush camping

Bush camping is allowed in the central and western blocks of the national park. You'll need a 4WD to tackle the terrain away from the established campgrounds and picnic areas. Consult the park ranger about conditions and guidelines before you camp out in the wild. If you camp in the central block, pay a visit to Yanipy School Reserve, where there's a self-guided walk. **Map refs: 173 B2, 194 D8**

506 Horseshoe Bend camping area

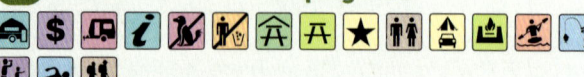

Horseshoe Bend is on the eastern boundary of Little Desert National Park, on the Wimmera River opposite Wail State Forest. North of here is the Pomponderoo Hill Nature Walk, which takes in a scenic lookout and some of the park's exceptional desert flora. Take Horseshoe Bend Rd south from Dimboola. Note: when swimming, take care to avoid snags in the river. **Map refs: 173 C2, 194 F8**

507 Kiata camping area

Kiata campground is in the eastern block of Little Desert National Park. It's at the end of Kiata South Rd, which runs off the Western Hwy between Nhill and Dimboola. Head to the nearby picnic area to take the half-hour Sanctuary–Keith Hateley Nature Walk, or spy on the thriving birdlife that includes mallee fowl and scrub robins. **Map refs: 173 C2, 194 E8**

MOUNT ARAPILES–TOOAN STATE PARK

Rockclimbers go weak at the knees at the mention of Mt Arapiles. This world-famous rock formation, 8 km west of the small town of Natimuk off the Wimmera Hwy, boasts several thousand free-climbing routes. The area also provides nesting sites for the endangered peregrine falcon. The park is embellished by the woodlands of the Tooan Block.

Who to contact: Parks Victoria 13 1963

508 Centenary Park camping area

The only camping site at Mt Arapiles, Centenary Park is accessed via Centenary Park Rd off the Wimmera Hwy – the spacious campground is about 2 km from the turn-off. Some sites require you to carry your gear in over some bollards. A walking track leads from here to the summit of Arapiles. Note: fires are only permitted May–Oct; bring your own wood. **Map refs: 173 C3, 194 E9**

ROCKLANDS STATE FORESTS

The large Rocklands Reservoir is at the centre of this grouping of forests, which lies just to the west of Grampians National Park. Most of the campsites here are spread out in the woodlands fringing the reservoir. Access is mainly from the Rocklands–Cherrypool Rd in the west, and the Henty Hwy in the east.

Who to contact: DSE 13 6186

509 Brodies camping area

Brodies is a popular campground on the north-western shoreline of Rocklands Reservoir, between Black Range State Park and the Claude Austin State Forest. If the redfin aren't biting here, head north to Toolondo Reservoir to try your luck hooking brown trout. To get here, follow the Rocklands–Cherrypool Rd from Balmoral. **Map refs: 173 C4, 194 F12, 196 F2**

510 Brookes Road camping area

This simple campground, which lies on the north-eastern shoreline of Rocklands Reservoir, is as close to nature as you can get, with no facilities to speak of. The access road passes through private property – take Brookes Rd off the Henty Hwy just south of Cherrypool. Don't forget to bring your own drinking water. **Map refs: 173 C4, 194 F12, 196 F1**

511 Bush camping (walk-in camping)

Those who want to go further afield than the established camping areas in Rocklands State Forests are permitted to go bush camping in the area. The only exceptions are where signage says otherwise. Contact the local ranger to talk about the regulations that apply to bush camping in this region. **Map refs:** 173 C4, 194 F12, 196 F2

512 Fergusons camping area

The only boat ramp on the eastern shoreline of Rocklands Reservoir is at Fergusons, so it's one of the area's most popular sites when there's enough water in the lake to make watersports possible. From the Henty Hwy, turn west on Gartons Rd, then north on Fergusons Rd. **Map refs:** 173 C4, 194 F12, 196 F2

513 Glendinning camping area

This campground is on the south-western edge of Rocklands Reservoir. It's permissible to collect firewood from the nearby Claude Austin State Forest for use here. Also nearby is the handsome Glendinning homestead, which you may be able to inspect by appointment. Glendinning can be reached from the west via Yarramyljup Rd, or from the south via Glendinning Rd, which forges north from the Henty Hwy at the town of Cavendish. **Map refs:** 173 C4, 194 F12, 196 F2

514 Henrys camping area

Henrys is a very basic campground located near the southernmost point of Rocklands Reservoir, where the shoreline of the sprawling water storage makes a ragged U-turn. From Henty Hwy, just south of Victoria Lagoon Wildlife Reserve, head west along East-West Rd, then turn north on Hallams Rd past Lookout Hill. Note: the access road traverses private property. **Map refs:** 173 C4, 194 F12, 196 F2

515 Mountain Dam camping area

Situated on the northern shore of Rocklands Reservoir and squeezed up against Black Range State Park, this campground has wood-fired BBQs, picnic tables and a boat ramp. Access is from Rocklands–Cherrypool Rd. Walkers should head further north along this road to the Black Range picnic ground, where a long, scenic walk on the Black Range commences. **Map refs:** 173 C4, 194 F12, 196 F1

WANNON FALLS SCENIC RESERVE

At Wannon Falls, the Wannon River washes down a 30 m lava cliff into a deep pool. Visitors can check out the cascading water from a cantilevered viewing platform and read up on the many colonial-era artists who attempted to capture this landscape on canvas. The falls are signposted off the Glenelg Highway, 18 km west of Hamilton.
Who to contact: Hamilton Visitor Information Centre (03) 5572 3746, 1800 807 056

516 Wannon River camping area

A short trail connects this campground with Wannon Falls, the end result of ancient lava flows, while another walking track leads to the nearby Thomas Clark Viewing Area, which also has views of the waterfall. The large shelter that overhangs some tables in the camping area provides shade when the sun is at its fiercest. This place is signposted off the Glenelg Hwy. **Map refs:** 173 C5, 196 E4

CAMPSITES LOCATED IN OTHER AREAS

517 Acacia Caravan Park

Located within walking distance of the centre of Ararat, just to the east of magnificent Grampians National Park, this family-friendly caravan park is ideal if things are busy in the Grampians. The Great Grape touring route will whisk you through many a winery cellar door in the area. Apart from the Grampians, it's a central location for touring nearby wilderness areas including Mt Cole, Mt Buangor and the Pyrenees Ranges. **Map refs:** 173 E4, 195 I12, 197 I2
How to book: 6 Acacia Ave, Ararat (03) 5352 2994 www.acaciatouristpark.com

518 Edenhope Lakeside Tourist Park

Right in the middle of the small township of Edenhope is Lake Wallace, on the southern shore of which you'll find a tourist park with shady campsites as well as on-site cabins and vans. When it has enough water, the lake offers decent redfin and trout fishing, and is frequented by nesting swans. Edenhope is off the Wimmera Hwy, out near the SA border. **Map refs:** 173 B3, 194 C11
Who to contact: bookings required during peak periods; Lake St, Edenhope (03) 5585 1659 www.edenhopelakeside.com.au

519 Halls Gap Caravan and Tourist Park

With the amenities of Halls Gap a short walk away, this caravan park is surrounded by the splendour of Grampians National Park on all sides. The plethora of activities in the area includes walking, hiking and mountain-biking, and don't forget to indulge in one of the area's fabulous wineries. The 250-plus campsites are level, well-grassed and come with fireplaces. **Map refs:** 173 D4, 194 H12, 196 H1

How to book: Grampians Rd, Halls Gap (03) 5356 4251 www.hallsgapcaravanpark.com.au

520 Hynes Reserve Camping Ground

Situated on the foreshore of the Rocklands Reservoir, this campground will suit those who enjoy watersports when there's enough water to fill the lake. There are lots of open spaces here, and plenty of level ground on which to set up camp. Best of all, the Grampians lie just over the Henty Hwy to the east. **Map refs:** 173 C4, 194 F12, 196 F1

How to book: (03) 5382 5080, 0429 138 008

521 Lake Bolac Caravan Park

Located 100 km west of Ballarat, Lake Bolac is popular with watersports enthusiasts when the water level is deep enough. The caravan park is situated on the lake foreshore, accessed off the Glenelg Hwy. All the park sites have town water and can accommodate big rigs, caravans or tents. There are also fully self-contained cabins, on-site vans with annexes, and normal on-site vans. The caravan park is close to Lake Bolac's activities, including a golf course, sports courts and a swimming pool. **Map refs:** 173 E5, 197 I4

How to book: bookings required during peak periods; 115 Frontage Rd, Lake Bolac (03) 5350 2329 www.lake-bolac-caravanpark.com.au

522 Lake Bolac Foreshore camping area

It's fine to camp on the foreshore at Lake Bolac, except where there are signs advising otherwise. Toilet facilities are located at various points around the lake, but hot showers are only available at Picnic Point on Main Beach. Local rangers collect the fees from campers. The foreshore is 2 km east of the township of Lake Bolac, and is reached via the Glenelg Hwy. **Map refs:** 173 E5, 197 I4

Who to contact: Lake Bolac Information Centre (03) 5350 2204

523 Lake Charlegrark Holiday Cottages and Caravan Park

Among the activities hosted at Lake Charlegrark are fishing, swimming and boating. Campsite availability is generally not an issue here, a major exception being in late Feb when a popular, long-running country music festival is set up on

the lake shore. The lake can be accessed off the Kaniva–Edenhope Rd near Booroopki, about 35 km north of Edenhope. **Map refs:** 173 B3, 194 C9

How to book: bookings recommended; 4532 Kaniva–Edenhope Rd, Minimay (03) 5386 6281

524 Lake Lonsdale camping area

Signposted on the Western Hwy about 4 km north of Stawell, just before Deep Lead, is the turn-off to Sandbar Rd. This road winds its way along the northern edge of compact Lake Lonsdale, providing access to a number of designated campsites on the foreshore. When the water level is high enough, people converge on the lake from the surrounding district to go swimming, waterskiing and fishing. Halls Gap, the main entry point for Grampians National Park, is only a short drive from here. **Map refs:** 173 D4, 194 H11

Who to contact: GMW Water 1300 659 961

525 Natimuk Lake Caravan Park

Travel 4 km north of the township of Natimuk to its namesake lake, reached via Lake Rd from the Wimmera Hwy. The caravan park sits at its southern tip. When the lake isn't dry it attracts attention from fishing folk and watersports aficionados. The cliffs and rock faces of Mt Arapiles, a sacred site to rockclimbers, are only 8 km down the road. **Map refs:** 173 C3, 194 F9

How to book: Lake Rd, Natimuk 0407 800 753

526 Toolondo Caravan Park

The Toolondo Reservoir is due west of Grampians National Park, on the other side of the Henty Hwy. On its south-eastern bank is a caravan park with an earthen boat ramp. There can be excellent fly fishing here, depending on the time of year and the reservoir's water holdings. Toolondo is a 40 km drive south of Horsham. The campground is off John McPhees Rd, which is accessed from Telangatuk Rd. **Map refs:** 173 C3, 194 F11

How to book: bookings required during peak periods for caravan sites; (03) 5388 2231

527 Wimmera Lakes Caravan Resort

The Wimmera Lakes Caravan Resort is out on the Western Hwy about 4 km south-east of Horsham. While the comfort and amenities offered by the park are already reasons to stay, the best rationale is that the spectacular terrain of the Grampians National Park is only a half-hour drive to the south of here. The resort has shaded grassy sites, plenty of sports facilities, and also wi-fi internet access for those who can't leave the computer at home. **Map refs:** 173 C3, 194 G9

How to book: 9161 Western Hwy, Horsham (03) 5382 4481 www.wimmeralakes.com

MALLEE COUNTRY

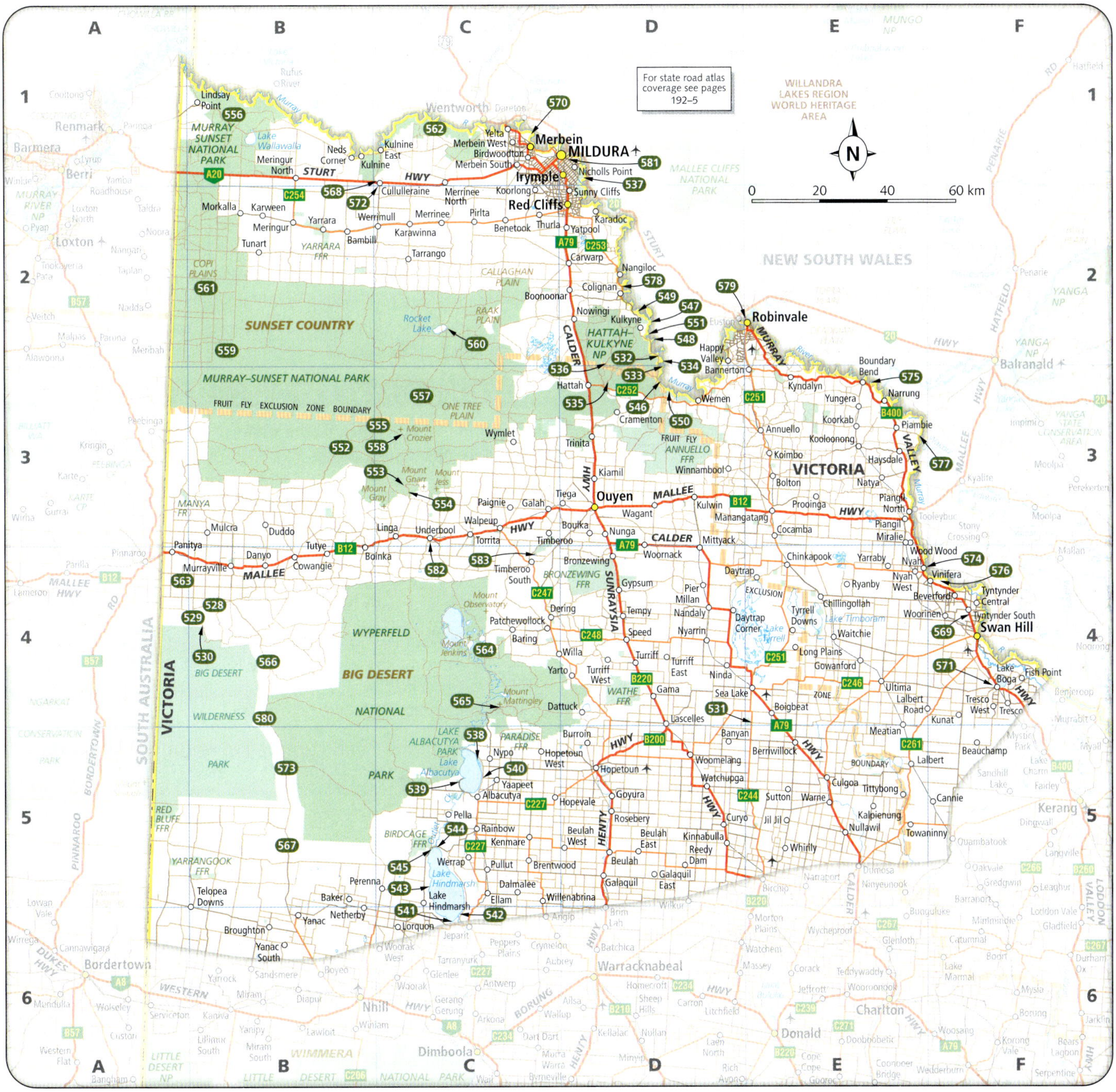

UP IN THE FAR north-western corner of Victoria is the iconic Mallee, a unique arid region that contains a pair of fantastically remote national parks, Murray–Sunset and Wyperfeld, the latter encompassing part of the wondrous Big Desert. After checking out the well-preserved colonial history at Swan Hill, including hitching a ride on an antique paddle-steamer, pursue the Murray River as it wends its way to the north-west, towards the SA border. Alongside the river, accessed by minor roads that snake off the highway between Swan Hill and Robinvale, are sundry bushland reserves where you can camp and cool yourself off with a freshwater dip.

South of Mildura is superb Hattah–Kulkyne National Park. The transformation that occurs here when the Murray decides to breach its banks, inundating the adjacent flood plain, is truly remarkable. Waterbirds descend on the area from far afield, and excited canoeists push off across the virgin wetlands. For a brilliant contrast, plunge into adjacent Murray–Sunset National Park to see the quartet of salty pools known as the Pink Lakes; they're at their blazing, colourful best in late summer. When you're done sightseeing at ground level, look up and take in the vastness of the Mallee sky – best done at night while sitting beside a sparkling campfire.

The magnificent vistas continue in Wyperfeld National Park, a patchwork of desert lakes that are continually dusted by passing 4WDs and trail bikes. Hikers also leave temporary markings on the sand dunes that have drifted across the Mallee here. The dunes get bigger and more intimidating in adjacent Big Desert Wilderness Park, which is so rugged that campsites and vehicles are banished to the eastern boundary. You'll have to head into the desert on foot to discover just how wonderful it really is.

CAMPSITES LOCATED IN PARKS AND RESERVES

BIG DESERT STATE FOREST

Its name sounds contradictory, but this forest is part of a broader habitat that includes sandy plains. Hundreds of plants and dozens of reptile species call this arid but striking region home. Wild dogs also live here, so leave pets at home. A 4WD is needed for the forest's black-soil floor, which is slippery when wet. From Murrayville on the Mallee Hwy, head south for 10 km down the Murrayville Track and take the signposted turning onto Firebreak Track.

Who to contact: DSE 13 6186

528 Blue Gums camping area

This is a big bush-camping site with some wood-fired BBQs – bring your own wood. Head west down Firebreak Track for almost 5.5 km from the Murrayville Track junction to reach the turning for Blue Gums Track. From the turning, which is about 6.7 km east of Coburns Track, drive for 350 m to the campground.
Map refs: 179 B4, 192 C12, 194 C1

529 Coburns Pines camping area (bush camping)

This big, open camping area, located in the west of the park, has a scattering of bush camp-sites. Bring everything with you as there are no facilities here. Head west on Firebreak Track for 12.5 km from the Murrayville Track junction, then turn south on Coburns Track and drive for just over 2 km to the campsites.
Map refs: 179 B4, 192 C12, 194 C2

530 Red Gums camping area

Like Coburns Pines, Red Gums is a dispersed bush campsite with no facilities, excepting some weathered picnic tables. Also in the western reaches of the state forest, and accessed via sandy tracks, you can reach it by turning west onto Firebreak Track from Murrayville Track, driving for 12.5 km, then turning south onto Coburns Track – Red Gums will be signposted off Coburns Track about 5.3 km south of the turning.
Map refs: 179 B4, 192 C12, 194 C2

GREEN LAKE REGIONAL PARK

Green Lake is adrift in the middle of a wheat-belt region. A natural depression, it looks at its best when the irrigation channels that run into it are flowing, allowing swimming, fishing and boating. It's located about 10 km south of the oddly named township of Sea Lake on the Calder Hwy.

Who to contact: Shire of Buloke (03) 5070 1448

531 Green Lake camping area

The campsites at Green Lake are surrounded by gum trees. There are also some BBQs here, which are coin-operated. Nearby is a patch of mallee woodland that makes for a nice walk. Follow the sign off the Birchip–Sea Lake Rd to get here.
Map refs: 179 E4, 195 J3

HATTAH–KULKYNE NATIONAL PARK

When the lakes system at the heart of Hattah–Kulkyne is in flood, this mallee region is transformed into wonderful wetlands that attract myriad bird species. Numerous 4WD tracks and bushwalks crisscross the area, or you can go canoeing into the sunset when the Murray overflows its banks. The park hugs the Murray River to the south of Mildura, and is accessed via the Hattah–Robinvale Rd; check road conditions inside the park with the rangers. All river camps are informal and many are surrounded by ancient river red gums. Note: always camp away from overhanging branches as they can fall without warning.

Who to contact: Parks Victoria 13 1963

532 Firemans Bend camping area (bush camping)

Firemans Bend is the northernmost of the trio of bush-camping spots allocated next to the Murray River, at the eastern border of the national park. Keen mountain-bikers can cycle along River Track, which links the 3 camping areas. As with nearby Jinkers Bend, you need to bring everything in with you as there are no facilities. Generators are permitted. **Map refs:** 179 D2, 192 H8

533 Jinkers Bend camping area (bush camping)

Jinkers Bend is another of the bush campsites alongside the Murray River in Hattah–Kulkyne. It's situated off the River Track between the 2 other bush-camping options – Ki Bend to the south and Firemans Bend to the north. There's nothing in the way of facilities here, but generators are allowed.
Map refs: 179 D3, 192 H9

534 Ki Bend camping area (bush camping)

If you're into fishing and you have a NSW fishing licence, you'll want to try one of the bush campsites down by the Murray River at Ki Bend. It's one of 3 places offering riverside campsites between Wemen and Colignan. But Ki Bend is the only one at which no generators are permitted, so tranquillity

Camping near the Murray River, Hattah–Kulkyne National Park (p. 180)

is usually assured here. Access is via the River Track.
Map refs: 179 D2, 192 H9

535 Lake Hattah camping area

Hattah–Kulkyne's main campground is located close to the visitor centre at Lake Hattah, near the national park's main entrance. Take the short, self-guided Hattah Nature Walk to check out the local landscape. For a taste of mallee dunes and flood plains, take the longer hike over to Lake Mournpall, which also loops around Lake Konardin. The Lake Hattah campground is a 4 km drive from Hattah township.

In times of drought, the lake can dry out completely. This is still a pleasant camping area, with grand river red gums surrounding many of the sites. Bring your own firewood and if you're throwing in a line don't forget a NSW fishing licence.
Map refs: 179 D3, 192 H9

536 Lake Mournpall camping area

Not the cheeriest name that's ever been bestowed on a place, but nonetheless a good place to camp. A leg-stretching 8 km track connects the campground to the national park visitor information centre. From Lake Mournpall, you can also strike out for Warepil Lookout, which affords great views over the surrounding mallee country. Be on the lookout for mallee fowl in the scrub and groups of gregarious apostlebirds, which usually travel by the dozen. Bring your own firewood with you and if you're throwing in a line don't forget a NSW fishing licence.
Map refs: 179 D2, 192 H9

KINGS BILLABONG PARK

Kings Billabong is a lovely little body of water that pools on the flood plain beside the equally lovely Murray River. There's excellent canoeing here after the water rises, or you can take a leisurely stroll along one of the walking tracks through the bird-filled gum trees. There's also a 120-year-old steam pump station to check out. The billabong is 8 km south-east of the centre of Mildura.

Who to contact: Parks Victoria 13 1963

537 Kings Billabong camping area (bush camping)

Bush camping is allowed around the billabong, as is the digging of pits for wood fires – check the guidelines with the rangers. There are toilets near the pump station, and there's a boat ramp at Bruces Bend. From the centre of Mildura, take Eleventh St off the highway, then turn right on Cureton Ave and left on Psyche Bend Rd, from where there's access to all the campsites. Note: some vehicle tracks may close in wet weather.
Map refs: 179 D1, 192 G6

LAKE ALBACUTYA PARK

Albacutya becomes an actual 'lake' only when floodwaters find their way here from the Wimmera River. Unfortunately, there's been no water for over 25 years. But in lieu of the watersports enjoyed here when Albacutya is full, you can do plenty of vigorous walking, including over some sand dunes north of the lake. The park is 14 km north of Rainbow and accessed via the Hopetoun–Rainbow Rd.

Who to contact: Parks Victoria 13 1963

538 OTIT camping area

This is a good place to camp if you're interested in taking an adventurous hike north of Lake Albacutya to Outlet Creek, and into the dunes beyond it; just remember that it gets too hot in summer to comfortably attempt this. A 2WD will get you here only in dry weather. From the Rainbow–Wyperfeld Park Road, turn west onto the OTIT Track. **Map refs:** 179 C5, 194 F4

539 Western Beach camping area

Western Beach is situated on the shoreline of Lake Albacutya amidst parrot-filled black box and river red gum woodlands. Stay here for a few days to enjoy the peace and quiet, or make it a stopover before visiting the fascinating semi-arid landscape of neighbouring Wyperfeld National Park. You can get here on sealed roads from Rainbow; turn off the Hopetoun–Rainbow Rd onto Albacutya Rd. **Map refs:** 179 C5, 194 F4

540 Yaapeet Beach camping area

On the eastern shore of Lake Albacutya, accessible from either Rainbow township or the nearby community of Yaapeet, is the Yaapeet Beach camping area. Water is only sometimes available here, so it's best to bring your own in. While a 4WD is needed for the rougher tracks in the park, a 2WD is adequate for reaching this campground. **Map refs:** 179 C5, 194 F4

LAKE HINDMARSH LAKE RESERVE

Lake Hindmarsh is the biggest freshwater lake in Victoria. Fed by the Wimmera River, it in turn nourishes a huge population of birds, including sea eagles and pelicans, as well as a large number of anglers, swimmers and waterskiers. The lake is 22 km north of Dimboola, just west of Jeparit on the Nhill–Jeparit Rd.

Who to contact: Parks Vic 13 1963 *How to book:* (03) 5391 4444 for campsite no. **541**

541 Four Mile Beach camping ground

Four Mile Beach has more facilities than any of the other campsites around Lake Hindmarsh, including powered sites and a kiosk selling basic foodstuffs; the trade-off is that this is the only place in the reserve where camping fees are charged. It's situated on the southern edge of the lake, about 5 km from Jeparit. **Map refs:** 179 C6, 194 F6

542 Picnic Point Beach camping ground

Picnic Point Beach, which lies just north of where the Wimmera River empties into Lake Hindmarsh, is a good place for some solitude. From the Nhill–Jeparit Rd, detour onto unsealed Lake Rd, which runs up along the eastern shoreline, and

then take the track to Picnic Point. Access is restricted to dry weather conditions. **Map refs:** 179 C6, 194 F6

543 Schulzes Beach camping area

This campground is located on the western shore of Lake Hindmarsh, where it has some impressive river red gums for company. South of here, at Antwerp on the road to Dimboola, you'll find what's left of the old Ebenezer Mission Station, the doors of which closed for the last time over a century ago. You can reach Schulzes from the Nhill–Rainbow Rd. **Map refs:** 179 C5, 194 F5

544 The Wattles camping area

After skirting the western edge of Lake Hindmarsh, the Nhill–Rainbow Rd crosses over Outlet Creek, heading east. It's here, at the northern foreshore of the lake, that you'll find the track leading down to the Wattles. There's dry weather access only, so check conditions with Parks Victoria. Campfires can be lit using the lake reserve's dead wood, but fuel stoves are preferred here. **Map refs:** 179 C5, 194 F5

545 Williamsons Beach camping area

Just off the Nhill–Rainbow Rd, at the northern tip of Lake Hindmarsh, is this serene campground. Note the lack of facilities here, and that the access road is sometimes inaccessible after rain; check before you visit. Adjacent Birdcage Flora and Fauna Reserve swaps river red gums for yellow gum and cypress pine woodlands. **Map refs:** 179 C5, 194 F5

MURRAY–KULKYNE PARK

The 2 sections of Murray–Kulkyne Park are squeezed between the Murray River to the east and the flood plains of Hattah–Kulkyne National Park to the west. It comprises some great riverfront land, with the added advantage that, unlike the neighbouring national park, dogs on leads and generators are permitted here. All camping sites are accessed from the River Track, which heads south from Colignan and north from the Hattah–Robinvale Rd; check road conditions if towing a caravan.

Who to contact: Parks Victoria 13 1963

546 The Boiler camping area

The camping area occupying the next riverbend up from the Paddlewheel is the Boiler. Like its neighbour to the south, it's a decent spot from which to contemplate the surrounding semi-arid wilderness. Anglers can try to hook yellow-belly, redfin and crayfish – but don't forget your fishing licence. **Map refs:** 179 D3, 192 H9

547 Britt Bend camping area

Britt Bend is situated up near the northern boundary of Murray–Kulkyne Park, just south of Tarpaulin Island. As with all campsites along the Murray, be careful not to park under any river red gums, whose large branches have a habit of dropping without any warning. **Map refs:** 179 D2, 192 H8

548 Deep Bend camping area (bush camping)

Deep Bend is an aptly named hook in the Murray River in the northern section of Murray–Kulkyne Park. As per the other bush campsites scattered alongside the River Track, you need to bring drinking water and firewood in with you. **Map refs:** 179 D2, 192 H8

549 Emmerts Bend camping area (bush camping)

Emmerts Bend is the first of the dispersed bush-camping areas you'll encounter in Murray–Kulkyne Park if you drive south down the River Track from nearby Colignan. Bring your own water, and some wood if you want to build a fire. **Map refs:** 179 D2, 192 H8

550 The Paddlewheel camping area (bush camping)

This is the first riverside bush-camping area you come to if you're driving into Murray–Kulkyne Park from the township of Wemen on Hattah–Robinvale Rd. Some of the protected species you may see when you're here include carpet pythons and the enigmatically named barking marsh frog. **Map refs:** 179 D3, 193 I9

551 Station Bend camping area (bush camping)

The twist of the Murray River called Station Bend is named after nearby Kulkyne Station, which was originally established in the mid-19th century. This bush-camping area is in the north of Murray–Kulkyne Park, accessed off the River Track. **Map refs:** 179 D2, 192 H8

MURRAY–SUNSET NATIONAL PARK

Wedged up in the far north-western corner of Victoria, this is a gloriously isolated, undisturbed region of sand dunes, salt lakes and wide-open mallee country. At 677 000 ha it is one of the state's biggest protected areas, and offers outback tracks suitable for a 4WD and bushwalking around the spectacular Pink Lakes. Access is off the Sturt Hwy and Millewa Rd from the north, the Calder Hwy in the east, and the Mallee Hwy in the south. A 4WD is needed for most of the park's tracks.

Who to contact: Parks Victoria 13 1963 **How to book:** (03) 5028 1212 for campsite no. **561**

552 Cattleyards camping area

The Cattleyards camping area is situated at the intersection of Underbool and Grub tracks at the southern edge of Murray–Sunset National Park. You can also get here via Sunset Rd from Cowangie on the Mallee Hwy, just east of Murrayville. Whichever route you choose to get to this isolated bush-camping spot, you'll need a 4WD. **Map refs:** 179 B3, 192 D10

553 Lake Becking camping area

Lake Becking is one of the captivating Pink Lakes. These dazzling salt lakes are a favourite of photographers visiting Murray–Sunset National Park, as are the wildflowers that break out in vivid colours here in the springtime. Walk along the eastern side of Lake Becking where there's a disused tramline, or head over to Lake Crosbie to do the Kline Nature Walk. This campground is 15 km from the Mallee Hwy, 2 km beyond Lake Crosbie. **Map refs:** 179 C3, 192 E10

554 Lake Crosbie camping area

The national park's main campground is on the southern shore of Lake Crosbie, the biggest of the 4 Pink Lakes that comprise one of the highlights of Murray–Sunset. The best way to see these colourful salt lakes is to drive or cycle between them along Pioneer Dr. The campground is 13 km along a gravel road from Linga on the Mallee Hwy, at the southern edge of the park. Access is for small caravans only. **Map refs:** 179 C3, 192 E10

555 Large Tank camping area

Travel 10 km west of Mt Crozier to Large Tank, a small bush campsite where you can admire the big open skies of north-western Victoria with few distractions. It's accessed via Mt Crozier Track, a trip that involves its fair share of deep sand and has to be tackled by 4WD. You can bring off-road camper trailers here. **Map refs:** 179 C3, 192 E9

556 Lindsay Island camping areas

Up in the park's far north, near where the NSW and SA borders meet, is Lindsay Island. Its flood plains, fed by Murray River overflow waters carried here along numerous creeks, sustain diverse birdlife and a mammal with the implausible name of paucident planigale. Pick your own shady campsite. Anglers will concentrate on the golden perch and Murray cod swimming in the Lindsay River and Mullaroo Creek, while others will seek the Murray lily, Victoria's biggest flower. Look for the signposted access road west of Meringur North on the Sturt Hwy. Note: all tracks on the island are accessible only in dry weather. **Map refs:** 179 B1, 192 C5

557 Mopoke Hut camping area

Lying just off the Mopoke Track, which runs along the western edge of the Mt Cowra Wilderness Zone, is Mopoke Hut. It was originally built as grazier's quarters and, like the Shearers Quarters located across the other side of the park, it's a reminder of the area's pastoral age. Mopoke Hut is 4 km south of the encouragingly named Last Hope Track, off which it's signposted; you'll need a 4WD to get here. **Map refs:** 179 C3, 192 E9

558 Mount Crozier camping area

There's a fine view from atop Mt Crozier of the surrounding plains. The camping area sticks to the basics: toilets, a fireplace and picnic table. To get here, steer your 4WD or off-road camper trailer along the sandy Mt Crozier Track that stretches 23 km north of Lake Becking. **Map refs: 179 C3, 192 E10**

559 Pheenys Track camping area

This campground is located in the remote far west of the national park and is a good spot from which to watch the hues of the surrounding landscape deepen during one of the park's famous desert sunsets. Needless to say, the trip here along Pheenys Track requires a 4WD. Carry plenty of water and fuel if you're going to head out this way. **Map refs: 179 B2, 192 C8**

560 Rocket Lake camping area

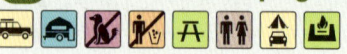

Rocket Lake is a salt lake situated in the north-eastern corner of the national park. You can get here from Nowingi on the Calder Hwy via the Nowingi Line Track, which crosses the Raak Plain. Alternatively, take a look at the Pink Lakes and then head north to link up with the Rocket Lake Track. On your way into or through Murray–Sunset, you may see groups of red kangaroos, which have flourished in the region. **Map refs: 179 C2, 192 F8**

561 The Shearers Quarters (hut accommodation)

This iron-hut hostel, originally built as sleeping quarters during the region's pastoral days, has over a dozen bunks, cooking equipment and that wilderness luxury – a hot shower. The Shearers Quarters can be reached from the Sturt Hwy via North–South Settlement Rd, a 4WD track. You'll need to book in advance to stay here. **Map refs: 179 B2, 192 C7**

562 Wallpolla Island camping area (bush camping)

Overnight visitors to Wallpolla Island take advantage of the dispersed bush camping on offer to spread themselves out. You may see whistling kites on the hunt around the river. If you're interested in fishing here, note that a Victorian licence will be required. The island is accessed via Old Mail Rd, which is only negotiable in dry weather. River access roads were due to be upgraded in 2012. **Map refs: 179 C1, 192 F5**

NGALLO PARK

It would be hard to camp any closer to the SA–Vic. border than at Ngallo Park. Established on the former site of a group of tennis courts, this small park can be accessed by driving west of Murrayville along the Mallee Hwy and turning south onto Ngallo South Rd.

Who to contact: Murrayville Newsagency (03) 5095 2181

563 Ngallo Park camping area

This compact, rustic camping area is located 2.5 km south of the Mallee Hwy down Ngallo South Rd. If you want to make use of the fireplace, bring your own wood. Further south of here are the vast reaches of Big Desert Wilderness Park, brimming with unexplored dunes and as peaceful a place as you'll find in Victoria. **Map refs: 179 A4, 192 B12, 194 B1**

WYPERFELD NATIONAL PARK

Etched into Wyperfeld's vast open plains is a series of dry lakes connected by the equally dry Outlet Creek. When water does arrive in this wilderness, however, the desert flowers come out to greet it. Terrain is excellent for a 4WD or for mountain-biking on rough-cut tracks, and there are hundreds of birds to observe, including wedge-tailed eagles and Major Mitchell cockatoos. Patchewollock Rd in the east and the road heading up from Yaapeet in the south provide the main access.

Who to contact: Parks Victoria 13 1963

564 Casuarina camping area

The Casuarina camping area is in the northern section of the national park – follow Patchewollock Rd from Baring and then turn south on Meridian Rd. The Casuarina Loop Walking Track forges through pine-buloke woodlands and across sand dunes and will take you roughly 3 hrs to complete. You can get to Casuarina from Baring in a conventional vehicle, but to traverse the park to reach Wonga you'll need a 4WD. **Map refs: 179 C4, 194 F2**

565 Wonga camping area

You'll find Wonga camping area on Main Entrance Rd after entering the national park from Yaapeet. A number of great walks start from here. Take the 4 km return Discovery Walk for an introduction to the mallee landscape; you can double your walking distance and head out to Lake Brambruk, crossing some sand dunes along the way. Day walkers should try the 13.5 km return option that tracks along Outlet Creek. **Map refs: 179 C4, 194 F3**

CAMPSITES LOCATED IN OTHER AREAS

566 Big Billy Bore camping area

Big Billy Bore is the first campground you reach if heading south down the Murrayville–Nhill Track. The signposted turning is 33 km from Murrayville, from where it's 650 m to the campsites. This stretch of the Murrayville–Nhill Track is unsealed, rough and very slippery after rain – it's accessible during dry weather only. **Map refs: 179 B4, 194 D2**

Who to contact: Parks Victoria 13 1963

567 Broken Bucket camping area

Despite the name, bore water is available at Broken Bucket, and there are toilets here as well. It's signposted some 53 km north of Nhill and almost 40 km south of The Springs camping area. Note: if you're driving south from Murrayville, access is restricted to dry weather due to the sandy track; the road between here and Nhill, however, is sealed. **Map refs:** 179 B5, 194 D5

Who to contact: Parks Victoria 13 1963

568 Bushmans Rest Caravan Park

This park offers plenty of grassy, well-shaded sites. It's situated on the pretty, peaceful shoreline of man-made Lake Cullulleraine, which means quick access to safe swimming and unhurried canoeing. The walking track that circumnavigates the lake is a good option if you want to keep fit but stay dry. From the Sturt Hwy at Cullulleraine, 58 km west of Mildura, take the signposted turn north onto Mullroo Dr. **Map refs:** 179 C1, 192 E6

How to book: bookings recommended at Easter and Christmas; Mullroo Dr, Lake Cullulleraine (03) 5028 2252 www.bushmansrest.com.au

569 HillTop Resort

Travel 5 km north of Swan Hill on the Murray Valley Hwy and, at Tyntynder South, you'll find the 13 ha HillTop Resort. There are several dozen spots here for tents and camper vans, with the rest of the complex occupied by cabins and motel units. The grounds are pleasant and the sports facilities allow you to lob tennis balls, swim laps and spike volleyballs. **Map refs:** 179 F4, 193 L12, 195 L2

How to book: 659 Murray Valley Hwy, Swan Hill (03) 5033 1515 www.hilltopresort.com.au

570 Horseshoe Bend camping area (bush camping)

Near the township of Merbein, 10 km north-west of Mildura, is Horseshoe Bend, also referred to as Merbein Common. There are a number of bush campsites along this stretch of the Murray River that will give you a sense of distance from town life while still being close enough to enjoy it. All of the sites are accessed via signposted Old Wentworth Rd (near the local racecourse and winery), which is accessed off River Ave in Merbein. **Map refs:** 179 C1, 192 G5

Who to contact: Parks Victoria 13 1963

571 Lake Boga Caravan Park

Lake Boga is part of a patchwork of lakes on either side of the Murray Valley Hwy to the north-west and south of Kerang. When water is plentiful, the Kerang Lakes, as they're known, form a significant wetlands area that attracts numerous bird species; they also attract humans keen on fishing, sailing and waterskiing. Lake Boga Caravan Park runs 3 camping areas at various points around the distinctly circular foreshore; access is from the highway in Lake Boga township. Note: observe any warning signs about potentially toxic algal blooms. **Map refs:** 179 F4, 195 M3

How to book: bookings essential during Christmas and New Year holiday period; Murray Valley Hwy, Lake Boga (03) 5037 2386 www.lakeboga.com.au

572 Lake Cullulleraine Holiday Park

Lake Cullulleraine is a man-made feature 59 km west of Mildura that owes its water stocks to Lock 9 on the Murray River. The holiday park sits on the lake's black box and reed-fringed foreshore, from where visitors launch sailboats and powerboats, or just throw themselves bodily into the water. Look for the Riverside Dr turn-off from the Sturt Hwy in Cullulleraine. **Map refs:** 179 C1, 192 E6

How to book: bookings required during peak periods; Sturt Hwy, Cullulleraine (03) 5028 2226, www.lakecullulleraineholidaypark.com.au

573 Moonlight Tank camping area

This is the most basic place for an overnight stop in the wilderness park, with space provided to camp for the night but no other facilities. It's situated off the unsealed section of the Murrayville–Nhill Track, about 10 km south of The Springs camping area, which means there's no access during or immediately after rain. **Map refs:** 179 B5, 194 D4

Who to contact: Parks Victoria 13 1963

Murray River – Robinvale to Swan Hill

Lying alongside the Murray River between the quaint town of Robinvale and the pioneering spirit of Swan Hill are a number of small reserves in which bush camping is permitted. Swimming off the Murray's sandy beaches is just the ticket on a hot day. Note: seasonal flooding can close some tracks, so check the road conditions before you pay a visit. Access roads are signposted off the Murray Valley Hwy. Bring your own firewood as there is a limited supply.

Who to contact: Parks Victoria 13 1963

574 Nyah camping area

This camping area is beside the township of Nyah, where the Murray River broadens its banks for a few kilometres. South-east of here, down the Murray Valley Hwy, is Tyntyndyer Homestead, which has the dubious honour of being Australia's first brick-veneer dwelling. **Map refs:** 179 E4, 193 L11, 195 L1

575 Passage Camp camping area

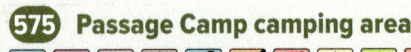

This was one of the places where Major Thomas Mitchell set up camp during his famous 1836 exploration of the country along the Murray River, a journey that prompted him to name what's now Victorian terrain 'Australia Felix' – fortunate Australia. There are fireplaces here. Look for the signposted access off the main road in Boundary Bend, 45 km south-east of Robinvale. **Map refs:** 179 E3, 193 K9

576 Vinifera camping area

The Vinifera Reserve is shared by forests of black box and river red gum, and is a pleasant place for a lazy picnic. The camping area is located about 20 km north of Swan Hill, south of Nyah near the town of Vinifera – the name comes from the grapevines that were planted here. Look for the sign off the Murray Valley Hwy. **Map refs:** 179 F4, 193 L12, 195 L1

577 Walkool Junction camping area

This dispersed bush-camping area is signposted off the Murray Valley Hwy, 7 km north of Piambie. It was another of Thomas Mitchell's stopovers on his ambitious trek down the Murray. Bring your own drinking water with you. **Map refs:** 179 E3, 193 L10

578 Nangiloc–Colignan camping area (bush camping)

Just 20 km south-east of Mildura, between the townships of Nangiloc and Colignan, are a series of parklands beside the Murray River where bush camping is allowed. Pitch a tent within river red gum and black box woodlands at Police Bend, Buxtons Bend and Graces Bend, and then concentrate on fishing, canoeing or swimming in the fresh water. South of Red Cliffs, turn off the Calder Hwy onto Kulkyne Way, and then take the Red Cliffs–Colignan Rd. **Map refs:** 179 D2, 192 H7

Who to contact: Parks Victoria 13 1963

579 Robinvale Riverside Caravan Park

If you'd like to throw a fishing line in from your caravan doorstep, this could be the spot for you. On the banks of the mighty Murray River just upstream from Euston Weir, this peaceful caravan park is a great spot to kick back. There's a handy boat ramp and fishing supplies are sold on-site. **Map refs:** 179 E2, 193 J8

How to book: Riverside Dr, Robinvale (03) 5026 4646 www.robinvaleaccommodation.com.au

580 The Springs camping area

The Springs unfortunately won't supply you with any water, but you will find a wood-fired BBQ and picnic table here. This site is signposted off the Murrayville–Nhill Track about 15 km south of Big Billy Bore. It's accessible in dry weather only. **Map refs:** 179 B4, 194 C3

Who to contact: Parks Victoria 13 1963

581 Sun City Caravan Park

Sun City is situated in Mildura, which occupies a series of snaking bends shaped by the Murray River as it flows past. The caravan park is on an orderly plot of land beside the town centre, which is convenient if you feel like strolling into town for a meal or a refreshing drink at a local pub. The amenities include free BBQs, a camp kitchen and a pool. **Map refs:** 179 D1, 192 G6

How to book: cnr Cureton and Benetook aves, Mildura East (03) 5023 2325

582 Underbool Recreational Reserve

The tiny township of Underbool is on the Murray Hwy and is notable for being sandwiched between two of Victoria's finest and most remote national parks: Murray–Sunset and Wyperfeld. Its recreational reserve is equipped with a football oval and tennis courts, and there's also a playground for the kiddies. To get to the campground, turn north off the Mallee Hwy in Underbool, cross the railway line and then follow Gnarr Rd. **Map refs:** 179 C3, 192 F11

Who to contact: Underbool General Store (03) 5094 6270
Camping fees: honesty box on-site (gold-coin donation)

583 Walpeup Lake camping area

When Walpeup Lake has high enough levels of water, it's a peaceful swimming and canoeing spot; however, due to water no longer being piped in here, it will be dry for the foreseeable future. The campsite is in an excellent sheltered area. It's located 14 km south-east of the town of Walpeup on the Mallee Hwy. Fringing the northern side of the lake is the extensive Timberoo Flora and Fauna Reserve. The lake is signposted off Hopetoun–Walpeup Rd. Bring in firewood and drinking water. **Map refs:** 179 C4, 192 G11, 194 G1

Who to contact: local management committee (03) 5084 1205

Eastern Victoria

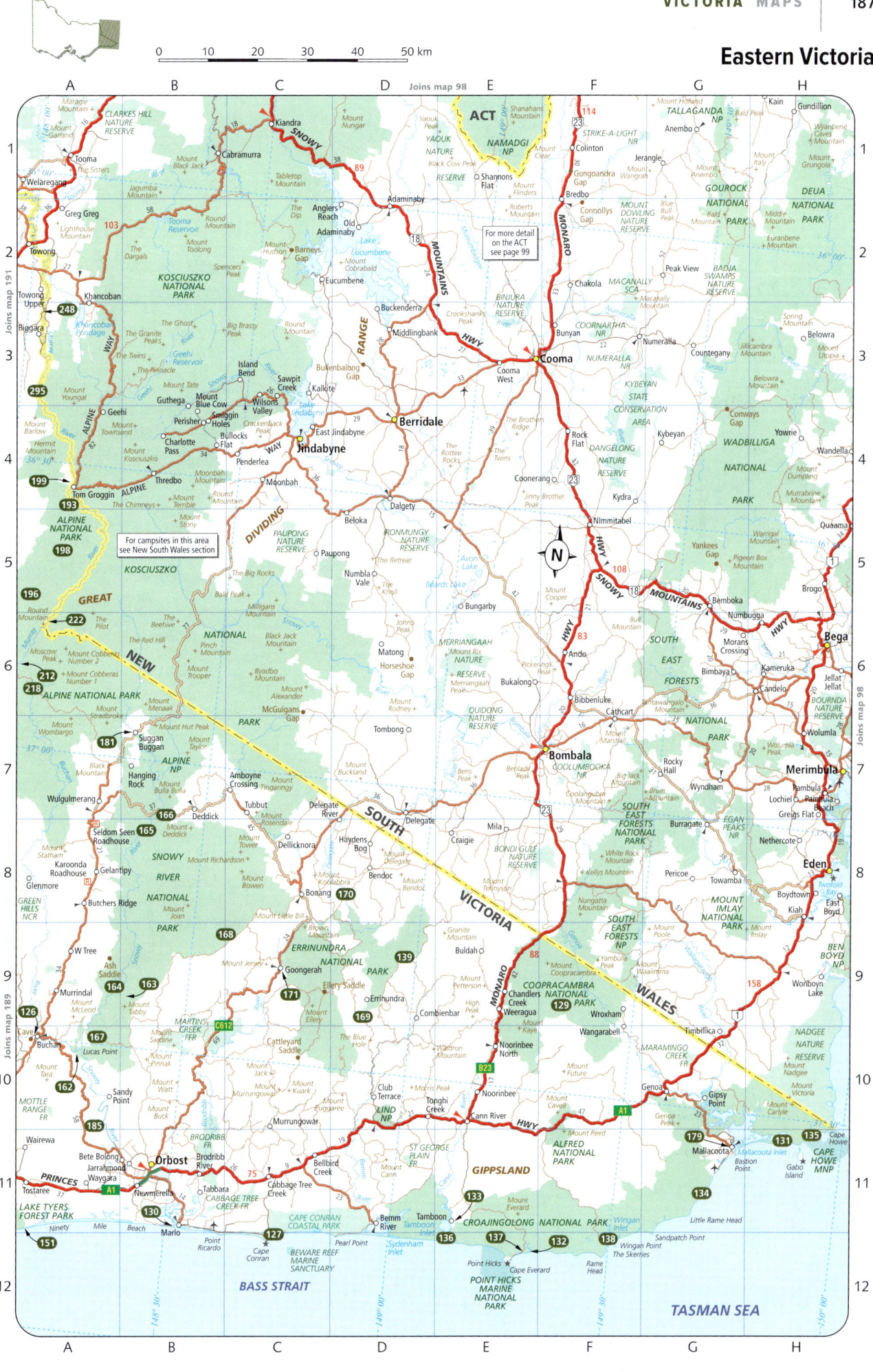

0 10 20 30 40 50 km

Joins map 98

For more detail on the ACT see page 99

For campsites in this area see New South Wales section

Joins map 191

Joins map 189

Joins map 98

Southern Central Victoria

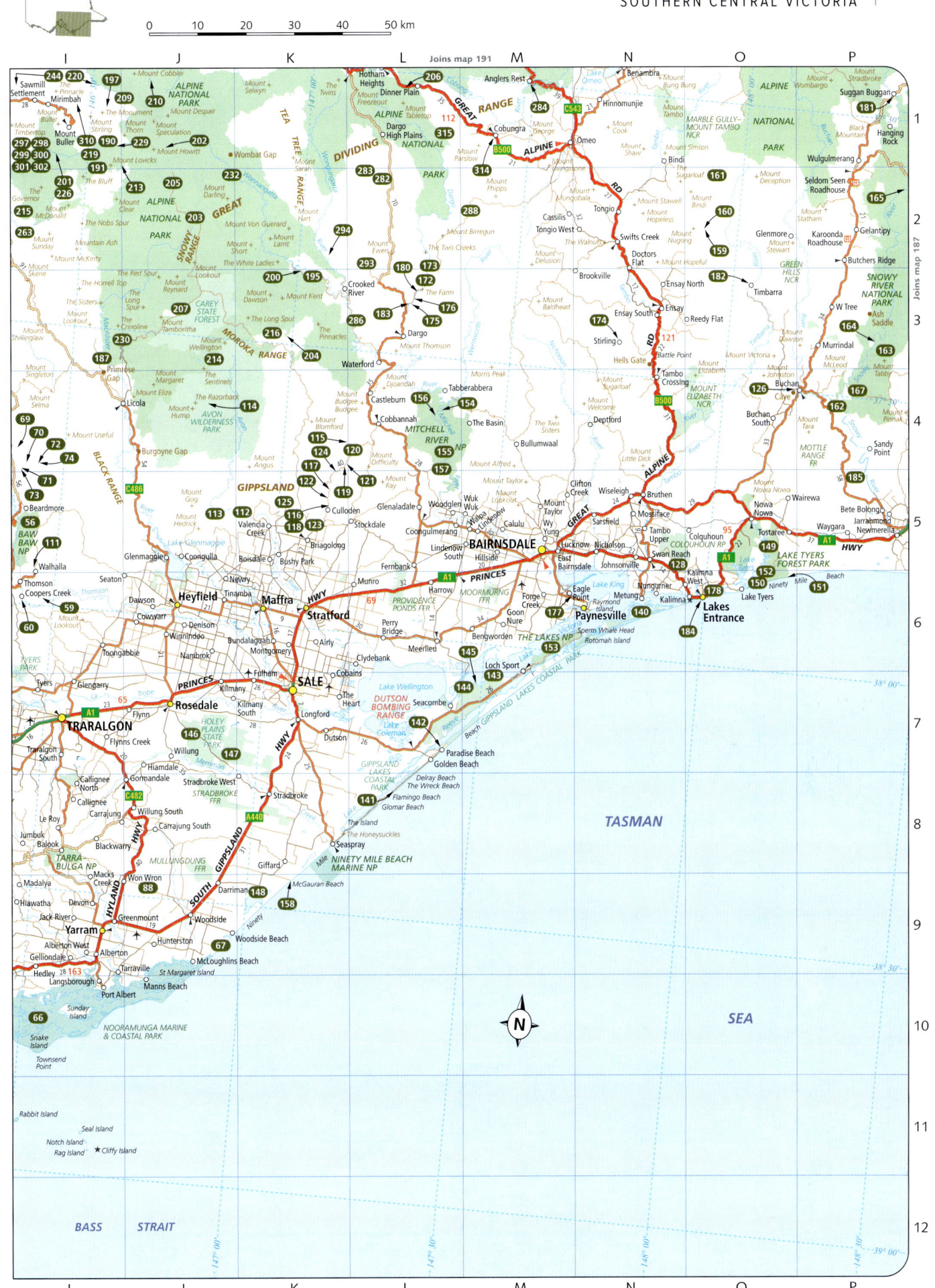

Northern Central Victoria

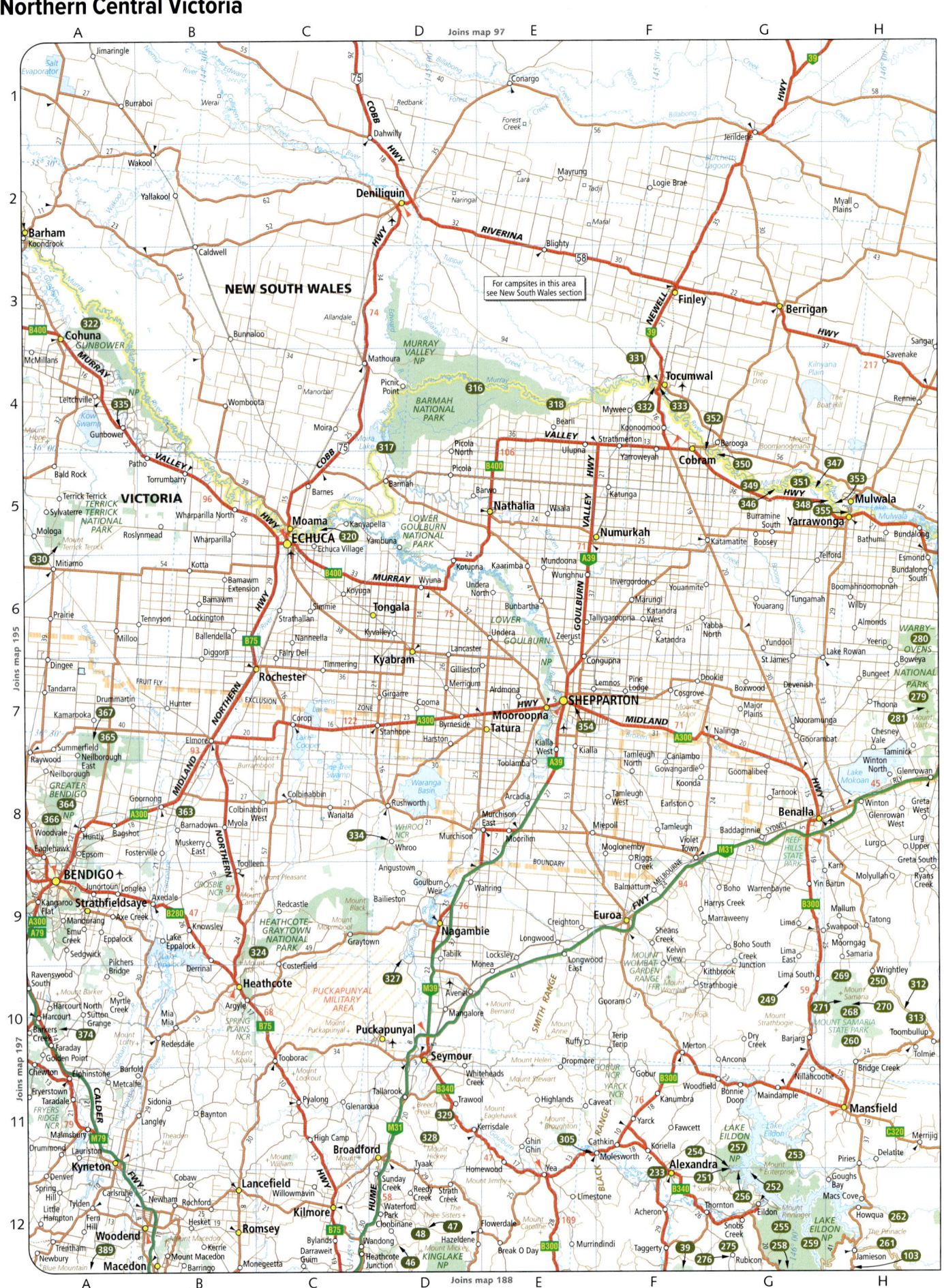

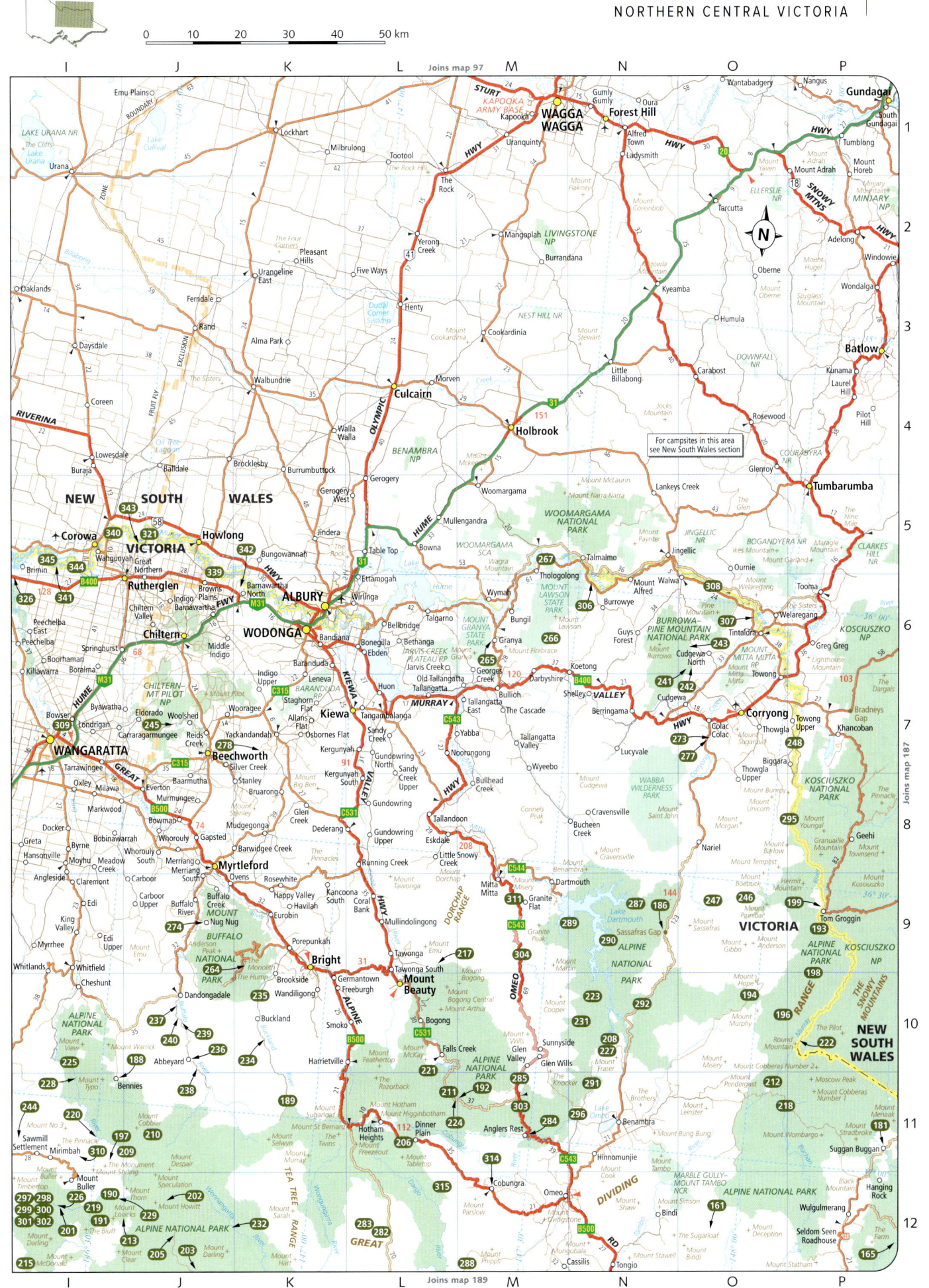

North-western Victoria

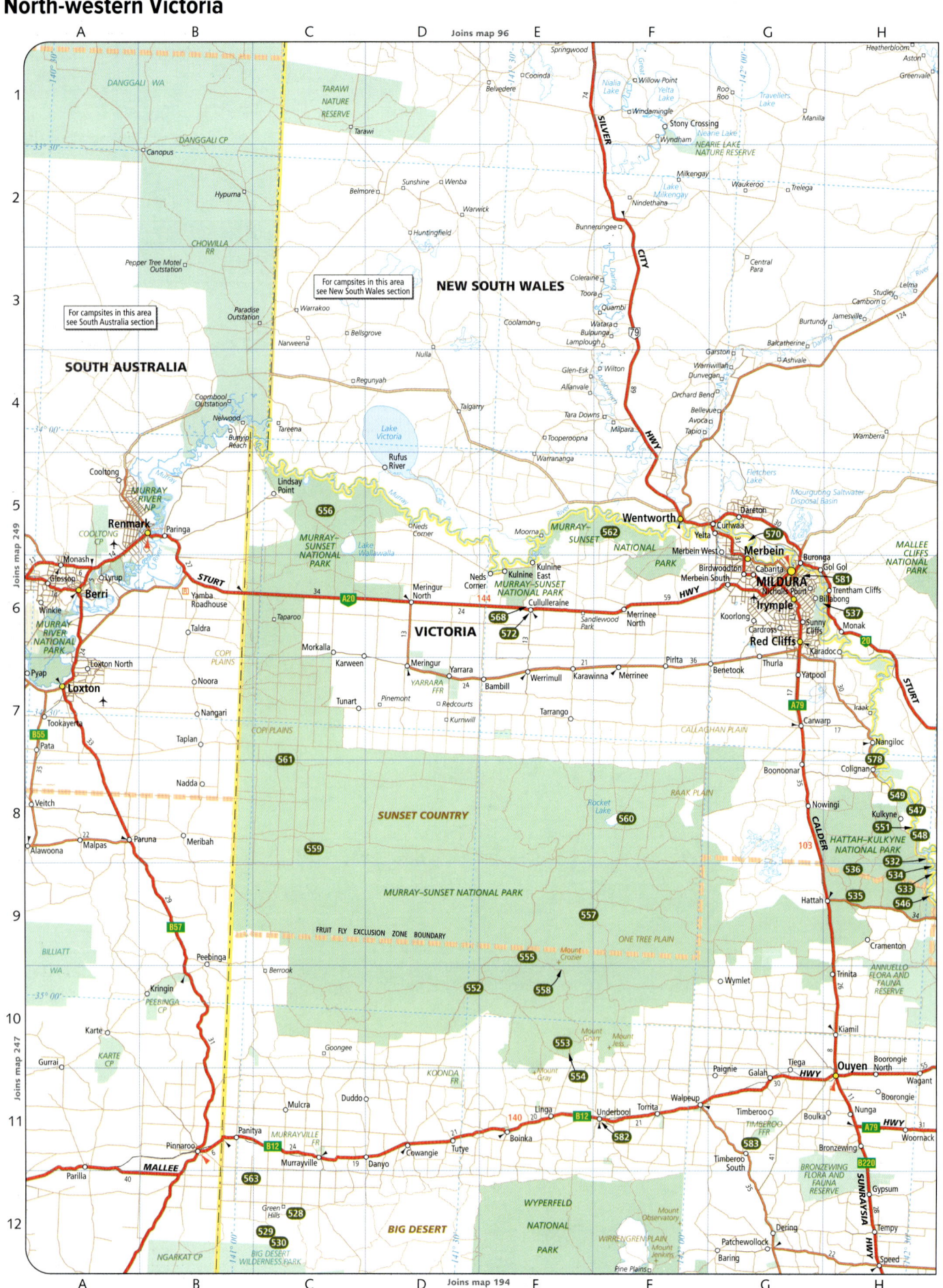

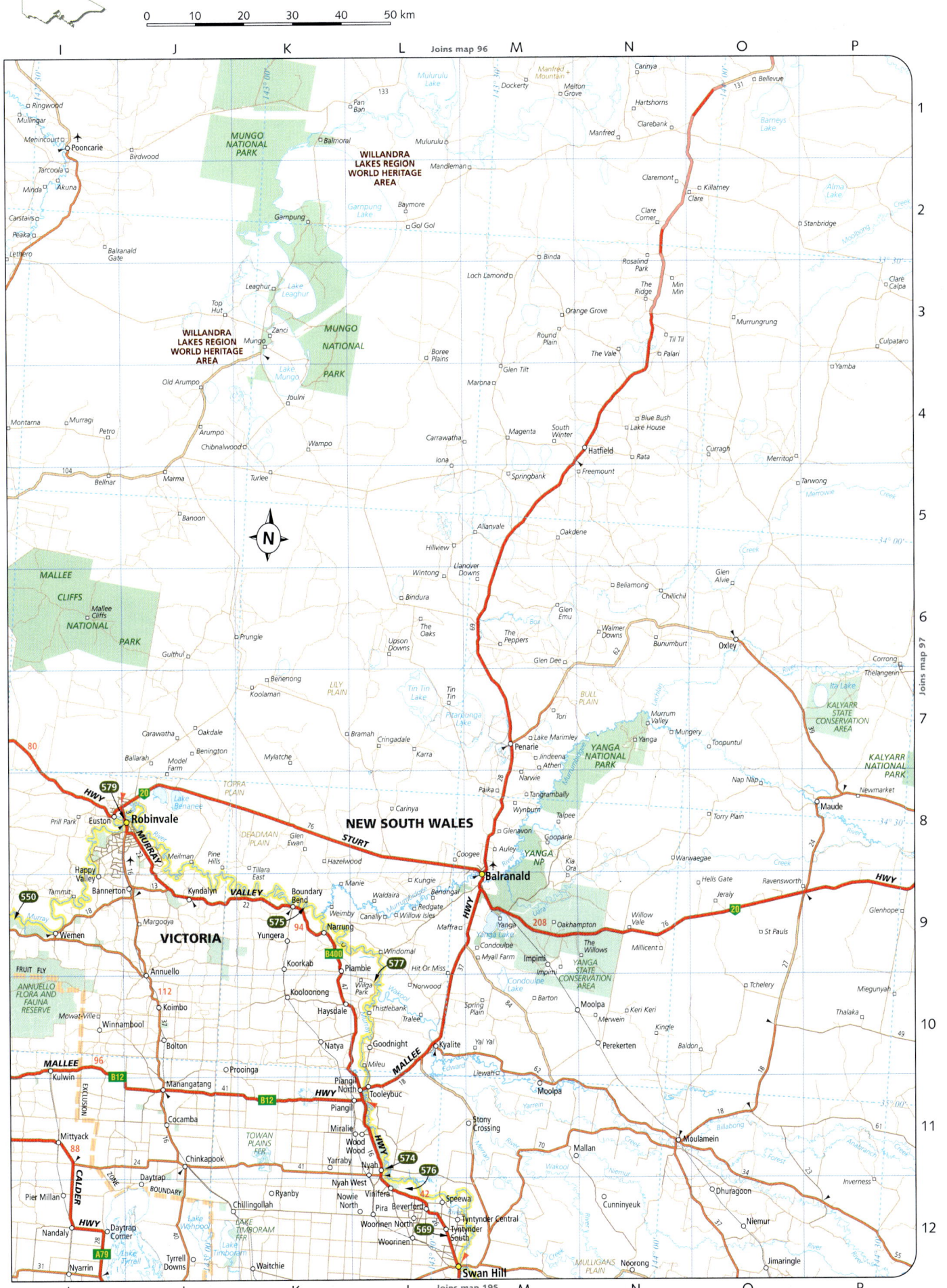

Joins map 96

Joins map 97

Central-western Victoria

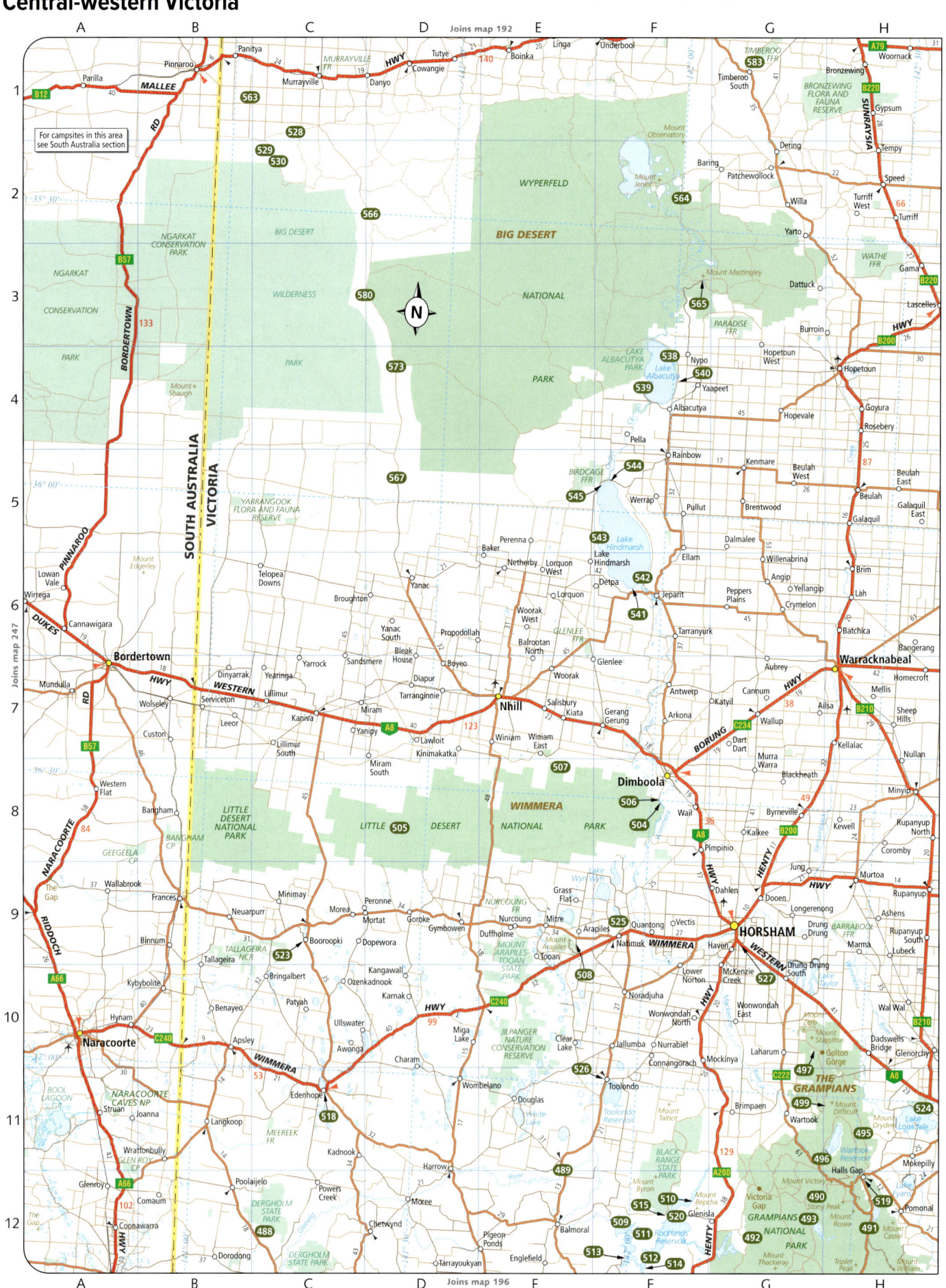

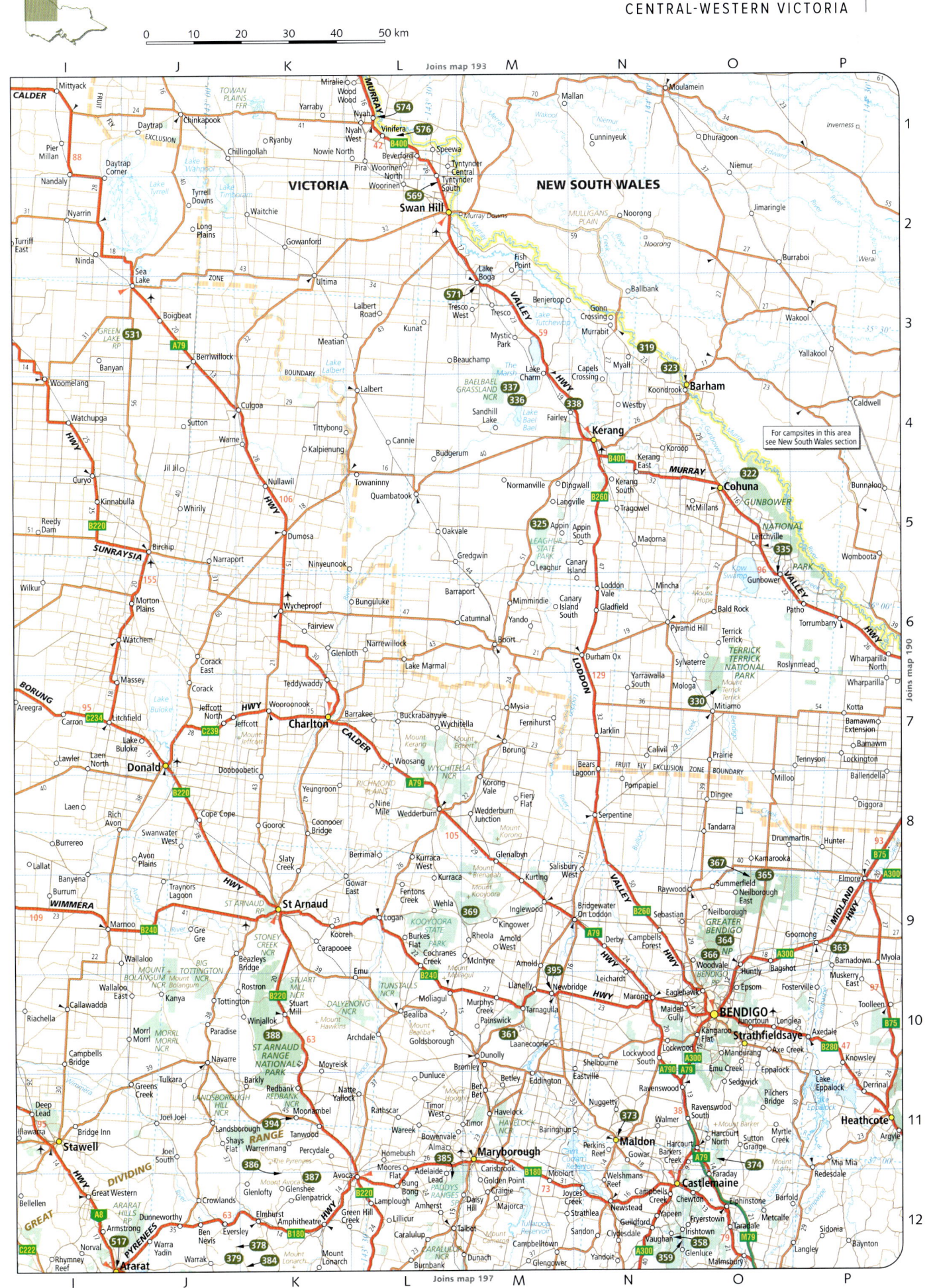

South-western Victoria

Joins map 195

Joins map 188

BASS STRAIT

TASMAN SEA

SOUTH AUSTRALIA

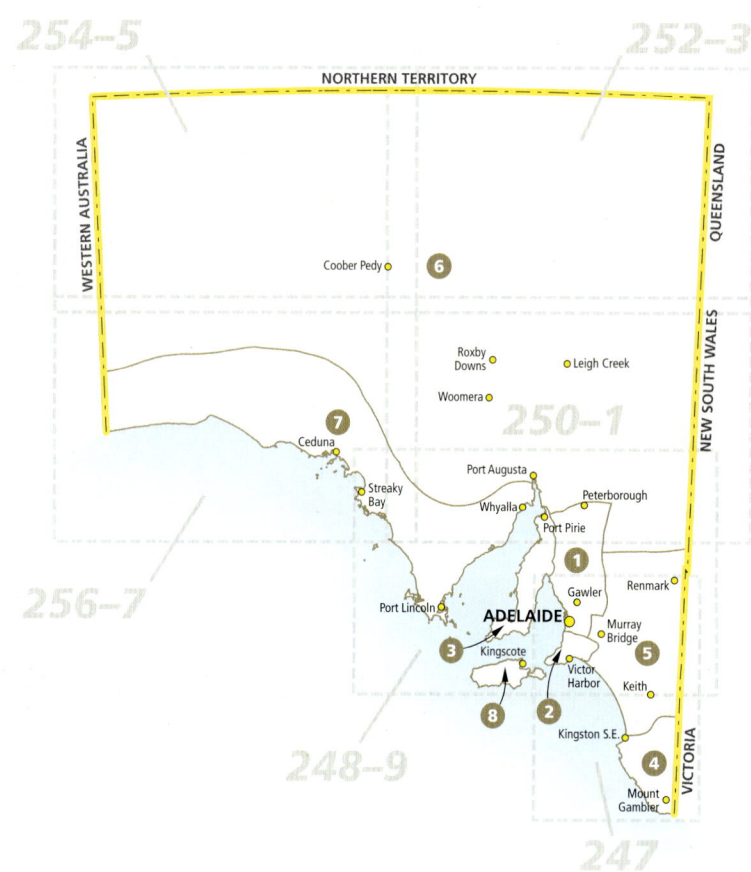

CONTENTS

BEST CAMPSITES

Cullyamurra Waterhole camping area
(Flinders Ranges and Outback), p. 226

Koolamon camping area
(Flinders Ranges and Outback), p. 225

Memory Cove camping area
(Eyre Peninsula and Nullarbor), p. 240

Shell Beach camping area
(Yorke Peninsula), p. 208

West Bay camping area
(Kangaroo Island), p. 245

USEFUL CONTACTS

Alert SA
www.alert.sa.gov.au

Country Fire Service
Fire Restrictions and Bushfire
Information Hotline
1300 362 361
www.cfs.sa.gov.au

**Department of Natural
Resources – Parks SA**
(08) 8204 1910
www.parks.sa.gov.au

Desert Parks Hotline
1800 816 078

Emergency
Dial 000 for police, ambulance
and fire brigade

**Fisheries – Department of
Primary Industries**
(08) 8204 1380
www.pir.sa.gov.au/fisheries

**Fossicking – Department of
Primary Industries**
(08) 8463 3000
www.pir.sa.gov.au/minerals

Transport SA
13 1084
Far North Road Conditions
1300 361 033
www.transport.sa.gov.au

*Camping at Brachina Gorge, Flinders
Ranges National Park, Flinders Ranges
and Outback region (p. 224)*

WINE COUNTRY

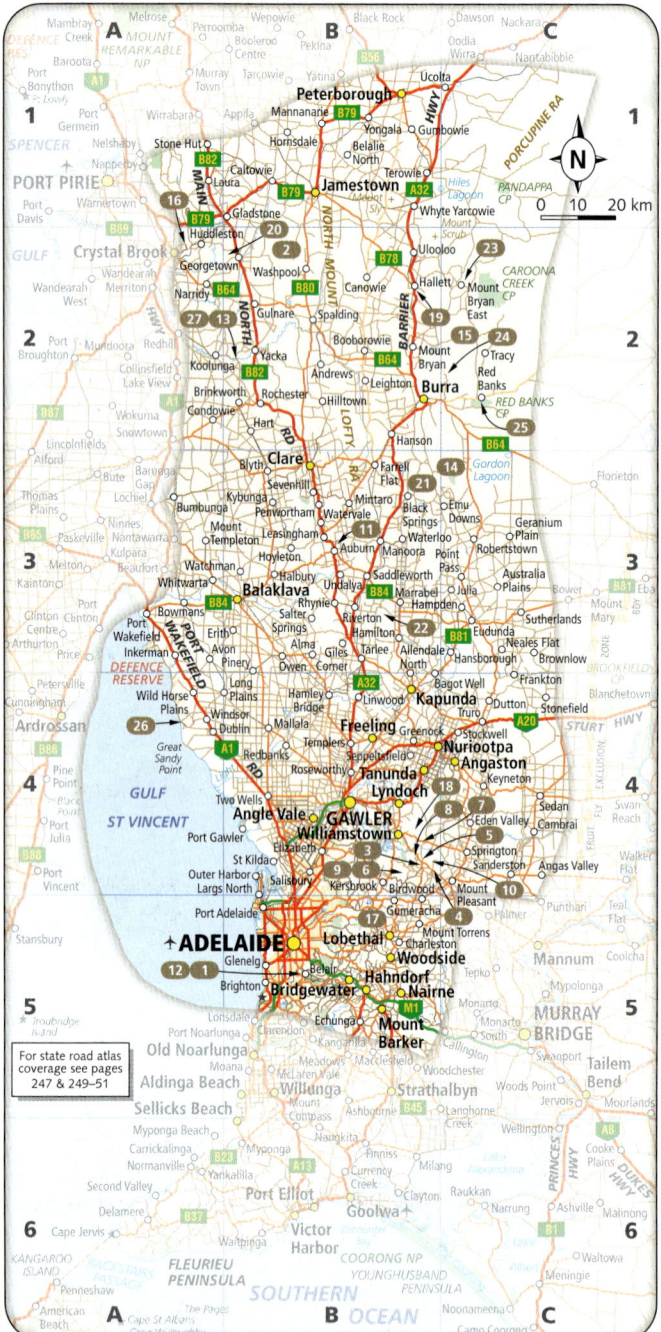

ADELAIDE'S HINTERLAND IS DEFINED by the Mt Lofty Ranges, a tumbling landscape patchworked with small farms. For lovers of wine, good food and the outdoors, this is paradise found. It's also easy to access. In half an hour's drive from downtown Adelaide you can be relaxing in a village cafe or a peaceful park dotted with river red gums. And no matter where you travel, it seems as if there's a vineyard around every bend. From the Piccadilly Valley below Mt Lofty itself and on through Lenswood, Eden Valley, the Barossa and Clare valleys, this is, unarguably, one of the world's premier wine regions.

The ranges are also a precious natural stronghold. Scattered along their length is a diverse collection of parks and reserves – great places to explore on foot, by bike or on horseback. Popular haunts include Belair National Park, Mt Crawford Forest and conservation parks such as Cleland, Morialta, Black Hill and Kaiserstuhl.

Linking many of the parks is the Heysen Trail, a long-distance walking route spanning 1200 km. Named after the artist Hans Heysen, the trail is also a reminder of the region's rich cultural heritage. While German traditions underpin locales like Hahndorf and the Barossa Valley, further north in Burra there are strong echoes of the 1840s' copper boom and the Cornish miners who made it happen.

Beyond Clare, the hills soften into the gently undulating farmland of SA's mid-north. This is classic sheep and cropping country, where life is unhurried and the roads that beckon are the ones less travelled.

CAMPSITES LOCATED IN PARKS AND RESERVES

BELAIR NATIONAL PARK

Just 13 km from the heart of Adelaide, SA's first national park is hugely popular. Its ovals, tennis courts and playgrounds are time-honoured family picnic spots. Belair also has an extensive network of trails for walking, horseriding and cycling. The park's upper reaches include pockets of secluded and surprisingly wild bushland. Through late winter and spring when the creeks run and wildflowers bloom, this park really comes alive.

Who to contact: (08) 8278 5477 **How to book:** Upper Sturt Rd, Belair (08) 8278 3540 www.belaircaravanpark.com.au

1 Belair Park Caravan Park

Just off Upper Sturt Rd, close to the national park's main entrance, this well-equipped caravan park has a playground and pool. Book ahead during peak holiday times, and bring a gas/fuel stove. **Map Refs:** 200 B5, 247 B3, 249 J9

BUNDALEER FOREST RESERVE

Covering 3200 ha, this forest reserve just south of Jamestown is a mix of plantation pine and native timbers, including sugar gum and red gum. It's a gentle, sheltered place to retreat to for a picnic or a walk. Both the Heysen and Mawson trails visit the reserve. Stone huts are for hire and camping is allowed from 1 Apr to 1 Dec. Permits and fees are needed for both camping and horseriding.

How to book: Forestry SA Wirrabara (08) 8668 5000

2 Curnow's Hut camping area

This restored 3-bedroom stone hut is in the south of the forest, 15 km south of Jamestown off Bundaleer Gardens Rd. You need to book, as the camping area is padlocked. Bring water and preferably a gas/fuel stove. Camping is allowed from 1 Apr to 1 Dec and you need a permit. This camping area is along the Heysen Trail. **Map refs:** 200 B2, 249 J4, 251 I12

MOUNT CRAWFORD FOREST

This sprawl of forest reserve an hour's drive north-east of Adelaide is a favourite escape for walkers, mountain-bikers and horseriders. Both the Heysen and Mawson trails weave through these forests and there are numerous camping locations to choose from, including more secluded hideaways. As well as the reserve's natural assets, it's also on the doorstep of the famed wine regions of the Eden and Barossa valleys. If you're horseriding, you'll need a permit, and there is now a camp that caters for horses at Starkeys Reserve.

Who to contact: Forestry SA Mt Crawford Forest (08) 8521 1700; or Friends of the Heysen Trail (08) 8212 6299

3 Chalks camping area

This expansive and popular grassed site is set among river gums on Chalks Rd, close to the corner of Warren and Forreston rds, 4 km from the information centre. There's a short walk from the parking area over bollards. The site can be closed during peak-summer fire danger periods. This camping area is along the Heysen Trail. **Map refs:** 200 B4, 247 C2, 249 K8

4 Cromer Shed camping area

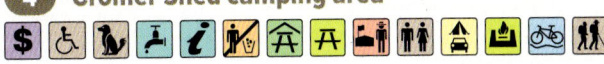

This recent addition to the forest's list of campsites features a large shelter shed among eucalypt woodland on the south-eastern edge of the forest. It's off Cricks Mill Rd, 7 km west of Mt Pleasant. It's reached through a gate, so you need to book. **Map refs:** 200 B4, 247 C2, 249 K8

5 Fromms Farm camping area

This former dairy is now a generous-sized shelter for group camping, with tent spaces close by. It's located on Mount Rd, 2 km from the information centre. You enter via a gate, so you need to book. This camping area is along the Heysen Trail. **Map refs:** 200 B4, 247 C2, 249 K8

6 Mount Crawford camping area (bush camping)

For self-sufficient walkers there are assorted bush camping options along the Heysen Trail, with walk-in access only, including 2 huts. The information office can provide details. Some have rainwater tanks, but bring a gas/fuel stove. **Map refs:** 200 B4, 247 C2, 249 K8

7 The Old School House camping area

On the Heysen Trail, this historic building in the north of the reserve sleeps 8 and has tent spaces close by. You'll find it 9 km east of Williamstown, from Springton Rd. Book ahead, as access is via a gate. **Map refs:** 200 B4, 247 C2, 249 K8

8 Rocky Paddock camping area

A large open campground set among rocky outcrops on the edge of the forest plantation, this site is 1 km from the information centre off Tower Rd. There is water here but it is not suitable for drinking, so carry in your own. **Map refs:** 200 B4, 247 C2, 249 K8

9 Scotts Shelter camping area

This site is located where the Heysen Trail leaves the south-western edge of Mt Crawford Forest. There is basic shelter and a toilet. Bring a gas/fuel stove. **Map refs:** 200 B4, 247 C2, 249 K8

10 Starkeys Horse Camp

Located along the Kidman Trail in Mt Crawford Forest is Starkeys campground, a relaxed spot set between native and plantation pine forest. It is perfect for those who want to camp with their horses. Popular with small or large groups, it offers plenty of room for tent camping. There is a fire pit, rainwater tanks (not suitable for drinking), a toilet, 4 horse yards and a shelter with picnic tables. You need to book, and riders are asked to check in with the Ranger. **Map refs:** 200 B4, 247 C2, 249 K8

CAMPSITES LOCATED IN OTHER AREAS

11 Auburn Caravan Park

This small park is in Auburn, the historic gateway town to the Clare Valley at the start of the popular Riesling Trail, on Saddleworth Rd, next to the oval and recreation grounds. Follow the sign from the Mid North Rd. You need to bring a gas/fuel stove. **Map refs:** 200 B3, 249 J6

How to book: Saddleworth Rd, Auburn (08) 8849 2186

12 Brownhill Creek Recreation Caravan Park

At this surprising natural nook just a few minutes south from Adelaide, mighty river red gums flank the creek, part of a major valley catchment. There are picnic areas and trails exploring the valley and beyond. To get here, take Brownhill Creek Rd from Blythewood Rd. The popular park has plenty of amenities, including a playground, pool, TV room, laundry and camp kitchen. There are several shady and grassy sites, and lots of pleasant walking trails along the creek. Book ahead during peak holiday periods. **Map refs:** 200 B5, 247 B3, 249 J9

How to book: Brownhill Creek Rd, Mitcham (08) 8271 4824
www.brownhillcreekcaravanpark.com.au

13 Bunyip Park camping area

Off the beaten track, Koolunga is a quiet farming town north of Clare. It's a handy overnight stop for north-bound travellers and, as the site's name suggests, the town is also renowned for sightings of the mythical bunyip. The park is on the southern edge of town, 200 m along the Yacka Rd. You need to be self-sufficient, with water, firewood and preferably a gas/fuel stove. There are 2 powered sites available. **Map refs:** 200 B2, 249 J5, 250 H12

Who to contact: Port Pirie Regional Tourism (08) 8633 8700

14 Burra Creek Gorge camping area

Mighty river red gums feature in this extensive reserve on Robertson Rd, 26 km south from Burra on the Heysen Trail. After winter rains the creek environment is a lush habitat for birds and other wildlife. It's a good spot for relaxed bush camping and nature walks, yet still within easy reach of Burra's attractions. Bring your own gas/fuel stove. **Map refs:** 200 C3, 249 K6

Who to contact: Burra Visitor Centre (08) 8892 2154

Heysen Trail

The middle section of the Heysen Trail takes you through some of the mid-north and Adelaide Hills, offering plenty of pleasant day walks or overnight stays. There are several rustic, but renovated, old huts and shelters available, most offering water and fireplaces.

Please note that campsites are listed in alphabetical order, not track order. Refer to the map on p. 200 for further information.

Who to contact: Parks SA Northern Lofty (08) 8336 0901; or Friends of the Heysen Trail (08) 8212 6299
www.heysentrail.asn.au

15 Black Jacks Shelter camping area

About 20 km north-east of Burra, just off White Hill Rd, is this basic site offering shelter, a rainwater tank and a toilet. Bring a gas/fuel stove. **Map refs:** 200 C2, 249 K5, 251 J12

16 Bowman Hut camping area

There is a locked hut (combination available from Friends of the Heysen Trail) with a camping area beside it. Nearby are historic ruins and a lookout. **Map refs:** 200 A2, 249 I4, 250 H12

14 Burra Creek Gorge camping area

See above.

3 Chalks camping area

See p. 201.

17 Cudlee Creek North camping area

Just north of Mt Crawford Forest, this bush campsite has a fire pit, water, a stone table and a small shelter. Bring a gas/fuel stove. **Map refs:** 200 B5, 247 C3, 249 K9

2 Curnow's Hut camping area

See p. 201.

18 Freeman's Hut camping area

Located just north of Warren Conservation Park, this hut was restored by volunteers from the Adelaide Central Mission's Day Centre in 1991. **Map refs:** 200 B4, 247 C2, 249 K8

5 **Fromms Farm camping area**

See p. 201.

19 **Hallett Railway Station camping area**

Just south of the small town of Hallett, this hut has bunks, a water tank, combustion stove, kitchen sink and toilets. **Map refs:** 200 B2, 249 K5, 251 I12

20 **Hiskey's Hut camping area**

On Slaughterhouse Rd, about 2 km west of Georgetown, this basic hut has water, a table, seats, a sink, bunks, a fireplace and a toilet. **Map refs:** 200 B2, 249 J4, 250 H12

21 **Huppatz Hut camping area**

This is a rough but charming shelter south of Burra, with a fireplace, sink, plumbed water, tables and chairs, beds and a drop toilet. **Map refs:** 200 B3, 249 K6

22 **Marschalls Hut camping area**

An excellent hut in a beautiful location, Marschall's is about 8 km south-west of Marrabel. Originally built in the mid 1850s, the hut is now a base for hikers and maintained by the Friends of the Heysen Trail. Bring a gas/fuel stove. **Map refs:** 200 B3, 247 C1, 249 K7

23 **Old Mount Bryan East School camping area**

This is a large old school building with a basic kitchen, about 10 km east of Hallett. There are bunks, water, a slow-combustion stove and toilets. **Map refs:** 200 C2, 249 K5, 251 J12

7 **The Old School House camping area**

See p. 201.

9 **Scotts Shelter camping area**

See p. 201.

24 **Wandallah Creek Shelter camping area**

This basic shelter with toilet and rainwater tank is about 10 km north-east of Burra, off Wandillah Rd. Bring a gas/fuel stove. **Map refs:** 200 C2, 249 K5

This track extends through both the Fleurieu Peninsula region (see p. 206) and the Flinders Ranges and Outback region (see p. 232).

25 **Mallee camping area**

Striking red cliffs are a feature of this camping spot in open mallee country, 15 km east of Burra. Follow the signpost from Eastern Rd, and come equipped with firewood and preferably a gas/fuel stove. **Map refs:** 200 C2, 249 K5

Who to contact: Burra Visitor Centre (08) 8892 2154

26 **Port Parham camping area**

Famed for its shallow waters and great crabbing beach, this small coastal settlement is a much-loved spot for family outings and boating. The camping is on a council reserve on the northern edge of town, with access 1 km north of Dublin from the Port Wakefield Rd. **Map refs:** 200 A4, 247 A1, 249 I7

Who to contact: District Council of Mallala (08) 8527 2006

27 **White Cliffs Reserve**

Come to White Cliffs for pleasant camping beside the Broughton River with its reed-fringed waterholes and stately river gums. You'll find it on Yacka Rd, 6 km east of Koolunga. Bring firewood and water, and preferably a gas/fuel stove. **Map refs:** 200 B2, 249 J5, 250 H12

Who to contact: Port Pirie Regional Tourism (08) 8633 8700

FLEURIEU PENINSULA

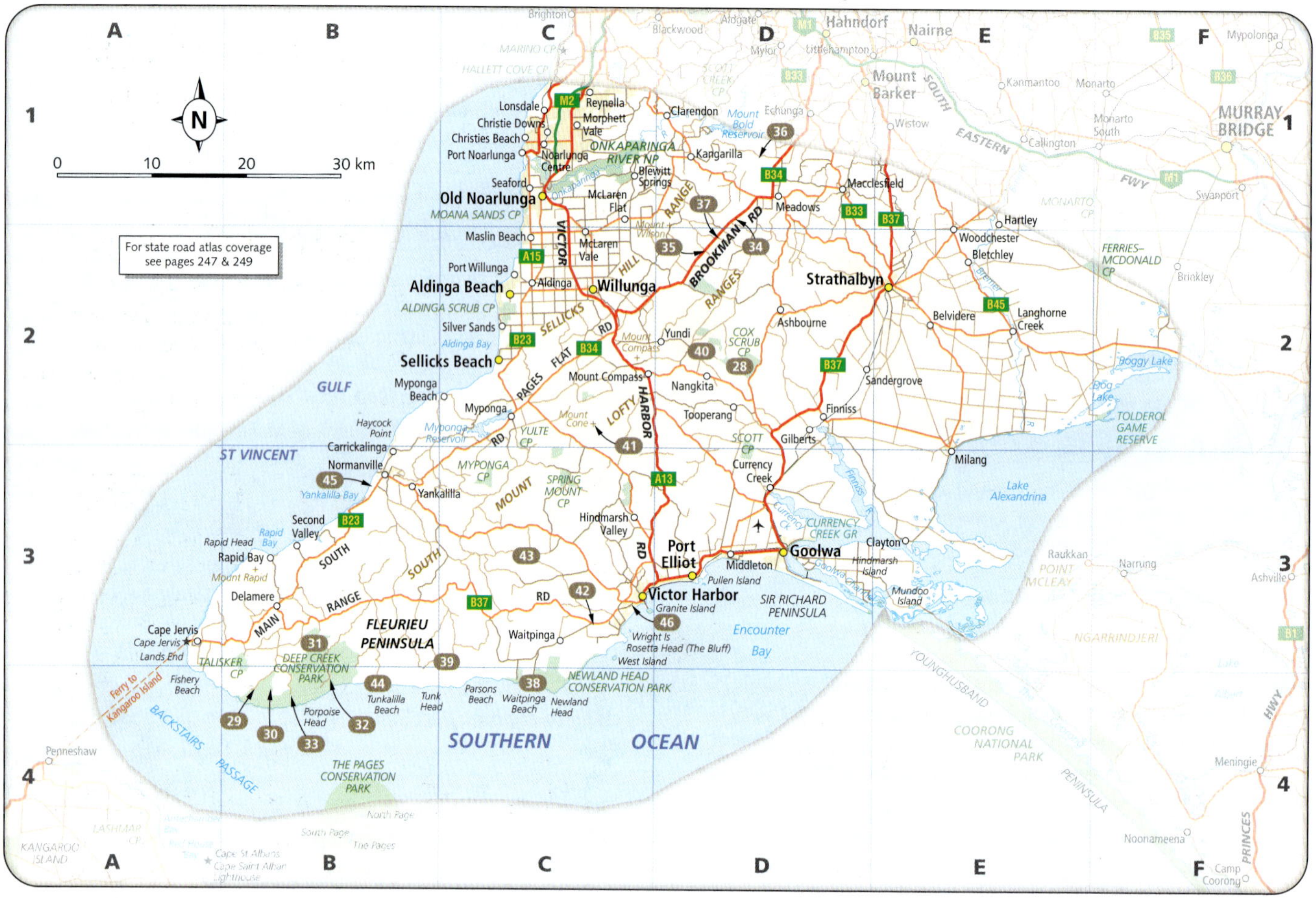

For state road atlas coverage see pages 247 & 249

IT MAY BE THE smallest of SA's big 3 peninsulas, but the Fleurieu still packs a punch. Being close to Adelaide, its coastline is home to the state's favourite holiday havens and much-loved beaches near Aldinga, Normanville, Victor Harbor and Goolwa.

Inland, there's a bounty of fine food and wine. The Fleurieu's rolling high country is a glorious patchwork of farms, orchards, forests and vineyards – including famous wine regions like McLaren Vale and Langhorne Creek. On this peninsula you're never far from a great bakery, cellar-door restaurant or beachfront cafe.

Further south, however, this region's wild side comes to the fore. Deep Creek Conservation Park is an impressive refuge of wave-lashed cliffs and deep ravines. There's excellent camping and walking here. The park is also traversed by the famous Heysen Trail, a well-marked walking route that kicks off at Cape Jervis and keeps rolling east past remote Tunkalilla Beach and Newland Head to the cliffs at Kings Head. From here it weaves north through the secluded parks and byways of the Mt Lofty Ranges – the start of the trail's marathon trek to the Flinders Ranges. Tucked along the Fleurieu's southern shores you can also find great beaches for surfing and fishing – plus, during winter, the bonus of perhaps spotting a southern right whale.

CAMPSITES LOCATED IN PARKS AND RESERVES

COX SCRUB CONSERVATION PARK

This small but captivating bushland hideaway on the eastern flanks of the Mt Lofty Ranges between Ashbourne and Goolwa is an important wildlife refuge. The park is a peaceful spot for nature walks and birdwatching among the stringybark and banksia scrub.

Who to contact: Parks SA Victor Harbor (08) 8552 3677

28 Cole Crossing camping area

Around 17 km north-east of Mt Compass, this peaceful camping area is reached from Cole Crossing Rd, 6 km south of Mt Magnificent Rd. No fires: only gas/fuel stoves are permitted.
Map refs: 204 D2, 247 B4, 249 J10

DEEP CREEK CONSERVATION PARK

This is a park with everything: wild beaches, hidden waterfalls, lush undergrowth and dramatic coastal cliffs. It's also home to the Fleurieu's largest remaining patch of native vegetation, which makes this a significant wildlife habitat. It's an engaging landscape to camp in and explore, though you need to be energetic to get the most out of the walking trails in this steep terrain. There's also excellent cabin and cottage accommodation available within the park.

Who to contact: Deep Creek Conservation Park (08) 8598 0263; or Friends of the Heysen Trail (08) 8212 6299

29 Cobbler Hill camping area

Ridgetop camping on the park's western boundary sits above wonderful Blowhole Beach, accessible by a steep 4WD track or walking trail. The campground is on Blowhole Creek Rd, 12 km south of Delamere, and is on the Heysen Trail. Pick up a permit from the self-registration station. **Map refs:** 204 B4, 247 A5, 249 I11

30 Eagle Waterhole camping area (walk-in camping)

Offering secluded bushland camping along the Heysen Trail, this walk-in site 2 km east of Cobber Hill also has a simple bushwalker's shelter. Bring a gas stove, water, and a permit from the self-registration station. **Map refs:** 204 B4, 247 A5, 249 I11

31 Stringybark camping area

Deep Creek's main camping area is sheltered by delightful stringybark forest, a feature of the park's higher ground. It's a comfortable base camp for daytrips and walks on Tapanappa Rd, 9 km south-east of Delamere. A permit is required from the self-registration station. **Map refs:** 204 B3, 247 A5, 249 I11

32 Tapanappa camping area

There are fantastic views along Tunkalilla Beach and over to Kangaroo Island from this lofty ridgetop campground on the Heysen Trail. It's also a staging post for challenging bushwalks to Deep Creek Cove and beautiful Boat Harbour Beach. You'll find it on Tapanappa Rd, 16 km south-east of Delamere. A permit is required from the self-registration station and you need to bring wood. **Map refs:** 204 B4, 247 A5, 249 I11

33 Trig camping area

This popular location in the heart of the park is sheltered and leafy, with good access to walking trails. It's at the end of the steep Tent Rock Rd, 12 km south of Delamere. Bring wood and pick up a permit from the self-registration station. **Map refs:** 204 B4, 247 A5, 249 I11

KUITPO FOREST

Above McLaren Vale and the Willunga Escarpment lies a hidden world of farmland, bush and forest. There are fine camping spots among the plantations, and long trails for horseriding (permit required), walking and mountain-biking. Camping is permitted from 1 Apr to 1 Dec.

Who to contact: Forestry SA Kuitpo Forest (08) 8391 8800; or Friends of the Heysen Trail (08) 8212 6299

34 Chookarloo camping area

Creekside camping is permitted just 1.5 km from Kuitpo's main information centre, 8 km south-west of Meadows on Brookman Rd. **Map refs:** 204 D1, 247 B4, 249 J10

35 Jacks Paddock camping area

Opposite Kuitpo Hall, with access from Christmas Hill Rd, this paddock campground is 11 km south of Meadows. With a restored barn and horseyards, it's recommended for group camping. Arrange your booking and permit in advance, as entry requires a key. **Map refs:** 204 D2, 247 B4, 249 J10

36 Rocky Creek Hut camping area

On the Heysen Trail, this camping area next to a cottage is on Razor Back Rd, 7 km north-west of Meadows. The stone cottage has a wood heater, sink, rainwater tank and sleeping platforms for 8. There is a short walk from the carpark. Bookings are essential for the hut; the Kuitpo Forest information centre provides the combination lock code. **Map refs:** 204 D1, 247 C3, 249 J10

37 Woodcutters Cottage

This former youth hostel is a 4-room stone cottage with a lounge, kitchen and sleeping room for 12, plus room nearby for tents. It is just 2 km from the information centre on Brookman Rd. Booking is necessary and a permit is required. **Map refs:** 204 D2, 247 B4, 249 J10

NEWLAND HEAD CONSERVATION PARK

For coastal splendour, this strip of southern Fleurieu shoreline includes 2 fine beaches, Parsons and Waitpinga, and a stunningly wild cliff-line traversed by the Heysen Trail. Popular for surfing and beach fishing, this park has fine coastal vegetation and an air of remoteness. It's a top spot for beach and bushwalks.

Who to contact: Parks SA Victor Harbor (08) 8552 3677; or Friends of the Heysen Trail (08) 8212 6299

38 Waitpinga camping area

Sheltered sites are set amongst coastal scrub a short stroll from Waitpinga Beach, 16 km south-west of Victor Harbor. Access is from Range and Dennis rds. A permit is required and cooking is by gas/fuel stove only. **Map refs:** 204 C4, 247 B5, 249 J11

CAMPSITES LOCATED IN OTHER AREAS

Heysen Trail

This section of the trail hits the coast, and offers spectacular scenery – from the inland forests to the stunning beach between Deep Creep Conservation Park and Newland Head Conservation Park.

Please note that campsites are listed in alphabetical order, not track order. Refer to the map on p. 204 for further information.

Who to contact: Parks SA Victor Harbor (08) 8552 3677; or Friends of the Heysen Trail (08) 8212 6299 www.heysentrail.asn.au

39 Balquhidder camping area

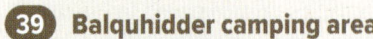

A picturesque campsite, at the junction of 2 creeks alongside Mt Scrub Rd, with new rainwater tanks. Bring a gas/fuel stove.
Map refs: 204 C3, 247 B5, 249 J11

34 Chookarloo camping area

See p. 205.

29 Cobbler Hill camping area

See p. 205.

30 Eagle Waterhole camping area (walk-in camping)

See p. 205.

40 Finniss River camping area

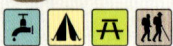

There are new facilities at this campsite immediately north-west of the road beside the Finniss River, 150 m down a small side road from an intersection off the Heysen Trail. Bring a gas/fuel stove. **Map refs:** 204 D2, 247 B4, 249 J10

41 Mount Cone Shelter camping area

This is a basic camping area with a day shelter on top of a hill. Bring a gas/fuel stove. **Map refs:** 204 C2, 247 B4, 249 J10

42 Newland Hill Road Reserve camping area

The Road Reserve is located 200 m from the stile at the junction of Range and Waitpinga rds. Limited tent space is available. Bring water and a gas/fuel stove. **Map refs:** 204 C3, 247 B5, 249 J11

43 Robinson Hill camping area

This area is about 1 km east of the ruined church, 800 m east along Hancock Rd from where the trail turns to the north off Hancock Rd. Bring a gas/fuel stove. **Map refs:** 204 C3, 247 B5, 249 J11

36 Rocky Creek Hut camping area

See p. 205.

32 Tapanappa camping area

See p. 205.

44 Tunkalilla Beach camping area

A good spot to camp is on the dunes above the beach, adjacent to the stile near the creek outlet. Note: there are no facilities.
Map refs: 204 B4, 247 B5, 249 I11

38 Waitpinga camping area

See p. 205.

This track continues through the Wine Country region (see p. 202).

45 Normanville Beachside Caravan Park

This well-appointed park is located on one of the best beaches in the state. The site is peaceful but close to great facilities, and only a short distance from the fantastic Deep Creek Conservation Park, Kangaroo Island and McLaren Vale. Tennis courts are next door and the Lady Bay golf course is 10 min down the road. There is 4WD access to the beach for boating and fishing, which is very popular. **Map refs:** 204 B3, 247 A4, 249 I10

How to book: Cape Jervis Rd, Normanville (08) 8558 2458 www.beachside.com.au

46 Victor Harbor Holiday and Cabin Park

A family park, with powered and unpowered sites, this place is close to attractions and just 5 min from the beach. There are plenty of sites, as well as villas and cabins. Good facilities for kids include a jumping pillow and go-karts for hire. Take a ride on the historic Victor Harbor horse-drawn tram to Granite Island, and check out the penguin tours. Whale watching, the nearby Urimbirra Wildlife Park and great beach walks are all on offer.
Map refs: 204 C3, 247 B5, 249 J11

How to book: Bay Rd, Victor Harbor (08) 8552 1949 www.victorharborholiday.com.au

YORKE PENINSULA

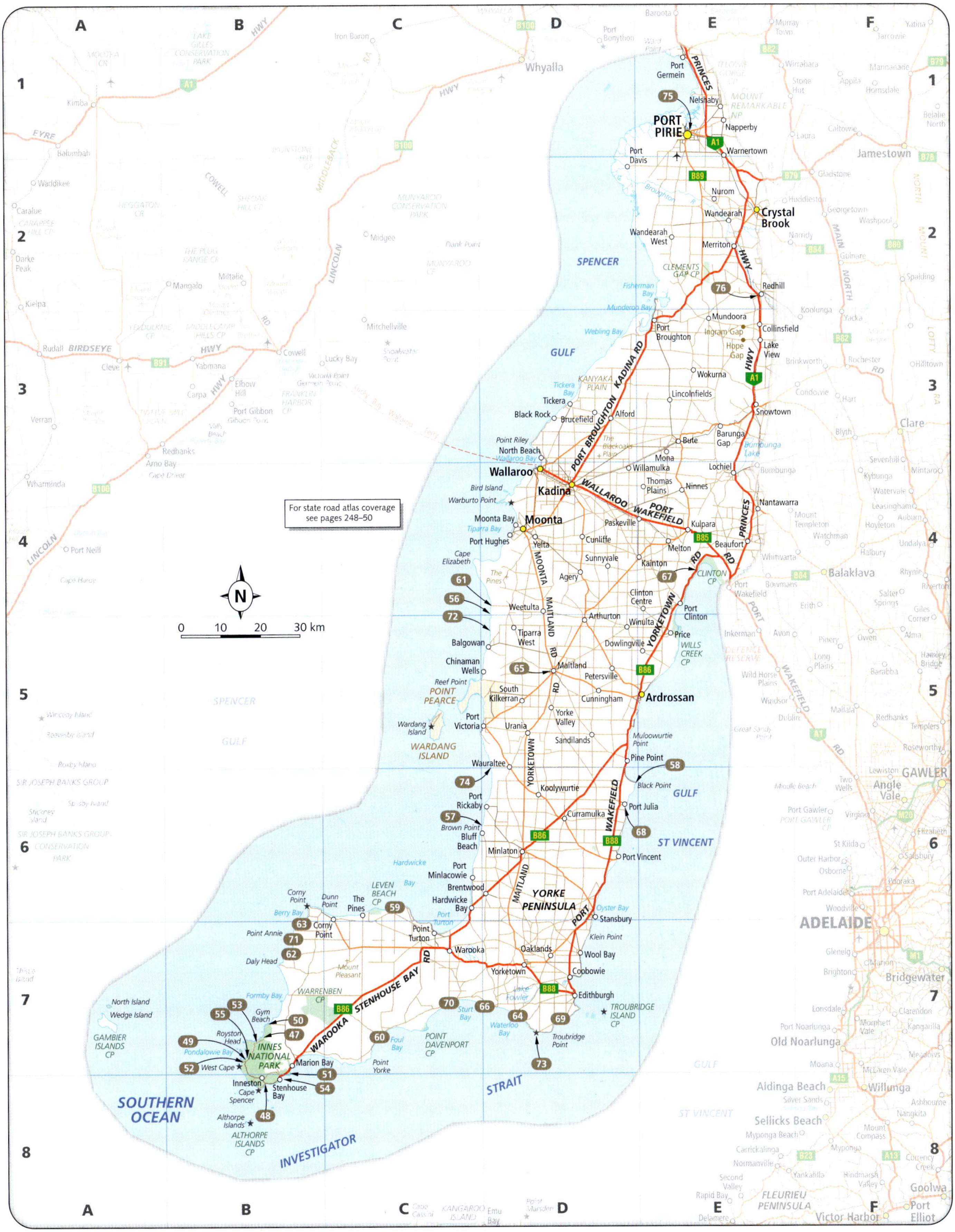

For state road atlas coverage
see pages 248–50

N

0   10   20   30 km

SPENCER

GULF

SPENCER

GULF

SOUTHERN
OCEAN

INVESTIGATOR   STRAIT

ST VINCENT
GULF

ST VINCENT
GULF

YORKE
PENINSULA

INNES
NATIONAL
PARK

WARDANG
ISLAND

SIR JOSEPH BANKS GROUP

GAMBIER
ISLANDS
CP

PORT
PIRIE

Crystal
Brook

Wallaroo

Kadina

Moonta

Ardrossan

ADELAIDE

GAWLER

Bridgewater

Victor Harbor

Port
Elliot

FLEURIEU
PENINSULA

WHATEVER THE SEASON – AND no matter which way the wind's blowing – 'Yorkes' has a calm bay to enjoy and a dune to tuck your tent behind. This distinctive boot-shaped peninsula is hugely popular with Adelaide locals looking to cast a line or relax on the beach with the family.

In the north, the former copper-mining hubs of Wallaroo, Kadina and Moonta are steeped in a proud Cornish heritage. Further south, the majority of the landscape was cleared for cropping. As a result, both sides of the peninsula are dotted with historic port towns where grain ships once loaded. The good news for holiday-makers is that these small, low-key settlements typically have a sheltered beach, caravan park, shops and – best of all – a jetty to fish from.

For those eager to get away from it all there's fine bush camping along the western shores of the peninsula. The facilities are few but you can almost always be guaranteed your own stretch of beach to fish and wander, as well as a sunset to remember.

The real excitement is down on 'the boot', with a succession of wild surf spots south of Corny Point, the seaside haven of Marion Bay and the natural delights of Innes National Park. Fortified on all sides by towering limestone cliffs, this park is a gem. Here you'll find walking trails to follow, historic cottage accommodation, shipwrecks and a bevy of excellent coastal campsites with easy beach access.

CAMPSITES LOCATED IN PARKS AND RESERVES

INNES NATIONAL PARK

A natural stronghold on the very toe of this farming peninsula, in contrast to the rolling fields of wheat and barley, this park is home to significant mallee scrub habitats and a spectacular coastline of limestone cliffs and secluded beaches. It's a great getaway spot for fishing, surfing, snorkelling and bushwalking. You need to be self-sufficient to camp here, bringing in your own firewood, water and preferably a gas/fuel stove, along with a permit to camp.

Who to contact: Parks SA Stenhouse Bay (08) 8854 3200

47 **Browns Beach camping area**

These 10 sites hunkered among the dunes and scrub close to a renowned salmon-fishing beach are found in the northern sector of the park, 26 km north-west of Marion Bay. **Map refs:** 207 B7, 248 F10

48 **Cable Bay camping area**

It's an easy walk to the beach from this camping area. Weather permitting, there's great snorkelling here and rockpools to explore. Being south-facing, the bay also has fine views of the offshore islands. It's just off Pondalowie Bay Rd, some 10 km from Marion Bay. **Map refs:** 207 B8, 248 G10

49 **Casuarina camping area**

At busy times this secluded site, 20 km to the west of Marion Bay, is a more peaceful alternative for enjoying Pondalowie Bay. It's a short walk to the beach and the wave action at Surfers is just up the road. Bookings are not required; pick up the key to the access gate. **Map refs:** 207 B7, 248 F10

50 **Gym Beach camping area**

Hidden away on the far northern outskirts of the park, 14 km north-west of Marion Bay, this small site offers solitude and easy access to the water. A 6 km bushwalking trail among dunes and mallee vegetation links this camp with Browns Beach. Note: the only vehicle access is via the Corny Point–Marion Bay Rd. **Map refs:** 207 B7, 248 G10

51 **Jollys Beach camping area**

There is basic seaside camping close to Willyama Bay at Jollys, 6 km south of Marion Bay. As the only east-facing site in the park, it offers shelter from the winter westerlies. Pick up a permit from the self-registration station here. **Map refs:** 207 B7, 248 G10

52 **Pondalowie camping area**

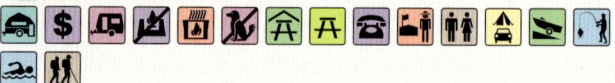

With close to 50 sites scattered among the coastal mallee vegetation, this is the biggest of the park's campgrounds. Pondalowie Bay is a famed surfing spot and home to an active lobster-fishing fleet. Tent-based camping is at the eastern end of the site, while campervans and caravans are catered for on the western side. The camping area is 18 km west of Marion Bay on Pondalowie Bay Rd. **Map refs:** 207 B7, 248 F10

53 **Shell Beach camping area**

This great unspoilt location tucked among the vegetation on the park's elevated north shores is a short walk to beautiful Shell Beach. Neighbouring Dolphin Beach is equally delightful, and the historic Shepherds Hut nearby is available for rent. The site is 24 km west of Marion Bay along Browns Beach Rd. **Map refs:** 207 B7, 248 F10

54 **Stenhouse Bay camping area**

This is the park's gateway site, close to the visitor centre, shops and tavern. The beach and the historic jetty, a favoured fishing haunt, are also just a short stroll away. The camping area is 6 km south of Marion Bay off Stenhouse Rd. **Map refs:** 207 B8, 248 G10

55 Surfers camping area

Campers who love to surf target this camping area, 20 km west from Marion Bay. To get here, follow the signs from Pondalowie Bay Rd. **Map refs:** 207 B7, 248 F10

YORKE PENINSULA RESERVES

At this broad array of coastal camping spots looked after by Yorke Peninsula's local council, there's a terrific selection of sites on all points of the compass. While they have few, if any, facilities, the bush locations are usually close to beach views and fishing spots – as well as being quiet and secluded. You need to be pretty self-sufficient, bringing your own firewood and water. You also need a permit (from the council office, or on sale in many local shops).

Who to contact: District Council of Yorke Peninsula (08) 8832 0000

56 The Bamboos camping area

There's a varied coastline to discover here – rocky headlands, seagrass shallows, and white sand beaches. The camping is behind the dunes, 12 km north of Balgowan. **Map refs:** 207 D4, 248 H7

57 Barkers Rocks camping area

Basic beachside camping is available on the narrow strip of coastal reserve between Port Rickaby and Bluff Beach. Being west-facing, it's great for sunsets and beachcombing but there's not much shelter in high summer. The camping area is 12 km north-west of Minlaton along Barkers Rocks Rd. **Map refs:** 207 D6, 248 H8

58 Black Point camping area

Black Point's sweep of north-facing beach is hugely popular at peak holiday periods. This small open area is right next to the boat ramp and main road at the western end of the housing strip; powered sites are available. It's a handy spot for boaties but peace and privacy are hard to find. The campground is 3 km south of Pine Point on the Main Coast Rd. **Map refs:** 207 D6, 247 A2, 249 I8

59 Burners Beach camping area

These beachfront sites are on the sheltered side of the peninsula's 'foot'. The north-facing shores catch the sun all year round and are home to some of the region's most popular holiday settlements. Located 12 km west of Point Turton on Point Souttar Rd, there is safe swimming here, toilets and a boat ramp. **Map refs:** 207 C6, 248 G9

60 Foul Bay camping area

Beachfront sites on this long, lonely stretch of beach are on the peninsula's southern fringe. There's easy access to swimming, fishing and snorkelling, coastal headlands to explore and Marion Bay's facilities are a short drive away. Foul Bay is 39 km south-west of Warooka, just off South Coast Rd. **Map refs:** 207 C7, 248 G10

61 The Gap camping area

Several beachfront sites huddle among the dunes here, on the remote north-west coast. The water is easy to access – including for boat launching – and the long, dazzling stretch of beach to the north is popular for 4WD visits. The camping is 15 km north of Balgowan. **Map refs:** 207 D4, 248 H7

62 Gleesons Landing camping area

Close to Daly Head and the crashing surf along Formby Bay, this is a popular lair for fishers. There are toilet facilities; the boat ramp is for 4WD only. The coastal reserve is reached via the Corny Point–Marion Bay Rd, 16 km south-west of Corny Point. **Map refs:** 207 B7, 248 G9

63 Gravel Bay camping area

The peninsula's wild west coast is a legendary haunt for fishers and experienced surfers. Take your pick from sites scattered along the coastal reserve from South Berry Bay carpark to Point Annie Rd. Access is via West Coast Rd, 6 km south-west of Corny Point. Camping is not permitted in the Berry Bay carpark areas. **Map refs:** 207 B7, 248 G9

64 Kemp Bay camping area

The beaches here are flanked by buffs and rocky points. There's good fishing to be had, along with swimming in lighter conditions. It is on the south coast of the peninsula, 13 km south of Yorketown off Diamond Lake Rd. **Map refs:** 207 D7, 248 H9

65 Maitland Overnight Camping Bay

This small overnight caravan stop in the centrally located town of Maitland is just opposite the hospital at the northern end of Robert St. **Map refs:** 207 D5, 248 H7

66 Mozzie Flat camping area

Camp at this secluded location on the far eastern end of Sturt Bay, 17 km south of Yorketown and 4 km west of Port Moorowie. There is easy beach access, plus extensive coastal dunes to explore and plenty of beach fishing spots to try. Access is via Green Hill and Mozzie Flats rds. **Map refs:** 207 D7, 248 H9

67 Port Arthur Roadside Rest Area

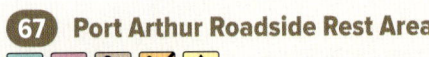

A shady, no-frills stop for weary travellers at the head of Gulf St Vincent, the rest area is close to mangrove flats where you might see wading birds at low tide. It's just off the Port Wakefield–Yorketown Rd, 9 km north of Port Clinton. **Map refs:** 207 E4, 249 I7

68 Port Julia Oval camping area

Basic community-supported camping is possible in the small coastal town of Port Julia, on the north-east coast. It's a popular fishing and seasonal crabbing spot, 17 km north of Port Vincent off the coast road. **Map refs:** 207 D6, 247 A2, 249 I8

69 Sheoak Flat camping area

Camping at Sheoak Flat is on the peninsula's southern coast, 10 km on from Edithburgh along Hancock Rd. **Map refs:** 207 D7, 248 H9

70 Sturt Bay camping area

A wide arc of dunes and south-facing beach stretches nearly 20 km from Point Davenport to Port Moorowie at Sturt Bay. The campsite is at the bay's midpoint, giving ample scope for fishing, swimming and snorkelling, especially towards Sandy Point on the western end of the bay. It is reached from Sturt Bay Rd, 13 km south of Warooka. **Map refs:** 207 C7, 248 H9

71 Swincers Rocks camping area

Remote cliff-top camping is possible at the end of Wurlie Rd, 13 km south-west of Corny Point. There are craggy headlands to explore and wave action on the 2 rocky islets offshore. **Map refs:** 207 B7, 248 G9

72 Tiparra Rocks camping area

This is the first of 3 coastal-reserve camping areas, 8 km north of the seaside settlement of Balgowan. A crust of vivid red cliffs marks the edge of the peninsula south of this site. You'll find lots of solitude here, plus ready access to swimming, fishing and the sandy point just north of the camp. Boats can be launched from the beach. **Map refs:** 207 D5, 248 H7

73 Troubridge Hill camping area

The rugged limestone shore on the peninsula's southern 'heel' was the scene of many a historic shipwreck. Nearby is the distinctive clay-brick Troubridge Hill Lighthouse. Camping is permitted all along the coastal reserve beside Diamond

Lake Rd, South Coast Rd and Troubridge Point Dr. The varied coastline includes beaches, bluffs and extensive reef platforms. You'll find it 19 km south of Yorketown and 15 km south-west of Edithburgh. **Map refs:** 207 D7, 248 H10

74 Wauraltee Beach camping area

Go camping beside the wild sprawl of beach south of Port Victoria, a low-key fishing and swimming destination with large areas of coastal reserve to wander. The camping area is on the peninsula's western flanks, 17 km south of Port Victoria on Wauraltee Beach Rd. **Map refs:** 207 D5, 248 H8

CAMPSITES LOCATED IN OTHER AREAS

75 Port Pirie Beach Caravan Park

This modern park on the banks of the Port Pirie River overlooks the picturesque Southern Flinders Ranges. There are generous grassed camping sites with a great garden feel. Fishers will have plenty to do, with whiting, snapper, mulloway, snook, salmon, squid and many other excellent table fish aplenty in the area. Pets are allowed on application. Campers can access a shared dishwashing and kitchen area. There are 2 amenities blocks, both with laundries and the main with a disabled bathroom. **Map refs:** 207 E1, 249 I4, 250 H11

How to book: Beach Rd, Port Pirie (08) 8632 4275 www.portpiriebeachcaravanpark.com.au

76 Redhill Recreation Ground

This overnight highway stop on the outskirts of the small farming town of Redhill is 50 km south of Port Pirie. It's just off the Princes Hwy along an access road to the west of the train line. **Map refs:** 207 E2, 249 I5, 250 H12

Who to contact: Redhill General Store (08) 8636 7020

LIMESTONE COAST

Map labels and grid references:

A, B, C, D, E, F (column headers top and bottom)
1, 2, 3, 4, 5, 6 (row numbers left and right)

COORONG NATIONAL PARK
Willalooka
Mundulla
Custon
RD B57
BORDERTOWN
Kahla
Yanipy
A8
PEACOCK RANGE
Western Flat
Bangham
BANGHAM CP
Minimay
LITTLE DESERT NATIONAL PARK
92 PADTHAWAY CP
Padthaway
RIDDOCH
NARACOORTE HWY
GEEGEELA CP
Morea
Mortat
Goroke
Kingston S.E.
Wyomi
Reedy Creek
MOUNT SCOTT CP
TALAPAR CP
Keppoch
Wallabrook
Frances
QUARRENA PLAIN
Boorooopki
Ozenkadnook
Kamak
BUTCHER GAP CP
B101
Mount + Scott
FAIRVIEW CP
86
Lodhaber Swamp
Binnum
Tallageira
Bringalbert
Cape Jaffa
Kings Camp
Avenue
Lucindale
Naracoorte
Hynam
A66
Kybybolite
Benayeo
Patyah
Apsley
Avonga
Charam
BERNOUILLI CR
Mount Benson
C240
NARACOORTE CAVES NP
Langkoop
Edenhope
Boatswain Point
Godfrey Islands
GUICHEN BAY CP
NARACOORTE
BIG HEATH CONSERVATION PARK
Moyhall Swamp
91
Struan
Joanna
Poolagelo
Kadnook
Powers Creek
C208
Moree
Robe
90
Cape Lannes
87
LITTLE DIP CP
88
Nora Creina
89
WOAKWINE
Lake Hawdon North
Conmurra
79
80
BOOL LAGOON GR
Wrattonbully
Comaum
Chetwynd
Greenways
KONETTA
Clay Wells
Wattle Range
Glenroy
Coonawarra
Moree
Dorodong
Deroholm
Bumboal
Bray Junction
Lake Eliza
Chinaman Wells
CLAY
WELLS
Furner
PENOLA
Penola
C198
Brumboal
Wando Bridge
P211
SOUTHERN
Lake St Clair
PORTS
Lakes George
77
78
BEACHPORT CP
Beachport
Cape Martin
HWY
Hatherleigh
PENOLA
Krongart
Nangwarry
A66
Lake Mundi
Casterton
C198
Wando Vale
Garapook
B160
Rivoli Bay
B101
Rendelsham
OLD
Mount Burr
Kalangadoo
Tarpeena
SOUTH AUSTRALIA
VICTORIA
Dunrobin
Sardford
Henty
Cape Buffon
Southend
94
Millicent
Mount Burr
Glencoe West
Glencoe
Wandilo
GLENELG HWY
Strathdownie
Merino
84 83
82
Geltwood Beach
Snuggery
Tantanoola
Lake Bonney S.E.
B1
HWY
RIDDOCH
Mil Lel
CANUNDA NATIONAL PARK
85
OCEAN
81
Cape Banks
Corattum
MOUNT GAMBIER
B160
Db Flat
Glenburnie
Yahl
A1
PRINCES
Puraika
Marp
Dartmoor
CRAWFORD RIVER CP
C187
Carpenter Rocks
Kongorong
B66
Caroline
Mumbannar
Winnap
Hotspur
Blackfellow Caves
NENE VALLEY CP
Nene Valley
Mount Schank
Attendale East
Donovans
Landing
Ewens Ponds
LOWER GLENELG NP
Nelson
Greenwald
Dok Drik
Lyons
HWY
Cape Northumberland
Port MacDonnell
PICCANINNIE PONDS CP
93
Discovery Bay
LOWER GLENELG NP
C198
COBBOBOONEE NATIONAL PARK
Kentbruck
Mount Richmond
Gorae West
Gorae

0 10 20 30 km (scale)

N (compass)

SOUTHERN OCEAN

For state road atlas coverage see page 247

THE SEA AND ITS legacies dominate this south-eastern quarter of the state. A series of parallel ranges – ancient dune rises from sea levels past – form natural corridors heading into the heart of the region.

The limestone that underlies so much of the landscape is responsible for the fossil-rich Naracoorte Caves, a World Heritage–listed drawcard with stunning caverns and formations to explore. Other natural limestone formations are on show all along the coast from Cape Jaffa to Port MacDonnell. These wind-lashed shores feature rugged coastal cliffs and surf beaches that offer

excellent fishing and camping hideaways, especially in Little Dip Conservation Park and Canunda National Park.

Tucked behind the dunes, there are numerous wetlands for birdwatching and bushwalking. Further inland, the sprawling Bool Lagoon Game Reserve is one of southern Australia's most significant freshwater habitats, giving refuge to some 150 bird species, including migratory waders.

The rich, free-draining soils formed on ancient limestone – the legendary terra rossa – are the secret to the success of the region's wine industry. While the Coonawarra is the historic heart of the grape industry here, significant vineyard plantings are also scattered from Padthaway and Wrattonbully in the east to Mt Benson, close to the coast near Robe. These shores are also famed for their fishing ports and hauls of southern rock lobster. Further south, the limestone landscape is dotted with reminders of Australia's most recent volcanic past, including the cones and craters in and around Mt Gambier.

CAMPSITES LOCATED IN PARKS AND RESERVES

BEACHPORT CONSERVATION PARK

On a slender peninsula just north of the Beachport township, this park is bounded by a wild ocean shore of ragged limestone cliffs on one side, and the relative calm of Lake George on the other. The park is a great spot for rambling the coast and enjoying the birdlife among the paperbarks and tea tree, while the lake is a haven for waterbirds. The lake is also a popular place for swimming, dinghy sailing and windsurfing. The coastal access tracks inside the park are for 4WD only. These sandy tracks, on the ocean side of the peninsula, give access to rocky headlands and secluded beaches.

Who to contact: Parks SA Mt Gambier (08) 8735 1177

77 Rooney Point camping area

A camping area for self-sufficient campers is found 7 km north of Beachport along Five Mile Drift Rd; the self-registration station for permits is on this road. **Map refs:** 211 C4, 247 E10

78 Three Mile Bend camping area

The campsites here, tucked among the paperbarks on the edge of Lake George, are large, sheltered and well separated. The camping area is 5 km north of Beachport along Five Mile Drift Rd. Bring wood and water and pick up a permit from the self-registration station. **Map refs:** 211 C4, 247 E10

BIG HEATH CONSERVATION PARK

A long strip of heathland in low-lying country west of Bool Lagoon, this is a real bush retreat with diverse plant communities including banksia scrub and pink gums, plus a range of woodland birdlife. This is an ideal destination for self-sufficient bushwalkers.

Who to contact: Parks SA Naracoorte (08) 8762 3412

79 Big Heath camping area (bush camping)

Located 35 km south-west of Naracoorte via Bool Lagoon Rd, there are no marked tracks or campsites here. Details and permits are available from Parks SA Naracoorte. **Map refs:** 211 D3, 247 G9

BOOL LAGOON GAME RESERVE

A birdwatcher's paradise, this extensive freshwater lagoon network with its basins, islands and swamps is one of southern Australia's most treasured wetlands. It's a refuge for more than 150 bird species, including many migratory waders. The reserve features scenic drives, lookouts and several boardwalks into the thick of the action.

Who to contact: Parks SA Naracoorte (08) 8762 3412

80 Hacks Peninsula camping area

Signposted access to this camping area is 27 km south of Naracoorte via Bool Lagoon Rd. Lagoon water levels vary seasonally. There is a self-registration station for permits; gas/fuel stoves only. **Map refs:** 211 E3, 247 G9

CANUNDA NATIONAL PARK

Spanning 40 km of wild coastline from Cape Buffon south to Cape Banks, this 9600 ha park offers tremendous variety. Weathered limestone cliffs, offshore islets and long stretches of beach and dune dominate these shores. Inland there are extensive pockets of tea-tree interspersed with coastal wattle and she-oaks. There are several easy bushwalks and scenic lookouts, as well as excellent fishing, with salmon and mulloway caught off the beaches. The park is accessible by conventional vehicle from the townships of Southend, Millicent and Carpenter Rocks, though to explore the full length of the coastline you'll need a 4WD.

Who to contact: Parks SA Mt Gambier (08) 8735 1177

81 Cape Banks Lighthouse camping area

Small clearings for self-sufficient camping are found in the coastal scrub at the southern end of the park. Access is from Cape Banks Rd, 3.2 km north of Carpenter Rocks. Self-registration stations have permits. **Map refs:** 211 D5, 247 F12

82 Geltwood Beach camping area

This campground offers coastal access for conventional vehicles, accessed from Oil Rig Square Track off Canunda Causeway Rd, 14 km west of Millicent. The 4 sites are 700 m west of the track. **Map refs:** 211 C4, 247 F11

83 Kotgee camping area

There are 7 sites here for self-sufficient campers, 2.6 km south-east of Southend via Boozy Gully access road. The sites are 400 m along Bevilaqua Ford Track. **Map refs:** 211 C4, 247 E11

84 Nal-a-wort camping area

There are more self-sufficient camping sites around 100 m further along the Bevilaqua Ford Track, next door to the Kotgee camping area. **Map refs:** 211 C4, 247 E11

Pine forest near Mount Gambier

85 Number Two Rocks camping area

There are 2 self-sufficient camping areas found 14.6 km and 14.8 km north of Carpenter Rocks. Access is 4WD-only along the marked coastal track. A permit is required from one of the self-registration stations in the park. **Map refs:** 211 D5, 247 F11

FAIRVIEW CONSERVATION PARK

This small, remote park protects Kangoora Lagoon, a wetland habitat north-west of Naracoorte. Tucked between the Stewart and Baker ranges, it features intact woodland flora and fauna.

Who to contact: Parks SA Naracoorte (08) 8762 3412

86 Fairview camping area (bush camping)

Remote wilderness camping for self-sufficient bushwalkers is situated 45 km north-west of Naracoorte, signposted from Wolumbool Rd. The Parks SA office at Naracoorte can provide further details and a permit. **Map refs:** 211 D2, 247 F9

LITTLE DIP CONSERVATION PARK

Wedged between the Southern Ocean and a network of lakes and wetlands, this coastal park is just south of Robe township. The shoreline is fretted by wild surf beaches and limestone headlands. Although key locations are accessible by conventional vehicles, a 4WD is needed to explore the full breadth of the park's coastal strip and dune systems. It's a popular getaway for fishing and beachcombing, while the mallee scrub and shoreline walks near Fresh Water and Big Dip lakes are more serene destinations.

Who to contact: Parks SA Mt Gambier (08) 8735 1177

87 The Gums camping area

The Gums self-sufficient camping area is reached from The Gums Track, off the Eastern Boundary Track, 5 km south of Robe. It is good for small vans. Pick up a permit from one of the self-registration stations in the park. **Map refs:** 211 B3, 247 E10

88 Long Gully camping area

A popular coastal site with all-vehicle access, Long Gully is on the Long Gully Track. It's off Nora Creina Dr, 10 km south of Robe. Bring wood and get a permit from one of the self-registration stations in the park. **Map refs:** 211 B3, 247 E10

89 Old Man Lake camping area

Sheltered spots are easily accessible from Nora Creina Dr, 14 km south of Robe. This is the spot with the best view. You need to be self-sufficient; pick up a permit from one of the self-registration stations in the park. **Map refs:** 211 C3, 247 E10

90 Stony Rise camping area

The northernmost camping area in the park is only 4 km south of Robe, reached from Stony Rise Track off Robe St. There is plenty of room for 4WDs and vans. Pick up a permit from one of the self-registration stations in the park. **Map refs:** 211 B3, 247 E10

NARACOORTE CAVES CONSERVATION PARK

Home to captivating natural formations and more than 100 fossil deposits collected over 500 000 years, this vast cave system is an unrivalled record of Australia's megafauna past. Species represented include the marsupial lion, thylacine and sthenurine kangaroos. Self-guided and guided tours of the caves are on offer, including to the Victoria Fossil Cave, and more adventurous excursions to the Cathedral Cave and Starburst Chamber. Highlights above ground include an informative visitor centre, a campground and adjacent caravan park, dormitory accommodation for groups, picnic grounds and a licensed cafe.

Who to contact: Parks SA Naracoorte Caves (08) 8762 2340

91 **Naracoorte Caves Caravan Park**

This fully equipped park with plenty of accommodation options, including extensive tent sites, is on Caves Rd, 14 km south of Naracoorte. Laundry facilities are available. **Map refs:** 211 E3, 247 G9

PADTHAWAY CONSERVATION PARK

This small park secures a block of original eucalypt woodland in the West Naracoorte Range. With dominant species including South Australian blue gum, manna gum and stringybarks, this is a winner for birdwatchers. The only access is via 4WD or on foot.

Who to contact: Parks SA Naracoorte (08) 8762 3412

92 **Padthaway camping area (bush camping)**

Bush camping with no facilities and limited access is reached from the Padthaway–Bordertown Rd, 4 km north-east of Padthaway. Access is by 4WD or on foot. Drinking water, accommodation and campsites are available in the adjacent caravan park. **Map refs:** 211 D1, 247 F8

PICCANINNIE PONDS CONSERVATION PARK

This park protects a long stretch of sandy beach backed by dunes and limestone ridges. The focus here is sinkholes filled with crystal-clear water plunging to depths of more than 70 m. These stunning limestone formations offer brilliant diving and snorkelling experiences, though you'll need a permit. The park also offers scope for bush and beach walks, fishing and birdwatching. The park is 32 km south of Mt Gambier on Discovery Bay, near the Victorian border.

Who to contact: Parks SA Mt Gambier (08) 8735 1177

93 **Piccaninnie Ponds camping area**

This camping area with 6 sites is 3.5 km south of Nelson Rd, 27.8 km south-east of Mt Gambier; the sites are 600 m past the access road to the ponds. Pick up a permit from the self-registration station. While you can't swim in the ponds, there's swimming and fishing in Discovery Bay. The sites are gas/fuel stove only. **Map refs:** 211 E6, 247 G12

CAMPSITES LOCATED IN OTHER AREAS

94 **Southend on Sea Tourist Park**

Relax right beside the beach in the casual surrounds of this friendly park. Absolute beachfront means you can set up a tent and listen to the waves roll in and out. Bush camping options are available if you want to skip on the mod cons. There's plenty of shade, and a nice touch for campers is the open fire with rock/cement surrounds near campsites. There's also a nearby jetty for people keen on a fishing outing. Ask at the kiosk for advice. **Map refs:** 211 C4, 247 E11

How to book: 1 Eyre St, Southend (08) 8735 6035
www.southendcaravanpark.com.au

MURRAY

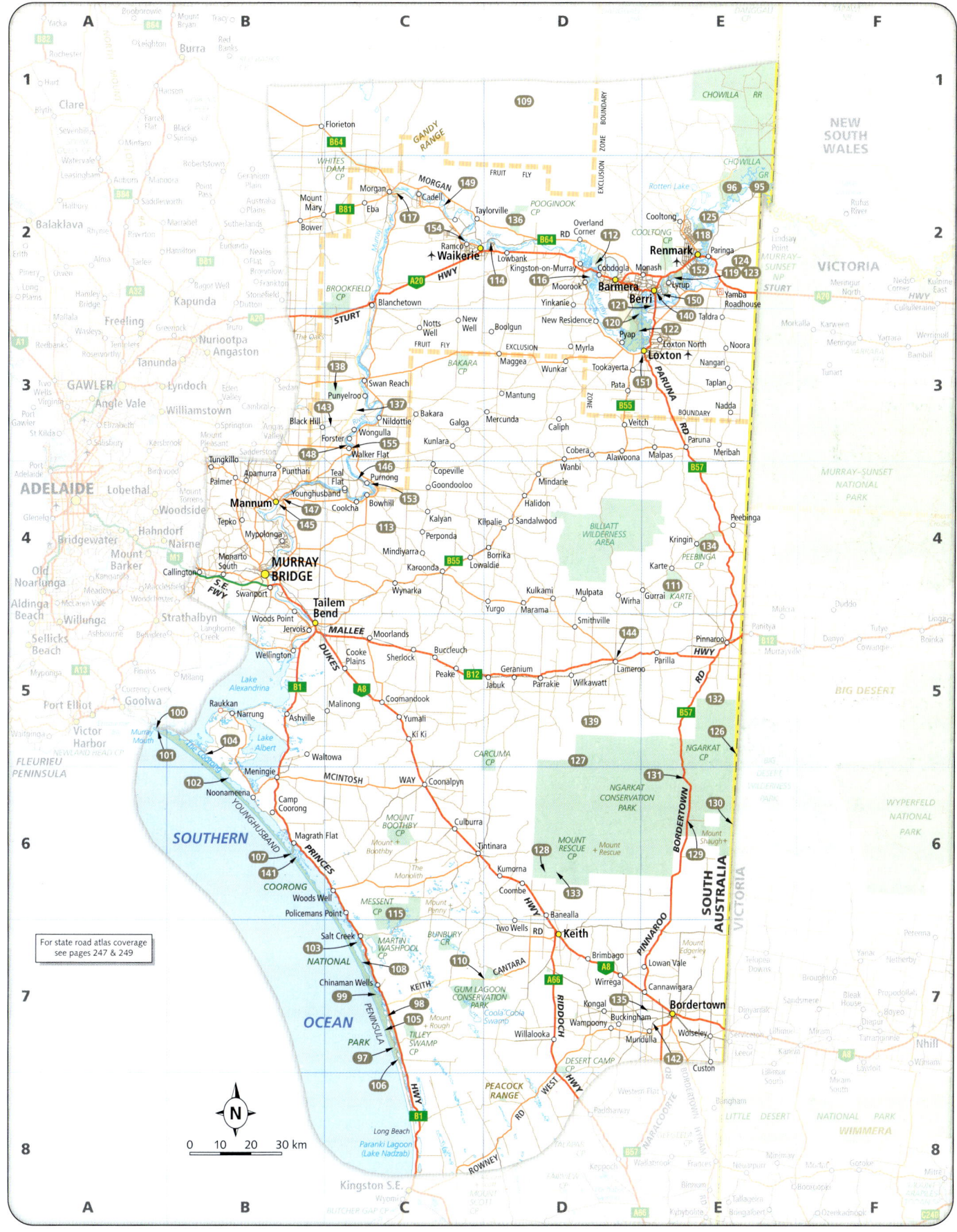

For state road atlas coverage
see pages 247 & 249

0 10 20 30 km

THE MIGHTY MURRAY IS SA's lifeline. All along its slow, snaking journey, the river brings much-needed water to a semi-arid environment – including the towns, farms and cities of the continent's driest state. While much of the landscape flanking the river is given over to irrigated agriculture, there are surviving stretches where the majesty of the natural order endures. There's also a real understanding that the region's many flood plains, lagoons, creeks and wetlands are vital habitats for the future health of the river.

The Murray has always been a meeting place. It's a region of living Aboriginal history and welcoming riverside towns with stories to share. As long as the waters keep flowing, there will be tales of paddlesteamers and river ports, of big floods and giant Murray cod, and families pioneering vast orchards and citrus groves.

Above all else, the river is known as a place for kicking back, a no-fuss holiday destination where families pitch a tent and fish, or spend a quiet week easing along the Murray in a houseboat. Highlights for camping, canoeing and birdwatching include Murray River National Park, Chowilla Game Reserve and – at the end of the river's run – Coorong National Park. And way beyond the colossal red gums and river cliffs there's another world to explore by 4WD – the vast mallee wildernesses of Ngarkat Conservation Park and Gluepot Reserve.

CAMPSITES LOCATED IN PARKS AND RESERVES

CHOWILLA GAME RESERVE AND REGIONAL RESERVE

A fascinating realm of big timber and secluded creeks hugging the border with Victoria, this is a key part of the vast Bookmark Biosphere Reserve. There are great opportunities for remote bush camping and canoeing the extensive backwaters, where large stands of river red gums, black box and mallee are home to myriad waterbirds and other woodland species. The reserve is 30 km east of Renmark along Murtho Rd, or 37 km following Wentworth Rd.

Who to contact: Parks SA Berri (08) 8595 2111

95 **Border Cliffs Customs House camping area**

Spend the night camping by the mighty Murray River, accessed along Murtho Rd. You need to be self-sufficient with wood and water. **Map refs:** 215 E2, 249 O6

96 **Chowilla camping area (bush camping)**

Off Renmark–Wentworth Rd, 32 km north-east of Renmark, this reserve has many sites along the Murray River for self-sufficient campers. Access may vary depending on river levels. **Map refs:** 215 E2, 249 O6

A narrow strip of coastal dunes, the Younghusband Peninsula extends for more than 100 km. It encloses an equally slender series of saline lagoons, a wetland habitat visited by more than 230 bird species. The homelands of the Ngarrindjeri people, this is a landscape of subtle natural wonders, and accordingly is an area of international ecological and historical significance. The beaches are accessible by 4WD, and are much-loved fishing and camping haunts. There are plenty of peaceful camping and walking destinations dotted along the park's mainland fringes. Exploring the lagoons by small boat or canoe is the ideal way to enjoy this region and the extraordinary sandscapes of the peninsula.

Who to contact: Parks SA Coorong (08) 8575 1200

97 **28 Mile Crossing camping area**

One of several locations for self-sufficient campers in the southern reaches of the park, 28 Mile Crossing is 30 km north of Kingston SE, with access off Old Coorong Rd. A permit is required from the self-registration station. **Map refs:** 215 C7, 247 E7

98 **32 Mile Crossing camping area**

An exposed coastal site close to the beach access track, this camping area for self-sufficient campers is reached from the Princes Hwy, 39 km north of Kingston SE. Pick up a permit from the self-registration station. **Map refs:** 215 C7, 247 E7

99 **42 Mile Crossing camping area**

The most popular entry to the main ocean beach, this camping area for self-sufficient campers is accessible to all vehicles in all weather, although the final 1.3 km to the beach is a 4WD and walking track. The camping area is 22 km south of Salt Creek and 48 km north of Kingston SE, off the Princes Hwy. A permit is required from the self-registration station. **Map refs:** 215 C7, 247 E7

100 **Barker Knoll camping area (boat-based camping)**

This is a great beach location for self-sufficient campers, right at the Murray Mouth and reached only by boat via Goolwa or Mundoo Channel, or from Hindmarsh Island. Pick up a permit from the self-registration station. **Map refs:** 215 A5, 247 C5, 249 K11

101 **Godfreys Landing camping area (boat-based camping)**

Beach camping just south of the Murray Mouth is accessible by boat only. Come equipped for self-sufficient camping, and pick up a permit from the self-registration station. There is a limit of 6 people per site. **Map refs:** 215 A5, 247 C5, 249 K11

102 Long Point camping area

There are good views of the northern lagoon from this site for self-sufficient campers on the eastern shore, and there's access to a small jetty. It's 26 km west of Meningie off Long Point Rd. A permit is required from the self-registration station. **Map refs:** 215 B6, 247 C5, 249 K11

103 Loop Road camping area

Pleasant bush sites are scattered among the mallee and tea-tree scrub close to Salt Creek, with good nature walks nearby. It is situated 60 km south of Meningie, 4 km south of Salt Creek, on Loop Rd. **Map refs:** 215 C7, 247 E6

104 Mark Point camping area

Close to the water, with a boat launch, Mark Point is reached from Mark Point Rd, 35 km west of Meningie. Permits are available from self-registration stations within the park. **Map refs:** 215 B5, 247 C5, 249 K11

105 Ocean Beach camping areas (bush camping)

Bush camping sites are available at different points along the ocean beach. Only designated sites can be used, and vehicles and tents must be kept within marked areas. Beach access by 4WD only is via 28 Mile Crossing, Wreck Crossing, 32 Mile Crossing, 42 Mile Crossing and Tea Tree Crossing. Use caution. Camping permits are available from self-registration stations within the park. Note: in order to protect nesting hooded plovers, the beach is closed to all traffic north of Tea Tree Crossing from 24 Oct to 24 Dec. **Map refs:** 215 C7, 247 E7

106 Old Coorong Road camping areas (bush camping)

In the far south of the park there are bush camping options along Old Coorong Rd, starting from 26 km north of Kingston SE. Follow the signs, bring water and wood as fires are allowed between high and low tides, and pick up a permit from a self-registration station within the park. **Map refs:** 215 C7, 247 E7

107 Parnka Point camping area

There are fine views and sheltered sites from this peninsula, 23 km south of Meningie, close to the narrows marking the boundary between the north and south lagoons. Accessed from the Princes Hwy, the camping area is 2.1 km off the road. Pick up a permit from the self-registration station and come equipped for self-sufficient camping. **Map refs:** 215 B6, 247 D6, 249 L12

108 Tea Tree Crossing camping area

This camping area for self-sufficient campers has 4WD access only in late summer, owing to lagoon levels. It's 9 km south of Salt Creek via Loop Rd; a permit is required. **Map refs:** 215 C7, 247 E7

GLUEPOT RESERVE

An expansive and much-loved sanctuary managed by Birds Australia, Gluepot Reserve occupies 50 000 ha of pristine mallee scrub. Home to some 197 bird species – including 6 that are nationally endangered – this must-see destination is surprisingly accessible, just 1.5 hr north of Waikerie. Facilities include a visitor information centre, campgrounds, birdhides, driving and walking tracks. Guided tours are also available. Note: in times of extreme heat, fire danger or heavy rains the reserve may be closed; check with rangers.

Who to contact: Gluepot Reserve Rangers (08) 8892 8600

109 Gluepot Reserve camping area

There are 5 separate sites for self-sufficient campers (gas/fuel stove only) located within the reserve, 64 km north of Waikerie. The reserve is accessed from Lunn Rd off Morgan–Renmark Rd. **Map refs:** 215 D1, 249 M6

GUM LAGOON CONSERVATION PARK

This 7000 ha reserve protects one of the many remnant wetlands in the south-east region. A wild area of paperbark forest, heathland and relic dune rises, it suits experienced wilderness walkers and campers equipped with 4WD vehicles.

Who to contact: Parks SA Naracoorte (08) 8762 3412

110 Gum Lagoon camping area (bush camping)

Self-sufficient bush camping is signposted off Keith–Cantara Rd, 44 km south-west of Keith. Access to the camping area requires a 4WD. **Map refs:** 215 D7, 247 F7

KARTE CONSERVATION PARK

This rolling dune landscape clad in mallee scrub and native pines, with a dense understorey of broom bush, is home to a diverse mix of wildlife, from western grey kangaroos and echidnas to mallee fowl and the endangered mallee whipbird. This is one of the more accessible mallee parks, popular for picnics and day walks among the steep dunes. It's 30 km north-west of Pinnaroo.

Who to contact: Parks SA Lameroo (08) 8576 3690

111 Karte camping area (bush camping)

Bush camping (permit required) is allowed in the northern corner of the park, with vehicle access off Karte Rd, 30 km north-west of Pinnaroo. It is popular with mallee-fowl watchers. **Map refs:** 215 E4, 247 G3, 249 N10

LOCH LUNA GAME RESERVE

Within easy reach of Barmera and Overland Corner, this wetland reserve is good for camping and as a base for canoeing, boating and fishing. There are many creeks and shallow swamps to explore, home to large populations of waterfowl and other birdlife. Signposted access – dry weather only for conventional vehicles – is off the Sturt Hwy 14 km north-west of Barmera.

Who to contact: Parks SA Berri (08) 8595 2111

112 Chambers Creek camping area

Several sites for self-sufficient camping (permit required) are dotted along Chambers Creek, reached from Nappers Bridge on Morgan Rd, 11 km north-west of Barmera. **Map refs:** 215 D2, 247 F1, 249 N7

LOWAN CONSERVATION PARK

A virtual island of intact mallee scrub amidst farmland just east of the Murray, halfway between Bow Hill and Karoonda, this quiet reserve is a nesting habitat for mallee fowl. It's also home to a diverse mix of wildlife, from echidnas and dunnarts to wedge-tailed eagles.

Who to contact: Parks SA Lameroo (08) 8576 3690

113 Lowan camping area (bush camping)

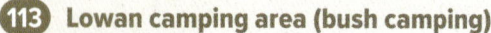

Offering self-sufficient bush camping, with no facilities, this camping area is reached from the park entrance on the northern boundary on Bow Hill–Karoonda Rd, 13 km south-east of Bow Hill. There's plenty of wildlife on show. **Map refs:** 215 C4, 247 E3, 249 L9

MAIZE ISLAND LAGOON CONSERVATION PARK

This is classic Murray River backwater country with lagoons overlooked by massive red gums. It's just 2 km out of Waikerie and offers great scope for canoeing, bird-spotting and fishing.

Who to contact: Parks SA Berri (08) 8595 2111

114 Maize Island camping area (bush camping)

This site offers bush camping with no facilities and is reached from Holder Settlement Rd. Note: you need a permit to camp here; gas fires are allowed. **Map refs:** 215 D2, 247 F1, 249 M7

MESSENT CONSERVATION PARK

One of the most diverse and significant reserves in the coastal hinterland of the south-east region, this conservation park features contrasting landscapes of old dune rises and limestone outcrops, with low-lying flats that become winter wetlands. It's a peaceful place for exploratory walks, wildlife-watching and spring wildflower displays. The Central Track provides 4WD access from the south-west to north-east corners of the park, which is 26 km south-west of Tintinara.

Who to contact: Parks SA Coorong (08) 8575 1200

115 Messent camping area (bush camping)

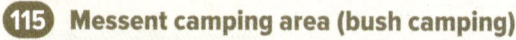

Remote bush camping is reached from Bellar Rd if you're coming from the north, or from Salt Creek Rd if accessing from the south. Contact Parks SA for camping details and a permit. **Map refs:** 215 C6, 247 E6, 249 L12

MOOROOK GAME RESERVE

Creeks, lagoons and flood plains take in the sweep of river west of Cobdogla. The reserve includes Wachtels Lagoon and several narrow channels suitable for canoeing and birdwatching.

Who to contact: Parks SA Berri (08) 8595 2111

116 Cooba camping area

Located 17 km south-west of Barmera, this area for self-sufficient campers is signposted off Moorook–Loxton Rd (a permit is required). **Map refs:** 215 D2, 247 F1, 249 N7

MORGAN CONSERVATION PARK

Directly opposite Morgan, on the eastern side of the Murray River, this reserve secures river flats that fill at times of high water. Inland the park features mallee-clad dune rises, with ruby saltbush and hop-bush. Take care swimming.

Who to contact: Parks SA Berri (08) 8595 2111

117 Morgan camping area (bush camping)

There is peaceful bush camping at this site (permits required), accessed by ferry from Morgan or via Cadell Rd on the eastern side of the river. There is also plenty of birdlife on display. **Map refs:** 215 C2, 249 L6

MURRAY RIVER NATIONAL PARK

Covering 13 000 ha, this extended archipelago of flood plains is traversed by a wonderful network of creeks and backwaters. It offers some of the finest canoe touring and riverside camping in the state. The park comprises 3 sections: the remote creek system of Katarapko, accessible Lyrup Flats, and the northern flood-plain outlier, Bulyong Island.

Who to contact: Parks SA Berri (08) 8595 2111

118 Bulyong Island camping area (boat-based camping)

Separated from the mainland by Ral Ral Creek, this island north-east of Renmark is only accessible by boat. Approach from Renmark and the nearby landings signposted off Ral Ral Ave. **Map refs:** 215 E2, 247 G1, 249 O7

119 Colligans camping area

Signposted off the Sturt Hwy, 12 km south-west of Renmark, numerous campsites for self-sufficient campers are scattered along the Murray River. **Map refs:** 215 E2, 247 G1, 249 N7

120 Eckerts Creek Section camping area

Sites for self-sufficient campers are scattered along Eckerts Creek, 12 km south-west of Berri off Lower Winkie Rd, reached from the Sturt Hwy. A permit is required from the self-registration station at the park entrance. Note: the site can be closed at times of high water. **Map refs:** 215 D3, 247 G1, 249 N7

121 Katarapko Extension Section camping area

There are 9 riverside campsites found here, 5 km south-west of Berri off Draper Rd. Pick up a permit from the self-registration station at the park entrance. This is self-sufficient camping, so bring wood and water. **Map refs:** 215 E2, 247 G1, 249 N7

122 Katarapko Section camping area

There is an array of sites set along Katarapko Creek, 16 km south-west of Berri off Katarapko Rd. Pick up a permit for self-sufficient camping from the park entrance at the self-registration station. **Map refs:** 215 D3, 247 G1, 249 N8

123 Murray River camping area (bush camping)

Self-sufficient bush camping is permitted beside the river in the Lyrup Flats section, off the Sturt Hwy, 12 km south-west of Renmark (a permit is required). The bush campsites here are dispersed along the river bank and pleasant sites abound. Fish, boat, swim, or just relax in the shade of the river red gums. **Map refs:** 215 E2, 247 G1, 249 N7

124 Tea Tree camping area

At Lyrup, near the ferry, off the Sturt Hwy 2 km south-west of Renmark, are a number of campsites for self-sufficient campers along the Murray River. This site is good for boating. A permit is required. **Map refs:** 215 E2, 247 G1, 249 N7

MURTHO FOREST RESERVE

Visitors enjoy spectacular river views from this bush site on the southern banks of the Murray River, 20 km north-east of Renmark. There are also amazing views of the crumbling red cliffs from the tower lookout at the top of the bluff.

Who to contact: Renmark Paringa Visitor Centre (08) 8586 6704

125 Headings Cliff–Murtho Forest Landing camping area

Self-sufficient camping beside the Murray River is signposted off Paringa–Murtho Rd, 16 km north-east of Renmark. This is a very pleasant bush camping site tucked in among the river red gums on the river bank, with the red and yellow bluffs as backdrop. Birdlife is plentiful here and it is a great spot for fishing or boating. There is lots of shade, and access to a boat ramp. **Map refs:** 215 E2, 249 O7

NGARKAT CONSERVATION PARK

The more than 270 000 ha of dense mallee woodlands hugging the Victorian border is a haven for wildlife. Best explored on extended overland trips, it offers serene bush camping and challenging 4WD options – especially along the Border Track. But it is a fragile environment, so drive responsibly. Buy self-serve permits at entrances to the park.

Who to contact: Parks SA Lameroo (08) 8576 3690

126 Border Track camping areas

There are 5 camping areas for well-prepared campers along the remote Border Track, on the SA–Vic. border. Only experienced drivers in high-clearance 4WD vehicles should attempt this one-way route; it's open 1 Apr to 30 Oct but contact Parks SA Lameroo before you set off. The Border Track is reached from Pine Hut Soak. **Map refs:** 215 E5, 247 H5, 249 O11

127 Box Flat camping area

This natural soak and seasonal wetland offers shaded campsites. Nearby ruins tell the tale of thwarted attempts to farm this area. Access is off Baan Hill Track, 38 km south of Lameroo. **Map refs:** 215 D5, 247 F5, 249 N11

128 Bucks Camp Soakage camping area

This is a good overnight option for those on the Dukes Hwy. Access is signposted off the hwy, 16 km north-west of Keith; drive for a further 9 km to this birdwatchers' site. **Map refs:** 215 D6, 247 F6, 249 N12

129 Comet Bore camping area

A birdwatchers' favourite, this site is also great for large groups. It is 60 km south of Pinnaroo, on the Bordertown–Pinnaroo Rd. **Map refs:** 215 E6, 247 G5, 249 O12

130 Doggers Hut camping area

Open all year round on the 2-way section of the Border Track, this is the last campsite as you head south along the track before exiting the park. Only accessible by 4WD, this shady campsite has sufficient room for a medium-size group. **Map refs:** 215 E6, 247 H5, 249 O12

131 Pertendi Hut camping area

All-vehicle access is possible to this popular site, a restored historic hut and picnic area. Walking trails explore the mallee vegetation. Signposted access is off Pinnaroo–Bordertown Rd, 48 km south of Pinnaroo. **Map refs:** 215 E6, 247 G5, 249 O11

132 Pine Hut Soak camping area

The start of many hikes, this site has a picnic table and toilets, and can handle caravans. Check road conditions with Parks SA if there has been rain. Follow the sign 5 km south of Pinnaroo via Rosy Pine Rd. **Map refs:** 215 E5, 247 G4, 249 O11

133 Rabbit Island Soak camping area

Good for smaller groups, and accessible with 4WD only, this site is also popular with birdwatchers. It's on the Mt Rescue Loop, 30 km north of Keith. **Map refs:** 215 D6, 247 F6, 249 N12

PEEBINGA CONSERVATION PARK

Originally set aside to protect the rare western whipbird, this isolated park features low-relief dunes with grassland and extensive mallee scrub. Bring everything you need to be self-sufficient. It's accessible for caravans.

Who to contact: Parks SA Lameroo (08) 8576 3690

134 **Peebinga camping area (bush camping)**

Bush camping is permitted 37 km north of Pinnaroo, reached from the Pinnaroo–Loxton Rd via the Kringin turn-off.
Map refs: 215 E4, 247 G3, 249 O9

POOCHER SWAMP GAME RESERVE

Poocher Swamp Game Reserve lies 8 km west of Bordertown, covering 77 ha. An attractive wetland area where mature river red gums grow, it is important as a habitat for many bird species – ducks, egrets and spoonbills are among the many to be seen when the swamp has filled after rain.

Who to contact: Parks SA Naracoorte (08) 8762 3412

135 **Poocher Swamp camping area**

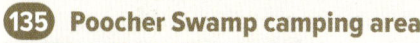

In the Poocher Swamp Game Reserve camping area, on Cannawigara Rd 9 km west of Bordertown, large river red gums and abundant birdlife feature. There are no facilities, so come prepared to be self-sufficient. **Map refs:** 215 E7, 247 G7

POOGINOOK CONSERVATION PARK

Rolling dune and mallee country lies off the beaten track north-east of Waikerie, protected by this 2852 ha park. The mix of original habitat and revegetation zones is home to mallee fowl, wombats, kangaroos and echidnas. Visit in spring to see wildflowers burst into colour.

Who to contact: Parks SA Berri (08) 8595 2111

136 **Pooginook camping area**

Conventional vehicles can access this basic campground, though other park tracks are 4WD only. It's situated 28 km north-east of Waikerie along the Morgan–Renmark Rd, 29 km west of the Nappers Bridge turn-off. **Map refs:** 215 D2, 249 M7

RIDLEY CONSERVATION PARK

This small, extremely slender park occupies a former stock route on the western side of the Swan Reach–Mannum Rd. The park was created for wombat conservation, and burrows are often in evidence on softer ground among the limestone plains. A mix of mallee vegetation, grassland and native pines creates a quiet haven for woodland birds.

Who to contact: Parks SA Lameroo (08) 8576 3690

137 **Ridley camping area (bush camping)**

Self-sufficient bush camping is permitted in the park, 8 km south of Swan Reach on the way to Mannum. **Map refs:** 215 C3, 247 D2, 249 L8

SWAN REACH CONSERVATION PARK

This grassland and mallee park is on the Swan Reach–Sedan Rd, 10 km west of Swan Reach. Species like mallee box and red mallee provide habitats for an array of birds. This is a quiet spot for walks and nature observation.

Who to contact: Parks SA Lameroo (08) 8576 3690

138 **Swan Reach camping area (bush camping)**

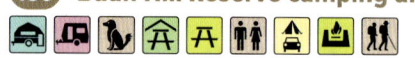

Sites for self-sufficient bush camping are signposted off Swan Reach–Sedan Rd, 10 km west of Swan Reach. Near here, on an unsealed road off the Swan Reach–Walker Flat Rd, are spectacular views of the Murray River and the cliffs at Big Bend. The area is great for birdwatching. The orange and yellow cliffs are especially impressive in the glow of late afternoon.
Map refs: 215 C3, 247 D2, 249 L8

CAMPSITES LOCATED IN OTHER AREAS

139 **Baan Hill Reserve camping area**

This is a popular picnic spot and overnight camp for self-sufficient 4WD parties overlanding through Ngarkat Conservation Park. It is situated 23.5 km south of Lameroo; take the Lameroo South Rd, turn west onto Trowbridge Rd and then south onto Baan Hill Rd. **Map refs:** 215 D5, 247 F5, 249 N11

Who to contact: Southern Mallee District Council (08) 8576 3002

140 **Berri Riverside Caravan Park**

This is an award-winning park with recently renovated amenities, including a solar-heated pool, school-holiday activities for the kids, a jumping pillow and plenty of space to camp alongside the great Murray River. The site is only a 10 min walk to the town centre, and the closest boat ramp is 250 m away. There is a well-equipped camp kitchen, and plenty of shaded sites to choose from. Animals are allowed at the manager's discretion, but not during peak periods. **Map refs:** 215 E2, 247 G1, 249 N7

How to book: Riverview Dr, Berri (08) 8582 3723
www.berricaravanpark.com.au

141 **Coorong Wilderness Lodge**

The lodge has top-line accommodation and modern cabins, camping sites and a bunkhouse. The Coorong is home to more than 230 species of waterbirds and shorebirds, and is a wetland of international importance. The Ngarrindjeri custodians run tours by 4WD or canoe, covering bush tucker, history, traditional crafts and environmental issues. **Map refs:** 215 B6, 247 D6, 249 L12

How to book: Hacks Pt, Meningie (08) 8575 6001
www.coorongwildernesslodge.com

142 Jimmies Waterhole camping area

There is self-sufficient camping off the beaten track in the small settlement of Mundulla, just minutes from the busy Dukes Hwy. This site is beside Mundulla Swamp with access off Rowney Rd, 10 km west of Bordertown. **Map refs:** 215 E7, 247 G7

Who to contact: Bordertown Visitor Information Centre (08) 8752 0700

143 John S Christian Reserve camping area

There's self-sufficient camping on Marne Valley Rd, 15 km north-west of Walker Flat, beside the Marne River. **Map refs:** 215 C3, 247 D2, 249 L8

Who to contact: Mid Murray Council (08) 8569 0100

144 Lameroo Lakeside Caravan Park

Camping is available at the caravan park in this small farming town. Contact the local hotel for bookings. Located next to Lake Roberts, this park has powered and unpowered sites. **Map refs:** 215 D5, 247 G4, 249 N10

How to book: 80 Railway Tce, Lameroo (08) 8576 3006 www.lameroohotelmotel.com.au

MURRAY RIVER

Opportunities to relax at a campsite beside the river are dotted along the Murray's banks in a variety of public picnic spots and reserves. Many are simple with few or no facilities, and you need to come with wood, water and a gas/fuel stove. Most give direct access to the water for fishing, swimming and boating.

Who to contact: Mid Murray Council (08) 8569 0100 for campsite nos **145**, **146**, **147**, **148**, **153**, **155**; Waikerie Tourist Information Centre (08) 8541 2332 for campsite no. **149**; Berri Visitor Centre (08) 8582 5511 for campsite no. **150**; District Council of Loxton-Waikerie (08) 8584 7221 for campsite nos **151**, **154**; Renmark Paringa Visitor Information Centre (08) 8586 6704 for campsite no. **152**

145 Bolto Reserve camping area

On Khartoum Rd, this camping area is south of the ferry on the east side of the river, in the Morgan-to-Mannum stretch of the Murray River. Pay fees to the council. **Map refs:** 215 B4, 247 D3, 249 L9

146 Caurnamont Riverside Reserve camping area

Just across the water from Purnong, Caurnamont is a small cluster of riverside shacks on the Morgan-to-Mannum stretch of the Murray River. The reserve is in the village, beside the ferry. **Map refs:** 215 C4, 247 E3, 249 L9

147 Haythorpe Reserve camping area

This reserve is in Mannum, on the eastern side of the river

on Bowhill Rd, north of the ferry. The site has a boat ramp. **Map refs:** 215 B4, 247 D3, 249 L9

148 Hettner Landing camping area

On the northern side of Walker Flat village on Walker Flat Rd, this camping area is on the Morgan-to-Mannum stretch of the Murray River. **Map refs:** 215 C3, 247 D2, 249 L8

149 Hogwash Bend camping area

This popular camping area, halfway between Morgan and Waikerie in the Renmark-to-Morgan stretch of the Murray River, is good for tents and vans. It is off Morgan–Waikerie Rd, 21 km north-west of Waikerie. **Map refs:** 215 C2, 249 M7

150 Martin Bend camping area

Located around 3 km east of Berri, this camping area is signposted off Martin Bend Rd from Riverview Dr, in the Renmark-to-Morgan stretch of the Murray River. **Map refs:** 215 E2, 247 G1, 249 N7

151 Moorook Reserve camping area

Riverfront camping is provided 7 km south of the Sturt Hwy on Moorook–Loxton Rd, in the Renmark-to-Morgan stretch of the Murray River. **Map refs:** 215 E3, 247 G2, 249 N8

152 Plushs Bend camping area

On the outskirts of Renmark in the Renmark-to-Morgan stretch of the Murray River, this camping area is reached from 23rd St. **Map refs:** 215 E2, 247 G1, 249 O7

153 Purnong Riverside Reserve camping area

In Purnong village beside the ferry on Purnong Rd, this camping area is on the Morgan-to-Mannum stretch of the Murray River. This is a large grassy clearing next to the ferry landing, shaded by mature river red gums. **Map refs:** 215 C4, 247 E3, 249 L9

154 Ramco Point camping area

This area is situated 5 km west of Waikerie on Ramco Point Rd in the Renmark-to-Morgan stretch of the Murray River. Access to this riverside camping area is signposted off Waikerie–Cadell Rd. **Map refs:** 215 C2, 247 E1, 249 M7

155 Walker Flat Boat Ramp Reserve camping area

On the southern side of Walker Flat village, 31 km north of Mannum, this campsite is on the Morgan-to-Mannum stretch of the Murray River, with great natural cliff views. **Map refs:** 215 C3, 247 D2, 249 L9

FLINDERS RANGES AND OUTBACK

AT THE HEAD OF Spencer Gulf one ocean ends and another begins. Beyond Port Augusta, a vast inland sea of dunes, gibber and mallee spreads north for nearly 1000 km to the heart of the continent. It's challenging country, home to the austere surfaces of the Simpson, Sturt Stony and Strzelecki deserts, not to mention the daunting salt-crust kingdoms of lakes Eyre, Torrens and Frome.

Yet hidden among all this there are many surprises, including some of Australia's greatest wetlands and waterholes. During years of bumper rains or incoming floodwaters, the desert blooms like nowhere else. It's a landscape that people have lived and travelled in for tens of thousands of years. Famed overland routes like the Birdsville, Ooodnadatta and Strzelecki tracks uphold this tradition. Along these tracks people have always gathered around campfires under skies full of stars for stories and songs. Now, with the advent of popular 4WD travel, a new generation of adventurers is voyaging inland.

For many, the magificent Flinders Ranges is the bridge to the outback. These steep sawtooth ridges stretch for 400 km, snaking from rolling wheat country to the desert's doorstep. It's a gritty, complex world of ravines and towering sandstone peaks. At the same time, the nearby valleys and open gorge country offer some of Australia's finest camping experiences, nestled among groves of native pine and mighty river red gums. Many such sites enjoy outstanding views of the surrounding ranges with their craggy, ochre-hued summits etched against brilliant blue skies.

The outback is a place just made for journeying and there's a rich history and living Aboriginal culture to connect with. It's great country to explore – whether you're tackling a rugged ridge-top drive, bushwalking deep into a gorge or paddling a canoe along the legendary Cooper Creek.

CAMPSITES LOCATED IN PARKS AND RESERVES

DANGGALI CONSERVATION PARK

Covering more than 253 000 ha, this vast sweep of dryland mallee hugs the border of NSW, 90 km north of Renmark. In 1977 it became Australia's first biosphere reserve, in recognition of the habitat's significance and scale. A great region for birdwatching, this remote park also has walking and vehicle tracks to explore. There are several options for bush camping around the huge park and sites with firepits near the camp HQ in the south. You need to be self-sufficient: bring all food, water and fuel.

Who to contact: Parks SA Danggali (08) 8595 8010

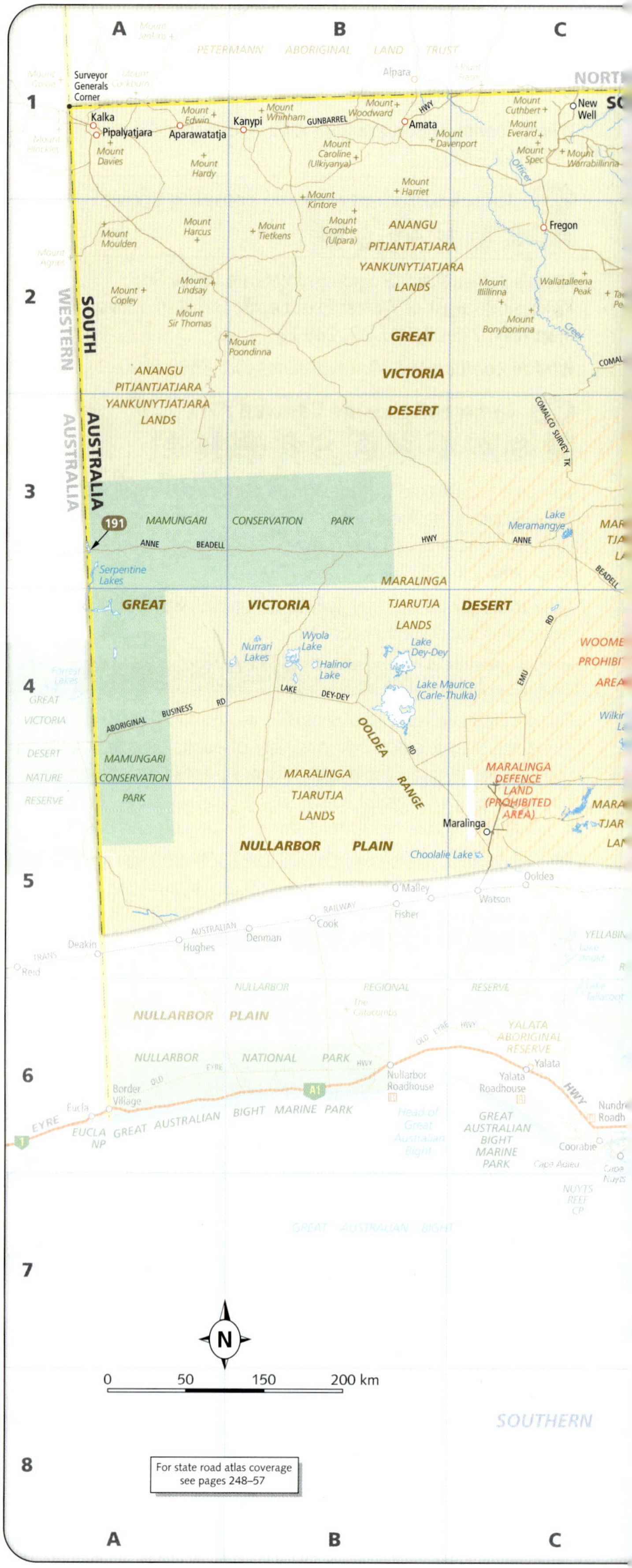

For state road atlas coverage see pages 248–57

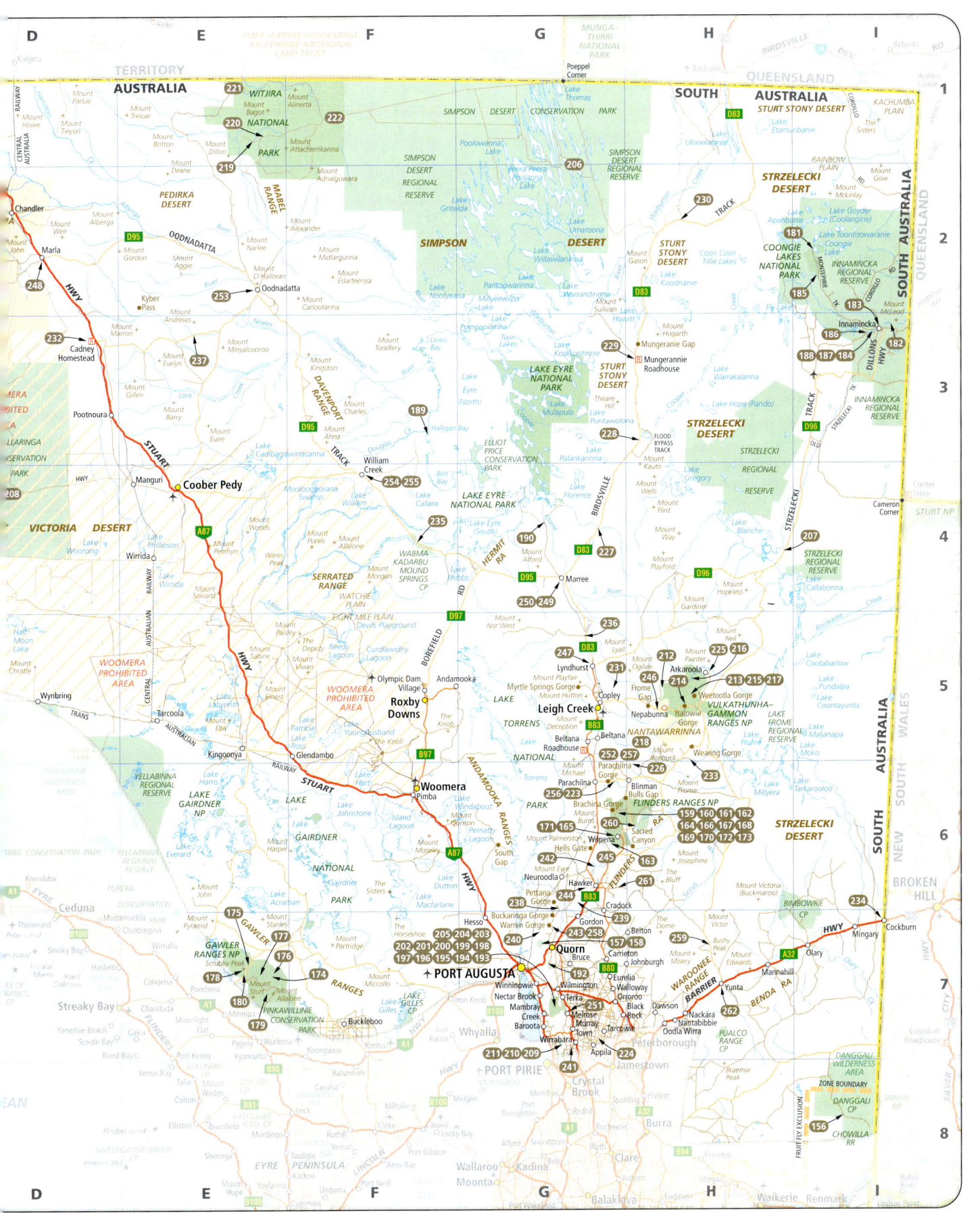

156 Canopus Homestead camping areas

Canopus has a large site located near the Ranger HQ with toilets and shelter, but there are 5 other bush camping options within a few km of the homestead. All have room for vans and pit fires, and are for self-sufficient campers only.
Map refs: 223 I8, 249 O5, 251 M12

THE DUTCHMANS STERN CONSERVATION PARK

Though small, this park has dramatic landforms and one of the best day-walks in the state. It's perched at the head of Spencer Gulf and is the northernmost stronghold of sugar gum woodland in the Flinders Ranges. The climb to the summit of the bluff reveals memorable views north and west. There is bush camping for self-sufficient walkers and the famed Heysen Trail also winds this way.

Who to contact: Parks SA Port Pirie (08) 8634 7068; or Friends of the Heysen Trail (08) 8212 6299

157 The Dutchmans Stern camping area (walk-in camping)

There is no vehicle-based camping here, so it's walk in and be self-sufficient. Many sites are provided west of the Dutchman Range, reached from Arden Vale Rd, 10 km north of Quorn.
Map refs: 223 G7, 249 I1, 250 G9

158 Old Homestead and Shearers Quarters camping area

Only walk-in camping is allowed in Dutchmans Stern Conservation Park, but these huts on the northern boundary track are a good option for overnight shelter if you aren't carrying a tent. This camping area is on the Heysen Trail.
Map refs: 223 G7, 249 I1, 250 G9

FLINDERS RANGES NATIONAL PARK

With astonishing Wilpena Pound as its centrepiece, this park packs tremendous visual punch. There's so much landscape laid bare that even taking a drive or relaxing in camp can be a captivating experience. Take to the Heysen Trail or jump on a mountain bike and an even richer story is revealed – a world of hidden waterholes, spring wildflowers, Aboriginal rock-art sites, abundant wildlife and geological grandeur.

Who to contact: Wilpena Pound Visitor Centre (08) 8648 0048; or Friends of the Heysen Trail (08) 8212 6299

159 Acraman camping area

Nestled in the ranges, this area for self-sufficient campers is a handy base for exploring the Heysen Trail, Bunyeroo Gorge and the scenic majesty of Bunyeroo Valley and Wilpena Pound. From the visitor centre it's 30 spectacular km along Bunyeroo Gorge Rd. There are only 4 sites and permits are required.
Map refs: 223 G6, 251 I6

160 Aroona Ruins camping area

Close to the historic Aroona Ruins, this site has fine outlooks to the Heysen and ABC ranges. It's also at the start of the Heysen Trail's final dash up the beautiful Aroona Valley to Parachilna Gorge. It's close to Aroona Hut, a basic shelter. Located 6 km along Aroona Rd from the Brachina Gorge track, there are limited caravan sites; van access is via Blinman Rd.
Map refs: 223 G6, 251 I6

161 Brachina East camping area

The gateway to all the Brachina action, this campground for self-sufficient campers is accessible from the east by 2WD and is pleasantly situated on the banks of Brachina Creek. Signposted along Brachina Gorge Rd, 48 km north-west of Wilpena Pound Visitor Centre, there are 2WD and 4WD sites.
Map refs: 223 G6, 251 I6

162 Brachina Gorge camping area (bush camping)

Through the twists and turns of the gorge there are several designated nooks for bush camping. Many have fine views of features like Heysen Hill and The Guardian, though in peak sightseeing times there can be a lot of vehicle traffic close by. Off-road camper trailers can access this area; you need to bring in your own water, firewood and preferably a gas/fuel stove.
Map refs: 223 G6, 251 I6

163 Bridle Gap camping area (walk-in camping)

On the Heysen Trail, at the very southern end of the Flinders Ranges park, this basic site has spectacular views over Elder Range. There are no facilities and no fires are allowed: bring water and a gas/fuel stove. A permit is required.
Map refs: 223 G6, 251 I7

164 Cambrian camping area

Self-sufficient campers will find 13 sites at this 4WD-access campground off Bunyeroo Gorge Rd, 37 km north-west of the park HQ. This is a pleasant campground and is near the western end of Bunyeroo Gorge. The drive between Bunyeroo and Brachina gorges offers impressive views of the rugged ranges.
Map refs: 223 G6, 251 I6

165 Cooinda camping area (walk-in camping)

This sheltered but no-frills walk-in site tucked within Wilpena Pound is 12 km from the visitor centre; a permit is required. This camping area serves as a base for bushwalks to St Mary Peak and Edeowie Gorge. The views from St Mary Peak are spectacular and the climb from this side, though longer, is much easier than the scramble up the eastern side.
Map refs: 223 G6, 251 I6

166 Dingley Dell camping area

There is basic camping here in the open hill country near Oraparinna, just off Blinman Rd, 31 km north-east of the visitor centre. A permit is required. **Map refs:** 223 H6, 251 I6

167 Koolamon camping area

For classic creek-side camping among the old river red gums in the beautiful Aroona Valley, follow Aroona Rd 46 km north of the visitor centre. There are sites here for both 2WD and 4WD vehicles with camper trailers. The scenery in the Aroona Valley is spectacular. **Map refs:** 223 G6, 251 I6

168 Middlesight Water Hut camping area

On the Heysen Trail, this is an open hut in the north end of the Flinders Ranges National Park on Yanyanna Track. There are basic sleeping platforms, water and a fireplace. **Map refs:** 223 G6, 251 I6

169 Teamsters camping area

Teamsters is at the western entrance to Brachina Gorge, a short walk from some of the steepest and most colourful gorge faces. It is 42 km from Wilpena, not far from the Hawker–Leigh Creek Rd, and suits off-road trailers. **Map refs:** 223 G6, 251 I6

170 Trezona camping area

This camping area on Brachina Gorge Rd, 44 km north of Wilpena, takes its name from the ancient shales and limestones of the craggy Trezona Range. There is a self-guided nature walk here as part of the Brachina Gorge Geological Trail and this is also a stop on the Heysen Trail. Caravan access is possible from the east only. **Map refs:** 223 G6, 251 I6

171 Wilpena Pound Campground

This is the main hub for visitors and bushwalkers exploring Wilpena Pound. The extensive facilities, easy access to the nearby resort and the magnificent river red gums along Wilpena Creek make this a very popular haunt – accordingly, it pays to book for holiday stays Apr–Oct. Follow the signs off Wilpena Rd, 52 km north of Hawker. A park entrance fee applies. **Map refs:** 223 G6, 251 I6

172 Yanyanna Hut camping area

On the Heysen Trail, the basic Yanyanna Hut and its surrounding stockyards were the central point of the Aroona pastoral run in the 1850s. It is on the Yanyanna Track, between Middlesight Water Hut camping area and Wilpena Pound. **Map refs:** 223 G6, 251 I6

173 Youngoona camping area

Self-sufficient camping is available on the eastern slopes of the Trezona Range, from where walking trails loop back through historic grazing country to Aroona Valley. The site is just off the Brachina Gorge Rd, 48 km north of the visitor centre. **Map refs:** 223 G6, 251 I6

GAWLER RANGES NATIONAL PARK

One of the most ancient landscapes on earth, these ranges on the northern fringes of the Eyre Peninsula feature dome-like hills shaped from 1500 million-year-old rhyolite, as well as wooded valleys, grasslands and dazzling salt lakes. Covering 120 000 ha, this park offers excellent bush camping and walking – especially when the wildflowers bloom in early spring. The ranges are readily accessible from Iron Knob, Kimba, Wudinna and Minnipa. While conventional vehicles can navigate the outskirts of the park, the inner track network is 4WD country and all roads here are dry-weather access only. Permits apply, and campers need to be self-sufficient with water, firewood and preferably a gas/fuel stove.

Who to contact: Parks SA Port Lincoln (08) 8688 3111

174 Chillunie camping area

This is secluded no-frills camping, 4WD only, in the north-east of the park. Follow the sign from the LP Track, 9.8 km north of Paney Homestead. From the turn-off it's 3.6 km west to the camp. **Map refs:** 223 E7, 248 D2, 250 B9

175 Kododo Hill camping area

Camping in the north of the park is signposted 12.8 km north along Minnipa–Yardea Rd from the western end of Old Paney Scenic Dr. The campsite with a hot-water donkey shower is 900 m north-west of this turn-off, and is suitable for 4WDs only. **Map refs:** 223 E7, 248 C2, 250 B9

176 Kolay Hut camping area

Small but shaded sites in open country are found on the north-east side of the park, with the organ-pipe formation of Kolay Falls close by. The hut access is 12.1 km north of Paney Homestead via the LP Track, and it is 4WD access only. The site has a hot-water donkey shower. **Map refs:** 223 E7, 248 D2, 250 B9

177 Mattera camping area

This valley, tucked away in the heart of the park, has an array of sheltered sites. Signposted access is along Mattera Track, 8.4 km north of Old Paney Scenic Dr, followed by a further 2.4 km drive west to the camping area. Access is for 4WDs only. **Map refs:** 223 E7, 248 D2, 250 B9

178 Scrubby Peak camping area

The signposted turn-off to Scrubby Peak is 8.1 km north of the western end of Old Paney Scenic Dr. It's another 900 m west to the camping area, which has a hot-water donkey shower and is suitable for off-road camper trailers. During wet weather, only 4WDs can reach it. **Map refs:** 223 E7, 248 C2, 250 B9, 257 P9

179 Waganny camping area

Pleasant open woodland camping is surrounded by dome-like granite hills to explore, and views of the Blue Sturts. Signposted access is 13 km west of Paney Homestead via the Old Paney Scenic Dr, which is suitable for off-road trailers and caravans; it's a further 3 km south from the turn-off to the camping area. **Map refs:** 223 E7, 248 D2, 250 B10

180 Yandinga camping area

For accessible camping near the western entrance to the park, take the signposted turn-off 3.1 km north of the western end of Old Paney Scenic Dr. It's another 600 m west to the sites; the road is suitable for off-road camper trailers and the site has a hot-water donkey shower. **Map refs:** 223 E7, 248 C2, 250 B9, 257 P9

INNAMINCKA REGIONAL RESERVE

This extensive reserve on SA's north-eastern border with Queensland is home to some of inland Australia's most varied habitats – from scorching gibber plains to lush waterholes and wetlands. It's also a dynamic landscape. During wet years, the network of dry creeks and flood plains erupts with plant and animal life. Yet even through drier seasons there are the permanent waters of Coongie Lakes and Cullyamurra Waterhole, both great haunts for camping, canoeing, fishing and birdwatching. A region rich in Aboriginal culture spanning thousands of years, it's also immortalised in the history of European exploration, largely due to the ill-fated Burke and Wills expedition. While conventional vehicles can access locations near Innamincka, much of the reserve can only be explored by 4WD. Dogs are allowed in some locations provided they are kept on a lead, but no pets are permitted in Coongie National Park. Check with rangers as some sites can be closed due to weather.

Who to contact: Desert Parks Hotline 1800 816 078

181 Coongie Lake camping area

This wonderfully remote wetland is birdwatching heaven, with a stunning array of waterbirds and raptors. There's a choice of idyllic lake-front campsites, and unlimited scope for canoeing, photography and nature walks. Access is via the 4WD-only Coongie Track, 106 km north-west of Innamincka. A permit is required and you need to bring water and a gas/fuel stove. As this camping area is within Coongie Lakes National Park, no fires, pets, fishing, generators or powerboats are allowed. **Map refs:** 223 I2, 253 M5

182 Cullyamurra Waterhole camping area

To reach one of Australia's grandest waterholes, with spectacular red gums and abundant birdlife, take the sign-posted turn-off 7 km east of Innamincka on the Innamincka–Nappamerrie Rd. It's another 7 km to an array of waterfront campsites along the south side of Cooper Creek; a permit is required. Powerboats up to 10 hp are allowed (but speed has to be kept under 10 knots). **Map refs:** 223 I3, 253 N7

183 Innamincka Town Common camping area

Basic camping in the heart of town is offered close to the pub and store, run by the local progress association. Hotel-style accommodation is also available. Coin-operated hot showers are opposite the store. **Map refs:** 223 I3, 253 N7

184 Kings Site camping area

Basic camping (permit required) is offered at the site where John King, the sole survivor of the Burke and Wills expedition, was found. It's 5 km south-west of Innamincka, off the Fifteen Mile Track. Powerboats with motors up to 10 hp are permitted (speeds under 10 knots only). **Map refs:** 223 I3, 253 N7

185 Kudriemitchie Outstation camping area

This historic pastoral outstation en route to Coongie Lakes National Park is 85 km north-west of Innamincka along the 4WD Coongie Track. You need a permit to camp here. **Map refs:** 223 I2, 253 M6

186 Minkie Waterhole camping area

This expansive waterhole, 9 km south-west of Innamincka, is a more secluded alternative to the ever-popular Cullyamurra sites; a permit is required. Birdlife is abundant and a quiet camp under the mature river red gums at this lesser-known waterhole is a great base from which to explore the area. Access is via the Fifteen Mile Track. **Map refs:** 223 I3, 253 N7

187 Policemans Waterhole camping area

Just 2 km south-west of Innamincka along Fifteen Mile Track, this camping area requires a permit and allows powerboats with motors up to 10 hp (speeds under 10 knots). **Map refs:** 223 I3, 253 N7

188 Ski Beach camping area

Located 4 km south-west of Innamincka, with signposted access from Fifteen Mile Track, this camping area permits powerboats with motors up to 10 hp (speeds under 10 knots); a permit is required to camp here. **Map refs:** 223 I3, 253 N7

LAKE EYRE NATIONAL PARK

Covering 8000 sq km, this colossal expanse – the world's largest salt pan – has only filled with water a handful of times in the past 150 years. Its blazing white crust is a sublime, dazzling spectacle and in flood years the surrounding dunes and shorelines come alive with waterbirds, raptors and reptiles. It has recently been returned to the area's traditional owners, the Arabuna people, after a long court battle. Access to the lake's edge is restricted to 4WD vehicles via signposted roads from the gateway towns of Marree and William Creek. Conventional vehicles can reach the camping sites at Muloorina Station. No boating is allowed on the lake.

Who to contact: Desert Parks Hotline 1800 816 078

189 Halligan Point camping area

The only designated camping area on the lake rim has sites along the western shores of Halligan Point, 71 km east of William Creek. A great place to birdwatch, relax and absorb the dazzling white open spaces. Access is off the Oodnadatta Track just south of William Creek and is suitable for 4WD vehicles only. Note: the last 10 km involves soft-sand driving. **Map refs:** 223 F3, 252 E9

190 Muloorina Homestead camping area

This bore-fed billabong on the Frome River, 51 km north of Marree, is a handy staging point for 4WD visits to Lake Eyre and Lake Eyre South. Signposted access is provided along the Muloorina Station road from Marree. It's privately owned, and you will need to come with your own water. Gas stoves only. **Map refs:** 223 G4, 252 G11

MAMUNGARI CONSERVATION PARK

Hugging the SA–WA border, this isolated park is jointly managed with traditional owners and encompasses a wild, challenging span of the Great Victoria Desert. Visits are restricted to permit holders with extensive experience in remote-area 4WD travel. Access is from Coober Pedy via Mabel Creek Station and the rugged Anne Beadell Hwy, or north from the Nullarbor via Cook through Aboriginal land. You must obtain permits to travel in the park – contact the Maralinga Tjarutja Administrator for further information.

Who to contact: Maralinga Tjarutja Administrator (08) 8625 2946

191 Bush camping areas

Self-sufficient bush camping is permitted in natural cleared areas within 100 m of the Anne Beadell Hwy. Permits are required and you need to lodge a detailed itinerary sheet. **Map refs:** 222 A3, 254 B9

MOUNT BROWN CONSERVATION PARK

Mt Brown is one of the highest peaks in the Flinders Ranges, at 964 m, and is popular with bushwalkers looking for wildlife and rugged landscapes. It has established walking tracks, including a section of the Heysen Trail as well as 2 other good walks. A 15 km loop walk (7–8 hrs) from Waukarie Falls, on the spur track to the Mt Brown summit, is a favourite with geologists, as the rocks and slopes along the way contain evidence of a 1 km deep canyon formed some 600 million years ago. Another hike is a 11.6 km return trek from the Olive Grove Trailhead to the summit. The lookout here commemorates Robert Brown, the naturalist aboard Matthew Flinders' *Investigator*, and offers great views over the southern ranges and Spencer Gulf.

Who to contact: Parks SA Mambray Creek (08) 8634 7068; or Friends of the Heysen Trail (08) 8212 6299

192 Waukarie Creek–Mount Brown North camping area

On the Heysen Trail, this is a basic camping area with a watertank and shelter. It is about 3 km east of the Hawker–Stirling North Rd. **Map refs:** 223 G7, 249 I2, 250 H9

MOUNT REMARKABLE NATIONAL PARK

All the elements that make the Flinders Ranges so appealing come to the fore in this diverse park. Mt Remarkable is a popular climb and there's an excellent walking-trail network among the gorges and rugged ridges to the west. Highlights include Hidden Gorge and Alligator Gorge. The park is 45 km north of Port Pirie, with access from Mambray Creek, Wilmington and Melrose.

Who to contact: Parks SA Mt Remarkable (08) 8634 7068; or Friends of the Heysen Trail (08) 8212 6299

193 Eaglehawk Dam camping area (bush camping)

This walk-in bush camp is on the Ring Route Track, 4 km north-west of the Alligator Gorge carpark. A permit is required from the self-registration station, and you need to use a gas/fuel stove. **Map refs:** 223 G7, 249 I3, 250 H10

194 Fricks Dam camping area (bush camping)

This elevated walk-in site is close to The Battery, with valley views. On Fricks Track, it is 10 km north of Mambray Creek. A permit is required from the self-registration station and you need to bring a gas/fuel stove. **Map refs:** 223 G7, 249 I3, 250 H10

195 Goat Rock camping area (bush camping)

A walk-in bush site (gas/fuel stove only), close to the junction of Woolfords and Racecourse tracks, this camping area requires a permit from the self-registration station. **Map refs:** 223 G7, 249 I3, 250 H10

196 Grays Hut camping area (walk-in camping)

On the Heysen Trail just west of the popular Racecourse camping area, this camping area is adjacent to a hut with sleeping benches, and there's a solar light. No fires are allowed; bring a gas/fuel stove. **Map refs:** 223 G7, 249 I3, 250 H10

197 Hidden Camp (bush camping)

This sheltered walk-in site is close to the dramatic ravine of Hidden Gorge, 8 km on foot north of Mambray Creek. The site is gas/fuel stove only, and a permit is required from the self-registration station. **Map refs:** 223 G7, 249 I3, 250 H10

198 Kingfisher Flat camping area (bush camping)

Delightful woodland walk-in camping is offered close to Alligator Creek. The facilities and ease of access make this a popular base for day walks to surrounding highlights. Situated 4 km south of the Alligator Gorge carpark, the site is gas/fuel stove only and requires a permit from the self-registration station. **Map refs:** 223 G7, 249 I3, 250 H10

199 Longhill Camp (bush camping)

Just 1 km south-west of Alligator, this walk-in camp (gas/fuel stove only) is at the start of the Ring Route Track. A permit is required from the self-registration station. **Map refs:** 223 G7, 249 I3, 250 H10

200 Mambray Creek Campground

The park's largest and most accessible campground is in a classic creek and river red gum setting. It offers a full range of facilities and ready access to the walking tracks heading east. Signposted access is off the Princes Hwy, 45 km north of Port Pirie, and cabin accommodation is also available. A permit is required from the self-registration station. **Map refs:** 223 G7, 249 I3, 250 H10

201 The Racecourse camping area (bush camping)

This walk-in site with a big water tank is near the junction of the Racecourse and Mungola Hut tracks, close to the modern Grays Hut camping area. It is also on the Heysen Trail. A permit is required from the self-registration station and the site is gas/fuel stove only. **Map refs:** 223 G7, 249 I3, 250 H10

202 Stony Creek Camp (bush camping)

The park's northernmost campground, this walk-in site is off the Stony Creek Track, 8 km north of the Alligator Gorge carpark. It is on the Heysen Trail. Only gas/fuel stoves are allowed and you need a permit from the self-registration station. **Map refs:** 223 G7, 249 I2, 250 H10

203 Stringers camping area (bush camping)

This walk-in camp is high on The Battery in the west of the park, 2 km north of the Hidden Gorge Hike. The site is gas/fuel stove only; pick up a permit from the self-registration station. Bring drinking water. **Map refs:** 223 G7, 249 I3, 250 H10

204 Sugar Gum Dam camping area (bush camping)

Secluded small sites are set in this walk-in area among high woodland on the Black Range Trek, 11 km east of Mambray Creek. A permit is required from the self-registration station, and the site is gas/fuel stove only. **Map refs:** 223 G7, 249 I3, 250 H10

205 Summit Camp (bush camping)

In an atmospheric bush setting on the high crest of Mt Remarkable, bush camping is permitted 6 km north-west of Melrose on the Mt Remarkable Summit Hike, also part of the Heysen Trail. The site is gas/fuel stove only and you need to pick up a permit from the self-registration station. **Map refs:** 223 G7, 249 I3, 250 H10

SIMPSON DESERT REGIONAL RESERVE AND CONSERVATION PARK

Straddling the borders of SA, Qld and the NT, this colossal expanse of dune-field desert – the world's largest – covers more than 3 million ha. It's home to some of the least visited terrain on the continent, and is a treasury of desert plants and wildlife. In recent years, desert crossings have become a popular excursion for experienced and well-equipped 4WD convoys. Note: parts of the park close from Dec to mid-Mar.

Who to contact: Parks SA Port Augusta (08) 8648 5300

206 Bush camping areas

Self-sufficient bush camping (permit required) is permitted anywhere within 50 m of public access tracks. Given the impact of desert wind and sun, low-lying areas with the shade of gidgee woodlands are recommended. Be aware of other vehicles when driving, and bring your own wood and water (and preferably a gas/fuel stove). **Map refs:** 223 G1, 252 H3

STRZELECKI REGIONAL RESERVE

This reserve covers a large sweep of dune fields and desert terrain either side of the Strzelecki Track, 200 km north of Lyndhurst. The track is generally navigable by conventional vehicles, but it's important to check road conditions prior to travel. Note: there is no fuel available in the 500 km stretch between Lyndhurst and Innamincka.

Who to contact: Parks SA Innamincka (08) 8675 9909

207 Montecollina Bore camping area

At this halfway stop for self-sufficient campers among the sand and saltbush along the Strzelecki Track, the bore spills water into a series of dams. It is 221 km north-east of Lyndhurst, with dry-weather access only. **Map refs:** 223 H4, 253 L12

TALLARINGA CONSERVATION PARK

Located 100 km west of Coober Pedy, this park abuts the Great Victoria Desert, Australia's largest desert landscape.

The only access to this remote area is via Coober Pedy along the Public Access Route (PAR) through Mabel Creek Station to the Anne Beadell Hwy – a rugged 4WD track that traverses the park heading west. All travellers must be well equipped for remote-area travel such as this, and a Desert Parks Pass is necessary.

Who to contact: Parks SA Port Augusta 8648 5300

208 Bush camping areas

Bush camping is permitted (with a permit) in Tallaringa in cleared areas within 50 m of the Anne Beadell Hwy. **Map refs:** 223 D4, 255 L10

TELOWIE GORGE CONSERVATION PARK

The southernmost park in the Flinders Ranges offers an authentic slice of the region's distinctive gorge and ridge terrain. Good bushwalks explore the park, which is home to a diversity of wildlife, including the charismatic yellow-footed rock wallaby. The park is 10 km east of Port Germain, with signposted access from the Princes Hwy.

Who to contact: Parks SA Port Pirie (08) 8634 7068; or Friends of the Heysen Trail (08) 8212 6299

209 Bush camping areas (walk-in camping)

Remote areas of the park are available for experienced, self-sufficient bushwalkers to use as walk-in campsites. Bring water and a gas/fuel stove. A permit is required. **Map refs:** 223 G7, 249 I3, 250 H11

210 Go-Cart Track Shelter camping area (walk-in camping)

On the Heysen Trail in Telowie Gorge Conservation Park, this is a new shelter, with water. Bring a gas/fuel stove. **Map refs:** 223 G7, 249 I3, 250 H11

211 Telowie Gorge camping area

Basic facilities are provided at this camping area, 27 km north of Port Pirie from the Princes Hwy. Come equipped with wood, water and a permit. **Map refs:** 223 G7, 249 I3, 250 H11

VULKATHUNHA–GAMMON RANGES NATIONAL PARK

The heart of this majestic wilderness park – a stronghold of Adnyamathanha culture – is an isolated 1000 m plateau fortified by rugged peaks and ravines. While this inner sanctum is the preserve of experienced wilderness walkers, there are many fine walks, drives and campsites on the plateau's fringes. The park headquarters are at Balcanoona, 100 km east of Leigh Creek along the Copley–Balcanoona Rd. Access for conventional vehicles is limited.

Who to contact: Parks SA Balcanoona (08) 8648 4829

212 Arcoona Creek camping area

Camp among the pines and red gums close to this major creek system draining the north-western corner of the park, which acts as a staging post for wilderness walks to the plateau and Gammon Hill. Signposted access is 23 km along the Mt Serle–Yankaninna Rd, 45 km east of Leigh Creek on Copley–Balcanoona Rd. It's accessed through private property, so leave the gates as you found them. The route is suitable for off-road camper trailers. **Map refs:** 223 H5, 251 J3

213 Grindells Hut camping area

A good base for exploring Weetootla Gorge and the various branches of Italowie Creek, this 4WD route via the Wortupa Loop Rd is 26 km north-west of park headquarters. The road is suitable for off-road camper trailers, but check current road conditions before heading out. Nearby Grindells Hut is available for rent. The track in can be rough and slow going, depending on when the grader last went through. There is a good walk from here to Weetootla Springs, following the creek through the gorge. **Map refs:** 223 H5, 251 J3

214 Italowie Gorge camping area

Two easily accessible sites – one a sheltered nook on the south-western side of the gap, the other to the north-east at the head of the Italowie Gorge Hike – are signposted off Copley–Balcanoona Rd, 82 km east of Leigh Creek and 17 km west of the park headquarters. There is only limited access for small caravans. A permit is required. **Map refs:** 223 H5, 251 J4

215 Lochness Well camping area

The closest vehicle-based camping to the plateau's major gorges and peaks is reached from Wortupa Loop Rd, 31 km north-west of the park headquarters. Access is 4WD only. Check road conditions and bring a permit plus equipment and supplies for self-sufficient camping. **Map refs:** 223 H5, 251 J3

216 Mainwater Well camping area

Secluded self-sufficient camping here on the park's northern fringe is a good kick-off point for exploring Mainwater Pound. Signposted access is 18.5 km along Idninna Rd from the Mt Serle–Yankaninna Rd. Alternative access from the east is provided via Wortupa Loop Rd. Access is 4WD only, but suitable for off-road camper trailers; check track conditions with the park office. **Map refs:** 223 H5, 251 J3

217 Weetootla Gorge camping area

Close to Balcanoona, this site for self-sufficient campers (permit required) gives easy access to the popular Weetootla Gorge hike. It's signposted along Weetootla Track, 7 km north-west of the park headquarters. **Map refs:** 223 H5, 251 J4

Dalhousie Springs camping area, Witjira National Park (p. 230)

WARRAWEENA CONSERVATION PARK

This former pastoral lease takes in a sweep of fine highland country in the northern Flinders Ranges. Now run as a private conservation estate, it offers an array of secluded bush camping, wildlife experiences and adventure 4WD options. Popular walks Include the outstanding summit of Mt Hack. It is dry-weather access only, and beyond the old homestead you'll need a 4WD to reach the highlights.

Who to contact: Warraweena Homestead (08) 8675 2770 www.warraweena.com

218 Warraweena camping areas

Take your pick from designated camping areas within the property, some with bush huts nearby; come with wood and water. The main homestead is 30 km east of Beltana Roadhouse, off the Leigh Creek Rd. Signposted access is provided from Old Beltana. Accommodation at the homestead and shearers' quarters is also available. **Map refs:** 223 H5, 251 I4

WITJIRA NATIONAL PARK

Famed for its mound springs – the largest collection in the Great Artesian Basin – this is a true oasis in a vast expanse of outback dunes and gibber plain. This country has a rich living heritage for the Lower Southern Arrernte and Wangkangurru people. The 7688 sq km park hugs the NT border and includes the western flanks of the Simpson Desert. As well as taking a dip in the soothing warm waters of Dalhousie Springs, enjoy the fine bushwalking and birdwatching opportunities here.

Who to contact: Desert Parks Hotline 1800 816 078

219 3 O'Clock Creek camping area

Relaxed self-sufficient camping is available 10 km west of Dalhousie Springs; it's a handy alternative if sites at the springs are busy. Access is via Mt Dare–Dalhousie Springs Rd. Firewood collection is permitted here, and there is a drinking-water tank, as well as pleasant, shady bush camping sites. **Map refs:** 223 E1, 252 B3

220 Dalhousie Springs camping area

You'll find this camping area for self-sufficient campers on the Purni Bore Access Rd, 180 km north of Oodnadatta via Pedirka Siding and 71 km south-east of Mt Dare. A swim in the warm (38–43°C) waters of the spring on a frosty winter morning is a magical experience, or try a night swim under the stars. The picturesque Dalhousie Homestead ruins are a short drive away and there are bush walks around the springs and surrounding country. **Map refs:** 223 E1, 252 B3

221 Mount Dare Homestead camping area

With the pub nearby, and fuel and food available (bring your own wood, though), this is a handy supply stop for outback travellers. It is 250 km north of Oodnadatta via the Oodnadatta–Witjira National Park Rd. Bookings are recommended. **Map refs:** 223 E1, 252 B2, 255 P2

222 Purni Bore camping area

This artificial bore on the threshold of the Simpson has created a wetland busy with birdlife. It's situated at the start of the French Line, 70 km east of Dalhousie Springs and 363 km west of Birdsville. You need a Desert Parks Permit to camp here, and it is best to bring wood, water and preferably a gas/fuel stove.
Map refs: 223 F1, 252 D2

CAMPSITES LOCATED IN OTHER AREAS

223 Angorichina Village camping area

This is an ideal base for campers wanting to explore the spectacular hills and gorges of this historic region, and is a perfect spot to discover the Flinders Ranges. From here you can set off on walks or 4WD adventures, or a hire a mountain bike and discover the delights of the area using pedal power.
Map refs: 223 G6, 251 I5

How to book: Brachina Gorge Rd, Parachilna (08) 8648 4842 www.angorichinavillage.com.au

224 Appila Springs camping area

A time-honoured traveller's stop 8 km north-east of Appila, this camping area is in the rolling farm country of the mid-north. Though on one of the region's backroads, it's central to several historic and appealing towns, including Laura, Wirrabara and Jamestown. The camping is in a quiet nook accessible off Appila–Tarcowie Rd. Bring your own firewood, water and stove. No camping is permitted during the Nov–Apr fire-ban season.
Map refs: 223 G7, 249 J3, 250 H11

Who to contact: Northern Areas Council (08) 8664 1139

225 Arkaroola Campground

Magnificent arid highlands in the far north of the Flinders Ranges are home to a special wilderness sanctuary, famous for its striking peaks and gorges. A geological marvel, Arkaroola is ideal for bushwalking, photography and 4WD exploring. As well as motel accommodation and caravan park sites, there is bush camping along Wywhyana Creek. Located 129 km north-east of Copley, the campground is 30 km north of Balcanoona along the Arkaroola–Balcanoona Rd. Check road conditions before travelling and come equipped for self-sufficient camping.
Map refs: 223 H5, 251 K3

Who to contact: Arkaroola Village (08) 8648 4848 www.arkaroola.com.au

226 Artimore Ruins camping area (bush camping)

This former homestead occupies a scenic and secluded valley, 28 km north-east of Blinman. Access is via PAR 4 on a tough track. Bring in your own firewood and water.
Map refs: 223 H6, 251 I5

Who to contact: DENR (08) 8648 5174

Birdsville Track

An outback icon covering 520 km, this once infamous track was founded in the 1860s for droving cattle from Queensland to the railhead at Marree. Over the years it's been a legendary mail route and now, with major improvements, it's a popular tourist trail to the gateway town of Birdsville. In dry weather the route is navigable by conventional vehicles, though travellers need to be well equipped and prepared for long stretches in remote, challenging terrain.

Please note that campsites are listed in alphabetical order, not track order. Refer to the map on p. 223 for further information.

Road conditions: DPTI 1300 361 033

227 Clayton Station camping area

See p. 232.

228 Cooper Creek camping area

See p. 232.

229 Mungerannie Hotel camping area

See p. 234.

230 Tippipila Creek camping area

See p. 235.

231 Boolyeroo Goldfields camping area

The hill country of the northern Flinders Ranges has a long history of small-scale mining. These goldfields and the associated bush camping are located 29 km east of Leigh Creek along the Copley–Balcanoona Road. For access details and other information it is necessary to contact Pasty Springs Station. Bring water and firewood but a gas/fuel stove is preferred. Dogs are welcome but must be kept on leads, as wild-dog baits are laid on the property. **Map refs:** 223 G5, 251 I3

Who to contact: (08) 8675 2553 (7–9pm)
Mail: Patsy Springs Station, via Copley, SA 5732

232 Cadney Homestead

Located 150 km north of Coober Pedy and about 80 km south-east of Marla, this remote location is an outback surprise. With the Cadney Roadhouse next door serving pub meals, it's a popular overnight stop on the Adelaide–Alice Springs drive. There are powered and unpowered sites, on-site vans and cabins to choose from. A feature of the area is the nearby 'Painted Desert', also known as the Arckaringa Hills, about

90 km east from Cadney Park. Famous movies such as *Mad Max: Beyond Thunderdome* and *Priscilla, Queen of the Desert* were filmed with the nearby Moon Plain as a backdrop. It is a must for keen photographers. **Map refs:** 223 D3, 255 N7

How to book: Stuart Hwy, Mount Willoughby (08) 8670 7994

233 Chambers Gorge camping area (bush camping)

This northern Flinders Ranges outlier is flanked by craggy summits and steep gorge walls. This is a handy stopover for travels further north, with good walks and significant Aboriginal rock-art sites. Access is signposted from the Blinman–Arkaroola Rd, 63 km north-east of Blinman. The campsites are located 9 km in from the turn-off. This is a remote area on private property and campers need to be self-sufficient. **Map refs:** 223 H5, 251 J5

Who to contact: Hawker Visitor Information Centre (08) 8648 4022

227 Clayton Station camping area

At this popular Birdsville Track stopover on a well-known pastoral property 44 km north of Marree and 466 km south of Birdsville, there is an oasis-like wetland with diverse vegetation and an array of birdlife to enjoy. Luxury cabin accommodation is available, along with sites for self-sufficient camping. **Map refs:** 223 G4, 253 I11

How to book: Clayton Station (08) 8675 8311 www.claytonstation.com

234 Cockburn Caravan and Camping Area

This is a handy highway stopover in the historic railway settlement of Cockburn, on the SA–NSW border. It's just off the Barrier Hwy, 148 km north-east of Yunta and 50 km west of Broken Hill. **Map refs:** 223 I7, 249 O1, 251 N8

Who to contact: Cockburn Telecentre (08) 8091 1999

228 Cooper Creek camping area

Camp beside the legendary Cooper Creek where it crosses the Birdsville Track on its final run to Lake Eyre. In flood years the transformation of the creek and influx of birdlife make a great spectacle. Access from the track is 137 km north of Marree and 383 km south of Birdsville. **Map refs:** 223 H3, 253 I9

Road conditions: DPTI 1300 361 033

235 Coward Springs Campground

This heritage-listed former railway siding on the old Ghan Line is now a comfortable stopover for self-sufficient campers on the Oodnadatta Track. It's surrounded by Wabma Kadarbu Conservation Park, a wetland fed by mound springs. Camel safaris are available on the property. Signposted access from the

Oodnadatta Track is 128 km west of Marree. Note: bookings are not taken for fewer than 4 vehicles. **Map refs:** 223 F4, 252 E11

How to book: Oodnadatta Track (08) 8675 8336 www.cowardsprings.com.au

236 Farina Campground

A popular stopover for travellers on the Oodnadatta and Birdsville tracks, the campsites are close to the historic ruins of the one-time railway town of Farina, just off the Lyndhurst–Marree Rd, 25 km north of Lyndhurst and 53 km south of Marree. The history of these picturesque ruins is now documented on signs in and around some of the old buildings. The campground is run by the owners of Farina Station and is set among the trees adjacent to Farina Creek. Firewood is available and there are flush toilets and shearers' quarters accommodation. Bring your own water here. **Map refs:** 223 G5, 250 H2

Who to contact: Lyndhurst–Marree Rd (08) 8675 7790 www.farinastation.com.au

237 Goorikiana Creek camping area (bush camping)

Self-sufficient bush camping beside Goorikiana Creek is 7 km east of the famous Painted Desert, a stark yet vividly hued landscape beloved by photographers and painters. Signposted access is provided along Oodnadatta–Cadney Park Rd. Alternative accommodation is available at the Pink Roadhouse, and Arckaringa Homestead, 15 km west of Goorikiana Creek. **Map refs:** 223 E3, 252 A7, 255 P7

Who to contact: Pink Roadhouse, Oodnadatta 1800 802 074 www.pinkroadhouse.com.au

Heysen Trail

The Flinders Ranges is the starting point of the magnificent Heysen Trail, one of the world's great walking tracks and the longest trail in Australia. If you start here – or at the other end in Deep Creek Conservation Park in the Fleurieu Peninsula – it can take around 60 days by foot to tackle the full 1200 km. But the whole trip is for experienced hikers only. Stick to the Flinders Ranges and you will experience breathtaking outback scenery. Although camping areas have water, be prepared to be self sufficent on this trail.

Please note that campsites are listed in alphabetical order, not track order. Refer to the map on p. 223 for further information.

Who to contact: Parks SA Wilpena Pound (08) 8648 0048; or Friends of the Heysen Trail (08) 8212 6299 www.heysentrail.asn.au

160 Aroona Ruins camping area
See p. 224.

163 Bridle Gap camping area (walk-in camping)
See p. 224.

238 Buckaringa North camping area

A very basic campsite, with a rainwater tank and shelter about 40 km south-west of Hawker. **Map refs:** 223 G6, 249 I1, 250 H8

239 Calabrinda Creek camping area

Just north of the Buckaringa site, this is a basic camping area with water and shelter. **Map refs:** 223 G6, 250 H8

240 Eyre Depot camping area

Just north of Dutchmans Stern Conservation Park, this basic stop on the Heysen Trail has a shelter and water. **Map refs:** 223 G7, 249 I1, 250 G8

210 Go-Cart Track Shelter camping area (walk-in camping)

See p. 229.

196 Grays Hut camping area (walk-in camping)

See p. 227.

241 Ippinitchie Campground

See p. 233.

242 Mayo Hut camping area

Just to the west of the Heysen Trail, about 15 km north of Hawker, this hut was built by William Mayo and his family in 1899. It has been restored and is now an overnight shelter for walkers. **Map refs:** 223 G6, 250 H7

168 Middlesight Water Hut camping area

See p. 225.

243 Mount Arden South camping area

This is a very basic site west of Warren Gorge, with a small shelter designed for catching rainwater. However, 250 m north there is another campsite (on private property) that has a BBQ and picnic table and is accessible by 4WD. **Map refs:** 223 G7, 249 I1, 250 G8

244 Mount Elm camping area

Located about 7 km west of Hawker, this a basic site but it does have a toilet and water. **Map refs:** 223 G6, 250 H8

158 Old Homestead and Shearers Quarters camping area

See p. 224.

201 The Racecourse camping area (bush camping)

See p. 228.

245 Red Range camping area

The next stop south from Bridle Gap camping area, this has a basic shelter, water and a toilet. **Map refs:** 223 G6, 251 I7

202 Stony Creek Camp (bush camping)

See p. 228.

205 Summit Camp (bush camping)

See p. 228.

170 Trezona camping area

See p. 225.

192 Waukarie Creek–Mount Brown North camping area

See p. 227.

171 Wilpena Pound Campground

See p. 225.

172 Yanyanna Hut camping area

See p. 225.

This track continues through the Fleurieu Peninsula region (see p. 206)

246 Iga Warta Campground

Set among the mountains in the northern Flinders Ranges in the north of SA, this privately owned property features cabins, safari tents, huts and campsites. It is owned and operated by the local Adnyamathanha people, who offer guided cultural tours and special meals to their guests. The campground has a big camp kitchen, a store and a pool for the hot days. **Map refs:** 223 H5, 251 J4

How to book: via Copley, Flinders Ranges (08) 8648 3737 www.igawarta.com

241 Ippinitchie Campground

Shady, creek-side camping is offered close to the appealing mid-north town of Wirrabara and the Heysen Trail, with its local forest, bush gardens and views from The Bluff. The campsite is just off Forest Rd, 8 km south-west of Wirrabara. A permit is required from the self-registration station at the forest headquarters, 4 km south of the campground. If you're riding in, fees and permits apply for horseriding. **Map refs:** 223 G7, 249 I3, 250 H11

Who to contact: Forestry SA (08) 8668 5000

247 Lyndhurst Hotel camping area

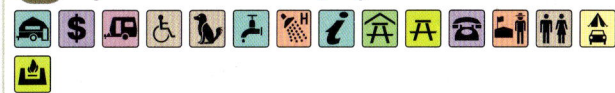

Both the Oodnadatta and Strzelecki tracks kick off from the one-time railway town of Lyndhurst, where the bitumen ends

and the fun begins. This camping area is right next to the hotel, and the vivid ochre pits just to the north of town are an important Aboriginal site. Hotel and cabin accommodation is also available. Lyndhurst is 33 km north of Leigh Creek. **Map refs:** 223 G5, 250 H3

How to book: 3 Short St, Lyndhurst (08) 8675 7781 www.lyndhurstthotel.com.au

248 Marla Travellers Rest

A sprawling roadhouse-cum-motel and caravan park, this travellers' hub is 233 km north of Coober Pedy on the busy junction of the Oodnadatta Track and Stuart Hwy. **Map refs:** 223 D2, 255 M5

How to book: Stuart Hwy, Marla (08) 8670 7001

249 Marree Caravan and Campers Park

You'll find this basic caravan park just south of Marree, 111 km north of Leigh Creek. Bring your own drinking water. **Map refs:** 223 G4, 250 H1, 252 H12

Who to contact: Lyndhurst–Maree Rd (08) 8675 8371

250 Marree Oasis Town Centre Caravan Park

In the heart of Marree's township, this central caravan park is 111 km north of Leigh Creek. Cabins are also available. **Map refs:** 223 G4, 250 H1, 252 H12

How to book: Marree town centre (08) 8675 8352 www.marreelakeeyreflights.com.au

251 Melrose Showgrounds camping area

Creekside camping is permitted on the outskirts of the delightful Flinders Ranges town of Melrose, the oldest settlement in the region. With sites among mighty river gums, this is a convenient base for enjoying the town or climbing nearby Mt Remarkable. Signposted access is off the Wilmington–Melrose Rd, 2 km north of Melrose. **Map refs:** 223 G7, 249 I3, 250 H10

Who to contact: District Council of Mt Remarkable (08) 8666 2014

229 Mungerannie Hotel camping area

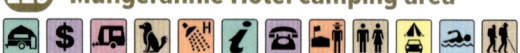

At this popular watering hole almost halfway along the Birdsville Track, you'll also find motel-style rooms and good no-frills camping beside the Derwent River. Permanent water means there are shade trees and a lively local bird population to observe, as well as a pool fed by hot artesian water to soak in. The Mungerannie Hotel is 205 km north of Marree and 315 km south of Birdsville. **Map refs:** 223 H3, 253 I8

How to book: Mungerannie Hotel (08) 8675 8317 www.mungeranniehotel.com.au

252 Nuccaleena Mine camping area

In a historic Flinders Ranges mine site, tucked among the sweep of hills north of Blinman, there are ruins to explore and hills to wander at this camping area on an elevated site near the ruins. Other accommodation is also available. Located on PAR 3, 42 km north-east of Parachilna, access is via Moolooloo Rd off Glass Gorge Rd. **Map refs:** 223 G5, 251 I5

Who to contact: Moolooloo Station (08) 8648 4861

253 Oodnadatta Caravan Park

Camping and van sites, along with cabin accommodation, are offered in the centre of this famous outback outpost 406 km north-west of Marree. Bring your own wood and water. **Map refs:** 223 E2, 252 B6

Who to contact: Oodnadatta Track (08) 8670 7822 www.pinkroadhouse.com.au

Oodnadatta Track

This rambling overland track follows the historic route of the old *Ghan Railway* from Marree to Marla on the Stuart Hwy. Highlights of this classic track include the outback outposts of William Creek, Coward Springs and Oodnadatta, the ochre pits near Lyndhurst, the ruined railway siding at Farina, the Strangways Telegraph Station ruins, the mound springs of Blanche Cup and The Bubbler at the Wabma Kadarbu Conservation Park near Coward Springs. There is plenty of history to explore in these arid expanses, and in good conditions it's accessible to conventional vehicles.

Please note that campsites are listed in alphabetical order, not track order. Refer to the map on p. 223 for further information.

Road conditions: DPTI 1300 361 033

256 Parachilna Gorge camping area (bush camping)

The road heading east from Parachilna to Blinman follows Parachilna Gorge as it snakes through the Heysen and ABC ranges. Spectacular summits and rock formations create a memorable atmosphere for the designated bush campsites dotted along this route, starting 9 km east of Parachilna. **Map refs:** 223 G6, 251 I5

Who to contact: Leigh Creek Tourist Information Centre (08) 8675 2723

257 Patawarta Gap camping area

This camping area lies in rugged terrain north of Artimore Ruins, with spectacular Patawarta Hill a commanding presence. It's 42 km north-east of Blinman via PAR 5. Bring wood and water, and preferably a gas/fuel stove. Do not camp in creekbeds. **Map refs:** 223 H5, 251 I5

Who to contact: Moolooloo Station (08) 8648 4861

230 Tippipila Creek camping area

Camp on the Birdsville side of this tree-lined creek, 336 km north of Marree and 180 km south of Birdsville, on the Birdsville Track. Come equipped for self-sufficient camping. **Map refs:** 223 H2, 253 J5

Road conditions: DPTI 1300 361 033

258 Warren Gorge camping area

A popular haunt for self-sufficient travellers touring the Flinders Ranges, this area has eye-catching rock formations and classic groves of native pines to wander through. It's 20 km north-west of Quorn via Arden Vale Rd. **Map refs:** 223 G7, 249 I1, 250 H8

Who to contact: Flinders Ranges Council (08) 8648 6031

259 Waukaringa Ruins camping area

For travellers on the Yunta–Arkaroola Rd, the picturesque ruins of this long-abandoned goldmining town, 35 km north of Yunta, make a convenient overnight spot. Camping is permitted in the vicinity of the ruins only; the surrounding areas are private property. Bring in wood and water. **Map refs:** 223 H7, 249 L1, 251 K9

Who to contact: Outback Areas Trust (08) 8648 5970

254 William Creek Campground

Basic camping is offered across the road from the pub in this tiny settlement on the old *Ghan Railway*. A popular lift-off point for scenic flights over Lake Eyre, it's 204 km west of Marree and halfway to Oodnadatta. **Map refs:** 223 F4, 252 D10

How to book: Oodnadatta Track, William Creek (08) 8670 7746

255 William Creek Hotel camping area

Dating from 1887, William Creek's classic timber-and-iron hotel is an SA outback legend – with an interior like no other. The camping area is tucked among scattered trees in the grounds behind the pub; bring your own firewood. William Creek is 202 km south of Oodnadatta. **Map refs:** 223 F4, 252 D10

How to book: Oodnadatta Track, William Creek (08) 8670 7880 www.williamcreekhotel.net.au

260 Willow Springs camping area (bush camping)

This family-run sheep property just north-east of Wilpena offers a range of camping options as well as cottage accommodation. It's also a popular destination for remote camping, bushwalking and adventure 4WD touring on the 70 km self-guided Skytrek into the Bunker Range. Signposted access is provided off Wilpena–Blinman Rd, 13 km north-east of the Wilpena Pound Resort turn-off. Camping is limited to 6 sites, so bookings are essential. **Map refs:** 223 H6, 251 I6

How to book: Willow Springs Homestead, off Wilpena–Blinman Rd (08) 8648 0016

261 Willow Waters camping area (bush camping)

A popular picnic spot on private land, 20 km east of Hawker, the camping area has a pleasant waterhole nearby. Campers need to be self-sufficient, use public access roads only, and observe minimum impact camping practices. Access is signposted off Orroroo–Hawker Rd. **Map refs:** 223 G6, 251 I8

Who to contact: Hawker Visitor Information Centre (08) 8648 4022

262 Yunta Recreational Ground

Camping is permitted in the heart of this small service town, 85 km north-east of Peterborough on the Barrier Hwy leading to Broken Hill. From here, a popular unsealed road heads north to Arkaroola and the northern Flinders Ranges. Bring water and a gas/fuel stove. **Map refs:** 223 H7, 249 L2, 251 K10

Who to contact: Yunta Rural Transaction Centre (08) 8650 5099

EYRE PENINSULA AND NULLARBOR

FOR SOUTH AUSTRALIANS, THE 'West Coast' is synonymous with ragged limestone shores, dazzling surf beaches and vast tracts of wheat. Above all else, it's famed for the tastiest gifts the sea can offer. Here you can sample everything from oysters and tuna to abalone, prawns, King George whiting and lobster.

Eyre Peninsula is vast. Covering more than 45 000 sq km, its farming traditions have been shaped by erratic seasons and the region's sheer scale and remoteness. In among the sheep paddocks there are ancient granite monoliths to scramble up and expanses of mallee bushland to enjoy. But the coast is where the main action lies. Thanks to the relentless power of the Southern Ocean, this is one of the most faceted shores on the continent. Wind and waves have carved elaborate peninsulas, island archipelagos and an array of coves, caverns and crescent-shaped bays. Further west, these same forces have sculpted the mighty cliff lines of the Great Australian Bight – where the desert meets the sea in the sublime spaces of the Nullarbor Plain.

Throughout national parks like Coffin Bay and Lincoln, opportunities abound to fish, swim, sail and dive. They are also great places simply to ramble. Whether you travel on foot, by boat or by 4WD, there's great wildlife and coastal scenery to discover. Head north-west and it's the same story, only the surf keeps getting bigger and the beaches seem to grow longer, whiter and even lonelier. The shores around Streaky Bay, Ceduna and Fowlers Bay are some of the best vantage points in the country to witness a passing parade of seals, dolphins, southern right whales and ocean birds.

While the region has destinations for travellers of every persuasion, for those who enjoy remote bush camping this is heaven. From outback dunes to raw coastal splendour, here you can revel in a special bounty of solitude and windswept freedom.

CAMPSITES LOCATED IN PARKS AND RESERVES

ACRAMAN CREEK CONSERVATION PARK

A wild sprawl of mallee scrub, dunes and mangroves framed by a windswept peninsula, this is an important refuge for migratory waders. An excellent birdwatching locale, it also offers abundant choices for fishing and swimming. The beach is accessible by conventional vehicles but to reach the creek and Point Lindsay – and to launch your boat off the beach – a 4WD is the go.

Who to contact: Parks SA (08) 8625 3144

263 **Acraman Creek camping area**

You'll find the camping area 16 km south of the Flinders Hwy and 53 km north of Streaky Bay. Camping here requires a permit, and you need to come equipped with water and preferably a gas/fuel stove. **Map refs:** 237 E3, 248 A2, 257 N9

BASCOMBE WELL CONSERVATION PARK

With its rare orchids and rich array of birdlife, this remote inland park conserves a swathe of mallee and dryland tea-tree habitats, ideal for nature-loving bush campers with a 4WD. Check ahead about track conditions.

Who to contact: Parks SA (08) 8688 3111

264 **Bascombe Well camping area (bush camping)**

There is bush camping for self-sufficient campers 22 km south-west of Lock, with dry-weather access only via Murdinga or Warrachie off the Tod Hwy. **Map refs:** 237 G4, 248 D5

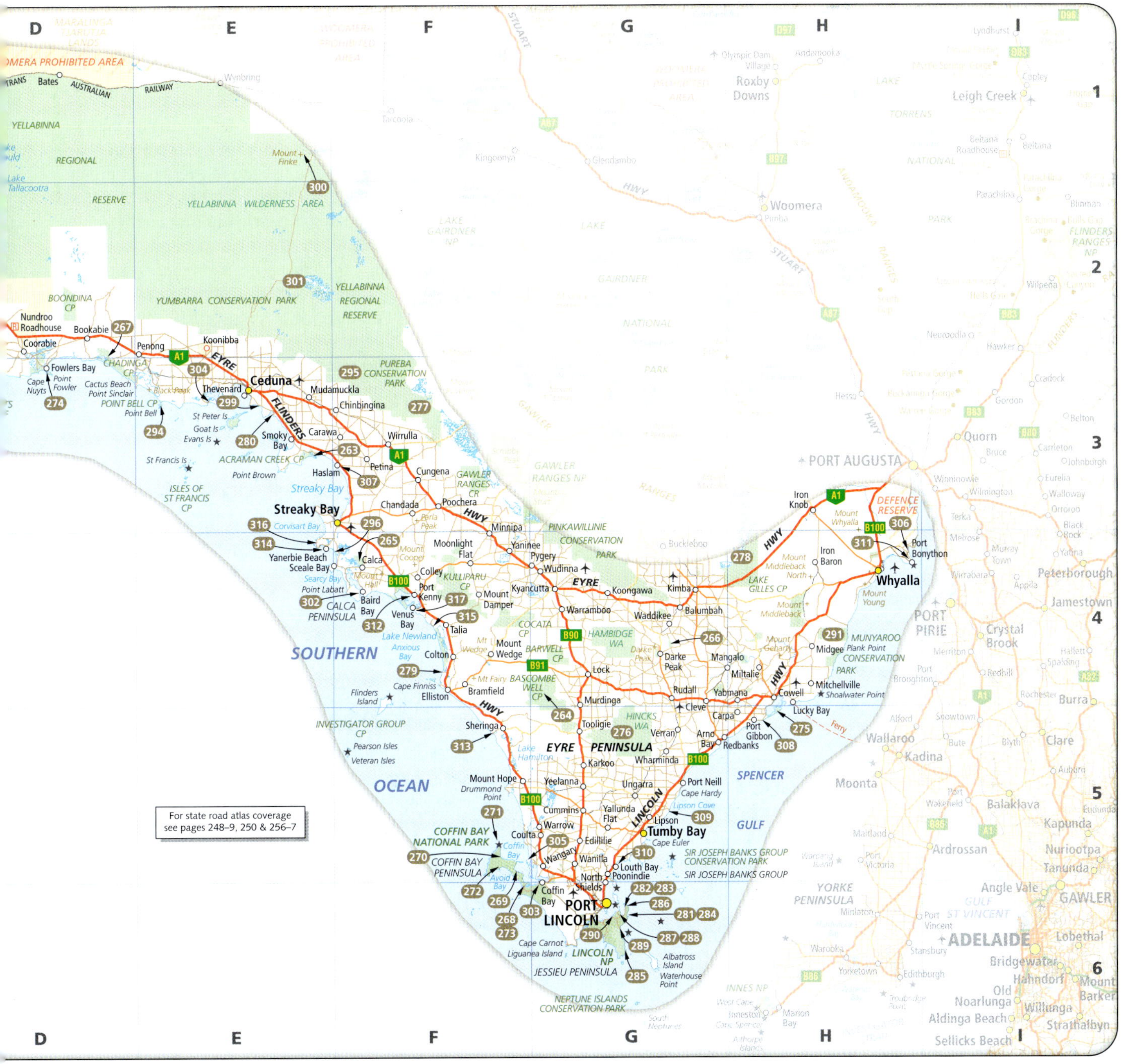

CALPATANNA WATERHOLE CONSERVATION PARK

Wedina Well was a life-sustaining landmark for Aboriginal people and early European settlers. With its stands of mallee, as well as swamp paperbark on the flats, this park is a great spot for birdwatching.

Who to contact: Parks SA (08) 8625 3144

 **Wedina Well camping area**

Wedina Well camping area is reached from Calca Rd off Flinders Hwy, 40 km south-east of Streaky Bay. Enter the gate with the

'Reserve' sign on Calca Rd, and come equipped with a gas/fuel stove, water and permit. Wood fires prohibited outside fire danger season. **Map refs:** 237 F4, 248 A3, 257 N11

CARAPPEE HILL CONSERVATION PARK

The peninsula's largest and loftiest rocky outcrop dominates this small park, 42 km south-west of Kimba. After winter rains you'll see wildflowers and rockpools on the 2 hr climb to the summit. Approach from the Darke Peak-Kimba Road.

Who to contact: Parks SA Port Lincoln (08) 8688 3111

266 Carappee Hill camping area (bush camping)

This site offers bush camping for self-sufficient campers. The approach from the Darke Peak–Kimba Rd can handle off-road trailers. **Map refs:** 237 G4, 248 E4, 250 D12

CHADINGA CONSERVATION PARK

This significant coastal reserve protects large tracts of mallee, coastal dune and samphire flats. The ocean beach is a wild strip of sand and surf, 25 km west of Penong.

Who to contact: Parks SA (08) 8625 3144

267 Tuckamore camping area (bush camping)

Bush camping for self-sufficient campers – 4WD access only – is available from Edwards Rd off the Eyre Hwy. Contact Parks SA at Ceduna for updates on track conditions. **Map refs:** 237 D2, 257 K8

COFFIN BAY NATIONAL PARK

A 4WD is the best way to enjoy everything this far-flung peninsula has to offer. Its southern beaches and limestone bluffs are wave-lashed and wild, but along the north side a series of broad, sheltered bays are ideal for swimming and canoeing. Meanwhile, the shores around distant Point Sir Isaac and beyond are wonderfully isolated and untrodden.

Who to contact: Parks SA (08) 8688 3111

268 Big Yangie camping area

These scalloped shorelines and beaches offer a feeling of sanctuary but with a little more remoteness and seclusion than Yangie Bay. This is a great camping hideout for coastal rambles, fishing, swimming and canoeing, just 1 km north of the Yangie Track. Bring in your own gas stove, wood and water; woodfires allowed, but restrictions apply. **Map refs:** 237 F6, 248 C8

269 Black Springs camping area

This is a well-protected headland site with a private shell beach below. Swim, fish off the rocks, take the walking trail to Black Springs Well or make the longer trek across the peninsula for views of the rugged south coast and Black Rocks. This is a great spot to take out a canoe or kayak, and dolphins are frequently seen just offshore. In calm conditions, snorkelling is good along the beach and rocks. Access is signposted off the main park road, 28 km north-west of ranger headquarters. Bring a stove, permit, firewood and water. **Map refs:** 237 F5, 248 C8

270 Morgans Landing camping area

With absolute-waterfront camping towards the western end of Seven Mile Beach, this marvellous stretch of golden sand and placid water is perfect for swimming, boating and fishing. The beach is the main 4WD track heading west, so expect passing traffic at busy holiday times. The site is situated 45 km north-west of park HQ along Seven Mile Beach. This is self-sufficient camping and a permit is required. **Map refs:** 237 F5, 248 C8

271 The Pool camping area

Nestled in the lee of distant Point Sir Isaac, this site for self-sufficient campers has a real 'out there' feeling. Being the northern side of the peninsula, the bay here is a protected haven for swimming, surfing and fishing. At every point of the compass there are dramatic headlands and deserted beaches to discover. You can walk along the beach and rocks out towards Point Sir Isaac from here. Plenty of 4WD tracks also give access to the far-western end of the peninsula, with amazing views over the sea from the bluffs above Mullalong Beach. This location is especially picturesque at sunset. The camp is 53 km north-west of the park HQ, with access by 4WD via Seven Mile Beach or by boat. **Map refs:** 237 F5, 248 C7

272 Sensation Beach camping area

Named after a tuna boat that ran aground here, this is a wonderfully isolated arc of crashing waves and dazzling sand. A popular base for beach fishing, these dune sites for self-sufficient campers are also on the doorstep to wilderness walks exploring the dramatic cliffs and coves near Boarding House Bay and Cape Whidbey. The beach is 49 km north-west of the ranger HQ with 4WD access via Seven Mile Beach. A permit is required. **Map refs:** 237 F5, 248 C8

273 Yangie Bay camping area

The most accessible and sheltered campsite on the peninsula, this is a tranquil bushland setting overlooking the bay. Walking trails are nearby and the wild surf shores of Almonta Beach and Point Avoid are within easy reach. It's 15 km west of the ranger HQ along the main park access road. A permit is required. Bring your own firewood and water. **Map refs:** 237 F6, 248 C8

FOWLERS BAY CONSERVATION PARK

The full gamut of coastal splendour is here: wild surf shores, craggy cliffs and headlands, sheltered bays and big dune systems. As well as a prime fishing and beach locale, this park, just west of Fowlers Bay township, is a prime habitat for seabirds.

Who to contact: Parks SA (08) 8625 3144

274 Fowlers Bay camping area (bush camping)

Go bush camping by the beach off the Coorabie–Fowlers Bay Rd, from the Eyre Hwy. A permit is required and you need to bring your own everything. **Map refs:** 237 D3, 257 J8

FRANKLIN HARBOUR CONSERVATION PARK

Though only 16 km due south of Cowell, this long arm of dunes and mangrove flats enclosing Franklin Harbour feels very isolated. There is scope for fishing and swimming along the ocean beach but the camping is for self-reliant 4WD parties only.

Who to contact: Parks SA (08) 8688 3111

275 Franklin Harbour camping area (bush camping)

Camping for self-sufficient campers is reached by 4WD via Wellington Rd. Bring your own everything. **Map refs:** 237 H5, 248 G5

HINCKS CONSERVATION PARK

Lots of bush hideaways can be found in this inland expanse of mallee, acacia and broombrush. Best visited by 4WD, this park has a bounty of flora and fauna, especially in spring.

Who to contact: Parks SA (08) 8688 3111

276 Nicholls Track camping area

On Nicholls Track, 54 km north-east of Cummins, this camping area is reached by 4WD via Reserve Rd from Mt Isabella. Check track conditions with Parks SA; a permit is required. Bring your own wood and water. **Map refs:** 237 G5, 248 E6

KOOLGERA CONSERVATION PARK

The first in a series of remote reserves north of the Eyre Hwy, this is 4WD country only and not for the faint-hearted. The outer reaches of these colossal expanses of mallee scrub and parallel dunes are defiant wildernesses.

Who to contact: Parks SA (08) 8625 3144

277 Koolgera camping area (bush camping)

Bush camping is available via the Gawler Ranges Rd, 27 km east of Wirulla. Check track conditions and site availability with Parks SA. **Map refs:** 237 F3, 248 B1, 257 O8

LAKE GILLES CONSERVATION PARK

Split by the Eyre Hwy, this park is one of the most accessible of the large mallee reserves on the Eyre Peninsula. Situated 17 km north of the Eyre Hwy, the lake is part of a complex environment of salt flats and dune rises with a surprising diversity of woodland birds. In good conditions it's accessible by conventional vehicle; check with Parks SA for details.

Who to contact: Parks SA (08) 8688 3111

278 Lakes Edge camping area (bush camping)

Access routes to this camping area for self-sufficient campers are signposted from Eyre Hwy, 87 km west of Iron Knob and 35 km east of Kimba. A 4WD is essential for areas north of the lake. A permit is required. **Map refs:** 237 H4, 248 F3, 250 E11

LAKE NEWLAND CONSERVATION PARK

Lake Newland Conservation Park has natural salt lakes and freshwater springs that extend for 20 km; it is the largest

wetland on the Eyre Peninsula. The park is home to various waterfowl and wading birds: birdwatchers should come prepared with binoculars. Fishing is permitted, so anglers should pack their rods. You need a 4WD to reach the lake itself, but Walkers Rocks camping area is accessible with a 2WD.

Who to contact: District Council of Elliston (08) 8687 9177

279 Walkers Rocks camping area

A brilliant beachside location close to Elliston, Walkers Rocks offers great fishing and safe swimming, with the occasional surf break too. Assorted sites are set among the dunes, some with shade. At low tide, experienced four-wheel drivers can explore the long strip of beach extending north, for salmon fishing. Access is signposted off Walkers Rocks Rd, 9 km north of Elliston via Flinders Hwy. Pick up a permit from the self-registration station. Gas BBQs are allowed. The park may be closed during days of extreme fire danger. **Map refs:** 237 F4, 248 B5, 250 A12, 257 O12

LAURA BAY CONSERVATION PARK

This compact coastal park is remarkably diverse, with everything from rocky headlands and mangrove creeks to sheltered bays and tidal pools. A sanctuary for seabirds, it's also a handy swimming and fishing stop, just off the Eyre Hwy.

Who to contact: Parks SA (08) 8625 3144

280 Laura Bay camping area (bush camping)

Situated 21 km south-east of Ceduna, there is alternative access to these sites for bush campers via Decres Bay Rd. Only use the designated sites. **Map refs:** 237 E3, 257 M8

LINCOLN NATIONAL PARK

Within easy reach of Port Lincoln, this many-faceted peninsula feels like a land apart. It's home to some of SA's finest beaches and coastal camping. As well as having fish to catch and beaches to swim from, the park is a priceless bushland refuge for native wildlife and seabirds, and plenty of sea lions and dolphins. The storm-ravaged southern shore has dramatic scenery, with a history to match. The camping areas are for self-sufficient campers equipped with firewood and water; permits are required. Some heritage accommodation is also available for rent in the park. For keen bushwalkers, the Investigator Trail is the highlight of the park; it can be done as a multi-day walk, or shorter sections can be completed as day or overnight walks.

Who to contact: Parks SA (08) 8688 3111

281 Carcase Rock camping area

There are 2 bush campsites in this small campground, south of the September Beach camping area. It is secluded and well sheltered in the coastal tea tree, near a beautiful beach. There is a walking track from here heading north to Yachties Beach, and on to either Fishermans Point or September Beach. It is not accessible for caravans. **Map refs:** 237 G6, 248 E8

282 Engine Point camping area

Entry is via the park access road, 25 km north-east of the park entrance. There are 4 sites overlooking Boston Bay.
Map refs: 237 G6, 248 E8

283 Fishermans Point camping area

There is access for small boats from the beach here by 4WD, 24 km north-east of the park entrance off the park access road. Many sites on the headland have great views over the bay. There is walking access from here to Yachties Beach to the east, as well as along the bay. **Map refs:** 237 G6, 248 E8

284 MacLaren Point camping area

It's tent sites only at this secluded site next to a sandy beach. Access is off the Lincoln National Park Access Rd, 27 km north-east of the park entrance. **Map refs:** 237 G6, 248 E8

285 Memory Cove camping area

Remote and beautiful, this is a pristine beach flanked by bushy headlands and massive granite boulders, signposted off Lincoln National Park Access Rd, 29 km south-east of the park entrance. Access is by key, so you need to book; this site is suitable for off-road camper trailers. **Map refs:** 237 G6, 248 E9

286 September Beach camping area

Access to this camping area is from Lincoln National Park Access Rd, 28 km north-east of the park entrance. There are toilets and there is wheelchair access to the beach.
Map refs: 237 G6, 248 E8

287 Spalding Cove camping area

Tent sites only are available on this sheltered bay. Look for the sign off Lincoln National Park Access Rd, 20 km north-east of the park entrance. **Map refs:** 237 G6, 248 E8

288 Surfleet Cove camping area

Surfleet Cove is reached from the national park access road, 22 km north-east of the park entrance. Good for tents, camper trailers and vans. **Map refs:** 237 G6, 248 E8

289 Taylors Landing camping area

Set back in bushland, this site is reached from Lincoln National Park Access Rd, 23 km east of the park entrance. There is boat-ramp access for 4WDs. **Map refs:** 237 G6, 248 E9

290 Woodcutters Beach camping area

There are only 2 sites at this camping area, signposted off Lincoln National Park Access Rd, 15 km east of the park entrance. The campsites are tucked back in the trees and are very sheltered, situated above Proper Bay, with views across the water to Port Lincoln. The Investigator Trail walking track passes through here and leads to the nearby climb up Stamford Hill. **Map refs:** 237 G6, 248 D8

MUNYAROO CONSERVATION PARK

A hefty tract of mallee and saltbush in the lonely stretch of country midway between Whyalla and Cowell, this park protects a diversity of terrain, from dunes and ironstone ridges inland to coastal salt flats and mangroves. Activities include fishing, birdwatching and nature walks to suit experienced wilderness travellers. Check the entry details with Parks SA, as access is via private property.

How to book: Parks SA (08) 8688 3111

291 Munyaroo camping area (bush camping)

The road to the camping area is signposted from the Lincoln Hwy, 44 km south of Whyalla. Bush camping here is for self-sufficient campers only, so bring everything with you. **Map refs:** 237 H4, 248 G4, 250 F12

NULLARBOR NATIONAL PARK

This tremendous span of coastal plain is a stronghold of Aboriginal culture and one of the world's largest – and flattest – limestone landscapes. Though seemingly featureless, it boasts an extraordinary complex of caverns and sinkholes. But the most conspicuous feature is the 80 m high stretch of coastal cliffs that arc for 200 km around the Great Australian Bight. This is a place of grand spectacle, with caves to explore and chance sightings of southern right whales from May to Oct.

Who to contact: Parks SA (08) 8625 3144

292 Highway camping area (bush camping)

Along the Eyre Hwy between the Nullarbor Roadhouse and Border Village there are several roadside bays in the scrub for overnight-only bush camping. Dogs on leads are allowed. **Map refs:** 236 B2, 256 D7

293 Koonalda Homestead camping area

The access track to this no-frills camping area near the homestead is off the Eyre Hwy, 100 km west of the Nullarbor Roadhouse and 90 km east of Border Village. The old homestead and outbuildings, built mainly from sleepers from the *Indian Pacific* railway, are unique and interesting. This homestead used to service traffic crossing the Nullarbor before the sealed Eyre Hwy was put in 15 km to the south in the 1970s. Nearby, to the north, is the entrance to Koonalda cave, a sinkhole with fruit trees growing at the bottom. The camping area is 15 km north of the highway; the homestead is available for rent. **Map refs: 236 B2, 256 E6**

POINT BELL CONSERVATION PARK

A striking cliff-edged promontory of granite, Point Bell is connected to the mainland by a slender isthmus. The wild beaches either side offer abundant choices for swimming, fishing and birdwatching. Access is by 4WD only.

Who to contact: Parks SA (08) 8625 3144; or Ceduna Gateway Visitor Information Centre (08) 8625 2780

294 Point Bell camping area

    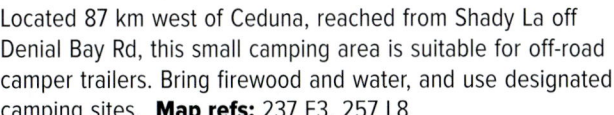

Located 87 km west of Ceduna, reached from Shady La off Denial Bay Rd, this small camping area is suitable for off-road camper trailers. Bring firewood and water, and use designated camping sites. **Map refs: 237 E3, 257 L8**

PUREBA CONSERVATION PARK

Part of the vast sweep of sand-dune and salt-flat country sprawling north-west of Eyre Peninsula, this conservation park is an important ecological corridor between the Great Victoria Desert and southern habitats. It's challenging terrain for exploration and natural-history enthusiasts. Access is by 4WD only.

Who to contact: Parks SA (08) 8625 3144

295 Pureba camping area (bush camping)

This camping area is 15 km north of the Eyre Hwy, reached from Mudamuckla. With no facilities, you need to be fully prepared for bush camping. **Map refs: 237 F3, 257 N8**

SCEALE BAY CONSERVATION PARK

This seafront reserve near Streaky Bay protects the northern reaches of dazzling Sceale Bay, including the key bird habitat of Seagull Lake and a wild stretch of coastal dunes. The beach fishing and rock-fishing here are excellent.

Who to contact: Parks SA (08) 8625 3144

296 Sceale Bay camping area (bush camping)

Located 15 km south of Streaky Bay, reached from Streaky Bay–Sceale Bay Rd, this area for bush camping has no facilities. **Map refs: 237 F4, 248 A3, 257 N10**

WAHGUNYAH CONSERVATION PARK

Wonderfully wild, this rambling shore of dunes backed by heath and mallee scrub is remote and little-trodden. A 4WD is required to get the most out of the beaches and backroads. Located 15 km south of the Eyre Hwy, this is a real surfing and fishing getaway spot, with Dog Fence Beach and Cheetima Beach among the most popular destinations. Contact Parks SA Ceduna for access details.

Who to contact: Parks SA (08) 8625 3144

297 Cape Adieu camping area

Situated 37 km south-west of Nundroo, off the Eyre Hwy, these camping areas for self-sufficient campers are set behind the main sand dunes. A 4WD is recommended. **Map refs: 237 D3, 257 J8**

298 Dog Fence Beach camping area

Located 40 km west of Nundroo, reached from the Eyre Hwy, this beach camping area is popular with self-sufficient surfers and anglers. **Map refs: 236 D2, 257 I7**

WITTELBEE CONSERVATION PARK

Here the slender headland of Point Wittlebee frames sheltered bays backed by dunes and mallee scrub. Though small, the park is only 10 km south-east of Ceduna and has a range of options for swimming, fishing and coastal walks, with cliff-top views to St Peter Island.

Who to contact: Parks SA (08) 8625 3144

299 Wittelbee camping area (bush camping)

A small camping area with designated sites for self-sufficient campers, follow the signposted route from Decres Bay Rd. Snorkelling in the sheltered bays around the headland can be good in calm conditions, and the rocky shore offers many opportunities for fossicking in the tide-pools. The sunset over Spencer Gulf can be quite spectacular from here. **Map refs: 237 E3, 257 M8**

YELLABINNA REGIONAL RESERVE

North of Ceduna a vast tract of SA is now a conservation and wilderness area. Red sand dunes with a sparse cover of fragile vegetation stretch to the horizon. Only 4WDs can access this area, which is home to rare birds such as scarlet-chested parrots, Major Mitchells cockatoos and mallee fowl.

Who to contact: Parks SA (08) 8625 3144

300 Mount Finke camping area (bush camping)

This is the northernmost of the 2 camping areas on the 4WD Googs Track. At 369 m high, Mt Finke is a major landmark in this desert landscape, with outstanding views from its craggy summit. It also has diverse plant communities, including a grevillea endemic to the area. Basic bush camping is available here; there are no facilities. It's 137.48 km north of Ceduna. **Map refs: 237 E1, 257 N5**

YUMBARRA CONSERVATION PARK

Red dune ridges in this park are traversed by the Googs Track, accessible to 4WDs only. Although the landscape may appear inhospitable, it contains a number of rockholes – including Childara Rock – that fill with rainwater and thus sustain many species of birds, making Yumbarra popular with birdwatchers.

Who to contact: Parks SA (08) 8625 3144

301 Googs Lake camping area (bush camping)

This is one of 2 camping areas on the 4WD Googs Track. It might be salt but this remote lake feels like an oasis in a sea of dunes. There's a surprising mix of vegetation and terrain to explore, plus some welcome shade. The lakes are 76.6 km north of the Eyre Hwy. A permit and all self-sufficient equipment are required. **Map refs:** 237 E2, 257 N6

CAMPSITES LOCATED IN OTHER AREAS

302 Baird Bay Campground

There's camping for self-sufficient campers on the northern side of Baird Bay, 50 km south-east of Streaky Bay. To get here, take Baird Bay Rd off Flinders Hwy. Boat tours of Baird Bay leave from the township near the campground, and take you for swims with wild dolphins and sea lions. This is an experience not to be missed. **Map refs:** 237 F4, 248 A4, 257 N11

Who to contact: Streaky Bay Visitor Information Centre (08) 8626 7033

303 Coffin Bay Caravan Park

Located only a stone's throw from the water's edge, this park is 16 ha and features big sites, so you won't feel hemmed in. There's lots of lawn and shaded areas, and the unpowered camping area is natural bushland with many native trees for shade. There are 2 amenities blocks, 1 with a modern laundry with coin-operated washing machines and dryers. The second amenities block includes excellent disabled facilities. There are 2 BBQ areas, in the middle of the park and near the playground. **Map refs:** 237 G6, 248 D8

How to book: The Esplanade, Coffin Bay (08) 8685 4170 www.coffinbay.net/caravanpark

304 Davenport Creek camping area

Home to some of the west coast's finest surfing and fishing, this remote spot 41 km west of Ceduna has it all: pristine beaches, beautiful dunes, wildlife-rich mangroves and glorious coastal landscapes. Conventional vehicles can access the Cocklebeds and Ocean Beach, while a 4WD is needed to launch a boat at the creek and navigate the dunes to the headland beyond. Check current conditions at Ceduna's visitor centre. Come with your own water, gas/fuel stove and firewood. **Map refs:** 237 E3, 257 L8

Who to contact: Ceduna Gateway Visitors Information Centre (08) 8625 2780

305 Farm Beach camping area

A west-coast icon, this magical strip of sand is famed for its tractor collection, excellent fishing and relaxed family camping in high summer. There is a 4WD boat launch from the beach. The camping area is 37 km north of Coffin Bay and 10 km west of Wangary, with access via Farm Beach Rd. Nearby Dutton Bay, with its historic jetty and stone woolshed, and Gallipoli Beach are well worth a look. Bring your own water and firewood. **Map refs:** 237 F5, 248 C8

Who to contact: Port Lincoln Visitor Information Centre (08) 8683 3544

306 Fitzgerald Bay camping area

A series of designated camping spots – some with toilets – can be found scattered along the shores of the bay for self-sufficient campers, 32 km north-east of Whyalla. Ocean views and beach access for swimming and fishing make these sites ideal. They are all found along the unsealed coast road between Point Lowly, with its iconic lighthouse, and the small settlement of Fitzgerald Bay. Approach via Point Lowly Rd off Lincoln Hwy, 10 km north of Whyalla. A boat ramp is nearby at Point Lowly. **Map refs:** 237 H4, 248 H3, 250 G10

Who to contact: Whyalla Visitor Centre (08) 8645 7900

Googs Track

Though less than 200 km long, this trek across the dune ridges spanning Yumbarra Conservation Park and Yellabinna Regional Reserve is a grand 4WD adventure. You need to be completely self-sufficient on this remote track, named in honour of John 'Goog' Denton, and his son Martin 'Dinger' Denton. South to north crossings are strongly recommended; take care when approaching other vehicles on crests.

Please note that campsites are listed in alphabetical order, not track order. Refer to the map on p. 237 for further information.

Who to contact: Parks SA (08) 8625 3144

301 Googs Lake camping area (bush camping)
See p. 241.

300 Mount Finke camping area (bush camping)
See p. 241.

307 Haslam Jetty camping area

This small camping area is just 100 m from the jetty in the historic port settlement of Haslam Jetty. You'll find it 40 km north of Streaky Bay and 33 km south-west of Wirulla, off Flinders Hwy. Bring your own firewood. **Map refs:** 237 F3, 248 A2, 257 N9

Who to contact: Streaky Bay Visitor Information Centre (08) 8626 7033

308 The Knob camping area

This popular fishing and swimming haunt is just 13 km south of Cowell and its oyster farms in Franklin Harbour, where the beach is a sheltered curve of sand bounded by rock flats and a low headland called the Knob. Camping is basic here, for self-sufficient campers. Look for the sign on Wellington–Beach Rd. **Map refs:** 237 H5, 248 F6

Who to contact: District Council of Franklin Harbour (08) 8629 2019

309 Lipson Cove camping area

This is an easygoing coastal hideout halfway between Tumby Bay and Port Neil, with fine ocean views and a beach that offers good swimming and fishing. There's a walk at low tide to explore Lipson Island Conservation Park. The camping is 24 km north of Tumby Bay, with signposted access from Lincoln Hwy via Lipson Cove Rd. Firewood, water and a gas/fuel stove are essential. **Map refs:** 237 G5, 248 E7

Who to contact: District Council of Tumby Bay (08) 8688 2101

310 Louth Bay camping area

No-frills camping for self-sufficient campers is possible on the fringe of the coastal township of Louth Bay, with views across the golf course. The rocky shoreline is not far away and there are plenty of opportunities for a fish and swim around town, plus you can launch the tinny off the beach. It's 21 km north of Port Lincoln with access via The Haven Dr off Lincoln Hwy. **Map refs:** 237 G5, 248 D8

Who to contact: District Council of Lower Eyre Peninsula (08) 8676 2106

311 Point Lowly camping area

There is an unpowered caravan/camping area at Port Bonython Rd near the boat ramp, with showers and toilets. Note: there are time limits on how long you can stay. **Map refs:** 237 H4, 248 H3, 250 G11

Who to contact: Whyalla Visitor Centre (08) 8645 7900

312 Port Kenny Caravan Park

This is a favourite for travellers looking for a quiet place to relax. There are shaded powered sites and ensuite cabins, a free BBQ area and open fire pits. The owner will launch your boat in the bay with the park tractor, and give you some local fishing tips. There is also a good fish-cleaning area and the adjoining roadhouse does hearty meals and takeaway if you have no luck fishing. **Map refs:** 237 F4, 248 B4, 257 O11

Who to contact: Flinders Hwy, Port Kenny (08) 8625 5076

313 Sheringa Coastal camping area

This classic west-coast surf beach is a legendary salmon-fishing haunt, with good catches of whiting also possible here. There's no shortage of wild coastline and scenery to the north; swim and surf with care. It's reached from Sheringa Beach Rd off Flinders Hwy, 39 km south of Elliston. Pick up a permit from the self-registration station, and come with firewood and water. **Map refs:** 237 F5, 248 C6

Who to contact: District Council of Elliston (08) 8687 9177

314 Speeds Point camping area (bush camping)

A popular camping haunt with sheltered nooks among the dunes near the protected waters off Yanerbie Beach, Speeds Point is 16 km south of Streaky Bay, off Westall Way Scenic Dr. This is bush camping, with no facilities. **Map refs:** 237 E4, 248 A3, 257 N10

Who to contact: Streaky Bay Visitor Information Centre (08) 8626 7033

315 Talia Caves camping area (bush camping)

Striking coastal cave formations here feature wave-hollowed limestone atop massive granite terraces. There's also good rock-fishing nearby and surf beaches just to the south. Watch the rip if swimming. Simple bush camping is offered, opposite Woolshed Cave, with not a lot of shelter. Take the signposted Talia Caves Rd off Flinders Hwy, 44 km north of Elliston. **Map refs:** 237 F4, 248 B4, 250 A12, 257 O12

Who to contact: District Council of Elliston (08) 8687 9177

316 Tractor Beach camping area (bush camping)

Just 9 km south of Streaky Bay, off Westall Way Scenic Dr, this coastal area for bush camping overlooks the coast and a safe swimming beach. **Map refs:** 237 E4, 248 A3, 257 N10

Who to contact: Streaky Bay Visitor Information Centre (08) 8626 7033

317 Venus Bay Caravan Park

This pretty park is situated on the beachfront, 6 km from Flinders Hwy. There are plenty of sites and cabins, with a fully equipped camp kitchen and spacious disabled facilities. The park rents out fibreglass boats in case you want to fish – or you can surf, explore or just relax. There are plenty of fish in the protected bay, including the much-loved King George whiting, tommy ruff, flathead, salmon trout, trevally, snook, garfish and squid. **Map refs:** 237 F4, 248 B4, 257 O11

How to book: 32 Matson Tce, Venus Bay (08) 8625 5073 www.venusbaycaravanparksa.com.au

KANGAROO ISLAND

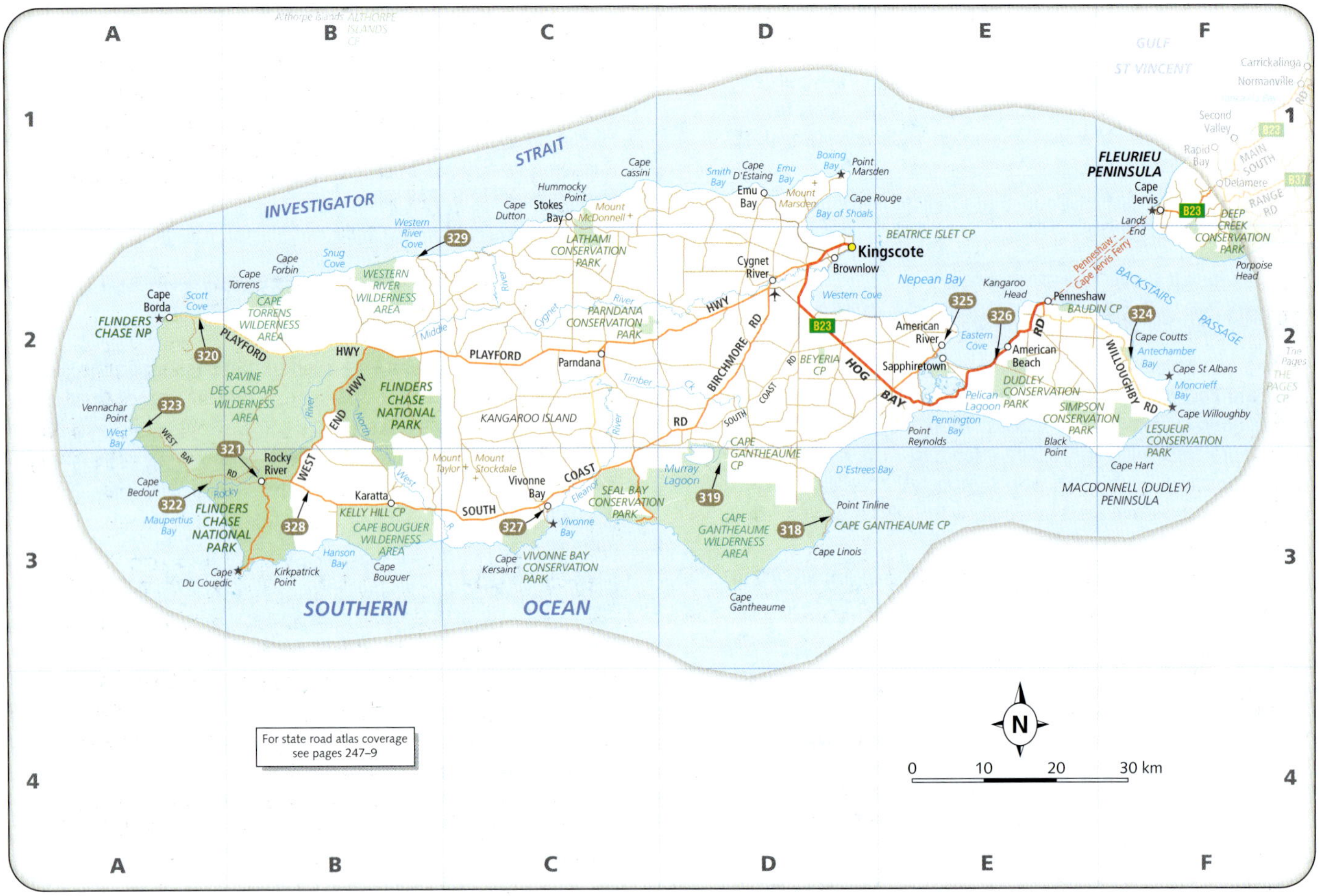

[Map of Kangaroo Island with grid reference coordinates A–F (columns) and 1–4 (rows)]

INVESTIGATOR STRAIT

Athorpe Islands ALTHORPE ISLANDS CP

Cape Cassini
Cape D'Estaing
Emu Bay
Boxing Bay
Point Marsden
Smith Bay
Cape Emu Bay
Mount Marsden
Cape Rouge
Bay of Shoals

Hummocky Point
Cape Dutton
Cape Stokes Bay
Mount McDonnell

329

Western River Cove
River

WESTERN RIVER WILDERNESS AREA

Snug Cove
Cape Forbin
Cape Torrens

CAPE TORRENS WILDERNESS AREA

Cape Borda
Scott Cove
FLINDERS CHASE NP

320 **PLAYFORD HWY**

RAVINE DES CASOARS WILDERNESS AREA

FLINDERS CHASE NATIONAL PARK

WEST END HWY

Vennachar Point
West Bay

323

321 Rocky River

WEST BAY RD

Cape Bedout
Rocky
322
Maupertius Bay
FLINDERS CHASE NATIONAL PARK
328
Cape Du Couedic
Kirkpatrick Point

Karatta
KELLY HILL CP
CAPE BOUGUER WILDERNESS AREA
Hanson Bay
Cape Bouguer

Mount Taylor
Mount Stockdale
Vivonne Bay
SOUTH
327
Cape Kersaint
VIVONNE BAY CONSERVATION PARK
Vivonne Bay

PLAYFORD
Parndana
PARNDANA CONSERVATION PARK
Cygnet River
Timber River
KANGAROO ISLAND
COAST RD
Elean
SEAL BAY CONSERVATION PARK
319
Murray Lagoon
CAPE GANTHEAUME CP
CAPE GANTHEAUME WILDERNESS AREA
318
Cape Linois
Cape Gantheaume
CAPE GANTHEAUME CP
Point Tinline

SOUTHERN OCEAN

BIRCHMORE RD
HWY
Kingscote
Brownlow
Cygnet River
BEATRICE ISLET CP
Nepean Bay
Western Cove
B23
American River
Sapphiretown
BEYERIA CP
Eastern Cove
American Beach
HOG BAY RD
DUDLEY CONSERVATION PARK
SIMPSON CONSERVATION PARK
Pelican Lagoon
Pennington Bay
Point Reynolds
Black Point
D'Estrees Bay
Cape Hart
MACDONNELL (DUDLEY) PENINSULA

GULF ST VINCENT
Carrickalinga
Normanville
Second Valley
B23
Rapid Bay
FLEURIEU PENINSULA
Cape Jervis
Lands End
DEEP CREEK CONSERVATION PARK
Porpoise Head
Penneshaw – Cape Jervis Ferry
BACKSTAIRS PASSAGE
Kangaroo Head
Penneshaw
325
326
BAUDIN CP
324
Cape Coutts
Antechamber Bay
Cape St Albans
Moncrieff Bay
Cape Willoughby
WILLOUGHBY RD
LESUEUR CONSERVATION PARK
MAIN SOUTH RANGE RD
Delamere
B37

For state road atlas coverage see pages 247–9

N

0 10 20 30 km

For state road atlas coverage see pages 247–9

AUSTRALIA'S THIRD LARGEST ISLAND is one of the world's most accessible wildlife havens, with more than half the island's original bushland intact. The pristine nature of its habitats, and the absence of foxes and rabbits, encourages an extraordinary abundance of native animals. If you want to be among kangaroos, wallabies, goannas, echidnas, koalas and possums in their natural settings, this is the place. It's also home to nearly 240 bird species and a parade of beguiling coastal visitors, from seals and sea lions to dolphins and little penguins.

Flinders Chase National Park at the island's wild western end is the major drawcard, with walks to secluded coves and woodlands, plus stunning rock formations like Admirals Arch and nearby Remarkable Rocks. But every corner of 'KI', as the locals call it, boasts its share of coastal splendour. Beyond the parks there is an array of reserves and expansive wilderness areas to explore.

And while the camping facilities might be basic, the spectacular scenery and seclusion at sites like Antechamber Bay, Western River Cove and Vivonne Bay are compensation aplenty. As well as the ever-present wildlife there is virtually unlimited scope to enjoy fine swimming beaches, bushwalks, fishing, surfing and diving.

Given the island's mild maritime climate, camping is possible all year round. Even mid-year there are sheltered bays and hideaways on the north and east coasts that catch the winter sun. Island landscapes and the power of the elements figure prominently in KI's vivid history of shipwrecks and settlement. Those same natural forces also continue to drive a strong local art tradition and a range of farming enterprises. As much as travellers treasure KI's wildlife, they increasingly revel in the island's emerging food and cafe culture – everything from premium lamb and sensational seafood to cheese, eggs, honey and award-winning wines.

CAMPSITES LOCATED IN PARKS AND RESERVES

CAPE GANTHEAUME CONSERVATION PARK

This vast chunk of coastal heath, dune hollows and mallee is mostly untracked wilderness. Coastal headlands and beaches overlook D'Estrees Bay, while experienced bushwalkers occasionally trek to the cape itself. Nearby Murray Lagoon is the island's largest freshwater enclosure and a great place to spot birds, while Seal Bay Conservation Park is a world-famous haven for Australian sea lions. Get your permits from the Murray Lagoon ranger station.

Who to contact: Parks SA (08) 8553 4444

318 D'Estrees Bay camping area

With beachside camping on the doorstep of some of the island's most windswept shores, this dramatic outpost comes with reefs, craggy headlands, shipwrecks and wild surf – and good fishing. It's 68 km south of Kingscote, off D'Estrees Bay Rd. Come with water and a gas/fuel stove. **Map refs:** 244 D3, 248 H12

319 Murray Lagoon camping area

The island's largest freshwater lagoon is a peaceful haunt for birdwatchers, nature photographers and wildflower enthusiasts, especially after winter rains. The camping area is off Seagers Rd, 46 km south of Kingscote. Cooking is gas/fuel stove only. **Map refs:** 244 D3, 248 H12

FLINDERS CHASE NATIONAL PARK

One of SA's wild gems, this 32 600 ha park includes dramatic coastal scenery, glorious bushland and compelling wildlife encounters. Admirals Arch and Remarkable Rocks are highlights, while the walks to Snake Lagoon and other hideouts along the west coast create a vivid sense of seclusion.

Who to contact: Parks SA (08) 8553 4490

320 Harveys Return camping area

In a remote and historic cliff-top location, this camping area is the old landing site for the lightkeepers at Cape Borda. Harveys Return is at the far western end of Playford Hwy, 63 km from Parndana. Bring water and a gas/fuel stove. Cottage and hut accommodation is also available near the lighthouse. **Map refs:** 244 A2, 248 F11

321 Rocky River camping area

The park's main campground is close to nature trails, facilities and the visitor centre and cafe. It's a pleasant woodland setting, though busy at peak holiday times. It is found on South Coast Rd, 4 km from the park entrance. There are hot showers and a gas BBQ on site. Bookings are essential. **Map refs:** 244 B3, 248 F12

322 Snake Lagoon camping area

Sheltered tent sites are nestled in the sugar gums by the lagoon, which is glorious in spring. This is also the start of an excellent walking track to the ravine and beach where Rocky River meets the sea. Bookings are required. The camping area is 8 km along West Bay Track from the park visitor centre. Bring water and a gas/fuel stove. **Map refs:** 244 A3, 248 F12

323 West Bay camping area

This site, perched atop the island's westernmost inlet, offers seclusion and spectacular views. While shipwrecks lie just beyond its rugged headlands, the bay's pristine beach is a delight for swimming and fishing. Camp at the end of West Bay Rd, 22 km from the the visitor centre. Bring water and a gas/fuel stove. **Map refs:** 244 A2, 248 F12

LASHMAR CONSERVATION PARK

Lashmar preserves a major patch of remnant coastal bush leading to beautiful Antechamber Bay, a sweep of white sand that offers the best swimming and fishing on the eastern end of Kangaroo Island. Nearby Lashmar Lagoon is great for canoeing and waterbirds.

Who to contact: Parks SA (08) 8553 4444

324 Antechamber Bay camping area

Various sites are tucked among the bush to the west of Chapman River, signposted off Willoughby Rd, 19 km south-east of Penneshaw. The tidal waters are safe for kids. Bring wood and water, and preferably a gas/fuel stove. **Map refs:** 244 F2, 247 A5, 249 I11

Boardwalk near the Remarkable Rocks, Flinders Chase National Park (p. 245)

CAMPSITES LOCATED IN OTHER AREAS

325   American River camping area

This pleasant council-owned waterfront site overlooking the channel leading to Pelican Lagoon and its abundant birdlife is an easy stroll to the boat ramp and good fishing spots on the town jetty. It's reached from Tangara Dr. **Map refs:** 244 E2, 248 H11

Who to contact: Kangaroo Island Council (08) 8553 4500
Camping fees: Pay at the self-registration site.

326   Browns Beach camping area

Assorted sites for self-sufficient campers are tucked close to this long beach, part of the sweeping shoreline facing Eastern Cove. It's suited to all ages, with sheltered swimming, beachcombing and good snorkelling. The camping area is just off Hog Bay Rd, 12 km south-west of Penneshaw. **Map refs:** 244 E2, 248 H11

Who to contact: Kangaroo Island Council (08) 8553 4500

327   Vivonne Bay camping area

These secluded sites are within easy reach of Harriet River and swimming areas by the town jetty, accessed from Jetty Rd.

Beyond lies a vast sweep of windswept beach to explore, which is also a great spot for whale-watching from May–Oct. **Map refs:** 244 C3, 248 G12

Who to contact: Kangaroo Island Council (08) 8553 4500
Camping fees: Pay at the self-registration box.

328   Western KI Caravan Park

Poised on the threshold to Flinders Chase, this leafy park is set in its own wildife reserve, so there is plenty of bird and animal life to enjoy. Log cabins are also available at the park, which is 65 km south-west of Kingscote on the South Coast Rd. No pets are allowed. **Map refs:** 244 B3, 248 F12

How to book: South Coast Rd (08) 8559 7201
www.westernki.com.au

329   Western River camping area

At this hideaway tucked alongside one of the north coast's more remote estuaries, a footbridge leads to the cove's enchanting sandy beach and nearby rockpools. It's a great place for swimming, fishing and fossicking. You'll find it on Western River Cove Rd, 44 km north-west of Parndana. Bring wood and a permit. **Map refs:** 244 B2, 248 G11

Who to contact: Kangaroo Island Council (08) 8553 4500

South-eastern South Australia

Southern Central South Australia

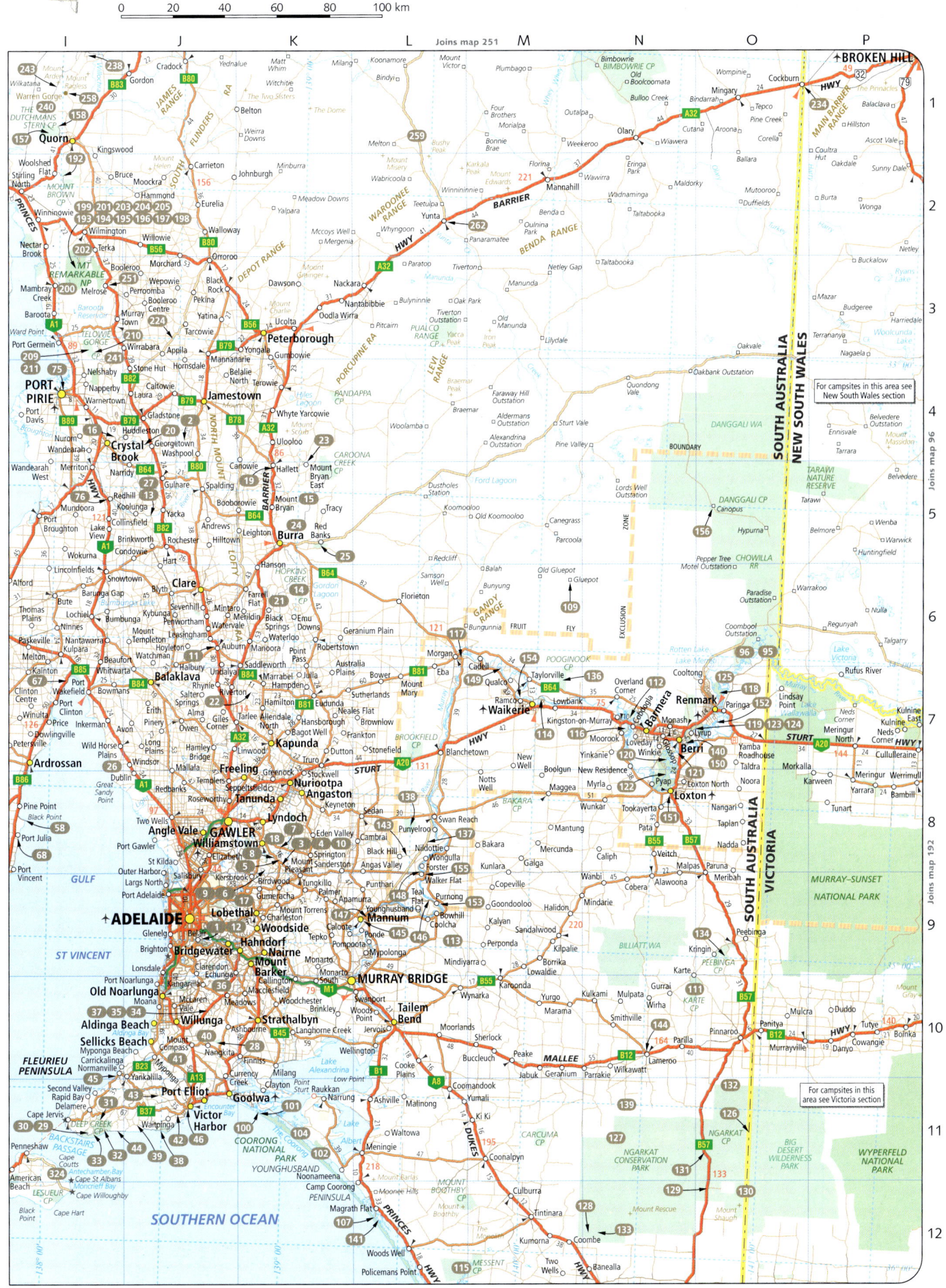

Central South Australia

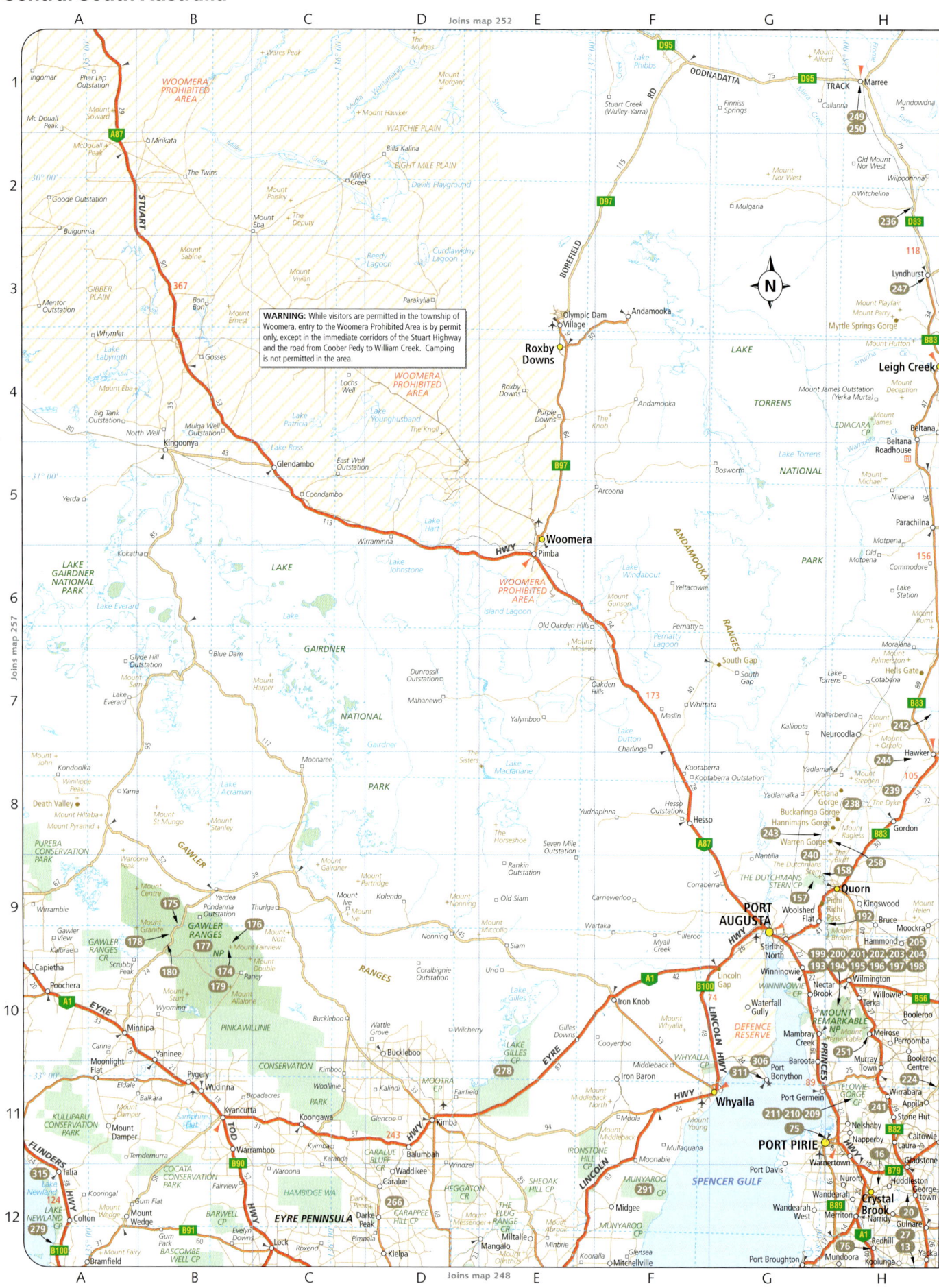

Joins map 252

Joins map 257

WARNING: While visitors are permitted in the township of Woomera, entry to the Woomera Prohibited Area is by permit only, except in the immediate corridors of the Stuart Highway and the road from Coober Pedy to William Creek. Camping is not permitted in the area.

Joins map 248

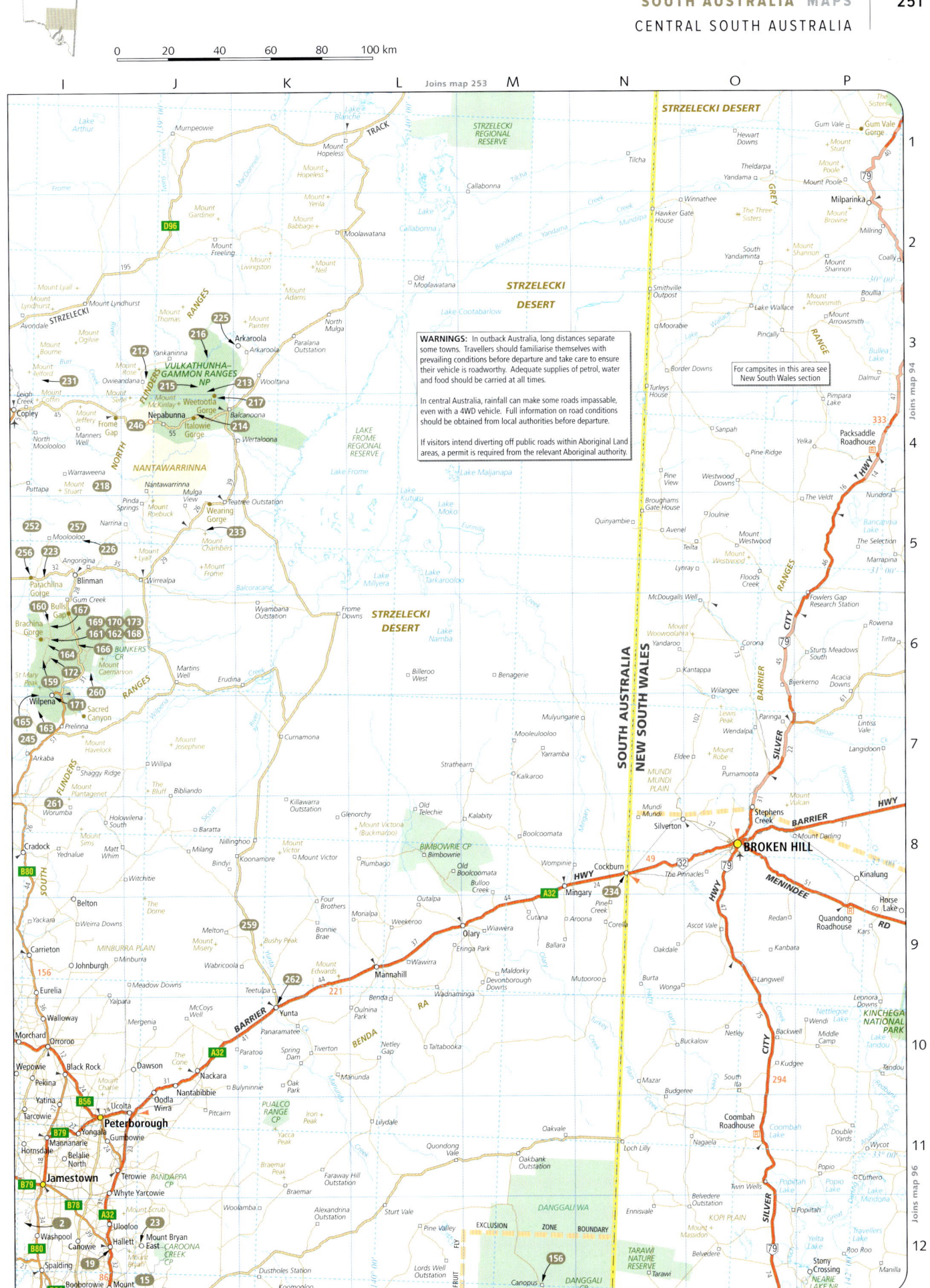

WARNINGS: In outback Australia, long distances separate some towns. Travellers should familiarise themselves with prevailing conditions before departure and take care to ensure their vehicle is roadworthy. Adequate supplies of petrol, water and food should be carried at all times.

In central Australia, rainfall can make some roads impassable, even with a 4WD vehicle. Full information on road conditions should be obtained from local authorities before departure.

If visitors intend diverting off public roads within Aboriginal Land areas, a permit is required from the relevant Aboriginal authority.

For campsites in this area see New South Wales section

North-eastern South Australia

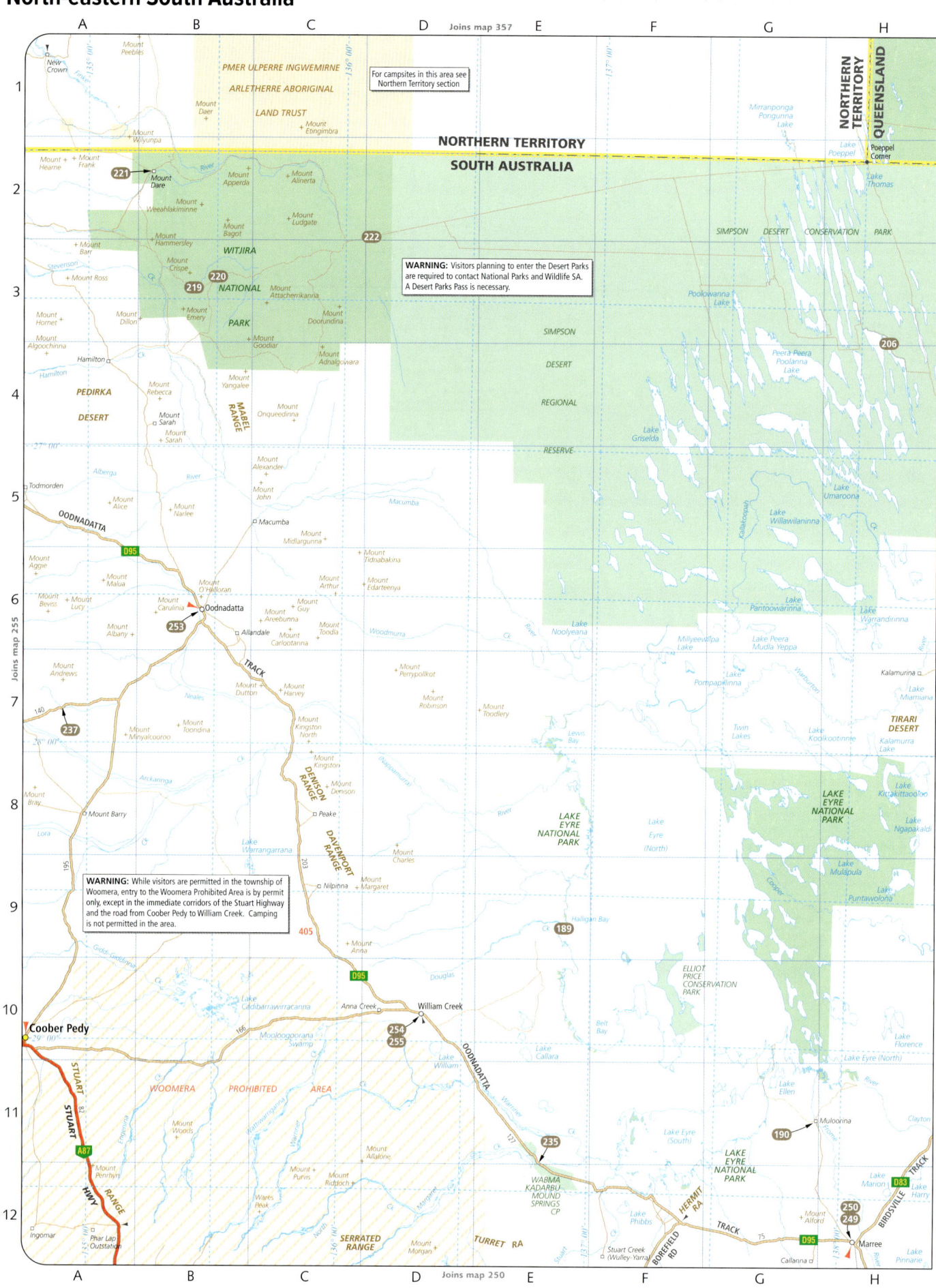

For campsites in this area see
Northern Territory section

NORTHERN TERRITORY
SOUTH AUSTRALIA

WARNING: Visitors planning to enter the Desert Parks
are required to contact National Parks and Wildlife SA.
A Desert Parks Pass is necessary.

WARNING: While visitors are permitted in the township of
Woomera, entry to the Woomera Prohibited Area is by permit
only, except in the immediate corridors of the Stuart Highway
and the road from Coober Pedy to William Creek. Camping
is not permitted in the area.

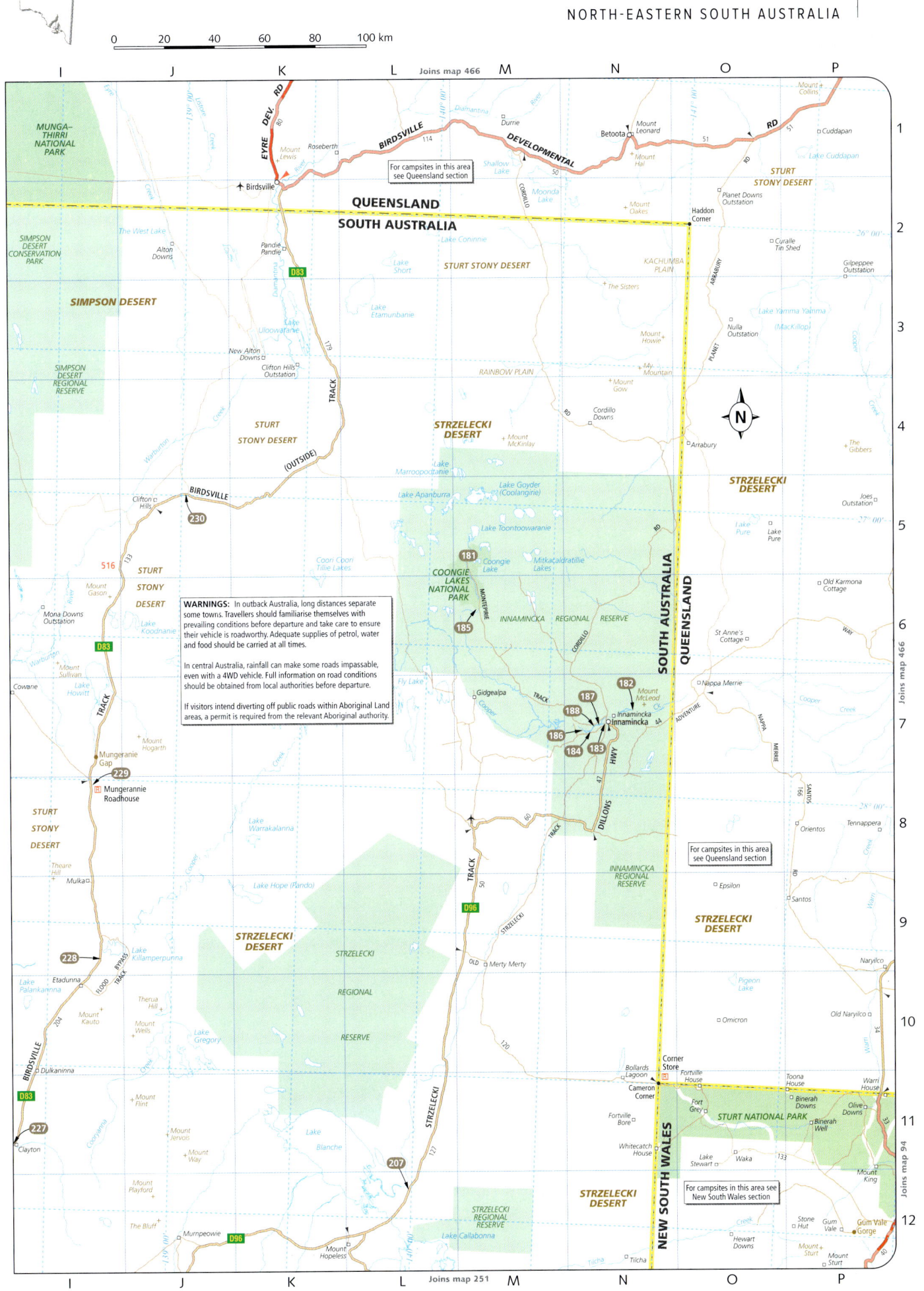

0 20 40 60 80 100 km

Joins map 466

WARNINGS: In outback Australia, long distances separate some towns. Travellers should familiarise themselves with prevailing conditions before departure and take care to ensure their vehicle is roadworthy. Adequate supplies of petrol, water and food should be carried at all times.

In central Australia, rainfall can make some roads impassable, even with a 4WD vehicle. Full information on road conditions should be obtained from local authorities before departure.

If visitors intend diverting off public roads within Aboriginal Land areas, a permit is required from the relevant Aboriginal authority.

For campsites in this area see Queensland section

QUEENSLAND
SOUTH AUSTRALIA

For campsites in this area see Queensland section

For campsites in this area see New South Wales section

Joins map 251

North-western South Australia

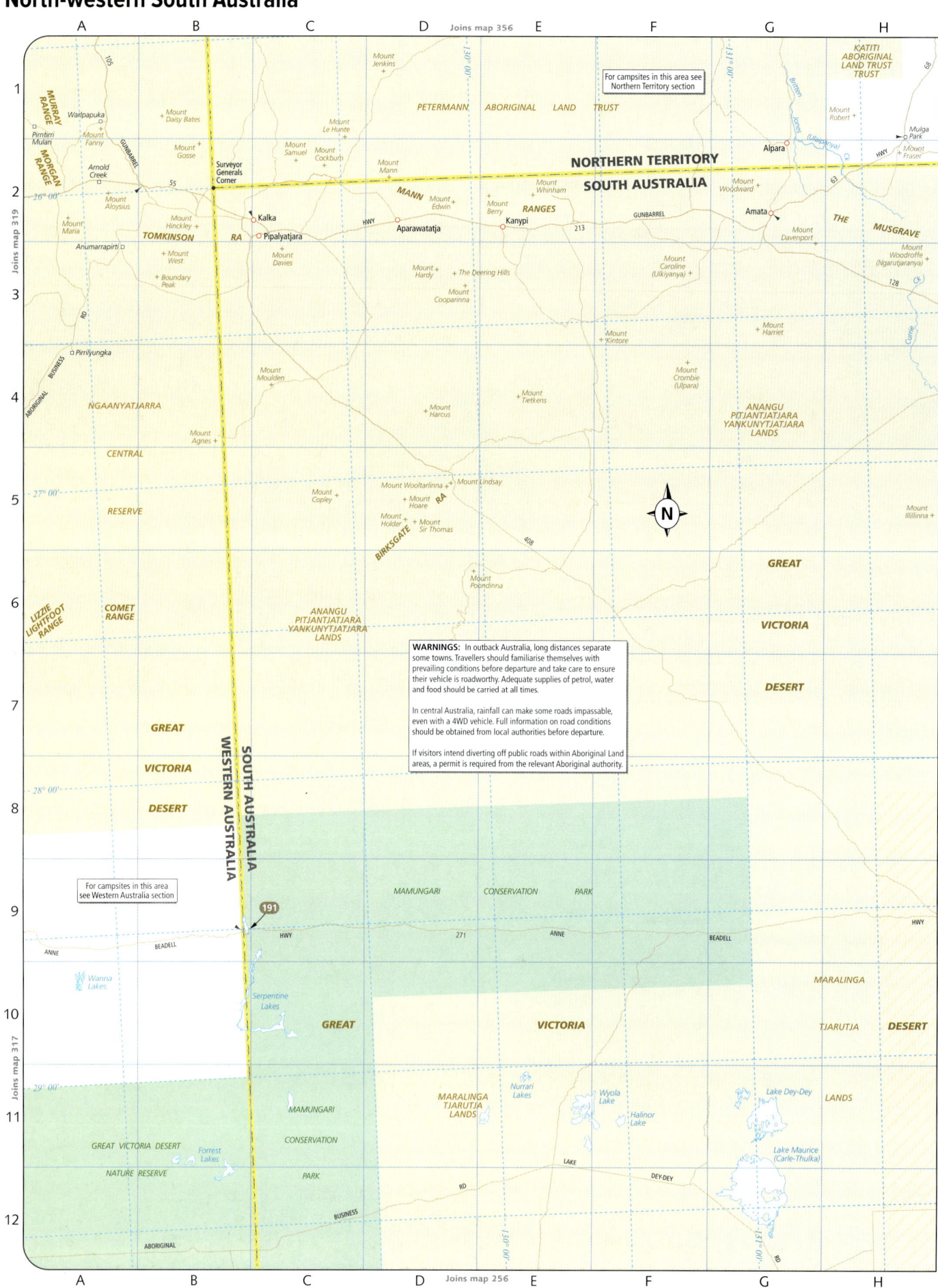

Joins map 356

Joins map 319

Joins map 317

Joins map 256

For campsites in this area see
Northern Territory section

KATITI
ABORIGINAL
LAND TRUST
TRUST

NORTHERN TERRITORY
SOUTH AUSTRALIA

PETERMANN   ABORIGINAL   LAND   TRUST

MURRAY
RANGE

Warlpapuka

Pirntiri
Mulan

MORGAN
RANGE

Mount
Maria

Anumarrapirti

Arnold
Creek

Mount
Aloysius

Mount
Fanny

Mount
Daisy Bates

Mount
Gosse

Surveyor
Generals
Corner

Mount
Hinckley

Kalka

Pipalyatjara

Mount
Davies

Mount
West

Boundary
Peak

TOMKINSON   RA

Mount
Samuel

Mount
Cockburn

Mount
Le Hunte

Mount
Jenkins

Mount
Mann

MANN

Mount
Edwin

Mount
Berry

Aparawatatja

Kanypi

RANGES

Mount
Whinham

Mount
Woodward

GUNBARREL

Amata

Mount
Davenport

THE

MUSGRAVE

Mount
Woodroffe
(Ngarutjaranya)

Mount
Hardy

The Deering Hills

Mount
Cooparinna

Mount
Caroline
(Ulkiyanya)

Mount
Harriet

Mount
Kintore

ANANGU
PITJANTJATJARA
YANKUNYTJATJARA
LANDS

Pirnlyungka

NGAANYATJARRA

Mount
Agnes

Mount
Moulden

Mount
Harcus

Mount
Tietkens

Mount
Crombie
(Ulpara)

CENTRAL

RESERVE

Mount
Copley

Mount Wooltarlinna

Mount
Hoare

Mount
Holder

Mount
Sir Thomas

Mount Lindsay

BIRKSGATE   RA

Mount
Illilinna

Mount
Poondinna

GREAT

VICTORIA

DESERT

LIZZIE
LIGHTFOOT
RANGE

COMET
RANGE

ANANGU
PITJANTJATJARA
YANKUNYTJATJARA
LANDS

WARNINGS: In outback Australia, long distances separate
some towns. Travellers should familiarise themselves with
prevailing conditions before departure and take care to ensure
their vehicle is roadworthy. Adequate supplies of petrol, water
and food should be carried at all times.

In central Australia, rainfall can make some roads impassable,
even with a 4WD vehicle. Full information on road conditions
should be obtained from local authorities before departure.

If visitors intend diverting off public roads within Aboriginal Land
areas, a permit is required from the relevant Aboriginal authority.

GREAT

VICTORIA

DESERT

SOUTH AUSTRALIA
WESTERN AUSTRALIA

For campsites in this area
see Western Australia section

MAMUNGARI   CONSERVATION   PARK

ANNE

BEADELL

ANNE

BEADELL

HWY

HWY

191

Wanna
Lakes

Serpentine
Lakes

GREAT

VICTORIA

MARALINGA

TJARUTJA   DESERT

MAMUNGARI

CONSERVATION

PARK

GREAT   VICTORIA   DESERT

NATURE   RESERVE

Forrest
Lakes

MARALINGA
TJARUTJA
LANDS

Nurrari
Lakes

Wyola
Lake

Halinor
Lake

LAKE

DEY-DEY

Lake Dey-Dey

Lake Maurice
(Carle-Thulka)

LANDS

RD

BUSINESS

ABORIGINAL

Alpara

Mount
Robert

Mulga
Park

Mount
Fraser

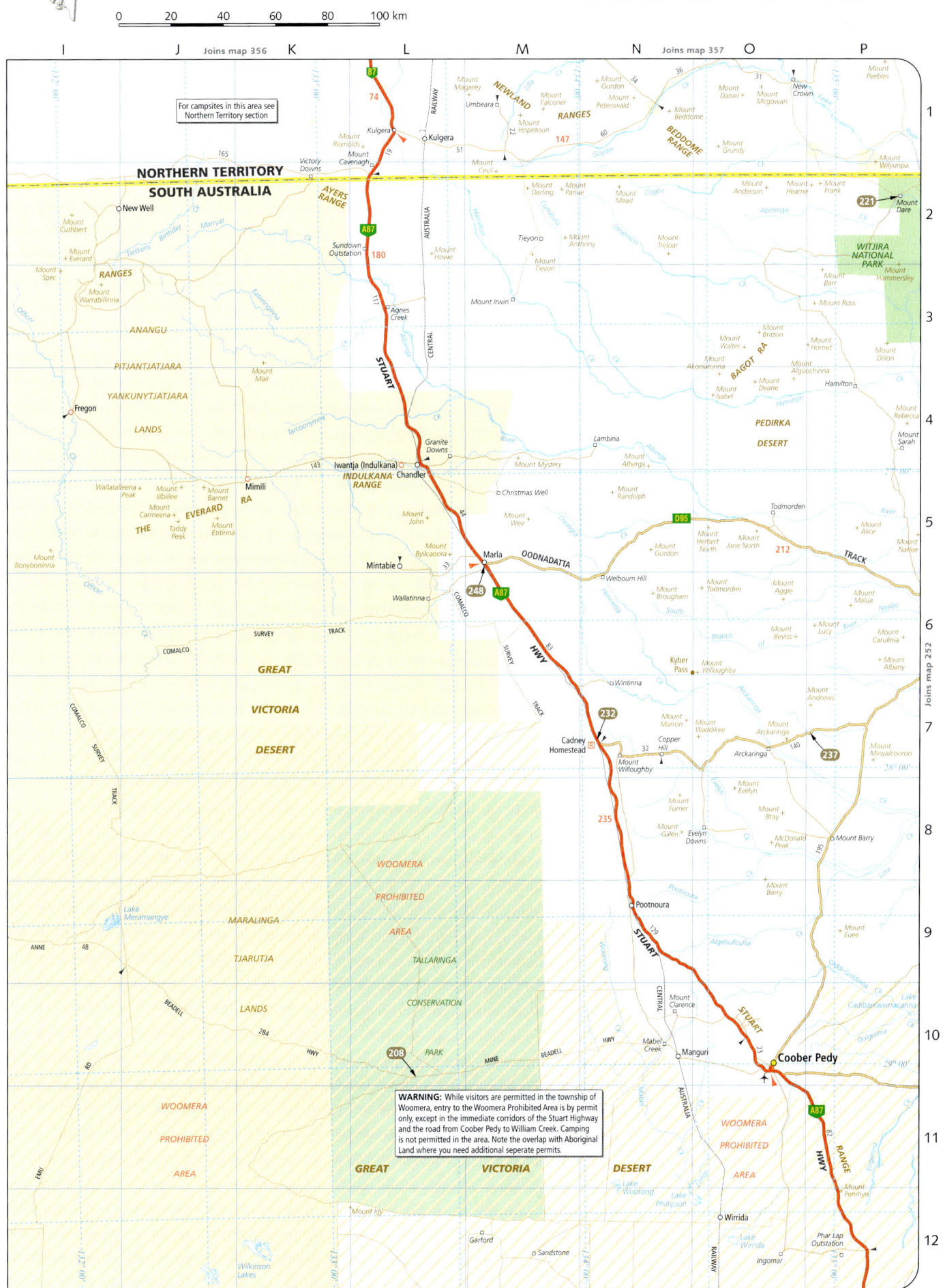

0   20   40   60   80   100 km

Joins map 356

Joins map 357

For campsites in this area see Northern Territory section

NORTHERN TERRITORY
SOUTH AUSTRALIA

WARNING: While visitors are permitted in the township of Woomera, entry to the Woomera Prohibited Area is by permit only, except in the immediate corridors of the Stuart Highway and the road from Coober Pedy to William Creek. Camping is not permitted in the area. Note the overlap with Aboriginal Land where you need additional seperate permits.

Joins map 257

Joins map 252

South-western South Australia

Joins map 254

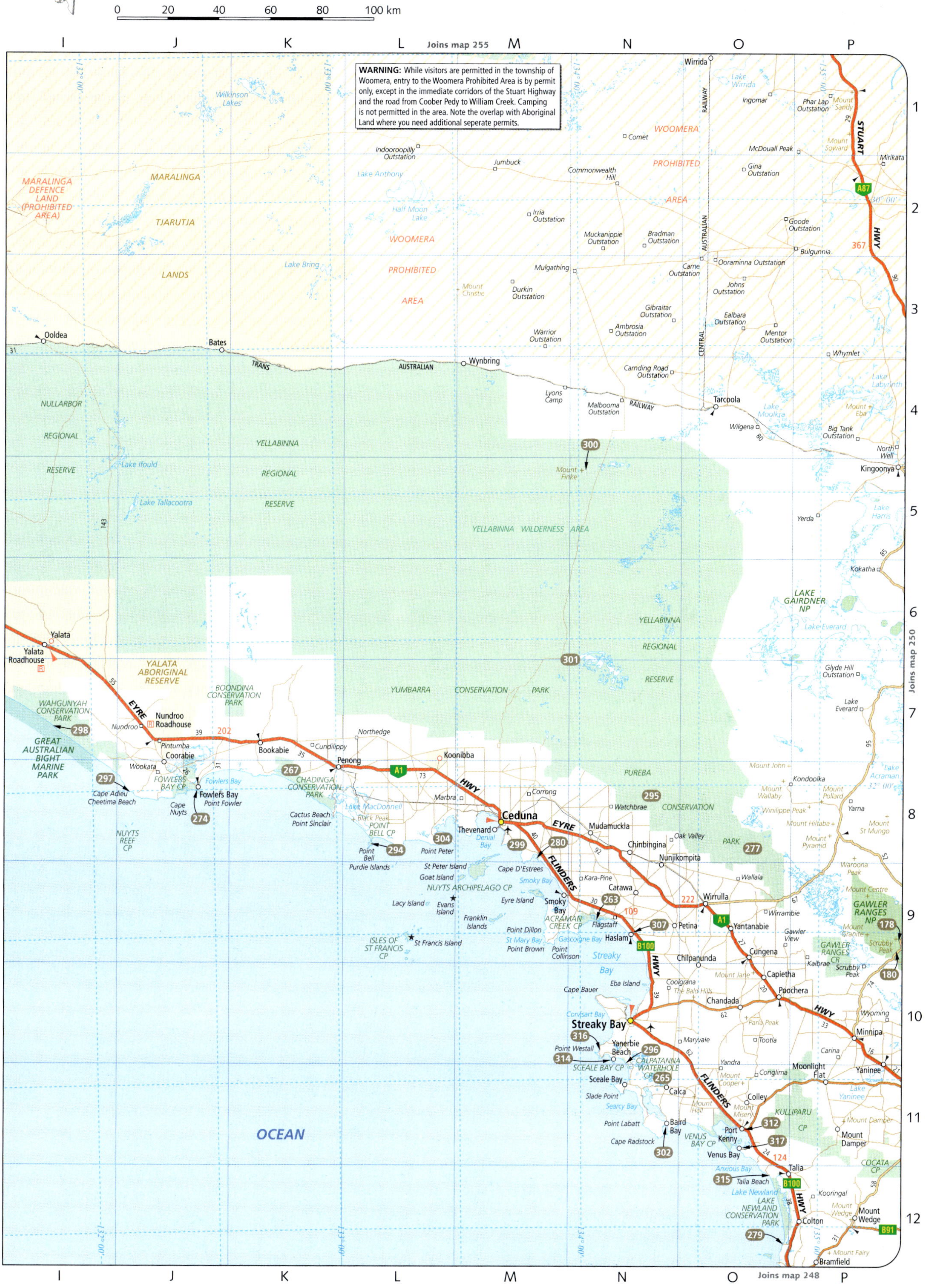

0   20   40   60   80   100 km

I   J   K   L   Joins map 255   M   N   O   P

WARNING: While visitors are permitted in the township of Woomera, entry to the Woomera Prohibited Area is by permit only, except in the immediate corridors of the Stuart Highway and the road from Coober Pedy to William Creek. Camping is not permitted in the area. Note the overlap with Aboriginal Land where you need additional seperate permits.

Wirrida

Wilkinson Lakes

WOOMERA

Ingomar
Phar Lap Outstation
Mount Sandy

STUART HWY

A87

Comet
McDouall Peak
Mount Soward
Mirikata

MARALINGA DEFENCE LAND (PROHIBITED AREA)

MARALINGA

TJARUTJA

LANDS

Indooroopilly Outstation
Jumbuck
Commonwealth Hill
PROHIBITED

Gina Outstation

367

Lake Anthony

Half Moon Lake

WOOMERA

Irria Outstation
Muckanippie Outstation
Bradman Outstation
AREA
Goode Outstation

Bulgunnia

Lake Bring

PROHIBITED

Mulgathing
Carne Outstation
Ooraminna Outstation

AREA

Mount Christie
Durkin Outstation

Johns Outstation
Gibraltar Outstation
Ealbara Outstation
Mentor Outstation

Ooldea
Bates

Warrior Outstation
Ambrosia Outstation

Whymlet

31
TRANS
AUSTRALIAN
Wynbring

Lyons Camp
Carnding Road Outstation

Lake Labyrinth

NULLARBOR

Malbooma Outstation
RAILWAY
Tarcoola

Mount Eba

REGIONAL

YELLABINNA

300

Wilgena
Big Tank Outstation

143

RESERVE

REGIONAL

Mount Finke

North Well

Lake Ifould

Kingoonya

Lake Tallacootra

RESERVE

Yerda
Lake Harris

85

Kokatha

LAKE GAIRDNER NP

Lake Everard

YELLABINNA WILDERNESS AREA

6

Yalata

YELLABINNA

Glyde Hill Outstation

Yalata Roadhouse

YALATA ABORIGINAL RESERVE

BOONDINA CONSERVATION PARK

301

REGIONAL

Lake Everard

WAHGUNYAH CONSERVATION PARK

55
EYRE

Nundroo Roadhouse

YUMBARRA
CONSERVATION
PARK

RESERVE

298

Nundroo
Pintumba
39
202

Northedge

Mount John
Kondoolka

Mount Wallaby

GREAT AUSTRALIAN BIGHT MARINE PARK

Coorabie
267
Bookabie
35
Cundilippy
Koonibba

Mount Pollard
Yarna

297

Wookata
31
Cactus Beach
Penong
A1
73

PUREBA

Winilippe Peak
Mount St Mungo

Cape Adieu
Cheetima Beach
FOWLERS BAY CP
Fowlers Bay

CHADINGA CONSERVATION PARK

HWY

Corrong

295

Mount Hiltaba
Mount Pyramid

NUYTS REEF CP

Cape Nuyts
274
Point Fowler

Lake MacDonnell
Black Peak
POINT BELL CP

Marbra
Ceduna
280
Mudamuckla
CONSERVATION
Waroona Peak

294
Point Bell
304
299
Thevenard
Denial Bay

EYRE
Watchbrae
Oak Valley
277
Mount Centre

Purdie Islands
Point Peter
St Peter Island
Goat Island
Cape D'Estrees
Smoky Bay
Kara-Pine
Chinbingina
Nunjikompita

PARK
Mount Granite
180

NUYTS ARCHIPELAGO CP
FLINDERS
Carawa
222
Wirrulla
Wirrabie
GAWLER RANGES NP
178

Lacy Island
Evans Island
Eyre Island
Smoky Bay
263
109
A1
Mount Centre

Franklin Islands
Point Dillon
ACRAMAN CREEK CP
Flagstaff
307
Petina
Yantanabie
Gawler View
GAWLER RANGES CR
Scrubby Peak

ISLES OF ST FRANCIS CP
St Francis Island
St Mary Bay
Point Brown
Haslam
B100
Chilpanunda
Cungena
Capietha
Kalbrae
Scrubby Peak
180

Gascoigne Bay
Point Collinson
Streaky Bay
Eba Island
Coolgrana
Mount Jane
Poochera

Cape Bauer
The Bald Hills
Chandada
HWY
Wyoming

Corvisart Bay
39
Paris Peak
Carina
Minnipa

Streaky Bay
316
Yanerbie Beach
296
Maryvale
Tootla
16

Point Westall
314
SCEALE BAY CP
CALPATANNA WATERHOLE CP
Yandra
Conglima
Moonlight Flat
Yaninee

Sceale Bay
265
Calca
Mount Cooper
Mount Misery
Colley
KULLIPARU CP
Mount Damper

Slade Point
Searcy Bay
FLINDERS
312
Mount Damper

OCEAN
Point Labatt
Baird Bay
VENUS BAY CP
Port Kenny
317
COCATA CP

Cape Radstock
302
Venus Bay
124

Talia
58

315
Anxious Bay
Talia Beach
B100

LAKE NEWLAND CONSERVATION PARK

Kooringal
Mount Wedge
Mount Wedge

279
Colton
B91

Bramfield

I   J   K   L   Joins map 248   M   N   O   P

Joins map 250

WESTERN AUSTRALIA

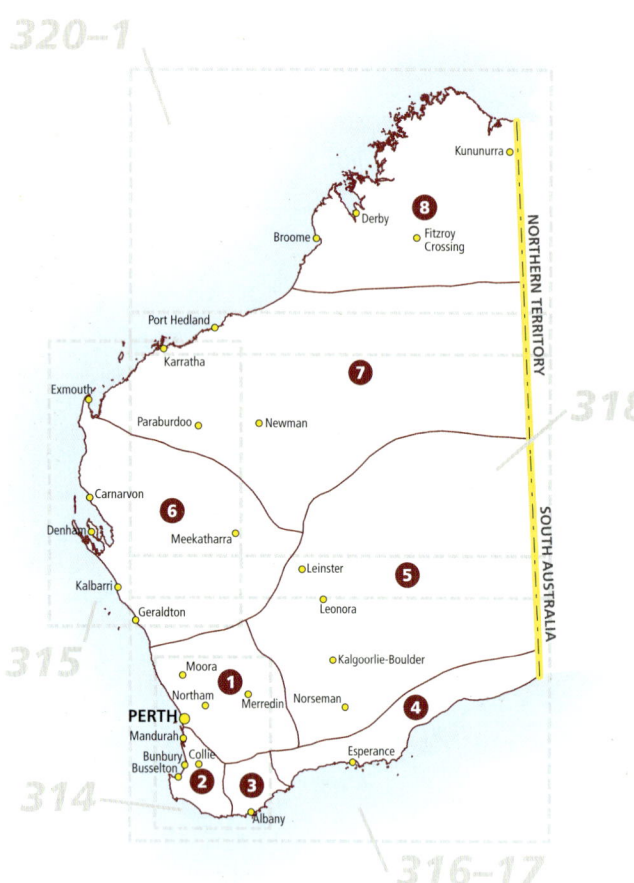

320–1

Kununurra

8

Derby

Broome   Fitzroy
                Crossing

NORTHERN TERRITORY

318–19

Port Hedland

Karratha

Exmouth

Paraburdoo   Newman   7

Carnarvon

Denham   SOUTH AUSTRALIA

6   Meekatharra

Kalbarri

Geraldton   Leinster   5

                  Leonora

                  Kalgoorlie-Boulder

315

Moora

Northam   1
         Merredin   Norseman
PERTH   4

Mandurah
Bunbury Collie
Busselton
         2   3   Esperance

314

Albany

316–17

BEST CAMPSITES

Allison camping area
Rottnest Island (Heartlands), p.262

Dales camping area
Karijini National Park (Pilbara), p. 301

Home Valley Station
Gibb River Road (Kimberley), p. 311

Lucky Bay camping area
Cape Le Grand National Park (Esperance and Nullarbor), p. 285

Red Bluff camping area
Quobba Station (Outback Coast and Mid-West), p. 300

USEFUL CONTACTS

Department of Environment and Conservation
(08) 6467 5000
www.dec.wa.gov.au

Department of Fisheries Western Australia
(08) 9482 7333
www.fish.wa.gov.au

Department of Indigenous Affairs
1300 651 077
www.dia.wa.gov.au

Department of Mines and Petroleum
(08) 9222 3333
www.dmp.wa.gov.au

Emergency
Dial 000 for police, ambulance and fire brigade

Fire and Emergency Services Authority
1300 657 209
www.fesa.wa.gov.au

Main Roads Western Australia
13 8138
Road Conditions
1800 013 314
www.mainroads.wa.gov.au

Camping in Purnululu (Bungle Bungle) National Park, the Kimberley region (p. 308)

HEARTLANDS

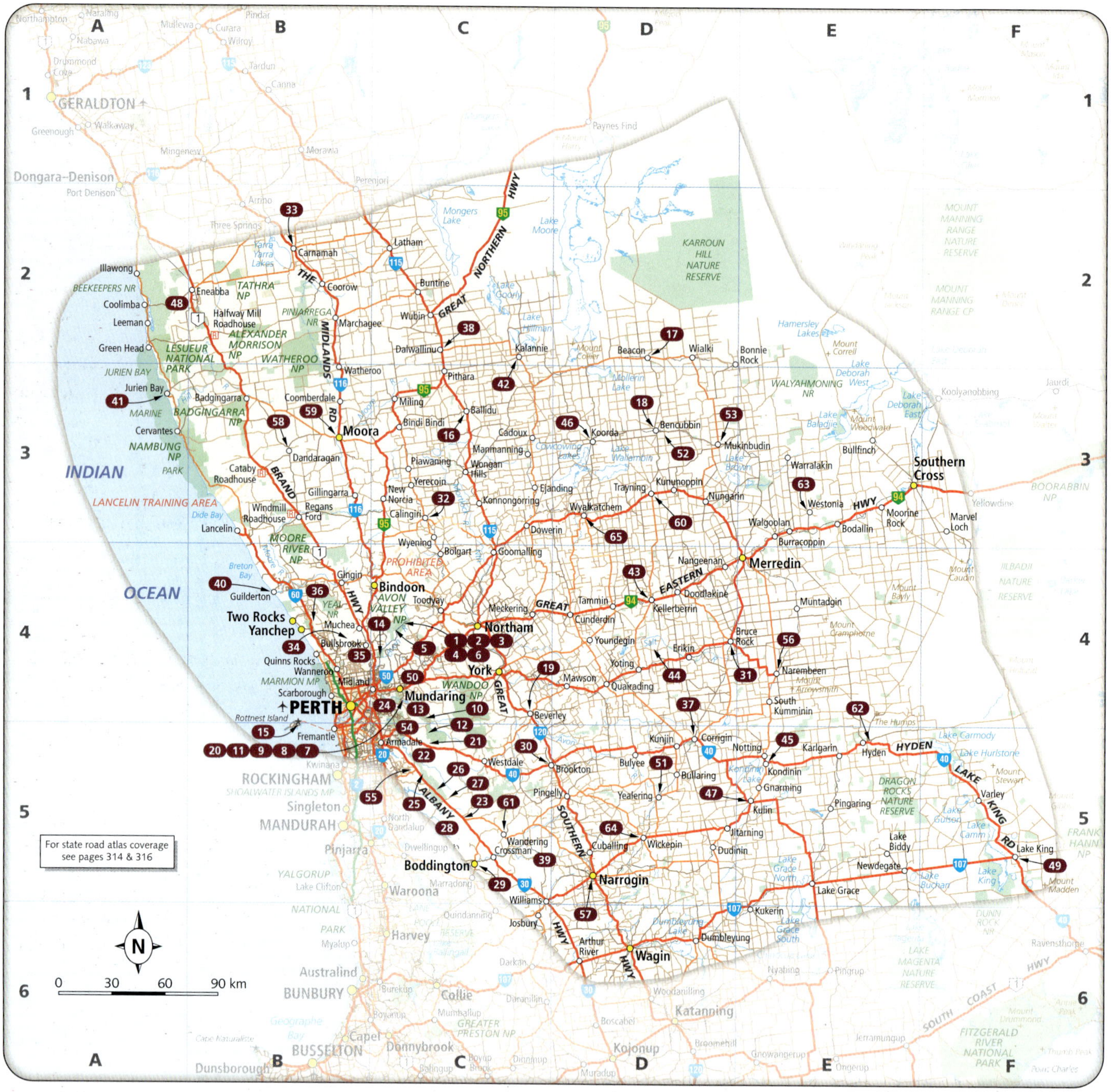

THE SMALL TOWNS, BEACHES and fishing villages of WA's heartlands are conveniently close to Perth, making exploration a breeze. Many of these small towns make a great base for discovering the region's historical and natural attractions. In spring, the most popular activity is taking a scenic drive to catch the annual wildflower displays.

The spiky Pinnacles of Nambung National Park are another highlight, along with the granite Wave Rock near Hyden. Bushwalkers and picnickers alike head to Dryandra Woodland, where unique wildlife is found.

Avon Valley National Park, less than an hour from Perth, is where the locals go to spend an afternoon bushwalking, whitewater rafting and canoeing. For island fun, stunning Rottnest Island is just offshore. Surrounded by coral reefs, the island is an idyllic spot where city dwellers can swim off white-sand beaches, snorkel over shipwrecks, go fishing or simply relax. Hiring a bike is the best way to explore Rotty's historic sites, and to find its famously secluded beaches and secret surf spots.

For state road atlas coverage see pages 314 & 316

CAMPSITES LOCATED IN PARKS AND RESERVES

AVON VALLEY NATIONAL PARK

From summer to winter, from north to south, and from high outcrops to deep river valleys, the forests of Avon Valley National Park are constantly changing. The Avon River flows in winter and spring, when the river churns over spectacular rapids. During summer and autumn, the river diminishes to a series of pools in a bed of granite boulders and tea-tree thickets. The park also offers the chance to see a wide variety of birds and other wildlife. A total fire ban applies from Nov to Apr, and the park is closed on days of Catastrophic Fire Danger. No camping is allowed here during the annual Avon Descent White Water race, which is usually held on the first weekend of Aug. Note: although firewood is supplied, it is provided for cooking use only, on a per-vehicle basis.

Who to contact: DEC Perth Hills (08) 9290 6100

Camping fees: fees payable at the park entrance stations on Quarry Rd and Plunket Rd

① Bald Hill camping area

Bald Hill camping area is near the top of a hill overlooking the Avon Valley to the west of Drummonds camping area, reached via Governors Dr off Quarry Rd. A short walk onto the stony outcrops provides spectacular views. **Map Refs:** 260 C4, 314 C4, 316 C7

② Drummonds camping area

Drummonds camping area is set among wandoo woodlands overlooking the Avon Valley. Access in is steep, so you'll need a 4WD tow if you're bringing in a campervan. The campsite is to the west of Homestead camping area, reached via Governors Dr off Quarry Rd. **Map refs:** 260 C4, 314 C4, 316 C7

③ Homestead camping area

Homestead camping area is adjacent to a small creek in wandoo forest. To find it, head 30 km west of Toodyay and 55 km north-east of Midland via Governors Dr, off Quarry Rd. **Map refs:** 260 C4, 314 C4, 316 C7

④ Sappers camping area

Sappers camping area is 25 km west of Toodyay on Sappers Rd, off Plunket Rd. Bring drinking water and come in a 4WD. Note: this camping area may be closed in winter. **Map refs:** 260 C4, 314 C4, 316 C7

⑤ Thirty-Seven Mile Road camping area

There's no surprise that this camping area is on Thirty-Seven Mile Rd. You'll find it off Plunket Rd, 40 km west of Toodyay. Bring your own supply of drinking water. **Map refs:** 260 C4, 314 C4, 316 C7

⑥ Valley camping area

Valley camping area is at the bottom of a valley near the Avon River. It's reached via Forty-One Mile Rd, off Quarry Rd. Note: access to the river is restricted due to the main east-west railway line. **Map refs:** 260 C4, 314 C4, 316 C7

BEELU NATIONAL PARK

Beelu National Park is 40 km from Perth in the shires of Mundaring and Kalamunda, situated west of Mundaring Weir Rd. Formerly known as Mundaring National Park, it offers visitors the opportunity to observe wildlife, go bushwalking and enjoy the many recreation sites within the park. The Fred Jacoby Park contains a boardwalk around a 140-year-old heritage-listed oak tree, and the Golden View Lookout provides views over Mundaring Weir and Helena River Valley, while at the Dell you can access walking and mountain-bike trails. The park provides toilets, wood BBQs and shaded picnic areas. Note: bring your own firewood.

Who to contact: DEC Perth Hills National Parks Centre (08) 9295 2244; or DEC Bibbulmun Track Office (08) 9334 0265 *How to book:* DEC Perth Hills National Parks Centre (08) 9295 2244 for campsite no. **8**; online booking at www.dec. wa.gov.au/campgrounds for campsite no. **9**

⑦ Hewetts Hill camping area

On the Bibbulmun Track, Hewetts Hill camping area is 10.3 km from Kalamunda and 10.6 km from Ball Creek camping area. **Map refs:** 260 C4, 314 C5, 316 C7

⑧ Patens Brook camping area (walk-in camping)

Patens Brook campsite is 3 km from the Perth Hills National Parks Centre on Patens Brook Trail, 6 km south of Mundaring via Mundaring Weir Rd and Allen Rd. Walk-in campers will find basic facilities in a beautiful bush setting and a range of nature-based activities to participate in. Note: bookings are essential and this site may be closed during fire danger season. **Map refs:** 260 C4, 314 C5, 316 C7

⑨ Perth Hills National Parks Centre camping area

Visitors here will find a range of nature-based activities, including the many scenic walks available throughout the area. There is a short walk from the carpark to the campsites. Perth Hills National Parks Centre is on the western edge of the Beelu National Park (formerly the Mundaring National Park). It is 6 km south of Mundaring on Allen Rd via Mundaring Weir Rd. The site has a good range of facilities in a beautiful forest setting. Bookings are essential. **Map refs:** 260 C4, 314 C5, 316 C7

HELENA NATIONAL PARK

Helena National Park is situated south-east of Mundaring Weir and encompasses the Mt Dale area. On the north side of

Mt Dale, visitors can experience spectacular views over Darkin River Valley and the Helena National Park from an animal-viewing hide. The park provides opportunities for bushwalking, wildlife observation, photography and picnicking. The lower recreational area is a good point for drop-off and pick-up access for walkers using the Bibbulmun Track.

Who to contact: DEC Mundaring (08) 9295 9100; or DEC Bibbulmun Track Office (08) 9334 0265

10 Beraking camping area

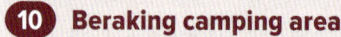

On the Bibbulmun Track, Beraking campsite is 8.5 km from Waalegh camping area and 11.5 km from Mt Dale camping area. **Map refs:** 260 C4, 314 C5, 316 C7

11 Helena camping area

On the Bibbulmun Track, Helena campsite is 8.6 km from Ball Creek campsite and 9.5 km from Waalegh campsite. **Map refs:** 260 C4, 314 C5, 316 C7

12 Mount Dale camping area

On the Bibbulmun Track, Mt Dale is 11.5 km from Beraking camping area and 8.3 km from Brookton camping area. **Map refs:** 260 C5, 314 C5, 316 C8

13 Waalegh camping area

On the Bibbulmun Track, Waalegh camping area is 9.5 km from Helena camping area and 8.5 km from Beraking campsite. **Map refs:** 260 C4, 314 C5, 316 C7

WALYUNGA NATIONAL PARK

Sensational wildflowers, prolific wildlife and untamed river valley landscapes form the backdrop at Walyunga National Park. There's whitewater action on the Avon River in winter, and placid pools along the valley floor in summer. Follow walking trails, go birdwatching and enjoy the national park's scenic views. Note: no camping Dec–Apr.

How to book: Perth Hills National Parks Centre (08) 9571 1371; or DEC Mundaring (08) 9295 9100

14 Walyunga camping area

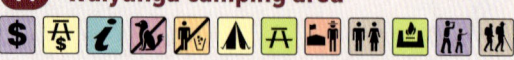

Walyunga camping area offers tent-based camping only, in a natural bush environment that is popular with bushwalkers and birdwatchers. To get here, head 17 km north of Midland via Walyunga Rd from the Great Northern Hwy. Bookings are essential. **Map refs:** 260 C4, 314 C4, 316 C7

CAMPSITES LOCATED IN OTHER AREAS

15 Allison camping area

On Rottnest Island at Thomson Bay, Allison camping area is the perfect place to relax and enjoy the beauty of this little patch of paradise just off the coast of Perth. Swimming, fishing, snorkelling and boating are hugely popular activities, and a bicycle will allow you to explore the island and its history at a leisurely pace. To get here, you need to take a ferry from Perth, Fremantle or Hillarys, then make your way to the accommodation centre at the jetty before you set up camp. Bring a gas/fuel stove with you. **Map refs:** 260 B4, 314 B5, 316 B7

Who to contact: Rottnest Island Authority (08) 9432 9111, 1800 111 111; or Rottnest Island Visitor and Information Centre (08) 9372 9732

16 Ballidu Caravan Park

This caravan park is close to town and visitors in spring have the opportunity to see dazzling displays of wildflowers in the surrounding countryside. An incredible variety of flora combines to craft a carpet of colour that stretches for kilometres. Nearby, the National Trust-classified Berkshire Valley Folk Museum is well worth a visit. **Map refs:** 260 C3, 314 D1, 316 C5

How to book: 7 Wallis St, Ballidu (08) 9674 1114; or Wongan–Ballidu Shire (08) 9671 1011

17 Beacon Caravan Park

The wheat-belt town of Beacon, 315 km north-east of Perth, is enormously popular with birdwatchers. This caravan park provides travellers with a good range of facilities in shady surroundings. Most birders head to the country around Karoon Hill, 50 km further along the track, which is a haven for a variety of birdlife. The cockatoos are especially colourful, including the brilliantly plumed red-tailed black and Major Mitchell varieties. This is the most north-easterly town in the wheat belt, and the ripening grain attracts birds from the goldfields region and other outlying areas beyond the emu-proof fence. **Map refs:** 260 D2, 314 F1, 316 D5

How to book: Lucas St, Beacon 0488 025 853; or Mt Marshall Shire Office (08) 9685 1202

18 Bencubbin Caravan Park

A minuscule wheat-belt town about 273 km north-east of Perth, Bencubbin's surrounds represent the last outposts of arable land before the desert exerts its desiccating influence on most non-indigenous plants. The caravan park is on the Bencubbin–Trayning Rd, providing travellers with a good range of facilities, including on-site accommodation. Visitors in spring will be treated to a spectacular wildflower display. Fire restrictions could be in place, so ask at the shire office for an update before setting a fire. **Map refs:** 260 D3, 314 F2, 316 D5

Who to contact: Mt Marshall Shire Office (08) 9685 1202
Camping fees: fees payable at council office 80 Monger St, Bencubbin

19 Beverley Caravan and Camping Ground

Beverley is a small historic town on the banks of the Avon River, 135 km east of Perth. Its main street features beautifully preserved examples of Edwardian, Federation and Art Deco architecture. As you wander around town, seek out the Dead Finish Museum on Hunt Rd (built as a hotel in 1872, and one of the oldest buildings in the present town) and St Paul's Church (built at the original town site, 5 km away, in 1862). The caravan park is on Council Rd in town. **Map refs:** 260 C4, 314 E5, 316 D7

How to book: Shire of Beverley Office (08) 9646 1200 *Camping fees:* fees payable at an on-site honesty box, and at the council office on weekdays, 136 Vincent St, Beverley

Bibbulmun Track – northern section

The Bibbulmun Track traverses some of the south-west's most scenic and beautiful areas for some 963 km, from Kalamunda on the outskirts of Perth all the way to the southern coast at Albany. The northern section begins at Kalamunda Trackhead, with a total of 27 campsites dotted along the track to Donnelly River Village, which is a private camping area 31 km south-east of Nannup. The campsites have a timber shelter, sleeping no more than 17 people, as well as a bush toilet, rainwater tank and picnic table. Tents can be erected at the campsites, but no camping is allowed in water catchment areas between Kalamunda and Collie, and south of the Blackwood River. With numerous vehicle access points along the way, the track can be tackled in sections; it would take 6–8 weeks to walk the entire track in one go. Water may not always be reliable so carry extra, and it's preferable to bring a gas/fuel stove. Fire restrictions are in place Oct–May. Walkers need to be self-sufficient and well-prepared, equipped with track maps and guides.

Please note that campsites are listed in alphabetical order, not track order. Refer to the map on p. 260 for further information.

Who to contact: DEC Bibbulmun Track Office (08) 9334 0265; or Bibbulmun Track Foundation (08) 9481 0551 www.bibbulmuntrack.org.au; or DEC Dwellingup (08) 9538 1078; or DEC Collie (08) 9735 1988; or DEC Kirup (08) 9731 6232

20 Ball Creek camping area

On the Bibbulmun Track, Ball Creek camping area is 10.6 km from Hewetts Hill camping area and 8.6 km from Helena camping area. **Map refs:** 260 C4, 314 C5, 316 C7

10 Beraking camping area
See p. 262.

21 Brookton camping area

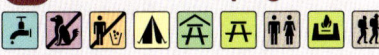

On the Bibbulmun Track, Brookton camping area is 8.3 km from Mt Dale camping area and 11.1 km from Canning camping area. **Map refs:** 260 C5, 314 C5, 316 C8

22 Canning camping area

On the Bibbulmun Track, Canning camping area is 11.1 km from Brookton camping area and 15.6 km from Monadnocks camping area. **Map refs:** 260 C5, 314 C5, 316 C8

23 Gringer Creek camping area

On the Bibbulmun Track, Gringer Creek camping area is 16.6 km from Nerang camping area and 17.6 km from White Horse camping area. **Map refs:** 260 C5, 314 D6, 316 C8

11 Helena camping area
See p. 262.

7 Hewetts Hill camping area
See p. 261.

24 Kalamunda Trackhead

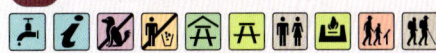

The Bibbulmun trackhead is in Kalamunda National Park and is the starting point of the walking trail for the northern section of the Bibbulmun Track. There are several trails within the park, but no camping. Kalamunda Trackhead is 10.3 km from Hewetts Hill camping area in Beelu National Park. **Map refs:** 260 C4, 314 C5, 316 C7

25 Monadnocks camping area

On the Bibbulmun Track, Monadnocks camping area is 15.6 km from Canning camping area and 12.7 km from Mt Cooke camping area. **Map refs:** 260 C5, 314 C6, 316 C8

26 Mount Cooke camping area

On the Bibbulmun Track, Mt Cooke camping area is 12.7 km from Monadnocks camping area and 12.6 km from Nerang camping area. **Map refs:** 260 C5, 314 D6, 316 C8

12 Mount Dale camping area
See p. 262.

27 Nerang camping area

On the Bibbulmun Track, Nerang camping area is 12.6 km from Mt Cooke camping area and 16.6 km from Gringer Creek camping area. **Map refs:** 260 C5, 314 D6, 316 C8

13 Waalegh camping area
See p. 262.

28 White Horse camping area

On the Bibbulmun Track, White Horse camping area is 17.6 km from Gringer Creek camping area and 14.5 km from Mt Wells camping area, which is within the South-West region of the

northern section of the Bibbulmun Track. **Map refs:** 260 C5, 314 D6, 316 C8

This track continues through the South-West region (see p. 275).

29 Boddington Caravan Park

Boddington Caravan Park provides a good range of facilities for travellers as it is close to the town and shops. The park is on the Hotham River, a popular fishing spot. Visitors can take a delightful excursion from here to Tullis Bridge, a trestle bridge and old timber mill which is a favourite spot for picnics and BBQs. The dense local forests abound with wildlife and birds, both native and introduced; in season a wide variety of wildflowers bloom. **Map refs:** 260 C5, 314 D7, 316 C8

How to book: Waraming Ave, Boddington (08) 9883 8018

30 Brookton Caravan Park

Set on the Brookton Hwy, 138 km south-east of Perth, this caravan park provides travellers with a good range of facilities in a town where the famous WA wildflowers bloom in colourful profusion in spring. Brookton's climate is Mediterranean, with cool to cold winters and hot, dry summers. Locally there are sheep, cattle and grain-growing industries. Of architectural and historical interest in the town are the railway station, the old police station and St Mark's Anglican Church. The Yenyening Lakes to the north-east of town are fed by the Avon River and provide a pleasant swimming, boating and fishing haven. **Map refs:** 260 C5, 314 E5, 316 D8

How to book: Brookton Hwy, Brookton (08) 9642 1434

31 Bruce Rock Caravan Park

Bruce Rock Caravan Park is on Dunstall St in this small wheatbelt town, 247 km east of Perth. Visitors to Bruce Rock can drop into Totadjin Dam Reserve, a favourite cooling-off spot for locals, and also view a large granite outcrop about 45 km west of town called Kokerbin, which is very impressive indeed. You can drive to the top of this rock for some terrific views. **Map refs:** 260 D4, 314 G4, 316 E7

How to book: Dunstall St, Bruce Rock; Bruce Rock Shire Council (08) 9061 1377

32 Calingiri Caravan Park

The town of Calingiri is 141 km north-east of Perth. This small park on Cavell St in the town centre has basic facilities, but the gravel surface is not suitable for tents. Visitors will find it a good base for exploring the regional attractions. **Map refs:** 260 C3, 314 C3, 316 C6

How to book: Cavell St, Calingiri; Shire of Victoria Plains (08) 9628 7004

33 Carnamah Caravan Park

This small caravan park is on King St, off McPherson St in Carnamah, a historic little country town with many of its old buildings intact. If you're into fossicking, you'll love visiting this area, which is rich in minerals and dotted with abandoned mines and ghost towns. Other accommodation is available. Carnamah is around 290 km north-east of Perth. **Map refs:** 260 B2, 316 B4

How to book: King St, Carnamah; Shire of Carnamah (08) 9951 7000

Coastal Plain Walk Trail

Walkers will experience a range of diverse flora on the Coastal Plain Walk Trail, taking in Yanchep National Park and Melaleuca Conservation Park. Each campsite has a hut sleeping up to 12, a rainwater tank, 3 tent sites, picnic tables, a bush toilet and fire pit; ideal for self-sufficient campers, who need to bring in their own water. Begin the walk at Ghost House Ruins in Yanchep National Park, and finish 55 km later at Cooper Rd in Melaleuca Conservation Park.

Please note that campsites are listed in alphabetical order, not track order. Refer to the map on p. 260 for further information.

Who to contact: Yanchep National Park (08) 9405 0759

34 Moitch camping area

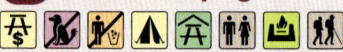

This small campsite is 19.9 km from Ridges camping area and 17 km from Prickly Bark camping area. Bring your own water, and a gas/fuel stove is preferred. **Map refs:** 260 B4, 314 B4, 316 C7

35 Prickly Bark camping area

This small campsite in the bush is 17 km from Moitch camping area and 2.7 km west of the trackhead in Melaleuca Conservation Park. A gas/fuel stove is preferred and you need to bring your own water. **Map refs:** 260 B4, 314 C4, 316 C7

36 Ridges camping area

This small campsite is 16 km from the Coastal Plain Walk trackhead at Ghost House Ruins and 19.9 km from Moitch camping area. You'll need to bring a gas/fuel stove. **Map refs:** 260 B4, 314 B4, 316 B7

37 Corrigin Caravan Park

Corrigin is widely regarded as one of WA's most attractive and tidy country towns. You'll be bewitched by the spring wildflower show and the granite outcrops that give an alien feel to the landscape, but don't miss the dog cemetery if you want to experience the quintessential Corrigin. **Map refs:** 260 D5, 314 F5, 316 E8

How to book: Kirkwood St, Corrigin (08) 9063 2515, 0427 632 515

38 Dalwallinu Caravan Park

Dalwallinu Caravan Park provides travellers with a good range of facilities and large, shady sites. The town is the first stop on the Wildflower Way, a world-famous tourist route. It's also renowned for its wattle trees, celebrated in Wattle Week in Sept. Interesting local attractions include the ancient agricultural machinery pieces displayed like sculptures on the main street; the Old Well at the entrance to town, from which the district's pioneers drew their water; and McIntosh Park at nearby Pithara, the site of the first fatal air crash in WA. **Map refs:** 260 C2, 314 D1, 316 C5

How to book: Dowie St, Dalwallinu (08) 9661 1253

39 Dryandra Woodland camping area

Dryandra Woodland camping area is 27 km north of Williams via York–Williams Rd, in a natural bush setting popular with bushwalkers, nature lovers and cyclists. Visitors can see a variety of flora, rare wildlife such as numbats and woylies, and learn about the region's history while taking the scenic drive through the area. Bring along firewood and drinking water. **Map refs:** 260 C5, 314 E7, 316 D8

Who to contact: DEC Narrogin (08) 9881 9200 *Camping fees:* pick up reply-paid envelopes from the information station

40 Guilderton Caravan Park

This little coastal town at the mouth of the Moore River, about 100 km north of Perth, stands guard over the wreck of the Dutch ship *Gilt Dragon*, which foundered on an offshore reef in 1656. The caravan park has large, grassed, shady sites on the foreshore. It is well-sited to take advantage of activities such as windsurfing, and Guilderton boasts some of the best windsurfing in the world. Anglers and canoeists will also enjoy their time here, and the area is noted for its safe swimming. **Map refs:** 260 B4, 314 B4, 316 B7

How to book: 2 Drewer St, Guilderton (08) 9577 1021

41 Jurien Bay Caravan Park

A haven for anglers, divers, snorkellers, surfers and boaters, Jurien Bay is around 266 km north of Perth. The beaches here are sheltered and pristine, thanks to loads of reefs and offshore islands that protect this part of the coast. The caravan park is set close to the beach and offers a good range of facilities for camping and other types of accommodation, and is an ideal base to enjoy the town's activities. **Map refs:** 260 A3, 316 A5

How to book: Roberts Rd, Jurien Bay (08) 9652 1595, 1800 119 239

42 Kalannie Caravan Park

About 300 km north-east of Perth, Kalannie lies in some of the best wildflower country in Australia, in the heart of WA's largest wheat-producing area. The district also claims more species of wattle (acacias) than anywhere else in the world. The caravan park offers basic facilities to campers. While you're here, don't miss a visit to the beautiful area around Petrudor Rock, about 17 km out of town. **Map refs:** 260 C2, 314 D1, 316 D5

How to book: Roche St, Kalannie (08) 9666 2068; or Dalwallinu Shire (08) 9661 0500

43 Kellerberrin Caravan Park

This small caravan park with basic facilities is at the sports ground on Connelly St in Kellerberrin, 202 km east of Perth via the Great Eastern Hwy. Visitors to this pastoral town should take a look at the old agricultural machinery and implements at the Pioneer Park in Leake St, and the Kellerberrin Folk Museum, which houses an interesting display of local bits and pieces. **Map refs:** 260 D4, 314 F4, 316 D7

How to book: Connelly St, Kellerberrin; Kellerberrin Shire (08) 9045 4006; or caretaker 0428 138 474

44 Kokerbin Rock camping area

Kokerbin Rock camping area is on Kwolyin West Rd, 10 km north of Kwolyin via Bruce Rock–Quairading Rd. Visitors to this large granite outcrop can enjoy panoramic views and explore caves and walking trails. Note: a fire ban applies Nov–Apr; check the dates with the council, and bring your own firewood if you're visiting outside the fire-ban season. **Map refs:** 260 D4, 314 F4, 316 D7

Who to contact: Bruce Rock Shire (08) 9061 1377

45 Kondinin Caravan Park

You'll find this caravan park in Kondinin, a town that presides over sheep country and the central wheat belt, about 278 km south-east of Perth. The gateway to Wave Rock, this is flat country that can get pretty hot and dry in summer. **Map refs:** 260 E5, 314 G5, 316 E8

How to book: Gordon St, Kondinin; Kondinin Shire (08) 9889 1006 *Camping fees:* pay fees at the shire office on Gordon St or at the Kondinin Hotel

46 Koorda Caravan Park

In Koorda, 235 km north-east of Perth, this council-run caravan park offers basic facilities in a bush setting. This is wonderful wildflower country, coming alive in spring with the vibrant colours of thousands of WA floral varieties. Bushwalkers will enjoy the nearby attractions of Mollerin Rock, Newcarlbeon, Badgerin Rock and Moningarin. These picturesque outcrops of granite each have their own mini-environments of wildflowers, birds and small animals. **Map refs:** 260 D3, 314 E2, 316 D6

How to book: Scott St, Koorda; Koorda Shire (08) 9684 1219
Camping fees: use the honesty box or pay fees at the shire office on Allenby St

47   Kulin Caravan Park

This caravan park is a popular stopover for floral fanciers who flock to this corner of the state's south-east to enjoy the abundant wildflowers in spring. The countryside is carpeted with vibrant colour as a swag of WA's more than 8000 varieties of wildflowers come into bloom. It's often the flowering Macrocarpa gums that capture much of the attention. There are several unusual rock formations outside of town, including a mammoth granite boulder and a particularly strange pink and white rock formation called Buckleys Breakaways. **Map refs:** 260 E5, 314 G6, 316 E8

How to book: Rankin St, Kulin (08) 9880 1053

48   Lake Indoon camping area

This large, freshwater lake covers 130 ha, with a depth varying from 1.5 m to 5 m depending on the seasons and rainfall. The lake is on the Brand Hwy, 12 km west of Eneabba. The birdlife is abundant and kangaroos and emus also use the lake as a watering hole. The camping area offers visitors a range of activities such as boating, waterskiing, sailing and canoeing. Visitors need to come equipped with a gas/fuel stove and drinking water. **Map refs:** 260 A2, 316 A5

Who to contact: Eneabba–Coolimba Rd, Carnamah; Shire of Carnamah (08) 9951 7000

49   Lake King Caravan Park

Lake King is a crossroads centre with a tavern and several stores, 70 km north-west of Ravensthorpe. The caravan park offers basic facilities to visitors travelling across this arid country. For those with a little time to spare, travel east along the fascinating Lake King Causeway to cross 10 km of salt lakes studded with natural scrub and wildflowers. Take the time to enjoy the scenery along the longest road built across a salt lake in WA. **Map refs:** 260 F5, 316 G8

How to book: Critchley Ave, Lake King (08) 9838 0052

50   Lake Leschenaultia camping area

Lake Leschenaultia, 2 km west of Chidlow via Rosedale Rd, dates to 1897, when it was constructed as a water supply for the railways. Nowadays it is a haven for birds and wildlife, and offers visitors activities such as swimming, canoeing and fishing. Lake Leschenaultia camping area has a good range of facilities and shady sites near the water. **Map refs:** 260 C4, 314 C5, 316 C7

Who to contact: ranger's office (08) 9572 4248

51   Lake Yealering Caravan Park

Yealering is a small town about 250 km south-east of Perth. The lake is on the edge of town via Wickepin–Corrigin Rd. Camping here is in a picturesque setting with BBQ facilities. It is an ideal place for a variety of watersports, including waterskiing, swimming, sailing and windsurfing. Relaxing with a good book under a tree by the lake would interest some, but there are also nature walks through the surrounding bushland for the more energetic. The caravan park has a good range of facilities with shady sites near the water. Cabin accommodation is also available. **Map refs:** 260 D5, 314 F6, 316 D8

How to book: Shire of Wickepin (08) 9888 1005; or Commercial Hotel (08) 9888 7014 **Camping fees:** fees payable at the Commercial Hotel, Yealering

52   Marshall Rock camping area

Marshall Rock camping area is 10 km south-east of Bencubbin and 273 km north-east of Perth. Access is via Mukinbudin and Marshall Rock rds. The area is noted for its wildflower displays in spring. There is plenty of shade available in the camping area between the 2 rocks but there are no facilities out here, so bring drinking water and a gas/fuel stove. **Map refs:** 260 D3, 314 F2, 316 E5

Who to contact: Mt Marshall Shire Office (08) 9685 1202

53   Mukinbudin Caravan Park

Mukinbudin is about 300 km north-east of Perth via Merredin on the Great Eastern Hwy. The caravan park has shady sites and a good range of facilities, including on-site accommodation. Nearby, you'll find a number of granite outcrops and, as this is wildflower country, it's a delight here in spring when they're in bloom. The fauna can be interesting and varied too: with a bit of luck you will see bush turkeys, wedge-tail eagles, echidnas, emus, red kangaroos and mallee fowl. **Map refs:** 260 D3, 314 G2, 316 E6

How to book: Cruickshank Rd, Mukinbudin (08) 9047 1103, 0429 471 103

Munda Biddi Trail

Eventually, this long-distance cycle trail will stretch from north-east of Perth at Mundaring, all the way to the south coast at Albany. Currently, it winds through forests and parks along bush and disused rail routes to Nannup. Well-equipped sites have toilets, tables, seats and shelters, and the trail passes through towns regularly enough to provide other accommodation options. Although water is available at campsites along the trail, you should bring water as well as route information and a gas/fuel stove.

- *Please note that campsites are listed in alphabetical order, not track order. Refer to the map on p. 260 for further information.*

Who to contact: DEC Munda Biddi Trail (08) 9334 0265; or Munda Biddi Trail Foundation (08) 9481 2483, 0422 112 229

54 Carinyah camping area

This campsite is nestled in a grove of she-oak trees 42 km south of Mundaring and 35 km north of Wungong camping area. **Map refs:** 260 C5, 314 C5, 316 C8

55 Wungong camping area

At this bush campsite surrounded by majestic jarrah trees, kangaroos may be sighted at early morning or dusk. Wungong is 26 km north-east of Jarrahdale and 35 km south of Carinyah camping area. **Map refs:** 260 C5, 314 C6, 316 C8

■ *This track continues through the South-West region*
■ *(see p. 279).*

56 Narembeen Caravan Park

Narembeen Caravan Park is on Curral St, 290 km east of Perth. It has basic camping facilities and limited on-site accommodation. Travellers through this predominantly grain-belt region can visit Roe Lookout, explore some unusual rock formations at nearby reserves, or indulge in some birdwatching at Roe Dam. **Map refs:** 260 E4, 314 G4, 316 E7

Who to contact: Curral St, Narembeen; Narembeen Shire (08) 9064 7308

57 Narrogin Caravan Park

Narrogin is at the heart of some of the best agricultural country in WA, about 190 km south-east of Perth. It is the major service centre for the Great Southern region. The caravan park has a good range of facilities for campers in a town renowned for its gardens, particularly its magnificent roses. Visitors can take a walk along nature trails in the bushland reserve across the road from the park. **Map refs:** 260 D5, 314 E7, 316 D9

How to book: Williams Rd, Narrogin (08) 9881 1260

58 Pioneer Park

Basic caravan park facilities are offered here in Dandaragan, a small town in the wheat-belt district that boasts lush pastures and golden crops, 180 km north of Perth. The characteristic red and white gums and a spectacular array of spring wildflowers complement the area, as do the historic buildings. **Map refs:** 260 B3, 314 B2, 316 B6

Who to contact: Danaragan Rd, Danaragan; Shire of Dandaragan (08) 9651 4010 *Camping fees:* pay fees at the shire office on Dandaragan Rd, or in the honesty box outside the office

59 Shire of Moora Caravan Park

On the Moore River in the Midlands district, about 180 km north of Perth, the town of Moora is at the centre of a mixed farming area of primarily wheat, wool and cattle. The main attractions here are the wildflowers which bloom in colourful abundance in spring – several wildflower varieties are unique to the area. The caravan park is centrally located on Dandaragan St and offers a good range of facilities with shady sites. **Map refs:** 260 B3, 314 B2, 316 B6

Who to contact: Dandaragan St, Moora; Shire of Moora (08) 9651 1401 or (08) 9651 1300 *Camping fees:* use the honesty box or pay fees at the council office, 34 Padbury St

60 Trayning Caravan Park

Visitors will see some interesting rock formations around Trayning, confined within a 2500 ha flora and fauna reserve that harbours a variety of rare plant species. Needless to say, the wildflowers in this part of the world are magnificent in the spring, when they bloom in all their multi-coloured glory. The caravan park has a good range of facilities in a shady setting. While you're here, get out and explore the area's gold-rush-era history. **Map refs:** 260 D3, 314 F2, 316 D6

Who to contact: Sutherland St, Trayning; Shire of Trayning (08) 9683 1001

61 Wandering Caravan Park

Wander into Wandering, south-east of Perth off the Albany Hwy, and you'll find the caravan park on Cheetaning St. It provides travellers with a good range of facilities and shady sites in a pleasant natural setting that attracts numerous birds and other wildlife. **Map refs:** 260 C5, 314 D6, 316 D8

Who to contact: Cheetaning St, Wandering; Shire of Wandering (08) 9884 1056 *Camping fees:* pay fees at the shire office, 22 Watts St, Wandering

62 Wave Rock Caravan Park

Wave Rock Caravan Park offers quiet and peaceful sites in a natural bush setting at the base of Wave Rock, one of the region's most impressive natural attractions. On Wave Rock Rd, 4 km east of Hyden and 340 km east of Perth via the Brookton Hwy, the park is ideally situated for visitors to go bushwalking among the local flora and fauna, or swim and canoe on nearby Lake Magic. Other accommodation is available at the nearby resort. **Map refs:** 260 E5, 314 H5, 316 F8

How to book: Wave Rock Rd (08) 9880 5022

Kangaroo at twilight in Walyunga National Park (p. 262)

63 Westonia Caravan Park

This caravan park has a good range of facilities in a location that has been preserved to reflect its days as a goldmining boom town. Old buildings have been restored and new ones have been constructed in a style that represents the past. The old Edna May mine site has a lookout that gives remarkable views over the surrounding landscape, the former mine workings and the open-cast mine, which has now filled with water. The nearby Sandford Rocks Nature Reserve, with its granite outcrops, pools, wildflowers, scrub and bushland, is a great spot for a picnic or a bit of bushwalking. Westonia is 316 km east of Perth. **Map refs:** 260 E3, 314 H3, 316 E6

How to book: Wolfram St, Westonia; Shire of Westonia (08) 9046 7063; or Westonia Community Resource Centre (08) 9046 7077

64 Wickepin Caravan Park

In the town of Wickepin, 38 km north-east of Narrogin on the Great Southern Hwy, there are some fine Edwardian buildings, including the house that Albert Facey made famous in his best-selling book, *A Fortunate Life*. Many of the sites mentioned in his book can still be seen today. The caravan park boasts one of the largest garden gnome collections you're ever likely to see. Other accommodation is available. **Map refs:** 260 D5, 314 F6, 316 D8

How to book: Wogolin Rd, Wickepin (08) 9888 1089

65 Wyalkatchem Caravan Park

Wyalkatchem is at the centre of WA's major wheat belt, 191 km north-east of Perth via Toodyay, and smack in the middle of some of Australia's best wildflower country. The town lies on the old Goldfields Track, the route taken by fortune seekers making their way toward Kalgoorlie–Boulder. It has most of the delights of a small country town and the caravan park here is a good base from which to explore the countryside. **Map refs:** 260 D3, 314 E3, 316 D6

How to book: Goomalling–Merredin Rd, Wyalkatchem 0427 814 042, 0429 814 042 or (08) 9681 4042

THE SOUTH-WEST

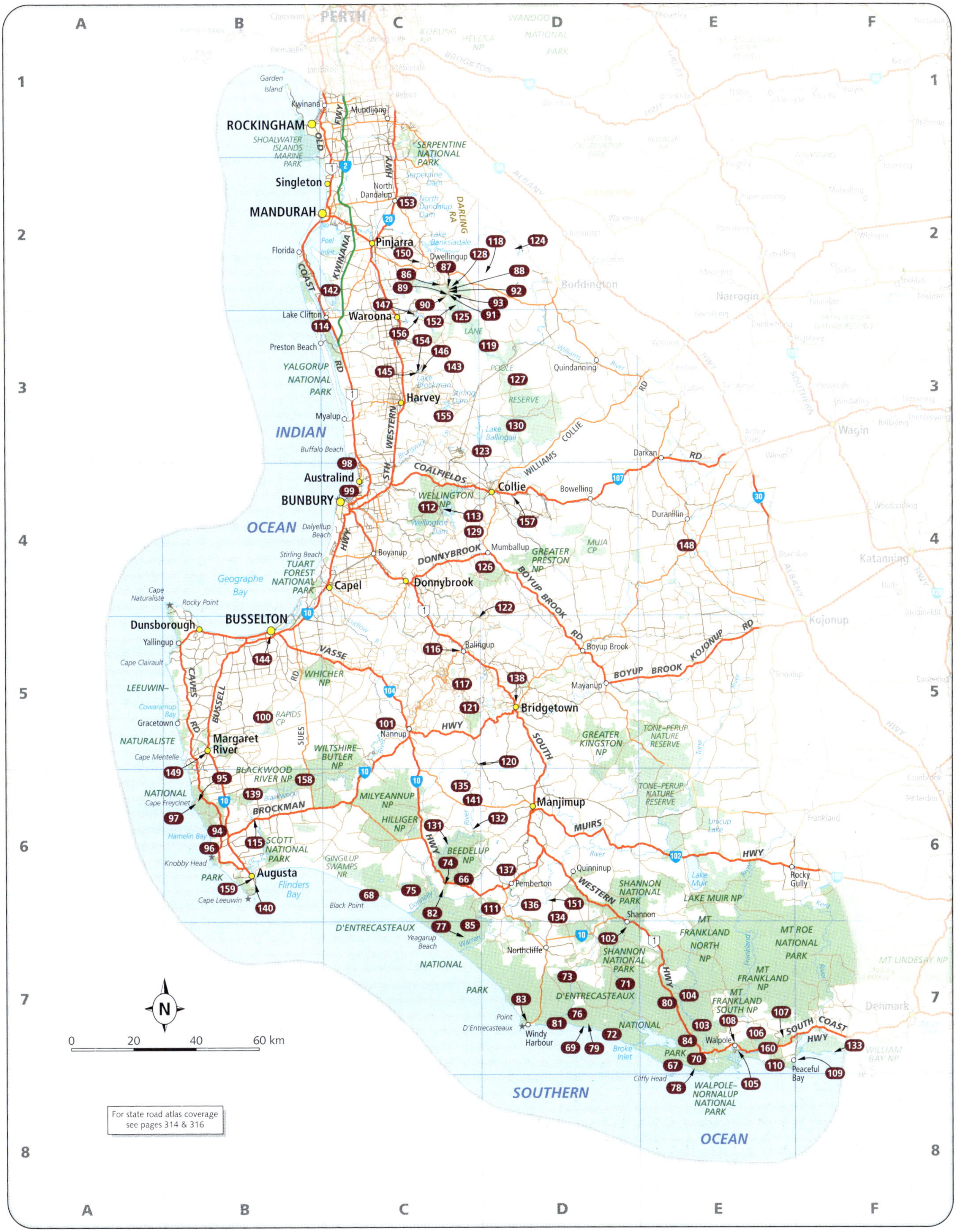

A **B** **C** **D** **E** **F**

PERTH

1

Garden
Island
Kwinana
ROCKINGHAM
SHOALWATER
ISLANDS
MARINE
PARK
Singleton
Mundijong
North
Dandalup

2
MANDURAH
Pinjarra
Florida
153
150
Peel
Inlet
North
Dandalup
Dam
Serpentine
Dam
SERPENTINE
NATIONAL
PARK
DARLING RA
Dwellingup
118
124
128
142
86
87
88
Lake
Banksiadale
Boddington
Narrogin

Lake Clifton
147
89
90
92
Waroona
152
125
93
91
114
156
154
119
LANE
Preston Beach
146
POOLE
YALGORUP
NATIONAL
PARK
145
143
Lake
Brockman
127
Quindanning
Myalup
155
Stirling
Dam
130
Lake
Ballingall
Buffalo Beach
123
Darkan
RD
Wagin

3
INDIAN
98
COALFIELDS
WILLIAMS
Australind
99
WELLINGTON
NP
Collie
Bowelling
107
BUNBURY
112
Wellington
Dam
113
157
Durahllin
30
OCEAN
Dalyellup
Beach
129
Mumballup
GREATER
PRESTON
NP
Katanning
148
Stirling Beach
TUART
FOREST
NATIONAL
PARK
Boyanup
DONNYBROOK
126
MUJA
CP

4
Cape
Naturaliste
Rocky Point
Geographe
Bay
Capel
Donnybrook
122
BOYUP BROOK
Kojonup
Dunsborough
116
Balingup
Boyup Brook
KOJONUP RD
Yallingup
BUSSELTON
144
VASSE
117
138
BOYUP BROOK
Cape Clairault
WHICHER
NP
104
121
Mayanup
Lingdale

5
LEEUWIN-
CAVES
BUSSELL
RD
SUES
RAPIDS
CP
101
Nannup
HWY
Bridgetown
SOUTH
GREATER
KINGSTON
NP
TONE-PERUP
NATURE
RESERVE
Cowaramup
Bay
100
WILTSHIRE-
BUTLER
NP
120
Gracetown
NATURALISTE
Margaret
River
BLACKWOOD
RIVER NP
158
10
MILYEANNUP
NP
135
TONE-PERUP
NATURE
RESERVE
Cape Mentelle
149
95
139
141
Manjimup
MUIRS
Frankland

6
NATIONAL
Cape Freycinet
97
BROCKMAN
115
HILLIGER
NP
131
132
102
Unicup
Lake
94
SCOTT
NATIONAL
PARK
GINGILUP
SWAMPS
NR
74
BEEDELUP
NP
137
Quinninup
SHANNON
NATIONAL
PARK
HWY
Rocky
Gully
96
66
Pemberton
LAKE MUIR NP
Knobby Head
PARK
159
Flinders
Bay
68
75
136
151
Shannon
MT
FRANKLAND
NORTH
NP
MT ROE
NATIONAL
PARK
140
Cape Leeuwin
82
111
134
MT
FRANKLAND
NP
MT LINDESAY NP
D'ENTRECASTEAUX
77
85
102
SHANNON
NATIONAL
PARK
MT
FRANKLAND
SOUTH NP
Denmark
Yeagarup
Beach
Warren
NATIONAL
Northcliffe
73
71
107
WESTERN
PARK
83
80
104
Point
D'Entrecasteaux
81
76
D'ENTRECASTEAUX
NATIONAL
72
103
108
106
SOUTH COAST
Windy
Harbour
69
79
Broke
Inlet
105
160
110
133
WILLIAM
BAY NP
67
70
109
Cliffy Head
78
Peaceful
Bay
WALPOLE-
NORNALUP
NATIONAL
PARK

7
N
0   20   40   60 km

SOUTHERN

8
For state road atlas coverage
see pages 314 & 316

OCEAN

A **B** **C** **D** **E** **F**

WA'S SOUTH-WESTERN POCKET IS a wonderfully diverse region washed by a fabulous coastline, dotted with magnificent forests and beribbonned with rivers. With such an abundance of natural features, it's little wonder the area is popular with tourists and locals alike as a premier camping destination.

The parks and reserves here have excellent facilities to suit all manner of campers, in pristine locations. Pitch a tent on the coastline in D'Entrecasteaux National Park or beside a gently flowing stream in Wellington National Park. Choose a secluded spot for your caravan in the forest of Shannon National Park or beside an idyllic pool in Rapids Conservation Park.

The range of activities available in this part of the state is limited only by your imagination. Depending on the season, when the weather can change quickly from very hot, dry summer to cold and wet winter, you can swim and canoe the rivers and streams of Lane Poole Reserve or walk countless trails through towering, shady forests and the open bushland of Walpole Wilderness Area.

Fish and surf along the spectacular coastline of Leeuwin–Naturaliste National Park, relax on a pristine stretch of sand, or indulge in the famous wines and gourmet produce of nearby Margaret River. You may even be lucky enough to find a natural pool in a blissfully secluded spot that you have all to yourself.

CAMPSITES LOCATED IN PARKS AND RESERVES

BEEDELUP NATIONAL PARK

Beedelup National Park is located on the Vasse Hwy about 22 km west of Pemberton. Its forests are mostly karri, but there are areas of jarrah and marri, and in spring wildflowers put on a show. One of its many features is Beedelup Falls, which are at their most spectacular in winter and spring. Here, Beedelup Brook flows 100 m over granite rock; there is a viewing point with wheelchair access but the best views are from the suspension bridge over the brook. Beedelup Falls is the starting point for several forest walking trails, including one around Lake Beedelup and another to the Walk-through Tree. The Bibbulmun Track also links to the park and offers a good pick-up and drop-off point for walkers.

Who to contact: DEC Pemberton (08) 9776 1207; or DEC Bibbulmun Track Office (08) 9334 0265

66 Beedelup camping area

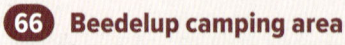

On the Bibbulmun Track, Beedelup is 19.5 km from Beavis camping area and 45.4 km from Warren camping area. **Map refs:** 269 C6, 314 C11, 316 C11

D'ENTRECASTEAUX NATIONAL PARK

A significant wilderness area of pristine natural beauty, D'Entrecasteaux National Park is a narrow strip hugging the coast for 130 km between Augusta and Walpole. With high dunes and spectacular coastal cliffs, the park's outstanding natural features include a series of hexagonal-shaped basalt columns to the west of Black Point, major streams and

rivers, including the Warren, Donnelly and Shannon, coastal heathlands, grasslands, low woodlands and scattered pockets of karri forest. Quokkas, western quolls, possums, wallabies and bandicoots are just some of the native animals you might spot, and southern right whales can be seen along the coast from Sept to Nov.

Who to contact: DEC Walpole (08) 9840 0400 for campsite nos **67**, **70**; DEC Walpole (08) 9840 0400 or DEC Pemberton (08) 9776 1207 for campsite nos **69**, **72**, **79**, **81**; DEC Nannup (08) 9756 0211 or DEC Pemberton (08) 9776 1207 for campsite nos **68**, **74**, **75**, **82**, **85**; DEC Bibbulmun Track Office (08) 9334 0265 for campsite nos **71**, **73**, **76**, **78**, **80**, **84** *How to book:* (08) 9776 8398 for campsite no. **83**; DEC Nannup (08) 9756 0211 or DEC Pemberton (08) 9776 1207 for campsite no. **77**

67 Banksia camping area

At 28 km west of Walpole via Mandalay Beach Rd, Banksia camping area is close to the water at a beach boasting spectacular coastal scenery. The popular surfing and fishing spot is very secluded and perfect for self-sufficient campers. Boil or treat the tank water, or bring your own drinking water. Bring firewood too. Access is 4WD only. **Map refs:** 269 E7, 314 E12, 316 D11

68 Black Point camping area

Black Point is the most northerly campsite in the park, with stunning coastal scenery providing the backdrop for keen anglers and surfers. It's 70 km south-west of Nannup via Black Point Rd, which is closed from May till after Jan; use Woodarburrup Rd off Milyeannup Coast Rd instead. From the access track 22 km south-east from Milyeannup Coast and Woodarburrup rds, it is 2 km south to the camping areas. Bring your own drinking water. **Map refs:** 269 C6, 314 C11, 316 C11

69 Coodamurrup Beach camping area (bush camping)

Behind the dunes 16 km south of Chesapeake Rd via Moores Track (3 km south of Moores Hut), Coodamurrup Beach offers dispersed bush camping for self-sufficient campers. Access is by 4WD only; bring drinking water and a fire bin or bucket. **Map refs:** 269 D7, 314 D11, 316 C11

70 Crystal Springs camping area

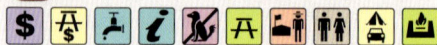

On Mandalay Beach Rd off the South Western Hwy, 13 km west of Walpole, Crystal Springs camping area is accessible to conventional vehicles and is located near the ranger station. Expect basic facilities in a shady, coastal scrub environment. Some firewood supplied. Note: no park pass required. **Map refs:** 269 E7, 314 E12, 316 D11

71 Dog Pool camping area

On the Bibbulmun Track, Dog Pool is 24.5 km from Lake Maringup campsite and 19.4 km from Mt Chance campsite. **Map refs:** 269 D7, 314 D11, 316 D11

72 Fish Creek camping area

Self-sufficient campers who enjoy fishing will make themselves at home at this basic beach campsite with no facilities. Fish Creek camping area is 13 km south of Chesapeake Rd via Moores Track and Fish Creek Track – 4WD access only. Bring drinking water, a fire bin or bucket, and firewood. **Map refs:** 269 D7, 314 D12, 316 D11

73 Gardner camping area

On the Bibbulmun Track, Gardner is 29.1 km from Schafer camping area and 15.9 km from Lake Maringup camping area. **Map refs:** 269 D7, 314 D11, 316 C11

74 Grass Tree Hollow camping area

Grass Tree Hollow camping area is on Boatlanding Rd, 2 km south of Vasse Hwy and 23 km west of Pemberton. It has basic facilities in 5 shady campsites among the trees on the edge of Carey Brook. Visitors enjoy fishing the crystal-clear waters of the brook, bushwalking and birdwatching in the area's lush forest. Bring drinking water. **Map refs:** 269 C6, 314 C11, 316 C11

75 Lake Jasper camping area

West of Pemberton via the Vasse Hwy, Scott Rd (9 km west of Beedelup Falls) and Lake Jasper Rd, this secluded camping area on the shores of the lake has basic facilities. Swimming and boating are popular pursuits. Bring drinking water. **Map refs:** 269 C6, 314 C11, 316 C11

76 Lake Maringup camping area

On the Bibbulmun Track, Lake Maringup is 15.9 km from Gardner camping area and 24.5 km from Dog Pool camping area. **Map refs:** 269 D7, 314 D11, 316 C11

77 Leaning Marri camping area

Leaning Marri is set among the dunes 2 km south of Yeagarup Lake, 22 km south-west of Pemberton via Ritter Rd and the Vasse Hwy. The camping area has a good range of facilities, including a hut for larger groups to enjoy beach-related activities. Bookings essential. **Map refs:** 269 C7, 314 C11, 316 C11

78 Long Point camping area

On the Bibbulmun Track, Long Point is 17.2 km from Woolbales camping area and 12.2 km from Mt Clare camping area. Bring a gas/fuel stove as no fires are permitted. **Map refs:** 269 E7, 314 E12, 316 D12

79 Moores Hut camping area

Moores Hut is 40 km south-east of Northcliffe via Chesapeake Rd and Moores Track – 4WD access only. It offers basic facilities near the beach in an area popular for fishing and swimming. Bring drinking water. **Map refs:** 269 D7, 314 D11, 316 C11

80 Mount Chance camping area

On the Bibbulmun Track, Mt Chance is 19.4 km from Dog Pool camping area and 20.4 km from Woolbales camping area. Bring a gas/fuel stove as no fires are permitted. **Map refs:** 269 E7, 314 E11, 316 D11

81 Mouth of Gardner camping area (bush camping)

This bush-camping area is set behind dunes next to the Gardner River. It has basic facilities in an area where fishing, swimming and canoeing are popular activities. The access track from Windy Harbour Rd is very sandy (4WD only) and seasonally closed. Bring drinking water. **Map refs:** 269 D7, 314 D11, 316 C11

82 Snottygobble Loop camping area

Snottygobble Loop camping area is 2 km south of the Vasse Hwy on Boatlanding Rd, 23 km west of Pemberton. With a good range of facilities at 9 small sites tucked away under the peppermint trees, there's also a larger site for groups or families. Bushwalkers and birdwatchers will enjoy the trails through the scrub, and anglers will find the brook a good spot for fishing. **Map refs:** 269 C6, 314 C11, 316 C11

83 Windy Harbour camping area

Windy Harbour camping area is 27 km south of Northcliffe and accessed from Windy Harbour Rd. It has a good range of facilities in a pleasant natural setting and is a popular surfing and fishing spot. Bookings advised at peak periods. **Map refs:** 269 D7, 314 D11, 316 C11

84 Woolbales camping area

On the Bibbulmun Track, Woolbales is 20.4 km from Mt Chance camping area and 17.2 km from Long Point camping area. Gas/fuel stove only; no fires are permitted. **Map refs:** 269 E7, 314 E12, 316 D11

85 Yeagarup Lake camping area

On Ritter Rd, 20 km south-west of Pemberton via the Vasse Hwy, Yeagarup Lake offers basic facilities in a coastal scrub setting near the lake. Cross the dunes to the beach for fishing, swimming and other sandy activities. **Map refs:** 269 C7, 314 C11, 316 C11

LANE POOLE RESERVE

Lane Poole Reserve, just south of Dwellingup, covers nearly 55 000 ha of steeply forested valley slopes and undulating woodlands inhabited by abundant wildlife, including diminutive quolls and quokkas. The Murray River runs through the reserve and its ever-changing landscape is ideal for swimming, fishing and canoeing. Bushwalking and picnicking are other popular activities in the reserve, where spring wildflower displays delight all those who visit. Note: a fire ban applies 15 Dec–31 Mar, when you need to bring your own gas/fuel stove; check with the DEC before lighting a fire as dates can change annually. Bring your own water and firewood, as wood must not be collected within the reserve. Fox baiting is common, so dogs need to be on leash.

Who to contact: DEC Dwellingup (08) 9538 1078 *How to book:* online bookings at www.dec.wa.gov.au/campgrounds for campsite nos **87**, **88**, **91**, **92**, **93**

86 Baden Powell camping area

You'll find Baden Powell campground 9 km south of Dwellingup on Nanga Rd, then a further 1.5 km east of the reserve entry along Park Rd. Drinking water is available, but best to bring your own. **Map refs:** 269 C2, 314 C7, 316 C8

87 Charlies Flat camping area

This secluded forest campsite is in a lovely setting beside the river, 14 km south of Dwellingup. It is suitable for smaller caravans and camper trailers. To get here, take Nanga Rd then head 7 km south-east of the reserve entry via Park and River rds. Bookings are essential. **Map refs:** 269 C2, 314 C7, 316 C8

88 Chuditch camping area

This forest site is suitable for small caravans or camper trailers and has a good range of facilities. It's 16 km from Dwellingup following Nanga and Park rds, 8.5 km south-east of the reserve entry off Murray Valley Rd. To get to the reserve entry, take Bobs Crossing off River Rd. Tank water is limited, and needs to be boiled or treated before use, so it's best to bring your own. No fires are allowed here. Bookings are essential. **Map refs:** 269 C2, 314 C7, 316 C8

89 Nanga Mill camping area

This secluded camping area in the forest near the old mill site is suitable for caravans, and just a pleasant stroll away from the river. The campground is 18 km south-east of Dwellingup; take Nanga, Park, River and Murray Valley rds; it's 11 km south-east of the reserve entry. **Map refs:** 269 C2, 314 C7, 316 C8

90 Nanga Townsite camping area

This is a secluded campsite in the forest with signposted access along Nanga Rd. It is 13.5 km south of Dwellingup and 6 km south of the reserve entry. **Map refs:** 269 C2, 314 C7, 316 C9

91 Stringers camping area

A small, secluded camping area, Stringers is beside the river on Murray Valley Rd, reached via Bobs Crossing off River, Park

and Nanga rds. The site is 19 km south-east of Dwellingup and 11.5 km south-east of the reserve entry. Bookings are essential. **Map refs:** 269 C2, 314 C7, 316 C8

92 Tonys Bend camping area

A delightfully secluded riverside camping area in the forest, Tonys Bend is 17 km south of Dwellingup via Nanga Rd. Turn off onto Park Rd 9 km south of Dwellingup, then travel 9.4 km south-east of the reserve entry via River Rd. Bookings are essential. **Map refs:** 269 C2, 314 C7, 316 C8

93 Yarragil camping area

On River Rd, off Park Rd, 20 km south of Dwellingup, this campground is 12 km south-east of the reserve entry via Nanga Rd. Bookings are essential. **Map refs:** 269 C2, 314 C7, 316 C8

LEEUWIN–NATURALISTE NATIONAL PARK

Leeuwin–Naturaliste National Park hugs the south-west coast of WA, stretching from Cape Naturaliste in the north to Cape Leeuwin in the south. The park boasts a stunning array of natural attractions, with wild and rugged coastal scenery, white-sand beaches, historic lighthouses, some of the state's best surfing breaks, great fishing, towering karri forests and magnificent cave formations.

Who to contact: DEC Busselton (08) 9752 5555 *How to book:* (08) 9757 7025 for campsite no. **95**; (08) 9758 5540 for campsite no. **96**

94 Boranup camping area

This small, shady camping area in the forest has access for small vans only. Follow the signpost on Boranup Dr, off Caves Rd, 10 km north-west of Karridale. Come equipped with drinking water. **Map refs:** 269 B6, 314 B10, 316 B11

95 Conto camping area

This camping area has a good range of facilities in natural surroundings. It's near the magnificent scenery and numerous activities offered by this beautiful stretch of coast, and also in close proximity to several of the park's renowned caves. You'll find it on Conto Rd, 18 km south-west of Margaret River and 2 km west of Caves Rd. Note: not suitable for large vans. **Map refs:** 269 B6, 314 B10, 316 B10

96 Hamelin Bay Holiday Park

Hamelin Bay Holiday Park is set on a sweeping section of a beautiful bay where ships once harboured in the timber-milling days. Catch the night's dinner from the ocean and cook it around the campfire in the evening, go cave- and wreck-diving, or just spend the days relaxing within this extraordinary natural environment. The holiday park is on Hamelin Bay West Rd, off Caves Rd, 8 km west of Karridale. **Map refs:** 269 B6, 314 B10, 316 B11

97 Point Road camping area

On Point Rd, 21 km south-west of Margaret River off Boranup Dr, this campground has 4WD access to a delightfully forested area with small campsites close to a fishing and surfing beach. You need to come equipped with drinking water. **Map refs:** 269 B6, 314 B10, 316 B10

LESCHENAULT PENINSULA CONSERVATION PARK

Leschenault Peninsula Conservation Park is bounded on one side by the Indian Ocean and by the Leschenault Estuary on the other. Its long, white beaches are very popular for fishing, snorkelling and diving. The park is renowned for birdwatching, with over 60 bird species recorded, and the peppermint and tuart woodlands are home to brushtail and ringtail possums. Access to Leschenault Peninsula Conservation Park is from the north via Buffalo Rd, 10 km north of Australind off the Old Coast Rd. The park is accessible by 2WD vehicles, but if you're bringing a caravan you need to check road conditions first.

Who to contact: DEC Collie (08) 9735 1988

98 Belvidere camping ground

Belvidere has a good range of facilities in a relaxing beach environment, 20 km north of Australind; you need to bring firewood and drinking water, though. An interpretation trail here explains the history of the area. The camping ground is south of Buffalo Rd off Old Coast Rd. **Map refs:** 269 C4, 314 C8, 316 C9

99 The Cut camping area (walk-in camping)

A small camping area at the end of a peninsula, 8.5 km south of the Belvidere camping ground, the Cut has walk-in, cycle or boat access only. Bring your own firewood and drinking water. **Map refs:** 269 C4, 314 C8, 316 C9

RAPIDS CONSERVATION PARK

Rapids Conservation Park is located 25 km north-east of Margaret River. The town was originally a retreat for surfers but has now evolved into the ultimate smorgasbord of good food, fine wine and spectacular scenery. Visitors can camp in beautiful natural forest along the banks of the Margaret River, yet still be able to enjoy the outstanding premium wines and food available in the region. Natural attractions in the area include underground caves, a rugged coastline, squeaky-clean sandy beaches, turquoise water and towering forests.

Who to contact: DEC Busselton (08) 9752 5555; or DEC Kirup (08) 9731 6232

100 Canebrake Pool camping area

A selection of peaceful sites in the forest beside the river, Canebrake Pool camping area is 5.5 km along Canebreak Rd. Swimming and canoeing are popular pastimes here. Rapids Conservation Park is 25 km north-east of Margaret River; leave the Bussell Hwy 4 km north of Margaret River at Osmington Rd, and bring your own drinking water. Access is possible for small vans or camper trailers but not large caravans. **Map refs:** 269 B5, 314 B9, 316 B10

ST JOHN BROOK CONSERVATION PARK

The Old Timberline Trail is the focus of this conservation park, highlighting remnants of the historic Timberline Railway. The trail can be walked or cycled before enjoying a refreshing swim in the cool waters of St John Brook, which is also suitable for a bit of fishing and canoeing.

Who to contact: DEC Kirup (08) 9731 6232; or Nannup Tourist Information Centre (08) 9756 1211 *Camping fees:* pay fees at self-registration station

101 Workmans Pool camping area

This camping area – also known as Workers Pool – is in the forest near a brook, 11 km west of Nannup. To get here, follow the Vasse Hwy and Mowen Rd; carry in your own firewood and drinking water. **Map refs:** 269 C5, 314 C9, 316 C10

SHANNON NATIONAL PARK

Shannon National Park protects karri, jarrah and marri forests over an area of around 53 500 ha. It's a peaceful place to linger by day, and to fall asleep to the sound of the southern boobook owl at night. Visitors can enjoy the park's wildflowers, several walks or the self-guided Great Forest Trees drive.

Who to contact: DEC Pemberton (08) 9776 1207

102 Shannon camping area

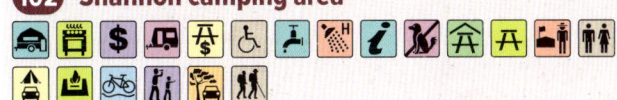

A spacious camping area in the forest, Shannon has a good range of facilities. It is just off the South Western Hwy, 53 km south of Manjimup and 41 km north-west of Walpole. For extra comfort, a 2-bedroom lodge is available for hire. **Map refs:** 269 D7, 314 D11, 316 D11

WALPOLE WILDERNESS AREA

Walpole Wilderness Area protects 363 000 ha to the north of Walpole and Denmark; an extent larger than some small countries. It embraces a number of current national parks, nature reserves and forest conservation areas. There are only 2 camping areas in this huge area, both of which offer basic facilities at secluded spots in pristine forest surroundings. It's the perfect place to experience a true wilderness adventure.

Who to contact: DEC Walpole (08) 9840 0400

103 Centre Road camping area

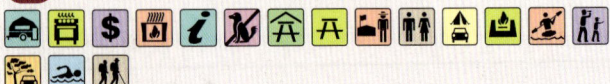

On Centre Rd, 5 km east of the South Western Hwy, this small camping area is on the western side of Deep River. Take the signposted turn-off 20 km north-west of Walpole. Surrounded by dense forest, the basic camping facilities include a shelter hut along with limited tent sites. A 3-night maximum stay applies. **Map refs:** 269 E7, 314 E11, 316 D11

104 Fernhook Falls camping area

Fernhook Falls is a small, secluded camping area in the forest. With limited sites for off-road camper trailers, you can stay here to explore the falls area or take a canoe trip on the pristine Deep River. The camping area is 6 km east of the South Western Hwy, with signposted access along Beardmore Rd, 35 km north-west of Walpole. Shelter huts are available and you need to bring your own drinking water. **Map refs:** 269 E7, 314 E11, 316 D11

WALPOLE–NORNALUP NATIONAL PARK

Surrounding the inlets of the same name, Walpole–Nornalup National Park is renowned for its giant red tingle trees in an area known as the Valley of the Giants. The breathtaking Tree Top Walk leads through the canopy. Bushwalking, coastal walks and a range of aquatic activities are available within the park. The Bibbulmun Track wends through this park, with 4 camping areas along the way.

Who to contact: DEC Walpole (08) 9840 0400; or DEC Bibbulmun Track Office (08) 9334 0265 *How to book:* 1800 670 026 for campsite no. **105**, bookings essential during peak periods; (08) 9840 8060 for campsite no. **109**

105 Coalmine Beach Holiday Park

On Knoll Dr off the South Coast Hwy, 3 km east of Walpole, Coalmine Beach Holiday Park has all the facilities of a good caravan park, in an ideal location. Choose from a wide range of water-based activities when not exploring the majestic forests of the national park. **Map refs:** 269 E7, 314 E12, 316 D11

106 Frankland camping area

On the Bibbulmun Track, Frankland is 27.5 km from Mt Clare camping area and 13.7 km from Giants camping area. Gas/fuel stove only as no fires are permitted. **Map refs:** 269 E7, 314 E12, 316 D11

107 Giants camping area

On the Bibbulmun Track, Giants is 13.7 km from Frankland camping area and 15.6 km from Rame Head camping area. Gas/fuel stove only as no fires are permitted. **Map refs:** 269 E7, 314 E12, 316 D11

108 Mount Clare camping area

On the Bibbulmun Track, Mt Clare is 12.2 km from Long Point camping area and 27.5 km from Frankland camping area. Gas/fuel stove only as no fires are permitted. **Map refs:** 269 E7, 314 E12, 316 D11

109 Peaceful Bay Caravan Park

Located on Peaceful Bay Rd off the South Coast Hwy, 34 km east of Walpole and 45 km west of Denmark, this shire-owned caravan park is on the eastern edge of the national park. Bordered by magnificent forest and pristine beaches, it offers all the facilities expected at a caravan park. **Map refs:** 269 E7, 314 E12, 316 D11

110 Rame Head camping area

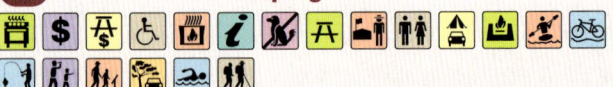

On the Bibbulmun Track, Rame Head is 15.6 km from Giants camping area and 33.2 km from Boat Harbour camping area. Gas/fuel stove only as no fires are permitted. **Map refs:** 269 E7, 314 E12, 316 D11

WARREN NATIONAL PARK

Warren National Park, 10 km south-west of Pemberton, is known for its towering karri trees, lush undergrowth and picturesque, meandering river. The Warren River rapids make fishing, swimming and canoeing very popular activities here. Other pastimes include strolling the Heartbreak Walk Trail, climbing the Dave Evans Bicentennial Tree and settling in for a relaxing night around the campfire.

Who to contact: DEC Pemberton (08) 9776 1207

111 Warren River camping area

There are 2 small, secluded campsites here in the forest near the river. Leave the Vasse Hwy at Old Vasse Rd, around 12 km south-west of Pemberton, or take Heartbreak Trail off Old Vasse Rd, 4.3 km east of the Vasse Hwy. Bring in your own drinking water. **Map refs:** 269 D6, 314 D11, 316 C11

WELLINGTON NATIONAL PARK

Whether you enjoy spending your summer days lazing by a gently flowing river or tranquil lake, or prefer the more athletic pursuits of cycling, swimming and bushwalking, then Wellington National Park is for you. To the west of Collie, the national park also offers fishing and canoeing, and in spring visitors can enjoy a wonderful wildflower display. The park's central feature is the beautiful Collie River valley, with its ancient gorge behind Wellington Dam. You'll need to bring a gas/fuel stove from Dec–Mar due to solid-fuel fire bans; dates can change annually, so check with the DEC before setting a fire.

Who to contact: DEC Collie (08) 9735 1988 *Camping fees:* fees collected on-site

112 Honeymoon Pool camping areas

These small camping areas set in the shady forest beside the Lower Collie River have a good range of basic facilities in a beautiful natural environment. Swimming and canoeing in the river are popular activities here, as is bushwalking through the magnificent jarrah forest. On River Rd via Wellington Dam and Coalfields rds, west of Collie. Bring your own firewood. **Map refs:** 269 C4, 314 C8, 316 C9

113 Potters Gorge camping area

Fishing, canoeing and bushwalking are popular activities at this forest camping area on the shoreline of Wellington Dam, 29 km west of Collie via Coalfields and Wellington Dam rds. A good range of facilities is provided. **Map refs:** 269 C4, 314 C8, 316 C9

YALGORUP NATIONAL PARK

Yalgorup National Park preserves the wetland system formed around a chain of 10 coastal lakes, with Lake Clifton and Lake Preston being the largest. Visitors with a scientific bent come here to view stromatolites and thrombolites, or to study birdlife at this very important habitat for native and migrating waterbirds.

Who to contact: DEC Mandurah (08) 9303 7750

114 Martins Tank camping area

Martins Tank camping area is arranged under a natural canopy of peppermint trees, 5 km from Preston Beach North Rd. Bring drinking water and firewood; Oct–Mar bring a gas/fuel stove as well, as a solid-fuel fire ban is in place. **Map refs:** 269 C3, 314 B7, 316 C9

CAMPSITES LOCATED IN OTHER AREAS

115 Alexandra Bridge camping area

Set beside the Blackwood River 26 km north-east of Augusta on Clarke Dr, this secluded campsite makes the most of the diverse forest landscape on the east side of Alexandra Bridge. With a good range of visitor facilities and activities such as boating, fishing and canoeing, it's very popular with campers year-round. Look for the sign off the Brockman Hwy, 10 km east of Karridale. **Map refs:** 269 B6, 314 B10, 316 B11

Who to contact: (08) 9758 2244

116 Balingup Caravan Transit Park

This small transit park with limited sites is arranged along the banks of Balingup Brook in Walter St, off Jayes Rd in Balingup.

Stays are limited to 3 nights. To get to this pretty crafts village nestled in the Blackwood River valley, follow the South Western Hwy between Donnybrook and Bridgetown. **Map refs:** 269 C5, 314 C9, 316 C10

Who to contact: Balingup General Store (08) 9764 1051

Bibbulmun Track – northern section

The Bibbulmun Track traverses some of the south-west's most scenic and beautiful areas for some 963 km, from Kalamunda on the outskirts of Perth all the way to the southern coast at Albany. The northern section begins at Kalamunda Trackhead, with a total of 27 campsites dotted along the track to Donnelly River Village, which is a private camping area 31 km south-east of Nannup. The campsites have a timber shelter sleeping no more than 17 people, as well as a bush toilet, rainwater tank and picnic table. Tents can be erected at the campsites, but no camping is allowed in water catchment areas between Kalamunda and Collie, and south of the Blackwood River. With numerous vehicle access points along the way, the track can be tackled in sections; it would take 6–8 weeks to walk the entire track in one go. Water may not always be reliable so carry extra, and it's preferable to bring a gas/fuel stove. Fire restrictions are in place Oct–May. Walkers need to be self-sufficient and well-prepared, equipped with track maps and guides.

Please note that campsites are listed in alphabetical order, not track order. Refer to the map on p. 269 for further information.

Who to contact: DEC Bibbulmun Track Office (08) 9334 0265; or Bibbulmun Track Foundation (08) 9481 0551 www.bibbulmuntrack.org.au; or DEC Dwellingup (08) 9538 1078; or DEC Collie (08) 9735 1988; or DEC Kirup (08) 9731 6232

117 Blackwood camping area

On the Bibbulmun Track, Blackwood is 40.1 km from Grimwade camping area and 18 km from Gregory Brook camping area. **Map refs:** 269 C5, 314 C9, 316 C10

118 Chadoora camping area

On the Bibbulmun Track, Chadoora is 14.8 km from Mt Wells camping area and 32.4 km from Swamp Oak camping area. **Map refs:** 269 D2, 314 C7, 316 C8

119 Dookanelly camping area

On the Bibbulmun Track, Dookanelly is 17.8 km from Murray camping area and 19.3 km from Possum Springs camping area. **Map refs:** 269 D3, 314 D7, 316 C9

120 Donnelly River Village

This privately operated campsite is located at the end of the northern section of the Bibbulmun Track and marks the start of its southern section. It is 20.6 km from the Gregory Brook camping area and 15.9 km from the Tom Rd camping area, which is in the southern section of the Bibbulmun Track. **Map refs:** 269 C5, 314 C10, 316 C10

121 Gregory Brook camping area

On the Bibbulmun Track, Gregory Brook is 18 km from Blackwood camping area and 20.6 km from Donnelly River Village. **Map refs:** 269 C5, 314 C9, 316 C10

122 Grimwade camping area

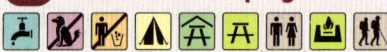

On the Bibbulmun Track, Grimwade is 21.9 km from Noggerup camping area and 40.1 km from Blackwood camping area. **Map refs:** 269 C5, 314 C9, 316 C10

123 Harris Dam camping area

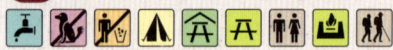

On the Bibbulmun Track, Harris Dam is 13.5 km from Yourdamung camping area and 41 km from Yabberup camping area. **Map refs:** 269 D3, 314 C8, 316 C9

124 Mount Wells camping area

On the Bibbulmun Track, Mt Wells is 14.5 km from White Horse camping area, which lies within the Heartlands region of the track, and 14.8 km from the Chadoora camping area. **Map refs:** 269 D2, 314 D6, 316 C8

125 Murray camping area

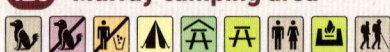

On the Bibbulmun Track, Murray is 18.6 km from Swamp Oak camping area and 17.8 km from Dookanelly camping area. **Map refs:** 269 C3, 314 C7, 316 C9

126 Noggerup camping area

On the Bibbulmun Track, Noggerup is 17.7 km from Yabberup camping area and 21.9 km from Grimwade camping area. **Map refs:** 269 D4, 314 C8, 316 C10

127 Possum Springs camping area

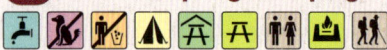

On the Bibbulmun Track, Possum Springs is 19.3 km from Dookanelly camping area and 18.7 km from Yourdamung camping area. **Map refs:** 269 D3, 314 D7, 316 C9

128 Swamp Oak camping area

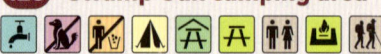

On the Bibbulmun Track, Swamp Oak is 32.4 km from Chadoora camping area and 18.6 km from Murray camping area. **Map refs:** 269 C2, 314 C7, 316 C8

129 Yabberup camping area

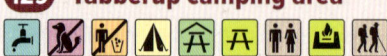

On the Bibbulmun Track, Yabberup is 41 km from Harris Dam camping area and 17.7 km from Noggerup camping area. **Map refs:** 269 C4, 314 C8, 316 C9

130 Yourdamung camping area

On the Bibbulmun Track, Yourdamung is 18.7 km from Possum Springs camping area and 13.5 km from Harris Dam camping area. **Map refs:** 269 D3, 314 D8, 316 C9

Bibbulmun Track – southern section

The southern section of the scenic Bibbulmun Track begins at Donnelly River Village, a private camping area 31 km south-east of Nannup. A total of 23 camping areas lie between Donnelly River and the trackhead at Albany; no fires are allowed at campsites from Mt Chance to Albany, so you'll need to carry in a gas/fuel stove to these areas. The campsites have a timber shelter sleeping no more than 17 people, as well as a bush toilet, rainwater tank and picnic table. Tents can be erected at the camping areas, but no camping is allowed in water catchment areas. With numerous vehicle access points along the way, the track can be tackled in sections; it would take 6–8 weeks to walk the entire track in one go. Water may not always be reliable so carry extra, and it's preferable to bring a gas/fuel stove. Fire restrictions are in place Oct–May. Walkers need to be self-sufficient and well-prepared, equipped with track maps and guides.

Please note that campsites are listed in alphabetical order, not track order. Refer to the map on p. 269 for further information.

Who to contact: DEC Bibbulmun Track Office (08) 9334 0265; or Bibbulmun Track Foundation (08) 9481 0551 www.bibbulmuntrack. org.au; or DEC Manjimup (08) 9771 7948; or DEC Pemberton (08) 9776 1207; or DEC Walpole (08) 9840 0400; or DEC Albany (08) 9841 9290

131 Beavis camping area

On the Bibbulmun Track, Beavis is 19.1 km from Boarding House camping area and 19.5 km from Beedelup camping area. **Map refs:** 269 C6, 314 C10, 316 C11

66 Beedelup camping area

See p. 270.

132 Boarding House camping area

On the Bibbulmun Track, Boarding House is 22.8 km from Tom Rd camping area and 19.1 km from Beavis camping area. **Map refs:** 269 C6, 314 C10, 316 C11

133 Boat Harbour camping area

Boat Harbour is 33.2 km from Rame Head camping area and 19.9 km from the William Bay camping area, which is located in the Great Southern region of the Bibbulmun Track. Gas/fuel stove only at this campsite. **Map refs:** 269 F7, 295 B1, 314 F12, 315 B4, 316 D11

71 Dog Pool camping area

See p. 271.

106 **Frankland camping area**

See p. 274.

73 **Gardner camping area**

See p. 271.

107 **Giants camping area**

See p. 274.

76 **Lake Maringup camping area**

See p. 271.

78 **Long Point camping area**

See p. 271.

80 **Mount Chance camping area**

See p. 271.

108 **Mount Clare camping area**

See p. 274.

110 **Rame Head camping area**

See p. 274.

134 **Schafer camping area**

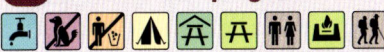

On the Bibbulmun Track, Schafer is 21.1 km from Warren camping area and 29.1 km from Gardner camping area.
Map refs: 269 D6, 314 D11, 316 C11

135 **Tom Road camping area**

On the Bibbulmun Track, Tom Rd is 15.9 km from Donnelly River Village and 22.8 km from Boarding House camping area.
Map refs: 269 C6, 314 C10, 316 C10

136 **Warren camping area**

On the Bibbulmun Track, Warren is 45.4 km from Beedelup camping area and 21.1 km from Schafer camping area.
Map refs: 269 D6, 314 D11, 316 C11

84 **Woolbales camping area**

See p. 271.

This track continues through the Great Southern region (see p. 282).

137 **Big Brook Arboretum**

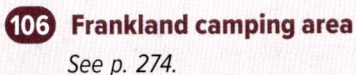

Big Brook Arboretum has a spacious camping area shaded by tall trees with abundant wildflowers. You'll find it 11 km north-west of Pemberton via Golf Links and Mullineaux rds. A walking trail here leads through the lovely arboretum, home to a varied collection of exotic trees. Bring your own drinking water.
Map refs: 269 D6, 314 D10, 316 C11

Who to contact: DEC Pemberton District Office (08) 9776 1207; or Pemberton Tourist Centre (08) 9776 1133

138 **Bridgetown Caravan Park**

Spend the night at this caravan park beside the Blackwood River. It's at the southern end of a town that's well-known for its old-world charm, warm hospitality and chilled, misty mornings. The rolling hills and stunning river scenery provide a beautiful backdrop to the galleries, wineries, cafes and restaurants that entice locals and visitors alike. **Map refs:** 269 D5, 314 D9, 316 C10

How to book: South Western Hwy, Bridgetown (08) 9761 1900; or Bridgetown Visitor Information Centre (08) 9761 1740

139 **Chapman Pool camping area**

This small camping area near the river is 25 km south-east of Margaret River via the Bussell Hwy and Warner Glen Rd. Good facilities are provided in a peaceful forest setting, with swimming, fishing and canoeing the main activities.
Map refs: 269 B6, 314 B10, 316 B10

Who to contact: DEC Busselton (08) 9752 5555; or DEC Kirup (08) 9731 6232

140 **Flinders Bay Caravan Park**

There's a range of sites in pleasant surroundings at this caravan park, 3 km south of the Augusta town centre, off Albany Tce. Surrounded by the Southern Ocean and native bushland, activities such as swimming, boating and fishing are popular, and nearby Leeuwin–Naturaliste National Park has a selection of hiking trails to satisfy those with a yen for bushwalking.
Map refs: 269 B6, 314 B11, 316 B11

How to book: Albany Tce, Augusta (08) 9758 1380 www.flindersbaypark.com.au

141 **Greens Island camping area**

Greens Island camping area is 2 km off Donnelly Dr, 23 km west of Manjimup via Graphite Rd. Set in a former family farm dating back to the 1921 settlement of the area, it provides easy bushwalking access to Four Acres and One Tree Bridge. You need to bring your own drinking water. **Map refs:** 269 C6, 314 C10, 316 C10

Who to contact: DEC Pemberton (08) 9776 1207; or Manjimup Tourist Bureau (08) 9771 1831

142 **Herron Point camping area**

Herron Point camping area is on Herron Point Rd, 7 km west of Old Bunbury Rd (turn off 16 km south of Pinjarra), on the shores of Peel Harvey Estuary. It's perfect for fishing, boating, swimming, sailing and other water-based activities in an area that abounds with birdlife. Bring drinking water and firewood.

A maximum stay of 2 nights applies. Although dogs are allowed, the area is baited, so you'll need to keep your pet on a lead. A fire ban applies Nov–Mar, when you'll need to use a gas/fuel stove. **Map refs:** 269 C2, 314 C7, 316 C8

Who to contact: Murray Shire Council (08) 9531 7777; or Pinjarra Tourist Centre (08) 9531 1438 *Camping fees:* fees apply Nov–Apr

143 Hoffman Mill camping area

This secluded camping area surrounds an old mill site on Clarke Rd, off the South Western Hwy. You'll find good facilities in a forest environment that is perfect for bushwalking and enjoying the natural surroundings. To get here, turn onto Logue Brook Dam Rd from the South Western Hwy, 6 km south of Yarloop, and onto Clarke Rd. Note: a fire ban applies Dec–Mar; check with authorities for exact dates. **Map refs:** 269 C3, 314 C7, 316 C9

Who to contact: DEC Collie (08) 9735 1988

144 Kookaburra Caravan Park

This caravan park is well-located, just a few minutes' walk to the town centre and the Busselton Jetty. The park has 3 separate areas and is ideal for club bookings or large groups. Here, you can experience the tuart and karri forests, and the still waters of Geographe Bay. Note: dogs are welcome but not in on-site accommodation. **Map refs:** 269 B5, 314 B9, 316 B10

How to book: 66 Marine Tce, Busselton (08) 9752 1516

145 Lake Brockman camping area (bush camping)

Foreshore bush camping is available at Lake Brockman, a beautiful lakeside environment 6 km east of the South Western Hwy. You need to bring your own drinking water. Popular activities include swimming, fishing, boating, canoeing and waterskiing. Access is via Logue Brook Dam Rd, 6 km south of Yarloop. **Map refs:** 269 C3, 314 C7, 316 C9

Who to contact: Lake Brockman Tourist Park (08) 9733 5402 www.lakebrockman.com.au

146 Lake Brockman Tourist Park

This extremely popular tourist park is on Logue Brook Dam Rd, 6 km east of the South Western Hwy. Head here for swimming, fishing, boating, waterskiing and canoeing. The lakeside environment is also perfect for bushwalking or cycling, which are ideal ways to enjoy the scenery. **Map refs:** 269 C3, 314 C7, 316 C9

How to book: Logue Brook Dam Rd (08) 9733 5402 www.lakebrockman.com.au

147 Lake Navarino Forest Resort

Until now, Lake Navarino Forest Resort was one of WA's best-kept secrets. Nestled in jarrah forest, it's the perfect place to

slip into the peaceful and unhurried pace of nature, or rush into one of the many activities available here, all while enjoying the good facilities of a caravan park. Don't tell anyone, but it's on Invarell Rd, off Scarp and Nanga Brook rds, 8 km east of Waroona. Bring a gas/fuel stove Dec–Mar. Bookings are essential at peak periods. **Map refs:** 269 C3, 314 C7, 316 C9

How to book: 147 Invarell Rd, Waroona (08) 9733 3000, 1800 650 626 www.navarino.com.au

148 Lakeside Camping

Lake Towerinning is a tranquil, ancient meteor crater filled with fresh, clear water off Darkin Rd South, 8 km south of Duranillin. The lake is a haven for waterbirds and lovers of boating, sailing, waterskiing and canoeing. Bookings are essential for peak periods. **Map refs:** 269 E4, 314 E8, 316 D9

How to book: Darkin Rd South (08) 9863 1040, 0428 631 040 www.lakesidecamping.com.au

149 Margaret River Tourist Park

Margaret River Tourist Park is 1 km from the centre of town, on Station Rd. It offers visitors shady, grassed sites with a good range of facilities for campers, who can set up their tents on the cloth pads provided, as well as other forms of accommodation. The park is well-placed to take advantage of the many attractions of the region. Whether you enjoy exploring caves and beaches or cafes and wineries, visiting Margaret River will surely be a delight. **Map refs:** 269 B5, 314 B10, 316 B10

How to book: 44 Station Rd, Margaret River (08) 9757 2180 www.margaretrivertouristpark.com.au

150 Marrinup camping area

Marrinup camping area is 5 km west of Dwellingup on Grey Rd, via Pinjarra Rd. It's a pleasant area in the forest beside Marrinup Brook. Nature lovers will enjoy the serenity of the forest and its flora and fauna while following trails along the creek to the falls or visiting the remnants of the old POW camp. Come equipped with firewood and drinking water. **Map refs:** 269 C2, 314 C7, 316 C8

Who to contact: Dwellingup Tourist Information Centre (08) 9538 1108

151 Moons Crossing camping area

This small, peaceful camping site is in the forest beside Warren River, which offers marroning and fishing opportunities. Come equipped with firewood and drinking water. To get here, take Moons Crossing Rd, off Spring Gully Rd from the Gloucester Tree, 16 km east of Pemberton. A 4WD is recommended, and is essential in wet weather. **Map refs:** 269 D6, 314 D11, 316 C11

Who to contact: DEC Pemberton (08) 9776 1207; or Pemberton Tourist Centre (08) 9776 1133

Munda Biddi Trail

Eventually, this long-distance cycle trail will stretch from north-east of Perth at Mundaring, all the way to the south coast at Albany. Currently, it winds through forests and parks along bush and disused rail routes to Nannup. Well-equipped sites have toilets, tables, seats and shelters, and the trail passes through towns regularly to provide other accommodation options. Although water is available at campsites along the trail, you should bring water as well as route information and a gas/fuel stove.

■ *Please note that campsites are listed in alphabetical order, not track order. Refer to the map on p. 269 for further information.*

Who to contact: DEC Munda Biddi Trail (08) 9334 0265; or Munda Biddi Trail Foundation (08) 9481 2483, 0422 112 229

152 Bidjar Ngoulin camping area

Towering forest shades this campsite, 28.5 km south of Dwellingup and 32 km from Lake Brockman. **Map refs:** 269 C2, 314 C7, 316 C9

153 Dandalup camping area

Stunning valley views and a ghostly stand of butter gums surround this campsite, 34 km south of Jarrahdale. Dwellingup is 44.9 km to the north. **Map refs:** 269 C2, 314 C6, 316 C8

154 Lake Brockman (Logue Brook Dam) camping area

There is camping in the bush lining the shore of the lake, 32 km south of Bidjar Ngoulin camping area and 46 km from Yarri camping area. **Map refs:** 269 C3, 314 C7, 316 C9

155 Yarri camping area

The Yarri campsite is on a hillside along a lovely tributary of the Harvey River. This shelter has been designed to take advantage of the slope of the site, with a stunning deck area that looks over the surrounding forest. The site is 46 km south of Lake Brockman. **Map refs:** 269 C3, 314 C8, 316 C9

■ *This track continues through the Heartlands region (see p. 266).*

156 Navarino Lakeside camping area

Accessed via the Navarino Forest Resort are numerous lake foreshore camping sites in beautiful, natural forest surroundings. These offer a more basic camping experience for those who don't require the full facilities of a caravan park. Expect shared fireplaces, toilets and access to all the activities available in the area. A total fire ban applies Dec–Mar, when you need to bring a gas/fuel stove. **Map refs:** 269 C3, 314 C7, 316 C9

How to book: 147 Invarell Rd, Waroona (08) 9733 3000, 1800 650 626 www.navarino.com.au

157 Stockton Lake camping area

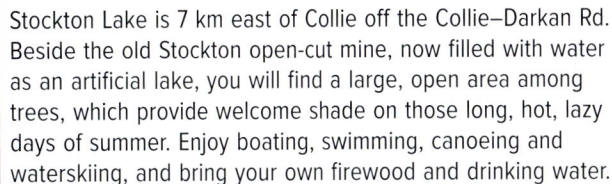

Stockton Lake is 7 km east of Collie off the Collie–Darkan Rd. Beside the old Stockton open-cut mine, now filled with water as an artificial lake, you will find a large, open area among trees, which provide welcome shade on those long, hot, lazy days of summer. Enjoy boating, swimming, canoeing and waterskiing, and bring your own firewood and drinking water. **Map refs:** 269 D4, 314 D8, 316 C9

Who to contact: DEC Collie (08) 9735 1988

158 Sues Bridge camping area

This small, secluded camping area is in the forest on Sues Rd, off the Brockman Hwy, 38 km east of Karridale. Campers will find a good range of facilities here while enjoying such activities as fishing, swimming and canoeing, or simply relaxing in the tranquil forest environment. **Map refs:** 269 B6, 314 B10, 316 B10

Who to contact: DEC Busselton (08) 9752 5555; or DEC Kirup (08) 9731 6232

159 Turner Caravan Park

Within walking distance of the Augusta town centre, the park is beside the Blackwood River and has easy access to the nearby beach, where swimming, fishing and boating are popular activities. Share your catch with the pelicans and stingrays, surf the swells, or explore the walking trails in the adjacent national park. **Map refs:** 269 B6, 314 B10, 316 B11

How to book: 1 Blackwood Ave, Augusta (08) 9758 1593 www.turnerpark.com.au

160 Valley of the Giants Ecopark

This caravan park with good facilities is nestled within forest and coastal hinterland. It is situated 6 km from the Tree Top Walk, which spans through giant tingle trees. The park is suitable for large vans or groups and is within easy reach of nearby beaches, rivers and nature walks. Bring your saw to collect the free firewood. **Map refs:** 269 E7, 314 E12, 316 D11

How to book: 6398 South Coast Hwy, Nornalup (08) 9840 1313, 1800 813 136 www.valleyofthegiantsecopark.biz

GREAT SOUTHERN

Map

A Narrogin B C D E F

1 Minninup Toolibin Harrismith Newdegate
Geeralying Boundain Tincurrin Lake Grace
Williams Dumberning Highbury ARTHUR RIVER NP DONGOLOCKING NATURE RESERVE TARIN ROCK NR NORTH TARIN ROCKS NP LAKE KING NP

2 Josbury Piesseville Kukerin Moulyinning LAKELAND NATURE RESERVE BREAKAWAY RIDGE NR DUNN ROCK NATURE RESERVE
Culbin Tarwonga Gundaring Nippering Wishbone Dumbleyung Lake Grace South CHINOCUP NATURE RESERVE Chinocup Lake Kuringup Pingrup 180 LAKE MAGENTA NATURE RESERVE SOUTH COAST HWY Mount Drummond
Wagin Ballaying Nyabing NYABING RD 178 CORNEECUP NR Lake Joy CAIRLOCUP NR FITZGERALD RIVER NATIONAL PARK

Boolading Hillman Arthur River Warup Woodanilling KATANNING Katanning Coyrecup COYRECUP NR GNOWANGERUP CHESTER Jerramungup Point Charles
Cordering Duranillin Boscabel Holly Broomehill 172 Gnowangerup Ongerup PASS 1 Tagelup Beach

3 Mayanup Muradup Kojonup Jingalup Tambellup Borden CORACKERUP NATURE RESERVE BREMER BAY RD HWY Bremer Tooreenukup Swamp
Dinninup Kulikup SOUTH JINGALUP NR Millyunup Lake Balicup Lake BORDEN Boxwood Hill Bremer Bay 171 Doubtful Islands
GREATER KINGSTON NP TONE-PERUP NATURE RESERVE Gordon River 30 120 Cranbrook CAMEL LAKE NR STIRLING RANGE PASS RANGE BORDEN BREMER BAY RD 176 Wray Bay Dillon Bay Bremer Bay Point Henry

4 Frankland 175 Tenterden STIRLING RANGE NATIONAL PARK 161 Kendenup Kalgan Wellstead SOUTH COAST BASIL ROAD NR Ledge Point Cape Riche 173 Cape Knob Smooth Rocks Beaufort Inlet Schooner Beach Willyun Beach Haul Off Rock
BOYNDAMINUP NP SHANNON NP LAKE MUIR NP MUIRS Rocky Gully MOUNT ROE NP Kamballup PORONGURUP PORONGURUP NP CHESTER South Stirling HASSELL NP Hassell Beach
Shannon MT FRANKLAND NORTH NP MT ROE NATIONAL PARK Mount Lindesay Mount Barker 102 Woodlands NORTH SISTER NR 162 Hassell Beach WAYCHINICUP NP

5 SHANNON STH MT FRANKLAND NP MT FRANKLAND SOUTH NP MOUNT LINDESAY NP Narrikup MILL BROOK NR Manypeaks 177 Cheyne Beach Bald Island MOUNT MANYPEAKS NR Two Peoples Bay
WESTERN Redmond 30 King River 1 182 Kalgan
Denmark 179 165 COAST Marbelup 167 ALBANY Nanarup TWO PEOPLES BAY NATURE RESERVE
D'ENTRECASTEAUX NATIONAL PARK WILLIAM BAY NP 170 174 Little Grove 166 For state road atlas coverage see pages 314 & 316
Walpole Nornalup HWY Wilson Inlet 169 Big Grove TORNDIRRUP NP
Peaceful Bay WEST CAPE HOWE NP 168 181 TORBAY 163 NP
WALPOLE-NORNALUP NP 164 West Cape Howe Torbay Head Eclipse Island

6 SOUTHERN OCEAN N 0 20 40 60 km

A B C D E F

STEP BACK IN TIME

STEP BACK IN TIME to explore convict lock-ups, old taverns, whaling ships, settlers' cottages and grand National Trust homes in beautifully landscaped grounds as you follow the dramatic Great Southern coastline from Denmark in the west to Bremer Bay in the east. The star of the coast is Albany on gorgeous Princess Royal Harbour.

There are several good coastal camping areas here, set against a backdrop of rugged granite cliffs and boasting a rare, wild beauty. The fishing in the bays and estuaries of the region is excellent, as are the beaches for surfing and lazing.

For those who prefer non-marine activities, numerous national parks dot the region, providing good camping, birdwatching and bushwalking opportunities. With its rugged peaks, the Stirling Range National Park is one of the world's most important areas for flora, with 1500 species packed within its boundaries. Not surprisingly, spring wildflower viewing is an incredible experience here.

Head west to Denmark and the many attractions include extraordinarily good fishing and surfing, along with great forests of towering karri and tingle. The trees are at their most imposing in the nearby Valley of the Giants.

Around 60 km north-west of Mt Barker is Lake Poorrarecup, a large freshwater lake with wide, white-sand beaches. It is used extensively for sailing and waterskiing, and its gently sloping shorelines make it ideal for young swimmers. The bushland near the lake is home to a variety of orchids and the camping area is excellent.

Bremer Bay, in the east of the region, is a wide expanse of crystal-clear azure water, edged by a long stretch of striking white sand. The bay is renowned for its great fishing, swimming and surfing. From July to Oct, southern right whales can be seen calving in the calm waters of the many sheltered bays. At times they can be as close as 6 m away!

CAMPSITES LOCATED IN PARKS AND RESERVES

STIRLING RANGE NATIONAL PARK

A mecca for hikers and climbers, this national park protects the breathtaking beauty of the Stirling Range, which rises abruptly to more than 1000 m above the surrounding flat, sandy plain. Its jagged peaks can sometimes be veiled in swirling clouds, with Bluff Knoll being the highest peak in WA's south-west region. The area is also renowned for its wildflowers in Sept–Nov, with many of the species being found nowhere else in the world.

Who to contact: DEC Stirling Range (08) 9827 9230, (08) 9827 9278; or DEC Albany (08) 9842 4500

161 Moingup Springs camping area

Moingup Springs camping area is on Chester Pass Rd, 76 km north-east of Albany. It has a good range of facilities in an area of breathtaking beauty that is very popular with hikers and climbers. Bring in a gas/fuel stove. **Map refs:** 280 D4, 314 G10, 316 E10

WAYCHINICUP NATIONAL PARK

Waychinicup National Park protects the Waychinicup River, stretching from Normans Beach in the west across to Cheyne Beach in the east. While the unspoilt coastal scenery is a delight, the deeply incised, tree-filled gullies that run down to the sea from boulder-strewn hilltops hide a secret world of streams, waterfalls and moss-covered boulders. Some rare and elusive animals have been isolated and protected here. Visitors will be delighted by the fishing, swimming and canoeing opportunities.

Who to contact: DEC Albany (08) 9842 4500; or Two Peoples Bay Visitor Centre (08) 9846 4276 *Camping fees:* fees collected on-site

162 Waychinicup Inlet camping area

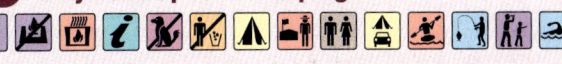

Off Cheyne Beach Rd, 60 km east of Albany, Waychinicup Inlet has 9 tent sites, some walk-in only. The facilities are basic (you need to bring drinking water and a gas/fuel stove) but the coastal location is picturesque. **Map refs:** 280 D5, 314 H11, 316 F11

WEST CAPE HOWE NATIONAL PARK

West Cape Howe National Park protects a rugged coastline of isolated beaches rimmed by pristine white sand and backed by coastal dunes. The varied flora ranges from karri forest and low coastal heath to peppermint trees and wildflowers. Go snorkelling and scuba diving at Shelley Beach, but be aware of strong rips in this area, or take a 4WD to search out some great fishing spots.

Who to contact: DEC Albany (08) 9842 4500; or DEC Bibbulmun Track Office (08) 9334 0265

163 Shelley Beach camping area

Shelley Beach camping area has basic facilities and limited space for trailers in a natural coastal environment where fishing, snorkelling and scuba diving are popular pastimes. The campsite is off Shelley Beach Rd, 38 km west of Albany via Lower Denmark and Cosy Corner rds. Not recommended for caravans. **Map refs**: 280 C5, 314 G12, 316 E11

164 West Cape Howe camping area

On the Bibbulmun Track, West Cape Howe is 16.5 km from Nullaki camping area and 16.4 km from Torbay camping area. Bring a gas/fuel stove as no fires are permitted. **Map refs:** 280 C5, 314 G12, 316 E12

WILLIAM BAY NATIONAL PARK

William Bay National Park is close to the town of Denmark. Renowned for its turquoise waters and sandy beaches, it is a great place for swimming or snorkelling. Attractions of the park include Green Pool, which is sheltered from the waves and is a safe swimming area for children, and Elephant Rocks. Known for its granite boulders and wildflowers in spring, the park provides many opportunities for photography, bushwalking and sightseeing.

Who to contact: DEC Walpole (08) 9840 0400; or DEC Bibbulmun Track Office (08) 9334 0265

165 William Bay camping area

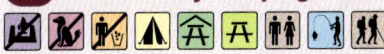

On the Bibbulmun Track, William Bay is 19.9 km from Boat Harbour camping area, within the South-West region of the track, and is 31.5 km from Nullaki camping area. Bring a gas/fuel stove as no fires are permitted. **Map refs:** 280 B5, 314 F12, 316 D11

CAMPSITES LOCATED IN OTHER AREAS

Bibbulmun Track – southern section

The southern section of the scenic Bibbulmun Track begins at Donnelly River Village, a private camping area 31 km south-east of Nannup. A total of 23 camping areas lie between Donnelly River and the trackhead at Albany; no fires are allowed at campsites from Mt Chance to Albany, so you'll need to carry in a gas/fuel stove to these areas. The campsites have a timber shelter sleeping no more than 17 people, as well as a bush toilet, rainwater tank and picnic table. Tents can be erected at the camping areas, but no camping is allowed in water catchment areas. With numerous vehicle access points along the way, the track can be tackled in sections; it would take 6–8 weeks to walk the entire track in one go. Water may not always be reliable so carry extra, and it's preferable to bring a gas/fuel stove. Fire restrictions are in place Oct–May. Walkers need to be self-sufficient and well-prepared, equipped with track maps and guides.

Please note that campsites are listed in alphabetical order, not track order. Refer to the map on p. 280 for further information.

Who to contact: DEC Bibbulmun Track Office (08) 9334 0265; or Bibbulmun Track Foundation (08) 9481 0551 www.bibbulmuntrack.org.au; or DEC Manjimup (08) 9771 7948; or DEC Pemberton (08) 9776 1207; or DEC Walpole (08) 9840 0400; or DEC Albany (08) 9841 9290

166 Albany Trackhead

The Albany Trackhead is 13 km from the Sandpatch campsite at the end of the southern section of the Bibbulmun Track. No camping is allowed here. **Map refs:** 280 C5, 314 G11, 316 E11

167 Muttonbird camping area

On the Bibbulmun Track, Muttonbird camping area is 12 km from Torbay camping area and 13 km from Sandpatch camping area. Bring a gas/fuel stove as no fires are permitted. **Map refs:** 280 C5, 314 G11, 316 E11

168 Nullaki camping area

On the Bibbulmun Track, Nullaki camping area is 31.5 km from William Bay camping area and 16.5 km from West Cape Howe camping area. Bring a gas/fuel stove as no fires are permitted. **Map refs:** 280 C5, 314 F12, 316 E11

169 Sandpatch camping area

On the Bibbulmun Track, Sandpatch camping area is 13 km from Muttonbird camping area and 13 km from the Albany Trackhead. Bring a gas/fuel stove as no fires are permitted. **Map refs:** 280 C5, 314 G12, 316 E11

170 Torbay camping area

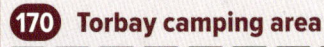

On the Bibbulmun Track, Torbay camping area is 16.4 km from West Cape Howe camping area and 12 km from Muttonbird camping area. Bring a gas/fuel stove as no fires are permitted. **Map refs:** 280 C5, 314 G12, 316 E11

164 West Cape Howe camping area

See p. 281.

165 William Bay camping area

See p. 281.

171 Bremer Bay Beaches Resort and Tourist Park

This caravan park caters for all budgets, from deluxe spa chalets, cabins and ensuite caravan sites, to basic tent sites. The park is nestled among shady peppermint trees, and a nature trail leads from the park. On the doorstep there is flora and fauna to see, as well as long, white-sand beaches and kilometres of four-wheel-driving. Fishing, snorkelling and scuba diving are popular here. **Map refs:** 280 F3, 316 G10

How to book: Wellstead Rd, Bremer Bay (08) 9837 4290 www.bremerbayaccommodation.com

172 Broomehill Village Caravan Park

On the corner of Morgan Rd and Journal St, Broomehill Village is perfectly positioned for visitors wanting to follow the town's Heritage Trail. The caravan park has good facilities and amenities. **Map refs:** 280 C3, 314 F9, 316 E10

Who to contact: Shire of Broomehill (08) 9825 3555, 0428 253 073 *Camping fees:* pay fees at shire office on Great Southern Hwy or to caretaker

173 Cape Riche camping area

Cape Riche is 118 km north-east of Albany via the South Coast Hwy and Sandalwood Rd, at Wellstead. A large camping area close to the beach, the campsites here are scattered through shady coastal scrub. Fishing, swimming or simply relaxing on the pristine beach are popular activities here, along with boating from the 4WD ramp. Bring firewood and drinking water. Generators are permitted between scheduled hours. **Map refs:** 280 E4, 316 F11

Who to contact: (08) 9847 3088

174 Cosy Corner (east) camping area

A secluded camping area near the foreshore, the cutely named Cosy Corner has 10 sites scattered around the trees in a coastal scrub environment. Off Cosy Corner Rd via Lower Denmark Rd, 30 km west of Albany, it is a good site for self-sufficient campers who enjoy a bit of fishing or swimming in a beautiful beach setting. Bring drinking water and firewood, though check with local authorities before lighting a fire as restrictions could be in place. Maximum stay is 7 nights. **Map refs:** 280 C5, 314 G12, 316 E11

Who to contact: City of Albany (08) 9841 9333; or Albany Visitor Centre (08) 9841 9290

175 Lake Poorrarecup camping area

Water-based activities abound at Lake Poorrarecup, 13 km east of Frankland on the Frankland–Cranbrook Rd. Boating, canoeing, waterskiing and sailing are just some of the diversions available to pass the time away at this large camping area on the northern side of the lake. Bring drinking water and firewood. Note: a solid-fuel fire ban applies Nov–Mar, when you need to bring a gas/fuel stove; check seasonal dates with local authorities. **Map refs:** 280 B4, 314 F10, 316 D11

Who to contact: Shire of Cranbrook (08) 9826 1008

176 Millers Point Reserve camping area

This small camping area is in Bremer Bay, 14 km east of Boxwood Hill via Borden–Bremer Bay Rd, then 6 km south via Millers Point Rd. Basic facilities (no firewood or drinking water) are provided in a coastal scrub environment near the beach. Anglers can try their luck at catching dinner or just swim and relax on the beach in an area renowned for its coastal scenery. **Map refs:** 280 E4, 316 F10

Who to contact: Shire of Jerramungup (08) 9835 1022

177 Normans Beach camping area

Fishing, swimming, walking or just relaxing on the beach are some of the activities available at this camping area 49 km east of Albany. The site is on the foreshore, reached via the South Coast Hwy, Homestead Rd and Normans Beach Rd. Basic facilities suit self-sufficient campers looking for a secluded beach setting surrounded by coastal scrub. The maximum stay is 3 days. **Map refs:** 280 D5, 314 H11, 316 E11

Who to contact: City of Albany (08) 9841 9333; or Albany Visitor Centre (08) 9841 9290

178 Nyabing Recreation Reserve camping area

Nyabing's Recreation Reserve is on Martin St, and offers welcome facilities for travellers. The area is noted for its string of shallow lakes: Magenta, Pingarup, Grace South, Grace North and Joy. This is also wildflower country and a good place to be July–Sept, when they add a colourful splash to the landscape. **Map refs:** 280 C2, 314 G8, 316 E9

Who to contact: Shire of Kent (08) 9829 1051 *Camping fees:* pay fees at shire office on Richmond St, Nyabing

179 Parry Beach Recreation Area

A very shady camping site under a canopy of trees close to the beach, this recreation area provides access to a range of water-based pastimes such as boating, fishing and sailing on the clear waters of William Bay. Parry Beach Recreation Area is 6 km off the South Coast Hwy at the end of Parry Beach Rd; the turn-off is 23 km west of Denmark. Bring your own firewood. **Map refs:** 280 B5, 314 F12, 316 D11

Who to contact: Shire of Denmark (08) 9848 1106; or Denmark Tourist Bureau (08) 9848 2055

180 Pingrup Caravan Park

This caravan park on Sanderson St in Pingrup is an ideal base for visiting the many historic and natural sites in and around the town. Birdwatchers head to Lake Bryde, an ephemeral wetland that is part of a chain of lakes running from Pingrup to Lake Grace, 50 km away to the north. In town, a giant replica of a shearer's handpiece stands out in all its glory on top of what locals call the Shears Shed, encouraging visitors to investigate further. **Map refs:** 280 D2, 314 H8, 316 F9

Who to contact: Community Resource Centre (08) 9820 1101

181 Torbay Inlet camping area

A very small camping area with basic facilities for self-sufficient campers, Torbay Inlet is surrounded by coastal scrub. The site is 28 km west of Albany via Lower Denmark, Perkins Beach and Torbay Inlet rds. A prime spot for fishing, swimming and canoeing. It also has a 4WD boat ramp. Minimum stay is 3 days. **Map refs:** 280 C5, 314 G11, 316 E11

Who to contact: City of Albany (08) 9841 9333; or Albany Visitor Centre (08) 9841 9290

182 Two Peoples Bay camping area

This secluded camping area is 52 km north-east of Albany on Two Peoples Bay. Fish and swim on a beautiful section of coastline or simply relax and take in the magnificent views. On East Bay Rd, the site is off Bettys Beach Rd via Homestead Rd, off the South Coast Hwy. The basic facilities suit self-sufficient campers; a 4WD is recommended. **Map refs:** 280 D5, 314 H11, 316 E11

Who to contact: City of Albany (08) 9841 9333; or Albany Visitor Centre (08) 9841 9290

ESPERANCE AND NULLARBOR

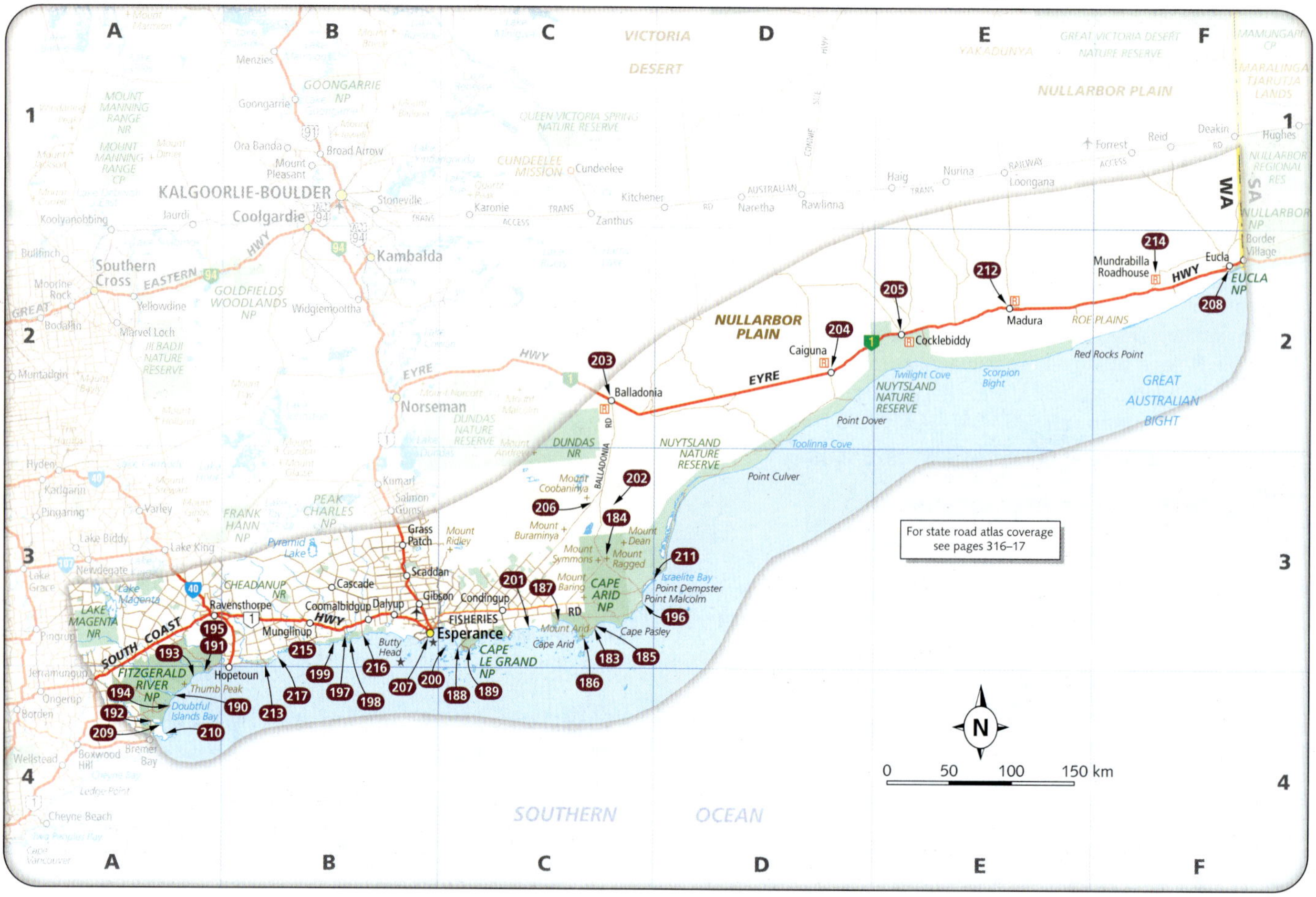

FOR SQUEAKY, WHITE BEACHES, getting off the beaten track and bunking down under the stars, head to Esperance. This place is so relaxed that even the kangaroos sunbake on the beach. Nestled on the shores of Esperance Bay, it's an ideal location for beach lovers who enjoy swimming, surfing, snorkelling and fishing against a backdrop of white-sand beaches, azure waters and expansive dunes.

Head east from here and you reach stunning Cape Le Grand National Park, a wonderland of rugged cliffs and perfect beaches for swimming and fishing. There are very good camping areas that make the most of their coastal environment, boasting such iconic drawcards as spring wildflowers and waters dotted with basking fur seals and southern right whales.

Quaalup Homestead Wilderness Retreat is approximately 45 km from Bremer Bay in Fitzgerald River National Park. The heritage-listed homestead was built in 1858 and guests can enjoy nature walks with views to West Mount Barren, spotting many species of wildflowers along the way. Campers can dream away under star-studded skies, wake up to bird calls and explore the attractions of Fitzgerald River National Park.

Venture even further east, almost to the SA border, and you reach Cape Arid National Park and Nuytsland Nature Reserve. Camping here puts you in the perfect position for wildflowers, fishing, bushwalking and four-wheel-driving.

CAMPSITES LOCATED IN PARKS AND RESERVES

CAPE ARID NATIONAL PARK

On WA's rugged south coast, Cape Arid National Park protects a stunning coastline of sweeping beaches rimmed by the intense blue waters of the Southern Ocean. An important park for the conservation of birds in WA, it harbours a number of restricted and threatened species, as well as some interesting inland birds. Coastal fishing from the beaches and headlands within the park is excellent year-round, and bushwalkers will be impressed by the display of wildflowers and birdlife.

Who to contact: DEC Cape Arid National Park (08) 9075 0055; or DEC Esperance (08) 9083 2100

183　Jorndee Creek camping area

Jorndee Creek camping area is 1.7 km off Poison Creek Rd, 24 km south of Merivale Rd. In a small area on the foreshore behind the dunes, it's 4WD only. Bring drinking water and a gas/fuel stove. **Map refs:** 284 C3, 317 J9

184 Mount Ragged camping area

Mt Ragged camping area is in the northern part of the park, 3.3 km east of Balladonia Rd and 131 km south of the Eyre Hwy (Balladonia Roadhouse). The road is 4WD access only and can be closed when wet. Bring drinking water and a gas/fuel stove. **Map refs:** 284 C3, 317 K8

185 Seal Creek camping area

On Poison Creek Rd, 26 km south-east of Merivale Rd reached via Fisheries Rd, Seal Creek camping area is in a coastal environment behind the dunes, with some shade and basic facilities available. A 4WD is recommended. Bring drinking water and a gas/fuel stove. **Map refs:** 284 C3, 317 J9

186 Thomas Fishery camping area

The very small camping area at Thomas Fishery is 9.8 km off Poison Creek Rd, 18 km south of Merivale Rd. It offers visitors basic facilities at a popular fishing spot on the coast. Access is 4WD only along a rough track, which may be closed if wet. Bring drinking water and a gas/fuel stove. **Map refs:** 284 C3, 317 J9

187 Thomas River camping area

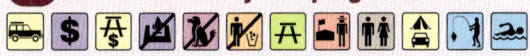

Thomas River camping area is 8.6 km along Thomas River Rd, off Merivale Rd, 105 km east of Esperance. The camping area is near the river, overlooking the ocean. Bring drinking water and a gas/fuel stove. **Map refs:** 284 C3, 317 J9

CAPE LE GRAND NATIONAL PARK

Lying to the east of Esperance on WA's rugged south coast, Cape Le Grand National Park is home to imposing granite peaks and undulating heathlands covered in wildflowers in spring. Rocky headlands and white-sand beaches are lapped by aquamarine waters, and scenic bays have evocative names such as Lucky Bay, Hellfire Bay and Thistle Cove. The islands of the Recherche Archipelago dot the horizon, making this area a mecca for swimming, fishing and boating enthusiasts.

Who to contact: DEC Cape Le Grand National Park (08) 9075 9072; or DEC Esperance (08) 9083 2100

188 Le Grand Beach camping area

Le Grand Beach camping area is in a coastal bush setting close to the water, 56 km south-east of Esperance via Merivale and Cape Le Grand rds. Visitors will find a good range of facilities here while they enjoy such activities as fishing, swimming and beach or bushwalks that highlight the park's stunning shoreline. Bring a gas/fuel stove. **Map refs:** 284 C3, 317 I9

189 Lucky Bay camping area

Lucky Bay camping area is 61 km south-east of Esperance via Merivale, Cape Le Grand and Lucky Bay rds; 4WD is recommended. There are 2 camping areas here, for tents (carry-in) and for trailers. You'll find a good range of facilities in a coastal scrub setting near the beach. The park offers visitors the opportunity to fish, swim or simply relax on one of the most pristine white-sand beaches in Australia. There's a beach boat launch. Bring a gas/fuel stove. **Map refs:** 284 C3, 317 I9

FITZGERALD RIVER NATIONAL PARK

Lying between Bremer Bay and Hopetoun on WA's south coast, Fitzgerald River National Park is renowned as one of the most diverse botanical regions in the world, and in turn supports a number of threatened animals. This vast, flora-rich area is one of only 2 national parks in WA to be gazetted by UNESCO as a World Biosphere Reserve. The spectacular coastline of sweeping beaches and rocky headlands provides an unbeatable location for fishing, bushwalking and whale-watching from Aug to Nov.

Who to contact: Fitzgerald River NP Ranger (08) 9835 5043; or Ranger Westside (08) 9837 1022 for campsite nos **190**, **194**; Ranger Eastside (08) 9838 3060 for campsite nos **191**, **192**
How to book: (08) 9837 4124 www.whalesandwildflowers.com.au for campsite no. **192**

190 Fitzgerald Inlet camping area

On Fitzgerald River Track, 20 km east of Pabelup Rd and 80 km north-east of Bremer Bay, this large, open clearing is around 2 km from the beach on the west side of Fitzgerald River National Park. It has basic facilities with some shade available and offers visitors swimming, fishing and bushwalking activities. Bring drinking water and a gas/fuel stove. There may be seasonal closures; check with rangers. **Map refs:** 284 A4, 316 G10

191 Hamersley Inlet camping area

Hamersley Inlet camping area on the east side of Fitzgerald River National Park is on Hamersley Inlet Rd off Hamersley Dr, 23 km west of Hopetoun. With basic facilities in a coastal environment, it is popular with anglers. Access in dry weather only. Bring drinking water and a gas/fuel stove. Check with rangers about seasonal closures. **Map refs:** 284 A4, 316 G10

192 Quaalup Homestead Caravan Park

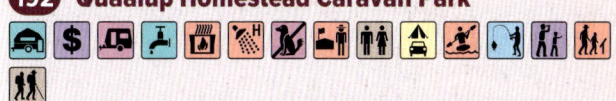

Quaalup Homestead is situated 75 km south-east of Jerrmungup via South Coast Hwy, Devils Creek Rd (turn-off 28 km south of

Jerramungup), then Collets and Gairdner rds. Visitors will find a good range of facilities in a shady, grassed area while enjoying the many activities available. Be amazed by the variety of flora and fauna in the area, fish and canoe the Gairdner River, or simply relax on the pristine white sand of Trigelow Beach before dreaming away under starry skies. Other accommodation is available at this privately run park. **Map refs: 284 A4, 316 G10**

193 Quoin Head camping area

Quoin Head camping area is on Telegraph Track off Hamersley Dr, 45 km west of Hopetoun, on the east side of Fitzgerald River National Park. It has basic facilities close to the foreshore. The steep access track is open in dry weather only. Bring drinking water and a gas/fuel stove. **Map refs: 284 A4, 316 G10**

194 St Marys Inlet camping area

St Marys Inlet camping area has basic facilities in a coastal setting on Point Ann Rd, off Pabelup Dr, 67 km north of Bremer Bay on the west side of Fitzgerald River National Park. Fishing and swimming are the main activities here, and lucky campers may even be treated to the haunting sounds of whales singing at night. Bring drinking water and a gas/fuel stove. **Map refs: 284 A4, 316 G10**

195 Shire Reserve camping area

Shire Reserve camping area is within Fitzgerald River National Park on Hamersley Inlet Rd, off Hamersley Dr, 26 km west of Hopetoun. This secluded area has basic facilities and shady campsites on the water's edge, making it a nice spot for swimming and fishing. Bring drinking water and a gas/fuel stove. No access in wet weather. **Map refs: 284 A4, 316 G10**

NUYTSLAND NATURE RESERVE

Nuytsland Nature Reserve embraces 400 000 ha and close to 500 km of coastline, incorporating the majestic cliffs and ocean beaches of the Great Australian Bight. Stretching from Cape Arid National Park eastward to Red Rock Point, the reserve contains a number of small caves and collapsed caverns known as dolines, as well as sections of the old Overland Telegraph Line, constructed in 1876. Also within the area is the Eyre Bird Observatory, a habitat for an abundance of native flora and fauna and a very popular location for birdwatchers. Another highlight is Twilight Cove, which is famous along the Nullarbor for its 70 m stretch of limestone cliffs overlooking the Bight. Anglers will find excellent fishing along this section of coast.

Who to contact: DEC Cape Arid National Park (08) 9075 0055; or DEC Esperance (08) 9083 2100

196 Point Malcolm camping area

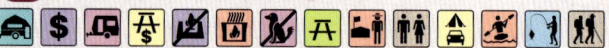

Point Malcolm camping area is 13 km south of Fisheries Rd and 59 km east of the signposted Poison Creek turn-off. The small site is near the beach, with a bit of shade and shelter from the coastal vegetation but no facilities. Self-sufficient campers who like a bit of fishing will enjoy a stay at this camping area, which has only limited camper-trailer space. Access is by 4WD through Cape Arid National Park; Fisheries Rd is very corrugated. **Map refs: 284 C3, 317 K9**

STOKES NATIONAL PARK

Stokes National Park is on the coast an hour west of Esperance, protecting Stokes Inlet and its surrounding heathland. The largest estuary in the region, and the only one with reasonably deep water, the inlet is a haven for waterbirds and a popular spot for canoeing and birdwatching. The fishing is excellent too, with black bream, salmon and King George whiting the main catch.

Who to contact: DEC Stokes National Park (08) 9076 8541; or DEC Esperance (08) 9083 2100

197 Benwenerup camping area

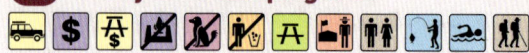

On Stokes Inlet Rd, 6 km south of the South Coast Hwy and 80 km west of Esperance, Benwenerup camping area is set among the scrub overlooking the inlet. You need to come equipped with a gas/fuel stove and drinking water. **Map refs: 284 B3, 316 H9**

198 Fanny Cove camping area

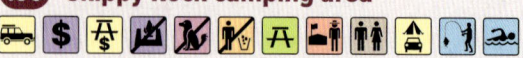

With only 3 sites, Fanny Cove is a very small camping area on the beach off Farrells Rd, reached via the South Coast Hwy west of Esperance. With basic facilities and accessed by 4WD only along a sandy track, it is a popular fishing, surfing and snorkelling spot. To get here from the South Coast Hwy, travel 7 km south on Farrells Rd to the turn-off. Bring a gas/fuel stove and drinking water. **Map refs: 284 B3, 316 H9**

199 Skippy Rock camping area

Skippy Rock camping area is in a well-protected environment of coastal scrub overlooking the ocean, in an area offering activities such as fishing and swimming. Access is 4 km off Springdale Rd, off the South Coast Hwy west of Esperance; a 4WD is required. Skippy Rock is 4 km from the park boundary. Bring a gas/fuel stove and drinking water. **Map refs: 284 B3, 316 H9**

WOODY ISLAND NATURE RESERVE

Woody Island Nature Reserve is a paradise for nature lovers and visitors looking for a diverse range of activities, including diving, snorkelling, fishing, birdwatching and going for bushwalks. To get here you need to join a boat cruise from Esperance, taking 1 hr 45 min. The island is only accessible Sept–May.

Who to contact: MacKenzies Island Cruises (08) 9071 5757

200 Woody Island Eco Stays

Camping at Woody Island Eco Stays is for tents only in a cleared area in the scrub, with access to a good range of facilities. It is a great base from which to explore the island and its attractions. **Map refs:** 284 C3, 317 I9

CAMPSITES LOCATED IN OTHER AREAS

201 Alexander Bay camping area

Alexander Bay camping area is on Alexander Rd, 85 km east of Esperance. A stunning coastline greets visitors to this shady camping area, which is situated in native bush just off the foreshore. The pristine beach is perfect for swimming, fishing or just relaxing while enjoying the panoramic views. Van sites are limited, the access road is unsealed, and you need to bring your own firewood and drinking water. **Map refs:** 284 C3, 317 J9

Who to contact: Esperance Shire rangers (08) 9083 1533; or Esperance Visitor Centre (08) 9083 1555

202 Balbinya Ruins camping area (bush camping)

Balbinya Ruins bush-camping area is reached by an access track 12.4 km south of the junction of Mt Ragged Track and Balladonia Rd. There are no facilities in this open grassland area, where the best campsites are set around the trees near the dam or in the vicinity of the ruins. This campsite is for self-sufficient campers only, and a 4WD is recommended. Bring firewood, though a gas/fuel stove is preferred, and drinking water. This area is not managed by DEC but it can assist with general enquiries. **Map refs:** 284 C3, 317 K8

Who to contact: DEC Esperance (08) 9083 2100

203 Balladonia Roadhouse Caravan Park

There are caravan facilities and other accommodation options at this iconic roadhouse on the Eyre Hwy at Balladonia, 191 km east of Norseman. Claypans typical of the region can be photographed, along with old stone walls built by pioneer farmers. Rocky outcrops and granite sheets collectively called Newmans Rocks, 50 km west of Balladonia, form a natural water catchment that supports a large array of wildlife, including donkeys, emus and kangaroos. Tank water is limited so visitors should bring their own drinking water. **Map refs:** 284 C2, 317 K7

How to book: Eyre Hwy, Balladonia (08) 9039 3453 www.balladoniahotelmotel.com.au

204 Caiguna Roadhouse Caravan Park

This roadhouse with caravan park facilities but no firewood is on the Eyre Hwy at Caiguna, 181 km east of Balladonia. Between Balladonia and Caiguna is the 90 Mile Straight, the longest stretch of straight road in Australia. Just 5 km west of Caiguna you can see the Blowhole, which blows when cool air escapes from the caverns and caves underground. **Map refs:** 284 D2, 317 M7

How to book: Eyre Hwy, Caiguna (08) 9039 3459

205 Cocklebiddy Roadhouse Caravan Park

Cocklebiddy Roadhouse has accommodation and caravan park facilities for visitors travelling along the Eyre Hwy, 66 km east of Caiguna. If you have a 4WD, take a detour to experience the pristine beauty of Nuytsland Nature Reserve. The Eyre Bird Observatory is 35 km from the highway, via a turn-off 17 km east of Cocklebiddy, housed in the wonderful old Eyre Telegraph Station. **Map refs:** 284 E2, 317 M6

How to book: Eyre Hwy, Cocklebiddy (08) 9039 3462

206 Deralinya Ruins camping area (bush camping)

Deralinya Ruins is 7 km west of Mt Ragged Track, a little west of Parmango Rd. Access is via a track 12.4 km south of the meeting of Balladonia Rd and Mt Ragged Track. Camping here is in woodland country that offers some welcome shade. There are no facilities, so it's for self-sufficient campers only and a 4WD is recommended. Bring drinking water and firewood, though a gas/fuel stove is preferred. **Map refs:** 284 C3, 317 J8

Who to contact: DEC Esperance (08) 9083 2100

207 Esperance Bay Holiday Park

This caravan park is well-situated close to the foreshore and has good facilities. Visitors enjoy fishing from the jetties or swimming in the clear waters off the white-sand beach, and can explore the foreshore via walkways and cycleways. A short drive east from Esperance are the wonders of Cape Le Grand National Park, including Lucky Bay beach, famed for its fine white sand. **Map refs:** 284 B3, 317 I9

How to book: 162 Dempster St, Esperance (08) 9071 2237, 1800 999 923 www.esperancebayholidaypark.com.au

208 Eucla Pass Caravan Park

These welcome caravan park facilities are on the Eyre Hwy at Eucla, 66 km east of Mundrabilla Roadhouse and 12 km west of the WA–SA border. Eucla was once home to the busiest telegraph station in Australia outside of the capital cities. Today, visitors can explore the ruins of this historic site, which are slowly being covered by shifting sand dunes. The remains of a jetty are a reminder of pioneering days, when supplies were transported by boat. Spend some time at the Eucla Museum or, for something a little different, pay a visit to the Bureau of Meteorology. **Map refs:** 284 F2, 317 P6

How to book: Amber Motor Hotel, Eyre Hwy, Eucla (08) 9039 3468

209 Gordon Inlet camping area

Estuarine Gordon Inlet sits on the mouth of the Gairdner River, which discharges about 9 400 000 cubic metres of water per annum. The estuary is transient and quite shallow, and salinity levels can be 4 times higher than seawater. The camping area is on Gordon Inlet Rd, off Gairdner Rd, 20 km north-east of Bremer Bay. With no facilities provided (bring water and gas/fuel stove), the site is tailor-made for self-sufficient campers who enjoy a secluded location for fishing and swimming. It's 4WD access only. **Map refs:** 284 A4, 316 G10

Who to contact: Shire of Jerramungup (08) 9835 1022

210 House Beach camping area

House Beach camping area is 43 km north-east of Bremer Bay via Gordon Inlet Rd, off Gairdner Rd. It offers secluded beach camping in a popular fishing and swimming spot. There are no facilities here so campers need to be self-sufficient. Access is 4WD only. **Map refs:** 284 A4, 316 G10

Who to contact: Shire of Jerramungup (08) 9835 1022

211 Israelite Bay camping area (bush camping)

Israelite Bay bush-camping area is set in coastal vegetation by the beach on Fisheries Rd, 204 km east of Esperance. A great spot for self-sufficient anglers, there are no facilities here and 4WD access through Cape Arid National Park can be extremely corrugated. Bring drinking water and firewood, though a gas/fuel stove is preferred. **Map refs:** 284 D3, 317 K9

Who to contact: Shire of Esperance (08) 9071 0666

212 Madura Pass Motel

This roadhouse with caravan park facilities is on the Eyre Hwy at Madura, 92 km east of Cocklebiddy. Bring firewood. A road opposite the Madura Roadhouse leads to a number of small blowholes; ask at the roadhouse for directions. **Map refs:** 284 E2, 317 N6

How to book: Eyre Hwy, Madura (08) 9039 3464

213 Mason Bay camping area

Mason Bay camping area is 34 km east of Hopetoun on Mason Bay Rd, 3.8 km south of the Southern Ocean Rd. It has campsites close to the beach in a large, shaded area, sheltered by coastal vegetation. And a very nice beach it is too, protected by an offshore reef that provides excellent, safe swimming and fishing. For the less adventurous, beachcombing or just relaxing on the sand is a great way to pass the time. There's a 4WD beach boat launch here. Bring drinking water. No fires are allowed during the fire danger season. **Map refs:** 284 B3, 316 H9

Who to contact: Shire of Ravensthorpe (08) 9839 0000; or Ravensthorpe Tourist Information (08) 9838 1277

214 Mundrabilla Roadhouse

Firewood is supplied at this roadhouse with caravan park facilities on the Eyre Hwy, 116 km east of Madura and 66 km west of Eucla. Take a detour to the tablelands above Mundrabilla for excellent views of the plains stretching far below. Other accommodation is also available here. **Map refs:** 284 F2, 317 O6

How to book: Eyre Hwy, Mundrabilla (08) 9039 3465

215 Munglinup Beach camping area

Munglinup Beach camping area is part of a caravan park facility 32 km south of Munglinup via Munglinup Beach Rd, off Springdale Rd. To get to Springdale Rd, take either Fuss Rd east of Munglinup or Doyal Rd to the west; both routes are off the South Coast Hwy. The camping area is a large, shady site on a beach that is ideal for swimming and fishing. Bring firewood. There are additional campsites and powered sites in the nearby caravan park. **Map refs:** 284 B3, 316 H9

Who to contact: Munglinup Beach Caravan Park (08) 9075 1155; or Esperance Visitor Centre (08) 9083 1555, 1300 664 455
Camping fees: pay fees at caravan park office

216 Quagi Beach camping area

South of the South Coast Hwy via Farrells Rd, 58 km west of Esperance and 48 km east of Munglinup, Quagi Beach camping area is a delightful spot in a bush setting on the beach. Fishing, swimming and snorkelling at the picturesque beach or around the rocky headlands are great ways to pass the time before cooking up the catch of the day at your campsite. Note: the access road is unsealed and you need to bring firewood and drinking water. **Map refs:** 284 B3, 316 H9

Who to contact: Shire of Esperance (08) 9071 0666

217 Starvation Boat Harbour camping area

This foreshore camping area is on a protected bay 50 km east of Hopetoun via Southern Ocean Dr, 8 km east of Mason Bay. The large camping area is sheltered by coastal vegetation, providing plenty of shade for campers. Activities include swimming, fishing and boating from the 4WD beach boat launch. Bring in your own drinking water. No fires during the fire danger season. **Map refs:** 284 B3, 316 H9

Who to contact: Shire of Ravensthorpe (08) 9839 0000; or Ravensthorpe Tourist Information (08) 9838 1277

GOLDFIELDS

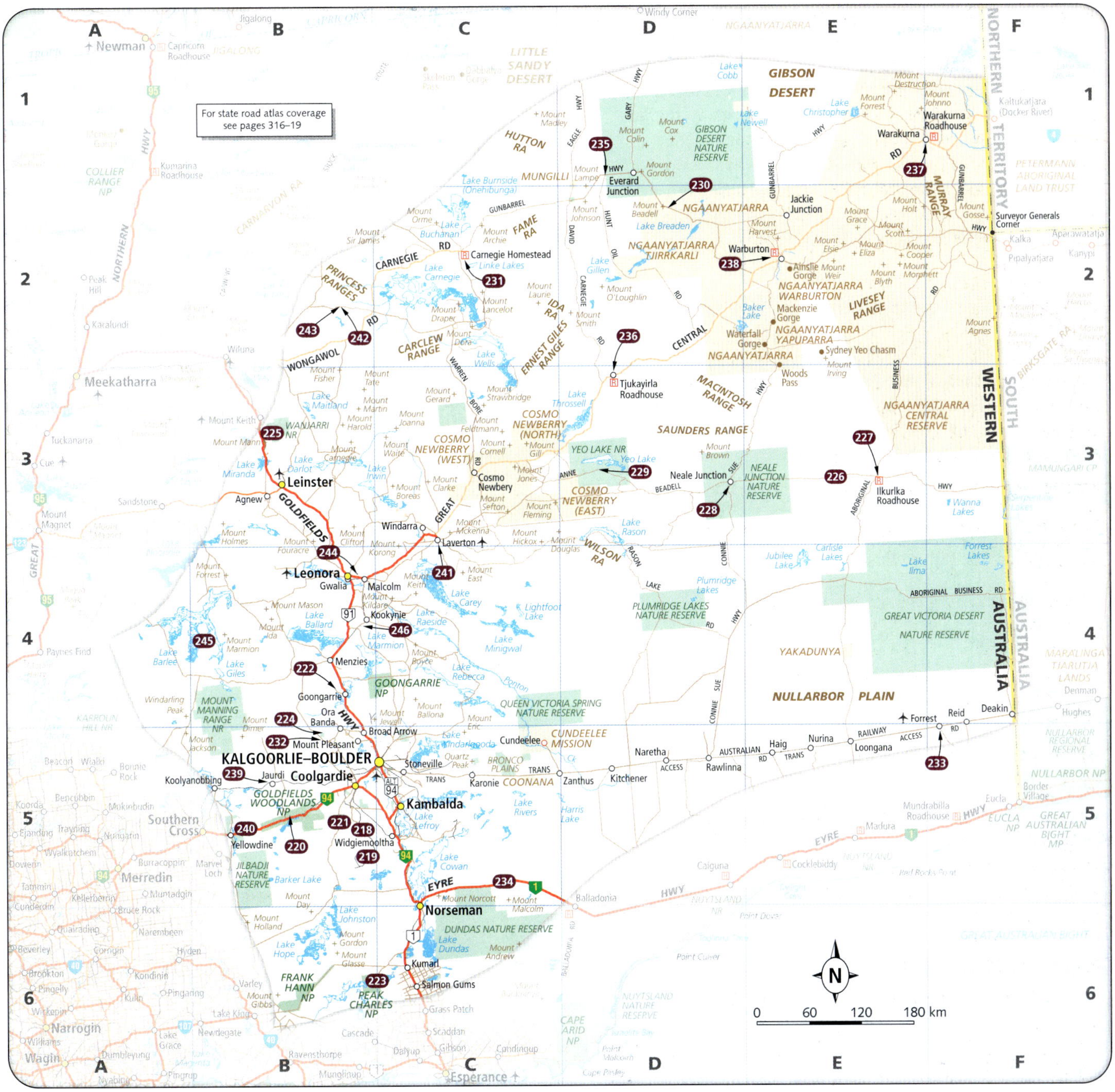

For state road atlas coverage see pages 316–19

KALGOORLIE, WA'S LARGEST GOLDFIELDS town, is famed for its fascinating gold-rush history, fabulous old buildings and miners' ghost towns. Both Kalgoorlie and Boulder are packed with lively pubs and colourful characters still living the prospecting dream. Visitors can share that dream by stepping back in time to the Australian Prospectors and Miners Hall of Fame – a historic precinct with a prospector's campsite and heritage buildings.

Norseman, the gateway to WA, is surrounded by dense bushland, ancient rock outcrops and large salt lakes. Leonora, a busy outback town 3 hr north of Kalgoorlie, has kept its character while providing modern facilities to adventurous travellers en route to Alice Springs or the northern parts of WA.

Remote desert camping experiences abound in this region. Take in panoramic views of salt lakes, woodlands and spring wildflowers from the very top of Peak Charles. Camp amongst granite outcrops in Burra Rock and Cave Hill nature reserves. Indulge in boating, waterskiing and birdwatching in the wetlands of Rowles Lagoon Conservation Park.

Campers in this region can also explore old pastoral leases at Jaurdi, Lorna Glen and Mount Elvire stations, experiencing life in the outback as it used to be, while making use of the old homesteads' range of facilities.

CAMPSITES LOCATED IN PARKS AND RESERVES

BURRA ROCK NATURE RESERVE

Burra Rock Nature Reserve, 58 km south of Coolgardie, is a great picnic or camping spot with a unique backdrop of granite rock, surrounded by regrowth woodland. In the late 1920s, the dam here supplied water to the steam engines taking timber to Kalgoorlie–Boulder via the narrow-gauge railway. From the summit of Burra Rock, bushwalkers are rewarded with views of the surrounding woodlands. There is conventional-vehicle access to the reserve.

Who to contact: DEC Kalgoorlie (08) 9080 5555

218 Burra Rock camping area

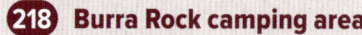

Burra Rock camping area is along Burra Rock Rd, 58 km south of Coolgardie via Hunt Rd. It provides campers with basic facilities (bring firewood and water) in a natural bush environment. **Map refs:** 289 B5, 316 H6

CAVE HILL NATURE RESERVE

For a taste of the Aussie outback and a goldfields adventure, head to Cave Hill Nature Reserve south of Coolgardie. Accessible only by 4WD, Cave Hill is known for its cave formation and spectacular granite outcrop, which is one of the biggest and highest granite monoliths in the region. On the western side of Cave Hill is a walking track leading to a large cave – an ideal excursion before relaxing back at camp under a star-filled sky.

Who to contact: DEC Kalgoorlie (08) 9080 5555

219 Cave Hill camping area

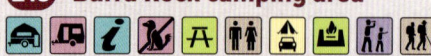

Cave Hill camping area is 50 km south-west of Widgiemooltha and 39 km south of Burra Rock via 4WD tracks. There are 2 camping areas on the western side of the granite outcrop, and another on the eastern side. Make the most of the secluded bush setting and basic facilities (bring firewood and water). **Map refs:** 289 B5, 316 H6

GOLDFIELDS WOODLANDS NATIONAL PARK

Goldfields Woodlands National Park straddles the Great Eastern Hwy 60 km west of Coolgardie, and runs for another 40 km beside the road. Protecting significant conservation values, the area includes a diversity of landforms and vegetation: habitats such as sand plains, freshwater swamps, salt lakes with saltbush and samphire surrounds, uncut and regrowth eucalypt woodlands, and granite complexes. There are historic sites within the park that are worth a look, such as remnants of the Kalgoorlie woodlines (narrow-gauge railways), the popular 4WD Holland Track that follows the route miners trod to the goldfields, and the Goldfields water pipeline.

Who to contact: DEC Kalgoorlie (08) 9080 5555

220 Boondi Rock camping area

Boondi Rock camping area is just off the Great Eastern Hwy, approximately 80 km west of Coolgardie. It provides campers with a few basic facilities (bring firewood and drinking water) near a granite rock outcrop in the bush. **Map refs:** 289 B5, 316 G6

221 Victoria Rock camping area

Victoria Rock camping area is on Victoria Rock Rd, 46 km south of Coolgardie via Gnarlbine Rock Rd, at the western end of town. Nestled beside the rock, visitors will find sites with basic facilities (bring drinking water and firewood) in an area that is home to many native animals, including emus, echidnas, ornate dragons and carpet pythons. It's well worth climbing Victoria Rock for spectacular views of the surrounding woodland. **Map refs:** 289 B5, 316 H6

GOONGARRIE NATIONAL PARK

Goongarrie National Park is 104 km north of Kalgoorlie. It encompasses an old homestead as well as the natural attractions of the salt lakes on Planto Rd and 25 Mile Rock. Visitors who venture here will be rewarded with the real outback experience: camping beside a fire under a star-filled sky, after a day exploring the surrounding bush and its remnants of a bygone era when the homestead flourished as a pastoral holding.

Who to contact: DEC Kalgoorlie (08) 9080 5555

222 Goongarrie Homestead camping area

Goongarrie Homestead camping area is 14 km west of the Menzies–Kalgoorlie Rd, 90 km north of Kalgoorlie. Use the homestead's facilities while exploring this old pastoral property. Note: roads may be closed after rain. **Map refs:** 289 B4, 316 H4

PEAK CHARLES NATIONAL PARK

This national park south-west of Norseman is laced with nature trails for observing the area's seasonal wildflowers and fascinating fauna. The ancient granite peaks of Peak Charles and its companion, Peak Eleanora, provide superb views of the sand plain heaths and salt lake systems, though the climb to the top is moderately hard.

Who to contact: DEC Stokes National Park (08) 9076 8541; or DEC Esperance (08) 9083 2100 *Road conditions:* Shire of Dundas (08) 9039 1205

223 Peak Charles camping area

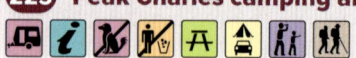

Self-sufficient campers and bushwalkers will enjoy staying at Peak Charles camping area, in a shady bush setting 105 km south-west of Norseman and 20 km south of the Lake King–Norseman Rd. The easy walk to the lookout gives a good view of the surrounding countryside, but the rewards for those who tackle the moderately difficult climb to the summit are far greater. Come equipped with a gas/fuel stove, preferably, and plenty of drinking water. **Map refs:** 289 B6, 316 H8

ROWLES LAGOON CONSERVATION PARK

If waterskiing in the desert appeals to you, then Rowles Lagoon is the place to go. A semipermanent set of lakes measuring 2 km across, it's no wonder this area is popular with watersports enthusiasts. In fact, it is the only Goldfields lake system with a gazetted waterski and jetski area. Nature lovers and birdwatchers will enjoy the area too, as the lakes are a conservation island within an arid zone. They provide habitat for more species of waterbirds than any other arid zone wetland south of the Kimberley.

Who to contact: DEC Kalgoorlie (08) 9080 5555

224 Rowles Lagoon camping area

Rowles Lagoon camping area is 6 km north-east of Coolgardie North Rd, 68 km north of Coolgardie. It has shady sites and a good range of facilities on the edge of the lagoon for campers who enjoy aquatic activities by day before settling in for the evening under outback stars. Bring firewood and drinking water with you. **Map refs: 289 B5, 316 H4**

WANJARRI NATURE RESERVE

Once a sheep station, Wanjarri Nature Reserve now protects a vast range of wildlife, including kangaroos, emus and wedge-tailed eagles. Camp near the old Wanjarri shearing shed and avail yourself of its facilities while exploring the old pastoral lease, and experience outback station life as it was once lived. The reserve is 74 km north of Leinster.

Who to contact: DEC Kalgoorlie (08) 9080 5555 **Camping fees:** pay fees at DEC Kalgoorlie office

225 Wanjarri Shearing Shed camping area

Wanjarri Shearing Shed camping area is 16 km north-east of the Goldfields Hwy; the turn-off is 58 km north of Leinster. Camping around the trees gives visitors the use of the shearing-shed facilities while they explore the remnants of this once-thriving pastoral venture. Bring your own water. **Map refs: 289 B3, 318 G11**

CAMPSITES LOCATED IN OTHER AREAS

Anne Beadell Highway

Traversing some of the most remote terrain Australia has to offer, the Anne Beadell Hwy was constructed by Len Beadell over a period of 9 years, commencing in 1953. He named the highway after his wife, Anne. However, the description 'highway' is a little misleading as the track is often very narrow, twisting and sandy, stretching from Laverton through the Great Victoria Desert to Coober Pedy in SA. There are several places along the way that are suitable for camping but few or no facilities are provided. You need to carry your own firewood and drinking water. The longest stretch without fuel is about 750 km from Coober Pedy to the Ilkurlka Roadhouse. Travellers need to be well-prepared and totally self-sufficient. The following permits are required for travel through this region.

WA: permit required to travel through Cosmo Newberry Aboriginal land (East), Reserve No. 20396, and Cosmo Newberry Aboriginal land (South), Reserve No. 25050; permit from Aboriginal Lands Trust in Perth (08) 9235 8000 or www.dia.wa.gov.au; allow up to 4 weeks for delivery of the free permit

SA: over the WA border, a camping permit is required to enter Unnamed Conservation Park; contact Parks SA Ceduna (08) 8625 3144; a permit is required to enter Maralinga Tjarutja land; contact Maralinga Tjarutja Inc (08) 8625 2946; a travel permit is required to travel through Woomera Prohibited Area; contact Defence Support Centre at Woomera (08) 8674 2311; a Desert Parks Pass is required to travel through Tallaringa Conservation Park 1800 816 078

Please note that campsites are listed in alphabetical order, not track order. Refer to the map on p. 289 for further information.

Who to contact: DEC Kalgoorlie (08) 9080 5555; or Ngaanyatjarra Council (08) 8950 1711 **Road conditions:** Shire of Laverton (08) 9031 1202

226 Bush camping

You can bush camp along the Anne Beadell Hwy, but campsites need to be no more than 30 m away from the roadside. There are a number of established sites with basic facilities. No. 1 is 124.1 km east of Neale Junction; No. 2 is 107.4 km east of No. 1 and 58.5 km east of Ilkurlka Roadhouse; No. 3 is 100.6 km east of No. 2 and 9.9 km west of the WA–SA border. **Map refs: 289 E3, 317 N1, 319 N11**

227 Ilkurlka Roadhouse camping area

See p. 292.

228 Neale Junction camping area

See p. 293.

229 Yeo Lake Homestead camping area

See p. 294.

230 Camp Beadell camping area

On the Gunbarrel Hwy, Camp Beadell camping area is 200 m south of the track, 95 km east of Geraldton Bore and 189 km north-west of Warburton. Visitors to this isolated and remote area will be treated to a stunning outback sunset as the last rays of the day fall on Mt Beadell in the distance. There are no facilities here so campers need to be totally self-sufficient. You can boil or treat water from Bore No. 3. **Map refs: 289 D2, 319 L8**

How to book: Shire of Wiluna (08) 9981 7010

231 Carnegie Station

On the Gunbarrel Hwy, Carnegie Station is 344 km north-east of Wiluna and 207.2 km west of Geraldton Bore. This is very remote country, suitable for totally self-sufficient travellers only. The route takes you through the Gibson Desert and offers shady sites with camping facilities near the homestead as well as basic supplies and fuel from the store. Other accommodation is available. **Map refs:** 289 C2, 319 I8

How to book: Carnegie Station (08) 9981 2991 www.carnegiestation.com.au

232 Credo Homestead camping area

Credo Homestead camping area is located 70 km north of Coolgardie on Coolgardie North Rd, opposite Rowles Lagoon. Visitors who set up camp near the old homestead will be able to make use of the facilities there as well as find some shade while they explore the remnants of this old pastoral lease. **Map refs:** 289 B5, 316 G5

Who to contact: DEC Kalgoorlie (08) 9080 5555

233 Forrest camping area

A refuelling location for aircraft, Forrest is 126 km north of the Eyre Hwy on the Transcontinental Railway Access Rd, via the 4WD Forrest–Mundrabilla Rd. Camping is permitted near the old weather station, which has been set up to provide facilities for intrepid 4WD-travellers through the area. Note that the Transcontinental Railway Access Rd is a private road from Rawlinna east to Tarcoola in SA. Forrest–Mundrabilla Rd leaves the Eyre Hwy 34 km west of Mundrabilla. **Map refs:** 289 F5, 317 O4

Who to contact: Forrest Airport (08) 9022 6403

234 Fraser Range Station

Fraser Range Station is 1.5 km south of the Eyre Hwy, 100 km east of Norseman. It offers weary travellers an unusual outback experience, with bushwalking, station tours, camping and other accommodation available. **Map refs:** 289 C5, 317 J7

How to book: Fraser Range Station (08) 9039 3210 www.fraserrangestation.com.au

235 Geraldton Bore camping area

On the Gunbarrel Hwy, the Geraldton Historical Society Bore camping area is 100 m south of the track on Hunt Oil Rd. To find it, head 207 km east of Carnegie Station, 32 km west of Everard Junction or 500 m west of the Len Beadell blazed tree. There are no facilities here, so travellers need to be totally self-sufficient to enjoy the solitude and seclusion this campsite offers. A gas/fuel stove is preferred. **Map refs:** 289 D1, 319 K7

How to book: Shire of Wiluna (08) 9981 7010

Great Central Road

Running east from Laverton to Yulara in the NT, the Great Central Road is a classic red centre route surrounded by the spinifex and red sand of the central Australian desert. A 4WD is recommended, and transit permits are required to travel through the Aboriginal land along its route.

WA: an Aboriginal Lands Trust permit is required; contact Department of Indigenous Affairs (08) 9235 8000 or www.dia.wa.gov.au

NT: a Central Land Council Permit to Transit is required; contact Central Land Council (08) 8951 6320

Please note that campsites are listed in alphabetical order, not track order. Refer to the map on p. 289 for further information.

Road conditions: Shire of Ngaanyatjarra, Warburton office (08) 8956 7966

236 Tjukayirla Roadhouse
See p. 294.

237 Warakurna Roadhouse
See p. 294.

238 Warburton Roadhouse
See p. 294.

Gunbarrel Highway

The Gunbarrel Hwy runs from the Warakurna Roadhouse to Wiluna, covering a distance of a little over 1000 km. Completed in 1958, the route has important historical significance, as it was the first road across Central Australia to the west. Visitors will travel through very remote desert country, so well-prepared vehicles and equipment are an absolute must. The magnificent desert scenery and sheer solitude of the environment make the journey worthwhile.

Please note that campsites are listed in alphabetical order, not track order. Refer to the map on p. 289 for further information.

Who to contact: DEC Kalgoorlie (08) 9080 5555 *Permits:* permit required to travel through this region; contact Aboriginal Lands Trust in Perth (08) 9235 8000 or www.dia.wa.gov.au *Pumps:* Bore No. 1, 500 m south of the Gunbarrel Hwy, 25 km south-east of Bore No. 2, follow the track opposite the Len Beadell Tree and plaque, GPS S:25 43.568 E:125 46.831; Bore No. 2, 30 km south-east of Camp Beadell, GPS S:25 40.620 E:125 35.162; if pumps are damaged or not functioning, contact DEC Kalgoorlie (08) 9080 5555; or Ngaanyatjarra Council (08) 8950 1711; or Shire of Wiluna (08) 9981 7011

230 Camp Beadell
See p. 291.

231 Carnegie Station
See p. 291.

235 Geraldton Bore
See above.

227 Ilkurlka Roadhouse camping area

Ilkurlka Roadhouse camping area is on the northern side of the Anne Beadell Hwy. Opposite the roadhouse, 173 km east of Neale Junction and 169 km west of the WA–SA border, it provides travellers through the Great Victoria Desert between

Laverton and Coober Pedy with a few basic facilities while they experience a real outback adventure. **Map refs:** 289 E3, 317 N1, 319 N11

Who to contact: Ilkurlka Roadhouse (08) 9037 1147
Camping fees: fees payable at roadhouse

239 Jaurdi Station Homestead camping area

Jaurdi Station Homestead camping area is 149 km north-east of Southern Cross via the Great Eastern Hwy, Mt Walton (Heath) and Ryans Find rds. Visitors have the use of a good range of facilities at the old homestead, a former pastoral lease now managed by DEC. Explore the old shearing shed and farm machinery to gain an appreciation of the station's pastoral history, and discover the rare flora and fauna of this granite country. Bring firewood and water (as supply may be unreliable), and choose from other accommodation available. Bookings are essential. **Map refs:** 289 B5, 316 G5

How to book: DEC Kalgoorlie (08) 9080 5555

240 Karalee Rock and Dam camping area

Karalee Rock and Dam camping area is 4 km north of the Great Eastern Hwy, 52 km east of Southern Cross. The large, shady site is set among trees near the 1897 dam, where an informative trail leads beside the old aqueduct. Capture good views of the surrounding area from the top of the rock before settling in for a tranquil night under the outback stars. A 3-night maximum stay applies and you need to come equipped with firewood and drinking water. **Map refs:** 289 B5, 316 G6

Who to contact: Shire of Yilgarn (08) 9049 1001

241 Laverton Caravan Park

The Laverton caravan park is on the edge of the Great Victoria Desert. It has a good range of facilities, shady, grassed camping sites and the convenience of on-site accommodation. Explore the region's nickel-mining history via the Mt Windarra Heritage Trail. **Map refs:** 289 C3, 317 I2, 319 I12

How to book: 211 Weld Dr, Laverton (08) 9031 1072

242 Lorna Glen camping area (bush camping)

You can bush camp on Lorna Glen station as long as you have the permission of the caretakers. Bush camping is suitable for self-sufficient campers only. **Map refs:** 289 B2, 318 H9

How to book: DEC Kalgoorlie (08) 9080 5555 *Camping fees:* pay fees at DEC Kalgoorlie or via on-site caretakers

243 Lorna Glen Homestead camping area

Lorna Glen Homestead camping area is 37 km east of Granite Peak Rd, north of the Gunbarrel Hwy and 150 km north-east of Wiluna. Visitors can avail themselves of the

homestead's facilities while they explore this isolated and remote region, which was formerly a cattle and sheep station. **Map refs:** 289 B2, 318 H9

How to book: DEC Kalgoorlie (08) 9080 5555 *Camping fees:* pay fees at DEC Kalgoorlie office or via on-site caretakers

244 Malcolm Dam camping area

Malcolm Dam camping area is a little oasis in the outback, with sites set in native bushland around the 1902 dam. Built to provide water for the outback trains, the dam is now a haven for birdlife and anglers. To get here, travel 3 km north of the Leonora–Laverton Rd, 10 km east of Leonora. While you're here, pay a visit to Leonora to admire its old buildings and gold-rush-era history. Come equipped with firewood and drinking water. **Map refs:** 289 B4, 316 H2

Who to contact: Leonora Information Centre (08) 9037 7016; orShire of Leonora (08) 9037 6044

245 Mount Elvire Homestead camping area

This homestead camping area is 40 km north of the Evanston–Menzies Rd, 175 km west of Menzies. Camping near the homestead or shearers' quarters gives visitors to this remote area access to very basic facilities while experiencing life on a station from a bygone era. Bring your own drinking water and firewood. **Map refs:** 289 B4, 316 F3

How to book: DEC Kalgoorlie (08) 9080 5555 *Camping fees:* pay fees at DEC Kalgoorlie office

246 Niagara Dam camping area

Niagara Dam camping area is 60 km north-east of Menzies via the Goldfields Hwy and Kookynie Rd. An oasis in the outback, it embraces a large, shady area among the trees on the edge of the dam. Visitors can explore the surrounding bush or swim and fish the waters of the dam, which was built to water the steam trains that serviced the nearby historic town of Kookynie. Today, Kookynie is a living ghost town, and not to be missed if you are visiting the northern Goldfields region. Note: baits are laid in this area, so keep your dog on a lead. Bring your own firewood and drinking water. **Map refs:** 289 B4, 316 H3

Who to contact: Shire of Menzies (08) 9024 2041; or Grand Hotel, Kookynie (08) 9031 3010

228 Neale Junction camping area

Neale Junction camping area is 200 m west of the junction of the Anne Beadell and Connie Sue hwys, 167 km east of Yeo Homestead and 309 km south of the Great Central Rd. Travellers through this rugged and remote country have the opportunity to enjoy a true desert experience. **Map refs:** 289 D3, 317 M1, 319 M11

Who to contact: DEC Kalgoorlie (08) 9080 5555; or Ngaanyatjarra Council (08) 8950 1711 *Road conditions:* Shire of Laverton (08) 9031 1202

Four-wheel driving along the Gunbarrel Highway (p. 292)

236 Tjukayirla Roadhouse

On the Great Central Rd, 305 km north-east of Laverton and 255 km south-west of Warburton, Tjukayirla Roadhouse caravan park provides travellers through this spectacularly desolate country with a good range of facilities within the roadhouse complex. Visitors will find shady trees to camp under and a swimming pool to relax in while enjoying a glorious desert sunset. Other accommodation is available, and you need to bring your own firewood. **Map refs:** 289 D3, 319 K10

How to book: Tjukayirla Roadhouse (08) 9037 1108
www.tjukayirlaroadhouse.com.au

237 Warakurna Roadhouse

Warakurna Roadhouse caravan park is on the Great Central Rd, 231 km north-east of Warburton Roadhouse and 92 km west of Docker River. It offers visitors a good range of facilities in an outback desert setting, though you need to carry your own firewood. Other accommodation is available. **Map refs:** 289 F1, 319 O7

How to book: Warakurna Roadhouse (08) 8956 7344
www.warakurnaroadhouse.com.au

238 Warburton Roadhouse

On the Great Central Rd and surrounded by a typical central Australian desert landscape, Warburton Roadhouse caravan park is 255 km north-east of Tjukayirla Roadhouse and 231 km south-east of Warakurna Roadhouse. There are green sites under shady trees within the roadhouse complex, where visitors can enjoy a desert camping experience as well as the basic facilities of an outback caravan park. Other accommodation is available and you need to bring firewood. **Map refs:** 289 E2, 319 M8

How to book: Warburton Roadhouse (08) 8956 7656
www.warburtonroadhouse.com.au

229 Yeo Lake Homestead camping area

Yeo Lake Homestead is on the Anne Beadell Hwy, 213 km north-east of Laverton, 67 km east of Yamarna Station ruins and 167 km west of Neale Junction. Camping near the homestead provides basic facilities and a bit of shade. Explore the remnants of this once-thriving pastoral lease by day, then experience the isolation and solitude of the outback by night. **Map refs:** 289 D3, 317 K1, 319 K11

Who to contact: DEC Kalgoorlie (08) 9080 5555; or Ngaanyatjarra Council (08) 8950 1711 *Road conditions:* Shire of Laverton (08) 9031 1202

OUTBACK COAST AND MID-WEST

DOLPHINS, TURTLES AND DUGONGS glide the ocean currents off WA's long outback coast. One of the best places to see these creatures at play is the Shark Bay area, renowned for the wild dolphins that come to shore at Monkey Mia, 26 km north-east of Denham.

There are other fascinating natural stories to be told in the area, such as the ancient algae fossil stromatolites at Hamelin Pool and the 110 km long Shell Beach, made up entirely of tiny shells. Splash out in the holiday towns that line the coast, or go bush in the national parks.

Francois Peron National Park offers visitors with a 4WD the opportunity to camp in pristine coastal locations while enjoying fishing and boating activities. Further north, Cape Range National Park is more accessible and has numerous campsites on the coast in an area renowned for its stunning scenery. No wonder pastimes such as fishing, swimming, sailing and canoeing are so popular in these parts.

Another highlight of the region is undoubtedly Ningaloo Marine Park. The reef, on WA's mid-north coast, has gained an impressive reputation as one of the earth's last ocean havens. Visitors can dive with hundreds of tropical fish, colourful coral and the world's biggest fish: the whale shark. Ningaloo is one of the largest fringing reefs in the world and, unlike many others, you can get to it by just stepping off the beach at places like Coral Bay.

The historic mines, Aboriginal art and varied vegetation of the inland round off this region's list of attractions. Self-sufficient campers will enjoy the true outback experience of Kennedy Range National Park, where ancient sandstone mesa, precipitous cliffs and spectacular gorges dominate the landscape.

CAMPSITES LOCATED IN PARKS AND RESERVES

CAPE RANGE NATIONAL PARK

A rugged landscape of rocky gorges edged by the stunning coastal environment of Ningaloo Marine Park, Cape Range National Park is 36 km from Exmouth on the western side of North West Cape. Ningaloo, the longest fringing coral reef in Australia, is a mecca for scubadivers, snorkellers and whale watchers. It is also an angler's delight, with beach and reef fishing providing rewarding catches in waters regarded as one of the top destinations in the state for game fishing. Walking trails lead to spectacular views from lookouts, enticing photographers, and the bird and fauna hides will captivate nature lovers.

Who to contact: DEC Exmouth (08) 9947 8000; or Milyering Visitor Centre (08) 9949 2808 *How to book:* online bookings www.dec.wa.gov.au/campgrounds for campsite nos **254**, **255**, **256**, **257**

247 Boat Harbour camping area

Boat Harbour camping area is 500 m west of Yardie Creek Rd, 5.2 km south of Yardie Creek crossing. Access is 4WD only, and you need to bring along a gas/fuel stove and drinking water. **Map refs: 269 F7, 295 B1, 314 F12, 315 B4, 316 D11**

248 Lakeside camping area

To get to Lakeside, take the turn-off at the Milyering Visitor Centre and travel 11 km from the park boundary to Yardie Creek Rd, then travel for a further 1.6 km. You will need to come equipped with a gas/fuel stove and drinking water. **Map refs: 295 B1, 315 B3**

249 Mesa Camp camping area

Flat coastal scrub surrounds this campsite 1.6 km west of Yardie Creek Rd. Bring a gas/fuel stove and drinking water to this camping area, 8 km south of the park boundary, where there is a self-registration station. **Map refs: 295 B1, 315 B3**

250 Neds Camp camping area

Carry a gas/fuel stove and plenty of drinking water with you when you come to camp at Neds, 600 m west of Yardie Creek Rd. It is 8 km south of the park boundary. **Map refs: 295 B1, 315 B3**

251 North Mandu camping area

A gas/fuel stove and drinking water are essential equipment when you camp at North Mandu, 400 m west of Yardie Creek Rd. Milyering Visitor Centre is 14 km away to the south. **Map refs: 295 B1, 315 B3**

252 North T Bone Bay camping area

Pack a gas/fuel stove and drinking water to camp here, and take the turn-off at the Milyering Visitor Centre. This campsite is 1.2 km west of Yardie Creek Rd and 11 km south from the park boundary. **Map refs: 295 B1, 315 B3**

253 One K Camp camping area

Access to One K Camp is 4.2 km north of the Boat Harbour track by 4WD only. Bring a gas/fuel stove and drinking water. The camping area is 100 m west of Yardie Creek Rd. **Map refs: 295 B1, 315 B4**

254 Osprey Bay camping area

Osprey Bay camping area is 800 m west of Yardie Creek Rd, 26 km south of Milyering Visitor Centre. Bring along a gas/fuel stove and drinking water. Bookings are required for peak season, Apr–Oct. **Map refs: 295 B1, 315 B3**

255 Pilgramunna camping area

Pack a gas/fuel stove and drinking water when you head to Pilgramunna camping area, 500 m west of Yardie Creek Rd and 20 km south of Milyering Visitor Centre. Bookings are required for peak season, Apr–Oct. **Map refs: 295 B1, 315 B3**

256 Tulki Beach camping area

Bring a gas/fuel stove and drinking water to Tulki Beach camping area, 800 m west of Yardie Creek Rd and 6 km south of the Milyering Visitor Centre. Bookings are required for peak season, Apr–Oct. **Map refs: 295 B1, 315 B3**

257 Yardie Creek camping area

Yardie Creek camping area is off Yardie Creek Rd, 36 km south of the Milyering Visitor Centre. Come equipped with a gas/fuel stove and drinking water. Bookings are required for peak season, Apr–Oct. **Map refs:** 295 B1, 315 B4

COALSEAM CONSERVATION PARK

This park is among the most botanically diverse bush areas in the region. The acacia shrub land, with its sparse understorey, comes alive with everlasting wildflowers after good winter rains; a delightful sight for those who enjoy a bit of bushwalking. Exploring the state's first coalmine, visiting old mine shafts and learning about the heritage of the area are some of the other attractions at Coalseam Conservation Park. The park is 32 km north of Mingenew, where fossil remnants are still visible in the rock strata today.

Who to contact: DEC Geraldton (08) 9921 5955

258 Breakaway camping area

Located just off Coalseam Rd from the Mingenew–Mullewa Rd, 34 km north of Mingenew, Breakaway camping area is set in a bush environment in an area noted for its wildflowers and mining heritage. Bring along a gas/fuel stove and drinking water. Toilets and picnic facilities are available at River Bend day use area, 1 km east of the camping area. **Map refs:** 295 C6, 315 E12, 316 B3

259 Miners Camp camping area

Basic facilities are provided in a natural bush setting that's perfect for bushwalking and exploring the heritage associated with WA's first coalmine. Come equipped with a gas/fuel stove and drinking water. Miners Camp is off Coalseam Rd, 35 km north of Mingenew and 5 km from the entrance to Coalseam Conservation Park. **Map refs:** 295 C6, 315 E12, 316 B3

FRANCOIS PERON NATIONAL PARK

Renowned for its scenic coastline, with its dramatically contrasting red cliffs, blue water and white beaches, Cape Peron offers visitors the chance to see bottlenose dolphins playing, dugongs feeding, green and loggerhead turtles coming up for air, and large manta rays gliding just beneath the water's surface. On the tip of the Peron Peninsula, this site was once a sheep station. Today, travellers can visit the old homestead by 2WD to experience what life would have been like on such a remote station. Beyond the homestead is a wilderness area suitable for high-clearance 4WD vehicles only. For those who venture there, the fishing can be rewarding.

Who to contact: DEC Denham (08) 9948 1208

260 Big Lagoon camping area

Big Lagoon camping area is 19 km north of the Monkey Mia Rd junction, 4 km north-east of Denham. This camp on the

foreshore has basic facilities; you need to bring in your own drinking water and gas/fuel stove. **Map refs:** 295 B4, 315 B8

261 Bottle Bay camping area

Bring drinking water and a gas/fuel stove to this camping area, 39 km north of the Monkey Mia Rd junction and 4 km north-east of Denham. Facilities are basic. **Map refs:** 295 B4, 315 B8

262 Gregories camping area

Facilities are coastal but basic at Gregories camping area, and you need to bring drinking water and a gas/fuel stove. The camping area is 39 km north of the Monkey Mia Rd junction, 4 km north-east of Denham. **Map refs:** 295 B4, 315 B8

263 Herald Bight camping area

Herald Bight camping area is 27 km north of the Monkey Mia Rd junction, 4 km north-east of Denham. In a coastal setting with basic facilities, camping here is gas/fuel stove only and you need to come equipped with drinking water. **Map refs:** 295 B4, 315 B8

264 South Gregories camping area

Off the main park road, 39 km north of the Monkey Mia Rd junction and 4 km north-east of Denham, this camping area has basic facilities on the foreshore. Bring along a gas/fuel stove and your own drinking water. **Map refs:** 295 B4, 315 B8

KENNEDY RANGE NATIONAL PARK

Just north of Gascoyne Junction, in the harsh and unforgiving interior of the state's north-west, lie the spectacular sandstone battlements of the Kennedy Range, beckoning visitors to explore and discover its natural attractions. This huge mesa, pushed up from an ancient seabed, has dominated the surrounding plains for millions of years. The park offers spectacular scenery of gorges and precipitous cliff faces, with a vast plateau of ancient dune fields on top of the range. The area still retains a wilderness feeling, and camping beneath the stark sandstone cliffs is an experience not to be missed.

Who to contact: DEC Carnarvon (08) 9941 3754 *Road conditions:* Shire of Upper Gascoyne (08) 9943 0988

265 Temple Gorge camping area

Temple Gorge camping area is 12 km west of Ullawarra Rd, 60 km north of Gascoyne Junction. The camping area has minimal facilities and is best suited for self-sufficient campers. Enjoy bushwalking and hiking to take in the spectacular scenery of this remote outback area. Bring firewood or preferably a gas/fuel stove, plus plenty of drinking water. **Map refs:** 295 C3, 315 D7, 318 A8

CAMPSITES LOCATED IN OTHER AREAS

266 The Blowholes camping area

The Blowholes camping area is off Blowholes Rd, 49 km from the North West Coastal Hwy. It is situated behind the dunes and close to a spectacular section of coastline, where fishing, swimming, diving and catching a wave are popular activities, along with boating from the 4WD ramp. Bring along firewood and drinking water to this park, 73 km north of Carnarvon. **Map refs:** 295 B3, 315 B7

Who to contact: Shire of Carnarvon (08) 9941 0030; or Carnarvon Tourist Bureau (08) 9941 1146; or ranger 0408 942 945 *Camping fees:* pay fees at the shire office in Francis St, Carnarvon; or to ranger

267 Blue Dolphin Caravan Park and Holiday Village

This caravan park has good facilities and is well-located, being within walking distance of town and a short drive from Monkey Mia and surrounding attractions. It's also only a short walk to a swimming beach, or a place where you can do a spot of fishing. **Map refs:** 295 B4, 315 B9

How to book: Lot 5, Hamelin Rd, Denham (08) 9948 1385

268 Bush Bay camping area

Camping at Bush Bay is in a coastal environment just off the beach, in a popular fishing area. Bring firewood and drinking water with you. The camping ground is 10 km from the North West Coast Hwy, 33 km south of Carnarvon. **Map refs:** 295 B3, 315 B7

Who to contact: Shire of Carnarvon (08) 9941 0030; or Carnarvon Tourist Bureau (08) 9941 1146

269 Coronation Beach camping area

Visitors here will find sites dispersed among the coastal vegetation on the beach, which is a great spot to swim, fish, snorkel or just relax to the sound of waves lapping the shore. You need to bring your own drinking water. The camping area is 8 km west of the North West Coastal Hwy on Coronation Beach Rd, 28 km north of Geraldton. **Map refs:** 295 C5, 315 D12, 316 A3

Who to contact: Shire of Chapman Valley (08) 9920 5011; or Geraldton Tourist Bureau (08) 9921 3999

270 Eagle Bluff camping area

With 4 sites among coastal vegetation on the foreshore, visitors will find a fine spot for birdwatching here, along with fishing and snorkelling. Bring in your own drinking water and a gas/fuel stove. The camping area is a small section on Eagle

Bluff Rd, off Shark Bay Rd, 18 km south-east of Denham. Note: stays are limited to 1 night. A permit is essential to camp here. **Map refs:** 295 B4, 315 B9

How to book: permit from Shark Bay World Heritage Discovery & Visitor Information Centre, 53 Knight Tce, Denham (08) 9948 1590

271 Ellendale Pool camping area

Ellendale Pool camping area is a delightful spot 47 km east of Geraldton via Ellendale Rd. Bring a gas/fuel stove and drinking water. Visitors will find a lovely freshwater pool that laps at a sheer cliff-face surrounded by shady gum trees. Campers can swim or canoe the waterways, or relax to the sounds of the abundant birdlife that inhabits the area. **Map refs:** 295 C6, 315 E12, 316 A3

Who to contact: Shire of Greenough (08) 9921 0500; or Geraldton Tourist Bureau (08) 9921 3999

272 Fowlers Camp camping area

There are no facilities provided here, but it's a good spot for beach fishing. You need to bring in a gas/fuel stove and drinking water. The camping area is on Fowlers Camp Rd, off Shark Bay Rd, 22 km south-east of Denham. It's a small area with 4 sites on the foreshore among coastal vegetation. A permit is required to camp here. Note: stays are restricted to 1 night only. **Map refs:** 295 B4, 315 B9

How to book: permit from Shark Bay World Heritage Discovery & Visitor Information Centre, 53 Knight Tce, Denham (08) 9948 1590

273 Gladstone camping area

In an open area in low coastal vegetation, close to a popular fishing beach, Gladstone camping area is 6 km west of the North West Coastal Hwy and 146 km south of Carnarvon. It's gas/fuel stove only and you need to bring in drinking water. **Map refs:** 295 B4, 315 C8

Who to contact: Shire of Carnarvon (08) 9941 0030; or Carnarvon Tourist Bureau (08) 9941 1146 *Camping fees:* pay fees at the shire office in Francis St, Carnarvon; or to ranger

274 Goulet Bluff camping area

Goulet Bluff camping area is off Goulet Bluff Rd from Shark Bay Rd, 36 km south-east of Denham. The small area has 4 sites dispersed among coastal vegetation on the foreshore. Stays are limited to 1 night only. A good spot for a quick swim or a bit of fishing, you need to bring drinking water and a gas/fuel stove. Note: a permit is required to camp here. **Map refs:** 295 B4, 315 C9

How to book: permit from Shark Bay World Heritage Discovery & Visitor Information Centre, 53 Knight Tce, Denham (08) 9948 1590

Red Bluff camping area, Quobba Station (p. 300)

275 Hamelin Pool Caravan Park

This park has shady, grassed sites near the foreshore, set around the old telegraph station established in 1884. Visitors have the opportunity to view some very interesting stromatolite structures only a short walk away. The caravan park is on Hamelin Pool Rd, off Shark Bay Rd, 37 km west of the North West Coastal Hwy. **Map refs:** 295 B4, 315 C9

How to book: Hamelin Pool Rd (08) 9942 5905

276 Kalbarri Tudor Holiday Park

This caravan park is centrally located in Kalbarri, just a short walk into town or to the beach for some fishing or swimming. Local attractions such as a drive to the Murchison Gorge are a must, and wildflowers are abundant in Aug–Oct. Note: dogs can be brought by arrangement, at off-peak periods only. **Map refs:** 295 B5, 315 C11

How to book: 10 Porter St, Kalbarri (08) 9937 1077
www.tudorholidaypark.com.au

277 Lake Mason camping area

Lake Mason camping area provides campers with a good range of facilities set around some shady trees; an ideal base from which to explore the old pastoral property nearby. Bring firewood and water to this site 56 km north of Sandstone off the Sandstone–Wiluna Rd. **Map refs:** 295 E4, 316 F1, 318 F11

Who to contact: DEC Kalgoorlie (08) 9080 5555

278 Monkey Mia Dolphin Resort

Monkey Mia Dolphin Resort is located on Monkey Mia Rd, 25 km north-east of Denham. The complex includes a resort and lodge as well as caravan and camping facilities, with some sites having a beachfront location. Dogs are allowed, but only in the caravan and camping areas. Visitors here will find a good range of facilities in the heart of the Shark Bay World Heritage Area and all of its attractions. But while some come to soak up the winter sun and others to catch fish, most come to see the famous Monkey Mia dolphins; a highlight not to be missed. **Map refs:** 295 B4, 315 B8

How to book: Monkey Mia Rd (08) 9948 1320
www.monkeymia.com.au

279 Mount Magnet Caravan Park

This caravan park is a handy base. You can follow a heritage walk through town, which offers an insight into the history of Mt Magnet, or range further afield, driving the 37 km Tourist Trail, which takes in an impressive rock formation called the

Amphitheatre, caves and old mining settlements. The abundant wildflower displays from July–Oct are an experience to remember. **Map refs:** 295 E5, 315 H11, 316 D2, 318 D12

How to book: Hepburn St, Mt Magnet (08) 9963 4198

280 New Beach camping area

Carry in firewood and drinking water to this camping area with no facilities, set close to the beach. You'll find it on New Beach Rd, 33 km south of Carnarvon and 8 km west of the North West Coastal Hwy. Note: you must have a chemical toilet to camp here. **Map refs:** 295 B3, 315 B7

Who to contact: Shire of Carnarvon (08) 9941 0030; or Carnarvon Tourist Bureau (08) 9941 1146

281 Ningaloo Caravan and Holiday Resort

This caravan park, situated opposite the visitor centre, offers facilities to suit every taste: from backpacking, camping and caravanning, to luxury accomodation. It is well-located for visitors to explore the magnificent Ningaloo Marine Park. The snorkelling here is spectacular, with abundant marine life around the coral, while Cape Range National Park is only a short drive away. **Map refs:** 295 B1, 315 B3

How to book: 1112 Murat Rd, Exmouth (08) 9949 2377, 1800 652 665 www.exmouthresort.com

282 Quobba Station

Quobba Station is at the southern tip of Ningaloo Marine Park. Visitors here can experience excellent land-based game fishing, snorkelling, isolated beaches, world-renowned surfing, whales, and abundant marine life and wildlife; all set in an arid outback landscape. Bring your own drinking water. Other accommodation is available. Quobba Station is on Gnaraloo Rd, off Blowholes Rd, 80 km north of Carnarvon. **Map refs:** 295 B3, 315 B6

How to book: Gnaraloo Rd, Carnarvon (08) 9948 5098 www.quobba.com.au

283 Red Bluff camping area

At Red Bluff you can revitalise your body and mind by immersing yourself in the turquoise waters or relaxing on the beach while taking in one of the most majestic sunsets you will ever see, followed by gazing into the star-filled desert sky. For the more energetic, surf the renowned Bluff Barrel, explore the abundant marine and wildlife, fish and swim off the pristine beach, or snorkel around the rocks. The marine wonderland of Red Bluff is on Quobba Station, a spectacularly rugged and authentic working station, 141 km north of Carnarvon via Gnaraloo Rd off Blowholes Rd. Bring along firewood and water, or choose from a wide range of other beachfront accommodation available. **Map refs:** 295 B3, 315 B6

Who to contact: Quobba Station (08) 9948 5001

284 Three Mile Camp camping area

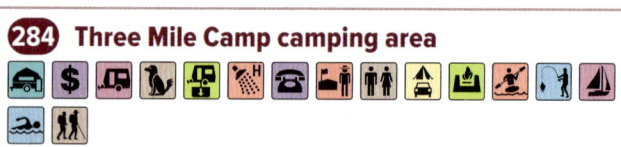

Three Mile Camp is on Gnaraloo Station, accessed via Blowholes Rd, 145 km north of Carnarvon. Right on the beach, this is a great spot for surfing and windsurfing, as well as swimming, boating and fishing. Bring firewood and drinking water, or choose cabin accommodation at the homestead. **Map refs:** 295 B2, 315 B6

Who to contact: Gnaraloo Station (08) 9948 5000

285 Warroora Station camping area

Warroora Station is an ideal place to experience the Australian outback in its most natural state. There are numerous sites for self-sufficient campers who enjoy surfing, diving, fishing and swimming in a pristine coastal environment. Bring along firewood and drinking water to this very special camping area with no facilities, 23 km off the Exmouth Rd and 160 km north of Carnarvon. Other accommodation is available. Note: you must have a chemical toilet to camp here. **Map refs:** 295 B2, 315 B5

How to book: (08) 9942 5920 *Camping fees:* pay fees at the homestead

286 Whalebone Bay camping area

There are 4 sites dispersed among coastal vegetation close to the beach at this camping area on Whalebone Rd, off Shark Bay Rd and 25 km south-east of Denham. Stays are limited to 1 night. It is a gas/fuel stove only camping site and you need to bring drinking water. Note: a permit is required to camp here. **Map refs:** 295 B4, 315 B9

How to book: permit from Shark Bay World Heritage Discovery & Visitor Information Centre 53 Knight Tce, Denham (08) 9948 1590

PILBARA

AUSTRALIA'S NORTH-WEST COUNTRY IS a land of extraordinary contrasts, where the red landscapes of the outback meet the turquoise waters of the Indian Ocean. Visitors to this remote region can walk through ancient gorges and swim in freshwater pools under plunging waterfalls, and encounter amazing native wildlife and fascinating local cultures.

This region has some of the world's most ancient natural landscapes, dating back two billion years and stretching over 400 000 sq km. At Karijini National Park you can camp near deep, rocky canyons that lead to dramatic gorges and peaceful pools; a haven for nature lovers, bushwalkers and photographers. An oasis of waterways and thriving vegetation contrasts with arid landscapes at Millstream–Chichester National Park.

Islands with dazzling white beaches and untouched coral gardens are yours to explore on the Dampier Archipelago, which offers world-class boating, fishing, diving and snorkelling. Should you visit in turtle nesting season, Sept–Apr, watch out for female turtles laying their eggs and newly hatched babies scrambling to the ocean. Another event on Mother Nature's calendar is the incredible Staircase to the Moon, occurring on full moon dates in Mar–Oct along the Pilbara coast.

Pilbara is also known as the engine room of Australia, as it is home to a massive mining industry in crude oil, salt, natural gas and iron ore. Among these operations along the coast around Roebourne and Dampier are bush-camping areas for self-sufficient campers who enjoy a bit of solitude along with their boating, swimming and fishing.

CAMPSITES LOCATED IN PARKS AND RESERVES

CAPE KERAUDREN COASTAL RECREATION RESERVE

Cape Keraudren Reserve is on a picturesque white-sand beach that stretches as far as the eye can see. The clear blue water is a spectacular welcome to the start of the famous Eighty Mile Beach. Follow one of several walking trails through the reserve to see the diverse flora and fauna native to this pristine coastline, or just sit back and relax on the magnificent beach. A good spot for fishing, you might be fortunate enough to be cooking your catch while watching a magnificent sunset over the ocean.

Who to contact: Shire East Pilbara (08) 9175 8000; or Newman Visitor Centre (08) 9175 2888 **Camping fees:** pay fees to the reserve ranger

287 Cape Keraudren camping area

Visitors will find dispersed camping sites in a large area behind the dunes on the foreshore at Cape Keraudren. You need to bring your own firewood and drinking water. Access is 14 km north of the Great Northern Hwy, opposite Pardoo Roadhouse, or 152 km north-east of Port Hedland. **Map refs:** 302 D2, 320 E11

KARIJINI NATIONAL PARK

Set in the Hamersley Range, in the heart of the Pilbara, vast Karijini National Park is an ancient landscape of massive mountains and steep escarpments cut by spectacular gorges more than 100 m deep. Within these sheer-sided chasms hide crystal-clear rockpools, cascading waterfalls and lush vegetation. Walking trails lead visitors to lookouts from which to marvel at the spectacular views, or to stunning gorges and freshwater pools for a dip. Enter the park 50 km east of Tom Price or 30 km west of the Great Northern Hwy along Karijini Dr.

Who to contact: Karijini National Park Visitor Centre (08) 9189 8121 **How to book:** Karijini Eco Retreat, Banjima Dr (08) 9189 8013, (08) 9425 5591 www.karijiniecoretreat.com.au for campsite no. **290**

288 Dales camping area

Dales camping area is in a gorge among lush, shady vegetation near the Fortescue River, 9 km east of Banjima Dr and 8.4 km north of Karijini Dr. Visitors need to bring a gas/fuel stove and drinking water. Swimming at the nearby Fortescue Falls is an absolute delight after trekking through the stunning natural features of this area. **Map refs:** 302 C3, 315 H3, 318 D4

289 Hamersley Gorge Truck Bay

There are no facilities at this truck bay and it is suitable for an overnight stop only, as long as you are equipped with your own gas/fuel stove and drinking water. It is at the junction of Nanutarra–Wittenoom Rd, 900 m north of Hamersley Rd and 20 km north of Hamersley–Mt Bruce Rd. **Map refs:** 302 C3, 315 G3, 318 C4

290 Karijini Eco Retreat camping area

This camping area, affiliated with the Eco Retreat, is on Banjima Dr, 20 km west of the visitor centre and 22 km north-east of the west entry point. Visitors will find a good range of facilities in a bush environment. Other accommodation is available, along with bar and restaurant facilities, guided tours and other activities. **Map refs:** 302 C3, 315 G3, 318 D4

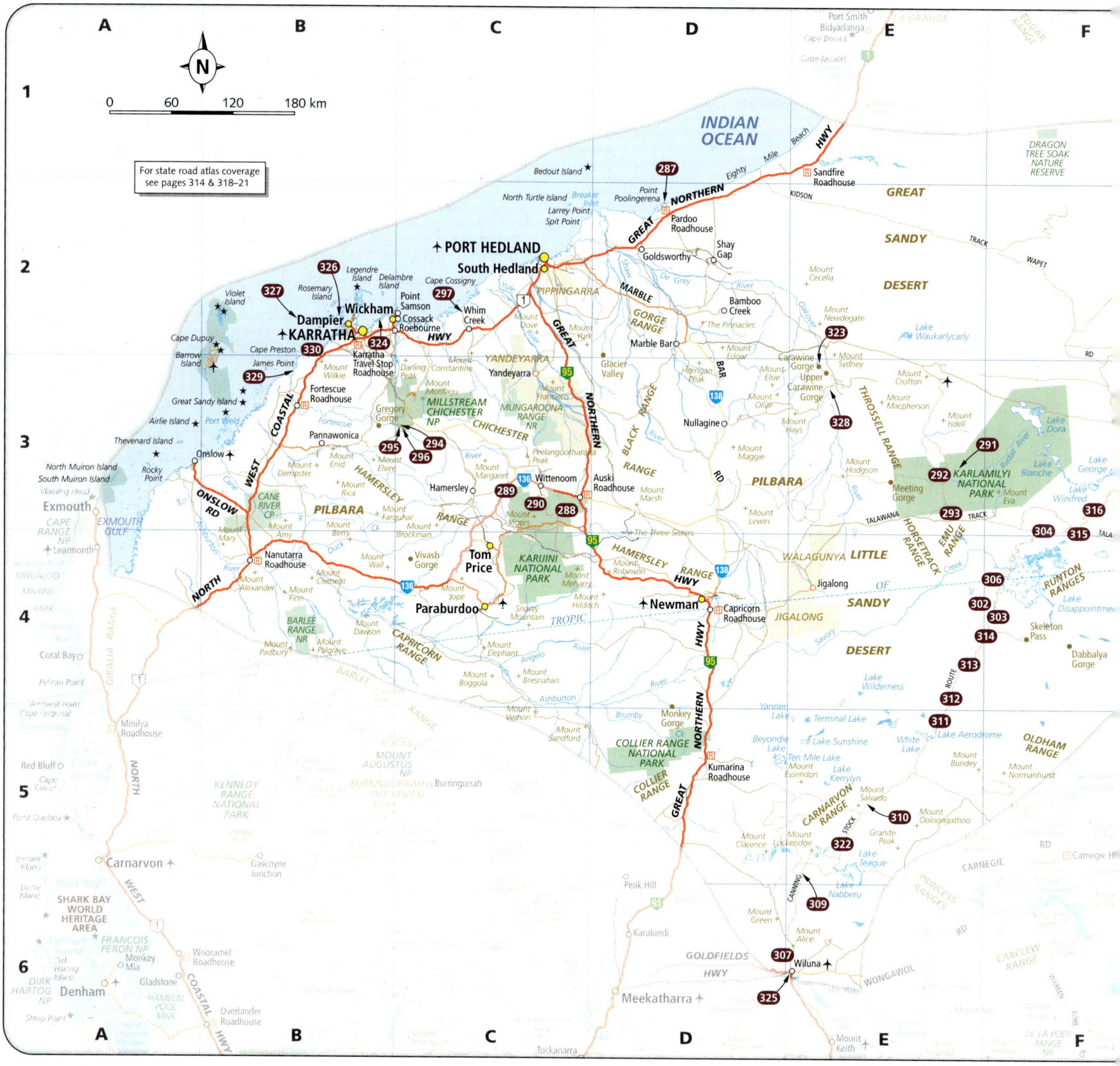

A   B   C   D   E   F

N

0   60   120   180 km

For state road atlas coverage
see pages 314 & 318–21

INDIAN OCEAN

1

2

3

4

5

6

A   B   C   D   E   F

KARLAMILYI NATIONAL PARK

Karlamilyi National Park is a beautiful and haunting place, rich in history and culture. This ancient land is one of the few areas in Australia that remain rarely visited. Its secrets are known only to a few hardy travellers, scientists, researchers and explorers, and, of course, the traditional Aboriginal groups who have lived there for tens of thousands of years. Karlamilyi National Park is the largest national park in WA and one of the largest in the world. As well as being vast, it is also one of the most remote places in the world, and features rugged wilderness and stunning natural beauty. Formerly known as Rudall River, it is the perfect place to experience the true isolation of the outback, but only for well-equipped, self-sufficient campers. You need a permit from the DEC in Karratha to gain access to the park's eastern section.

Who to contact: DEC Pilbara (08) 9182 2000; or Telfer Mine gatehouse 0419 042 292

291   **Desert Queen Baths camping area (bush camping)**

Desert Queen Baths camping area is reached via Marble Bar. Take the Ripon Hills and Telfer rds, then turn south on Telfer Mine Rd, which becomes the main north-south track through the park. The campsite is 18.2 km south-east of the main track via a turn-off after entering the park. Bring firewood and drinking water with you. The main pool is a 30–40 min walk each way through the gorge from the camping area.   **Map refs:** 302 E3, 318 H4

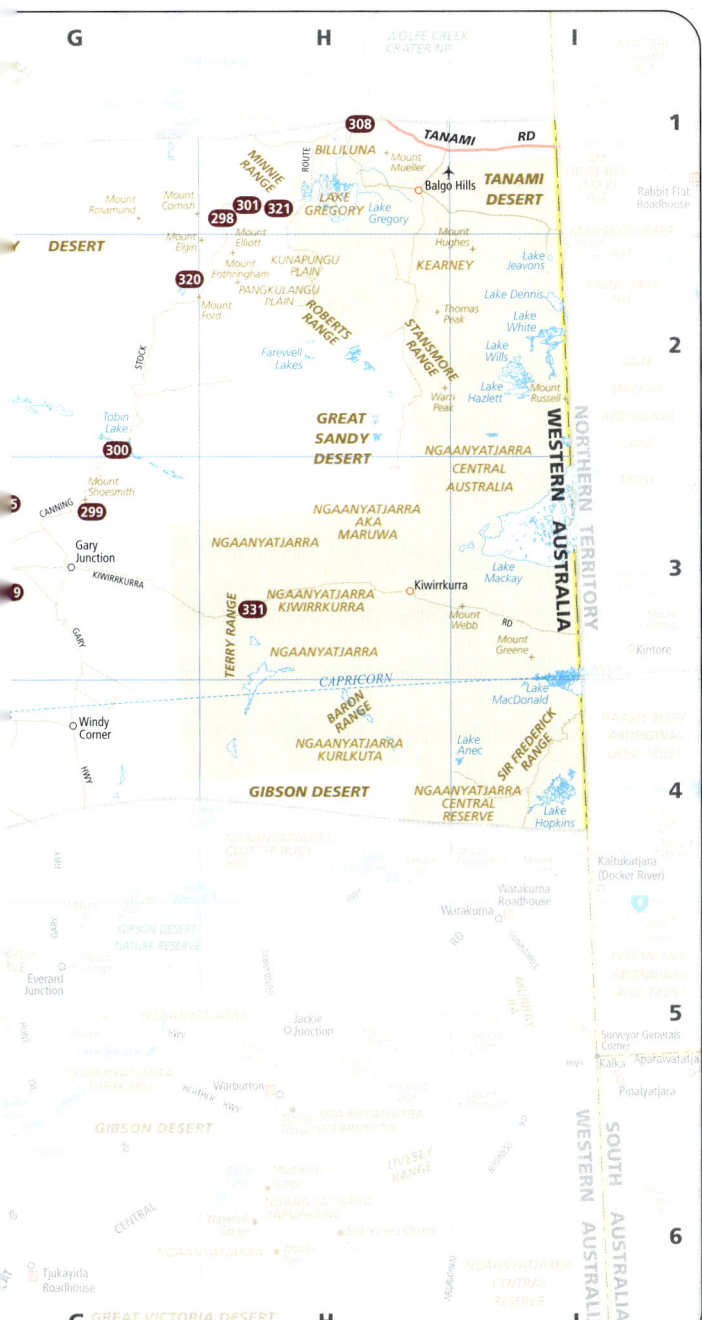

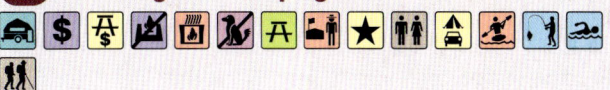

293 White Gum Bore camping area (bush camping)

Water is available from the bore at White Gum, but you need to boil or treat it before use. The camping area is 100 m east of the main park track and 9 km north of the Talawana Track off Marble Bar Rd, 325 km north-east of Newman. **Map refs:** 302 E3, 318 H4

MILLSTREAM–CHICHESTER NATIONAL PARK

Millstream–Chichester National Park in the western Pilbara protects some very different landscapes. In the north lies the rocky, sparsely vegetated Chichester Range, while in the south you'll find winding, tree-lined watercourses and the oasis-like Millstream. Here, a natural freshwater spring feeds lily-covered pools surrounded by paperbark and palm trees. The visitor centre at Millstream has informative displays on Aboriginal culture, early settlers and the environment. Fishing, canoeing and swimming are all possible at Deep Reach Pool and Crossing Pool, while bushwalking or scenic drives are a great way to take in the superb scenic beauty of the park.

Who to contact: Millstream–Chichester Visitor Centre (08) 9184 5144; or DEC Karratha (08) 9182 2000

294 Crossing Pool camping area

Crossing Pool camping area has a good range of facilities around large, shady gum trees on the banks of the Fortescue River; a great spot for fishing, swimming and canoeing. Bring drinking water with you. It's on Snappy Gum Dr via the Millstream–Yarraloola Rd, 11.5 km west of the Roebourne–Wittenoom Rd and 98 km south of the North West Coastal Hwy. Note: access is not suitable for caravans. **Map refs:** 302 C3, 315 F2, 318 B3

295 Miliyanah camping area

Bring your own drinking water to Miliyanah camping area. It is opposite the park visitor centre, and offers a good range of facilities in a bush setting. **Map refs:** 302 C3, 315 F2, 318 B3

296 Stargazers camping area

The area is an overflow campsite with only basic facilities; come equipped with drinking water. The camping area is on Snappy Gum Dr, north of the Millstream–Yarraloola Rd. It is on the western side of the Fortescue River, reached via the Millstream–Yarraloola Rd, 14.7 km west of the Roebourne–Wittenoom Rd, which in turn is 98 km south of the North West Coastal Hwy. **Map refs:** 302 C3, 315 F2, 318 B3

292 Tjingkulatjatjarra Pool camping area (bush camping)

Tjingkulatjatjarra camping area is 21 km south off the Desert Queen Baths track and 7.2 km west of the main Karlamilyi National Park track. The campsite is on the southern side of the Rudall River, 38.7 km north of the track to White Gum Bore and 500 m north of the river crossing. Bring your own firewood and drinking water. **Map refs:** 302 E3, 318 H4

CAMPSITES LOCATED IN OTHER AREAS

297 Balla Balla (Bulla Bulla) camping area

This small camping area is 20 km north of North West Coastal Hwy, set among trees on the river. It suits self-sufficient campers who enjoy fishing. You need to bring firewood, drinking water and, preferably, a portable toilet. To get here, leave the hwy at Whim Creek, 85 km east of Roebourne. **Map refs:** 302 C2, 315 F1, 318 C2, 320 C12

Who to contact: Karratha Tourist Bureau (08) 9144 4600

Canning Stock Route

The 1900 km Canning Stock Route takes travellers through harsh and remote desert country, from Wiluna north to Billiluna, with very little in the way of fuel and supplies available along the way. The spectacular landscapes and history of the region appeal to modern-day adventurers, many of whom choose to camp at the old well sites. This is some of the most isolated and desolate country in Australia, and although water should be available en route at some of the wells, bring a supply of your own as well as firewood, a gas/fuel stove and a detailed route description. You need to be self-sufficient, well-prepared and well-equipped, with fuel supplies arranged well in advance. Note: the Canning Stock Route is not suited to camper trailers, and some sections of the route require a permit; Well 5 (no camping) is on private property, contact (08) 9981 2983 to ask about entering or leaving the route via Well 5.

Please note that campsites are listed in alphabetical order, not track order. Refer to the map on p. 302–3 for further information.

Who to contact: Newman Tourist Information Centre (08) 9175 2888; or Wiluna Police (08) 9981 7024; or Halls Creek Police (08) 9168 6000 **How to book:** (08) 9176 9040 for campsite no. **305**; Mindibungu Aboriginal Community (08) 9168 8988 or (08) 9168 8076 for campsite no. **308 Permits:** permits can be bought online at http://permits.canningstockroute.net.au (08) 9425 2099

298 Breaden Valley camping area (bush camping)

Breaden Valley has a small camping area near the carpark for Breaden Pool and Godfreys Tank, 4.5 km from the route. It is 24.4 km north of the access track to Well 47 and 1.3 km south of the Well 48 track. **GPS** S:20 14.793 E:126 34.169 **Map refs:** 303 H1, 321 M10

299 Campsite east of Well 36 (bush camping)

Trees surround this well-regarded campsite, 22.2 km east of the track to Well 36 and 0.3 km west of Well 37. **GPS** S:22 09.121 E:125 27.335 **Map refs:** 303 G3, 319 L3

300 Campsite north of Well 39 (bush camping)

Camp in an area shaded by desert oaks, 4 km north of Well 39 and 0.4 km south of Tobin Lake. Follow the track on

the lake's southern edge. **GPS** S:22 44.802 E:125 40.160 **Map refs:** 303 G2, 319 L2, 321 L12

301 Campsites east of 'Notice to Travellers' sign (bush camping)

Bush campsites are located off tracks leading north, 0.1 km and 0.5 km east of the 'Notice to Travellers' sign. **GPS** S:20 10.346 E:126 44.260 **Map refs:** 303 H1, 321 M10

302 Diebel Spring camping area (bush camping)

Pick up the track to Diebel Spring camping area 20 km north of the Durba Springs crossroads. After following the track for 15.2 km to another crossroads, turn right then right again after 1.4 km, and travel a further 4.2 km. **GPS** S:23 37.752 E:122 21.155 **Map refs:** 302 E4, 318 H5

303 Durba Springs camping area (bush camping)

Pick up the 5.3 km track to Durba Springs camping area from the crossroads 24 km north of Calvert Range. **GPS** S:23 45.268 E:122 31.039 **Map refs:** 302 F4, 319 I5

304 Georgia Bore camping area (bush camping)

Georgia Bore has camping and water, and is 300 m north of the route. Find it 8.6 km north of the Well 22 access and 0.5 km south of the Talawana Track. **GPS** S:23 03.532 E:123 01.066 **Map refs:** 302 F3, 319 I4

305 Kunawarritji Aboriginal Community camping area

Kunawarritji Aboriginal Community camping area is on the Kidson Track, 4 km west of the Canning Stock Route. It has basic facilities for campers as well as a store for supplies and fuel; but not firewood, so bring your own. Kunawarritji is a restricted access community, so visitors need to contact the Shire of Wiluna before entering the area. For camper-trailer access, use the Kidson Track. There are additional types of accommodation available at this camping area, 985 km north of Wiluna and 636 km south of Billiluna. **GPS** S:22 19.762 E:124 43.613 **Map refs:** 303 G3, 319 K3

306 Lake Disappointment camping area (bush camping)

Travel 3.4 km or 5.5 km north of the Savory Creek crossing to camp on the lake's western shore. **Map refs:** 302 F4, 318 H5

307 North Pool camping area (bush camping)

This small site is found 10.4 km north of Wiluna. **GPS** S:26 26.772 E:120 08.868 **Map refs:** 302 D6, 318 F9

308 Nyarna–Lake Stretch camping area

Visitors will find a large, open area on the banks of a lagoon at this camping area, 2.4 km south-east of the route. Bring your own drinking water to camp under the shade of the trees by day and millions of stars by night. Access for trailers is from the north only. The signed access point is 19.3 km south of Tanami Rd and 17.3 km south of the Billiluna store. Bookings are essential. *GPS* S:19 40.773 E:127 33.973 **Map refs:** 303 H1, 321 N9

309 Well 3 (bush camping)

Well 3 has water and a small camping area to the east of the route, 71.1 km from the turn-off north of Wiluna. No camping is permitted between Well 3 and Windich Springs, as this is private property. *GPS* S:25 46.541 E:120 24.819. **Map refs:** 302 E5, 318 F8

310 Well 6 – Pierre Spring (bush camping)

There is water at this camp near river red gums, 48.1 km north-east of Windich Springs. *GPS* S:25 14.453 E:121 05.967 **Map refs:** 302 E5, 318 G8

311 Well 12 (bush camping)

Well 12 is 500 m west of the route. The camping area is under desert oaks near a restored well, which that has water available. Find it 133.3 km north-east of Well 6. *GPS* S:24 35.651 E:121 52.361 **Map refs:** 302 E5, 318 H7

312 Well 13 (bush camping)

Be careful not to get stuck in the mud if it has been raining at Well 13 and its camping area, 2.1 km west of the route and 20.8 km north of Well 12. *GPS* S:24 25.318 E:121 59.294 **Map refs:** 302 E4, 318 H6

313 Well 15 (bush camping)

Well 15 campsite is 200 m east of the route and has welcome water available. You will find it 42.7 km north of Well 13. *GPS* S:24 08.475 E:122 12.120 **Map refs:** 302 E4, 318 H6

314 Well 16 (bush camping)

With a small area for camping, Well 16 is 500 m west of the route and 38.2 km north of Well 15. *GPS* S:23 54.491 E:122 23.009 **Map refs:** 302 F4, 318 H6

315 Well 24 (bush camping)

Well 24 camping area is 400 m south-east of the Canning Stock Route. Well 23 is 14 km to the east. *GPS* S:23 06.567 E:123 20.606 **Map refs:** 302 F3, 319 I4

316 Well 26 (bush camping)

Well 26 has water and camping out in the open. You will find it 45.2 km north of Well 24. *GPS* S:22 54.967 E:123 30.334 **Map refs:** 302 F3, 319 J4

317 Well 30 (bush camping)

Well 30 has treed campsites 6.3 km east of the track leading to Nangabbittajarra Native Well. *GPS* S:22 30.169 E:124 08.315 **Map refs:** 302 F3, 319 J3

318 Well 31 (bush camping)

Well 31 camping area is 4 km south of the Canning Stock Route. Well 30 is 26.2 km to the east. *GPS* S:22 31.539 E:124 24.425 **Map refs:** 303 G3, 319 J3

319 Well 33 (bush camping)

Camping at Well 33 is in a large and open area with water available, 3.6 km north of the crossroads with Jenkins Track. *GPS* S:22 20.513 E:124 46.512 **Map refs:** 303 G3, 319 K3

320 Well 46 (bush camping)

There is water at Well 46, along with a large, shady camping area. The well is 31.6 km north of Well 45 and 14.4 km west of the Canning Stock Route. *GPS* S:20 38.510 E:126 17.258 **Map refs:** 303 G2, 319 L1, 321 L11

321 Well 50 (bush camping)

Camp in the shade at Well 50, 2 km south of the route. Find it 20.2 km south-west of Weriaddo Well and 26.2 km east of the 'Notice to Travellers' sign. *GPS* S:20 12.531 E:126 58.079 **Map refs:** 303 H1, 321 M10

322 Windich Springs (No. 4A Water) camping area (bush camping)

Windich Springs has camping beside a large waterhole, 76.6 km north-east of Well 3. *GPS* S:25 33.432 E:120 49.541 **Map refs:** 302 E5, 318 G8

323 Carawine Gorge camping area

Self-sufficient campers here will find shady sites on the banks of the Oakover River. Relax in the shade while trying to catch dinner or refresh in the cool waters of this beautiful waterhole. You need to bring your own firewood and drinking water. Signposted access along Woodie Woodie Rd is 162 km east of Marble Bar, or 8.9 km east of the Woodie Woodie/Telfer/Ripon Hills rds junction. The camping area is a further 22.5 km south-west. This land is private property, owned by the Mills family, and is a working cattle station. Call ahead before visiting and take your rubbish away with you. **Map refs:** 302 E3, 318 G2

Who to contact: Mills family (08) 9176 5900

324 Cleaverville camping area

Cleaverville camping area is an ideal spot for self-sufficient campers who enjoy the beach. Visitors will find dispersed sites in a large area behind the dunes on the foreshore of a pristine beach, which offers good swimming, fishing and boating. Bring firewood, drinking water and, preferably, a portable toilet to this site 14 km west of Roebourne via the North West Coastal Hwy, followed by a further 13 km north. Note: camping is permitted Apr–Oct only. **Map refs:** 302 B2, 315 E1, 318 B2, 320 B12

Who to contact: Shire of Roebourne (08) 9186 8555; or Roebourne Tourist Bureau (08) 9182 1060 *Camping fees:* fees collected on-site

325 Club Hotel Caravan Park

Wiluna, on the Goldfields Hwy between Meekatharra and Leonora, is the start and finish point for the Canning Stock Route and the famous Gunbarrel Hwy. For many intrepid adventurers, it is the first or last sign of civilisation for some time. The caravan park is behind the Club Hotel, with shady, grassed sites for campers and other accommodation available. **Map refs:** 302 E6, 318 F10

How to book: Wotton St, Wiluna (08) 9981 7012

326 Dampier Archipelago camping areas (boat-based camping)

This string of 42 islands off the Dampier coast is home to a large and diverse range of marine species, making it one of WA's best diving and snorkelling spots. With 25 of the islands protected as part of the Dampier Archipelago Marine Park, the islands' white-sand beaches and blue waters also make them an ideal location for swimming or just lazing the day away. Beach camping here is for self-sufficient visitors equipped with a gas/fuel stove, but drinking water is available. Access is by boat only. A 5-night maximum stay applies. **Map refs:** 302 B2, 315 E1, 318 B2, 320 B12

Who to contact: DEC Pilbara (08) 9143 1488; or Karratha Tourist Bureau (08) 9144 4600

327 Dampier Transit Caravan Park

Dampier is one of those pivotal places where visitors begin to get a handle on the ancient ark that is Australia. Large shell middens and magnificent rock art are found throughout the area; the significant, prehistoric rock carvings standing as testament to the timeless occupation of the land. The

Dampier Transit Caravan Park provides a good base to explore the ancient history of the region. Stays are limited to 3 days. **Map refs:** 302 B2, 315 E1, 318 B2, 320 B12

How to book: The Esplanade, Dampier (08) 9183 1109

328 Eel Pool (Running Waters) camping area

West of Woodie Woodie Rd and 34 km south of the Woodie Woodie/Telfer/Ripon Hills rds junction, self-sufficient campers here will find a shady camping area on the banks of the Oakover River. This is a good spot for a bit of fishing and swimming, but bring your own firewood and drinking water. Note: this land is private property, owned by the Mills family, so you need to call ahead before visiting and ensure that you take your rubbish away with you. **Map refs:** 302 E3, 318 G3

Who to contact: Mills family (08) 9176 5900

329 Fortescue River Mouth camping area

Self-sufficient campers who enjoy boating and fishing should pack their firewood, portable toilet and drinking water, and set up camp here for a spell. Leave the North West Coastal Hwy 105 km south-west of Roebourne, 80 km south of Karratha, and travel north-west for a further 24 km. The small camping area is set among trees at the mouth of the river; check the tide before launching your boat. **Map refs:** 302 B3, 315 D1, 318 A2

Who to contact: Karratha Tourist Bureau (08) 9144 4600; or Council Ranger Service (08) 9186 8528

330 Forty Mile camping area

Forty Mile camping area is 83 km south-west of Roebourne via the North West Coastal Hwy, followed by a further 13 km north. The large open camping area is in the dunes on the foreshore. There are no facilities here, but self-sufficient campers equipped with firewood, a portable toilet and drinking water will find it a pleasant spot for fishing, swimming and boating on a delightful stretch of coast. You can camp here only Apr–Oct. **Map refs:** 302 B2, 315 E1, 318 A2, 320 A12

Who to contact: Shire of Roebourne (08) 9186 8555; or Roebourne Tourist Bureau (08) 9182 1060 *Camping fees:* fees payable on-site

331 Jupiter Well camping area

Jupiter Well is a large, open area around a few she-oak trees on Gary Junction Rd, 157 km east of Gary Junction. Isolated and remote, it is 223 km east of the Canning Stock Route and 260 km west of the WA–NT border. You'll find water here but no facilities, and you need a permit. **Map refs:** 303 H3, 319 M4

Who to contact: Kiwirrkurra Aboriginal Community (08) 8956 8612 *Permit:* Ngaanyatjarra Council (08) 8950 1741

KIMBERLEY

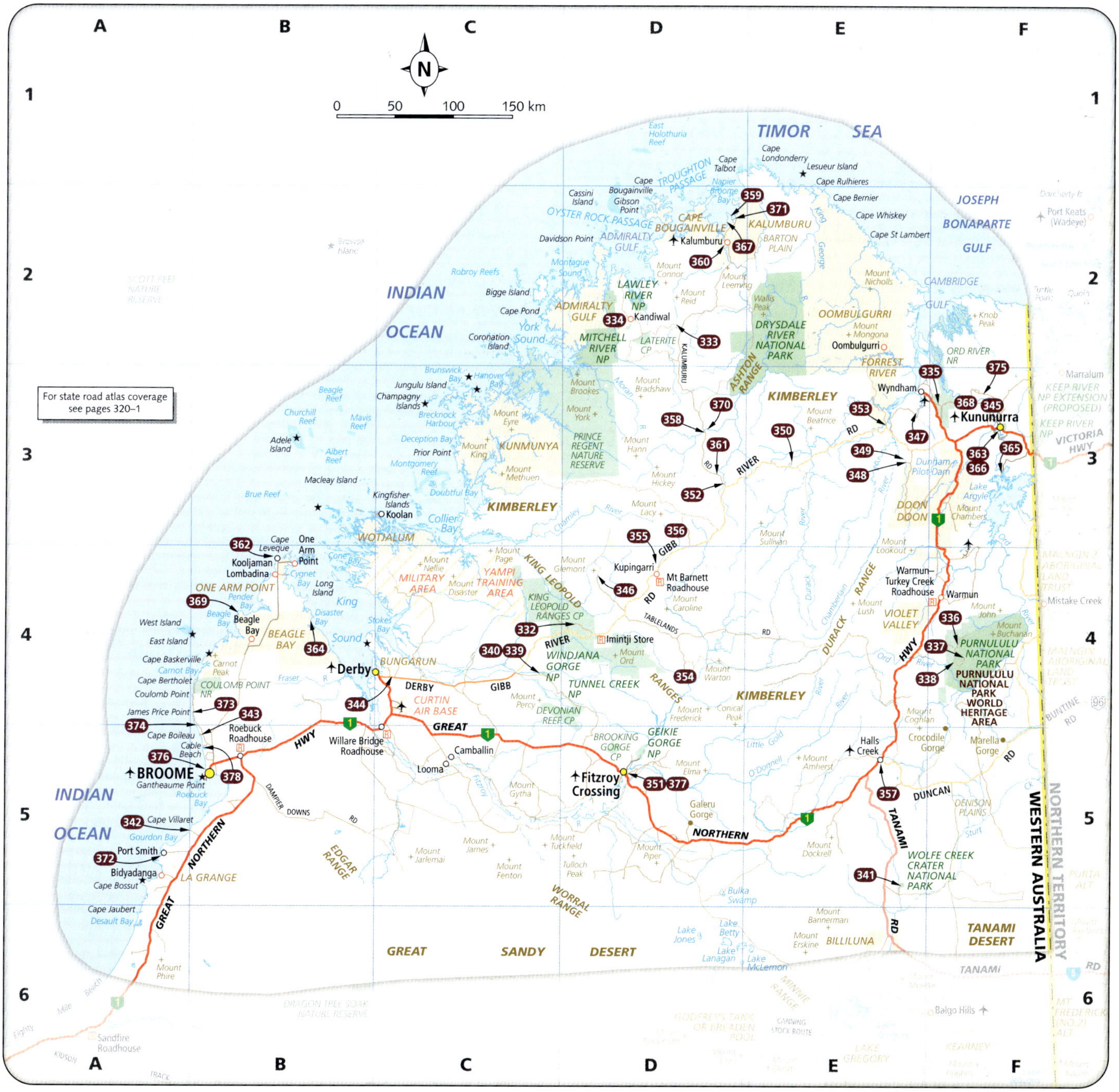

For state road atlas coverage see pages 320–1

A **B** **C** **D** **E** **F**

1

0 50 100 150 km

N

TIMOR SEA

East Holothuria Reef

Cape Talbot
Cape Londonderry
Lesueur Island
Cape Rulhieres

TROUGHTON PASSAGE

Cape Bougainville
Napier Broome Bay

Cassini Island
Bougainville
Gibson Point

359
371

Cape Bernier
Cape Whiskey
Cape St Lambert

JOSEPH
BONAPARTE
GULF

Port Keats (Wadeye)

INDIAN OCEAN

2

OYSTER ROCK PASSAGE

CAPE BOUGAINVILLE
ADMIRALTY GULF

Kalumburu
KALUMBURU

367
360

BARTON PLAIN

Mount Connor

Mount Leeming

Mount Nicholls

CAMBRIDGE GULF

Knob Peak

Davidson Point

Montague Sound

Bigge Island

Bonaparte Archipelago

Cape Pond

York Sound

Coronation Island

Kandiwal

334

LAWLEY RIVER NP

Mount Reid

Mount Bradshaw

DRYSDALE RIVER NATIONAL PARK

Oombulgurri

Oombulgurri

FORREST RIVER

ORD RIVER NR

375

335

Brunswick Bay

Jungulu Island
Champagny Islands
Hanover Bay

Brecknock Harbour

MITCHELL RIVER NP

LATERITE CP

333

ASHTON RANGE

KIMBERLEY

353

Mount Beatrice

Wyndham

368 345

347

KEEP RIVER NP EXTENSION (PROPOSED)

KEEP RIVER NP

Kununurra

VICTORIA HWY

Martalum

3

Roebuck Reefs

Beagle Reef

Mavis Reef

Deception Bay

Prior Point

Mount King

Mount Methuen

Doubtful Bay

370

361

358

RD

RIVER

352

Mount Hann

Mount Hickey

348

349

363
366

365

DOON DOON

Turkle Creek

VICTORIA HWY

4

Churchill Reef

Adele Island

Brue Reef

Macleay Island

Kingfisher Islands

Koolan

Collier Bay

Charnley

WOTJALUM

KIMBERLEY

River

Mount Lacy

Mount Sullivan

356

355

GIBB

Kupingarri

Mt Barnett Roadhouse

346

Mount Caroline

King

Durack

Mount Lookout

Warmun-Turkey Creek Roadhouse

Warmun

VIOLET VALLEY

336

Mistake Creek

MALNYIN ABORIGINAL LAND TRUST

BUNTINE

96

NORTHERN TERRITORY

WESTERN AUSTRALIA

Cape Leveque

One Arm Point

362

Kooljaman
Lombadina

369

ONE ARM POINT

Pender Bay

Cone Bay

Cygnet Bay

Long Island

King

Disaster Bay

Stokes Bay

MILITARY AREA

YAMPI TRAINING AREA

Mount Nellie

Mount Disaster

KING LEOPOLD RANGES CP

332

Mount Glenont

WINDJANA GORGE NP

Imintji Store

TABLELANDS

RANGES

Mount Warton

KIMBERLEY

Mount Frederick

DURACK

RANGE

Mount Lush

PURNULULU NATIONAL PARK

337

PURNULULU NATIONAL PARK WORLD HERITAGE AREA

West Island

East Island

Cape Baskerville

Carnot Peak

Cape Bertholet

Coulomb Point

COULOMB POINT NR

James Price Point

373

343

364

BEAGLE BAY

Beagle Bay

Derby

BUNGARUN

DERBY

CURTIN AIR BASE

344

GREAT

Willare Bridge Roadhouse

GIBB

DEVONIAN REEF CP

340 339

RIVER

TUNNEL CREEK NP

Mount Percy

354

GEIKIE GORGE NP

BROOKING GORGE NP

Mount Elma

Conical Peak

Mount Ord

338

Little Gold

O'Dognell

Mount Amhurst

Halls Creek

357

Crocodile Gorge

DUNCAN

Marella Gorge

DENISON PLAINS

RD

Stuart

374

Cape Boileau

Cable Beach

376

BROOME

Gantheaume Point

378

Roebuck Roadhouse

HWY

DAMPIER DOWNS

Willare Bridge Roadhouse

Camballin

Looma

Mount Gytha

Fitzroy Crossing

351 377

Galeru Gorge

NORTHERN

Mount Piper

Mount Dockrell

341

WOLFE CREEK CRATER NATIONAL PARK

INDIAN OCEAN

342 Cape Villaret

Gourdon Bay

372

Port Smith

Bidyadanga

Cape Bossut

Cape Jaubert

Desault Bay

GREAT NORTHERN

LA GRANGE

EDGAR RANGE

RD

Mount James

Mount Jarlemai

Mount Fenton

Mount Tuckfield

Tulloch Peak

WORRAL RANGE

Mount Bannerman

Mount Erskine

BILLILUNA

TANAMI DESERT

5

Mount Phire

GREAT SANDY DESERT

Lake Jones

Lake Lanagan

Lake McLemon

Lake Betty

TANAMI

RD

MT

6

Eighty Mile Beach

Sandfire Roadhouse

DRAGON TREE SOAK NATURE RESERVE

KIDDERDOO TARN OR BREADEN POOL

CANNING STOCK ROUTE

Balgo Hills

KEARNEY

WINNIE RANGE

LAKE GREGORY

A **B** **C** **D** **E** **F**

THE KIMBERLEY REGION OFFERS some of WA's most unique wilderness experiences. Covering nearly 423 000 sq km and larger than the United Kingdom and New Zealand combined, this ancient region has fewer people per square kilometre than almost any other place on earth.

At the heart of the Kimberley are vast wildlife sanctuaries and thundering waterfalls that provide the perfect backdrop for adventurous travellers looking to explore this region. A visit to the isolated Aboriginal communities on the north-west coast will enhance your appreciation of the antiquity of the region, while enjoying the hospitality and facilities of the locals.

This coast has some of the world's most beautiful beaches, untouched coral atolls and rugged islands, with an amazing variety of marine life to astound nature lovers and entice anglers. Set between the vast red desert and azure sea lies the charismatic town of Broome. If you like to unwind, stroll along the world-famous 22 km of pristine white sand that is Cable Beach and take in a glorious sunset.

Camping along the Gibb River Rd, a world-renowned tourist drive from Derby to Kununurra, is a highlight not to be missed. Lake Argyle covers an area of 812 sq km and could perhaps be called an inland sea. A little over 70 km south of Kununurra, the lake was formed by the damming of the Ord River. It is the largest freshwater storage in mainland Australia, containing the volume equivalent of 9 Sydney Harbours; what were once mountains are now just islands dotting the lake. Further inland is a photographer's delight for 4WD campers: the unique sandstone domes and palm-fringed gorges of the Bungle Bungle Range in Purnululu National Park.

CAMPSITES LOCATED IN PARKS AND RESERVES

KING LEOPOLD RANGE CONSERVATION PARK

King Leopold Range Conservation Park is situated in some of the most inaccessible country in Australia, making it ideal for a 4WD adventure. The park covers nearly 400 000 ha of sandstone mountains, palm groves, granite outcrops and stunning gorges. Camp out under the stars after exploring nearby Bell and Lennard gorges, which are among the most magnificent gorges in the Kimberley. The folded rock formations of these and other gorges were millions of years in the making.
Who to contact: DEC West Kimberley (08) 9195 5500

332 Silent Grove camping area

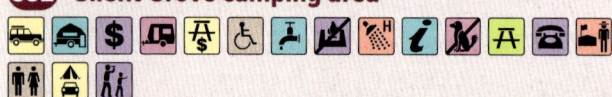

The turn-off to Silent Grove camping area is 8 km west of Imintji Roadhouse and 20 km north of the Gibb River Rd. It has a good range of facilities for visitors and its shady setting provides the ideal camp from which to explore the magnificent Bell Gorge. Bring along a gas/fuel stove. Silent Grove is only accessible by 4WD. **Map refs:** 307 D4, 321 K6

MITCHELL RIVER NATIONAL PARK

For outback scenery and Aboriginal culture, Mitchell River National Park is among the best in Australia. In full flood, the Mitchell Falls are an amazing sight. A bushwalking track leads to the falls, where you can enjoy a refreshing dip. The Mitchell Plateau abounds in wildlife and plants, and is home to many ancient rock-art sites, most of which have remained untouched for thousands of years.
Who to contact: DEC Kimberley, Kununurra (08) 9168 4200
Camping fees: pay fees on-site

333 Munurru (King Edward River Crossing) camping area

Munurru camping area is on the access road, 2.5 km west of Kalumburu Rd. The camping area has basic facilities in a shady bush setting near the river. Travellers to this isolated area have a welcome chance to wash the dust off with a refreshing swim, and perhaps even catch dinner. A gas/fuel stove is preferred, and you need to bring drinking water. **Map refs:** 307 D2, 321 L3

334 Punamii-unpuu (Mitchell Falls) camping area

Situated in a very isolated region, this area provides campers with basic facilities among shady trees on the banks of Mertens

Creek. Bring a gas/fuel stove, preferably, along with drinking water. A 3.3 km walk leaves the camping area for Mitchell Falls, where it is possible to swim in the upper falls. The camping area is 88 km west of Kalumburu Rd via the Mitchell Plateau access road, 101.8 km north of the Drysdale River Station access road. **Map refs:** 307 D2, 321 K3

PARRY LAGOONS NATURE RESERVE

Parry Lagoons Nature Reserve, 20 km south of Wyndham, is a wet season stopover point for many migratory birds; some from as far away as Siberia. The wet season floods bring food in abundance to the area, and as the water dries up it leaves concentrations of lagoons and billabongs that provide perfect breeding grounds for crocodiles. Camping is only permitted in the privately owned land within the reserve.
How to book: Parry Creek Farm (08) 9161 1139
www.parrycreekfarm.com.au

335 Parry Creek Farm camping area

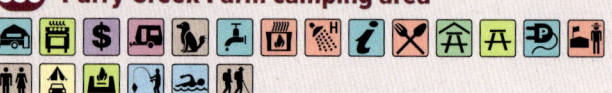

Parry Creek Farm camping area, off the Great Northern Hwy, is surrounded by the reserve and provides visitors with an ideal base for birdwatching. A bar, restaurant (open April–September) and other accommodation are available. Note: although dogs are allowed at the camping area, they are not allowed in the reserve. **Map refs:** 307 F3, 321 N4

PURNULULU (BUNGLE BUNGLE) NATIONAL PARK

The Bungle Bungle Range in Purnululu National Park is one of the most imposing landmarks in WA. The orange and black stripes across the beehive-like mounds, encased in a skin of silica and algae, are clearly visible as you approach from the south by air. As you sweep further over the range, a hidden world of gorges, creeks and pools is revealed, with fan palms clinging precariously to walls and crevices in the rocks. The park is open Apr–15 Dec (weather permitting); check with DEC at Kununurra before you travel. The park is accessible to 4WD vehicles only; there is no access for caravans due to road conditions, but off-road camper trailers are permitted.
Who to contact: DEC Kimberley, Kununurra (08) 9168 4200
How to book: online bookings www.dec.wa.gov.au/campgrounds for campsite nos **336**, **338**

336 Kurrajong camping area

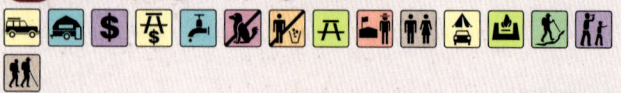

Explore the fascinating geological features by day, and relax under a canopy of millions of stars by night. Bring your own drinking water to this campsite, which is north of the visitor centre and 53 km east of the Great Northern Hwy via Spring Creek Track. Bookings are required. Note: no generators are allowed at this camping area. **Map refs:** 307 F4, 321 O6

337 Piccaninny Gorge camping area

If you are an experienced and self-sufficient camper, go camping along the Piccaninny Gorge walking trail; a 30 km return walk

of moderate to difficult standard, where the deeper you go the more spectacular it gets. Register at the visitor centre before you head off, and carry a gas/fuel stove and drinking water with you. **Map refs:** 307 F4, 321 O6

338 Walardi camping area

Walardi makes a good base for exploring the amazing geological features of the area and gaining an appreciation of the ecological importance of the park. On-site water must be boiled before drinking, or bring drinking water to this camping area, which is around 20 km south of the visitor centre. Bookings are required. Note: generators are allowed at Walardi. **Map refs:** 307 F4, 321 O6

WINDJANA GORGE NATIONAL PARK

The walls of Windjana Gorge rise abruptly from the wide alluvial floodplain of the Lennard River, reaching 100 m high in some places. The Lennard River runs through the 3.5 km gorge in wet weather, but during the dry season it forms pools surrounded by trees and shrubs. The range is part of an ancient barrier reef, formed 350–375 million years ago, and hosts fossils of extinct creatures in its caves. The park is a great place for photography, observing nature and bushwalking while enjoying a true Kimberley outback adventure.

Who to contact: DEC West Kimberley, Broome (08) 9195 5500; or DEC Windjana/Tunnel Creek (08) 9191 7076

339 The Generator Campground

This camping area, set among shady trees, has a good range of facilities. It is 1.2 km off the Fairfield–Leopold Downs Rd, 20 km east of the Gibb River Rd and 35 km west of the access road to Tunnel Creek National Park. You can use a generator here and, preferably, a gas/fuel stove. **Map refs:** 307 C4, 321 K7

340 Quiet Campground

This campground is set among shady trees by the gorge, and has good facilities. You will find it 1.2 km off Fairfield–Leopold Downs Rd, 20 km east of the Gibb River Rd. It is preferable to use a gas/fuel stove. **Map refs:** 307 C4, 321 K7

WOLFE CREEK CRATER NATIONAL PARK

On the edge of the Great Sandy Desert and the extensive spinifex grasslands of the East Kimberley lies the Wolfe Creek meteorite crater; the second largest crater in the world from which fragments of a meteorite have been collected. The crater measures 880 m across and is roughly circular in shape. A steep climb leads to the rim of the crater which was formed, according to Aboriginal legend, by a powerful rainbow serpent during the Dreamtime.

Who to contact: DEC Kimberley, Kununurra (08) 9168 4200

341 Wolfe Creek Crater camping area

This camping area has only minimal facilities in a barren and desolate landscape. Check the road conditions before heading here with a trailer or caravan, and bring a gas/fuel stove and drinking water. The national park is 23 km off Tanami Rd, 130 km south of Halls Creek. **Map refs:** 307 E5, 321 N9

CAMPSITES LOCATED IN OTHER AREAS

342 Barn Hill Beachside Station Stay

Barn Hill is located 120 km south of Broome (95 km south of Roebuck Plains Roadhouse) and 9 km off the Great Northern Hwy. The park faces the sea and has become very popular with anglers – and others who just want to soak up the warm winter sunshine. Its special features include a lawn bowls green. There is limited power to powered sites; not sufficient to run air conditioners or microwaves. **Map refs:** 307 B5, 320 G8

How to book: Barn Hill Station (08) 9192 4975
www.barnhill.com.au

343 Barred Creek camping area

This is a good spot for self-sufficient campers who enjoy a bit of fishing. There are no facilities, so bring firewood or, preferably, a gas/fuel stove, as well as drinking water. The camping area is 9.2 km north of Willie Creek Rd, then a further 1.4 km west, and is set along the banks of Barred Creek. Check if there are fire bans in place before lighting a fire. The maximum stay is 3 nights. **Map refs:** 307 B5, 320 G7

Who to contact: Shire of Broome (08) 9191 3456; or Broome Visitor Centre (08) 9192 2222

344 Birdwood Downs Station

Birdwood Downs Station is north of the Gibb River Rd and 17.6 km east of Derby. The camping area, which is frequented by numerous bird species and other wildlife, is situated in a nature park setting near the homestead. It has a good range of facilities and shady sites. You need to bring a gas/fuel stove. You can take a tour of this working station. Meals and accommodation other than camping are available. **Map refs:** 307 C4, 321 I7

How to book: Gibb River Rd (08) 9191 1275
www.birdwooddowns.com.au

345 Buttons Crossing camping area

Buttons Crossing camping area is by scrub near the Ord River and Kununurra township, where visitors have a large range of activities and attractions to choose from. Facilities here are limited: use the fireplaces and bring in your own firewood and drinking water. The camping area is 18.3 km north of the Victoria Hwy via Parry Creek Rd; 4WD is recommended. **Map refs:** 307 F3, 321 O4

Who to contact: Kununurra Visitor Centre (08) 9168 1177 *Road conditions:* Shire of Wyndham–East Kimberley (08) 9168 1677

346 Charnley River Station

Charnley River Station is a working cattle station off the Gibb River Rd, 49.6 km south-west of Mt Barnett Roadhouse and 4.1 km north-east of the Mornington Wilderness Camp access. It is a further 43 km north-west to the camping area near the homestead, which has a good range of facilities and shady sites among the trees near the river. **Map refs:** 307 D4, 321 K6
How to book: Gibb River Rd (08) 9191 4646

347 Diggers Rest Station

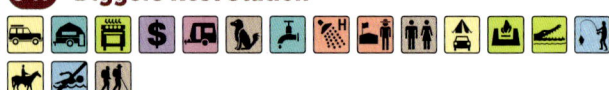

Diggers Rest is an authentic, working cattle station, nestled on the banks of the tidal King River in the King River Valley. It is on King River Rd, 40 km south-west of Wyndham, with the majestic Cockburn and Erskine ranges providing a stunning backdrop to the station accommodation and adjacent camping area. The atmosphere is relaxed and ageless, offering a rare opportunity to step back in time and become part of the ancient landscape and traditions. From horseriding to fishing tours, and bushwalking to birdwatching, there's plenty to do for those looking for an incredible adventure. **Map refs:** 307 E3, 321 N4
How to book: King River Rd (08) 9161 1029
www.diggersreststation.com.au

348 El Questro Station – Black Cockatoo camping area

El Questro Station township is 16.5 km from the Gibb River Rd. The Black Cockatoo camping area is set in a diverse landscape of rugged ranges, tidal flats, rainforest, gorges and waterfalls. Boating on the Chamberlain Gorge, relaxing in the thermal pools of Zebedee Springs, or horse-trekking to observe the Kimberley wildlife are just some of the activities available here. Wine and dine at the on-site bar and restaurant, or stay overnight in a range of accommodation other than camping. The access point off the Gibb River Rd is 33.7 km west of the Great Northern Hwy and 24 km east of the Pentecost River crossing. A Wilderness Park Permit, available at the property, is required. **Map refs:** 307 E3, 321 N4
Who to contact: Gibb River Rd (08) 9161 4318
www.elquestro.com.au

349 El Questro Station – Riverside camping area

Riverside camping area is on the Pentecost River near El Questro Station township. Campers will find secluded sites on the riverbank but no facilities; these are only available back at the homestead. This is an ideal spot for self-sufficient campers who like to feel a sense of discovery at every turn while they explore this ancient land. A Wilderness Park Permit, available at the property, is required. **Map refs:** 307 E3, 321 N4
Who to contact: Gibb River Rd (08) 9161 4318
www.elquestro.com.au

350 Ellenbrae Station

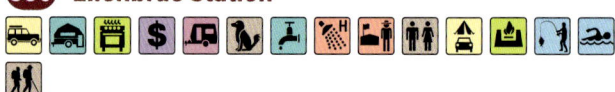

Leaving the Gibb River Rd, it is 4.9 km north to this homestead and camping area, where visitors will find basic facilities near a deep, cool waterhole. Fishing and swimming are popular pastimes here, as is relaxing in the pure serenity of the place at day's end. Leave the Gibb River Rd 69.9 km east of the Kalumburu Rd junction, 106.5 km west of Home Valley Station or 115.3 km west of the Pentecost River crossing. **Map refs:** 307 E3, 321 M4
How to book: Gibb River Rd (08) 9161 4325

351 Fitzroy River Lodge camping area

Fitzroy River Lodge camping area is on the Great Northern Hwy, 2.3 km east of Fitzroy Crossing. Visitors here will find a good range of facilities spread around shady, grassed sites on the bank of the Fitzroy River, where activities such as swimming, fishing and canoeing are popular. Other accommodation, a bar and restaurant, tennis court, swimming pool and other resort facilities are available to campers. **Map refs:** 307 D5, 321 K8
How to book: Great Northern Hwy, Fitzroy Crossing (08) 9191 5141 www.fitzroyriverlodge.com.au

352 Gibb River Crossing camping area

Bring a gas/fuel stove and drinking water to this rest area, 3.2 km north of the Gibb River Rd. It is suitable for an overnight stop only. **Map refs:** 307 D3, 321 L5
Who to contact: Shire of Wyndham–East Kimberley (08) 9168 1677 *Road conditions:* WA Main Roads 1800 013 314, 13 8138

Gibb River Road

The Gibb River Rd was originally built to transport cattle from the surrounding stations to Derby and Wyndham. Since those stations opened their doors to travellers, it has become one of Australia's most popular tourist routes. It provides access to the magnificent Kimberley region and its very diverse landscapes, which range from lush, tropically vegetated river gorges and rainforests, to vast savannah woodlands and open plains, all of which have stood the test of time and prospered despite human intervention. The road covers a distance of about 650 km and should only be travelled in the dry season, May–Nov.

■ *Please note that campsites are listed in alphabetical*
■ *order, not track order. Refer to the map on p. 307 for*
■ *further information.*

Who to contact: Derby Visitor Centre (08) 9191 1426, 1800 621 426; or Kununurra Visitor Centre (08) 9168 1177; or Wyndham Tourist Information Centre (08) 9161 1281 *Road conditions:* WA Main Roads 1800 013 314, 13 8138

344 Birdwood Downs Station
See p. 309.

346 Charnley River Homestead
See p. 310.

347 Diggers Rest Station
See p. 310.

348 El Questro Station – Black Cockatoo camping area
See p. 310.

349 El Questro Station – Riverside camping
See p. 310.

350 Ellenbrae Station
See p. 310.

353 Home Valley Station
See below.

354 Mornington Wilderness Camp
See p. 312.

355 Mount Barnett Roadhouse – Manning Gorge camping area
See p. 313.

356 Mount Elizabeth Station
See p. 313.

357 Halls Creek Caravan Park

This caravan park offers visitors basic facilities near the site of the first gold rush in WA, back in 1855. **Map refs:** 307 E5, 321 N7
How to book: Roberta Ave, Halls Creek (08) 9168 6169

353 Home Valley Station

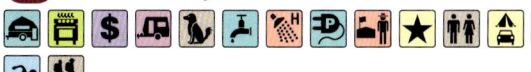

Set at the foot of the majestic Cockburn Range, Home Valley Station is an outback adventure playground. It features a breathtaking combination of towering gorges, sparkling waterholes, billabongs, waterfalls and ancient landforms. From gentle gorge walks and relaxing boating to adventurous horse treks and cattle mustering, Home Valley Station has an inspiring range of tours and activities available. Shady campsites are on offer at the homestead for those who enjoy relaxing by the lagoon-style pool, and there is riverside camping on the mighty Pentecost a few kilometres away, offering more basic charm. Home Valley Station is off the Gibb River Rd, 8.8 km west of the Pentecost River crossing and 106.5 km east of the road to Ellenbrae Station. **Map refs:** 307 E3, 321 N4
How to book: Gibb River Rd (08) 9161 4322 www.hvstation.com.au

358 Homestead Camp camping area

Adventurers in this isolated outback region will find an oasis in Homestead Camp, where a good range of services and facilities are provided. Scenic flights over the Kimberley's natural attractions are available here, and a chat with other visitors over a cold brew in the shady beer garden is a great way to end

the day. Homestead Camp is reached via Kalumburu Rd, 59 km north from the Gibb River Rd. **Map refs:** 307 D3, 321 L4
Who to contact: Drysdale River Station (08) 9161 4326
www.drysdaleriver.com.au

359 Honeymoon Beach camping area

Honeymoon Beach camping area is 26 km north of Kalumburu and offers basic facilities at either the beach or near the homestead, where there is some shade. Fishing and boating are the main activities here. **Map refs:** 307 D2, 321 L2
Who to contact: Kalumburu Mission (08) 9161 4300

360 Kalumburu Mission camping area

Kalumburu Mission camping and accommodation area is set in the picturesque Aboriginal community of Kalumburu, 413 km east of Derby and 265 km north of the Gibb River Rd. Visitors to this area can explore places of historic interest and try their luck at fishing and mudcrabbing at several nearby beaches. **Map refs:** 307 D2, 321 L2
How to book: Kalumburu Mission (08) 9161 4333

Kalumburu Road

Travellers to this remote region need to be well-prepared and only visit the area during the dry season. This long road stretches from the Gibb River Rd to Kalumburu on the north coast of WA; a distance of about 250 km through the more isolated and remote areas of the Kimberley region.

▪ *Please note that rest areas are listed in alphabetical order, not track order. Refer to the map on p. 307 for further information.*

Who to contact: Shire of Wyndham–East Kimberley (08) 9168 1677 *Road conditions:* WA Main Roads 1800 013 314, 13 8138

352 Gibb River Crossing camping area
See p. 310.

361 Plain Creek camping area
See p. 313.

362 Kooljaman camping area

Kooljaman camping area at Cape Leveque is part of an award-winning Aboriginal-owned wilderness camp, 208 km north of Broome. A beautiful and remote paradise, it offers visitors a quiet place to get away from it all. Cape Leveque is a popular spot to fish, swim and snorkel, or just sit back and relax on the pristine white-sand beach. A store, restaurant and other accommodation are available; bookings are essential. **Map refs:** 307 B4, 320 H5
How to book: Cape Leveque (08) 9192 4970
www.kooljaman.com.au

363 Kununurra Agricultural Society Showgrounds

Only visitors with pets and large camping rigs can stay at this showgrounds caravan park. Within walking distance of town, it offers basic camping facilities but is closed in July, when the local show takes over the site. **Map refs:** 307 F3, 321 O4

How to book: cnr Ivanhoe Rd and Coolibah Dr, Kununurra 0417 823 693

364 La Djardarr Bay Community camping area

With basic facilities for campers who enjoy solitude and fishing, La Djardarr Bay Community camping area is 42 km east of the Broome–Cape Leveque Rd. The small camping area is under the shade of some gum trees near the beach, 149 km north of Broome. **Map refs:** 307 B4, 320 H6

Who to contact: (08) 9192 4891

365 Lake Argyle Caravan Park

Lake Argyle is Australia's largest body of fresh water, covering over 800 sq km at normal full-supply level and in excess of 2000 sq km at flood capacity. Adjacent to the lake, 70 km south-east of Kununurra, Lake Argyle Caravan Park provides visitors with a good range of facilities, a choice of accommodation and grassed, shady sites, as well as water-based pastimes such as fishing, boating, canoeing and swimming. **Map refs:** 307 F3, 321 O4

How to book: Lake Argyle Rd (08) 9168 7777 www.lakeargyle.com.au

366 Lakeside Resort

Lakeside Resort's caravan park offers travellers shady, grassed sites with water views in a tranquil, relaxing environment. It is an ideal base from which to explore the raw wilderness of the Kimberley. A swimming pool, store, bar and restaurant facilities are available for visitors, as is other accommodation. The resort is 2 km south-east of Kununurra on the eastern side of town via Casuarina Way, off Victoria Hwy. **Map refs:** 307 F3, 321 O4

How to book: Casuarina Way, Kununurra (08) 9169 1092, 1800 786 692 www.lakeside.com.au

367 McGowans Beach camping area

North of Kalumburu, McGowans Beach provides basic facilities for visitors who like to camp close to a beach where boating and fishing are the main activities. **Map refs:** 307 D2, 321 L2

Who to contact: Kalumburu Mission (08) 9161 4300

368 Mambi Island camping area

This camping area has dispersed sites set among paperbark trees near the boat ramp on the bank of the Ord River, in an area that is popular for fishing. Bring firewood and drinking water. Mambi Island is 45.9 km north of Kununurra via the Victoria Hwy, then a turn-off to Parry Creek Rd. **Map refs:** 307 F3, 321 O4

Who to contact: Kununurra Visitor Centre (08) 9168 1177 *Road conditions:* Shire of Wyndham–East Kimberley (08) 9168 1677

369 Middle Lagoon Natures Hideaway camping area

This camping area is 32 km west of the Cape Leveque Rd, sited in shady native scrub near the foreshore. It has basic facilities and is a good spot for fishing, swimming or just relaxing on the beach. Bring your own firewood. Take the turn-off from the Cape Leveque Rd, 145 km north of Broome. **Map refs:** 307 B4, 320 H6

How to book: Cape Leveque Rd (08) 9192 4002 www.middlelagoon.com.au

370 Miners Pool camping area

Miners Pool camping area on Drysdale River Station is 5 km from the homestead and 59 km north of the Gibb River Rd, on the banks of the Drysdale River. Basic facilities are provided in a large area among the trees. Fishing and swimming in a natural outback environment are the highlights here, but it's only a short drive to the homestead, where a range of services and facilities are available. Bring drinking water and drop into the homestead to check in when you arrive. **Map refs:** 307 D3, 321 L4

Who to contact: Drysdale River Station (08) 9161 4326 www.drysdaleriver.com.au

354 Mornington Wilderness Camp

Mornington Wilderness Camp is 95 km south-east of the Gibb River Rd. The turn-off is 53.7 km south-west of Mt Barnett Roadhouse and 25.5 km north-east of Imintji Roadhouse. The camping area is set in a wildlife sanctuary, with shady sites in the bush alongside a creek. Visitors will be delighted by the wildlife that frequents the camping area. As well as basic camping facilities, there is also a bar, restaurant and other accommodation available. **Map refs:** 307 D4, 321 L7

How to book: Gibb River Rd (08) 9191 7406, 1800 631 946

355 Mount Barnett Roadhouse – Manning Gorge camping area

The camping area at Manning Gorge is 7 km north of the roadhouse, with shady sites on the riverbank and a good range of facilities. Its swimming hole is reputedly the best in the region, so it's a very popular spot in the dry season. Additional accommodation is available at the roadhouse. Bring firewood and drinking water to this camping area on the Gibb River Rd, 406 km west of Kununurra, 108 km south-west of the Kalumburu Rd junction and 309 km east of Derby. **Map refs:** 307 D4, 321 L5

How to book: Gibb River Rd (08) 9191 7007

356 Mount Elizabeth Station

This working cattle station welcomes visitors to its homestead and shady camping area, as do the dozens of wallabies and kangaroos that come out to graze. The station is 30 km off the Gibb River Rd, 38 km north-east of Mt Barnett Roadhouse and 70 km south of the Kalumburu Rd junction. Most days here finish with impressive sunsets followed by a wonderful view of the stars. Day tours, swimming and fishing are also on offer. **Map refs:** 307 D3, 321 L5

How to book: Gibb River Rd (08) 9191 4644
www.mountelizabethstation.com

371 Pago Mission camping area (bush camping)

Pago Mission camping area is 25 km north of Kalumburu and offers secluded camping for self-sufficient campers only. Bring your own drinking water. **Map refs:** 307 D2, 321 L2

Who to contact: Kalumburu Mission (08) 9161 4300

361 Plain Creek camping area

Suitable for an overnight stop, this rest area on the Kalumburu Rd is 15.9 km north of the Gibb River Rd on the eastern side of the river. A gas/fuel stove is preferred and you need to bring your own drinking water. **Map refs:** 307 D3, 321 L4

Who to contact: Shire of Wyndham–East Kimberley (08) 9168 1677 *Road conditions:* WA Main Roads 1800 013 314, 13 8138

372 Port Smith Lagoon Caravan Park

This park is about 160 km south of Broome off the Great Northern Hwy, where a clearly signposted turn-off takes you 23 km down a well-maintained dirt road. The park has good facilities and shaded sites, as well as diesel and unleaded fuel. Anglers can try their luck at fishing or mudcrabbing, or you can have a round of bush golf. **Map refs:** 307 A5, 320 G8

How to book: via Great Northern Hwy (08) 9192 4983
www.portsmithcaravanpark.com.au

373 Prices Point camping area

No facilities are provided here, so self-sufficient campers might find a secluded spot for a bit of fishing. A gas/fuel stove is preferred and you need to bring drinking water. The camping area is 13.4 km north of the access track to Quondong Point. A 3-night maximum stay applies. **Map refs:** 307 B4, 320 G7

Who to contact: Shire of Broome (08) 9191 3456; or Broome Visitor Centre (08) 9192 2222

374 Quondong Point camping area

A good spot for self-sufficient campers who enjoy fishing, the track to this camping area is 7.6 km north of Barred Creek. You need to come equipped with drinking water and firewood, or preferably a gas/fuel stove, as fire bans can apply. There are 3 camping areas here, 1.6 km, 2.7 km and 3 km from Manari Rd. Maximum stay is 3 nights. **Map refs:** 307 B4, 320 G7

Who to contact: Shire of Broome (08) 9191 3456; or Broome Visitor Centre (08) 9192 2222

375 Skull Rock camping area

This area floods in the wet season so the campsite is very rocky and sandy. There are basic facilities here as well as the chance to catch a good feed of fish. Come with your own firewood and drinking water. The camping area is a large open site on the banks of the Ord River, 36.6 km north of Kununurra via Carlton Hill and Weaber Plains rds. **Map refs:** 307 F3, 321 O4

Who to contact: Kununurra Visitor Centre (08) 9168 1177 *Road conditions:* Shire of Wyndham–East Kimberley (08) 9168 1677

376 Tarangau Caravan Park

This park has good facilities and is located within walking distance of the famous Cable Beach, as well as restaurants and cafes, although it is about 5 km from Broome's major shopping centre. Enjoy walks along the glorious white sand or take a camel ride along the beach; be sure to experience the fantasic sunsets over the water. **Map refs:** 307 B5, 320 H8

How to book: 66 Millington Rd, Cable Beach, Broome (08) 9193 5084 www.tarangaucaravanpark.com

377 Tarunda Caravan Park

Visitors to Fitzroy Crossing can explore the nearby national park at Geike Gorge or access the Fitzroy River for fishing and swimming. The small town on the edge of the Great Sandy Desert is between Derby and Halls Creek on the Great Northern Hwy. Tarunda Caravan Park offers travellers a good range of facilities, with grassed sites among shady trees. **Map refs:** 307 D5, 321 K8

How to book: 272 Forrest Rd, Fitzroy Crossing (08) 9191 5330

378 Willie Creek camping area

Bring drinking water and a gas/fuel stove to this small area on the beach north of Broome. It is a good spot for boating and fishing but has no facilities, so is better suited to self-sufficient campers. The camping area is 7.1 km along Willie Creek Rd, off Manari Rd. Maximum stay 3-nights. **Map refs:** 307 B5, 320 G7

Who to contact: Shire of Broome (08) 9191 3456; or Broome Visitor Centre (08) 9192 2222

South-western Western Australia

0 20 40 60 80 km

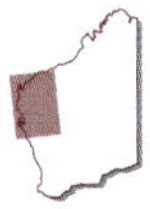

Central-western Western Australia

0   50   100   150   200 km

WITTENOOM: The blue asbestos dust present in and around Wittenoom may cause cancer if inhaled. While the risk from such fibres to short term visitors is significantly less than to residents, the Ashburton Shire Council advocates avoidance of the Wittenoom area.

INDIAN OCEAN

KARRATHA
Dampier
Wickham
Point Samson
Cossack
Roebourne
Whim Creek
Karratha Travel Stop Roadhouse

MILLSTREAM–CHICHESTER NATIONAL PARK

Yandeyarra
MUNGAROONA RANGE NATURE RESERVE

Wittenoom
Auski Roadhouse

KARIJINI NP
Tom Price
KARIJINI NATIONAL PARK

Paraburdoo

PILBARA
HAMERSLEY RANGE

Fortescue Roadhouse
Pannawonica
Onslow

Nanutarra Roadhouse

BARLEE RANGE NATURE RESERVE

CAPRICORN

Exmouth
Learmonth
EXMOUTH GULF
CAPE RANGE NP
SANDALWOOD PENINSULA
NINGALOO MARINE PARK
Ningaloo Reef

Coral Bay
NINGALOO MARINE PARK
Pelican Point
Warroora
Amherst Point
Cape Farquhar
Gnaraloo Bay

Red Bluff
Cape Cuvier
Quobba
Point Quobba
Carnarvon

BARLEE RANGE

MOUNT AUGUSTUS NP
Burringurrah
BURRINGURRAH (MT JAMES)

COLLIER RANGE NP

KENNEDY RANGE NATIONAL PARK

Gascoyne Junction

Bernier Island
Dorre Island
BERNIER AND DORRE ISLANDS NR
SHARK BAY WORLD HERITAGE AREA
Cape St Cricq
Cape Inscription
West Point
DIRK HARTOG
Dirk Hartog Island
Quoin Head
NATIONAL PARK
FRANCOIS PERON NP
PERON PENINSULA
Monkey Mia
Faure Is
Denham
Gladstone
Peron

Meekatharra

Wooramel Roadhouse

Steep Point
Thunder Bay
False Entrance
Carrarang
CARARANG PENINSULA
Tamala

Nanga Station
Nilemah
Hamelin
Coburn
HAMELIN POOL MARINE NATURE RESERVE

Overlander Roadhouse
Billabong Roadhouse
Murchison

TOOLONGA NATURE RESERVE

SHARK BAY WORLD HERITAGE AREA
ZUYTDORP NATURE RESERVE

Cue
Tuckanarra
WILGIE-MIA
NICHOLSON RANGE
PIA WADJARRI

KALBARRI NP
Kalbarri
Bluff Point

WANDANA NATURE RESERVE
Yalgoo
Mount Magnet
Paynes Find

Binnu
Hutt
Ogilvie
Gregory
Horrocks
Northampton
Naraling
Mullewa
Pindar
Curara
Tardun
Canna

GERALDTON
Mount Pleasant
Walkaway
Cape Burney

INDIAN OCEAN

HOUTMAN ABROLHOS
WALLABI GROUP
EASTER GROUP
North Island

Joins map 320
Joins map 318

Southern Western Australia

0   50   100   150   200 km

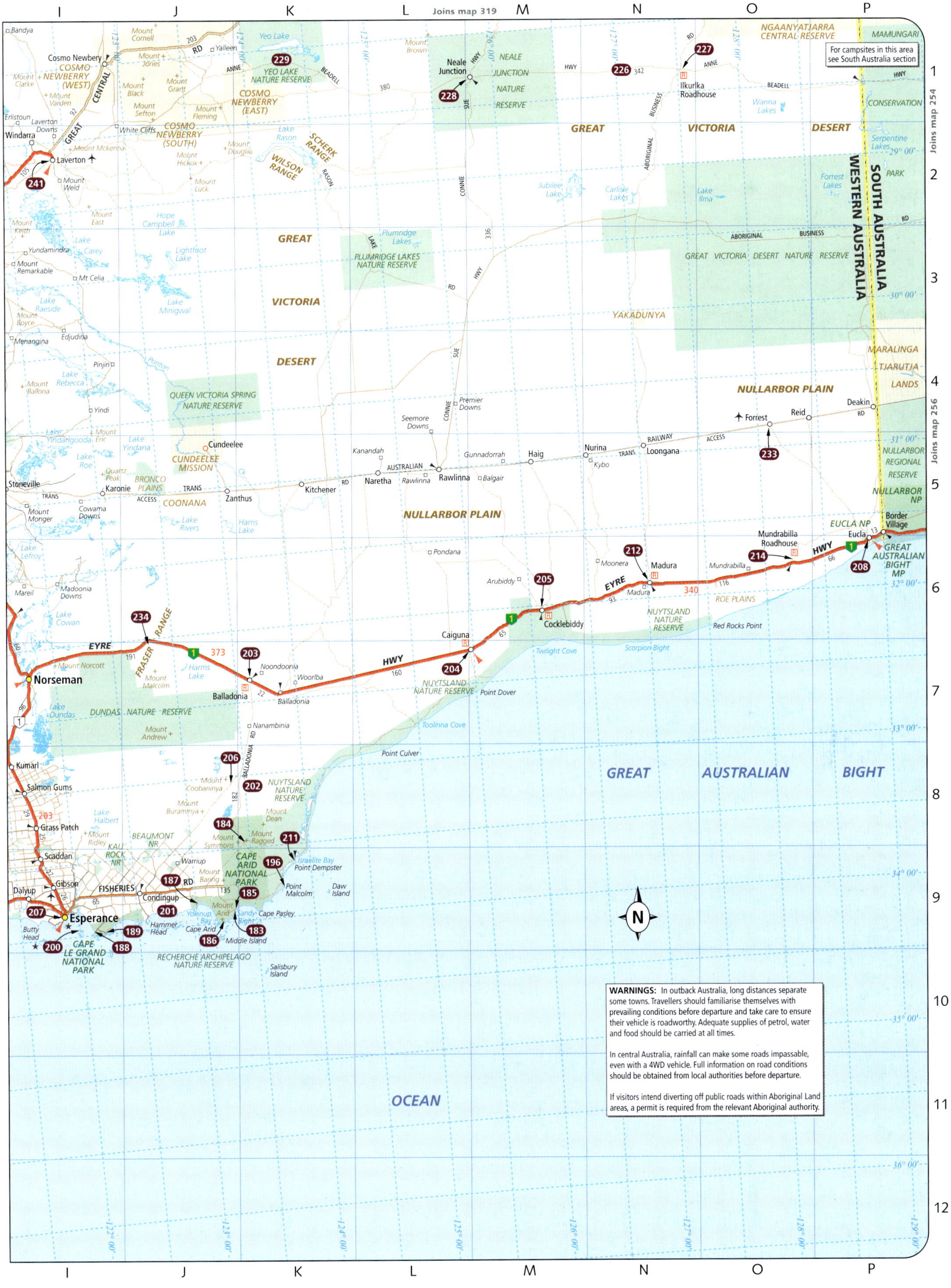

WARNINGS: In outback Australia, long distances separate some towns. Travellers should familiarise themselves with prevailing conditions before departure and take care to ensure their vehicle is roadworthy. Adequate supplies of petrol, water and food should be carried at all times.

In central Australia, rainfall can make some roads impassable, even with a 4WD vehicle. Full information on road conditions should be obtained from local authorities before departure.

If visitors intend diverting off public roads within Aboriginal Land areas, a permit is required from the relevant Aboriginal authority.

Central Western Australia

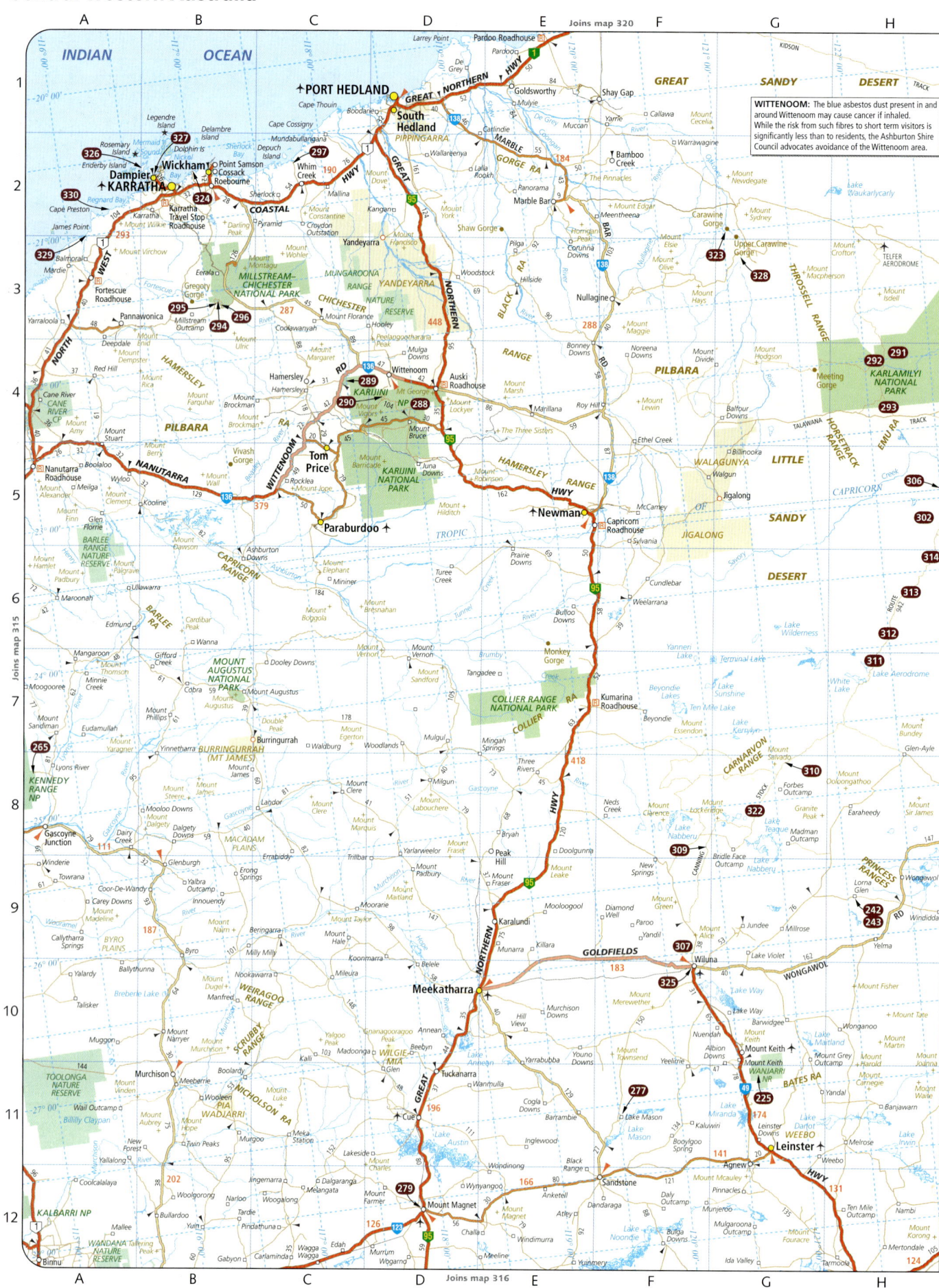

WITTENOOM: The blue asbestos dust present in and around Wittenoom may cause cancer if inhaled. While the risk from such fibres to short term visitors is significantly less than to residents, the Ashburton Shire Council advocates avoidance of the Wittenoom area.

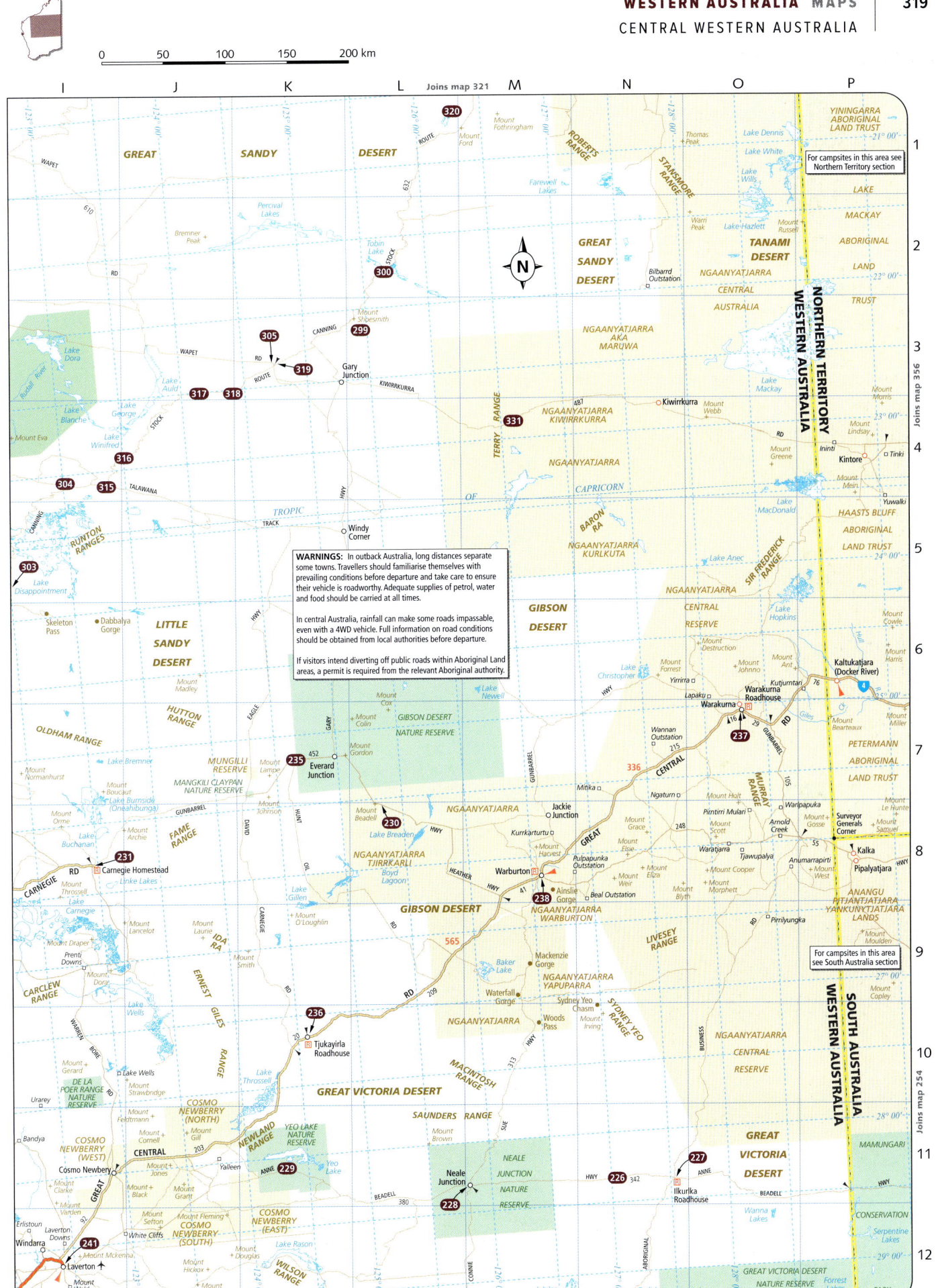

0   50   100   150   200 km

For campsites in this area see
Northern Territory section

WARNINGS: In outback Australia, long distances separate
some towns. Travellers should familiarise themselves with
prevailing conditions before departure and take care to ensure
their vehicle is roadworthy. Adequate supplies of petrol, water
and food should be carried at all times.

In central Australia, rainfall can make some roads impassable,
even with a 4WD vehicle. Full information on road conditions
should be obtained from local authorities before departure.

If visitors intend diverting off public roads within Aboriginal Land
areas, a permit is required from the relevant Aboriginal authority.

For campsites in this area
see South Australia section

Joins map 356

Joins map 254

Northern Western Australia

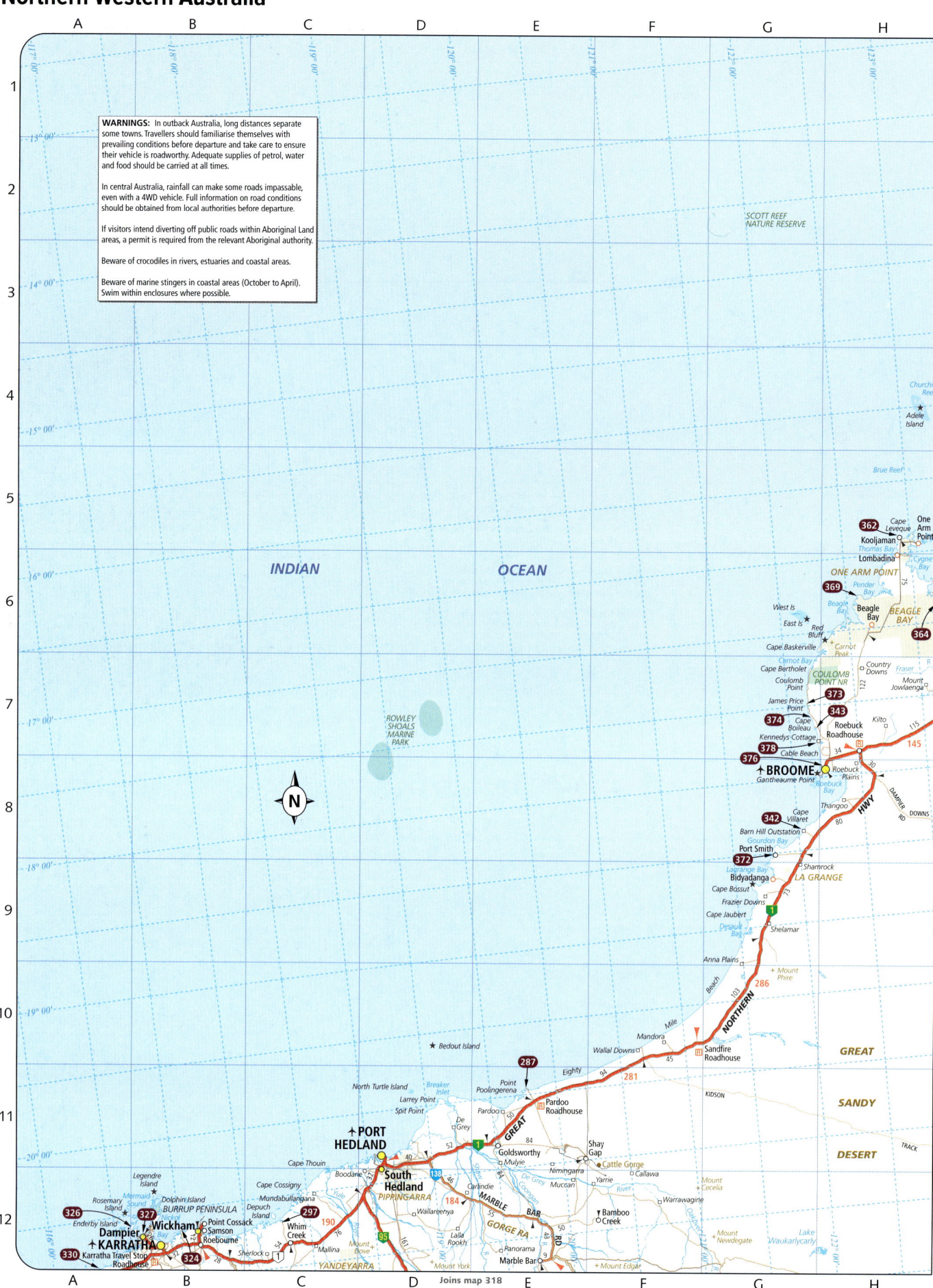

WARNINGS: In outback Australia, long distances separate some towns. Travellers should familiarise themselves with prevailing conditions before departure and take care to ensure their vehicle is roadworthy. Adequate supplies of petrol, water and food should be carried at all times.

In central Australia, rainfall can make some roads impassable, even with a 4WD vehicle. Full information on road conditions should be obtained from local authorities before departure.

If visitors intend diverting off public roads within Aboriginal Land areas, a permit is required from the relevant Aboriginal authority.

Beware of crocodiles in rivers, estuaries and coastal areas.

Beware of marine stingers in coastal areas (October to April). Swim within enclosures where possible.

INDIAN OCEAN

Joins map 318

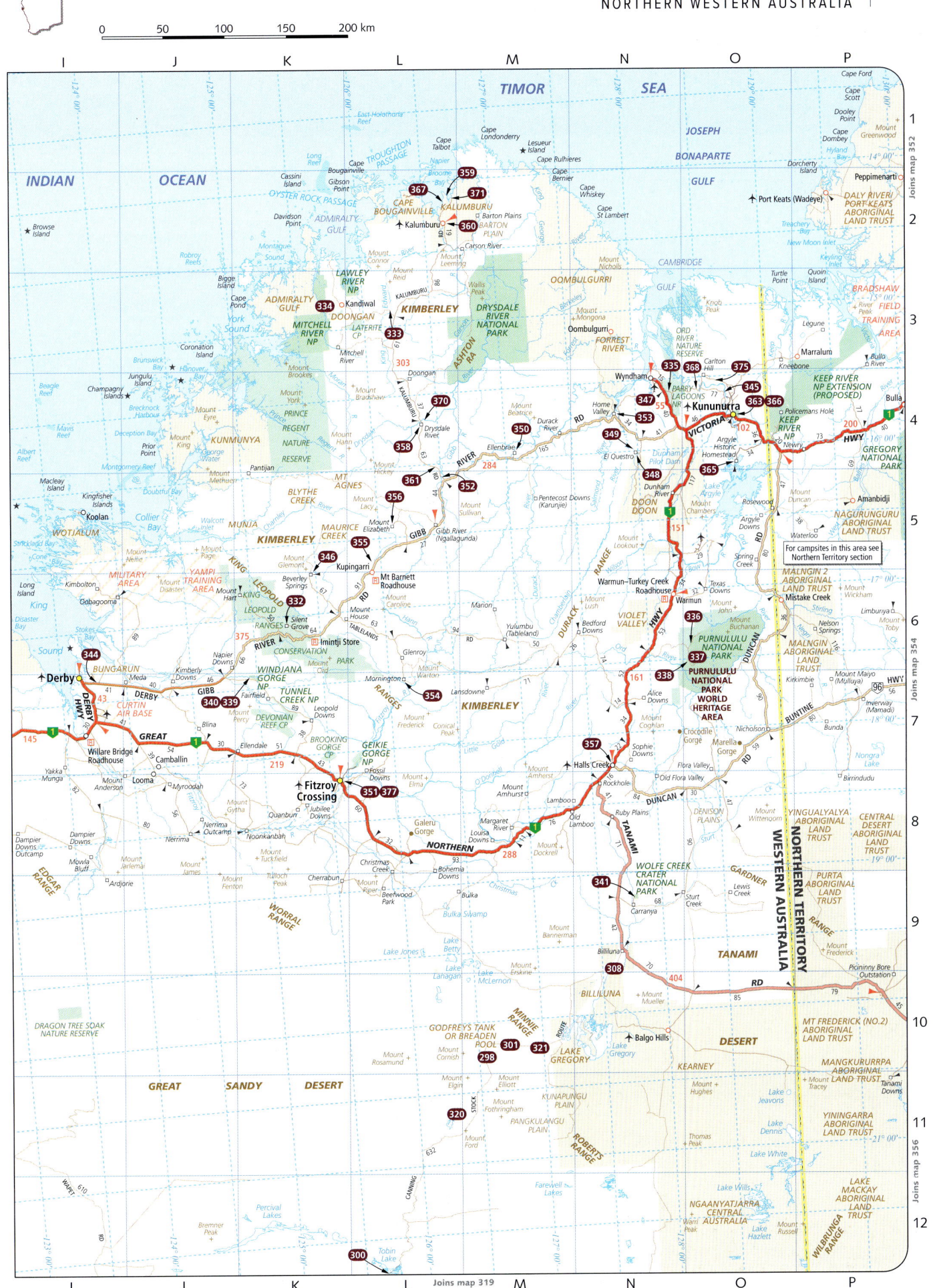

NORTHERN TERRITORY

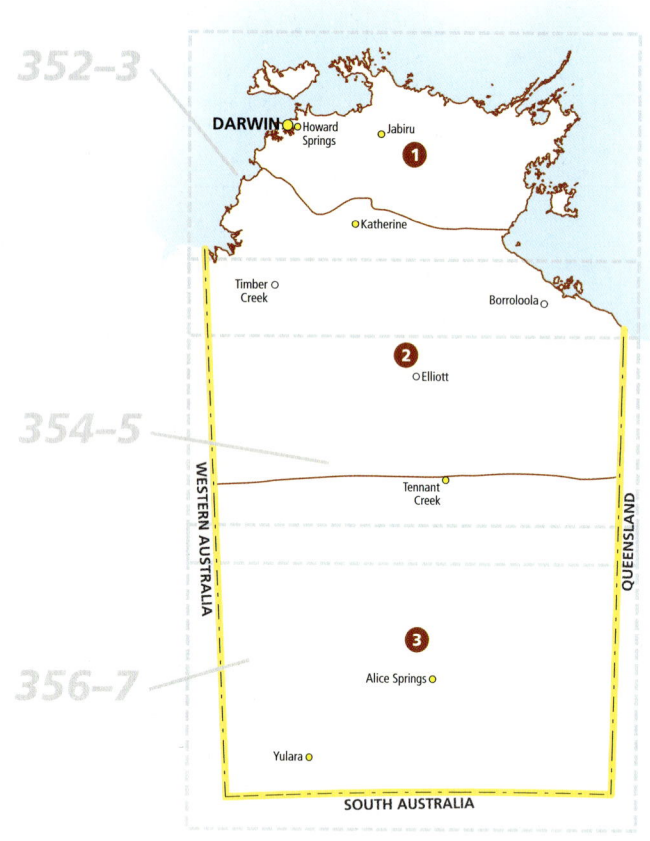

352–3

DARWIN

Howard Springs

Jabiru

1

Katherine

Timber Creek

Borroloola

2

Elliott

354–5

WESTERN AUSTRALIA

Tennant Creek

QUEENSLAND

356–7

3

Alice Springs

Yulara

SOUTH AUSTRALIA

BEST CAMPSITES

Douglas Daly Tourist Park
(Darwin, Kakadu and Arnhem Land), p. 327

John Hayes Rockhole camping area
Trephina Gorge Nature Park (Red Centre), p. 345

Old Police Station Waterhole camping area
Davenport Range National Park (Red Centre), p. 344

**Paradise Bay camping area
(boat-based camping)**
Barranyi (North Island) National Park (Gulf to Gulf), p. 333

**Sweetwater Pool camping area
(walk-in camping)**
Nitmiluk National Park (Gulf to Gulf), p. 338

USEFUL CONTACTS

Bushfires Council NT
(08) 8922 0844
http://www.nretas.nt.gov.au/natural-resource-management/bushfires

Central Land Council
(08) 8951 6211
www.clc.org.au

Emergency
Dial 000 for police, ambulance and fire brigade

Fisheries – Department of Primary Industry, Fisheries and Resources
(08) 8999 2144
www.nt.gov.au/d/Fisheries

Fossicking – Department of Primary Industry, Fisheries and Resources
(08) 8999 5322
http://www.nt.gov.au/d/Minerals_Energy

Northern Land Council
(08) 8920 5100
www.nlc.org.au

Northern Territory Land Information System – Road Report
1800 246 199
www.ntlis.nt.gov.au/roadreport

Parks and Wildlife Service
(08) 8999 5511
http://www.nretas.nt.gov.au/national-parks-and-reserves

Uluṟu–Kata Tjuṯa National Park Information Centre
(08) 8956 1128
www.environment.gov.au/parks/uluru

Curtin Springs Roadhouse, Red Centre region (p. 348)

DARWIN, KAKADU AND ARNHEM LAND

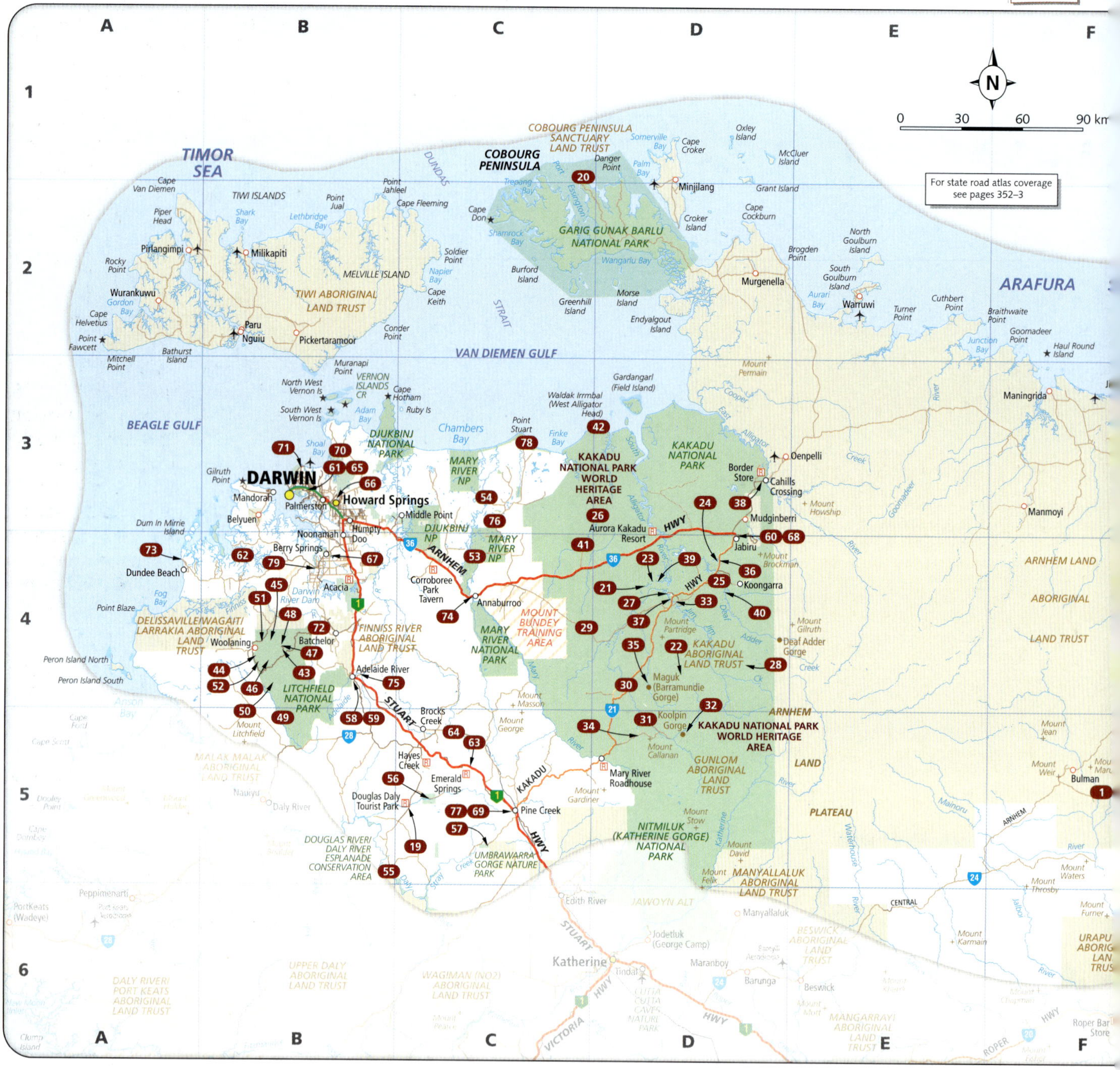

STEAMY AND BROODING, SOAKED in natural wonders and hidden delights, the Top End is ideal for adventurous campers. There is great fishing for barramundi and saratoga almost everywhere you go, and wildlife oozes out of every landscape – from the hidden presence of saltwater crocodiles to the rich birdlife, with more than one-third of Australia's birds found in the Top End's national parks.

Delve into the bountiful Aboriginal history of this area for yet more rewards, with stunning, multi-layered artworks dating back 20 000 years or more, as well as some of contemporary Australia's richest cultural experiences. Learn to play a didgeridoo or throw a spear, or listen as Aboriginal rangers tell ancient stories of the creation of the landscape and the law.

Kakadu remains the most iconic national park in this area, and it has plenty of campsites to choose from. But don't let your experience of the Top End stop there – venture out into Litchfield National Park, or into the enormous basin of the Douglas and Daly rivers. You'll find beautiful and safe swimming holes, thermal springs and places to just let the wildlife come to you.

The most popular time for camping in this area is during the Dry (Apr–Sept), when temperatures are slightly cooler and the humidity is bearable. During the build-up (Oct–Dec) the humidity

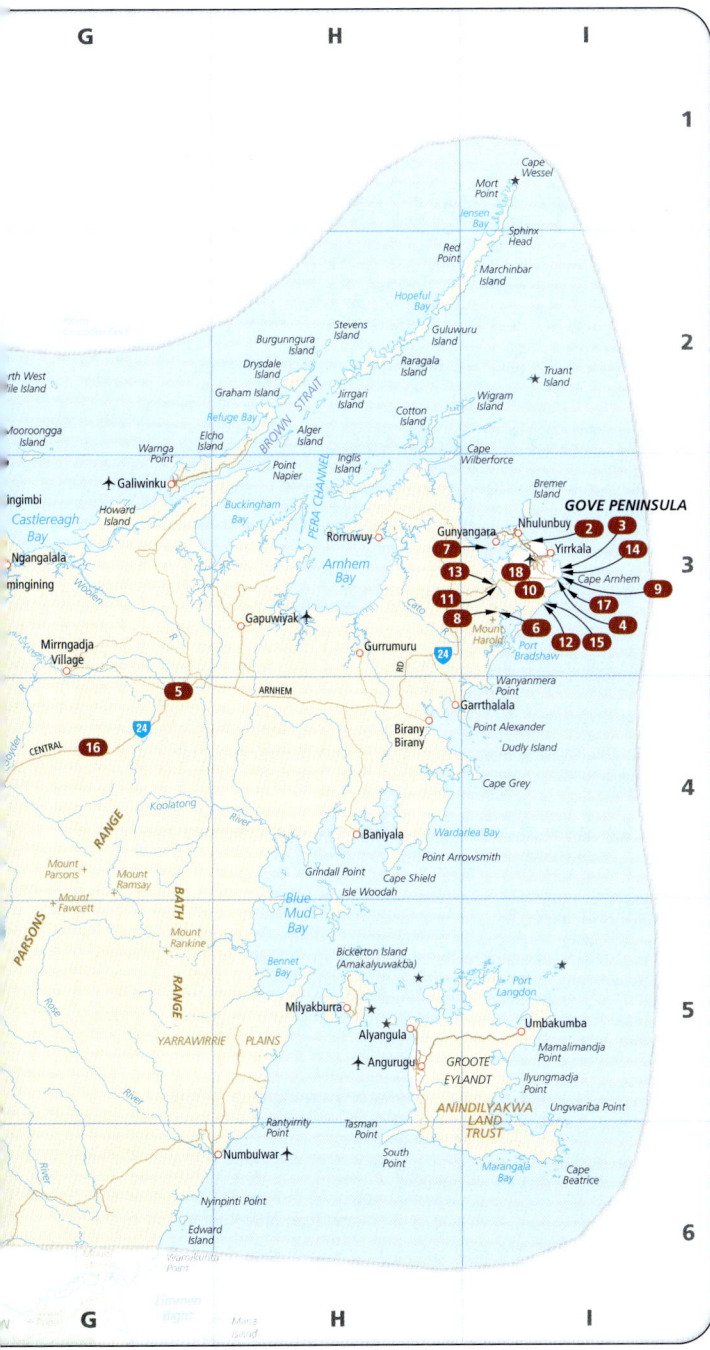

can be uncomfortable, and during the Wet (Dec–Apr) some remote areas can be inaccessible, although the country is probably at its most spectacular at this time. Mosquitoes and other insects can be a problem, so do up your tents, and bring a good mozzie net and plenty of insect repellent.

CAMPSITES LOCATED IN PARKS AND RESERVES

ARNHEM LAND

Arnhem Land is becoming more and more accessible for people who want a unique camping experience. Permits are required to travel the Central Arnhem Rd to east Arnhem Land and there are limited places to stay on the way. The journey is an adventure: it's a 710 km 4WD journey from Katherine to Nhulunbuy, and travellers need to be self-sufficient. The road has river crossings, corrugations and sandy stretches. But it's all worthwhile: there are several great stops en route – in particular, Baghetti Homeland near Bulman. Once at Nhulunbuy, there are some magnificent pristine and remote camping areas to explore; contact Lirrwi Tourism for more information.

Who to contact: Northern Land Council (08) 8920 5100 for permission to travel Central Arnhem Rd; Lirrwi Tourism (08) 8987 2828 for Baghetti Homeland and Gulkula Campground; Dhimurru Aboriginal Corporation (08) 8939 2700 for all other camping areas
Permits: permission is needed from Northern Land Council (08) 8920 5100 to travel the Central Arnhem Rd and to access Baghetti Homeland and Gulkula Campground, a Visitor's Permit from Dhimurru Aboriginal Corporation (08) 8939 2700 is required to access recreational areas on Aboriginal land, and special permits are required for Cape Arnhem, Wonga Creek, Memorial Park and Scout Camp

1 Baghetti Homeland camping area

Bagetti Homeland is 48 km from Bulman – on the Central Arnhem Hwy – along a 4WD track which can be sandy. Camping is on a lovely stretch of river alongside a paperbark forest for shade and with riverside fishing. There is a camp kitchen, toilets and shower. The traditional owners offer guided walks and bush-food walks along the river and lagoon and through the forest. Basic provisions are available from the Bulman store. Note: alcohol is not allowed. **Map refs:** 324 F5, 353 J7

2 Banambarrnga (Rainbow Cliffs) camping area (bush camping)

This camping area is 9 km from Nhulunbuy on a rough 4WD track. Campers need to be self-sufficient and bring their own water. **Map refs:** 325 I3, 353 N4

3 Baringura (Little Bondi Beach) camping area (bush camping)

Out in the northern beaches area, this camping site is 41 km from Nhulunbuy via a sandy 4WD track. There are toilets but you need to bring your own drinking water. **Map refs:** 325 I3, 353 N4

4 **Binydjarrna (Daliwuy Bay) camping area**

Binydjarrna is 35.5 km from Nhulunbuy, on the northern beaches, along a rough 4WD track. Trailers are permitted and there is a boat ramp. Bring your own drinking water. **Map refs:** 325 I3, 353 N4

5 **Flat Rock Creek Crossing camping area (bush camping)**

This small site with no facilities is on the Central Arnhem Rd, 108 km north of the Ramingining Rd junction. It is to the east of the road, on the south side of the creek crossing. Bring your own drinking water. **Map refs:** 325 G4, 353 L5

6 **Ganami (Wonga Creek) camping area (bush camping)**

In the inland waterways region, this camping site is 57 km from Nhulunbuy along a rough dirt 4WD track which is sometimes closed due to flooding. Bring your own drinking water. **Map refs:** 325 I3, 353 N4

7 **Ganinyara (The Granites) camping area (boat-based camping)**

There is a basic camping site at Ganinyara (Granite Islands). Bring your own everything. **Map refs:** 325 I3, 353 N4

8 **Gapuru (Memorial Park) camping area (bush camping)**

Gapuru is in the inland waterways, 65 km from Nhulunbuy along a rough 4WD track. Bring your own drinking water. **Map refs:** 325 I3, 353 N4

9 **Garanhan (Macassan Beach) camping area (bush camping)**

Part of the northern beaches, this camping site is 37.5 km from Nhulunbuy along a sandy 4WD track. There are toilets but bring your own drinking water. **Map refs:** 325 I3, 353 N4

10 **Gulkula Campground**

This is the site of the Garma Festival, normally held in the first week of August. For the dry season unpowered camping is available. The site is on the edge of an escarpment with views out to the coast and it is close to the northern beaches and Cape Arnhem. **Map refs:** 325 I3, 353 N4

11 **Guwatjurumurru (Giddy River) camping area (bush camping)**

This camping area is in the inland waterways area, approximately 50 km from Nhulunbuy along a rough 4WD track. There are no facilities. **Map refs:** 325 I3, 353 N4

12 **Lurrupukurru (Oyster Beach) camping area (bush camping)**

Lurrupukurru is on Cape Arnhem, 43.5 km from Nhulunbuy via a soft sand 4WD track. Bring your own drinking water. **Map refs:** 325 I3, 353 N4

13 **Mananggaymi (Scout Camp) camping area**

Mananggaymi is in the inland waterways, 48 km from Nhulunbuy along a 4WD track with a shallow creek crossing. Bring your own drinking water. **Map refs:** 325 I3, 353 N4

14 **Ngumuy (Turtle Beach) camping area (bush camping)**

Camping here is on the northern beaches 40 km from Nhulunbuy via 4WD over dirt and sand. Bring your own drinking water. **Map refs:** 325 I3, 353 N4

15 **Rangura (Caves Beach) camping area (bush camping)**

On Cape Arnhem, 39 km from Nhulunbuy, this site is accessed via a sandy 4WD track. Bring your own drinking water. **Map refs:** 325 I3, 353 N4

16 **Rocky Bottom Creek Crossing camping area (bush camping)**

On the north side of the road, on the east side of the crossing, this small site with no facilities is on the Central Arnhem Rd, 60 km north of the Ramingining Rd junction. **Map refs:** 325 G4, 353 L5

17 **Wanuwuy (Cape Arnhem) camping area (bush camping)**

Wanuwuy is on Cape Arnhem, 50 km from Nhulunbuy along a soft sandy 4WD track. Bring your own drinking water. **Map refs:** 325 I3, 353 N4

18 **Wathawuy (Latham River and Goanna Lagoon) camping areas (bush camping)**

These areas are approximately 30 km from Nhulunbuy along a rough 4WD track. Bring your own drinking water. **Map refs:** 325 I3, 353 N4

DOUGLAS RIVER/DALY RIVER ESPLANADE CONSERVATION AREA

This conservation area is a favourite spot for travellers visiting the hot springs and thermal pools at Tjuwaliyn (Douglas) Hot Springs Park and the beautiful Butterfly Gorge.

19 Douglas Daly Tourist Park

Base yourself here for an adventure in this less-travelled part of the Top End. The well-equipped park has fuel, alcohol, a restaurant and supplies, as well as a pool and beautiful river cascades to swim (observe crocodile warning signs within the area). Camp in the main area alongside the facilities or bush camp further up the Daly River near the Arches. **Map refs:** 324 C5, 352 E7

How to book: Oolloo Rd, off Stuart Hwy (08) 8978 2479
www.douglasdalypark.com.au

GARIG GUNAK BARLU NATIONAL PARK

A 4500 sq km combination of land and sea, this isolated national park has a stunning coastline perfect for sunsets, and wildlife galore. Tour the old Victoria Settlement for an insight into the past. The park is accessible by 4WD track or by boat.

How to book: PWCNT Black Point Ranger Station (08) 8979 0244
Permits: separate permission from the Northern Land Council is required if you wish to explore Arnhem Land; contact PWCNT for road access and camping permission (08) 8999 4814

20 Smith Point camping area

The park campground is 6 km north-east of the ranger station at Black Point. There are composting toilets, solar hot-water showers and bore water, BBQs and picnic tables. The campground has areas for those with generators and those without. There is great fishing but no craypots are allowed. There are beautiful coastal views but no swimming. Collect firewood before arriving at the campsite. **Map refs:** 324 C1, 352 F1

KAKADU NATIONAL PARK

Legendary for its wildlife, Indigenous culture, beautiful wetlands and sensational views from plunging escarpments, Kakadu is an iconic World Heritage Area, with plenty of scope for camping. It is huge, with a multitude of landscapes, habitats and wildlife. There are many thousands of plant species and insects as well as animals, reptiles and frogs. Camping opportunities range from managed campgrounds to free bush camping. Check the availability of facilities and make sure to take enough water. National Park rangers offer free guided walks and talks during the Dry, May–Oct. Many campsites close during the Wet, so it is best to check accessibility. A park pass is required for each person over the age of 16 who is not a NT resident; purchase the pass online or from the visitor centre.

Who to contact: PWCNT Kakadu (08) 8938 1120 *Permits:* required for campsite nos **22** and **32**, information and application forms are available online at www.environment.gov.au/parks/permits/kakadu-camping.html (campsite no. **22**) and at www.environment.gov.au/parks/permits/kakadu-jarrangbarnmi.html (campsite no. **32**)

21 Alligator Billabong camping area (bush camping)

Reached via the track to Red Lily Billabong by 4WD, this campsite is 26 km south of the Arnhem Hwy. There are no facilities, toilets or drinking water. **Map refs:** 324 D4, 352 G5

22 Bilkbilkmi (Graveside Gorge) camping area (bush camping)

You need to obtain a permit and book this basic bush site, which has no toilets or other facilities. The track in is suitable for experienced 4WD drivers only. You will find the camping area 44 km south-east of the Kakadu Hwy, with access 73 km south of the Bowali Visitor Centre. The site is sometimes closed to allow for cultural use by Aboriginal traditional owners. **Map refs:** 324 D4, 352 G6

23 Bucket Billabong camping area (bush camping)

No toilets or drinking water are available at this site, just 2 km past Red Lily Billabong camping area. You will need a 4WD. **Map refs:** 324 D4, 352 G5

24 Burdulba camping area

This camping area is near the turn-off for Nourlangie Rock, which has a number of impressive rock-art sites. Various walks link these sites, and there is also a track to the Nawurlandja Lookout, which gives good views over the surrounding countryside. There is no caravan access to Burdulba, and some campsites require a short carry-in, so are suitable for tents only. You will need to bring drinking water. Look for the sign 15 km south of the Bowali Visitor Centre. **Map refs:** 324 D4, 352 G5

25 Djarradjin Billabong (Muirella Park) camping area

One of the largest camping areas in Kakadu, this campground has showers and drinking water, and separate areas allowing generators and generator-free. Kakadu Culture Camp is also based here – it runs cruises on the billabong in the Dry (reservations are required). The camping area is about 6 km off the Kakadu Hwy, 26 km south of the Bowali Visitor Centre. **Map refs:** 324 D4, 352 G5

26 Four Mile Hole camping area (bush camping)

This 4WD site may be inaccessible in the Wet and has no toilets or drinking water. To get here, continue past Two Mile Hole for another 22 km. **Map refs:** 324 D3, 352 F4

27 Gagudju Camping Cooinda

The camping here is right on the doorstep of Yellow Water Billabong. Camp in powered or unpowered sites with access to

Gagudju Lodge Cooinda's pools and dining facilities. Spectacular wetland cruises run from here, and there are bush walks; tours are also available to Jim Jim Falls. The centre is 54 km from Jabiru down the Kakadu Hwy towards Pine Creek. Fires are not allowed but there are BBQ facilities. **Map refs: 324 D4, 352 G5**

28   Garnamarr (Jim Jim Falls) camping area

This is the closest campsite to the spectacular Jim Jim Falls. It can cater for 200 people, with showers and drinking water. It's accessible only in the dry season, and is a 60 km journey by 4WD on gravel roads. Turn east off the Kakadu Hwy, 43 km south of the Bowali Visitor Centre. **Map refs: 324 D4, 352 G6**

29   Giyamungkurr (Black Jungle Springs) camping area

You will need a 4WD to reach this basic site on the Old Jim Jim Rd, which links the Arnhem Hwy to the Kakadu Hwy, 18 km east of Bark Hut Inn. There are composting toilets but no drinking water. **Map refs: 324 C4, 352 F5**

30   Gungurul camping area

There is all-year-round access for camping and caravans here. There are picnic tables and toilets but bring drinking water and firewood. It is a 4 km bushwalk to the South Alligator River. Access is signposted off the Kakadu Hwy, 47 km north of the Mary River Roadhouse. **Map refs: 324 D4, 352 G6**

31   Gunlom camping area

This is a great camping spot with access to Gunlom Falls and a swimming hole (observe crocodile warning signs within the area), as well as a bushwalk to the top of the waterfall. There are separate generator and non-generator areas, BBQs, hot showers and drinking water. Follow Gunlom Rd for 22 km past the Kambolgie camping area to reach this site. Note: it is on a gravel road so check suitability for 2WD and caravans. **Map refs: 324 D5, 352 G6**

32   Jarrangbarnmi (Koolpin Gorge) camping area

You will need a special permit from the visitor's centre to camp here, beside Koolpin Creek. Take the Gunlom Rd off the Kakadu Hwy, 11 km north of Mary River Roadhouse, and follow it for 44 km, past Kambolgie and Gunlom camping sites. There are toilets but no showers or drinking water. **Map refs: 324 D5, 352 G6**

33   Jim Jim Billabong camping area

Jim Jim Billabong is near Yellow Waters (not close to Jim Jim Falls). You will need to bring firewood and drinking water to

this camping area. To get here, take the signposted access off Kakadu Hwy, 47 km south of the Bowali Visitor Centre, and drive for about 5 km. **Map refs: 324 D4, 352 G5**

34   Kambolgie camping area

Camp near the creek on the way to Gunlom. The site has toilets but no drinking water. To get here, take Gunlom Rd, 11 km north of the Mary River Roadhouse, and follow it for 13 km. **Map refs: 324 D5, 352 G6**

35   Maguk camping area

This basic campsite has a 2 km return bushwalk through monsoon forest to a plunge pool and waterfall (observe crocodile warning signs). There are toilets but no drinking water. Take the signposted turn-off from the Kakadu Hwy, 60 km north of the Mary River Roadhouse, and drive for 10 km. A 4WD is recommended. **Map refs: 324 D4, 352 G6**

36   Malabanjbanidju camping area

This site has 2 areas: one suitable for tents only, with a small carry-in from the carpark, and one for camper trailers and caravans. There is signposted access off the Kakadu Hwy, about 13 km south of the Bowali Visitor Centre. There are no showers or drinking water. During the Dry there is a 3.8 km hike, Ilgadjarr Walk, along the billabong. **Map refs: 324 D4, 352 G5**

37   Mardugal camping area

This large campsite has separate areas for tents and caravans/camper trailers with generators. It has showers and a boat ramp. Follow the signpost off the Kakadu Hwy, 50 km south of the Bowali Visitor Centre. Nearby attractions include the boardwalk on Home Billabong and cruises on Yellow Water Billabong. Sunrise cruises are magnificent and popular, so book ahead. You may spot a saltwater crocodile, and the birdlife is spectacular. **Map refs: 324 D4, 352 G5**

38   Merl camping area

Make the most of the good facilities at this large camping area. Take the Central Arnhem Rd, 36 km north of Jabiru, then turn onto the Ubirr–Oenpelli Rd. This camping area is close to the Ubirr rock-art site. There are great views from the escarpment at Ubirr and it is well worth the short hike up, especially for the sunset. **Map refs: 324 D3, 352 H4**

39   Red Lily Billabong camping area (bush camping)

Popular with anglers with a tinnie, this site has no toilets or drinking water and is 20 km off the Arnhem Hwy. Take the signposted turn-off, 90 km east of Bark Hut. **Map refs: 324 D4, 352 G5**

40 Sandy Billabong camping area

There is great birdwatching and just a few campsites at this 4WD area set alongside a billabong. Drive a further 6 km from Djarradjin Billabong to get here. **Map refs:** 324 D4, 352 G5

41 Two Mile Hole camping area (bush camping)

There are no toilets or drinking water at this site. Follow the sign from the Arnhem Hwy, 55 km east of Bark Hut, for 12 km. **Map refs:** 324 C4, 352 F5

42 Waldak Irrmbal (West Alligator Head) camping area

Continue by 4WD past the Two Mile Hole and Four Mile Hole camping areas to reach this remote site, 81 km north of the Kakadu Hwy. There are 2 camping areas: at Pokok's Beach, which has toilets; and at Middle Beach, which has no facilities. Bring your own drinking water. **Map refs:** 324 D3, 352 F4

LITCHFIELD NATIONAL PARK

Less visited than Kakadu, but equally spectacular, Litchfield National Park is only 1.5 hr south of Darwin. It has spring-fed waterfalls creating beautiful, crocodile-free swimming holes, and plains dotted with massive termite mounds. There are many short bushwalking trails plus the exceptional 39 km Tabletop Track circuit that links many of the park attractions. A sealed road allows easy access, although it is 4WD access only to the Lost City and Surprise Falls. Generators are not allowed anywhere in the park, firewood should be collected outside of the camping areas and water should be boiled. Caravans are only allowed at Wangi Falls, but note that there is no power.

Who to contact: PWCNT Batchelor (08) 8976 0282 *Permits:* if the Tabletop Track is closed (for example, during the Wet) a permit is required; contact PWCNT Batchelor (08) 8976 0282

43 Buley Rockhole camping area

Swim in the pools and cascades that tumble down the rocks. To get here, take the signposted turn-off from Litchfield Park Rd, 42 km south-west of Batchelor towards Florence Falls, and follow it for 2.5 km. Note: crocodiles may inhabit the area, observe warning signs. **Map refs:** 324 B4, 352 D5

44 Bush camp 1 – Tabletop Track (walk-in camping)

This camping area's only facility is toilets. The site is 4 km from Wangi Falls (clockwise around the track). **Map refs:** 324 B4, 352 D6

45 Bush camp 2 – Tabletop Track (walk-in camping)

This is a basic camping area 1.8 km from the end of the Walker Creek Link Walk. Toilets are provided. **Map refs:** 324 B4, 352 D5

46 Bush camp 3 – Tabletop Track (walk-in camping)

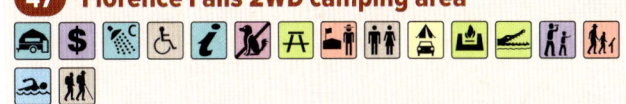

This basic camping area with toilets is 12.4 km from Florence Falls and 4.2 km from Wangi Falls. **Map refs:** 324 B4, 352 D6

47 Florence Falls 2WD camping area

Florence Falls is accessible down 160 steps or along Shady Creek Walk, about 1 km. At the bottom of the gorge there is a magnificent plunge pool and waterfall. Note: observe crocodile warning signs for other nearby waterways. Camping for 2WD vehicles is 4.5 km off Litchfield Park Rd, via the turn-off 42 km south-west of Batchelor. **Map refs:** 324 B4, 352 D5

48 Florence Falls 4WD camping area

This 4WD campsite is 1 km up the road from the area for 2WD vehicles. To reach it take the signposted turn-off, 42 km south-west of Batchelor. Note: you can swim in nearby waterways, but observe crocodile warning signs. **Map refs:** 324 B4, 352 D5

49 Surprise Creek Falls camping area

Walk through the bush to a beautiful waterhole with plunge pools hidden in the rocks (observe crocodile warning signs in the area). This is the most remote campsite in the park, is without drinking water and is off the Reynolds River 4WD track, about 16 km north of Daly River Rd and about 29 km south of Litchfield Park Rd. **Map refs:** 324 B5, 352 D6

50 Tjaynera (Sandy Creek) Falls camping area

A 3.4 km return walk takes you from here through cycads to a large plunge pool (observe crocodile warning signs within the area). This site off the Reynolds River 4WD track is 9 km south of Litchfield Park Rd. **Map refs:** 324 B4, 352 D6

51 Walker Creek camping area (walk-in camping)

Suitable only for tents, this walk-in camping area has just 6 sites along Walker Creek. Stroll along the creek to reach a quiet swimming hole (observe crocodile warning signs in the area). Bring drinking water. It's just off Litchfield Park Rd, 82 km west of Batchelor and 16 km past Wangi Falls. **Map refs:** 324 B4, 352 D5

52 Wangi Falls camping area

At Wangi Falls multiple waterfalls cascade down the escarpment. There is a beautiful swimming hole, boardwalk lookouts and a ridgetop walk. Swimming is only possible during the Dry (observe crocodile warnings) but there are magnificent views during the

Wet. This large campsite is only 1.5 km off Litchfield Park Rd. It's signposted 66 km west of Batchelor. **Map refs:** 324 B4, 352 D6

MARY RIVER NATIONAL PARK

Gentle bushwalks, great birdlife and some of the Top End's best fishing spots are some of the highlights of this national park. The landscape includes the Mary River, floodplains, billabongs, rainforest and paperbark forests. There are several walking trails and 4WD tracks. The park is 150 km east of Darwin on the Arnhem Hwy.

Who to contact: PWCNT Wildman (08) 8978 8986

53 Couzen's Lookout camping area

Take a walk by the river or stroll up to the lookout to witness spectacular Top End sunsets. You need to bring drinking water. To get here, take the Point Stuart Rd turn-off from the Arnhem Hwy then turn onto Rockhole Rd. **Map refs:** 324 C4, 352 E5

54 Shady Camp camping area

Shady Camp is a popular fishing and crocodile-spotting place. Bring your own drinking water. The site is 45 km from the Arnhem Hwy, off Point Stuart Rd. **Map refs:** 324 C3, 352 E4

OOLLOO CROSSING CONSERVATION AREA

This is a top spot for fishing enthusiasts who don't mind roughing it, and is situated along the picturesque Daly River. Keep an eye out for turtles, crocodiles, agile wallabies and myriad birdlife. A 4WD is recommended.

Who to contact: PWCNT Batchelor (08) 8976 0282

55 Oolloo Crossing camping area (bush camping)

Travel in a 4WD and bring your own gas/fuel stove and water to this bush camping site on Oolloo Rd by the Daly River, a 77 km drive south of Hayes Creek. **Map refs:** 324 B5, 352 E7

TJUWALIYN (DOUGLAS) HOT SPRINGS PARK

There is great wildlife here, everything from little red flying foxes to rich birdlife and unusual fish, but the main reason people come here is for the extraordinary hot springs. The best place to enjoy them is a few hundred metres downstream from the camping area, where the hot waters mingle with refreshing cool streams. Note: areas may be closed for cultural reasons, please respect these sacred places.

Who to contact: PWCNT Batchelor (08) 8976 0282

56 Douglas Hot Springs camping area

This reasonably large camping area has pit toilets and bore water and a designated area for generators. The park is about 50 km south of Hayes Creek off the Oolloo–Douglas Daly Rd. The last 7 km is a gravel road suitable for conventional vehicles as long as you take care. **Map refs:** 324 C5, 352 E7

Popular with Top End rockclimbers, this park has a deep gorge with sand-rimmed rockpools suitable for swimming. There are small nature walks and Aboriginal rock-art sites to explore.

Who to contact: PWCNT Batchelor (08) 8976 0282

57 Umbrawarra Gorge camping area

Camp near to the gorge entrance with easy walking and beautiful swimming in rocky pools and off the beach. The area is located 25 km south-west of Pine Creek off the Stuart Hwy. Bring your own drinking water and firewood. **Map refs:** 324 C5, 352 F7

CAMPSITES LOCATED IN OTHER AREAS

58 Adelaide River Inn Tourist Park

The park is part of the Adelaide River Inn, which has a bistro, bar and service station. The campground is quiet, with large, shady, grassed areas in a tropical garden. There are powered and unpowered sites and free BBQs. Dogs are allowed if on leash. Adelaide River is 1 hr south of Darwin with good access to Litchfield National Park and the historic Goldfields Loop. **Map refs:** 324 B4, 352 D6

How to book: Stuart Hwy, Adelaide River (08) 8976 7047 www.adelaideriverinn.com.au

59 Adelaide River Show Society Caravan Park

About 500 m off the Stuart Hwy and within an easy drive of Litchfield, this park is dog- and horse-friendly. It's a good stop-off on the way back from the Douglas Daly region. Note: no generators. **Map refs:** 324 B4, 352 D6

Who to contact: Dorat Rd, Adelaide River (08) 8976 7032

60 Aurora Kakadu Lodge

This is a convenient base to visit the rock-art sites of Ubirr and Nourlangie. Camping is in spacious, grassed areas, and powered and unpowered areas are available. There is a shaded swimming pool with a bistro alongside it. **Map refs:** 324 D4, 352 G5

How to book: Jabiru Dr, Jabiru (08) 8979 2422 www.auroraresorts.com.au

61 Aurora Shady Glen Tourist Park

This caravan park is the closest camping spot to Darwin's city centre. There is powered camping on grass or concrete sites

and plenty of shady, grassed areas for tents and trailers. Across the road is the Aviation Museum. **Map refs:** 324 B3, 352 D4

How to book: Farrell Cr, Winnellie (08) 8984 3330 www.shadyglen.com.au

62 Crab Claw Island Resort

Crab Claw is 130 km from Darwin and is almost completely surrounded by water. It has excellent fishing and is a laid-back, relaxing place to camp. There is a small campground with power to all sites (power is limited to 6 amps, which is enough to run air-con and the normal array of fridges) and access to a restaurant and bar that overlook the beach and the sea. There are 2 swimming pools and a boat ramp. **Map refs:** 324 B4, 352 D5

How to book: Bynoe Harbour (08) 8978 2313 www.crabclawisland.com.au

63 Emerald Springs Roadhouse

Emerald Springs is a bit of a surprise. There is just a small camping area with powered and unpowered sites, and camping is on large, grassy shaded sites with plenty of access for large trailers. The Bent Bull Bar and Grill is the local meeting place, serving great pub food in a lovely setting overlooking the bush. Emerald Springs has all the usual roadhouse facilities, such as fuel. Use this as a base to explore Butterfly Gorge, Douglas Daly and the Goldfields Loop. Emerald Springs is 160 km from Darwin. **Map refs:** 324 C5, 352 E6

How to book: Stuart Hwy, Emerald Springs (08) 8976 1169 www.emeraldsprings.com.au

64 Grove Hill Heritage Hotel

Grove Hill Heritage Hotel is located on the northern Goldfields Loop, which runs between the Stuart Hwy north of Emerald Springs and the Kakadu Hwy south of Pine Creek. It is one of the oldest pubs in the NT and everything about the place has character. It incorporates an amazing museum reflecting the hardships of life on the goldfields. Camping is behind the pub, with basic facilities and a communal spa. Free camping with live music is a fun event that takes place on the last Sat of each month. **Map refs:** 324 C5, 352 E6

How to book: Grove Hill Siding, near Adelaide River (08) 8978 2489

65 Hidden Valley Tourist Park

Only 10 km south of Darwin and off the Stuart Hwy, this quiet park has powered sites – ensuite bathrooms available – as well

as unpowered sites. The park has a cafe, swimming pool, BBQs and an internet kiosk. **Map refs:** 324 B3, 352 D4

How to book: 25 Hidden Valley Rd, Berrimah (08) 8984 2888, 1300 727 937 www.hiddenvalleytouristpark.com.au

66 Howard Springs Holiday Park

With Howard Springs National Park just up the road and extensive facilities on-site, this 6 ha Big4 caravan park is ideal for a relaxing stay in Darwin. It has 3 saltwater pools, 3 spas, squash courts, a TV room, games room and camp kitchen, as well as lots of trees. The park is 15 km south of Darwin. **Map refs:** 324 B3, 352 D4

How to book: 170 Whitewood Rd, Darwin (08) 8983 1169, 1800 831 169 www.howard-springs-holiday-park.nt.big4.com.au

67 Lakes Resort Caravan Park

Lakes Resort is well located for exploring the outer Darwin attractions, situated close to the Territory Wildlife Park, Berry Springs and Litchfield National Park. Powered and unpowered camping and caravan spots are on grassed or drive-through concrete sites. The camping areas are shady and surrounded by lovely grounds. **Map refs:** 324 B4, 352 D5

How to book: Doris Rd, Berry Springs (08) 8988 6277 www.lakesresortcaravanpark.com.au

68 Lakeview Park Kakadu

Lakeview offers easy access to Nourlangie and Ubirr rock-art sites and walking trails. There are powered and unpowered camping sites, some with ensuite toilet and shower facilities. It's a short walk to dining and supermarket facilities. **Map refs:** 324 D4, 352 G5

How to book: Lakeside Dr, Jabiru (08) 8979 3144 www.lakeviewkakadu.com.au

69 Lazy Lizard Tavern and Van Park

The caravan park at the Lazy Lizard has tropical landscaped grounds with powered and unpowered sites. The pub does good food, has a pool and is the information centre for local attractions. **Map refs:** 324 C5, 352 F7

Who to contact: Millar Tce, Pine Creek (08) 8976 1019 www.lazylizardpinecreek.com.au

70 Leaders Creek Fishing Base

The name says it all. On Leaders Creek, 40 km north of Howard Springs along Gunn Point Rd, this is an ideal base for anglers

as they fish 15 km of sheltered waterways, the mouth of the Adelaide River, or Vernons, Melville and Ruby islands. Bring your own boat or hire one here. Gunn Point Rd is dirt, but accessible to conventional vehicles. There are both powered and unpowered sites here. **Map refs: 324 B3, 352 D4**

How to book: Gunn Point Rd, Howard Springs (08) 8983 5009 www.leaderscreek.com

71 Lee Point Village Resort

Lee Point Village Resort is a large caravan park with ensuite sites as well as grassy powered and unpowered sites, plus camping areas. It is 14 km from the centre of Darwin, close to Casuarina Coastal Reserve and Lee Point beach. Facilities include 2 swimming pools, laundries and wood BBQs. **Map refs: 324 B3, 352 D4**

How to book: Lee Point Rd, Darwin (08) 8945 0535 www.leepointvillageresort.com.au

72 Litchfield Tourist Park

This camping area is just outside Litchfield National Park with its waterfalls, bushwalks and plunge pools. There are over 70 powered sites, plus unlimited unpowered ones. The park also has a bar and a restaurant. **Map refs: 324 B4, 352 D5**

How to book: Litchfield Park Rd, Rum Jungle (08) 8976 0070 www.litchfieldtouristpark.com.au

73 The Lodge of Dundee

The lodge is at the end of the road, about 150 km from Darwin and right on the beach, where fishing is the main activity. The setting is spectacular; enjoy magnificent sunsets. The camping area has powered and unpowered sites, basic facilities and a pool. There is also a bistro and bar. **Map refs: 324 A4, 352 C5**

How to book: Dundee Beach, Cox Peninsula (08) 8978 2557 www.thelodgeofdundee.com.au

74 Mary River Wilderness Retreat and Caravan Park

Mary River Wilderness Park is 110 km from Darwin en route to Kakadu National Park. There is a large, shady grassed area for powered and unpowered camping and there are great facilities, including a pool and a restaurant. The park is on the banks of the river. **Map refs: 324 C4, 352 E5**

How to book: Arnhem Hwy, Annaburroo (08) 8978 8877 www.maryriverpark.com.au

75 Mount Bundy Station

Historic Mt Bundy Station is a working cattle farm with camping alongside Adelaide River. It is very picturesque, set in a valley with the old farm buildings restored for accommodation surrounding a billabong. There are grassed, shady sites; some have power. There is also a pool (crocs inhabit the river). Fires are allowed and campfire social nights are organised in the dry season. **Map refs: 324 B4, 352 E6**

How to book: Haynes Rd, Adelaide River (08) 8976 7009 www.mtbundy.com.au

76 Point Stuart Wilderness Lodge

Point Stuart Wilderness Lodge is well situated for exploring the wetlands and 4WD tracks of Mary River National Park; it is also close to Shady Camp, a renowned fishing spot. It has a small camping area with powered and unpowered sites bordering Jimmy Creek monsoon forest. **Map refs: 324 C3, 352 F4**

How to book: Point Stuart Rd, off Arnhem Hwy (08) 8978 8914 www.pointstuart.com.au

77 Pussy Cat Flats Caravan Park

This olde worlde place is in a great location at Pine Creek, alongside the local racetrack and golf course. It is cheap and cheerful, with only basic facilities, but it is very social – the bar opens at 4pm daily, just for campers. **Map refs: 324 C5, 352 F7**

How to book: Kakadu Hwy, Pine Creek (08) 8976 1355

78 Stuarts Tree Fishing Camp

There's a 4WD track into Stuarts Tree Fishing Camp, at the end of Point Stuart Rd, which is usually only open during the Dry. This is a privately run camp with basic facilities, but the fishing is great. A daily fee applies and it is necessary to book in advance. **Map refs: 324 C3, 352 F4**

How to book: Point Stuart Rd, off Arnhem Hwy (08) 8978 8863

79 Tumbling Waters Holiday Park

Tumbling Waters is more than just a stopover. It is near the northern access to Litchfield National Park (gravel road) and also close to Berry Springs and Cox Peninsula. There are powered sites set in a lush tropical landscape; grassy unpowered sites are scattered through the trees and have open fireplaces. There is also a licensed restaurant and 'movies under the stars'. **Map refs: 324 B4, 352 D5**

How to book: Cox Peninsula Rd, Berry Springs (08) 8988 6255 www.tumblingwatersholidaypark.com.au

GULF TO GULF

THIS IS PERHAPS THE most forgotten stretch of the Northern Territory, with a majority of visitors focusing on the Top End or the Red Centre. Yet in its vast area there are many superb camping spots and a wealth of natural wonders to explore. Don't miss the beautiful waterfalls and plunge pools in Nitmiluk National Park, which has excellent car and walk-in camping, and is quite accessible. Explore the peaceful beauty of this park and its dramatic gorges by canoe, or stride out on the 66 km multi-day Jatbula Trail.

Many other top spots in this region are more remote, offering isolated camping and serenity for those who are well prepared. Delve into Judbarra/Gregory National Park, Keep River National Park or go looking for endangered Gouldian finches in one of their last strongholds in Limmen National Park. There are remote 4WD tracks, and plenty of European and Aboriginal history to explore.

Other treasures in this region might be underground – you can fossick for riches near Kalkaringi and enjoy thermal springs set among paperbarks and palms in Elsey National Park.

As with the Top End, the most popular time to explore this area is in the dry season. The humidity and unrelenting heat in the build-up to the Wet (Oct–Dec) can be unbearable for the uninitiated, and the wet season (Dec–Apr), although spectacular, can cut many roads and make some areas inaccessible.

CAMPSITES LOCATED IN PARKS AND RESERVES

BARRANYI (NORTH ISLAND) NATIONAL PARK

You can only access this spectacular haven in the Sir Edward Pellew islands group by boat and visitors must be self-sufficient. Once there you'll find superb fishing for species such as northern bluefin tuna, spanish mackerel, queenfish and trevally. There are long white sandy beaches great for walking and beachcombing, and plenty of birdwatching opportunities; 4 species of sea turtle also nest along these beaches.
Who to contact: PWCNT Borroloola (08) 8975 8792

80 Mud Bay camping area (boat-based camping)

Mud Bay is in the southern part of the island and is an excellent fishing spot. Access is by boat and there are no facilities, so bring in everything. **Map refs:** 335 H4, 353 N10, 355 N1

81 Paradise Bay camping area (boat-based camping)

In the north of the island, this camping area has toilets and bore water on tap, but it needs to be boiled or treated before drinking. A couple of bushwalks lead from here. Campers are encouraged to use gas/fuel stoves rather than fires.
Map refs: 335 H4, 353 N10, 355 N1

ELSEY NATIONAL PARK

Enjoy swimming in thermal pools and fishing or canoeing on the Roper River. There are also 21 km of riverside walking tracks. This beautiful national park of 13 840 ha is 100 km south-east of Katherine. The birdlife is prolific. Boat ramps and canoe launching areas are found at 12 Mile Yards, near the camping area, and at Mataranka Homestead, but outboard motors are limited to a maximum of 15 hp. The park is closed if conditions are too wet; call the parks office to be sure of access. Bitter Springs is reached via a sealed road leading north-east from the Mataranka township. To access the rest of the park, head 1.5 km south of Mataranka on the Stuart Hwy and take Homestead Rd.
Who to contact: PWCNT Mataranka (08) 8975 4560

82 Jalmurark camping area

Enjoy great facilities here, including solar showers, in a peaceful environment (no generators). Swimming is allowed during the Dry, but observe crocodile warning signs. Bring your own firewood. Turn off Homestead Rd to the right after 4 km, onto John Hauser Dr, and follow it to the end. **Map refs:** 334 E3, 352 H9

GIWINING/FLORA RIVER NATURE PARK

The main attraction in this park, 122 km south of Katherine, is the 25 km of protected river way. It has tufa dams, springs, portages and plenty of areas to explore by canoe. Look for rare pig-nosed turtles, as well as salt- and freshwater crocodiles, and riverbanks lined with palms, melaleucas and pandanus.
Who to contact: PWCNT Katherine (08) 8973 8888

83 Djarrung camping area

Set in a beautiful spot near the river, this is a great isolated camping spot for birdwatchers, canoeists and anglers. There is a boat-launching area, but motors must be 15 hp or less, and anglers are asked to use lures not bait, to protect the turtles. The last 30 km is a dirt road that's usually quite rough, so 4WD is recommended. **Map refs:** 334 C3, 352 E9

JUDBARRA/GREGORY NATIONAL PARK

At 13 000 sq km, this park is nearly as big as the mighty Kakadu, and lies in the transitional zone between tropical and semi-arid regions. As a result it has a vast range of habitats, including soaring escarpments, thickly vegetated gorges, flat tropical woodlands and magnificent river systems. There are plenty of significant Aboriginal sites, evidence of early European pastoral history, and campsites galore. Some parts of the park off the Victoria Hwy are accessible to conventional vehicles but in the Wet most areas are inaccessible to all. The other park entrances, off the Buntine and Buchanan hwys, are suitable for 4WD only.
Who to contact: PWCNT Timber Creek (08) 8975 0888

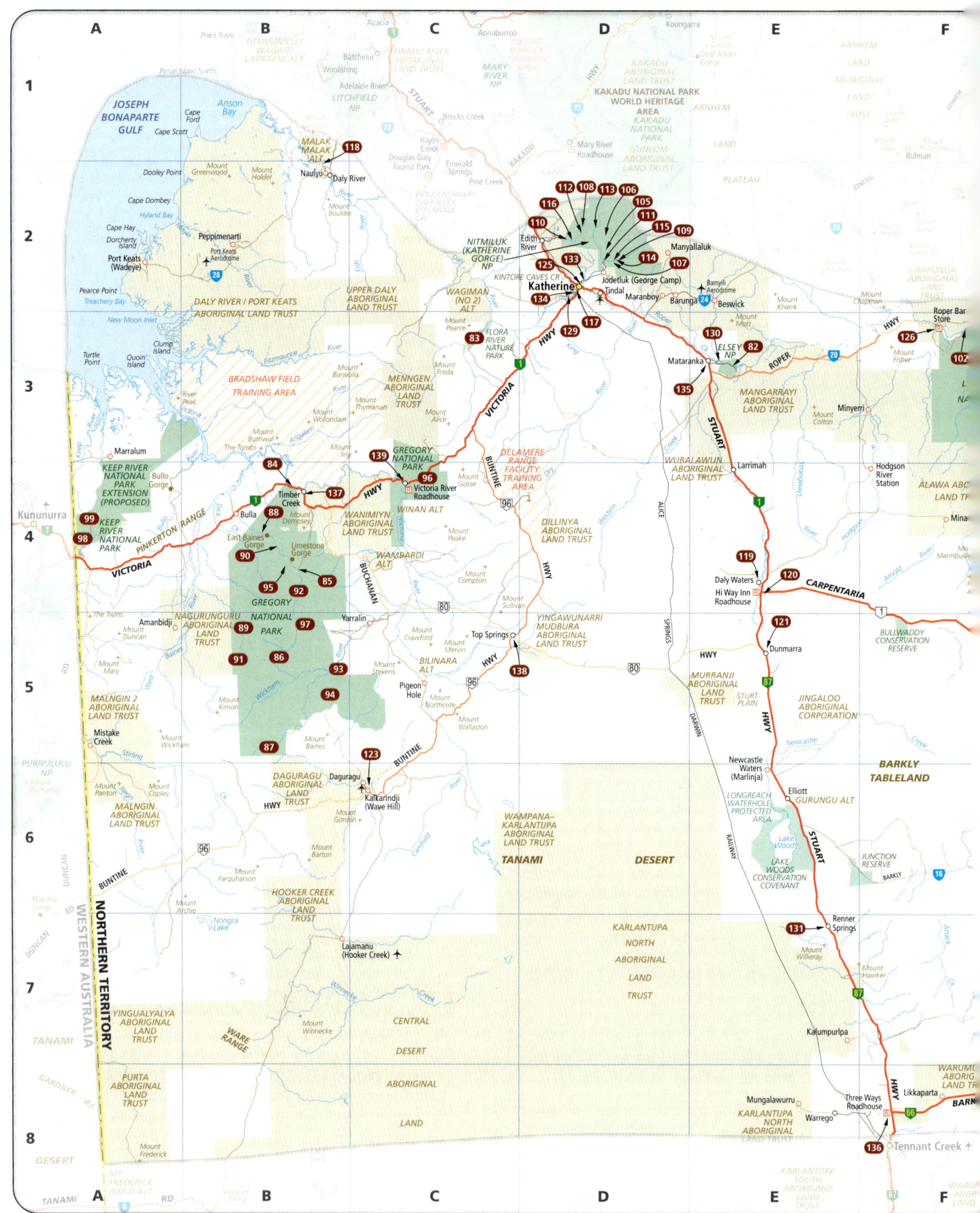

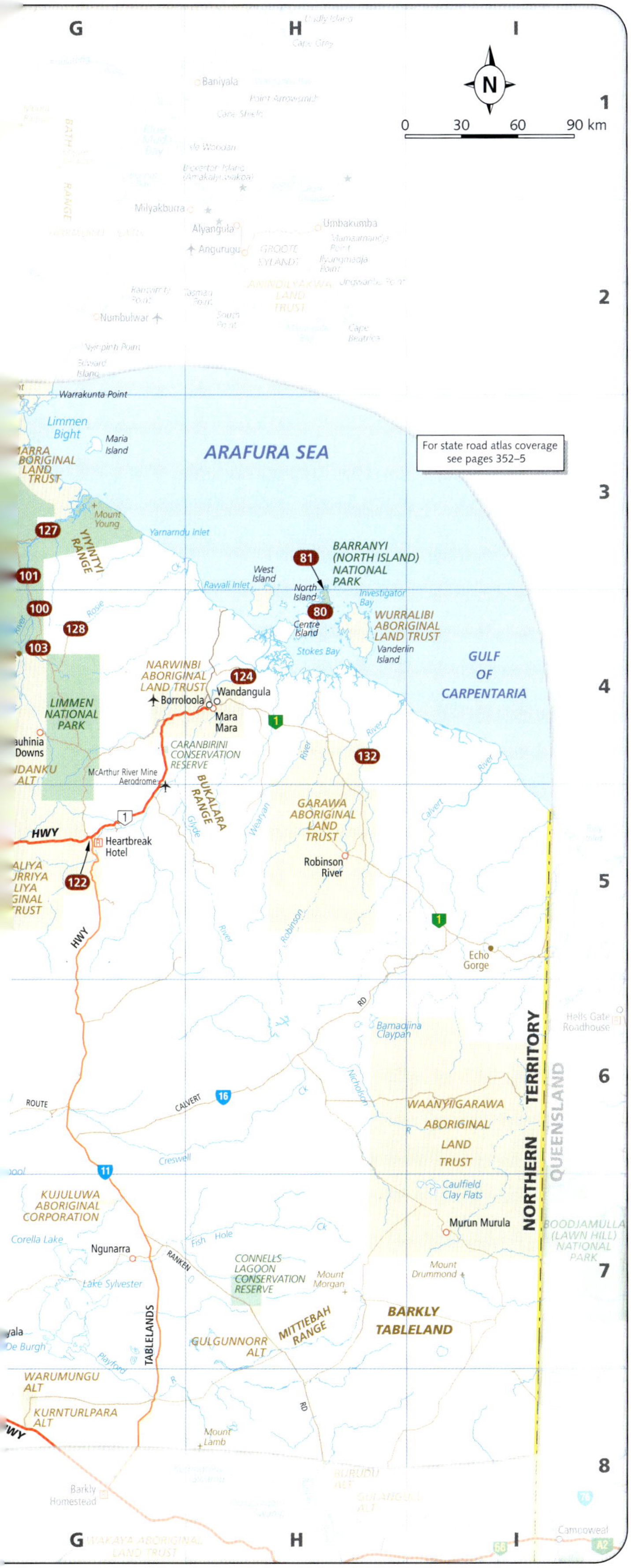

84 Big Horse Creek camping area

This is just off the Victoria Hwy, 10 km west of Timber Creek, on the banks of the river. It's a great base for fishing and as a stopover between Kununurra and Katherine. Caravans are not permitted. Facilities are good but there is only limited drinking water. **Map refs:** 334 B4, 352 C10, 354 C1

85 Bullita camping area

On the banks of the East Baines River, this campsite is near the historic Bullita Homestead and stockyards. 4WD access is via a turn-off from the Victoria Hwy, 10 km south of Timber Creek; the track may be closed during the Wet. The restored Bullita Homestead and stockyards are a good place to learn about the challenges faced by early settlers. Both the Humbert 4WD track and the Bullita Stock Route start here. **Map refs:** 334 B4, 352 C11, 354 C2

86 Camel Point camping area

The first campsite along the 4WD Broadarrow Track from the Buntine Hwy, this camping area is about 27 km from the Wickham Track. **Map refs:** 334 B5, 352 C12, 354 C3

87 Depot Creek camping area

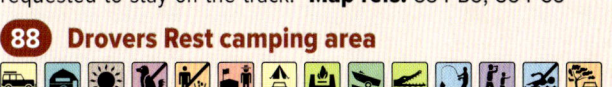

The last campsite along the 4WD Broadarrow Track is about 45 km from the Buntine Hwy. From the park boundary to the highway, the route goes through 38 km of private property and you are requested to stay on the track. **Map refs:** 334 B5, 354 C5

88 Drovers Rest camping area

Boasting a boat ramp, this site on the East Baines River is 13 km from the Bullita Stock Route. **Map refs:** 334 B4, 352 C11, 354 C2

89 East Baines camping area

This site, on the Broadarrow Track, is 30 km west of Camel Point on the East Baines River. It is only suitable for 4WD vehicles. **Map refs:** 334 B5, 352 C12, 354 C3

90 East Baines Crossing camping area

This site is about 400 m north of the East Baines River crossing on the Bullita Stock Route. **Map refs:** 334 B4, 352 C11, 354 C2

91 Escarpment Lookout camping area

The third of the 4 campsites on the Broadarrow Track, this is about 75 km from East Baines. **Map refs:** 334 B5, 352 C12, 354 C3

(Map content)

G   H   I

N

0   30   60   90 km

ARAFURA SEA

For state road atlas coverage
see pages 352–5

Baniyala

Point Arrowsmith

Cape Grey

Milyakburra

Alyangula

GROOTE
EYLANDT

Umbakumba

Angurugu

ANINDILYAKWA
LAND
TRUST

Numbulwar

127

YIYINTJI
RANGE

Mount
Young

Yarnarndu Inlet

BARRANYI
(NORTH ISLAND)
NATIONAL
PARK

81

101

West
Island

Rawali Inlet

North
Island

Investigator
Bay

80

WURRALIBI
ABORIGINAL
LAND TRUST

100

128

Stokes Bay

Vanderlin
Island

103

NARWINBI
ABORIGINAL
LAND TRUST

124

Wandangula

GULF
OF
CARPENTARIA

LIMMEN
NATIONAL
PARK

Borroloola

Mara
Mara

1

CARANBIRINI
CONSERVATION
RESERVE

McArthur River Mine
Aerodrome

BUKALARA
RANGE

132

Bauhinia
Downs

IDANKU
ALT

HWY

Heartbreak
Hotel

1

GARAWA
ABORIGINAL
LAND
TRUST

Robinson
River

ALIYA
JRRIYA
LIYA
RUST

122

Echo
Gorge

1

Hells Gate
Roadhouse

NORTHERN TERRITORY

QUEENSLAND

RD

Barranna
Claypan

ROUTE

CALVERT

16

WAANYI/GARAWA
ABORIGINAL
LAND
TRUST

Creswell

Caulfield
Clay Flats

KUJULUWA
ABORIGINAL
CORPORATION

11

Corella Lake

Ngunarra

RANKEN

Fish
Hole

CONNELLS
LAGOON
CONSERVATION
RESERVE

Murun Murula

BOODJAMULLA
(LAWN HILL)
NATIONAL
PARK

Mount
Drummond

Lake Sylvester

TABLELANDS

GULGUNNORR
ALT

MITTIEBAH
RANGE

Mount
Morgan

BARKLY
TABLELAND

WARUMUNGU
ALT

KURNTURLPARA
ALT

RD

Mount
Lamb

HWY

Barkly
Homestead

92 Fig Tree Yard camping area

About 1 km off the Humbert Track, this campsite is signposted 18 km south of the start of the 4WD route. **Map refs: 334 B4, 352 C12, 354 C3**

93 Fish Hole Yard camping area

In a lovely spot on the Wickham River, 58 km south of Top Humbert Yard and 24 km north of Paperbark Yard, this campsite is on private property just outside the park boundary; it is accessed through the park via the 4WD Gibbie or Humbert tracks. There are no facilities here. **Map refs: 334 B5, 354 D4**

94 Paperbark Yard camping area

This camping area is on the Gibbie Track 4WD route, 20 km south of the junction with the Wickham Track. **Map refs: 334 B5, 354 D4**

95 Spring Creek Yard camping area

This small site is on the 4WD Bullita Stock Route, 14 km west of the beginning of the route. Camp beside the boab trees and the nearby waterhole and enjoy the peace and quiet. **Map refs: 334 B4, 352 C11, 354 C2**

96 Sullivan Creek camping area

Easily accessed from the Victoria Hwy and a good stopover on the way to WA, this campsite is set on the banks of a permanent waterhole, 17 km east of the Victoria River Roadhouse. **Map refs: 334 C4, 352 E10, 354 E1**

97 Top Humbert Yard camping area

This camping area is just off the Humbert Track in a clearing by the Humbert River, 28 km south of Fig Tree Yard. **Map refs: 334 B5, 352 D12, 354 D3**

KEEP RIVER NATIONAL PARK

Some of the best short walks in the country await you in Keep River National Park. Right on the border with WA, it's the start of the Kimberley, so there are some magnificent Bungle Bungle rock formations, ravines full of towering livistona palms, spinifex plains and eucalypt woodlands. Water is in short supply, but there is a public water tank about 5 km off the Victoria Hwy, just past the ranger station. An information board is situated at the ranger station, and a few small walks go from there, including to a stone structure used by Aboriginal people to hunt birds. Roads are inaccessible during the Wet, and can be quite difficult immediately after the Wet.

Who to contact: PWCNT (08) 9167 8827

98 Gurrandalng camping area

This campsite is 18 km past the ranger station. Generators are permitted within certain times. There is no drinking water here but it is available at Jarnem and the ranger station. A 2 km walk gives magnificent views of sandstone rock formations. **Map refs: 334 A4, 352 A11, 354 A2**

99 Jarnem camping area

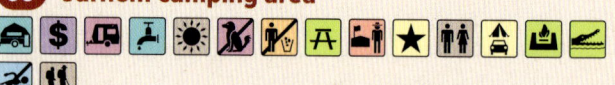

From this isolated campsite, about 30 km off the highway, you can do the Jarnem Walk. This excellent 7.5 km hike is the highlight of a stay here, with eroded sandstone beehive formations reminiscent of the Bungle Bungle Range, as well as open savannah and, in more sheltered areas, stands of livistona palms. Depending on the time of year, there can be good birdlife and wildflowers as well. Rock art at Nigli Gap is another nearby attraction. Generators are not permitted at this site, but there is a tank – for drinking water only (not showers). **Map refs: 334 A4, 352 A11, 354 A2**

LIMMEN NATIONAL PARK

This wild, remote and rugged park has 'lost city' geological formations of spires and columns of stratified sandstone, isolated thermal springs, lofty escarpments and billabongs aplenty. There are some bushwalking tracks, great birdwatching and you can swim at Butterfly Springs in the south of the park. The park is some 300 km south-east of Katherine and 76 km north-west of Borroloola; a 4WD is required. Turn off the Roper Hwy, 3 km west of Roper Bar, onto the Point Roper Rd.

Who to contact: PWCNT Limmen Ranger Station (08) 8975 9940

100 Butterfly Springs camping area

Just a couple of km off the Savannah Way, this is the most popular campsite in the park, as it is the only safe spot for swimming. Towards the end of the dry season the water can become stagnant though. Look for the sign on the Savannah Way, 20 km south of the Limmen Bight River Crossing. **Map refs: 335 G4, 353 L10, 355 L1**

101 Limmen River Campground

Just off the Savannah Way, 20 km north of Butterfly Springs, this spot has reasonable facilities but you will need to bring your own drinking water. **Map refs: 335 G3, 353 L10, 355 L1**

102 Munbililla (Tomato Island) camping area

At the time of writing, this area was predominantly bush camping with no facilities except a boat ramp. It is very popular with fishermen. Plans are in place to create a brand-new facility with powered and unpowered sites and a solar ablution block; it is expected to be completed by the end of 2012. **Map refs:** 334 F3, 353 K9

103 Southern Lost City camping area

Four kilometres off the Savannah Way, 30 km south of Butterfly Springs, you'll see the turn-off to this campsite, which is near the 2.5 km walking track among the sandstone pillars of the Southern Lost City rock formations. **Map refs:** 335 G4, 353 L11, 355 L2

104 Towns River Crossing camping area

Come equipped with firewood and water to this simple campsite on the Towns River, 38 km north of the Limmen Bight River Crossing. There is a boat ramp. **Map refs:** 335 G3, 353 K9

NITMILUK NATIONAL PARK

This extraordinarily beautiful 300 000 ha park has stunning waterfalls, spectacular gorges and plunging escarpments, and is rich with plants and animals. It's heavenly for hikers, canoeists and swimmers, with safe and delightful swimming holes at Southern Rockhole, Northern Rockhole, 17 Mile Falls, Biddlecombe Cascades, Crystal Falls and Leliyn (not all waterways are safe for swimming as crocodiles inhabit the area, observe warning signs). There are boat-launching facilities, but only boats without motors are allowed. There is an excellent network of short bushwalks, or you could tackle the 66 km Jatbula Trail; you need to book all the campsites along the Jatbula. The park's main entrance is 30 km north-east of Katherine on the sealed Gorge Road; Leliyn (Edith Falls) is 40 km north-west of Katherine.

Who to contact: Nitmiluk Visitor Centre (08) 8972 1253, 1300 146 743 *How to book:* (08) 8972 1886 for campsite nos **105**, **106**, **108**, **112**, **113**, **116** *Permits:* Overnight walkers are required to register and pay a deposit at the visitor centre; note: numbers permitted are limited

105 Biddlecombe Cascades camping area (walk-in camping)

The seasonal cascades are a perfect place to relax and cool off. This is a flat camping site 11 km along the Jatbula Trail. **Map refs:** 334 D2, 352 G8

106 Crystal Falls camping area (walk-in camping)

About 20 km along the Jatbula Trail you will find Crystal Falls. There is great swimming in Crystal Creek but be careful of the river crossing. **Map refs:** 334 D2, 352 G7

107 Dunlop Swamp camping area (bush camping)

With no toilets, and drinking water only available some of the year, this is a site for the experienced. There is swimming

below Dunlop Swamp. It's 9 km along the Smitt Rocks Walk. **Map refs:** 334 D2, 352 G8

108 Edith River Crossing camping area (walk-in camping)

This campsite is 45 km along the Jatbula Trail and is the start of the walk along the river. Top up your drinking water here. **Map refs:** 334 D2, 352 G7

109 Eighth Gorge camping area (bush camping)

A campsite popular among overnight canoeists, this site is 16 km east of the visitor centre via Eighth Gorge Walk. It has no toilets. **Map refs:** 334 D2, 352 G8

110 Leliyn (Edith Falls) camping area

This large campground is signposted off the Stuart Hwy, 40 km north-west of Katherine. Generators and fires are not permitted and all sites are unpowered. It is a pleasant camping ground with grassy sites and ample shade. A swim in the pool below the falls is a refreshing way to end the day. There is a kiosk here where you can pay camping fees and purchase food and drinks. **Map refs:** 334 D2, 352 F8

111 Nitmiluk Centre Campground

Centrally positioned near Nitmiluk Visitor Centre, walking tracks, canoe hire and the cruise boat, this privately run campsite has pretty much everything you need, including a pool, and is the main camping area in the park. Generators are not permitted, and although wood is sometimes supplied you will need to bring your own timber from outside the park if a campfire is essential. The campground has 40 powered sites as well as unpowered ones. A rewarding way to see the Nitmiluk Gorge is to hire a canoe: book ahead in peak season, as canoe numbers are limited. **Map refs:** 334 D2, 352 G8

112 Sandy Camp Pool camping area (walk-in camping)

This pleasant spot is 51 km along the Jatbula Trail. It's on the Edith River beside a great swimming hole. **Map refs:** 334 D2, 352 F7

113 Seventeen Mile Falls camping area (walk-in camping)

You'll find this campsite not 17 miles, but 35 km along the Jatbula Trail. It is an opportunity for swimming and rockhopping. **Map refs:** 334 D2, 352 G7

114 **Sixth Gorge camping area (boat-based camping)**

There are no walking tracks at Sixth Gorge but overnight access is available to canoeists. There are toilets but no other facilities. **Map refs:** 334 D2, 352 G8

115 **Smitt Rocks camping area (walk-in camping)**

Suitable for canoeists or hikers, this site is 11 km east of the visitor centre, and accessible by the Katherine River or the Smitt Rocks Walk. Swimming, toilets and drinking water are available. **Map refs:** 334 D2, 352 G8

116 **Sweetwater Pool camping area (walk-in camping)**

Sweetwater Pool is reached via a walking trail, 4 km east of the Leliyn camping ground, or near the end of the Jatbula Trail. Last opportunity for a swim. **Map refs:** 334 D2, 352 F8

CAMPSITES LOCATED IN OTHER AREAS

117 **BIG4 Katherine Holiday Park**

This caravan park has a large grassy space for tent and camper trailers and shady grassed powered areas, with facilities, for caravans and motorhomes. There are even separate sites for people camping on their own. There's a swimming pool and a bistro, and visitors can wander down to the nearby Low Level Nature Park or the Katherine River for a spot of fishing. **Map refs:** 334 D2, 352 F8

How to book: Shadforth Rd, Katherine (08) 8972 3962 big4katherinecaravanpark.com.au

118 **Daly River Barra Resort**

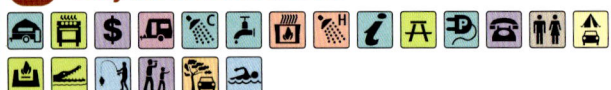

The Daly River is renowned for its fishing opportunities, so much so that the Barra Classic and the Barra Nationals are both held here. The caravan park is on the banks of the river (observe crocodile warning signs); fish for yourself or join a fishing charter. Also close by is the Merrepen Art Centre at the Nauiyu Community (ring first to confirm they are open). Camping is under 30-year-old mango trees on large sites that are shady and grassed. There is powered and unpowered camping, plus all facilities, including a camp kitchen, pool and free BBQ. Daly River is 223 km from Darwin. **Map refs:** 334 B2, 352 D7

How to book: Daly River (08) 897 81193 www.dalyriverbarra.com.au

119 **Daly Waters Historic Pub**

Established in 1930, the Daly Waters Pub is a local institution, built to service the drovers and settlers in the area. Visitors to the Territory flock here during the dry season, but bookings are not taken so it's best to arrive early. There is a great restaurant, beer on tap and free entertainment nightly. The camping area has powered and unpowered sites and there is a pool. It's 4 km off the Stuart Hwy, 275 km south of Katherine. **Map refs:** 334 E4, 352 H12, 354 H3

Who to contact: Stuart St, Daly Waters (08) 8975 9927 www.dalywaterspub.com

120 **Daly Waters Hi-way Inn**

The convenience of the location and the pool are the key attractions at this site. It's also a convenient stop for those heading out on the Savannah Way for fishing or camping trips. You can pay a small fee to use the pool and facilities if you are just passing through. **Map refs:** 334 E4, 352 H12, 354 H3

How to book: cnr Stuart and Carpentaria hwys, Daly Waters (08) 8975 9925

121 **Dunmarra Wayside Inn**

It's a bit of a wildlife experience when you stay at Dunmarra Wayside Inn, conveniently situated halfway between Katherine and Tennant Creek. On the Stuart Hwy, 8 km south of the Buchanan Hwy intersection, the roadhouse has a reptile enclosure with snakes and lizards, water buffalo out the back, and the lagoon across the road can have up to 50 species of birds. The roadhouse has fuel, a swimming pool, bar and some reasonable murals. Firewood is supplied occasionally and there are 32 powered sites as well as a large unpowered camping area. **Map refs:** 334 E5, 352 H12, 354 H3

How to book: Stuart Hwy, Dunmarra (08) 8975 9922

122 **Heartbreak Hotel**

With easy access to the spectacular Lost City in Limmen National Park, this Aussie institution has a beer garden with its own pool, and 44 powered as well as unpowered campsites. The hotel is 117 km south of Borroloola. **Map refs:** 335 G5, 353 L12, 355 L3

How to book: cnr Carpentaria and Tablelands hwys, Cape Crawford (08) 8975 9928 www.heartbreakhotel.com.au

123 **Kalkaringi Service Station and Store**

There are 2 new cabins, as well as powered and unpowered sites at this spot near Wave Hill, on the Buntine Hwy about

140 km south-west of Top Springs. The road can sometimes become impassable after heavy rain. The water here has a high calcium content so you are advised to bring your own drinking water. **Map refs:** 334 C6, 354 D5

Who to contact: Buntine Hwy, Victoria River (08) 8975 0788

124 King Ash Bay Fishing Club

The King Ash Bay Fishing Club runs a caravan park and camping area open to members and non-members. It's beside the McArthur River and has powered and unpowered sites. From Borroloola, head north on the sealed hwy towards Bing Bong Station until you reach the King Ash Bay turn-off to the right. There is about 25 km of dirt road accessible to conventional vehicles and caravans for most of the dry season. **Map refs:** 335 H4, 353 M11, 355 M2

Who to contact: (08) 8975 9800 www.kingashbay.com.au

125 Knotts Crossing Resort

A 5-time winner of the NT Brolga Award for tourism, this resort has a range of accommodation options, including powered and unpowered sites, and sites with ensuites. Set by the river, it has a bistro, bar and pool and is the closest resort to Katherine Gorge. **Map refs:** 334 D2, 352 F8

How to book: cnr Giles and Cameron sts, Katherine (08) 8972 2511 www.knottscrossing.com.au

126 Leichhardts Caravan Park

Anglers flock to Leichhardts Caravan Park at Roper Bar, and its well-used boat ramp has seen many a good catch come in. The water on-site must be boiled before use so you are advised to bring your own drinking water, and your own firewood too (though there is usually plenty in the nearby area). Dogs must be tied up at all times and exercised outside the park. **Map refs:** 334 F3, 353 J9

Who to contact: Roper Bar Store (08) 8975 4636 www.roperbar.com.au

127 Limmen Bight Fishing Camp

Limmen Bight Fishing Camp is definitely off the beaten track. Its facilities are very basic but the location is worth the rough track in. Unpowered sites are available along the bank of the Limmen River, which flows into the Limmen Bight; there are also a few powered sites. This is the perfect location for relaxing, birdwatching or fishing – and there is a boat ramp. **Map refs:** 335 G3, 353 L10, 355 L1

Who to contact: it is best to just drop in

128 Lorella Springs Wilderness Camping and Caravan Park

It's a bit of a trek but Lorella Springs is worth the drive. It's an oasis in the middle of outback Australia between Roper Bar and Borroloola, 29 km down a gravel road off the Savannah Way. The property is family run, over 400 000 ha of wilderness with camping either at the Homestead or bush-style down at the Rosie River. Apart from the wonderful hospitality, the camping area is right next to Lorella thermal spring. Choose to laze around in the warm waters or explore the local gorges and 4WD tracks. Lorella Springs is also a good stopover on the way to the Lost City at Limmen River National Park. **Map refs:** 335 G4, 353 L10, 355 L2

How to book: (08) 8975 9917 www.lorellasprings.com.au

129 Manbulloo Homestead Caravan Park

Manbulloo is a working cattle station 12 km south-west of Katherine, off the Victoria Hwy. It is in a quiet, rural location on the banks of the Katherine River. Popular activities here include bushwalking, birdwatching and fishing. There are large, shady grassed sites, both powered and unpowered, and a camp kitchen and free BBQs. This caravan park is a great alternative to staying in town. **Map refs:** 334 D2, 352 F8

How to book: Murnburlu Rd, Katherine (08) 8972 1559 www.manbulloohomesteadcaravanpark.com.au

130 Mataranka Homestead Tourist Resort

Mataranka Homestead is close to the border of Elsey National Park. Surrounded by lush tropical vegetation, it's a short walk from the resort to the attractions of the park, in particular the Rainbow Springs thermal pool. This is a delight, especially early in the morning when the birds keep you company. There is a large camping area here with over 100 powered sites and unlimited unpowered sites, all within walking distance of the thermal pool. Pets are allowed if arranged in advance. The Homestead is open all year round; it serves meals and has a bar. In the Dry there is regular entertainment at night. **Map refs:** 334 E3, 352 H9

How to book: Homestead Rd, Mataranka (08) 8975 4544 www.matarankahomestead.com.au

131 Renner Springs Desert Inn

Ideally located between Darwin, Alice Springs and Mt Isa, 160 km north of Tennant Creek, the camping area is beside a bird-filled lagoon. There are 15 powered and 60 unpowered sites. A 4 km return walk to the lookout at Labyrinth Point gives

you a view over the whole area. Firewood is usually supplied.
Map refs: 334 E7, 355 I7

How to book: Stuart Hwy, Renner Springs (08) 8964 4505
www.rennerspringshotel.com.au

132 Seven Emu Station

Seven Emu Station is a working cattle station. Camping is available here throughout the dry season, and the well-spaced sites overlook the magnificent Robinson River, giving visitors stunning views. There is plenty to do here, including birdwatching, fishing, 4WD trails and Aboriginal culture tours to the 'beach with no name'. The station is 100 km south-east of Borroloola. **Map refs:** 335 H4, 353 N12, 355 N3

How to book: Savannah Way, via Borroloola (08) 8975 9904
www.sevenemustation.com.au

133 Shady Lane Tourist Park

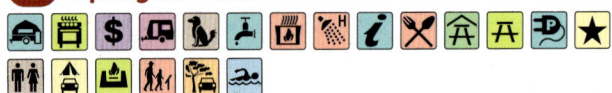

This quiet spot just out of Katherine has great facilities. Take a short stroll to the river and do some fishing, or lounge in the pool. It is conveniently close to Katherine Gorge.
Map refs: 334 D2, 352 G8

How to book: 257 Gorge Rd, Katherine (08) 8971 0491,
1800 043 043 www.shadylanetouristpark.com.au

134 Springvale Homestead Tourist Park

Camp alongside the billabong near the oldest standing homestead in NT, built in the 1880s. Most days during the Dry there is a Devonshire tea, and at night a crocodile adventure. The park has budget accommodation, a bistro and kiosk, a swimming pool and waterslide, as well as unpowered and powered sites. Follow the Victoria Hwy (Savannah Way) south of Katherine for 8 km, then turn right into Zimin Dr, cross the river and turn left. **Map refs:** 334 D2, 352 F8

How to book: Shadforth St, Katherine (08) 8972 1355

135 Territory Manor Motel and Caravan Park

Territory Manor Caravan Park is on the junction of the Stuart Hwy and the road to Bitter Springs, which has thermal pools and a swimming hole. There are powered and unpowered camping sites, a pool and an outdoor restaurant. Twice a day there is a barramundi feeding show at the billabong – go along to find out more about this elusive fish. **Map refs:** 334 E3, 352 H9

How to book: 51 Martin Rd, Mataranka (08) 8975 4516
www.matarankamotel.com

136 Threeways Roadhouse and Tourist Park

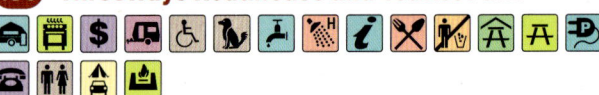

Threeways was the winner of the NT 2008 Roadhouse of the Year. There are powered sites and the tent areas are shaded by trees. The facilities include a camp kitchen and laundry. From the roadhouse it's just a 3 min walk to a memorial commemorating the Reverend John Flynn, legend of the outback and founder of the Royal Flying Doctor Service. It's advisable to bring your own drinking water, as supplies are limited. **Map refs:** 334 F8, 355 J9

How to book: cnr Stuart and Barkly hwys, Tennant Creek (08) 8962 2744 www.threewaysroadhouse.com.au

137 Timber Creek Hotel Fogarty's Store

Circle F Caravan Park is part of the Timber Creek Hotel and Fogarty's Store complex, which offers accommodation options for all, from air-conditioned motel rooms through to camping areas. There are powered and unpowered campsites on large grassy and shady areas. The complex has dining and bar facilities, plus a pool, spa and supermarket, as well as the usual campground BBQs. It's a good stopover between Katherine and Kununurra or Gregory National Park. Firewood is usually supplied, and there is bore water which will need to be treated, or you can bring your own drinking water. It's on the Victoria Hwy at Timber Creek, 285 km west of Katherine. **Map refs:** 334 B4, 352 D11, 354 D2

How to book: Victoria Hwy, Timber Creek (08) 8975 0722
www.timbercreekhotel.com.au

138 Top Springs Hotel

With everything from fuel and supplies to a bar and motel, Top Springs offers a vital resupply stop at the junction of the Buchanan and Buntine hwys. The campground has rainwater tanks and a refreshing swimming pool. There is plenty of information about explorers of the area, and legendary road-train operator Noel Buntine, after whom the road is named. The recently developed long-distance 4WD route, the Binns Track, goes past Top Springs. **Map refs:** 334 C5, 352 F12, 354 F3

How to book: Buntine Hwy, Top Springs (08) 8975 0767
www.topspringshotel.com.au

139 Victoria River Roadhouse Caravan Park

This is a pleasant stopover between Katherine and Kununurra, with lovely views of the escarpment. There is a large area for camping, where there is also a group campfire. The caravan park is part of the roadhouse, which offers dining, bar and fuel facilities. **Map refs:** 334 C4, 352 E10, 354 E1

How to book: Victoria Hwy, Victoria River (08) 8975 0744

RED CENTRE

THE GEOGRAPHICAL AND SPIRITUAL heart of the country, the Red Centre is, for many, the defining Australian landscape. Black kites and wedge-tailed eagles soar over sienna sand dunes, where flowers bloom after rain and little dragons scurry about. Iconic features, such as the awesome monolith Uluru and the Kata Tjuta domes, attract pilgrims from all over the country and the rest of the world.

But there are so many other natural treasures hidden in this vast landscape: the stunning multi-hued rock face of Rainbow Valley; the tranquil waterholes in Iytwelepenty/Davenport Range National Park; the much-photographed boulders of the Karlu Karlu/ Devils Marbles. And deeply gouged into the red earth are other dramatic features: spectacular Watarrka/Kings Canyon, the hidden oasis of Palm Valley and the craters in the Henbury Meteorites Conservation Reserve.

In the cooler months of the year (Apr–Oct), the Red Centre is perfect for camping, with plenty of warm, clear days and cold nights great for snuggling by a campfire. Nights can get below freezing, so don't forget your beanie and a decent sleeping bag. In the hotter months, the area is usually much quieter, but the heat in the middle of the day can become very taxing.

There are plenty of activities to keep all ages occupied. Bushwalks go from short strolls and nature trails to one of the longest and best arid-country walking tracks in the world, the 223 km Larapinta Trail. But there are also camel rides and station tours, fossicking opportunities, swimming spots and 4WD routes. Those interested in history will find plenty of reminders of early settlers and explorers, as well as thousands of years of Aboriginal occupation and culture, which is still very much alive today.

Sometimes the best way to see this area, however, is to set up camp in a beautiful spot, such as in West Macdonnell or Trephina Gorge national parks, and just sit and soak up the beauty of this ancient landscape.

CAMPSITES LOCATED IN PARKS AND RESERVES

ANNAS RESERVOIR CONSERVATION RESERVE

With homestead ruins and other relics from the 19th century, this is a great location to immerse yourself in history. Access is via the Stuart Hwy, 160 km north of Alice Springs. You need to get permission from Aileron Station before taking the private road, 5 km before Aileron.

Who to contact: PWCNT Alice Springs (08) 8952 0113; or Aileron Station (08) 8956 9706

140 Annas Reservoir camping area (bush camping)

There are no facilities for camping, but the recommended camping area is 200 m before the ruins of the station homestead and blacksmith's hut. Do not camp near the waterhole. **Map refs:** 342 D4, 356 H4

CHAMBERS PILLAR HISTORICAL RESERVE

The 50 m tower of sandstone here is the main attraction – both for its natural beauty and for the historic graffiti carved into it; early European visitors from the exploring party for the Overland Telegraph Line, including John Ross and Alfred Giles, carved their initials in the soft stone in 1870. At sunset it appears to glow. There are walking tracks around the pillar and the surrounding area.

Who to contact: PWCNT Alice Springs Telegraph Station (08) 8952 1013

141 Chambers Pillar camping area

Camping is permitted about 500 m before the pillar. The reserve is 160 km south of Alice Springs, along the Old South Rd. Turn west at Maryvale Station onto a 4WD track with deep sand drifts. Easy walking tracks give access to various views of Chambers Pillar, as well as other interesting rock formations nearby, including Castle Rock, Window Rock and Eagle Rock. **Map refs:** 342 E7, 357 I9

FINKE GORGE NATIONAL PARK

The highlight of this beautiful park of red rock and the often dry Finke River is the hidden gorge of Palm Valley, where rare red cabbage palms flourish. Campers may also see rock wallabies and plentiful birdlife. The park is 138 km west of Alice Springs; turn south off Larapinta Dr just west of Hermannsburg. A 4WD is necessary to get into the park, and the track may be impassable after rain.

Who to contact: PWCNT Finke Gorge (08) 8956 7401

142 Boggy Hole camping area (bush camping)

You can fish and swim here, but there are no facilities and generators are not allowed. It is on the Finke River 4WD route, 33 km south of Larapinta Dr. **Map refs:** 342 D6, 356 H7

143 Palm Valley camping area

The main campground has good facilities and is 22 km south of Hermannsburg. You will need to bring your own firewood or use the gas BBQs. Many sites are under trees along Palm Creek, which usually has some water in it but does not often flow. A short walk from the campsite leads to Kalaranga Lookout, which is spectacular at sunset. **Map refs:** 342 D6, 356 H7

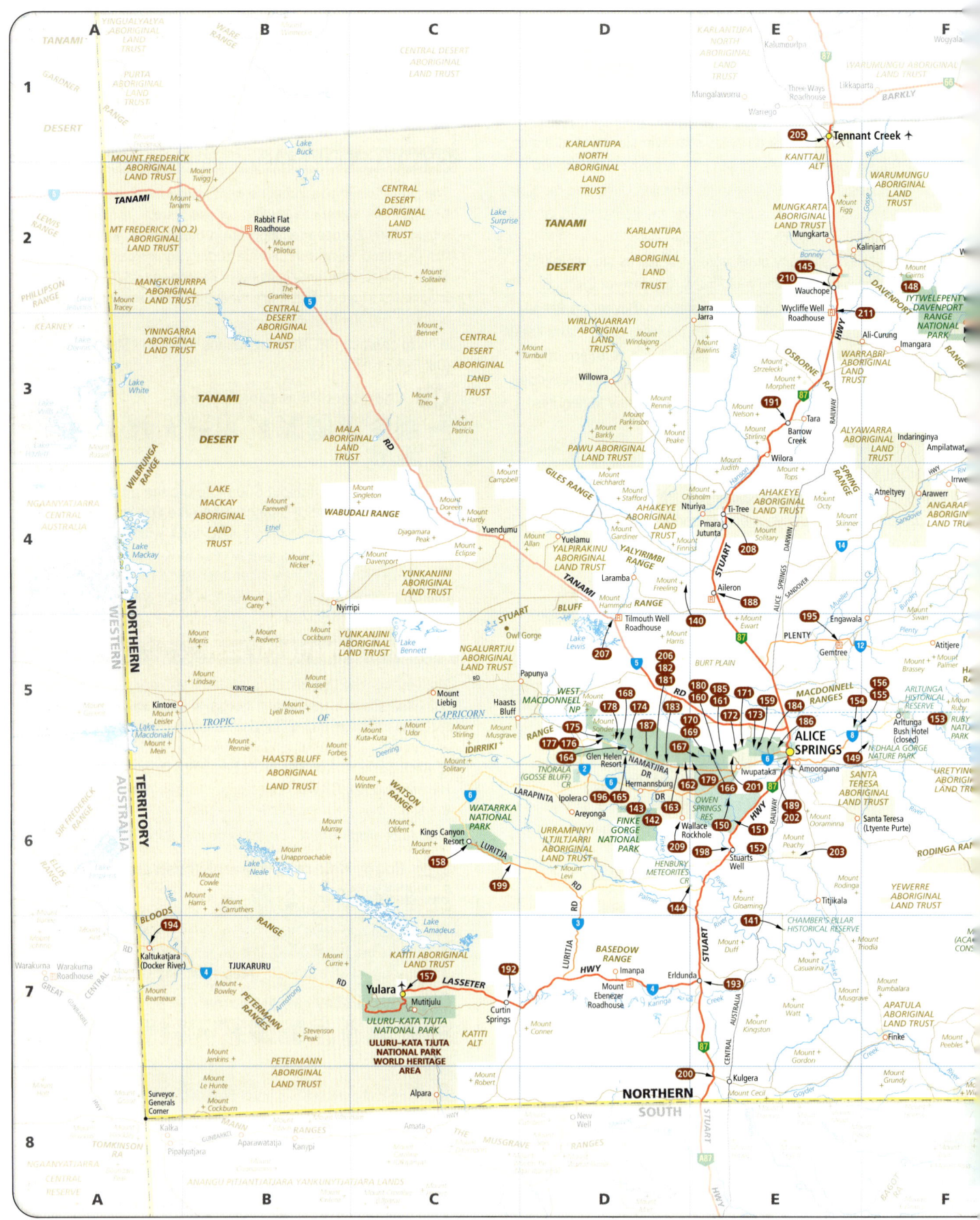

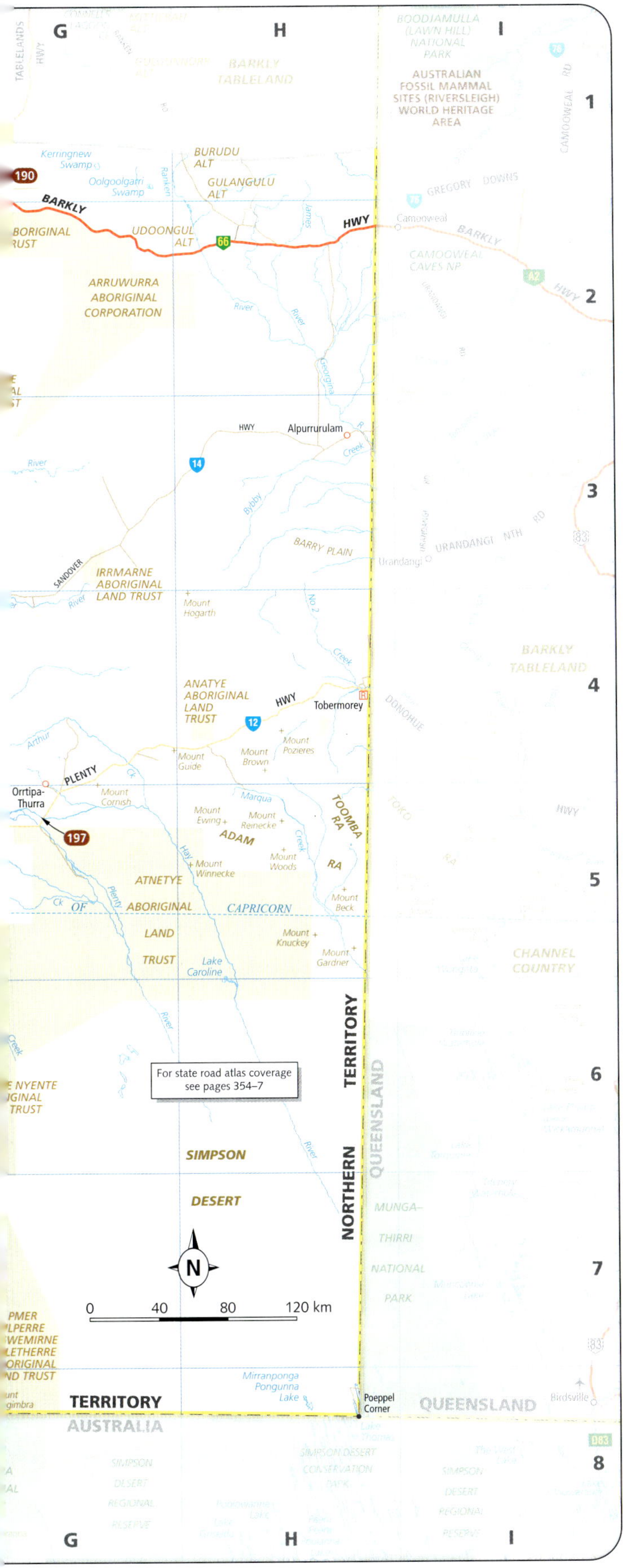

The map on the left side shows map grid references G, H, I across columns 1-8, including features such as BARKLY TABLELAND, BURUDU ALT, GULANGULU ALT, UDOONGUL ALT, ARRUWURRA ABORIGINAL CORPORATION, BOODJAMULLA (LAWN HILL) NATIONAL PARK, AUSTRALIAN FOSSIL MAMMAL SITES (RIVERSLEIGH) WORLD HERITAGE AREA, GREGORY DOWNS, Camooweal, CAMOOWEAL CAVES NP, BARKLY HWY, Kerringnew Swamp, Oolgoolgatti Swamp, ABORIGINAL TRUST, Alpurrurulam, BARRY PLAIN, Urandangi, URANDANGI NTH RD, IRRMARNE ABORIGINAL LAND TRUST, Mount Hogarth, ANATYE ABORIGINAL LAND TRUST, Tobermorey, DONOHUE, BARKLY TABLELAND, Mount Guide, Mount Brown, Mount Pozieres, PLENTY HWY, Mount Cornish, Marqua, ADAM, TOOMBA RA, Orrtipa-Thurra, Mount Ewing, Mount Renecke, Mount Woods, ATNETYE ABORIGINAL LAND TRUST, CAPRICORN, Mount Winnecke, RA, Mount Beck, Mount Knuckey, Lake Caroline, Mount Gardner, CHANNEL COUNTRY, NYENTE ABORIGINAL TRUST, NORTHERN TERRITORY, QUEENSLAND, SIMPSON DESERT, MUNGA-THIRRI NATIONAL PARK, PMER LPERRE WEMIRNE LETHERRE ABORIGINAL LAND TRUST, Mirranponga Pongunna Lake, Poeppel Corner, Birdsville, TERRITORY, QUEENSLAND, SIMPSON DESERT, AUSTRALIA, SIMPSON DESERT CONSERVATION PARK, SIMPSON DESERT REGIONAL RESERVE.

For state road atlas coverage see pages 354–7

Scale: 0 — 40 — 80 — 120 km (with N compass)

HENBURY METEORITES CONSERVATION RESERVE

When the Henbury meteorite split into chunks and hit the earth at 40 000 kph, it left 12 large craters. Marvel at the impact when you take the self-guided walk around the craters.

Who to contact: PWCNT Alice Springs Telegraph Station (08) 8952 1013

144 Henbury Meteorites camping area

The park can be reached in a conventional vehicle. Take the Stuart Hwy south of Alice Springs for 130 km, then turn onto the gravel road leading to Watarrka National Park and drive for 8 km, then take the turn-off north for 5 km to reach the reserve's entrance. You'll need to bring your own drinking water and collect firewood before entering the park. Dogs are allowed on leads in the carpark only. Do not remove any of the meteorite fragments.

Map refs: 342 E6, 356 H8

KARLU KARLU/DEVILS MARBLES CONSERVATION RESERVE

Enjoy the spectacular piles of red and orange granite boulders here, best observed at sunset and sunrise, when they seem to glow from within. There is a self-guided walk, and budding landscape photographers will be in heaven. There is no specific location from which to view or photograph the rock formations, so a wander around well in advance of sunset is recommended if you wish to scope out a pleasing scene. The 1802 ha reserve spreads over both sides of the Stuart Hwy, nearly 400 km north of Alice Springs.

Who to contact: PWCNT Tennant Creek (08) 8962 4599

145 Devils Marbles camping area

The simple camping area is 1 km east of the hwy, with signposted access 9 km north of Wauchope. No generators are allowed; bring in your own firewood and water, and note that dogs are only permitted in the campground (not on walking tracks). The campsites all surround a large carpark/turnaround and there is little shade, but a stopover here is still worthwhile for viewing or photographing the rock formations at sunset and sunrise. There is a 15 min self-guided walk from the carpark.

Map refs: 342 E2, 355 J11

IYTWELEPENTY/DAVENPORT RANGE NATIONAL PARK

Described by many who go there as one of the most beautiful parks in the Red Centre, Itwelepenty/Davenport Range National Park has rolling ranges and a network of permanent waterholes that provide a refuge for animals. A day's drive north of Alice Springs, it doesn't get the number of visitors as other parks, such as West MacDonnell National Park, so is perfect for those who want to soak up its quiet beauty. There are some easy walks and it is possible to swim at the Old Police Station Waterhole when the water level is high. Access from the Stuart Hwy can be rough and quite corrugated and the road from the Barkly Hwy can have extensive bulldust holes.

Who to contact: PWCNT Tennant Creek (08) 8962 4599

146 Frew River camping area

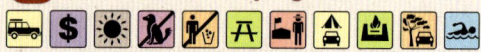

This isolated spot is on a rough 4WD track, the 17 km Frew River Loop, and is recommended for dry weather only. The basic campsite is 5 km from the Old Police Station Waterhole camping area. **Map refs:** 342 F2, 355 K11, 357 K1

147 Old Police Station Waterhole camping area

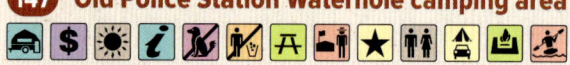

This waterhole has abundant birdlife and is great for swimming if the water levels are up, but beware of submerged logs and rocks. A 4WD is recommended to reach the campsite, and the road may be impassable in wet weather. Campsites here are widely spaced and next to the waterhole, but you will need to bring your own drinking water and firewood. It is a remote and peaceful location, and you may have it all to yourself. Take the road to Hatches Creek off the Stuart Hwy, 44 km north of Barrow Creek. Travel along this road for 165 km, then follow the signposted turn-off for 8 km. **Map refs:** 342 F2, 355 K11, 357 K1

148 Whistleduck Creek camping area

A 4WD is not essential but is recommended to reach this site, and the road may be unsuitable in wet weather. Camping facilities are limited and you'll need to bring your own firewood and drinking water. From the Stuart Hwy, 27 km north of Wauchope, take the Kurundi Rd east for 70 km, then follow the sign for 23 km. **Map refs:** 342 F2, 355 K11, 357 K1

N'DHALA GORGE NATURE PARK

A cultural treasure-house, N'Dhala Gorge contains nearly 6000 petroglyphs, or Aboriginal rock carvings, some of which could be 10 000 years old. There is a 1.5 km walk into the gorge with interpretive signs. Take the Ross Hwy for about 90 km east of Alice Springs and then the turn-off to the right to Ross River Homestead.

Who to contact: PWCNT Trephina Gorge (08) 8956 9765

149 N'Dhala Gorge Nature Park camping area

From the Ross River Homestead there is 11 km of 4WD track to the gorge, and the track becomes impassable after heavy rain. The small campsite is near the park entrance. Generators are not permitted and you will need to bring your own water. A 1.5 km walking track leads into the gorge. **Map refs:** 342 F5, 357 J6

OWEN SPRINGS RESERVE

This 1780 sq km reserve just 50 km out of Alice Springs has many attractive points along the Hugh River, with spreading river red gums and large waterholes. The reserve is also packed with evidence of European explorer and settler history. A self-drive information sheet is available online or on-site. You will need a 4WD.

Who to contact: PWCNT Owen Springs (08) 8956 7300

150 Lawrence Gorge camping area (bush camping)

Bush camping is permitted between the signposts within the gorge, along the river. Access is via the Owen Springs Reserve Tourist Dr, 20 km north of Redbank Gorge. Take time to explore the historic Old Owen Springs Homestead. Dogs are not allowed at this camping area. **Map refs:** 342 E6, 357 I7

151 Redbank Waterhole camping area (bush camping)

Enter the park from the Stuart Hwy, travel along Owen Springs Reserve Tourist Dr for 4 km, then take the left turn for a further 2 km. Dogs are permitted here. There are no facilities, so bring everything you need. **Map refs:** 342 E6, 357 I7

RAINBOW VALLEY CONSERVATION RESERVE

This spectacular site displays a wide array of colour at sunset and in the early morning. Occasionally after rain a shallow claypan fills with water, providing wonderful reflections of the rocks. The reserve is signposted 100 km south of Alice Springs, off the Stuart Hwy and 4WD is recommended.

Who to contact: PWCNT Alice Springs Telegraph Station (08) 8952 1013

152 Rainbow Valley Conservation Reserve camping area

You'll need to bring your own drinking water and firewood to this campsite. The access road is sandy and recommended for 4WD only. All sites have a view of the brightly coloured cliffs; in winter both sunrise and sunset light up the rocks – in other seasons this only happens at sunset. There is good birdlife along the marked trail to the cliffs. **Map refs:** 342 E6, 357 I8

RUBY GAP NATURE PARK

Swim, wander and enjoy peaceful camping in this park, 150 km east of Alice Springs and 40 km east of the Artlunga Historical Reserve. A high-clearance 4WD is essential for Ruby Gap.

Who to contact: PWCNT Trephina Gorge (08) 8956 9765

153 Ruby Gap camping area (bush camping)

There are no camping facilities, but plenty of nice spots along the river between the park entrance and Ruby Gap. There are also no walking tracks, but experienced walkers can follow the riverbed upstream on a beautiful walk to Glen Annie Gorge. Garnets (not rubies) can be found in the sand of the river bed. Ruby Gap has few visitors and you may be undisturbed here. **Map refs:** 342 F5, 357 K6

TREPHINA GORGE NATURE PARK

One of the most delightful quiet spots in the Red Centre, Trephina Gorge Nature Park has beautiful swimming holes lined with river red gums and surrounded by cliffs. There are some excellent bushwalks, including the Chain of Ponds and Ridgetop Trail. The nature park is 85 km east of Alice Springs, and is accessible to all vehicles.

Who to contact: PWCNT Trephina Gorge (08) 8956 9765

154 John Hayes Rockhole camping area

A popular swimming spot in summer, this site is accessible only by 4WD. Bring your own drinking water to the campground.
Map refs: 342 E5, 357 J6

155 Trephina Bluff camping area

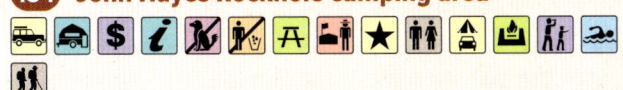

Set on Trephina Creek, about 1 km before the Gorge campground at the end of the unsealed road, this site is unsuitable for trailers or caravans. Swimming holes are extremely cold and there may be submerged rocks and logs.
Map refs: 342 E5, 357 J6

156 Trephina Gorge camping area

Take one of the great walks from this pleasant campground at the end of the unsealed road that is suitable for conventional vehicles. Also, for experienced walkers there is Trephina Ridgetop Trail. If swimming, note that the water may be extremely cold. **Map refs:** 342 E5, 357 J6

ULURU–KATA TJUTA NATIONAL PARK

This is probably the most iconic of all Australia's national parks, and the one best recognised internationally. The majestic monolith called Uluru, which appears to magically change colour at sunset and sunrise, is the main attraction in the park, but the domes of Kata Tjuta, or the Olgas, are equally beautiful. There are a variety of walks in the park (the flat walk around Uluru is particularly recommended), and an excellent cultural centre that describes the Anangu people and their way of life. You can also take cultural walks, learning about Dreamtime stories, bush tucker and other aspects of Anangu life. There is no camping in the park, which is reached via the Lasseter Hwy, 255 km west of the Stuart Hwy.

157 Ayers Rock Resort Campground

See p. 348.

WATARRKA NATIONAL PARK

This park of rugged ranges includes one of the most spectacular sites in the Red Centre – Kings Canyon, with its 100 m sheer rock walls protecting a lush gorge. The 3–4 hr Kings Canyon Rim Walk is one of the best half-day walks in the country, and at sunset the gorge cliffs light up. The detour to the Garden of Eden is worthwhile, and on hotter days provides welcome shade. There are several shorter walks, as well as the 22 km Giles Track which is suitable for overnight

walkers carrying everything. Access to the park is via Luritja Rd, from the south-east, or the 4WD Mereenie Loop Rd.

Who to contact: PWCNT Watarrka (08) 8956 7460
How to book: Kings Canyon Resort, Luritja Rd (08) 8956 7442
www.kingscanyonresort.com.au

158 Kings Canyon Resort Caravan Park and Campground

This privately owned resort is inside Watarrka National Park, 7 km north-east of Kings Canyon, off Luritja Rd. The camping area has powered and unpowered sites, in shady, grassed surrounds. The resort offers a wide range of facilities including bars, restaurants, swimming pool and tennis courts. Fuel is also available. There is a short walk to a spectacular sunset lookout with wonderful views to the escarpment. No fires are permitted.
Map refs: 342 C6, 356 F8

WEST MACDONNELL NATIONAL PARK

Stretching 170 km across the West MacDonnell Ranges west of Alice Springs, this is one of the most visited parks in the Red Centre. Its highest peak is 1531 m Mount Zeil, in the far west, and its gorges contain beautiful waterholes, startling white ghost gums, and retreats for wildlife. The park is connected by the 223 km Larapinta Trail, as well as by a multitude of shorter walks. A world-class bicycle path also leads through the park from Alice Springs. Most of the park trailheads are accessible by 2WD.

Who to contact: PWCNT Ormiston Gorge (08) 8956 7799

159 Arenge Bluff camping area (walk-in camping)

On the Larapinta Trail, this basic site overlooking Arenge Bluff is 10 km west of Simpsons Gap. Bring water and a gas/fuel stove.
Map refs: 342 E5, 357 I7

160 Birthday Waterhole camping area

A high-clearance 4WD is required to access the trailhead. This site is on the Larapinta Trail 18 km west of Standley Chasm. Bring a gas/fuel stove. **Map refs:** 342 E5, 356 H7

161 Brinkley Bluff camping area (walk-in camping)

On the Larapinta Trail, this bush camp with no facilities is 10 km west of Standley Chasm. Bring water and a gas/fuel stove.
Map refs: 342 E5, 357 I7

162 Bush camping area (walk-in camping)

On the Larapinta Trail, this basic camping area is between Ellery Creek and Rocky Gully. Bring water and a gas/fuel stove.
Map refs: 342 D5, 356 H7

163 Ellery Creek Big Hole camping area

This campsite is on the Larapinta Trail. It is also popular with those not hiking and is accessible with conventional 2WD vehicles. It is a short walk from a permanent waterhole surrounded by river red gums. There are also pleasant shady walks along the creek, which is usually dry. It is signposted off Namatjira Dr, 88 km west of Alice Springs. Bring drinking water. Note: generators are not permitted. **Map refs:** 342 D6, 356 H7

164 Finke River camping area (walk-in camping)

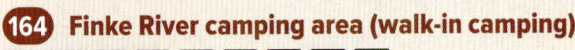

This trailhead for the Larapinta Trail has no vehicle access. It's 4WD to Finke River Two Mile camping and then a walk. The camping area has water and toilets, but you need to bring a gas/fuel stove. **Map refs:** 342 D5, 356 G7

165 Finke River Two Mile camping area

On the Larapinta Trail, this very basic site has no facilities and vehicle access is 4WD only. It is reached north of Namatjira Dr between the Glen Helen Resort access and the Finke River crossing. After heavier rains the Finke River can sometimes flow, and you can enjoy the sound of a river in the desert. Glen Helen Resort is easily accessible from here, for meals and helicopter flights over the West MacDonnell Ranges. Bring water and a gas/fuel stove. **Map refs:** 342 D5, 356 G7

166 Fringe Lily Creek camping area (walk-in camping)

On the Larapinta Trail, this basic campsite is between Windy Saddle and Rocky Saddle, and is 5.1 km from Hugh Gorge. Bring water and a gas/fuel stove. **Map refs:** 342 E5, 356 H7

167 Ghost Gum Flat camping area (walk-in camping)

On the Larapinta Trail, this camping area is 7 km from Hugh Gorge. There are no facilities and you must bring water and a gas/fuel stove. **Map refs:** 342 E5, 356 H7

168 Hilltop Lookout camping area (walk-in camping)

On the Larapinta Trail, this bush campsite has no facilities but a great lookout. Bring water and a gas/fuel stove. **Map refs:** 342 D5, 356 G6

169 Hugh Gorge camping area (walk-in camping)

On the Larapinta Trail, high-clearance 4WD vehicles can gain access to the carpark here, which is 15 km west of Birthday Waterhole. There is drinking water but no other facilities. Bring a gas/fuel stove. **Map refs:** 342 E5, 356 H7

170 Hugh Gorge Junction camping area (walk-in camping)

On the Larapinta Trail, this basic campsite is 3.5 km from Hugh Gorge. Bring water and a gas/fuel stove. **Map refs:** 342 E5, 356 H7

171 Jay Creek camping area (walk-in camping)

This is a section trailhead on the Larapinta Trail, and 4WDs can reach to within 1 km of it. There are gas BBQs, toilets and drinking water. **Map refs:** 342 E5, 357 I6

172 Millers Flat camping area (walk-in camping)

On the Larapinta Trail, this site is 9 km west of Jay Creek. It has no facilities and you need to bring water and a gas/fuel stove. **Map refs:** 342 E5, 357 I7

173 Mulga Camp camping area (walk-in camping)

On the Larapinta Trail, Mulga Camp is 13 km west of Simpsons Gap. Bring a gas/fuel stove. **Map refs:** 342 E5, 357 I7

174 Ormiston Gorge camping area

On the Larapinta Trail, this popular campsite can be reached by conventional 2WD vehicles and has good facilities. The site is 7 km off Namatjira Dr, 128 km west of Alice Springs. A number of walking trails start and finish here, including the Ormiston Pound Circuit and the Ghost Gum Lookout walk, which finishes at a viewing platform over Ormiston Gorge. **Map refs:** 342 D5, 356 G6

175 Redbank Gorge camping area (bush camping)

This bush camping area is for walkers on the Larapinta Trail only. There are no facilities: bring water and a gas/fuel stove. **Map refs:** 342 D5, 356 G6

176 Redbank Gorge – Ridgetop camping area

This campsite is on the Larapinta Trail, 3.5 km north of Namatjira Dr, 152 km west of Alice Springs. Vehicles can access this site but 4WD is recommended. Bring drinking water. Note: no generators are allowed. This campsite has good views of the ranges. A short drive takes you to the walking access to Redbank Gorge itself. There are permanent waterholes at the top of the gorge and in dry times the trail follows the sandy river bed. When wet there is still access via a track along the bank. **Map refs:** 342 D5, 356 G6

Camping along the Finke River, Finke Gorge National Park (p. 341)

177 Redbank Gorge – Woodland camping area

On the Larapinta Trail, this camping area has large sites amongst mulga shrubs. There are facilities including a free gas BBQ. It is the trailhead for Section 11. Bring drinking water. **Map refs:** 342 D5, 356 G6

178 Rocky Bar Gap camping area (walk-in camping)

On the Larapinta Trail, this site is 15 km west of the Finke River trailhead and has no facilities except drinking water. Bring a gas/fuel stove. **Map refs:** 342 D5, 356 G6

179 Rocky Gully camping area (walk-in camping)

On the Larapinta Trail, Rocky Gully, with toilets and water, is 15.3 km from Ellery Creek. Bring a gas/fuel stove. **Map refs:** 342 E5, 356 H7

180 Section 4 & 5 Junction camping area (walk-in camping)

On the Larapinta Trail, this bush camping area has no facilities. Bring water and a gas/fuel stove. It is between Birthday Waterhole and Mintbush Spring. **Map refs:** 342 E5, 356 H7

181 Serpentine Chalet camping area

This 4WD-access camping area is off Namatjira Dr. No generators are allowed and you need to bring firewood, a gas/fuel stove and drinking water. Quiet and secluded, it has dispersed bush camping sites along the track to Serpentine Chalet Ruins. The walk from the end of the road is pleasant and ends at an old dam and reservoir near the mouth of the gorge. **Map refs:** 342 D5, 356 H7

182 Serpentine Chalet Dam camping area (walk-in camping)

On the Larapinta Trail, this bush campsite requires a 4WD to access the carpark. It is then a 750 m walk to the camping area. Bring a gas/fuel stove. **Map refs:** 342 D5, 356 H7

183 Serpentine Gorge camping area (walk-in camping)

This trailhead is 14 km west of Ellery Creek Big Hole. The campsite is located about 500 m along the trail from the carpark to the gorge. The view from the lookout further along this trail is quite spectacular and worth the steep climb. **Map refs:** 342 D5, 356 H7

184 Simpsons Gap camping area (walk-in camping)

On the Larapinta Trail, this camping area is only available to walkers of the trail. **Map refs:** 342 E5, 357 I7

185 Stuarts Pass camping area (walk-in camping)

On the Larapinta Trail, this camping area 3 km from Brinkley Bluff has no facilities. Bring water and a gas/fuel stove. **Map refs:** 342 E5, 357 I7

186 Wallaby Gap camping area (walk-in camping)

On the Larapinta Trail, just 300 m from Wallaby Gap, this site is 13 km west of Alice Springs Telegraph Station. **Map refs:** 342 E5, 357 I7

187 Waterfall Gorge camping area (walk-in camping)

On the Larapinta Trail, Waterfall Gorge has no facilities and is 1.6 km from the nearby lookout. Bring water and a gas/fuel stove. **Map refs:** 342 D5, 356 H7

CAMPSITES LOCATED IN OTHER AREAS

188 Aileron Roadhouse

As well as all the necessities, such as fuel and supplies, this roadhouse has an Aboriginal art gallery, pool, bar and BBQ picnic area. It's 135 km north of Alice Springs, and you can't really miss it now that giant statues of Aboriginal people have been constructed. First was the Big Man, with the tip of his spear 17 m off the ground, and more recently the Big Woman and Child was added. **Map refs:** 342 E4, 356 H5

How to book: Stuart Hwy, Aileron (08) 8956 9703 www.aileronroadhouse.com.au

189 Alice Springs Heritage Caravan and Tourist Park

Although a little out of the main part of Alice, this 4-star park is in a peaceful location near an old date farm. It has a cracking great pool, shade trees and even includes a library. Head south out of Alice Springs on the Stuart Hwy. **Map refs:** 342 E5, 357 I7

How to book: Ragonesi Rd, Alice Springs (08) 8952 3135 www.heritagecaravanpark.com.au

157 Ayers Rock Resort Campground

The Ayers Rock campground has a very large shady camping area, with powered and unpowered sites. Cabins are also available, and there are bicycles to hire. The campsite includes a pool, 2 tennis courts and a wireless internet kiosk. The resort itself has all the facilities of a 5-star hotel, with easy access to tours. Look for the signpost 8 km before the park entrance. **Map refs:** 342 C7, 356 E10

How to book: Lasseter Hwy, Yulara (08) 8957 7001 www.ayersrockresort.com.au

190 Barkly Homestead

The last fuel stop before crossing over into Queensland on the Barkly Hwy, the homestead is about 210 km east of Tennant Creek. There isn't much to do in the area – the Devils Marbles are probably the closest attraction, and they're more than 200 km away. However, there are powered and unpowered campsites, and a licensed pub. Some firewood is supplied. **Map refs:** 343 G1, 355 L9

How to book: Barkly Hwy, Tennant Creek (08) 8964 4549 www.barklyhomestead.com.au

191 Barrow Creek Hotel

On the Stuart Hwy, about 290 km north of Alice Springs, this historic building was the earliest hotel constructed along the north–south road between Alice Springs and Tennant Creek. Its original features include the cellar, pressed-tin ceilings, and most of the windows and doors. Grab a key and inspect the old telegraph station next door, or go for a hike up to the lookout to see the sunset. Bring your own drinking water and firewood if you are staying here. **Map refs:** 342 E3, 357 I2

How to book: Stuart Hwy, Barrow Creek (08) 8956 9753

192 Curtin Springs Roadhouse

There are plenty of free unpowered campsites at this roadhouse, conveniently located on the Lasseter Hwy, 85 km east of the entrance to the Uluru–Kata Tjuta National Park. There are also 8 powered sites, a pub and a store. Take tours of the working cattle station or of Mt Conner, or daytrips into the national park. Bring your own firewood. Drinking water is bore water, and you can purchase bottled water. A small fee is charged for showers. **Map refs:** 342 C7, 356 F10

How to book: Curtin Springs Station, Lasseter Hwy (08) 8956 2906 www.curtinsprings.com

193 Desert Oaks Resort

Packed with facilities, including a pool, tennis court, playground and licensed restaurant, the Desert Oaks Resort is 200 km south of Alice Springs. It is another 2.5 hr drive to Uluru–Kata Tjuta National Park, but campers with 4WD can explore places such as Rainbow Valley and Chambers Pillar in the area. Firewood can be supplied, but you will need to bring your own drinking water. There are powered and unpowered sites. **Map refs:** 342 E7, 356 H9

How to book: cnr Stuart and Lasseter hwys, Erldunda (08) 8956 0984 www.desertoaksresort.com

194 Docker River Campground

Camp almost on the WA border in a grove of shady desert oaks with views of sand dunes and the stunning Petermann

Ranges. You'll need to be well prepared: the road is unsealed and probably not suitable for caravans, with at least 180 km of rough, sandy road. The campsite, which is signposted 1 km west of Docker River community, is managed by the community. **Map refs:** 342 A7, 356 B9

Who to contact: Docker River Council (08) 8956 7337
Permits: A transit permit is required to travel the Outback Way; contact Central Land Council (08) 8950 6320, Ngaanyatjarra Council (08) 8950 1711, or apply online at www.clc.org.au

195 Gemtree Caravan Park

The primary reason to camp at Gemtree, 70 km east of the Stuart Hwy, is the great fossicking for garnet and zircon. Fossicking tours can be booked, but only by prior arrangement in the summer months. There is also a nature trail and opportunities for birdwatching. During the main Apr–Sept season you'll need to book to camp among the mulga trees. There are powered and unpowered sites, fuel, a general store and you can rent 2-person tents with airbeds. Firewood is available for sale and you can pick oranges, lemons and mandarins from the orchard. Note: no portable generators. **Map refs:** 342 E5, 357 J5

How to book: Plenty Hwy, Alice Springs (08) 8956 9855
www.gemtree.com.au

196 Glen Helen Resort

Glen Helen Resort is surrounded by the West MacDonnell Ranges and is within walking distance of the Larapinta Trail. Palm Valley, Hermannsberg and the gorges and canyons of the national park are only short drives away. There is powered and unpowered camping, many sites with views of the escarpment. Most grassy sites have fireplaces but bring your own wood. BYO alcohol is not allowed and you need to bring your own drinking water. The resort has all facilities, including restaurants, swimming pool and tour bookings. **Map refs:** 342 D5, 356 G7

How to book: Namatjira Dr, West MacDonnell Ranges
(08) 8956 7489 www.glenhelen.com.au

197 Jervois Station

This working cattle station has fuel and a shop, as well as a simple camping area 1 km off the Plenty Hwy, some 277 km east of the Stuart Hwy. There are no powered sites, but there are eco-cabins with power to hire (booking required). The road is recommended for 4WD only and can be impassable after rain, although many people do bring caravans. There is plenty of firewood to collect in the area. **Map refs:** 343 G5, 357 M5

How to book Plenty Hwy (08) 8956 6307

198 Jim's Place/Stuarts Well Roadhouse

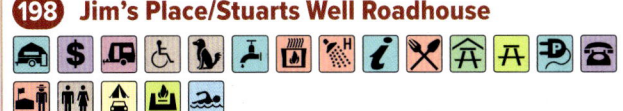

With a pool, fuel, restaurant and bar, and camel tours and safaris next door, Jim's Place is a welcome stopover 90 km south of Alice Springs. You'll need to bring your own firewood, but everything else is available, and there are extensive information panels about the history of the area. **Map refs:** 342 E6, 357 I8

Who to contact: Stuarts Well, Stuart Hwy (08) 8956 0808

199 Kings Creek Station

The largest exporter of camels in Australia, this is one of the best spots to go for a camel safari across an outback station. There are also quad-bike rides and helicopter tours, and a live 'stock camp' show. The camping area has trees and a swimming pool, and there is a station shop with cooked food and supplies, but the camp kitchen is only for those staying in the cabins. You will need to bring your own firewood. It's 35 km south-east of the Watarrka National Park, off Luritja Rd. **Map refs:** 342 C6, 356 F8

How to book: online at www.kingscreekstation.com.au

200 Kulgera Roadhouse

Just 20 km north of the NT–SA border, on the Stuart Hwy, this is an intermediate stop for many travellers. The roadhouse has supplies and eating facilities, and the camping area has powered and unpowered sites. You can boil the water and drink it, or you may want to bring your own. You will also need your own firewood. **Map refs:** 342 E8, 356 H11

How to book: Stuart Hwy, Kulgera (08) 8956 0973

Larapinta Trail

One of the premier arid-land walks in the world, this 223 km route goes over rugged ranges and through sheltered gorges in West MacDonnell National Park. The whole route will take 1–2 weeks, but it is designed in sections so you can choose shorter overnight trips or even day walks; you will need to organise your own transport. Most campsites have picnic tables and hardened tent sites, all the trailheads have a water supply and some have free gas BBQs. You will need to carry in a portable gas/fuel stove.

Please note that campsites are listed in alphabetical order within section, not track order. Refer to the map on p. 342 for further information.

Who to contact: PWCNT Alice Springs (08) 8951 8211

Section 1

184 Simpsons Gap camping area (walk-in camping)
See p. 347.

186 Wallaby Gap camping area (walk-in camping)
See p. 348.

Section 2

159 **Arenge Bluff camping area (walk-in camping)**
See p. 345.

171 **Jay Creek camping area (walk-in camping)**
See p.346.

173 **Mulga Camp camping area (walk-in camping)**
See p. 346.

Section 3

172 **Millers Flat camping area (walk-in camping)**
See p. 346.

201 **Standley Chasm camping area**

Standley Chasm is privately owned and operated and there is a fee to access the gorge. There is unpowered camping here plus 2 powered sites, and basic facilities. The area is predominantly a carpark but there are also picnic tables and BBQs. Drinking water is available at the kiosk. **Map refs:** 342 E5, 357 I7

How to book: Larapinta Dr (08) 8956 7440
www.standleychasm.com.au

Section 4

160 **Birthday Waterhole camping area**
See p. 345.

161 **Brinkley Bluff camping area (walk-in camping)**
See p. 345.

180 **Section 4 & 5 Junction camping area (walk-in camping)**
See p. 347.

185 **Stuarts Pass camping area (walk-in camping)**
See p. 347.

Section 5

166 **Fringe Lily Creek camping area (walk-in camping)**
See p. 346.

169 **Hugh Gorge camping area (walk-in camping)**
See p. 346.

170 **Hugh Gorge Junction camping area (walk-in camping)**
See p. 346.

Section 6

162 **Bush camping area (walk-in camping)**
See p. 345.

163 **Ellery Creek Big Hole camping area**
See p. 346.

167 **Ghost Gum Flat camping area (walk-in camping)**
See p. 346.

179 **Rocky Gully camping area (walk-in camping)**
See p. 347.

Section 7

183 **Serpentine Gorge camping area (walk-in camping)**
See p. 347.

Section 8

181 **Serpentine Chalet camping area**
See p. 347.

182 **Serpentine Chalet Dam camping area (walk-in camping)**
See p. 347.

Section 9

174 **Ormiston Gorge camping area**
See p. 346.

187 **Waterfall Gorge camping area (walk-in camping)**
See p. 348.

Section 10

164 **Finke River camping area (walk-in camping)**
See p. 346.

Section 11

168 **Hilltop Lookout camping area (walk-in camping)**
See p. 346.

175 **Redbank Gorge camping area (bush camping)**
See p. 346.

176 **Redbank Gorge – Ridgetop camping area**
See p. 346.

177 **Redbank Gorge – Woodland camping area**
See p. 347.

178 **Rocky Bar Gap camping area (walk-in camping)**
See p. 347.

202 **MacDonnell Range Holiday Park**

This caravan park is set in picturesque surroundings in the MacDonnell Ranges, 4 km south of Alice Springs. There is plenty to do: hire a bike and cycle into town or visit the recreation room with pool tables, table tennis and video games. Youngsters enjoy the pedal-powered go-carts, BMX track, half-court basketball and jumping pillows. There are villas, cabins, ensuite powered sites and unpowered sites, as well as 2 swimming pools and a children's wading pool. Follow the Stuart Hwy just south of Alice Springs through the gap in the MacDonnell Ranges. **Map refs:** 342 E5, 357 I7

How to book: Palm Pl, Alice Springs (08) 8952 6111, 1800 808 373 www.macrange.com.au

203 Oak Valley camping area

Experience a guided tour of Aboriginal rock-art sites and fossil fields from this simple campground owned and run by the local Aboriginal community. Follow the Old South Rd, near the Alice Springs Airport, south for 87 km, and then take the signposted turn-off west for 10 km. A 4WD is advisable. **Map refs:** 342 E6, 357 I8

How to book: (08) 8956 0959

204 Old Andado Homestead

On the fringe of the Simpson Desert, 330 km south-east of Alice Springs, you can look through the 1920s homestead, which has been restored as a museum. Caretakers are usually on hand to discuss the history of the old homestead and life prior to electricity, running water and phones. Camping is permitted, and there are shower facilities (heated with a donkey boiler), but you'll need to bring all your own drinking water, supplies and firewood. There is only 4WD access from the north via the Old Andado Track, or via the Stuart Hwy to Kulgera and then in through Finke Community (Apatula), through New Crown and Andado stations. **Map refs:** 342 F7, 357 L10

How to book: (08) 8956 0812 www.oldandado.com

205 Outback Caravan Park

Explore the region's 4WD tracks and experience Aboriginal and European history. This park is renowned for its tropical gardens, shaded swimming pool and spa. The park has cabins as well as powered and unpowered sites. **Map refs:** 342 E1, 355 J9

How to book: Peko Rd, Tennant Creek (08) 8962 2459

206 Serpentine Chalet Bush Camp

This is a quiet spot off the hwy. The camping area here is accessible for 2WDs but you will need 4WD to reach Serpentine Chalet Dam and link into the Larapinta Trail. It is not recommended for caravans or motorhomes. **Map refs:** 342 D5, 356 H7

Who to contact: Namatjira Dr, Alice Springs (08) 8951 8250

207 Tilmouth Well Roadhouse

Here you can take part in cattle work, study the local art in the Wirmbrandt Gallery, play golf, go for walks or lounge around the pool. You will also find a restaurant and bar, air-conditioned cabins and 2 powered campsites, plus plenty of unpowered sites. There is a sealed road all the way from Alice Springs to Tilmouth Well, which is on the edge of Napperby Station. Take the Tanami Track off the Stuart Hwy, 20 km north of Alice Springs, and follow it for 166 km. **Map refs:** 342 D5, 356 G5

Who to contact: Tanami Track via Stuart Hwy (08) 8956 8777 www.tilmouthwell.com

208 Ti-Tree Roadhouse

Although mainly a stop for people passing through, there are a few attractions in the local area, including a mango farm, tea-tree farm, grape farm, gem prospecting and an Aboriginal art gallery. Central Mt Stuart is nearby, indicating the approximate geographical centre of Australia. The roadhouse has a pool, restaurant and bar. It's on the Stuart Hwy, 193 km north of Alice Springs, about 60 km past Aileron. **Map refs:** 342 E4, 357 I4

How to book: Stuart Hwy, Ti Tree (08) 8956 9741

209 Wallace Rockhole Tourist Park

Take part in dot-painting workshops and Aboriginal rock-art tours at this cosy campground nestled among trees that provide reasonable shade in summer. You will need to bring your own firewood. Signposted off the Larapinta Dr, 100 km west of Alice Springs, the campground is 17 km from the turn-off. It is best to book if you would like a powered site. **Map refs:** 342 D6, 356 H7

How to book: Larapinta Dr (08) 8956 7993 www.wallacerockholetours.com.au

210 Wauchope Hotel

Just 8 km from the Devils Marbles, 114 km south of Tennant Creek, this historic pub and roadhouse dates back to the 1930s. You can hire bikes and ride to the Devils Marbles, lounge around the pool, or enjoy the other facilities such as the cafe and licensed restaurant. Fires are permitted but you will need to bring your own firewood. **Map refs:** 342 E2, 355 J11, 357 J1

How to book: Stuart Hwy, Wauchope (08) 8964 1963 www.wauchopehotel.com.au

211 Wycliffe Well Holiday Park

One wonders if the fact that this is one of the highest ranking sites for reported UFO activity in the world has anything to do with the huge range of beers on offer. This well-catered park, with 24 ha of parkland, has an indoor swimming pool, 50 powered sites, restaurants, cabins and often hosts a 2 hr country and western singalong for free! It's just 25 km from the Devils Marbles on the Stuart Hwy, 131 km south of Tennant Creek. **Map refs:** 342 E2, 355 J11, 357 J1

How to book: Stuart Hwy, Wycliffe (08) 8964 1966, 1800 222 195 www.wycliffe.com.au

Top End

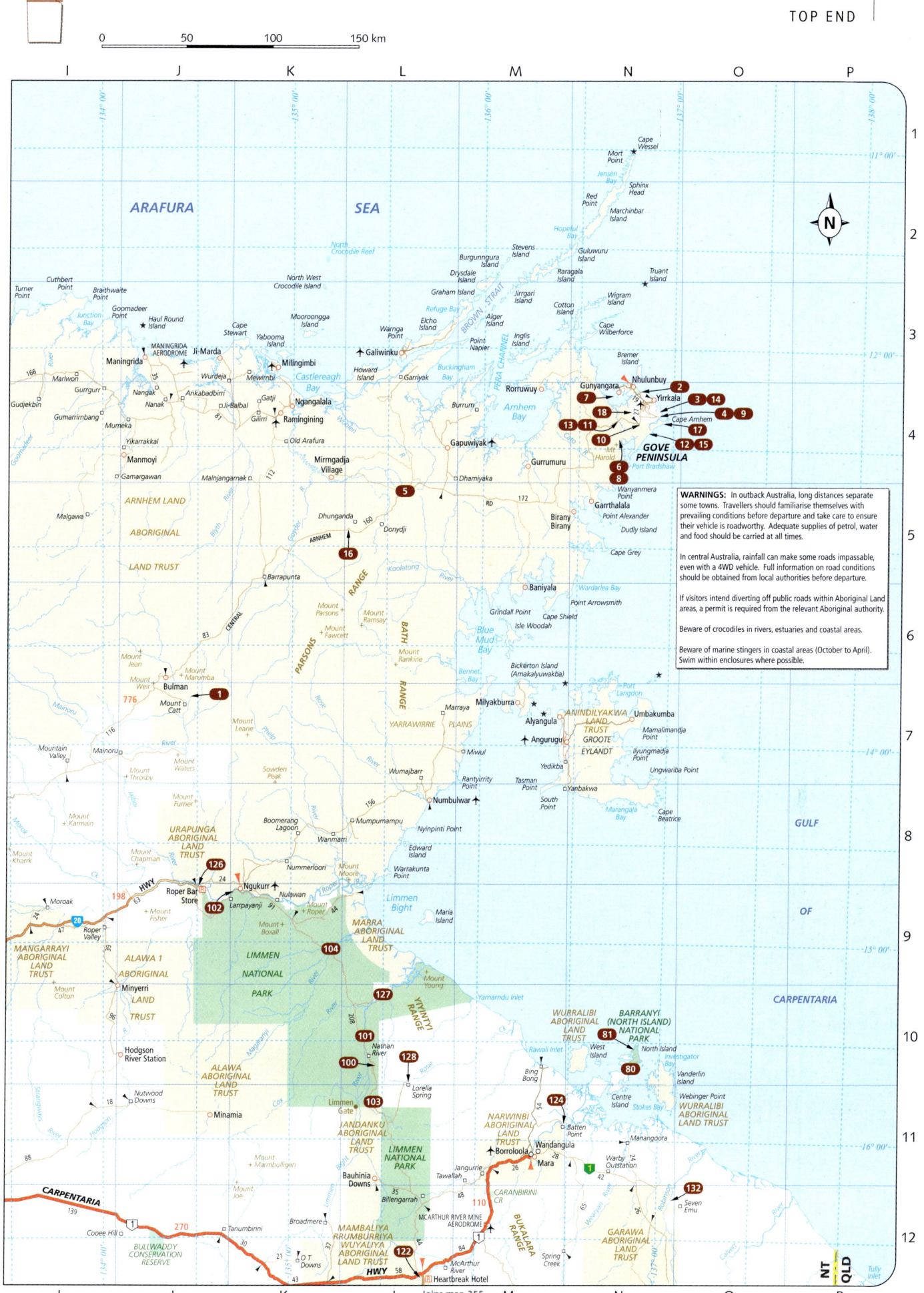

0   50   100   150 km

I   J   K   L   M   N   O   P

ARAFURA   SEA

1

2

North
Crocodile Reef

Cape
Wessel
Mort
Point
Jensen
Bay
Sphinx
Head
Red
Point
Marchinbar
Island

Turner
Point
Cuthbert
Point
Braithwaite
Point
Burgunngura
Island
Stevens
Island
Guluwuru
Island
Truant
Island

3

Junction
Bay
Goomadeer
Point
Haul Round
Island
Cape
Stewart
Yabooma
Island
Mooroongga
Island
North West
Crocodile Island
Warnga
Point
Drysdale Island
Elcho Bay
Jirrgari
Island
Cotton
Island
Wigram
Island
Cape
Wilberforce
Bremer
Island

166
Marlwon
MANINGRIDA
AERODROME
Ji-Marda
Wurdeja
Mewinbi
Howard
Island
Graham Island
Point Napier
Alger
Island
Inglis
Island
Nhulunbuy
Cape Arnhem

Maningrida
Gurrgurr
Nangak
Nanak
Ankabadbirri
Gatji
Ji-Balbal
Gilirri
Ramingining
Garriyak
Burrum
Roruwuy
Gunyangara
Yirrkala
2
3 **14**
7
18
4 **9**

Gudjekbin
Gumarrirnbang
Mumeka
Yikarrakkal
Old Arafura
Gapuwiyak
Arnhem
Bay
13 **11**
10
17
12 **15**
**GOVE
PENINSULA**

4

Manmoyi
Gamargawan
Mirrngadja
Village
Malnjangarnak
112
Dhamiyaka
Gurrumuru
Mt
Harold
6
8
Port Bradshaw

ARNHEM LAND

Malgawa
Dhunganda
Donydji
RD
172
Birany
Birany
Garrthalala
Point Alexander
Wanyanmara
Point
Dudly Island

5

ABORIGINAL

5

160
ARNHEM
16
Cape Grey

LAND TRUST

Barrapunta
Koolatong
Baniyala
Wardarlea Bay
Point Arrowsmith

6

Mount
Parsons
Mount
Fawcett
Mount
Ramsay
Mount
Rankine
Grindall Point
Cape Shield
Isle Woodah
Blue
Mud
Bay
Bennet
Bay
Bickerton Island
(Amakalyuwakba)
Port
Langdon

Mount
Jean
Mount
Marumba
Bulman
Mount
Leane
Milyakburra
Maraya
Marraya
ANINDILYAKWA
LAND
TRUST
Umbakumba
Mamalimandja
Point

776
1
Mount
Catt
116
Mount
Throsby
Mount
Waters
Mount
Furner
Yarrawirrie
Plains
Alyangula
Angurugu
GROOTE
EYLANDT
Ilyungmadja
Point

7

Mountain
Valley
Mainoru
Sowden
Peak
Wumajbarr
Miwul
Yedikba
Yanbakwa
Ungwariba Point

Mount
Kharrk
Mount
Karmain
Boomerang
Lagoon
Wanmarri
Mumpumampu
Rantyirrity
Point
Tasman
Point
South
Point
Cape
Beatrice

8

URAPUNGA
ABORIGINAL
LAND
TRUST
Mount
Chapman
Nummerloori
Mount
Moore
Edward
Island
Numbulwar
Marangala
Bay

GULF

OF

Moroak
126
Ngukurr
Nulawan
Warrakunta
Point
Limmen
Bight
Maria
Island

9

HWY
198
24
Roper Bar
Store
102
Larrpayanji
Mount
Roper
44
MARRA
ABORIGINAL
LAND
TRUST

20
Roper
Valley
Mount
Fisher
104
Mount
Boxall

CARPENTARIA

MANGARRAYI
ABORIGINAL
LAND
TRUST
ALAWA 1
ABORIGINAL
LIMMEN
NATIONAL
Mount
Young
Yarnamdu Inlet
WURRALIBI
ABORIGINAL
LAND
TRUST
BARRANYI
(NORTH ISLAND)
NATIONAL
PARK

Mount
Colton
Minyerri
LAND
TRUST
PARK
127
YYINYTYI
RANGE
Rawali Inlet
West
Island
North Island
Investigator
Bay
81

10

Hodgson
River Station
101
Nathan
River
Bing
Bong
80
Vanderlin
Island

Nutwood
Downs
ALAWA
ABORIGINAL
LAND
TRUST
100
128
Lorella
Spring
NARWINBI
ABORIGINAL
LAND
TRUST
Centre
Island
Stokes Bay
Webinger Point
WURRALIBI
ABORIGINAL
LAND
TRUST

18
Downs
Minamia
Limmen
Gate
103
Batten
Point
124
Manangoora

11

88
Mount
Mambulligan
JANDANKU
ABORIGINAL
LAND
TRUST
LIMMEN
NATIONAL
PARK
Jangurrie
Tawallah
Borroloola
Wandangula
Mara
Warby
Outstation
42
54

Bauhinia
Downs
35
Billengarrah
26
CARANBIRINI
CR
110
132
Seven
Emu

CARPENTARIA
139
GARAWA
ABORIGINAL
LAND
TRUST

Cooee Hill
270
Tanumbirini
Broadmere
MCARTHUR RIVER MINE
AERODROME
BUKALARA
RANGE
Spring
Creek

12

Mount
Joe
MAMBALIYA
RRUMBURRIYA
WUYALIYA
ABORIGINAL
LAND TRUST
122
McArthur
River
HWY
58
Heartbreak Hotel

BULLWADDY
CONSERVATION
RESERVE
O T
Downs
43
NT
QLD

Joins map 355

I   J   K   L   M   N   O   P

Joins map 355

WARNINGS: In outback Australia, long distances separate some towns. Travellers should familiarise themselves with prevailing conditions before departure and take care to ensure their vehicle is roadworthy. Adequate supplies of petrol, water and food should be carried at all times.

In central Australia, rainfall can make some roads impassable, even with a 4WD vehicle. Full information on road conditions should be obtained from local authorities before departure.

If visitors intend diverting off public roads within Aboriginal Land areas, a permit is required from the relevant Aboriginal authority.

Beware of crocodiles in rivers, estuaries and coastal areas.

Beware of marine stingers in coastal areas (October to April). Swim within enclosures where possible.

Central Northern Territory

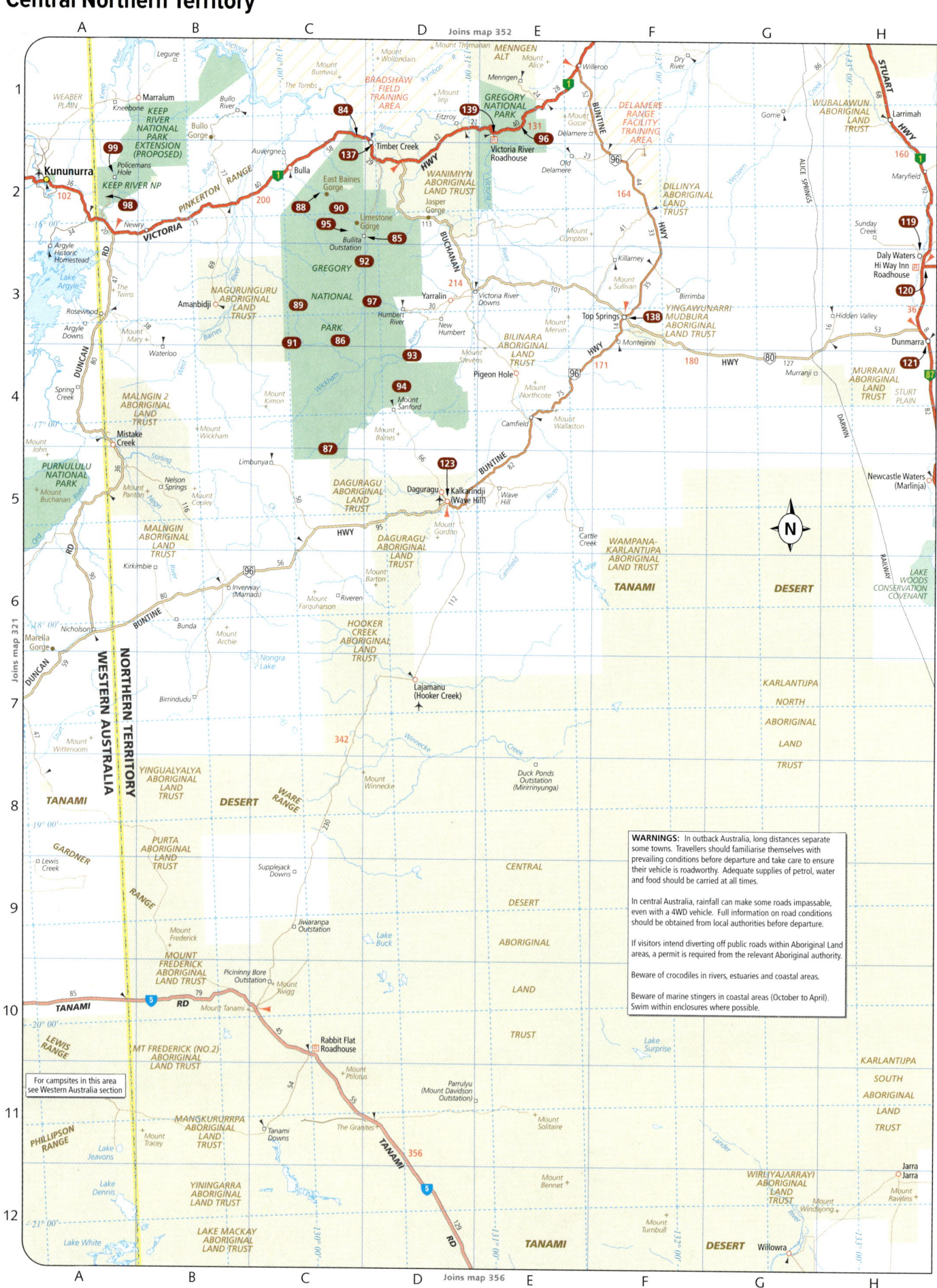

Joins map 352
Joins map 321
Joins map 356

WARNINGS: In outback Australia, long distances separate some towns. Travellers should familiarise themselves with prevailing conditions before departure and take care to ensure their vehicle is roadworthy. Adequate supplies of petrol, water and food should be carried at all times.

In central Australia, rainfall can make some roads impassable, even with a 4WD vehicle. Full information on road conditions should be obtained from local authorities before departure.

If visitors intend diverting off public roads within Aboriginal Land areas, a permit is required from the relevant Aboriginal authority.

Beware of crocodiles in rivers, estuaries and coastal areas.

Beware of marine stingers in coastal areas (October to April). Swim within enclosures where possible.

For campsites in this area see Western Australia section

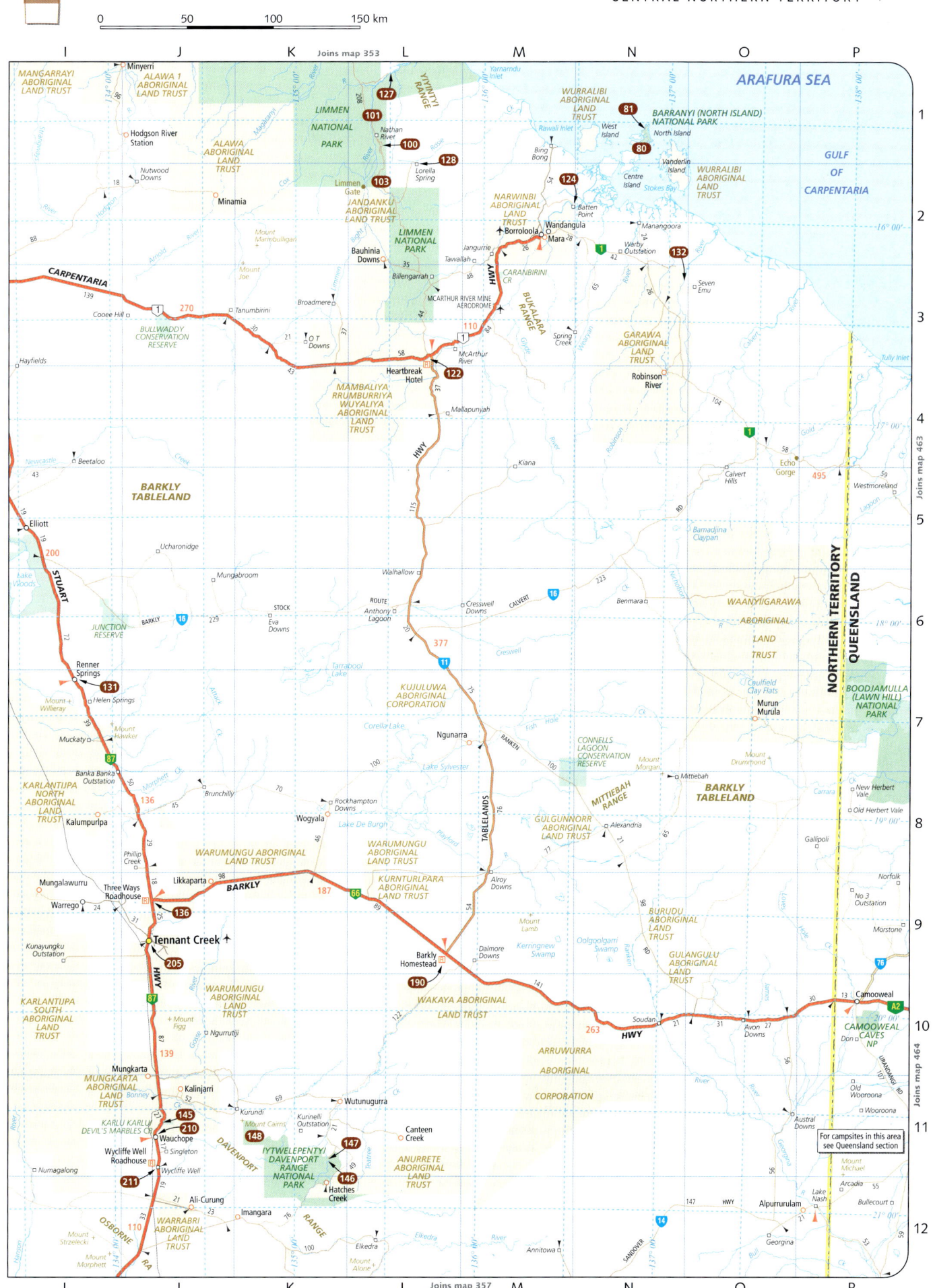

ARAFURA SEA

GULF
OF
CARPENTARIA

NORTHERN TERRITORY

QUEENSLAND

Joins map 463

Joins map 464

For campsites in this area
see Queensland section

Southern Northern Territory

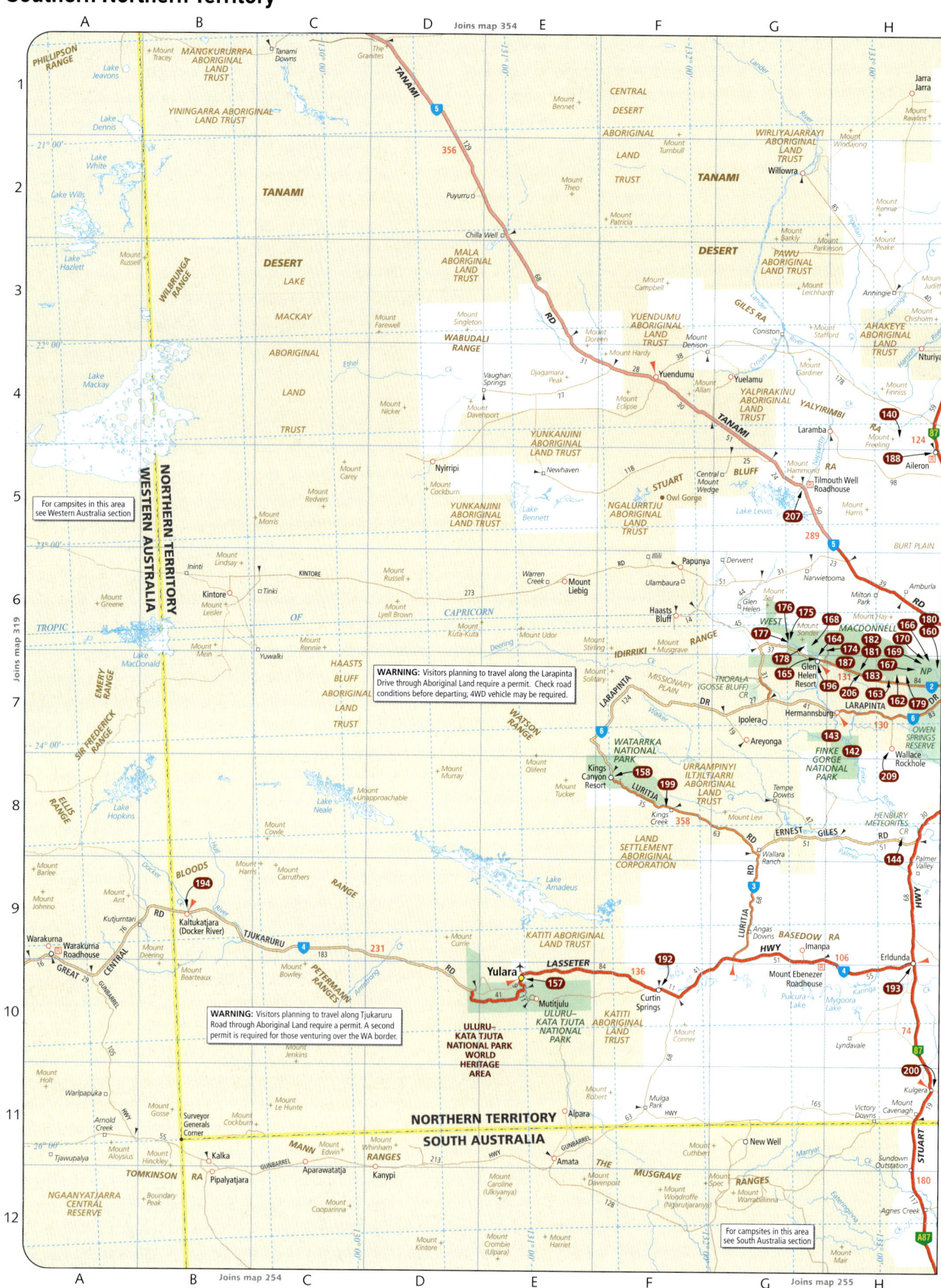

Joins map 354

Joins map 319

For campsites in this area see Western Australia section

WARNING: Visitors planning to travel along the Larapinta Drive through Aboriginal Land require a permit. Check road conditions before departing; 4WD vehicle may be required.

WARNING: Visitors planning to travel along Tjukaruru Road through Aboriginal Land require a permit. A second permit is required for those venturing over the WA border.

For campsites in this area see South Australia section

Joins map 254

Joins map 255

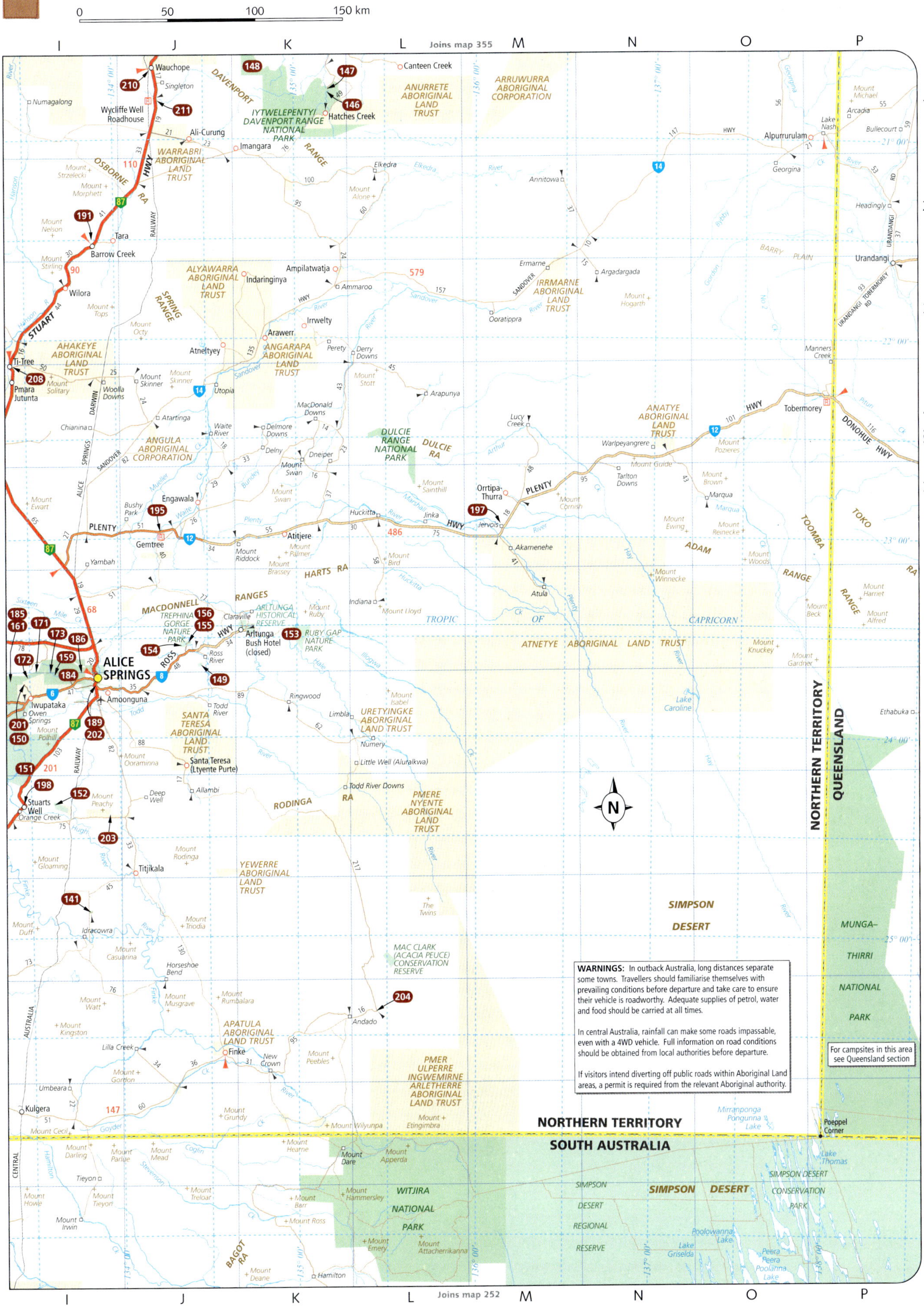

0   50   100   150 km

Joins map 355

WARNINGS: In outback Australia, long distances separate some towns. Travellers should familiarise themselves with prevailing conditions before departure and take care to ensure their vehicle is roadworthy. Adequate supplies of petrol, water and food should be carried at all times.

In central Australia, rainfall can make some roads impassable, even with a 4WD vehicle. Full information on road conditions should be obtained from local authorities before departure.

If visitors intend diverting off public roads within Aboriginal Land areas, a permit is required from the relevant Aboriginal authority.

For campsites in this area see Queensland section

NORTHERN TERRITORY

SOUTH AUSTRALIA

Joins map 464

Joins map 466

QUEENSLAND

NORTHERN TERRITORY

SOUTH AUSTRALIA

NEW SOUTH WALES

462

460–1

463

458–9

464–5

466–7

456–7

Weipa

Cooktown

Karumba

Cairns

Innisfail

Mount Isa

Townsville

Bowen

Hughenden

Charters Towers

Mackay

Winton

Moranbah

Barcaldine

Emerald

Rockhampton

Gladstone

Charleville

Bundaberg

Maryborough

Gympie

Maroochydore

Roma

Caboolture

Cunnamulla

Toowoomba

St George

BRISBANE

Warwick

Nerang

CONTENTS

BEST CAMPSITES

Cania Gorge Tourist Retreat
(Capricorn), p. 395

Granite Gorge Nature Park
(The Far North), p. 451

Platypus Bush Camp
(The Mid-Tropics), p. 435

Seisia Holiday Park
(The Far North), p. 454

**Whitehaven Beach camping area
(boat-based camping)**
Whitsunday Islands National Park
(The Mid-Tropics), p.433

USEFUL CONTACTS

**Department of Agriculture,
Fisheries and Forestry**
13 2523
www.daff.qld.gov.au

**Department of National Parks,
Recreation, Sport and Racing**
13 7468
www.nprsr.qld.gov.au

**Department of Transport
and Main Roads**
(07) 3834 2011
www.tmr.qld.gov.au

Emergency
Dial 000 for police, ambulance
and fire brigade

Fire and Rescue Service
(07) 3247 8100
www.fire.qld.gov.au

**Great Barrier Reef Marine
Park Authority**
(07) 4750 0700
www.gbrmpa.gov.au

*Camping on Fraser Island, Great
Sandy National Park, Sunshine Coast
and Fraser Island region (p. 374)*

BRISBANE ISLANDS AND HINTERLAND

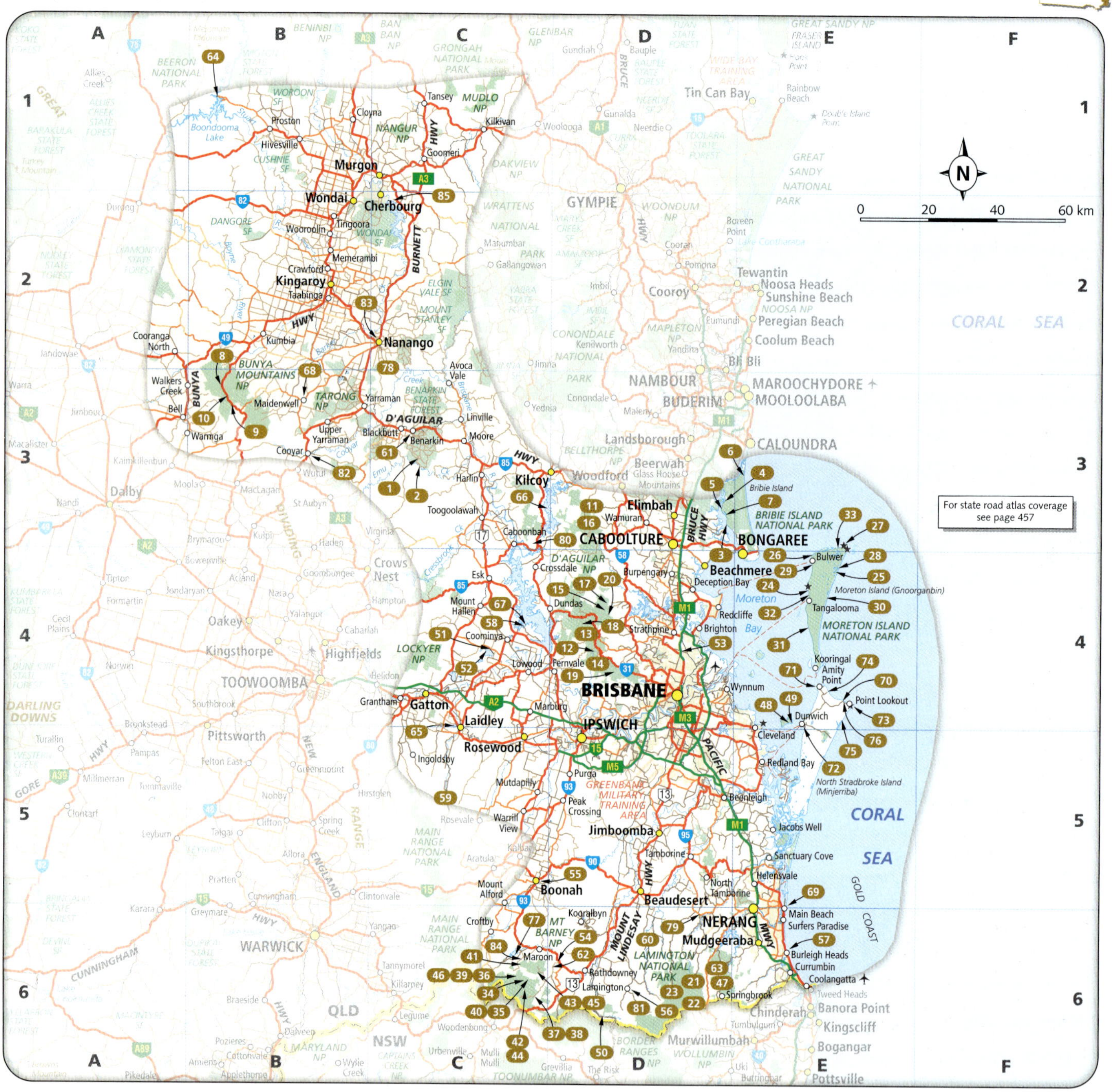

DON'T BOTHER PACKING THAT extra jacket or scarf – you're heading for the state of never-ending summers, sensational surf beaches and an average 300 days of sunshine per year. South-east Queensland's wonderfully mild and temperate climate, gorgeous tropical islands and stunning inland protected forests give it the edge as one of the best camping regions in the country.

Moreton Bay's magnificent islands – North Stradbroke, Bribie and Moreton – are easily accessed from Brisbane and offer postcard-perfect foreshore campgrounds. Camp on a surf beach on North Stradbroke, by a beautiful lagoon on Moreton or at a secluded site on Bribie accessible only by boat.

Half an hour's drive inland from the Gold Coast lie the spectacular rainforests, waterfalls, mountains and hiking trails of Springbrook and Lamington national parks. The tranquil national park hinterland campgrounds are a world away from the theme parks and tourist traps on the coast – you can camp near the dramatic cliffs of Binna Burra in Lamington or chill out at the secluded Settlement campground in Springbrook. Whatever you choose, it's sure to be peaceful and relaxing.

The lakeside campgrounds in south-east Queensland are perfect for thrill-seeking jetskiers, waterskiers, boaties and keen anglers. North of Brisbane, Lake Somerset and Lake Wivenhoe are fantastic watersports playgrounds, and further north you can spend your days fishing, sailing or canoeing on Lake Boondooma. Maroon Dam, Bjelke-Peterson Dam and Atkinson Dam also have popular lakeside campgrounds.

Other national parks in the region offer everything from scenic drives and picnicking spots to challenging bushwalks on rugged terrain for experienced hikers. Check out Bunya Mountains, Mt Barney, D'Aguilar or Benarkin State Forest.

CAMPSITES LOCATED IN PARKS AND RESERVES

BENARKIN STATE FOREST

Known for its towering hoop pines and eucalypt forests, Benarkin is a stunning subtropical rainforest near the regional town of Blackbutt. The forest is popular with wilderness bushwalkers seeking amazing views on the National Bicentennial Trail. Vehicle access to the forest is from Benarkin Forest Dr (be wary of logging trucks). Advance bookings are required for camping.

How to book: NPRSR 13 7468 www.nprsr.qld.gov.au
Permits: camping permit required

1 Clancys camping area

Beside Emu Creek (a tributary of the Brisbane River) and adjacent to the Bicentennial National Trail, this campground has sizeable, open grassy areas suitable for large groups. The site is accessible with conventional vehicles via a gravel road, around 11 km south of D'Aguilar Hwy. Note: there is no mobile phone coverage. Bring your own firewood and drinking water – or treat or boil the tap water at this campsite. **Map refs:** 360 C3, 457 L8

2 Emu Creek camping area

Great for families, with enough space for up to 200 campers, you need to bring firewood and drinking water to this camping area (or treat or boil the water provided before drinking). The gravel road can be steep, narrow and winding at times, but is accessible for caravans, motorhomes and even buses. The camping area is around 13 km south of the D'Aguilar Hwy. Note: at the time of printing this campsite was closed owing to flood damage. The NPRSR website will advise when the site has reopened. **Map refs:** 360 C3, 457 L8

BRIBIE ISLAND NATIONAL PARK

Linked to the mainland by bridge via the Caboolture–Bribie Island Rd, beautiful Bribie is a popular weekend getaway for Brisbane residents and a relaxed holiday spot for tourists seeking sun, sand and a chilled-out vibe. There's no shortage of activities on the island: 2 golf courses, scenic cruises, heritage walks and lawn bowls are on offer. The array of wildlife includes dolphins, dugongs and turtles. Bribie is east of Caboolture in the north of Moreton Bay. Advance bookings are required for camping here.

How to book: NPRSR 13 7468 www.nprsr.qld.gov.au
Permits: permits are required for both camping and 4WD access

3 Gallagher Point camping area

One of Bribie's smallest campsites, with just 6 numbered sites, this camping area is typically popular with backpackers who can easily access the grounds, just 3 km north of White Patch Ranger Headquarters. There is boat access via Pumicestone Passage and 4WD access via White Patch Espl. Note: there is no toilet block. Bring your own drinking water and firewood. **Map refs:** 360 D3, 457 N8

4 Lime Pocket camping area (boat-based camping)

This tiny campsite (6 numbered sites) is Bribie's most secluded and tranquil, but also one of its most basic. Access is only by boat from Pumicestone Passage, and campers must bring their own drinking water and firewood. Lime Pocket is north of Mission Point and Poverty Creek on western Bribie. Note: there is no toilet block. Fishing is permitted near the campsite but not in nearby Tipcony Bight. **Map refs:** 360 D3, 457 N8

5 Mission Point camping area (boat-based camping)

Accessible only by boat from Pumicestone Passage, there are 12 numbered sites at Mission Point, along with toilets, picnic tables and fireplaces; bring your own drinking water and firewood. Mission Point is north of Poverty Creek on western Bribie. **Map refs:** 360 D3, 457 N8

6 Ocean Beach camping area

Bribie's biggest camping area, the 64 sites are set behind sand dunes and reached via defined tracks. Access is 4WD only from the Eighth Ave carpark off North St, Woorim, but you'll need to check tide times before departing. Visitors are required not to take their 4WD vehicles on the dunes or to create new tracks. Note: toilet facilities are provided at the camping area accessed by track P. Bring your own drinking water and a gas/fuel stove. **Map refs:** 360 E3, 457 N8

7 Poverty Creek camping area

Poverty Creek campsite is a popular family area, with 12 numbered sites and a group camping area suitable for camper trailers. Bring your own drinking water and firewood. Access is via White Patch Espl (navigable by 4WD only), or by boat from Pumicestone Passage. **Map refs:** 360 D3, 457 N8

BUNYA MOUNTAINS NATIONAL PARK

The Bunya Mountains, peaking at 1135 m, rise abruptly from the surrounding Darling Downs and South Burnett Valley. The most westerly rainforest park in southern Queensland, it protects more than 30 rare and threatened species of flora and fauna. Here you will find the largest remaining area of bunya pines in the world, along with cool subtropical rainforests, dry rainforests, and grasslands known as 'balds', containing rare grass species. There are 35 km of walking tracks, ranging from a 500 m stroll to a 10 km hike. The winding roads in the area are not recommended for large camper trailers or caravans. Advance bookings are required for camping.

How to book: NPRSR 13 7468 www.nprsr.qld.gov.au
Permits: camping permit required

8 Burtons Well camping area (walk-in camping)

Camp among the ancient grass trees with beautiful forest surrounds at this large tent-only site, 8.5 km north-west of the QPWS information centre. The carpark is a short walk from the open camping area with room for up to 50 campers. Fires are permitted, but the park prefers gas/fuel stoves. A donkey boiler is available to heat water for showers. The tap water here must be treated before drinking, or bring your own. You'll find Burtons Well 4 km north of Westcott camping area on Bunya Mountains Rd. **Map refs:** 360 B3, 457 K7

9 Dandabah camping area

Dandabah has large, open grassy areas conveniently close to a small general store, restaurant and public phone. There are sites for up to 70 campers and it can be reached by conventional vehicle. The site is on Bunya Ave, signposted off Bunya Mountains Rd. Tap water must be treated before drinking, or bring your own. Note: there is an information centre close to Dandabah, at the southern entrance to the park. **Map refs:** 360 B3, 457 K7

10 Westcott camping area (walk-in camping)

Suitable for tents only, there is no vehicular access to this small (up to 30 people), partly shaded campground, but parking is just 20 m away. There are fireplaces but use the firewood sparingly. Tap water must be treated before drinking, or bring your own. The site is 4 km north of Dandabah on Bunya Mountains Rd. **Map refs:** 360 B3, 457 K7

D'AGUILAR NATIONAL PARK

D'Aguilar National Park consists of 2 distinct areas: the southern section (formerly Brisbane Forest Park) and the northern (formerly Mt Mee State Forest). The southern section features open eucalypt woodlands, lush subtropical rainforests and more than 800 plant species – all just a short drive from the Brisbane city centre. The southern section's

Walkabout Creek complex has an information centre, cafe and details about the amazing wildlife in the park, which includes endangered giant barred frogs and yellow-bellied gliders. Other features to enjoy include scenic lookouts, picnic and BBQ areas, bushwalking tracks, horseriding and cycling trails. The northern section extends all the way to Woodford and boasts lookouts and excellent walking tracks. For those less active, there's a popular half-day mountain drive covering The Gantry, Rocky Hole and the relaxing picnic spot at Broadwater. The Falls lookout over D'Aguilar is another must-see in the northern section. Advance bookings are required for all camping in the park.

How to book: NPRSR 13 7468 www.nprsr.qld.gov.au
Permits: camping permit required

11 Archer camping area

Camp in open woodland near a creek at this lovely grassy site just 1 km from the Rasmussen Rd entry to the northern section of the park. It can be accessed by car from Rasmussen Rd, but if you are entering via Mt Mee and The Gantry you'll need a 4WD. There are 9 designated sites and enough space to accommodate large groups. Fire rings are provided but you must bring your own firewood, as collecting wood in the forest is prohibited. Tank water must be treated before drinking, or bring your own. **Map refs:** 360 D3, 457 M8

12 Dundas Road camping area (walk-in camping)

This 15-person bush camp is a 1.6 km walk from Mt Nebo Rd. There are no facilities provided aside from tank water, which must be boiled or treated before drinking, or bring your own; also bring a gas/fuel stove. It is within striking distance of the Westridge outlook. **Map refs:** 360 D4, 457 M9

13 England Creek camping area (walk-in camping)

This 9-person campsite lies deep within D'Aguilar, next to the picturesque England Creek. No facilities at all are provided and the camp lies at the end of a 10.5 km hike from Mt Glorious Rd. It's for experienced self-sufficient campers only. Bring water and a gas/fuel stove. **Map refs:** 360 D4, 457 M9

14 Light Line Road camping area (walk-in camping)

This tiny campsite (maximum 6 people) provides a small shelter and a water tank (treat or boil water before drinking). It is located 1.7 km from the park boundary at Forestry Rd, Mt Nebo. Bring a gas/fuel stove. **Map refs:** 360 D4, 457 M9

15 Middle Kobble camping area (walk-in camping)

This campsite near the Kobble Creek waterfall is accessed via a 4.7 km uphill track featuring some steep climbs. Bring your own drinking water, as none is provided and Kobble Creek is often dry; also bring a gas/fuel stove. **Map refs:** 360 D4, 457 M9

16 Neurum Creek camping area

A 4WD is recommended for accessing this medium-size campsite off Neurum Creek Rd, about 6 km from the Salin Rd entry (The Gantry) to the northern section of the park and about 13.5 km from the Rasmussen Rd entry (Woodford end). There are 13 numbered sites with raised dirt pads, septic toilets, fireplaces (bring your own firewood) and water to be boiled or treated before drinking. Note: mobile phone coverage is unreliable.
Map refs: 360 D3, 457 M8

17 North Kobble camping area (walk-in camping)

This campsite, north of Middle Kobble, can be accessed only by unmarked trails through steep terrain. Campers must be physically fit, capable of navigating the bush unaided, and prepared for emergencies. There are no facilities and Kobble Creek is often dry, so bring your own drinking water and a gas/fuel stove. **Map refs:** 360 D4, 457 M9

18 Northbrook Mountain camping area (walk-in camping)

This small clearing on a high ridge overlooking Kipper Creek hosts only 9 people and provides no facilities whatsoever (bring your own drinking water and a gas/fuel stove). The 4.7 km walk to camp from Lawton Rd is only for experienced hikers.
Map refs: 360 D4, 457 M9

19 Scrub Road camping area (walk-in camping)

This 9-person bush camp is a 4 km hike within D'Aguilar's southern section from Mt Nebo Rd. Like other campsites in the southern half of D'Aguilar, it is for self-sufficient campers only. There is a small shelter. Boil or treat the tank water before drinking. Bring a gas/fuel stove. **Map refs:** 360 D4, 457 M9

20 South Kobble camping area (walk-in camping)

Like North Kobble, this campsite is very remote and accessible only by unmarked trails through steep terrain. Campers must be physically fit, capable of navigating the bush unaided, and prepared for emergencies. There are no facilities and Kobble Creek is often dry, so bring your own drinking water, and a gas/fuel stove. **Map refs:** 360 D4, 457 M9

LAMINGTON NATIONAL PARK

The World Heritage–listed Lamington National Park, cresting the McPherson Range, is renowned for its natural beauty, panoramic views, lush rainforests, ancient trees, picturesque waterfalls, prolific birdlife and over 150 km of well-maintained walking trails. It is also famous for 2 exceptional guesthouses (Binna Burra and O'Reillys), where hospitality is combined with informative activities aimed to give all who stay there an appreciation of the precious environment. Bookings are required for all camping in the park.

Green Mountains camping area, Lamington National Park (p. 364)

Who to contact: QPWS Lamington National Park Green Mountains (07) 5544 0634 for access information about bush camping areas **How to book:** Binna Burra Mountain Lodge (07) 5533 3622, 1300 246 622 for campsite no. **21**; or NPRSR 13 7468 www.nprsr.qld.gov.au for all other campsites **Permits:** camping permit required for all camping areas except campsite no. **21**

21 Binna Burra camping area

A south-east Queensland gem, this privately managed mountain-top site has long been a favourite with campers for its stunning panoramic views of the Numinbah Valley. Activities at Binna Burra include guided bushwalks, abseiling, flying fox, a kids' club and superb dining at the Binna Burra Tea House or Clifftop Dining Room. Also on offer are furnished safari-style tents (2–6 people) with beds, tables and chairs, lighting and your own private verandah with beautiful valley or rainforest views. This campsite is part of the Gold Coast Hinterland Great Walk. The location is Binna Burra Rd, 28 km south of Canungra. Bookings are essential for weekends and peak periods.
Map refs: 360 D6, 457 N11

22 Bush camping areas (walk-in camping)

For experienced, self-sufficient campers with good navigational skills, there are 10 remote camping sites (Bithongabel, Darlington, Echo Point, Illinbah, Lost World Creek, Lost World Saddle, Point Lookout, Rat-a-tat, Running Creek and Stinson) in the bush along the walking trails in the national park. These are walk-in only, limited to around 6 people per site, and for a single-night stay. Allow 10 business days for processing bookings. Note: these bush-camping sites are closed every year Dec–Jan. For access instructions and locations, contact QPWS Lamington. **Map refs:** 360 D6, 457 N11

23 Green Mountains camping area

Close to O'Reillys Rainforest Resort, this hillside campground in forest surrounds has designated campsites on terraces on the slope and a separate area designated for those doing the Gold Coast Hinterland Great Walk. It is suitable for camping beside your car, walk-in camping and campervans, but not for caravans or camper trailers. The nearby day-use area contains BBQs, picnic facilities and wheelchair-accessible toilets. A public phone is available past O'Reillys reception office. You'll find the campground at the end of the 36 km narrow and winding Lamington National Park Rd (depart from Canungra), just 200 m from the information centre outside O'Reillys. Bookings are essential for weekends and peak periods. Tap water must be boiled or treated before drinking. **Map refs:** 360 D6, 457 N11

MORETON ISLAND NATIONAL PARK AND RECREATION AREA

Regarded as the jewel of Moreton Bay's sandy islands, Moreton Island is a haven for off-road adventurers (it's 4WD only) looking for a wilderness experience within easy reach of Brisbane. Here, only a 2 hr barge trip from the mainland, are long sandy beaches, clear freshwater lagoons, wildflower heaths and some of the highest sand dunes in the world. Anglers should check the Moreton Bay Marine Park map before casting off, as fishing is prohibited in some areas of the coast. Advance booking is required for camping.

How to book: NPRSR 13 7468 www.nprsr.qld.gov.au
Permits: camping permit required

24 Ben-Ewa camping area

A favourite with families and school groups, Ben-Ewa's valley location provides protection from strong winds and offers many a shady tree. The site is on the western side of the island, 1.5 km north of The Wrecks. There are only 12 camping plots available, but it is accessible for camper trailers. Open fires are permitted in existing fire sites, but you must BYO firewood. Treat or boil the water before drinking, or bring your own. **Map refs:** 360 E4, 457 N8

25 Blue Lagoon camping area

With beautiful walking trails to the nearby lake and close proximity to the surf beach, this camping area is in a gorgeous spot on the eastern side of the island between Middle Rd and Cape Moreton. Trailers and caravans are permitted, but due to the soft sand on the one-way track they are not recommended. Bring your own firewood and treat or boil the water before drinking, or bring that along too. **Map refs:** 360 E4, 457 N8

26 Comboyuro Point camping area

Within walking distance of the Bulwer township on the island's west coast, this site has 49 camping plots marked with totem poles and plenty of shade. There is water available, but it must be treated or boiled before consumption. Open fires are allowed, but you must bring all firewood from the mainland, as Moreton's natural environment is protected. Note: mobile phone coverage is poor in this area. **Map refs:** 360 E4, 457 N8

27 North Point camping area

On the northern tip of the island between Yellow Patch and Cape Moreton, this is a large grassy site close to the surf beach and within walking distance of Honeymoon Bay. The area is not accessible with a caravan or trailer and is reached by 4WD only. There is a maximum of 17 sites available. Bring a gas/fuel stove from the mainland and treat or boil water before drinking. **Map refs:** 360 E3, 457 O8

28 North-east camping area (bush camping)

Self-sufficient campers can stay in areas marked with totem poles on this stretch of beach on the east coast of Moreton, spanning between Middle Rd and Spitfire Creek (excluding Blue Lagoon camping area). There are no facilities, so bring your own drinking water and firewood (for use in existing fire sites only) and take all rubbish with you. **Map refs:** 360 E4, 457 O8

29 North-west camping area (bush camping)

Self-sufficient campers can stay in areas marked with totem poles on this stretch of beach on the west coast of Moreton, spanning the area between Ben-Ewa and Comboyuro Point camping areas. There are no facilities, so bring your own drinking water and firewood (for use in existing fire sites only) and take all rubbish with you. **Map refs:** 360 E4, 457 N8

30 South-east camping area (bush camping)

Self-sufficient campers can stay in areas marked with totem poles on this stretch of beach on the east coast of Moreton, spanning the area between Middle Rd and Rous Battery. There are no facilities in this camping area, so bring your own drinking water and firewood (for use in existing fire sites only) and take all rubbish with you. **Map refs:** 360 E4, 457 N8

31 South-west camping area (bush camping)

Self-sufficient campers can stay in areas marked with totem poles on this stretch of beach on the west coast of Moreton, spanning the area between Tangalooma Bypass and Toulkerrie. There are no facilities in this camping area, so bring your own drinking water and firewood (for use in existing fire sites only) and take all rubbish with you. **Map refs:** 360 E4, 457 N9

32 The Wrecks camping area (walk-in camping)

The Wrecks is a walk-in camping area just a short stroll from Tangalooma near the main barge landing point. There are 21 sites available; the surface is sand (not grassy) and is surrounded by native shrubs and trees. Vehicles can park on the beach a short distance from the campground. The water must be boiled or treated before use. **Map refs:** 360 E4, 457 N8

33 Yellow Patch camping area (bush camping)

Self-sufficient campers can stay in areas marked with totem poles on this stretch of beach at the northern end of Moreton, spanning the area between North Point and Heath Island. There are no facilities in this camping area, so bring your own drinking water and firewood (for use in existing fire sites only) and take all rubbish with you. **Map refs:** 387 G2, 459 N11

MOUNT BARNEY NATIONAL PARK

As one of the state's largest areas of pristine vegetation, World Heritage–listed Mt Barney National Park on the Qld–NSW border is a mecca for experienced bushwalkers and climbers. Out of this rugged wilderness rise 7 peaks, of which Mt Barney is the highest. The Yellow Pinch picnic area at the base of Mt Barney provides wheelchair-accessible toilets, BBQs and tables. Bush camping areas have no facilities. Advance bookings are required to camp here.

How to book: QPWS Boonah (07) 5463 5041 for campsite no. **35**, **45**; or NPRSR 13 7468 www.nprsr.qld.gov.au for campsite nos **34**, **36**, **37**, **38**, **39**, **40**, **41**, **42**, **43**, **44**, **46** *Permits:* camping permit required; pay fees and arrange permit 3–6 weeks in advance

34 Barney Gorge Junction camping area (walk-in camping)

This basic bush camping area, as its name might suggest, is located in tall eucalypt forest at the junction of Mt Barney Creek and Barney Gorge. There are no facilities and fires are prohibited, so bring all self-sufficient gear, including drinking water and a gas/fuel stove. **Map refs:** 360 C6, 457 M11

35 Bush camping areas (walk-in camping)

Experienced hikers looking for additional challenges can camp in 10 designated bush camping zones in the remotest areas of

Mt Barney National Park. Hikers are required to book permits and discuss their itinerary directly with QPWS Boonah. There are no facilities and fires are prohibited, so bring all self-sufficient gear, including drinking water and a gas/fuel stove. **Map refs:** 360 C6, 457 M11

36 Cleared Ridge camping area (walk-in camping)

This campsite is located at the top of a ridge on a fire trail, and is a 1.5 hr walk from the carpark of the same name on Waterfall Creek Rd (4WD access only). There are no facilities and fires are prohibited, so bring all self-sufficient gear, including drinking water and a gas/fuel stove. **Map refs:** 360 C6, 457 M11

37 Cronan Creek Site 9 camping area (walk-in camping)

This campsite is reached by a 50 min walk from the Yellow Pinch Reserve day-use area on the east side of the national park, and consists of a clearing in the open eucalypt forest near the upper reaches of the Logan River. There are no facilities and fires are prohibited, so bring all self-sufficient gear, including drinking water and a gas/fuel stove. **Map refs:** 360 C6, 457 M11

38 Cronan Creek Site 10 camping area (walk-in camping)

A 10 min walk from Cronan Creek Site 9, this camping area is accessed from the Yellow Pinch Reserve on Upper Logan Rd. There are no facilities and fires are prohibited, so bring all self-sufficient gear, including drinking water and a gas/fuel stove. **Map refs:** 360 C6, 457 M11

39 Hoop Pines camping area (walk-in camping)

This camping area offers room for a relatively large number of campers (30 people), and is accessed via a 1 hr downhill walk from the Cleared Ridge carpark on Waterfall Creek Rd (4WD only). There are no facilities and fires are prohibited, so bring all self-sufficient gear, including drinking water and a gas/fuel stove. **Map refs:** 360 C6, 457 M11

40 Lower Portals camping area (walk-in camping)

This campsite near Mt Barney Creek is accessed via a 3.7 km walk from the carpark of the same name off Upper Logan Rd. There are no facilities and fires are prohibited, so bring all self-sufficient gear, including drinking water and a gas/fuel stove. **Map refs:** 360 C6, 457 M11

41 Mount May Saddle camping area (walk-in camping)

Thrillseekers will revel in the challenge of accessing this campsite in the 'saddle' between the north and south peaks of Mt May (836 m). Access is via a steep climb including rock

scrambles off Waterfall Creek Rd. There are no facilities and fires are prohibited, so bring all self-sufficient gear, including drinking water and a gas/fuel stove. **Map refs:** 360 C6, 457 M11

42 Old Hut Site camping area (walk-in camping)

This small campsite is located beside a small patch of remnant rainforest in the 'saddle' between the east and west peaks of Mt Barney. It is a 4–5 hr challenging hike (including exposed rock climbs) from Yellow Pinch Reserve on Upper Logan Rd, and is closed Dec–Jan every year. There are no facilities and fires are prohibited, so bring all self-sufficient gear, including drinking water and a gas/fuel stove. **Map refs:** 360 C6, 457 M11

43 Paddys Plain camping area (walk-in camping)

This relatively large campsite (30 people) is located in open eucalypt forest near Paddys Gully, between Mt Maroon and Mt May. Contact QPWS Boonah for access instructions. There are no facilities and fires are prohibited, so bring all self-sufficient gear, including drinking water and a gas/fuel stove. **Map refs:** 360 C6, 457 M11

44 Rum Jungle camping area (walk-in camping)

Like Old Hut Site camping area, this campsite is located in the 'saddle' between the east and west peaks of Mt Barney, and is surrounded by remnant rainforest. It is a 4–5 hr challenging hike (including exposed rock climbs) from Yellow Pinch Reserve on Upper Logan Rd, and the campsite is closed every year through Dec–Jan. There are no facilities and fires are prohibited, so bring all self-sufficient gear, including drinking water and a gas/fuel stove. **Map refs:** 360 C6, 457 M11

45 Skull Camp camping area (walk-in camping)

This relatively large campsite (30 people) is located in open eucalypt forest south of Mt Maroon. Contact QPWS Boonah for access instructions. There are no facilities and fires are prohibited, so bring all self-sufficient gear, including drinking water and a gas/fuel stove. **Map refs:** 360 C6, 457 M11

46 Yamahra Creek camping area (walk-in camping)

This campsite is a moderate 1.5 hr downhill walk from the Cleared Ridge carpark on Waterfall Creek Rd (4WD access only). There are no facilities and fires are prohibited, so bring all self-sufficient gear, including drinking water and a gas/fuel stove. **Map refs:** 360 C6, 457 M11

SPRINGBROOK NATIONAL PARK

A winding drive up into the Gold Coast hinterland leads to a pristine landscape of deep valleys, splendid waterfalls and forests of ancient beech trees. A World Heritage–listed park, Springbrook protects subtropical, warm temperate and cool temperate rainforests, open eucalypt forest and heath. Advance bookings are required for camping.

How to book: NPRSR 13 7468 www.nprsr.qld.gov.au
Permits: camping permit required

47 The Settlement camping area

The 11 well-defined sites at this newly established campsite are suitable for tents and campervans, but the area is not well shaded. Hikers should note that walking tracks near this site lead to the Gold Coast Hinterland Great Walk. Each campsite has a well-grassed area approximately 10 m in diameter and an individual parking bay. Numbered sites 1–4 have longer parking bays that could accommodate a camper trailer. Tap water must be treated or boiled before drinking, or bring your own. The campground is 30 km south-west of Mudgeeraba, signposted off Springbrook Rd from the Springbrook–Nerang Rd. **Map refs:** 360 D6, 457 N11

TEERK ROO RA NATIONAL PARK

Located 4 km west of the Brisbane suburb of Cleveland, between the mainland and North Stradbroke Island, Teerk Roo Ra National Park covers the entire 519 ha of Peel Island in Moreton Bay. The island is a significant historical site both for its traditional owners, the Quandamooka people, and as a quarantine station and leprosy lazaret for European settlers. Most of the park, except for Horseshoe and Platypus bays, is a restricted-access area closed to the public. Access to the park's camping areas is via private boat only, and advance bookings are required.

How to book: NPRSR 13 7468 www.nprsr.qld.gov.au
Permits: camping permit required

48 Horseshoe Bay camping area (boat-based camping)

This campsite, on the foreshore of Horseshoe Bay, can only be accessed by boat. It provides an excellent base for swimming, fishing and exploring the other islands of Moreton Bay. Access is restricted to the foreshore only, and fines apply. There are few facilities other than composting toilets, so bring all self-sufficient gear, including drinking water and a gas/fuel stove. **Map refs:** 360 E4, 457 N9

49 Platypus Bay camping area (boat-based camping)

This small campsite, near the stone causeway at Platypus Bay, offers no facilities, but it provides excellent access to snorkelling in the shipwrecks of the bay. Bring all self-sufficient gear, including drinking water and a gas/fuel stove. Note: the QPWS-registered mooring near this campsite is for authorised vessels only. **Map refs:** 360 E4, 457 N9

CAMPSITES LOCATED IN OTHER AREAS

50 Andrew Drynan Park camping area

At this well-grassed area backing onto beautiful rainforest, campers can enjoy a splash in Running Creek or a relaxing picnic at one of the shaded tables. (Note: the creek's water needs to be boiled before drinking.) You'll need to travel 19 km south-east from Rathdowney to get here; it's on Running Creek Rd (Lions Tourist Rd). Bookings are advisable over the Easter period. **Map refs:** 360 D6, 457 M11

How to book: Running Creek Rd, Running Creek (07) 5544 1281

51 Atkinson Dam Cabin Village and Shoreline Camping

Watersports enthusiasts can enjoy access to the shoreline of Atkinson Dam at this site, 8 km south-west of Coominya. There's a general store for supplies, fuel and gas bottle refills, plus laundry facilities. Look out for the signpost on Atkinson Dam Rd. Bookings are advisable at peak periods. **Map refs:** 360 C4, 457 M9

How to book: 381 Atkinson Dam Rd, Atkinson Dam (07) 5426 421

52 Atkinson Dam Waterfront Caravan Park

Anglers will like this freshwater sportfishing hotspot, and holiday-makers will enjoy the kitchen, kiosk, cabins and other park facilities. An officially sanctioned local group has plans to stock the water with sufficient saratoga to make a breeding population, plus big eye trevally, Australian tarpon and mangrove jack, as breeding stock become available. Powerboat numbers are limited to 15 on the 550 ha lake. **Map refs:** 360 C4, 457 M9

How to book: 545 Atkinson Dam Rd, Atkinson Dam (07) 5426 4151 www.lakeatkinson.com.au

53 BIG4 Brisbane Northside Caravan Village

This holiday park in Brisbane's north offers excellent access to the city's cosmopolitan features and the Redcliffe area's marine attractions. The well-appointed grounds include a laundry, tennis courts, a camp kiosk and a lending library. Bookings are recommended for peak periods. **Map refs:** 360 D4, 457 N9

How to book: cnr Dorville and Zillmere rds, Aspley (07) 3263 4040, 1800 060 797 http://brisbane-northside-caravan-village.qld.big4.com.au

54 Bigriggen Park camping area

There's plenty of room to sprawl on this 40 ha ground known for its peaceful surroundings and proximity to national parks. Wildlife is aplenty here: tree frogs, possums, wallabies and, if you're lucky, maybe even platypus. The kiosk is open daily for bread, milk, ice, firewood and gas bottle refills (cash only). Bigriggen is 9 km west of Rathdowney, signposted on Bigriggan Rd from Upper Logan Rd. Bookings are required year round. **Map refs:** 360 D6, 457 M11

How to book: 196 Bigriggan Rd, Rathdowney (07) 5463 6190 www.bigriggen.com.au

55 Boonah Showground camping area

The showground is a top spot for powered sites, only a 3 min walk from Boonah town centre. There's a camp kitchen and laundry facilities, but BYO firewood. The showground provides excellent access to the attractions of the Scenic Rim and Lake Moogerah. Boonah is 50 km west of Beaudesert and 56 km south of Ipswich. **Map refs:** 360 C5, 457 M10

How to book: Melbourne St, Boonah (07) 5463 4080

56 Burgess Park camping area

Much smaller than its sister site at Darlington Park, this flat and grassy 1.2 ha camping area backs onto Christmas Creek, a good spot for swimming and fishing. To find it, head for Christmas Creek Rd, 37 km south of Beaudesert; the road is signposted off Mt Lindesay Hwy at Laravale, 14 km south of Beaudesert. Note: tap water needs to be treated or boiled before drinking. Bookings are recommended for peak periods. **Map refs:** 360 D6, 457 M11

How to book: Christmas Creek Rd, Laravale (07) 5544 8120

57 Burleigh Beach Tourist Park

Set on a prime location directly opposite Burleigh Beach, this tourist park has 73 powered sites and 16 unpowered sites. Facilities include a modern amenities block, laundry, free wireless broadband access and tour desk. Other attractions include the public swimming pool and gym across the street, surf lessons on Burleigh Beach and access to cafes and restaurants at the nearby Burleigh Theatre Arcade. **Map refs:** 360 E6, 457 N11

How to book: 37 Goodwin Tce, Burleigh Heads 1300 672 750 www.goldcoasttouristparks.com.au/park/burleigh-beach

58 Captain Logan Camp

With as much water as 2.5 Sydney Harbours, Wivenhoe Dam is a major water storage reserve for south-east Queensland and a hub for watersports enthusiasts (however boat motors are not to be used on the lake). With 57 unpowered sites, Captain Logan Camp suits both tent and trailer camping. Hot showers are available. You'll find it on Hay Rd, off the Brisbane Valley Hwy, 11 km north of Coominya. The boat ramp is nearby at Lumley Hill. Bookings are recommended for peak periods. **Map refs:** 360 C4, 457 M9

How to book: Logan Inlet Rd, Wivenhoe Hill (07) 5426 4729 www.seqwater.com.au/public/recreation/camping
Permits: permits needed to fish (under-18s excepted) and to take boats requiring trailers on Lake Wivenhoe

59 Centenary Park camping area

This campground features 8 powered sites, a laundry and an electric BBQ. Campers can stay for a maximum of 7 nights, and the second night is free. Visitors can throw a line in at nearby Lake Dyer or enjoy the walking trails. To get here, follow the signpost on Mulgowie Rd in Thornton, 15 km south of Laidley. Treat or boil tap water before drinking. Advance bookings are required. **Map refs:** 360 C5, 457 L10

How to book: cnr Mulgowie and Thornton School rds, Thornton (07) 5465 3698, 0439 368 561

60 Darlington Park camping area

Sensational for families, this well-shaded campsite has the added bonus of a cricket oval (with artificial turf pitch) and kids' playground on a glorious 12 ha site. The kiosk is handy for basic supplies, including firewood. You'll need to buy drinking water there, bring your own, or treat the water provided. Follow the signposted access on Kerry Rd, 25 km south of Beaudesert. Bookings are recommended for peak periods. **Map refs:** 360 D6, 457 N10

How to book: Kerry Rd, Beaudesert (07) 5544 8120

61 First Settlers Park camping area

Available for a single-night stopover, this free site has surprisingly good facilities. There's a powered site suitable for caravans and camper trailers, showers (bring $2 coins for hot water) and a public phone at the general store across the road. It is in Benarkin, signposted off the D'Aguilar Hwy south-east of Nanango. **Map refs:** 360 C3, 457 L8

Who to contact: South Burnett Energy and Information Centre (07) 4171 0100 www.southburnett.qld.gov.au

62 Flanagan Reserve camping area

The natural bush setting makes this one of the most peaceful family-oriented spots in the Scenic Rim. The Logan River offers fantastic bass and mullet fishing, there's an assortment of wildlife (turtles, lorikeets, kookaburras) and at night you can relax around the warmth of the campfire. To get to this reserve, head south from Rathdowney on the Mt Lindesay Hwy and turn right onto Boonah–Rathdowney Rd. Follow this road for 7 km and then turn left into Upper Logan Rd. Follow this road for 4 km to a T-intersection and turn right into the reserve. Bookings are recommended for peak periods. **Map refs:** 360 D6, 457 M11

How to book: Flanagan Reserve Rd, Barney View (07) 5544 3128, 0408 759 928 www.flanaganreserve.com.au

Gold Coast Hinterland Great Walk

This 54 km hiking trail traverses 2 World Heritage–listed national parks, over the top of a dormant volcano and behind a waterfall. It is best approached from west to east, starting at Green Mountains camping area and finishing at The Settlement. Note: Binna Burra is a privately operated campsite, and bookings for it must be made separately from those made through NPRSR. Walkers are required to purchase a topographic map of the Great Walk before embarking.

Please note that campsites are listed in alphabetical order, not track order. Refer to the map on p. 360 for further information.

How to book: Binna Burra Mountain Lodge (07) 5533 3622, 1300 246 622 for campsite no. **21**; NPRSR 13 7468 for campsite nos **23**, **47**, **63** *Permits:* permits required for all campsites except Binna Burra camping area

21 Binna Burra camping area
See p. 363.

23 Green Mountains camping area
See p. 364.

47 The Settlement camping area
See p. 366.

63 Woonoongoora camping area (walk-in camping)

This campsite, on Gold Coast Council land, offers no facilities besides composting toilets. Bring your own drinking water and a gas/fuel stove, as open fires are prohibited. It is 23.6 km from Binna Burra camping area and 9 km from The Settlement camping area. **Map refs:** 360 D6, 457 N11

64 Lake Boondooma Caravan and Recreation Park

An angler's paradise, the lake camping area features powered sites, hot showers, a dump point and laundry facilities. Other

facilities include a kiosk, playground, tennis court and boats for hire. The site is 20 km north-west of Proston, via Boondooma Dam Rd. Bookings are recommended for powered sites. **Map refs:** 360 B1, 457 K6

How to book: 40 Bushcamp Rd, Lake Boondooma (07) 4168 9694 www.lakeboondooma.com.au

65 Lake Dyer Camping and Caravan Ground

The caretakers at Lake Dyer recently renovated the toilet block, installed new gas BBQs and a washing machine, and built a new playground. There are 16 powered sites at the campground. Visitors can enjoy the scenery at nearby Cunninghams Crest or Schultz lookouts, take a drive around the popular Antiques Trail or discover the historic Spring Bluff Railway Station. The lakeside site is 1.5 km west of Laidley. Note: pets must be approved by management in advance. Advance bookings are required. **Map refs:** 360 C4, 457 M9

How to book: Gatton–Laidley Rd, Laidley (07) 5465 3698, 0439 368 561

66 Lake Somerset Holiday Park

Set on a 45 ha property, this holiday park has excellent facilities for campers, caravans and camper trailers, and the option of a log or waterfront cabin for those seeking a little extra comfort. The area is known for its wineries, craft shops and watersports, and there are weekend markets at Esk, Kilcoy and Woodford. The park is on Kirkleagh Rd, 10 km south of Kilcoy off Esk–Kilcoy Rd. Note: bring your laptop as there is free wireless internet available. Bookings are recommended for peak periods. **Map refs:** 360 C3, 457 M8

How to book: Kirkleagh Rd, Hazeldean (07) 5497 1093, 1800 689 679 www.lakesomerset.com.au

67 Lumley Hill camping area

Just a short distance from Captain Logan Camp, Lumley Hill has powered sites. The campground is on Logan Inlet Rd, off Hay Rd, signposted off the Brisbane Valley Hwy. Lake Wivenhoe is a major water storage reserve with canoeing, sailing and fishing popular pastimes (do not operate boat motors on Lake Wivenhoe). Bookings are required for powered sites. **Map refs:** 360 C4, 457 M9

How to book: Logan Inlet Rd, Wivenhoe Hill (07) 5426 4729 www.seqwater.com.au/public/recreation/camping
Permits: permits required to fish (under-18s excepted) and to take boats requiring trailers on Lake Wivenhoe

68 Maidenwell camping area

This free stopover (maximum 24 hr) has a BBQ, toilets and picnic tables on Coomba Falls Rd in Maidenwell, 25 km south-west of Nanango. Have a hot shower in the town hall (pick up the key from the general store), and bring your own firewood and drinking water (tap water must be treated or boiled before drinking). **Map refs:** 360 B3, 457 L7

Who to contact: South Burnett Energy and Information Centre (07) 4171 0100 www.southburnett.qld.gov.au

69 Main Beach Tourist Park

This large, busy tourist park – across the road from Main Beach and 2 min drive from Surfers Paradise – has 100 powered sites and an additional 24 ensuite powered sites. Facilities include a swimming pool, BBQ areas, kids' playground and free wireless broadband internet. Also available are laundry facilities, a tour desk, surfboard hire and gas refills. **Map refs:** 360 E6, 457 N10

How to book: 3600 Main Beach Pde, Main Beach 1300 672 720 www.goldcoasttouristparks.com.au/park/main-beach

North Stradbroke Island

Called Minjerribah by the Indigenous Quandamooka people, and affectionately known as 'Straddie' among locals, the laid-back vibe and subtropical beauty of Stradbroke Island will have you blissfully relaxed from the moment you arrive. Spot dolphins and manta rays on the North Gorge Headlands Walk, take a scuba-diving adventure, hike through bushland to magnificent freshwater lakes, enjoy a 4WD tour on the beach, go fishing or simply sit back at the Point Lookout pub and enjoy the glorious sunsets. Several areas of North Stradbroke Island are now part of Naree Budjong Djara National Park and Minjerribah Recreation Area, jointly administered by the Quandamooka and NPRSR. All campsites must be booked and paid for in advance of travel.

Who to contact: for Minjerribah Recreation Area contact NPRSR 13 7468 www.nprsr.qld.gov.au *How to book:* Straddie Holiday Parks (07) 3409 9602, 1300 551 253 www.straddieholidayparks.com.au *Permits:* an annual permit is required to drive 4WDs on Flinders and Main beaches

70 Adder Rock camping area

Sheltered in the bushland behind a cove, Adder Rock is a shady campground with 26 powered sites and plenty of room for tents. There's a general store and public phone within 100 m, and you have the option of hiring a 2-bedroom cabin on-site. The campground is on East Coast Rd at Point Lookout, around 20 km north-east of Dunwich. **Map refs:** 360 E4, 457 O9

71 Amity Point camping area

A lovely, quiet spot for swimming and dropping in a line, Amity is ideal for camping with the family. It is suitable for conventional vehicles and has 23 powered sites; there's also cabin accommodation at the campground. It is on Claytons Rd at Amity, 18 km north of Dunwich. **Map refs:** 360 E4, 457 N9

72 Bradbury's Beach camping area

Popular with boaties and fishing enthusiasts, this small campsite is just 1 km from the ferry terminal. Go past the information centre and turn left into Ballow Rd, follow it around to the right where it becomes Bingle Rd, then turn left into Flinders Ave (just before the cemetery). The park is 200 m on the right. **Map refs:** 360 E4, 457 N9

73 Cylinder Beach camping area

Straddie's most popular campground is metres from Cylinder's patrolled surf beach and close to Point Lookout's shops and pub. There are 60 unpowered sites, 8 powered sites and plenty of shade. From the ferry at Dunwich, take East Coast Rd about 19 km to Point Lookout, and follow the signs to Cylinder Beach. The park is on the left-hand side at the bottom of the hill. Note: there are electric BBQs in the adjacent public park. **Map refs:** 360 E4, 457 O9

74 Flinders Beach camping area

Accessible by 4WD only, the camping areas are behind the sand dunes and designated with blue tent signs. The only facilities on Flinders Beach are 4 composting toilets, so bring all of your self-sufficient camping equipment and supplies, including firewood and drinking water. From the ferry, follow the signs to Flinders Beach or drive out to Point Lookout and enter the beach at the Adder Rock Beach access (the first street on your left at Point Lookout, opposite the bus stop/Tramican St). **Map refs:** 360 E4, 457 N9

75 Main Beach camping area

You'll need a 4WD to access this area and there are no facilities – not even composting toilets. Bring drinking water and a gas/fuel stove. Camping areas commence 7.5 km south of the causeway and tracks are designated by red numbered zone signs. From the ferry, follow Tazi Rd past the turn-offs to Brown Lake and the North Stradbroke Golf Course until you reach Main Beach. Or from East Coast Rd turn right onto George Nothling Dr at Point Lookout; the beach is 2 km further. **Map refs:** 360 E4, 457 O9

76 Thankful Rest camping area

Adjacent to Home Beach at Point Lookout, this secluded campground is only open during peak periods. Nearby you'll find a general store, restaurants, a bowls club, library, community markets and skater's half-pipe. It is on East Coast Rd, 20 km north-east of Dunwich. **Map refs:** 360 E4, 457 O9

77 Pointro camping area

A 1 min walk from the water's edge of Maroon Dam, Pointro is a mown site with plenty of clear spaces and a few gum trees if you prefer shade. The dam is popular for fishing and watersports. You'll need to bring drinking water (or treat/boil the on-site water) and stock up on supplies at the stores in Boonah or Rathdowney, but firewood can be obtained on-site. The campground is on Burnett Creek Rd, 28.5 km south of Boonah. Bookings are advised during peak periods. **Map refs:** 360 C6, 457 M11

How to book: Ministry Education Commission (07) 5463 6209

78 Seven Mile Diggings camping area

You can still dig around in this old fossicking area 11 km south of Nanango, though it's unlikely you'll find any gold. The campgrounds at the end of the sealed section of Old Esk North Rd are drive-in, but if you want to camp further down in the diggings themselves you'll have to carry your equipment in. This site has no facilities and suits self-sufficient campers (bring water and firewood). Camping is free but visitors must obtain a permit from the South Burnett Energy and Information Centre. **Map refs:** 360 C2, 457 L7

Who to contact: South Burnett Energy and Information Centre (07) 4171 0100 www.southburnett.qld.gov.au *Permits:* camping permit required

79 Sharp Park River Bend Bush Camping

Only 30 min from the Gold Coast's theme parks, this no-frills family site is split into 2 areas by the Coomera River. It's 4 km south of Canungra, which in turn is 27 km east of Beaudesert. Ideal for daytrips to Mt Tamborine, Lamington National Park or O'Reillys, you'll find it on Beechmont Rd off the Beaudesert–Nerang Rd. Bookings are recommended for peak periods. **Map refs:** 360 D6, 457 N10

How to book: 3095 Beechmont Rd, Canungra 0409 550 745

80 Somerset Park camping area

Waterskiing enthusiasts and keen anglers enjoy staying at this basic site, 25 km north-east of Esk and 26 km south of Kilcoy. The camping ground is on the western shore of the lake, reached via the Esk–Kilcoy Rd. There is a boat ramp 1.2 km away and a shop on-site. Advance bookings are required for peak periods. **Map refs:** 360 C3, 457 M8

How to book: Esk–Kilcoy Rd, Somerset Dam (07) 5426 0176 www.seqwater.com.au/public/recreation/camping
Permits: permits are required to fish (under-18s excepted)

81 Stinson Park camping area

In 1937 local legend Bernard O'Reilly led the Stinson air crash survivors to safety from this historic site. O'Reilly found the wreckage in dense rainforest and saved the lives of 2 men who had been lost in the mountains for 2 days. Experienced, well-equipped bushwalkers can take the 'stretcher track' to the site of the crash. To get to the campsite, take the Mt Lindesay Hwy at Beaudesert (towards Rathdowney). At Laravale (14 km) turn left into Christmas Creek Rd. Note: tap water needs to be treated or boiled before drinking. **Map refs:** 360 D6, 457 M11

How to book: Christmas Creek Rd, Christmas Creek (07) 5544 8008

82 Swinging Bridge Park camping area

This site has no showers or toilets, but public toilets are available nearby and the Cooyar Hotel is happy for you to use their facilities; they charge a small fee for showers. If you are using one of the powered sites, collect the key to the power box from the pub (a small fee applies). The campground is beside Cooyar Creek on Fergus St (off Munro St). Cooyar is on the New England Hwy, 90 km north of Toowoomba. **Map refs:** 360 B3, 457 L8

Who to contact: Toowoomba Regional Council 13 1872

83 Tipperary Flat camping area

This spot on the D'Aguilar Hwy in Nanango offers free overnight camping with a few surprising mod cons, including a dump point for caravans, and disabled toilets. Grab a key to the town hall from the Nanango information centre (open every day of the year except Christmas) for a free hot shower. **Map refs:** 360 C2, 457 L7

Who to contact: South Burnett Energy and Information Centre (07) 4171 0100

84 Waterfall Creek Reserve camping area

On the edge of Mt Barney National Park, this very basic campsite with no facilities is suitable for self-sufficient campers and experienced bushwalkers. You'll find it on Waterfall Creek Rd, 35 km south of Boonah and 28 km west of Rathdowney. Access is via Newmans Rd off the Boonah–Rathdowney Rd. Note: during wet weather the reserve can only be access by 4WD vehicles. Fires are only permitted in the fire rings provided; bring your own firewood. Advance bookings are required. **Map refs:** 360 C6, 457 M11

How to book: Scenic Rim Regional Council Customer Service (07) 5540 5222 www.scenicrim.qld.gov.au *Permits:* camping permit required

85 Yallakool Caravan Park on Bjelke-Petersen Dam

Outdoor movies and friendly tennis competitions might not be typical tourist park activities, but Yallakool offers more bang for your buck. Situated 13 km south-east of Murgon, there are sheltered swimming areas, good fishing at Bjelke-Petersen Dam, kayaks available for hire and wildlife such as koalas, wallabies and kangaroos are often spotted in the grounds. The camp kitchen includes a fridge, hotplates, oven and microwaves. The park is signposted off Barambah Rd, from the Burnett and Bunya hwys. **Map refs:** 360 C2, 457 L6

How to book: Haager Dr, Moffatdale (07) 4168 4834 www.yallakoolpark.com.au

SUNSHINE COAST AND FRASER ISLAND

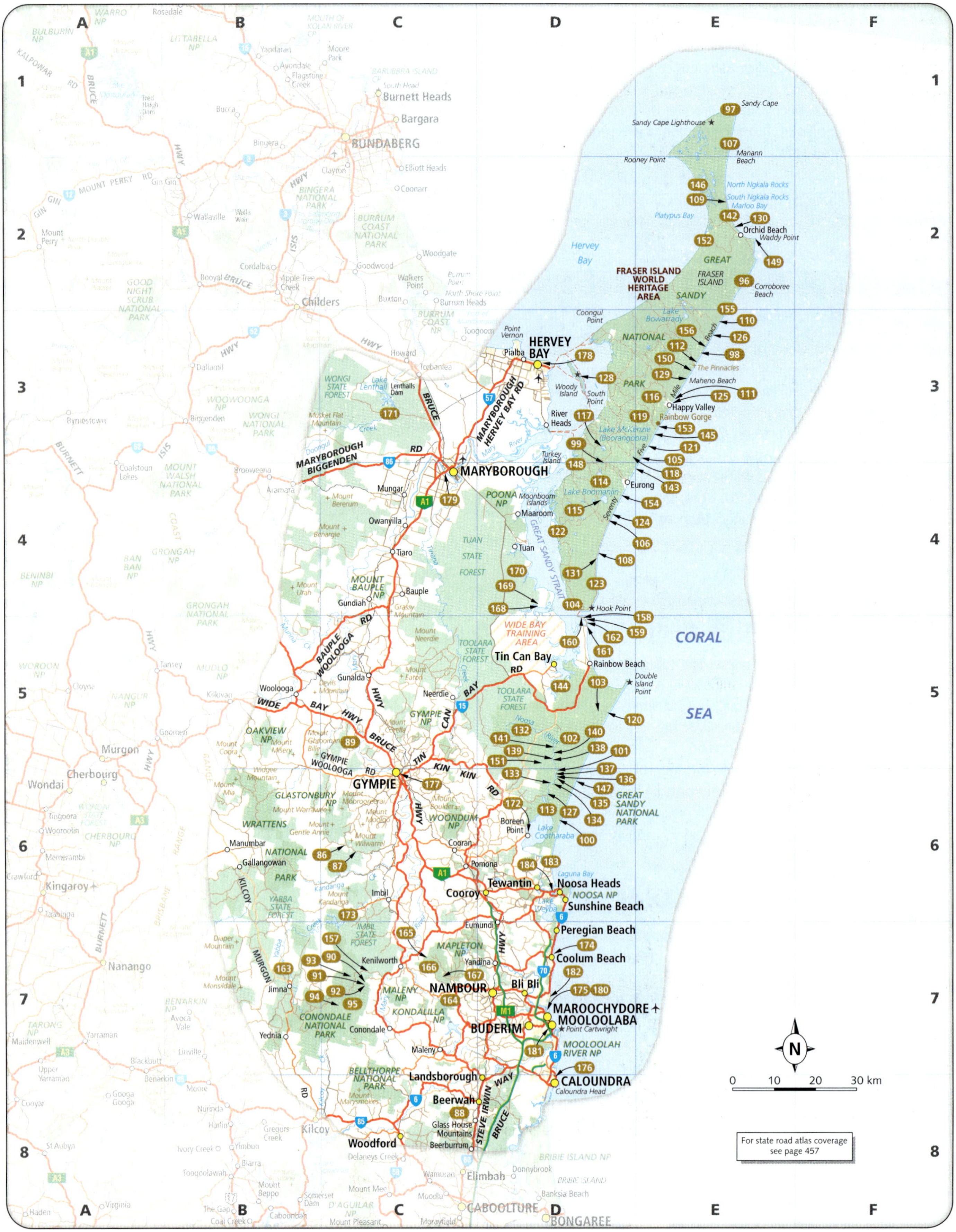

STRETCHING FROM CALOUNDRA TO Cooloola north of Brisbane, the Sunshine Coast's pristine coastline and year-round warm weather are a magnet for surfers, holidaying families and anyone seeking the laid-back seaside lifestyle. Venture just a few kilometres inland from the sunny coast to find the region's national parks shaped by forested mountains, rocky outcrops and spectacular waterfalls – the perfect location to relax, unwind and enjoy scenic camping.

North of Noosa, the Cooloola section of Great Sandy National Park features a range of beachfront and riverside campsites offering superb bushwalking, fishing, four-wheel driving, canoeing and boating. Further inland, the Amamoor, Beerburrum and Brooyar state forests have picturesque camping and day-use areas, as well as swimming holes and creeks for taking a leisurely paddle or dropping a line in.

World Heritage–listed Fraser Island, part of Great Sandy National Park, is the world's largest sand island, with 184 000 ha of exceptional beauty. You can go four-wheel driving on the beach, fish for whiting and bream on the famous 75 Mile Beach, or visit the coloured sands of The Pinnacles. Fraser is a must-see for wildlife-watchers; the long sandy beaches and beautiful rainforests provide a valuable habitat for dingoes, wallabies, flying foxes, echidnas and possums. The waters surrounding Fraser Island are home to dolphins and dugongs, and the region off Hervey Bay is one of the world's best known whale-watching spots. There are numerous bush camping sites on the island and well-established campgrounds at Central Station, Dundubara and Waddy Point.

Back on the mainland, state forests and reserves such as Imbil, Jimna, Tuan and Wongi are popular with campers and daytrippers. Imbil has scenic forest tracks for four-wheel driving, several bushwalking circuits and is one of the few protected reserves in Queensland that permits horseriding.

CAMPSITES LOCATED IN PARKS AND RESERVES

AMAMOOR STATE FOREST

Known for its riverine rainforests, hoop and bunya pine plantations and scenic walking tracks, Amamoor State Forest is 180 km north of Brisbane. Popular walks include a short path (with wheelchair access) to a platypus-viewing platform, a 1 km return rainforest walk and, for experienced hikers, the 4.6 km (4 hr) Cedar Grove trail. The forest is the traditional home of the Gubbi Gubbi, Wakka Wakka, Jinibara and Kabi Kabi peoples. The traditional owners maintain strong cultural links and strive to protect the land by sharing their culture. Advance bookings are required for all camping.

How to book: NPRSR 13 7468 www.nprsr.qld.gov.au
Permits: camping permit required

86 Amamoor Creek camping area

A rare find for pet owners, this camp is dog friendly. Take care though, as the creek is home to platypus and a variety of frogs. The flat, grassy campsites are suitable for tents and caravans, and surrounded by majestic ironbark and blue gum forest. Toilets and showers are wheelchair-accessible and there is a public phone. The campsite is closed to the public for the annual Country Music Muster for a week each Aug. Bring a gas/fuel stove or your own firewood, as collecting wood in the forest is illegal. Tap water needs to be boiled or treated before drinking. **Map refs:** 372 C6, 457 M6

87 Cedar Grove camping area

Cedar Grove camping area in Amamoor State Forest has tent and caravan campsites in open grassy areas beside riverine rainforest of white and red cedars, as well as tall open forest and Amamoor Creek. Bring along a gas/fuel stove or your own firewood, as collecting wood in the forest is illegal. Tap water needs to be boiled or treated before drinking, or bring your own. **Map refs:** 372 C6, 457 M6

BEERBURRUM STATE FOREST

A 1 hr drive north of Brisbane, Coochin Creek camping area in the north-east of Beerburrum State Forest is a renowned spot for fishing and boating. It is close to the site of Campbellville, an 1880s timber town. To get here, take Roys Rd from the Bruce Hwy. Advance bookings are required for camping.

How to book: NPRSR 13 7468 www.nprsr.qld.gov.au
Permits: camping permit required

88 Coochin Creek camping and day-use area

A great find for those who enjoy fishing and boating, this flat and grassy site beside Coochin Creek is on Roys Rd, 3 km upstream from the Pumiceton Passage. Access is 9 km east of Beerwah and 4 km east of the Bruce Hwy. There are 23 numbered campsites, various surfaces (sand, dirt, concrete, grass) and access for all vehicles. Open fires are not permitted except in provided fireplaces; bring firewood. **Map refs:** 372 C8, 457 N8

BROOYAR STATE FOREST

West of Gympie, Brooyar State Forest is known for having some of Queensland's best hoop pine plantations and cliff-top lookouts. Visitors can take rainforest walks or kick through the shallows of Glastonbury Creek. Northern access is from Petersen Rd from the Wide Bay Hwy 20 km west of Gympie. From the south, follow the sign from Glastonbury on Gympie–Woolooga Rd. Bookings must be made in advance for all camping.

How to book: NPRSR 13 7468 www.nprsr.qld.gov.au
Permits: camping permit required

89 Glastonbury Creek camping area

This large grassy camping area with a maximum capacity of 120 people is on the south-eastern edge of Brooyar State Forest. There is a day-use area with picnic tables and wood BBQs, and open fires are allowed in the designated fire rings. From the south, the campground is on the right just past the entrance to the forest; from the north it is on the left, 2 km past the entrance. Bring your own firewood, as gathering wood is prohibited. **Map refs:** 372 C5, 457 M6

CONONDALE NATIONAL PARK

The beautiful forests and gorges of Conondale National Park are reached by Booloumba Creek Rd, off Maleny–Kenilworth Rd 6 km south of Kenilworth. The park has waterfalls and lookouts, plus more than 120 bird species. Serious hikers will appreciate the challenge of the Conondale Range Great Walk, a 56 km hiking trail with 3 designated campsites, and its reward of stunning lookouts. Advance bookings are required for camping.

How to book: NPRSR 13 7468 www.nprsr.qld.gov.au
Permits: camping permit required

90 Booloumba Creek no. 1 camping area

This area offers secluded camping in a rainforest setting, ideal for tents but not for caravans or trailers, which are not permitted here. To reach it, go through Maleny and follow the signs to Kenilworth. You'll pass through the small town of Conondale; the turn-off to Booloumba is about 13 km past Conondale. Bring your own firewood and treat or boil the water before drinking. Conventional vehicle access is only possible in dry weather; there is 4WD access at all times. **Map refs:** 372 C7, 457 M7

91 Booloumba Creek no. 3 camping area

Much like site no. 1, no. 3 offers secluded tent camping in a rainforest setting. No caravans or camper trailers are permitted. To get there, go through Maleny and follow the signs to Kenilworth; the turn-off to Booloumba is about 13 km past Conondale. Bring your own firewood and treat or boil the water before drinking. Conventional vehicle access is only possible during dry weather; there is 4WD access at all times. **Map refs:** 372 C7, 457 M7

92 Booloumba Creek no. 4 camping area

Booloumba Creek's no. 4 campground is suitable for campervans, caravans and trailers. To get there, go through Maleny and follow the signs to Kenilworth; the turn-off to Booloumba is about 13 km past Conondale. Bring your own firewood and use existing fire sites. Treat or boil the water before drinking. Conventional vehicle access is only possible during dry weather; there is 4WD access at all times. **Map refs:** 372 C7, 457 M7

Conondale Range Great Walk

 *Please note that campsites are listed in alphabetical order, not track order. Refer to the map on p. 372 for further information.*

93 Summer Falls camping area (walk-in camping)

This campsite near the picturesque Summer Falls offers simple facilities for a maximum of 24 campers. Boil or treat the water before drinking and bring a gas/fuel stove, as fires are prohibited. Summer Falls is 15.2 km from Tallowwood camping area and 12 km from the Booloumba Creek day-use area. **Map refs:** 372 C7, 457 M7

94 Tallowwood camping area (walk-in camping)

As the name might suggest, Tallowwood camping area is located in a section of Conondale National Park dominated by the tallowwood. It offers simple facilities for a maximum of 24 campers. Boil or treat the water provided before drinking and bring a gas/fuel stove, as fires are prohibited. Tallowwood is 15.2 km from Summer Falls camping area and 17 km from Wongai camping area. **Map refs:** 372 C7, 457 M7

95 Wongai camping area (walk-in camping)

This camping area in the grassy open forest offers simple facilities for a maximum of 24 campers. Boil or treat the water provided before drinking and bring a gas/fuel stove, as fires are prohibited. Wongai is 11 km from the Booloumba Creek day-use area and 17 km from Tallowwood camping area. **Map refs:** 372 C7, 457 M7

GREAT SANDY NATIONAL PARK

Great Sandy National Park encompasses World Heritage–listed Fraser Island, the largest sand island in the world; nearby Woody Island, offering bush camping for self-sufficient visitors; and Cooloola on the mainland. This national park is 4WD only. Bookings are required in advance for all camping sites.

Fraser Island is famous for its giant dunes, some reaching 230 m in height, and its magnificent sand cliffs. Huge sand blows – dunes that continually move and regenerate – are a feature. It is also distinguished by its 40 perched dune lakes, of which Lake Boomanjin, at 200 ha, is the largest in the world. Ringed by white beaches, the water's colour in these freshwater lakes varies, from the sparkling blue of Lake McKenzie to the reddish-brown of Lake Boomanjin, which is stained by tannins from surrounding plants. The Fraser Island Great Walk traverses a 90 km stretch and takes in many of the island's attractions. Note: campfires are prohibited on Fraser Island, except at Dilli Village, Dundubara and Waddy Point. For these sites you need to bring your own firewood; collection of wood locally is prohibited. Many wild dingoes live on Fraser Island; these are dangerous, so read NPRSR's dingo safety information before visiting.

Cooloola offers a scenic experience amid open forests and fringing mangroves, placid waterways and coloured sands. This section of Great Sandy National Park is on the coast north of Noosa Heads, west of Gympie and south of Rainbow Beach. It contains the Cooloola Great Walk, a 102 km long track that traverses rainforest, dry scrubby regions, waterways and coastal heath. Take time to visit Double Island Point Lighthouse while you're here.

How to book: Fraser Island Learning and Research Centre (07) 4127 9130 for campsite no. **106**; (07) 4127 9177 www.cathedralsonfraser.com.au for campsite no. **98**; NPRSR 13 7468 www.nprsr.qld.gov.au for all other campsites
Permits: camping permit required for all NPRSR campsites, and 4WD permits required for all vehicles

96 Burad camping area (bush camping)

Bush camping for self-sufficient campers is available behind the dunes on this stretch of beach south of Corroboree Beach on Fraser Island's east coast. Bring drinking water and a gas/fuel stove (fires are prohibited), and place all rubbish and scraps in containers in your 4WD to avoid attracting dingoes. **Map refs:** 372 E2, 457 O4

97 Carree camping area (bush camping)

This semi-remote camping area at the far north of Fraser Island near Sandy Cape Lighthouse is suitable only for experienced wilderness campers. Bring drinking water and a gas/fuel stove (fires are prohibited), and place all rubbish and scraps in containers in your 4WD to avoid attracting dingoes. **Map refs:** 372 E1, 457 O3

98 Cathedrals on Fraser

This privately managed camping area, part of the Cathedrals on Fraser resort, offers some creature comforts missing from other campgrounds on the island, including fuel sales, a convenience store with bottle shop, and laundry facilities. It is a short distance from some of Fraser Island's key attractions, including the multicoloured sand cliff faces of The Pinnacles and the wreck of the SS *Maheno*. **Map refs:** 372 E3, 457 O4

99 Central Station camping area

This fenced family campground in central Fraser Island's rainforest setting has 44 tent sites, 16 camper trailer sites and a group area for 20–40 people. Accessible by 4WD or hiking trails only, it is 13 km east of the Wanggoolba Creek barge landing area and 9 km west of Eurong. Bring coins for the hot showers and use a gas/fuel stove (open fires are prohibited). It is a designated campsite on the Fraser Island Great Walk, and is 7.5 km from Lake Benaroon and 6.6 km from Lake McKenzie. **Map refs:** 372 D3, 457 N5

Cooloola Great Walk

Please note that campsites are listed in alphabetical order, not track order. Refer to the map on p. 372 for further information.

100 Brahminy camping area (walk-in camping)

This clearing in the coastal heath of Cooloola boasts stunning views of Lake Cootharaba and some modest facilities. It is 17 km from the southern entrance to Cooloola Great Walk and 20 km from Dutgee camping area. Note: water provided at this campsite must be boiled or treated before drinking. Bring a gas/fuel stove. **Map refs:** 372 D6, 457 N6

101 Dutgee camping area (walk-in camping)

This sandy campsite next to the Noosa River is named after the local Indigenous word for the boronia flowers that are abundant in the area. Like Brahminy, it has modest facilities, including water (treat or boil before drinking). It is 20 km from Brahminy camping area and 16.5 km from Litoria camping area. Bring a gas/fuel stove. **Map refs:** 372 D6, 457 N6

102 Kauri camping area (walk-in camping)

The Kauri camping area is so named because it lies at the very southern edge of the kauri pine's range. This camp on a lush forested ridge offers modest facilities, including drinking water (must be treated or boiled before use). Bring a gas/fuel stove. It is 20 km from Litoria camp and 15 km from the northern entrance to Cooloola Great Walk at Carlo Sandblow. **Map refs:** 372 D5, 457 N6

103 Litoria camping area (walk-in camping)

This campsite, near the shores of the mildly acidic Lake Coolamera, is named after the Cooloola sedgefrog, and you can hear its distinctive call. Boil or treat the water provided here before drinking. Bring a gas/fuel stove. It is 16.5 km from Dutgee camping area and 20 km from Kauri camping area. **Map refs:** 372 D5, 457 N6

104 Coolooloi Creek camping area (bush camping)

Bush camping for self-sufficient campers is available at this area to the west of the Hook Point barge terminal on Fraser Island, accessible by 4WD or boat. Bring drinking water and a gas/fuel stove (fires are prohibited), and place all rubbish and scraps in sealed containers to avoid attracting dingoes. **Map refs:** 372 D4, 457 N5

105 Cornwells camping area (bush camping)

Bush camping for self-sufficient campers is available behind the dunes on this stretch of beach at the eastern end of Fraser Island's central lakes scenic drive. Bring drinking water and a gas/fuel stove (fires are prohibited), and place all rubbish and scraps in containers in your 4WD to avoid attracting dingoes. **Map refs:** 372 E3, 457 N5

106 Dilli Village camping area

This privately managed camping area is attached to University of the Sunshine Coast's Fraser Island Research and Learning Centre, and offers reasonable facilities enclosed in a dingo-proof fence. Bring your own firewood for the provided campfire sites, and boil or treat water before drinking. Dilli Village is the southern trailhead for Fraser Island Great Walk, and is 6.3 km from Lake Boomanjin camping area. **Map refs:** 372 D4, 457 N5

107 Diray camping area (bush camping)

Semi-remote bush camping for self-sufficient campers is available behind the dunes on this stretch of beach south of Sandy Cape on Fraser Island's east coast. Bring drinking water and a gas/fuel stove (fires are prohibited), and place all rubbish and scraps in containers in your 4WD to avoid attracting dingoes. **Map refs:** 372 E1, 457 O3

108 Dulara camping area (bush camping)

Bush camping for self-sufficient campers is available behind the dunes on this stretch of beach at the northern end of Hook Point Inland Rd. Generators are prohibited and campers are required to bring a portable toilet (waste disposal facilities are available at Garulim). Bring drinking water and a gas/fuel stove (fires are prohibited), and place all rubbish and scraps in containers in your 4WD to avoid attracting dingoes. **Map refs:** 372 D4, 457 N5

109 Duling camping area (bush camping)

Bush camping for self-sufficient campers is available behind the dunes on this stretch of beach south of Ngkala Rocks on the northern east coast of Fraser Island. Bring drinking water and a gas/fuel stove (fires are prohibited), and place all rubbish and scraps in containers in your 4WD to avoid attracting dingoes. **Map refs:** 372 E2, 457 O3

110 Dundubara camping area

This popular family campground on Fraser Island has 40 tent sites, 5 camper trailer sites and a separate group camping area for up to 40 people. Accessed by 4WD, it's on the central east coast, about 75 km north of the Hook Point barge landing area and 19 km south of Indian Head. There is a payphone and post box near the campground, plus a waste transfer station 1 km from the site. You'll need to bring coins for the hot showers and to boil or treat the water before drinking. Note: there is a 9pm noise curfew. Bring your own firewood from the mainland. **Map refs:** 372 E3, 457 O4

111 Eli camping area (bush camping)

Bush camping for self-sufficient campers is available behind the dunes on this stretch of beach halfway between Dilli Village and Eli Creek on Fraser Island's east coast. Bring drinking water and a gas/fuel stove (fires are prohibited), and place all rubbish and scraps in containers in your 4WD to avoid attracting dingoes. **Map refs:** 372 E3, 457 O4

112 Eugarie camping area (bush camping)

Bush camping for self-sufficient campers is available behind the dunes on this stretch of beach north of Knifeblade Sandblow on Fraser Island's east coast. Bring drinking water and a gas/fuel stove (fires are prohibited), and place all rubbish and scraps in containers in your 4WD to avoid attracting dingoes. **Map refs:** 372 E3, 457 O4

113 Fig Tree Point camping area

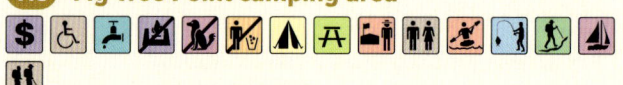

This campground beside Lake Cootharaba in the Cooloola section has basic facilities and a maximum capacity of 25 campers. It can be reached by boat or canoe from the Noosa River, 2 km north of Kinaba, or a 10 km walk from Elanda Point. Boil or treat water before using, and bring a gas/fuel stove. **Map refs:** 372 D6, 457 N6

Fraser Island Great Walk

Please note that campsites are listed in alphabetical order, not track order. Refer to the map on p. 372 for further information.

99 Central Station camping area

See p. 375.

106 Dilli Village camping area

See opposite.

114 Lake Benaroon camping area (walk-in camping)

There is a maximum stay of 2 nights and groups should number no more than 8 at this hikers' campsite. Lake Benaroon camping area is 7.2 km from Lake Boomanjin camping area and 6.3 km from Dilli Village. Water from the lake is drinkable but you need to boil or treat it. Bring a gas/fuel stove. **Map refs:** 372 D4, 457 N5

115 Lake Boomanjin camping area (walk-in camping)

See p. 378.

116 Lake Garawongera camping area (walk-in camping)

This site is 13.1 km from Valley of the Giants camping area and about 6.6 km from the Fraser Island Great Walk trailhead at

Happy Valley. Treat or boil water before drinking and use gas/fuel stoves only (no open fires are permitted). A maximum 2-night stay applies. **Map refs:** 372 E3, 457 N4

117 Lake McKenzie camping area (walk-in camping)

This basic clearing with few facilities is 6.6 km from Central Station camping area and 11.9 km from Lake Wabby camping area. The maximum stay is 2 nights and groups should be no bigger than 8. Boil or treat water before drinking, and bring a gas/fuel stove. **Map refs:** 372 D3, 457 N5

118 Lake Wabby camping area (walk-in camping)

This walkers' camp has a maximum 2-night stay and is suitable for groups no larger than 8. Water is available on-site (treat or boil first) and there is a toilet. Use only a gas/fuel stove. It is 11.9 km from Lake McKenzie camping area and 16.2 km from Valley of the Giants camping area. **Map refs:** 372 D3, 457 N5

119 Valley of the Giants camping area (walk-in camping)

This walkers' camp, 16.2 km from Lake Wabby and 13.1 km from Lake Garawongera, has a toilet and tap water (treat or boil water before drinking). A 2-night maximum stay applies. Bring a gas/fuel stove as fires are prohibited. **Map refs:** 372 E3, 457 N4

120 Freshwater Campground

Accessible by 4WD only, this campground with 59 sites is 8 km south of Double Island Point off Teewah Beach in Great Sandy's Cooloola section. The camping area is 500 m from the beach in scribbly gum woodland. Travel here via Teewah Beach or Freshwater Rd from the Bymien picnic area, 19 km east of Rainbow Beach Road, 1 km west of the beach. Sites must be pre-booked. Note: bring $1 coins for hot showers. Treat or boil tap water before drinking. Gas BBQs are available at the nearby day-use area. **Map refs:** 372 D5, 457 N6

121 Gabala camping area (bush camping)

Bush camping for self-sufficient campers is available behind the dunes on this stretch of beach between Poyungan Rocks and Cornwells camping area on Fraser Island's east coast. Bring drinking water and a gas/fuel stove (fires are prohibited), and place all rubbish and scraps in containers in your 4WD to avoid attracting dingoes. **Map refs:** 372 E3, 457 N5

122 Garrys Anchorage camping area

Unfenced campsites and picnic tables in a very quiet, remote location are 19 km south of Ungowa on Fraser Island's south-west coast. Access is by 4WD or boat. Bring drinking water and a gas/fuel stove (fires are prohibited), and place all rubbish and

scraps in containers in your 4WD to avoid attracting dingoes. **Map refs:** 372 D4, 457 N5

123 Garulim camping area (bush camping)

Bush camping for self-sufficient campers is available behind the dunes on this stretch of beach halfway between Hook Point and Dilli Village on Hook Point Inland Rd. Generators are prohibited and campers are required to bring a portable toilet (waste disposal facilities available on site). Bring drinking water and a gas/fuel stove (fires are prohibited), and place all rubbish and scraps in containers in your 4WD to avoid attracting dingoes. **Map refs:** 372 D4, 457 N5

124 Govi camping area (bush camping)

Bush camping for self-sufficient campers is available behind the dunes on this stretch of beach north of Dilli Village on Fraser Island's east coast. Bring drinking water and a gas/fuel stove (fires are prohibited), and place all rubbish and scraps in containers in your 4WD to avoid attracting dingoes. **Map refs:** 372 D4, 457 N5

125 Guluri camping area (bush camping)

Bush camping for self-sufficient campers is available behind the dunes on this stretch of beach directly to the north of Happy Valley on Fraser Island's east coast. Bring drinking water and a gas/fuel stove (fires are prohibited), and place all rubbish and scraps in containers in your 4WD to avoid attracting dingoes. **Map refs:** 372 E3, 457 O4

126 Guruman camping area (bush camping)

Bush camping for self-sufficient campers is available behind the dunes on this stretch of beach south of Dundubara camping area on Fraser Island's east coast. Bring drinking water and a gas/fuel stove (fires are prohibited), and place all rubbish and scraps in containers in your 4WD to avoid attracting dingoes. **Map refs:** 372 E3, 457 O4

127 Harrys camping area

This is the only campground in the Cooloola section with vehicle (4WD only) and Upper Noosa River access. It is 10 km east of Cooloola Way on Harrys Hut Rd. Campers should be aware that goannas and brush turkeys often scrounge for food in the area, so do not leave any scraps at the site. Boil or treat drinking water and use a gas/fuel stove. Note: you do not require a 4WD permit to drive along Harrys Hut Rd. **Map refs:** 372 D6, 457 N6

128 Jeffries Beach camping area (boat-based camping)

This bush campground with no facilities is the only camping area on Woody Island. You'll find Jeffries Beach on the south-east side of the island, about 5 min south of the gas shed. Experienced sea kayakers will find the waters of the Great Sandy Strait a delight to paddle in, but beware of the strong currents. You'll need to bring your own water, gas/fuel stove and rubbish bags. Note: mobile phone coverage here is poor. Camping is not permitted on Little Woody Island. **Map refs: 372 D3, 457 N4**

115 Lake Boomanjin camping area (walk-in camping)

This fenced campground suitable for tent camping (walk-in only) is in open forest between the carpark on Birrabeen Rd and Lake Boomanjin on Fraser Island. It is 6.3 km north of Dilli Village on the Fraser Island Great Walk, or 10 km north-west of Dilli Village on Birrabeen Rd (4WD only). Bring a gas/fuel stove and drinking water. **Map refs: 372 D4, 457 N5**

129 Maheno camping area (bush camping)

Bush camping for self-sufficient campers is available behind the dunes on this stretch of beach directly to the north of Eli Creek near the wreck of the *SS Maheno* on Fraser Island's east coast. Bring drinking water and a gas/fuel stove (fires are prohibited), and place all rubbish and scraps in containers in your 4WD to avoid attracting dingoes. Eli Creek is suitable for swimming, but do not swim in the ocean. **Map refs: 372 E3, 457 O4**

130 Marloo camping area (bush camping)

Bush camping for self-sufficient campers is available behind the dunes on this stretch of beach between Orchid Beach and Ocean Lake on Fraser Island's east coast. Bring drinking water and a gas/fuel stove (fires are prohibited), and place all rubbish and scraps in containers in your 4WD to avoid attracting dingoes. **Map refs: 372 E2, 457 O4**

131 Midyim camping area (bush camping)

Bush camping for self-sufficient campers is available behind the dunes on this stretch of beach between Dulara and Garulim on Hook Point Inland Rd. Generators are prohibited and campers are required to bring a portable toilet (waste disposal facilities are available at Garulim). Bring drinking water and a gas/fuel stove (fires are prohibited), and place all rubbish and scraps in containers in your 4WD to avoid attracting dingoes. **Map refs: 372 D4, 457 N5**

132 Neebs Waterhole camping area (walk-in camping)

Bush camping for self-sufficient hikers is permitted at Neebs Waterhole, 8.1 km (3 hr walk) south of Mullens carpark on Rainbow Beach Rd in the Cooloola section. It is around 12.5 km north of the Wandi Waterhole camping area. Access is walk-in only from the Cooloola Wilderness Trail. Bring in drinking water and a gas/fuel stove (no fires are permitted). **Map refs: 372 D5, 457 N6**

133 Noosa River camping area – no. 1 (boat-based camping)

Take a paddle down the Noosa River in the Cooloola section to this remote campsite, accessible only by small boat or canoe (jetty provided). It holds a maximum of 8 campers and offers few facilities. Boil or treat the provided water before using. Fires are banned, so bring a gas/fuel stove. **Map refs: 372 D6, 457 N6**

134 Noosa River camping area – no. 2 (boat-based camping)

This campsite, further up the Noosa River in the Cooloola section than camping area no. 1, is similarly low-key and tranquil. It can be accessed by canoe or small boat (canoe landing area provided). It holds a maximum of 8 campers and offers few facilities. Boil or treat the provided water before using. Fires are banned, so bring a gas/fuel stove. **Map refs: 372 D6, 457 N6**

135 Noosa River camping area – no. 3 (boat-based camping)

This campsite, further up the Noosa River in the Cooloola section than camping areas nos 1 and 2, marks the limit of how far motorised vessels can travel up the Noosa. It camps 25 people and has an access jetty, although there are no toilet facilities. Bring your own drinking water – or boil or treat the water here – and a gas/fuel stove. Note: the Cooloola Great Walk passes by this campsite. **Map refs: 372 D6, 457 N6**

136 Noosa River camping area – no. 4 (boat-based camping)

This campsite, just to the north of camping area no. 3 on the Noosa River in the Cooloola section, is the first of a series of isolated bush camps for self-sufficient campers. Accessible only by canoe (no motorised boats), there are no facilities on-site and it holds a maximum of 8 people. Boil or treat water from the river, or preferably bring in your own water. Fires are banned, so also bring a gas/fuel stove. Note: the Cooloola Great Walk passes by this campsite. **Map refs: 372 D6, 457 N6**

137 Noosa River camping area – no. 5 (boat-based camping)

This campsite, a few bends up the Noosa River in the Cooloola section from camping area no. 4, is the last of the riverside camping areas that the Great Walk passes by before turning north-east towards Lake Cooloomera. Like the other campsites, it has no facilities. Boil or treat the river water, or bring your own drinking water as well as a gas/fuel stove. **Map refs: 372 D6, 457 N6**

138 Noosa River camping area – no. 8 (boat-based camping)

This campsite is in the semi-remote north of Noosa River in the Cooloola section, 5 km north of camping area no. 5. (The numbered camping areas between are currently closed.) Like the other campsites, it has no facilities. Boil or treat the river water, or bring your own drinking water, and bring a gas/fuel stove. **Map refs:** 372 D5, 457 N6

139 Noosa River camping area – no. 9 (boat-based camping)

This campsite is in the semi-remote north of Noosa River in the Cooloola section, 1 km upstream of camping area no. 8. Like the other campsites, it has no facilities. Boil or treat the river water, or bring your own drinking water, as well as a gas/fuel stove. **Map refs:** 372 D5, 457 N6

140 Noosa River camping area – no. 13 (boat-based camping)

This campsite is in the semi-remote north of Noosa River in the Cooloola section, 2 km upstream of camping area no. 9. Like the other campsites, it has no facilities. Boil or treat the river water, or bring your own water, and carry in a gas/fuel stove. **Map refs:** 372 D5, 457 N6

141 Noosa River camping area – no. 15 (boat-based camping)

If you want to get away from it all, head far up the Noosa River in the Cooloola section to this, the final campsite on the river. Like the other campsites, it has no facilities. Boil or treat the river water, or bring your own water, and bring a gas/fuel stove. **Map refs:** 372 D5, 457 N6

142 Ocean Lake camping area (bush camping)

Bush camping for self-sufficient campers is available behind the dunes between Ocean Lake and the beach on Fraser Island's east coast. Some facilities are available at the nearby Ocean Lake day-use area. Bring drinking water and a gas/fuel stove (fires are prohibited), and place all rubbish and scraps in containers in your 4WD to avoid attracting dingoes. **Map refs:** 372 E2, 457 O3

143 One Tree Rocks camping area (bush camping)

Bush camping for self-sufficient campers is available behind the dunes on this stretch of beach north of Eurong QPWS Information Centre on Fraser Island's east coast. Bring drinking water and a gas/fuel stove (fires are prohibited), and place all rubbish and scraps in containers in your 4WD to avoid attracting dingoes. **Map refs:** 372 E4, 457 N5

144 Poverty Point camping area

This simple campground overlooking Tin Can Bay is 13 km south of Rainbow Beach off Rainbow Beach Rd in the Cooloola section. Follow the 4WD access road a further 6 km to reach the site. Bring your own water and firewood (for use only in the fire rings provided). There are no facilities on-site. **Map refs:** 372 D5, 457 N6

145 Poyungan camping area (bush camping)

Bush camping for self-sufficient campers is available behind the dunes on this stretch of beach north of Poyungan Rocks on Fraser Island's east coast. Bring drinking water and a gas/fuel stove (fires are prohibited), and place all rubbish and scraps in containers in your 4WD to avoid attracting dingoes. **Map refs:** 372 E3, 457 N5

146 Teebing camping area (bush camping)

This very large remote camping area stretches south from Sandy Cape Lighthouse on Fraser's west coast down to Wathumba camping area. 4WD vehicles are not permitted in this delicate area (boat or walk-in access only), and there are no facilities; bring water and a gas/fuel stove. Note: as this area is remote and difficult to reach in case of emergency, it is suitable only for experienced wilderness campers. Place rubbish and scraps in sealed containers to avoid attracting dingoes. **Map refs:** 372 E2, 457 O3

147 Teewah Beach camping area

You can camp on Teewah Beach in the 15 km zone between Noosa Shire boundary and Little Freshwater Creek in the Cooloola section, but there are no facilities provided. Access is 4WD only, with room for off-road caravans and camper trailers. Beach camping is not permitted from Double Island Point west to Rainbow Beach, north of Little Freshwater Creek, or south of the Noosa Shire boundary. Bring your own water and firewood. Note: use existing tent and fire sites to minimise your impact. **Map refs:** 372 D6, 457 N6

148 Ungowa camping area

Expect plenty of open, shady spots for tents, and defined camper trailer sites, at Ungowa, 12 km south-west of Central Station on the south-west coast of Fraser Island. The facilities are relatively basic but include a sink for washing up. Access is by 4WD or boat. Bring drinking water and a gas/fuel stove, and also insect repellent, as mosquitoes and sandflies are active year-round. **Map refs:** 372 D4, 457 N5

Teewah Beach camping area, Great Sandy National Park (p. 379)

149 Waddy Point camping area

The camping area at Waddy Point on Fraser Island contains a fenced clearing with 30 tent sites and 3 camper trailer sites, a fenced group-camping area for up to 40 people, and unfenced beachfront camping for 90 people. It is on the north-east coast of Fraser Island, about 5 km north of Indian Head, and is accessible only by 4WD. Facilities include flushing toilets, hot showers (coin-operated) and a waste transfer system 500 m from the campground. Use the communal fire rings for campfires – bring your own firewood. Generators are not permitted. **Map refs:** 372 E2, 457 O4

150 Wahba camping area (bush camping)

Bush camping for self-sufficient campers is available behind the dunes on this stretch of beach south of The Pinnacles on Fraser Island's east coast. Bring drinking water and a gas/fuel stove (fires are prohibited), and place all rubbish and scraps in containers in your 4WD to avoid attracting dingoes. **Map refs:** 372 E3, 457 O4

151 Wandi Waterhole camping area (bush camping)

Wandi has clearings for bush camping suitable for self-sufficient hikers, around 12.5 km south of Neebs Waterhole in the Cooloola section. Access is walk-in only from the Cooloola Wilderness Trail. Carry in drinking water and a gas/fuel stove (no fires are permitted). **Map refs:** 372 D5, 457 N6

152 Wathumba camping area

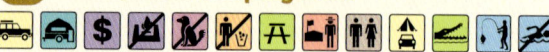

Nearby mangroves ensure mosquitoes and sandflies are ever-present, especially in summer, so come prepared! There are 20 designated sites and plenty of grass at this Fraser Island site, 16 km west of Waddy Point and accessible by 4WD or boat only. Bring drinking water and a gas/fuel stove. **Map refs:** 372 E2, 457 O4

153 Winnam camping area (bush camping)

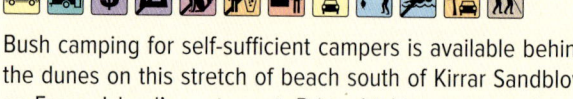

Bush camping for self-sufficient campers is available behind the dunes on this stretch of beach south of Kirrar Sandblow on Fraser Island's east coast. Bring drinking water and a gas/fuel stove (fires are prohibited), and place all rubbish and scraps in containers in your 4WD to avoid attracting dingoes. **Map refs:** 372 E3, 457 N4

154 Wongai camping area (bush camping)

Bush camping for self-sufficient campers is available behind the dunes on this stretch of beach south of Eurong Beach Resort on Fraser Island's east coast. Bring drinking water and a gas/fuel stove (fires are prohibited), and place all rubbish and scraps in containers in your 4WD to avoid attracting dingoes. **Map refs:** 372 D4, 436 D5, 457 N5, 462 G11

155 Wyuna camping area (bush camping)

Bush camping for self-sufficient campers is available behind the dunes on this stretch of beach south of Burad camping area on Fraser Island's east coast. Bring drinking water and a gas/fuel stove (fires are prohibited), and place all rubbish and scraps in containers in your 4WD to avoid attracting dingoes. **Map refs:** 372 E2, 457 O4

156 Yurru camping area (bush camping)

Bush camping for self-sufficient campers is available behind the dunes on this stretch of beach north of Cathedrals on Fraser resort on Fraser Island's east coast. Bring drinking water and a gas/fuel stove (fires are prohibited), and place all rubbish and scraps in containers in your 4WD to avoid attracting dingoes. **Map refs:** 372 E3, 457 O4

IMBIL STATE FOREST

Adjacent to both Jimna State Forest and Conondale National Park, this state forest provides access to a range of different landscapes – lush rainforests, imposing eucalypts, creeks and waterfalls. It is a popular locale for horseriding, walking through bush, mountain-biking and relaxing with a picnic. Campsites must be booked in advance.

How to book: NPRSR 13 7468 www.nprsr.qld.gov.au
Permits: camping permit required

157 Charlie Moreland camping area

This sizeable campground is suitable for large groups and is accessible for caravans, trailers and campervans. You'll need to bring your own firewood and use existing fire sites. Treat or boil water before drinking. Horses are welcome to stay overnight in the adjoining horse paddock. To get there, go through Maleny and follow the signs to Kenilworth; the turn-off to Charlie Moreland is about 13.5 km past Conondale. **Map refs:** 372 C7, 457 M7

INSKIP PENINSULA RECREATION AREA

Looking onto the southern tip of Fraser Island, north of Rainbow Beach, the peninsula is washed by the Pacific Ocean on its eastern side and by Tin Can Bay and Great Sandy Strait to the west. Fishing and birdwatching are popular pursuits. Note: check road conditions for caravan access. Inskip's beaches are unpatrolled and sharks are common, so swimming is not recommended. Boaties should familiarise themselves with Great Sandy Marine Park's zones and regulations before launching. Campsites must be booked in advance.

How to book: NPRSR 13 7468 www.nprsr.qld.gov.au
Permits: camping permit required

158 MV Beagle camping area

This small campground is accessible from the road or beach by 4WD only, and is not suitable for caravans, trailers or buses. There are hybrid toilets, and water is available at the service facility on Clarkson Dr in Rainbow Beach. Open fires are permitted in fire sites (bring your own firewood). The sandy campsites are set amid coastal vegetation of casuarina, heath and eucalypt woodland. **Map refs:** 372 D5, 457 N5

159 MV Natone camping area

Accessible from the road or the beach by 4WD only, this campsite is not suitable for caravans, trailers or buses. You can set up camp behind the foredunes and it's only a short walk to the beach. Water is available at the service facility on Clarkson Dr in Rainbow Beach. Bring your own firewood for use in defined fire sites. **Map refs:** 372 D5, 457 N5

160 MV Sarawak camping area

Popular with large groups, this campground off Clarkson Rd is the furthest from the entrance to Inskip Peninsula Recreation Area and can be accessed by road (conventional vehicles, when dry) or beach (4WD). It is accessible for trailers and caravans, but not buses. Water is available at the service facility on Clarkson Dr in Rainbow Beach. Open fires are permitted in fire sites; bring your own firewood. **Map refs:** 372 D5, 457 N5

161 The Oaks camping area

This basic campsite offers only rubbish bins and fire sites; there are no predefined sites, so camping is on a first-come, first-served basis. The campsite is within walking distance of the surf beach, and a boat launch is located close by at Bullock Point. Bring your own firewood, and you can pick up water at the service facility on Clarkson Dr in Rainbow Beach. **Map refs:** 372 D5, 457 N5

162 SS Dorrigo camping area

Within walking distance of the surf beach, this is the closest campground to the entrance of Inskip Peninsula Recreation Area. It is accessible for trailers, caravans and buses, but 4WD is recommended, especially in wet weather. Open fires are permitted in fire sites; bring your own firewood. Water is available at the service facility on Clarkson Dr in Rainbow Beach. The boat launch is nearby on Bullock Point. **Map refs:** 372 D5, 457 N5

JIMNA STATE FOREST

At the western edge of Upper Mary Valley, 140 km north of Brisbane and 40 km north of Kilcoy, this state forest has mountains, swimming holes and walking trails to keep visitors occupied. Bookings are required for all camping.

How to book: NPRSR 13 7468 www.nprsr.qld.gov.au
Permits: camping permit required

163 Peach Trees camping and day-use area

This is one for wildlife-watchers; you can spot eastern grey kangaroos, possums and maybe even platypus near here, 45 km north-west of Kilcoy along the Kilcoy–Murgon Rd (access via Peach Trees Rd). Horses can stay overnight in the horse paddock beside Peach Trees; a registered horse trail passes through Jimna State Forest. Grassy sites are beside Yabba Creek, with a cold shower on-site and drinking water from a tank (boil or treat it first). Bring your own untreated firewood. **Map refs:** 372 B7, 457 M7

KONDALILLA NATIONAL PARK

Kondalilla National Park, high in the Blackall Ranges, offers a cool retreat for bushwalkers looking to escape Queensland's heat. The park is named after Kondalilla Falls, where Skene Creek takes a 90 m plunge into the rainforest valley below. The park protects several important native species, including the pouched frog and the vulnerable Macadamia ternifolia. Camping in the park is prohibited except for hikers taking the Sunshine Coast Hinterland Great Walk. Bookings are required in advance for camping.

How to book: NPRSR 13 7468 www.nprsr.qld.gov.au
Permits: camping permit required

164 Flaxton camping area (walk-in camping)

This campsite, set amongst ferns, is on the Sunshine Coast Hinterland Great Walk. It offers simple facilities for up to 48 hikers. Boil or treat the water provided before drinking, and bring a gas/fuel stove, as fires are prohibited. Flaxton camping area is 16.5 km from the walk's trailhead at Baroon Pocket Dam and 13.1 km from Ubajee camping area in Mapleton National Park. **Map refs:** 372 C7, 457 N7

MAPLETON NATIONAL PARK

Just over 100 km north of Brisbane, Mapleton is at the northern end of the Blackall Range in the Sunshine Coast Hinterland. The area has magnificent bushwalks, picnic and day-use areas, and abseiling points. Trail-bike riders can make use of 26 km of circuits, provided you have a registered motorcycle. The Sunshine Coast Hinterland Great Walk passes through Mapleton; the campsites at Thilba Thalba and Ubajee are for hikers only. Bookings are required in advance for camping.

How to book: NPRSR 13 7468 www.nprsr.qld.gov.au
Permits: camping permit required

165 Gheerulla camping area

The Gheerulla creekside camping area is 8 km north-east of Kenilworth, accessed 6 km north-east of Kenilworth along the Eumundi–Kenilworth Rd (4WD only). It is illegal to collect firewood from the forest, so bring your own wood for the BBQs on-site, as well as drinking water. **Map refs:** 372 C7, 457 M7

166 Thilba Thalba camping area (walk-in camping)

This campsite, set high on a ridge above the Gheerulla Valley, is on the Sunshine Coast Hinterland Great Walk. It offers simple facilities for up to 48 hikers. Boil or treat the water provided before drinking, and bring a gas/fuel stove, as fires are prohibited. Thilba Thalba camping area is 16.1 km from the walk's trailhead at Delicia Rd and 13.5 km from Ubajee camping area. **Map refs:** 372 C7, 457 N7

167 Ubajee camping area (walk-in camping)

This campsite, in a blackbutt forest at the edge of the Gheerulla Valley, is on the Sunshine Coast Hinterland Great Walk. It offers simple facilities for up to 48 hikers. Boil or treat the water provided before drinking, and bring a gas/fuel stove, as fires are prohibited. Ubajee camping area is 13.5 km from Thilba Thalba camping area and 13.1 km from Flaxton camping area in Kondalilla National Park. **Map refs:** 372 C7, 457 N7

TUAN STATE FOREST

Around a 20 min drive south-east of Maryborough, the Tuan forest conserves a large range of plant species and is home to diverse wildlife. Visitors can go canoeing along the creeks, enjoy the flower displays in late winter and spring, and set up in one of the campgrounds with water frontage. The entrance to the forest is off Tinnanbar Rd, reached from Maryborough–Cooloola Rd. Bookings are required in advance for campsites.

How to book: NPRSR 13 7468 www.nprsr.qld.gov.au
Permits: camping permit required

168 Hedleys Campground

If you've never accessed a campsite via canoe, here's your chance. Set on a creek, Hedleys also has road access through a private property (fees apply, and the road is suitable for conventional vehicles only in dry weather). It's 3.4 km south of Tinnanbar Rd, signed 11.7 km east of Maryborough–Cooloola Rd on Tinnanbar Rd. Bring drinking water and untreated firewood, or a gas/fuel stove. **Map refs:** 372 D4, 457 N5

169 Log Dump Campground

The Log Dump on Kauri Creek is the only camping area in the region with a toilet; bring drinking water and untreated firewood, or a gas/fuel stove. You'll find it 1 km south-east of Tinnanbar Rd, signposted 7 km east of the Maryborough–Cooloola Road along Tinnanbar Rd. **Map refs:** 372 D4, 457 N5

170 Poona Creek camping area

This very basic clearing for self-sufficient campers can be accessed by entering Tuan State Forest from Cooloola Coast Rd. Campers must bring their own untreated wood for campfires, as gathering wood in the forest is not permitted. Use the fire rings provided and bring in water. Note: this campsite currently operates on a self-registration basis, but will be incorporated with NPRSR's online booking system in future; check NPRSR's webpage for Tuan State Forest before embarking. **Map refs:** 372 D4, 457 N5

WONGI STATE FOREST

Wongi State Forest has several waterholes fringed by paperbarks and surrounded by eucalypt forest. Wongi protects hoop pine rainforest, open eucalypt forest, open woodland with a heath understorey and exotic pine plantations. Visitors can follow a section of the Bicentennial National Trail in the forest. Advance bookings are required for camping.

How to book: NPRSR 13 7468 www.nprsr.qld.gov.au
Permits: camping permit required

171 Wongi camping area

Chill down with a dip in the beautiful waterholes at Wongi, but note that fishing is not allowed and jumping or diving is not recommended. There is conventional vehicle access and plenty of space for caravans, motorhomes and large groups. Signposted access is along Warrah Rd, 10 km west of the Bruce Hwy. Bring a gas/fuel stove. **Map refs:** 372 C3, 457 M4

CAMPSITES LOCATED IN OTHER AREAS

172 Boreen Point Campground

This neat and tidy campground, on the shores of Lake Cootharaba, offers an oasis of civilisation next door to the wilds of Cooloola. These well-appointed grounds include a laundry, camp kitchen, hot showers and sporting facilities (basketball, BMX, skateboarding and tennis) to keep the kids amused. The hamlet of Boreen Point is 20 km north-east of Pomona on Louis Bazzo Dr. Fires are only allowed in the designated wood BBQs. Note: bring your own firewood. Bookings are required. **Map refs:** 372 D6, 457 N6

How to book: The Esplanade, Boreen Point (07) 5485 3244 www.sunshinecoastholidayparks.com.au

173 Borumba Deer Park

Kids adore this friendly family-owned park where you can take tours of the grounds and feed the deer. Set on 6 ha of bush along the banks of Yabba Creek, there are powered sites, a kiosk, laundromat, 2 amenities blocks, playgrounds, plus boats and kayaks for hire. Nearby Borumba Dam (3 km west) offers a boat ramp, fishing and waterskiing. To reach the park from Imbil, 12 km away, follow the signs for Borumba Dam and cross Yabba Creek 5 times (9 km); the driveway is 200 m after the fifth crossing. **Map refs:** 372 C6, 457 M7

How to book: 1133 Yabba Creek Rd, Imbil (07) 5484 5196 www.borumbadeerpark.com

174 Coolum Beach Holiday Park

This popular tourist spot right on the beach at Coolum has room for legions of campers, with 133 powered caravan sites and 101 tent sites. The facilities are very advanced, and include a brand-new camp kitchen with wireless internet access, dump points and hot showers. Coolum beach's excellent surfing, swimming and fishing spots are moments away, and intrepid hikers can tackle Mt Coolum for its stunning views. Note: pets are welcome, but must be cleared in advance by the park. Advance bookings are required. **Map refs:** 372 D7, 457 N7

How to book: David Low Way, Coolum Beach (07) 5446 1474 www.sunshinecoastholidayparks.com.au

175 Cotton Tree Holiday Park

This park is the largest operated by the Sunshine Coast Council, with 264 powered sites suitable for caravans and camper trailers, and 139 camping sites. Conveniences include amenities blocks with laundry facilities, dump points and a sheltered camp kitchen. Cotton Tree is conveniently located between the holiday meccas of Maroochydore and Mooloolaba. Bookings are required in advance. **Map refs:** 372 D7, 457 N7

How to book: Cotton Tree Pde, Cotton Tree (07) 5459 9070 www.sunshinecoastholidayparks.com.au

176 Dicky Beach Family Holiday Park

If you're after family-friendly beaches, it doesn't get much better than Dicky Beach, 3 km north of Caloundra. This cosy holiday park offers access not only to the patrolled waters of its namesake but is also within striking distance of a host of others, including Kings, Bullock, Golden, Shelly and Moffat beaches. If the kids haven't exhausted themselves with sand and sun there's an on-site recreation room. Laundry facilities are available. Advance bookings are required. **Map refs:** 372 D8, 457 N8

How to book: Beerburrum St, Dicky Beach (07) 5491 3342 www.sunshinecoastholidayparks.com.au

177 Gympie Caravan Park

This pleasant caravan park offers access to a wide variety of the Sunshine Coast's attractions; it is within easy driving distance of Tin Can Bay, Boreen Point, Pomona and the Cooloola section of Great Sandy National Park. On-site facilities include a laundry, pool and LPG filling station. Bookings are recommended for peak periods. **Map refs:** 372 C6, 457 M6

How to book: 1 Jane St, Gympie (07) 5483 6800

178 Happy Wanderer Village Caravan Park

This well-appointed and modern caravan park offers all the creature comforts you'd expect from a 4.5 star park, including internet access, pool and spa, games room and laundromat. Its central location in Hervey Bay allows access to the Sunshine Coast's great tourist attractions, including whale-watching and coral-viewing tours. Bookings are recommended. **Map refs:** 372 D3, 457 N4

How to book: 105 Truro St, Torquay (07) 4125 1103 www.happywanderer.com.au

179 Huntsville Caravan Park

Maryborough, 40 km south of Hervey Bay, offers an excellent base to explore the natural attractions of the Sunshine Coast – especially during the whale-watching season, when campsites can be difficult to find in Hervey Bay. This caravan park offers easy access to Maryborough's central shopping district, a saltwater pool and laundry facilities. Bookings are recommended at peak periods. **Map refs:** 372 C4, 457 N5

How to book: 23 Gympie Rd, Maryborough (07) 4121 4075
www.huntsvillecaravanpark.com.au

180 Maroochydore Beach Holiday Park

This moderately sized holiday park (117 sites) is smaller than many of its fellow council-operated parks, but what it lacks in size it makes up for with its absolute waterfront location. Campers looking for a fix of civilisation will be pleased to find wireless internet and a shopping precinct with cafes and restaurants across the road, while swimmers and surfers will revel in Maroochy's iconic golden sands. Advance bookings are required. **Map refs:** 372 D7, 457 N7

How to book: Melrose Pde, Maroochydore (07) 5443 1167
www.sunshinecoastholidayparks.com.au

181 Mooloolaba Beach Holiday Park

This small campsite on Parkyn Pde in Mooloolaba is so popular that it extends to a separate area 1 km up the road at Ocean Beach. Both these locations offer absolute beachfront camping for tents, caravans and camper trailers, as well as modern facilities including laundry and wireless internet. Note: visitors at Ocean Beach need to visit the Parkyn Pde reception area before setting up camp. Bookings are required in advance.
Map refs: 372 D7, 457 N7

How to book: Parkyn Pde, Mooloolaba (07) 5444 1201
www.sunshinecoastholidayparks.com.au

182 Mudjimba Beach Holiday Park

Mudjimba, across the river to the north of Maroochydore, is home to this quiet haven of a holiday park. Visitors are minutes away from the beach and excellent surfing, but if the surf is too rough you can take a dip in the park's pool. Dogs are permitted on application, so mention your canine friend when booking. There's also a laundry and wireless internet. Bookings are required in advance. **Map refs:** 372 D7, 457 N7

How to book: Cottonwood St, Mudjimba (07) 5448 7157
www.sunshinecoastholidayparks.com.au

183 Noosa North Shore Beach Campground

Entirely surrounded by Great Sandy National Park and the Coral Sea, Noosa North Shore is the most rustic of the council-operated camping areas, but also one of the most charming. Being surrounded by nature doesn't mean giving up modern conveniences: this park features a well-stocked kiosk, hot showers and a laundry. Campfires are prohibited here and there are no gas or electric BBQs, so bring your own portable cooker or rent one from reception. Bookings are required in advance. **Map refs:** 372 D6, 457 N7

How to book: 240 Wilderness Track, Noosa North Shore (07) 5449 8811 www.sunshinecoastholidayparks.com.au

184 Noosa River Holiday Park

This campsite on the banks of Noosa River and Weyba Creek has one of the most enviable positions in Noosa real estate, including stunning views from the camp kitchen and BBQ area. Anglers, boaties and kayakers will find excellent access to Noosa's waterways from this site. A comprehensive kiosk, laundry and wireless internet provide creature comforts. Bookings are required in advance. **Map refs:** 372 D6, 457 N7

How to book: 4 Russell St, Noosaville (07) 5449 7050
www.sunshinecoastholidayparks.com.au

Sunshine Coast Hinterland Great Walk

This 58 km hiking trail traverses Kondalilla, Mapleton and Mapleton Falls national parks. It is best approached from south to north, starting at Baroon Pocket Dam and looping back through Gheerulla Valley to finish at the Delicia Rd entrance. Campsite bookings are required in advance. Note: walkers are required to purchase a topographic map of the Great Walk before embarking.

Please note that campsites are listed in alphabetical order, not track order. Refer to the map on p. 372 for further information.

How to book: NPRSR 13 7468 www.nprsr.qld.gov.au
Permits: camping permit required

164 Flaxton camping area (walk-in camping)
See p. 382.

166 Thilba Thalba camping area (walk-in camping)
See p. 382.

167 Ubajee camping area (walk-in camping)
See p. 382.

CAPRICORN

THE DIVERSE CHARMS OF the Capricorn region will have you discovering the country charm of coastal centres such as Bundaberg, Gladstone and Rockhampton, exploring the spectacular gorges and waterfalls out west, or setting sail for the southernmost tropical islands of the Great Barrier Reef.

The region is dotted with dozens of wonderfully diverse national parks, state forests, dams and lakes, with some of the best camping locations the state has to offer. Carnarvon National Park is one of the gems. Shaped by dramatic sandstone cliffs, pillars, arches and featuring rare Aboriginal rock art, the 16 000 ha Carnarvon Gorge is the most popular section of the park for campers. Vehicle-based camping is also permitted at the Mt Moffatt, Ka Ka Mundi and Salvator Rosa sections. For experienced hikers, the 86 km Carnarvon Great Walk leads through the gorge and across the rugged plateaus and valleys of the Consuelo Tableland and Mt Moffatt sections of the national park.

Another unique highlight of the region is Capricornia Cays National Park at the southern end of the Great Barrier Reef, north-east of Gladstone and the town of Seventeen Seventy. Camping is permitted on the coral cays of Masthead Island, North West Island and Lady Musgrave Island. Off the coast of Rosslyn Bay Harbour, camping is allowed on the islands of Keppel Bay Islands National Park – up to 75 people can camp on North Keppel Island at any one time.

Back on the mainland, Lake Murphy Conservation Park, north-west of Taroom, is a great site for birdwatchers. Keen anglers should head for Broadwater Conservation Park, Deep Water National Park or one of the popular water reserves such as Wuruma Dam, Lake Awoonga or Glebe Weir. Only very experienced bushwalkers should attempt to traverse the rugged landscapes and vegetation in Mount Walsh National Park.

CAMPSITES LOCATED IN PARKS AND RESERVES

AUBURN RIVER NATIONAL PARK

Massive granite boulders and steep gorges leading to the Auburn River give this national park a scenic quality like no other. Situated 225 km west of Maryborough, a highlight is the 600 m (15 min) walk to the Gorge Lookout for spectacular views. Bookings are required for all camping.

How to book: NPRSR 13 7468 www.nprsr.qld.gov.au
Permits: camping permit required

185 Auburn River camping area

On the northern bank of the Auburn River, this site has 5 camping clearances close to bushwalking tracks. Don't drink the river water; the tank water available on-site must be treated or boiled, and you need to bring milled firewood. To get there from Mundubbera, take Duron Rd for 13 km, then take Hawkwood Rd for 20 km to the signposted park access road. A 4WD is recommended in wet weather. Stay on the road, as soils are treacherous when wet. **Map refs: 386 F5, 457 K5**

BARAKULA STATE FOREST

Expect to see logging trucks on the access roads at Barakula, as this forest is a major supplier of cypress pine. Despite the presence of industry, the forest (about 45 km north of Chinchilla) is known for providing good fishing opportunities after rains, and there's plenty on display for wildlife-watchers. Go west on the Warrego Hwy from Chinchilla, then take Auburn Rd north to Barakula. Advance bookings are required for all camping.

How to book: NPRSR 13 7468 www.nprsr.qld.gov.au
Permits: camping permit required

186 Bush camping areas

Both drive-up and walk-in bush camping for self-sufficient campers is permitted at various locations throughout Barakula. There are no facilities, so bring your own drinking water, a gas/fuel cooker, rubbish bags for taking waste with you and all other necessaries. Camping is prohibited in signposted logging areas. Note: cattle herds are common throughout Barakula. For your safety, do not camp near feeding lots, cattle trails or livestock watering dams. **Map refs: 386 E6, 457 J6**

187 Dogwood Creek camping area

This old sawmill site is now a clearing for campers, but offers no facilities. It is reached from Barakula State Forest Rd off Auburn Rd. Go past the Department of Primary Industries area and look for the forestry camp signs to Dogwood Creek. Bring drinking water and a gas/fuel stove. Open fires are permitted when there are no fire bans, but exercise caution, as there are no formal fire areas. **Map refs: 386 E6, 457 I6**

BLACKDOWN TABLELAND NATIONAL PARK

The traditional home of the Ghungalu people, Blackdown Tableland National Park is in the north-east corner of the central Queensland sandstone belt. Its gorges and waterfalls offer spectacular scenery, and rock faces with Ghungalu artwork highlight the wonderful cultural significance of the land. The signed turn-off on the Capricorn Hwy is 11 km west of Dingo or 110 km east of Emerald. Advance bookings are required for all camping.

How to book: NPRSR 13 7468 www.nprsr.qld.gov.au
Permits: camping permit required

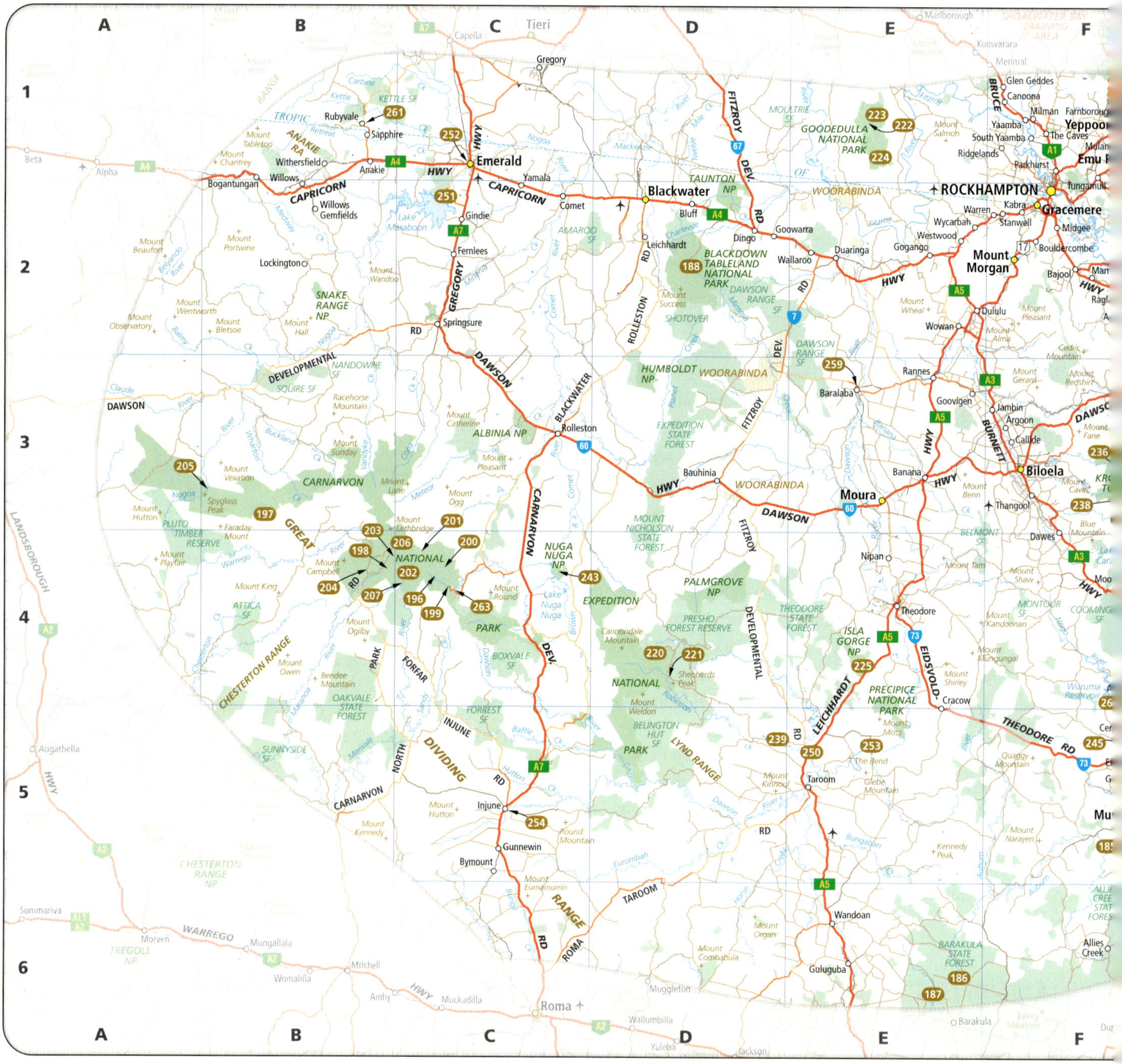

(map of Queensland Capricorn region showing towns including Emerald, Blackwater, Rockhampton, Gracemere, Mount Morgan, Biloela, Moura, Theodore, Taroom, Injune, Roma, and national parks including Carnarvon National Park, Blackdown Tableland National Park, Goodedulla National Park, Expedition National Park, Isla Gorge NP, Precipice National Park, Palmgrove NP)

---

188 Munall camping area

Also known as Mimosa Creek, this camping area is 8 km from the park entrance and can be reached with a conventional vehicle. There are 16 numbered sites with a maximum of 6 per site, ideal for camping beside your car, or for small camper trailers (no caravans). Bring drinking water and firewood.
Map refs: 386 D2, 459 J11

BROADWATER CONSERVATION PARK

Broadwater Conservation Park lies between Baffle and Deepwater creeks. Visitors can swim at the beach, but note that it is unpatrolled and marine stingers are present

Oct–May. There is 4WD beach access at low tide; check tides and access points before proceeding onto the beach. Anglers need to familiarise themselves with the rules and zones of Great Barrier Reef Marine Park before casting off. Advance bookings are required for all camping.
How to book: NPRSR 13 7468 www.nprsr.qld.gov.au
Permits: camping permit required

189 Mitchell Creek camping area

Fantastic for fishing and wildlife-watching, the campground is accessible by 4WD or boat along Rules Beach; check tides and entry points before proceeding to the beach. There are no

For state road atlas coverage see pages 456–9

190 Bush camping areas

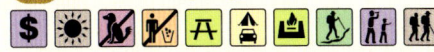

Bush camping is permitted anywhere throughout the bunya pines of Bulburin, but the most popular site is a former forestry barracks on Granite Creek Forest Rd. There are no facilities here besides a picnic platform, so campers must be totally self-sufficient. Bring your own drinking water and firewood (open fires are permitted, but no sites are provided). Scenic drives through the forest are recommended; a 4WD loop road passes through the rainforest. **Map refs: 387 G4, 457 L2**

BURRUM COAST NATIONAL PARK

Covering more than 23 000 ha, Burrum Coast National Park boasts a stunning natural environment with mangrove-lined riverbanks, wallum heath wildflowers and tea-tree swamps. Also known for its rare wildlife and quiet beaches, the park is divided into 3 main sections: Woodgate, Kinkuna and Burrum River. Advance bookings are required for all camping.

How to book: NPRSR 13 7468 www.nprsr.qld.gov.au
Permits: camping permit required

191 Burrum Point camping area

Whether you prefer swimming at the beach or boating on a river, you're blessed with the choice of both at Burrum Coast National Park. The sandy camping area is just a short walk from the beach at Burrum Point, and Burrum River is also close by. The campground has 13 numbered sites, cold showers and toilets. It is 8 km south of Woodgate; access is signposted on Walkers Point Rd from Woodgate. Note: it is 4WD access only, and roads may be closed during extreme wet weather. **Map refs: 387 H5, 457 N4**

192 Kinkuna camping area (bush camping)

Take your pick from 40 sandy sites behind the beach foredunes in the Kinkuna section. There are no facilities but open fires are allowed (except when fire bans apply). Bring drinking water. Note: the Woodgate–Palm Beach Rd through Kinkuna is closed during wet conditions. **Map refs: 387 H5, 457 M4**

CAPRICORNIA CAYS NATIONAL PARK

Part of the Great Barrier Reef World Heritage area, Capricornia Cays is a stunning group of coral cays, islands and reefs off the coast of Gladstone and Seventeen Seventy. The park protects several vegetated coral cays, including Lady Musgrave, North West, Masthead, Wilson, Heron, Erskine and Tryon islands. Commercial operators run daily services to Lady Musgrave Island, and provide charter boats to other islands. Advance bookings are required for all camping.

How to book: NPRSR 13 7468 www.nprsr.qld.gov.au
Permits: camping permit required

facilities so you'll need to bring water, a gas/fuel stove and all self-sufficient camping equipment. **Map refs: 387 H3, 457 M2**

BULBURIN NATIONAL PARK

Formerly a forest reserve and now a national park, Bulburin features vast subtropical rainforests and eucalypt woodlands, home to a variety of wildlife, including the red-eyed tree frog and the rare long-nosed potoroo. Bulburin is 50 km north-east of Monto, with conventional vehicle access from Builyan on the Monto–Gladstone Rd. Advance bookings are required for all camping.

How to book: NPRSR 13 7468 www.nprsr.qld.gov.au
Permits: camping permit required

193 Lady Musgrave Island camping area (boat-based camping)

Lady Musgrave has space for up to 40 campers at any one time from Easter school holidays until Australia Day in Jan (the campsite is closed in Feb and Mar each year). The campground has composting toilets, an information shelter and emergency radio. Lady Musgrave is the southernmost island in the national park, just south of the Tropic of Capricorn – a great spot for snorkellers. You need to bring drinking water and a gas/fuel stove. **Map refs: 387 H3, 457 M1, 459 P12**

194 Masthead Island camping area (boat-based camping)

Up to 50 people can camp at this site on the north-west corner of the island. Suitable only for self-sufficient campers, there are no facilities and no generators permitted. Masthead Island is known as an important rookery for green turtles and endangered loggerhead turtles; avoid disturbing them. Activities include snorkelling, fishing, birdwatching and reef walking in designated areas. Bring drinking water and a gas/fuel stove. Note: the camping area is closed for regeneration from mid-Oct to Easter each year. **Map refs: 387 G2, 459 O11**

195 North West Island camping area (boat-based camping)

Camping is permitted on the island from Easter until the end of the summer school holidays in Jan each year. The campground has enough space for up to 150 people. Bring drinking water and a gas/fuel stove. There are composting toilets and information displays but no generators are permitted on the island. **Map refs: 387 G2, 459 O11**

CARNARVON NATIONAL PARK

Tucked away in this vast, rambling park in Queensland's Central Highlands is the magnificent Carnarvon Gorge. Boasting towering white sandstone cliffs, breathtaking side gorges and some of the finest Aboriginal rock art in Australia, this 160-million-year-old natural wonder is the region's most popular tourist attraction. The Mt Moffat section of the park features grassy woodlands and magnificent sandstone outcrops. Further west, the isolated and unspoiled Ka Ka Mundi and Salvator Rosa sections of the park offer wildlife watching and bush camping areas. Bookings are required in advance for all sites except Bunbuncundoo Springs and Nogoa River.

How to book: NPRSR 13 7468 www.nprsr.qld.gov.au
Permits: camping permit required **Camping fees:** fees can be paid and permits acquired for Bunbuncundoo Springs and Nogoa River at the self-registration stations

196 Big Bend camping area (walk-in camping)

Great for experienced walkers and campers, this site is reached by a 9.7 km walk from the visitor information centre through the gorge; there's no access for vehicles. Once there, you'll find a small campground (the maximum number of campers is 10) in a rainforest setting with a cliff backdrop. A composting toilet and a picnic table are the only facilities, so you'll need to bring all self-sufficient goods and equipment. Note: record your trip details in the registration book at the park's information centre, and log out when you return. Big Bend is a designated campsite on the Carnarvon Great Walk and is 14.8 km from Gadd's camping area. **Map refs: 386 C4, 456 F3**

197 Bunbuncundoo Springs camping area (bush camping)

This campsite, deep inside Carnarvon's Ka Ka Mundi section, is suitable for self-sufficient campers only: bring water and a gas/fuel stove. There is good wildlife watching in the area so look out for king parrots and red-necked wallabies. It is 130 km south-west of Springsure. Travel west on the Springsure–Tambo Rd for 50 km, then turn south into Buckland Rd; the campsite is accessible by 4WDs in dry weather only. **Map refs: 386 B3, 456 E2**

198 Bush camping areas (walk-in camping)

Walk-in bush camping is permitted in all areas of the Mt Moffat section of Carnarvon National Park except restricted-access areas. There are no facilities and fires are prohibited, so bring all self-sufficient gear, including drinking water and a gas/fuel stove. **Map refs: 386 B4, 456 E2**

199 Carnarvon Gorge camping area

Camping is permitted here only during certain Queensland school holidays: Easter, winter and spring. There are 35 numbered campsites, plenty of room for large groups, and good shade under gum trees and cabbage palms. Visitors should note that the site can be reached by conventional vehicle, but the last 20 km of the access road is unsealed and could be impassable in wet weather. The site is 45 km west of the Carnarvon Developmental Rd. **Map refs: 386 C4, 456 F3**

Carnarvon Great Walk

Please note that campsites are listed in alphabetical order, not track order. Refer to the map on p. 386 for further information.

196 Big Bend camping area (walk-in camping)
See opposite.

200 Cabbage Tree camping area (walk-in camping)

This open grassy campsite high on the Consuelo Tableland is the last stop on the recommended Carnarvon Great Walk itinerary. It is 13.8 km from Consuelo camping area and 15.3 km from the Carnarvon Gorge information centre. Water is provided from an underground tank, but it must be treated or boiled before drinking. Bring a gas/fuel stove. Note: do not camp

Takaru Bush Resorts, Carnarvon Gorge (p. 397)

within 20 m of the water collection point, to avoid damaging the underground tank. **Map refs:** 386 C4, 456 F2

201 Consuelo camping area (walk-in camping)

High up on the Consuelo tableland – known as 'the roof of Queensland' – this campsite offers no facilities other than water from an underground tank (boil or treat water before drinking). Bring a gas/fuel stove. It is 17.3 km from West Branch camping area and 13.8 km from Cabbage Tree camping area. Note: do not camp within 20 m of the water collection point, to avoid damaging the underground tank. **Map refs:** 386 C4, 456 F2

202 Gadd's camping area (walk-in camping)

This site is situated among the remains of an old cattle station, past the stunning views of Battleship Spur lookout. There are no facilities other than water from an underground tank, which must be boiled or treated before drinking. Bring a gas/fuel stove. It is 14.8 km from Big Bend camping area and 15.8 km from West Branch camping area. Note: do not camp within 20 m of the water collection point, to avoid damaging the underground tank. **Map refs:** 386 C4, 456 F3

203 West Branch camping area

See p. 390.

204 Dargonelly Rock Hole camping area

This campground is beside the rock hole at Marlong Creek and can be accessed by conventional vehicles and off-road caravans in dry weather only. Up to 35 people can camp at the site at any one time, and there is a water supply for drinking and cooking only (treat or boil first). Unlike many other national park campgrounds, this one permits generators during the day. You need to bring your own firewood but a gas/fuel stove is preferred. **Map refs:** 386 B4, 456 E2

205 Nogoa River camping area (bush camping)

This bush camping site in the Salvator Rosa section of Carnarvon National Park is for entirely self-sufficient campers. Orange-barked yellow-jacket trees and beautiful wildflower displays are some of the highlights of the area. You can reach the campsite in a conventional vehicle, but need 4WD to explore the park any further. Use a gas/fuel stove for cooking, treat or boil the creek water before drinking, and remove your rubbish. To get to Salvator Rosa from Springsure, head 114 km west along Tambo Rd to the park turn-off. **Map refs:** 386 B3, 456 D2

206 Rotary Shelter Shed camping area

This camping area about 17 km north-east of the park office is accessible only by 4WD (suitable for high-clearance camper trailers). There are no defined sites, but a maximum of 15 people can camp at any one time. Bring all self-sufficient goods and equipment, including firewood, and treat or boil the water before drinking. A gas/fuel stove is preferred. **Map refs:** 386 C4, 456 F2

207 Top Moffatt camping area

Accessible only by 4WD and high-clearance camper trailers, this site is at the east branch of the Maranoa River. A maximum of 20 people can use the area at any one time, and it suits self-sufficient campers as the only facilities are a pit toilet and communal fire rings. Bring water and firewood, or a gas/fuel stove. **Map refs:** 386 C4, 456 F3

203 West Branch camping area

This site is near the west branch of the Maranoa River and can be reached by conventional vehicles and off-road caravans in dry weather only. Open fires are permitted only at existing fire rings; check for fire bans. No generators are permitted. The camping area is 9 km north-east of the park office. West Branch is a designated campsite on the Carnarvon Great Walk with a separate area for great walkers; it is 15.8 km from Gadd's camping area and 17.3 km from Consuelo camping area. **Map refs:** 386 B4, 456 F2

CASTLE TOWER NATIONAL PARK

Experienced bush hikers and climbers will relish the challenges in Castle Tower National Park, 35 km south of Gladstone. The dramatic peaks of Mt Castle Tower and Mt Stanley rise out of open eucalypt woodland, and those with the skill and endurance to scale these peaks are rewarded with views over the Boyne Valley and north to Gladstone. Access to the park is on foot only through private property, or via boat across the Awoonga Dam and on foot through Gladstone Area Water Board land. Permission is required from relevant property owners or GAWB before accessing the park. Advance bookings are required for camping.

How to book: NPRSR 13 7468 www.nprsr.qld.gov.au
Permits: GAWB (07) 4976 3000 www.gawb.qld.gov.au for camping permit and permission to access the park; or request permission from private property owners

208 Bush camping areas (walk-in camping)

Bush camping is permitted throughout Castle Tower National Park, wherever hikers can find a suitable site. No facilities are provided and open fires are prohibited, so bring all self-sufficient camping gear, including drinking water and a gas/fuel stove. **Map refs:** 387 G3, 457 K1

CURTIS ISLAND NATIONAL PARK

This national park is at the north-eastern end of Curtis Island, off the Queensland coast between Gladstone and Rockhampton. There is a historic lighthouse at Cape Capricorn, but no other notable facilities. Fishing, swimming, snorkelling and wildlife-watching are all popular activities here, although swimmers and snorkellers should wear protective clothing during stinger season (Oct–May). Travel to the island is by private boat from Gladstone, The Narrows, Port Alma or Rosslyn Bay. Advance bookings are required for camping.

How to book: NPRSR 13 7468 www.nprsr.qld.gov.au
Permits: camping permit required

209 Joey Lees camping area (bush camping)

This secluded campsite north of Turtle Street offers no facilities, but it comes with a lovely view, beach access and shady trees – perfect for self-sufficient campers looking for a quiet getaway. Bring your own drinking water, a gas/fuel stove (open fires are prohibited) and all other necessities. **Map refs:** 387 G2, 459 N11

210 Turtle Street camping area (bush camping)

This campsite, the closest to the Southend ferry terminal, is the most accessible of Curtis Island's campsites – although it's still very remote and can only be reached by 4WD. There are no facilities, so bring your own drinking water, a gas/fuel stove (open fires are prohibited) and all other necessities. **Map refs:** 387 G2, 459 N11

211 Yellow Patch camping area (boat-based camping)

There is bush camping at the north-eastern end of Curtis Island at Yellow Patch, known for its bright yellow sand. It is suitable for self-sufficient campers, with no facilities on-site, and can only be accessed by boat. Bring your own drinking water and a gas/fuel stove (open fires are prohibited). **Map refs:** 387 G2, 459 N11

DAWES RESOURCES RESERVE

Located 109 km south of Gladstone and 58 km north-east of Monto, this resources reserve and the surrounding national park preserve the remains of Glassford, an abandoned mining town whose fortunes waned as the Glassford Creek copper lode was diminished. Glassford's ruins are surrounded by Sydney blue gums and and blackbutt forests. To access the park, turn west onto Childs Rd (4WD and dry-weather access only) off the Gladstone–Monto Rd 9 km south of Many Peaks or 16 km north of Kalpowar.

Who to contact: QPWS Gladstone (07) 4971 6505
Permits: camping permit required *Camping fees:* fees can be paid and permits arranged at QPWS Gladstone

212 Bush camping areas

Bush camping is permitted throughout Dawes National Park and Resources Reserve, wherever campers can find a suitable site. No facilities are provided and open fires are prohibited, so bring all self-sufficient camping gear, including drinking water and a gas/fuel stove. **Map refs:** 387 G4, 457 K2

213 Old Mine camping area (bush camping)

Those with an interest in history will find this campsite, near the well-preserved remains of a copper smelter and mine workings from the early 1900s, a fascinating experience. No facilities are provided, so bring all self-sufficient camping gear and your own drinking water. Open fires are permitted here; bring your own firewood or a gas/fuel stove. **Map refs:** 387 G4, 457 K2

DEEPWATER NATIONAL PARK

Deepwater National Park, about 100 km north-west of Bundaberg, features diverse vegetation, creeks, beaches and a variety of wildlife. Access to the park is 4WD only, via Wreck Rock Rd from Agnes Water or Tableland Rd from Berajondo. Advance bookings are required for camping.

How to book: NPRSR 13 7468 www.nprsr.qld.gov.au
Permits: camping permit required

214 Middle Rock camping area (bush camping)

At the north-eastern side of Deepwater National Park, this sand and woodchip bush camp has undefined sites behind the foredunes and is accessible only by 4WD. There are no facilities provided and you need to take a gas/fuel stove, drinking water and rubbish bags. Also bring along a pair of binoculars and a bird field guide to help identify the diverse birdlife. From Jan–Apr, marine turtle hatchlings emerge, usually at night, from their nests. The beach is unpatrolled and there may be rips and sharks. Beware of marine stingers Oct–May. **Map refs:** 387 G3, 457 M2

215 Wreck Rock camping area

This small campsite behind the frontal dunes at the south-eastern end of Deepwater National Park has 14 sites for a maximum of 6 people each. It provides excellent beachfront camping with sand and woodchip surfaces and is just a skip across the sand dunes to the beach. The park is near the tiny town of Seventeen Seventy where you can join a range of tours and boat trips to Lady Musgrave Island and Fitzroy Reef. Agnes Water and Seventeen Seventy are the closest mainland points to the outer Great Barrier Reef. **Map refs:** 387 G3, 457 M2

EURIMBULA NATIONAL PARK

Protecting tropical forests and coastal mangroves, Eurimbula National Park lies about 110 km north-west of Bundaberg. The park is just 10 km from Seventeen Seventy and 13 km from Agnes Water; both towns are ideal jumping-off points to reach the outer Barrier Reef. Access to the park is signposted off Agnes Water–Seventeen Seventy Rd, west of Agnes Water. Take the short but steep walk to Ganoonga Noonga Lookout for beautiful views over Bustard Bay. Bookings are required in advance for camping.

How to book: NPRSR 13 7468 www.nprsr.qld.gov.au
Permits: camping permit required

216 Bustard Beach camping area

Set behind the foredunes on the eastern side of the park, this campground with a sand-and-woodchip surface has 17 defined camping sites with a maximum of 6 per site. You're just a short stroll to the beach, but remember that it's unpatrolled and there may be rips and sharks. Beware of marine stingers Oct–May. The campsite is signposted off the Eurimbula Access Rd, which is signposted off the Agnes Water–Seventeen Seventy Rd, 10 km west of Agnes Water. **Map refs:** 387 G3, 457 L1

217 Bustard Head camping area (boat-based camping)

Self-sufficient campers can boat into this camping area on Bustard Head. There are no facilities and open fires are not permitted, so bring your own water, a gas/fuel stove and all other necessaries. **Map refs:** 387 G3, 457 L1, 459 O12

218 Middle Creek camping area

About 35 km north-west of Agnes Water, this campsite can be accessed by boat or by 4WD (off the Eurimbula Access Rd). Bring your own drinking water, rubbish bags and a gas/fuel stove, as fires are prohibited. **Map refs:** 387 G3, 457 L1

219 Rodds Peninsula camping area (boat-based camping)

A second boat-only campsite in Eurimbula exists on Rodds Peninsula. There are no facilities and open fires are not permitted, so bring your own water, a gas/fuel stove and all other necessaries. **Map refs:** 387 G3, 457 L1, 459 O12

EXPEDITION NATIONAL PARK

Part of the Central Queensland Sandstone Belt, Expedition National Park's eucalypt and gum forests are about 130 km west of Taroom. There are 3 main sections: Robinson Gorge, Lonesome and Beilba. Stencil art indicates that Aboriginal people have lived in the area for thousands of years. Signposted access to Robinson Gorge is 18 km north of Taroom from the Leichhardt Hwy; both Lonesome and Beilba sections are accessed via Carnarvon Developmental Rd north of Injune.

Who to contact: NPRSR 13 7468 www.nprsr.qld.gov.au
Permits: camping permit required *Camping fees:* fees can be paid and permits acquired at the self-registration stations

220 Bush camping areas

Bush camping is permitted throughout the Robinson Gorge section and in certain areas of Beilba and Lonesome sections for self-sufficient and experienced campers. For a unique outback Queensland experience, set up camp inside the house at the old cattle station in the Beilba section, or camp by the banks of the Dawson River in the Lonesome section. There are no facilities, so bring your own drinking water and all other necessaries. Open fires are allowed when fire bans do not apply, but a gas/fuel stove is recommended. **Map refs:** 386 D4, 456 G3

221 Starkvale camping area

Self-sufficient campers with 4WD vehicles can access this grassy clearing in the Robinson Gorge section of Expedition, 4 km south-east of Robinson Gorge lookout (dry-weather access only). There are approximately 8 campsites suitable for walk-in camping, high-clearance camper trailers, or camping beside your car. No generators are permitted. Note: tank water is provided (it must be treated or boiled before use) but supply is unreliable, so bring your own water. **Map refs:** 386 D4, 456 H3

GOODEDULLA NATIONAL PARK

Located 80 km west of Rockhampton, this national park protects a large number of rare and threatened species, including the black ironbox and the greater glider. This hilly, semi-remote park is perfect for birdwatching. To get there, take the Capricorn Hwy south-west from Rockhampton to Gogango, then follow the signs north to Rookwood Station. Follow further signs to the park from Rookwood along a rough, unsealed and difficult road (4WD only). Advance bookings are required for camping.

How to book: NPRSR 13 7468 www.nprsr.qld.gov.au
Permits: camping permit required

222 Kings Dam camping area (bush camping)

This bush campsite is 35 km north of Goodedulla's southern entrance. There are no facilities here, so campers must bring their own water, rubbish bags and other necessaries. Open fires are allowed when fire bans do not apply, but a gas/fuel stove is recommended. **Map refs:** 386 E1, 459 L10

223 The Palms camping area (bush camping)

This bush campsite is located in open woodland next to a waterhole on the seasonal Melaleuca Creek, 50 km north of the park entrance. There are no facilities here, so campers must bring their own water, rubbish bags and other necessaries. Open fires are allowed when fire bans do not apply, but a gas/fuel stove is recommended. **Map refs:** 386 E1, 459 L10

224 Wadlow Yards camping area (bush camping)

This bush campsite is located in open woodland next to a waterhole on the seasonal Melaleuca Creek, 6 km north of the park entrance. There are no facilities here, so campers must bring their own water, rubbish bags and other necessaries. Open fires are allowed when fire bans do not apply, but a gas/fuel stove is recommended. **Map refs:** 386 E1, 459 L10

ISLA GORGE NATIONAL PARK

This park of rugged landscapes lies 36 km south-west of Theodore, in central Queensland's sandstone belt. It protects not only Isla Gorge, created by erosion from Gorge Creek, but also remnants of dry rainforest, mulga and brigalow scrub, eucalypts and natural grasslands. Access to the park is off the Leichhardt Hwy 55 km north of Taroom and 35 km south of Theodore.

Who to contact: NPRSR 13 7468 www.nprsr.qld.gov.au
Permits: camping permit required *Camping fees:* fees can be paid and permits acquired at the self-registration station

225 Isla Gorge camping area

If you're seeking a campsite with a view, you'll love watching the sun set over the orange-coloured cliffs of Isla Gorge at this camping area. There are undefined walking tracks for experienced walkers. Bring your own firewood, and treat or boil the tank water before drinking. The site is just over 1 km off the Leichhardt Hwy and can be reached by conventional vehicles. Note: the campsite is next to an unfenced cliff face; be cautious when walking and supervise children closely. **Map refs:** 386 E4, 457 I3

KALPOWAR STATE FOREST

More than 150 plant species exist amongst rainforest, eucalypt forest and hoop pine plantations in Kalpowar State Forest, 38 km north-east of Monto. The 20 km Kalpowar Forest Drive is a good way to get around and see the forest. The forest is reached by Fireclay Rd or the Kalpowar–Gin Gin Rd, both off the Monto–Gladstone Rd. Advance bookings are required for camping.

How to book: NPRSR 13 7468 www.nprsr.qld.gov.au
Permits: camping permit required

226 Kalpowar camping area

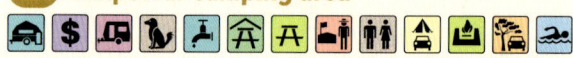

This campground beside Crane Creek has plenty of grassy sites for camping beside your car, and also accommodates those with caravans and trailers. To get there from Monto, travel 37 km north-east on the Monto–Gladstone Rd and take the gravel road turn-off. You need to be self-sufficient, preferably with a gas/fuel stove, and bring your own firewood. The water here must be treated or boiled before use. **Map refs:** 387 G4, 457 L2

KEPPEL BAY ISLANDS NATIONAL PARK

This national park covers the region from Curtis Island to Corio Bay off the central Queensland coast and includes 15 islands. Travel to the islands is by private boat or water taxi from Rosslyn Bay Harbour, 15 km east of Yeppoon. Access to Barren and Peak islands is restricted. Note: swimmers should take precautions against marine stingers, particularly from Oct–May. Advance bookings are required for camping.

How to book: NPRSR 13 7468 www.nprsr.qld.gov.au
Permits: camping permit required; campers are required to notify QPWS Rosslyn Bay (07) 4933 6595 immediately before departure from the mainland

227 Conical Island camping area (boat-based camping)

Conical Island has a small camping area with space for 6 campers. There are picnic tables but no other facilities, so you need to be self-sufficient, bringing water and a gas/fuel stove. Coral reefs to the west of the island are within easy snorkelling distance of the beach. **Map refs:** 386 F1, 459 N10

228 Divided Island camping area (boat-based camping)

Self-sufficient campers can pitch at tent at this small campground. The maximum number of people permitted to camp at the site is 6; there are no facilities. The beach on the western side is a recommended spot for picnicking. Bring water and a gas/fuel stove. **Map refs:** 386 F1, 459 N11

229 Humpy Island camping area (boat-based camping)

The national park's most popular camping area, Humpy Island has space for up to 60 self-sufficient campers. The campground is on the island's northern beach; taps throughout the site provide bore water not suitable for drinking, so bring water and a gas/fuel stove. **Map refs:** 387 F1, 459 N10

230 Miall Island camping area (boat-based camping)

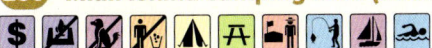

This tiny camping site behind the foredunes only has space for 6 self-sufficient campers and there are no facilities besides picnic tables. Bring water and a gas/fuel stove. Reefs on the south-eastern and northern sides of the island are recommended for divers and snorkellers. **Map refs:** 386 F1, 459 N10

231 Middle Island (Northeastern Beach) camping area (boat-based camping)

Only 6 self-sufficient campers are permitted at any one time in this bush campsite behind the dunes of Middle Island's north-eastern beach. Reefs at nearby Olive Point headland provide excellent snorkelling and diving. The only facilities on the island are picnic tables, so bring your own water, garbage bags and a gas/fuel stove. Note: fishing is prohibited in the waters around Middle Island. **Map refs:** 386 F1, 459 N10

232 Middle Island (Northwestern Beach) camping area (boat-based camping)

This bush campsite behind the dunes of Middle Island's north-western beach offers room for 6 self-sufficient campers. The only facilities on the island are picnic tables, so bring your own water, garbage bags and a gas/fuel stove. Note: fishing is prohibited in the waters around Middle Island. **Map refs:** 386 F1, 459 N10

233 Middle Island (Southeastern Beach) camping area (boat-based camping)

This campsite, behind the dunes of the smallest of Middle Island's 3 beaches, offers excellent access to the large reef to the west of the island. Picnic tables are the only facilities on the island, so this site suits self-sufficient campers only (maximum of 6 people); bring water, rubbish bags and a gas/fuel stove. Note: fishing is prohibited in the waters around Middle Island. **Map refs:** 386 F1, 459 N10

234 North Keppel Island (Considine Beach) Campground (boat-based camping)

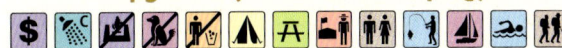

This site with space for 75 self-sufficient campers is at the southern end of Considine Beach on the western side of North Keppel Island. Bring water, rubbish bags and a gas/fuel stove. Sandflies and mosquitoes are common so come prepared, and secure your food well to avoid attracting brushtail possums. **Map refs:** 386 F1, 459 N10

235 Pelican Island camping area (boat-based camping)

Camping is restricted to 6 people at any one time on rugged, isolated Pelican Island, and no facilities are provided. It is suitable for self-sufficient campers only. Bring water and a gas/fuel stove. **Map refs:** 386 F1, 459 N10

KROOMBIT TOPS NATIONAL PARK

Home to many rare and threatened plants and animals, Kroombit Tops National Park offers excellent bushwalks, a 4WD circuit, a lookout over the Boyne Valley, and day-use areas. The park is 85 km south-west of Gladstone, at the meeting point of the Dawes, Calliope and Milton ranges. Note: falling trees and branches pose a danger in this park, so avoid camping under dead or dying trees, and during periods of high winds. Advance bookings are required for camping.

How to book: NPRSR 13 7468 www.nprsr.qld.gov.au
Permits: camping permit required

236 The Barracks camping area (bush camping)

A clearing suitable for bush camping is located opposite the old forestry barracks (now a ranger station), 4 km south of the Tableland Rd entrance. It can be reached with 2WD only in dry weather. There is a maximum of 10 campers permitted at the site; no facilities are provided. Bring water, firewood and preferably a gas/fuel stove. While in the area, visit the lookout for excellent views over the Boyne Valley. **Map refs:** 386 F3, 457 K2

237 Bush camping areas

Bush camping is permitted in most areas of Kroombit Tops, excluding The Barracks, the lookout, and the intersection of Griffiths Creek and Tableland Rd. There are no facilities, so bring your own water, rubbish bags, and milled firewood or a gas/fuel stove. **Map refs:** 386 F3, 457 K2

238 The Wall camping area (bush camping)

This grassy clearing on the south bank of Annie Creek can be reached on the 4WD loop road near the bomber crash site. There is a maximum of 20 campers allowed, but there are no defined sites and no facilities. Bring everything you will need. **Map refs:** 386 F3, 457 K2

LAKE MURPHY CONSERVATION PARK

Beneath Murphy's Range in the central highlands, Lake Murphy fills only when nearby Robinson Creek overflows. It's a peaceful, relaxing location – even when the lake is dry. The park is 13 km along Glenhaughton Rd, off the Leichhardt Hwy 18 km north of Taroom.

Who to contact: NPRSR 13 7468 www.nprsr.qld.gov.au
Permits: camping permit required *Camping fees:* fees can be paid and permits acquired at the self-registration station

239 Lake Murphy camping area

This large camping area has plenty of space for motorhomes and large groups looking for a shady spot near the lake, which is a seasonal refuge for waterbirds. You'll need to bring firewood and drinking water. Access is via the main road into the park, near the picnic area. Note: this campsite can only be accessed by conventional vehicles during dry weather. **Map refs:** 386 D5, 456 H4

MOUNT WALSH NATIONAL PARK

Known for its exposed granite cliffs, the craggy landscape of Mt Walsh National Park offers excellent hiking for bushwalkers. It takes just 2.5 hrs to reach the summit of Mt Walsh, but the ascent should only be attempted by experienced walkers. Reach the park via the Biggenden–Maryborough Rd, 2 km east of Biggenden.

Who to contact: NPRSR 13 7468 www.nprsr.qld.gov.au
Permits: camping permit required *Camping fees:* fees can be paid and permits acquired at QPWS Maryborough (07) 4121 1800

240 Bush camping areas (walk-in camping)

Bush camping is permitted at Mt Walsh for self-sufficient campers; no facilities are provided. It is recommended that walkers bring along a topographic map and compass. Campers are required to meet with the park ranger at QPWS Maryborough to discuss their itinerary before embarking; there are no self-registration facilities at Mt Walsh. **Map refs:** 387 G5, 457 L5

MOUTH OF BAFFLE CREEK CONSERVATION PARK

Mouth of Baffle Creek Conservation Park is on the northern shore of Rules Beach, 1 hr north of Bundaberg. Behind the sandy beaches are low, open she-oak woodlands and paperbark woodlands. The park is off Rules Beach Rd, from the Bundaberg–Agnes Water Rd. There is 4WD beach access at low tide only. Advance bookings are required for camping.

How to book: NPRSR 13 7468 www.nprsr.qld.gov.au
Permits: camping permit required

241 Mouth of Baffle Creek camping area

Visitors to this park can camp behind the dunes, 2 km south of the beach access point. There are no facilities and it is recommended for self-sufficient campers only: bring everything. Beware of marine stingers Oct–May. **Map refs:** 387 H4, 457 M2

MOUTH OF KOLAN RIVER CONSERVATION PARK

Located 25 km north-west of Bundaberg, Mouth of Kolan River Conservation Park protects a diverse array of wildlife and vegetation. Fragile saltplain plants line the river banks, and migratory birds – including pied oystercatchers, eastern curlews and red-necked stints – travel here annually to nest. Advance bookings are required for camping.

How to book: NPRSR 13 7468 www.nprsr.qld.gov.au
Permits: camping permit required

242 Mouth of Kolan River camping area (bush camping)

This bush camping area for self-sufficient campers lies behind the dunes at Moore Park Beach, and can be accessed by 4WD or private boat only. To get there, take the beach access road off Sylvan Dr in Moore Park at low tide. No facilities are provided and fires are prohibited, so bring all self-sufficient camping gear, including drinking water, rubbish bags and a gas/fuel cooker. **Map refs:** 387 H4, 457 M3

NUGA NUGA NATIONAL PARK

At the northern end of Arcadia Valley, Nuga Nuga National Park is a popular destination for fishing, canoeing, kayaking and bushwalking. It is about 400 km west of Gladstone, approximately 150 km north of Injune via Mulcahy Rd from the Carnarvon Developmental Rd. Check the road conditions, as there is access in dry weather only.

Who to contact: NPRSR 13 7468 www.nprsr.qld.gov.au
Permits: camping permit required *Camping fees:* fees can be paid and permits acquired at the self-registration station

243 Nuga Nuga camping area (bush camping)

Self-sufficient visitors can camp at this site on the banks of Lake Nuga Nuga. Access (in dry weather only) is via the main road to the park, 7 km from Arcadia Valley Access Rd. The surface is a combination of dirt and grass and there are no defined sites. Bring water, firewood and preferably a gas/fuel stove. **Map refs:** 386 C4, 456 G2

RUNDLE RANGE NATIONAL PARK

Approximately 40 km north-west of Gladstone, Rundle Range National Park protects areas of dry rainforest and open forests, with more than 280 plant species recorded. The park is about 60 km south-east of Rockhampton. Access is off the Bruce Hwy at Ambrose by 4WD in dry weather only.

Who to contact: NPRSR 13 7468 www.nprsr.qld.gov.au; *Permits:* camping permit required *Camping fees:* fees can be paid and permits acquired at QPWS Gladstone (07) 4971 6500

244 Sandfly Point camping area (bush camping)

This site for self-sufficient campers is on the western boundary of the national park. As the name suggests, sandflies and mosquitoes are a major problem here, so bring repellent and wear appropriate clothing. The boat ramp and creek nearby are suitable for small vessels and fishing. Bring water, firewood and a gas/fuel stove. **Map refs: 386 F2, 459 N11**

TOLDERODDEN CONSERVATION PARK

Beside the Burnett River, this small park is suitable for brief stays. Take the track from the camping area up a ridge (700 m) for a view over the park. It is on the Cracow Rd, just 4.5 km west of Eidsvold. Bookings are required in advance.

How to book: NPRSR 13 7468 www.nprsr.qld.gov.au *Permits:* camping permit required

245 Tolderodden Conservation Park camping area (bush camping)

This grassy site beside the river has good accessibility for all types of vehicles. Tank water is available but should be boiled or treated before drinking. Bring your own firewood, as collecting wood in the park is not permitted. **Map refs: 386 F5, 457 K4**

WILD CATTLE ISLAND NATIONAL PARK

Wild Cattle Island National Park takes up most of its eponymous island – a small, unspoiled sand island located near the sleepy hamlet of Tannum Sands, 15 km south-east of Gladstone. Access to this picturesque island is by boat, or on foot from Tannum Sands at low tide.

Who to contact: QPWS Gladstone (07) 4971 6500 *Permits:* camping permit required *Camping fees:* fees can be paid and permits acquired at QPWS Gladstone (07) 4971 6500

246 Bush camping areas (boat-based camping)

Camping is permitted at certain areas on Wild Cattle Island – check with QPWS Gladstone. There are no facilities provided and fires are prohibited, so bring all self-sufficient camping gear, including drinking water, rubbish bags and a gas/fuel stove. **Map refs: 387 G3, 457 L1, 459 N12**

CAMPSITES LOCATED IN OTHER AREAS

247 1770 Camping Ground

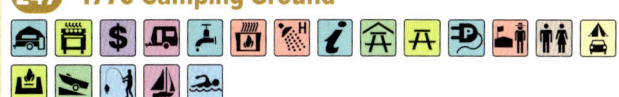

Those looking for absolute beachfront access will adore this commercial camping area in the hamlet of Seventeen Seventy. All of the camp's 100 sites are within a short walk of the water and its activities, and 27 of them are absolute beachfront. The facilities here are basic but well maintained, and the lack of on-site cabins means that the 1770 Camping Ground is a favourite with seasoned campers. Bookings are recommended. **Map refs: 387 G3, 457 M1**

How to book: 641 Captain Cook Dr, Seventeen Seventy (07) 4974 9286 www.1770campingground.com.au

248 BIG4 Cania Gorge

The friendly and welcoming folks at this tourist park offer a high standard of accommodation and facilities for the whole family. Campers have the option of powered and unpowered sites, or you can upgrade to a cabin or hillside villa. The park is very close to the spectacular cliffs, ancient caves and bright-coloured sandstone of Cania Gorge National Park. Activities on-site include bird feeding, outdoor movies, a swimming pool, tennis court and even a 9-hole golf course. It is 4 km from Lake Cania, 35 km north of Monto and 25 km north of the Burnett Hwy. Bookings are recommended for peak periods. **Map refs: 386 F4, 457 K2**

How to book: Phil Marshall Dr, Monto (07) 4167 8188 www.caniagorge.com.au

249 Cania Gorge Tourist Retreat

In a sandstone gorge at the entrance to the Cania Gorge National Park, this excellent eco-friendly tourist park packed with top-notch facilities has 40 powered sites, 20 unpowered sites and a modern amenities block. There's a pool, laundry, grocery shop, cabins, gas re-fills and a fish-cleaning area. Popular activities include taking a hike on the national park walking tracks, fishing in Lake Cania and taking a scenic drive on a 4WD track. From Monto, follow the Burnett Hwy for 12 km, then take the bitumen road a further 12 km to the national park. Bookings are recommended for peak periods. **Map refs: 386 F4, 457 K2**

How to book: 1253 Cania Rd, Monto (07) 4167 8110 www.caniagorgeretreat.com.au

250 Chain Lagoons camping area

This free campsite with no facilities is 15 km north-east of Taroom, reached via the Old Theodore Rd from the Leichhardt Hwy. Taroom, on the Dawson River, is 120 km north of

Miles on the Warrego Hwy and 153 km south of Banana on the Dawson Hwy. **Map refs:** 386 E5, 457 I4

Who to contact: Banana Shire Council (07) 4992 9500

251 Discovery Holiday Parks – Lake Maraboon

Said to be 3 times the size of Sydney Harbour, Lake Maraboon is a major destination for fishing and boating enthusiasts year-round. The caravan park has excellent facilities: swimming pool, cabins, licensed restaurant, boat hire, and a kiosk for bait, ice, gas and fuel. Access to the lake is via Selma Rd from Emerald (18 km) or the Fairbairn Dam Access Rd from the Gregory Hwy. Bookings are recommended for peak periods. **Map refs:** 386 C2, 459 I11

How to book: Selma Rd, Emerald (07) 4982 3677, 1800 627 226 www.discoveryholidayparks.com.au/qld/central_highlands/lake_maraboon

252 Emerald Cabin and Caravan Village

Overlooking Emerald's 18-hole golf course, this caravan park has an range of facilities including drive-through powered sites, a laundry, and a camp kitchen with gas BBQ, microwave and fridge. The camping area offers plenty of grass and shade. Visitors can get supplies in Emerald, go fossicking in the gem fields, or take a day trip to Carnarvon Gorge. **Map refs:** 386 C1, 459 I10

How to book: 64 Opal St, Emerald (07) 4982 1300 www.emeraldcabinandcaravanvillage.com.au

253 Glebe Weir camping area

A hugely popular spot for fishing and waterskiing, Glebe Weir is a 54 km drive from Taroom. To get to the campground, take the Leichhardt Hwy 28 km north of Taroom, turn right onto Glebe Weir Rd and travel for a further 26 km. Bring your own firewood and drinking water. Sites are allocated on a first-come, first-served basis. **Map refs:** 386 E5, 457 I4

Who to contact: Banana Shire Council (07) 4992 5900
Camping fees: fees can be paid at the self-registration station

254 Injune Caravan Park

This campground on Station St in Injune, about 90 km north of Roma, has laundry facilities, BBQs and other modern conveniences. Winter is the busiest period, so book ahead if you're travelling at this time. The Injune district is known for its natural wonders, including beautiful lakes and volcanic rocks, and Aboriginal paintings. **Map refs:** 386 C5, 456 F4

How to book: cnr Station St and Third Ave, Injune (07) 4626 1881 www.injunecaravanpark.com.au

255 Lake Awoonga Caravan Park

Catching huge barramundi is easy at Lake Awoonga – or so the locals say. If you fancy yourself as an angler, this caravan park provides a comfortable base. Set on the lake's edge, there are plenty of bonus extras such as a kiosk, laundry facilities, a bait and tackle shop, and a playground nearby. There's also the option of staying in permanent tents, a bunkhouse, canvas cabins or family cabins. You'll find the caravan park on Awoonga Dam Rd, 8 km west of the Bruce Hwy. Bookings are recommended for peak periods. **Map refs:** 387 G3, 457 L1, 459 N12

How to book: 865 Awoonga Dam Rd, Benaraby (07) 4975 0155 www.lakeawoonga.net

256 Lake Monduran Holiday Park

A fantastic spot for big barramundi fishing, Lake Monduran is 20 km north-west of Gin Gin and 4.5 km east of the Bruce Hwy. The campground, on Claude Wharton Dr, has free wireless internet, laundry facilities, a kiosk, fish-cleaning tables, a tackle shop and boat hire. There's also a golf course nearby at Gin Gin and it's less than an hour's drive to Bundaberg's distillery and shopping. Bookings are recommended for powered sites and cabins. **Map refs:** 387 G4, 457 L3

How to book: 1 Claude Wharton Dr, Lake Monduran (07) 4157 3881, 1800 228 754 www.lakem.com.au

257 Lilley's Beach camping area

A popular spot with locals, camping is permitted in the fenced enclosed area at the north end of Lilley's Beach on Boyne Island. No facilities are provided, so bring your own drinking water, rubbish bags, and firewood or a gas/fuel cooker. Wherever possible, camp in an existing site rather than creating a new one. Access is 4WD only via Handley Dr and the Boyne Island Sewerage Treatment Plant. **Map refs:** 387 G3, 457 L1, 459 N12

Who to contact: Gladstone Regional Council (07) 4970 0700
Permits: 4WD access permit required

258 Mingo Crossing camping area

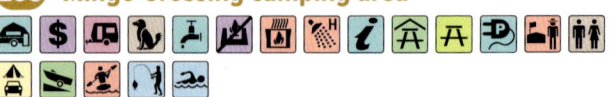

A popular spot for local anglers, Mingo Crossing camping area is located on the shores of Paradise Dam in Mt Perry. The park is recovering after damage incurred during the 2011 Queensland floods, but progress has been swift. To get here, travel 30 km south of Mt Perry on Gayndah–Mt Perry Rd and turn left just before Mingo Crossing Bridge. **Map refs:** 387 G5, 457 L4

How to book: 2670 Gayndah–Mt Perry Rd, Mt Perry (07) 4161 6200

259 Neville Hewitt Weir camping area

Hugely popular in the winter months, this beautiful riverside campground in the town of Baralaba is a favourite with campers from southern Australian states looking to escape the cold weather in a picturesque spot. There's a dump point for caravan waste 500 m away at the showground. The town is on the Dawson River, 96 km north-west of Biloela and 141 km south-west of Rockhampton. You'll need to bring your own water and firewood. **Map refs:** 386 E3, 457 I1, 459 L12

Who to contact: Baralaba Land Care and Community Resource and Development Centre (07) 4998 1142

260 The Oaks camping area

This campground has 35 sites for self-sufficient campers within a skip of Oaks Beach on the north-west side of Facing Island. It is 2 km from the ferry drop-off point and suits self-sufficient campers. Bring a gas/fuel stove. The island is 12 km from the Gladstone mainland, accessible by private vessel or the Curtis Ferry Services barge; book ferry services on (07) 4972 6990. **Map refs:** 387 G2, 459 N12

How to book: Gladstone Visitor Information Centre (07) 4972 9000 www.gladstoneregion.info/destinations/facing-island/accommodation/the-oaks-on-facing-island
Permits: camping permit required

261 Rubyvale Caravan Park

This camping area is a short stroll from the Rubyvale town centre, and is located within easy distance of tourist mines and fossicking areas. There are powered and unpowered sites, and a range of good facilities. Rubyvale is about 60 km north-west of Emerald. **Map refs:** 386 B1, 458 H10

How to book: 16 Main St, The Gemfields (07) 4985 4118

262 South End Settlement

South End Settlement is just over 1 km from the ferry drop-off point on Curtis Island and is suitable for small caravans and camper trailers. It's an open grassy area with plenty of shade and 20 allocated campsites, just a short walk to Front Beach. Tank water on-site needs to be treated before drinking. The island is 12 km from the Gladstone mainland, accessible by private vessel or the Curtis Ferry Services barge; pre-book the ferry trip if you're bringing a vehicle, (07) 4972 6990. You need to bring a gas/fuel stove. **Map refs:** 387 G2, 459 N12

How to book: Gladstone Visitor Information Centre (07) 4972 9000 www.gladstoneregion.info/destinations/curtis-island/accommodation/southend-at-curtis-island
Permits: camping permit required

263 Takaru Bush Resorts Carnarvon Gorge

Located on the boundary of Carnarvon National Park's Carnarvon Gorge section, this commercial resort offers access to the natural wonders of the gorge without having to battle for a spot in the school-holidays-only camping area or having to lug your gear to Big Bend. The modern facilities include a convenience store, gas bottle refills and a laundry. Note: there is no petrol for sale near Carnarvon Gorge; fill up at Injune or Rolleston before embarking. Advance bookings are recommended. **Map refs:** 386 C4, 456 F3

How to book: Carnarvon Gorge via Rolleston (07) 4984 4535 www.takaru.com.au/takaru

264 Workmans Beach Campsite

Just a short stroll to the unpatrolled surf beach, this campground is 1 km from the Agnes township and across the road from a skatepark. There are cold-water beach showers and free gas BBQs. Signposted access is off Springs Rd, just south of Agnes Water. The town is 57 km east of Miriam Vale on the Bruce Hwy and 130 km north of Bundaberg. **Map refs:** 387 G3, 457 M2

Who to contact: Agnes Water Rural Transaction Centre (07) 4902 1515

265 Wuruma Dam camping area

Well stocked with perch, bass and saratoga, Wuruma Dam is an angler's paradise. The dam is also popular for a range of watersports: canoeing, sailing, swimming and waterskiing. The area is 48 km north-west of Eidsvold along Wuruma Dam Rd. Note: watersports are permitted only when the dam is above 15% capacity. **Map refs:** 386 F4, 457 K4

Who to contact: (07) 4167 5177 **Permits:** a Stocked Impoundment Permit is required for fishing, from DAFF 13 7468 www.daff.qld.gov.au

DARLING DOWNS

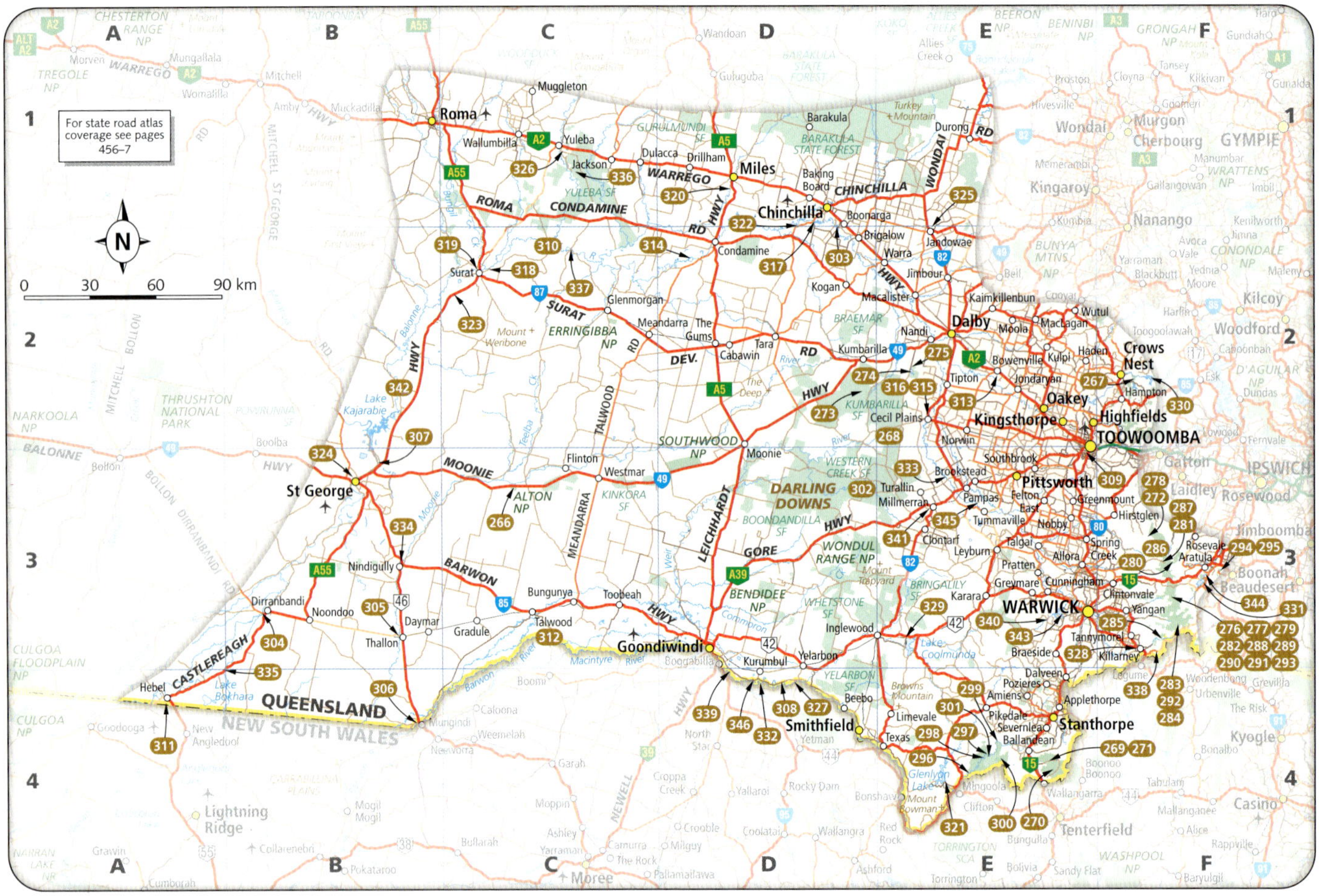

For state road atlas coverage see pages 456–7

N

0   30   60   90 km

THE DARLING DOWNS, ON the western slopes of the Great Dividing Range, has long been known as the food bowl of southern Queensland, with its rich soil for crops, livestock and magnificent gardens.

Look beyond the main centres of Toowoomba and Warwick and you'll find the green rolling hills, spectacular mountain scenery and lush rainforests that attract adventurous hikers and camping enthusiasts from far and wide. South of Toowoomba, Main Range National Park has some of the region's best-known campgrounds and natural attractions: Cunninghams Gap, Spicers Gap, Mt Roberts, Goomburra and the Queen Mary Falls. Collectively, these sections offer more than 20 bushwalking trails with various gradings and surfaces for easy strolls through to physically demanding hikes. The 2 km Queen Mary Falls circuit gives you the opportunity to watch Spring Creek plunge over the 40 m falls – a must-see for visitors.

Further west, the St George region is swiftly recovering from the effects of 3 devastating floods – in Mar 2010, Jan 2011 and Feb 2012 – and continues to offer lovely riverside campgrounds along the Barwon, Narran, Moonie and Bokhara rivers. East of St George, the border town of Goondiwindi – another major centre for agriculture – has some relaxing reserves ideal for overnight stays.

Watersports enthusiasts are spoilt for choice in the Darling Downs, with various lakes and dams across the region. Coolmunda Dam, Glenlyon Dam, Lake Broadwater, Lake Cressbrook, Lake Moogerah and Leslie Dam are popular destinations for fishing, canoeing, sailing, waterskiing and other activities.

If you prefer dry land, national parks and reserves such as Girraween, Sundown and Crows Nest offer secluded bush camping where you're likely to encounter rare and protected wildlife. Expect to see native species such as koalas, echidnas, possums and an array of colourful birdlife.

CAMPSITES LOCATED IN PARKS AND RESERVES

ALTON NATIONAL PARK

This undeveloped national park, approximately 100 km west of Moonie on the Moonie Hwy, protects 558 ha of brigalow-belah forest. It is remote and there are no facilities, so it is suited only to self-sufficient and experienced bush campers with 4WD vehicles.

Who to contact: QPWS Culgoa Floodplain (07) 4625 0942
Permits: camping permit required *Camping fees:* fees can be paid and permits acquired at any QPWS office

266 Bush camping areas

Self-sufficient campers are welcome to camp in Alton National Park, but be aware that there are no facilities or amenities and that open fires are prohibited. Bring all self-sufficient gear, including drinking water, rubbish bags and a gas/fuel stove. There is no self-registration facility in the park, so acquire your permit before camping. **Map refs:** 398 C3, 456 G9

CROWS NEST NATIONAL PARK

Crows Nest National Park, on the edge of the Great Dividing Range west of Brisbane, features the picturesque Crows Nest Falls with its 20 m drop into a granite rockpool. Downstream is the Valley of Diamonds, a deep gorge surrounded by cliffs up to 120 m high through which the Crows Nest Creek flows. These natural attractions are set in a landscape of dry eucalypt forest, in which stringybarks, bloodwoods and ironbarks flourish. Advance bookings are required for camping.

How to book: NPRSR 13 7468 www.nprsr.qld.gov.au
Permits: Camping permit required

267 Crows Nest camping area

The eucalypt forests of Crows Nest provide a beautiful setting for wildlife-watching, hiking and bush camping. You can look for platypus in the creek, spot brush-tailed rock wallabies, or take a walk across the gorge to Crows Nest Falls. Other wildlife in the region include rosellas, sugar gliders and ringtail possums. The campground has showers operating on a self-serve donkey boiler system, and you should treat or boil the water before drinking. Follow the signs on Three Mile Rd, 6 km from Crows Nest. **Map refs:** 398 F2, 457 L8

DUNMORE STATE FOREST

This undeveloped state forest, about 15 km west of Cecil Plains on Cecil Plains–Tara Rd, exists primarily as a logging reserve, but can be accessed by intrepid bush campers. The forest fills with attractive wildflowers in spring, and the trails inside the forest are suitable for mountain-biking and horseriding. Advance bookings are required for camping.

How to book: NPRSR 13 7468 www.nprsr.qld.gov.au
Permits: camping permit required

268 Bush camping areas

Self-sufficient campers are welcome to camp in Dunmore State Forest, but be aware that there are no facilities or amenities and that open fires are prohibited. Bring all self-sufficient gear, including drinking water, rubbish bags and a gas/fuel stove. Exercise caution when driving in the forest, as logging trucks may be active. **Map refs:** 398 E2, 457 J9

GIRRAWEEN NATIONAL PARK

Situated between Stanthorpe and Tenterfield (NSW), Girraween National Park lies in Queensland's Granite Belt and features pristine forests interspersed with towering granite outcrops. Picturesque creeks flow past teetering boulders, and there is an abundance of wildlife and wildflowers – Girraween is an Indigenous word meaning 'place of flowers'. Only a few campsites, and markings on trees and rocks, remain as evidence of the Kambuwal people who once lived in this area. Girraween is signposted from Pyramids Rd off the New England Hwy, 11 km north of Wallangarra and 7 km south of Ballandean. Advance bookings are required for camping.

How to book: NPRSR 13 7468 www.nprsr.qld.gov.au
Permits: camping permit required

269 Bald Rock Creek camping area

Bald Rock Creek camping area is the first turning on the left as you enter the national park from the New England Hwy, and can be reached by conventional vehicle. The area is semi-grassed, has no designated sites and provides some shade. Firewood for BBQs can be purchased at the Ballandean Store, on the hwy 15 km from the park. **Map refs:** 398 E4, 457 K12

270 Bush camping areas (walk-in camping)

Self-sufficient and experienced walkers can make use of the remote walk-in bush campsites throughout the park. Open fires are prohibited and camping permits are required. You'll need to lodge a bush camping form in advance at the Girraween park office or by phoning QPWS Girraween on (07) 4684 5157. **Map refs:** 398 E4, 457 L12

271 Castle Rock camping area

Just 400 m from Bald Rock Creek, the forest setting at Castle Rock is suitable for walk-in or vehicle-based camping and there's plenty of room for large groups. You need to come equipped with firewood. Boil or treat the water provided before drinking. **Map refs:** 398 E4, 457 K12

GLEN ROCK PARK

This open park area at the head of the Tenthill Valley was purchased by the Queensland state government in 1996 to provide open spaces for public use. It adjoins the

World Heritage–listed Main Range National Park (whose Glen Rock outcrop gives the park its name) and offers riding trails for both bikes and horses, as well as walking trails. Fauna in the area include the brush-tailed rock-wallaby, powerful owl and glossy black-cockatoo. Advance bookings are required for camping.

How to book: NPRSR 13 7468 www.nprsr.qld.gov.au
Permits: camping permit required

272 Casuarina camping area

This open, grassy campsite, close to a creek, offers excellent access to Glen Rock Park's network of walking, horseriding and biking trails. A horse corral is provided for riders. To get here, take Mt Sylvia Rd south from Gatton, through Tenthill, then continue south to Junction View. Turn left at Junction View Primary School and follow East Haldon Rd to its southern end in Glen Rock Park. Note: if you'd like to use the provided campfires, bring your own firewood. **Map refs:** 398 F3, 457 L10

KUMBARILLA STATE FOREST

This undeveloped state forest, around 46 km south-west of Dalby on the Moonie Hwy, exists primarily as a logging reserve, but is open to intrepid bush campers. Fishing is permitted at Wilkie Creek. Advance bookings are required for camping.

How to book: NPRSR 13 7468 www.nprsr.qld.gov.au
Permits: camping permit required

273 Bush camping areas

Self-sufficient campers are welcome to camp in Kumbarilla State Forest, but be aware that there are no facilities or amenities and that open fires are prohibited. Bring all self-sufficient gear, including drinking water, rubbish bags and a gas/fuel stove. Exercise caution when driving in the forest, as logging trucks may be active. **Map refs:** 398 D2, 457 J8

LAKE BROADWATER CONSERVATION PARK

An important refuge for waterbirds and other wildlife, Lake Broadwater is surrounded by cypress pine, eucalypt and brigalow open woodland. The park, 30 km south-west of Dalby, preserves valuable remnants of the vegetation types that once covered the western Downs. Access to the lake is signposted off the Moonie Hwy, 20 km west of Dalby.

Who to contact: NPRSR 13 7468 www.nprsr.qld.gov.au *Permits:* camping and boating permits required; call Lake Broadwater on (07) 4663 3562 to arrange boating permit *Camping fees:* fees can be paid and permits acquired at the self-registration station

274 Lake Broadwater camping area

This camping area among the shady red and blue gums of Lake Broadwater Conservation Park lies 30 km south-west of Dalby.

The lake is a popular watersports venue and the surrounding forests are great for birdwatching. The camping area is 10 km along Lake Broadwater Rd, off the Moonie Hwy. Bring your own firewood and treat or boil the water provided before drinking. **Map refs:** 398 E2, 457 J8

275 Wilga Bush camping area

On the northern side of Lake Broadwater, this secluded campground is linked to Lake Broadwater camping area via a 2 km track. You can learn about the park's vegetation along the walking track and see the remains of an old dingo fence built in the 1860s. The site is 8 km along Lake Broadwater Rd, off the Moonie Hwy. Treat or boil the water provided before drinking and bring your own firewood. **Map refs:** 398 E2, 457 J8

MAIN RANGE NATIONAL PARK

Covering 29 730 ha along the Great Dividing Range, World Heritage–listed Main Range National Park forms the western part of a crescent of mountains in south-east Queensland known as the Scenic Rim. The park boasts impressive peaks and escarpments, and the delightful Queen Mary Falls. There are 3 main types of vegetation: rainforest in the moist, sheltered areas; open eucalypt forest on the high ridges and slopes; and mountain heath on the cliffs and rocky outcrops. Picnic spots are plentiful and there are spectacular views from Governors Chair (to the NSW border), and Sylvesters and Fassifern Valley lookouts. The park is divided into 3 sections with separate access routes: Cunninghams Gap, Goomburra and Queen Mary Falls. Advance bookings are required for camping.

Who to contact: QPWS Main Range (07) 4666 1133 for access information for bush camping areas *How to book:* NPRSR 13 7468 www.nprsr.qld.gov.au *Permits:* camping permit required

276 Bush camping areas (walk-in camping)

There are 11 bush campsites in Main Range National Park (Davies Ridge, Knoll E12, Knoll T30, Lizard South, Lower Panorama Point, Mt Huntley Saddle, Mt Steamer Saddle, Mt Superbus – South Peak, Panorama Point, Ramparts South and South Branch) for self-sufficient campers, located in remote areas of the park. These sites can only be reached by walking. For access instructions and locations, contact QPWS Main Range. **Map refs:** 398 F3, 457 L10

277 Double Top camping area (walk-in camping)

Thrillseekers and experienced climbers will delight in this tiny campsite (up to 4 people) on the edge of a razorback on the southern side of the north peak of Mt Spicer. There are no facilities provided and fires are prohibited, so bring all self-sufficient equipment, including drinking water, rubbish bags and a gas/fuel stove. Note: extreme caution should be taken in this area, owing to the site's proximity to unfenced clifftops. **Map refs:** 398 F3, 457 L10

Walking in Main Range National Park (p. 400)

278 Glen Rock camping area (walk-in camping)

Those looking for a scenic campsite will relish the views from this campsite (up to 8 people) on top of Glen Rock, in the far north of the Goomburra section. There are no facilities provided and fires are prohibited, so bring all self-sufficient equipment, including drinking water, rubbish bags and a gas/fuel stove. **Map refs:** 398 F3, 457 L10

279 Huntley – Sentinel Saddle camping area (walk-in camping)

This open forest site west of Mt Huntley in the Cunninghams Gap section offers camping for up to 8 experienced bush hikers. There are no facilities provided and fires are prohibited, so bring all self-sufficient equipment, including drinking water, rubbish bags and a gas/fuel stove. **Map refs:** 398 F3, 457 L10

280 Laidley Creek Falls camping area (walk-in camping)

This open forest site at the headwaters of Laidley Creek in the Goomburra section offers camping for up to 8 experienced bush hikers. There are no facilities provided and fires are prohibited, so bring all self-sufficient equipment, including drinking water, rubbish bags and a gas/fuel stove. **Map refs:** 398 F3, 457 L10

281 Manna Gum camping area

This large grassy campsite in the Goomburra section is shaded by manna gums, making it perfect for the warmer months. Many of the Goomburra section's walking trails begin at its eastern end. Bring your own firewood if you wish to use the wood BBQs (collecting firewood within the park is prohibited). Manna Gum is roughly 250 m past Poplar Flat at the end of Forestry Reserve Rd. **Map refs:** 398 F3, 457 L10

282 Mount Huntley camping area (walk-in camping)

This elevated open forest site next to rainforest in the Cunninghams Gap section offers camping for up to 8 experienced bush hikers. There are no facilities provided and fires are prohibited, so bring all self-sufficient equipment, including drinking water, rubbish bags and a gas/fuel stove. **Map refs:** 398 F3, 457 L10

283 Mount Superbus – North Peak camping area (walk-in camping)

This rough rainforest campsite on the north peak of Mt Superbus offers camping for up to 8 experienced bush hikers. There are no facilities provided and fires are prohibited, so bring all self-sufficient equipment, including drinking water, rubbish bags and a gas/fuel stove. Note: there is limited protection from the elements in windy weather. **Map refs:** 398 F3, 457 M11

284 Mount Superbus – Raspberry Saddle camping area (walk-in camping)

This pleasant, sheltered rainforest site in the saddle between the peaks of Mt Superbus offers camping for up to 8 experienced bush hikers. There are no facilities provided and fires are prohibited, so bring all self-sufficient equipment, including drinking water, rubbish bags and a gas/fuel stove. **Map refs:** 398 F3, 457 M11

285 Paddy's Knob camping area (walk-in camping)

This newly created site, 400 m from Paddy's Knob in the Queen Mary Falls section, offers expansive views of the Condamine gorge for up to 8 experienced bush hikers. There are no facilities provided and fires are prohibited, so bring all self-sufficient equipment, including drinking water, rubbish bags and a gas/fuel stove. **Map refs:** 398 F3, 457 L11

286 Point Pure camping area (walk-in camping)

This newly created site in the Goomburra section, near Glen Rock, offers good views to the west over Glen Rock Park. There are no facilities provided and fires are prohibited, so bring all self-sufficient equipment, including drinking water, rubbish bags and a gas/fuel stove. **Map refs:** 398 F3, 457 L10

287 Poplar Flat camping area

On the banks of Dalrymple Creek in the Goomburra section, this large grassy campsite is big enough for 100 campers. You'll need to bring your own firewood if you want to use the BBQs, or purchase it locally, as firewood must not be collected from the park or roadside (fines apply). The site is on Forestry Reserve Rd, 35 km east of Allora, reached from the New England Hwy via Inverramsay Rd. **Map refs:** 398 F3, 457 L10

288 Spicers – Double Top Saddle camping area (walk-in camping)

This open forest site in the saddle between the peaks of Mt Spicer offers more room – and less risk – than the nearby Double Top camping area. There are no facilities provided and fires are prohibited, so bring all self-sufficient equipment, including drinking water, rubbish bags and a gas/fuel stove. **Map refs:** 398 F3, 457 L10

289 Spicers Gap camping area (walk-in camping)

Spicers Gap is a small walk-in campground on the eastern side of the gap, with good walking trails nearby. A maximum of 50 campers is allowed, but there's the freedom of setting up anywhere in the mown area. Boil or treat water before drinking and bring your own firewood or a gas/fuel stove. It is on East Spicers Gap Rd, 17.5 km south-west of Aratula. **Map refs:** 398 F3, 457 M10

290 Spicers Peak (East) camping area (walk-in camping)

Climbers tackling Mt Spicer can rest at this small site (up to 4 people) on the margin between rainforest and heath. There are no facilities provided and fires are prohibited, so bring all self-sufficient equipment, including drinking water, rubbish bags and a gas/fuel stove. **Map refs:** 398 F3, 457 L10

291 Spicers Peak (West) camping area (walk-in camping)

Climbers tackling Mt Spicer can rest at this site (up to 8 people) on the margin between rainforest and heath. There are no facilities provided and fires are prohibited, so bring all self-sufficient equipment, including drinking water, rubbish bags and a gas/fuel stove. **Map refs:** 398 F3, 457 L10

292 Stern camping area (walk-in camping)

This newly created campsite in the Cunninghams Gap section offers bush camping for up to 8 experienced hikers. There are no facilities provided and fires are prohibited, so bring all self-sufficient equipment, including drinking water, rubbish bags and a gas/fuel stove. **Map refs:** 398 F3, 457 L10

293 Swan Knoll camping area (walk-in camping)

This open forest site in the Cunninghams Gap section offers bush camping for up to 8 experienced hikers. There are no facilities provided and fires are prohibited, so bring all self-sufficient equipment, including drinking water, rubbish bags and a gas/fuel stove. Note: there is limited protection from the elements in windy weather. **Map refs:** 398 F3, 457 L10

MOOGERAH PEAKS NATIONAL PARK

This small national park includes a number of isolated mountain peaks, such as Mt Edwards (632 m), Mt French (579 m), Mt Greville (770 m) and Mt Moon (784 m), the result of volcanic activity in the area some 22 million years ago. The vegetation on the mountains is mainly open eucalypt forest, with spotted gum, grey gum and stringybark. Advance bookings are required for camping.

How to book: NPRSR 13 7468 www.nprsr.qld.gov.au
Permits: camping permit required

294 Frog Buttress camping area (walk-in camping)

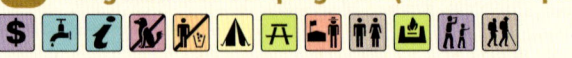

This small campground in Moogerah Peaks, suitable for walk-in camping only, is located 11 km west of Boonah on Mt French Rd, signposted 1 km south of Boonah off the Boonah–Rathdowney Rd. Bring your own firewood. There is a carpark and day-use area close to the campsites. **Map refs:** 398 F3, 457 M10

295 Mount French camping area

Although Frog Buttress is unsuited to vehicular camping, 2 vehicle campsites suitable for caravans or camper trailers (but not tents) are available in the carpark of the Mt French section of the park. No facilities are provided, but the carpark is a short stroll from the Mt French day-use area's facilities, which include BBQs, toilets and picnic tables. Bring your own firewood for use in the wood BBQs or a gas/fuel cooker. Note: this camping area is allocated on a first-come, first-served basis and you need to book a permit in advance for Frog Buttress to access it. **Map refs:** 398 F3, 457 M10

SUNDOWN NATIONAL PARK

South-west of Brisbane on the Qld–NSW border, Sundown National Park is known for its rugged gorge scenery around the Severn River and its wilderness trails for experienced walkers. The park is popular for swimming, fishing and canoeing, and there's access for conventional vehicles signposted off Glenlyon Dam Rd. Advance bookings are required for camping.

How to book: NPRSR 13 7468 www.nprsr.qld.gov.au
Permits: camping permit required

296 The Broadwater camping area

These grassy sites on the banks of the Severn River are on Permanents Rd, signposted from Glenlyon Dam Rd. Visitors with caravans longer than 4 m are recommended not to attempt entering the site due to narrow sections of track. There are donkey boiler hot-water showers on-site. **Map refs:** 398 E4, 457 K12

297 Burrows Waterhole camping area

This site has a maximum capacity of 60 people, with a maximum group size of 6. It is reached from the park's eastern boundary, 18 km from the park entrance gate and signposted along the Sundown National Park access road. Bring drinking water, firewood or a gas/fuel stove. **Map refs:** 398 E4, 457 K12

298 Bush camping areas (walk-in camping)

Bush campsites throughout the park are for experienced and self-sufficient walkers only. Campers should discuss their planned itinerary with the park ranger and check conditions before setting out. Open fires are permitted with firewood brought in from outside the park, but a gas/fuel stove is recommended. **Map refs:** 398 E4, 457 K12

299 Nundubbermere Falls camping area (bush camping)

Bush camping for self-sufficient campers is available at Nundubbermere Falls, at the northernmost point of Sundown. There are no facilities provided, but you can swim, fish and canoe along the Severn River. Access is via Stanthorpe–Texas and Nundubbermere rds and is suitable for conventional vehicles. Bring your own water and firewood or a gas/fuel stove. **Map refs:** 398 E4, 457 K12

300 Red Rock Gorge camping area

There are few facilities other than pit toilets at Red Rock Gorge, but this remote campsite is close to a marvellous lookout over

the gorge. Access is 4WD only via Curr and Sundown rds from Ballandean. Bring your own drinking water and firewood or a gas/fuel stove. **Map refs:** 398 E4, 457 K12

301 Reedy Waterhole camping area (bush camping)

This campsite on the Severn River offers no facilities and is suitable for self-sufficient campers only. Campers can swim, fish, and canoe in the Severn, or take a walk up to the natural lookout at Rats Castle. It is 18 km into Sundown, accessible by 4WD only via Curr and Sundown rds from Ballandean. Bring your own drinking water and firewood or a gas/fuel cooker. **Map refs:** 398 E4, 457 K12

WESTERN CREEK STATE FOREST

This undeveloped state forest, about 30 km west of Millmerran on the Gore Hwy, exists primarily as a logging reserve but can be accessed by intrepid bush campers. The forest was previously a grazing selection; curious explorers may find abandoned log huts and other historical artefacts here. Advance bookings are required for camping.

How to book: NPRSR 13 7468 www.nprsr.qld.gov.au
Permits: camping permit required

302 Bush camping areas

Self-sufficient campers are welcome to camp in Western Creek State Forest, but be aware that there are no facilities or amenities and that open fires are prohibited. Bring all self-sufficient gear, including drinking water, rubbish bags and a gas/fuel stove. Exercise caution when driving in the forest, as logging trucks may be active. **Map refs:** 398 D3, 457 J9

CAMPSITES LOCATED IN OTHER AREAS

303 Archers Crossing camping area

A great spot for fishing, Archers Crossing has a boat ramp on the southern side of the Condamine River. Suitable for self-sufficient campers, the only facilities are the shelter shed, tables and BBQs. The site is 24 km south-east of Chinchilla, reached by Hopelands Rd. **Map refs:** 398 D1, 457 J7

Who to contact: Chinchilla Visitor Information Centre (07) 4679 4491

304 Balonne Minor Bridge camping area (bush camping)

Self-sufficient campers can stay at this site, 3 km west of Dirranbandi on Dirranbandi–Bollon Rd, around 94 km south of St George. **Map refs:** 398 B3, 456 E10

Who to contact: Balonne Visitor Information Centre (07) 4620 8877

305 Barney's Beach camping area (bush camping)

You'll find this campground beside the Moonie River, on Thallon–Dirranbandi Rd, 3 km west of Thallon. There are no facilities at the site. Thallon is 76 km south-east of St George. **Map refs:** 398 B3, 456 F11

Who to contact: Balonne Visitor Information Centre (07) 4620 8877

306 Barwon River camping area (bush camping)

This basic camping area is set on the north bank of the Barwon River in Mungindi, 118 km south-east of St George. **Map refs:** 398 B4, 456 F11

Who to contact: Balonne Visitor Information Centre (07) 4620 8877

307 Beardmore Dam Turnoff camping area (bush camping)

This campground is 13 km north of St George, on the turn-off to Beardmore Dam. You'll need to bring drinking water, as there are no facilities. St George is at the junction of the Carnarvon, Balonne and Moonie hwys, 200 km west of Goondiwindi and 290 km east of Cunnamulla. **Map refs:** 398 B3, 456 F9

Who to contact: Balonne Visitor Information Centre (07) 4620 8877

308 Bengalla Reserve camping area (bush camping)

This area is about 34 km from Goondiwindi, with good river access for dropping in a line. You need to bring firewood and water. From the Goondiwindi post office, travel east on Marshall St to the large roundabout. Take the Border Rivers Tourist Dr exit, then travel 33 km to the reserve sign and follow the bush track to the river. Note: conventional vehicle access is only possible in dry weather. **Map refs:** 398 D4, 457 I11

Who to contact: Goondiwindi Regional Council (07) 4671 7400

309 BIG4 Toowoomba Garden City Holiday Park

Toowoomba is known as the 'Garden City', and this holiday park certainly takes that reputation to heart, offering award-winning landscaped gardens to its guests. Other facilities include a library, laundry, baby-care facilities and a fresh herb garden for guests to add a little zest to their cooking. The attractions of Toowoomba's central district are nearby. Advance bookings are recommended. **Map refs:** 398 E3, 457 L9

How to book: 34A Eiser St, Harristown (07) 4635 1747, 1800 333 667 www.big4toowoombagchp.com.au

310 Bingi Crossing camping area (bush camping)

This site, suitable for self-sufficient campers (bring drinking water), is 45 km east of the town of Surat. Take the Surat–Tara Rd from the Carnarvon Hwy. Surat is 78 km south of Roma and 116 km north of St George. **Map refs:** 398 C2, 456 H7

Who to contact: Surat Visitor Information Centre (07) 4626 5136

311 Bokhara River camping area (bush camping)

This site with no facilities is set beside the Bokhara River in Hebel, 162 km south of St George and 65 km south of Dirranbandi. **Map refs:** 398 A4, 456 D11

Who to contact: Balonne Visitor Information Centre (07) 4620 8877

312 Boonanga Reserve camping area (bush camping)

This site is just over 90 km from Goondiwindi near Talwood. You can camp beside the Barwon River, but you'll need to bring your own drinking water and firewood. From Talwood, travel 15 km on the Talwood–Boomi Rd to Barwon River. **Map refs:** 398 C3, 456 H11

Who to contact: Goondiwindi Regional Council (07) 4671 7400

313 Bowenville Reserve camping area

This large, shady campground is on the southern banks of Oakey Creek – perfect for fishing or taking a dip. Bring your own drinking water. To get here, follow Bowenville–Norwin Rd, 4 km south of the Warrego Hwy. **Map refs:** 398 E2, 457 K8

Who to contact: Toowoomba Regional Council 13 1872

314 Caliguel Lagoon camping area

Very popular with waterskiers, this site is 7 km south of Condamine and 33 km south of Miles. Bring your own firewood and water (or boil/treat the tank water provided) to the camping area, reached from Condamine–Meandarra Rd. **Map refs:** 398 D2, 457 I7

Who to contact: Miles Visitor Information Centre (07) 4627 1492

315 Cecil Plains Rural Retreat Caravan Park

This basic campground with a toilet block and hot showers is on Taylor St in Cecil Plains, opposite Henry Stuart Russell Park. There is a black-water dump here but you need to bring your own drinking water. From Toowoomba, take the Cecil Plains–Toowoomba Rd west for about 90 km. **Map refs:** 398 E2, 457 K9

Who to contact: Toowoomba Regional Council 13 1872

316 Cecil Plains Weir camping area

The Condamine River flows through the Millmerran area, where a number of campsites are available, ideal for fishing and boating. This site is 1 km east of Cecil Plains, reached via Cecil Plains–Toowoomba Rd. Millmerran is on the Gore Hwy, 82 km south-west of Toowoomba. **Map refs:** 398 E2, 457 K9

Who to contact: Toowoomba Regional Council 13 1872

317 Chinchilla Weir camping area

Catch some perch, catfish or Murray cod in the Condamine River near this campsite, where a maximum 2-night stay applies. There is a boat ramp on-site but fishing is not permitted within 200 m of the weir wall. BYO firewood and drinking water. From Chinchilla, travel 8 km south on Chinchilla–Tara Rd. **Map refs:** 398 D1, 457 J7

Who to contact: Chinchilla Visitor Information Centre (07) 4679 4491

318 Cow Paddocks camping area (bush camping)

This site with no facilities is 2 km east of Surat on Sawmill Rd. Surat is on the Carnarvon Hwy, 78 km south of Roma and 116 km north of St George. Bring all necessary supplies. **Map refs:** 398 C2, 456 G7

Who to contact: Surat Visitor Information Centre (07) 4626 5136

319 Fishermans Park camping area

This basic campground with toilets and picnic tables is on the Carnarvon Hwy at the Balonne River, on the north side of the town of Surat. You need to bring firewood and drinking water. It's 78 km south of Roma and 116 km north of St George. **Map refs:** 398 C2, 456 G7

Who to contact: Surat Visitor Information Centre (07) 4626 5136

320 Gil Weir camping area

This basic campsite by the Gil Weir, south of Miles, offers good fishing opportunities. Bring your own drinking water and firewood for the BBQs. The campsite is located on the Leichhardt Hwy, 4 km south of Miles. **Map refs:** 398 D1, 457 I7

Who to contact: Miles Visitor Information Centre (07) 4627 1492

321 Glenlyon Dam Tourist Park

A popular destination for watersports, Glenlyon Dam is also a top spot for fishing for perch, eel-tailed catfish and Murray cod. The tourist park has laundry facilities, a kiosk, boat hire and fuel. Follow the signs off the Glenlyon–Texas Rd,

93 km south of Stanthorpe, or the Bruxner Hwy, 67 km north-west of Tenterfield. Bookings are advised for peak periods. **Map refs:** 398 E4, 457 K12

How to book: Glenlyon–Texas Rd, Glenlyon Dam (02) 6737 5266

322 Grays Reserve camping area (bush camping)

This small site has no facilities and suits self-sufficient campers only. From Chinchilla, travel 16 km south along Chinchilla–Tara Rd. After a large dip in the road, travel 200 m and turn right onto the bush track that leads to the river, opposite the property called Chinta. **Map refs:** 398 D1, 457 J7

Who to contact: Chinchilla Visitor Information Centre (07) 4679 4491

323 Green Timbers camping area (bush camping)

This site is for self-sufficient campers only, as there are no facilities. It is 18 km south of Surat off the Carnarvon Hwy, and is accessible in dry weather only. Surat is 78 km south of Roma and 116 km north of St George. **Map refs:** 398 C2, 456 G8

Who to contact: Surat Visitor Information Centre (07) 4626 5136

324 Jack Taylor Weir camping area (bush camping)

This site is on the western side of the weir in St George. There are no facilities but it is close to town. St George is at the junction of the Carnarvon, Balonne and Moonie hwys, 200 km west of Goondiwindi and 290 km east of Cunnamulla. **Map refs:** 398 B3, 456 F9

Who to contact: Balonne Visitor Information Centre (07) 4620 8877

325 Jandowae Accommodation Park

You'll find a good range of facilities at this park, 50 km north of Dalby, but bring your own firewood. There's a swimming pool, camp kitchen, laundry facilities, kiosk and the option of self-contained cabins. It's on High St in Jandowae. The nearby dam is ideal for picnicking, boating and fishing. **Map refs:** 398 E2, 457 K7

How to book: 104 High St, Jandowae (07) 4668 5071

326 Judd's Lagoon camping area

Great for fishing, this quiet and tidy campsite is on Mongool Rd, 5 km south-east of Yuleba. There are few facilities on-site, so bring drinking water and firewood. Yuleba is on the Warrego Hwy, 60 km east of Roma and 80 km west of Miles. Note: the signage on the hwy is poor. **Map refs:** 398 C1, 456 H6

Who to contact: Maranoa Regional Council 1300 007 662

327 Keetah Reserve camping area (bush camping)

This campsite, close to the NSW border, offers great fishing. Take the Border Rivers Tourist Dr exit from Goondiwindi, then travel 52 km to an intersection. Follow the road marked Yelarbon to the camping area in an open paddock on your right. **Map refs:** 398 D4, 457 I11

Who to contact: Miles Visitor Information Centre (07) 4627 1492

328 Killarney View Cabins and Caravan Park

This award-winning caravan park outside the quiet hamlet of Killarney offers remarkably modern amenities, including a laundry and camp kitchen. It is a short distance from Queen Mary Falls and the natural splendour of Main Range National Park. Advance bookings are recommended. **Map refs:** 398 F3, 457 L11

How to book: cnr O'Maras and Claydons rds, Killarney (07) 4664 1522, 0418 789 531 www.killarneyview.com.au

329 Lake Coolmunda Caravan Park

Waterskiing and fishing for silver perch, cod and catfish are popular pursuits on Coolmunda Dam, on the dam access road 13 km east of Inglewood. The caravan park has drive-through campsites, 8 cabins and an excellent range of facilities, including a swimming pool and tennis courts. Bookings are recommended at peak periods. **Map refs:** 398 E3, 457 J11

How to book: 38 Access Rd, Coolmunda (07) 4652 4171

330 Lake Cressbrook camping area

With excellent fishing, canoeing, kayaking, sailing and windsurfing on offer, it's a watersports wonderland at Lake Cressbrook. For walkers, a 5 km circuit starts at the camping ground and loops around the lake shore. The camping ground has a self-registration system and no bookings are taken at any time. It is suitable for small caravans and trailers and is situated 13 km north-east of Pechey and 50 km north of Toowoomba. There is signposted access off the New England Hwy from Crows Nest and Pechey. Note: there is an access fee, to be paid at the boomgate. **Map refs:** 398 F2, 457 L8

Who to contact: Toowoomba Regional Council 13 1872

331 Lake Moogerah Caravan Park

On the shores of Lake Moogerah, this large caravan park is packed with top-grade facilities for a comfortable stay in the region. There's a kiosk, 2 boat ramps, laundry, campfire pits, 2 amenities blocks, cabins and a playground, plus it's close to

the tennis courts, restaurants, pubs and cafes at Boonah. Local attractions include wineries, scenic drives and rock climbing. To get there, follow the signs from the Cunningham Hwy and turn off near Aratula. **Map refs:** 398 F3, 457 M10

How to book: 1 Muller Park Rd, Moogerah (07) 5463 0141 www.moogerah.com

332 Lees Reserve camping area (bush camping)

Another anglers' favourite, this free campsite on the Dumaresq River is pet-friendly and allows open fires. Take the Border Rivers Tourist Dr exit from Goondiwindi, then travel 29 km east. A narrow access road takes you to the campsite and the banks of the Dumaresq. **Map refs:** 398 D4, 457 I11

Who to contact: Miles Visitor Information Centre (07) 4627 1492

333 Lemontree Weir

The lack of facilities ensures this spot is suitable for self-sufficient campers only. It's 20 km north of Millmerran. Access is via Lemon Tree Rd, off the Gore Hwy, in dry weather only. **Map refs:** 398 E3, 457 K9

Who to contact: Toowoomba Regional Council 13 1872

334 Moonie River camping area (bush camping)

There are no facilities at this site beside the Moonie River in Nindigully, 44 km south-east of St George. St George is at the junction of the Carnarvon, Balonne and Moonie hwys, 200 km west of Goondiwindi and 290 km east of Cunnamulla. **Map refs:** 398 B3, 456 F10

Who to contact: Balonne Visitor Information Centre (07) 4620 8877

335 Narran River camping area (bush camping)

This campground beside the Narran River has no facilities. To get here, take Dirranbandi–Hebel Rd, 37 km south of Dirranbandi. **Map refs:** 398 A4, 456 E11

Who to contact: Balonne Visitor Information Centre (07) 4620 8877

336 Old Yuleba Town camping area

Suitable for self-sufficient stopover camping, there are no facilities at this site 13 km east of Yuleba. From the Warrego Hwy, go south onto Forestry Rd, then right onto Mongool Rd and right again after the fourth grid. Yuleba is 60 km east of Roma and 80 km west of Miles. **Map refs:** 398 C1, 456 H7

Who to contact: Maranoa Regional Council 1300 007 662

337 Pialaway Reserve camping area

This no-frills site is 85 km north of Surat. From the Surat–Condamine Rd, head along the Warkan Rd for 18 km. Surat is on

the Carnarvon Hwy, 78 km south of Roma and 116 km north of St George. **Map refs:** 398 C2, 456 H7

Who to contact: Maranoa Regional Council 1300 007 662

338 Queen Mary Falls Caravan Park and Cabins

Great for kids, you can handfeed king parrots, take a twilight animal-viewing walk or stroll to beautiful Queen Mary Falls opposite this caravan park. The office has an adjoining cafe, there's a laundry and campfires are allowed in designated areas. The caravan park is on Spring Creek Rd, 11 km east of Killarney. Bookings are recommended for powered sites. **Map refs:** 398 F3, 457 L11

How to book: 676 Spring Creek Rd, Killarney (07) 4664 7151 www.queenmaryfallscaravanpark.com.au

339 Rainbow Reserve camping area (bush camping)

Camp by the McIntyre River at this site just outside Goondiwindi, a great spot for fishing and camping, with a boat ramp too. From the Goondiwindi post office, travel east on Marshall St to the large roundabout. Take the Border Rivers Tourist Dr exit and travel 17 km to the site. **Map refs:** 398 D4, 457 I11

Who to contact: Goondiwindi Regional Information Centre (07) 4671 2653 www.goondiwindi.qld.au

340 Rocklands Camping Reserve

This 8 ha campground is a little more secluded than nearby Washpool Camping Reserve, and is suitable for tents, camper trailers and small caravans. It is 18 km west of Washpool on Rocklands Rd, off Glen Rd. Campers are encouraged to use existing fire sites; bring your own firewood and drinking water. **Map refs:** 398 E3, 457 K10

Who to contact: (07) 4661 7844, 0418 870 354
Camping fees: pay fees at the self-registration station

341 Walpole Park camping area

This pull-up area is suitable only for self-contained caravans or camper trailers. It is located at Walpole Park on Charles St in Millmerran, with a grey-water dump point opposite. **Map refs:** 398 E3, 457 K9

Who to contact: Toowoomba Regional Council 13 1872

342 Warroo Bridge camping area (bush camping)

Camping is permitted on the north side of the bridge at this site 60 km north of St George. Bring your own drinking water. To get here, follow the Wycombe School–Warroo Bridge Rd from the Carnarvon Hwy, then travel 9 km to the bridge. **Map refs:** 398 B2, 456 F8

Who to contact: Balonne Visitor Information Centre (07) 4620 8877

343 Washpool Camping Reserve

Washpool's 25 ha campground is well grassed, shady and has 40 powered sites. The scenic Leslie Dam nearby is well known as a good fishing spot for golden perch and is popular for canoeing and sailing. The camping area is on Leslie Dam Rd, off the Cunningham Hwy, 13 km west of Warwick. **Map refs:** 398 E3, 457 L10

Who to contact: (07) 4661 7844, 0418 870 354 *Camping fees:* fees can be paid at the camp office or self-registration station

344 Yarramalong Camping and Outdoor Recreation Centre

There's no shortage of space for comfortable camping at this 65 ha property, with 2 campgrounds: The Main and The Island. Both have private fireplaces (bring your own wood) and shady trees. There are 8 hot showers on-site and a kiosk, and Aratula's bakery, pub and service station is close by. Reynold's Creek nearby is ideal for swimming, canoeing and fishing. Yarramalong, on Lake Moogerah Rd, is signed from the Aratula turn-off adjacent to the pub and from the road to Boonah, Kalbar and Aratula. Pets are permitted except during public holidays and long weekends. **Map refs:** 398 F3, 457 M10

How to book: 688 Lake Moogerah Rd, Kalbar (07) 5463 7369

345 Yarramalong Weir

Camp on the riverbank at this basic site, 30 km east of Millmerran on the Condamine River; bring along firewood and drinking water. It's on Shire Rd (No. 96) off the Millmerran–Leyburn Rd. Millmerran is 82 km south-west of Toowoomba. **Map refs:** 398 E3, 457 K9

Who to contact: Toowoomba Regional Council 13 1872

346 Yellowbank Reserve camping area (bush camping)

This campsite by the Dumaresq River is a little more difficult to access than others in the region, but it offers excellent fishing. Take the Border Rivers Tourist Dr exit from Goondiwindi and travel 25 km east. The campsite is on a bush track that leads towards the Dumaresq (dry-weather access only for conventional vehicles). **Map refs:** 398 D4, 457 I11

Who to contact: Miles Visitor Information Centre (07) 4627 1492

OUTBACK AND THE GULF

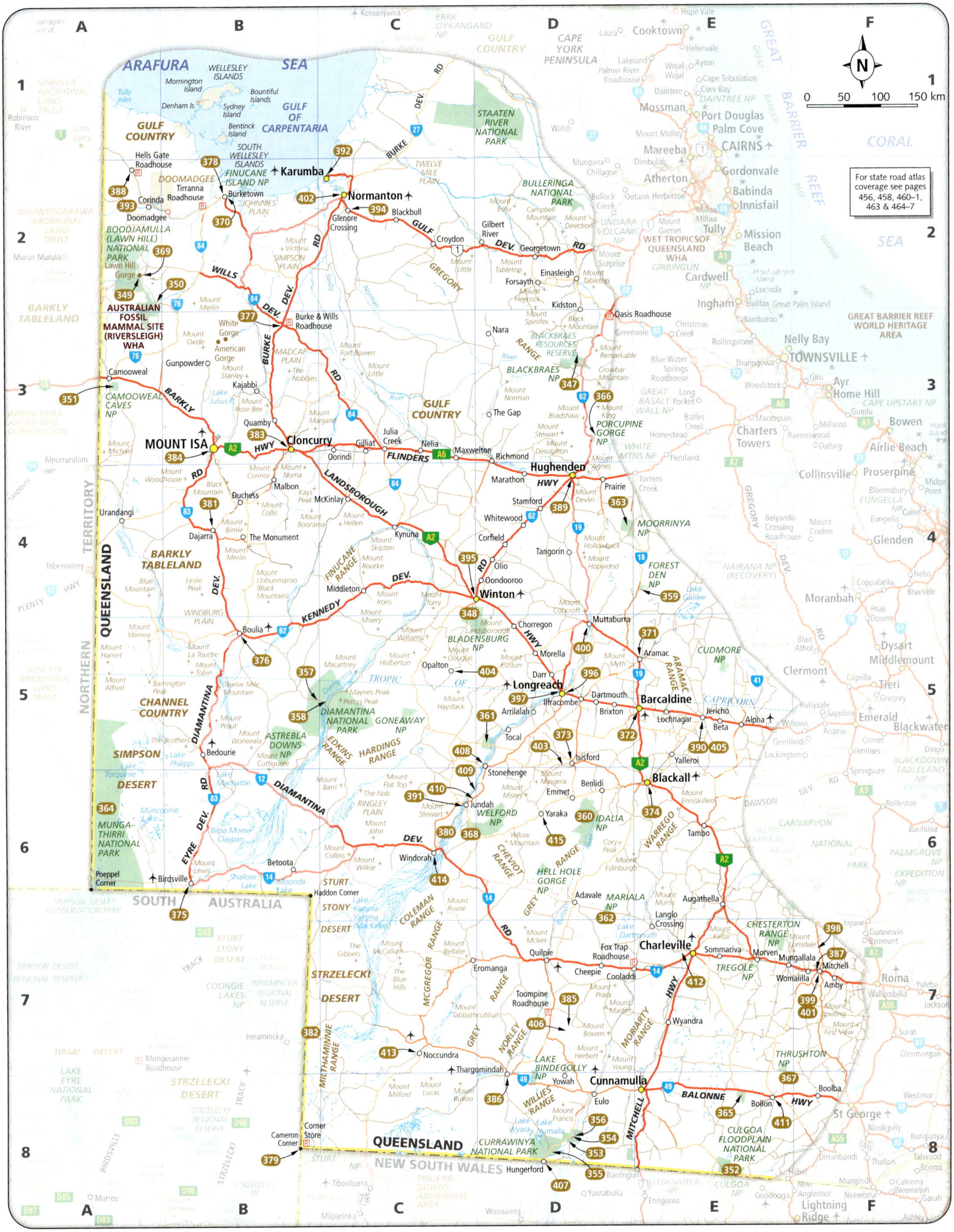

REMOTE AND REVERED, PICTURESQUE and pristine, isolated and iconic – camping in Queensland's outback and gulf country is a unique experience. Historic country towns such as Mt Isa, Birdsville, Charleville, Longreach and Blackall are a springboard for campers to discover numerous national parks, reserves and fossicking fields. Winton, Cunnamulla, Cloncurry, Hughenden, Barcaldine and Normanton are the other major centres to use as bases for trekking into this vast region.

In the north-west corner, Boodjamulla (Lawn Hill) National Park is spectacular gorge country, shaped by sandstone ranges and laden with World Heritage–listed fossils. Campgrounds such as Adels Grove and Lawn Hill Gorge have excellent facilities and are heavily booked Apr–Aug.

Further south in the Channel Country lie the red sand dunes of Diamantina National Park, which has 2 campgrounds close to waterholes for excellent fishing and canoeing. Closer to Winton is Bladensburg National Park, known for its scenic drives and spectacular views at Scrammy Gorge.

South-east of Winton, campers can pitch a tent by the waterhole at Longreach and discover Australia's aviation history at the Qantas Founders Museum or visit the Stockman's Hall of Fame. Birdsville – home of the famous Birdsville Races every Sept – is in the south-west corner of the state.

Further west is Queensland's largest national park, at 1 million ha: Munga-Thirri National Park, where bush camping is permitted within 500 m of the unsealed QAA Line track. In the southern pocket, history buffs can follow the footsteps of explorers Burke and Wills at the Dig Tree camping area on Cooper Creek. Other popular camping destinations across the region include the Barcoo Riverside Camp in Blackall (home to legendary shearer Jackie Howe), bush camping by the Thompson River in Lochern National Park near Longreach, and the Normanton Tourist Park in the Carpentaria Shire.

CAMPSITES LOCATED IN PARKS AND RESERVES

BLACKBRAES RESOURCES RESERVE

This resources reserve is part of a larger complex of reserves that, combined with Blackbraes National Park, protects 52 000 ha of outback highlands. The scenery in these reserves and parks includes sandstone plateaus and escarpments, granite hills and woodlands of lemon-scented gums and ironbarks. It is 520 km north-east of Mt Isa or 380 km west of Townsville, on the Kennedy Developmental Rd.

Who to contact: NPRSR 13 7468 www.nprsr.qld.gov.au
Permits: camping permit required *Camping fees:* fees can be paid and permits acquired at the self-registration station

347 Emu Swamp camping area (bush camping)

Bush camping is permitted beside Emu Swamp dam, 20.5 km from the park entrance on the Kennedy Developmental Rd. There are no facilities or amenities and open fires are prohibited, so bring all self-sufficient gear, including drinking water, rubbish bags and a gas/fuel stove. **Map refs:** 408 D3, 458 B1, 461 I11, 465 N1

BLADENSBURG NATIONAL PARK

Situated 17 km south-west of Winton, Bladensburg National Park is a great place for a scenic drive along the River Gum route or the Scrammy Dr to the spectacular lookout. Conventional vehicles can access Bladensburg during dry weather only; a high-clearance 4WD is recommended. Most of the driving roads in the park are suitable for mountain-bikers. Advance bookings are required for camping.

How to book: NPRSR 13 7468 www.nprsr.qld.gov.au
Permits: camping permit required

348 Bough Shed Hole camping area

This campground is accessed via the Route of River Gums. Campers are encouraged not to tie ropes to trees or drape things over vegetation, and to set up camp away from animal nests and burrows. Bring self-sufficient supplies, including drinking water and a gas/fuel stove. The campsite offers good access to Scrammy Lookout and Bladensburg Homestead. **Map refs:** 408 C4, 465 L7

BOODJAMULLA (LAWN HILL) NATIONAL PARK

In Queensland's arid far north-west lies a place of such unexpected and arresting beauty that its remoteness appears to be no impediment to travellers. Lawn Hill Gorge, with its multicoloured sandstone cliffs towering over a palm-fringed, emerald-green river, is the oasis-like centrepiece of Boodjamulla National Park. The park also contains the Riversleigh World Heritage Site, an important trove of fossils. Advance bookings are required for camping.

How to book: NPRSR 13 7468 www.nprsr.qld.gov.au
Permits: camping permit required

349 Lawn Hill Gorge camping area

This campground for self-sufficient campers has 20 campsites adjacent to Lawn Hill Creek, about 4 km from the park entrance. Conventional vehicles can access the park May–Oct, but 4WD is recommended at all times. Only 1 vehicle per campsite is permitted; the campground is not suitable for vehicles wider than 6 m. **Map refs:** 408 A2, 463 B6

350 Miymba camping area (bush camping)

On the banks of the Gregory River, Miymba is 3.5 km south of Riversleigh D Site. Conventional vehicles can access the Riversleigh section May–Sept, but 4WD is recommended at all times. Open fires and generators are prohibited; bring a gas/fuel stove and drinking water, as the tank-water supply is unreliable. **Map refs:** 408 A2, 463 B7

CAMOOWEAL CAVES NATIONAL PARK

The traditional country of the Indjilandji people, Camooweal Caves National Park lies about 180 km north-west of Mt Isa, 8 km south of Camooweal along Urandangi Rd. The caves, or sinkholes as they're known, are not accessible to visitors and there are only 2 short walking tracks in the park. The park is dry-weather access only and a 4WD is recommended. Advance bookings are required for camping.

How to book: NPRSR 13 7468 www.nprsr.qld.gov.au
Permits: camping permit required

351 **Caves Waterhole camping area**

Set beside Nowranie Waterhole, about 14 km from the park entrance, the Caves Waterhole campground can be reached by conventional vehicle with difficulty only – a 4WD is strongly recommended. Open fires and generators are prohibited. Bring all self-sufficient supplies, including rubbish bags, drinking water and a gas/fuel stove. **Map refs:** 408 A3, 463 A9, 464 C1

CULGOA FLOODPLAIN NATIONAL PARK

Lying on the Qld–NSW border about 130 km south-west of Dirranbandi, this national park is known for its diverse woodlands, flood plains and stony ridges. Wildlife-watchers can spot kangaroos, goannas and various bird species. Access to the park is via Goodooga in NSW.

Who to contact: NPRSR 13 7468 www.nprsr.qld.gov.au **Permits:** camping permit required **Camping fees:** fees can be paid and permits acquired at the park office **Road conditions:** call Culgoa Floodplains (07) 4625 0942 before embarking

352 **Bush camping areas**

For self-sufficient campers only, bush camping is permitted at various sites throughout the park. To get there from St George, travel 160 km south to Hebel on a sealed road then 45 km south to Goodooga (impassable after rain). From Goodooga, turn right into Brenda Rd then take the left fork after the cattle grid and follow the 'Byra 7 km' sign. **Map refs:** 408 E8, 456 C11, 467 P11

CURRAWINYA NATIONAL PARK

Currawinya National Park, set in rugged mulga country, protects a significant wetland system. There are 2 large lakes, Numalla and Wyara which, together with the Paroo River and its seasonal waterholes and other smaller semi-permanent lakes, are a significant bird habitat and a wildlife refuge during drought. More than 200 bird species have been recorded here – around 280 000 birds have been recorded on the lakes at one time. In this national park you can canoe and swim in the lakes, picnic on the shores of Lake Numalla and fish at sites specified by the ranger (it is an 85 km 4WD return trip from the ranger station to the lakes). Farming relics dot the landscape, reminders of the 1860s when the area was a pastoral property.

Who to contact: NPRSR 13 7468 www.nprsr.qld.gov.au
Permits: camping permit required **Camping fees:** fees can be paid and permits acquired at the self-registration station

353 **Caiwarro Waterhole camping area (bush camping)**

This bush camping area on the south bank of the Paroo River, west of the Caiwarro Homestead ruins, is suitable only for self-sufficient and experienced bush campers. Bring your own water, rubbish bags and firewood or a gas/fuel stove. To access Caiwarro Waterhole, turn right after reaching Caiwarro Homestead from Hungerford Rd, cross the Paroo River, then turn right once more and follow the road south-west. **Map refs:** 408 D8, 467 M10

354 **Corni Paroo Waterhole camping area (bush camping)**

This bush campsite is located next to the ruins of Caiwarro Homestead, and it offers some modest facilities, such as toilets (located in the ruins) and picnic tables. Bring your own water, rubbish bags and firewood or a gas/fuel stove. Access to Corni Paroo is via Hungerford Rd, 20 km north of Hungerford, then a further 3 km east. **Map refs:** 408 D8, 467 M10

355 **Ourimperee Waterhole camping area**

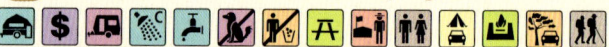

Behind the Currawinya Woolshed, the Ourimperee Waterhole is accessed off the Hungerford Rd, 20 km north of Hungerford. The campground, for self-sufficient campers only, is accessible by 2WD in dry weather only. **Map refs:** 408 D8, 467 L10

356 **Pump Hole camping area (bush camping)**

This bush camping area east of the Caiwarro Homestead ruins offers no facilities, although history buffs will find some fascinating remnants of settler life in the nearby old pump and bough shed. Bring your own water, rubbish bags and firewood or a gas/fuel stove. To access Pump Hole, turn right after reaching Caiwarro Homestead from Hungerford Rd, cross the Paroo River, then turn left and follow the Paroo east until the bough shed. Turn left again and drive down to the camping area. **Map refs:** 408 D8, 467 M10

DIAMANTINA NATIONAL PARK

Shaped by sandstone ranges, grass plains, waterholes and wetlands, this 500 000 ha national park lies about 300 km south-west of Winton. The scenic Warracoota Circuit drive (around 150 km) takes in historic sites and birdwatching and fishing hot spots. Travel via the Kennedy Developmental Rd if you're coming from the north; from the south, take the Diamantina Developmental Rd.

Who to contact: NPRSR 13 7468 www.nprsr.qld.gov.au
Permits: camping permit required **Camping fees:** fees can be paid and permits acquired at the self-registration stations

357 Gum Hole camping area

This campground is 11 km past the turn-off to Hunters Gorge, about 21 km west of the ranger station on Boulia Rd. A pit toilet and self-registration station are the only facilities; pick up a drive guide brochure from the self-registration station. Bring your own drinking water and a gas/fuel stove. **Map refs:** 408 B5, 464 H10

358 Hunters Gorge camping area

The turn-off to this campground is 10 km along the Boulia–Springvale Rd from the Diamantina National Park HQ. A further 4 km along is the Mundewerra Waterhole, a channel of the Diamantina River. A pit toilet and self-registration station are the only facilities. This is a great spot for fishing, canoeing and birdwatching; bring your own drinking water and a gas/fuel stove. **Map refs:** 408 C5, 464 H10

FOREST DEN NATIONAL PARK

The grass plains and woodlands of Forest Den National Park are 100 km north of Aramac, reached via the Corinda turn-off from Torrens Creek Rd. The Four Mile Waterhole camping area, accessible by 4WD, is a great spot for viewing wildlife. Forest Den is relatively small by national park standards, at only 6000 ha. Advance bookings are required for camping.

How to book: NPRSR 13 7468 www.nprsr.qld.gov.au
Permits: camping permit required

359 Four Mile Waterhole camping area

Campers must be totally self-sufficient to use this site near the banks of Torrens Creek; there are no facilities. Take the Corinda turn-off from Torrens Creek Rd; travel for 5 km to the park entrance, plus a further 5 km north to the camping area. A 4WD is strongly recommended. **Map refs:** 408 E4, 458 D7, 465 P7

IDALIA NATIONAL PARK

Set in the Gowan Range in central western Queensland, Idalia National Park is a dry, remote wilderness. Although the park encompasses the headwaters of the Bulloo River and the tributaries of the Barcoo River, the waterways have wide, sandy beds that are usually dry, except following big rains. There are a number of pastoral relics, including Old Idalia, the site of an abandoned musterer's hut and stockyards. Visitors must be self-reliant. Advance bookings are recommended for camping.

How to book: NPRSR 13 7468 www.nprsr.qld.gov.au
Permits: camping permit required *Camping fees:* if you have not booked ahead, fees can be paid and permits acquired at the self-registration station

360 Monks Tank camping area (bush camping)

Monks Tank has a clearing for self-sufficient camping, with permits available from a self-registration station. To reach Idalia National Park, follow Isisford Rd from Blackall for 42 km

then turn left onto Yaraka Rd. At the Benlidi siding, turn left and follow the Idalia–Benlidi Rd for 34 km to the park boundary. The park has several easy walks through rocky gorges and tablelands. Bring water and a gas/fuel stove. **Map refs:** 408 D6, 467 M2

LOCHERN NATIONAL PARK

Protecting more than 24 000 ha of habitat rich with lagoons and waterholes, Lochern National Park is 150 km south-west of Longreach and 330 km south of Winton. Take a drive along the 40 km (2–4 hr) scenic route through woodlands to the flood plains of the Thomson River. To get here, follow the signposted access off Longreach–Jundah Rd, 100 km south of Longreach.

Who to contact: NPRSR 13 7468 www.nprsr.qld.gov.au
Permits: camping permit required *Camping fees:* fees can be paid and permits acquired at the self-registration station

361 Broadwater Waterhole camping area (bush camping)

Camping for self-sufficient campers is permitted at Broadwater Waterhole, 2 km north of the access road. There are no walking tracks, but the waterhole is a great spot for watching wildlife such as birds and turtles. Fires are prohibited; bring drinking water and a gas/fuel stove. **Map refs:** 408 D5, 465 L11

MARIALA NATIONAL PARK

Mariala, 128 km north-west of Charleville, is a small, remote national park known for its abundance of birdlife. Walking trails are not marked in the park, so bushwalkers need to be well equipped with a compass and maps. 4WDs are recommended on the unsealed roads.

Who to contact: NPRSR 13 7468 www.nprsr.qld.gov.au
Permits: camping permit required *Camping fees:* fees can be paid and permits acquired at QPWS Charleville (07) 4654 4777

362 Bush camping areas

Bush camping is permitted along Adavale–Charleville Rd in the park for self-sufficient campers. Be aware that there is no ranger in the park (a permit is required before entering), the local water supply is unsuitable for drinking, and there are no facilities. Bring drinking water and a gas/fuel stove. **Map refs:** 408 D6, 467 N4

MOORRINYA NATIONAL PARK

Shaped by dry, flat plains and crucial water catchments, Moorrinya National Park is about 90 km south of Torrens Creek or 180 km north of Aramac on Torrens Creek–Aramac Rd. It is accessible only by 4WD during dry weather. Expect to see plenty of wildlife in the region including kangaroos, koalas, emus and dingoes. Note: the park may be closed Nov–Apr.

Who to contact: NPRSR 13 7468 www.nprsr.qld.gov.au
Permits: camping permit required *Camping fees:* fees can be paid and permits acquired at the self-registration station

363 Moorrinya camping area (bush camping)

Self-sufficient bush camping (with a permit) is allowed near the old shearing shed, about 4.5 km from the homestead, accessible by 4WD only. Open fires and generators are not permitted. Bring water and a gas/fuel stove. **Map refs:** 408 D4, 458 C5, 465 O5

MUNGA-THIRRI NATIONAL PARK

The largest national park in Queensland, Munga-Thirri National Park is part of the remote and unforgiving Simpson Desert, a destination for experienced outback adventurers only. Covering the intersecting borders of 3 states – Augustus Poeppel in 1884 established the corner point now known as Poeppel Corner – the park is characterised by huge sand dunes up to 50 m high, which run parallel to each other, around 1 km apart, and extend for up to 200 km. The park is closed 1 Dec–15 Mar annually due to high temperatures. Note: visitors must keep to the QAA Line. Advance bookings are required for camping.

How to book: NPRSR 13 7468 www.nprsr.qld.gov.au
Permits: camping permit required

364 Bush camping areas

Camping is permitted in the national park only within 500 m either side of the QAA Line. Munga-Thirri is extremely remote: visitors must take a 2-way radio, spare vehicle parts, fuel and a week's worth of food and water in case of emergency. Only very experienced, self-sufficient visitors should explore the Simpson Desert. The park boundary is about 75 km west of Birdsville.
Map refs: 408 A6, 466 B1

NARKOOLA NATIONAL PARK

This recently gazetted national park consists of 11 799 ha of mulga and brigalow scrub 20 km west of Bollon near the Balonne Hwy. Several sections of the park are currently recovering from their former use as farming land, and park facilities, including access roads, are still being developed.

Who to contact: QPWS Culgoa Floodplain (07) 4625 0942
Permits: camping permit required *Camping fees:* fees can be paid and permits acquired at any QPWS office *Road conditions:* QPWS Culgoa Floodplain (07) 4625 0942

365 Bush camping areas

Self-sufficient campers are welcome to camp in Narkoola National Park, but be aware that there are no facilities or amenities. Fires are prohibited. Bring drinking water, rubbish bags and a gas/fuel stove. **Map refs:** 408 E8, 456 C9

PORCUPINE GORGE NATIONAL PARK

Appearing like an oasis in the dry, flat plains north of Hughenden, Porcupine Gorge National Park features towering sandstone cliffs and a ribbon of greenery lining Porcupine Creek. Over millions of years, this stream has eroded the surrounding basalt-capped sandstone into the deep gorge we see today; it changes from a string of pools in winter to a cascade in the wet season. The best time to visit this national park is in the cooler months of the year, as the summers can be extremely hot. Come with a 4WD in wet weather. Advance bookings are recommended for camping.

How to book: NPRSR 13 7468 www.nprsr.qld.gov.au
Permits: camping permit required *Camping fees:* if you have not booked ahead, fees can be paid and permits acquired at the self-registration station

366 Pyramid Campground

Over time, Porcupine Creek has carved sculptures and potholes in the natural rock, the most famous of which is the Pyramid, an isolated monolith of multicoloured sandstone rising from the floor of the gorge. Pyramid Campground, with 22 sites for self-sufficient campers, is in the upper level of the gorge at the starting point for the 2.4 km return Pyramid track that leads down into the gorge. It is 500 m from the park entrance and 2.5 km from Mt Emu Plains Rd. Bring drinking water. Note: open fires and generators are not permitted. Half of the sites can be booked in advance; the other half are first-come, first-served.
Map refs: 408 D3, 458 C3, 465 O3

THRUSHTON NATIONAL PARK

About 40 km north-east of Bollon in southern Queensland, Thrushton National Park is a popular reserve for nature lovers. About 130 km north-west of St George and 190 km south of Mitchell, the park is accessible only in dry weather, and 4WD vehicles are recommended.

Who to contact: QPWS Culgoa Floodplain (07) 4625 0942
Permits: camping permit required *Camping fees:* fees can be paid and permits acquired at any QPWS office

367 Bush camping

Self-sufficient campers are welcome to camp in Thrushton National Park, but be aware that there are no facilities or amenities and it is very rarely patrolled. Come equipped with drinking water and a gas/fuel stove, as fires are prohibited. There are no self-registration facilities at this park.
Map refs: 408 E8, 456 D9

WELFORD NATIONAL PARK

On the Barcoo River, Welford National Park protects 124 000 ha and can be accessed from either Jundah, Windorah, Blackall or Quilpie. Access roads are unsealed and a 4WD is recommended; the roads are impassable when wet. The park's northern boundary is 30 km south-east of Jundah. Advance bookings are required for camping.

How to book: NPRSR 13 7468 www.nprsr.qld.gov.au
Permits: camping permit required

368 Little Boomerang Waterhole camping area

On the banks of the Barcoo River, this is a remote campground for experienced, self-sufficient campers. To get there, turn west off the Jundah–Quilpie Rd; the campground is about 10 km from the turn-off. Conventional vehicles can access this campsite in dry weather only, and 4WD is recommended at all times. Open fires are prohibited, so bring a gas/fuel stove and drinking water. **Map refs:** 408 C6, 467 J2

CAMPSITES LOCATED IN OTHER AREAS

369 Adels Grove

Most sites at this campground, 10 km north of Boodjamulla (Lawn Hill) National Park, have water, a fireplace and a BBQ plate, but no power is available. There is a modern amenities block and a laundry with 2 machines. Other accommodation options on-site include permanent tents and rooms with beds and linen provided. Popular activities in the area include swimming, canoeing, fishing, birdwatching and bushwalking. Note: the bar and restaurant on-site is open for breakfast, lunch and dinner. **Map refs:** 408 A2, 463 B6

How to book: Lot 3 Lawn Hill Rd, Lawn Hill (07) 4748 5502 www.adelsgrove.com.au

370 Albert River camping area (bush camping)

Bush camping for self-sufficient campers is permitted on the banks of the Albert River north-east of Burketown; there are no designated sites and no facilities. The Western Gulf Region of Queensland has a mixture of sealed and maintained unsealed roads; checking with local authorities for road conditions is recommended. The best time to travel is during the dry season (May–Oct). **Map refs:** 408 B2, 460 A7, 463 D4

Who to contact: Burketown Visitor Information Centre (07) 4745 5111

371 Aramac Caravan Park

This campground is next to the Aramac Showgrounds on Booker St in Aramac. There are some powered sites and laundry facilities are available. Aramac is part of the Barcaldine Regional Council, 440 km west of Rockhampton, one of the largest cattle-producing regions in central west Queensland. **Map refs:** 408 E5, 458 D9, 465 P9

Who to contact: Barcaldine Regional Council (07) 4651 3311
Camping fees: fees can be paid at the council offices in Gordon St, Aramac

372 Barcaldine Tourist Park

About 1.5 km from the centre of town on Box St (Matilda Hwy), this tourist park with drive-through grassy sites has an excellent range of facilities including wireless internet, and free use of the washing machines and iron. The town centre offers plenty of restaurants and shops. Barcaldine is about 100 km east of Longreach and about 100 km north of Blackall. Ensuite cabins are also available on-site. **Map refs:** 408 E5, 458 D10, 465 P10

How to book: 51-65 Box St, Barcaldine (07) 4651 6066, 1300 658 251 www.barcaldinetouristpark.com.au

373 Barcoo River camping area

Camping is permitted beside the Barcoo River in Isisford. The camping area has a toilet block; the nearby park has an amenities block with showers. The Barcoo River offers excellent fishing, camping, canoeing and birdwatching. Isisford is about 120 km west of Blackall and about 85 km south of Ilfracombe. **Map refs:** 408 D5, 458 B11, 465 N11

Who to contact: Longreach Regional Council, Isisford branch (07) 4658 8900

374 Barcoo Riverside Camp

Caravan-based campers with self-contained facilities can use the clearing on the northern side of the Barcoo River, about 500 m from the centre of Blackall. All visitors must register at the information centre on Shamrock St. On the Landsborough Hwy, 108 km south of Barcaldine, Blackall features a statue of sheep shearer Jackie Howe, who in 1892 set a world record by shearing 321 sheep with hand shears in under 8 hours. **Map refs:** 408 E6, 456 A1, 458 D12, 465 P12, 467 O1

Who to contact: Blackall Visitor Information Centre (07) 4657 4637 *Camping fees:* fees can be paid at the visitor centre, 145A Shamrock St, or at the self-registration station

375 Birdsville Caravan Park

Make sure to book well ahead (at least 6 months) for powered sites at this caravan park during the Birdsville Races in Sept, and bookings are recommended Mar–Nov. The park, on Florence St, covers an area of about 12 ha, with plenty of unpowered sites if you miss out. No pets are allowed during race week. Birdsville is reached from the north via Bedourie (187 km), from the east via Windorah (380 km) and from the south along the Birdsville Track from Marree in SA (519 km). Note: the internet cafe has 2 computers; BBQs are coin-operated. **Map refs:** 408 B6, 466 D3

How to book: 1 Florence St, Birdsville (07) 4656 3214 www.birdsvillecaravanpark.com

376 Boulia Caravan Park

This spacious, grassy caravan park with 40 powered sites is on the eastern banks of the Burke River, on the Diamantina Developmental Rd. In addition to caravan and camping sites, the park offers unit accommodation with ensuites, 1 self-contained cabin and laundry facilities. Boulia is 288 km south of Mt Isa and 363 km west of Winton. Note: bring your own firewood. **Map refs:** 408 B5, 464 F8

How to book: Winton Rd, Boulia (07) 4746 3320

377 Burke and Wills Roadhouse

This roadhouse with 12 powered sites sits at the junction of Wills Developmental Rd and Burke Developmental Rd, about 180 km north of Cloncurry and about 200 km south of Normanton. The camping surface is a mixture of grass and dirt; bring your own firewood. **Map refs:** 408 B3, 460 B10, 463 F8

Who to contact: Burke Developmental Rd, Four Ways (07) 4742 5909

378 Burketown Caravan Park

This caravan park in Burketown, about 225 km west of Normanton, has excellent facilities: tourist and fishing information, 2 amenities blocks, laundry facilities, EFTPOS and a kiosk. There are also self-contained air-conditioned units and standard rooms for 4–6 people. Crocodiles make the waterways dangerous for all activities except fishing, but you can cool off in the council-owned pool. The Western Gulf Region of Queensland has a mixture of sealed and maintained unsealed roads; check road conditions before heading off. **Map refs:** 408 B2, 460 A7, 463 D4

How to book: Sloman St, Burketown (07) 4745 5118

379 Cameron Corner camping area

An expansive camping area covering about 240 ha, Cameron Corner fees go to the Royal Flying Doctor Service. Firewood and other basic supplies are available at the on-site store. Cameron Corner is where the Qld, NSW and SA borders meet. A 4WD is recommended. **Map refs:** 408 B8, 466 F10

How to book: Cameron Corner Store (08) 8091 3872

380 Cooper Creek camping area (bush camping)

Bush camping for self-sufficient campers is offered 6 km east of the Thomson Developmental Rd, north-east of Windorah in Barcoo Shire. The shire's primary river systems are the Thomson and Barcoo, which join above Windorah to flow into Cooper Creek. This site can be accessed by conventional vehicles in dry weather only. **Map refs:** 408 C6, 467 J2

Who to contact: Windorah Visitor Information Centre (07) 4656 3063

381 Dajarra Campground

This basic campground with an amenities block including hot showers is on the Diamantina Developmental Rd at Dajarra, a small community 140 km south of Mt Isa. Bring in your own drinking water. **Map refs:** 408 B4, 464 F5

Who to contact: Jimberella Co-Op (07) 4748 4828

382 Dig Tree camping area

Hugely popular with tourists passing through, this historic site is where explorers Burke and Wills were expecting to meet the remainder of their 1861 expedition party; however, all they found was a blazed tree and a limited amount of supplies buried. Burke later died under the tree. The campground is beside Cooper Creek with signposted access off the Adventure Way. For supplies, including drinking water, travel 55 km south-west to Innamincka, SA. Dogs are permitted if you advise the ranger in advance. **Map refs:** 408 B7, 466 G7

Who to contact: Dig Tree Ranger (07) 4655 4323

383 Discovery Holiday Parks – Cloncurry

Those looking for a taste of outback history will revel in Cloncurry, the town famous for launching the first-ever Royal Flying Doctor Service flight. This hoiday park offers a range of modern conveniences, including a kiosk, laundry and swimming pool. Advance bookings are recommended. **Map refs:** 408 B3, 463 F11, 464 H3

How to book: McIlwraith St (Flinders Hwy), Cloncurry (07) 4742 2300, 1800 635 559 www.discoveryholidayparks.com.au/qld/outback_queensland/cloncurry

384 Discovery Holiday Parks – Mount Isa

This caravan park in the heart of Mt Isa, with a swimming pool, internet access and laundry, offers a refreshing slice of civilisation deep in the outback. Nearby attractions include mine tours and the Riversleigh Fossil Centre. Advance bookings are recommended. **Map refs:** 408 B3, 463 D11, 464 F3

How to book: 185–195 Little West St, Mt Isa (07) 4743 4676, 1800 456 661 www.discoveryholidayparks.com.au/qld/outback_queensland/mount_isa

385 Duck Creek camping area (bush camping)

Self-sufficient bush camping is permitted in the opal fields of Duck Creek, about 60 km south-east of Toompine and 130 km south of Quilpie. Check road conditions before setting off, as access is dry weather only for conventional vehicles. **Map refs:** 408 D7, 467 M7

Who to contact: Quilpie Visitor Information Centre
(07) 4656 0540 **Permits:** camping and fossicking permits
required **Camping fees:** fees can be paid and permits acquired
from the Quilpie Visitor Information Centre

386 Explorers Caravan Park

This campground has 25 powered sites, more than
20 unpowered sites, plus the option of 6 ensuite cabins or
4 standard rooms. Thargomindah is 185 km west of Cunnamulla
and 195 km south of Quilpie. The camp kitchen is well equipped,
but you need to bring firewood. Note: laundry facilities are
available. **Map refs:** 408 D8, 467 K8

How to book: 88 Dowling St, Thargomindah (07) 4655 3307

387 Fishermans Rest camping area

This riverside campground for self-sufficient campers is 4 km
west of Mitchell, 500 m off the Warrego Hwy. Mitchell is on
the Maranoa River, 90 km west of Roma and 180 km east of
Charleville. **Map refs:** 408 F7, 456 E6

Who to contact: Mitchell Visitor Information Centre
(07) 4624 6923

388 Hells Gate Roadhouse

Open only during the dry season (Apr–Sept/Oct), this roadhouse
is 180 km west of Burketown and 48 km east of the NT
border. The Western Gulf region has a mixture of sealed and
maintained unsealed roads; check with the roadhouse for
road conditions. Note: visitors have access to laundry facilities.
Map refs: 408 A2, 463 B3

How to book: Savannah Way (07) 4745 8258 **Road conditions:**
(07) 4745 8258

389 Hughenden Allan Terry Caravan Park

This charming council-owned caravan park in the small town
of Hughenden offers modern, clean amenities and facilities,
including a laundry, kiosk and even carwash facilities. Resolution
St is off the Flinders Hwy. **Map refs:** 408 D4, 458 B4, 465 N4

How to book: Resolution St, Hughenden (07) 4741 1190

390 Jericho Showground Caravan Park

Campers passing through the hamlet of Jericho will be
delighted to find a campsite with comprehensive facilities at the
showground. It is on Showground Rd, off the Capricorn Hwy.
Map refs: 408 E5, 458 E10

Who to contact: Barcaldine Regional Council, Jericho office
(07) 4651 4188 **Camping fees:** fees can be paid at the self-
registration station

391 Jundah Caravan Park

You'll find this caravan park on Miles St in Jundah, near the
town park and swimming pool. There are laundry facilities on-
site; a dump point is availble 800 m away on Longreach Rd.
Jundah is part of Barcoo Shire, a remote council in central
western Queensland. **Map refs:** 408 C6, 467 J1

Who to contact: Jundah Visitor Information Centre
(07) 4658 6930

392 Karumba Point Tourist Park

This caravan park has an excellent range of facilities, including
a swimming pool, craft shop, 2 amenities blocks, fish-cleaning
areas and laundry facilities. Air-conditioned on-site caravans are
available. You'll find it on Col Kitching Dr (the road to Karumba
Point) in Karumba, a popular destination for barramundi fishing
at the mouth of the Norman River. Bookings are required for
May–Aug. **Map refs:** 408 C2, 460 C6, 463 G4

How to book: 2 Col Kitching Dr, Karumba (07) 4745 9306
www.karumbapoint.com.au

393 Kingfisher Camp

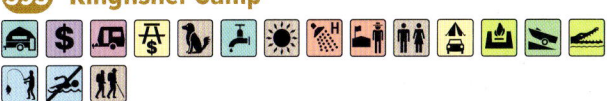

Kingfisher Camp is 42 km west of the Savannah Way, and
a further 126 km from Burketown. The campground has
30 grassed, shaded sites at one end of a 5 km waterhole.
Each campsite has its own fireplace and water tap (boil or treat
before drinking). Generators are permitted. The Western Gulf
region of Queensland has a mixture of sealed and maintained
unsealed roads; checking with local authorities for road
conditions is recommended. The best time to travel is during the
dry season. **Map refs:** 408 A2, 463 B4

How to book: Bowthorn Station Rd, Lawn Hill (07) 4745 8212
www.kingfisherresort.com.au

394 Leichhardt Camping Park

About 800 m from the Norman River on the Normanton–
Croydon Rd (Savannah Way), 26 km east of Normanton. There
are no powered sites here but campers are encouraged to
bring their own generators. Normanton, the major commercial
centre of the Carpentaria Shire, is popular with barramundi
anglers. The town is about 380 km north of Cloncurry and
680 km west of Cairns. Note: boil or treat water before drinking.
Map refs: 408 C2, 460 D7, 463 G5

How to book: Savannah Way (07) 4745 1330, 0487 675 173

395 Long Waterhole camping area (bush camping)

Self-sufficient campers can stay at this site, but be aware
that there is no power, water or facilities. The camping area

is reached from the Winton–Jundah Rd, about 2 km south of Winton. While you're here, head into town to visit the Waltzing Matilda museum. **Map refs:** 408 D4, 465 L7

Who to contact: Winton Visitor Information Centre (07) 4657 1466

396 Longreach Caravan Park

This holiday park provides a comfortable stay in one of central Queensland's popular tourist towns. Facilities include 2 swimming pools, 3 spas, a mini mart, wireless broadband internet or internet kiosks, free electric BBQs and 3 amenities blocks. Caravan sites have electricity, water and sullage points. Note: check out the Stockman's Hall of Fame and the Qantas Founders Museum. **Map refs:** 408 D5, 458 B10, 465 N10

How to book: 180 Ibis St, Longreach (07) 4658 1770 www.longreachcaravanpark.com.au

397 Longreach Waterhole camping area

The Longreach Waterhole is reached from the Landsborough Hwy, about 4 km north-west of Longreach. There's a toilet block, picnic tables and shelters in the adjacent day-use area, but you need to be totally self-sufficient to stay here. To get here from Longreach, take the hwy towards Winton, then turn east to the motorcross track; the camping area is north, by the river. **Map refs:** 408 D5, 458 B10, 465 N10

Who to contact: Longreach Visitor Information Centre (07) 4658 3555

398 Major Mitchell Campground

This campsite, 45 km north of Mitchell on Forestvale Rd, is of tremendous historical significance to the Maranoa region, as it is where Sir Thomas Livingstone Mitchell based his camp while exploring the region during his fourth expedition. Toilet facilities and sheltered wood BBQs are provided, but you will need to bring your own drinking water and firewood. **Map refs:** 408 F7, 456 E5

Who to contact: Mitchell Visitor Information Centre (07) 4624 6923

399 Major Mitchell Caravan Park

This caravan park has a total of 67 sites, including 47 powered sites and 16 ensuite sites. On the Warrego Hwy in Mitchell, close to town, the park's other on-site accommodation options include 3 cabins and 2 overnight vans. Mitchell is beside the Maranoa River, 90 km west of Roma and 180 km east of Charleville. **Map refs:** 408 F7, 456 E6

How to book: Warrego Hwy, Mitchell (07) 4623 6600 www.majormitchellcaravanpark.com.au

400 Muttaburra Caravan Park

Muttaburra Caravan Park is on Bridge St in Muttaburra, about 85 km north-west of Aramac. Muttaburra is part of the Barcaldine Regional Council, one of the largest cattle-producing regions in central western Queensland. **Map refs:** 408 D5, 458 C8, 465 O8

Who to contact: Barcaldine Regional Council (07) 4658 7191 **Camping fees:** pay at the Muttaburra Library, Bridge St

401 Neil Turner Weir camping area

This camping area is on River St in Mitchell by the Maranoa River. If you're a keen angler, check out Fishermans Rest. Mitchell is 90 km west of Roma and 180 km east of Charleville on the Warrego Hwy. **Map refs:** 408 F7, 456 E6

Who to contact: Maranoa Regional Council 1300 007 662

402 Normanton Tourist Park

This park has 55 powered sites, 25 unpowered sites, 12 ensuite cabins and 5 budget rooms. Facilities include a lap pool, artesian spa bath and 3 amenities blocks. Normanton is about 380 km north of Cloncurry and 680 km west of Cairns. Bookings are recommended for Apr–Aug. **Map refs:** 408 C2, 460 D7, 463 G4

How to book: 14 Brown St, Normanton (07) 4745 1121, 1800 193 469 www.normantontouristpark.com.au

403 Oma Waterhole camping area

The Oma Waterhole for self-sufficient campers is set beside the Barcoo River on Yaraka Rd, 13 km south of Isisford. The river offers excellent fishing, camping, canoeing and birdwatching. Isisford is about 120 km west of Blackall and 85 km south of Ilfracombe. **Map refs:** 408 D5, 458 B11, 465 N11

Who to contact: Longreach Regional Council, Isisford branch (07) 4658 8900

404 Opalton Field camping area

The Opalton Field is one of the largest and most extensively worked opal deposits in Queensland. The camping area is about 110 km south of Winton; the turn-off is signposted on Jundah Rd, 15 km south of Winton (dry weather access only for conventional vehicles). Bring firewood and drinking water. If you wish to fossick, obtain a permit through Queensland Mining and Safety's Winton office, (07) 4657 1727. **Map refs:** 408 C5, 465 K9

Who to contact: Opalton Outpost (07) 4657 1418 **Permits:** fossicking permit required **Camping fees:** fees can be paid at the honesty box

405 Redbank Park camping area

Jericho's free campsite is by the banks of the Jordan Creek. Turn onto Davy St from Edison St (Blackall–Jericho Rd) and follow it over the levee. A donation system helps cover the cost of maintaining the facilities. **Map refs:** 408 E5, 458 E10

Who to contact: Barcaldine Regional Council, Jericho office (07) 4651 4188

406 Sheep Station Creek camping area (bush camping)

Self-sufficient bush camping is permitted in the opal fields of Sheep Station Creek, about 60 km south-east of Toompine and 130 km south of Quilpie. Check road conditions before arriving, as access is dry weather only. **Map refs:** 408 D7, 467 M7

Who to contact: Quilpie Visitor Information Centre (07) 4656 0540 ***Permits:*** camping and fossicking permits required ***Camping fees:*** fees can be paid and permits acquired from the Quilpie Visitor Information Centre

407 Southern Cross Caravan Park

Southern Cross Caravan Park is in the tiny settlement of Hungerford, on the Qld–NSW border. The campground is in the centre of town near the pub, which doubles as a general store and fuel station. Hungerford is about 120 km south of Eulo on the Thargomindah–Cunnamulla Rd and about 100 km north of Wanaaring in NSW. **Map refs:** 408 D8, 467 L11

Who to contact: Royal Mail Hotel, Hungerford (07) 4655 4093

408 Stonehenge Caravan Park

This caravan park is on the corner of Salisbury and Stratford sts in Stonehenge, part of Barcoo Shire, a remote council in central western Queensland. Bring your own firewood. **Map refs:** 408 D5, 465 L12

Who to contact: Stonehenge Visitor Information Centre (07) 4658 5857

409 Thomson River camping area (bush camping)

This site for self-sufficient campers is beside the Thomson River, west of Jundah on Thomson Developmental Rd. **Map refs:** 408 C6, 465 L12, 467 J1

Who to contact: Jundah Visitor Information Centre (07) 4658 6930

410 Top Six Mile camping area (bush camping)

This bush site for self-sufficient campers is beside the Thomson River, 14 km north of Jundah on the Thomson Developmental Rd. **Map refs:** 408 C6, 465 L12, 467 J1

Who to contact: Jundah Visitor Information Centre (07) 4658 6930

411 Wallam Creek camping area

This campground for self-sufficient campers is by the creek in Bollon, on the Balonne Hwy, 112 km west of St George. Hot showers are located a short walk away, opposite the Bollon pub. **Map refs:** 408 E8, 456 D9

Who to contact: St George Shire Visitor Information Centre (07) 4625 4996

412 Ward River camping area (bush camping)

The Ward River bush camping area is on the east side of the river on the Quilpie Rd, about 20 km west of Charleville. Visitors must be totally self-sufficient; there is no amenities block and no powered sites. To get there, follow Quilpie Rd west from Charleville for 19 km, then turn right onto the dirt track to the camping area (dry-weather access only for conventional vehicles). **Map refs:** 408 E7, 456 B5, 467 O5

Who to contact: Charleville Visitor Information Centre (07) 4654 3057

413 Wilson River camping area

This campground is beside the Wilson River, just across the road from the Noccundra Hotel, 141 km west of Thargomindah. The amenities block with toilet and hot showers is next to the hotel. Campers must be totally self-sufficient. **Map refs:** 408 C7, 467 I8

Who to contact: Thargomindah Information Centre (07) 4655 3399 ***Camping fees:*** gold-coin donation for use of amenities block

414 Windorah Caravan Park

There are laundry facilities at this caravan park on Diamantina Developmental Rd (Maryborough St) in Windorah, part of Barcoo Shire. The primary river systems here are the Thomson and Barcoo, which merge above Windorah to become Cooper Creek. Note: there is a dump point 800 m away. **Map refs:** 408 C6, 467 I3

Who to contact: Windorah Visitor Information Centre (07) 4656 3063

415 Yaraka Town Caravan Park

This small caravan park for self-sufficient visitors is behind the Yaraka Town Hall, next to the Yaraka Hotel. There are 3 sites available (free of charge) with concrete slabs, power and water. Yaraka is about 100 km south-west of Isisford and 160 km west of Blackall. **Map refs:** 408 D6, 467 L2

Who to contact: Longreach Regional Council, Isisford branch (07) 4658 8900

THE MID-TROPICS

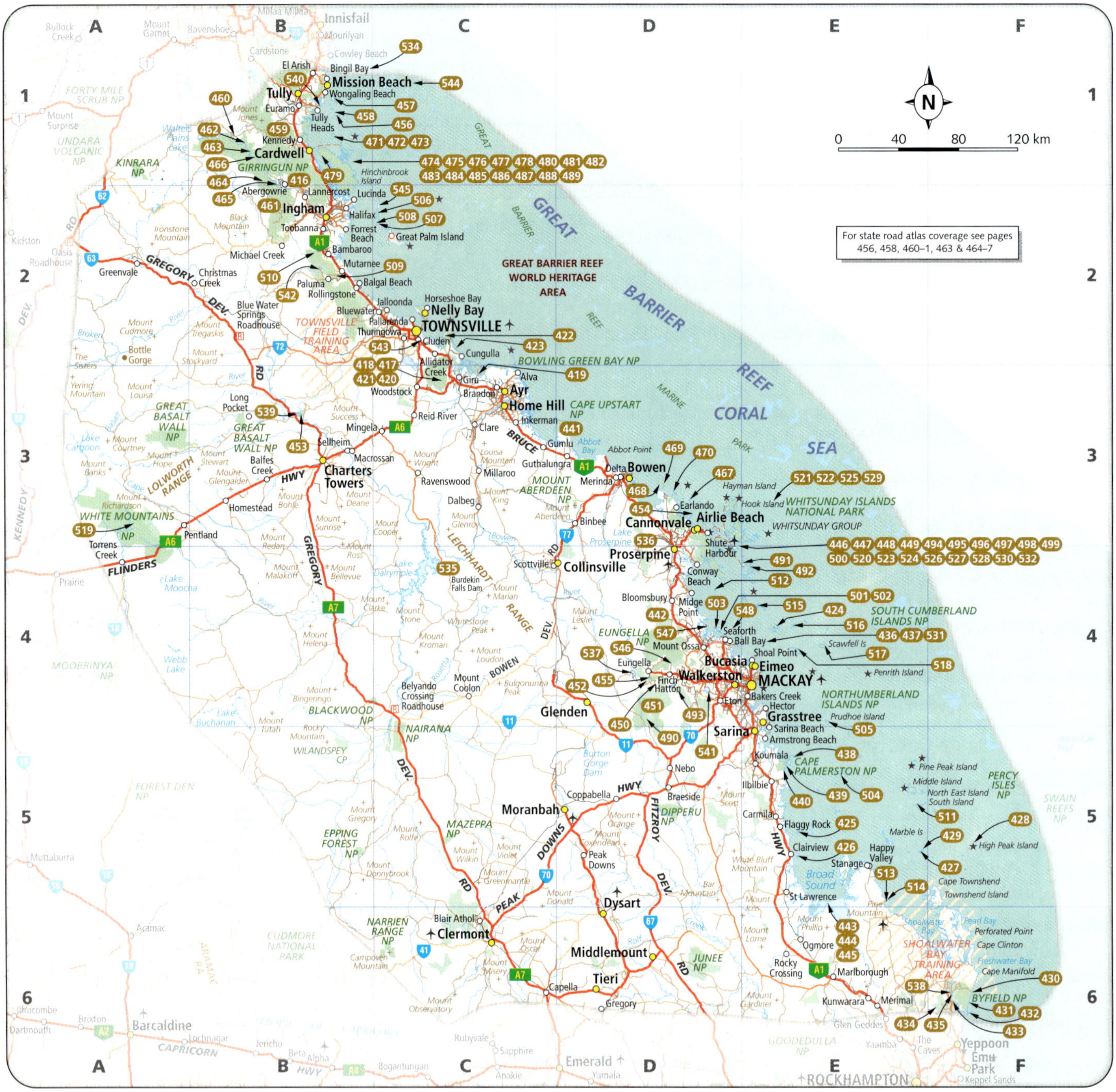

GRAB YOUR SNORKEL AND flippers – the Mid-Tropics is the jumping-off point for the magical tropical islands of the Whitsundays and Great Barrier Reef. Plush resorts and hotels are scattered along the coastline, but many campgrounds in this region have prime positions even closer to the beaches and offshore reefs that you'll be exploring. Campers can pitch a tent behind the dazzling white silica sands of Whitehaven Beach on Whitsunday Island – a completely undeveloped beach typically visited via boat or helicopter daytrip – or set up camp on Hinchinbrook Island, Australia's largest island national park.

Visitors to the region can go snorkelling amid kaleidoscopic corals, brightly coloured fish, turtles and dugongs, or take a daytrip to the outer reef for once-in-a-lifetime scuba diving. The beaches are sensational for soaking up the sunshine, and sail-boat cruises take you around the islands to some of the best snorkelling locations. Beach camping clearings such as those on Hook Island are quiet, secluded, mostly free from tourist traffic and offer sensational snorkelling just metres from your tent. Other national parks with island-based campgrounds include Family, Gloucester, Goold, Hinchinbrook, Lindeman, Molle, Newry and Orpheus islands.

On the mainland, the southern section of Eungella National Park near Mackay is a popular destination for daytrippers and campers. Visitors can set up camp beside Broken River, go bushwalking or try spotting a platypus in the river. North-west of Eungella is the large Eungella Dam, a popular camping and fishing venue for barramundi. About 50 km north of Mackay, Cape Hillsborough National Park has scenic walking tracks to lookouts, picnic areas and broad beaches. Other highly recommended camping spots on the mainland include Mission Beach Caravan Park south of Innisfail, Ball Bay Campground north of Mackay and Platypus Bush Camp at Finch Hatton Gorge.

CAMPSITES LOCATED IN PARKS AND RESERVES

ABERGOWRIE STATE FOREST

The tropical rainforests and pine plantations of Abergowrie State Forest, in the Herbert River Valley, lie about 45 km west of Ingham via Trebonne. Visitors enjoy the 1.6 km return Rainforest Walk (30 min) and the 3 km return Creek Walk (1 hr), where you can cool off in pools along Broadwater Creek near the Wet Tropics World Heritage Area boundary. Advance bookings are required for camping.

How to book: NPRSR 13 7468 www.nprsr.qld.gov.au
Permits: camping permit required *Road conditions:* 13 1905

416 Broadwater camping area

Endangered riparian rainforest lines the clear waters of Broadwater Creek, and open eucalypt forest dominates the visitor areas in Broadwater campground, 47 km west of Ingham and 16 km of unsealed road from the forest entrance. This is a cool and pleasant place for family camping, with a large grassy picnic area and plenty of wildlife, including the vulnerable rufous owl and the spectacular, but endangered, southern cassowary. Bring old sneakers if you want to take a dip – poisonous bullrout fish inhabit the creek. You need to treat or boil the water before use, and bring firewood. Check road conditions during the wet season (Dec–Apr), when roads may be closed temporarily, and drive carefully, as logging trucks also use access roads. **Map refs:** 418 B1, 461 M9

BOWLING GREEN BAY NATIONAL PARK

A spectacular nature reserve with more than 55 000 ha of rugged landscapes, Bowling Green Bay National Park is 28 km south of Townsville. Highlights include the Alligator Creek area, a popular spot for family picnics, and for serious hikers there's the challenging 17 km return track to Alligator Falls, with stunning mountain views along the way. Advance bookings are required for camping.

How to book: NPRSR 13 7468 www.nprsr.qld.gov.au
Permits: camping permit required

417 Alligator Creek camping area

Just 600 m from the main access gate, near the day-use picnic area, this site is a great base to explore around the creek area, hike along the Alligator Falls track, or go fishing – all the while keeping an eye out for wildlife such as rock wallabies and brush-tail possums. The campground is only suitable for tents and small campervans. Gas BBQs are located in the day-use picnic area. Tap water needs to be boiled or treated before use. This camping area can be very crowded in holiday periods. Note: the main gate to the camping and picnic area is open 6.30am to 6.30pm daily. **Map refs:** 418 C2, 458 G1, 461 N12

418 Alligator Falls camping area (walk-in camping)

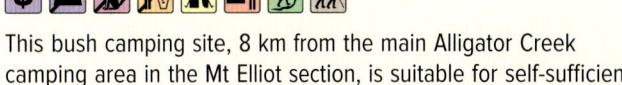

This bush camping site, 8 km from the main Alligator Creek camping area in the Mt Elliot section, is suitable for self-sufficient campers only. It has room for a maximum of 6 campers. Bring water and a gas/fuel stove. **Map refs:** 418 C3, 458 G1, 461 N12

419 Barratta Creek camping area (bush camping)

This bush camping site, near the town of Jerona in the Bowling Green Bay section, is suitable for self-sufficient campers only. There are 7 campsites, and 8 campers are permitted per site. It can only be accessed by 4WD. Check tide times before embarking and avoid travelling 2 hrs either side of high tide. Bring water and a gas/fuel stove. **Map refs:** 418 C3, 458 H1, 461 O12

420 Bush camping areas (walk-in camping)

Remote bush camping in undefined spots is available for experienced and self-sufficient hikers in the Mt Elliot and Mt Cleveland areas of the park. There is a limit of 6 hikers per group and hikers must set up camp at least 1 km from other camping areas and other groups. Bring water and a gas/fuel stove. **Map refs:** 418 C3, 458 G1, 461 N12

421 Cockatoo Creek camping area (walk-in camping)

This bush camping site, 2 km from the main Alligator Creek camping area in the Mt Elliot section, is suitable for self-sufficient campers only. It has room for a maximum of 6 campers. Bring water and a gas/fuel stove. **Map refs:** 418 C2, 458 G1, 461 N12

422 Cocoa Creek camping area (bush camping)

This bush camping area, off Cape Cleveland Rd in the Cape Cleveland section, is suitable for self-sufficient campers only. There are 7 campsites, and 8 campers are permitted per site. It can be accessed by conventional vehicles only during dry weather. Bring water and a gas/fuel stove. **Map refs:** 418 C2, 458 G1, 461 N11

423 Salmon Creek camping area (bush camping)

This bush camping area, 6 km along the beach from the town of Cungulla in the Cape Cleveland section, is suitable for self-sufficient campers only. There are 6 campsites, and 8 campers are permitted per site. It can only be accessed by 4WD. Check tide times before embarking and avoid travelling 2 hrs either side of high tide. Bring water and a gas/fuel stove. **Map refs: 418 C2, 458 H1, 461 N12**

BRAMPTON ISLANDS NATIONAL PARK

Located 32 km north of Mackay, Brampton Islands National Park encompasses 2 islands, Brampton and Carlisle. These traditional lands of the Indigenous Ngaro people are rich with wildlife, from open eucalypt forests on the islands' ridges to the fringing coral reefs. Beware of marine stingers Oct–May. Advance bookings are required for camping.

How to book: NPRSR 13 7468 www.nprsr.qld.gov.au
Permits: camping permit required

424 Neils camping area (boat-based camping)

Bush camping is permitted on Carlisle Island, at the entrance to the Whitsunday Passage. Toilets and picnic shelters are the only facilities, so bring all self-sufficient supplies. The surrounding coral reefs provide excellent snorkelling but beware of marine stingers Oct–May. **Map refs: 418 E4, 459 K5**

BROAD SOUND ISLANDS NATIONAL PARK

The 116 km long string of 48 islands that comprises Broad Sound Islands National Park stretches east from Flock Pigeon Island, 116 km south-east of Mackay. The park protects a variety of wildlife and environments, including most of the flatback turtle's east coast nesting habitat. Access to Broad Sound Islands is by private boat only; the more far-flung islands are rarely patrolled and should be tackled only by seasoned sailors. Advance bookings are required for camping.

How to book: NPRSR 13 7468 www.nprsr.qld.gov.au
Permits: camping permit required

425 Aquila Island camping area (boat-based camping)

Camping is permitted on Aquila Island, 16 km north-east of the town of Clairview. There are no facilities provided and fires are prohibited, so bring all self-sufficient camping gear, including drinking water, rubbish bags and a gas/fuel stove. **Map refs: 418 E5, 459 L7**

426 Flock Pigeon Island camping area (boat-based camping)

Camping is permitted on Flock Pigeon Island, 3 km east of Clairview. There are no facilities provided and fires are prohibited, so bring all self-sufficient camping gear, including drinking water, rubbish bags and a gas/fuel stove. **Map refs: 418 E5, 459 L8**

427 Hexham Island camping area (boat-based camping)

Camping is permitted on Hexham Island, 35 km north-east of Stanage Bay, adjacent to Shields Island. There are no facilities provided and fires are prohibited, so bring all self-sufficient camping gear, including drinking water, rubbish bags and a gas/fuel stove. Note: as this campsite is remote, bring extra supplies and plan for all eventualities. **Map refs: 418 E5, 459 M8**

428 High Peak Island camping area (boat-based camping)

Camping is permitted on High Peak Island, 180 km south-east of Mackay. There are no facilities provided and fires are prohibited, so bring all self-sufficient camping gear, including drinking water, rubbish bags and a gas/fuel stove. Note: as this campsite is very remote, bring extra supplies and plan for all eventualities. **Map refs: 418 F5, 459 N8**

429 Shields Island camping area (boat-based camping)

Camping is permitted on Shields Island, 35 km north-east of Stanage Bay, adjacent to Hexham Island. There are no facilities provided and fires are prohibited, so bring all self-sufficient camping gear, including drinking water, rubbish bags and a gas/fuel stove. Note: as this campsite is remote, bring extra supplies and plan for all eventualities. **Map refs: 418 E5, 459 M8**

BYFIELD CONSERVATION PARK

Adjacent to Byfield National Park, this conservation park is noted for its coastal scenery, enormous sand dunes and eucalypt woodlands. It is accessible by 4WD through Byfield National Park's main section. A popular walking activity is the Five Rocks track (up to 2 hr return) that follows Findlays Creek and leads to the beach. Advance bookings are required for camping.

How to book: NPRSR 13 7468 www.nprsr.qld.gov.au
Permits: camping permit required

430 Five Rocks camping area

This is the only campground in both the Byfield National Park and Conservation Park with facilities; generators are permitted. There are 12 numbered campsites; timber pallets are available to use as a camp surface. It is 28 km east of Water Park Creek and accessed through the national park's main section; a 4WD vehicle is required. From here you can go fishing or take a dip in the surf. The water should be boiled or treated before drinking. **Map refs: 418 F6, 459 N9**

BYFIELD NATIONAL PARK

Known for its massive sand dunes that stretch up to 6 km inland, Byfield National Park protects 15 000 ha of scenic and diverse landscapes. It is about 70 km north-east of Rockhampton and 43 km north of Yeppoon. Experienced bushwalkers have a range of signed trails to explore, and fishing enthusiasts can throw a line in at Nine Mile Beach, Water Park Point or at the end of Sandy Point Rd. Advance bookings are required for camping.

How to book: NPRSR 13 7468 www.nprsr.qld.gov.au
Permits: camping permit required

431 Nine Mile Beach camping area (bush camping)

Nile Mile Beach is a top spot for fishing, but there are no facilities at this campground so you need to be totally self-sufficient. Accessible by 4WD or boat, it is 27 km east of Water Park Creek and about 6 km south of the Nine Mile Access Track. Small generators (65 dBA or quieter) are permitted between 8am and 7pm. **Map refs:** 418 F6, 459 N10

432 Scouts camping area (bush camping)

Accessible only by boat or walking at low tide from Corio Bay carpark, this small campground on the northern side of Corio Bay has room for just 20 campers and has no facilities. It's suitable for self-sufficient campers only; small generators (65 dBA or quieter) are permitted between 8am and 7pm. Note: if you're walking along the beach, it takes about 2 hrs to reach the campground. **Map refs:** 418 F6, 459 N10

BYFIELD STATE FOREST

Go bushwalking through magnificent rainforests, view rare wildlife or have a relaxing picnic by the creek – Byfield State Forest offers a beautiful natural setting for a range of recreational activities. About 34 km north of Yeppoon, the forest has scenic easy-to-moderate walking tracks, some good spots for fishing, and excellent day-use areas. Note: swimming is not permitted in some areas, as estuarine crocodiles have been seen in Water Park Creek. Advance bookings are required for camping.

How to book: NPRSR 13 7468 www.nprsr.qld.gov.au
Permits: camping permit required

433 Red Rock camping area

Camp under the pine trees at this grassy campground 1 km along the turn-off signed on Byfield Rd, just before the Byfield Forestry office. Small generators (65 dBA or quieter) are permitted between 8am and 7pm and open fires are allowed in existing fireplaces – bring your own wood. Water is available here but must be boiled or treated before drinking. Note: this is the only campground in the forest that allows pets; dogs must be on a leash at all times. **Map refs:** 418 F6, 459 M10

434 Upper Stony camping area

Adjacent to Stony Creek, this campground is in a great location close to swimming and bushwalking. There are 18 numbered sites and some are suitable for vans and camper trailers. Automated BBQs are in the day-use area or you can use the built-in fireplaces (bring your own milled timber). The campground is 11 km from Byfield Rd, along a gravel road turn-off. Bring plenty of insect repellent and sunscreen, and treat or boil the water before drinking. **Map refs:** 418 F6, 459 M10

435 Water Park Creek camping area

Water Park Creek has 14 secluded walk-in campsites close to the Bowenia rainforest bushwalking circuit (1.2 km return, 2 hrs). Swimming is not permitted here. The campground is 4 km from the turn-off signed on Byfield Rd, and a short walk from the carpark area. Small generators (65 dBA or quieter) are permitted between 8am and 7pm; bring your own firewood as well as a gas/fuel stove. The water should be boiled or treated before use. The nearest shop is in Byfield township, 2 km north of the turn-off to Water Park Creek. **Map refs:** 418 F6, 459 M9

CAPE HILLSBOROUGH NATIONAL PARK

Cape Hillsborough National Park is renowned for its beautiful beaches nestled between rocky headlands. Rhyolite boulders are scattered over the sand, the result of volcanic activity millions of years ago. Home to the Yuipera people for thousands of years, the cape got its European name in 1770 when Captain James Cook named it after the Earl of Hillsborough. Advance bookings are required for camping at Smalleys Beach.

How to book: Cape Hillsborough Nature Resort (07) 4959 0152 www.capehillsboroughresort.com.au; or NPRSR 13 7468 www.nprsr.qld.gov.au for Smalleys Beach camping area
Permits: camping permit required for Smalleys Beach

436 Cape Hillsborough Nature Resort

This private enterprise tucked away inside Cape Hillsborough National Park offers a pocket of modern amenities and creature comforts while surrounded by wilderness. There's a laundry, internet access and book exchange, as well as unparalleled access to the park's walking trails. To get there, turn off the Bruce Hwy at Yakapari, Kuttabul or Mt Ossa and follow the signs. **Map refs:** 418 D4, 459 K5

437 Smalleys Beach camping area

The gravel road to Smalleys Beach is signposted about 6 km along Cape Hillsborough Rd, 50 km north-west of Mackay.

The campground offers plenty of shade under eucalypt trees and there are 11 numbered sites. The nearby Great Barrier Reef Marine Park permits boating and fishing, but beware of estuarine crocodiles, box jellyfish and marine stingers, which are common Oct–May. Generators are not permitted at the campground. Fires are allowed in off-ground fire containers only – bring your own wood – but a gas/fuel stove is preferred. **Map refs:** 418 D4, 459 K5

CAPE PALMERSTON NATIONAL PARK

The rocky headlands, rainforests and sand dunes of Cape Palmerston National Park lie 115 km south-east of Mackay. There are 3 bush campgrounds in the park, some great spots for fishing, and you can walk to Cape Palmerston for beautiful views of Northumberland Isles and Mt Funnel. Access is by 4WD only via Cape Palmerston Rd, off Greenhill Rd from Ilbilbie, on the Bruce Hwy. Advance bookings are required for camping.

How to book: NPRSR 13 7468 www.nprsr.qld.gov.au
Permits: camping permit required

438 Bush camping areas

Bush camping is permitted in the fore dunes along the eastern coast of Cape Palmerston. There are no facilities or amenities provided, so bring all self-sufficient camping gear, including drinking water, rubbish bags and a raised fire container/brazier – bring your own wood – or a gas/fuel stove. **Map refs:** 418 E5, 459 L6

439 Cape Creek campsite

Cape Creek is to the south-west of Cape Palmerston. For self-sufficient campers, it is accessible by 4WD only via a sandy track. Fires are permitted if you bring your own raised fire container/brazier – bring your own wood; gas/fuel stoves are recommended. **Map refs:** 418 E5, 459 K6

440 Windmill Bay campsite

This basic site for self-sufficient campers is south of Cape Palmerston on the eastern edge of the park. Access is by 4WD only via a sandy track. Fires are permitted in raised fire containers/braziers – bring your own wood – but gas/fuel stoves are preferred. **Map refs:** 418 E5, 459 K7

CAPE UPSTART NATIONAL PARK

Known for its granite outcrops and sandy beaches, Cape Upstart National Park is a large headland north of Bowen and south of Ayr. With no access for vehicles, camping is boat-based only. There are ramps at Elliot River near Guthalungra and at Molongle Creek, south of Gumlu. Advance bookings are required for camping.

How to book: NPRSR 13 7468 www.nprsr.qld.gov.au
Permits: camping permit required

441 Coconut Beach camping area (boat-based camping)

Coconut Beach has no facilities and suits self-sufficient campers. Access is by boat only; beware of marine stingers Oct–May and beware of estuarine crocodiles year-round. The campground is surrounded by the waters of the Great Barrier Reef Marine Park; anglers should check zoning and regulations before casting off. **Map refs:** 418 D3, 459 I2

CATHU STATE FOREST

Take a scenic drive to the Clarke Range Lookout, enjoy a relaxing bush picnic or simply sit back and enjoy views of the Whitsunday islands – Cathu State Forest has much to offer campers and daytrippers. Cathu is 72 km north of Mackay or 51 km south of Proserpine, and Jaxut is 12 km off the Bruce Hwy.

Who to contact: NPRSR 13 7468 www.nprsr.qld.gov.au
Permits: camping permit required *Camping fees:* fees can be paid and permits acquired at the self-registration station

442 Jaxut camping area

This camping area is next to Pandanus Creek at Jaxut, about 200 m past the old forest station. Access is via the Cathu–O'Connell River Rd, a very steep road suitable for small caravans and camper trailers only. Campers should bring firewood and water, or treat/boil the tap water provided. Cathu State Forest is known as a particularly good location for birdwatching, with more than 100 species inhabiting the area. **Map refs:** 418 D4, 459 J5

CHARON POINT CONSERVATION PARK

Located 44 km north of Marlborough, Charon Point Conservation Park encompasses the southern side of the mouth of the Styx River, famous for its massive tides and fast tidal currents. These features make it an attractive spot for professional fishers and crabbers. Advance bookings are required for camping.

How to book: NPRSR 13 7468 www.nprsr.qld.gov.au
Permits: camping permit required

443 Beach camping area (bush camping)

Bush camping for up to 6 self-sufficient campers is available on the beachfront at the northern tip of Charon Point. No facilities are provided, so bring your own drinking water, rubbish bags and firewood or (preferably) a gas/fuel stove. **Map refs:** 418 E5, 459 L8

444 Boat Ramp camping area (bush camping)

As its name might suggest, Boat Ramp camping area is located near the beach next to one of Charon Point's 2 boat ramps. Up to 6 self-sufficient campers can stay here. No facilities are provided, so bring your own drinking water, rubbish bags and firewood or (preferably) a gas/fuel stove. **Map refs:** 418 E5, 459 L8

445 Meadow Camp (bush camping)

Meadow campsite is located slightly inland, to the south of Boat Ramp campsite, but still very close to its own boat launch. Up to 6 self-sufficient campers can stay here. No facilities are provided, so bring your own drinking water, rubbish bags and firewood or (preferably) a gas/fuel stove. **Map refs:** 418 E5, 459 L8

CONWAY NATIONAL PARK

Bushwalking trails through beautiful, lush rainforests and beach tracks with scenic ocean views can be explored in Conway National Park. In particular, the Mt Rooper track has excellent views of the Whitsunday Passage; allow 2.5 hrs for the 5.4 km circuit. To reach the national park from Airlie Beach, follow Shute Harbour Rd south-east for 6.5 km. Conway State Forest was incorporated into Conway National Park in July 2012, and the park now contains the entirety of the Whitsunday Great Walk, a challenging 30 km, 3-day, 1-way walk for experienced hikers and campers. Advance bookings are required for camping.

How to book: NPRSR 13 7468 www.nprsr.qld.gov.au
Permits: camping permit required

446 Swamp Bay camping area (walk-in camping)

Walk 2.1 km from the Swamp Bay/Mt Rooper carpark to this campground overlooking Daydream Island (accessible only by foot or boat). A pit toilet, shelter shed and picnic tables are the only facilities, so you need to bring all self-sufficient goods and equipment. Keen bushwalkers should check out the Swamp Bay walking track (2.1 km, 1 hr), which links to the scenic Mt Rooper track. Beach fishing is permitted at Swamp Bay and Coral Beach (check the regulations). **Map refs:** 418 D3, 459 K3

Whitsunday Great Walk

Please note that campsites are listed in alphabetical order, not track order. Refer to the map on p. 418 for further information.

447 Bloodwood camping area (walk-in camping)

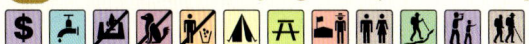

Hikers on the Whitsunday Great Walk can camp at this site, 11.5 km (5–6 hrs) from Repulse Creek camp and 8.5 km from the end of the walk at Airlie Beach. The track from Repulse Creek follows a ridge to the summit of Mt Hayward and continues to Bloodwood Camp, with picturesque views beyond Jubilee Pocket to the Whitsunday islands. Bring a gas/fuel stove. **Map refs:** 418 D3, 459 J3

448 Bush camping areas (walk-in camping)

Experienced and self-sufficient hikers looking for a little extra challenge on the Whitsunday Great Walk can camp at 2 bush

campsites, 1.8 and 3 km beyond Repulse Creek campsite (or 11.3 and 10.1 km respectively from Bloodwood campsite). No facilities are supplied, so bring your own water and a gas/fuel stove. **Map refs:** 418 D3, 459 J4

449 Repulse Creek camping area (walk-in camping)

Experienced hikers and campers can walk 8.3 km from the Brandy Creek carpark along the Whitsunday Great Walk to reach this site (allow 3.5–4.5 hr). Along the way, look out for rare wildlife such as the buff-breasted paradise-kingfisher and leaf-tail gecko. Toilets, picnic tables and tank water are the only facilities; bring all self-sufficient goods and equipment. **Map refs:** 418 D3, 459 J4

CREDITON STATE FOREST

Protecting stately rose gums and relics of gold mining from the 1880s, Crediton State Forest possesses a quiet rural charm. The Mackay Highlands Great Walk passes through this forest. Crediton is 80 km west of Mackay and 8 km south of Eungella. Advance bookings are required for camping.

How to book: NPRSR 13 7468 www.nprsr.qld.gov.au
Permits: camping permit required

450 Crediton Hall camping area

This spacious campsite on a grassy hill, 14.7 km south-east of Eungella, offers camping for up to 24 people. To reach it, turn off Eungella Dam Rd 8 km south of Eungella and follow Crediton Loop Rd 6.7 km to the camping area. Crediton Hall is a designated campsite on the Mackay Highlands Great Walk, and is 11.2 km from Fern Flat camping area and 19.5 km from Denham Range camping area. The water must be boiled or treated before drinking. **Map refs:** 418 D4, 459 J5

451 Denham Range camping area

This camping area, near the border of Homevale National Park, offers cooling breezes and excellent views from its ridge-top location. There are few facilities, so bring self-sufficient camping equipment, including water (or boil/treat the water provided) and a gas/fuel stove. To reach it, turn off Eungella Dam Rd 14.7 km south of Eungella and follow Cockies Creek Rd 23.7 km to the campsite. Denham Range is a designated campsite on the Mackay Highlands Great Walk, and is 19.5 km from Crediton Hall camping area and 16.2 km from Moonlight Range camping area. **Map refs:** 418 D4, 459 J6

452 The Diggings camping area

The forest here still contains relics from goldmining exploration during the 1880s. Self-sufficient campers can use this site near Eungella Dam Rd. There are no facilities, so bring drinking water, rubbish bags and firewood or a gas/fuel stove. **Map refs:** 418 D4, 459 J5

DALRYMPLE NATIONAL PARK

Situated 42 km north of Charters Towers, Dalrymple National Park's main feature is the Burdekin River, which provides a seasonal habitat for waterbirds and makes the spot ideal for birdwatchers. The old Dalrymple township, one of the first inland settlements in northern Australia, can also be found in the park. Advance bookings are required for camping.

How to book: NPRSR 13 7468 www.nprsr.qld.gov.au
Permits: camping permit required

453 Burdekin River camping area (bush camping)

Camp on the banks of the Burdekin River here, just 700 m from the entrance to the park. This site suits self-sufficient campers only; there are no facilities. Open fires are prohibited and generators are not permitted. Note: the road is often impassable for conventional vehicles in wet weather, Nov–Mar. **Map refs:** 418 B3, 458 F2, 461 M12

DRYANDER NATIONAL PARK

Accessible by boat from Airlie Beach or Dingo Beach, this national park overlooks the Whitsunday islands and Great Barrier Reef Marine Park. Visitors should check fishing and boating permissions in the marine park and beware of marine stingers Oct–May. Advance bookings are required for camping.

How to book: NPRSR 13 7468 www.nprsr.qld.gov.au
Permits: camping permit required

454 Grimstone Point camping area (boat-based camping)

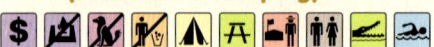

This low-key, quiet campground is accessible by boat only. Pit toilets and picnic tables are the only facilities here so bring all self-sufficient goods and equipment (including insect repellent). **Map refs:** 418 D3, 459 J3

EUNGELLA NATIONAL PARK

In the rugged Clarke Range, high above the surrounding plains, this mountainous national park is rent by deep gorges and contains large tracts of both tropical and subtropical rainforest. Isolated from similar forests for at least 30 000 years, this important rainforest refuge supports around 860 plant species and some unique wildlife, including the critically endangered Eungella day frog, the rare Eungella tinkerfrog and the Eungella honeyeater. Advance bookings are required for camping.

How to book: NPRSR 13 7468 www.nprsr.qld.gov.au
Permits: camping permit required

455 Fern Flat camping area (walk-in camping)

This campground, 5 km south of Eungella, is just 600 m from the carpark and picnic area at Broken River. The site has toilets and water (which must be boiled or treated before use), but you'll need to visit the picnic area for information, BBQs and picnic tables. It is a designated campsite on the Mackay

Highlands Great Walk, 10 km from Pine Grove carpark, the walk's trailhead, and 11.2 km from Crediton Hall camping area. **Map refs:** 418 D4, 459 J5

FAMILY ISLANDS NATIONAL PARK

Part of the Great Barrier Reef World Heritage Area, this national park embraces a group of islands off the coast north of Cardwell, accessible via boat from Mission Beach. The park is about 130 km south-east of Cairns. The Bandjin and Djiru Aboriginal people are the traditional owners of the land. Advance bookings are required for camping.

How to book: NPRSR 13 7468 www.nprsr.qld.gov.au
Permits: camping permit required

456 Coombe Island camping area (boat-based camping)

Fancy staying at your own exclusive, secluded bush campground? This site, about 13 km east of Tully Heads, only permits 1 group at a time. There are, however, no facilities here so you'll need to be completely self-sufficient. Note: private boat access is from Mission Beach. **Map refs:** 418 B1, 461 M8

457 Dunk Island camping area

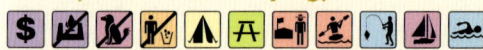

This campground is on the west coast of Dunk Island, with 9 designated sites provided. Dunk has 13 km of scenic walking tracks; you can trek through rainforests, complete a circuit of the island or enjoy beautiful views from the summit of Mt Kootaloo. The island also offers excellent swimming and snorkelling opportunities. Note: at the time of printing this campsite was closed owing to cyclone damage. The NPRSR website will advise when the site has re-opened. **Map refs:** 418 B1, 461 M8

458 Wheeler Island camping area (boat-based camping)

Located 12 km east of Tully Heads, Wheeler Island is accessible by private boat from Mission Beach. The campground's only facilities are pit toilets and picnic tables, so campers will need to bring all self-sufficient goods and equipment, including drinking water and a gas/fuel stove. **Map refs:** 418 B1, 461 M8

GIRRAMAY NATIONAL PARK

Girramay National Park lies in the foothills of the Kirrama Range, and consists of 2 sections: Edmund Kennedy, 5 km north of Cardwell, and Murray Falls, 41 km north-west of Cardwell. One of the region's prettiest waterfalls, the 10 m Murray Falls can be admired from a river boardwalk leading from the camping area. The campground is signposted off the Bruce Hwy, 14 km south of Tully. Advance bookings are required for camping.

How to book: NPRSR 13 7468 www.nprsr.qld.gov.au
Permits: camping permit required

459 Murray Falls camping area

Campers here can enjoy the 930 m walk through a rainforest gully that leads into open forest and finishes with amazing views over the falls and Murray Valley. The first 75 m section of the boardwalk at the top end of the campground is wheelchair accessible. There is swimming at the day-use area. Bring drinking water and firewood. **Map refs:** 418 B1, 461 L9

GIRRINGUN NATIONAL PARK

Girringun National Park, part of the traditional lands of the Warrgamaygan people, comprises 4 sections: Wallaman Falls, Mt Fox, Blencoe Falls and Dalrymple Gap Walking Track. The Wallaman Falls section in the Herbert River Valley is the most accessible; Wallaman Falls plunges 300 m off the Seaview Range, making it the longest single-drop waterfall in Australia. The gorge here supports rainforest with palms, umbrella trees and figs, while around the rim grow casuarinas, eucalypts and grasstrees. Camping is not permitted along Dalrymple Gap Walking Track; the nearest campsite is Broadwater camping area in Abergowrie State Forest. The Wet Tropics Great Walk, a network of 5 connected walking tracks, winds through this park. Advance bookings are required for camping.

How to book: NPRSR 13 7468 www.nprsr.qld.gov.au
Permits: camping permit required

460 Blencoe Falls camping area

This remote site for totally self-sufficient campers is set beside Blencoe Creek, 81 km west of Cardwell. 4WD is recommended, but stay on the marked tracks, as damaging vegetation can incur penalties. Bring drinking water and firewood. To get here, travel along Kirrama Range Rd, off Kennedy Creek Rd from the Bruce Hwy at Kennedy. Blencoe Falls is a designated campsite on the Wet Tropics Great Walk; it is 10.5 km from Blanket Creek camping area on the Juwun and Jambal walks. **Map refs:** 418 B1, 461 L9

461 Wallaman Falls camping area

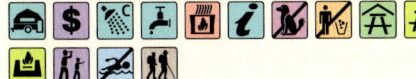

This campground is beside the Stony Creek picnic area – a great place for spotting platypus. It's 51 km west of Ingham, off the Abergowrie Rd at Trebonne. Check out the Banggurru circuit walk while you're here, an easy 1 km track, or try the 4 km Djyinda walk. Bring your own firewood or, preferably, a gas/fuel stove. Water here must be boiled or treated before use. **Map refs:** 418 B2, 461 L10

Wet Tropics Great Walk

Please note that campsites are listed in alphabetical order, not track order. Refer to the map on p. 418 for further information.

462 Blanket Creek camping area (walk-in camping)

This bush campsite for self-sufficient hikers by the Herbert River is shaded by she-oaks. No facilities are provided and open fires are prohibited, so bring all self-sufficient gear, including drinking water, rubbish bags and a gas/fuel stove. It is 10.5 km from Blencoe Falls camping area and 33.5 km from Yamanie camping area on the Juwun and Jambal walks. Note: do not swim in the river, as crocodiles inhabit it. **Map refs:** 418 B1, 461 L9

460 Blencoe Falls camping area

See opposite.

463 Herbert River Gorge camping area (walk-in camping)

Intrepid hikers taking the strenuous Juwun walk can camp anywhere along the 26.5 km stretch of the Herbert River Gorge between Blanket Creek and Orange Tree. No facilities are provided and open fires are prohibited, so bring all self-sufficient gear, including drinking water, rubbish bags and a gas/fuel stove. Note: do not swim in the river, as crocodiles inhabit it. **Map refs:** 418 B1, 461 L9

464 Pack Trail camping area (walk-in camping)

This campsite on the Buujan Quiinbiira and Djagany walks offers sweeping views over the Herbert River Valley, but few facilities aside from composting toilets. Open fires are prohibited, so bring all self-sufficient gear, including drinking water, rubbish bags and a gas/fuel stove. It is 15.2 km from Yamanie camping area, 23.3 km from Wallaman Falls camping area and 13.9 km from Stony Creek camping area. **Map refs:** 418 B1, 461 L9

465 Stony Creek camping area (walk-in camping)

This campsite on the Djagany and Gugigugi walks is in open woodland beside Stony Creek. There are no facilities except for a composting toilet and open fires are prohibited, so bring all self-sufficient gear, including drinking water, rubbish bags and a gas/fuel stove. It is 13.9 km from Pack Trail camping area, 18.7 km from Yamanie camping area and 19.6 km from the Henrietta gate pick-up point. **Map refs:** 418 B1, 461 L9

461 Wallaman Falls camping area

See opposite.

466 Yamanie camping area (bush camping)

Bush camping along the banks of the Herbert River is permitted at this site, 54 km west of Ingham. Access to the area is by 4WD or via the Wet Tropics Great Walk only, and campers need to be completely self-sufficient. Fires and generators are not permitted and no rubbish bins are provided. The campsite functions as a collection point for hikers on the Wet Tropics Great Walk, and is 7 km from the southern end of Herbert River Gorge camping area at Orange Tree on the Juwun walk, 15.2 km from Pack

Trail camping area on the Buujan Quiinbiira walk and 18.7 km from Stony Creek camping area on the Gugigugi walk. Note: estuarine crocodiles inhabit the waters surrounding Yamanie camping area. **Map refs: 418 B1, 461 L9**

GLOUCESTER ISLANDS NATIONAL PARK

One of the most remote national parks in the Whitsunday region, the Gloucester Islands are east of Bowen and north of Airlie Beach. Camping is allowed at 3 of the islands – Gloucester, Saddleback and Armit. To get here, catch a commercial or private boat from Shute Harbour at Airlie Beach or Dingo Beach. Advance bookings are required for camping.

How to book: NPRSR 13 7468 www.nprsr.qld.gov.au
Permits: camping permit required

467 Armit Island camping area (boat-based camping)

This campground in the south-west corner of the island has space for 12 totally self-sufficient campers. Access to the southern beach and Little Armit Island is prohibited Oct–Mar each year, for regeneration. Remember to go slow when boating, report marine strandings and not collect coral or shells. **Map refs: 418 D3, 459 J3**

468 Bona Bay camping area (boat-based camping)

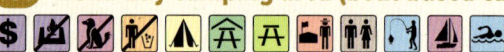

This large shaded campground, with beach views, is on the south-west side of Gloucester Island. The site can hold up to 36 campers, making it suitable for large groups, but you need to be completely self-sufficient. The surrounding waters are part of the Great Barrier Reef World Heritage Area; some fishing and collecting activities are not permitted. **Map refs: 418 D3, 459 J3**

469 East Side Bay camping area (boat-based camping)

This site is on the east side of Gloucester Island between 2 rocky headlands and adjacent to a seasonal freshwater lagoon. It's a small campground suitable for a maximum of 6 people and there are no facilities. **Map refs: 418 D3, 459 J3**

470 Saddleback Island camping area (boat-based camping)

On the western side of Saddleback Island, this campground has space for 12 people. The only facilities are picnic tables, so you need to bring all self-sufficient goods and equipment. **Map refs: 418 D3, 459 J3**

GOOLD ISLAND NATIONAL PARK

Goold Island's close proximity to Cardwell (17 km north-east) makes it a good choice for camping. The surrounding waters are great for waterskiing and boating, but be wary, as estuarine crocodiles are present in the area. Fishing is not permitted in the freshwater creeks on the island. Access to Goold Island is by private boat or ferry service from Cardwell. Advance bookings are required for camping.

How to book: NPRSR 13 7468 www.nprsr.qld.gov.au
Permits: camping permit required

471 Southern Beach camping area (boat-based camping)

Intrepid adventurers can reach this secluded spot (up to 6 campers) on the east side of Goold Island only by sea kayak – there are no ferry services and powered boats are forbidden. There are no facilities and open fires are prohibited, so bring all self-sufficient gear, including drinking water, rubbish bags and a gas/fuel stove. **Map refs: 418 B1, 461 M9**

472 The Spit (Western Beach) camping area (boat-based camping)

This site on the island's west coast has a maximum capacity of 50 campers; the surface is sand and grass and there are some shady trees. Walkers can attempt the beach walk around the coastline of Goold Island, extending for 13 km (5 hr), at low tide only. Note: generators are not permitted at the campground. Bring drinking water and a gas/fuel stove, as the BBQ should not be relied upon. **Map refs: 418 B1, 461 M9**

473 Wilderness Cove camping area (boat-based camping)

Boaties will relish this secluded beach campsite, accessible only to private boats (no ferry services). There's room for 12 campers on the dunes here, but there are no facilities and open fires are prohibited, so bring all self-sufficient gear, including drinking water, rubbish bags and a gas/fuel stove. **Map refs: 418 B1, 461 M9**

HINCHINBROOK ISLAND NATIONAL PARK

A tropical island with stunning postcard-perfect scenery, Hinchinbrook is Australia's largest island national park. Off the north Queensland coast, 8 km east of Cardwell, Hinchinbrook is home to sweeping sandy beaches, rainforests and rugged mountains, dugongs, green turtles and other marine life. For hikers, one of the main attractions is the 32 km (3–5 day) Thorsborne Trail on the island's east coast. Advance bookings are required for camping.

How to book: NPRSR 13 7468 www.nprsr.qld.gov.au
Permits: camping permit required

474 Agnes Beach camping area (boat-based camping)

This campsite for self-sufficient campers, accessible only by boat, lies between Little Ramsay Bay and Zoe Bay. It is closed Apr–Sept to protect nesting seabirds. There are no facilities and fires are prohibited; bring all self-sufficient camping gear, including drinking water, rubbish bags and a gas/fuel stove. **Map refs: 418 B1, 461 M9**

475 Banksia Bay camping area (bush camping)

This campsite for self-sufficient campers, accessible only by boat or via the Thorsborne Trail, lies between Little Ramsay Bay and Zoe Bay, close to Agnes Beach. There are no facilities and fires are prohibited; bring all self-sufficient camping gear, including drinking water, rubbish bags and a gas/fuel stove. **Map refs:** 418 B1, 461 M9

476 Banshee Bay camping area (boat-based camping)

This campsite for self-sufficient campers, accessible only by boat, is on the north-east of the island, just south of Cape Sandwich. There are no facilities and fires are prohibited; bring all self-sufficient camping gear, including drinking water, rubbish bags and a gas/fuel stove. **Map refs:** 418 B1, 461 M9

477 Blacksand Beach camping area (boat-based camping)

This campsite for self-sufficient campers, accessible only by sea kayak, is at the southern end of Ramsay Bay, near Nina Peak. There are no facilities and fires are prohibited; bring all self-sufficient camping gear, including drinking water, rubbish bags and a gas/fuel stove. **Map refs:** 418 B1, 461 M9

478 George Point camping area

This campground for self-sufficient campers is 7.5 km south of Mulligan Falls at the southern trackhead of the Thorsborne Trail. It can also be accessed by private boat or sea kayak. Water can be collected from Mulligan Falls. A maximum 2-night stay applies. **Map refs:** 418 B2, 461 M9

479 The Haven (Scraggy Point) camping area (boat-based camping)

The Haven is on the west coast of the island in Hinchinbrook Channel. Access is by charter or private boat and there is a maximum 7-night stay. Bring all supplies for self-sufficient camping. **Map refs:** 418 B1, 461 M9

480 Mulligan Bay camping area (boat-based camping)

This campsite for self-sufficient campers, accessible only by boat, is on the south-east of the island, north of George Point. There are no facilities and fires are prohibited; bring all self-sufficient camping gear, including drinking water, rubbish bags and a gas/fuel stove. **Map refs:** 418 B2, 461 M9

481 North Macushla camping area (boat-based camping)

This campsite, on the north of the island, is a 100 m walk away from South Macushla, and has less well-developed facilities.

It can only be accessed by boat. Bring drinking water, rubbish bags and a gas/fuel stove. **Map refs:** 418 B1, 461 M9

482 North Zoe Bay camping area (boat-based camping)

The North Zoe Bay camping area has no facilities and there is a maximum 2-night stay. Access is by private boat only, subject to weather conditions. Bring all self-sufficient supplies. **Map refs:** 418 B1, 461 M9

483 South Macushla camping area (boat-based camping)

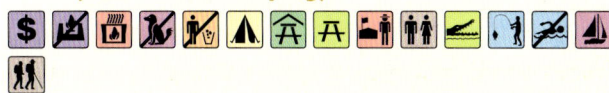

North and South Macushla camping areas are just 100 m apart in the north of the island, on the east coast of Missionary Bay, and are accessed by boat. A maximum 7-night stay applies here. Bring drinking water and a gas/fuel stove. **Map refs:** 418 B1, 461 M9

484 South Zoe Bay camping area

South Zoe Bay is 10.5 km south of Little Ramsay Bay and 7.5 km north of Mulligan Falls on the Thorsborne Trail. Water from the nearby creek must be boiled or treated before use. There is a maximum 2-night stay. Bring all self-sufficient supplies with you. **Map refs:** 418 B1, 461 M9

485 Sunken Reef Bay camping area (bush camping)

There are no facilities at this campground, on the Thorsborne Trail between South Zoe Bay and Mulligan Falls, so be prepared to be self-sufficient. Sunken Reef Bay can also be accessed by sea kayak. Water from the nearby creek must be boiled or treated before drinking. The maximum stay is 2 nights. **Map refs:** 418 B1, 461 M9

486 Sunset Beach camping area (boat-based camping)

This campsite on the north-east of the island, just west of Cape Sandwich, is accessible only by boat. There are no facilities and fires are prohibited; bring all self-sufficient camping gear, including drinking water, rubbish bags and a gas/fuel stove. **Map refs:** 418 B1, 461 M9

Thorsborne Trail

Please note that campsites are listed in alphabetical order, not track order. Refer to the map on p. 418 for further information.

475 Banksia Bay camping area (bush camping)
See opposite.

478 George Point camping area
See opposite.

487 Little Ramsay Bay camping area (walk-in camping)

This site on the Thorsborne Trail is 2.5 km south of Nina Bay camping area and 10.5 km north of South Zoe Bay camping area. Water from the nearby creek must be boiled or treated before drinking. A maximum 2-night stay applies. The site is gas/fuel stove only. **Map refs:** 418 B1, 461 M9

488 Mulligan Falls camping area (walk-in camping)

With a 1-night maximum stay, Mulligan Falls campground is 7.5 km south of South Zoe Bay camping area, 1 km south of Diamantina Creek and 7.5 km north of George Point camping area on the Thorsborne Trail. Water from the nearby creek must be boiled or treated before drinking. Bring all self-sufficient supplies. **Map refs:** 418 B2, 461 M9

489 Nina Bay camping area (walk-in camping)

Nina Bay has a maximum 2-night stay. It is 4 km south of the Ramsay Bay trackhead for the Thorsborne Trail and 2.5 km north of Little Ramsay Bay. Creek water must be boiled or treated before drinking. **Map refs:** 418 B1, 461 M9

484 South Zoe Bay camping area

See p. 427.

485 Sunken Reef Bay camping area (bush camping)

See p. 427.

HOMEVALE NATIONAL PARK

The dramatic landscape of Homevale National Park – full of cliffs, peaks and spires – was formed through volcanic activity over 30 million years ago. Older still are the fossil sites from the Permian period (225–280 million years ago) that the park protects. The park currently houses dry softwood scrub, open eucalypt forests and brigalow trees. Advance booking is required for camping.

How to book: NPRSR 13 7468 www.nprsr.qld.gov.au
Permits: camping permit required

490 Moonlight Dam camping area

This tranquil camping area lies at the edge of Moonlight Dam, 70 km south-west of Mackay. There are few facilities besides pit toilets and tap water (treat or boil before drinking), but it offers spectacular wildlife-watching as birds descend on the dam at dusk to drink. To get there, head north 6 km along the Peak Downs Hwy from Nebo, turn left onto Nebo–Glenden Rd, then right onto Turrawulla Rd, and follow this to the signed intersection for Moonlight Dam. Moonlight Dam is a designated campsite on the Mackay Highlands Great Walk and is 16.2 km from Denham Range camping area and 5.5 km to the Great Walk entry at Mt Britton. **Map refs:** 418 D4, 459 J6

LINDEMAN ISLANDS NATIONAL PARK

With humpback whales and dolphins often spotted from the shore, Lindeman Island is a tropical paradise surrounded by waters with stunning marine life that is sure to make your stay memorable. Lindeman Islands National Park is within the Great Barrier Reef Marine Park and is accessible via boat from Shute Harbour or Laguna Quays. Advance bookings are required for camping.

How to book: NPRSR 13 7468 www.nprsr.qld.gov.au
Permits: camping permit required

491 Boat Port camping area (boat-based camping)

Once used as a location for cleaning sailing vessels, this quiet campground on Lindeman Island with room for 12 campers is a world away from Club Med. Backing onto rainforest, there are no facilities here, so you'll need to bring all self-sufficient supplies, including drinking water and a gas/fuel stove, with you on the 25 km boat ride from Shute Harbour. There is, however, 20 km of walking tracks to explore – perfect for keen hikers. **Map refs:** 418 E4, 459 K4

492 Neck Bay camping area (boat-based camping)

A good stopover for kayakers, this small campground on the north-west side of Shaw Island has space for about 12 campers. All visitors must be completely self-sufficient, as there are no facilities at the site; bring drinking water and a gas/fuel stove. Shaw Island is approximately 40 km south-east of Shute Harbour. **Map refs:** 418 E4, 459 K4

MIA MIA STATE FOREST

Scenic drives, trail-bike tracks, creek swimming and peaceful bush camping are some of the attractions in Mia Mia State Forest, in the foothills of the Clarke Range west of Mackay. Access is by 4WD only; the gravel access road is closed in wet weather and high fire-danger periods.

Who to contact: QPWS Mackay (07) 4944 7800 *Permits:* camping permit required *Camping fees:* fees can be paid and permits acquired at QPWS Mackay

493 Captain's Crossing camping area

Camp beside lovely Teemburra Creek at this campground and picnic spot. There are no facilities; bring all self-sufficient supplies, including drinking water, rubbish bags and a gas/fuel stove. Access is by 4WD only. **Map refs:** 418 D4, 459 J6

MOLLE ISLANDS NATIONAL PARK

Lying 10 km from Airlie Beach off the Queensland coast, Molle Islands National Park has superb walking tracks and circuits with beautiful views and lookouts, picturesque swimming spots and, best of all, excellent snorkelling, particularly off South Molle Island. Access is by private or commercial boat from Airlie Beach or Shute Harbour. Advance bookings are required for camping.

How to book: NPRSR 13 7468 www.nprsr.qld.gov.au
Permits: camping permit required

494 Cockatoo Beach camping area (boat-based camping)

This campground is at the southern end of North Molle Island. The site holds a maximum of 24 people and suits self-sufficient campers only; bring water and a gas/fuel stove. **Map refs:** 418 D3, 459 K3

495 Denman Island camping area (boat-based camping)

Denman Island, east of South Molle Island, has a small campsite with a sand and rubble surface suitable for a maximum for 4 people. The island is 6.5 km east-north-east of Shute Harbour and can be accessed at low or high tide. Bring water and a gas/fuel stove. Note: fishing is not permitted. **Map refs:** 418 D3, 459 K3

496 Paddle Bay camping area (boat-based camping)

Overlooking Daydream Island, Paddle Bay is a well-shaded site connected to the 11.5 km walking track system at the north-western tip of South Molle Island, 500 m from Bauer Bay resort. The maximum number of campers is 12. Generators are not permitted; bring water and a gas/fuel stove. South Molle Island's Mt Jeffreys walk is 5.6 km return (3 hr) taking you to the island's highest point. **Map refs:** 418 D3, 459 K3

497 Planton Island camping area (boat-based camping)

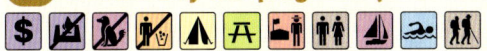

Planton Island, east of South Molle Island, has a small campground behind the beach for 4 people. Composting toilets are the only facilities, so you need to bring all self-sufficient supplies. **Map refs:** 418 D3, 459 K3

498 Sandy Bay, Long Island camping area (boat-based camping)

Not to be confused with the Sandy Bay campground on South Molle Island, this small campground on Long Island is close to a mangrove creek – bring insect repellent! Also bring all self-sufficient supplies, including drinking water and a gas/fuel stove. **Map refs:** 418 D4, 459 K4

499 Sandy Bay, South Molle Island camping area (boat-based camping)

Reachable only by boat at mid-high tide, this campground on the west side of South Molle Island is connected to the rest of the island by a 11.5 km walking track system. One of South Molle's most popular walks is the Spion Kop track, a 2 hr, 4.4 km return walk taking you through rainforest to spectacular

lookouts. The clearing can hold a maximum of 36 self-sufficient campers; bring water and a gas/fuel stove. Note: generators are not permitted. **Map refs:** 418 D3, 459 K3

500 Tancred Island camping area (boat-based camping)

Just 1 km from Shute Harbour, this campground has no facilities and suits self-sufficient campers only. A maximum of 6 campers per night is permitted. **Map refs:** 418 D3, 459 K3

NEWRY ISLANDS NATIONAL PARK

The exposed headlands, sandstone cliffs and sandy beaches of Newry Islands National Park lie off the coast of Seaforth, about 48 km north of Mackay. The islands are teeming with wildlife and its surrounding waters, home to dugongs, are part of the Great Barrier Reef World Heritage Area. Access to the park is via private boat only, with nearby boat ramps located at Seaforth, Mackay Marina, Murray Creek and Laguna Keys. Advance bookings are required for camping.

How to book: NPRSR 13 7468 www.nprsr.qld.gov.au
Permits: camping permit required

501 Newry Island camping area (boat-based camping)

This open campsite had a past life as the grounds of a resort, but now offers splendid camping for up to 36 people. Visitors can explore the remains of the resort or use the campsite as a base for exploring the other islands of the Newry group. Campers should take drinking water, rubbish bags and a gas/fuel stove. **Map refs:** 418 D4, 459 K5

502 Outer Newry Island camping area (boat-based camping)

This campground is on Outer Newry Island's south-west coast. If you're lucky you might see some amazing birdlife on the island, including brahminy kites, ospreys and white-bellied sea eagles. Campers should take fresh water, a gas/fuel stove and insect repellent. Note: generators are prohibited and all rubbish should be taken back to the mainland. **Map refs:** 418 D4, 459 K5

503 Tug's Point camping area (boat-based camping)

Camping is permitted on Rabbit Island's south-east coast, where you'll find a gas BBQ and a few other basic facilities such as picnic tables and a shelter shed. Bring drinking water. There's excellent wildlife-watching on the island – try spotlighting for possums at night. Note: insect repellent is a must for Rabbit Island. Beware of marine stingers and estuarine crocodiles. **Map refs:** 418 D4, 459 K5

NORTHUMBERLAND ISLANDS NATIONAL PARK

Ranging 45–90 km off the coast of Mackay, this undeveloped and little-known national park protects several islands of the Northumberland Islands group (which also includes the Percy Isles and Broad Sound Islands). Access is via private boat only, and should only be attempted by those with high levels of seagoing ability – there are significant navigational challenges. Advance bookings are required for camping.

How to book: NPRSR 13 7468 www.nprsr.qld.gov.au
Permits: camping permit required

504 North Beach camping area (boat-based camping)

This site on Curlew Island, 82 km south-east of Mackay, offers camping for up to 6 self-sufficient campers. There are no facilities, so bring all self-sufficient gear, including drinking water, rubbish bags and a gas/fuel stove. **Map refs:** 418 E5, 459 L7

**505 Prudhoe Island camping area
(boat-based camping)**

This site on Prudhoe Island, 54 km south-east of Mackay, offers camping for up to 6 self-sufficient campers. There are no facilities, so bring all self-sufficient gear, including drinking water, rubbish bags and a gas/fuel stove. **Map refs:** 418 E4, 459 L6

ORPHEUS ISLAND NATIONAL PARK

The caves, headlands and rock formations in Orpheus Island National Park, 110 km north of Townsville and 45 km east of Ingham, have been a source of fascination for geologists for many years. The park offers picturesque picnic and day-use areas, superb wildlife-watching and lovely camping areas. The closest boat ramp is at Taylors Beach, 25 km from Ingham, and charter boat access is from Dungeness (Lucinda), 23 km to the north-west. Advance bookings are required for camping.

How to book: NPRSR 13 7468 www.nprsr.qld.gov.au
Permits: camping permit required

506 Pioneer Bay camping area (boat-based camping)

This small campground on the north-west coast has a clearing for up to 12 people. Composting toilets and picnic tables are the only facilities, so bring all self-sufficient supplies, including drinking water and a gas/fuel stove. Note: stinging jellyfish may be present in the surrounding waters during the warmer months. Fishing is not permitted in certain areas. **Map refs:** 418 C2, 461 N10

507 South Beach camping area (boat-based camping)

This campground on the south-east coast has no facilities and suits self-sufficient campers only. Generators and open fires are not permitted: bring everything necessary. Note: the reefs and waters surrounding Orpheus Island National Park are protected within the Great Barrier Reef Marine Park, so check for permission before boating or fishing. **Map refs:** 418 C2, 461 N10

508 Yanks Jetty camping area (boat-based camping)

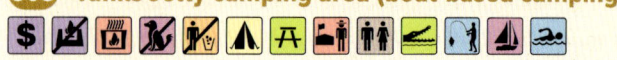

Yanks Jetty campground is just north of Harrier Point on the south-west coast of the island. The gas BBQ is free but open

fires are prohibited; bring a gas/fuel stove and drinking water. The campground has space for up to 30 self-sufficient campers. **Map refs:** 418 C2, 461 N10

PALUMA RANGE NATIONAL PARK

Lying within the Wet Tropics World Heritage Area, Paluma Range National Park offers mountain-top views and picturesque waterfalls. The Mt Spec section encompasses the summit and escarpment of the Paluma Range, while the Jourama Falls section, in the foothills of the Seaview Range, features cascades, rapids and the impressive Jourama Falls on Waterview Creek. Both sections offer picnic areas, lookouts, bushwalks and campsites. Advance bookings are required for camping.

How to book: NPRSR 13 7468 www.nprsr.qld.gov.au
Permits: camping permit required

509 Big Crystal Creek camping area

This popular swimming and picnic area is off the Old Bruce Hwy; the 4 km road to the campground is partially unsealed. Bring a gas/fuel stove and drinking water, or treat the creek water before drinking. The summit of Mt Spec, rising 1000 m above the Big Crystal Creek flood plain, receives 3 times the average rainfall of the surrounding area and is often cloaked in mist or low cloud. Vegetation changes from open eucalypt forests in the park's lower areas to dense rainforest on the higher slopes. **Map refs:** 418 B2, 461 M11

510 Jourama Falls camping area

This campground, beside Waterview Creek, is about 300 m from the entrance to the national park. Nearby Jourama Falls Lookout Walk (3 km return, 1 hr) leads through dry open forest of poplar gum, bloodwood and Moreton Bay ash. Rainforest grows on the higher slopes and lines the banks of Waterview Creek. Wildlife-watchers may spot the azure kingfisher, satin flycatcher and northern fantail during the day and the southern boobook, large-tailed nightjar and tawny frogmouth by torchlight at night. Other nocturnal residents include sugar gliders and endangered mahogany gliders. Note: the camping area can flood during heavy rain. **Map refs:** 418 B2, 461 M10

PERCY ISLES NATIONAL PARK

The Percy Isles, 128 km south-east of Mackay, have long been known as a yachties' paradise and are famous in the sailing world for their stunning beaches, unspoilt waters – and isolation. The isles found fame outside the sailing world recently after several legal battles over ownership of Middle Percy Island, which is now firmly part of the Percy Isles National Park, with the exception of the Middle Percy Island Conservation Park, a small, privately managed section.

Who to contact: NPRSR 13 7468 www.nprsr.qld.gov.au
Permits: camping permit required

511 **North West Beach camping area (boat-based camping)**

This site on South Percy Island offers camping for up to 12 self-sufficient campers. There are no facilities, so bring all self-sufficient gear, including drinking water, rubbish bags and a gas/fuel stove. Owing to South Percy Island's distance from the mainland and the navigational challenges posed, sailing there should only be attempted by seasoned sailors. Note: as this campsite is very remote, bring extra supplies and plan for all eventualities. **Map refs:** 418 E5, 459 M7

REPULSE ISLANDS NATIONAL PARK

Repulse Islands National Park protects 3 small islands south of Cape Conway, about 35 km south-east of Airlie Beach. The deep blue waters surrounding the islands are ideal for boating and fishing. Private boat access is from Shute Harbour or Abel Point Marina. Advance bookings are required for camping.

How to book: NPRSR 13 7468 www.nprsr.qld.gov.au
Permits: camping permit required

512 **South Repulse Island camping area (boat-based camping)**

This sheltered campground for self-sufficient campers – a maximum of 12 – is on the west side of the island, with views of Conway Range. Generators are not permitted and the site is gas/fuel stove only; also bring drinking water. There is good anchorage at the site; remember to go slow when boating, report marine strandings and not collect coral or shells.
Map refs: 418 D4, 459 K4

SHOALWATER BAY CONSERVATION PARK

Located at the northern end of Shoalwater Bay, 23 km south-east of the hamlet of Stanage and 62 km north-east of Marlborough, Shoalwater Bay Conservation Park is a remote area protecting coastal heathland. Access to the park is by boat only; owing to its remoteness, the voyage should only be tackled by experienced sailors.

Who to contact: NPRSR 13 7468 www.nprsr.qld.gov.au
Permits: camping permit required

513 **Chips Hut camping area (boat-based camping)**

There are no facilities provided at Chips Hut and fires are prohibited, so bring all self-sufficient camping gear, including drinking water, rubbish bags and a gas/fuel stove. Note: as this campsite is remote, bring extra supplies and plan for all eventualities. **Map refs:** 418 E5, 459 M8

514 **Macdonalds Point camping area (boat-based camping)**

There are no facilities provided at Macdonalds Point and fires are prohibited, so bring all self-sufficient camping gear, including drinking water, rubbish bags and a gas/fuel stove. Note: as

this campsite is remote, bring extra supplies and plan for all eventualities. **Map refs:** 418 E5, 459 M8

SMITH ISLANDS NATIONAL PARK

For a truly secluded mid-tropics experience, head to Smith Islands National Park, 45 km north of Mackay. This isolated group of 16 islands lies halfway between Mackay and the Lindeman Islands of the Whitsundays, and the islands share many of the features of the Whitsundays, but without the hordes of tourists. Access to the islands is by boat only; the nearest boat ramp is in Seaforth. Advance bookings are required for camping.

How to book: NPRSR 13 7468 www.nprsr.qld.gov.au
Permits: camping permit required

515 **Roylen Bay camping area (boat-based camping)**

Camping is permitted on Goldsmith Island, part of the Great Barrier Reef World Heritage Area off the coast of Mackay. Toilets and picnic tables are the only facilities, so you'll need to bring all self-sufficient supplies. The surrounding coral reefs provide excellent snorkelling but beware of marine stingers Oct–May.
Map refs: 418 E4, 459 K4

SOUTH CUMBERLAND ISLANDS NATIONAL PARK

Located 60 km north-east of Mackay and 50 km from Seaforth by boat, the 9 islands that comprise South Cumberland Islands National Park are characterised by rugged, hoop pine–clad headlands, long sandy beaches and hidden pockets of remnant dry rainforest. The islands are an important breeding site for flatback and green turtles. Access to the islands is by private or charter boat only. Advance bookings are required for camping.

How to book: NPRSR 13 7468 www.nprsr.qld.gov.au
Permits: camping permit required

516 **Cockermouth Island camping area (boat-based camping)**

Bush camping is permitted for up to 12 people at Cockermouth Island's south-western bay. There are no facilities provided, so bring all self-sufficient camping gear, including drinking water, rubbish bags and a gas/fuel stove. **Map refs:** 418 E4, 459 L5

517 **Refuge Bay camping area (boat-based camping)**

Bush camping is permitted at Refuge Bay on Scawfell Island. Toilets and a shelter shed are the only facilities, so you'll need to bring all self-sufficient supplies, including drinking water and a gas/fuel stove. The island is an important turtle rookery, and the surrounding coral reefs provide excellent snorkelling but beware of marine stingers Oct–May. **Map refs:** 418 E4, 459 L5

518 **Turtle Beach camping area (boat-based camping)**

Bush camping is permitted for up to 24 people at this area, on the north shore of the steep and rugged St Bees Island. There are no facilities provided, so bring all self-sufficient camping gear, including drinking water, rubbish bags and a gas/fuel stove. **Map refs:** 418 E4, 459 L5

WHITE MOUNTAINS NATIONAL PARK

The white sandstone gorges of White Mountains National Park lie 140 km south-west of Charters Towers and 80 km north-west of Hughenden. Lovers of flora and fauna will be attracted by the flowering native vegetation and various reptiles, birds and wallabies found in the park. Note: there are no signed walking trails in the park. Advance bookings are required for camping.

How to book: NPRSR 13 7468 www.nprsr.qld.gov.au
Permits: camping permit required

519 Canns Camp Creek camping area (bush camping)

This campground is 11 km west of the Burra Range lookout and 19 km east of Torrens Creek. The road is sometimes closed to conventional vehicles Dec–Apr, due to wet weather. Generators and fires are not permitted; bring drinking water and a gas/fuel stove. **Map refs:** 418 A3, 458 D3, 465 P3

WHITSUNDAY ISLANDS NATIONAL PARK

Protecting one of Queensland's most beautiful and popular holiday destinations, this national park features 32 islands, including Whitsunday Island and its famous Whitehaven Beach. Whitsunday Island has 2 excellent walking trails well worth exploring. The Tongue Point track (400 m, 15 min) leads to a beautiful view of Whitehaven Beach, and the Dugong Beach to Sawmill Beach track (1.5 km, 45 min) features gorgeous bay outlooks. Other protected islands include Hook Island, with its stunning coral reef just metres offshore from 2 campgrounds, and Black and Langford islands. Access to various islands is via Shute Harbour or Airlie Beach. If boating in the region, remember to go slow, report marine strandings, not collect coral or shells, and check for permissions before fishing. Advance bookings are required for camping.

How to book: NPRSR 13 7468 www.nprsr.qld.gov.au
Permits: camping permit required

520 Chance Bay camping area (boat-based camping)

The sandy Chance Bay campground is on the south coast of Whitsunday Island, about 27 km east-south-east of Shute Harbour. A composting toilet and picnic tables are the only facilities, so bring all self-sufficient supplies. The site can only be reached at mid-high tide. **Map refs:** 418 E3, 459 K4

521 Crayfish Beach camping area (boat-based camping)

This campground on the east coast of Hook Island is sheltered by a large rocky headland to the east, and mountains to the north and west. Hook Island has some of the Whitsundays' most accessible coral reefs, just metres from the shore, providing magnificent snorkelling. The site suits self-sufficient campers; bring drinking water and a gas/fuel stove.
Map refs: 418 D3, 459 K3

522 Curlew Beach camping area (boat-based camping)

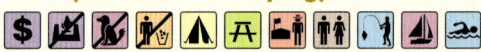

This small campground on the south coast of Hook Island at Macona Inlet has space for 12 campers. Open fires and generators are not permitted, and you need to bring drinking water and a gas/fuel stove. **Map refs:** 418 D3, 459 K3

523 Dugong Beach camping area (boat-based camping)

Ideal for larger groups, Dugong Beach campground on the west coast of Whitsunday Island has space for up to 36 people. A 1 km walking track links it to nearby Sawmill Beach. Access is best at mid-high tide. Bring drinking water and a gas/fuel stove. **Map refs:** 418 D3, 459 K3

524 Joe's Beach camping area (boat-based camping)

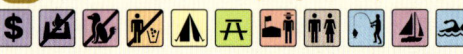

The reef off Joe's Beach on Whitsunday Island is ideal for snorkelling and there are superb views of nearby islands. The campground has space for 12 campers. Generators and open fires are not permitted; bring drinking water and a gas/fuel stove. **Map refs:** 418 D3, 459 K3

525 Maureen's Cove camping area (boat-based camping)

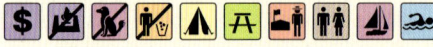

Maureen's Cove is a coral rubble beach on the north coast of Hook Island with excellent snorkelling opportunities at the fringing coral reef. The site, for a maximum of 24 people, has great views of the Coral Sea, and a small creek runs behind the campground. Bring all self-sufficient supplies.
Map refs: 418 D3, 459 K3

526 Nari's Beach camping area (boat-based camping)

Nari's Beach is a small campground on the west coast of Whitsunday Island with space for 6 self-sufficient campers. The area has magnificent views of Cid Island. The site is gas/fuel stove only; bring drinking water. **Map refs:** 418 D3, 459 K3

527 Northern Spit camping area (boat-based camping)

This campground for totally self-sufficient campers is in a secluded spot behind the beach on the northern side of Henning Island, overlooking Whitsunday and Hamilton islands. Open fires and generators are not permitted. **Map refs:** 418 D3, 459 K4

528 Peter Bay camping area (boat-based camping)

This picturesque campground on the north-east coast of Whitsunday Island has views across the bay to Border and Dumbell islands. It can only be reached at mid-high tide

and is for a maximum of 12 totally self-sufficient campers.
Map refs: 418 D3, 459 K3

529 Steens Beach camping area (boat-based camping)

This campground on the north-west coast of Hook Island overlooks Hayman Island. The fringing coral reef provides excellent snorkelling. Bring drinking water and a gas/fuel stove.
Map refs: 418 D3, 459 K3

530 Whitehaven Beach camping area (boat-based camping)

Famous for its postcard-perfect white sandy beach and azure waters, Whitehaven on Whitsunday Island is one of Queensland's most beautiful protected camping spots. The area is busy with hundreds of tourists during the day, but campers at this site can enjoy being the only visitors with permission to stay overnight – there are no hotels, bars or restaurants at Whitehaven. Set in the eucalyptus woodland behind the beach, there are 7 defined sites for a maximum of 36 people. A new toilet block was recently built on-site. Open fires and generators are prohibited. Bring all self-sufficient supplies.
Map refs: 418 E3, 459 K4

CAMPSITES LOCATED IN OTHER AREAS

531 Ball Bay Campground

Ball Bay is a basic campground (no powered sites) off Cape Hillsborough Rd, about 48 km north of Mackay. Camping attendants visit the site daily to collect fees. Mackay is on the Bruce Hwy, about 125 km south of Proserpine, with more than 30 sandy beaches and access to several tropical islands in the Great Barrier Reef World Heritage Area.
Map refs: 418 D4, 459 K5

How to contact: (07) 4959 0695

532 BIG4 Adventure Whitsunday Resort

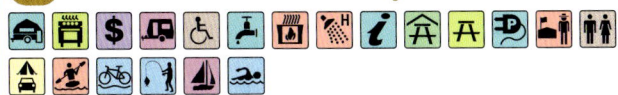

This modern 26 ha camping and caravan park is located in Cannonvale, 4 km from Airlie Beach's town centre. The facilities are top class: ensuite powered sites, plenty of shade, concrete slabs, and 3 amenities blocks with coin-operated laundry facilities. Other features include free electric BBQs and a large undercover camp kitchen with microwave and fridge.
Map refs: 418 D3, 459 J3

How to book: 25–29 Shute Harbour Rd, Cannonvale (07) 4948 5400, 1800 640 587 www.adventurewhitsunday.com.au

533 BIG4 Airlie Cove Resort Van Park

This modern tourist park with excellent facilities is located 2.5 km from Airlie Beach town centre on Shute Harbour Rd. The campground features a Polynesian-style camp kitchen with fridge, microwave, hotplates and other conveniences. Other benefits include a pool with waterslide and spa, a mini market, television room, laundry and free gas BBQs. All caravan sites have cement slabs, sullage, water and electricity points.
Map refs: 418 D3, 459 J3

How to book: Lot 2, Shute Harbour Rd, Jubilee Pocket (07) 4946 6727, 1800 653 445 www.airliecove.com.au

534 Bingil Bay camping area

This campground is about 3 km north of Mission Beach on Bingil Bay Rd. There is no power available here. Mission Beach is 2 hr drive from Cairns or 3 hr from Townsville, and is known for its 14 km stretch of sandy beaches. Take precautionary measures against marine stingers Oct–May. **Map refs:** 418 B1, 461 M8

Who to contact: Tully Visitor Information Centre (07) 4068 2288

535 Burdekin Falls Dam Caravan Park

Well stocked with barramundi for excellent fishing, Burdekin Falls Dam on Lake Dalrymple is 120 km south of Mingela on the Flinders Hwy, with signposted access via Ravenswood Rd. The caravan park has good facilities and gets very busy in holiday periods, as the dam is also a popular spot for canoeing, sailing and waterskiing. **Map refs:** 418 C4, 458 G4

How to book: SunWater Burdekin Dam (07) 4770 3177

536 Camp Kanga

Powered sites are available at this campground, 24 km north-west of Proserpine on Crystal Brook Rd. It's just 1.5 km from Lake Proserpine (also known as Peter Faust Dam) and offers handy extras such as laundry facilities and a camp kitchen. The lake is well stocked with fish for excellent sportfishing, and is also a popular spot for waterskiing and boating.
Map refs: 418 D3, 459 J4

How to book: 2396 Crystal Brook Rd, Crystal Brook (07) 4947 2600 www.campkanga.com.au

537 Eungella Dam camping area

Eungella Dam, 40 km north-west of Eungella, is a popular place for all manner of watersports. The fishing is good

too, as the dam is well stocked with sooty grunter and barramundi. You need to be totally self-sufficient if you are camping here; bring your own firewood and drinking water. **Map refs:** 418 D4, 459 J5

Who to contact: SunWater Mackay (07) 4954 2220
Permits: a permit is required to fish in Eungella Dam
Camping fees: fees can be paid at the ranger station

538 Ferns Hideaway Resort

The camping facilities at this resort, 39 km north of Yeppoon, are relatively basic, but the lush rainforest surrounds more than make up for that. Campers looking for a touch of civilisation will find the resort's pool, restaurant and bar a godsend, while outdoors adventurers can paddle down Sandy Creek in a canoe (provided free of charge to camping guests). Bookings are essential at peak periods. **Map refs:** 418 F6, 459 M9

How to book: 67 Cahills Rd, Byfield (07) 4935 1235 www.fernshideaway.com.au

539 Fletcher Creek Camping Reserve

This camping reserve is beside Fletcher Creek, 45 km north of Charters Towers near the entrance to Dalrymple National Park; access is via Gregory Developmental Rd from the Flinders Hwy. The Charters Towers region is noted for its diverse landscapes, with rainforests in the north-east and desert plains in the south-west. **Map refs:** 418 B3, 458 F2, 461 M12

Who to contact: Charters Towers Regional Council (07) 4761 5300

540 Hull Heads camping area

Estuary and reef fishing from an all-weather boat ramp and pontoon makes Hull Heads an excellent destination for anglers. The campground is next to the coastguard on Luff St in Hull Heads, 15 km east of the Bruce Hwy. There are 7 sites with a 4-night maximum stay, and generators are permitted during the day. The access road is 6 km south of Tully at Silky Oak, on the Bruce Hwy. **Map refs:** 418 B1, 461 M8

Who to contact: Tully Visitor Information Centre (07) 4068 2288

541 Kinchant Waters Leisure Resort

Popular with waterskiers and anglers, the Kinchent Waters Leisure Resort includes a 4 ha camping area, offering a range of accommodation options including cabins and backpacker rooms, plus a bar, restaurant and laundry facilities. Kinchant Dam is about 40 km west of Mackay, off the Peak Downs Hwy at Eton. Fishing permits are available on-site. **Map refs:** 418 D4, 459 K6

How to book: 841 Kinchant Dam Rd, Eton North (07) 4954 1453

542 Lake Paluma camping area

Surrounded by World Heritage rainforest, Lake Paluma (12 km north-west of Paluma) is a popular spot for swimming, canoeing and kayaking, so bookings are essential. The lake is a well-known wildlife-watching area, with opportunities to see platypus, peregrine falcons and eastern water dragons. The day-use area has BBQs and weatherproof shelters, and there's a drinking-water storage area. Heavy rain and strong winds can lead to road closures, and the gravel access road is unsuitable for caravans. Note: motorised boating is not permitted on the lake. **Map refs:** 418 B2, 461 M10

How to book: Townsville City Council 1300 878 001 www.townsville.qld.gov.au *Camping fees:* fees can be paid online, at a Townsville City Council customer service centre or at the self-registration station

Mackay Highlands Great Walk

This 56 km, 3–5 day walk allows experienced and self-sufficent hikers to see everything from rugged cliffs and cool rainforests to open eucalypt woodland and an 1880s gold-mining hamlet. Some sections of the track require a high level of physical fitness, and the track is easier to manage if approached north to south, from Pine Grove in Eungella National Park to Mt Britton township. Advance bookings are required for all camping on the walk.

Please note that campsites are listed in alphabetical order, not track order. Refer to the map on p. 418 for further information.

How to book: NPRSR 13 7468 www.nprsr.qld.gov.au
Permits: camping permit required

450 Crediton Hall camping area
See p. 423.

451 Denham Range camping area
See p. 423.

455 Fern Flat camping area (walk-in camping)
See p. 424.

490 Moonlight Dam camping area
See p. 428.

543 Magnetic Gateway Holiday Village

Situated on the Bruce Hwy at Cluden, just 8 km from Townsville, this tourist park has plenty of shady tent sites and an excellent range of facilities. Visitors can enjoy the swimming pool, spa, TV room and book exchange, laundry, internet facilities and a kiosk with gas refills and ice. Air-conditioned ensuite cabins are also available on-site. Note: access is from Racecourse Rd via Abbott St. **Map refs:** 418 C2, 458 G1, 461 N11

Who to contact: Racecourse Rd (Bruce Hwy), Cluden (07) 4778 2412

544 **Mission Beach Caravan Park**

This caravan park with laundry facilities is on Porters Promenade in Mission Beach, about 2 hr drive from Cairns or 3 hr from Townsville. Known for its 14 km stretch of sandy beaches, the town is a jumping-off point to reach Dunk Island or Bedarra Island and it's just a 1 hr boat trip to the Great Barrier Reef. **Map refs:** 418 B1, 461 M8

Who to contact: Tully Visitor Information Centre (07) 4068 2288

545 **Pelorus Island camping area (boat-based camping)**

No permits or bookings are required for this free camping ground known as a great jumping-off point to fantastic snorkelling around the coral reefs of Pelorus Island's west coast. The island is in the Great Barrier Reef Marine Park. If you're snorkelling, take note that there could be fast currents. The island is reached by private boat or commercial operator from Taylor's Beach. Wood fires are permitted, but campers must be self-sufficient, bringing all supplies, including drinking water. **Map refs:** 418 C2, 461 N10

Who to contact: Tyto Wetlands Visitor Information Centre (07) 4776 5211

546 **Platypus Bush Camp**

Hot showers with rainforest views and a superb open-air camp kitchen are some of the excellent facilities at this popular campground. The camping area has plenty of space for groups, or you can stay in the tree-house huts nestled in the rainforest. Finch Hatton Gorge is 40 km east of Eungella. From the picnic area, a 2 km rainforest walk leads through the gorge to Araluen Falls. **Map refs:** 418 D4, 459 J5

How to book: Gorge Rd, Finch Hatton (07) 4958 3204 www.bushcamp.net

547 **St Helens Beach camping area**

This basic campground is in the township of St Helens Beach, 68 km north of Mackay, and is accessed via Murrays Rd. Firewood is supplied and camping attendants visit the site daily to collect fees. Mackay is on the Bruce Hwy about 125 km south of Proserpine, offering more than 30 sandy beaches and access to several tropical islands in the Great Barrier Reef World Heritage Area. **Map refs:** 418 D4, 459 K5

Who to contact: Mackay Regional Council 1300 622 529; or Mackay Visitor Information Centre 1300 130 001

548 **Seaforth camping area**

This campground is 45 km north of Mackay along the Seaforth–Yakapari Rd. It has coin-operated showers. Camping attendants visit the site daily to collect fees. Mackay is on the Bruce Hwy about 125 km south of Proserpine, with more than 30 sandy beaches and access to several tropical islands in the Great Barrier Reef World Heritage Area. **Map refs:** 418 D4, 459 K5

Who to contact: (07) 4966 4359, 0427 373 358

Whitsunday Ngaro Sea Trail

The Whitsunday Ngaro Sea Trail is the most unusual of Queensland's Great Walks for one simple reason – there's more sailing than walking involved. Keen sailors and sea kayakers who follow this trail between island campsites will discover gorgeous beaches, brilliant azure seas and challenging mountain climbs, as well as gaining insight into the Ngaro people's traditional way of life. Advance bookings are required for all camping.

▦ *Please note that campsites are listed in alphabetical order.*
▦ *Refer to the map on p. 418 for further information.*

How to book: NPRSR 13 7468 www.nprsr.qld.gov.au
Permits: camping permit required

520 **Chance Bay camping area (boat-based camping)**
See p. 432.

522 **Curlew Beach camping area (boat-based camping)**
See p. 432.

523 **Dugong Beach camping area (boat-based camping)**
See p. 432.

527 **Northern Spit camping area (boat-based camping)**
See p. 432.

496 **Paddle Bay camping area (boat-based camping)**
See p. 429.

528 **Peter Bay camping area (boat-based camping)**
See p. 432.

499 **Sandy Bay, South Molle Island camping area (boat-based camping)**
See p. 429

530 **Whitehaven Beach camping area (boat-based camping)**
See p. 433.

THE FAR NORTH

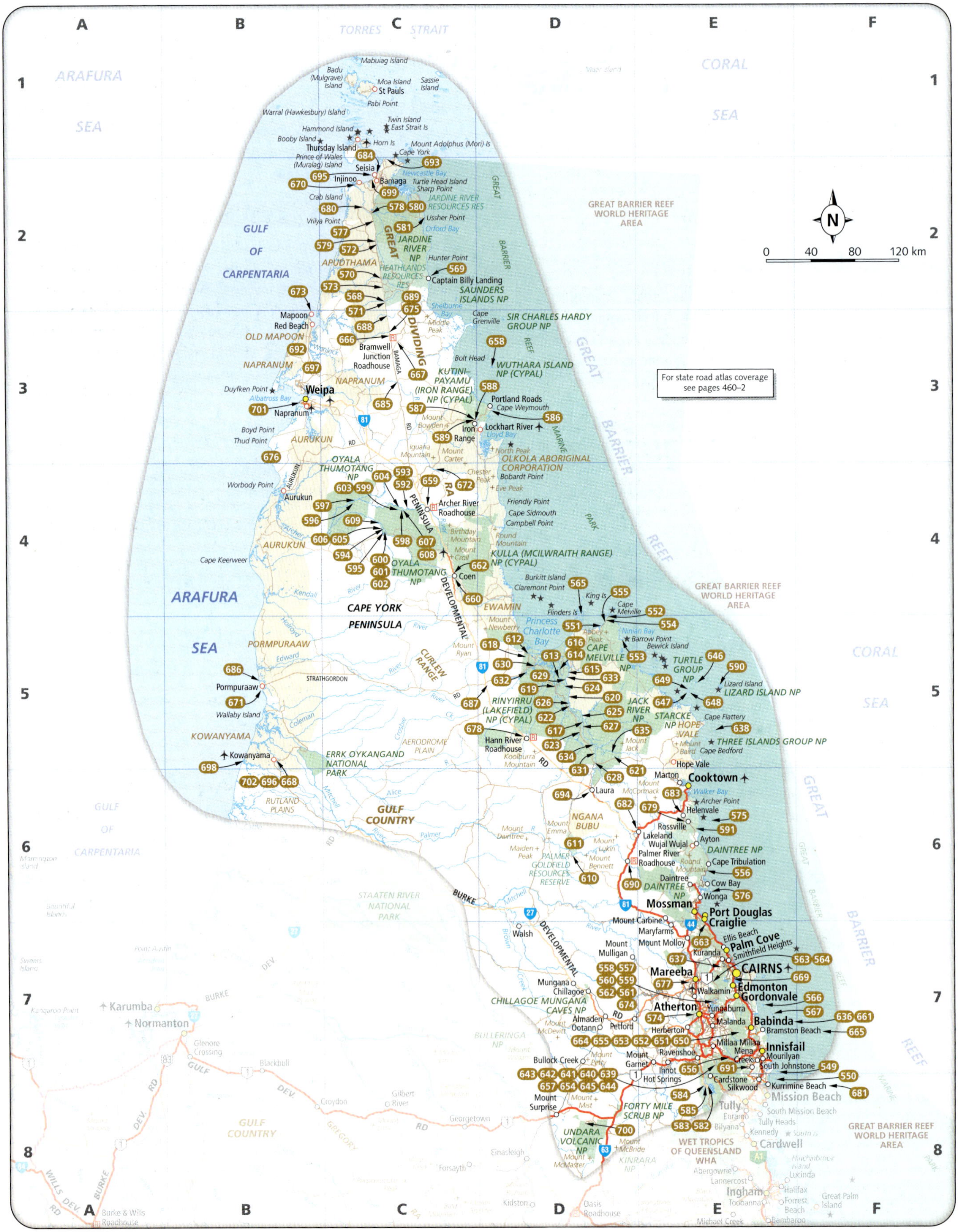

STRETCHING FROM CAIRNS TO the Torres Strait islands off the tip of Cape York, Far North Queensland's unique remoteness and stunning natural beauty is a boon for adventurous campers. Rugged 4WD tracks lead you through densely forested national parks to isolated waterholes and lagoons, tiny villages, outback roadhouses, riverside camping areas and beautiful unspoiled coastlines.

Watersports fanatics can make their way to Lake Tinaroo, south-west of Cairns, for sensational boating, fishing, canoeing, waterskiing and windsurfing. Visitors stay at the popular Lake Tinaroo Holiday Park or head for the peaceful lakeside camping areas in Danbulla State Forest, where you can take short walks to impressive crater lakes and enormous strangler fig trees.

North of Cairns near Cooktown, Rinyirru (Lakefield) National Park is Queensland's second largest national park, covering the area from the town of Laura to Princess Charlotte Bay. Anglers can set up camp at one of the many waterholes and fish for barramundi or catfish in the lakes and creeks – but beware of crocs! The park is also a significant traditional land for Indigenous people, a place for ceremonies and stories of ancestral spirits.

Famous hospitable roadhouses such as those at Hann River, Musgrave, Archer River and Bramwell Junction provide spacious campgrounds, tasty meals, fuel and supplies for those heading through Cape York, past Weipa to Australia's most northerly point on the mainland. Close to the tip is Jardine River National Park, known for its magnificent waterfalls, lookouts, rainforests and amazing wildlife.

At Northern Cape York, relaxing campgrounds such as Seisia Holiday Park and Punsand Bay Camping Resort – both with excellent facilities – are the perfect reward for making the trek all the way to the top. Offshore, campers can discover the wonders of the Great Barrier Reef and stay on Flinders, Lizard, Snapper, the Turtle Group and other island-based national parks.

Note: alcohol restrictions apply in certain areas of Cape York Peninsula, and it is illegal to bring alcohol into dry communities, even if you are only travelling through. Ensure that you have up-to-date information about alcohol restrictions before travelling by calling 13 7468.

CAMPSITES LOCATED IN PARKS AND RESERVES

BARNARD ISLAND GROUP NATIONAL PARK

The Barnard Island Group National Park is around 15 km offshore from Kurrimine Beach and about 90 km south of Cairns. The islands include Bresnahan, Hutchinson, Jessie, Kent and Lindquist (North Barnard group) and Sisters and Stephens (South Barnard group). Mainland access is from Mourilyan Harbour or Kurrimine Beach. Advance bookings are required to camp on Stephens Island.

How to book: NPRSR 13 7468 www.nprsr.qld.gov.au *Permits:* camping permit required *Camping fees:* fees can be paid and permits acquired for Kent Island at NPRSR Cairns business centre

549 Kent Island camping area (boat-based camping)

Self-sufficient camping is found on the west coast of Kent Island, part of the North Barnard group. This site is ideal for anglers and wildlife-watchers. There are 3 sites with a maximum of 5 people per site; bring all necessaries, including a gas/fuel stove. Be aware of marine stingers when swimming, particularly during Oct–May. **Map refs:** 436 E7, 461 M8

550 Stephens Island camping area (boat-based camping)

This campground for self-sufficient campers is on the western side of Stephens Island, part of the South Barnard group. There are 3 separate sites, each with a maximum of 4 people. Open fires and generators are not permitted; bring a gas/fuel stove. Access to some sections of the island is prohibited Sept–Mar to protect nesting seabirds. **Map refs:** 436 E8, 461 M8

CAPE MELVILLE NATIONAL PARK

Some gruelling 4WD tracks lead to this national park on Cape York Peninsula. At journey's end is a wild and rugged coastline of rocky headlands and sandy beaches bordered by wetlands and eucalypt woodlands stretching inland to the Melville and Altanmoui ranges. This is the land of the Daarba, Junjuu, Muli, Bagaarrmugu, Wurri, Manyamarr, Yiirrku and Gambiilmugu people. The ruins of homesteads, testament to early European pastoral settlement, are scattered throughout the region. Travel here from the west via Rinyirru (Lakefield) National Park (280 km, 6 hr) or from the south from Cooktown and Starcke Homestead along the Coast Rd (250 km, 12 hr). Note: this park is closed for the wet season, Dec–Jul each year; access is 4WD only. Advance bookings are required for camping.

How to book: NPRSR 13 7468 www.nprsr.qld.gov.au
Permits: camping permit required

551 Crocodile camping area (bush camping)

This camping area covers a 2 km stretch of beach on Bathurst Bay, between the Muck River estuary and the Nookai day-use area. There are no facilities, so bring all self-sufficient camping gear, including drinking water and rubbish bags. Open fires are permitted (bring your own firewood), but a gas/fuel stove is preferred. **Map refs:** 436 D5, 462 G11

552 Granite camping area (bush camping)

This camping site on the beach at Bathurst Bay stretches across the 4 km span between Oystercatcher camping area and the northernmost point of Cape Melville. Accessing the site requires 4 creek crossings, including a difficult and dangerous tidal creek crossing at the boundary between Oystercatcher and Granite camping areas – bring vehicle recovery equipment. There are no facilities, so bring all self-sufficient camping gear, including drinking water and rubbish bags. Open fires are permitted (bring your own firewood), but a gas/fuel stove is preferred. **Map refs:** 436 D5, 462 G10

553 Ninian Bay camping area (bush camping)

This camping area lies on the east coast of Cape Melville National Park, 88 km from the camping areas at Bathurst Bay. A 1 km stretch of beach, it contains no facilities, so bring all self-sufficient camping gear, including drinking water and rubbish bags. The road into Ninian Bay is difficult and should be attempted only by experienced 4WD operators. Open fires are permitted (bring your own firewood), but a gas/fuel stove is preferred. **Map refs:** 436 D5, 462 H11

554 Oystercatcher camping area (bush camping)

This camping area covers a 2 km stretch of beach on Bathurst Bay, between the Wongai and Granite camping areas. There are no facilities, so bring all self-sufficient camping gear, including drinking water and rubbish bags. Open fires are permitted (bring your own firewood), but a gas/fuel stove is preferred. **Map refs:** 436 D5, 462 G11

555 Wongai camping area (bush camping)

This camping area covers a 2 km stretch of beach on Bathurst Bay, between the Nookai day-use area and Oystercatcher camping area. There are no facilities, so bring all self-sufficient camping gear, including drinking water and rubbish bags. Open fires are permitted (bring your own firewood), but a gas/fuel stove is preferred. **Map refs:** 372 D4, 436 D5, 457 N5, 462 G11

DAINTREE NATIONAL PARK

With its stunning scenery of rainforest-clad mountains sweeping down to long sandy beaches, Daintree National Park is one of the most revered parks in Australia. Its Cape Tribulation section, 100 km north of Cairns, is the only place on earth where 2 World Heritage areas exist side by side, as the Wet Tropics area meets the Great Barrier Reef. Advance bookings are required for camping.

How to book: NPRSR 13 7468 www.nprsr.qld.gov.au
Permits: camping permit required

556 Noah Beach camping area

Noah Beach campground is in a secluded spot just 50 m from the beach, about 8 km south of Cape Tribulation village. Throughout the Cape Tribulation section visitors will find facilities such as picnic areas, boardwalks to scenic sites, and viewing platforms. Conventional-vehicle access is via Cape Tribulation Rd after crossing the Daintree River via ferry. Note: open fires and generators are not permitted at this campsite. Bring all self-sufficient supplies; the tap water must be boiled or treated before drinking. **Map refs:** 436 E6, 461 L4

DANBULLA STATE FOREST

Less than 2 hrs' drive from Cairns, wildlife-rich Danbulla State Forest is on the north-east side of Lake Tinaroo on the Atherton Tablelands. Visitors can take the scenic Danbulla Forest Dr, have a picnic at one of 4 day-use areas, or go bushwalking on one of 5 tracks with varying degrees of difficulty. To get here, take the Danbulla Forest Dr north-east of Tinaroo Dam. Advance bookings are required for camping.

How to book: NPRSR 13 7468 www.nprsr.qld.gov.au
Permits: camping permit required

557 Curri Curri camping areas (boat-based camping)

Bush camping is available on the shores of Lake Tinaroo, to the east of the public boat ramp in Tinaroo township. There are 5 numbered campsites, each equipped with a fire ring (bring your own firewood). There are no other facilities, so bring all self-sufficient gear, including drinking water and rubbish bags. Gas/fuel stoves are preferred. **Map refs:** 436 E7, 461 L6

558 Downfall Creek camping area

This campground is 7 km from the western entrance and 21 km from the eastern entrance of the Danbulla Forest Dr. Campers can take the 2.4 km walk through the forest to Kauri Creek. Note: open fires are permitted in fire rings. Bring all self-sufficient supplies, including firewood. **Map refs:** 436 E7, 461 L6

559 Fong-On Bay camping area

A favourite with waterskiers, this campground is divided into 2 sections with good water access: Bulmba and Gungul. To get there, turn off Danbulla Forest Dr 16.5 km from the western entrance, or 11.5 km from the eastern entrance, and continue 4.7 km to the camping area. Open fires are permitted in fire rings; no generators. Bring all self-sufficient supplies, including firewood. **Map refs:** 436 E7, 461 L6

560 Kauri Creek camping area

A great spot for swimming and canoeing, Kauri Creek is 9 km from the western entrance and 19 km from the eastern entrance of Danbulla Forest Dr. Open fires are allowed in fire rings; generators are not permitted. Visitors are advised to bring insect repellent, firewood and drinking water. A shower room is provided for campers who want to bring their own bush showers. **Map refs:** 436 E7, 461 L6

561 Platypus camping area

Platypus campground, 4 km from the western entrance, has 18 numbered sites for small tents, large tents and vans. Open fires are allowed here in the provided fire rings and BBQs (except when fire bans apply); bring your own firewood as well as all other self-sufficent supplies. **Map refs:** 436 E7, 461 L6

562 School Point camping area

School Point can be reached by 2WD or boat. It has has 8 numbered campsites with a gravel surface. To get there, turn off Danbulla Forest Dr 16 km from the western entrance, or 12 km from the eastern entrance, and follow the road 1 km to the campground. Bring all self-sufficient supplies, including firewood. **Map refs:** 436 E7, 461 L6

DAVIES CREEK NATIONAL PARK

The rugged boulder-lined Davies Creek is a popular region for scenic hikes, picnics and wildlife-watching. The access road to the national park is 21 km from Kuranda; follow it for another 7 km to reach the campground. The Davies Creek Falls circuit is an easy 1.1 km (20 min) track worth checking out; platypus are often spotted in the area.

Who to contact: NPRSR 13 7468 www.nprsr.qld.gov.au
Permits: camping permit required *Camping fees:* fees can be paid and permits acquired at the self-registration station

563 Davies Creek camping area

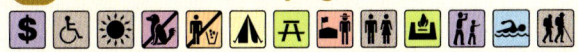

Camp beside the creek at this clearing 6 km from the Kennedy Hwy, accessible by conventional vehicles. There are 8 sites with space for 10 campers per site. Bring firewood for the allocated fireplaces, and all self-sufficient supplies. Note: Davies Creek Rd is sometimes closed due to flooding. **Map refs:** 436 E7, 461 L6

DINDEN NATIONAL PARK

About 20 km south-west of Cairns, Dinden National Park is on the Atherton Tableland, just south of Davies Creek National Park. The park's eucalypt forests are threaded with excellent walking trails, including the Kahlpahlim Rock trail (12 km return, 6–7 hr) and Turtle Rock trail (8 km, 3–4 hr). Drive 22 km south of the Kennedy Hwy to the sites, preferably in a 4WD. Advance bookings are required for camping.

How to book: NPRSR 13 7468 www.nprsr.qld.gov.au
Permits: camping permit required

564 Dinden camping area (bush camping)

A 4WD is advisable for accessing these 6 bush campsites, 5 km along Davies Creek Rd from Davies Creek National Park. It is preferable to visit in the dry season (Apr–Oct); bring your own water, rubbish bags, and a gas/fuel stove. The Kahlpahlim Rock walking trail follows a former logging trail through rainforest and leads to views over the Davies Creek catchment. **Map refs:** 436 E7, 461 L6

FLINDERS GROUP NATIONAL PARK

Located 340 km north of Cairns, the remote islands of the Flinders Group National Park are part of the sea country of the Yiithuwarra 'saltwater people', and have important Indigenous sites. The group is east of the Cape York Peninsula between Cape Melville and Princess Charlotte Bay, accessible by private boat. Advance bookings are required for camping.

How to book: NPRSR 13 7468 www.nprsr.qld.gov.au
Permits: camping permit required

565 Flinders Island camping area (boat-based camping)

This is the only island in the group that permits camping; bring all self-sufficient supplies; the water available here needs to be boiled or treated before use. The site is on the northern side of Flinders Island at Fredrick Point, accessible by private boat only. Respect cultural sites. **Map refs:** 436 D4, 462 G10

FRANKLAND GROUP NATIONAL PARK

About 45 km south of Cairns, this island group is known for its fringing reefs, rocky outcrops and varied wildlife. Access to the islands is by private boat from the Mulgrave and Russell rivers. Beware of the sandbar at the mouth of the Mulgrave River at Russell Heads. Advance bookings are required for camping.

How to book: NPRSR 13 7468 www.nprsr.qld.gov.au *Permits:* camping permit required *Camping fees:* for Russell Island, fees can be paid and permits acquired at NPRSR Cairns business centre

566 High Island camping area (boat-based camping)

This campground on the north-west side of High Island has space for 14 self-sufficient campers. Open fires and generators are not permitted, so bring a gas/fuel stove. **Map refs:** 436 E7, 461 M6

567 Russell Island camping area (boat-based camping)

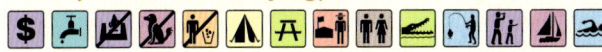

This sandy campground is on the north-east side of Russell Island, accessible by private boat. There are 6 numbered sites; open fires and generators are not permitted and you need to be self-sufficient. There are a few small walking tracks around the campground, but to protect nesting seabirds some areas have restricted access. **Map refs:** 436 E7, 461 M7

HEATHLANDS RESOURCES RESERVE

This large reserve, directly south of Jardine River National Park, protects a diverse array of wildlife, including Torresian crows and red-winged parrots. It is also the home of several stunning waterfalls, including Fruit Bat Falls, Eliot Falls and Twin Falls. Access is 4WD only via the Telegraph Rd or the Southern Bypass Rd. Advance bookings are required for camping.

Who to contact: Heathlands Ranger Station (07) 4060 3421 for the Telegraph Track *How to book:* NPRSR 13 7468 www.nprsr.qld. gov.au *Permits:* camping permit required

568 Bertie Creek camping area (bush camping)

Bush camping is permitted at this site on the 4WD Telegraph Track, 1.4 km north of Dulhunty River camping area and 14.1 km

south of Gunshot Creek. There are no facilities; bring all self-sufficient gear. **Map refs:** 436 C2, 462 D5

569 Captain Billy Landing camping area

Captain Billy Landing is on the eastern side of Heathlands Resources Reserve, about 27 km east of the bypass road and 55 km north-east of the ranger headquarters. The campground is quite large, suitable for up to 10 groups. Note: open fires are permitted in the provided fire rings, but BYO firewood. **Map refs:** 436 C2, 462 D4

570 Cockatoo Creek camping area (bush camping)

Bush camping is permitted at this site on the 4WD Telegraph Track, 9.5 km north of Gunshot Creek camping area and 12 km south of the Eliot Falls turn-off. There are no facilities; bring all self-sufficient gear. **Map refs:** 436 C2, 462 C4

571 Dulhunty River camping area (bush camping)

On the 4WD Telegraph Track, bush camping is permitted at 2 sites either side of the Dulhunty River, 11.2 km north of North Alice Creek camping area and 1.4 km south of Bertie Creek. There are no facilities; bring all self-sufficient gear. **Map refs:** 436 C2, 462 D5

572 Eliot Falls camping area

This campground is known for its 3 short but scenic walking tracks that lead through the forest along creeks to Twin Falls and Eliot Falls. All tracks are suitable for inexperienced bushwalkers. The campground, with 31 numbered sites, is between Canal and Eliot creeks, close to the northern boundary of Heathlands Resources Reserve. Open fires are permitted (bring firewood) but gas/fuel stoves are preferred. **Map refs:** 436 C2, 462 C4

573 Gunshot Creek camping area (bush camping)

Bush camping is permitted at this site on the 4WD Telegraph Track, 14.1 km north of Bertie Creek camping area and 9.5 km south of Cockatoo Creek. There are no facilities; bring all self-sufficient gear. **Map refs:** 436 C2, 462 C5

HERBERTON RANGE STATE FOREST

Directly west of Atherton, on the Atherton Tableland, Herberton Range State Forest protects some of the little remaining cloud forest in Queensland. Cloud forests harvest water directly from clouds (in the form of fog, mist and rain), and their abundance of mosses and ferns makes them unique. The high elevation of Herberton Range yields great views over Atherton and the surrounding areas. Advance bookings are required for camping.

How to book: NPRSR 13 7468 www.nprsr.qld.gov.au
Permits: camping permit required

574 Bush camping areas

Self-sufficient campers can bush camp in most areas of Herberton Range State Forest, excluding the Herberton Range Ridge Rd. Vehicle-based campers (4WD only) are required to select sites adjacent to established roads. There are no facilities and fires are banned, so bring all self-sufficient camping gear, including drinking water, rubbish bags and a gas/fuel stove. **Map refs:** 436 E7, 461 L7

HOPE ISLANDS NATIONAL PARK

The traditional sea country of the Kuku Yalanji Indigenous people, East Hope Island is a sand cay 37 km south-east of Cooktown. Access is by boat only and it can be reached within a day's sailing from Cairns. Wildlife-watchers can view several species of sea and woodland birds on the islands, and there are good fishing opportunities. Advance bookings are required for camping.

How to book: NPRSR 13 7468 www.nprsr.qld.gov.au
Permits: camping permit required

575 East Hope Island camping area (boat-based camping)

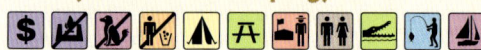

This small sandy campground is on the western side of East Hope Island, accessible by private or commercially operated boat. Each of the 3 separate sites holds up to 4 people. There are no walking tracks on the island, but visitors can walk around the beach perimeter. Bring all self-sufficient supplies, including drinking water and a gas/fuel stove. **Map refs:** 436 E6, 461 L3

576 West Point camping area (boat-based camping)

A favourite with sea kayakers, this sandy campground on Snapper Island, 20 km north of Port Douglas, has space for up to 24 campers. The day-use area on the south-west side of the island has picnic tables and a pit toilet; open fires and generators are not permitted. Campers should be aware that estuarine crocodiles are in the waters around the island. West Point is suitable for self-sufficient campers only. **Map refs:** 436 E6, 461 L4

JARDINE RIVER NATIONAL PARK

Inhabited for thousands of years by Indigenous 'sandbeach people', Jardine River National Park sprawls across 237 000 ha between Telegraph Rd and Cape York Peninsula's northern tip. The park includes the state's largest perennial waterway, the Jardine River, and provides a habitat for numerous bird species, such as the palm cockatoo and yellow-billed kingfisher. Access is by 4WD vehicles only. Advance bookings are required for camping.

Who to contact: Heathlands Ranger Station (07) 4060 3421 for the Telegraph Track *How to book:* NPRSR 13 7468 www.nprsr.qld.gov.au *Permits:* camping permit required

577 Bridge Creek camping area (bush camping)

Bush camping is permitted at this site, 19 km north of Sam Creek camping area at the far north end of the 4WD Telegraph Track. There are no facilities; bring all self-sufficient gear. **Map refs:** 436 C2, 462 C3

578 North Jardine River camping area (bush camping)

The Jardine River separates 2 camping areas, each within sight of each other. (The nearest crossing is the Jardine River ferry.) The camp on the northern side has 6 sites and is accessible via Telegraph Rd, south of the junction between Bamaga and Northern Bypass rds. Bring all self-sufficient supplies, including firewood or a gas/fuel stove. **Map refs:** 436 C2, 462 C3

579 Sam Creek camping area (bush camping)

Bush camping is permitted at this site on the 4WD Telegraph Track, 4.1 km north of the Eliot Falls turn-off and 19 km south of Bridge Creek. There are no facilities; bring all self-sufficient gear. **Map refs:** 436 C2, 462 C4

580 South Jardine River camping area (bush camping)

This campsite, on the southern side of the Jardine River facing the North Jardine River camping area, is accessible via Telegraph Rd. No facilities are provided, so bring all self-sufficient camping gear, including drinking water, rubbish bags firewood and a gas/fuel stove. **Map refs:** 436 C2, 462 C3

JARDINE RIVER RESOURCES RESERVE

Jardine River Resources Reserve is a large reserve to the north-east of Jardine River National Park. Several species of frogs, including the iconic white-lipped tree frog, can be spotted here. Access is 4WD only, via an infrequently maintained track off Bamaga Rd. Advance bookings are required for camping.

How to book: NPRSR 13 7468 www.nprsr.qld.gov.au
Permits: camping permit required

581 Ussher Point camping area (bush camping)

This remote camping area, on the eastern boundary of the Jardine River Resources Reserve, offers a true sense of isolation and remoteness – an authentic Cape York experience. No facilities are provided, so bring all self-sufficient gear, including firewood, water and rubbish bags. Note: quiet generators (less than 65 dBA at 7 m) are permitted. **Map refs:** 436 C2, 462 D3

KOOMBOOLOOMBA CONSERVATION PARK

Located on the shores of Koombooloomba Dam, 29 km south-east of Ravenshoe, Koombooloomba Conservation Park is surrounded on all sides by Koombooloomba National Park. The general region is part of the World Heritage–listed Wet Tropics Area, and is home to the endangered Lumholtz's tree-kangaroo. Access to the conservation park is via Koombooloomba National Park. Advance bookings are required for camping.

How to book: NPRSR 13 7468 www.nprsr.qld.gov.au
Permits: camping permit required

582 Koombooloomba Conservation Park camping area

This campsite, on the cricket oval of the former town of Koombooloomba, offers enviable access to the attractions of Koombooloomba Dam (including fishing, boating and waterskiing). There are 9 separate numbered sites, each with capacity for up to 6 campers. Bring drinking water, rubbish bags and firewood. **Map refs:** 436 E8, 461 L8

KOOMBOOLOOMBA NATIONAL PARK

Koombooloomba National Park, 27 km south-east of Ravenshoe and 53 km south-west of Innisfail, is part of the Wet Tropics World Heritage Area. The traditional land of the Jirrbal people, the land is rich with a diverse array of wildlife, including the rare golden bowerbird and the yellow-bellied glider. To get here, travel south from Raveshoe on Tully Falls Rd, through Tully Falls National Park. Advance bookings are required for camping.

How to book: NPRSR 13 7468 www.nprsr.qld.gov.au
Permits: camping permit required

583 Koombooloomba National Park camping area (bush camping)

This area adjacent to Koombooloomba Dam offers no facilities, but it has excellent access to the water and its attractions via the Koombooloomba Conservation Park. Bring all self-sufficient camping gear, including drinking water, rubbish bags and firewood or a gas/fuel stove. To get here, follow the sign marked 'bush camping' before reaching the former Koombooloomba town site. **Map refs:** 436 E8, 461 L8

584 Nitchaga Creek Road camping area (bush camping)

Bush camping is permitted in the areas adjacent to Nitchaga Creek Rd, west of the bush camping area by Koombooloomba Dam. No facilities are provided and fires are prohibited, so bring all self-sufficient camping gear, including drinking water, rubbish bags and a gas/fuel stove. **Map refs:** 436 E8, 461 L8

585 Wall Creek Road camping area (bush camping)

Bush camping is permitted in the areas adjacent to Wall Creek Rd, south of the bush camping area by Koombooloomba Dam. No facilities are provided and fires are prohibited, so bring all self-sufficient camping gear, including drinking water, rubbish bags and a gas/fuel stove. **Map refs:** 436 E8, 461 L8

KUTINI–PAYAMU (IRON RANGE) NATIONAL PARK (CYPAL)

Protecting a range of magnificent wildlife, including the palm cockatoo and green python, Kutini–Payamu (Iron Range) National Park is a stunning natural reserve on the east coast of Cape York Peninsula. William Bligh landed here in 1792, goldminers came through in the 1930s and American troops were sent here during World War II. Access to the national park is by 4WD only. Advance bookings are required for camping.

How to book: NPRSR 13 7468 www.nprsr.qld.gov.au
Permits: camping permit required

586 Chilli Beach camping area

Chilli Beach is near the north-east boundary of the park, reached by 4WD off Portland Roads Rd. From this campsite for self-sufficient campers you can take the 5 km walk to the mouth of Chilli Creek at the southern end of the beach. Chilli Beach is 32 km north of the ranger headquarters and 24 km east of the Gordon Creek camping area. **Map refs:** 436 D3, 462 E7

587 Cooks Hut camping area

Cooks Hut is near the Rainforest camping area on the banks of the Claudie River, near the junction of Portland Roads and Lockhart River rds. The campsite surface is a combination of dirt and grass and there are 4 defined campsites within the space. There is a hybrid toilet but the site is for self-sufficient campers only. A recommended activity is the 10 km return bushwalking track from the Rainforest camping ground through open woodland. **Map refs:** 436 C3, 462 E7

588 Gordon Creek camping area (bush camping)

This campground is on the banks of Gordon Creek at the Portland Roads Rd, about 8 km north of the ranger HQ and less than a kilometre west of the Cooks Hut camping area. There are no facilities so you need to bring self-sufficient supplies, including water and a gas/fuel stove. **Map refs:** 436 C3, 462 E7

589 Rainforest camping area (bush camping)

Accessible by 4WD only, the Rainforest campsite is set in riverine rainforest on the banks of the Claudie River. The campsite surface is a combination of dirt and grass and there are 4 defined campsites available within the space. There are no facilities; bring all self-sufficient supplies, including drinking water and a gas/fuel stove. **Map refs:** 436 C3, 462 E7

LIZARD ISLAND NATIONAL PARK

Situated 93 km north-east of Cooktown, Lizard Island National Park comprises 6 islands in the Great Barrier Reef World Heritage Area. The islands contain sacred sites of the Dingaal Aboriginal people and are known for being covered with thick grasslands. There are regular flights to Lizard Island from Cairns, and commercial charter vessels depart from Cairns,

Port Douglas and Cooktown. Advance bookings are required for camping.

How to book: NPRSR 13 7468 www.nprsr.qld.gov.au
Permits: camping permit required

590 Watsons Bay camping area

This campground is just over 1 km from the airstrip at the northern end of Watsons Bay on Lizard Island, and is a great spot for snorkelling and swimming. The camping area is next to the day-use area and close to several walking tracks. Bring all self-sufficient supplies, including pots and pans – the gas BBQ in the campground is an open-flame burner without a hotplate. Water is available from a pump but must be boiled or treated before use. **Map refs:** 436 E5, 461 L1

NGALBA BULAL NATIONAL PARK

About 40 km south of Cooktown, Ngalba Bulal National Park attracts visitors with its beautiful sandy beaches. Getting to its Mangkalba (Cedar Bay) section is a little more challenging than most national parks; you can reach it by boat or along 2 difficult-grade walking tracks. The Home Rule track (16 km one-way, 6–8 hrs) begins at Home Rule Rainforest Lodge, a private property 3 km off the Cooktown–Bloomfield Rd from Rossville. The Gap Creek track (6 km one-way, 4–6 hrs) begins further south on the eastern side of the Cooktown–Bloomfield Rd. Note: access to Rattlesnake Point is restricted to members of the Eastern Kuku Yalanji people.

Who to contact: QPWS Mossman 13 7468 *Permits:* camping permit required *Camping fees:* fees can be paid and permits acquired at QPWS Mossman; or NPRSR Atherton and Cairns business centres

591 Cedar Bay camping area (bush camping)

This campground is just east of Centre Garden at the southern end of the beach. Access is via the Home Rule or Gap Creek walking tracks, or by boat. Generators are not permitted and gas/fuel stoves are preferred. Bring all self-sufficient supplies. Wildlife-watchers can look out for Bennett's tree-kangaroo, the endangered southern cassowary and beach stone-curlew. **Map refs:** 436 E6, 461 L3

OYALA THUMOTANG NATIONAL PARK (CYPAL)

An enormous wilderness park in central Cape York Peninsula, Oyala Thumotang National Park (CYPAL) covers 381 000 ha between the Coen and Archer rivers. The region is the home of the Wik Mungkan, Southern Kaanju and Ayapathu Indigenous peoples. 4WD access is from the Peninsula Developmental Rd, 24 km north of Coen; the ranger headquarters is 72 km west of the Peninsula Developmental Rd. Note: the park is closed Dec–Apr each year for the wet season. Advance bookings are required for camping.

How to book: NPRSR 13 7468 www.nprsr.qld.gov.au
Permits: camping permit required

592 10 Mile Junction 7 camping area (bush camping)

A maximum of 6 self-sufficient campers are permitted to stay at this sandy site by the Archer River in the Langi section of the park. No facilities are provided, so bring all self-sufficient camping gear, including drinking water, rubbish bags and firewood or a gas/fuel stove. **Map refs:** 436 C4, 462 D9

593 10 Mile Junction 8 camping area (bush camping)

A maximum of 6 self-sufficient campers are permitted to stay at this sandy site by the Archer River in the Langi section of the park. No facilities are provided, so bring all self-sufficient camping gear, including drinking water, rubbish bags and firewood or a gas/fuel stove. **Map refs:** 436 C4, 462 D9

594 Chong Swamp camping area (bush camping)

A maximum of 6 self-sufficient campers are permitted to stay at this clearing by the Chong Swamp in the Coen River section of the park. No facilities are provided, so bring all self-sufficient camping gear, including drinking water, rubbish bags and firewood or a gas/fuel stove. **Map refs:** 436 C4, 462 C9

595 First Coen River camping area (bush camping)

A maximum of 8 self-sufficient campers are permitted to stay at this shady clearing by the Coen River in the Coen River section of the park. No facilities are provided, so bring all self-sufficient camping gear, including drinking water, rubbish bags and firewood or a gas/fuel stove. **Map refs:** 436 C4, 462 C9

596 Governors Waterhole camping area (bush camping)

A maximum of 12 self-sufficient campers are permitted to stay in open woodland by Governors Waterhole in the Archer Bend section of the park. No facilities are provided, so bring all self-sufficient camping gear, including drinking water, rubbish bags and firewood or a gas/fuel stove. **Map refs:** 436 C4, 462 C8

597 Horsetailer Waterhole camping area (bush camping)

A maximum of 10 self-sufficient campers are permitted to stay by the bank of the Archer River in the Archer Bend section of the park. No facilities are provided, so bring all self-sufficient camping gear, including drinking water, rubbish bags and firewood or a gas/fuel stove. **Map refs:** 436 C4, 462 C8

598 Jerry Lagoon camping area (bush camping)

A maximum of 6 self-sufficient campers are permitted to stay in the open woodland beside Jerry Lagoon in the Langi section of the park. No facilities are provided, so bring all self-sufficient

camping gear, including drinking water, rubbish bags and firewood or a gas/fuel stove. **Map refs:** 436 C4, 462 D9

599 Langi Lagoon camping area (bush camping)

A maximum of 8 self-sufficient campers are permitted to stay in the open woodland beside Langi Lagoon in the Langi section of the park. No facilities are provided, so bring all self-sufficient camping gear, including drinking water, rubbish bags and firewood or a gas/fuel stove. **Map refs:** 436 C4, 462 D9

600 Mango Lagoon 9 camping area (bush camping)

A maximum of 8 self-sufficient campers are permitted to stay in this open woodland campsite beside Mango Lagoon in the Coen River section of the park. No facilities are provided, so bring all self-sufficient camping gear, including drinking water, rubbish bags and firewood or a gas/fuel stove. **Map refs:** 436 C4, 462 D9

601 Mango Lagoon 10 camping area (bush camping)

A maximum of 8 self-sufficient campers are permitted to stay in this open woodland campsite beside Mango Lagoon in the Coen River section of the park. No facilities are provided, so bring all self-sufficient camping gear, including drinking water, rubbish bags and firewood or a gas/fuel stove. **Map refs:** 436 C4, 462 D9

602 Mango Lagoon 11 camping area (bush camping)

A maximum of 8 self-sufficient campers are permitted to stay in this open woodland campsite beside Mango Lagoon in the Coen River section of the park. No facilities are provided, so bring all self-sufficient camping gear, including drinking water, rubbish bags and firewood or a gas/fuel stove. **Map refs:** 436 C4, 462 D9

603 Night Paddock Lagoon camping area (bush camping)

A maximum of 6 self-sufficient campers are permitted to stay in the open woodland beside Night Paddock Lagoon in the Langi section of the park. No facilities are provided, so bring all self-sufficient camping gear, including drinking water, rubbish bags and firewood or a gas/fuel stove. **Map refs:** 436 C4, 462 D9

604 Old Archer Crossing camping area (bush camping)

A maximum of 8 self-sufficient campers are permitted to stay in this shady campsite on the banks of the Archer River in the Langi section of the park. No facilities are provided, so bring all self-sufficient camping gear, including drinking water, rubbish bags and firewood or a gas/fuel stove. **Map refs:** 436 C4, 462 D9

605 Second Coen River 14 camping area (bush camping)

A maximum of 8 self-sufficient campers are permitted to stay in this clearing by the Coen River in the Coen River section of the park. No facilities are provided, so bring all self-sufficient camping gear including drinking water, rubbish bags and firewood or a gas/fuel stove. **Map refs:** 436 C4, 462 C9

606 Second Coen River 15 camping area (bush camping)

A maximum of 8 self-sufficient campers are permitted to stay in this clearing by the Coen River in the Coen River section of the park. No facilities are provided, so bring all self-sufficient camping gear, including drinking water, rubbish bags and firewood or a gas/fuel stove. **Map refs:** 436 C4, 462 C9

607 Twin Lagoons 5 camping area (bush camping)

A maximum of 8 self-sufficient campers are permitted to stay in this open woodland campsite by Twin Lagoons in the Langi section of the park. No facilities are provided, so bring all self-sufficient camping gear, including drinking water, rubbish bags and firewood or a gas/fuel stove. **Map refs:** 436 C4, 462 D9

608 Twin Lagoons 6 camping area (bush camping)

A maximum of 8 self-sufficient campers are permitted to stay in this open woodland campsite by Twin Lagoons in the Langi section of the park. No facilities are provided, so bring all self-sufficient camping gear, including drinking water, rubbish bags and firewood or a gas/fuel stove. **Map refs:** 436 C4, 462 D9

609 Vardons Lagoon camping area (bush camping)

A maximum of 6 self-sufficient campers are permitted to stay in this cleared area by Vardons Lagoon in the Coen River section of the park. No facilities are provided, so bring all self-sufficient camping gear, including drinking water, rubbish bags and firewood or a gas/fuel stove. **Map refs:** 436 C4, 462 C9

PALMER GOLDFIELD RESOURCES RESERVE

About 280 km north-west of Cairns, Palmer Goldfield Resources Reserve was the site of a major gold rush from 1873. The goldfields have been inactive since the 1880s, but today visitors can view the old sites and reminders of the gold rush. Take the Whites Creek turn-off to Granite and Cannibal creeks from the Peninsula Developmental Rd, then turn north to Dog Leg Creek Junction south-east of Maytown.

Who to contact: NPRSR 13 7468 www.nprsr.qld.gov.au
Permits: camping permit required **Camping fees:** fees can be paid and permits acquired at NPRSR Cairns business centre

610 Dog Leg Crossing camping area (bush camping)

This campsite is located by the Palmer River's Dog Leg Crossing, past the Ida Mine complex. There are 2 main access routes for this area; contact NPRSR for information. No fires are allowed; bring everything you will need. **Map refs:** 436 D6, 461 J4

611 Palmer River camping area (bush camping)

This campground beside the North Palmer River is accessible by 4WD and suits self-sufficient campers only. As with Dog Leg Crossing camping area, there are 2 main access routes for the campground; contact NPRSR for information. **Map refs:** 436 D6, 461 J4

RINYIRRU (LAKEFIELD) NATIONAL PARK (CYPAL)

Rinyirru (Lakefield) National Park (CYPAL) on the Cape York Peninsula is Queensland's second largest park. Stretching from the small outback town of Laura in the south to Princess Charlotte Bay in the north, it is renowned for its vast river systems and spectacular wetlands. Gallery rainforest grows along parts of the Normanby and Kennedy rivers, and monsoonal scrub is found on sections of the park's sandstone escarpments. Rinyirru is a favourite fishing destination of the Cape York Peninsula: anglers can target barramundi, tarpon, catfish and archerfish in the freshwater regions; and mangrove jack, fingermark, cod, trevally, queenfish and salmon in the saltwater areas. Note: the park is closed during the wet season, usually from Dec to the end of Apr, and camping areas north of the Lakefield ranger base are closed until the end of May. Advance bookings are required for camping.

How to book: NPRSR 13 7468 www.nprsr.qld.gov.au
Permits: camping permit required

612 Annie River camping area (bush camping)

The 4WD access track to Annie River, the park's most northerly campground, is off Marina Plains Rd, about 14 km north of Lakefield Rd. Bring drinking water, firewood and a gas/fuel stove. Never swim, canoe, clean fish or prepare food at the water's edge, or camp close to deep waterholes, as estuarine crocodiles live in these waters. **Map refs:** 436 D5, 462 F11

613 Basin Hole camping area (bush camping)

This basic campsite for self-sufficient campers only is on Jam Tin Creek, 28 km north of Lakefield ranger base and 9 km north-east of Hann Crossing. Bring all self-sufficient gear, including drinking water, rubbish bags and firewood or a gas/fuel stove. **Map refs:** 436 D5, 461 J1, 462 G12

614 Bizant River camping area (bush camping)

This bush camp is located on a flat patch adjacent to the Bizant River boat ramp – an unformed boat launch that offers access to the tidal Bizant River and Princess Charlotte Bay. It is 25 km north-north-east of Hann Crossing by road. Bring all self-sufficient gear, including drinking water, rubbish bags and firewood or a gas/fuel stove. **Map refs:** 436 D5, 462 G11

615 Bottom Whiphandle Waterhole camping area (bush camping)

Just a few km north of Top Whiphandle, Bottom Whiphandle Waterhole is about 29 km north-east of Hann Crossing, reached from Bizant Outstation. Recreational fishing is permitted at all camping areas. Check with a ranger for current fishing restrictions and regulations. Note: canoeing is not recommended due to the presence of crocodiles. **Map refs:** 436 D5, 461 J1, 462 G11

616 Brown Creek camping area (bush camping)

This campsite, close to the Bizant River boat ramp and camping area, lies at the junction of Brown Creek and Bizant River, 26 km north-north-east of Hann Crossing by road. Bring all self-sufficient gear, including drinking water, rubbish bags and firewood or a gas/fuel stove. **Map refs:** 436 D5, 462 G11

617 Dingo Waterhole camping area (bush camping)

Dingo Waterhole is 33 km north of New Laura Ranger Station and a further 9 km from the Lakefield Rd turn-off. Open fires are allowed but generators are not permitted. **Map refs:** 436 D5, 461 J1, 462 G12

618 Five Mile Creek camping area (bush camping)

This small site is about 5 km south-west of Annie River camping area, and suits self-sufficient campers only. Use the existing fire sites, and preferably bring a gas/fuel stove. **Map refs:** 436 D5, 462 F11

619 Hann Crossing camping area

Most campers visiting Rinyirru stay at either Kalpowar or this campground at Hann Crossing on Lakefield Rd, 29 km north of Lakefield Ranger Station. Accessible by 4WD only, there are 17 numbered sites for general use and 2 for commercial operators. Bring drinking water, firewood, rubbish bags and a gas/fuel stove. William Hann made a crossing of the North Kennedy River here during his expedition to Cape York in 1872. He also discovered gold on the Palmer River, initiating the rush of 1873, which resulted in the tracks through the southern end of the park. **Map refs:** 436 D5, 461 J1, 462 F12

620 Hanush's Waterhole camping area (bush camping)

To reach Hanush's Waterhole, take the access track signposted about 7 km north of Lakefield Ranger Station, then travel a further 7.5 km to the camping area. This site suits self-sufficient campers only; use existing fire sites (a gas/fuel stove is preferred). **Map refs:** 436 D5, 461 J1, 462 G12

621 Horseshoe Lagoon camping area (bush camping)

To reach this campground for self-sufficient campers, head for Old Laura Homestead then turn onto Battle Camp Rd and travel 29 km east of Old Laura to the turn-off. Check with a ranger for current fishing restrictions and regulations. Canoeing is not recommended in some areas of the park due to the presence of crocodiles. **Map refs:** 436 D5, 461 K2

622 Kalpowar Crossing Campground

Rinyirru's most popular camping ground, with the best facilities, Kalpowar is 3 km east of the Lakefield Ranger Station, next to an 8 km stretch of permanent fresh waterholes on the Normanby River. Accessible by 4WD only, there are 14 numbered sites for general use and 4 numbered sites set aside for commercial operators. Wildlife-watchers can explore the 4 km walking track and boaties can launch their craft from the causeway. Water provided here must be boiled or treated before use. Bring your own firewood. Note: generators are not permitted. **Map refs:** 436 D5, 461 J1, 462 G12

623 Kennedy Bend Waterhole camping area (bush camping)

Kennedy Bend Waterhole is on Lakefield Rd, 8 km north of New Laura Ranger Station. Rinyirru (Lakefield) National Park protects a number of threatened species, including the golden-shouldered parrot, star finch, red goshawk, Lakeland Downs mouse and spectacled hare-wallaby. A variety of fish inhabit the rivers, including barramundi. Campers need to use the existing fire sites and preferably bring a gas/fuel stove. **Map refs:** 436 D5, 461 J2, 462 G12

624 Melaleuca Waterhole camping area (bush camping)

This waterhole's access track is signposted about 7 km north-west of Lakefield Ranger Station; approximately 19 km further on you'll find the camping area with 4 sites. Rinyirru has an extensive river system comprising the Normanby, Morehead and North Kennedy rivers and their tributaries. During the wet season, these waterways join to flood vast areas, eventually draining into Princess Charlotte Bay. Bring all self-sufficient supplies. **Map refs:** 436 D5, 461 J1, 462 G12

625 Mick Fienn Waterhole camping area (bush camping)

Mick Fienn Waterhole is 33 km north of New Laura Ranger Station and a further 9 km from the Lakefield Rd turn-off, just north of Dingo Waterhole. There are 5 numbered sites; campsites 1, 2 and 5 provide good shade and access to permanent deep holes in the river. During the dry season, the rivers and creeks in the region shrink, leaving large permanent waterholes, lakes and lagoons interspersed with flood plains, ridges and riverbeds. Bring all self-sufficient supplies. **Map refs:** 436 D5, 461 J1, 462 G12

626 Midway Waterhole camping area (bush camping)

The access track to Midway Waterhole is signposted about 6 km north-west of Lakefield Ranger Station; then it's a further 3.7 km to the camping area. This site suits self-sufficient campers only; use existing fire sites (gas/fuel stove preferred). For wildlife-watchers, in the open woodland and grassland areas of Rinyirru (Lakefield) National Park, agile wallabies are abundant; the northern nailtail wallaby and Australian bustard are harder to find. **Map refs:** 436 D5, 461 J1, 462 G12

627 Old Faithful Waterhole camping area (bush camping)

Turn off about 23 km north of New Laura Ranger Station to reach this campground, about 6 km east of Lakefield Rd. There are 3 numbered campsites next to the waterhole on the Normanby River, an ideal spot for fishing. Open fires and generators are allowed; a gas/fuel stove is preferred. **Map refs:** 436 D5, 461 J2, 462 G12

628 Old Laura Homestead camping area (bush camping)

This campsite is next to the historical Old Laura Homestead, a cattle homestead recently restored from years of decay and vandalism and now protected by the Queensland Heritage Register. There are no facilities, so bring all self-sufficient gear, including drinking water, rubbish bags and firewood or a gas/fuel stove. **Map refs:** 436 D5, 461 J2

629 Orange Plain Waterhole camping area (bush camping)

This waterhole is about 18 km north-east of Hann Crossing via Bizant Outstation. Campers must be totally self-sufficient; bring drinking water, firewood and preferably a gas/fuel stove. During the dry season, the rivers and creeks shrink, leaving large permanent waterholes, lakes and lagoons interspersed with flood plains, ridges and riverbeds. **Map refs:** 436 D5, 461 J1, 462 G12

630 Saltwater Crossing camping area (bush camping)

This campground is on Lakefield Rd, about 32 km north-west of Hann Crossing and about 8 km east of Marina Plains Rd. There are 2 areas – on the east and west side of the causeway – both with 2 campsites for self-sufficient campers only. **Map refs:** 436 D5, 462 F11

631 Six Mile Waterhole camping area (bush camping)

Six Mile Waterhole is about 15 km south of the New Laura Ranger Station, 3 km east of Lakefield Rd. The park's wetlands attract

---

a diversity of animals, particularly waterbirds. Look for brolgas, sarus cranes, black-necked storks, comb-crested jacanas, magpie geese and ducks. It is for self-sufficient campers only; use the existing fire sites. **Map refs:** 436 D5, 461 J2

632 Sweetwater Lake camping area (bush camping)

At the northern section of the park near Nifold Plain, Sweetwater Lake is 2 km south of Marina Plains Rd near the information station. It is for self-sufficient campers only; use fire sites (a gas/fuel stove is preferred). Termite mounds – both magnetic and cathedral constructions – are a common sight on the grasslands, particularly on the Nifold Plain. **Map refs:** 436 D5, 461 I1, 462 F11

633 Top Whiphandle Waterhole camping area (bush camping)

Top Whiphandle Waterhole is about 20 km north-east of Hann Crossing via Bizant Outstation. Campers must be totally self-sufficient, and preferably bring a gas/fuel stove; use existing fire sites. **Map refs:** 436 D5, 461 J1, 462 G12

634 Twelve Mile Lagoon camping area (bush camping)

Twelve Mile Lagoon is near the Normanby River about 12 km east of Lakefield Rd; take the turn-off opposite New Laura Ranger Station. There are 9 numbered sites; open fires are allowed in the provided rings and generators are permitted. Bring all self-sufficient supplies. Rinyirru (Lakefield) has an extensive river system comprising the Normanby, Morehead and North Kennedy rivers and their tributaries. During the wet season, these waterways join to flood vast areas, eventually draining into Princess Charlotte Bay. **Map refs:** 436 D5, 461 J2

635 Welcome Waterhole camping area (bush camping)

The Welcome Waterhole is about 7 km from Horseshoe Lagoon and about 6 km north of Battle Camp Rd. The turn-off from Battle Camp Rd is about 30 km east of Old Laura Homestead. Bring all self-sufficient supplies. **Map refs:** 436 D5, 461 K2

RUSSELL RIVER NATIONAL PARK

Situated about 83 km south-east of Cairns, Russell River National Park is a small coastal park within the Wet Tropics World Heritage Area. The park occupies a section of the Graham Range between the Russell River and the coastal mangroves. There is a high incidence of estuarine crocodiles in the region.

Who to contact: NPRSR 13 7468 www.nprsr.qld.gov.au
Permits: camping permit required ***Camping fees:*** fees can be paid and permits acquired at the self-registration station

636 Graham Range camping area (bush camping)

This sandy campground with 5 separate sites is next to the beach and accessible only by 4WD. To get here, turn off the

Bruce Hwy at Miriwinni, 65 km south of Cairns, and follow the road for 17 km to Bramston Beach. At Bramston Beach, turn left onto Sassafras St and follow the track for 5.5 km to Bluemetal Creek. From the mouth of Bluemetal Creek, follow the unsealed road 1.5 km to the self-registration stand. This camping area is suitable for self-sufficient campers only; fires are permitted (bring firewood) but a gas/fuel stove is preferred. **Map refs:** 436 E7, 461 M7

SPEEWAH CONSERVATION PARK

Speewah Conservation Park is a small (15.2 ha) park on the western border of Barron Gorge National Park, 42 km north-west of Cairns. It provides excellent access to Barron Gorge's tropical wonderland of rainforests, butterflies and waterfalls. The Skyrail and scenic train provide picturesque jaunts through the area, reached from Kuranda on the Kennedy Hwy.

Who to contact: NPRSR 13 7468 www.nprsr.qld.gov.au
Permits: camping permit required *Camping fees:* fees can be paid and permits acquired at the self-registration station

637 Speewah Campground

This campground is in the conservation park adjacent to Barron Gorge National Park's western boundary. It is reached from the Kennedy Hwy, 10 km west of Kuranda, then a further 6 km east to the site. You can also get here from Stoney Creek Rd, off Speewah Rd. Fires are prohibited, so bring a gas/fuel stove along with all other self-sufficient supplies (water is provided). Take the 570 m bush boardwalk to the falls, or check out Wrights Lookout, a 1 km (30 min) walk from the Barron Falls carpark. **Map refs:** 436 E7, 461 L6

THREE ISLANDS GROUP NATIONAL PARK

An archipelago stretching 44–72 km north-east of Cooktown, Three Islands Group National Park is one of the most remote and unspoiled national parks in Queensland. These islands are particularly significant as breeding sites for seabirds, including the wedge-tailed shearwater. Access is by private boat or accredited tour company only. Advance bookings are required for camping.

How to book: NPRSR 13 7468 www.nprsr.qld.gov.au
Permits: camping permit required

638 Two Islands camping area (boat-based camping)

Bush camping is permitted on Two Islands A, the larger western island in the Two Islands group, between Apr and Aug each year. Camping outside these times is prohibited, to protect nesting seabirds. There are no facilities and open fires are not permitted; bring all self-sufficient camping gear, including drinking water, rubbish bags and a gas/fuel stove. **Map refs:** 436 E5, 461 L2

TULLY FALLS NATIONAL PARK

Bring an umbrella or raincoat with you when you visit Tully Falls National Park – part of the Wet Tropics World Heritage

Area, it is one of the wettest places in Australia, receiving approximately 400 cm of rain per annum. Tully Falls protects a dazzling variety of wildlife, including species found only in the Wet Tropics, such as Lumholtz's tree-kangaroo and the golden bowerbird. Camping in the park is prohibited except for hikers taking the Misty Mountains Wilderness Walking Tracks. Advance bookings are required for camping.

How to book: NPRSR 13 7468 www.nprsr.qld.gov.au
Permits: camping permit required

639 Cannabullen Creek camping area (walk-in camping)

This campsite on the Cardwell Range track is 11 km from Hinson Creek trailhead, 10 km from Hinson Creek camping area and 9.5 km from Cardwell Range trailhead. There are no facilities provided; bring all self-sufficient camping gear, including drinking water, rubbish bags and a gas/fuel stove. **Map refs:** 436 E7, 461 L7

640 Carter Creek camping area (walk-in camping)

This campsite on the Cannabullen Creek track is 8 km from the Hinson Creek trailhead, 6.5 km from Hinson Creek camping area, and 6.5 km from Cochable Creek camping area. There are no facilities provided; bring all self-sufficient camping gear, including drinking water, rubbish bags and a gas/fuel stove. **Map refs:** 436 E7, 461 L8

641 Hinson Creek camping area (walk-in camping)

This campsite near the intersection of the Cannabullen Creek and Cardwell Range tracks is 1 km from Hinson Creek trailhead, 19 km from Cardwell Range trailhead, 10 km from Cannabullen Creek camping area and 6.5 km from Carter Creek camping area. There are no facilities provided; bring all self-sufficient camping gear, including drinking water, rubbish bags and a gas/fuel stove. **Map refs:** 436 E7, 461 L8

642 Koolmoon Creek Headwaters camping area (walk-in camping)

This campsite on the Koolmoon Creek track is 1.3 km from Koolmoon Creek Headwaters trailhead and 12.3 km from Walters Waterhole camping area. There are no facilities provided; bring all self-sufficient camping gear, including drinking water, rubbish bags and a gas/fuel stove. **Map refs:** 436 E7, 461 L8

643 Walters Waterhole camping area (walk-in camping)

This campsite on the Koolmoon Creek track is 3.4 km from Djilgarrin trailhead, 12.3 km from Koolmoon Creek Headwaters and 12 km from Cochable Creek camping area. There are no facilities provided; bring all self-sufficient camping gear, including drinking water, rubbish bags and a gas/fuel stove. **Map refs:** 436 E8, 461 L8

TULLY GORGE NATIONAL PARK

Famous for the whitewater rafting on the Tully River, Tully Gorge National Park is 35 km north-west of the town of Tully. Home to the Jirrbal Indigenous people, the park offers bushwalking, swimming and panoramic lookouts. The park can be accessed by conventional vehicle along Cardstone and Gulnay rds. The Misty Mountains Wilderness Walking Tracks pass through Tully Gorge; the campsite at Cochable Creek is for hikers only. Advance bookings are required for camping.

How to book: NPRSR 13 7468 www.nprsr.qld.gov.au
Permits: camping permit required

644 Cochable Creek camping area

This campsite at the intersection of the Koolmoon Creek and Cannabullen Creek tracks is 15.4 km from Djilgarrin trailhead, 12 km from Walters Waterhole and 14.5 km from Hinson Creek trailhead. It is one of the few camping areas on the Misty Mountains tracks that can be accessed by car. Basic facilities are provided; bring all self-sufficient camping gear, including drinking water, rubbish bags and a gas/fuel stove.
Map refs: 436 E8, 461 L8

645 Tully Gorge camping area

Accessible by 2WD via a bitumen road, this grassy site is the only campground in the national park available to non-hikers. A 375 m return wheelchair-accessible rainforest walk starts from the picnic and camping area. Watch the whitewater rafters from the Flip Wilson lookout, 2 km beyond the campground. Note: open fires are prohibited and bring all self-sufficient supplies.
Map refs: 436 E8, 461 L8

TURTLE GROUP NATIONAL PARK

Turtle Group National Park protects 4 very small islands in the Great Barrier Reef Marine Park, about 30 km west of Lizard Island. Access is by private boat only. Visitors should be aware that estuarine crocodiles live in the surrounding waters and that marine stingers are present Oct–May. Advance bookings are required for camping.

How to book: NPRSR 13 7468 www.nprsr.qld.gov.au
Permits: camping permit required

646 Nymph Island camping area (boat-based camping)

Camping is permitted on the northern edge of Nymph Island, 35 km east of Murdoch Point. There are no facilities on-site; bring all self-sufficient supplies. Note: fishing is prohibited in the waters of the Turtle Group. **Map refs:** 436 E5, 461 L1

647 Turtle Group A camping area (boat-based camping)

Camping is permitted anywhere on Turtle Group A, the second largest islet in the Turtle Group, west of Turtle Group B. There are no facilities on-site; bring all self-sufficient supplies. Note: fishing is prohibited in the waters surrounding the Turtle Group. **Map refs:** 436 E5, 461 L1

648 Turtle Group B camping area (boat-based camping)

Camping is permitted anywhere on Turtle Group B, the largest and southernmost islet in the Turtle Group. There are no facilities on-site; bring all self-sufficient supplies. Note: fishing is prohibited in the waters surrounding the Turtle Group. **Map refs:** 436 E5, 461 L1

649 Turtle Group F camping area (boat-based camping)

Camping is permitted anywhere on Turtle Group F, the second most northerly islet in the Turtle Group. There are no facilities on-site; bring all self-sufficient supplies. Note: fishing is prohibited in the waters surrounding the Turtle Group. **Map refs:** 436 E5, 461 L1

WOOROONOORAN NATIONAL PARK

Part of the Wet Tropics World Heritage Area, Wooroonooran National Park boasts the 2 highest mountains in Queensland, including Mt Bartle Frere, along with wild rivers, spectacular waterfalls and lush rainforests, which blanket the landscape from foothills to summits. Widely regarded as one of the most scenic areas of the Wet Tropics, yet receiving few visitors, Wooroonooran is one of Queensland's best-kept secrets. The Misty Mountains Wilderness Walking Tracks pass through Wooroonooran; the campsite at Downey Creek is for hikers only. A small number of self-registration sites are available at Goldsborough Valley, but advance bookings are required for all other areas.

How to book: NPRSR 13 7468 www.nprsr.qld.gov.au
Permits: camping permit required **Camping fees:** fees can be paid and permits acquired for Goldsborough Valley at the self-registration station

Bartle Frere Trail

Please note that campsites are listed in alphabetical order, not track order. Refer to the map on p.436 for further information.

650 Big Rock camping area (walk-in camping)

The Big Rock camp clearing is a 3 km walk north-west of the Josephine Falls parking area, and is suitable for self-sufficient campers only. For experienced walkers, Josephine Falls is the starting point for the difficult Mt Bartle Frere Trail (15 km one-way, 2 days), which leads to the summit and back. Broken Nose Track (10 km return, 8 hr) offers a shorter but equally steep alternative. The summit can also be approached from the Atherton Tableland, again a challenging 2-day walk.
Map refs: 436 E7, 461 M7

651 Eastern Summit camping area (walk-in camping)

This campground for self-sufficient campers only has excellent views over Innisfail and the undulating Atherton Tableland. The site is 4 km north-west of Big Rock camping area and 7 km from the Josephine Falls parking area. Make sure you check weather conditions with the ranger before undertaking the Bartle Frere Trail, as clouds can move in quickly on the upper reaches of the mountain and rainstorms are common all year. The dry season, May–Oct, is the best time to walk the trail. **Map refs:** 436 E7, 461 M7

652 Junction camping area (bush camping)

At the western end of the Mt Bartle Frere walking trail, campers can walk in or access the site via road (unsuitable for conventional vehicles when wet). Go birdwatching during the day and search for possums by spotlight at night. The many beautiful waterfalls along the national park's walking tracks are a photographer's delight. Note: there are no facilities on-site; campers must be self-sufficient. **Map refs:** 436 E7, 461 L7

653 Western Summit camping area (walk-in camping)

Accessible only on foot, this campground is an 8 km walk from the Junction camping area at the Atherton Tableland (west) end of the walking trail. The Bartle Frere summit is just 750 m from this camp. There are no facilities. The Mt Bartle Frere area is the spiritual home of the Noongyanbudda Ngadjon and the place their spirits return to when they die. **Map refs:** 436 E7, 461 L7

654 Downey Creek camping area (walk-in camping)

This campsite on the Gorrell track, one of the Misty Mountain Wilderness Walking Tracks, is 15.5 km from eastern Gorrell trailhead and 10.3 km from western Gorrell trailhead. There are no facilities provided; bring all self-sufficient camping gear, including drinking water, rubbish bags and a gas/fuel stove. **Map refs:** 436 E7, 461 L8

655 Goldsborough Valley camping area

This grassy, shady site for self-sufficient campers is on the banks of the Mulgrave River, 25 km south-west of Gordonvale. There are 4 numbered sites for e-permit holders, each with its own alcove. Open fires are permitted in the existing fire rings. Check out the Goldfield trail, a 19 km one-way (7–9 hr) track following the footsteps of the gold prospectors from the camping area along the Mulgrave River. Bring firewood and drinking water. **Map refs:** 436 E7, 461 L7

656 Henrietta Creek camping area

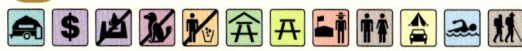

Accessible by 2WD, this grassy camping area is signposted off the Palmerston Hwy, 38 km from Innisfail. There are 3 numbered

and 20 unnumbered sites. The park's Wet Tropics' endemics include the tiny musky rat-kangaroo, double-eyed fig-parrot and chowchilla. At Henrietta Creek there are also platypus and freshwater turtles. Golden bowerbirds, which only live at elevations above 900 m between Paluma and Cooktown, can be seen Nov–Jan in this section of the park. Bring drinking water. **Map refs:** 436 E7, 461 L7

657 South Johnstone camping area

This small spot on the banks of the South Johnstone River offers room for about 5 tents (camper trailers are accommodated in the nearby carpark). The main activities here are swimming and short walks, and it connects with the Misty Mountains Wilderness Walking Tracks. It is 12.3 km from Palmerston Hwy on K-Tree Rd, or 2.4 km from the western Gorrell track trailhead. Fires are prohibited: bring water and a gas/fuel stove. **Map refs:** 436 E7, 461 L8

WUTHARA ISLAND NATIONAL PARK (CYPAL)

Located 58 km north of Lockhart River, Wuthara Island National Park (CYPAL) comprises 3 islands of the Wuthara Group. These steep, high continental islands are covered in melaleuca scrub and dramatic headlands. Access is by private boat from Lockhart River or accredited tour company only. Advance bookings are required for camping.

How to book: NPRSR 13 7468 www.nprsr.qld.gov.au
Permits: camping permit required

**658 Wuthara Island camping area
(boat-based camping)**

Bush camping is permitted above the high-water mark on the main beach on the north-west of the main Wuthara Island. There are no facilities and open fires are not permitted; bring all self-sufficient camping gear, including drinking water, rubbish bags and a gas/fuel stove. **Map refs:** 436 D3, 462 E6

CAMPSITES LOCATED IN OTHER AREAS

659 Archer River Roadhouse

Archer River Roadhouse is open Apr–Dec and closed at other times due to the wet season. The licensed roadhouse offers meals, fuel and basic mechanical repairs. In addition to the camping facilities, 10 single air-conditioned rooms and 4 twin rooms are also available on-site. The roadhouse is on the Peninsula Developmental Rd, 64 km north of Coen. **Map refs:** 436 C4, 462 D9

How to book: Peninsula Developmental Rd, Archer River (07) 4060 3266

660 Armbrust & Co camping area

Across the road from the Exchange Hotel on Regent St in the centre of the town of Coen, this campground has 14 campsites and space for 2 vehicles per site; bring your own firewood. Due to the summer wet season and impassable roads, the campground is open Apr–Dec. Coen is about 100 km north of the Musgrave Roadhouse and 65 km south of the Archer River Roadhouse. **Map refs:** 436 C4, 462 E10

How to book: Regent St, Coen (07) 4060 1134

661 Babinda Creek camping area

This campground beside the creek is a great spot for camping with kids. It's east of the Bruce Hwy on Howard Kennedy Dr in Babinda, 24 km north of Innisfail. Note: there is a maximum stay of 72 hr. **Map refs:** 436 E7, 461 M7

Who to contact: Babinda Information Centre (07) 4067 1008

662 The Bend camping area

This small campground has space for 6 caravans or camper trailers, so make it an overnight stop only. It is set beside the Coen River on the Peninsula Developmental Rd, 3 km north of Coen. In the centre of the Cape York Peninsula, Coen is part of the large Cook Shire Council. Note: there are no showers at the toilet block. **Map refs:** 436 C4, 462 E10

Who to contact: Cooktown Tourist Information Centre (07) 4069 6004

663 BIG4 Port Douglas Glengarry Holiday Park

This holiday park offers campers a quiet getaway tucked in the undisturbed Mowbray River Valley, 6 km from Port Douglas. It offers a variety of creature comforts, including free wireless internet, a laundry and a jumping pillow. It also offers caravan and vehicle storage for those who wish to explore the cape in a rented 4WD. Bookings are recommended. **Map refs:** 436 E7, 461 L5

How to book: Mowbray River Rd, Craiglie (07) 4098 5922, 1800 888 134 www.glengarrypark.com.au

664 The Boulders camping area

This campground beside a creek is 6 km west of Babinda on Boulders Rd, with signposted access off the Bruce Hwy. There are 5 sites with no more than 5 people per site. Note: there is a maximum stay of 48 hr. **Map refs:** 436 E7, 461 M7

Who to contact: Babinda Information Centre (07) 4067 1008

665 Bramston Beach Campground

This campground in a small village with just a general store provides a quiet, relaxing stopover or weekend getaway. Bramston Beach is on the coast, 10 km north-east of Miriwinni on the Bruce Hwy, with excellent coastal scenery. The campground is on Evans Rd. There are no powered sites, but a washing machine is available for use. There is a boat ramp 1.5 km down the road. Bookings are required for peak periods. **Map refs:** 436 E7, 461 M7

How to book: Evans Rd, Bramston Beach (07) 4067 4121

666 Bramwell Junction camping area

Refuel with hamburgers and beverages at the roadhouse, then set up camp at this site at the junction of the Telegraph Track and Bypass Rd, about 40 km north of Cape York's Old Moreton Telegraph Station. Note: fireplaces are provided but you will need to bring your own firewood. **Map refs:** 436 C3, 462 D5

Who to contact: cnr Telegraph Track and Bypass Rd (07) 4060 3230

667 Bramwell Station Tourist Park

The most northerly cattle station in Australia, Bramwell Station is east of Cape York's Peninsula Developmental Rd, signposted 12 km south of Bramwell Junction. The campground is grassy and shady, with several mango and frangipani trees; bring your own firewood. The station has a licensed bar and serves meals; unit accommodation is also available on-site. **Map refs:** 436 C3, 462 D6

Who to contact: Bramwell Station (07) 4060 3300 www.bramwellstationtouristpark.com.au

668 Bull Crossing camping area

This campground is east of the Kowanyama Aboriginal community, a traditional land open for camping and barramundi fishing June–Sept. There is a boat launch suitable for small boats. Due to limited space, permission from the Kowanyama Land Office is essential for camping here; advance bookings are recommended. Bring all self-sufficient supplies. Note: alcohol is prohibited on Kowanyama lands; heavy fines apply. **Map refs:** 436 B5, 460 E2

How to book: Kowanyama Land Office (07) 4060 5187
Permits: camping permit required

669 Cairns Coconut Holiday Resort

This holiday park, located just outside the hustle and bustle of Cairns, offers excellent facilities and enviable access to the region's attractions. Facilities include a water park for the kids, an 18-hole minigolf course and outdoor movies under the stars. Advance bookings are recommended. **Map refs:** 436 E7, 461 L6

How to book: 23–51 Anderson Rd, Woree (07) 4054 6644 www.coconut.com.au

670 Cape York camping areas (bush camping)

It isn't an easy route, with river crossings to navigate and unstable road conditions, but driving to the tip of Cape York is one of Australia's most sensationally scenic 4WD trips. You'll find a number of bush campsites throughout the Cape, north from the Dulhunty River on Injinoo Community Council land. The best time to visit is June–Sept. Note: alcohol restrictions apply in the far north cape; check limits and zoned areas before embarking. **Map refs:** 436 C2, 462 C3

Who to contact: Northern Peninsula Area Regional Council (07) 4069 3252 **Camping fees:** included in the Jardine River Ferry fee

671 Chapman River camping area

This camping area at the mouth of the river near the airstrip is a great spot for fishing. The Pormpuraaw Aboriginal Community is on the western coast of Cape York on the Gulf of Carpentaria, about 200 km west of Musgrave. The access road is open from late May, depending on the wet season; a 4WD is recommended. Note: alcohol is strictly prohibited in Pormpuraaw; heavy penalties apply. **Map refs:** 436 B5, 460 E1, 462 A12

How to book: Pormpuraaw Shire Council (07) 4060 4600 www.pormpuraaw.qld.gov.au **Permits:** camping and vehicle permits required in advance

672 Chuulangun Aboriginal Corporation Campgrounds

A great spot for birdwatching and enjoying the natural surrounds, Chuulangun Aboriginal Corporation Campgrounds are about 5 km from the upper Wenlock crossing on Portland Roads Rd. There are no facilities besides the amenities block. No alcohol is permitted on-site and you need to bring your own drinking water. **Map refs:** 436 C4, 462 D8

Who to contact: Kaanju Chuulangun Aboriginal Corporation (07) 4060 3240 www.kaanjungaachi.com.au **Permits:** a permit may be required for activities other than camping; contact Kaanju Chuulangun Aboriginal Corporation to discuss your proposed itinerary **Camping fees:** fees can be paid at the self-registration station or to the ranger

673 Cullen Point camping area

Self-sufficient campers can stay at Cullen Point, 10 km north of Mapoon and 95 km north of Weipa, with access via Mapoon Rd. Note: alcohol restrictions are enforced in Mapoon Shire and heavy penalties apply; check current limits before embarking. This campsite is closed during the wet season. **Map refs:** 436 B3, 462 B5

Who to contact: Weipa Camping Ground (07) 4069 7871 **Permits:** camping and vehicle access permits required **Camping fees:** fees can be paid and permits acquired at Weipa Camping Ground

674 Discovery Holiday Parks – Lake Tinaroo

Just 150 m from Lake Tinaroo, this caravan park has an excellent range of facilities for a comfortable stay after a day of boating or waterskiing on the lake. Other activities include fishing for barramundi or sooty grunter, or driving through Danbulla State Forest nearby. The caravan park is on Tinaroo Falls Dam Rd, about 16 km north-east of Atherton. There's a general store on-site, laundry facilities, a swimming pool and the option of staying in villas or cabins. Bookings are recommended at peak periods. **Map refs:** 436 E7, 461 L6

How to book: 4–28 Tinaroo Falls Dam Rd, Tinaroo (07) 4095 8232, 1300 727 044 www.discoveryholidayparks.com.au/qld/atherton_tableland/lake_tinaroo

675 Ducie Creek camping area (bush camping)

Bush camping is permitted at this site on the 4WD Telegraph Track, 2.6 km north of Palm Creek camping area and 12.5 km south of North Alice Creek. There are no facilities; bring all self-sufficient gear. **Map refs:** 436 C3, 462 D5

Who to contact: Bramwell Junction (07) 4060 3230; or Northern Peninsula Regional Council (07) 4069 6800

676 False Pera Head camping area

This campground for self-sufficient campers is north of the Aurukun Community, reached from Aurukun Rd, off the Peninsula Developmental Rd. Camping and vehicle permits are required and you need to bring all self-sufficient camping gear. Alcohol is prohibited; heavy fines apply. **Map refs:** 436 B3, 462 A8

How to book: Aurukun Land and Sea Management (07) 4060 6831 **Permits:** camping and access permit required **Camping fees:** acquire permits and pay fees in advance through Aurukun Land and Sea Management

677 Granite Gorge Nature Park

Formed millions of years ago by ancient volcanoes, the boulders at Granite Gorge are a natural wonder well worth checking out. Some, allegedly, are shaped like animals. The tent sites are shady; safari tent accommodation is also available and there's a kiosk serving light lunches. Take a walk beside the creek, go fishing or feed the wallabies. Granite Gorge Nature Park is 12 km west of Mareeba on Chewko Rd. Note: laundry facilities are available. **Map refs:** 436 E7, 461 L6

How to book: Chewko Rd, Chewko (07) 4093 2259 www.granitegorge.com.au

678 Hann River Roadhouse

This riverside camping ground is a great spot for watching wildlife such as birds and wallabies. It is next to the roadhouse on Peninsula Developmental Rd, 74 km north-west of Laura and 62 km south of Musgrave. The roadhouse serves food daily and stocks basic food supplies. **Map refs:** 436 D5, 461 I2

Who to contact: (07) 4060 3242

679 Home Rule Rainforest Lodge

Camp on the riverbank at this site on the Cooktown–Bloomfield Rd in Rossville. From Cape Tribulation, drive 50 km to Bloomfield (across the Bloomfield River) and along the edge of Cedar Bay National Park to reach Rossville. On-site facilities include a coin-operated washing machine and dryer, licensed bar, canoe hire and budget meals. **Map refs:** 436 E6, 461 L3

How to book: Home Rule Rd, Rossville (07) 4060 3925 www.home-rule.com.au

680 Jardine River Ferry camping area

This basic campsite is located near the Jardine River ferry crossing at the Northern Bypass Rd, 290 km north of the Archer River Roadhouse. Bring your own drinking water or treat or boil the river water before using. **Map refs:** 436 C2, 462 C3

Who to contact: Jardine River Ferry (07) 4069 1369

681 Kurrimine Beach Caravan Park

This very basic council campground is on Robert Johnson Pde in Kurrimine Beach, about 9 km east of the Bruce Hwy, accessed from Silkwood. The closest major town is Innisfail, about 30 km north of Kurrimine. The nearby Kurrimine Conservation Park features a 600 m walking track through a vine forest that's great for wildlife-watching. There are laundry facilities on-site, and you need to bring a gas/fuel stove. **Map refs:** 436 E8, 461 M8

Who to contact: Tully Visitor Information Centre (07) 4068 2288

682 Lakeland Caravan Park

Lakeland Caravan Park is at the junction of the Mulligan Hwy and Peninsula Development Rd in the town of Lakeland, between the Laura and Normanby rivers. On site you'll find a small internet cafe with 3 coin-operated computers, and a shop for groceries and fuel. Backpacker rooms are also available. **Map refs:** 436 E6, 461 K3

How to book: 1 Sesame St, Lakeland (07) 4060 2033 www.lakelandcaravanpark.com.au

683 Lions Den Hotel

One of Cape York's iconic pubs, the Lions Den offers excellent riverside camping on its spacious property with plenty of shade and natural surrounds. Powered campsites have access to an amenities block and drinkable water, as well as washing machines and dryers. Unpowered sites are near cool swimming holes and semi-rainforest settings. The Lions Den is at Helenvale, 32 km south of Cooktown on the Bloomfield Track. Note: safari lodges and air-conditioned 'donga' demountable accommodation are also available. Bookings are essential June–Oct. **Map refs:** 436 E6, 461 L3

How to book: 398 Shiptons Flat Rd, Helenvale (07) 4060 3911 www.lionsdenhotel.com.au

684 Loyalty Beach Campground and Fishing Lodge

Loyalty Beach is a 500 m strip of beachfront campsites just 45 min from Australia's most northerly point. The region is a popular place for fishing, 4WD tours and scenic flights over the islands. The campground has laundry facilities and a kiosk with gas and ice, and pets are permitted under supervision. Other accommodation options include the air-conditioned fishing lodge and 2-storey, open-air guesthouse. It is 3 km north of Seisia Wharf, signposted from Seisia. Note: this campsite is a designated 'wet' area, but alcohol restrictions apply in the surrounding areas; check current restrictions before embarking. **Map refs:** 436 C2, 462 C3

How to book: 1 Loyalty Beach Rd, New Mapoon (07) 4069 3372 www.loyaltybeach.com.au

Misty Mountains Wilderness Walking Tracks

This 130 km network of walking tracks takes hikers through high-altitude tropical rainforests with crystal-clear creeks and stunning views. There are 4 main walking tracks (Koolmoon Creek, Cannabullen Creek, Cardwell Range and Gorrell) which wind their way through several national parks (Millstream Falls, Tully Falls, Tully Gorge and Wooroonooran) in a region roughly bounded by Tully, Innisfail, Mena Creek, Millaa Millaa and Ravenshoe. Advance bookings are required for camping.

Please note that campsites are listed in alphabetical order, not track order. Refer to the map on p. 436 for further information.

How to book: NPRSR 13 7468 www.nprsr.qld.gov.au
Permits: camping permit required

639 Cannabullen Creek camping area (walk-in camping)

See p. 447.

640 Carter Creek camping area (walk-in camping)

See p. 447.

644 **Cochable Creek camping area**

See p. 448.

654 **Downey Creek camping area (walk-in camping)**

See p. 449.

641 **Hinson Creek camping area (walk-in camping)**

See p. 447.

642 **Koolmoon Creek Headwaters camping area (walk-in camping)**

See p. 447.

657 **South Johnstone camping area**

See p. 449.

643 **Walters Waterhole camping area (walk-in camping)**

See p. 447.

685 **Moreton Telegraph Station**

Moreton Telegraph Station is an ideal stopover if you're travelling to the tip of Cape York. It is just under 300 km south of the tip, about 130 km from the nearest town of Weipa. The 6 ha grounds are spacious and shady for comfortable camping, and there are on-site safari tents with beds, towels and linen provided. A kiosk has basic supplies and souvenirs; firewood is not supplied. Road conditions can vary throughout the year; call ahead for up-to-date access information. **Map refs:** 436 C3, 462 D6

How to book: Telegraph Rd, Wenlock (07) 4060 3360 www.moretonstation.com.au

686 **Mungkun River camping area**

This camping area for self-sufficient campers is 7.5 km north of the Pormpuraaw Aboriginal Community of approximately 600 people, on the western coast of Cape York – the Gulf of Carpentaria – about 200 km west of Musgrave. The access road is open from late May, depending on the wet season. Access by 4WD is recommended. There is a boat launch on-site. Note: alcohol is strictly prohibited in Pormpuraaw; heavy penalties apply. **Map refs:** 436 B5, 460 E1, 462 A12

How to book: Pormpuraaw Shire Council (07) 4060 4600 www.pormpuraaw.qld.gov.au *Permits:* camping and vehicle permits required in advance

687 **Musgrave Roadhouse**

Owned and operated by the same local family for generations, this popular old roadhouse – formerly a telegraph station, dating back to 1887 – serves up food and fuel daily. The camping area is spacious and grassy and there is plenty of shade. The licensed kiosk provides basic food supplies, ice, fuel and souvenirs. Musgrave Roadhouse is 136 km north of

Laura on the Peninsula Developmental Rd. The roads from Lakefield, Kowanyama and Pormpuraaw all meet at Musgrave. **Map refs:** 436 D5, 461 I1, 462 E12

How to book: Peninsula Developmental Rd, Musgrave (07) 4060 3229 www.musgraveroadhouse.com.au

688 **North Alice Creek camping area (bush camping)**

Bush camping is permitted at this site on the 4WD Telegraph Track, 12.5 km north of Ducie Creek camping area and 11.2 km south of Dulhunty River. There are no facilities; bring all self-sufficient gear. **Map refs:** 436 C3, 462 D5

Who to contact: Bramwell Junction (07) 4060 3230; or Northern Peninsula Regional Council (07) 4069 6800

689 **Palm Creek camping area (bush camping)**

Bush camping is permitted at this site on the 4WD Telegraph Track, 3.4 km north of Bramwell Junction at the southern end of the Telegraph Track, and 2.6 km south of Palm Creek. There are no facilities; bring all self-sufficient gear. **Map refs:** 436 C3, 462 D5

Who to contact: Bramwell Junction (07) 4060 3230; or Northern Peninsula Regional Council (07) 4069 6800

690 **Palmer River Roadhouse**

This scenic campground on an old 1870s goldmining site is on the Mulligan Hwy (Peninsula Developmental Rd), about 150 km north-west of Mareeba and 30 km south of Lakeland. Up to 17 000 diggers lived in the area in the mid 1870s – check out the artefacts at the pub. Mainly unsealed, the Peninsula Developmental Rd heads north from Mareeba for 750 km to Weipa, and is the main Cape York road. **Map refs:** 436 D6, 461 K4

How to book: Mulligan Hwy, Palmer River (07) 4060 2020 http://palmerriverroadhouse.com.au

691 **Paronella Park Caravan Park**

This basic caravan park is located beside the fascinating Paronella Park, a slowly decaying castle and grounds created by José Paronella, Catalonian emigrant canecutter, in the 1930s. Guided tours through the site are recommended. You can get there via the Old Bruce Hwy south of Innisfail. Bookings are recommended for peak periods. **Map refs:** 436 E7, 461 M8

How to book: Japoonvale Rd (Old Bruce Hwy), Mena Creek (07) 4065 3225 www.paronellapark.com.au

692 **Pennefather River camping area**

This basic campground for self-sufficient campers is 71 km north of Weipa, signposted off Mapoon Rd. Camping and

vehicle permits can be obtained from the Weipa Camping Ground. Note: alcohol restrictions are enforced in Mapoon Shire and heavy penalties apply; check current limits before embarking. This campsite is closed during the wet season. **Map refs:** 436 B3, 462 B6

Who to contact: Weipa Camping Ground (07) 4069 7871
Permits: camping and vehicle access permits required
Camping fees: fees can be paid and permits acquired at Weipa Camping Ground

693 Punsand Bay Camping Resort

Punsand Bay provides beachfront camping a short distance from popular ocean and river fishing locations. The campground has powered and unpowered sites, cabins with air-conditioning, on-site tents (with or without ensuite) and a laundry. There's a swimming pool, licensed bar and restaurant, kiosk and internet facility. The campground is on the esplanade, 30 km north of Bamaga. A ferry to Thursday Island operates May–Oct. Note: alcohol restrictions apply in the areas around Punsand Bay; check current limits before embarking. Bookings are recommended for June–Dec. **Map refs:** 436 C2, 462 D2

How to book: Lot 11, Punsand Bay (07) 4069 1722 www.punsand.com.au

694 Quinkan Hotel

Camping is permitted on the grounds of this hotel in the remote township of Laura, about 140 km west of Cooktown. Hotel accommodation with air-conditioning and laundry facilities is also available on-site. Meals are available at the pub, open daily to midnight. The region's biggest annual drawcard is the Laura Aboriginal Dance Festival, one of the nation's largest Indigenous cultural events. The festival is staged in June and features dance, song, workshops and films. **Map refs:** 436 D6, 461 J3

How to book: Terminus St, Laura (07) 4060 3393

695 Seisia Holiday Park

This holiday park in the Torres Strait Islander community of Seisia has powered and unpowered sites in beachfront and garden settings, suitable for everything from a swag to a luxury caravan. Other accommodation options on-site include self-contained A-frame villas and cottages with air-conditioning. Access is via the Development Rd or the Telegraph Track; both require a 4WD and both have varying road conditions – vehicle damage is common. Several airlines and ferries regularly go to Seisia or nearby. Note: there is a kiosk and restaurant on-site. The holiday park is a designated 'wet' area but alcohol restrictions apply in the surrounding areas; check current limits before embarking. **Map refs:** 436 C2, 462 C3

How to book: Koraba Rd, Seisia (07) 4069 3243 www.seisiaholidaypark.com

696 Shelso camping area

This campground is on Kowanyama–Pormpuraaw Rd, north-east of the Kowanyama Indigenous community, a traditional land open for camping and barramundi fishing Aug–Sept. Due to limited space, permission from the Kowanyama Land Office is essential for camping. There is a boat launch suitable for small boats. Bring all self-sufficient supplies. Note: alcohol is prohibited on Kowanyama lands; heavy penalties apply. Advance bookings are recommended. **Map refs:** 436 B5, 460 E2

How to book: Kowanyama Land Office (07) 4060 5187
Permits: camping permit required

697 Stoneys Crossing camping area (bush camping)

This basic campground for self-sufficient campers is 30 km east of Mapoon Rd and 58 km north-east of Weipa. Camping and vehicle permits can be obtained from the Weipa Camping Ground. Note: alcohol restrictions are enforced in Mapoon Shire and heavy penalties apply; check current limits before embarking. This campsite is closed during the wet season. **Map refs:** 436 B3, 462 B6

Who to contact: Weipa Camping Ground (07) 4069 7871
Permits: camping and vehicle access permits required
Camping fees: fees can be paid and permits acquired at Weipa Camping Ground

Telegraph Track

The Telegraph Track is an icon of wild Cape York. The track, which follows a nearly straight line from Bramwell Junction to Punsand Bay, used to be a service route for maintaining the telegraph line that connected Cape York to the rest of the world. The telegraph itself has been retired, but its service route lives on as this notorious 4WD challenge. The tradition is to take the Telegraph Track on the way north and return via the easier bypass roads. Owing to the difficulty of several creek crossings, the Telegraph Track should only be attempted during the dry season (May–Nov) by seasoned 4WD operators with vehicle recovery equipment and spare parts. Off-road caravans and camper trailers can be towed as far north as Eliot Falls, but are not recommended beyond this point.

Please note that campsites are listed in alphabetical order, not track order. Refer to the map on p. 436 for further information.

Who to contact: Bramwell Junction (07) 4060 3230; or Northern Peninsula Regional Council (07) 4069 6800; or Heathlands Ranger Station (07) 4060 3421

568 Bertie Creek camping area (bush camping)
See p. 439.

577 Bridge Creek camping area (bush camping)
See p. 441.

570 Cockatoo Creek camping area (bush camping)
See p. 440.

675 **Ducie Creek camping area (bush camping)**

See p. 451.

571 **Dulhunty River camping area (bush camping)**

See p. 440.

573 **Gunshot Creek camping area (bush camping)**

See p. 440.

688 **North Alice Creek camping area (bush camping)**

See p. 453.

689 **Palm Creek camping area (bush camping)**

See p. 453.

579 **Sam Creek camping area (bush camping)**

See p. 441.

698 **Topsy Creek camping area**

Hundreds of anglers make the annual trip to Kowanyama every year during barramundi season to experience some of the best fishing the Far North has to offer. Topsy Creek, about 45 km west of the Kowanyama Aboriginal community, is open June–Sept. There is a boat launch for small boats. Bring all self-sufficient supplies. Note: due to limited space, permission to camp is essential on this traditional land and advance bookings are recommended. Alcohol is prohibited on Kowanyama lands; heavy penalties apply. **Map refs:** 436 B5, 460 E2

How to book: Kowanyama Land Office (07) 4060 5187
Permits: camping permit required

699 **Umagico Camping Ground**

This beachfront campground is on Umagico Beach, 4 km south-west of Bamaga. Visitors should be aware that the roads through the Cape York region can be difficult and challenging, with numerous river crossings and changing conditions. The dry season, June–Sept, is the peak period and preferred time to visit. Note: laundry facilities are available at the campground. **Map refs:** 436 C2, 462 C3

Who to contact: Northern Peninsula Area Regional Council (07) 4069 3266

700 **Undara Experience**

Next to Undara Volcanic National Park and its lava-tube cave system, the Undara Experience has a spacious caravan park and campground with laundry, swimming pool, bar and restaurant. Other accommodation options on-site include restored railway carriages, swag tents, a wilderness lodge and safari shelter. Activities include evening wildlife-spotlighting walks, campfires and bushwalking, while qualified Savannah guides conduct

tours of the lava tubes. The Undara Experience is 275 km south-west of Cairns. Advance bookings are recommended. **Map refs:** 436 D8, 461 J9

How to book: Savannah Way, Undara Volcanic National Park (07) 4097 1900, 1800 990 992 www.undara.com.au

701 **Weipa Camping Ground**

A 5.5 ha beachfront camping ground on Kerr Point Rd, this site has a pool, general supplies kiosk and laundry facilities. If upgrading, an accommodation block on-site has 12 air-conditioned units. Weipa is at the northern end of the unsealed Peninsula Developmental Rd, about 200 km north-west of the Archer River Roadhouse. Ask about fishing and mining tours. Note: alcohol restrictions apply in the areas surrounding Weipa; check current limits before embarking. **Map refs:** 436 B3, 462 B7

How to book: Kerr Point Rd, Weipa (07) 4069 7871 www.campweipa.com

702 **Wonya camping area (bush camping)**

This campground is north-east of the Kowanyama Aboriginal community, a traditional land open for camping and barramundi fishing June–Sept. Due to limited space, permission from the Kowanyama Land Office is essential for camping here and advance bookings are recommended. There is a boat launch for small boats. Bring all self-sufficient supplies. Note: alcohol is prohibited on Kowanyama lands; heavy penalties apply. **Map refs:** 436 B5, 460 E2

How to book: Kowanyama Land Office (07) 4060 5187
Permits: camping permit required Larapinta Trail

South-eastern Queensland

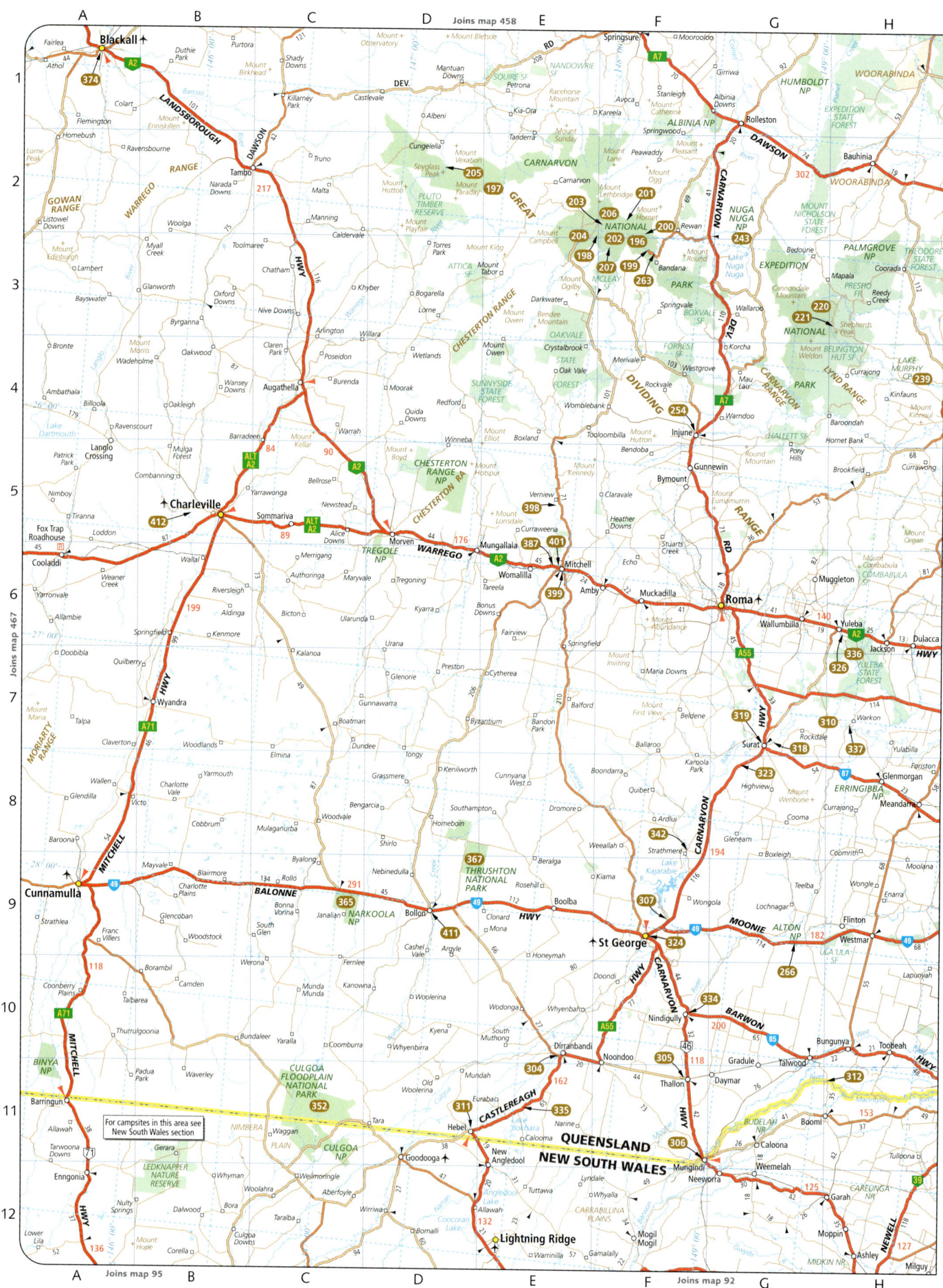

Joins map 458

Joins map 467

Joins map 95

Joins map 92

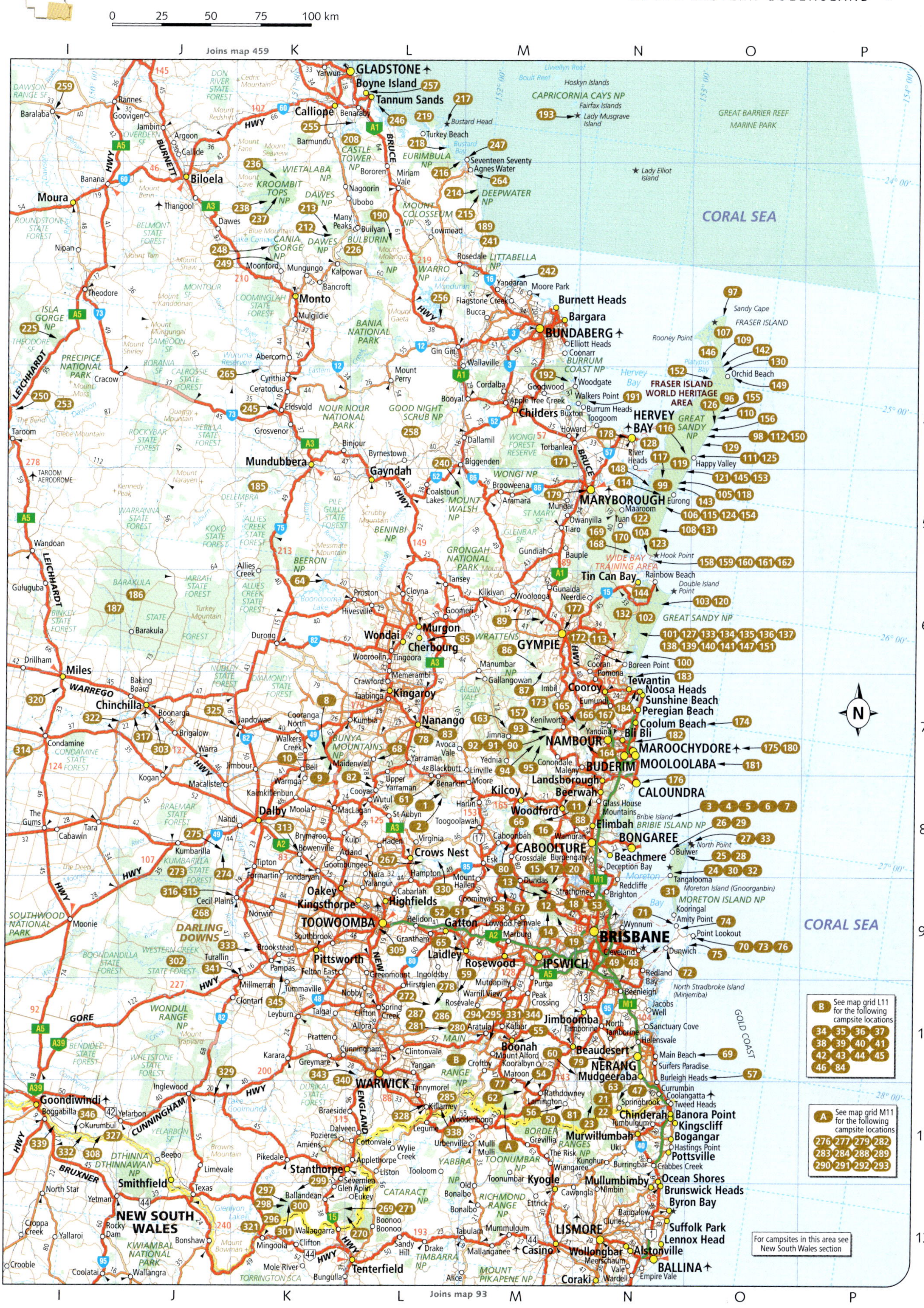
0 25 50 75 100 km
Joins map 459
Joins map 93
CORAL SEA
GREAT BARRIER REEF MARINE PARK
CAPRICORNIA CAYS NP
Hoskyn Islands
Fairfax Islands
Lady Musgrave Island
Lady Elliot Island
GLADSTONE
Boyne Island
Tannum Sands
Calliope
Biloela
Moura
Banana
Baralaba
Theodore
Monto
Mundubbera
Gayndah
Eidsvold
Taroom
Wandoan
Miles
Chinchilla
Dalby
Oakey
Kingsthorpe
TOOWOOMBA
Highfields
Crows Nest
Pittsworth
Millmerran
Goondiwindi
Texas
Inglewood
Stanthorpe
Tenterfield
WARWICK
Kingaroy
Nanango
Murgon
Wondai
Cherbourg
GYMPIE
Tin Can Bay
Rainbow Beach
MARYBOROUGH
HERVEY BAY
Childers
Bargara
Burnett Heads
BUNDABERG
FRASER ISLAND
FRASER ISLAND WORLD HERITAGE AREA
GREAT SANDY NP
Sandy Cape
Noosa Heads
Tewantin
Sunshine Beach
Peregian Beach
Coolum Beach
Bli Bli
NAMBOUR
MAROOCHYDORE
MOOLOOLABA
BUDERIM
CALOUNDRA
Landsborough
Beerwah
Kilcoy
Woodford
Elimbah
CABOOLTURE
BONGAREE
BRIBIE ISLAND NP
Beachmere
MORETON ISLAND NP
Moreton Island (Gnoorganbin)
BRISBANE
IPSWICH
Gatton
Laidley
Rosewood
Boonah
Jimboomba
Beaudesert
NERANG
Mudgeeraba
Surfers Paradise
Main Beach
Burleigh Heads
Coolangatta
Tweed Heads
GOLD COAST
North Stradbroke Island (Minjerriba)
Murwillumbah
Chinderah
Banora Point
Kingscliff
Bogangar
Pottsville
Ocean Shores
Brunswick Heads
Byron Bay
Mullumbimby
Kyogle
LISMORE
Casino
Wollongbar
Alstonville
Lennox Head
Suffolk Park
BALLINA
NEW SOUTH WALES
Smithfield
DARLING DOWNS
BUNYA MOUNTAINS NP
Gin Gin
Bundaberg
See map grid L11 for the following campsite locations
34 35 36 37 38 39 40 41 42 43 44 45 46 84
See map grid M11 for the following campsite locations
276 277 279 282 283 284 288 289 290 291 292 293
For campsites in this area see New South Wales section
I J K L M N O P
1 2 3 4 5 6 7 8 9 10 11 12

North-eastern Queensland

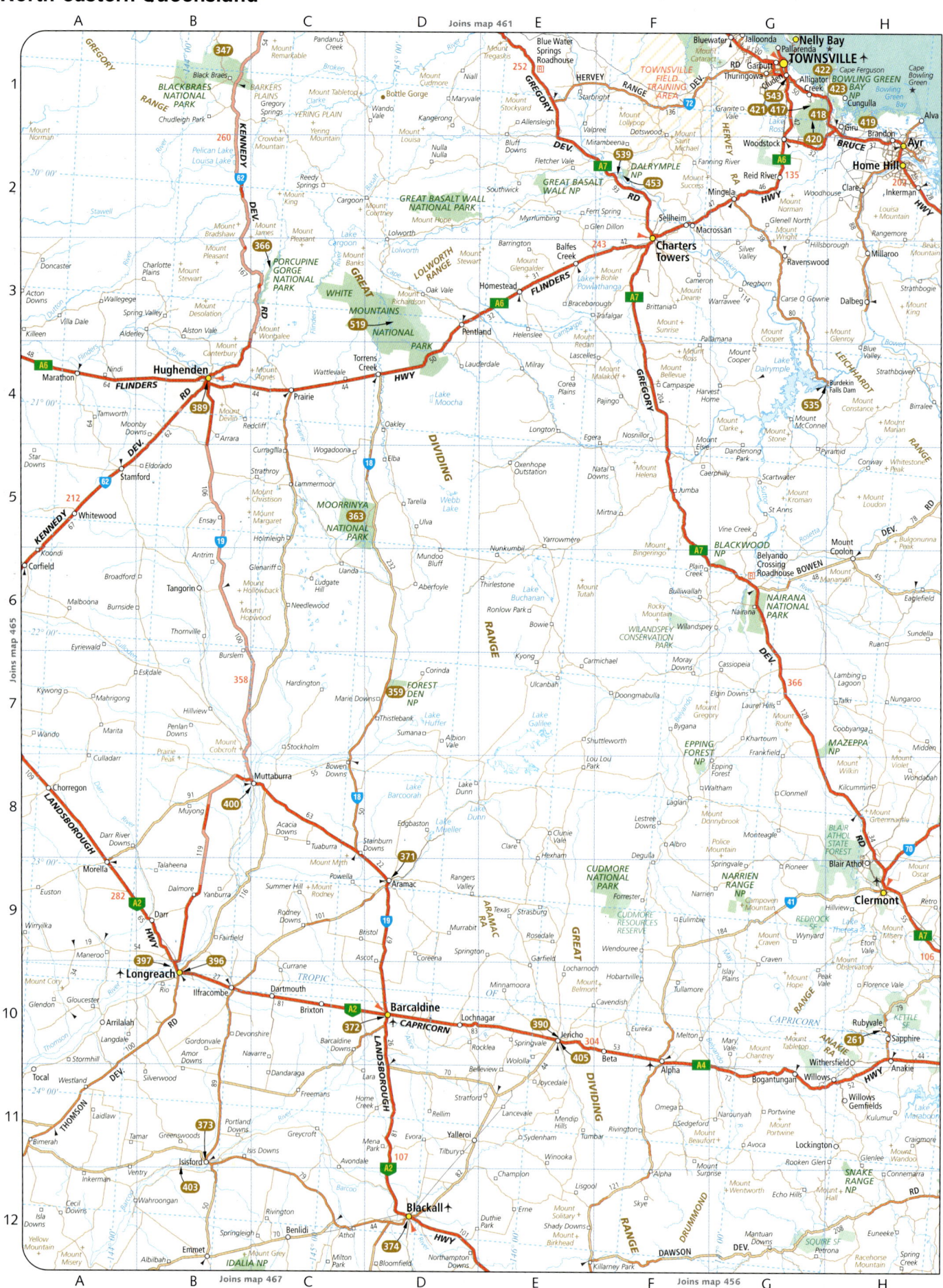

Joins map 461

Joins map 465

Joins map 467

Joins map 456

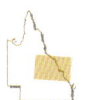

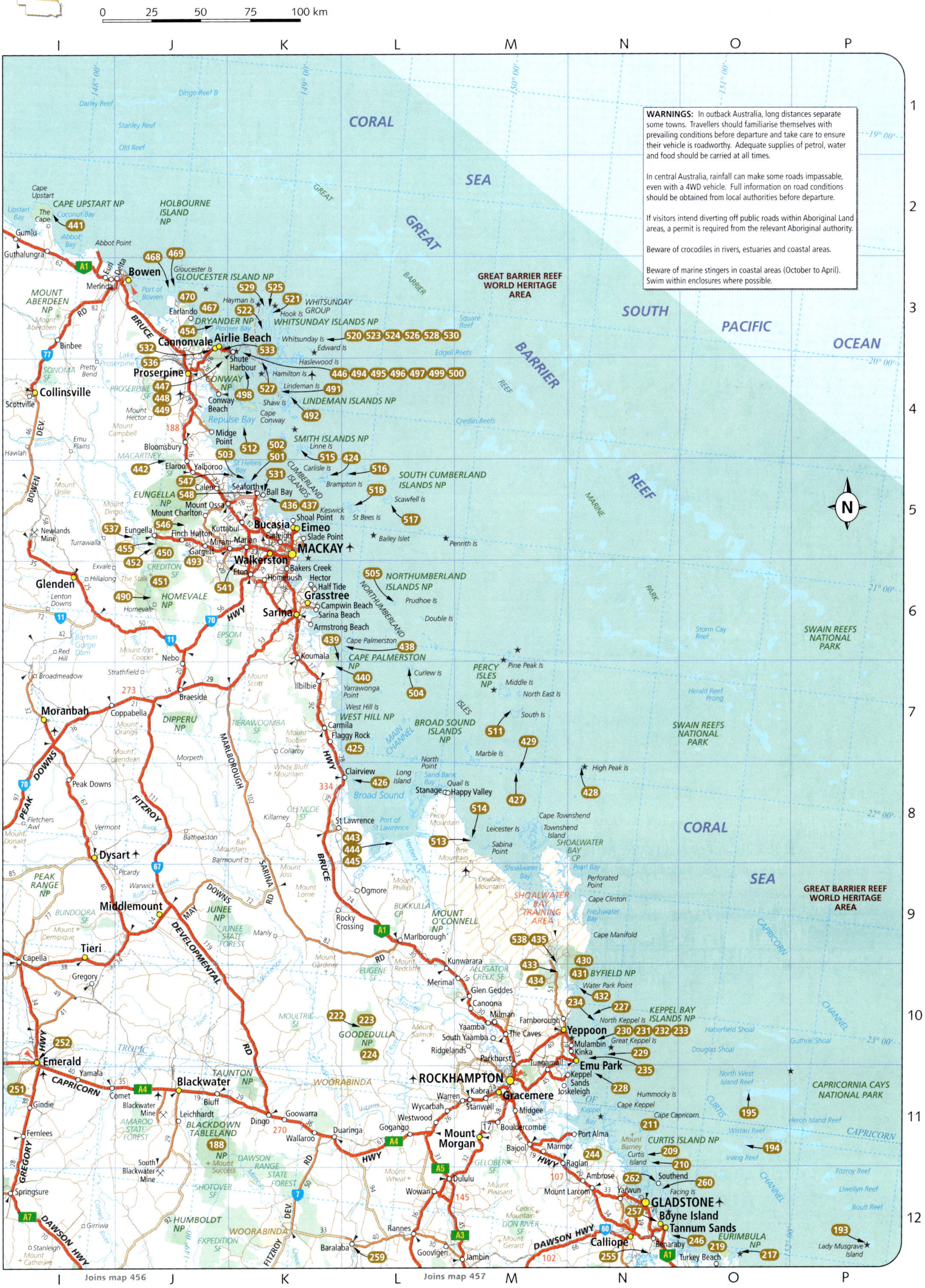
0 25 50 75 100 km
WARNINGS: In outback Australia, long distances separate some towns. Travellers should familiarise themselves with prevailing conditions before departure and take care to ensure their vehicle is roadworthy. Adequate supplies of petrol, water and food should be carried at all times.
In central Australia, rainfall can make some roads impassable, even with a 4WD vehicle. Full information on road conditions should be obtained from local authorities before departure.
If visitors intend diverting off public roads within Aboriginal Land areas, a permit is required from the relevant Aboriginal authority.
Beware of crocodiles in rivers, estuaries and coastal areas.
Beware of marine stingers in coastal areas (October to April). Swim within enclosures where possible.
CORAL SEA
GREAT BARRIER REEF
GREAT BARRIER REEF WORLD HERITAGE AREA
SOUTH PACIFIC OCEAN
BARRIER REEF
REEF
MARINE PARK
CORAL SEA
SWAIN REEFS NATIONAL PARK
CAPRICORNIA CAYS NATIONAL PARK
CAPRICORN CHANNEL
CURTIS CHANNEL
CAPE UPSTART NP
HOLBOURNE ISLAND NP
GLOUCESTER ISLAND NP
DRYANDER NP
WHITSUNDAY ISLANDS NP
CONWAY NP
LINDEMAN ISLANDS NP
SMITH ISLANDS NP
SOUTH CUMBERLAND ISLANDS NP
EUNGELLA NP
HOMEVALE NP
NORTHUMBERLAND ISLANDS NP
CAPE PALMERSTON NP
PERCY ISLES NP
WEST HILL NP
BROAD SOUND ISLANDS NP
DIPPERU NP
PEAK RANGE NP
JUNEE NP
MOUNT O'CONNELL NP
BYFIELD NP
KEPPEL BAY ISLANDS NP
CURTIS ISLAND NP
EURIMBULA NP
GOODEDULLA NP
BLACKDOWN TABLELAND NP
HUMBOLDT NP
TAUNTON NP
SHOALWATER BAY TRAINING AREA
Bowen
Collinsville
Proserpine
Cannonvale
Airlie Beach
MACKAY
Walkerston
Sarina
Glenden
Moranbah
Dysart
Middlemount
Tieri
Emerald
Blackwater
ROCKHAMPTON
Gracemere
Yeppoon
Emu Park
Mount Morgan
GLADSTONE
Boyne Island
Tannum Sands
Calliope
BRUCE HWY
PEAK DOWNS
FITZROY DEVELOPMENTAL RD
MAY DOWNS RD
MARLBOROUGH SARINA RD
CAPRICORN HWY
GREGORY HWY
DAWSON HWY
BOWEN DEV. RD
Joins map 456
Joins map 457

Far North-eastern Queensland

WARNINGS: In outback Australia, long distances separate some towns. Travellers should familiarise themselves with prevailing conditions before departure and take care to ensure their vehicle is roadworthy. Adequate supplies of petrol, water and food should be carried at all times.

In central Australia, rainfall can make some roads impassable, even with a 4WD vehicle. Full information on road conditions should be obtained from local authorities before departure.

If visitors intend diverting off public roads within Aboriginal Land areas, a permit is required from the relevant Aboriginal authority.

Beware of crocodiles in rivers, estuaries and coastal areas.

Beware of marine stingers in coastal areas (October to April). Swim within enclosures where possible.

Joins map 462

Joins map 463

Joins map 464

Joins map 465

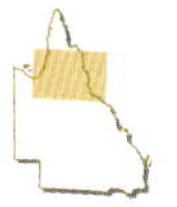

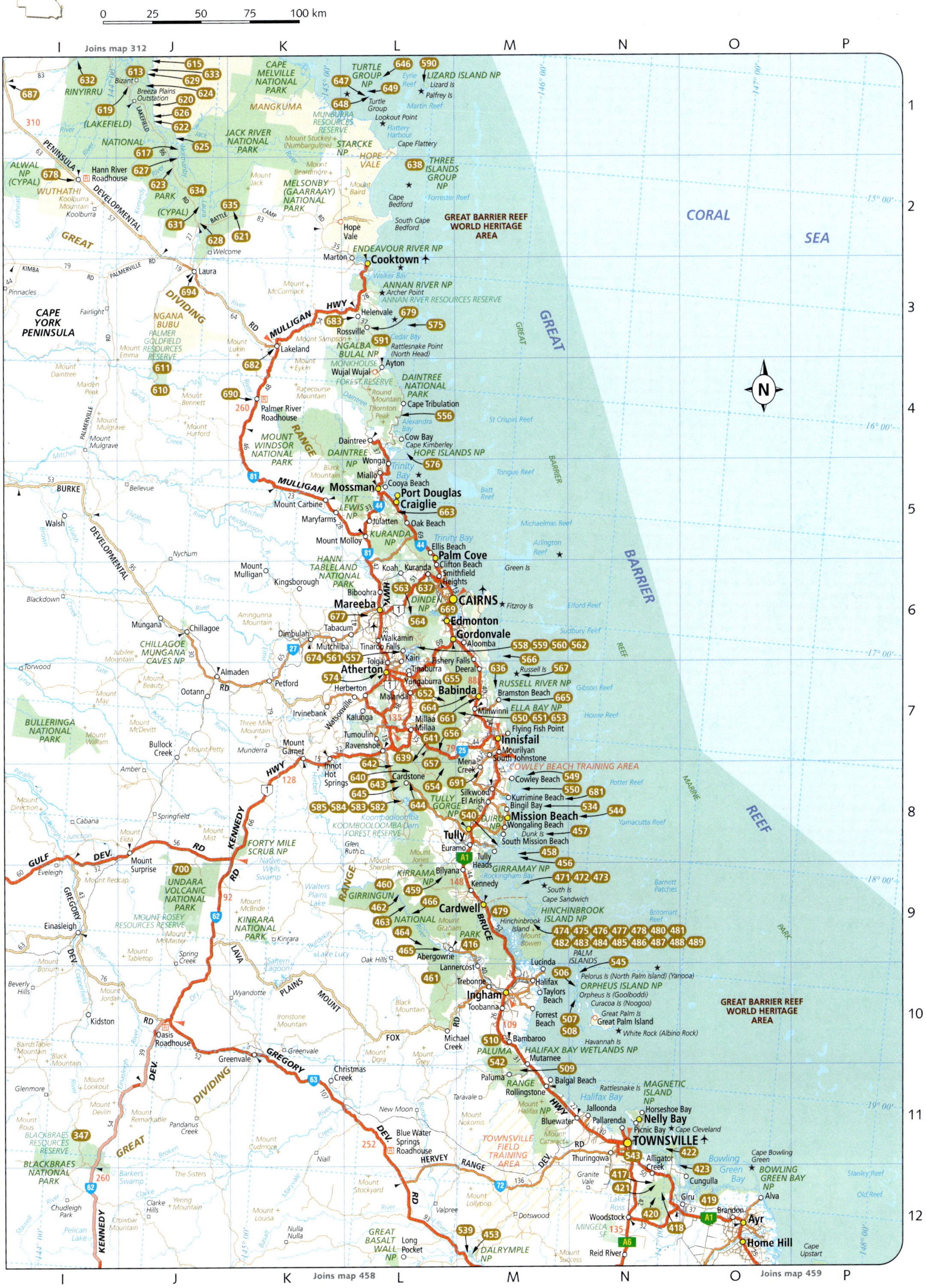
0 25 50 75 100 km
Joins map 312
Joins map 458
Joins map 459
I J K L M N O P
1 2 3 4 5 6 7 8 9 10 11 12
CORAL
SEA
GREAT BARRIER REEF WORLD HERITAGE AREA
GREAT
BARRIER
REEF
GREAT BARRIER REEF MARINE PARK
CAPE YORK PENINSULA
CAPE MELVILLE NATIONAL PARK
TURTLE GROUP NP
LIZARD ISLAND NP
Lizard Is
Palfrey Is
Turtle Group
Lookout Point
Martin Reef
Flattery Harbour
Cape Flattery
MANGKUMA
MUNBURRA RESOURCES RESERVE
Mount Stuckey (Numbargulmel)
STARCKE NP
HOPE VALE
THREE ISLANDS GROUP NP
Forrester Reef
JACK RIVER NATIONAL PARK
MELSONBY (GAARRAAY) NATIONAL PARK
Mount Jack
Mount Beardmore
Mount Baird
Cape Bedford
South Cape Bedford
Hope Vale
RINYIRRU (LAKEFIELD) NATIONAL PARK
Bizant
Breeza Plains Outstation
LAKEFIELD
Hann River Roadhouse
ALWAL NP (CYPAL)
WUTHATHI
Koolburra Mountain
Koolburra
PENINSULA DEVELOPMENTAL
GREAT
BATTLE CAMP
Welcome
Laura
KIMBA
Pinnacles
Fairlight
PALMERVILLE RD
ENDEAVOUR RIVER NP
Marton
Cooktown
Walker Bay
ANNAN RIVER NP
Archer Point
ANNAN RIVER RESOURCES RESERVE
Mount McCormack
DIVIDING
NGANA BUBU PALMER GOLDFIELD RESOURCES RESERVE
Palmer
Mount Emma
Mount Lukin
MULLIGAN HWY
Helenvale
Rossville
Cedar Bay
Mount Sampson
NGALBA BULAL NP
Rattlesnake Point (North Head)
Lakeland
Mount Eykin
MONKHOUSE
Wujal Wujal
Ayton
FOREST RESERVE
DAINTREE NATIONAL PARK
Racecourse Mountain
Round Mountain
Thornton Peak
Cape Tribulation
Mount Daintree
Maiden Peak
Mount Bennett
Palmer River Roadhouse
PALMERVILLE
Mount Mulgrave
Mount Hurford
Mount Mulgrave
MOUNT WINDSOR NATIONAL PARK
RANGE
Daintree
Cow Bay
Cape Kimberley
HOPE ISLANDS NP
Alexandra Bay
St Crispin Reef
DAINTREE NP
Black Mountain
Wonga
Miallo
Trinity Bay
Cooya Beach
Mossman
Port Douglas
Craiglie
Tongue Reef
Batt Reef
MULLIGAN
Mount Carbine
MT LEWIS NP
Maryfarms
Julatten
Oak Beach
Mount Molloy
KURANDA NP
Trinity Bay
Ellis Beach
Palm Cove
Clifton Beach
Smithfield Heights
Michaelmas Reef
Arlington Reef
Green Is
BURKE
DEVELOPMENTAL
Bellevue
Walsh
Elizabeth
Mitchell
Hodgkinson
Nychum
Mount Mulligan
Kingsborough
HANN TABLELAND NATIONAL PARK
Koah
Kuranda
Biboohra
DINDEN NP
CAIRNS
Fitzroy Is
Blackdown
Mareeba
Elford Reef
Mungana
Chillagoe
Arringunna Mountain
Dimbulah
Tabacum
Edmonton
Gordonvale
Aloomba
Sudbury Reef
CHILLAGOE MUNGANA CAVES NP
Jubilee Mountain
Mutchilba
Walkamin
Tinaroo Falls
Kairi
Tolga
Atherton
Fishery Falls
Deeral
Tinaburra
Yungaburra
Russell Is
Torwood
Almaden
Petford
Ootann
Mount Beauty
Mount May
Herberton
Malanda
Babinda
RUSSELL RIVER NP
Bramston Beach
Gibson Reef
Miriwinni
ELLA BAY NP
Flying Fish Point
Innisfail
Mourilyan
South Johnstone
Howie Reef
BULLERINGA NATIONAL PARK
Mount McDevitt
Mount William
Three Mile Mountain
Irvinebank
Watsonville
Kalunga
Millaa Millaa
Tumoulin
Ravenshoe
Bullock Creek
Mount Petty
Munderra
Mount Garnet
Innot Hot Springs
Cardstone
Mena Creek
COWLEY BEACH TRAINING AREA
Cowley Beach
Potter Reef
Amber
Silkwood
El Arish
Kurrimine Beach
Bingil Bay
Mission Beach
Wongaling Beach
DJIRU NP
Dunk Is
South Mission Beach
Yamacutta Reef
Mount Direction
Cabana
Springfield
KENNEDY HWY
TULLY GORGE NP
KOOMBOOLOOMBA Dam
Koomboolooomba
FOREST RESERVE
Tully
Euramo
Tully Heads
Mount Eliza
Mount Mist
FORTY MILE SCRUB NP
Glen Ruth
GULF
DEV.
RD
Mount Surprise
Eveleigh
Mount Redcap
UNDARA VOLCANIC NATIONAL PARK
Native Wells Swamp
Mount Sharples
KIRRAMA NP
Bilyana
GIRRAMAY NP
Rockingham Bay
Kennedy
South Is
Cape Sandwich
Barnett Patches
GREGORY
Einasleigh
MOUNT ROSEY RESOURCES RESERVE
Mount McBride
Mount McMaster
KINRARA NATIONAL PARK
Kinrara
Walters Plains Lake
GIRRINGUN
Cardwell
BRUCE
Mount Graham
NATIONAL PARK
HINCHINBROOK ISLAND NP
Hinchinbrook Island
Mount Bowen
Britomart Reef
Mount Bonum
Mount Tabletop
Spring Creek
LAVA
Saltern Lagoon
Lake Lucy
Oak Hills
Abergowrie
Lannercost
Trebonne
Lucinda
PALM ISLANDS
Halifax
Pelorus Is (North Palm Island) (Yanooa)
ORPHEUS ISLAND NP
Orpheus Is (Goolboddi)
Curacoa Is (Noogoo)
Great Palm Is
Great Palm Island
White Rock (Albino Rock)
Taylors Beach
Forrest Beach
Ingham
Toobanna
Beverly Hills
Mount Jordan
Wyandotte
PLAINS
MOUNT
Black Mountain
Ironstone Mountain
Kidston
Oasis Roadhouse
FOX
Michael Creek
Bambaroo
Havannah Is
PALUMA
HALIFAX BAY WETLANDS NP
Mutarnee
Bairdstable Mountain
Black Mountain
Greenvale
Greenvale
GREGORY
Mount Dora
Mount Grey
Paluma
RANGE
Rollingstone
Balgal Beach
Rattlesnake Is
MAGNETIC ISLAND NP
Glenmore
Mount Lookout
DIVIDING
Christmas Creek
Taravale
Halifax Bay
Mount Halifax NP
Jalloonda
Bluewater
Horseshoe Bay
Nelly Bay
Picnic Bay
Cape Cleveland
Pallarenda
Mount Rous
Mount Devlin
Mount Remarkable
Pandanus Creek
New Moon
Mount Nokomis
BLACKBRAES RESOURCES RESERVE
GREAT
Mount Cudmore
DEV.
Blue Water Springs Roadhouse
TOWNSVILLE FIELD TRAINING AREA
Mount Cataract
TOWNSVILLE
Alligator Creek
Bowling Green Bay
Cape Bowling Green
BOWLING GREEN BAY NP
Stanley Reef
Old Reef
BLACKBRAES NATIONAL PARK
Barkers Swamp
The Sisters
Broken
Niall
HERVEY
RANGE
DEV.
Thuringowa
Granite Vale
Cungulla
Mount Stockyard
Mount Lollypop
Giru
Alva
Brandon
Ayr
Home Hill
Cape Upstart
Chudleigh Park
Clarke Hills
Yering Mountain
Crowbar Mountain
Pelican Lake
KENNEDY
Mount Louisa
Nulla Nulla
Valpree
Dotswood
Lake Ross
Woodstock
MINGELA SF
Reid River
GREAT BASALT WALL NP
Long Pocket
DALRYMPLE NP
Mount Success
15° 00'
16° 00'
17° 00'
18° 00'
19° 00'
144° 00'
145° 00'
146° 00'
147° 00'
148° 00'
N

Cape York

0 25 50 75 100 km

WARNINGS: In outback Australia, long distances separate some towns. Travellers should familiarise themselves with prevailing conditions before departure and take care to ensure their vehicle is roadworthy. Adequate supplies of petrol, water and food should be carried at all times.

In central Australia, rainfall can make some roads impassable, even with a 4WD vehicle. Full information on road conditions should be obtained from local authorities before departure.

If visitors intend diverting off public roads within Aboriginal Land areas, a permit is required from the relevant Aboriginal authority.

Beware of crocodiles in rivers, estuaries and coastal areas.

Beware of marine stingers in coastal areas (October to April). Swim within enclosures where possible.

N

TORRES STRAIT

ARAFURA SEA

GREAT BARRIER REEF WORLD HERITAGE AREA

CORAL SEA

GULF OF CARPENTARIA

GREAT BARRIER REEF WORLD HERITAGE AREA

CAPE YORK PENINSULA

Joins map 460
Joins map 461

Far North-western Queensland

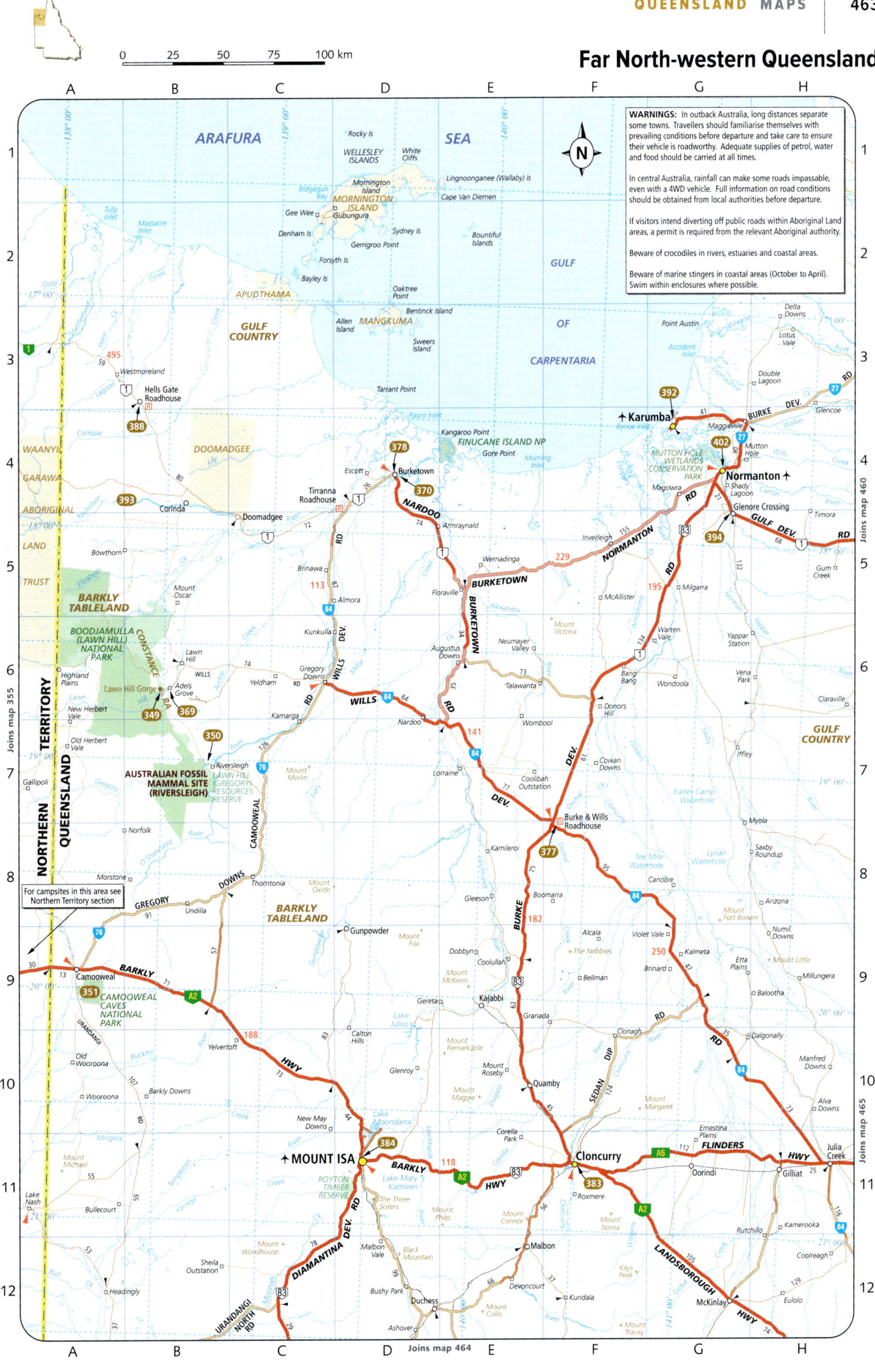

Joins map 355
Joins map 460
Joins map 465
Joins map 464

WARNINGS: In outback Australia, long distances separate some towns. Travellers should familiarise themselves with prevailing conditions before departure and take care to ensure their vehicle is roadworthy. Adequate supplies of petrol, water and food should be carried at all times.

In central Australia, rainfall can make some roads impassable, even with a 4WD vehicle. Full information on road conditions should be obtained from local authorities before departure.

If visitors intend diverting off public roads within Aboriginal Land areas, a permit is required from the relevant Aboriginal authority.

Beware of crocodiles in rivers, estuaries and coastal areas.

Beware of marine stingers in coastal areas (October to April). Swim within enclosures where possible.

For campsites in this area see Northern Territory section

North-western Queensland

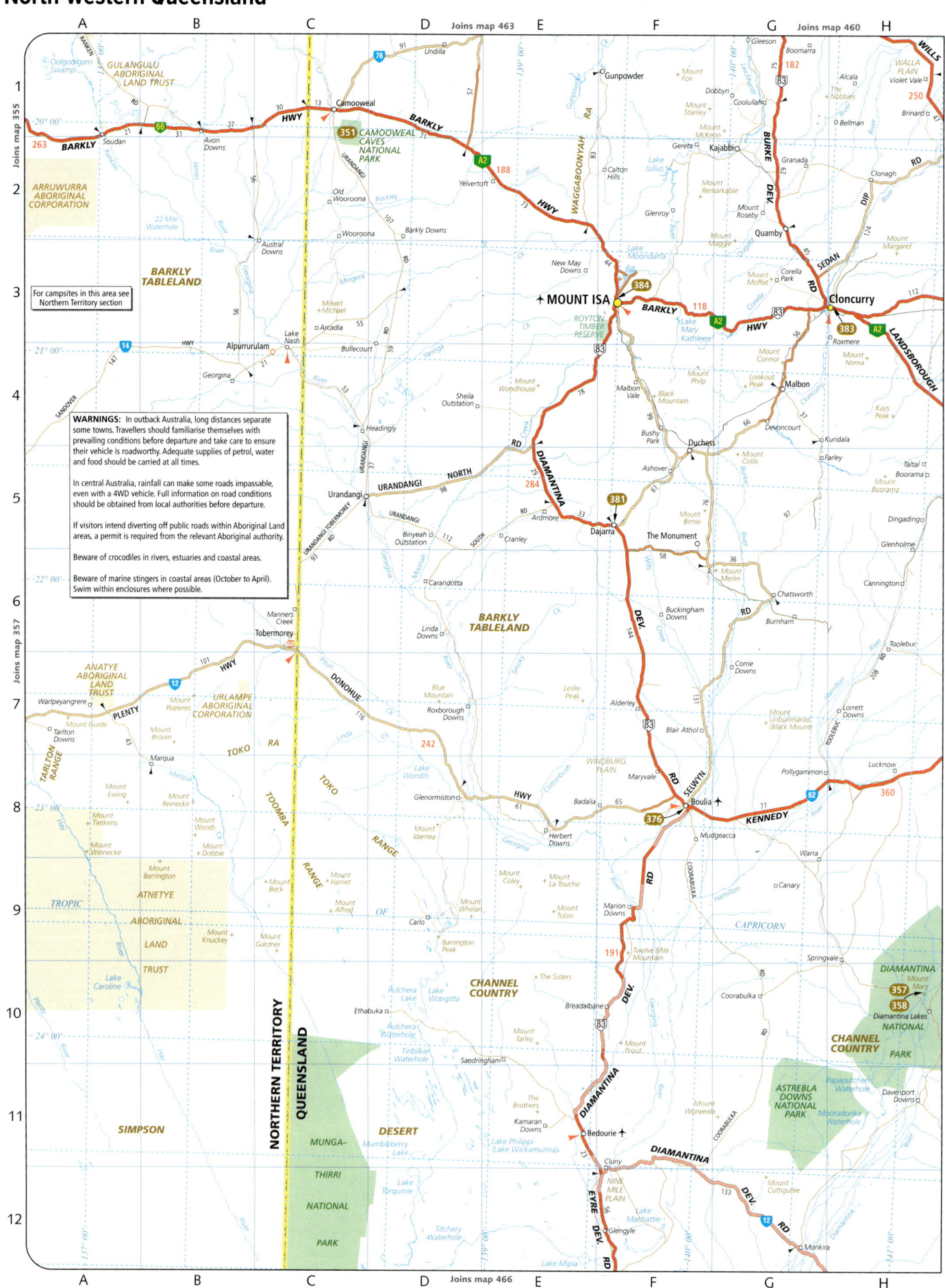

Joins map 355

Joins map 357

Joins map 466

WARNINGS: In outback Australia, long distances separate some towns. Travellers should familiarise themselves with prevailing conditions before departure and take care to ensure their vehicle is roadworthy. Adequate supplies of petrol, water and food should be carried at all times.

In central Australia, rainfall can make some roads impassable, even with a 4WD vehicle. Full information on road conditions should be obtained from local authorities before departure.

If visitors intend diverting off public roads within Aboriginal Land areas, a permit is required from the relevant Aboriginal authority.

Beware of crocodiles in rivers, estuaries and coastal areas.

Beware of marine stingers in coastal areas (October to April). Swim within enclosures where possible.

For campsites in this area see Northern Territory section

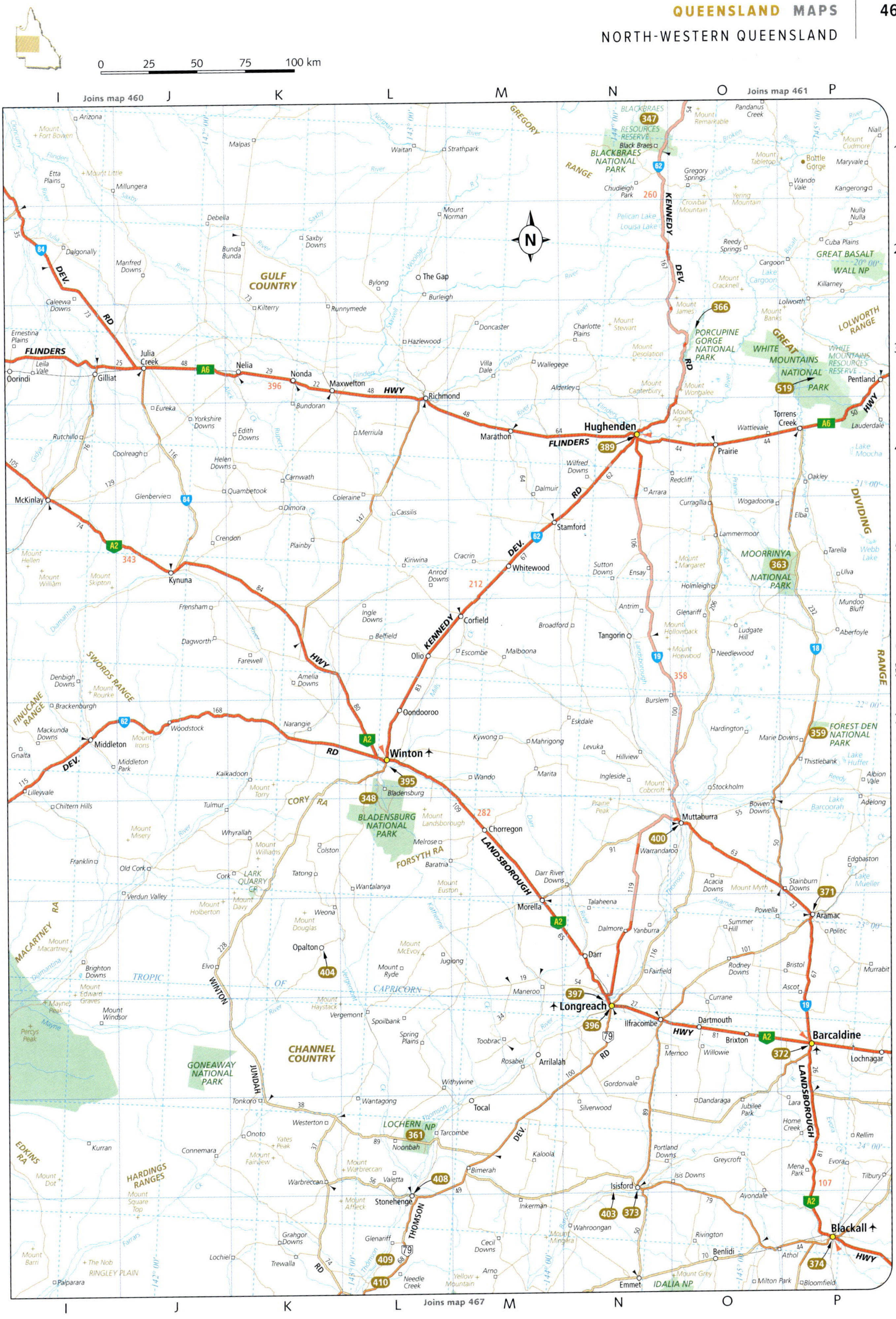
0 25 50 75 100 km
Joins map 460
Joins map 461
Joins map 458
Joins map 467
I J K L M N O P
1 2 3 4 5 6 7 8 9 10 11 12
Arizona
Mount Fort Bowen
Malpas
Waitan
Strathpark
GREGORY
BLACKBRAES RESOURCES RESERVE
Black Braes
BLACKBRAES NATIONAL PARK
Mount Remarkable
Pandanus Creek
Niall
Mount Cudmore
Bottle Gorge
Mount Tabletop
Maryvale
Etta Plains
Mount Little
Millungera
Gregory Springs
Chudleigh Park
Wando Vale
Kangerong
RANGE
KENNEDY
Crowbar Mountain
Yering Mountain
Debella
Mount Norman
Pelican Lake
Louisa Lake
Nulla Nulla
Dalgonally
Bunda Bunda
Saxby Downs
Reedy Springs
Cuba Plains
Manfred Downs
GULF COUNTRY
The Gap
Bylong
Cargoon
Lake Cargoon
GREAT BASALT WALL NP
DEV.
Burleigh
Mount Cracknell
Killarney
Caleewa Downs
Kilterry
Runnymede
Mount James
Lolworth
Mount Banks
LOLWORTH RANGE
RD
Doncaster
Charlotte Plains
Mount Stewart
PORCUPINE GORGE NATIONAL PARK
Ernestina Plains
Hazlewood
Mount Desolation
GREAT WHITE MOUNTAINS NATIONAL PARK
WHITE MOUNTAINS RESOURCES RESERVE
FLINDERS
Julia Creek
Leila Vale
Oorindi
Gilliat
Nelia
Nonda
Maxwelton
Villa Dale
Wallegege
HWY
Richmond
Alderley
Mount Canterbury
Mount Wongalee
Pentland
Eureka
Bundoran
Yorkshire Downs
Edith Downs
Merriula
Marathon
Hughenden
Mount Agnes
Wattlevale
Torrens Creek
Lauderdale
Rutchillo
Coolreagh
FLINDERS
Prairie
Lake Moocha
Helen Downs
Wilfred Downs
Redcliff
Carnwath
Oakley
Glenbervie
Quambetook
Dalmuir
Arrara
McKinlay
Coleraine
Curragilla
Wogadoona
DIVIDING
Dimora
Cassilis
Elba
Stamford
Crendon
Lammermoor
Plainby
MOORRINYA NATIONAL PARK
Tarella
Webb Lake
Mount Helen
Kiriwina
Cracrin
Whitewood
Sutton Downs
Ensay
Mount Margaret
Mount William
Mount Skipton
Kynuna
Anrod Downs
Holmleigh
Ulva
Frensham
Antrim
Glenariff
Mundoo Bluff
Ingle Downs
Corfield
Broadford
Mount Hollowback
Ludgate Hill
Aberfoyle
Dagworth
Belfield
Tangorin
Mount Hopwood
Needlewood
SWORDS RANGE
Farewell
Escombe
Malboona
Olio
RANGE
Denbigh Downs
Mount Rourke
Amelia Downs
Burslem
FINUCANE RANGE
Brackenburgh
Oondooroo
Eskdale
FOREST DEN NATIONAL PARK
Mackunda Downs
Middleton
Mount Irons
Woodstock
Narangie
Hardington
Marie Downs
Gnalta
Winton
Kywong
Mahrigong
Levuka
Hillview
Thistlebank
Lake Huffer
Middleton Park
Kalkadoon
Mount Torry
Bladensburg
Wando
Marita
Ingleside
Mount Cobcroft
Albion Vale
Lilleyvale
Stockholm
Reedy
Chiltern Hills
Tulmur
CORY RA
BLADENSBURG NATIONAL PARK
Mount Landsborough
Chorregon
Prairie Peak
Muttaburra
Bowen Downs
Lake Barcoorah
Adelong
Mount Misery
Whyrallah
Mount Williams
Colston
Melrose
Warrandaroo
Franklin
FORSYTH RA
Baratria
Old Cork
Cork
LARK QUARRY CP
Tatong
LANDSBOROUGH
Darr River Downs
Acacia Downs
Mount Myth
Stainburn Downs
Edgbaston
Lake Mueller
Verdun Valley
Wantalanya
Mount Euston
Morella
Talaheena
Mount Holberton
Mount Davy
Powella
Aramac
RA
Weona
Mount Douglas
Dalmore
Yanburra
Summer Hill
Politic
MACARTNEY RA
Mount Macartney
Opalton
Mount McEvoy
Darr
Rodney Downs
Bristol
Murrabit
Brighton Downs
TROPIC
Elvo
OF
CAPRICORN
Mount Ryde
Jugiong
Fairfield
Ascot
Mount Edward Graves
Mayne Peak
Mount Haystack
Maneroo
Longreach
Currane
Mount Windsor
Vergemont
Spoilbank
Ilfracombe
Dartmouth
Percys Peak
Mayne
WINTON
Spring Plains
Toobrac
Brixton
Barcaldine
CHANNEL COUNTRY
Rosabel
Arrilalah
Mermoo
Willowie
Lochnagar
GONEAWAY NATIONAL PARK
JUNDAH
Withywine
Gordonvale
Tonkoro
Wantagong
Tocal
Silverwood
Dandaraga
Jubilee Park
Lara
Westerton
LOCHERN NP
Tarcombe
Home Creek
Rellim
EDKINS RA
Kurran
Onoto
Yates Peak
Noonbah
Kaloola
Portland Downs
Greycroft
Connemara
Mount Fairview
Mount Warbrecan
Bimerah
Isis Downs
Mena Park
Evora
HARDINGS RANGES
Mount Dot
Warbrecan
Valetta
Tilbury
Mount Square Top
Stonehenge
Mount Affleck
Inkerman
Isisford
Avondale
Grahgor Downs
Wahroongan
Blackall
Mount Mingera
Rivington
Glenariff
THOMSON
Cecil Downs
Athol
Lochiel
Trewalla
Benlidi
Mount Barri
The Nob
RINGLEY PLAIN
Needle Creek
Arno
Yellow Mountain
Mount Grey
IDALIA NP
Emmet
Milton Park
Bloomfield
Palparara

South-western Queensland

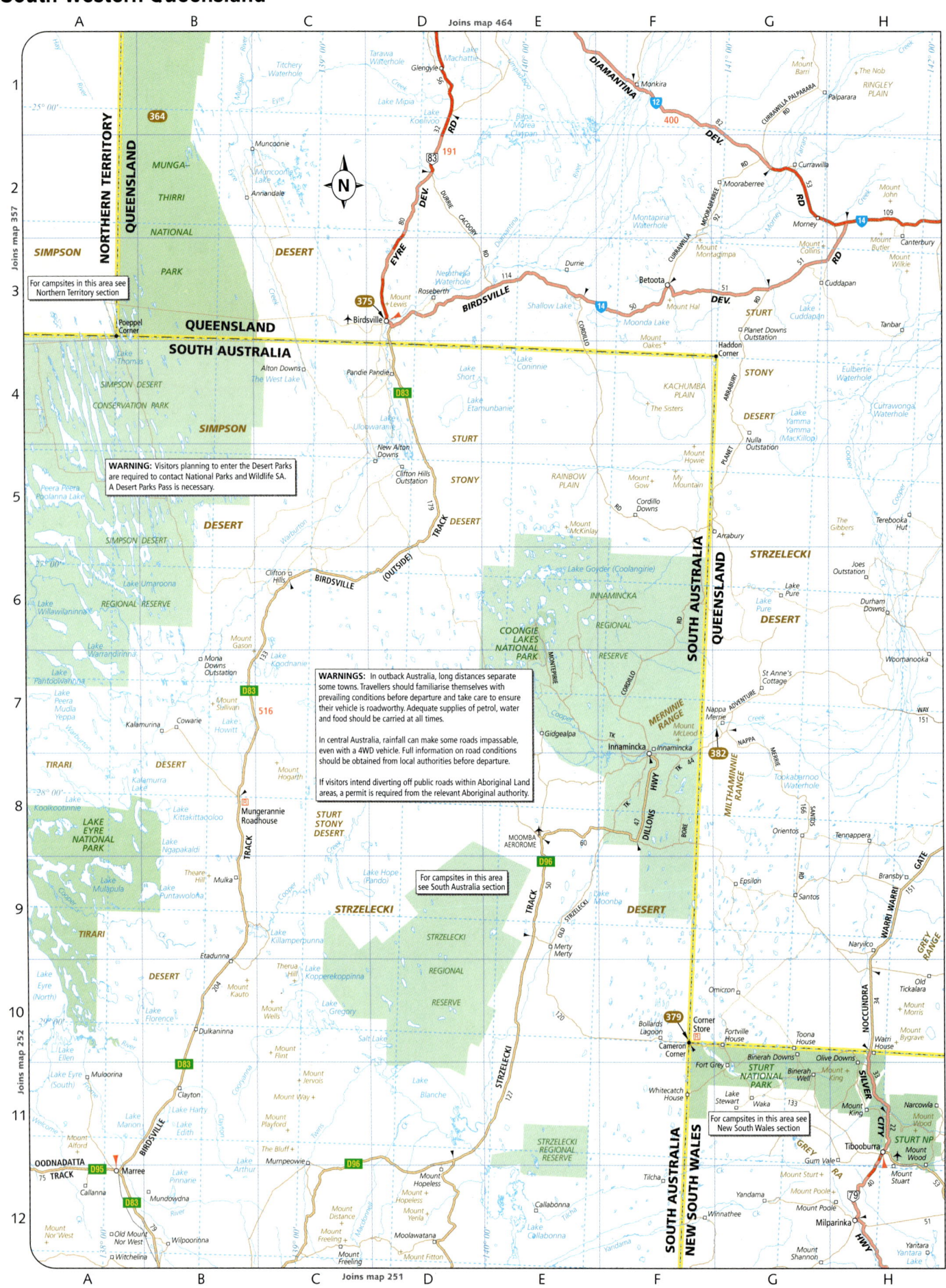

Joins map 464

Joins map 357

Joins map 252

Joins map 251

For campsites in this area see Northern Territory section

WARNING: Visitors planning to enter the Desert Parks are required to contact National Parks and Wildlife SA. A Desert Parks Pass is necessary.

WARNINGS: In outback Australia, long distances separate some towns. Travellers should familiarise themselves with prevailing conditions before departure and take care to ensure their vehicle is roadworthy. Adequate supplies of petrol, water and food should be carried at all times.

In central Australia, rainfall can make some roads impassable, even with a 4WD vehicle. Full information on road conditions should be obtained from local authorities before departure.

If visitors intend diverting off public roads within Aboriginal Land areas, a permit is required from the relevant Aboriginal authority.

For campsites in this area see South Australia section

For campsites in this area see New South Wales section

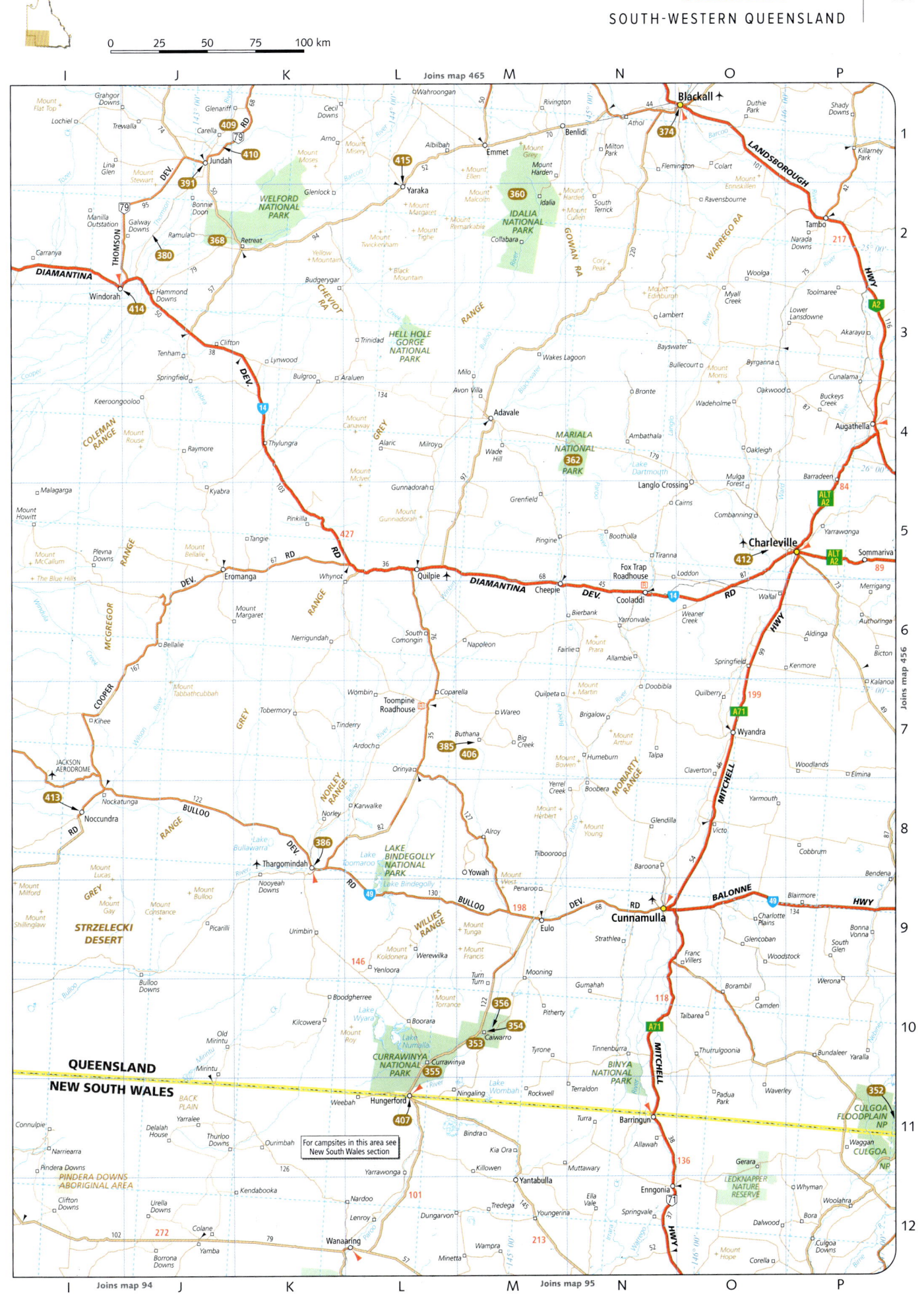

TASMANIA

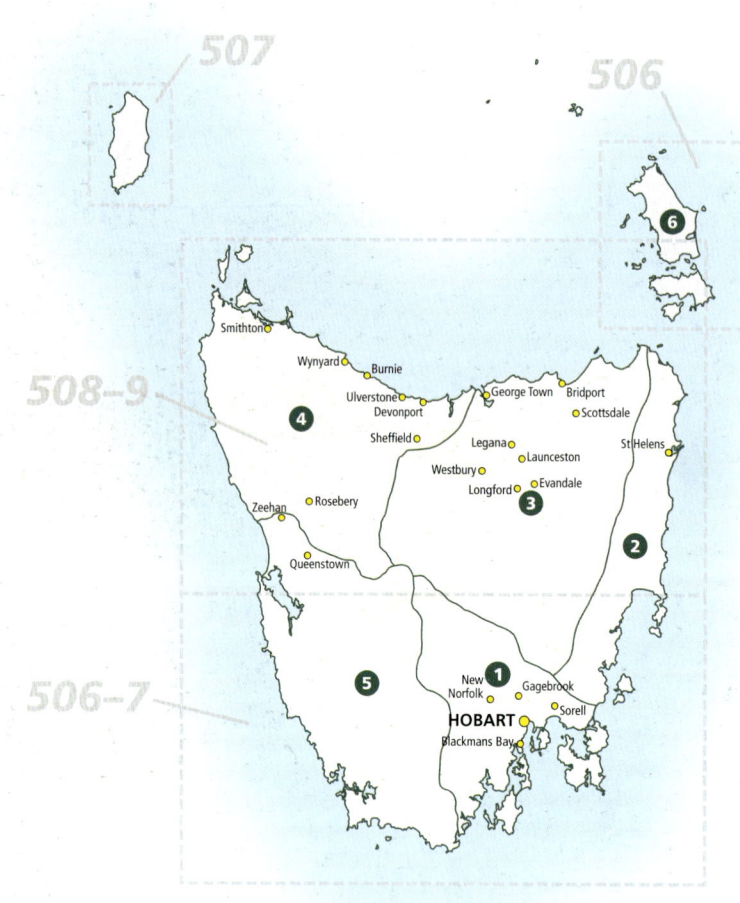

CONTENTS

BEST CAMPSITES

Gilhams Beach camping area
Recherche Bay Nature Recreation Area (South-West), p. 500

Jeanneret Beach camping area
Bay of Fires Conservation Area (East Coast), p. 477

Myrtle Park Recreation Ground
Targa (Midlands and the North), p. 490

Neck Reserve camping area
South Bruny National Park (South-East), p. 472

Springlawn camping area
Narawntapu National Park (North-West), p. 495

USEFUL CONTACTS

Emergency
Dial 000 for police, ambulance and fire brigade

Forestry Tasmania
(03) 6235 8333 or 1800 367 378 (Tasmania only)
www.forestrytas.com.au

Hydro Tasmania
(03) 6271 6221 or 1300 360 441
www.hydro.com.au

Inland Fisheries Service
(03) 6261 8050 or 1300 463 474
www.ifc.tas.gov.au

Parks and Wildlife Service
1300 135 513
www.parks.tas.gov.au

Spirit of Tasmania – Information and Reservations
1800 634 906
www.spiritoftasmania.com.au

Tasmania Fire Service
(03) 6230 8600
www.fire.tas.gov.au

Arve River Picnic Ground camping area, South-East region (p. 473)

SOUTH-EAST

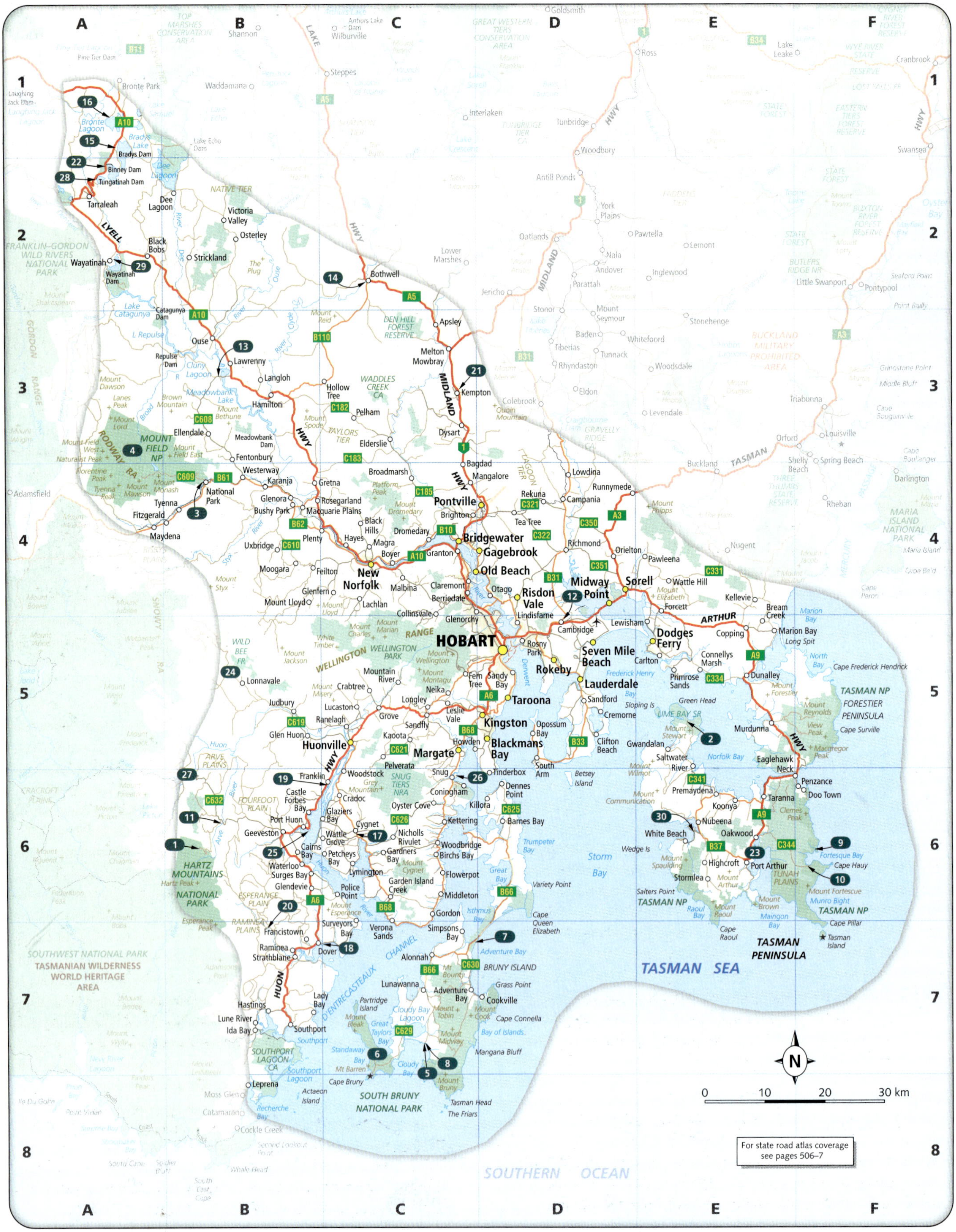

For state road atlas coverage
see pages 506–7

A **B** **C** **D** **E** **F**

1
2
3
4
5
6
7
8

B11

Laughing Jack Dam
Pine Tier Dam
Bronte Park
16
Bronte Lagoon
A10
Bradys Lake
15
Bradys Dam
22
Binney Dam
28
Tungatinah Dam
Tarraleah
Dee Lagoon

FRANKLIN-GORDON WILD RIVERS NATIONAL PARK
LYELL
Black Bobs
Wayatinah **29**
Wayatinah Dam
Catagunya Dam
A10
Ouse
L Repulse
Repulse Dam
Cluny Lagoon
13
Lawrenny
Langloh
Hamilton

GORDON RANGE

Victoria Valley
Osterley
Strickland
The Plug

Waddamana
Shannon
Steppes
Wilburville
Arthurs Lake Dam
GREAT WESTERN TIERS CONSERVATION AREA
Lake Fenton

NATIVE TIER

Interlaken
Lake Sorell
14 Bothwell
A5
Apsley
Melton Mowbray
21
Kempton
Dysart

Ross
Tunbridge
Woodbury
Antill Ponds
York Plains
Oatlands
Lovett Marshes
Jericho
Stonor
Baden
Tiberias
Tunnack
Rhyndaston
Colebrook
Woodsdale

MIDLAND

HWY

A5

Goldsmith
Lake Leake
STATE FOREST
Cranbrook
Swansea
A34

WYE RIVER STATE RESERVE
EASTERN TIERS FOREST RESERVE
HWY
BUTLERS RIDGE NR
Seaford Point
Point Bailly
Little Swanport
Pontypool
Gunstone Point
Middle Bluff
Cape Bougainvilie

BUCKLAND MILITARY PROHIBITED AREA
A3

MOUNT FIELD NP
RODWAY RA
4
Mount Field East
Naturaliste Peak
Mount Mawson
C608
C609
B61
3
National Park
Tyenna
Fitzgerald
Maydena
Ellendale
Fentonbury
Westerway
Karanja
Glenora
Bushy Park
Rosegarland
Macquarie Plains
Gretna
Black Hills
Hayes
Magra
B62
Plenty
Boyer
A10
Granton

WADDLES CREEK CA
C182
TAYLORS TIER
C183
Pelham
Broadmarsh
Platform Peak
Mount Dromedary
C185
Brighton
Pontville
Tea Tree
C321
Bagdad
Mangalore
Rekuna
Campania
Lowdina
Runnymede

Dennistoun
Gravelly Ridge
Mount Phipps
Buckland
TASMAN HWY

Orford
Louisville
Rheban
Cape Bernier

THREE THUMBS STATE RESERVE
MARIA ISLAND NATIONAL PARK
Maria Island
Cape Boullanger
Darlington
MERCURY
Cape Peron
Cape Bald

SNOWY RANGE
Mount Styx
Ellendale
Uxbridge
C610
Moogara
Feilton
Glenfern
Mount Lloyd
Lachlan
New Norfolk
Malbina
Claremont
Berriedale
Collinsvale
Glenorchy

WILD BEE FR
Lonnavale
24
Judbury
Lucaston
C619
Ranelagh
Glen Huon
Grove
Kaoota
Neika
Longley
Leslie Vale
Crabtree
Mountain River
Fern Tree
Sandy Bay
A6

WELLINGTON RANGE
WELLINGTON PARK
Mount Wellington
Mount Montagu
HOBART
Rosny Park
Risdon Vale
Lindisfarne
12
Midway Point
Cambridge
Lewisham
Forcett
ARTHUR
Sorell
Wattle Hill
Orielton
Pawleena
C331
Kellevie
Bream Creek
Copping
A9
Marion Bay
Long Spit

MARION BAY
Cape Frederick Hendrick
North Bay
Cape Surville
TASMAN NP FORESTIER PENINSULA
Mount Reynolds
View Peak
Macgregor Peak
Murdunna
2

Richmond
C350
C351
C322
Old Beach
Gagebrook
Bridgewater
B10
B31
B37
Midway Point
Seven Mile Beach
Rokeby
Taroona
A6
Kingston
Blackmans Bay
Margate
C621
C626
Woodstock
Cradoc
19
Franklin
27
Castle Forbes Bay
Glaziers Bay
Cygnet
17
Nicholls Rivulet
Gardners Bay
11
Port Huon
Geeveston
25
Cairns Bay
Waterloo
Surges Bay
Glendevie
20
A6
Police Point
Francistown
Raminea
Strathblane
18 Dover
HUON HWY
C632
FOURFOOT PLAIN
ARVE PLAINS
CRACROFT PLAINS
HARTZ MOUNTAINS NATIONAL PARK
1
Hartz Peak

Kettering
B33
Clifton Beach
Primrose Sands
Connellys Marsh
Carlton
Dodges Ferry
Lauderdale
Opossum Bay
Sandford
Cremorne
Dunalley
Eaglehawk Neck
Penzance
Doo Town
Taranna
A9
C341
Premaydena
Koonya
Nubeena
30
White Beach
Oakwood
B37
Highcroft
23
Port Arthur
Stormlea
TASMAN NP
9
Fortescue Bay
Cape Hauy
10
Mount Fortescue
Cape Pillar
Tasman Island
TASMAN PENINSULA

Frederick Henry Bay
Sloping Is
LIME BAY SR
Green Head
Saltwater River
Gwandalan
Norfolk Bay
Mount Stewart
Betsey Island
Wedge Is
Storm Bay
Mount Spaulding
Salters Point
Raoul Bay
Cape Raoul
Maingon Bay
Munro Bight
TASMAN SEA

Woodbridge
Birchs Bay
Mount Cygnet
Flowerpot
Garden Island Creek
Lymington
Gordon
Verona Sands
Middleton
B68
B66
7
Simpsons Bay
Alonnah
Adventure Bay
B66
C630
C629
Lunawanna
Partridge Island
Cloudy Bay Lagoon
Great Taylors Bay
6
5
8
Mount Bruny
SOUTH BRUNY NATIONAL PARK
Cape Bruny
Tasman Head
The Friars
BRUNY ISLAND
Barnes Bay
C625
Dennes Point
Tinderbox
26
Snug
Coningham
Oyster Cove
Howden
Pelverata
SNUG TIERS NRA
GREY MOUNTAIN
D'ENTRECASTEAUX CHANNEL
South Arm
Mount Wilmot
Communication
Mount Direction
Trumpeter Bay
Variety Point
Cape Queen Elizabeth
Adventure Bay
Grass Point
Cookville
Cape Connella
Bay of Islands
Mangana Bluff
Cloudy Bay
Mount Midway

HUON
Hastings
Lune River
Ida Bay
Southport
Leprena
Catamaran
Cockle Creek
SOUTHPORT LAGOON CA
SOUTHWEST NATIONAL PARK
TASMANIAN WILDERNESS WORLD HERITAGE AREA
ESPERANCE PLAIN
RAMINEA PLAINS
Lady Bay
Recherche Bay
Actaeon Island
Mt Barren
Standaway Bay
Great Taylors Bay
South Cape
South East Cape

SOUTHERN OCEAN

0 10 20 30 km

N

THIS EXTRAORDINARILY SCENIC REGION is dominated by the rural valleys of the Derwent and Huon rivers. Against a backdrop of forested hills, the farms here produce an abundance of fruits and vegetables, as well as cheeses, hops, saffron, wine grapes, fine wool, salmon and gourmet meats. It is no surprise to find a roadside stall advertising anything from local pink-eye spuds to goats cheese, rhubarb jam or just-picked cherries and blueberries. Around this thriving farming community a gourmet food culture has emerged, and now the Huon Valley boasts some of Tasmania's best restaurants.

The region's coastline is a rugged and spectacular strip of peninsulas, islands, inlets and channels. Bruny Island lies just offshore and is a perfect touring destination, with long ocean beaches, penguin viewings at the Neck each evening, cliff-top walking trails in South Bruny National Park and pretty swimming beaches at Jetty Beach, Adventure Bay and Dennes Point.

In the south and west, Tasmania's unique forests wow visitors with their grandeur. The impressive Tahune AirWalk takes you on a cantilevered walkway high in the forest canopy, while at Mt Field National Park the fern-fringed walk to Russell Falls displays the soft beauty of the forest floor. High in the Derwent Valley there are dozens of trout-stocked lakes – an angler's delight in season.

The region's biggest attraction is the Port Arthur Historic Site, offering an insight into the notoriously cruel treatment of convicts transported here from the other side of the world. It lies amid some of the area's most dramatic natural landforms, with blowholes, arches and cliff-top lookouts teetering over ocean swells far below. Closer to Hobart at the delightful historic village of Richmond, you can dawdle along the main street poking your nose into every little antique shop and cafe, before taking that picture-postcard photograph at Australia's oldest bridge.

CAMPSITES LOCATED IN PARKS AND RESERVES

HARTZ MOUNTAINS NATIONAL PARK

Far from the main tourist route, this World Heritage Area park preserves a spectacular alpine landscape. Uncrowded and with only basic facilities, it has some of Tasmania's best day walks. Tracks lead to shimmering tarns, cascading waterfalls and dolerite peaks, where the views are truly panoramic. The road into the park is unsealed and subject to snow and ice, so check conditions before travel.

Who to contact: PWS Huonville (03) 6264 8460 *Permits:* Parks Pass is required to enter national parks (03) 6233 2621 www.parks.tas.gov.au *Road conditions:* Forest and Heritage Centre, Geeveston (03) 6297 1821

1 Bush camping (walk-in camping)

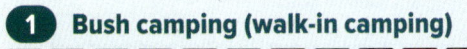

Walk-in bush camping is allowed almost anywhere in the park, except close to roads, in day-use areas or around Osborne and Esperance lakes and Ladies Tarn. You will need to be

self-sufficient: bring drinking water and a gas/fuel stove (fires are only allowed in the day-use shelter fireplace). Walkers should carry warm, protective clothing because the weather can turn dangerously cold with little warning, even in summer. To get here, head along the rough (and occasionally snow-covered) Hartz Rd from a signposted left turn off Arve Rd, 15 km from its junction with the Huon Hwy west of Geeveston. A day-use picnic shelter, tables, gas BBQ, fireplace and toilet are near the Waratah Lookout track entrance. **Map refs: 470 B6, 507 I9**

LIME BAY STATE RESERVE

Lime Bay State Reserve is a beautiful 1300 ha secluded reserve of sheltered beaches and pretty eucalypt woodlands at the end of Coal Mines Rd, on the north-west tip of the Tasman Peninsula. There are 2 tranquil beaches: Lime Bay is next to the camping area, while the gorgeous Lagoon Beach lies in the lee of Sloping Island, an easy 40 min walk. Nearby are remnants of the 1833 coal mines where Port Arthur's most hardened convicts were sent for punishment. Underground cells and mine entrances are still visible.

Who to contact: PWS Southeast District (03) 6214 8100

2 Lime Bay camping area

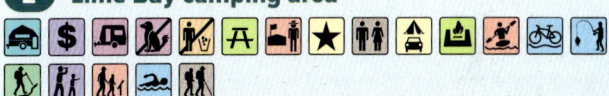

This picturesque, grassed camping area is 4 km beyond the historic mining site and is the starting point for an easy, scenic walk to Greens Point cliffs and Lagoon Beach. Gas/fuel stoves are recommended, and you need to bring firewood and drinking water. To get here, take the C341 from Premaydena, through Saltwater River. **Map refs: 470 E5, 507 L8**

MOUNT FIELD NATIONAL PARK

Ever since the 1860s, when the area attracted its first tourists, visitors to Mt Field National Park have been captivated by its sublime grandeur. The park's entrance is in its lower section: here you'll find forests of swamp gums – the world's tallest flowering plant – and rainforest walks through moss-covered fern glades leading to multi-tiered waterfalls. The alpine region of the park is reached via a 15 km narrow, unsealed road winding to Lake Dobson, a pretty lake surrounded by snow gums. There is a day shelter here and nearby are 4 huts offering basic accommodation, which can be hired. For the hardier bushwalker or skier, tracks lead to the ski runs above Lake Dobson and then out along Tarn Shelf, or higher still to the glacier-carved crags and peaks of the park's mountainous heart.

Who to contact: PWS Mt Field National Park (03) 6288 1149 *Camping fees:* payable by self-registration *Permits:* Parks Pass is required to enter national parks (03) 6233 2621 www.parks.tas.gov.au *Road conditions:* road to Lake Dobson subject to snow (03) 6288 1319

3 Mount Field Campground

This pretty caravan park and campground next to the Tyenna River has sites suitable for every camper, from big rigs to

2-person tents. Set up on the neat lawns underneath giant swamp gums and, as evening draws in, watch dozens of wallabies come out of the surrounding bush to nibble. Turn right into the park at the sign on the B61, 8 km north of Westerway. Drive 1 km to the visitor centre, then turn left to the camping area. **Map refs:** 470 B4, 507 I6

4 Twilight Tarn camping area (walk-in camping)

At the northern end of the exquisitely beautiful Tarn Shelf are a few small camping sites near the Twilight Tarn hut. Campers must be fully equipped, prepared for alpine weather and carrying water and a gas/fuel stove. In autumn, this area is especially popular with admirers of the fagus – a deciduous alpine shrub which turns bright golden orange as the season changes. Moderate to steep tracks lead up from Lake Dobson to Twilight Tarn via Lake Webster or Tarn Shelf (6 hr circuit). **Map refs:** 470 A3, 506 H5

SOUTH BRUNY NATIONAL PARK

This wild and spectacular coastal national park takes in southern Bruny Island's rugged shoreline and parts of its hinterland from Fluted Cape to Great Taylors Bay. It is dominated by massive dolerite sea cliffs and windswept heaths but there are also superb beaches and sheltered coves, these being the main attraction for campers. In summer, the camping areas are popular with visitors coming to fish, surf and laze away their holidays. Gas/fuel stoves are recommended and no water or firewood is supplied.

Who to contact: PWS Bruny Island Field Centre (03) 6293 1419
Permits: Parks Pass is required to enter national parks (03) 6233 2621 www.parks.tas.gov.au

5 Cloudy Corner camping area

At the far end of Cloudy Bay, this isolated campsite is accessible only to 4WD vehicles and involves driving 3 km along the beach at low tide. Camping is a short walk from the beach. The creek water must be boiled or treated before use. Boats can be launched from the beach, but vehicles and trailers can't be parked at the campsite or on the beach. From Lunawanna, take the C629 then Cuthberts Rd to Cloudy Bay Beach. Once on the beach, a limit of 40 kph applies and drivers should stay below the high-tide mark. **Map refs:** 470 C7, 507 J10

6 Jetty Beach camping area

Behind the gentle curve of Jetty Beach, this camping ground among the trees is very popular – and deservedly so. Sheltered from the south-west, it faces a sandy cove with clear water, safe swimming, great snorkelling and excellent fishing. The 6 hr circuit walk around Labillardiere Peninsula starts from the campsite, and Australia's second oldest lighthouse is at Cape Bruny, 3 km south. Turn right onto the C629 at Lunawanna and then right into Jetty Rd, 17 km further on. Most of this road is

gravel and affords fantastic views of Cape Bruny just before the turn-off. Bring insect repellent as well as water and firewood. **Map refs:** 470 C7, 507 J10

7 Neck Reserve camping area

The Neck is a narrow, sandy isthmus joining north and south Bruny. Halfway along it is a must-see lookout with 360-degree views, and at night the sand dunes below come alive with penguins. The camping area is sheltered among trees behind the dunes at the southern end of the beach. Arriving by ferry, head towards south Bruny then turn left into the camping area off the B66, 3 km past the lookout. Neck Beach is beautiful and you will more than likely have it to yourself, but care is needed when swimming in the surf as conditions can occasionally be treacherous and the water is cold. Note: a Parks Pass is not required here. **Map refs:** 470 C7, 507 K10

8 The Pines camping area

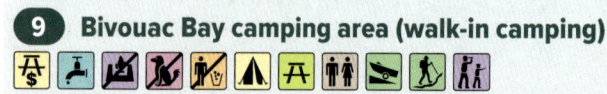

This sheltered camping area is a popular spot for surfers attracted to Cloudy Bay's beach and point breaks. It is very small, so campers have to take their chances finding a site. While surfing is the main attraction, there are also scenic coastal walks and excellent beachcombing, as well as kayaking nearby in beautiful Cloudy Bay Lagoon. To get here, turn south at Lunawanna along the C629, then right into Cuthberts Rd, 3 km further on. The turn-off to the campground is 6 km south (500 m before the road ends at Cloudy Bay). **Map refs:** 470 C7, 507 J10

TASMAN NATIONAL PARK

Needle-like rock spires, towering sea cliffs, blowhole caves and pounding surf make up the awe-inspiring gothic landscape of this coastal park, which spans the remote southern regions of the Tasman and Forestier peninsulas. It offers some of the most spectacular coastal scenery in Australia, and sits alongside some of the country's most brutal history in the slowly crumbling remains of Port Arthur's convict heritage. To reach the park, take the Arthur Hwy (A9), turning left along Blowhole Rd just past Eaglehawk Neck, to the park's thumping blowholes in its eastern section; or continue towards Port Arthur, turning left along the 12 km unsealed Fortescue Bay Rd to a lovely white-sand beach and camping area. Further west, access tracks to Cape Raoul and the world-renowned big-wave surfing site at Shipstern Bluff are reached from Stormlea Rd.

Who to contact: PWS Seven Mile Beach (03) 6214 8100; or Fortescue Bay Campground manager (03) 6250 2433
Permits: Parks Pass is required to enter national parks (03) 6233 2621 www.parks.tas.gov.au

9 Bivouac Bay camping area (walk-in camping)

This beautiful bay is a 2 hr hike north from Fortescue Bay on the Tasman Coastal Trail, following the coastline along beaches and over steep-sided headlands. The views are worth the effort and the campsite is in a very scenic spot with a freshwater creek and toilets. From here you can continue on the Tasman Coastal Trail to Waterfall Bay (6 hr) or head back to Fortescue. To access the Tasman Trail, drive 12 km along the unsealed Fortescue Bay Rd from the Arthur Hwy and walk to the northern end of the beach, where the track is signposted. **Map refs:** 470 F6, 507 M9

10 Fortescue Bay Campground

A few steps from the sun, sand and surf of lovely Fortescue Bay, this camping area is a popular summer destination and bookings are necessary for peak times. Camping sites are grouped into 2 areas – Mills Creek for vans and Banksia for tents – tucked into shady forest clearings at the end of Fortescue Bay Rd, 12 km from the Arthur Hwy turn-off, which is signposted 4 km south of Taranna. The road is unsealed but fine for 2WD vehicles and mountain bikes. Bring your own drinking water. Campfires are allowed and wood is available for sale, but the rest of the park is a gas/fuel stove-only area. Walking tracks from here lead to Canoe Bay (2 hr return), Mt Fortescue (7 hr return) and the spectacular Cape Hauy (5 hr return). **Map refs:** 470 F6, 507 M9

CAMPSITES LOCATED IN OTHER AREAS

11 Arve River Picnic Ground camping area

Along the Arve Rd, 14 km west of Geeveston, this streamside picnic and camping area is tucked away in a forest reserve beside the pretty Arve River. There are lovely spots to put up your tent among the ferns, as well as limited space for smaller campervans or caravans. Soak up the atmosphere of the surrounding tall, wet forests along the nearby Arve River Nature Walk. The river water here should be boiled or treated before drinking. **Map refs:** 470 B6, 507 I8

Who to contact: Forestry Tasmania Huon District Office, Geeveston (03) 6295 7111

12 Barilla Holiday Park

Just 5 min from Hobart airport and 15 min from Hobart CBD, this cabin and caravan park is a very convenient stopover for travellers. There are all the usual facilities on-site, plus an indoor spa pool, wood-fired pizzeria, minigolf and children's playground. Historic Richmond is only a 10 min drive away and the vineyards of the lovely Coal River Valley are right on your doorstep. To top it off, there's a Saturday shuttle bus to take you to Hobart's famous Salamanca Market. **Map refs:** 470 D5, 507 K7

How to book: 75 Richmond Rd, Cambridge (03) 6248 5453 www.barilla.com.au

13 Bethune Park camping area

Beside Meadowbank Lake, this grassy camping and picnic area has sites that can accommodate big rigs. Perfect for waterskiers and anglers, there's a launching ramp close by on the eastern side of Dunrobin Bridge. The lake is the final section of the Derwent River Hydro-electricity Scheme and the last of the catchment's 10 power stations is at the foot of the Meadowbank Dam downstream. As the campground is on Hydro land, campers can stay for a maximum of 7 days. Access is through a gate on Ellendale Rd (the C608), just west of Dunrobin Bridge, 2 km from the Lyell Hwy. Bring water and firewood. **Map refs:** 470 B3, 507 I5

Who to contact: Central Highland Council, Hamilton (03) 6286 3202 **Permits:** an Inland Angling Licence is required to fish here and this lake has a year-round season; check regulations www.ifs.tas.gov.au

14 Bothwell Camping Ground

Right in the centre of town, this unshaded gravel park in Market Pl is set up mainly for vans rather than tents. Bothwell is off the beaten track but well worth a visit for its history and craft, not forgetting it is home to Australia's oldest golf course, which dates back to 1837. The Australian Golf Museum is a must-see and is almost next-door to the camping area. There is a park opposite with BBQs and picnic tables. **Map refs:** 470 C2, 507 J4

How to book: Central Highlands Council, Bothwell (03) 6259 5503; or Bothwell Garage (03) 6259 5599 **Camping fees:** fees payable at Bothwell Garage, keys from council office in Alexander St, Bothwell

15 Bradys Lake camping area (bush camping)

The camping sites at Bradys are at the northern end of the lake from Whitewater Point (near the boat ramp), around Claypit and Kangaroo bays to the Dee Tunnel inlet. All are undeveloped bush-camping sites, but suitable for big rigs and accessible via tracks from the Lyell Hwy (A10) north and south of the canal. Your camping stay can be up to 7 days and there is accommodation at Bronte Park Village and Tarraleah nearby if you prefer a break from outdoor living. You need to bring a portable toilet and water, and preferably a gas/fuel stove. Access is signposted off the Lyell Hwy, 6 km south of the B11. **Map refs:** 470 A1, 506 H3, 508 H12

Who to contact: Hydro Tasmania (03) 6271 6221, 1300 360 441; check lake levels at www.hydro.com.au/water/lake-levels **Permits:** an Inland Angling Licence is required to fish here; check regulations and seasons www.ifs.tas.gov.au

16 Bronte Lagoon camping area

Bronte Lagoon lies amid sub-alpine woodland beside the Lyell Hwy (A10). Its tussocky shallows offer some of the most treasured fly fishing in Tasmania and its waters are reserved for artificial lures and flies. Camping is near the boat ramp and on the far

side of the dam wall. Because this is Hydro Tasmania land, stays are limited to 7 days. There are no facilities so campers need to be self-sufficient, bringing their own water, firewood and gas/fuel stoves. To get here, turn off the A10 at the signs and travel 2 km to the boat ramp. **Map refs:** 470 A1, 506 H2, 508 H12

Who to contact: Hydro Tasmania (03) 6271 6221, 1300 360 441
Permits: an Inland Angling Licence is required; check regulations and seasons www.ifs.tas.gov.au

17 Cygnet Holiday Park

Cygnet is the Huon Valley's top foodie destination and accommodation can be hard to find at peak times. On top of that, each Jan thousands of music lovers come to town for Cygnet's lively folk festival. This council park has good amenities and is central to everything Cygnet has to offer. Bookings are essential at peak times. There's a dump point at nearby Burtons Reserve. The park is on Mary St behind the RSL Club, near the recreation ground, and signposted from the highway. **Map refs:** 470 C6, 507 J9

How to book: 77 Mary St, Cygnet 0418 532 160

18 Dover Beachside Tourist Park

This popular beachside caravan park has everything from cabins and campsites to wifi access, and it ticks all the boxes for family fun. The kids will love the playground and the sheltered beach across the road, while all the facilities you might need are in the park or at the Dover shops 500 m away. The Ida Bay Vintage Railway, Hastings Caves and Thermal Springs, and the Tahune AirWalk are all within easy reach if you can drag yourself away from this idyllic spot. Bookings are recommended in summer. When you get to Dover, turn left into Station Rd, then left again into Kent Beach Rd. **Map refs:** 470 C7, 507 J10

How to book: 27 Kent Beach Rd, Dover (03) 6298 1301 www.dovertouristpark.com.au

19 Franklin Foreshore Reserve RV Camping Ground

After a day touring the gourmet delights of the Huon Valley, this riverside park is a good central location to camp. There are sites all along the foreshore just a short walk from Franklin's main street. Facilities (including a dump point) are at the southern end of the park. Fees are collected each evening and the maximum stay is 4 nights. Driving south through Franklin, turn left off the Huon Hwy at the sign near the Franklin Fire Station. **Map refs:** 470 C6, 507 J8

Who to contact: Huon Valley Council (03) 6264 0300

20 Hastings Forest Picnic Area camping area

Beside the Esperance River, these forest campsites have fireplaces, soft, mossy ground and a babbling brook to lull you to

sleep after your walk to Duckhole Lake or Adamsons Falls nearby. You will need to carry your gear to the campsites and there are toilets close by. Although the river is clean, it is recommended that its water is boiled or treated before drinking. The camping area is 8 km along Esperance Rd, following a right-hand turn off the Huon Hwy, 4 km south of Dover. **Map refs:** 470 B7, 507 I9

Who to contact: Forestry Tasmania Huon District Office, Geeveston (03) 6295 7111

21 Kempton Overnight Bay camping area

This sizeable layover is ideal for travellers looking for a quiet overnight stop between Hobart and Launceston. Tiny Kempton has an old-world village atmosphere with galleries, cafes, churches and heritage houses to explore. Take the well-signposted side road off the Midland Hwy, between Pontville and Oatlands. The camping area is easy to find, on the main street next to a blue church. Keys are at the council office, doctor's surgery and shop. Vehicle wash-down facilities are here and there is a dump point at the nearby public toilets. **Map refs:** 470 C3, 507 K5

Who to contact: Southern Midlands Council, Kempton office (03) 6259 3011

22 Lake Binney camping area (bush camping)

Lake Binney's main camping area is at Camp Corner between the boat ramp and the dam wall, just off the highway. There are also bush sites along the North Shore across the dam wall. The whole area is Hydro Tasmania land, so you can stay for up to a week. You will need to bring your own water, firewood, portable toilet and a gas/fuel stove in case of fire bans. The campsite is signposted off the Lyell Hwy (A10), 3 km south of Bradys Lake. **Map refs:** 470 A2, 506 H3

Who to contact: Hydro Tasmania (03) 6271 6221, 1300 360 441
Permits: an Inland Angling Licence is required; check regulations and seasons www.ifs.tas.gov.au

23 Port Arthur Holiday Park

Although this park is big, each spacious campsite is screened with shrubs, so it feels sheltered and private. Visit Port Arthur Historic Site (1 km along the road, or take the walking track along Stewarts Beach), then settle in by your fireplace while the kids and young-at-heart organise an all-in cricket match on the oval. If it is warm there is a safe swimming beach nearby, otherwise there is a pretty walking track to Garden Point. For a spectacular cliff-top day walk nearby, head out to Cape Raoul from the trailhead on Stormlea Rd off B37. The park has a camp kitchen if you don't fancy cooking on your campfire, or frock up and head to one of Port Arthur's restaurants for dinner. Turn into Garden Point Rd at the large sign on the Tasman Hwy (A9), 1 km north of the Historic Site turn-off. **Map refs:** 470 E6, 507 M9

How to book: Garden Point Rd, Garden Point (03) 6250 2340, 1800 607 057 www.portarthurhp.com.au

24 Rivers Edge Wilderness Camping and RV

As the name suggests, this grassy camping area is nestled beside the lovely Russell River. The river's pools are perfect for a dip in summer and offer great fishing spots for trout and blackfish, and the surrounding forest is home to abundant wildlife. This place is family friendly, with plenty of room for the kids to kick a football while you relax in the lounge chairs or around the fire pots provided. Take the Judbury turn-off on the south side of the river at Huonville. At Judbury, turn left along the unsealed road towards Lonnavale and then follow the signs a further 7 km to the campsite. **Map refs:** 470 B5, 507 I7

How to book: 1322 Lonnavale Rd, Lonnavale 0439 760 007, 0402 332 468 *Permits:* an Inland Angling Licence is required to fish; check season and regulations www.ifs.tas.gov.au

25 Shipwrights Point Regatta Ground Recreation Reserve camping area

Within an hour's drive from both the Tahune AirWalk and Hastings Caves, this informal foreshore camping area has plenty of room for the kids to run around, as well as a new playground to keep them occupied. The nearby jetty offers good fishing and a boat ramp. Most of the shady, grassed sites have lovely views over the water. There is also the added convenience of a dump point. Turn off the Huon Hwy on a sweeping bend 1 km north of Port Huon. A short access track leads to the campsites. Maximum stay is 4 days. **Map refs:** 470 B6, 507 I9

Who to contact: Huon Valley Council (03) 6264 0300

26 Snug Beach Cabin and Caravan Park

This landscaped caravan park is just 20 min south of Hobart, so it is an easy commute to the city's attractions. On the other hand, if you are looking for a relaxed and picturesque holiday spot it ticks that box too. There are caravan and tent sites set among pretty waterside gardens, as well as an all-weather BBQ and camp kitchen. There is a delightful sandy cove for safe swimming, and for travellers heading to Bruny Island, the ferry terminal at Kettering is only 5 min away. **Map refs:** 470 C6, 507 K8

How to book: 35 Beach Rd, Snug (03) 6267 9138 www.seasidetouristparks.com.au/snug.asp

27 Tahune camping area

In the forest beside the Tahune AirWalk carpark, there are a handful of sites where you can set up camp in a campervan or caravan to enjoy this magnificent riverside forest and its teetering, cantilevered canopy walkway. The surface is gravel so although you could pitch a tent here it would be nicer to camp back at the Arve River Picnic Ground. There are facilities at the visitor centre and some firewood is supplied. River water should be boiled or treated before drinking. Tahune AirWalk is at the junction of the Huon and Picton rivers, deep in the forest 28 km west of Geeveston, along the scenic Arve Rd. **Map refs:** 470 B6, 507 I8

Who to contact: Tahune Forest AirWalk and Visitor Centre (03) 6297 0068

28 Tungatinah Lagoon camping area

There are sheltered, grassed camping areas here on either side of the inlet canal, as well as next to the boat ramp in the western corner of the lagoon. These areas are informal bush campsites and there are no facilities provided, so campers must be fully self-sufficient. Bring water, firewood and a portable toilet. Access to the boat ramp is signposted from the Lyell Hwy (A10) south of the lagoon, and the canal is reached via a gravel road off the Lyell Hwy between Binney and Tungatinah. **Map refs:** 470 A2, 506 H3

Who to contact: Hydro Tasmania (03) 6271 6221, 1300 360 441 *Permits:* an Inland Angling Licence is required; check regulations and seasons www.ifs.tas.gov.au

29 Wayatinah Lakeside Caravan Park

Wayatinah started life as a workers' village but these days it is a popular holiday spot with anglers because the nearby lagoon offers excellent trout fishing. Turn off the Lyell Hwy at the Wayatinah sign, 23 km north of Ouse (pronounced 'ooze'), and you'll find the park in Second Ave – take the third left after turning left into Centreway Ave. A kids' swimming pool, games room and tennis court will keep the family entertained, and there is a laundry plus a camp kitchen to cook your catch at the end of the day. You need to bring your own firewood and bookings are essential at peak holiday times. **Map refs:** 470 A2, 506 H4

How to book: 6 Second Ave, Wayatinah (03) 6289 3317 www.wayatinah.net *Permits:* an Inland Angling Licence is required to fish; check season and regulations www.ifs.tas.gov.au

30 White Beach Tourist Park

If you are travelling with the family and a boat, this park is ideal. It is on a safe swimming beach and has every amenity you will need, from a laundry and kiosk to a playground and rec room. They will even refill your scuba tanks and there is a boat lock-up area. The Port Arthur Historic Site is only 10 min drive away, so if the Ghost Tour is on your agenda, it is only a short drive 'home' in the dark. Turn off the Tasman Hwy (A9) at Taranna onto the B37. Turn right 2 km past Nubeena and the park is 1.5 km along White Beach Rd. **Map refs:** 470 E6, 507 L9

How to book: 128 White Beach Rd, White Beach (03) 6250 2142 www.whitebeachtouristpark.com.au

EAST COAST

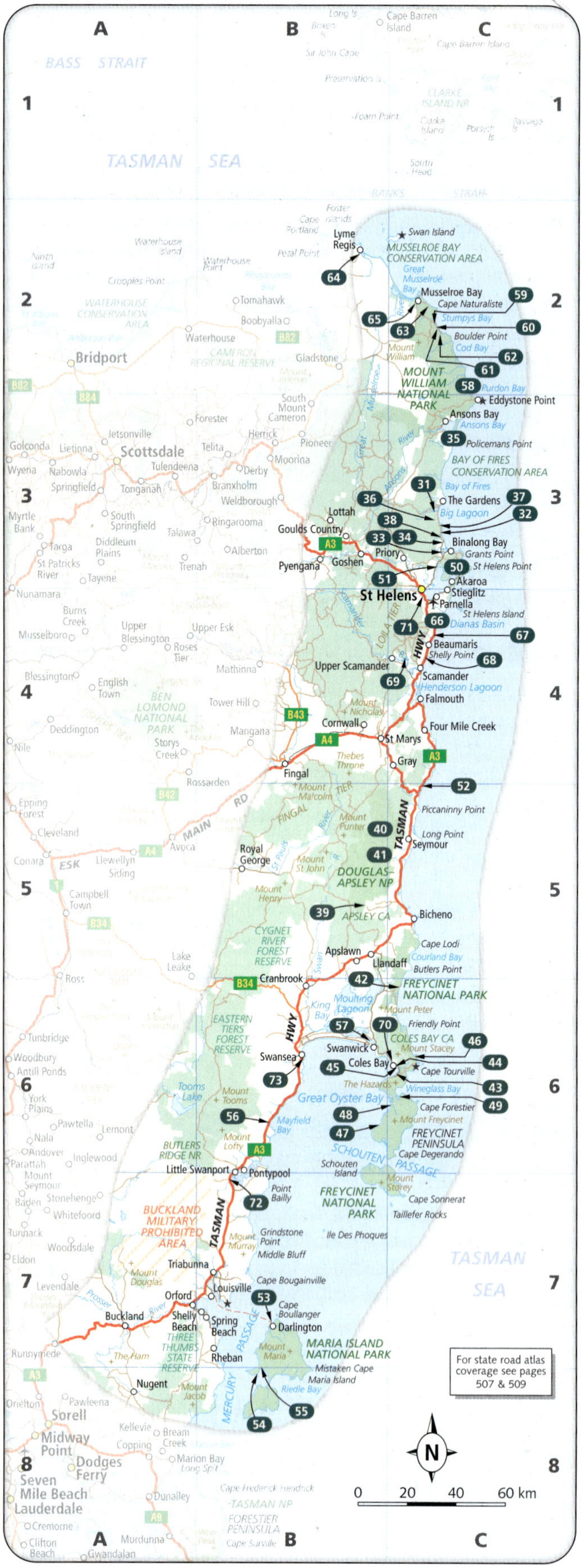

TASMANIA'S EAST COAST IS the state's summertime playground. Its mild climate, blue skies and countless pretty beaches bring so many holiday-makers here that the little towns of Orford, Swansea, Coles Bay, Bicheno and St Helens burst at the seams in warm weather. There are easily accessible campgrounds all along the coast, where you can spend days lazing on a sandy beach or paddling in a crystal-clear lagoon, or a week or more winding your way leisurely from one end of the region to the other, sampling the scenic delights as you go.

The heart of the coast is Freycinet National Park, with its spine of pink-granite mountains and famously perfect Wineglass Bay. It's an energetic 1 hr climb to the Wineglass Bay viewing platform, but the picture-postcard view from the lookout is worth the effort. Camping sites in the park are balloted out each year in August, but don't despair if you miss out as there are plenty of other beautiful beachside camping areas up and down the coast.

South of Freycinet, the coast's jewel is Maria Island. Here, without cars or phones, you can immerse yourself in nature. Climb to the dizzying heights of Bishop and Clerk for panoramic seascape views, returning to Darlington campground in time to watch the wildlife come out to feed. Or take to your bicycle and pedal to scenic camping sites in the remote south of the island.

From Bicheno north to St Helens, and beyond to the world-renowned Bay of Fires, there is plenty of camping at idyllic white-sand beaches. At Mount William National Park and Musselroe Bay you can camp in the dunes under shady casuarinas, next to beaches where you can walk for hours and not meet another soul.

CAMPSITES LOCATED IN PARKS AND RESERVES

BAY OF FIRES CONSERVATION AREA

Travellers have always been drawn to this ribbon of white sand and azure sea. Aborigines were the first, their campfires giving Europeans a name for their maps, while today's travellers know it as one of Lonely Planet's favourite destinations. Despite its fame, you're still likely to have these wide ocean beaches and shell-strewn coves to yourself. The maximum stay in any of the campsites is 4 weeks, and you need to bring in your own firewood and water. Access is via Binalong Bay Rd (C850) and then Gardens Rd (C848), which runs north along the shore and ends at the Gardens. Tracks lead to the coast along its length.

Who to contact: PWS St Helens Field Centre (03) 6376 1550; or St Helens Visitor Centre (03) 6376 1744

31 **Big Lagoon camping area**

This is a camping area with no facilities on the southern side of Big Lagoon, just south of the Gardens. Beautiful Taylors Beach is nearby, but no camping is allowed there. Turn left off

Gardens Rd (C848) onto Old Gardens Rd either at Cosy Corner or halfway along Taylors Beach. **Map refs:** 476 C3, 509 O7

32 Cosy Corner camping area

This camping area is right behind the beautiful Cosy Corner Beach. The northern end is best suited to bigger vans and the southern end has sheltered sites among trees. Access is signposted off Gardens Rd (C848) and there are entrances 5.4 and 5.6 km north of the Binalong Bay Rd intersection. Facilities are limited, but the views are superb. **Map refs:** 476 C3, 509 P7

33 Grants Lagoon camping area

This is an open, grassy area with boat access to the lagoon and sites suitable for larger rigs. Nearby is a day-use area with access to the beach. Head along Binalong Bay Rd (C850), turning left after 8 km to the Gardens. Grants Lagoon track is signposted 1.3 km past the turn-off. **Map refs:** 476 C3, 509 P7

34 Jeanneret Beach camping area

This gorgeous cove has secluded and well-sheltered camping sites at its northern end, nestled in the trees at Round Hill Point. These sites are accessible to larger vans. Swim and snorkel to your heart's content, or hike along the Binalong Bay Coastal Walk. Turn off Gardens Rd (C848), 3.2 km from the Binalong Bay turn-off. **Map refs:** 476 C3, 509 P7

35 Policemans Point camping area

There are plenty of beachside camping sites among shady trees at this isolated camping area on the southern side of Ansons Bay. You need to bring a portable toilet. Access is 35 km north of St Helens along the gravel Ansons Bay Rd (C843), via the Priory (watch out for wildlife at dusk). Or you can take the 32 km unsealed Eddystone Rd (C843) from Gladstone, turning east along South Ansons Rd, then a further 5 km takes you into the camping ground. **Map refs:** 476 C3, 509 P6

36 Sloop Lagoon camping area

Behind the southern end of Taylors Beach, this very basic camping area is between Sloop Lagoon and the sea. There are no facilities here. Access is 2.5 km along Old Gardens Rd. Turn left off Gardens Rd (C848) at Cosy Corner. **Map refs:** 476 C3, 509 O7

37 Sloop Reef camping area

This spot on the point between Taylors Beach and Seaton Cove is everything you imagine Bay of Fires to be: clear blue waves and a deserted curve of pure white beach. There are no toilets

here and it is suited to small vehicles only. Take the signposted track off Gardens Rd, 7.4 km from the Binalong Bay intersection. Head left 200 m to a small camping area overlooking the water, or head right 200 m to another small camping area best suited to tents. **Map refs:** 476 C3, 509 P7

38 Swimcart Beach camping area

There are sandy camping sites accessible to smaller vehicles all along this renowned surf-fishing beach, and a picnic area at the northern end near a small lagoon. Take care swimming as the beach drops away steeply. Access is signposted off Gardens Rd (C848), 4 km from the Binalong Bay Rd intersection. **Map refs:** 476 C3, 509 P7

DOUGLAS–APSLEY NATIONAL PARK

This rugged national park of forested hills and sheltered gorges, dominated by the Nichols Needle dolerite spire, protects a diverse remnant of beautiful eucalypt forests. There are easy walks to tranquil freshwater pools, or longer treks to secluded waterfalls and lookouts with views to take your breath away. The park contains the largest area of undisturbed dry eucalypt forest in the state, as well as groves of Oyster Bay pine and rare Esk pines. It is a biodiversity hot spot, with 67 bird species and 26 species of mammal recorded there. The Leeaberra Track – named for the Aboriginal word for Douglas River – is a moderate-grade, 28 km (3-day) walk traversing the park from north to south via waterfalls, lookouts and gorges.

Who to contact: PWS Freycinet Visitor Centre (03) 6256 7000
Permits: Parks Pass is required to enter national parks (03) 6233 2621 www.parks.tas.gov.au

39 Apsley Waterhole camping area (walk-in camping)

For camping spots in dappled shade a short walk from the delightful Apsley River swimming hole, in the south of the park, turn inland from the Tasman Hwy (A3), 4 km north of Bicheno, onto Rosedale Rd. Drive 7 km to the carpark, then take a 10 min walk to the camping area. No campfires are allowed Oct–Apr, when gas/fuel stoves should be used. The river water should be boiled or treated before drinking. **Map refs:** 476 B5, 507 O1, 509 O11

Leeaberra Track

Please note that campsites are listed in alphabetical order, not track order. Refer to the map on p. 476 for further information.

40 Heritage Falls camping area (walk-in camping)

This sheltered site sits on the bank beside the Douglas River, with the Heritage and Leeaberra waterfalls nearby. Campers need to be completely self-sufficient and carry a gas/fuel stove; no fires may be lit Oct–Apr. River water should be boiled or treated before drinking. The trailhead is accessed from the Tasman Hwy (A3), turning inland at the sign onto the unsealed

Thompsons Marshes Rd (E road) 26 km north of Bicheno, between Seymour and Piccaninny Point. After 5 km turn left into the park. The last 2 km is rough, steep and requires a 4WD. The camping area is a 2 hr walk from the trailhead. **Map refs:** 476 B5, 509 O10

41 Tevelein Falls camping area (walk-in camping)

This sheltered camping area is on the southern side of the Douglas River crossing. Campers must be self-sufficient and carry a gas/fuel stove. Water from the river should be boiled or treated before drinking. **Map refs:** 476 B5, 507 O1, 509 O10

FREYCINET NATIONAL PARK

Tasmania's first national park is also its most spectacular. Even driving towards the park is a visual treat, as soaring granite peaks come into view. Once there you will be mesmerised by the park's spectacular cliff-top lookouts, azure water and pure white beaches; especially the iconic Wineglass Bay. Camping sites for the summer and Easter holidays at Richardsons Beach and Honeymoon Bay are allocated by an online ballot drawn on 1 Aug each year. Tracks lead into the park from a trailhead at the end of Coles Bay Rd, ranging from a 1 hr return walk to the Wineglass Bay lookout to a climb up Mt Amos. Both are rewarded with bird's-eye views over Wineglass Bay and the Freycinet Peninsula. The 3-day, 30 km Freycinet Peninsula Circuit heads to glorious beaches and the mountainous southern part of the peninsula. The park is a gas/fuel stove-only area and although water is available it should be boiled or treated before drinking. Brushtail possums and wallabies are common in the park and likely to raid your food if it isn't stowed securely.

Who to contact: PWS Freycinet Visitor Centre (03) 6256 7000
Permits: Parks Pass is required to enter national parks
(03) 6233 2621 www.parks.tas.gov.au

42 Friendly Beaches camping area (bush camping)

Head to Friendly Beaches to get away from it all along this wild stretch of shoreline. There is bush camping near Isaacs Point in the northern corner of the beach and a much smaller area at South Friendly, which is accessible only by 4WD. Facilities at both are limited and campers will need to bring drinking water and a gas/fuel stove. Turn east off Coles Bay Rd (C302), 9 km from the A3. Drive 2 km along the unsealed road then head left to Isaacs Point or right to South Friendly. **Map refs:** 476 C6, 507 O2, 509 O12

43 Honeymoon Bay camping area

This scenic spot is only open for the summer season and sites are allocated by ballot due to overwhelming demand. If you win a spot, you can pitch your tent above this deliciously enticing cove and enjoy one of Tasmania's nicest camping experiences. Access is 1.6 km past the visitor centre. Some

sites are 4WD access only, and all are a quite a long walk from amenities. Water here should be boiled or treated before use. **Map refs:** 476 C6, 507 O3

44 Richardsons Beach (powered sites) camping area

There are 18 powered sites suitable for vans here, set on firm ground near the visitor centre and just metres from the beach. A day-use area nearby has a BBQ and picnic tables. If you are lucky enough to win a spot here in the annual ballot, you can stay up to 10 nights, giving you plenty of time to explore Freycinet's scenic delights. Boil or treat the water before use. Access to the park is signposted off the Tasman Hwy (A3), 33 km north of Swansea. Drive 28 km along the C302 and enter the park 1 km past Coles Bay township. Coles Bay has petrol, stores, ice, gas refills and a number of good restaurants. **Map refs:** 476 C6, 507 O3

45 Richardsons Beach (the Sand Dunes) camping area

In the dunes behind the southern end of Richardsons Beach are 25 tent sites (fewer in winter), allocated by ballot for the peak summer season each year. These are lovely sites with tracks to the beach and space for 1 car in each. There is no shortage of things to do, with many of the park's superb walking tracks starting 2 km along the road, as well as summer activities and an outdoor cinema at the visitor centre. Boil or treat the water before use. Access is off Freycinet Dr, past the visitor centre. **Map refs:** 476 C6, 507 O3

46 Whitewater Wall camping area (bush camping)

This camping area is a favourite with rockclimbers attracted to the area's granite sea cliffs. Turn left from Cape Tourville Rd, 2 km before the lighthouse, but be sure to check out the amazing view from the cape's cliff-top boardwalk. The camping area is on a bluff between Bluestone and Little Bluestone bays, accessed 2 km along a rough 4WD track. Bring water and a gas/fuel stove. **Map refs:** 476 C6, 507 O3, 509 O12

Freycinet Peninsula Circuit Track

The 30 km Freycinet Peninsula Circuit bushwalk to the spectacular southern part of the park is best done in an anti-clockwise direction, to prevent spreading plant root-rot fungus via your boots or tent pegs. Register in and out, check if water is available during dry spells and bring a gas/fuel stove (and your camera). The track starts at a carpark 4 km past the visitor centre.

Please note that campsites are listed in alphabetical order, not track order. Refer to the map on p. 476 for further information.

Who to contact: PWS Freycinet Visitor Centre (03) 6256 7000

Camping ground in Freycinet National Park (p. 478)

47 **Cooks Beach camping area (walk-in camping)**

This camping area is 2 hr from Hazards Beach and a 5–6 hr walk to Wineglass Bay over Mt Graham. The side track to Bryans Beach (1 hr) is well worth the effort. There is tank water here, at Cooks Hut, which should be treated or boiled before use.
Map refs: 476 B6, 507 O3

48 **Hazards Beach camping area (walk-in camping)**

This lovely camping area is at the southern end of Hazards Beach, reached after an easy 2 hr walk across the isthmus from Wineglass Bay, or 2 hr from the carpark trailhead via the Hazards Beach Track and Lemana Lookout. From here it is another 2 hr to the Cooks Beach camping area.
Map refs: 476 C6, 507 O3

49 **Wineglass Bay camping area (walk-in camping)**

There is a small camping area at this unforgettably beautiful bay, 1.5 hr from the carpark trailhead. Drinking water is not always available here. **Map refs:** 476 C6, 507 O3

HUMBUG POINT NATURE RECREATION AREA

The 1600 ha Humbug Point is a hot spot for birds and wildlife. Lying on the northern side of Georges Bay, it encompasses delightful coastal woodland from sheltered Moulting Bay to sparkling ocean beaches. Opportunities for easy bushwalking abound, and there is safe swimming, fishing, boating and paddling.

Who to contact: PWS St Helens Field Centre (03) 6376 1550

50 **Dora Point camping area**

This delightful camping area looks out over the Georges Bay narrows to St Helens Point. There are plenty of sheltered sites next to a safe swimming beach, and the kids will love exploring the rockpools at low tide. Come equipped with drinking water and firewood, although gas/fuel stoves are preferred, and bring your binoculars if you enjoy birdwatching. The turn-off is signposted from Binalong Bay Rd, 8 km north of St Helens. Turn right onto unsealed Dora Point Rd, 2 km from the intersection.
Map refs: 476 C3, 509 P7

51 Moulting Bay camping area

There is space here under the trees for the biggest of big rigs and, with the convenience of a boat-launching place, this is a fantastic spot to set up camp close to the excellent fishing at Georges Bay. Bring water and firewood. Turn right off Binalong Bay Rd at the sign to Moulting Bay, 7 km north of St Helens. The camping area is on an access track to the right, 1 km from the turn-off. **Map refs:** 476 C3, 509 P7

LAGOONS BEACH CONSERVATION AREA

This long, thin coastal reserve was declared in 1981 to preserve a scenic stretch of ocean beach backed by gently sloping dunes, tranquil lagoons and pretty forest glades. Home to black swans and an abundance of nocturnal wildlife, it offers some of Tasmania's best beach fishing, with plentiful Australian salmon.

Who to contact: PWS Freycinet Visitor Centre (03) 6256 7000

52 Lagoons Beach camping area

Between a long lagoon and a beautiful white beach, this extensive camping area has enough sites to accommodate everyone and is rarely full. Although it is very popular with families, the beach is wide and you will still be able to find a quiet spot in the dunes away from everyone. Swim, fish for salmon in the surf or just get your feet wet in the crystal-clear lagoon. You need to bring water and firewood. Turn onto access tracks 2 km north of the junction between the Tasman Hwy (A3) and the A4 at the base of Elephant Pass. **Map refs:** 476 C5, 509 O10

MARIA ISLAND NATIONAL PARK

This remarkable car-free island has a history as wide-ranging as its landscape. Daily ferry services (fewer in winter) run between Triabunna on the mainland and Darlington. The island's main camping area and most of its historic ruins are at Darlington, but there are also fascinating sites further afield. If you enjoy natural beauty, there are precipitous sea crags and sheltered coves with 'painted' cliffs, while the hike or pedal south to the island's sandy isthmus is well worth the effort. Ferries can be booked online.

Who to contact: Triabunna Visitor Centre (03) 6256 4772; or PWS Maria Island (03) 6257 1420 *How to book:* Maria Island Ferry 0419 746 668 www.mariaislandferry.com.au; or East Coast Cruises (03) 6257 1300 www.eastcoastcruises.com.au *Permits:* Parks Pass is required to enter national parks (03) 6233 2621 www.parks.tas.gov.au

53 Darlington Campground (walk-in camping)

Although it might be peaceful during the day, this large, grassy campground between Darlington Penitentiary and Bernacchi Creek comes alive at night, when it is a top spot for wildlife-watching. The campground is a 500 m walk from the jetty and shares laundry, shower and toilet facilities with the Penitentiary bunkhouse. **Map refs:** 476 B7, 507 N5

54 Encampment Cove camping area (walk-in camping)

This very remote campsite overlooking Chinamans Bay and McRaes Isthmus is a 13 km, 4 hr hike south of Darlington, and is about 2 km from Frenchs Farm. Although there is no jetty access, it is often used by boating parties. The access track along the isthmus is sandy, so cyclists will need to push rather than ride their bikes. **Map refs:** 476 B8, 507 N6

55 Frenchs Farm camping area (walk-in camping)

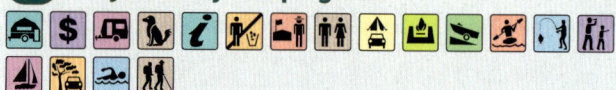

Camping areas here are in cleared paddocks around an old farmhouse at the northern end of remote Chinamans Bay, 11 km south of Darlington, but there is a 3 hr hike to reach it. The track is rocky or sandy in parts and there are some creek crossings, so if you are on a bike, be prepared to walk some of the way. **Map refs:** 476 B7, 507 N6

MAYFIELD BAY CONSERVATION AREA

This picturesque 16 ha coastal reserve south of Swansea is a popular summertime holiday destination, with shaded beachside campsites. The sweeping curve of Mayfield Beach is accessible in the north at Brickfield Beach and via a gated track to Mayfield Jetty at its southern end.

Who to contact: PWS Freycinet Visitor Centre (03) 6256 7000

56 Mayfield Bay camping area

Space for seaside camping is tucked in beside the Tasman Hwy (A3) at the southern end of Mayfield Bay, 15 km south of Swansea. There is plenty of room for big rigs here, and with boat-launching access as well, chances are you will be able to catch your dinner. If you are not into fishing, there is a lovely beach, good snorkelling and the 1845 convict-built Three Arch Bridge nearby. Bring your own firewood and drinking water. **Map refs:** 476 B6, 507 N3

MOULTING LAGOON GAME RESERVE

Declared in 1959 to conserve waterfowl habitat, Moulting Lagoon is now an internationally recognised RAMSAR-listed wetland and home to about 100 bird species, including Tasmania's largest flocks of common greenshanks and black swans. With an eye to sustainable management, a duck-hunting season Mar–June brings shooters to the wetland, but for the rest of the year it is a birdwatcher's and paddler's paradise.

Who to contact: PWS Freycinet Visitor Centre (03) 6256 7000

57 Buckleys Rocks camping area

Named for the piles of black swan feathers that can sometimes be seen along its shoreline, Moulting Lagoon Game Reserve is an internationally recognised wetland. Camping here is restricted to a site at Buckleys Rocks. The massive lagoon is a haven for birdwatchers and duck-shooters (in season), as well as an important cultural place for the Aboriginal community. Turn onto unsealed River and Rocks Rd off Coles Bay Rd (C302), 18.5 km from the Tasman Hwy (A3), and drive 500 m to the camping area by the lagoon. Bring water and firewood. **Map refs:** 476 B6, 507 O3, 509 O12

MOUNT WILLIAM NATIONAL PARK

Abutting the northern edge of Bay of Fires Conservation Area, this remote coastal park of pure white beaches, deserted granite headlands and sheltered lagoons is also home to an incredible abundance of animal life. A slow drive around the park at dusk will have you convinced that Tasmania's wallaby population is thriving, and by day the birdlife is delightful. The 1889 Eddystone Lighthouse, situated on a lichen-encrusted granite point in the southern part of the park, is a dramatic sight. In 2012, this headland was returned to the Tasmanian Aboriginal community and it is now known as larapuna. Access to the park is unsealed and tracks into the camping areas are unsuitable for large caravans and motorhomes due to overhanging branches. Bring drinking water and firewood, but gas/fuel stoves are preferred.

Who to contact: PWS Mt William (03) 6357 1043; or PWS St Helens Field Centre (03) 6376 1550 *Camping fees:* fees payable at deposit boxes in each campground *Permits:* Parks Pass is required to enter national parks (03) 6233 2621 www.parks.tas.gov.au

58 Deep Creek camping area

This out-of-the-way camping area is in the south of the park, 9 km along Eddystone Point Rd (C846) off Ansons Rd, turning left 3 km before the lighthouse. Camping areas are 3 km along this track. Be sure to detour along Eddystone Point Rd and check out the spectacular sand dunes at Abbotsbury Beach, as well as great views of the lighthouse and Bay of Fires. **Map refs:** 476 C2, 509 P6

59 Stumpys Bay – campsite no. 1

The first of 4 campsites in Stumpys Bay, this one gives access to the middle of the beach. Take the second right turn off Musselroe Rd (C845), 5 km past the self-registration booth, onto Forester Kangaroo Dr. After 2 km, turn into a signposted track to all 4 campsites. Campsite no. 1 is the largest, but the beach is steep and swimmers should take care. Suitable for small vans only. Bore water is available but not suitable for drinking. **Map refs:** 476 C2, 509 O5

60 Stumpys Bay – campsite no. 2

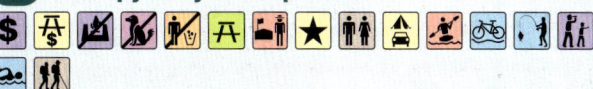

Smaller than campsite no. 1, this is the best site for tents and it has safer swimming. Access is off Forester Kangaroo Dr, 400 m past the access track to campsite no. 1. Tent sites are scattered among trees in an open forest and there is plenty of shade to relax in after a day's beachcombing. This camping area is gas/fuel stove-only as fires are prohibited. **Map refs:** 476 C2, 509 P5

61 Stumpys Bay – campsite no. 3

If you are planning on boating then head to this campsite, which has the only beach launching site in the Stumpys area. Beach access requires 4WD. Generators can be used here, so you can set up with all mod cons. Take the track 1 km past the campsite no. 2 turn-off. Do not drink the bore water. The site is suitable for small vans only. **Map refs:** 476 C2, 509 P5

62 Stumpys Bay – campsite no. 4

This is the most developed camping ground in the Stumpys area, with shady spots for about 25 tents or small vans. The beach is close and there is some excellent beachcombing to be had if you head south towards Cobler Rocks. You need to bring water and firewood. Continue along Forester Kangaroo Dr, 1.4 km past the turn-off to campsite no. 3. **Map refs:** 476 C2, 509 P5

63 Top Camp camping area

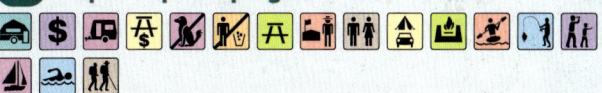

There is every chance you will have the beautiful beach next to this campsite to yourself, as few people venture to the northern edge of the park. There are a small number of rather exposed sites behind the beach. Access for small vans only is via the unsealed C845 through Musselroe Bay township, then 4 km along a signposted track. Bring water and firewood. **Map refs:** 476 C2, 509 O5

MUSSELROE BAY CONSERVATION AREA

This long coastal reserve stretches from Little Musselroe Bay south-east along Great Musselroe Bay to Poole at the northern edge of Mt William National Park. The incredibly scenic coastline of deserted white-sand beaches punctuated by windswept headlands, sheltered lagoons and estuaries is a haven for anglers and birdwatchers.

Who to contact: PWS St Helens Field Centre (03) 6376 1550; or PWS Mt William (03) 6357 1043

64 **Little Musselroe Bay camping area**

This is a stunningly beautiful bay with views to the Furneaux Islands and an abundance of birdlife. Drive along Cape Portland Rd, 27 km north of Gladstone, and then 200 m into the sheltered bayside camping area. Best to come here between Christmas and Easter, when there is 4WD access to the camping area; otherwise access is on foot from the road. Bring drinking water and firewood. **Map refs: 476 B2, 509 O4**

65 **Musselroe Bay camping area**

There is camping suited to big rigs in this remote coastal conservation area north of Mt William National Park. Drive north-east of Gladstone along the Musselroe Bay Rd (C845), 8 km past the park information booth. The access road is 100 m past the track to Top Camp in the national park. Note: maximum stay is 4 weeks, and you need to bring firewood and drinking water. **Map refs: 476 C2, 509 O5**

ST HELENS POINT CONSERVATION AREA

This 1066 ha reserve on the southern side of Georges Bay encompasses scenic St Helens Point, and offers excellent fishing, paddling, shoreline walks and birdwatching, as well as great surfing and swimming at Beerbarrel Beach. The extensive dunes stretching south along Maurourard Beach are a photographer's paradise and great fun for bodyboarders, plus there is an area set aside at Peron Dunes for 4WD action.

Who to contact: PWS St Helens Field Centre (03) 6376 1550; or St Helens Visitor Centre (03) 6376 1744

66 **Dianas Basin camping area**

This lovely camping area has a lagoon on one side and Beaumaris Beach on the other. Swim, surf, fish or head north or south along the beach for hours of beachcombing. You may bring your dog to the camping area but not to the beach. The camping sites, sheltered amongst the coastal scrub, are large enough for big rigs. Turn off the Tasman Hwy (A3) onto a dirt road at the sign to Dianas Basin, 9 km south of St Helens. The road forks 500 m further on; go left to campsites beside the lagoon or continue right another 900 m to campsites with better shade closer to the beach. You will need to bring your own firewood and water. **Map refs: 476 C4, 509 P8**

SCAMANDER CONSERVATION AREA

Beside the highway, midway between St Helens and St Marys, this thin coastal reserve stretches along 12 km of glorious, unspoilt ocean beaches from Dianas Basin south along Beaumauris, Wrinklers and Steels beaches to Hendersons Lagoon. With fishing one of the biggest drawcards, there

are launching places at Scamander River, Paddys Island and Hendersons Lagoon.

Who to contact: PWS St Helens Field Centre (03) 6376 1550

67 **Paddys Island camping area**

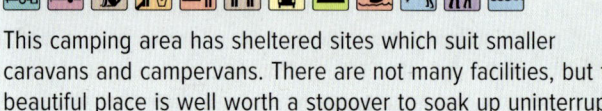

With white-sand beaches stretching to the horizon north and south, this camping area between the highway and the sea is ideal if you love long beach walks. All along this coast there is evidence of Aborigines having lived here, and no wonder they did: it's not only beautiful but has a mild climate and bountiful seafood. Turn off the Tasman Hwy into the small parking area 2.5 km north of Beaumaris. There is a beach boat-launching place here. Bring drinking water and firewood. **Map refs: 476 C4, 509 O8**

68 **Shelly Point camping area**

This camping area has sheltered sites which suit smaller caravans and campervans. There are not many facilities, but this beautiful place is well worth a stopover to soak up uninterrupted ocean views and explore beaches which go on forever. Turn in off the Tasman Hwy, 3 km north of Scamander. You can camp in the clearings beside the road but not at the beachside day-use area. You need to bring your own water and firewood. **Map refs: 476 C4, 509 O8**

SCAMANDER FOREST RESERVE

Among the forested hills to the west of Scamander, this peaceful reserve offers a lovely contrast to the wide-open ocean beaches of the coast. Get here along winding roads off the Tasman Hwy (A3), or by boat 6 km upstream from Scamander. There is plenty of excellent fishing and the campsites are set among the trees, where you can do as much or as little as you like.

Who to contact: Forestry Tasmania Scottsdale Forest EcoCentre (03) 6352 6520

69 **Trout Creek camping area**

This leafy camping area beside Trout Creek has perfect spots to set up your deckchair for an afternoon's fishing in comfort. With a bit of luck you will have a nice bream, trout, mullet or cocky salmon to throw in the pan for dinner. Turn inland off the Tasman Hwy (A3) at Beaumaris Tavern along Skyline Rd, then take Eastern Creek Rd and turn left into Trout Rd. The campsite is 3 km further on. Or, from Scamander, follow the Upper Scamander Rd (C421) and turn north across the bridge. After 7 km, turn onto Eastern Creek Rd, then turn right 5 km along into Trout Rd. Come equipped with firewood and drinking water. **Map refs: 476 C4, 509 O8**

CAMPSITES LOCATED IN OTHER AREAS

70 BIG4 Iluka on Freycinet Holiday Park

This is a park for families: it has great facilities for all ages, with a playground, tennis courts nearby and a beautiful safe swimming beach opposite. The kids can bounce, swing and see-saw while you relax around the BBQ or enjoy the family-friendly bistro dining room. The entry gate to Freycinet's famous national park is only 1 km along the road, while closer at hand there are shops and a bakery. At Coles Bay turn right onto Jetty Rd, then left on Garnet Ave and 100m further on turn left into Esplanade. **Map refs:** 476 C6, 507 O3

How to book: Esplanade, Coles Bay (03) 6257 0115, 1800 786 512 www.ilukaholidaycentre.com.au

71 BIG4 St Helens Holiday Park

Although it gets busy in summer, this spacious cabin and van park is perfect for a quiet few days. With all the amenities you could expect and extras such as a lounge area with a large flat screen television, a bouncy jumping pillow for the kids and a fully equipped indoor camp kitchen, this family-friendly park is a convenient base from which to explore the beautiful coastal region around St Helens and the Bay of Fires. The park is 1 km south of St Helens township, off the Tasman Hwy. **Map refs:** 476 C4, 509 O8

How to book: 2 Penelope St, St Helens (03) 6376 1290, 1300 559 745 www.sthelenscp.com.au

72 Gumleaves Bush Holidays

This large cabin park and holiday centre is set among pretty woodland with its own little lake, pioneer display and adventure playground. It caters for large groups in cabin-style accommodation and there is camping for vans and motorhomes too. On-site there is tennis, minigolf and a flying fox, while further afield there are beaches, vineyards and great fishing spots. Turn inland off the Tasman Hwy at the sign on Swanston Rd, 26 km north of Orford. **Map refs:** 476 B7, 507 N4

How to book: Tasman Hwy, Little Swanport (03) 6244 8147 www.gumleaves.com.au

73 Swansea Holiday Park – Schouten Beach

With picture-postcard views across Great Oyster Bay to the mountains of Freycinet Peninsula, this family-friendly cabin and caravan park is in a great spot next to Swansea's golf course. It is right on Schouten Beach and just a short walk to main street cafes and restaurants. Close by is the Loon.tite.ter.mair. re.le.hoin.er walk, which wends its way around scenic Waterloo Point. Further afield there are vineyards and berry farms, and Freycinet National Park is a 55 min drive from the park. Turn into Wellington St towards the ocean at the sign on the Tasman Hwy, on the southern side of Swansea. Pets are permitted after Easter. **Map refs:** 476 B6, 507 N3, 509 N12

How to book: 2 Bridge St, Swansea (03) 6257 8148 www.swansea-holiday.com.au

MIDLANDS AND THE NORTH

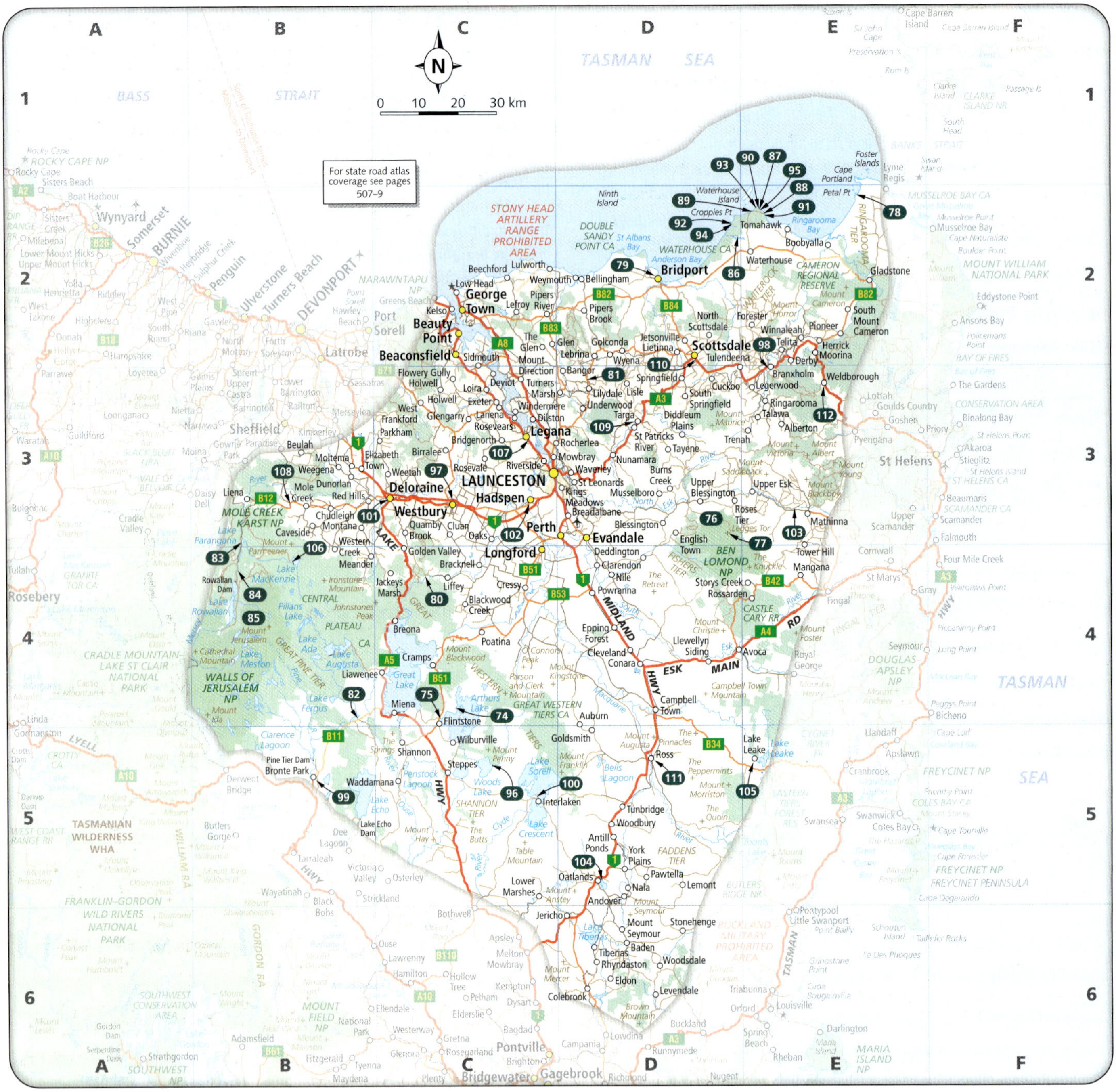

THIS LARGE REGION CENTRED on Launceston includes Tasmania's earliest settlements. The main north-south highway cuts through the broad sweep of its wheat and sheep-farming plains, where grand manor houses at Longford, Evandale and Westbury hint at the success of the first European settlers. The area's colonial history is preserved in almost every town and village, with convict-made bricks and hand-hewn sandstone part of many houses, bridges and churches.

Launceston is Tasmania's second city and a food- and wine-lover's delight, nestled in hilly country where the Tamar, North Esk and South Esk rivers meet. From here, you can explore the scenic

Tamar Valley's wine estates or head east through hilly timber country and small fruit orchards to Scottsdale. Touring west of Launceston towards Devonport, the road passes through a scenic English landscape, where the vibrant little village of Deloraine sits amid pretty fields and meandering rivers. A detour from here takes you up into limestone cave country and the forested foothills of the Central Plateau.

The midland plains end abruptly at the Great Western Tiers to the west and Ben Lomond National Park in the east. Driving up from the valley floors, the roads into both these areas take you through dizzying switchback corners to magical landscapes of dolerite spires, alpine lakes and swirling mists. The lakes of the Western Tiers offer superb angling in season and most have camping grounds accessible to 2WD vehicles, while further west the Walls of Jerusalem National Park offers a truly remote camping experience accessible only on foot.

The region's north coast has a mild, summery climate and beautiful beaches. There are delightful seaside holiday towns at Weymouth and Bridport, while further east you can get off the beaten track at the vast dune fields, isolated camping sites and deserted ocean beaches either side of Waterhouse Point and Cape Portland.

CAMPSITES LOCATED IN PARKS AND RESERVES

ARTHURS LAKE LAKESIDE RESERVE

Like many other lakes in Tasmania's central highlands, Arthurs Lake was formed to store water for hydro-electricity generation. Water from Arthurs is pumped to Great Lake and then piped through massive conduits to the Poatina power station on the northern face of the Central Plateau. These extraordinary engineering works have created lakes which are now home to some of the world's best inland fishing. Anglers come to Arthurs Lake more than any other in Tasmania for its wild brown trout. The average catch rate is 2 fish per angler per day, so few go away disappointed.

Who to contact: Bothwell Tourism Association (03) 6287 1313
Camping fees: fees payable at the self-registration station
Permits: an Inland Angling Licence is required to fish; check regulations and season www.ifs.tas.gov.au **Road conditions:** Gunns Marsh Rd is closed to the public June–July

74 Jonah Bay camping area

Most of the camping is around the boat ramp but there are also some more isolated campsites on the edge of the scrub at the other end of Jonah Bay, accessed via a track 100 m from the ramp. Turn east along Gunns Marsh Rd off Poatina Rd (B51), 10 km north of its junction with the Lake Hwy (A5). **Map refs:** 484 C4, 507 J1, 509 J11

75 Pumphouse Bay camping area

This beautifully maintained, scenic campground beside Arthurs Lake has open, grassed areas among the trees that are perfect for larger rigs. The lake is not just for anglers: campers of all kinds love this place, especially the mealtime get-togethers around the communal BBQs (even though there are campsite fireplaces and free firewood). Turn east off Poatina Rd, pass the not-so-scenic hydro pumphouse and the 'no camping' sign, and take the first turn to the left. Be sure to take advantage of the wood-heated showers after your day out on the lake. View lake conditions via the Pumphouse Bay webcam at www.coastview.com.au **Map refs:** 484 C4, 507 J1, 509 J11

BEN LOMOND NATIONAL PARK

Ben Lomond is a Tolkienesque world of sheer dolerite cliffs, scree slopes and swirling mists. Winter snows attract skiers, while in all seasons there are splendid lookouts and scenic walks for those brave enough to tackle the drive up Jacobs Ladder, a steep switchback road leading to the park's alpine heart. June–Sept all vehicles must carry snow chains.

Who to contact: PWS Tamar Field Centre (03) 6336 5391
Permits: Parks Pass is required to enter national parks (03) 6233 2621 www.parks.tas.gov.au

76 Ben Lomond camping area

At the picnic area beside the road, 1 km inside the park boundary, there are 6 camping sites in an area of beautiful lowland gums, mountain pepper bushes and snowberries. The water here should be boiled or treated before drinking. Bring firewood. To get to the park, take the C401 towards Upper Blessington and turn right onto gravel at the signposted C432. **Map refs:** 484 D3, 509 M8

77 Bush camping

Bushwalkers can camp anywhere in the park, as long as they are at least 500 m from any road. You'll need to carry drinking water and a gas/fuel stove, and be prepared for all weather conditions. Walkers should register at the village before departure and deregister on return. **Map refs:** 484 D3, 509 M9

BOOBYALLA CONSERVATION AREA

Abutting Musselroe Bay Conservation Area, this newly designated 10 km strip of coastal reserve spans the windswept dunes of Ringarooma Bay, from the tiny shack settlement of Tomahawk to the end of the Boobyalla Beach at Petal Point. It is a beautiful, isolated corner of Tasmania with a pristine white-sand surf beach, striking coastal vegetation and few visitors.

Who to contact: PWS Scottsdale Field Centre (03) 6352 6421

78 Petal Point camping area

If you like to be alone on a windswept beach, with only seabirds for company, then this remote coastal camping area is for you. Head to the far north-east corner of Tasmania, where there are campsites tucked into the scrub at the eastern end of Boobyalla Beach. Take the Cape Portland Rd (C844), 21 km north of Gladstone, and then turn left to Petal Point. You will need to be completely self-sufficient for water and a gas/fuel stove is recommended. Camp only in existing sites. There are no dump sites in the reserve. **Map refs:** 484 E2, 509 N4

GRANITE POINT CONSERVATION AREA

Granite Point Conservation Area is 100 ha of diverse coastal heath and includes the lovely Bridport Wildflower Reserve alongside Bridport Caravan Park. A meandering shared pathway leads through the reserve to Granite Point and Adams Beach. There is a wonderful display of flowering heath here in spring.

Who to contact: Bridport Caravan Park, 83 Bentley St, Bridport (03) 6356 1227

79 Bridport Caravan Park

This is like one of those caravan parks you remember from the past, when summer was just sun, sand and swimming. Set up camp among the trees, nip over to the beach for a long lazy swim with the kids, then enjoy the evening around your campfire (bring firewood and fire pot). Bridport is 50 km east of George Town on the B82. Head left onto Emily Rd, then The Espl, which becomes Main St. The park is on Bentley St, a right turn towards the beach. **Map refs:** 484 D2, 509 L5

LIFFEY FALLS STATE RESERVE

The gorgeous Liffey Falls area spans a forestry reserve with a delightful picnic and BBQ area, while the pretty waterfall itself lies within a 100 ha state reserve of sassafras, myrtle and leatherwood rainforest managed by the Parks and Wildlife Service. If green is your favourite colour, you will love it here amongst the ferns.

Who to contact: PWS Tamar Field Centre (03) 6336 5391

80 Lower Liffey camping area

Liffey Falls is a series of beautiful waterfalls – all of which can be viewed from observation decks – cascading through dense myrtle rainforest on the edge of the Great Western Tiers. Access is via Lake Hwy (A5) south of Deloraine, or from the east via Bracknell on the C513. The narrow, winding Riversdale Rd to the top carpark and falls walk is not accessible by trailers and vans, and there is no camping at this day-use area. A small, sheltered, grassy campground is at the Gulf Rd picnic area, off the signposted Liffey Falls/Lower Track rd, and is best accessed from Liffey to the east if you are driving a big rig. The 1.5 hr Liffey Falls Track links the upper and lower picnic areas. Bring firewood and water. **Map refs:** 484 C4, 509 I9

LILYDALE FALLS RESERVE

This little council reserve was set aside in 1923 to preserve 2 pretty waterfalls and their surrounding ferny forest. The picnic area is a delightful shady glen and has 2 huge oak trees, which were planted on the day of Queen Elizabeth's coronation, in 1953, from acorns collected at Windsor's Great Park in England.

Who to contact: Lilydale Newsagent and Takeaway (03) 6395 1156
Camping fees: pick up keys to the amenities block from the newsagent

81 Lilydale Falls Reserve camping area

In the middle of Tasmania's north-eastern wine region, 2.5 km north of the little township of Lilydale on Golconda Rd (B81), this pleasant campground has shady sites beneath mature trees. The playground, picnic shelter and free firewood make this a desirable place to camp. However, the grassed area is beyond bollards, for tents only, and you have to carry in your gear; van sites are in the adjoining gravel carpark. Note: the maximum stay is 2 nights and small pets may be allowed if you ask first. **Map refs:** 484 D3, 509 K7

LITTLE PINE LAGOON LAKESIDE RESERVE

This reserve circles Little Pine Lagoon, which, to those in the know, is the best fly-fishing water in Australia, with wild brown trout the main attraction. When full, the lagoon is 220 ha of shallow water surrounded by open, grassy banks. There is boat launching at Montpeelyata Canal, but to protect the lagoon's precious population of trout, boating speeds are restricted and there is a no-boating area 100 m from Little Pine Dam.

Who to contact: Inland Fisheries Service 1300 463 474
Camping fees: fees payable at the self-registration station
Permits: an Inland Angling Licence is required to fish; check season and regulations www.ifs.tas.gov.au

82 Little Pine Lagoon Lakeside Reserve camping area

The lagoon is right beside the Marlborough Hwy (B11), 7 km west of Miena, in Tasmania's central highlands. From the highway, it is a further 500 m to the grassed camping areas located along Cricket Pitch Shore beyond the shacks; there are separate areas for tents and trailers. No fires may be lit here, so gas/fuel stoves are a must. **Map refs:** 484 B4, 507 I1, 509 I11

MERSEY STATE FOREST

This forest reserve abutting Cradle Mountain National Park, Walls of Jerusalem National Park and Central Plateau Conservation Area is one of several tucked under the Great Western Tiers between Tasmania's rich coastal farmlands and its rugged uplands. The Mersey River at its centre is dammed to form 2 long, thin lakes sheltered by steep, forested hills. Both lakes offer excellent angling, with Lake Rowallan being stocked yearly with rainbow trout.

Who to contact: Forestry Tasmania, Devonport (03) 6424 8388 www.forestrytas.com.au **Permits:** an Inland Angling Licence is required to fish; check regulations and season www.ifs.tas.gov.au

83 Lake Parangana camping area (bush camping)

Peaceful, scenic camping sites are dispersed in the bush along the western shore of this long, skinny lake. It is a lovely spot to fish, swim and boat – or just relax. From Mole Creek take the Liena Rd to the winding Mersey Forest Rd (C171), or from Gowrie Park take the C138. Turn left just south of the dam wall and drive through the picnic area to reach the bush camping area. You will need your own firewood and drinking water, or you can boil or treat water from the lake. **Map refs:** 484 B3, 508 G9

84   Lake Rowallan camping area (bush camping)

A few kilometres south of Lake Parangana, Lake Rowallan has extensive bush-camping areas next to the river by the dam wall and on the lake's eastern shore, accessible along 4WD tracks. Take the Mersey Forest Rd up into the Mersey Valley, turning left to cross the river where the road forks at West Rowallan Track. The lake's main attraction is its rainbow trout and as it can be fished in season (Aug–Apr) with lures, flies or bait, all the family can have a go. You will need to bring firewood and water. **Map refs:** 484 B4, 508 G9

WALLS OF JERUSALEM NATIONAL PARK

This park is a pristine alpine plateau accessible only to dedicated bushwalkers. It is an unforgettably beautiful landscape of lakes and tarns, some surrounded by ancient pencil pines, others ringed by cushion plants. Scenic highlights include the pencil pine-fringed Pool of Bethesda and the delightful Dixons Kingdom Hut, which is also set in a grove of pencil pines, some over 1000 years old. Trails up to Solomons Throne and Mt Jerusalem offer stunning vistas across Tasmania's central plateau. The park entrance is a 30 min walk from the carpark on the rocky, unsealed Fish River Rd. Turn off the Mersey Forest Rd (C171) at Lake Rowallan.

Who to contact: PWS Great Western Tiers Field Centre (03) 6363 5133 ***Permits:*** Parks Pass is required to enter national parks (03) 6233 2621 www.parks.tas.gov.au

85   Wild Dog Creek camping area (walk-in camping)

Tent sites on timber platforms beside Wild Dog Creek are reached 3 hr from the carpark, after negotiating a moderately steep and muddy track. You will need to be fully equipped and capable of sitting out extreme cold weather. You must also carry a gas/fuel stove as campfires are not allowed. The huts in the park are for emergency shelter only. From Wild Dog Creek it is a short climb to Herods Gate and Lake Salome. Bring your camera. **Map refs:** 484 B4, 508 G10

WATERHOUSE CONSERVATION AREA

This 25 km stretch of dune-backed beach and coastal lagoons is reached from the B82 via Blackmans Lagoon and Homestead rds. A network of rough and sandy tracks – some only passable with a 4WD vehicle – leads to beach launching sites, sheltered camping areas and rocky headlands. Campers can stay for up to 4 weeks and need to be self-sufficient for water, firewood and food; they should also bring a portable toilet. There are no dump sites here.

Who to contact: PWS Scottsdale Field Centre (03) 6352 6421 ***Road conditions:*** check before travel as tracks are sandy in parts and conditions vary (03) 6352 6421

86   Big Waterhouse Lake camping area

A few cleared camping sites are provided here on the northern shore of the lake, but there are no facilities at this location. Access is signposted 4 km along Homestead Rd, then it is a further 3 km to the camping area. Bring drinking water and firewood. **Map refs:** 484 D2, 509 M5

87   Brads camping area

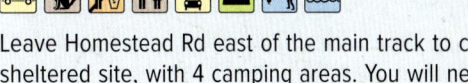

This beachside camping area faces gorgeous Ringarooma Bay and the Furneaux Islands. It is reached via a track off Homestead Rd, 1.4 km east of the Herbies Landing turn-off, then right where the track splits after about 1 km. Camping is 400 m further on towards the beach, where there is a boat-launching site. Bring drinking water and firewood. **Map refs:** 484 E2, 509 M4

88   Casuarina Hill camping area

Leave Homestead Rd east of the main track to camp at this sheltered site, with 4 camping areas. You will need a 4WD to cope with the steep, sandy track. Bring drinking water and firewood. **Map refs:** 484 E2, 509 M4

89   Herbies Landing camping area

If you continue north along Homestead Rd past the South Croppies Rd turn-off, 5 km further on there is a signpost to a very small camping area with just 3 sites and no facilities. There is a boat-launching place at Blizzards Landing, 2 km east. Bring drinking water and firewood. **Map refs:** 484 E2, 509 M4

90   Mathers camping area

This site has sheltered, shady nooks among coastal vegetation where you can set up out of the wind. Head out towards Waterhouse Point via the track off Homestead Rd, 1.4 km east of the Herbies Landing turn-off. Where the track splits, about 1 km in, continue 100 m to a small number of campsites by the beach, where there is a boat-launching site. Bring drinking water and firewood. **Map refs:** 484 E2, 509 M4

91   Ransons Beach camping area

At the eastern end of Homestead Rd, there is a small camping area and beach boat-launching place near a couple of fishing shacks. This is a popular spot for off-roaders as it has 4WD and bike access for surf-fishers between Easter and 1 Dec each year. Bring drinking water and firewood. **Map refs:** 484 E2, 509 M5

92   South Croppies Point camping area

These campsites are at the northern side of this scenic point. They have spectacular ocean outlooks but are relatively exposed to the weather. From Homestead Rd, turn left 2 km north of the Big Waterhouse Lake track, then take the right fork 2 km further

on through the scrub to windswept Croppies Point. No facilities are provided and no firewood collecting is allowed: bring water and wood or a gas/fuel stove. Track conditions vary and it is best to check before travel. **Map refs:** 484 D2, 509 M5

93 Village Green camping area

On the western side of Waterhouse Point, this camping area has magnificent views across Waterhouse Passage but no shade. Access is from Homestead Rd, turning off 1.4 km east of the Herbies Landing turn-off. About 1 km in, the track splits; take the left fork, then it is 800 m to the camping area. A beach boat-launching site is nearby. Bring drinking water and firewood. **Map refs:** 484 E2, 509 M4

94 Waterhouse Beach camping area

North of Waterhouse, these campsites sit behind the beach and are sheltered by coastal scrub. Head towards the coast along Homestead Rd, turning left to Croppies Point, then left again at the Y-junction. No facilities are provided: bring drinking water and firewood. **Map refs:** 484 D2, 509 M5

95 Waterhouse Point camping area

At the remote northern tip of this conservation area, there are campsites scattered among scrub next to sandy tracks. Head out to the magnificently scenic Waterhouse Point via a track off Homestead Rd, 1.4 km east of the Herbies Landing turn-off. About 1 km in, the track splits; camping is in this area as well as along a track heading east. A 4WD boat-launching site is nearby. Bring drinking water and firewood. **Map refs:** 484 E2, 509 M4

WOODS LAKE LAKESIDE RESERVE

This lakeside reserve encircles Woods Lake in the central highlands. It is one of the state's most exciting trout fisheries, with high catch rates, especially for early season anglers. The lake offers fly-fishing, trolling or casting. Locals suggest the delightfully named squidgy flick baits or woolly bugger flies as your top choices here, or maybe an evil minnow or shimmy shrimp. The road from Arthurs Lake to Woods Lake has been upgraded and now offers better access.

Who to contact: Inland Fisheries Service (03) 6261 8050, 1300 463 474 *Permits:* an Inland Angling Licence is required to fish; check regulations specific to Woods Lake www.ifs.tas.gov.au

96 Woods Lake camping area (bush camping)

There are bush-camping sites between the boat ramp and the dam wall, as well as around the north-eastern edge of the lake. No facilities are provided, so you need to bring firewood and water. Because this is a popular camping area, special care should be taken to bury waste away from the shore. To get here, turn off Poatina Rd (B51) to Arthurs Lake Dam, heading along 15 km of steep gravel road past the dam. If you are towing a boat, you may need a 4WD on this road, even though it has been upgraded. **Map refs:** 484 C5, 507 J2, 509 J12

CAMPSITES LOCATED IN OTHER AREAS

97 Andy's Motorhome and Caravan Park

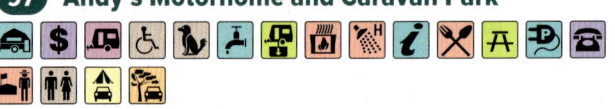

Behind Westbury's 24 hr bakery cafe, this motorhome park is a convenient stopover 30 min from Launceston. Its great facilities include a laundry, dump point and wireless hotspot. While you're here, check out Westbury's interesting attractions, especially the hedge maze, steam museum and Andy's prize-winning latte gelato. Westbury is well signposted off the Bass Hwy between Launceston and Deloraine; Andy's is on the main street, the B54. **Map refs:** 484 C3, 509 J8

How to book: Andy's Bakery Cafe, 45 Meander Valley Rd, Westbury 03) 6393 1846 www.andystasmania.com

98 Branxholm Centenary Park camping area

Branxholm is a sleepy little timber town on the Ringarooma River, east of Scottsdale. The camping ground is near the Red Bridge in the middle of town, close to the start of the historic Briseis Race walking track, and it is a great spot to relax while the kids enjoy the pool and playground. There is a shop across the road, the grand old Imperial Hotel close by, excellent sightseeing at nearby Mt Horror lookout and fascinating mining history evident in the town's graveyard. Bring firewood and fire pot, and phone ahead for permission to bring your dog. **Map refs:** 484 E3, 509 M7

Who to contact: Branxholm Supermarket (03) 6354 6168
Camping fees: pick up keys from the supermarket

99 Bronte Park Village

This delightful township was built in the 1940s to house workers constructing the Tungatinah hydro-electricity scheme. The old hydro houses have been converted to cabin accommodation for visitors to the area's famous angling waters. Bronte Park is set in open farmland with 11 lakes within 20 min drive, and anglers are drawn by the variety of excellent trout fishing on offer. The caravan park has gravel sites and is conveniently close to a store and tavern. Bronte Park is on the Marlborough Hwy (B11) 4 km north of the Lyell Hwy intersection. **Map refs:** 484 B5, 506 H2, 508 H12

How to book: 376 Marlborough Hwy, Bronte Park (03) 6289 1126 www.bronteparkvillage.com.au *Permits:* an Inland Angling Licence is required and available from Bronte Park General Store (03) 6289 1129; check angling regulations and season www.ifs.tas.gov.au

100 Dago Point camping area

Among tall trees along the Lake Sorell foreshore are about 100 gloriously secluded camping spots. It is more than likely

you'll be the only one here. There is plenty of firewood, an old water tank (boil or treat the water before use), playground and toilet facilities, but there are no shops in the area and Lake Sorell is closed for fishing. To get here, head to tiny Interlaken, 28 km from both the Midland and Lake hwys, and the campground is 300 m from the turn-off, signposted on the unsealed C527. **Map refs:** 484 C5, 507 K2, 509 K12

Who to contact: PWS Great Western Tiers Field Centre (03) 6363 5133

101 Deloraine Apex Caravan Park

This caravan park beside the picturesque Meander River is just a short walk from National Trust–classified Deloraine's main street. There are grassy sites along the river bank, and while there is a playground and swimming pool nearby to keep the kids happy, you will need to keep an eye on them because there is no fencing between the park and a nearby railway track. The caretaker lives across the road and the office is easy to miss, but the facilities here are topnotch and it is a great base within easy distance of some of the most scenic parts of Tasmania. **Map refs:** 484 C3, 509 I8

How to book: 51 West Pde, Deloraine (03) 6362 2345
Camping fees: fees payable to caretaker opposite park

102 Discovery Holiday Parks – Hadspen

In the little riverside village of Hadspen, this cabin park and camping area is within easy reach of Launceston, which is just 10 min along the highway. It is renowned for its convivial atmosphere: aim to be here on a Friday, when the owner hosts a friendly BBQ get-together for campers. The kids will love the playground, games room and half tennis court, while Hadspen itself and the nearby villages of Evandale and Longford will entrance history buffs. Further afield are the Tamar Valley's wineries and the region's gourmet cheeseries, chocolatiers and berry farms. Access Hadspen via Meander Valley Hwy off Bass Hwy, either from Travellers Rest or Illawarra Rd. At Hadspen you will find the park on the corner of Main St. **Map refs:** 484 C3, 509 K8

How to book: cnr Main St and Meander Valley Hwy, Hadspen (03) 6393 6391, 1800 281 885 www.discoveryholidayparks.com.au/tas/tamar_valley/hadspen

103 Griffin camping area

Along the banks of the South Esk River are pleasant, grassed camping sites close to a network of tracks heading into the North East Forests, so this place is ideal if you are into trail bikes or ATVs. There is good trout fishing and safe swimming in the river. Close by is the 30 min return walking track to Mathinna Falls, while Evercreech Forest Reserve, home to the world's tallest white gums, is a short drive away. Griffin Rd is

signposted off the C423, 2 km north of Mathinna. There are numerous campsites at this intersection and further along Griffin Rd. Campsites are closed during forest harvesting. **Map refs:** 484 E3, 509 N8

Who to contact: Scottsdale Forest EcoCentre (03) 6352 6520; or Forestry Tasmania, Fingal (03) 6374 2102 *Road conditions:* access roads are closed during forestry operations

104 Lake Dulverton Roadside Stopover camping area

A stopover here is worthwhile to check out the historic town of Oatlands. Visit the restored working Callington Mill, or take a walking tour around the town, nature walk around the lake or drive around the district on the drystone wall tour. The camping area is signposted from The Esplanade; you can have a shower at the pool or pub and there is a 24 hr laundromat. Don't leave without sampling artisan sourdough from the town's very good bakery. The maximum stay here is 1 night. **Map refs:** 484 D5, 507 K3

Who to contact: Heritage Highway Tourism Centre, the Stables, 85 High St, Oatlands (03) 6254 1212

105 Lake Leake camping area

Back in the 1880s, this lake was created for Campbell Town's water supply. Today it is a premium trout water, regularly stocked with brook and rainbow trout, and said to offer some of Tasmania's best early- and late-season wet fly-fishing. There's a small camping area between the boat ramp and the dam wall, and you'll need to be self-sufficient with your own firewood and drinking water. Turn north off the B34, 34 km east of Campbell Town, or 30 km west of the Tasman Hwy (A3). Drive 4 km along an unsealed access road to the boat ramp. **Map refs:** 484 E5, 507 M2, 509 M12

Who to contact: Lake Leake caretaker (03) 6381 1319

106 Lake Mackenzie camping area (bush camping)

Camping at this remote hydro lake is only for the dedicated angler or bushwalker. Accessed via 21 km of unsealed – and occasionally snow-covered – winding road south of Mole Creek Karst National Park, it is likely that the only visitors here are hiking up into Tasmania's alpine central plateau or after a wild trout, or both. The small, exposed camping area is at the end of the road and there are no facilities. The turn-off to Lake Mackenzie Rd is 20 km west of Mole Creek on the Mersey Forest Rd (C171). **Map refs:** 484 B4, 508 H9

Who to contact: Hydro Tasmania (03) 6271 6221, 1300 360 441

107 Launceston Holiday Park

This well-equipped cabin park and camping area is perfectly located for travellers visiting Launceston and the beautiful Tamar

Camping in Walls of Jerusalem National Park (p. 487)

Valley. There are plenty of sites in a parkland setting with great amenities, including a laundry, rec room, playground, camp kitchen and kiosk. An added attraction is the park's wine bar, where you can relax with a glass of great Tasmanian wine at the end of your day touring the valley's vineyards. The park is on the west side of the West Tamar Hwy (A7), 10 km from Launceston. **Map refs:** 484 C3, 509 K7

How to book: 711 West Tamar Hwy, Legana (03) 6330 1714 www.islandcabins.com.au/launceston

108 Mole Creek Caravan Park

This riverside caravan park, just west of Mole Creek township, has plenty of attractions close by. There are Australia's finest cave systems at Marakoopa and King Solomons Cave, as well as honey farms, a cheesery, and a salmon and a ginseng farm to visit. The park has laundry facilities and wifi, and is happy to provide you with firewood on request. From Mole Creek, take Liena Rd west, turning right into Union Bridge Rd past the bridge, 4 km from town. **Map refs:** 484 B3, 508 H8

How to book: 2 Union Creek Rd, Mole Creek (03) 6363 1150 www.molecreek.net.au

109 Myrtle Park Recreation Ground

This delightful camping area is next to the pretty St Patricks River at Targa, about halfway between Launceston and Scottsdale on the Tasman Hwy (A3). The camping area is beside riverbank willows, and there's plenty of room for large rigs. If there is energy to burn after a long drive, the kids will love the playground while you enjoy a game of tennis. There is also a small kiosk on site. Bookings are recommended if you want a site with a fireplace. **Map refs:** 484 D3, 509 L7

How to book: 38250 Tasman Hwy, Targa (03) 6399 3368

110 Northeast Park camping area

Surrounded by beautiful parkland, trees and lakes, this pretty camping ground is 1 km east of Scottsdale on the A3. There is a playground on-site and you can stay at the park for up to 7 days, giving you plenty of time to meet the other residents – ducks, wallabies, platypus or the rare burrowing crayfish. Scottsdale's modern Forest Eco Centre in King St has a wealth of information about the area and is well worth a look. Scottsdale is a 1 hr scenic drive from Launceston over the Sideling Range. **Map refs:** 484 D2, 509 M6

Who to contact: Scottsdale Visitor Information Centre (03) 6352 6520; or Dorset Council (03) 6352 6500

111 Ross Caravan Park

This riverside cabin and van park is set among lovely, mature trees close to the beautiful sandstone Ross Bridge – the third oldest in Australia. The children will love the swimming pool and playground across the road, and you will enjoy this fascinating historic town with its interesting street junction (see if you can pick the temptation, recreation, salvation and damnation corners) and 2 scrumptious bakeries a short walk from the park. Not surprisingly, bookings are recommended for peak times. It is on Bridge St, beside the river. **Map refs:** 484 D5, 507 L2, 509 L12

How to book: Ross Motel, Bridge St, Ross (03) 6381 5224 www.rossmotel.com.au/park

112 Weldborough Hotel Campground

Tiny Weldborough (blink and you'll miss it) has shaded, grassed camping sites with good amenities out the back of its delightful historic pub. Before you get too comfortable with a cold beer in the pub, be sure to have a look at the ancient myrtle and fern forest at the Weldborough Pass Scenic Reserve, or take to a mountain bike on the 14 km Blue Tier track down to the campground. Bring your own firewood. Weldborough is 42 km inland from St Helens on the Tasman Hwy (A3). **Map refs:** 484 E3, 509 N7

How to book: Weldborough Hotel, Tasman Hwy (03) 6354 2223 www.hotel.weldborough.com.au

NORTH-WEST

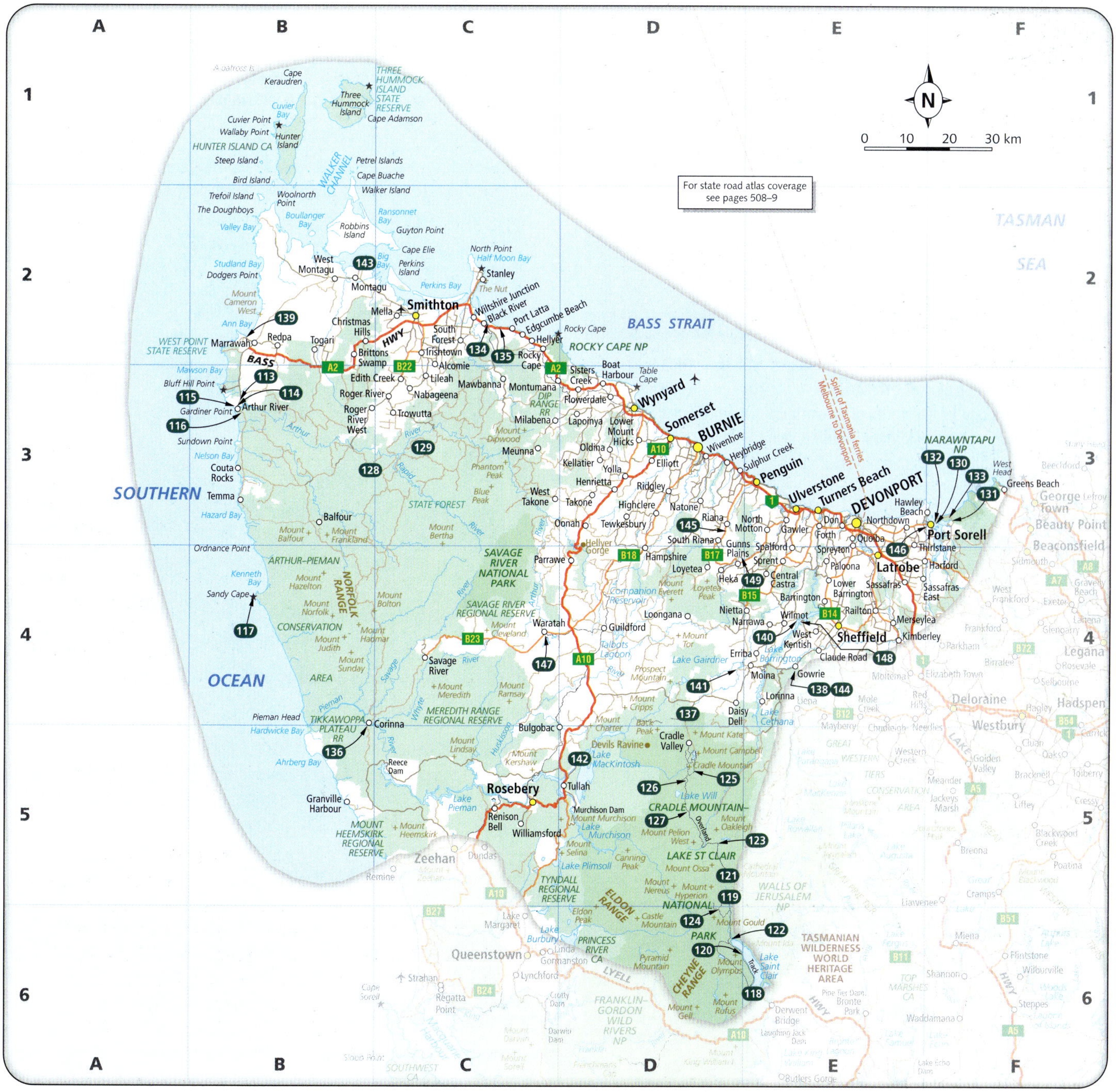

For state road atlas coverage
see pages 508–9

A B C D E F

1 2 3 4 5 6

Albatross Is
Cape Keraudren
Cape Adamson
THREE HUMMOCK ISLAND STATE RESERVE
Three Hummock Island
Cuvier Point
Cuvier Bay
Wallaby Point
Hunter Island
HUNTER ISLAND CA
Steep Island
Bird Island
Petrel Islands
Cape Buache
Walker Island
Trefoil Island
Woolnorth Point
The Doughboys
Boullanger Bay
Robbins Island
Ransonnet Bay
Guyton Point
Valley Bay
Studland Bay
Dodgers Point
West Montagu
Big Bay
Perkins Island
Perkins Bay
Cape Elie
North Point
Half Moon Bay
Stanley
The Nut
Montagu
Mount Cameron West
Ann Bay
WEST POINT STATE RESERVE
Mawson Bay
Marrawah
Bluff Hill Point
Gardiner Point
Arthur River
Sundown Point
Nelson Bay
Couta Rocks
Temma
Hazard Bay
Ordnance Point
Kenneth Bay
Sandy Cape
Pieman Head
Hardwicke Bay
Ahrberg Bay
SOUTHERN OCEAN
BASS HWY
A2
139
113
114
115
116
117
143
Smithton
Mella
Christmas Hills
South Forest
Trishtown
Alcomie
Edith Creek
Roger River
Nabageena
Trowutta
Roger River West
Brittons Swamp
Togari
Redpa
B22
134
135
129
128
136
Wiltshire Junction
Black River
Port Latta
Edgcumbe Beach
Rocky Cape
Hellyer
Boat Harbour
Sisters Creek
Rocky Cape
Table Cape
ROCKY CAPE NP
BASS STRAIT
Flowerdale
Lapoinya
Lower Mount Hicks
Montumana
Mawbanna
Milabena
Oldina
Kellatier
Henrietta
Ridgley
Yolla
Natone
Wynyard
Somerset
BURNIE
Wivenhoe
Heybridge
Sulphur Creek
Penguin
Ulverstone
Turners Beach
DEVONPORT
A10
1
132
130
133
131
Greens Beach
West Head
NARAWNTAPU NP
Hawley Beach
Northdown
Port Sorell
Thirlstane
George Town
Beauty Point
Beaconsfield
Don
Forth
Spreyton
Quoiba
Paloona
Latrobe
Hadford
Sassafras
Sassafras East
146
148
Sheffield
Kimberley
Claude Road
Gowrie
Moina
Lorinna
Railton
Lower Barrington
Barrington
Wilmot
West Kentish
Nietta
Narrawa
Loongana
Heka
Central Castra
Gunns Plains
B14
B15
B17
B18
140
141
138
144
DIP RANGE RR
Mount Hicks
Elliott
North Motton
Gawler
Sprent
Spalford
Riana
South Riana
Hampshire
Loyetea
Companion Reservoir
Loyetea Peak
Mount Everett
Tewkesbury
Highclere
Oonah
West Takone
Takone
Mount Dipwood
Phantom Peak
Blue Peak
STATE FOREST
Meunna
Parrawe
Guildford
Waratah
SAVAGE RIVER NATIONAL PARK
SAVAGE RIVER REGIONAL RESERVE
Savage River
Balfour
Mount Balfour
Mount Frankland
Mount Bertha
ARTHUR-PIEMAN CONSERVATION AREA
NORFOLK RANGE
Mount Hazelton
Mount Norfolk
Mount Judith
Mount Hadmar
Mount Sunday
Mount Meredith
MEREDITH RANGE REGIONAL RESERVE
TIKKAWOPPA PLATEAU RR
Corinna
Reece Dam
Granville Harbour
MOUNT HEEMSKIRK REGIONAL RESERVE
Zeehan
Remine
Dundas
Rosebery
Renison Bell
Williamsford
Murchison Dam
Lake Murchison
Tullah
Lake MacKintosh
Lake Plimsoll
Lake Rolleston
Canning Peak
TYNDALL REGIONAL RESERVE
ELDON RANGE
Bulgobac
Mount Cripps
Mount Charter
Daisy Dell
Cradle Valley
Devils Ravine
Mount Kate
Mount Campbell
CRADLE MOUNTAIN–LAKE ST CLAIR
Lake Will
Lake Windermere
Mount Oakleigh
Mount Pelion West
Mount Ossa
Mount Pelion East
Mount Thetis
Mount Nereus
Mount Hyperion
WALLS OF JERUSALEM NP
Mount Gould
TASMANIAN WILDERNESS WORLD HERITAGE AREA
NATIONAL PARK
CHEYNE RANGE
Lake St Clair
Mount Olympus
Mount Gell
Mount Rufus
Pyramid Mountain
Castle Mountain
Eldon Bluff
Lake Petrarch
Overland Track
Derwent Bridge
126
125
127
123
121
119
124
122
120
118
142
147
149
145
137
149
Queenstown
Strahan
Lynchford
Regatta Point
Cape Sorell
FRANKLIN-GORDON WILD RIVERS NP
PRINCESS RIVER CA
LYELL HWY
A10
B23
B24
B27

SPANNING TASMANIA FROM ITS populated north-west coast across a hinterland of rolling hills to the storm-swept and almost deserted west coast, this diverse region is a perfect destination for car touring and camping. Around any corner the road might reveal a patchwork of lush farmland, a pretty seaside town, a blue Bass Strait horizon or a rainforest valley. You can spend the night under canvas in a pristine alpine wilderness, park your campervan alone at a west-coast beach to watch the Southern Ocean swells, or lay out a gourmet feast in your caravan after a day touring local farm outlets.

There are 2 very different but easily accessible national parks in this region. In the east, Narawntapu National Park's wildlife-packed grassy plains have it dubbed 'little Serengeti', and it is one of the best places in the state to see kangaroos and wombats in the wild. Here you can camp in the dunes behind wide swimming beaches, or beside a calm, picturesque estuary with excellent fishing.

To the south, the famously scenic Cradle Mountain–Lake St Clair National Park wows visitors with incredibly rugged mountains and ever-changing weather. For the fit and well-prepared, there is the Overland Track 6-day walk through the park's alpine centre, or you can just set up camp in the forest near the park and enjoy leisurely scenic walks to rainforest glades and alpine lakes. At night, grab your camera to snap the local wildlife, which is out and about every evening in rain, hail or snow.

Along the region's Bass Strait coast are delightful towns to explore, such as Stanley with its doll's house row of historic cottages nestled under the 'Nut'. For lovers of wild, natural places, the forests of the Tarkine south of Smithton and the Arthur–Pieman Conservation Area should not be missed.

CAMPSITES LOCATED IN PARKS AND RESERVES

ARTHUR–PIEMAN CONSERVATION AREA

Between the Tarkine rainforest wilderness and the wild Southern Ocean, this remote strip of heathland, dunes and forest lies directly in the path of relentless ocean storms. Once the home of the Tarkiner people, it has an incredibly rich concentration of archaeological sites dating back some 30 000 years. Apart from the Western Explorer route, access is only possible via 4WD tracks, so it remains mostly uninhabited, with only a handful of fishing shacks along its windswept coast. The area's tracks and beaches are perfect for horseriding and there are holding yards at Arthur River and Rebecca Creek.

Who to contact: PWS Arthur River (03) 6457 1225 *How to book:* Arthur River Cabin Park, 1239 Arthur River Rd (03) 6457 1212 www.arthurrivercabinpark.com *Camping fees:* fees payable at ranger station *Permits:* an Arthur–Pieman Off-Road permit is required to drive south of Temma *Road conditions:* recreational vehicle access to the area is under review and may change; check closures and track conditions before travel www.parks.tas.gov.au

113 Arthur River Cabin Park

This camping area is part of a privately run cabin park at Arthur River. The park has good facilities, plenty of resident local wildlife and offers a great information service for travellers in the region. The road from Smithton is sealed as far as Arthur River; further south to Strahan it is unsealed but well maintained and suitable for ordinary vehicles. There are several walks nearby where you can view the magnificent natural surroundings. The park is close to boat and canoe hire businesses, as well as excellent fishing and surfing spots. **Map refs:** 491 B3, 508 A5

114 Manuka Campground

At remote Arthur River, this large campground is the nicest of the 3 in the area and has sheltered spots for large rigs. Keeping out of the wind is a priority here, but if you want to feel the true force of west-coast weather head to 'The Edge of the World' at Gardiner Point. Gather firewood from the beach for your campfire, but make sure you light it in a fire pot and not on the

ground. The water should be boiled or treated before drinking. From Marrawah, Arthur River is 14 km south on the unsealed Arthur River Rd (C214); the campsite is just before the ranger station on the right. **Map refs:** 491 B3, 508 A5

115 Peppermint Campground

This camping area in the township of Arthur River has the BBQ you will need to cook that freshly caught salmon, even if the weather is too wet to get the fire going. These sites are on the smallish side, so large rigs will need to find a spot in the neighbouring campgrounds (Manuka or Prickly Wattles). Bring drinking water or boil/treat the water supplied, and only use collected driftwood for campfires. The sites are next to the ranger station, off Arthur River Rd. **Map refs:** 491 B3, 508 A5

116 Prickly Wattles Campground

There are plenty of secluded, sheltered sites at this extensive camping ground next to the road, 2 km south of Arthur River. Reputed to be a very good fishing destination, the beach at Arthur River has firm sand and boat-launching places, but you can also fish off the beach. Collect driftwood for fires and light them only in the fireplaces provided. Boil or treat the water before drinking, or bring your own. **Map refs:** 491 B3, 508 A5

117 Sandy Cape camping area (bush camping)

The largest sand dunes in the state are at Sandy Cape, but they are hard to reach and this unserviced camping ground on Tasmania's remote west coast is only accessible by 4WD. Tracks in the area should be attempted by experienced drivers only, and you'll need to check track conditions and organise your Arthur–Pieman Off-Road permit with the ranger at Arthur River before you head out. Access is via the Temma or Balfour 4WD tracks off the Western Explorer (C249), 50 km south of Arthur River. The beach drive from Greenes Creek to Sandy Cape is rated hard due to quicksand and should not be attempted alone. Bring drinking water and all self-sufficient supplies. **Map refs:** 491 B4, 508 A7

CRADLE MOUNTAIN–LAKE ST CLAIR NATIONAL PARK

This mountainous park is part of 1 500 000 ha of World Heritage wilderness in the heart of Tasmania. It is an unforgettable alpine landscape of peaks, lakes, moors and ancient forests, attracting thousands of walkers yearly to its famous 65 km Overland Track. Vehicle access is only to the northern and southern extremities; otherwise the park is the preserve of bushwalkers.

Who to contact: PWS Cradle Mountain Visitor Centre (03) 6492 1110; or PWS Lake St Clair Visitor Centre (03) 6289 1172 *How to book:* (03) 6289 1137 for campsite no.**118** *Permits:* Parks Pass is required to enter national parks (03) 6233 2621 www.parks.tas.gov.au

118 Cynthia Bay Campground

This popular campground at the southern end of the national park is part of the privately run Lake St Clair Wilderness Lodge. It has shady sites for big rigs on the southern shore of Australia's deepest lake. Check out the park's impressive visitor centre, take the ferry to Narcissus Bay or walk the 1.5 hr Larmairremener tabelti Aboriginal cultural walk. At night, enjoy visits from resident wildlife or, if the weather is clear, admire the amazing night sky – fitting that Cynthia was the Greek goddess of the moon. Turn north off the Lyell Hwy at Derwent Bridge. The camping area is signposted 5 km along Lake St Clair Rd. **Map refs: 491 E6, 506 G2, 508 G12**

The Overland Track

The Overland Track is Australia's most famous bushwalk. During the summer walking season, trekkers start at the Cradle Mountain end of the track and take around 6 days – longer depending on the weather and side tracks – to finish at Cynthia Bay at the southern end of Lake St Clair. The track leads through Tasmania's alpine heart and although there are huts and an upgraded path, walkers must be reasonably fit and fully equipped with a gas/fuel stove and tent. They should also be prepared to sit out bad weather, which can occur in any season. Camping is at the huts along the track; each has tank water and gas or coal heaters, with fuel supplied and camping platforms nearby. Walkers must book departure dates in the peak season (Nov–Apr).

Please note that campsites are listed in alphabetical order, not track order. Refer to the map on p. 491 for further information.

119 Bert Nichols Hut (walk-in camping)

This hut replaced the Windy Ridge hut in 2008. It sleeps 24 in bunks and is 10 km from Kia Ora (allow 4 hr). **Map refs: 491 D5, 506 G1, 508 G10**

120 Echo Point Hut (walk-in camping)

This lakeside hut is 6.5 km south of Narcissus Hut. Walking north to south, this is the last hut and camping area on the trail before the end of the Overland Track at Cynthia Bay (11 km south). **Map refs: 491 D6, 506 G1, 508 G11**

121 Kia Ora Hut (walk-in camping)

The delightful Kia Ora hut is nestled below the Du Cane Range, 9 km south of Pelion Hut (allow 3 hr). It sleeps 20 in bunks. **Map refs: 491 D5, 508 F10**

122 Narcissus Hut (walk-in camping)

Narcissus is the last hut and camping area on the north-south route if you choose to take the ferry 13 km along Lake St Clair to

the trailhead at Cynthia Bay. It sleeps 18 and is 9 km south of the Bert Nichols hut (allow 3 hr). **Map refs: 491 D6, 506 G1, 508 G11**

123 Pelion Hut (walk-in camping)

Pelion Hut is the halfway point on the Overland Track and the largest hut, sleeping 36. It is 16.5 km south of Windermere Hut (allow 6 hr). **Map refs: 491 D5, 508 F10**

124 Pine Valley Hut (walk-in camping)

This hut is a possible side-trip between Bert Nichols Hut and Narcissus Bay. **Map refs: 491 D6, 506 F1, 508 F11**

125 Scott-Kilvert Memorial Hut (walk-in camping)

This hut was built as a memorial to 13 yr old David Kilvert and his teacher, Ewan Scott, who died in a blizzard here in 1965. It is beside Lake Rodway and involves a side-trip from the main Overland route. Access is via the Cradle Cirque or Lake Dove walking tracks. Sleeping accommodation is an upstairs loft. **Map refs: 491 D5, 508 F9**

126 Waterfall Valley Hut (walk-in camping)

From the northern trailhead at Waldheim, it is 10 km (allow 6 hr) to this large hut. **Map refs: 491 D5, 508 F9**

127 Windermere Hut (walk-in camping)

This rustic hut sleeps 16 and is 7.5 km (3 hr) south of Waterfall Valley hut. **Map refs: 491 D5, 508 F9**

JULIUS RIVER FOREST RESERVE

Deep in Tasmania's north-west, this reserve is a tiny sample of the vast, ancient rainforest wilderness that lies between the Arthur–Pieman Conservation Area and the untracked Savage River Regional Reserve and National Park. Access is possible in a standard vehicle along the scenic, unsealed South Arthur Forest Drive (C218), which loops through the remote forest south of the Arthur River between the Tayetea and Kanunnah bridges.

Who to contact: Forestry Tasmania, Smithton (03) 6452 9100

128 Julius River Forest camping area

On the northern edge of the huge Tarkine rainforest wilderness, this forest camping area is 10 km east of the Kanunnah Bridge and Sumac Lookout on the South Arthur Forest Dr (C218). At Julius River Reserve, there are 6 sites suitable for vans (not tents) located 600 m past the picnic area. Take an interpretive rainforest walk among ferns, bush orchids, mosses and fungi to a limestone sinkhole, or head to nearby Lake Chisholm for a walk through old-growth myrtle forest to an even more spectacular flooded sinkhole. **Map refs: 491 B3, 508 C5**

Tents pitched near Waterfall Valley Hut, Cradle Mountain–Lake St Clair National Park (p. 493)

MILKSHAKE HILLS FOREST RESERVE

This pretty forest reserve is one of several in the remote wet forests south of Smithton. Access is along the unsealed South Arthur Forest Dr (C218) – a 130 km loop from Smithton – which winds through deep forest valleys and past scenic lookouts, offering visitors fantastic views of this remote region.

Who to contact: Forestry Tasmania, Smithton (03) 6452 9100
Permits: an Inland Angling Licence is required to fish; check regulations and season www.ifs.tas.gov.au

129 **Milkshake Hills camping area**

This sheltered camping area is nestled in a ferny glade near the reserve's picnic facilities. There are a number of walks nearby, ranging from an easy 10 min stroll through a rainforest loop to the more strenuous 45 min return climb to the top of one of the Milkshake Hills, which give the reserve its unusual name. Turn left onto the South Arthur Forest Dr at Roger River, 23 km south of Smithton; the reserve is 16 km along this unsealed road.
Map refs: 491 C3, 508 C5

NARAWNTAPU NATIONAL PARK

Within this long coastal park – the first in Tasmania to adopt its Aboriginal name – there are wide beaches, lagoons packed with birdlife, open plains crowded with animals and an excellent information centre. The abundance of wildlife to be seen here at dusk is remarkable, with dozens of wallabies and wombats coming out to feed each evening. It is also significant for its human history, with evidence that people have lived here for perhaps 30 000 years. Most camping areas in the park have fireplaces with some firewood supplied, although gas/fuel stoves are recommended. Narawntapu is 40 km east of Devonport via the B71, or 85 km north of Launceston via the West Tamar Hwy (A7).

Who to contact: PWS Narawntapu (03) 6428 6277 **Permits:** Parks Pass is required to enter national parks (03) 6233 2621 www.parks.tas.gov.au

130 **Bakers Point camping area**

On the point by Springlawn Beach, this large camping area has 36 sites – 16 suitable for larger rigs – a portable toilet waste collection point and a boat-launching area. There's excellent fishing in the estuary, and from Nov–Apr part of nearby Springlawn Beach is reserved for waterskiing. Drive past the ranger station, turning right to Bakers Point. The sites are clearings among the coastal vegetation. **Map refs:** 491 F3, 509 I6

131 Horse Yards camping area

A 26 km horseriding trail leads from this camping area, but you must camp nearby and give the ranger 48 hours notice before you can bring your horse into the park. Narawntapu is 40 km east of Devonport via the B71, or 85 km north of Launceston via the West Tamar Hwy (A7). Follow the unsealed C740 into the park, and Horse Yards is 600 m past the park entrance. **Map refs: 491 F3, 509 I6**

132 Koybaa camping area

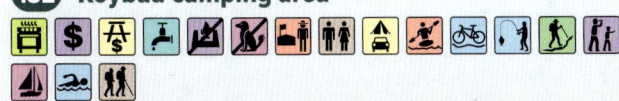

This camping area at Griffiths Point, 4 km past the ranger station, has 12 small sites surrounded by scrub. They are only suitable for tent-based camping because you have to carry your gear in past a row of bollards. From these sites it is only a short walk to the beach, but you need to be careful of strong currents around the rocks or in the estuary, especially when the tide is going out. **Map refs: 491 F3, 509 I6**

133 Springlawn camping area

This is the place to head to in the park if you have a large rig and need power. It also has the best facilities and is only 100 m past the ranger station and visitor centre, so it is just a short walk to join one of the ranger's spotlight walks or to check out the Springlawn nature walk to the lagoon bird hide. **Map refs: 491 F3, 509 I6**

PEGGS BEACH CONSERVATION AREA

This 208 ha conservation area lies on the coast between Stanley and Rocky Cape National Park. It takes in the beachfront and coastal vegetation of the scenic Peggs Beach, from the Black River inlet to the Little Peggs Beach State Reserve. Camping is at the Peggs Beach end or beside the estuary, and with 4WD boat-launching areas at both camping sites, it is popular spot for a fishing holiday.

Who to contact: PWS Stanley Field Centre (03) 6458 1480
Camping fees: fees payable by self-registration at the entrances to camping areas

134 Black River camping area

These secluded sites are nestled in coastal vegetation next to the Black River estuary. There is safe swimming at lovely Brickmakers Beach and a boat-launching ramp into the river. This large campground is part of the beautiful Peggs Beach Conservation Area, so you must bring firewood and a fire pot because campfires should not be lit on the ground. Tank water is available but should be boiled or treated for drinking. There are plenty of spaces – secluded or open – including sites that

can accommodate large rigs. Turn at the sign off the Bass Hwy, 8.5 km east of the Stanley turn-off, and head along a dirt track for 700 m. **Map refs: 491 C2, 508 D4**

135 Peggs Beach camping area

This small campground is very popular with locals, so you will be lucky to find a spot here in the summer holiday season. Although it is close to the highway, it is right next to a gorgeous, wide beach with boat-launching places nearby. There are sites sheltered among the coastal vegetation and a separate, more open area, but few facilities. The tank water should be boiled or treated for drinking. A shower cubicle is available to hang solar showers. Turn off the Bass Hwy 11 km east of the Stanley turn-off, or 14 km west of the Rocky Cape turn-off. **Map refs: 491 C2, 508 D4**

PIEMAN RIVER STATE RESERVE

Declared in 1936, this long, thin reserve protects magnificent riverside rainforests of Huon pine. It extends along both sides of the Pieman River from the Reece Dam at the base of Lake Pieman to the Pieman Heads in Hardwicke Bay, where the river empties into the Southern Ocean. The tiny hamlet of Corinna is halfway along the reserve.

How to book: Tarkine Hotel and Corinna Wilderness Experience (03) 6446 1170 www.corinna.com.au

136 Corinna Wilderness Experience camping area

Tiny Corinna – named for the Tasmanian tiger – lies on the southern edge of the vast, heritage-listed Tarkine rainforest wilderness at the Pieman River crossing. Limited camping and riverside van sites are at the Tarkine Hotel, close to the beautiful Huon Pine walk. There are more walks through ferny forest to Lovers Falls or Donaldsons Peak, while the Pieman River Cruise is not to be missed. Corinna is 133 km south of Arthur River on the winding, unsealed Western Explorer (C249), or 69 km from Waratah on the B23, then the unsealed C247. From the south, take the Western Explorer from Zeehan, reaching the Pieman River after 153 km, then the Fatman Barge across the river to Corinna. **Map refs: 491 B4, 508 C8**

CAMPSITES LOCATED IN OTHER AREAS

137 Discovery Holiday Park – Cradle Mountain Campground

This is the only camping area at the northern end of Cradle Mountain–Lake St Clair National Park, so it gets busy in summer and bookings are essential. Sites are in bush alcoves 2 km outside the park. Most people are here to see the awe-inspiring

scenery but there are also horse rides, ATVs and night-time spotlight tours on offer. This alpine country is notorious for its rapidly changing weather, so even in summer you'll need to be equipped for rain and snow. The route is signposted from Sheffield. Take the C136 to Moina, turn left onto the C132 and left again after 21 km. The campground is 3 km along on the right. **Map refs:** 491 D4, 508 F8

How to book: 3832 Cradle Mountain Rd (03) 6492 1395, 1800 068 574

138 Gowrie Park Wilderness Village

This caravan and van park is across the creek from the O'Neills Creek Reserve camping area and offers more facilities and longer stays. It has a range of accommodation and the convenience of a licensed restaurant, which is open every day. Sheffield is a short drive to the north and it is only 40 km from here to the northern end of Cradle Mountain–Lake St Clair National Park. You will find this caravan park on the C136 (Claude Rd) 15 km south of Sheffield. **Map refs:** 491 E4, 508 G8

How to book: 1447 Claude Rd (03) 6491 1385 www.gowriepark.com.au

139 Green Point camping area

Green Point is the end of the road heading west. This grassy camping ground faces onto wild surf beaches, where huge ocean swells roll in uninterrupted from South Africa. Bring good shelter as the campground is open and exposed. Head to Marrawah, 51 km west of Smithton on the Bass Hwy (A2). Turn right into Comeback Rd (C215) and then left onto Green Point Rd, which leads downhill to the beachside campground, 2 km from the turn-off. **Map refs:** 491 B2, 508 A4

Who to contact: Circular Head Council (03) 6452 4800

140 Lake Barrington West camping area

Lake Barrington is famous for its world-class rowing course, and while there are big crowds here for rowing championships, the rest of the time there is peaceful camping, all-year angling and beautiful scenery. Camping sites are just off Lake Barrington Rd, 8 km south of Lower Wilmot. Bring firewood and drinking water, or treat/boil the water here. **Map refs:** 491 E4, 508 G7

Who to contact: Kentish Council (03) 6491 2500; or Sheffield Visitor Information Centre (03) 6491 1760 *Permits:* an Inland Angling Licence is required to fish; check regulations and season www.ifs.tas.gov.au

141 Lake Gairdner camping area

There is a free camping area with no facilities on the banks of this hydro lake, so if the campground at Cradle Mountain is full

(as it often is), this may be a good alternative, provided you are completely self-sufficient (come with firewood and drinking water). Turn west off the Cradle Mountain Rd (C132), 1 km south of Moina, then follow a dirt road to a gate signposted 'camping but please shut the gate', just before a white bridge. The area is an unshaded, open paddock on private land. There is another small site beneath the bridge. **Map refs:** 491 D4, 508 G8

Permits: An Inland Angling Licence is required to fish; check regulations and season www.ifs.tas.gov.au

142 Lake Mackintosh camping area

If you are a self-sufficient camper and enjoy trout fishing and lovely scenery, this camping ground 6 km north of Tullah is ideal. It is best suited to caravans and camper trailers, as there are few tent sites. Turn east off the Murchison Hwy (A10) onto the signposted Mackintosh Dam Rd. Take the single-lane road across 2 dams (provided the spillway is not flooding), then turn down gravel tracks to the lakeside camping areas. There are no facilities so bring your own firewood and drinking water. There are excellent bushwalks nearby, including the spectacular, but challenging, Mt Farrell. **Map refs:** 491 D5, 508 E9

Who to contact: Hydro Tasmania (03) 6271 6221, 1300 360 441
Permits: an Inland Angling Licence is required to fish; check regulations and season www.ifs.tas.gov.au

143 Montagu Recreation Reserve camping area

This very picturesque campground on the edge of remote Robbins Passage is only open Nov–Apr each year, so if you want to camp under the shade of these beautiful gums, it is a good idea to book ahead. There are 46 sites catering for all types of campers, including big rigs; you need to bring firewood and water. There is a boat ramp, making this a popular spot for anglers and boating enthusiasts. Head west along Montagu Rd (C215), just after crossing the bridge at Smithton. Travel 16 km, passing through Scopus and Montagu, then turn right onto Old Port Rd, arriving at the camping ground after 4 km. **Map refs:** 491 B2, 508 C3

Who to contact: Stanley Visitor Information Centre (03) 6458 1330, 1300 138 229; or Circular Head Council caretaker 0428 524 843 *Camping fees:* fees payable to the caretaker on-site

144 O'Neills Creek Reserve camping area

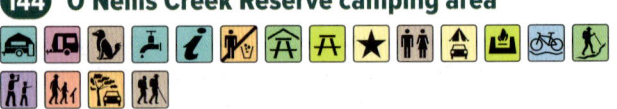

Next to the creek and rodeo ground, this pretty forest reserve has places for vans for short stays (2 nights maximum), making it a perfect overnight stop on your way to Cradle Mountain–Lake St Clair National Park. It is close to the Mt Roland hiking trail and there is a nice 15 min nature walk you can take from the campground to the start of the track. Across the creek, the Gowrie Park Wilderness Village has cabins and powered van sites for longer stays. Access is along the C136, 16 km south-west of Sheffield. **Map refs:** 491 E4, 508 G8

Who to contact: Kentish Council (03) 6491 2500; or Sheffield Visitor Information Centre (03) 6491 1760

145 Pioneer Park camping area

Set among farmland and forested hills 15 km from Penguin, the tiny settlement of Riana is picture-postcard pretty. Its quiet little campground is on the left-hand side of the main road (B17), just past the cricket oval and service station. There are shaded sites on a first-come, first-served basis, and it is one of those unhurried places where you can sit back and take it easy in very peaceful surroundings. While you are here, take a look at Gunns Plains Caves and the spectacular Leven Canyon. **Map refs:** 491 D3, 508 F6

Who to contact: 1399 Pine Rd, Riana (03) 6437 6137

146 Port Sorell Lions Caravan Park

This large caravan park is close to shops and just a short walk from the foreshore of the Rubicon estuary, with its sheltered beach and lovely views of Narawntapu National Park. The safe swimming beach and kids' playground will keep the little ones happy, and there is golf, tennis and excellent fishing nearby. Further afield there are nice scenic drives through pretty farmland. Head east from Devonport, turning off the Bass Hwy (A1) onto Port Sorell Rd (B74). Port Sorell is 14 km from the turn-off, and the park is on Meredith St. Bring your own fire pot. There is a dump point at the jetty. **Map refs:** 491 F3, 509 I6

How to book: 42 Meredith St, Port Sorell (03) 6428 7267 www.portsorellcaravanpark.com.au

147 Waratah camping area

Formerly the location of the world's leading tin mine, Waratah now welcomes tourists not miners, although there is still gold to be panned in nearby creeks. In the middle of town, there is a lake and waterfall; this council-run campground is right next to them, behind the council chambers on Smith St. There are 20 van sites on both grass and gravel, and a dump point in Annie St. There is a shop nearby and the hotel does very good meals. Cradle Mountain and Corinna are within easy driving distance. Waratah is on the B23, 7 km from its junction with the Murchison Hwy (A10), 63 km south of Somerset and 55 km north of Rosebery. **Map refs:** 491 C4, 508 E7

Who to contact: Visitor Information Centre, Smith St, Waratah (03) 6439 7100; or Waratah Roadhouse (03) 6439 1110

148 West Kentish Park camping area

This informal camping area on the eastern shore of beautiful Lake Barrington is 6 km from West Kentish. Busy when there are rowing events at the lake, at other times it is a peaceful campground amid pretty scenery. Bring your own firewood. Access is from the C140 south of Sheffield. **Map refs:** 491 E4, 508 G7

Who to contact: Kentish Council (03) 6491 2500; or Sheffield Visitor Information Centre (03) 6491 1760 *Permits:* an Inland Angling Licence is required to fish; check regulations and season www.ifs.tas.gov.au

149 Wings Wildlife Park

Gunns Plains is a picturesque rural valley surrounded by forested hills and spectacular cliffs. It is close to some of Tasmania's most scenic natural attractions, such as Leven Canyon, Gunns Plains Caves and the renowned Cradle Mountain. As well as providing cabin and camper accommodation, this park is also home to an extensive menagerie of exotic and native animals, from koalas and Tasmanian devils to water buffalo and bison. The grassed camping areas are alongside the Leven River. The park has good facilities and offers a gas bottle exchange service. Winduss Rd runs off South Riana Rd (B17) at a signposted hairpin bend 1 km from the turn-off from Gunns Plains Rd. **Map refs:** 491 D4, 508 G6

How to book: 137 Winduss Rd, Gunns Plains (03) 6429 1151 www.wingswildlife.com.au

SOUTH-WEST WILDERNESS

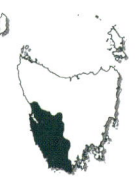

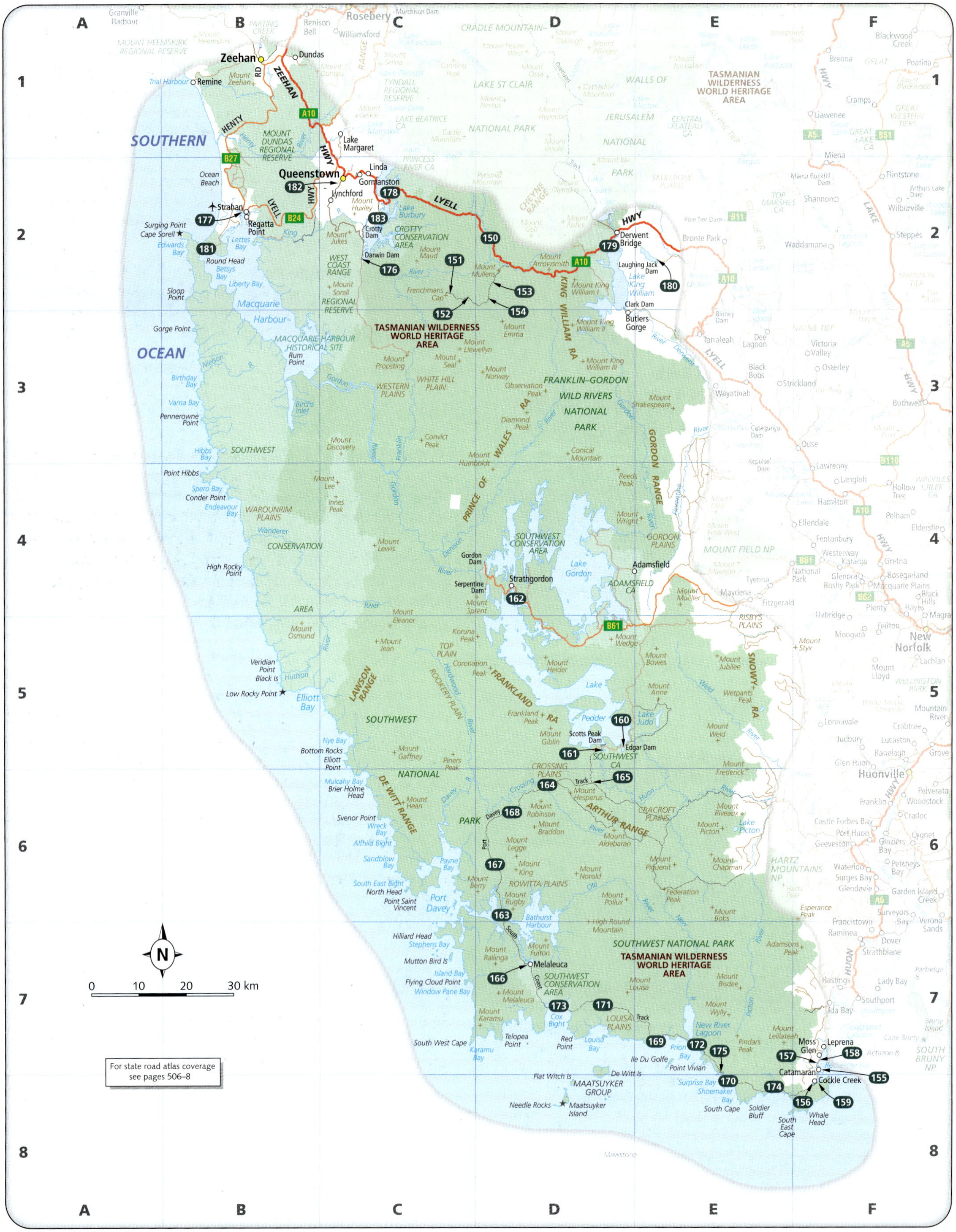

For state road atlas coverage see pages 506–8

THIS REMOTE PART OF Tasmania is a vast wilderness of craggy peaks and windswept moors, edged by rugged coastline to the south and west and by forested valleys in the east. It is almost entirely protected in 2 huge national parks and its pristine ecology is recognised internationally with a World Heritage listing.

But it was not always so. This majestic area has been the centre of Tasmania's most bitterly fought conservation battles, the first over the flooding of the original, tiny Lake Pedder for a power scheme in 1972, and the second saving the Franklin River from a similar fate 10 years later. Today, the Gordon and Pedder hydro lakes offer world-class angling amid stunningly beautiful mountain scenery, while the Franklin River's whitewater gorges and idyllic pools lure adventurers to its challenging, week-long paddle-and-portage journey.

Most travellers to this region experience its beauty in 21st-century comfort from the deck of a cruise boat, gliding through the Gordon River's rainforest valleys from Strahan. There are few roads into the area but you can catch a glimpse of its wild horizons from the Lyell Hwy, Cockle Creek Rd or Gordon River Rd.

But the real south-west wilderness is the preserve of bushwalkers, and the only way to experience the true wonder of this place is to venture deep into its heart on foot. There are dozens of trails, from gentle coast-hugging walks to gruelling treks over steep and muddy terrain. For dedicated and well-prepared bushwalkers, there are 2 great treks which meet at remote Melaleuca, deep in the wilderness near Bathurst Harbour. From Scotts Peak, the 5-day, 70 km Port Davey Track cuts through the middle of Southwest National Park, and from Cockle Creek, the 85 km, 5–10 day South Coast Track skirts the beaches, headlands and lagoons of the south coast.

CAMPSITES LOCATED IN PARKS AND RESERVES

FRANKLIN–GORDON WILD RIVERS NATIONAL PARK

Carrying the iconic name of Tasmania's most famous wild river, this vast Wilderness World Heritage Area is a region of rainforest, mountain peaks and pristine river valleys. The Lyell Hwy cuts through its north, providing access to trails, waterfalls and lookouts, and there are river cruises from Strahan in the west, while the most adventurous come here to paddle or raft the Franklin River's legendary gorges. One of the park's most challenging tracks is the 4-day hike to Frenchmans Cap, a prominent quartzite-topped peak which can be seen from the Lyell Hwy.

Who to contact: PWS Queenstown Field Centre (03) 6471 2511; or PWS Strahan Office (03) 6472 6020 *Permits:* Parks Pass is required to enter national parks (03) 6233 2621 www.parks.tas.gov.au

150 **Collingwood River camping area**

This small camping area with no facilities is in the ferny rainforest on the eastern side of the Lyell Hwy (A10), where it crosses the Collingwood River, 40 km west of Derwent Bridge. This is where seasoned adventurers set out for rafting trips on the Franklin River, and it is also a great spot for some challenging paddling in the river's Grade 6 rapids. This is a gas/fuel stove-only area and the river water should be boiled or treated before drinking. **Map refs: 498 D2, 506 F2, 508 F12**

Frenchmans Cap Track

The track to Frenchmans Cap is a challenging 4-day hike that's best suited to experienced, fit bushwalkers, so the rest of us must settle for capturing glimpses of this prominent white peak from the highway. The trailhead and walker registration is on the Lyell Hwy (A10), 3 km west of the Franklin River Bridge. Note: sturdy, worn-in boots, a gas/fuel stove and large-scale maps are essential.

Please note that campsites are listed in alphabetical order, not track order. Refer to the map on p. 498 for further information.

151 **Lake Tahune hut camping area (walk-in camping)**

This hut, 9 km (4 hr) from Lake Vera, is heated with methylated spirit, which you will need to bring as supplies are limited. The hut sleeps 12 and there are tent sites just past the helipad. From here it is a 2 hr climb to the summit of Frenchmans Cap, but no camping is allowed there. This is a gas/fuel stove-only area. **Map refs: 498 C2, 506 E3, 508 E12**

152 **Lake Vera hut camping area (walk-in camping)**

This coal-heated bushwalker hut sleeps 20 and is 16 km (6 hr) from the trailhead on the Lyell Hwy. There are tent sites across the bridge just past the hut. No fire allowed: gas/fuel stove-only area. **Map refs: 498 C2, 506 F3, 508 F12**

153 **Loddon River camping area (walk-in camping)**

This camping site is on the first leg of the track to Frenchmans Cap. There are no facilities here and it is a gas/fuel stove-only area. **Map refs: 498 D2, 506 F3, 508 F12**

154 **Philps Creek camping area (walk-in camping)**

This walk-in bush campsite between the Frenchmans Cap trailhead and Lake Vera has no facilities. No fires: use a gas/fuel stove only. **Map refs: 498 D2, 506 F3, 508 F12**

RECHERCHE BAY NATURE RECREATION AREA

Almost at the end of Australia's road network, 2 hr south of Hobart, this forested reserve surrounds Recherche Bay. It offers some of the state's most scenic camping, with a snow-capped mountain backdrop and a pure white sandy beach in front. Firewood and drinking water are not available in the reserve. Maximum stay is 1 month.

Who to contact: PWS Huonville (03) 6264 8460

155 Catamaran camping area

This free roadside camping area is next to the boat-launching ramp. It has a good selection of secluded sites but is best suited to vans and trailers. There are few facilities and you will need to bring all your supplies with you, including water and firewood. The last chance to buy food is at Dover, 35 km north. Signposted access is 1 km south of Finns Beach on Cockle Creek Rd (C636). **Map refs:** 498 F7, 507 I11

156 Cockle Creek camping area

Alongside the last few potholed kilometres of Australia's most southerly road, these undeveloped campgrounds suit those who don't mind roughing it a bit. There is no camping on the ocean side of the road, but on the other side there are good grassed sites opposite a sheltered white-sand beach. Bring water, firewood and all self-sufficient supplies. Access is via Hastings Caves Rd (C635), then the gravel Cockle Creek Rd (C636). Cockle Creek is about 25 km after turning west off the Huon Hwy (A6) south of Dover. **Map refs:** 498 F8, 507 I11

157 Finns Beach camping area

This undeveloped, free camping area has its own forest-fringed beach and – being so far south – a night sky you will never forget. Turn right off the Huon Hwy (A6) 19 km south of Dover, onto the C635 then C636 to Lune River, where the road becomes gravel; 11 km further on, turn left to Catamaran. The campground is on the right-hand side of the road, 800 m south of Gilhams Beach. Bring firewood and water. **Map refs:** 498 F7, 507 I11

158 Gilhams Beach camping area

What this free camping area lacks in facilities it more than makes up for in magnificent surroundings. Dense green forest, white sand and crystal-clear water attract plenty of visitors in summer, but at other times you might have it all to yourself. Spend your day swimming, fishing or exploring the area's whaling history, and your nights marvelling at the stars or watching the local wildlife. The campground is on the right-hand side of Cockle Creek Rd (C636) at Catamaran. Bring water and firewood. **Map refs:** 498 F7, 507 I11

SOUTHWEST NATIONAL PARK

Tasmania's largest national park is 600 000 ha of rugged, unspoilt coastline, mountain wilderness and trout-stocked lakes. Accessible by car via the Gordon River Rd in the north and Cockle Creek Rd in the south, there are also dozens of walks, from 10 min nature trails to the epic 85 km South Coast track. Fire places are provided in roadside picnic/camping areas along the Gordon River Rd, but not at other places in the park. Bushwalkers should bring a gas/fuel stove.

Who to contact: PWS Mt Field National Park (03) 6288 1149; or PWS Huonville Office (03) 6264 8460 *How to book:* for bushwalker transport to trailheads Evans Coaches (03) 6297 1335; or Par-Avion Wilderness Tours www.paravion.com.au *Camping fees:* fees payable at self-registration stations at some sites *Permits:* Parks Pass is required to enter national parks (03) 6233 2621 www.parks.tas.gov.au; an Inland Angling Licence is required to fish, check regulations and season www.ifs.tas.gov.au

159 Boltons Green camping area

There is room for 10 tents at this campground, which is south of the bridge at the very end of the unsealed and potholed Cockle Creek Rd. Come equipped with a gas/fuel stove and be prepared to carry your gear 100 m or so because vehicles are not allowed at the camping sites. The terminus of the South Coast Track is nearby. The site has pit toilets and a public telephone. **Map refs:** 498 F8, 507 I11

160 Edgar Campground

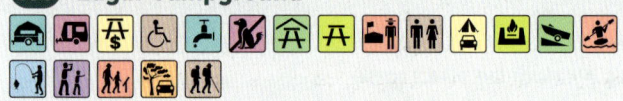

This is the larger of 2 camping areas on the Scotts Peak Dam Rd. It has 20 sites beside the road, 31 km from a well-signposted left turn from the Gordon River Rd (B61). The site is relatively exposed to the weather so you will need a sturdy waterproof shelter for a comfortable stay here. It is popular with anglers, as there is a convenient boat ramp accessible via a short track opposite the campsite. Firewood and tank water are provided but you will need to bring insect repellent. **Map refs:** 498 D5, 506 G8

161 Huon Campground

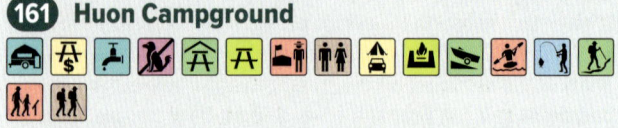

This camping area 7 km past the Edgar Campground is also the trailhead for the 70 km Port Davey walking track, which heads deep into Tasmania's southern wilderness. The 10 sheltered sites at the end of a 1 km gravel entrance road are conveniently close to boat-launching facilities at Scotts Peak Dam, giving access to Lake Pedder's world-class trout waters. On your way here along the Scotts Peak Rd (C607), take a look at the Creepy Crawly rainforest nature trail just after the turn-off from the Gordon River Rd. Firewood and tank water are supplied. **Map refs:** 498 D5, 506 G8

Melaleuca camping area along the Port Davey Track, Southwest National Park (p. 501)

162 Teds Beach Campground

Although there is an abundance of magnificent mountain scenery all around and the spectacular Gordon Dam is only 15 km away, most campers here have their sights set on the water. Lake Pedder is one of the world's great trout-fishing lakes and this site is set up for anglers' vans and trailers: there is no grass to pitch a hiking tent. This is the only campsite along the Gordon River Rd. Access is via a short signposted access road to the left, 39 km beyond the Scotts Peak Dam Rd intersection, which is 29 km from Maydena. There is a boat ramp nearby.
Map refs: 498 D4, 506 F6

Port Davey Track

Passing through the heart of Tasmania's awe-inspiring south-west, this 70 km, 5-day trek from Scotts Peak to Melaleuca is only for the fittest, most experienced hikers. The track is rough, steep and muddy; it rains on average every second day in summer, and icy storms are common in all seasons. Walkers must be equipped for weather delays and able to wait for suitable tides at river crossings. Gas/fuel stoves must be carried. Note: walker registration is at Huon Campground and Melaleuca.

▓ *Please note that campsites are listed in alphabetical*
▓ *order, not track order. Refer to the map on p. 498 for*
▓ *further information.*

Who to contact: PWS Mt Field National Park (03) 6288 1149

163 Bathurst Narrows camping area (walk-in camping)

This large campsite is near the Bathurst Channel boat crossing, 12 km (allow 5 hr) before the track end at Melaleuca. There are great views to Mt Rugby. Hikers must be completely self-sufficient, carrying water and a gas/fuel stove.
Map refs: 498 D6, 506 F9

164 Crossing River camping area (walk-in camping)

This pretty riverside campsite with a pebble beach is 10 km from Junction Creek (allow 6 hr). The camping area is surrounded by lots of tracks so take, care when heading out in the morning. It can be muddy here and the river can rise quickly during rain. Bring a gas/fuel stove. **Map refs:** 498 D6, 506 F8

161 Huon Campground

See p. 500.

165 Junction Creek camping area (walk-in camping)

This walk-in campsite on the southern side of the creek is 7 km from the Huon Campground trailhead at Scotts Peak (allow 3 hr). The tent sites are small clearings among trees. Bring a gas/fuel stove. **Map refs:** 498 D6, 506 G8

166 Melaleuca camping area (walk-in camping)

Deep in Tasmania's south-west, at Bathurst Harbour, this campsite is at the end of the South Coast and Port Davey walking track. Trekkers can arrange to fly in from Hobart to start their walks here, or be picked up after completing them. Some hardy souls use the relatively comfortable hut accommodation at Melaleuca as a layover before heading off on the second leg of these 2 tracks, to traverse the entire Southwest National Park. The nearby Denny King Memorial Hide is your best chance of spotting an orange-bellied parrot, Tasmania's most endangered bird. **Map refs: 498 D7, 506 F10**

167 Spring River camping area (walk-in camping)

This is a sometimes muddy campsite among leaning old trees, 14 km from Watershed Camp. Allow 5 hr for the hike and bring a gas/fuel stove. **Map refs: 498 D6, 506 F9**

168 Watershed Camp (walk-in camping)

The small Watershed Camp is 11 km from Crossing River (allow up to 8 hr, with lots of creek crossings) and has space for 4 tents. This site can be wet. Be warned: there are plenty of leeches. **Map refs: 498 D6, 506 F8**

South Coast Track

There are 6 camping areas on the 85 km, 5–10 day trek around Tasmania's wild southern coastline, from Cockle Creek to Melaleuca at Bathurst Harbour. Walkers must be experienced, well-equipped and able to sit out weather delays. Gas/fuel stoves are required. Note: walkers should register at Cockle Creek or Melaleuca.

Please note that campsites are listed in alphabetical order, not track order. Refer to the map on p. 498 for further information.

Who to contact: PWS Huonville (03) 6264 8460

159 Boltons Green camping area

See p. 500.

169 Deadmans Bay camping area (walk-in camping)

This camp at the eastern side of the Ironbound Range has plenty of sheltered sites among trees next to a creek. The 12 km track from Louisa River over the Ironbound Range is rough, steep and muddy on its descent into the camp, so allow 10 hr. To the east, the New River Lagoon stage is also a muddy 9 km (allow 4 hr). Bring a gas/fuel stove. **Map refs: 498 E7, 506 G11**

170 Granite Beach camping area (walk-in camping)

Granite Beach's large, sheltered camping area is up off the beach at the eastern end, 3 km (1 hr) from Surprise Bay. The 9 km leg between here and South Cape Rivulet is the toughest of the whole track due to muddy conditions (allow 7 hr), and a creek crossing may require waiting for the tide. Bring a gas/fuel stove. **Map refs: 498 E8, 506 H11**

171 Louisa River camping area (walk-in camping)

Campsites here are scattered along both sides of the river at the foot of the 900 m high Ironbound range. From Point Eric, it is a 17 km (6 hr) trek over Red Point Hills. Or, from Deadmans Bay, take the moderately hard 12 km (10 hr) track over the rugged Ironbounds. Bring a gas/fuel stove. **Map refs: 498 D7, 506 G10**

166 Melaleuca camping area (walk-in camping)

See p. 501.

172 New River Lagoon camping area (walk-in camping)

There is camping at the Prion Beach boat crossing of New River Lagoon, but no reliable drinking water. New River Lagoon is 9 km of muddy track from Deadmans Bay (allow 4 hr) or 9 km (4 hr) from Surprise Bay. A side-trip to the spectacular Precipitous Bluff is a 22 km (2–3 day return) trek from here. Bring water and a gas/fuel stove. **Map refs: 498 E7, 506 H11**

173 Point Eric camping area (walk-in camping)

This pretty camping area overlooks Coxs Bight. The best sites are on sheltered, grassy flats right behind the beach. There is fresh water along the beach at Goring Creek, 200 m east. This campsite is 13 km (an easy 5 hr) from Melaleuca camping area and 17 km over Red Point Hills (allow 6 hr) from Louisa River camping area. Bring a gas/fuel stove. **Map refs: 498 D7, 506 F10**

174 South Cape Rivulet and Lion Rock camping area (walk-in camping)

This is the first – or last – camp on the track. There are some campsites at Lion Rock, 8 km (3 hr) from the Cockle Creek trailhead, while the main camping area, beside South Cape Rivulet lagoon, is a further 3 km west, sheltered beside the rivulet 100 m up from the beach. South Cape Rivulet is a moderately hard and muddy 9 km (7 hr) from Granite Beach. Bring a gas/fuel stove. **Map refs: 498 E8, 506 H11**

175 Surprise Bay camping area (walk-in camping)

This scenic elevated campsite and another at nearby Osmiridium Beach both have nice views over the beach. Surprise Bay is 9 km from New River Lagoon crossing, or 3 km from Granite Beach going the other way. Bring a gas/fuel stove. **Map refs: 498 E7, 506 H11**

CAMPSITES LOCATED IN OTHER AREAS

176 Darwin Dam camping area

This remote camping area at the southern tip of Lake Burbury is located deep within the forest, 25 km south of Queenstown along the unsealed Mt Jukes Rd. There is free camping beside the dam and in clearings bedside the road. A boat-launching facility makes this a popular spot for anglers. Head out of Queenstown along Lynchford Rd, turning right into Mt Jukes Rd. **Map refs:** 498 C2, 506 E2, 508 E12

Who to contact: West Coast Council, Queenstown (03) 6471 4700; or Lake Burbury groundskeeper (not always available) (03) 6471 2762 *Permits:* an Inland Angling Licence is required to fish; check regulations and season www.ifs.tas.gov.au

177 Discovery Holiday Parks – Strahan

Located in Strahan township, a short walk from the quayside, this large caravan and van park has a range of accommodation options. All the facilities you would expect are here and it is a very convenient base for touring, with the Gordon River cruise boats on your doorstep. At Strahan, follow the main road (B24) as it becomes Esplanade, then Bay St, then Innes St. The park is at the intersection of Innes and Andrew sts. **Map refs:** 498 B2, 506 C2, 508 C12

How to book: 8 Innes St, Strahan (03) 6471 7442 www.discoveryholidayparks.com.au

178 Lake Burbury Camping Ground

This vast scenic lake is the west coast's aquatic playground, with watersports and excellent seasonal trout fishing (licences are required). Lake levels vary, reducing boat access in some years. Grassed picnic and camping areas (gas/fuel stove-only) are 700 m from a signposted access road off the Lyell Hwy, 21 km east of Queenstown. **Map refs:** 498 C2, 506 E2, 508 E11

Who to contact: West Coast Council, Queenstown (03) 6471 4700; or Lake Burbury groundskeeper (not always available) (03) 6471 2762 *Permits:* an Inland Angling Licence is required to fish; check regulations and season www.ifs.tas.gov.au

179 Lake King William camping area (bush camping)

These undeveloped lakeside camping areas are in bush clearings along narrow tracks, and are not accessible to larger rigs. Accessed from the Lyell Hwy (A10), 5 km west of Derwent Bridge, there are sites among trees near the boat ramp overlooking a vista of stark – but very photogenic – dead tree stumps. A more scenic area at Butlers Gorge in the south is reached along Butlers Gorge Rd, 15 km from its turn-off on the Lyell Hwy, 3 km south of Tarraleah. There are fireplaces but gas/fuel stoves are preferred. Trout fishing is seasonal and a licence is needed. The nearby Cradle Mountain–Lake St Clair National Park is well worth a visit. **Map refs:** 498 D2, 506 G2, 508 G12

Who to contact: Hydro Tasmania 1300 360 441 *Permits:* an Inland Angling Licence is required to fish; check regulations and season www.ifs.tas.gov.au

180 Laughing Jack Lagoon camping area

Popular with anglers during the Aug–May season, there are sites in the bush to the left of the dam wall and additional sites across the bridge. You can stay for up to 7 days and it is advisable to bring portable toilets, drinking water, gas/fuel stoves and firewood. The access road (C602) turns left off the Lyell Hwy (A10), 25 km north of Tarraleah; follow the left-hand fork after the Clarence River bridge. **Map refs:** 498 E2, 506 G2, 508 G12

Who to contact: Hydro Tasmania 1300 360 441
Permits: an Inland Angling Licence is required to fish; check regulations and season www.ifs.tas.gov.au

181 Macquarie Heads camping area

Strahan is a must-see destination in Tasmania, and the starting point for cruises along the iconic Gordon River. This grassed, shady camping area is 15 km west of town; follow Ocean Beach Rd, then head left along a rough – but passable – unsealed road (C251) that leads past the picnic area. Make sure you visit nearby Ocean Beach to watch the sun set over the sea. **Map refs:** 498 B2, 506 C2, 508 C12

How to book: West Coast Visitor Information and Booking Centre, Strahan (03) 6472 6800

182 Queenstown Cabin and Tourist Park

This cabin park in Queenstown's south has a full list of facilities and is a good central site from which to explore the region's mining history and extraordinary natural features. There is everything you might need, from laundry facilities to a games room, and there is a dump point in town. At Queenstown, turn south off the Lyell Hwy onto Driffield St, which becomes Urquart St and then Grafton St. The park is on your left. **Map refs:** 498 C2, 506 D1, 508 D11

How to book: 17 Grafton St (03) 6471 1332 www.westcoastcabins.com.au

183 Thureau Hills camping area

This remote spot on the edge of pretty Lake Burbury is used by campervans, motorhomes and caravans, but there are no facilities so you need to bring your own everything. The lake offers fishing and boating, with a stunningly scenic mountain backdrop. The area is reached 4 km along a sealed road from the Lyell Hwy (A10), via a well-signposted turn-off to the south, 15 km from Queenstown. **Map refs:** 498 C2, 506 E2, 508 E12

Who to contact: West Coast Council, Queenstown (03) 6471 4700 *Permits:* an Inland Angling Licence is required to fish; check regulations and season www.ifs.tas.gov.au

FLINDERS ISLAND

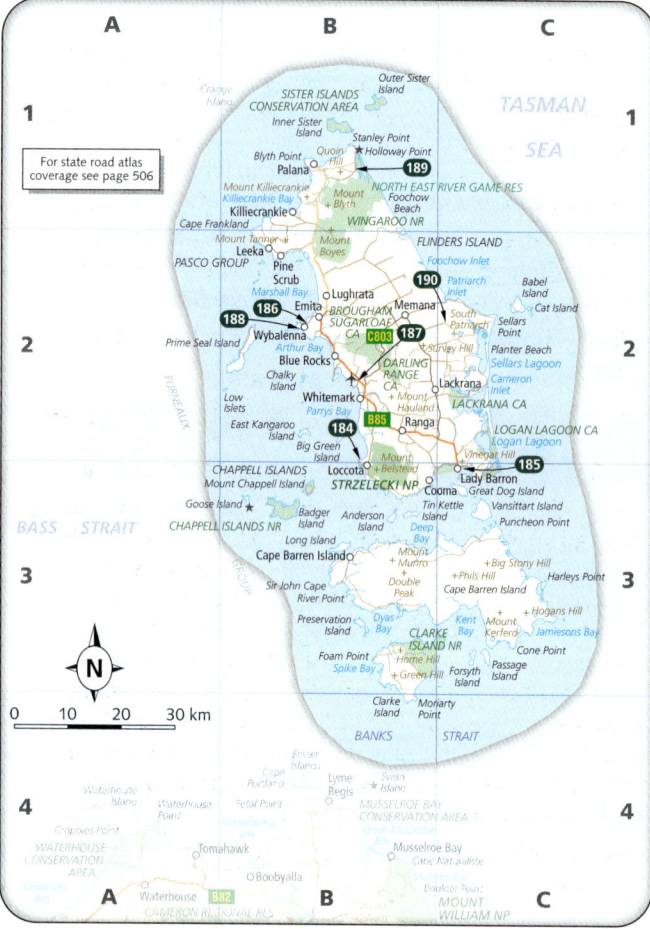

For state road atlas coverage see page 506

FLINDERS ISLAND LIES IN eastern Bass Strait, between Tasmania and mainland Australia, among the Furneaux group of islands. It is remote and beautiful, offering visitors magnificent scenery, a mild climate, superbly fresh seafood and a taste of laid-back island life. You can spend unhurried days beachcombing, fossicking for Killiecrankie 'diamonds' or exploring the fascinating history of the island. There is world-class fishing offshore, while the island's bays and reefs offer all sorts of fun, from kayaking to wreck diving.

From high vantage points, the Furneaux Islands look like stepping stones across the sea, and it is easy to see how they would have formed a land bridge allowing Ice Age people to walk between Tasmania and Australia when sea levels were lower. Now surrounded by ocean, they are refuges for abundant wildlife and plants, with over 200 species of birds alone. Cape Barren geese and short-tailed shearwaters (muttonbirds) are here in their thousands, and any evening you will see dozens of wallabies and wombats coming out to feed, no matter where you are on the island.

In the island's south-east, Strzelecki National Park dominates the landscape. Its massive granite peak rises to over 750 m directly from the foreshore at Trousers Point, and although the track to the summit is a challenge, it takes you through delightful forest and the views from the climb are sensational.

The best way to get to Flinders Island is by air from Launceston or Melbourne. On the island, you will need to cycle or hire a car as there is no public transport, but distances are short and there is plenty to see. Camping is free and if you have your own water and gas/fuel stove, you can set up almost anywhere around the island's beautiful coastline.

CAMPSITES LOCATED IN PARKS AND RESERVES

STRZELECKI NATIONAL PARK

This beautiful little park is named for the Polish explorer Strzelecki, who climbed the island's highest peak in 1847. You can follow in his footsteps on the challenging 5 hr (return) hike to the summit, which will reward your effort with fabulous views, or you can simply relax by paddling, swimming or fishing in the park's cool, clear waters.

Who to contact: Flinders Island Visitor Information Centre (03) 6359 5002; or PWS Furneaux (Flinders) Islands, Whitemark (03) 6359 2217 **Permits:** Parks Pass is required to enter national parks (03) 6233 2621 www.parks.tas.gov.au

184 Trousers Point camping area

With its own tiny swimming beach, this camping area has to be one of the most delightful places to pitch a tent. Clear waters offer spectacular diving and snorkelling, and there are lovely scenic coastal walks nearby. Access is via the gravel Trousers Point Rd, turning right to Trousers Point Beach. The campground is 100 m past the picnic area. Campers should bring their own firewood and drinking water. **Map refs:** 504 B2, 506 B11, 509 O1

YELLOW BEACHES COASTAL RESERVE

Yellow Beaches Coastal Reserve lies along the curving shoreline of Adelaide Bay at Flinders Island's southernmost settlement of Lady Barron. It offers sheltered beaches, easily accessed, which are tucked in behind Little Green Island. There is safe swimming and the surroundings are pretty. There is also brilliant scenery below the waterline, so bring your camera and snorkelling gear.

Who to contact: Flinders Island Visitor Information Centre (03) 6359 5002; or PWS Furneaux (Flinders) Islands, Whitemark (03) 6359 2217

185 Yellow Beaches Coastal Reserve camping area

Looking out over island-dotted Franklin Sound, this small camping area is set in a coastal reserve within walking distance

of the settlement of Lady Barron. Being so close to the town has its advantages; if arrangements are made, campers can fill up their water supplies and get hot showers at the nearby Furneaux Tavern, where accommodation and very good seafood counter meals are also available. From Lady Barron, head 1 km east along Franklin Pde, which becomes Pot Boil Rd. The camping area is 500 m along on the right and stays are limited to 1 night. **Map refs:** 504 C3, 506 B11, 509 P1

CAMPSITES LOCATED IN OTHER AREAS

186 Allports Beach camping area

This pretty beachside camping area is near the historic Wybalenna chapel and cemetery, which now sit fully restored on Aboriginal land, marking the place where Tasmania's Aborigines were exiled in miserable conditions in the 1830s. History is also on display at nearby Emita, with a small museum housing relics from the island's many shipwrecks. Follow the signposts from Palana Rd, heading towards the coast along Port Davies Rd, and find a sheltered spot out of the wind off Allports Beach Rd. Bring your own everything. **Map refs:** 504 B2, 506 A10

Who to contact: Flinders Island Visitor Information Centre (03) 6359 5002; or PWS Furneaux (Flinders) Islands Field Centre, Whitemark (03) 6359 2217

187 Flinders Island Cabin Park and Car Hire

This place, just south of the airport, offers a range of options to visitors, from bicycle camping to self-catering cabins for the whole family. The park hires out kayaks, campervans and mountain bikes, as well as all the camping and fishing gear you will need to enjoy the island at your own pace. There is a lovely nature walk opposite and pretty Killicrankie Bay, where you can scour the beach at low tide for the topaz known locally as Killicrankie diamond, is a 30 min drive north. **Map refs:** 504 B2, 506 B10

How to book: 1 Bluff Rd, Whitemark (03) 6359 2188, 0427 592 188 www.flindersislandcp.com.au

188 Lillies Beach camping area

This coastal site has only the most basic facilities but provides camping areas where you can really get away from it all. Set on a gently sloping point next to pretty Lillies Beach, it is close to boat-launching facilities at nearby Port Davies. You will need to be self-sufficient here as there is no water or firewood. Head along Port Davies Rd from Palana Rd, passing Wybalenna historic site, until you reach the rough track to Lillies Bay. Lillies is suitable for tent camping but not for larger vehicles. **Map refs:** 504 B2, 506 A10

Who to contact: Flinders Island Visitor Information Centre (03) 6359 5002

189 North East River camping area

The remote and beautiful northern tip of Flinders Island is a haven for lovers of wild coastal scenery. There are plenty of secluded camping spots among trees beside the inlet and no shortage of excellent snorkelling, surfing and fishing. To get here, head north along Palana Rd, turning right into North East River Rd just a few km from the coast. Negotiate your way along this track to the river mouth at the northern tip of the remarkable 30 km Foochow Beach. You will need to bring firewood and water. **Map refs:** 504 B1, 506 B9

Who to contact: Flinders Island Visitor Information Centre (03) 6359 5002

190 The Patriarchs Wildlife Sanctuary camping area

Surrounding 3 granite hills on the island's eastern flanks, the forests, lagoons and swamps of this sanctuary offer unspoilt wildlife habitat and a chance to get to know Flinders Island's unique animals. Access is 6 km east along Lees Rd from Lackrana Rd. Attractions include fantastic nature walks and spotting the refuge's wallabies, wombats and Cape Barren geese. The refuge is lovingly cared for by the Friends of the Patriarchs and donations to their cause are appreciated. There is a heated A-frame camp shelter but you will need to bring your own drinking water and firewood, and take care as the access track can be boggy after rain. **Map refs:** 504 C2, 506 B10

Who to contact: Flinders Island Visitor Information Centre (03) 6359 5002

Southern Tasmania

Joins map 508

Joins map 509

0   10   20   30   40   50 km

SOUTHERN OCEAN

TASMAN SEA

BASS STRAIT

TASMAN SEA

0   10   20 km

Northern Tasmania

INDEX

This index includes all campsites, towns, localities, roadhouses and national parks shown on the maps and mentioned in the text. For easy reference, campsite names include the national park, state forest or reserve in which they are located.

Campsite names are followed by a map page number and grid reference, and the text page number on which that campsite is mentioned. A page number set in **bold** type indicates the text entry for that campsite. For example:

Barranyi (North Island) NP NT 353 N10, 355 N1, **333**
    Paradise Bay camping area NT 335 H4, 353 N10, 355 N1, **333**

Barranyi (North Island) NP	– National Park name
NT	– State
353 N10, 355 N1	– Barranyi (North Island) National Park appears on these map pages
333	– Barranyi (North Island) National Park appears on this text page
Paradise Bay camping area	– This campsite is located within Barranyi (North Island) National Park
335 H4, 353 N10, 355 N1	– Paradise Bay camping area appears on these map pages
333	– Paradise Bay camping area appears on this text page

The alphabetical order followed in the index is that of 'word-by-word' – a space is considered to come before 'A' in the alphabet, and the index has been ordered accordingly. For example:

White Hills
White Mountains National Park
Whitefoord
Whiteheads Creek
Whitemark

Names beginning with Mc are indexed as Mac and those beginning with St as Saint.

The following abbreviations and contractions are used in the index:

ACT	– Australian Capital Territory		SF	– State Forest
CA	– Conservation Area		SP	– State Park
CR	– Conservation Reserve		SF	– State Reserve
JBT	– Jervis Bay Territory		Tas.	– Tasmania
NSW	– New South Wales		Vic.	– Victoria
NP	– National Park		WA	– Western Australia
NR	– Nature Reserve			
NT	– Northern Territory			
Qld	– Queensland			
SA	– South Australia			

Acknowledgements

The publisher would like to acknowledge the help of the following individuals and organisations in the production of this edition:

Publications manager
Astrid Browne

Managing editor
Melissa Krafchek

Editors
Clare Coney, Jane Thompson, Clare Marshall, Alison Proietto

Writers
Liz Ginis, Alan Murphy, Jenny Turner, Jeremy Edwards, Sue Moffitt, Chad Parkhill, Sue Medlock

Cartography
Bruce McGurty, Emily Maffei, Claire Johnston

Cover design
Phil Campbell

Internal page design
Peter Dyson of desertpony

Layout
Megan Ellis

Index
Max McMaster

Pre-press
Splitting Image

Photography credits
Front Cover: Campsite in Brachina Gorge, Flinders Ranges and Outback region, South Australia (Jeff Drewitz)

Back cover: Cycle-tourers relaxing at camp on Gibb River Road, Kimberley region, Western Australia (Tim Hughes/Lonely Planet Images)

Title page: Little Beach, Two Peoples Bay Nature Reserve, Great Southern region, Western Australia (Orien Harvey/Lonely Planet Images)

Other images: Page 2 Ross Dunstan/Australian Geographic; 11 Nick Rains; 18 Manfred Gottschalk/Lonely Planet Images; 65 Tony Bee/Photolibrary/Getty Images; 88 courtesy Destination New South Wales; 101 Glenn Van der Knijff/Lonely Planet Images; 110 Tourism Victoria; 116 Bethune Carmichael/Lonely Planet Images; 125 Rory McGuinness/Australian Geographic; 158 Tourism Victoria; 128 Jeff Drewitz; 199 Mike Langford/Australian Geographic; 213 South Australian Tourism Commission; 230 Tim Webster/Australian Geographic; 246 South Australian Tourism Commission; 259 Nick Rains; 268 Joel Day/Alamy; 294 Blue Gum Pictures/Alamy; 299 Suzanne Long/Auscape International; 323 Mitch Reardon/Australian Geographic; 347 Barry Skipsey/Ozstock Images Pty Ltd; 359 Johnny Haglund/Lonely Planet Images; 363 Tourism Queensland; 380 Jeff Drewitz; 389 Tourism Queensland; 401 Tourism Queensland; 469 Sue Medlock; 479 Tourism Tasmania; 494 Tourism Tasmania; 501 Andrew Bain/Lonely Planet Images

Explore Australia Publishing Pty Ltd
Ground Floor, Building 1, 658 Church Street,
Richmond, VIC 3121

Explore Australia Publishing Pty Ltd is a division of Hardie Grant Publishing Pty Ltd

hardie grant publishing

Published by Explore Australia Publishing Pty Ltd, 2013

Concept, text, maps, form and design © Explore Australia Publishing Pty Ltd, 2013

A Cataloguing-in-Publication entry is available from the catalogue of the National Library of Australia at www.nla.gov.au

The maps in this publication incorporate data © Commonwealth of Australia (Geoscience Australia), 2006. Geoscience Australia has not evaluated the data as altered and incorporated within this publication, and therefore gives no warranty regarding accuracy, completeness, currency or suitability for any particular purpose.

Maps contain Aboriginal Land data (2010), which is owned and copyright of the relevant Queensland, Northern Territory, South Australia and Western Australia state government authorities. The authorities give no warranty in relation to the data (including accuracy, reliability, completeness or suitability) and accept no liability (including without limitation, liability in negligence) for any loss, damage or costs (including consequential damage) relating to any use of the data.

ISBN-13 9781741174014 (paperback edition)
ISBN-13 9781741174113 (spiral-bound edition)

10 9 8 7 6 5 4 3 2 1

Printed and bound in China by 1010 Printing International Ltd

Publisher's note: Every effort has been made to ensure that the information in this book is accurate at the time of going to press. The publisher welcomes information and suggestions for correction or improvement. Email: info@exploreaustralia.net.au

www.exploreaustralia.net.au
Follow us on Twitter: @ExploreAus
Find us on Facebook: www.facebook.com/exploreaustralia